Full pronunciation key

The pronunciation of each word is shown just after the word, in this way:
ab bre vi ate (ə brē′vē āt).

The letters and signs used are pronounced as in the words below.

The mark ′ is placed after a syllable with primary or heavy accent, as in the example above.

The mark ′ after a syllable shows a secondary or lighter accent, as in
ab bre vi a tion (ə brē′vē ā′shən).

a	hat, cap	p	paper, cup
ā	age, face	r	run, try
ä	father, far	s	say, yes
		sh	she, rush
b	bad, rob	t	tell, it
ch	child, much	th	thin, both
d	did, red	ŦH	then, smooth
e	let, best	u	cup, butter
ē	equal, be	u̇	full, put
ėr	term, learn	ü	rule, move
f	fat, if	v	very, save
g	go, bag	w	will, woman
h	he, how	y	young, yet
		z	zero, breeze
		zh	measure, seizure
i	it, pin		
ī	ice, five		
j	jam, enjoy	ə	represents:
k	kind, seek		a in about
l	land, coal		e in taken
m	me, am		i in pencil
n	no, in		o in lemon
ng	long, bring		u in circus
o	hot, rock		
ō	open, go		
ô	order, all		
oi	oil, voice		
ou	house, out		

Scott, Foresman
Beginning Dictionary

Scott, Foresman Beginning Dictionary

by E.L. Thorndike / Clarence L. Barnhart

Scott, Foresman and Company

Editorial Offices: Glenview, Illinois

Regional Offices: Palo Alto, California ·
Tucker, Georgia · Glenview, Illinois ·
Oakland, New Jersey · Dallas, Texas

ISBN: 0-673-12380-4

910-RRW-91908988

Contents

Introduction

Children have a natural interest in using and learning about words. The Beginning Dictionary has been designed to encourage this interest. During the last forty years, millions of children have used dictionaries by E. L. Thorndike and Clarence L. Barnhart, edited and published by Scott, Foresman. This dictionary continues that tradition and combines with it a fresh design and carefully chosen illustrations. The result is a book that young people will want to browse through and will find rewarding when they do so.

To prepare this book, a wide variety of contemporary children's textbooks and other literature was read to check for new words and meanings. Current word frequency counts were reviewed to ensure that the dictionary contains all of the words and meanings likely to be encountered by its users. This reading is backed up by Scott, Foresman's citation files, which contain about one million examples of words in use collected from newspapers, children's and general magazines, books, and other publications.

Every dictionary entry was reexamined for simplicity and clarity by a staff of editors long experienced in writing dictionaries for young people. Changes were made as necessary. Revisions were based on testing of children in many parts of the country on their ability to use a dictionary. Many definitions, sentences showing words in use, and word histories have been rewritten as a direct result of this testing.

Great care has been taken to make this dictionary visually attractive to its users. The purpose of the improved format is to stimulate young people to notice and retain interesting facts and impressions about words. The variety of illustrations—color and black-and-white photographs, drawings, cartoons, movie stills, collages—encourages browsing and incidental learning in which the user absorbs more than the specific information being sought. Fine art such as paintings, sculpture, and etchings provides an introduction to the arts, exposing young people to cultural values without obviously emphasizing them. Picture captions give the size of animals both in the customary way and in the metric system.

Words that express feelings, ideas, and actions deserve to be illustrated as much as words for things. Art can be very effective when called on to express *melancholy, gleeful, affection, blacken, breathtaking,* and similar words. Dramatizing such words broadens and deepens young people's conversational and written vocabulary. This new approach to dictionary illustration is pioneered in the Beginning Dictionary.

This book was specifically designed so that the user can readily find the information being sought. The type was chosen for its readability. Large guide words make entries easy to find. A short, easy-to-use pronunciation key appears at the top of each right-hand page. In addition, the varying line length in the right-hand margin of each column helps guide the user's attention to the entry words at the left, allows even spacing between words, and eliminates hyphens at the end of lines, thus improving readability.

To help develop basic skills in dictionary use, self-teaching lessons are included in the front of the book. These colorfully illustrated lessons are designed to appeal to young people. Stories, puzzles, games, and riddles teach the fundamentals of dictionary use—how to find a word, how to find and understand a definition, how to use the pronunciation symbols to pronounce a word, and the other skills necessary to derive the greatest benefit from a dictionary. An answer key for the lesson section is in the back of the book on page 709.

Throughout the Beginning Dictionary, pictures and sentences showing words in use have been carefully chosen to reflect the richness and diversity of our world. Girls and boys and men and women of many cultures appear in a wide variety of occupations and activities.

The Beginning Dictionary is truly a basic dictionary. Scott, Foresman offers it as the best possible book of its kind for young people.

The Editors

zoo—This view of a zoo was drawn by an eleven-year-old girl.

USING THIS DICTIONARY

"Wow! Look at those polar bears splashing!" cried Laura.

"Did you hear those roars?" asked Tim. "The lions and leopards are really wild."

"I thought I'd seen long necks before," laughed Jean as she eyed the giraffe, "but this is ridiculous!"

"What I liked best was seeing the elephant taking a bath," said Mariko. "The zoo keeper used a hose to pour water over him. It was just like washing a Volkswagen."

The whole class was enjoying the trip to the zoo. They had already seen lots of animals. And there was more excitement to come.

Everyone wondered what they should see next. Several signs showed people where to go. Laura saw one that said, "Reptiles." She knew there would be snakes there. She asked her teacher, Mr. Lopez, if they could see the reptiles next.

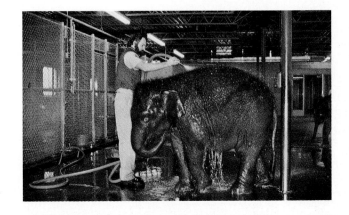

But Tim saw another sign. It said "Primates." "I think we should go there," he said. "We've all seen some snakes, but I don't think I've ever seen a primate before."

Mr. Lopez smiled. "Let's go to see the primates next," he said. "I believe you'll find that you really know much more about them than you think. And we'll all have lots of fun watching them."

Read what your dictionary says about a primate. On page 464 of this book you will find:

> **pri mate** (prī′māt), one of a group of mammals that have very advanced brains, and hands with thumbs that can be used to hold on to things. Primates are the most highly developed mammals. Apes, monkeys, and human beings are primates. *noun.*

The first thing after the word *primate* is (prī′māt). This shows you how the word is pronounced. Then the dictionary explains the meaning of the word. What kind of animals do you think Tim found when he reached the zoo's primate house?

Like Tim, you may have wondered what a primate is. You found out by reading what the dictionary says about the word *primate.* A dictionary is a book that tells about words. When you know how to use this dictionary, you can find out many things about many words. You can find out how words are spelled and how they are pronounced. You can find out what words mean and how to use them. You can even find out the history of some words. These lessons will help you learn how to use this dictionary to find out all this information about words.

gorilla

shrew

Gorillas and shrews are both **primates.**

The words that a dictionary tells about are called entry words. Entry words are printed in heavy black type.

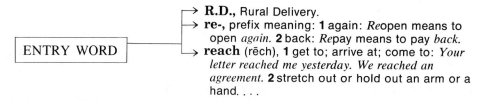

ENTRY WORD

> **R.D.,** Rural Delivery.
> **re-,** prefix meaning: **1** again: *Re*open means to open *again.* **2** back: *Re*pay means to pay *back.*
> **reach** (rēch), **1** get to; arrive at; come to: *Your letter reached me yesterday. We reached an agreement.* **2** stretch out or hold out an arm or a hand. . . .

Sometimes entry words are made up of more than one word.

ENTRY WORD

> **jack rabbit,** a large hare of western North America, having very long legs and ears.

All the entry words in this dictionary are listed in alphabetical order. All the words beginning with the letter *a* come first. All the words beginning with the letter *z* come last.

HOW TO FIND A WORD

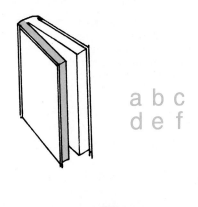

a b c
d e f

g h i j k
l m n o p

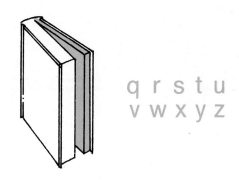

q r s t u
v w x y z

▶TEACH YOURSELF

Open your dictionary to the words beginning with the letter *g.* You have opened your dictionary about one third of the way through.

1. Which of the animals in group A to the right will you find in the first third of your dictionary?

  Open your dictionary to the words beginning with *q.* Notice that you are about two thirds of the way through your dictionary.

2. Which of the animals in group B to the right will you find in the second third of your dictionary?
3. Which of the animals in group B will you find in the last third of your dictionary?

A.	anteater	elephant
	cobra	hedgehog

B.	hyena	turtle
	kangaroo	walrus
	ostrich	

Egirt, the tiger cub

Exercise 1

On a piece of paper, copy all the numbers in the blank spaces below. After each number, rewrite the letters of the animal's name in alphabetical order. You will then have the name of each baby animal.

The zoo keeper told the children that the new lion cub had been named by alphabetizing the letters in the word *lion*. "Oh, ___(1)___! What a funny name!" cried Tim. "Is the wolf cub called ___(2)___?" asked Laura.

"Yes, and the bear cub is named ___(3)___, and the tiger cub is named ___(4)___."

"If you have a baby rat, I'll bet its name is ___(5)___," said Tim. "And the baby owl must be ___(6)___."

"Right," said the zoo keeper. "We also have a baby ocelot named ___(7)___ and a young stork named ___(8)___."

"Well, I hope the walrus pup is not named ___(9)___," said Mr. Lopez. "If so, we'd have to call him Al."

Exercise 2

Can you put the words in these groups in alphabetical order? Write them on a piece of paper. Each one you do right will mean something.

1. my
   call
   name

2. the
   see
   whale

3. toy
   her
   find

4. some
   him
   toast
   give

5. now
   go
   don't
   home

6. tall
   every
   is
   giraffe

7. lent
   me
   the
   wagon
   he

8. with
   me
   let
   play
   you

9. nice
   feed
   rabbit
   pet
   my

WITH BUMBLEBEE ME LET PLAY YOU?

DANDELION, DO YOU MEAN, "BUMBLEBEE, LET ME PLAY WITH YOU?"

Suppose you want to look up the words *circle, cub,* and *cab* in your dictionary. All three words begin with the letter *c.* You know you will find them with the words beginning with *c* in your dictionary. But which word comes first? To find out, you must look at the second letter in each word. Words that have the same first letter are put in alphabetical order by their second letters. Now you know that *cab* will come first, then *circle,* then *cub.*

▶ **TEACH YOURSELF**

1. Look at list A at the right. What are the first and second letters in all the words?
2. What letter in each word must you look at to alphabetize the words?
3. Are the words in the list in alphabetical order?

   Look at list B at the right. The first three letters of each word are *s, h,* and *e.*

4. What letter must you look at to alphabetize these words?
5. The word *she* has only three letters. If you alphabetized the words, where would you put *she?*
6. On a piece of paper write the words in alphabetical order.

A. draw
   dress
   drink
   drop
   drum
   dry

B. sheep
   shell
   sheriff
   she
   shed
   shepherd

Exercise 3

The words listed and numbered below are in alphabetical order, but the list is not complete. The words at the side were left out. Put each of these words in its proper place in the list below.

1. cabin	13. _____	cash
2. _____	14. card	car
3. cake	15. _____	cane
4. calf	16. care	catch
5. _____	17. _____	cage
6. calm	18. careful	call
7. camel	19. case	cardboard
8. _____	20. _____	cape
9. candy	21. cast	can
10. _____	22. cat	carefree
11. cap	23. _____	
12. _____	24. catkin	

Guide words

Mr. Lopez told about the first time he visited a zoo. He was only a child. His father had read him a story about a unicorn. While at the zoo, Mr. Lopez begged his parents to take him to see the unicorns. He cried when his parents told him they couldn't see any unicorns.

Some of the class laughed at Mr. Lopez's story. Others didn't understand it. They didn't know what a unicorn was. Jan and Anita decided to look up *unicorn* in the dictionary. They found nine pages of words beginning with the letters *un-*.

Jan started to look down all the columns of these words. It took her a long time to find *unicorn.* Anita found the word a faster and easier way. Let's try to find *unicorn* Anita's way.

▶TEACH YOURSELF

Turn to the first page in the dictionary that has words on it beginning with *un-*. It is page 652.

There are two large words printed in very dark type at the top of the page. These words are called guide words. The first guide word is **U.** Notice that it is the first entry word on the page too. The other guide word is **unchanged.** It is the last entry word on the page. You know that the words in the dictionary are listed in alphabetical order.

1. Does *unicorn* come between **U** and **unchanged** in alphabetical order?
2. Then would *unicorn* come on this page of the dictionary?

Look at the guide words at the top of each page that has words on it that begin with *un-*. Stop when you come to the page that has *unicorn* on it.

3. What are the guide words on this page?
4. What is the first entry word on this page?
5. What is the last entry word on this page?

Anita found the word *unicorn* by using the guide words. Guide words tell you the first and last entry words on each page. Anita knew that *unicorn* would be on the page with the guide words **unhitch** and **unkind,** because *unicorn* comes between **unhitch** and **unkind** in alphabetical order.

Exercise 4

Each animal in a zoo has a cage or area where it belongs. By using the guide words, put each animal in the correct cage. Write each number, and after it write the letter of the cage with the correct guide words.

1. a. tick | tie   b. tier | time   c. timely | tip   tiger

2. a. C | cage   b. cake | call   c. caller | can   camel

3. a. liftoff | lily   b. line | lit   c. liter | lively   lion

4. a. crinkle | crochet   b. crock | crossbones   c. crossbow | crowd   crocodile

5. a. gnome | goblin   b. god | gone   c. gong | gouge   gorilla

6. a. be | beaver   b. became | beetle   c. befall | belligerent   bear

Words that aren't entry words

Many words that end in *s, es, ed, ing, er,* and *est* are not entry words in your dictionary. To find the meaning of such a word, you usually have to look up the word that the ending was added to.

To find the meaning of *ousted* or *ousting,* you look up *oust.*

> **oust** (oust), force out; drive out: *The sparrows have ousted the bluebirds from their nest. verb.*

To find the meaning of *loped* or *loping,* you look up *lope.*
To find the meaning of *ponies,* you look up *pony.*
To find the meaning of *glossier* or *glossiest,* you look up *glossy.*
To find the meaning of *glummer* or *glummest,* you look up *glum.*

▶TEACH YOURSELF

Read what your dictionary says about the entry words *lope, pony, glossy,* and *glum.*

> **lope** (lōp), **1** run with a long, easy stride: *The horse loped along the trail in an easy gallop.* **2** a long, easy stride. 1 *verb,* **loped, lop ing;** 2 *noun.*
>
> **po ny** (pō′nē), kind of small horse. Ponies are usually less than 5 feet (1¹⁄₂ meters) tall at the shoulder. *noun, plural* **po nies.**
>
> **gloss y** (glô′sē), smooth and shiny. *adjective,* **gloss i er, gloss i est.**
>
> **glum** (glum), gloomy; dismal; sullen: *I felt very glum when my friend moved away. adjective,* **glum mer, glum mest.**

1. Do you see *loped* and *loping* in the entry for *lope?*
2. What letter is dropped from *lope* before *ed* and *ing* are added?
3. Do you see *ponies* in the entry for *pony?*
4. What letter of *pony* changes before *es* is added?
5. Do you see *glossier* and *glossiest* in the entry for *glossy?*
6. What letter of *glossy* changes before *er* and *est* are added?
7. Do you see *glummer* and *glummest* in the entry for *glum?*
8. What letter of *glum* is doubled before *er* and *est* are added?

The spelling of each of the words *lope, pony, glossy,* and *glum* is changed before the endings are added. Any time there is a change in the spelling of a word when an ending is added, this spelling is shown in dark type after the definitions.

Exercise 5

To find the meaning of each numbered word below, which entry word would you look up in your dictionary? Write each number on a piece of paper, and after it write the entry word. Use your dictionary to check your work.

1. thrushes
2. fiercest
3. animals
4. grazing
5. rhinoceroses
6. aviaries
7. grizzlier
8. caged
9. swimming
10. hibernated

BUTTERFLIES

HOW DO WE SPELL YOUR NAME WHEN THERE ARE TWO OF YOU?

► *TEST YOURSELF*

A. The following questions will be answered when you put the listed words in alphabetical order.

  1. Why is a dictionary like a king?
     both   have
     many   pages
  2. What do you do if you want to paint a gray rabbit?
     spray   get
     gray   hare
  3. If a runner gets athlete's foot, what does an astronaut get?
     gets   toe   missile
     an   astronaut
  4. What kind of coat has no buttons, looks like a piece of fruit, and is put on wet?
     a   oozing   coat
     of   paint   orange
  5. What is worse than finding four white worms in your apple?
     white   of   worms
     four   finding   halves
  6. Do you know how long skinny skunks can be caged?
     skunks   skinny   like
     just   short
  7. What is the most important use of thin tiger skin?
     together   the   thin
     tiger   holding tightly

B. Each numbered word below occurs alphabetically between one of the eight pairs of guide words in the second column. Write the number of each word listed. Then match it with the guide words in the second column.

     1. ale   actor/adjacent
     2. amuse   adjective/adore
     3. address   airway/alfalfa
     4. antler   allege/aloft
     5. allow   ample/anchor
     6. admire   anchorage/angry
     7. Arab   anticipation/apart
     8. andiron   April/arctic

C. Look up each numbered word in your dictionary to find its plural form. Write each number, and after it write the plural.

     1. moose   6. hippopotamus
     2. ostrich   7. dormouse
     3. flamingo   8. canary
     4. goose   9. walrus
     5. mongoose   10. grizzly

HOW TO FIND A MEANING

While walking around the zoo, the class came to a large field. The fence had a sign that said "Zebu." But not a single animal was there. Tim had never seen a zebu, and he waited to see if one would come in view. After about five minutes he had to move on, disappointed.

All the way home in the bus, Tim wondered what he had missed. As soon as he could, he looked in the dictionary to see if it could help him. This is what he found:

> **ze bu** (zē′bü *or* zē′byü), an animal like an ox but with a large hump. The zebu is a domestic animal in Asia and eastern Africa. See picture. *noun.*

Now Tim knew what he had missed.

Part of the dictionary entry described the zebu. That part of the entry is called the definition, or meaning.

Next, a sentence told Tim that in some parts of the world the zebu is a domestic animal. That gave him more information.

Lastly, a picture showed Tim exactly what a zebu looked like, and its caption told him the zebu's size.

zebu—up to 5 feet (1½ meters) high at the shoulder

Understanding what you read and hear

"In less than 400 years, about 200 kinds of wild animals have vanished from the earth," the zoo keeper said. "And today, many more are in danger of becoming extinct."

Jean had never heard the word *extinct* before. But she did not think she would have to look it up. The words used with it made its meaning clear to her. She decided that becoming extinct had something to do with vanishing from the earth.

Look up *extinct* in your dictionary, and you will see that she was right.

Jean asked the zoo keeper why certain animals had vanished. "There are several reasons," he replied. "Some animals are hunted for food, or for their fur or feathers. So many are killed that they become rare and gradually disappear.

"Other animals can no longer survive because their habitat has been destroyed."

Jean did not know what *habitat* meant, and the words used with it did not give her a clue. She did not have a dictionary, so she could not look up the word. But you can.

▶TEACH YOURSELF

Look up the entry word *habitat* and read its definition.
1. Now tell what a habitat is in your own words.
2. Write a sentence using the word *habitat.*

Exercise 6

Read the sentences below. See if you can guess the meaning of each underlined word by using clues given by the words used with it. Write each number, and after it write the letter of the meaning you think is right. You can check your answers by looking up the word in your dictionary.

1. People who visit Woburn Abbey in England can see a <u>unique</u> sight—the only herd of Père David's deer in the world.

   a. beautiful   b. one of a kind   c. united

2. Père David was a French priest and <u>naturalist</u> with a great knowledge of plants and animals. He lived in China for a number of years.

   a. student of plants and animals   b. citizen   c. famous person

3. In 1865 he saw some strange-looking deer <u>isolated</u> behind the walls of the emperor's park near Peking. He told European scientists about the deer, which were later named in his honor.

   a. kept apart from others   b. in good health   c. happy

4. The deer's Chinese name meant "four <u>characters</u> that do not fit together." The animal was thought to have the antlers of a deer, the neck of a camel, the tail of a donkey, and the feet of a cow.

   a. kinds of things   b. people in a book   c. puzzles

5. The Chinese were asked many times to send some of the deer to zoos in Europe, and <u>eventually</u> they did so.

   a. right away   b. sadly   c. finally

6. Afterwards, <u>catastrophes</u> including a flood and a war killed all the deer in the emperor's park.

   a. great misfortunes   b. waterfalls   c. deaths

7. The few deer in European zoos were the only <u>survivors</u>. Unless they could be bred, the Père David's deer would disappear.

   a. heroes   b. good ones   c. ones left living

8. An English duke had a <u>vast</u> estate called Woburn Abbey, which contained a very large deer park.

   a. quick   b. tiny   c. extremely large

9. <u>Zoologists</u> agreed that Père David's deer from zoos should be brought there to form a herd.

   a. teachers   b. scientists who study animals   c. zoo animals

10. Young deer were born and the herd <u>expanded</u> until in the 1940's a few deer were given to zoos.

    a. grew larger   b. grew smaller   c. stayed the same

11. In 1956 four Père David's deer were <u>dispatched</u> to the Peking zoo in China.

    a. spotted   b. sent   c. repaired

12. It was an important day when they came back to their first home. They had been saved from <u>extinction</u> halfway around the world.

    a. happening   b. disappearing from the earth   c. sickness

Père David's deer crossing a stream

THE NAME OF THE DEER IS PRONOUNCED (per´ dä vēdz´ dir´).

I DIDN'T ASK BUT THANKS ANYWAY.

Sentences and phrases that help meaning

Sentences and phrases are an important part of the definition of many words in this dictionary. Sentences and phrases help you to understand what a word means by showing how the word is used.

> **con coct** (kon kokt′), prepare; make up: *She concocted a drink made of grape juice and ginger ale. He concocted an excuse to explain his lateness. verb.*

Read the two sentences in the definition of *concoct*. They help you to understand the meaning of *concoct*. They show you how *concoct* is used.

> **mag nif i cent** (mag nif′ə sənt), richly colored or decorated; grand; stately; splendid: *a magnificent palace, a magnificent view of the mountains.*

The two phrases, *a magnificent palace* and *a magnificent view of the mountains*, help you to understand the meaning of *magnificent* by showing you how it is used.

Exercise 7

Look up the definition of each word at the left. Then choose the sentence that illustrates the use of the word. Write each number. Then copy the sentence, filling in the blank with the missing word.

heal
hideous
hilarious
peerless
squander
sparkle

1. The winner of the debate was a _____ speaker.
2. The tiger's paw will _____ in a few days.
3. _____ sounds of laughter came from the next room.
4. See how the jewels in the crown _____.
5. People at the movie screamed when the _____ monster attacked the hero.
6. We must not _____ our natural resources.

Using definitions

While the children ate a snack in the zoo cafeteria, they told stories about animals they had seen.

First Jane told about seeing a moose in Yellowstone Park. Allen had also visited Yellowstone, and told about watching bears beg for food there. Tim topped this with a tale about his family's summer vacation in Ireland.

"We were driving down a narrow dirt road when we saw a donkey pulling a cart ahead of us," he said. "We had to slow down. The donkey mustn't have liked the noise of the car, because it ran right into a bog. It started to sink right away. Its owner tried to get it out, and we offered to help too. Several farmers brought ropes and pieces of timber. But the donkey's struggles only made it sink lower.

"I got really worried when I could only see the donkey's head," Tim continued. "We had to get it out in the next few minutes, or it would die. In the nick of time, the farmers got some timbers underneath the donkey that prevented it from sinking further. Then they used the rope to haul it out."

According to Tim, the donkey showed how grateful it was by sending a shower of mud over everyone!

Jane had brought a notebook to jot down information about the zoo. Since she wasn't sure what a bog was, she wrote this sentence in her notebook:

The donkey ran into a bog.

Later, she checked the dictionary and found this definition:

bog (bog), **1** soft, wet, spongy ground; marsh; swamp.

Jane tried using the definition in place of the word she didn't know in the sentence. There are three parts to the definition. They are separated by semicolons. Each part means almost the same thing. Each part could be used instead of *bog* in the sentence, like this:

The donkey ran into a *bog.*
The donkey ran into *soft, wet, spongy ground.*
The donkey ran into a *marsh.*
The donkey ran into a *swamp.*

Now Jane knows three more ways to say the idea of the sentence she wrote.

▶ **TEACH YOURSELF**

Look up the entry word *precarious* and read its definition. Now read the following sentence:

The donkey was in a precarious position.

1. How many parts does the definition of *precarious* have?
2. On a piece of paper, rewrite the sentence using another word with the same meaning as *precarious.*

Exercise 8

In the following exercise, look up the underlined words in your dictionary. Then choose which of the three meanings listed is the correct one.

1. How would you like to make dinner for thousands of <u>ravenous</u> animals?
   a. noisy   b. very hungry   c. excited
2. Preparing meals for many different kinds of zoo animals is an <u>exacting</u> job.
   a. needing hard work   b. high in rank   c. correct
3. Some animals are <u>carnivorous</u> and others are not.
   a. amusing   b. wild   c. meat-eating
4. Each animal needs the same kind of food it gets in its natural <u>environment.</u>
   a. surroundings   b. diet   c. cage
5. People who plan the animals' meals know that vitamins are <u>essential.</u>
   a. nice   b. good to eat   c. necessary
6. However, the most important thing is to be <u>punctual</u> with the meals.
   a. brave   b. polite   c. on time

I should never have said, "come and get it!"

More than one meaning

"Do chickens have combs?" Sue asked Tony. Tony replied, "Why would a chicken need a comb? Chickens don't have hair."

Tony was only joking. He knew that Sue expected him to answer yes to her question. But Tony knew that the word *comb* has more than one meaning.

This dictionary gives six meanings or definitions for the word *comb.* Here they are.

> **comb** (kōm), **1** piece of metal, rubber, plastic, or bone with teeth, used to arrange or straighten the hair or to hold it in place. **2** anything shaped or used like a comb. One kind of comb cleans and takes out the tangles in wool or flax. **3** straighten; take out tangles in; arrange with a comb: *You should comb your hair every morning.* **4** search through: *We had to comb the whole city before we found our lost dog.* **5** the red, fleshy piece on the top of the head of chickens and some other fowls. **6** honeycomb. 1,2,5,6 *noun,* 3,4 *verb.*

Each definition is numbered to help you find the meaning you're looking for.

▶TEACH YOURSELF

Read the definitions of *comb* again. Tell or write on a piece of paper which definition fits the meaning of *comb* in each of the following sentences.

1. We bought some honey that was still in the comb.
2. We combed and brushed the cat until it was shiny.
3. Some teeth fell out of my pocket comb.
4. Some roosters have very large combs.

Exercise 9

On a piece of paper, write the number of each sentence. Then look up and read the entry for the underlined word. Write the number of the definition used in the sentence.

1. The <u>birth</u> of the twin orangutans took place on Halloween.
2. It was easy for the zoo to <u>name</u> them—Trick and Treat, of course.
3. Trick and Treat live in the zoo <u>nursery</u>.
4. The baby orangutans need a great <u>amount</u> of care, and in many ways they must be treated like human babies.
5. Trick and Treat drink milk from bottles and play with <u>toys</u>
6. They even have their <u>own</u> playpen.
7. A veterinarian checks them often to see that they are getting the <u>proper</u> food and care.
8. They have to be protected from catching <u>colds</u> and other sicknesses from people.
9. Trick and Treat are very <u>playful</u>.
10. Everyone who passes by stops to <u>watch</u> them, and they are one of the biggest attractions in the zoo.

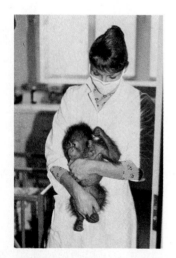

Trick and Treat

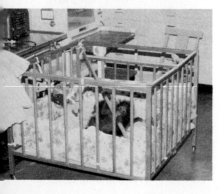

Different words with the same spelling

Ann said she watched a game of cricket on TV. John said he caught a cricket. Did you know that there are two different words that are both spelled *c-r-i-c-k-e-t?* This dictionary shows that these are really two different words by entering them separately.

"I JUST RAN INTO A BIG, BLACK Cricket[1]!"

ANYONE FOR Cricket[2]?

> **crick et[1]** (krik′it), a black insect related to the grasshopper. Male crickets make a chirping noise by rubbing their front wings together. *noun.*

> **crick et[2]** (krik′it), an English outdoor game played by two teams of eleven players each, with ball, bats, and wickets. *noun.*

The small numbers after the entry words tell you that there is at least one other entry word spelled the same way. You may not find the meaning you are looking for in one entry. The small number reminds you to look in another entry for the meaning you want.

▶TEACH YOURSELF

Read the entries for the words spelled *c-r-i-c-k-e-t* again.
>   1. Which cricket was Ann talking about, *cricket[1]* or *cricket[2]?*
>   2. Which cricket was John talking about?

You may wonder what makes *cricket[1]* and *cricket[2]* different words. They are different words because they have different histories. You will learn more about word histories later in these lessons. This dictionary does not give histories for all words. That doesn't mean that some words don't have histories.

Exercise 10

Each of the words underlined below is spelled the same as another word. Look up each word and decide which entry is used in the sentence. Do it this way: 1. last[1]

1. The world's <u>last</u> passenger pigeon died in 1914 in the Cincinnati zoo.
2. Great numbers of these birds used to <u>fly</u> in large flocks.
3. The passenger pigeon was <u>found</u> in most of the United States and was the most common <u>bird</u> in eastern North America.
4. Alexander Wilson, a scientist, <u>saw</u> and studied these birds in the early 1800's.
5. He figured out that a single flock was 240 miles <u>long</u> and contained more than two billion birds.
6. How could such a common <u>kind</u> of bird disappear completely in a hundred years?
7. Hunters <u>shot</u> thousands of passenger pigeons at a time.
8. Sometimes a baited <u>net</u> was used to catch them on the ground.
9. The zoos that had passenger pigeons did not pay attention to the <u>plight</u> of the birds.
10. They were slaughtered so <u>fast</u> that when scientists realized how few were left, it was too late.

the world's last passenger pigeon

► *TEST YOURSELF*

A.   Look up each numbered word and read the entry. Write each number on a piece of paper and answer each question by writing yes or no.

Would you be happy if someone called you:

1. repulsive?	6. extravagant?
2. nonchalant?	7. straightforward?
3. relentless?	8. ludicrous?
4. extraordinary?	9. judicious?
5. melancholy?	10. plucky?

B.   Turn to page 210 and look at the illustration for **fall.** Match each picture to the definition it illustrates.

1. woman falling in space	definition 1
2. trees in fall	definition 5
3. falls of a river	definition 17

C.   Turn to page 62 and look at the illustration for **bonnet.** Match each picture to the definition it illustrates.

1. bonnet worn by a girl	
2. bonnet worn by a baby	definition 1
3. bonnet worn by a man	definition 2
4. Indian bonnet	definition 3

D.   For each of the following groups, look up all the entries spelled the same as the underlined word. Decide which entry is used in each sentence.

1. a. A <u>bear</u> usually sleeps through most of the winter.
   b. These apple trees <u>bear</u> lots of fruit.

2. a. The <u>calf</u> stayed near its mother.
   b. The <u>calf</u> of his leg was bruised.

3. a. Many people hunt <u>quail</u>.
   b. The angry tiger made me <u>quail</u>.

4. a. I tried to <u>duck</u> when I saw the snowball.
   b. Many <u>ducks</u> lived on the lake.

5. a. <u>Bats</u> flew around the haunted house.
   b. He got a new baseball <u>bat</u>.

Crossword puzzle

Use the dictionary to help you solve this crossword puzzle. If you look up a clue word, you will find the answer somewhere in its definition.

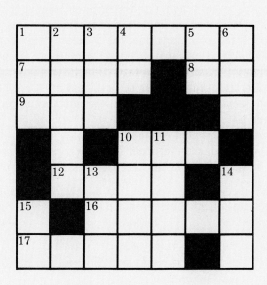

ACROSS

1 sincere
7 hatchets
8 upon
9 dab
10 weep
12 real
16 upright
17 pattern

DOWN

1 opening
2 true
3 seine
4 ourselves
5 nay
6 finish
10 remedy
11 stagger
13 scarlet
14 consumed
15 I'm means "I ____."

HOW TO USE THE PRONUNCIATIONS

Allen handed a piece of paper to each person in the class. "It's a secret message," he said. "The first one who figures it out gets something special."

Laura looked at the paper. This is what she saw:

R rmergv zoo lu blf gl xlnv levi gl nb slfhv uli
xzpv zmw rxv xivzn zg gsivv gsrh zugvimllm.
                                    Zoovm Xifa.

She showed it to her teacher and asked, "What can it mean?" Mr. Lopez said, "This is written in a code in which one letter stands for another letter. Once you know how the code is set up, it will be easy to figure out. Each letter always stands for the same thing."

"Wait a minute," said Laura. "Two capitalized words, *Zoovm Xifa,* are on the third line by themselves. That must be the signature. It must mean *Allen Cruz.* If I write out the alphabet in order, and write the code letters I know underneath, it may tell me something."

Laura wrote the alphabet on one line. Then she thought a bit. She wrote *z* underneath *a, o* underneath *l, v* underneath *e,* and *m* underneath *n.* She did the same with the second part of the name. It looked like this:

a b c d e f g h i j k l m n o p q r s t u v w x y z
z   x   v   o   m   i   f   a

Over every *z* in the secret message she wrote an *a.* Over every *x* she wrote a *c.* Over every *v* she wrote an *e.* She did the same with the other letters she had figured out.

"I found out one whole word," she told Mr. Lopez. "The third word of the message is *all.*"

"I see something else," said Mr. Lopez. "The first word has only one letter. Since you already know what letter stands for *a,* this must stand for *I.*"

Laura looked at the alphabet again. Suddenly she got an idea. She thought she knew what the code was.

She worked for a few minutes, and then read the secret message to the class.

"I invite all of you to come over to my house for
cake and ice cream at three this afternoon.
                                    Allen Cruz."

Mr. Lopez said, "That was very good, Laura. And Allen, that was certainly an interesting way to write out your invitations. I'm glad this happened today, because we are going to learn about a different kind of code. When you can figure out this code, you can *say* any word in the English language."

In a code, one thing acts as a symbol for another. It may be a letter that acts as a symbol for another letter, as in Allen's code. It may be a picture that stands for a word or a sound, as in ancient Egyptian writing. It may be another type of symbol.

CHALLENGE:
Now that you know the message, can you guess what Laura's idea was?

Once you know what each symbol stands for, you can understand the meaning. Each symbol stands for only one thing.

Your dictionary uses a type of code. Do you know where?

cough (kôf) **call** (kôl)

Your dictionary tells you how to pronounce words by using symbols for sounds.

Symbols that stand for sounds

In this dictionary, the pronunciations come right after the entry word like this:

cat (kat) ← PRONUNCIATION

In pronunciations, letters of the alphabet are used to stand for sounds. When letters are used in pronunciations, they are called pronunciation symbols.

Here are some words followed by their pronunciations.

jam (jam)	**lip** (lip)	**gulf** (gulf)	**vend** (vend)
drop (drop)	**wag** (wag)	**yak** (yak)	**hunt** (hunt)
plan (plan)	**bend** (bend)	**hot** (hot)	**win** (win)
nut (nut)	**wisp** (wisp)	**zip** (zip)	**rend** (rend)
pad (pad)	**must** (must)	**trim** (trim)	**bat** (bat)
fan (fan)	**mask** (mask)	**yelp** (yelp)	**bulk** (bulk)

If you looked carefully at the words and their pronunciations, you may have noticed something interesting. Each word is pronounced just as it is spelled.

If you are able to pronounce all the words above, you already know 23 pronunciation symbols. In this dictionary, 23 letters of the alphabet are used as pronunciation symbols. Each letter stands for only one sound. It is the sound that the letter usually spells.

If all words were pronounced just as they are spelled, a dictionary would not have to give pronunciations. But all words are not pronounced as they are spelled. Here are some words along with their pronunciations. You probably know the words. Notice how much easier the pronunciation of each word is than its spelling.

edge (ej) **knock** (nok) **lamb** (lam) **wrap** (rap)

The pronunciation key

You may not remember what sound every pronunciation symbol stands for. You don't have to. Open your dictionary to the inside of the front or back cover. Here you will see the pronunciation key. It is a list of all the pronunciation symbols used in this dictionary.

You already know 23 pronunciation symbols. They are the same as letters of the alphabet. Let's see how the key can help you remember what sound some of these symbols stand for.

Look at the symbol (g). Pronounce the words *go* and *bag*. They follow the symbol. *Go* and *bag* are called key words. The sound that the symbol (g) stands for is the sound that you hear in *go* and *bag*.

Now look at the symbol (a). Pronounce the key words *hat* and *cap*. The sound (a) is the same sound you hear in *hat* and *cap*.

THIS KEY IS AT THE TOP OF EVERY RIGHT-HAND PAGE.

THESE SYMBOLS ARE IN THE SHORT PRONUNCIATION KEY.

a	hat
ā	age
ä	far
e	let
ē	equal
ėr	term
i	it
ī	ice
o	hot
ō	open
ô	order
oi	oil
ou	out
u	cup
ù	put
ü	rule
ch	child
ng	long
sh	she
th	thin
ŦH	then
zh	measure

ə = { a in about
e in taken
i in pencil
o in lemon
u in circus

▶**TEACH YOURSELF**

1. Look at the symbol (e). Pronounce its key words *let* and *best*. Which of the following words has the sound (e) in it?

    bat   bet   but   bit

2. Look at the symbol (j). Pronounce its key words *jam* and *enjoy*. Which of the following words has the sound (j) in it?

    ridge   rig   rug

When you become familiar with the pronunciation key inside the covers of your book, turn to any right-hand page of your dictionary. Look at the top of the outside column. Here is a short pronunciation key. It, too, shows pronunciation symbols with a key word. If you forget what a pronunciation symbol stands for, you may find it here.

Exercise 11

From the two words at the right, choose the one in which you hear the sound on the left. Do it like this: 1. man

1.	(a)	main	man
2.	(b)	lab	lamb
3.	(o)	got	goat
4.	(i)	pin	pine
5.	(k)	cent	can't
6.	(u)	cut	cute
7.	(g)	germ	get
8.	(e)	met	meat
9.	(f)	laugh	bough
10.	(s)	his	hiss

Vowels with special marks

When you looked at the pronunciation key, you saw more than 23 pronunciation symbols. All but one of the remaining pronunciation symbols are letters of the alphabet, too. Eight of them are the vowel letters *a, e, i, o,* and *u* with special marks over them.

You already know that the vowel letters *a, e, i, o,* and *u* without marks over them are used as pronunciation symbols. They stand for the short vowel sounds. Four vowel letters with marks over them are used as pronunciation symbols for the long vowel sounds. These symbols are (ā), (ē), (ī), and (ō). The long *u* is actually a combination of two sounds. It takes two symbols to show the long *u* pronunciation.

▶ **TEACH YOURSELF A**

1. Look at the pronunciation key and find the symbol (ā).
   Pronounce its key words *age* and *face.* Which one of the words
   below has the sound (ā) in it?

   bat   bait

2. Look at the pronunciation key and find the symbol (ē).
   Pronounce its key words *equal* and *be.* Which one of the words
   below has the sound (ē) in it?

   fell   feel

3. Look at the pronunciation key and find the symbol (ī). Pronounce
   its key words *ice* and *five.* Which one of the words below has the
   sound (ī) in it?

   kite   kit

4. Look at the pronunciation key and find the symbol (ō).
   Pronounce its key words *open* and *go.* Which one of the words
   below has the sound (ō) in it?

   note   not

Four other pronunciation symbols are vowel letters with marks
over them. They are (ä) as in *father* and *far*, (ô) as in *order* and *all*,
(u̇) as in *full* and *put*, and (ü) as in *rule* and *move*.

▶ **TEACH YOURSELF B**

1. Say the key words for the sound (ä) again. Which of these words
   has the sound (ä) in it?

   farm   form

2. Say the key words for the sound (ô). Which of these words has
   the sound (ô) in it?

   born   barn

3. Say the key words for the sound (u̇). Which of these words has
   the sound (u̇) in it?

   buck   book

4. Say the key words for the sound (ü). Which of these words has
   the sound (ü) in it?

   pool   pole

5. Pronounce the word *mule* (myül). The word *mule* is pronounced
   with a long *u.* The symbols (yü) together stand for this
   pronunciation. Which of the following words has (yü) in its
   pronunciation?

   cube   cub

Exercise 12

Some of the birds the class saw in the zoo's aviary are pictured below. Each bird is numbered and its name is given in pronunciation symbols. The spellings of the names are given at the side. Write each number. Pronounce the bird's name, using the pronunciation key to help you. Then choose from the list at the side the word you have pronounced.

lark
hawk
teal
kite
loon
crow
snipe
rook
quail
goose
stork
jay

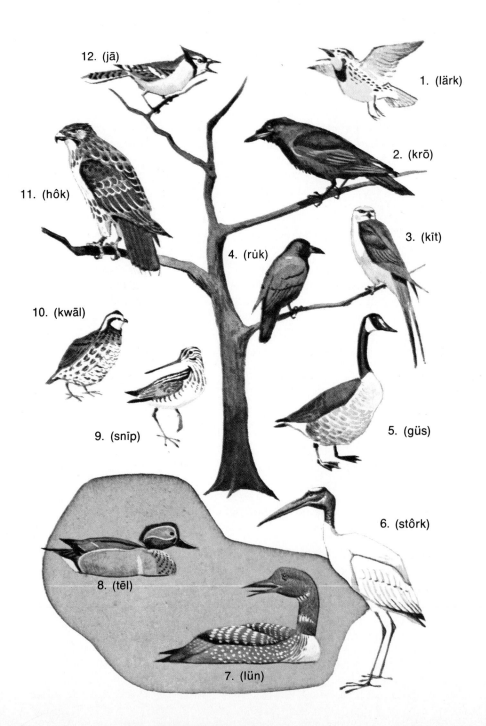

12. (jā)
1. (lärk)
2. (krō)
11. (hôk)
3. (kīt)
4. (ruk)
10. (kwāl)
9. (snīp)
5. (güs)
6. (stôrk)
8. (tēl)
7. (lün)

Two-letter symbols

All but one of the rest of the pronunciation symbols are made up of two letters. Two of these pronunciation symbols are for vowel sounds. They are (oi) and (ou). The sound (oi) is the sound you hear in the words *oil* and *voice.* The sound (ou) is the sound you hear in *house* and *out.*

▶TEACH YOURSELF A

1. Which one of the following words has the sound (oi) in it?

toy   toe   town

2. Which one of the following words has the sound (ou) in it?

coat   count   cot

Another two-letter pronunciation symbol is (ėr). It has the sound you hear in *term* and *learn.* It has the sound you hear in the words *fir, fur, word,* and *journey,* too. You can see from these words that the sound (ėr) is spelled many ways.

The two-letter symbol (ng) stands for the sound that the letters *ng* usually spell. It is the sound you hear in *long* and *bring.*

You are used to seeing the letters *ch* together in words. You are used to seeing *sh* and *th,* too. Each of these letter combinations usually spells a certain sound. These letter combinations are used as pronunciation symbols. Each symbol stands for the sound it usually spells. The symbol (ch) stands for the sound you hear in *child* and *much.* The symbol (sh) stands for the sound you hear in *she* and *rush.* The symbol (th) stands for the sound you hear in *thin* and *both.*

There are two more symbols that are made up of two letters. They are (ᴛʜ) and (zh). The sound (ᴛʜ) is closely related to the sound (th). The word *thin* begins with the sound (th). The word *both* ends with the sound (th). The word *then* begins with the sound (ᴛʜ). The word *smooth* ends with the sound (ᴛʜ). Can you hear the difference between the sounds (th) and (ᴛʜ)?

▶TEACH YOURSELF B

1. Which words below have the sound (th) in them?

think   this   breathe   breath   those   throw

2. Which words above have the sound (ᴛʜ) in them?

The sound (zh) is very close to the sound (sh). The word *mesh* has the sound (sh) in it. The word *measure* has the sound (zh) in it. Can you hear the difference between these two sounds? The sound (zh) usually comes in the middle of a word.

hat shep'sŭt

Exercise 13

In each sentence below, pick the correct pronunciation for the underlined word. Write the number of each sentence, and then write the letter of the correct pronunciation. Do it like this: 1. a.

a. (jēn) b. (zhēn)   1. <u>Jean</u> had a fine time at the zoo.

a. (lėrn) b. (lēn)   2. She wanted to <u>learn</u> more about the history of zoos.

a. (thinz) b. (thingz)   3. A book in the library told her many interesting <u>things</u>.

a. (doun) b. (dun)   4. Zoos have existed <u>down</u> through the years since the beginning of history.

a. (four) b. (fôr)   5. More than <u>four</u> thousand years ago the rulers of Egypt collected animals.

a. (ᴛHat) b. (thangk)   6. At <u>that</u> time Egypt had a queen called Hatshepsut who loved animals.

a. (kash) b. (kach)   7. She sent people on trips to <u>catch</u> wild animals and bring them back for her zoo.

a. (fond) b. (found)   8. On one trip they <u>found</u> monkeys, leopards, and a giraffe.

a. (fėrst) b. (firs)   9. The giraffe was the <u>first</u> of its kind to be seen in Egypt.

a. (jėrnd) b. (joind)   10. It caused a great sensation when it <u>joined</u> the zoo.

a. (lông) b. (lōn)   11. A very <u>long</u> time ago, a Chinese emperor had a zoo called "the garden of intelligence."

a. (thēm) b. (ᴛHem)   12. Jean learned that people have always liked to look at animals and to learn about <u>them</u>.

▶ TEST YOURSELF

A.   On a piece of paper, write each of the numbers below. Then say each pronunciation, using the pronunciation key if you need help. After each number, write the word you have pronounced. Spellings of the words used are given at the left.

all	pile
car	pill
cave	rock
chew	rough
laugh	says
look	these
luck	think
phone	

1. (laf)   6. (pīl)   11. (kär)
2. (pil)   7. (lùk)   12. (ôl)
3. (rok)   8. (fōn)   13. (ᴛHēz)
4. (sez)   9. (luk)   14. (chü)
5. (ruf)   10. (thingk)   15. (kāv)

B. Tell which word on the right rhymes with the numbered word on the left. Use the dictionary to help you. Then write each number and after it write the word that rhymes. Do it like this: 1. mile

1. aisle	sail	mile	hazel
2. shoe	toe	show	through
3. plaid	pad	said	paid
4. whir	hear	poor	purr
5. cough	trough	bough	rough
6. pear	fear	bear	fir
7. feign	mean	sign	rain
8. suite	feet	fruit	put

Syllables and accent

Each part of a word that has one vowel sound in it is called a syllable.

day (dā)   **dai ly** (dā′lē)

The word *day* has one vowel sound (ā). *Day* has one syllable. The word *daily* has two vowel sounds (ā) and (ē). *Daily* has two syllables.

▶TEACH YOURSELF

Say each word below and look at its pronunciation.

arm (ärm)   **ar my** (är′mē)
mouth (mouth)   **mouth ful** (mouth′fúl)
tax (taks)   **tax i** (tak′sē)
high (hī)   **O hi o** (ō hī′ō)

1. How many syllables do the words in the first list have?
2. How many syllables do the first three words in the second list have?
3. How many syllables does the word *Ohio* have?

The words *army, mouthful,* and *taxi* all have two syllables. The word *Ohio* has three syllables. If you look at the way the entry word is written, you can tell how many syllables a word has. There is a space left between syllables in the entry word.

You can usually tell how many syllables a word has by looking at its pronunciation, too. Look again at the words above that have more than one syllable. You see either a space between syllables or a mark (′). This mark is called an accent mark. An accent mark comes after an accented syllable. You say an accented syllable with more force than you say the other syllables.

Exercise 14

Listed below are the entry words and pronunciations of some animals the class saw at the zoo. Write each number, and after it write the number of syllables in the word. For each word of more than one syllable, tell which syllable is accented.

1. **py thon** (pī′thon)
2. **ba boon** (ba bün′)
3. **moose** (müs)
4. **os trich** (ôs′trich)
5. **o ri ole** (ôr′ē ōl)

6. **jag uar** (jag′wär)
7. **deer** (dir)
8. **pen guin** (pen′gwin)
9. **rac coon** (ra kün′)
10. **par tridge** (pär′trij)

baboon

oriole

The schwa

There is one pronunciation symbol we haven't talked about. It looks like this: (ə). This symbol is called the *schwa* (shwä). It is a vowel sound. It is heard only in unaccented syllables. The sound (ə) is spelled many different ways, as you can see from its key words.

The sound (ə) is the sound of:

a in **a bout** (ə bout′)
e in **tak en** (tā′kən)
i in **pen cil** (pen′səl)
o in **lem on** (lem′ən)
u in **cir cus** (sėr′kəs)

Exercise 15

The schwa (ə) sound is used in pronouncing each of the following words. Write down each word, and underline the letter or letters that stand for the sound represented by (ə).

favor	pursue	leopard
giraffe	tower	mountain
tortoise	buffalo	curious

▶ *TEST YOURSELF*

Look at each picture. Then pick out the correct pronunciation. Write the number of each picture, and after it write the letter before the correct pronunciation. Do it like this: 1. b.

1.   a. (grin)   b. (grēn)   c. (krēm)

2.   a. (oks)   b. (ōks)   c. (ôks)

3.   a. (klōk)   b. (kluk)   c. (klok)

4.   a. (wôrm)   b. (werm)   c. (wôrn)

5.   a. (brēd)   b. (breth)   c. (bred)

6.   a. (ə pēl′)   b. (ap′əl)   c. (ə pôl′)

7.   a. (san′dē)   b. (san′dl)   c. (sand′wich)

8.   a. (pik′chər)   b. (pich′ər)   c. (pik′əl)

Secondary accents

Many words have more than one accented syllable. The words below, which are compound words, have two accented syllables. Say the words and look at their pronunciations.

hand spring (hand′spring′)   **bas ket ball** (bas′kit bôl′)

You already know that the mark (′) comes after the syllable you say with the most force. The accent mark (′) is a primary accent mark. The lighter mark (′) is an accent mark, too. It is a secondary accent mark. It comes after a syllable that you say with more force than a syllable with no accent mark, but not as forcefully as a syllable with a primary accent mark.

Sometimes a compound word has two syllables that are pronounced with equal force. Both syllables will be followed by a primary accent mark in the pronunciation.

jet-pro pelled (jet′prə peld′)

Many words besides compound words have more than one accented syllable.

►TEACH YOURSELF

hel i cop ter (hel′ə kop′tər)

1. Which syllable in the word *helicopter* has a primary accent?
2. Which syllable in the word *helicopter* has a secondary accent?

Exercise 16

At the left below are the pronunciations of six words. Write each
number, then say the word from its pronunciation, and write the
spelling of the word. The spellings are listed at the right.

1. (hip′ə pot′ə məs)	copperhead
2. (pē′kok′)	orangutan
3. (lā′dē bug′)	salamander
4. (ô rang′ù tan′)	peacock
5. (kop′ər hed′)	hippopotamus
6. (sal′ə man′dər)	ladybug

(hip′ə pot′ə məs)

Pronunciation and meaning

Sometimes when the meaning of a word changes, its pronunciation
changes, too.

> **per mit** (pər mit′ *for 1;* pėr′mit *for 2*), **1** let; allow:
> *My parents will not permit me to stay up late. The
> law does not permit smoking in this store.* **2** a formal
> written order giving permission to do something:
> *Have you a permit to fish in this lake?* 1 *verb,*
> **per mit ted, per mit ting;** 2 *noun.*

Notice that the pronunciation tells you that the word is
pronounced (pər mit′) when you use it with the first meaning. The
word is pronounced (pėr′mit) when you use it with the second
meaning.

►TEACH YOURSELF

How is *permit* pronounced in the following sentence?
a. (pər mit′)   b. (pėr′mit)
My parents signed a permit so that I could go on the field trip.

Exercise 17

Read each of the following sentences. Then check your dictionary and decide which pronunciation of the underlined word you would use. Write your answer like this: 1. b.

1. Mr. Lopez likes to <u>conduct</u> his class on trips like the one to the zoo.

    a. (kon′dukt)
    b. (kən dukt′)

2. He told the students to notice how the zoo is able to <u>confine</u> each type of animal in its own area.

    a. (kən fīn′)
    b. (kon′fīn)

3. This takes away the possibility of <u>conflict</u> between animals of different kinds.

    a. (kon′flikt)
    b. (kən flikt′)

4. When animals of the same family, such as lions and leopards, are located in one area it is easy to <u>contrast</u> them.

    a. (kon′trast)
    b. (kən trast′)

5. Modern zoos, by using moats instead of cages, <u>present</u> a very realistic view of how wild animals live in nature.

    a. (pri zent′)
    b. (prez′nt)

6. Zoos have made great <u>progress</u> from the days when a zoo animal spent its life in a tiny cage.

    a. (prog′res)
    b. (prə gres′)

7. However, people who build zoos are still working to design the <u>perfect</u> zoo.

    a. (pėr′fikt)
    b. (pər fekt′)

Which way do you say it?

How do you say the word *either?* Have you ever heard anyone say it another way? Did you wonder if one pronunciation is right and one is wrong? You can find out by looking up the pronunciation of *either* in your dictionary. Here's what it says.

ei ther (ē′ᵺər *or* ī′ᵺər)

When you see two pronunciations given for a word, you know that either one is correct.

Here are some more words that have two pronunciations. Which way do you say these words?

Col o rad o (kol′ə rad′ō *or* kol′ə rä′dō)
car a mel (kar′ə məl *or* kär′məl)
a dult (ə dult′ *or* ad′ult)
creek (krēk *or* krik)
route (rüt *or* rout)
to ma to (tə mā′tō *or* tə mä′tō)

Exercise 18

The names of these zoo animals can be pronounced more than one way. Write down the number that appears before each name. After it write the letter that appears before the pronunciation you use.

ocelot

1. chimpanzee	a. (chim′pan zē′)	or	b. (chim pan′zē)
2. ocelot	a. (ō′sə lot)	or	b. (os′ə lot)
3. coyote	a. (kī ō′tē)	or	b. (kī′ōt)
4. zebu	a. (zē′bü)	or	b. (zē′byü)
5. bison	a. (bī′sn)	or	b. (bī′zn)

MORE ABOUT MEANING

Mr. Lopez read a story to the class in the bus as they were going home from the zoo. Here it is:

> "It's <u>raining cats and dogs</u> outside," said Mrs. Jones, "but Lynn and Jim are not home yet."
> Just then the children came in, wet and laughing. Mrs. Jones <u>smelled a rat</u>, and decided to find out what had happened.
> "We were just <u>horsing around</u>," said Lynn. But Jim <u>let the cat out of the bag.</u>
> "Jerry Smith <u>got my goat</u> in school today. So we decided to <u>cook his goose</u>. Lynn and I filled two buckets with water. Then we threw it all over him as he walked up his driveway. You'll think our manners have <u>gone to the dogs</u>, but we really <u>made a monkey out of him</u>."
> "When the joke was on him," said Lynn, "he thought it was a <u>horse of a different color</u>. But after we <u>talked turkey</u>, he decided to <u>eat crow</u>, and said he was sorry. So now we're friends again."

"Did you notice anything strange about the story?" Mr. Lopez asked.

"There are a lot of different animals in it," said Tim.

"That's not quite it," said Laura. "Different animals are mentioned, but the people are not really talking about the animals."

"That's it," said Mr. Lopez. "Sometimes words are used together to mean something different from what you would expect. For instance, the meaning of *let the cat out of the bag* has nothing to do with cats or bags. The phrase, or group of words, has a meaning of its own. We use such phrases to make our speech livelier."

To help you locate these phrases in the story above, they have been underlined. To locate them in your dictionary, look under the most important word in the phrase. Sometimes you will have to look in more than one place, if several words seem important.

These special meanings are called idioms. They are usually listed at the end of the dictionary entry, in dark type:

> **cat** (kat), **1** a small, furry animal, often kept as a pet or for catching mice and rats. **2** any animal of the group including cats, lions, tigers, and leopards. *noun.*
> **let the cat out of the bag,** tell a secret.
> **rain cats and dogs,** pour down rain very hard.

What did Jim really do when he let the cat out of the bag?

Exercise 19

1. Write down each of the underlined idioms in the story above. Then find each idiom in your dictionary. After each idiom on your list write the entry word under which you found it.

2. Look up the idioms at the right in your dictionary. Then use each of them in a sentence.

1. meet halfway
2. lend a hand
3. rough it
4. beat around the bush
5. brush up on
6. drink in
7. at a loss
8. roll up

replay
playful
playfully
un**play**ful
playfulness
player

Prefixes and suffixes

Many words with prefixes and suffixes are entry words in your dictionary.

> **re build** (rē bild′), build again or anew. *verb,*
> **re built, re build ing.**

> **build er** (bil′dər), **1** person or animal that builds:
> *The pioneers were the builders of the West. Beavers*
> *are builders.* **2** person whose business is
> constructing buildings. *noun.*

Some words with prefixes and suffixes are not entry words in your dictionary. But you can find out what these words mean.

Let's say that you do not know the meaning of the word *nontoxic* in the following sentence.

> This paint is nontoxic.

You look for *nontoxic* in your dictionary and find that it is not an entry word. So you look up *toxic* and find the meaning:

> poisonous: *Fumes from an automobile are toxic.*

Now you look up the prefix *non-*. You find:

> **non-,** prefix meaning: **1** not; not a: *Non*breakable
> means *not* breakable. *Non*member means *not a*
> member. **2** opposite of; lack of: *Non*agreement
> means the *opposite of* or *lack of* agreement.

Now you can figure out that the sentence "This paint is nontoxic" means "This paint is not poisonous."

You can find out the meaning of a word with a suffix in the same way. You look up the meaning of the word to which the suffix was added. Then you look up the suffix. You put the two meanings together to get the meaning of the whole word.

▶ TEACH YOURSELF

1. The word *scoffer* is not an entry word in your dictionary. If you didn't know the meaning of *scoffer,* what word would you look up?
2. What suffix would you look up?

> **scoff** (skôf), make fun to show one does not
> believe something; mock: *We scoffed at the idea of*
> *swimming in three inches of water. verb.*

> **-er**[1]**,** suffix meaning person or thing that _____s:
> Follow*er* means a *person or thing that* follow*s.*

3. Is a scoffer a person?
4. What does a person who scoffs do?
5. Write your own definition for the word *scoffer.*

Exercise 20

The underlined words in the sentences below are not entry words in your dictionary. To find the meaning of each word, you may have to look up the meaning of its prefix or suffix. You may also have to look up the meaning of the word to which the prefix or suffix is added. Write each number, and after it write the meaning of the sentence in your own words.

1. These curtains are made of <u>nonflammable</u> cloth.   non-
2. Mother is going to <u>repaint</u> my room.   re-
3. Even in the scary part of the movie, I was <u>unafraid</u>.   un-
4. We had been <u>forewarned</u> that a storm was coming.   fore-
5. There was <u>disunity</u> among the members of the club.   dis-
6. The queen gave a <u>splendorous</u> ball.   -ous
7. This pudding is <u>lumpy</u>.   -y
8. Our car's seat belts are <u>adjustable</u>.   -able
9. What is the name of that large bird with the <u>pinkish</u> feathers?   -ish
10. His <u>frankness</u> helped him win the election.   -ness

painful

nonstop

powerful

deeply   unlock

wealthy

preschool

dangerous

Word histories

Saki was an old cat who spent his days sleeping in the sun. He had just curled up in his favorite chair for his afternoon nap.

Suddenly he had an idea. He packed his lilac pajamas in a suitcase. "I'm going on a journey to visit my wild cat relatives in the jungle," he meowed. "I'm tired of being treated like a robot."

The sky was blue as he ran outdoors. He passed several houses, sniffing the aroma of gumbo, yams, and spaghetti. He wondered how far the jungle was, and if he would need a yacht to get there. Saki could not swim. He hoped he would not run into a typhoon.

He heard loud roars. "I'm not sure what that is," he thought. "It can't be a dinosaur, and it isn't a spaniel or a dachshund." He ran toward the sound, and soon he came to a zoo. Saki thought he had reached the jungle. He passed a rhinoceros, a hippopotamus, a yak, a moose, and an alligator. Then he passed a walrus and an orangutan. "Where are the big cats?" he asked. "Next door," answered an elephant, "but I'd stay out of there if I were you. You might end up in an ambulance."

Saki ran to the next building. He went into the tiger's cage to introduce himself. The tiger growled and flexed his muscles. Still, Saki did not panic. After all, the tiger was a relative! Saki began to yowl as the tiger got ready to pounce. Before he could foil the attack the tiger grabbed him and——
The old cat woke with a start. He stretched himself, looked at the clock, and walked over to his food dish. Time for another meal—and tonight he was having a barbecue.

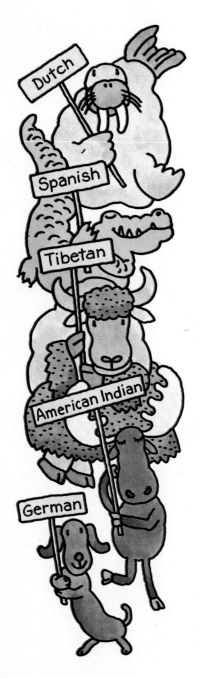

Mr. Lopez read the story above to the class. "If you can understand this," he said, "you know words from at least 17 different languages. Every word has its own history. Some started as English words spelled just as they are now, and have always meant the same thing. Some words have come to us from other languages. Some came from more than one word. Some came from people's names, and some came from the names of places."

Dinosaur is one of the words used in the story. Some entries in this dictionary, including dinosaur and all the other underlined words in the story, include word histories. The history is at the end of the entry. It is inside square brackets like this [ ].

> **di no saur** (dī/nə sôr), one of a group of extinct reptiles that lived many millions of years ago. Some dinosaurs were bigger than elephants. Some were smaller than cats. *noun.* [*Dinosaur* comes from Greek words meaning "terrible lizard."]

The word history tells you that dinosaur came from Greek words meaning "terrible lizard."

Exercise 21

1. Pick ten words that are underlined in the story and write them on
   a piece of paper. Look each of them up in the dictionary and read
   the word history. After each word, write the language that it
   came from.
2. How many languages are on your list?

DANDELION COMES FROM
FRENCH WORDS MEANING
"LION'S TOOTH."

THAT'S BECAUSE YOU
HAVE TOOTHED LEAVES.

HOW TO USE THIS DICTIONARY FOR SPELLING AND WRITING

HOW
DO YOU
SPELL
THISTLE?

LOOK
IT UP!

When Mr. Lopez assigned a class report, Kevin decided to write his on the balance of nature. The trip to the zoo had given him a lot of ideas. But Kevin was not good at spelling. As soon as he started to write, he began to ask his mother how to spell first one word and then another.

"How do you spell *balance?*"

"B-a-l-a-n-c-e," Kevin's mother replied.

"How do you spell *nature?*"

"N-a-t-u-r-e."

"Thanks. Now how do you spell—"

Kevin's mother interrupted him right there. "Please, Kevin, I'm busy right now," she said. "Why don't you go ahead and write the report. If you don't know how to spell a word, leave a blank. Then, after I finish what I'm doing, I'll help you spell the words you don't know."

When Kevin had finished, his report looked funny. It was full of blanks! The report is printed below. Each blank in it is numbered. To the left are three spellings for the word Kevin wanted to put in each blank. One of the three spellings is correct. The others are wrong.

If you use your dictionary to help you, you can complete Kevin's report and spell every word correctly. Try it.

Exercise 22

1. feild, field, feeled
2. usually, usally, usualy
3. effect, affecked, affect
4. influance, influans, influence
5. whether, weather, wether
6. enemies, enamies, ennemies
7. weazels, weezels, weasels
8. increase, encrease, increese
9. environement, environment, invirenment
10. altar, allter, alter
11. extinkt, extinct, exstinked
12. speeshies, spechies, species

The Balance of Nature

In each area, such as a ___(1)___ or a pond, many kinds of plants and animals live. The number of each kind of plant or animal ___(2)___ stays about the same. This is called the balance of nature.

The air, the water, the soil, and the climate ___(3)___ plants and animals. Plants and animals also ___(4)___ each other. When the ___(5)___ is good during the year, lots of plants grow. Then animals like rabbits, which eat the plants, are well fed. The rabbit population becomes larger. After a while there are too many rabbits, and all of them have a hard time finding food. Some rabbits become weak and sick. They also become easier targets for such natural ___(6)___ as hawks, ___(7)___, cats, and dogs. This causes the rabbit population to drop. Then the rabbits start to ___(8)___ again until they are in balance with their ___(9)___. When something happens to ___(10)___ the balance of nature, animals may become ___(11)___.

Keeping nature in balance is important. If we can do this, zoos will not have to use the words "Vanishing ___(12)___" to describe so many kinds of wild animals.

Words with more than one spelling

Sue decided to write her report about North American wild animals. She had to look up several animals in her dictionary. Here are some of the entries she looked up:

wol ve rine or **wol ve rene** (wûl′və rēn′), a heavily built, meat-eating animal living in the northern parts of the world. See picture. *noun.*

wolverine—about 3½ feet (1 meter) long with the tail

rac coon (ra kün′), **1** a small, grayish animal with a bushy ringed tail, that lives in wooded areas near water, and is active at night. See picture. **2** its fur. *noun.* Also spelled **racoon.**

ra coon (ra kün′), raccoon. *noun.*

raccoon (definition 1)
32 inches (80 centimeters) long with the tail

Most words are correctly spelled in only one way. But these words have more than one correct spelling. The entries above show you how the dictionary treats words that have more than one correct spelling.

Sometimes the spellings are listed together and defined as one entry, like the first entry above. The more commonly used spelling is given first. Sometimes the spellings of words are listed separately, like *raccoon* and *racoon.* Then the definitions are given after the more common spelling. After the definitions come the words "Also spelled" followed by the other spelling.

Exercise 23

Here are some of the other words Sue looked up for her report. Use your dictionary to find another correct spelling for each word. Write each number on a piece of paper, and after it write the other spelling you found.

1. gray
2. fulfill
3. inclose
4. skillful
5. although
6. through
7. quartet
8. O.K.

I CAN DIVIDE YOUR NAME IN TWO PLACES, BUMBLE BEE.

DANDELION CAN BE DIVIDED IN THREE PLACES.

Dividing words in writing

Sue wanted her report to look very neat. As she got near the end of a line, the next word she wanted to write was *wolverine.* Even if she made her writing smaller, there wasn't room for her to get nine more letters on that line. If she started the word on the next line, a big gap would be left on the line she was on.

Then Sue remembered something Mr. Lopez had said. He told the class that it was all right to divide a long word between syllables. She could put the first part of the word on one line and the rest on the next line. She checked her dictionary to find out how the word is divided. This is how the entry word looked:

wol ve rine

There were two places where she could divide the word. She finished the line by writing *wol-* and started the next line with *verine.* The hyphen would show Mr. Lopez that the rest of the word was written on the next line.

When Sue came near the end of another line, her next word was *hilly.* She looked it up, and the dictionary divided it like this:

hill y

She saw that she could not divide it. Mr. Lopez had said that one letter should not be separated from the rest of the word.

Sue decided to make a chart showing how to divide words. It would help her to remember the rules the next time she had a report to write. She remembered all the things Mr. Lopez had mentioned. She wrote them down, with a few examples of each one. Here is the chart Sue made:

RULES	EXAMPLES		
1. Check words in the dictionary and divide between syllables.	rein- deer	an- imal	ani- mal
2. Don't divide words the dictionary does not divide.	flight		through
3. A word with a hyphen should be divided only at the hyphen.	good- natured		baby- sitter
4. Don't separate a single letter from the rest of the word.	adult		idea

1. o pos sum
2. musk rat
3. a dult
4. bi son
5. cot ton tail
6. four-foot ed
7. al li ga tor
8. cop per head

Exercise 24

Use the rules in Sue's chart to show where each numbered word can be divided in writing. The words have been divided into syllables for you. Copy each word, leaving spaces between the syllables. Then underline any letter after which you can divide the word at the end of a line.

▶ *TEST YOURSELF*

A. Your dictionary tells you interesting things about many subjects. Look up the entry word in parentheses after each question below. Write each number on a piece of paper, and after it give the answer to the question. Sometimes the answer will be found in the entry, sometimes in a picture caption or illustration.

1. How thick is a dime? (metric system)
2. Where is the abacus used? (abacus)
3. Is Africa the largest continent? (Africa)
4. What person was the month of July named after? (July)
5. About how long is an alligator? (alligator)
6. Who was Sequoya? (sequoia)
7. How tall is the Sears Tower? (skyscraper)
8. Where was the first Ferris wheel located? (Ferris wheel)
9. Do you need any special equipment to see an ameba? (ameba)
10. How many basic kinds of fingerprints are there? (fingerprint)
11. What did *Alabama* originally mean? (Alabama)
12. Which is larger, a bald eagle or an armadillo? (armadillo, bald eagle)

B. Look up each entry underlined below. Then on a piece of paper, answer each numbered question *yes* or *no* and give the reason for your answer.

1. Would you buy a dishwasher in a machine shop?
2. Does hearing ghosts in the cellar mean you have low spirits?
3. Do daisies grow in a magnetic field?
4. Are hot dogs allowed in restaurants?
5. Can a person have a square foot?
6. Would you buy a spinning wheel for your family car?
7. Would a veterinarian treat a monkey wrench?
8. When a sick man wants to leave his money to someone, does he write an ill will?
9. Does a lymphatic vessel sail the sea?
10. Would a camper sleep in an oxygen tent?
11. Do ice-cream shops sell nose cones?
12. If you lived in the Rocky Mountains, would you cook with a mountain range?
13. Would you drink milk from a magnifying glass?
14. Would you like to have sweet peas for dinner?
15. Can a sea horse gallop?
16. Would you eat spaghetti with a tuning fork?
17. If your father likes to jog, does your mother have a running mate?
18. Could you learn to play a powder horn?
19. Does a prairie schooner have sails?

The puzzles on this page may be reproduced for classroom use.

STEP PUZZLE
Start this game at PLAY. See if you can reach the GOAL in five steps. Only one letter will change in each step. The definitions below give you a clue to the words.

Clues
1. used to make bricks
2. another word for clothed
3. happy
4. spur

P	L	A	Y

1. | | | | |

2. | | | | |

3. | | | | |

4. | | | | |

G	O	A	L

WORD SQUARE
Look up the clue words below. In their definitions you will find the answers you need to solve the puzzle. The answer for each number should be written both down and across.

Clues
1. resound
2. mince
3. residence
4. unfold

1	2	3	4
2			
3			
4			

The Parts of a Dictionary Entry

1. **The entry word** is printed in heavy black type. It shows how the word is spelled and how it may be divided in writing.

2. **The small raised number** appears when two or more entry words have the same spelling.

3. **The pronunciation** is enclosed in parentheses. In the pronunciation, each letter or other symbol stands for a certain sound. These symbols are explained in the pronunciation key.

4. **The definition** of a word tells its meaning. A word with more than one meaning has numbered definitions, one for each meaning.

5. **A sentence or phrase** to show how the word may be used is printed in slanted type following the definition.

6. **The part-of-speech label** is printed in slanted type. It tells the part of speech of the entry word. When the word is used as more than one part of speech, definition numbers appear before each label.

7. **Word endings and special forms** of entry words are printed in heavy black type. They are given whenever their spelling might cause you trouble.

8. **The word history** appears in square brackets. It tells what language the English word came from and what the word meant in that language.

9. **Idioms** are printed in heavy black type. Each idiom starts a new line. Idioms are word combinations having special definitions that cannot be understood from the meanings of the individual words.

10. **A picture** helps to show what a word means. Some pictures have captions that give additional information or show how the word can be used in a sentence.

at las (at′ləs), book of maps. A big atlas has maps of every country. *noun,* plural **at las es.** [*Atlas* comes from the name of a giant in Greek myths, who held up the sky on his shoulders. His picture often appeared in early books of maps.]

crow[1] (krō), **1** the loud cry of a rooster. **2** make this cry: *The cock crowed as the sun rose.* **3** a happy sound made by a baby. **4** make this sound. **5** boast; show one's happiness and pride: *The winning team crowed over its victory.* 1,3 *noun,* 2,4,5 *verb,* **crowed** (or **crew** for 2), **crowed, crow ing.**

crow[2] (krō), a large, glossy, black bird with a harsh cry. *noun.*

eat crow, be forced to do something very disagreeable.

flex i ble (flek′sə bəl), able to be bent without breaking; not stiff; easily bent in all directions. Leather, rubber, and wire are flexible. See picture. *adjective.*

guin ea pig (gin′ē pig′), a burrowing animal with short ears and no tail. Guinea pigs are kept as pets and used in scientific experiments. See picture.

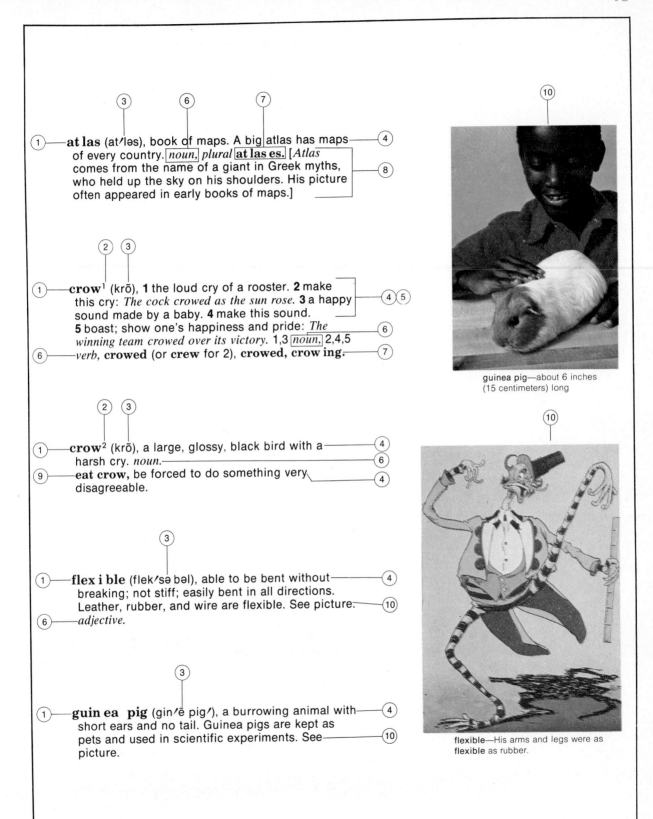

guinea pig—about 6 inches (15 centimeters) long

flexible—His arms and legs were as flexible as rubber.

A a

a hat	i it	oi oil	ch child		a in about
ā age	ī ice	ou out	ng long		e in taken
ä far	o hot	u cup	sh she	ə =	i in pencil
e let	ō open	u̇ put	th thin		o in lemon
ē equal	ô order	ü rule	ŦH then		u in circus
ėr term			zh measure		

A or **a**¹ (ā), the first letter of the English alphabet. There are two *a*'s in *afraid. noun, plural* **A's** or **a's.**

a² (ə *or* ā), **1** any: *Is there a pencil in the box?* **2** one: *Buy a dozen eggs.* **3** every: *Thanksgiving comes once a year. adjective* or *indefinite article.*

a back (ə bak′). **taken aback,** suddenly surprised: *I was taken aback by her angry answer. adverb.*

ab a cus (ab′ə kəs), frame with rows of counters or beads that slide back and forth. Abacuses are used in China, Japan, and Korea for counting. See picture. *noun, plural* **ab a cus es.**

a ban don (ə ban′dən), **1** give up entirely: *We abandoned the idea of a picnic because of the rain.* **2** desert, forsake, or leave without intending to return: *The crew abandoned the sinking ship. verb.*

a ban doned (ə ban′dənd), deserted: *The children often played in the abandoned house. adjective.*

a bashed (ə basht′), embarrassed and confused: *I was abashed by their laughter. adjective.*

a bate (ə bāt′), make or become less: *The storm has abated. verb,* **a bat ed, a bat ing.**

ab bess (ab′is), woman who is the head of an abbey of nuns. *noun, plural* **ab bess es.**

ab bey (ab′ē), **1** the building or buildings where monks or nuns live a religious life. **2** the monks or nuns living there. *noun, plural* **ab beys.**

ab bot (ab′ət), man who is the head of an abbey of monks. *noun.*

ab bre vi ate (ə brē′vē āt), make shorter: *We can abbreviate "hour" to "hr." verb,* **ab bre vi at ed, ab bre vi at ing.**

ab bre vi a tion (ə brē′vē ā′shən), a shortened form: *"Dr." is an abbreviation for "Doctor." noun.*

ab di cate (ab′də kāt), give up (office, power, or authority); resign: *When the king abdicated his throne, his brother became king. verb,* **ab di cat ed, ab di cat ing.**

ab di ca tion (ab′də kā′shən), resigning. *noun.*

ab do men (ab′də mən), **1** the part of the body that contains the stomach, the intestines, and other digestive organs; belly. See picture. **2** the last of the three parts of the body of an insect. See picture. *noun.*

ab dom i nal (ab dom′ə nəl), of the abdomen: *abdominal muscles. adjective.*

ab duct (ab dukt′), kidnap. *verb.*

ab duc tion (ab duk′shən), kidnaping. *noun.*

ab hor (ab hôr′), shrink away from with horror; feel disgust for; hate very, very much: *Many people abhor snakes. verb,* **ab horred, ab hor ring.**

a bide (ə bīd′), put up with; endure: *I can't abide their always being late. verb,* **a bid ed, a bid ing.**

abide by, 1 accept and follow out: *Both teams will abide by the umpire's decision.* **2** remain faithful to: *Abide by your promise.*

a bil i ty (ə bil′ə tē), **1** power: *A horse has the ability*

abacus—When the beads are pushed toward the middle bar, the top ones count as 5 and the bottom ones as 1 each. The number shown is 964,708.

to work. **2** skill: *He has great ability in making jewelry.* **3** power to do some special thing; talent: *Musical ability often shows itself early in life. noun, plural* **a bil i ties.**

ab ject (ab′jekt), wretched; miserable: *Many people still live in abject poverty. adjective.*

a blaze (ə blāz′), on fire; blazing. *adjective.*

a ble (ā′bəl), **1** having enough power, skill, or means: *A cat is able to see in the dark.* **2** having more power or skill than most others have: *She is an able teacher. adjective,* **a bler, a blest.**

-able, suffix meaning: **1** that can be _____ed: An enjoy*able* party means a party *that can be* enjoy*ed.* **2** able, liable, or likely to _____: Break*able* means *liable* to break.

a bly (ā′blē), in an able manner; with skill; well. *adverb.*

ab nor mal (ab nôr′məl), not as it should be; very different from the ordinary conditions; unusual: *It is abnormal for a person to have six fingers on each hand. adjective.*

a board (ə bôrd′), on board; in or on a ship, train, bus, or airplane. *adverb, preposition.*

a bol ish (ə bol′ish), do away with; put an end to: *Many wish that nations would abolish war. verb.*

ab o li tion (ab′ə lish′ən), putting an end to; abolishing: *The abolition of slavery in the United States occurred in 1865. noun.*

a bom i na ble (ə bom′ə nə bəl), **1** hateful;

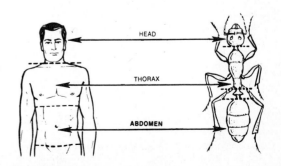

disgusting: *Kidnaping is an abominable act.* **2** very unpleasant: *The weather for the picnic was abominable—rainy, windy, and cold. adjective.*

a bound (ə bound′), be plentiful: *Fish abound in the ocean. verb.*

a bout (ə bout′), **1** of; having something to do with: *"Black Beauty" is a story about a horse.* **2** nearly; almost: *She has about finished her work.* **3** around: *A collar goes about the neck. Look about and tell me what you see.* **4** one after another; by turns: *Turn about is fair play.* **1,3** *preposition,* **2-4** *adverb.*

about to, on the point of; ready to: *The plane is about to take off.*

a bove (ə buv′), **1** in a higher place; overhead: *The sky is above.* **2** higher than; over: *Look above the tall building to see the sun. A captain is above a sergeant.* **3** more than: *Our club has above thirty members—thirty-five, to be exact.* **4** beyond: *Turn at the first corner above the school.* **5** too great in importance for; superior to: *The spoiled child felt above washing dishes.* **1** *adverb,* **2-5** *preposition.*

a breast (ə brest′), side by side. *adverb, adjective.*

a bridge (ə brij′), make shorter, especially by using fewer words: *A long story can be abridged by leaving out unimportant parts. verb,* **a bridged, a bridg ing.**

a broad (ə brôd′), **1** outside one's country: *She is going abroad next year to study in Italy.* **2** out in the open air; outdoors: *My grandfather walks abroad only on warm days.* **3** widely: *The news of the tornado damage was quickly spread abroad. adverb.*

a brupt (ə brupt′), **1** sudden: *The driver made an abrupt turn to avoid another car.* **2** very steep: *The road made an abrupt rise up the hill.* **3** short, sudden, and blunt: *She answered me with an abrupt remark and left. adjective.*

ab scess (ab′ses), a collection of pus in the tissues of some part of the body. An abscess results from an infection and usually makes a painful sore. *noun, plural* **ab scess es.**

ab sence (ab′səns), **1** being away: *My absence from school was caused by illness.* **2** time of being away: *I returned to school after an absence of two days.* **3** being without; lack: *Darkness is the absence of light. noun.*

ab sent (ab′sənt), **1** away; not present: *Three members of the class are absent today.* **2** lacking: *Snow is absent in some countries. adjective.*

ab sen tee (ab′sən tē′), person who is away or stays away. *noun.*

ab sent-mind ed (ab′sənt mīn′did), forgetful; not paying attention to what is going on: *The absent-minded man put salt in his coffee and sugar on his egg. adjective.*

ab so lute (ab′sə lüt), **1** complete; entire: *Try to tell the absolute truth.* **2** not limited in any way: *Long ago some rulers had absolute power. adjective.*

ab so lute ly (ab′sə lüt′lē), **1** completely: *My broken bicycle was absolutely useless.* **2** without doubt; certainly: *This is absolutely the best cake I've ever eaten. adverb.*

ab solve (ab solv′), **1** declare free from sin or blame: *We thought she caused the accident, but the police absolved her after they investigated it.* **2** set free: *I absolve you from your promise to go. verb,* **ab solved, ab solv ing.**

ab sorb (ab sôrb′), **1** take in or suck up (liquids): *The sponge absorbed the spilled milk.* **2** take in and hold: *Rugs absorb sounds and make a house quieter.* **3** take up all the attention of; interest very much. See picture. *verb.*

ab sorb ent (ab sôr′bənt), taking in, or able to take in, moisture, light, or heat: *Absorbent paper is used to dry the hands. adjective.*

ab sorb ing (ab sôr′bing), extremely interesting: *I watched an absorbing program about dolphins on TV last night. adjective.*

ab sorp tion (ab sôrp′shən), **1** act or process of absorbing: *A blotter dries ink by absorption.* **2** condition of being absorbed; great interest: *The absorption of the children in their game was so complete that they did not notice the first few drops of rain. noun.*

ab stain (ab stān′), do without something; hold oneself back: *If you want to lose weight, abstain from eating candy and rich foods. verb.*

ab sti nence (ab′stə nəns), partly or entirely giving up certain pleasures, food, or drink: *Abstinence from candy and desserts helped my father lose weight. noun.*

ab stract (ab′strakt *for 1 and 2;* ab strakt′ *for 3*), **1** thought of apart from any object or real thing: *Sweetness is abstract; a lump of sugar is concrete.* **2** hard to understand; difficult: *The atomic theory of matter is so abstract that it can be fully understood only by advanced students.* **3** take away; remove: *Iron is abstracted from ore.* **1,2** *adjective,* **3** *verb.*

ab surd (ab sėrd′), plainly not true or sensible; foolish; ridiculous: *The idea that the number 13 brings bad luck is absurd. adjective.*

ab surd i ty (ab sėr′də tē), **1** lack of sense; foolishness: *You can see the absurdity of wearing shoes on your head and hats on your feet.* **2** something absurd; something foolish or ridiculous. See picture. *noun, plural* **ab surd i ties.**

a bun dance (ə bun′dəns), great plenty; quantity that is more than enough: *There is an abundance of apples this year. noun.*

a bun dant (ə bun′dənt), more than enough; very plentiful: *The trapper had an abundant supply of food for the winter. adjective.*

a buse (ə byüz′ *for 1,3, and 6;* ə byüs′ *for 2,4,5, and 7*), **1** make bad or wrong use of: *Don't abuse the privilege of using the library by talking too loud.* **2** bad or wrong use: *The people hated the wicked king for his abuse of power.* **3** treat cruelly or roughly: *The children abused the dog by throwing rocks at it.* **4** cruel or rough treatment: *I stopped their abuse of the dog.* **5** a bad practice or custom: *Slavery is an abuse.* **6** scold very severely. **7** a severe scolding. **1,3,6** *verb,* **a bused, a bus ing;** **2,4,5,7** *noun.*

a byss (ə bis′), a bottomless or very great depth; a

a hat	**i** it	**oi** oil	**ch** child	⎧ a in about
ā age	**ī** ice	**ou** out	**ng** long	⎪ e in taken
ä far	**o** hot	**u** cup	**sh** she	**ə** = ⎨ i in pencil
e let	**ō** open	**ù** put	**th** thin	⎪ o in lemon
ē equal	**ô** order	**ü** rule	**ŦH** then	⎩ u in circus
ėr term			**zh** measure	

absorb (definition 3)—She was **absorbed** in reading a good book most of the afternoon.

Courtesy of The Museum of Modern Art

absurdity (definition 2)
I thought the fur-covered dishes were an **absurdity**.

very deep crack in the earth: *They stood at the edge of a cliff overlooking an abyss four thousand feet deep.* See picture. *noun, plural* **a byss es.**

a.c. or **A.C.,** alternating current.

a cad e my (ə kad′ə mē), **1** place for instruction. **2** a private high school. **3** school where some special subject can be studied: *West Point is a military academy. noun, plural* **a cad e mies.**

ac cel e rate (ak sel′ə rāt′), speed up: *The engineer accelerates a train by turning on more power. Sunshine, fresh air, and rest often accelerate a person's recovery from sickness. verb,* **ac cel e rat ed, ac cel e rat ing.**

ac cel e ra tion (ak sel′ə rā′shən), speeding up: *the acceleration of a train. Acceleration of tooth decay is caused by lack of care. noun.*

ac cel e ra tor (ak sel′ə rā′tər), thing that causes an increase in the speed of anything. The pedal or lever that controls the flow of gasoline to an automobile engine is an accelerator. *noun.*

ac cent (ak′sent), **1** the greater force or stronger tone of voice given to certain syllables or words: *In "letter," the accent is on the first syllable.* **2** a mark (′) written or printed to show the spoken force of a syllable, as in *to day* (tə dā′). Some words have two accents, a stronger accent (′) and a weaker accent (′), as in *ac cel e ra tor* (ak sel′ə rā′tər). **3** pronounce or mark with an accent: *Is "acceptable" accented on the first or second syllable?* **4** a different way of pronouncing heard in different parts of the same country, or in the speech of a person speaking a language not his or her own: *My father was born in Germany and speaks English with a German accent.* **5 accents,** tone of voice: *We soothed the child by speaking in tender accents.* 1,2,4,5 *noun,* 3 *verb.*

ac cept (ak sept′), **1** take what is offered or given to one; consent to take: *The teacher accepted our gift.* **2** consent to; say yes to: *She asked me to go to the party and I accepted her invitation.* **3** take as true or satisfactory; believe: *The teacher accepted our excuse.* **4** receive with liking and approval: *I soon accepted the new student as a friend. verb.*

ac cept a ble (ak sep′tə bəl), **1** likely to be gladly received; agreeable: *Flowers are an acceptable gift.* **2** satisfactory: *The singer gave an acceptable performance but it was not outstanding. adjective.*

ac cept ance (ak sep′təns), **1** taking what is offered or given to one: *The teacher's acceptance of the flowers they brought delighted the children.* **2** being accepted: *She was excited by the acceptance of her story by the magazine. noun.*

ac cess (ak′ses), approach to places, things, or persons: *Access to mountain towns is often difficult because of poor roads. All children have access to the library during the afternoon. noun.*

ac ces si ble (ak ses′ə bəl), easy to get at; easy to reach: *A telephone should be put where it will be accessible. adjective.*

ac ces sor y (ak ses′ər ē), **1** something added to help something of more importance: *Her new car has many accessories, including an air conditioner.* **2** added; extra: *His tie supplied an accessory bit of color.* **3** person who has helped in a crime: *By not reporting the theft she became an accessory.* **1,3** *noun, plural* **ac ces sor ies;** **2** *adjective.*

ac ci dent (ak′sə dənt), **1** something harmful or unlucky that happens: *She was hurt in an automobile accident.* **2** something that happens without being planned, intended, wanted, or known in advance: *A series of lucky accidents led the explorer to his discovery. noun.*
by accident, by chance; not on purpose: *I met an old friend by accident.*

ac ci den tal (ak′sə den′tl), happening by chance: *Breaking the lamp was accidental; I did not do it on purpose. adjective.*

ac ci den tal ly (ak′sə den′tl ē), without being planned; by chance; not on purpose. *adverb.*

ac claim (ə klām′), **1** applaud; shout welcome; show approval of: *The crowd acclaimed the winning team.* **2** applause; welcome: *The astronaut was welcomed with great acclaim.* **1** *verb,* **2** *noun.*

ac com mo date (ə kom′ə dāt), **1** hold; have room for: *This airplane is large enough to accommodate 120 passengers.* **2** help out; oblige: *I wanted change for five dollars, but no one could accommodate me.* **3** supply with a place to sleep or live for a time: *Tourists are accommodated here. verb,*
ac com mo dat ed, ac com mo dat ing.

ac com mo dat ing (ə kom′ə dā′ting), obliging: *My teacher was accommodating enough to lend me a dollar. adjective.*

ac com mo da tion (ə kom′ə dā′shən), **1** a help, favor, or convenience: *It will be an accommodation to me if you will meet me tomorrow instead of today.* **2 accommodations,** room or lodging for a time: *Can we find accommodations at a motel for tonight? noun.*

ac com pa ni ment (ə kum′pə nē mənt), anything that goes along with something else: *The rain was an unpleasant accompaniment to our ride. We sang with piano accompaniment. noun.*

ac com pa ny (ə kum′pə nē), **1** go along with: *May we accompany you on your walk? She accompanied the singer on the piano.* **2** be or happen along with: *The rain was accompanied by a high wind. verb,* **ac com pa nied, ac com pa ny ing.**

ac com plice (ə kom′plis), person who aids another in committing a crime: *Without an accomplice to open the door the thief could not have got into the building so easily. noun.*

ac com plish (ə kom′plish), do; carry out: *Did you accomplish your purpose? She can accomplish more in a day than anyone else in class. verb.*

ac com plished (ə kom′plisht), **1** done; carried out: *With their work accomplished the children went out to play.* **2** expert; skilled: *Only an accomplished dancer can perform this ballet. adjective.*

ac com plish ment (ə kom′plish mənt), **1** something that has been done with knowledge, skill, or ability: *The teacher was proud of her pupils' accomplishments.* **2** special skill: *She was a girl of many accomplishments; she could play the guitar, paint a picture, and change a tire equally well.* **3** doing; carrying out: *The accomplishment of his purpose took two months. noun.*

ac cord (ə kôrd′), **1** agree: *His account of the accident accords with yours.* **2** agreement: *Most people are in accord in their desire for peace.* **1** *verb,* **2** *noun.*
of one's own accord, without being asked or without suggestion from anyone else: *We didn't ask for help; they helped of their own accord.*

ac cord ance (ə kôrd′ns), agreement: *What she did was in accordance with what she said. noun.*

ac cord ing ly (ə kôr′ding lē), **1** in agreement with something that has been stated: *These are the rules; you can act accordingly or leave the club.* **2** therefore: *I was told to speak briefly; accordingly I cut short my talk. adverb.*

ac cord ing to (ə kôr′ding tü), **1** in agreement with: *He came according to his promise.* **2** in proportion to: *You will be ranked according to the work you do.* **3** on the authority of: *According to this book a tiger is really a big cat.*

ac cor di on (ə kôr′dē ən), a musical wind instrument with a bellows, metal reeds, and keys. See picture. *noun.*

ac count (ə kount′), **1** a statement telling in detail about an event or thing; explanation: *She gave her parents an account of everything that happened on the class trip.* **2** value: *This torn notebook is of little account.* **3** statement of money received and spent; record of business dealings: *I decided to keep a written account of the way I spend my allowance. All stores, banks, and factories keep accounts. noun.*
account for, 1 tell what has been done with; answer for: *The treasurer of the club had to account for the money paid to her.* **2** explain: *Late frosts accounted for the poor fruit crop.*
on account of, because of; for the reason of: *The game was put off on account of rain.*
on one's account, for one's sake: *Don't wait on*

accordion

my account, I may be late.

take into account, make allowance for; consider: *You must take into account the wishes of all the class in planning a picnic.*

ac count ant (ə koun′tənt), person who examines or manages business accounts. *noun.*

ac cu mu late (ə kyü′myə lāt), pile up; collect: *Dust and cobwebs had accumulated in the empty house. verb,* **ac cu mu lat ed, ac cu mu lat ing.**

ac cu mu la tion (ə kyü′myə lā′shən), **1** material collected; mass: *Their accumulation of old papers filled the attic.* **2** collecting; amassing: *The accumulation of useful knowledge is one result of reading. noun.*

ac cu ra cy (ak′yər ə sē), exactness; correctness; being without errors or mistakes: *Arithmetic problems must be solved with accuracy. noun.*

ac cur ate (ak′yər it), exactly right; correct: *You must be accurate in arithmetic. An airplane pilot must have an accurate watch. adjective.*

ac cu sa tion (ak′yə zā′shən), a charge of being or doing something bad: *The accusation against them was that they had cheated on the exam. noun.*

ac cuse (ə kyüz′), charge with being or doing something bad: *The driver was accused of speeding. verb,* **ac cused, ac cus ing.**

ac cus er (ə kyü′zər), person who accuses another. *noun.*

ac cus tom (ə kus′təm), make familiar by use or habit; get used: *You can accustom yourself to almost any kind of food. verb.*

ac cus tomed (ə kus′təmd), usual: *By Monday I was well again and was back in my accustomed seat in class. adjective.*

accustomed to, used to; in the habit of: *I am accustomed to getting up early.*

ace (ās), a playing card with one spot on it. It is the highest card in most card games. *noun.*

ache (āk), **1** continuous pain: *My cousin ate too much candy and got a stomach ache.* **2** suffer continuous pain; be in pain; hurt: *My arm aches.* **3** be eager; wish very much: *During the hot days of August we all ached to go swimming.* 1 *noun,* 2,3 *verb,* **ached, ach ing.**

a chieve (ə chēv′), **1** do; carry out: *Did you achieve all that you expected to today?* **2** reach by one's own efforts: *She achieved fame as a swimmer. verb,* **a chieved, a chiev ing.**

a chieve ment (ə chēv′mənt), **1** thing achieved; some plan or action carried out with courage or with unusual ability. See picture. **2** an achieving: *the achievement of good grades, the achievement of success. noun.*

ac id (as′id), **1** a chemical substance that unites with a base to form a salt. The water solution of an acid turns blue litmus paper red. **2** sour; sharp or biting to the taste: *Lemons are an acid fruit.* **3** sharp in manner or temper: *My teacher made an acid comment about my frequent tardiness.* 1 *noun,* 2,3 *adjective.*

ac knowl edge (ak nol′ij), **1** admit to be true: *He acknowledges his own faults.* **2** recognize the authority or claims of: *Everyone in the chorus*

a hat	**i** it	**oi** oil	**ch** child	a in about
ā age	**ī** ice	**ou** out	**ng** long	e in taken
ä far	**o** hot	**u** cup	**sh** she	ə = i in pencil
e let	**ō** open	**u̇** put	**th** thin	o in lemon
ē equal	**ô** order	**ü** rule	**ᴛH** then	u in circus
ėr term			**zh** measure	

acknowledged the twins to be the best singers. **3** make known that one has received (a favor, service, or message): *She acknowledged the gift with a pleasant letter. verb,* **ac knowl edged, ac knowl edg ing.**

ac knowl edg ment (ak nol′ij mənt), **1** something given or done to show that one has received a favor, service, or message: *A thank-you note is an acknowledgment of a gift.* **2** admitting that something is true: *I made acknowledgment of my mistake to my parents.* **3** recognition of authority or claims. *noun.*

achievement (definition 1)
Landing astronauts on the moon was a great **achievement.**

ac ne (ak′nē), a skin disease in which the oil glands in the skin become clogged, sore, and swollen. It often causes pimples. *noun.*

a corn (ā′kôrn), the nut of an oak tree. *noun.*

ac quaint (ə kwānt′), make aware; let know; inform: *Acquaint me with your plans for next summer. verb.*

be acquainted with, be familiar with or know: *I have heard about your friend, but I am not acquainted with him.*

ac quaint ance (ə kwān′təns), **1** person known to you, but not a close friend: *We have many acquaintances in our neighborhood.* **2** knowledge of persons or things gained from experience with them: *I have some acquaintance with French, but I do not know it well. noun.*

ac quire (ə kwīr′), gain or get as one's own; get: *I acquired a strong liking for sports at camp. verb,* **ac quired, ac quir ing.**

ac qui si tion (ak′wə zish′ən), **1** acquiring or getting as one's own: *He spent hundreds of hours in the acquisition of skill at the piano.* **2** something acquired or gained: *The museum's new acquisitions included two very old vases.* noun.

ac quit (ə kwit′), declare not guilty: *Both of the prisoners accused of the robbery were acquitted.* verb, **ac quit ted, ac quit ting.**

acquit oneself, do one's part; behave: *You acquitted yourself well during the game.*

a cre (ā′kər), a unit of area equal to 160 square rods or 43,560 square feet. Land is measured in acres. See picture. noun.

a cre age (ā′kər ij), number of acres: *The acreage of this park is over 800.* noun.

ac rid (ak′rid), sharp, bitter, or stinging: *Smoke from a bonfire feels acrid when you breathe it in. The quarrelsome man had an acrid disposition.* adjective.

ac ro bat (ak′rə bat), person who can swing on a trapeze, turn handsprings, walk a tightrope, or do other feats of bodily skill and strength. See picture. noun.

a cross (ə krôs′), **1** from one side to the other of; over: *The cat walked across the street.* **2** from one side to the other: *What is the distance across?* **3** on the other side of; beyond: *The woods are across the river.* **1,3** preposition, **2** adverb.

come across or **run across,** find: *We come across hard words in some books.*

act (akt), **1** something done; deed: *Sharing the candy with your friends was a generous act.* **2** doing: *I was caught in the act of taking my sister's sweater.* **3** do something: *The firemen acted promptly and saved the burning house.* **4** have effect: *The medicine failed to act.* **5** behave: *I'm sorry I acted badly in school today.* **6** perform on the stage, in motion pictures, on television, or over the radio; play a part: *He acts the part of a doctor in a TV series.* **7** a main division in a play or opera: *This play has three acts.* **8** one of several performances on a program: *We stayed to see the trained dog's act.* **9** law. An act of Congress is a bill that has been passed by Congress. **1,2,7-9** noun, **3-6** verb.

act for, take the place of; do the work of: *While the principal was gone, the assistant principal acted for her.*

act on, 1 follow; obey: *I will act on your suggestion.* **2** have an effect or influence on: *Yeast acted on the dough and made it rise.*

ac tion (ak′shən), **1** doing something: *The quick action of the firemen saved the building from being burned down.* **2** something done; act: *Giving the dog food was a kind action.* **3** way of working: *A child can push our lawn mower, because it has such an easy action.* **4** battle; part of a battle: *My uncle was wounded in action.* **5 actions,** conduct or behavior: *Her actions revealed her thoughtfulness.* noun.

ac tive (ak′tiv), **1** showing much action; moving rather quickly much of the time; lively: *Most children are more active than grown people.* **2** acting; working: *An active volcano may erupt at any time.* adjective.

ac tiv i ty (ak tiv′ə tē), **1** being active; use of power; movement: *Children engage in more physical activity than old people.* **2** action: *The activities of groups of interested citizens have brought about*

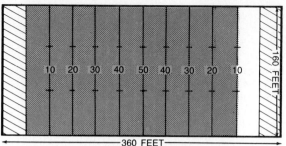

acre—An acre is smaller than a football field. The green part of this football field is an acre.

acrobat

ACUTE ANGLE   RIGHT ANGLE

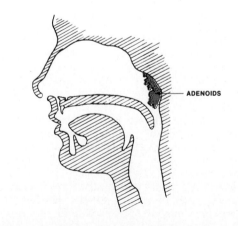

ADENOIDS

many new laws. **3** thing to do: *My favorite outdoor activity is playing football. noun, plural* **ac tiv i ties.**

ac tor (ak′tər), person who acts on the stage, in motion pictures, on television, or over the radio. *noun.*

ac tress (ak′tris), girl or woman actor. *noun, plural* **ac tress es.**

ac tu al (ak′chü əl), real; existing as a fact: *What he told us was not a dream but an actual happening. adjective.*

ac tu al ly (ak′chü ə lē), really; in fact: *Are you actually going to camp this summer or just wishing to go? adverb.*

a cute (ə kyüt′), **1** sharp and severe: *A toothache can cause acute pain.* **2** keen; sharp: *Dogs have an acute sense of smell. adjective.*

acute angle, angle less than a right angle. See picture.

ad (ad), advertisement. *noun.*

A.D., after the birth of Christ. A.D. 100 is 100 years after the birth of Christ. [The abbreviation *A.D.* stands for the Latin words *Anno Domini,* meaning "in the year of the Lord."]

ad a mant (ad′ə mənt), firm; unyielding: *Columbus was adamant in refusing all requests to turn back. adjective.*

a dapt (ə dapt′), make fit or suitable; adjust: *The children adapted the barn for use by the club. verb.*

a dapt a ble (ə dap′tə bəl), easily changed or changing easily to fit different conditions: *I have an adaptable schedule; I can see you at any time. She is an adaptable person. adjective.*

ad ap ta tion (ad′ap tā′shən), **1** changing to fit different conditions: *She made a good adaptation to her new school.* **2** something made by changing to fit different conditions: *A motion picture is often an adaptation of a novel. noun.*

add (ad), **1** find the sum of: *Add 3 and 4 and you have 7.* **2** say further; go on to say or write: *She said good-by and added that she had had a pleasant visit.* **3** join (one thing to another): *Add a stone to the pile. verb.*

add to, make greater: *The fine day added to our pleasure.*

add up to, amount to: *What do your sales add up to?*

ad dend (ad′end *or* ə dend′), number to be added to another: *In 2 + 3 + 4 = 9, the addends are 2, 3, and 4. noun.*

ad dict (ad′ikt), person who is a slave to a habit: *A drug addict finds it almost impossible to stop using drugs. noun.*

ad dict ed (ə dik′tid), enslaved by a habit or by regular use: *Many people are addicted to alcohol or other drugs. adjective.*

ad di tion (ə dish′ən), **1** process of adding one number to another: *2 + 3 = 5 is a simple addition.* **2** adding one thing to another: *The addition of flour will thicken gravy.* **3** thing added: *Cream is a tasty addition to many desserts. noun.*

in addition or **in addition to,** besides: *In addition to her work in school, our teacher gives music lessons after school hours.*

a hat	**i** it	**oi** oil	**ch** child	a in about
ā age	**ī** ice	**ou** out	**ng** long	e in taken
ä far	**o** hot	**u** cup	**sh** she	ə = i in pencil
e let	**ō** open	**u̇** put	**th** thin	o in lemon
ē equal	**ô** order	**ü** rule	**ŦH** then	u in circus
ėr term			**zh** measure	

ad di tion al (ə dish′ə nəl), extra; more: *Can you give me the additional help I need? adjective.*

ad di tive (ad′ə tiv), substance added to another substance to keep it from spoiling or make it more effective. *noun.*

ad dress (ə dres′), **1** a speech, either spoken or written: *The President gave an address to the nation over television.* **2** speak to or write to: *The king was addressed as "Your Majesty."* **3** the place to which mail is directed: *Write your name and address on this envelope.* **4** write on (an envelope or package) where it is to be sent: *Please address this letter for me.* **5** apply (oneself): *She addressed herself to the task of learning her lessons.* **1,3** *noun,* **2,4,5** *verb.*

ad e noids (ad′n oidz), growths in the upper part of the throat, just back of the nose. Adenoids can swell up and make breathing and speaking difficult. See picture. *noun plural.*

a dept (ə dept′), very skillful; expert. See picture. *adjective.*

ad e quate (ad′ə kwit), enough; sufficient; as much as is needed: *an adequate diet. adjective.*

ad here (ad hir′), stick fast: *Mud adheres to your shoes. He adhered to his plan even though others thought it foolish. verb,* **ad hered, ad her ing.**

ad he sive (ad hē′siv), **1** sticky tape used to hold bandages in place. **2** glue, paste, or other substance for sticking things together. **3** sticky. **1,2** *noun,* **3** *adjective.*

ad ja cent (ə jā′snt), near; adjoining; next: *The house adjacent to ours has been sold. adjective.*

adept
This woman is **adept** at carrying jugs of water on her head.

ad jec tive (aj′ik tiv), word that describes more fully the name of a person, animal, or thing. In "a tiny brook," "The day is warm," "great happiness," and "this pencil," *tiny, warm, great,* and *this* are adjectives. *noun.*

ad join (ə join′), be next to; be close to; be side by side: *His yard adjoins ours. verb.*

ad journ (ə jėrn′), **1** put off until a later time: *The members of the club voted to adjourn the meeting until two o'clock.* **2** stop business for a time: *The court adjourned from Friday until Monday. verb.*

ad just (ə just′), arrange; set just right; change to make fit: *These desks and seats can be adjusted to the height of any child. verb.*

ad just ment (ə just′mənt), settlement; changing to make fit; setting right to fit some standard or purpose: *The adjustment of seats to the right height for children is necessary for their comfort. Try to make some adjustment of your differences so that you can work together without quarrels. noun.*

ad min is ter (ad min′ə stər), **1** manage; direct: *The Secretary of Defense administers a department of the government. A housekeeper administers a household.* **2** give out; apply: *The coach administered first aid to the injured player. Judges administer justice and punishment. verb.*

ad min is tra tion (ad min′ə strā′shən), **1** the managing of a business or an office; management: *The administration of a big business requires skill in dealing with people.* **2** group of persons in charge: *The principal and teachers are part of the administration of the school.* **3** the **Administration,** people in charge of running the government of the United States. The Administration includes the President, the cabinet appointed by the President, and the departments of the government headed by cabinet members. **4** the time during which a government holds office. *noun.*

ad min is tra tor (ad min′ə strā′tər), person who administers; manager. *noun.*

ad mir a ble (ad′mər ə bəl), **1** worth admiring: *Lincoln had an admirable character.* **2** very good; excellent: *The doctor took admirable care of the patient. adjective.*

ad mir al (ad′mər əl), officer having the highest rank in the navy. *noun.*

ad mi ra tion (ad′mə rā′shən), **1** the feeling we have when we admire; delight or satisfaction at something fine or beautiful or well done: *I expressed my admiration for the artist's beautiful painting.* **2** person or thing that is admired: *Her new bicycle is the admiration of her friends. noun.*

ad mire (ad mīr′), **1** look at or think of with wonder, pleasure, or satisfaction: *We all admired the beautiful painting.* **2** think highly of; respect: *Everyone admired the explorer's courage. verb,* **ad mired, ad mir ing.**

ad mis sion (ad mish′ən), **1** act of allowing (a person or animal) to enter: *His admission into the hospital was delayed for lack of beds.* **2** price paid for the right to enter: *Admission to the show is one dollar.* **3** an admitting to be true; acknowledging:

adorn
an African woman adorned with bead jewelry

Their admission that they were to blame kept others from being punished. noun.

ad mit (ad mit′), **1** say (something) is real or true; acknowledge: *I admit now that I made a mistake.* **2** allow to enter: *She was admitted to law school. Windows admit light and air to the room. verb,* **ad mit ted, ad mit ting.**

ad mit tance (ad mit′ns), right to enter; permission to enter: *There is no admittance to the park after dark. noun.*

ad mon ish (ad mon′ish), warn or advise (a person) about a fault in order to encourage improvement: *The policeman admonished him not to drive so fast. The teacher admonished the students for their careless work. verb.*

a do (ə dü′), action; stir; fuss; bustle: *There was much ado about the party by all the family. noun.*

a do be (ə dō′bē), **1** brick made of clay baked in the sun. **2** built or made of adobe: *Our friends in Arizona live in an adobe house.* **1** *noun,* **2** *adjective.*

ad o les cent (ad′l es′nt), person growing up from childhood to adulthood, especially a person from about 12 to about 20 years of age. *noun.*

a dopt (ə dopt′), **1** take for your own or as your own choice: *I liked your idea and adopted it.* **2** take (a child of other parents) and bring up as one's own child: *The judge permitted the family to adopt the child. verb.*

a dop tion (ə dop′shən), **1** adopting: *Our club voted for the adoption of some new rules.* **2** being adopted: *The children were offered for adoption. noun.*

a dor a ble (ə dôr′ə bəl), attractive; delightful: *What an adorable kitten! adjective.*

ad o ra tion (ad′ə rā′shən), **1** the highest love and admiration. **2** worship. *noun.*

a dore (ə dôr′), **1** love and admire very greatly: *She* *adores her mother.* **2** like very much: *I just adored that movie!* **3** worship: *"O! Come, let us adore Him," sang the choir. verb,* **a dored, a dor ing.**

a dorn (ə dôrn′), add beauty to; decorate. See picture. *verb.*

a drift (ə drift′), drifting; floating without being guided: *During the storm our boat was adrift on the lake. adjective.*

a droit (ə droit′), skillful: *Monkeys are adroit climbers. A good teacher is adroit in asking questions. adjective.*

a dult (ə dult′ *or* ad′ult), **1** full-grown; grown-up; having full size and strength: *an adult person.* **2** a grown-up person. **3** plant or animal grown to full size and strength. **1** *adjective,* **2,3** *noun.*

ad vance (ad vans′), **1** move forward: *The angry crowd advanced toward the building.* **2** forward movement; progress: *The explorer's advance was very slow.* **3** help forward: *The President's speech advanced the cause of peace.* **4** put forward; suggest: *What plan to win the game can you advance?* **5** promote: *The colonel advanced him from lieutenant to captain.* **6** raise; increase: *The store advanced the price of milk by two cents. Milk advanced two cents a quart.* **7** rise in price or value: *There was an advance of two cents a quart in the price of milk.* **8 advances,** approach made to gain something: *My sister made the first advances toward making up our quarrel.* **1,3-6** *verb,* **ad vanced, ad vanc ing; 2,7,8** *noun.*

in advance, 1 in front: *The leader of the band marched in advance.* **2** ahead of time: *I paid for my ticket in advance.*

ad vanced (ad vanst′), **1** in front of others: *Our army is in an advanced position.* **2** ahead of most others: *The advanced class has studied history three years.* **3** very old: *Her grandmother lived to the advanced age of ninety years. adjective.*

ad vance ment (ad vans′mənt), **1** a moving forward; improvement: *Hard work brought him an advancement in pay.* **2** promotion: *Good work won her advancement to a higher position. noun.*

ad van tage (ad van′tij), anything that is a benefit or a help in getting something wanted: *Good health is always an advantage. noun.*

take advantage of, 1 use to help or benefit oneself: *We took advantage of the beautiful day by working in our garden.* **2** use unfairly: *Don't take advantage of me by asking me to run errands.*

to one's advantage, to one's benefit or help: *It will be to your advantage to study Spanish before you visit Mexico.*

ad van ta geous (ad′vən tā′jəs), favorable; helpful: *From our advantageous position we were able to see the whole valley. adjective.*

ad ven ture (ad ven′chər), **1** an unusual or exciting experience: *The trip to Alaska was quite an adventure for her.* **2** a bold and difficult undertaking, usually exciting and somewhat dangerous: *Sailing across the Pacific on a raft was a daring adventure. noun.*

ad ven tur er (ad ven′chər ər), person who has or seeks adventures. *noun.*

a	hat	i	it	oi	oil	ch	child		a in about
ā	age	ī	ice	ou	out	ng	long		e in taken
ä	far	o	hot	u	cup	sh	she	ə =	i in pencil
e	let	ō	open	ů	put	th	thin		o in lemon
ē	equal	ô	order	ü	rule	ᴛʜ	then		u in circus
ėr	term					zh	measure		

ad ven tur ous (ad ven′chər əs), **1** fond of adventures; ready to take risks: *The adventurous family sailed around the world in a small boat.* **2** full of danger: *Sailing around the world in a small boat is an adventurous thing to do. adjective.*

ad verb (ad′vėrb′), word that tells how, when, or where something happens. In "He walked slowly," "He came late," "I saw her there," and "She sings well," *slowly, late, there,* and *well* are adverbs. Adverbs also tell how much or how little is meant. In "This soup is very good" and "I am rather tired," *very* and *rather* are adverbs. *noun.*

ad ver sar y (ad′vər ser′ē), **1** enemy: *The United States and Japan were adversaries in World War II.* **2** person or group on the other side in a contest: *Which school is our adversary in this week's football game? noun, plural* **ad ver sar ies.**

ad verse (ad′vėrs′ *or* ad vėrs′), **1** unfriendly in purpose; hostile: *Their adverse criticism discouraged me.* **2** unfavorable; harmful: *A poor diet and lack of sleep had an adverse effect on his health.* **3** acting in a contrary direction; opposing: *Adverse winds hinder planes. adjective.*

ad ver si ty (ad vėr′sə tē), distress; misfortune; hardship. *noun, plural* **ad ver si ties.**

ad ver tise (ad′vər tīz), give public notice of; announce: *Stores often advertise in newspapers. verb,* **ad ver tised, ad ver tis ing.**

advertise for, ask for by public notice: *He advertised for a job.*

ad ver tise ment (ad′vər tīz′mənt *or* ad vėr′tis mənt), public announcement; printed notice: *The furniture store has an advertisement in the newspaper of a special sale. noun.*

ad vice (ad vīs′), opinion about what should be done: *I followed my teacher's advice and joined the dramatic club. noun.*

ad vis a ble (ad vī′zə bəl), wise; sensible; suitable: *It is not advisable for you to go to school while you are still sick. adjective.*

ad vise (ad vīz′), **1** give advice to: *He advised me to put my money in the bank.* **2** inform: *We were advised of the dangers before we began our trip. verb,* **ad vised, ad vis ing.**

ad vis er *or* **ad vi sor** (ad vī′zər), person who gives advice. *noun.*

ad vo cate (ad′və kāt *for* 1; ad′və kit *for* 2), **1** speak in favor of; recommend publicly: *The mayor advocates using the land along the river for a public park.* **2** person who speaks in favor; supporter: *She is an advocate of equal rights for all people.* **1** *verb,* **ad vo cat ed, ad vo cat ing; 2** *noun.*

adz *or* **adze** (adz), tool somewhat like an ax, used for shaping heavy timbers. The blade is set across the end of the handle and curves inward. *noun, plural* **adz es.**

aer i al (er′ē əl *or* ar′ē əl), a long wire or set of wires or rods used in television or radio for sending out or receiving sounds and pictures; antenna. *noun.*

aer o nau tics (er′ə nô′tiks *or* ar′ə nô′tiks), science or art that deals with the design, manufacture, and operation of aircraft. *noun.*

aer o space (er′ō spās *or* ar′ō spās), the earth's atmosphere and the space beyond it, especially the space in which rockets, satellites, and other spacecraft operate. *noun.*

a far (ə fär′). **from afar**, from far off; from a distance: *I saw them from afar. adverb.*

af fa ble (af′ə bəl), easy to talk to; courteous and pleasant: *She is very friendly and affable. adjective.*

af fair (ə fer′ *or* ə far′), **1** thing to do; job; business: *Their lawyer looked after their affairs while they were gone.* **2** any thing, matter, or happening: *The costume party was a delightful affair. noun.*

af fect[1] (ə fekt′), **1** produce a result on; have an effect on; influence: *The small amount of rain last year affected the growth of crops.* **2** touch the heart of: *The stories of starving children so affected him that he gave all his money to their aid. verb.*

af fect[2] (ə fekt′), pretend to have or feel: *She affected ignorance of the fight, but we knew that she had seen it. verb.*

af fect ed[1] (ə fek′tid), acted upon; influenced: *Everyone felt affected by the war. adjective.*

af fect ed[2] (ə fek′tid), not natural; pretended; artificial: *The speaker's affected way of talking annoyed us. adjective.*

af fec tion (ə fek′shən), friendly feeling; love. See picture. *noun.*

af fec tion ate (ə fek′shə nit), loving; fond; showing affection: *an affectionate hug. adjective.*

af firm (ə fėrm′), say firmly; declare to be true; assert: *The prisoner affirmed his innocence. verb.*

af firm a tive (ə fėr′mə tiv), saying yes; affirming: *Her answer to my question was affirmative. adjective.*

af fix (af′iks), a sound or group of sounds added to a word to change its meaning or use. Affixes are either prefixes like *un-* and *re-* or suffixes like *-ly, -ness, -s,* or *-ed. noun, plural* **af fix es.**

af flict (ə flikt′), cause pain to; trouble very much; distress: *She is afflicted with rheumatism. verb.*

af flic tion (ə flik′shən), **1** pain; trouble; distress: *The country suffered from the affliction of war.* **2** cause of pain, trouble, or distress; misfortune: *Blindness is an affliction. noun.*

af flu ence (af′lü əns), wealth; riches. *noun.*

af flu ent (af′lü ənt), having wealth; rich. *adjective.*

af ford (ə fôrd′), **1** have the means; have the money, time, or strength: *Can we afford to buy a new car? He cannot afford to waste time.* **2** yield; give: *Reading this story will afford pleasure. verb.*

af front (ə frunt′), **1** an open insult: *To be called a coward is an affront.* **2** insult openly and purposely: *The boy affronted his teacher by making a face at her.* **1** *noun,* **2** *verb.*

a field (ə fēld′), away; away from home: *She wandered far afield in foreign lands. adverb.*

affection

agile dancers

agate (definition 1)—a polished agate

a fire (ə fīr'), on fire. *adverb, adjective.*

a flame (ə flām'), in flames; on fire. *adverb, adjective.*

a float (ə flōt'), **1** floating on the water or in the air. **2** flooded: *After the heavy rain the basement was afloat. adverb, adjective.*

a foot (ə füt'), **1** on foot; by walking. **2** going on; in progress: *Great preparations for the dinner were afoot in the kitchen. adverb, adjective.*

a fraid (ə frād'), **1** frightened; feeling fear: *afraid of the dark, afraid of heights.* **2** sorry: *I'm afraid I must ask you to leave now. adjective.*

a fresh (ə fresh'), again: *If you spoil your drawing, start afresh. adverb.*

Af ri ca (af'rə kə), continent south of Europe and east of the Atlantic Ocean. Only one other continent, Asia, is larger than Africa. Egypt, Ghana, and Tanzania are countries in Africa. *noun.*

Af ri can (af'rə kən), **1** of Africa; having something to do with Africa or its people; from Africa. **2** person born or living in Africa. 1 *adjective,* 2 *noun.*

Af ro (af'rō), a bushy hairdo like that worn in parts of Africa. *noun.*

Af ro-A mer i can (af'rō ə mer'ə kən), **1** of or having to do with American Negroes. **2** an American Negro. 1 *adjective,* 2 *noun.*

aft (aft), at or toward the rear of a ship, boat, or aircraft. *adverb.*

af ter (af'tər), **1** later in time than; following: *After dinner we can go.* **2** later; following: *I ran so hard I panted for five minutes after. Day after day I waited for a letter from my friend.* **3** behind: *You come after me in the line. Jill came tumbling after.* **4** in search of: *The dog ran after the rabbit.* 1-4 *preposition,* 2,3 *adverb.*

af ter noon (af'tər nün'), the time from noon to evening. *noun.*

af ter ward (af'tər wərd), afterwards; later. *adverb.*

af ter wards (af'tər wərdz), later: *The bud was small at first, but afterwards it became a large flower. adverb.*

a gain (ə gen'), another time; once more: *Come again to play. Say that again. adverb.*

a gainst (ə genst'), **1** in opposition to: *It is against the law to cross the street when the light is red.* **2** upon: *Rain beats against the window.* **3** in preparation for: *Squirrels store up nuts against the winter. preposition.*

ag ate (ag'it), **1** a kind of quartz with colored stripes or cloudy colors. See picture. **2** a marble used in games that looks like agate. *noun.*

age (āj), **1** time of life: *His age is ten.* **2** length of life: *Turtles live to a great age.* **3** a particular period of life: *She has reached old age.* **4** period in history: *We live in the age of jet planes.* **5 ages,** a long time: *I haven't seen you for ages!* **6** grow old: *He is aging fast.* **7** make old: *Worry can age a person.* 1-5 *noun,* 6,7 *verb,* **aged, ag ing** or **age ing.**
of age, at the time of life when a person is considered legally an adult, usually 18 years old.

a ged (ā'jid *for 1;* ājd *for 2*), **1** old; having lived a long time: *an aged woman.* **2** of the age of: *Children aged six must go to school. adjective.*

a hat	i it	oi oil	ch child	a in about
ā age	ī ice	ou out	ng long	e in taken
ä far	o hot	u cup	sh she	ə = i in pencil
e let	ō open	ů put	th thin	o in lemon
ē equal	ô order	ü rule	ŦH then	u in circus
ėr term			zh measure	

a gen cy (ā'jən sē), **1** the office or business of some person or company that acts for another: *An agency rented our house for us. Employment agencies help people to get jobs.* **2** means; action: *Snow is drifted by the agency of the wind. noun, plural* **a gen cies.**

a gent (ā'jənt), **1** person or company that acts for another: *She is a real estate agent and can help you sell your house.* **2** any power or cause that produces an effect: *Yeast is an agent that causes bread to rise. noun.*

ag gra vate (ag'rə vāt), **1** make worse; make more severe: *His headache was aggravated by all the noise.* **2** annoy; irritate: *She aggravated me by asking questions. verb,* **ag gra vat ed, ag gra vat ing.**

ag gre gate (ag'rə git *for 1;* ag'rə gāt *for 2*), **1** total: *The aggregate of all the gifts was over $100.* **2** amount to: *The money collected will aggregate $1000.* 1 *noun,* 2 *verb,* **ag gre gat ed, ag gre gat ing.**

ag gres sion (ə gresh'ən), the first step in an attack or a quarrel: *A country that sends its army to seize another country is guilty of aggression. noun.*

ag gres sive (ə gres'iv), **1** taking the first step in an attack or a quarrel; attacking: *An aggressive country is always ready to start a war.* **2** very active; energetic: *The police are making an aggressive campaign against driving too fast. adjective.*

ag gres sor (ə gres'ər), **1** one that begins an attack or a quarrel. **2** nation that starts a war. *noun.*

ag grieved (ə grēvd'), feeling unjustly treated; troubled; distressed: *He was aggrieved at the insult from his friend. adjective.*

a ghast (ə gast'), struck with surprise or horror: *I was aghast when I saw the destruction caused by the earthquake. adjective.*

ag ile (aj'əl), moving quickly and easily; nimble: *An acrobat has to be agile. You need an agile mind to solve puzzles. See picture. adjective.*

a gil i ty (ə jil'ə tē), ability to move quickly and easily: *He has the agility of a monkey. noun.*

ag i tate (aj'ə tāt), **1** move or shake: *The slightest wind will agitate the leaves of some trees.* **2** disturb; excite: *He was agitated by the news of his friend's serious illness. verb,* **ag i tat ed, ag i tat ing.**

ag i ta tion (aj'ə tā'shən), **1** a moving or shaking: *The agitation of the sea almost turned over the little boat.* **2** disturbance; excitement: *Because of her agitation, she could not sleep. noun.*

a go (ə gō'), **1** gone by; past: *I met her two years ago.* **2** in the past: *He lived here long ago.* 1 *adjective,* 2 *adverb.*

a gog (ə gog'), very excited; eager: *The children were agog to see their presents. adjective.*

ag o niz ing (ag′ə nī′zing), causing very great pain or suffering. *adjective.*

ag o ny (ag′ə nē), very great suffering of body or mind: *Nobody can stand for long the agony of a severe toothache. noun, plural* **ag o nies.**

a gree (ə grē′), **1** have the same opinion: *We all agree in liking the teacher. I agree with your argument.* **2** be in harmony: *Your story agrees with mine.* **3** get along well together: *Brothers and sisters don't always agree as well as they should.* **4** say that one is willing; consent: *He agreed to go with us. verb,* **a greed, a gree ing.**

agree with, have a good effect on: *This food does not agree with me; it makes me sick.*

a gree a ble (ə grē′ə bəl), **1** pleasant; pleasing: *The boy had an agreeable manner.* **2** willing: *If she is agreeable, we can all meet tonight. adjective.*

a gree ment (ə grē′mənt), **1** an understanding reached by two or more persons, groups of persons, or nations. Nations make treaties; certain persons make contracts. Both are agreements. **2** harmony: *There was perfect agreement between the two friends. noun.*

ag ri cul tur al (ag′rə kul′chər əl), of agriculture; having something to do with farming: *The Middle West is an important agricultural region. adjective.*

ag ri cul ture (ag′rə kul′chər), farming; cultivating the soil to make crops grow; the raising of crops and farm animals. *noun.*

a ground (ə ground′), on the shore; on the bottom in shallow water: *The ship ran aground and stuck in the sand. adverb, adjective.*

ah (ä), exclamation of pain, sorrow, regret, pity, admiration, surprise, joy, dislike, or contempt. *interjection.*

a ha (ä hä′), exclamation of triumph, satisfaction, surprise, or joy. *interjection.*

a head (ə hed′), **1** in front; before: *Walk ahead of me. Road repairs ahead!* **2** forward: *Go ahead with this work for another week.* **3** in advance: *He was ahead of his class in reading. adverb.*

be ahead, 1 be winning: *Our team is ahead by 6 points.* **2** have more than is needed: *We're ahead $10 on the budget.*

get ahead, succeed: *I worked hard at my job in the hope that I would get ahead.*

get ahead of, do or be better than: *She worked hard and got ahead of the others in her class.*

a hoy (ə hoi′), call used by sailors to attract attention. Sailors say, "Ship, ahoy!" when they call to a ship. *interjection.*

aid (ād), **1** give support to; help: *The Red Cross aids flood victims.* **2** a help; assistance: *When my arm was broken, I could not dress without aid.* **3** helper; assistant: *a nurse's aid, a teacher's aid.* **1** *verb,* **2,3** *noun.*

aide (ād), helper; assistant. *noun.*

ail (āl), **1** be the matter with; trouble: *What ails the child?* **2** be ill; feel sick: *She has been ailing for a week. verb.*

ail ment (āl′mənt), illness; sickness: *His ailment was only an upset stomach. noun.*

aim (ām), **1** point or direct (a gun or a blow) in order to hit: *She aimed carefully at the target.* **2** act of pointing or directing at something: *She hit the target because her aim was good.* **3** direct words or acts so as to influence a certain person or action: *The teacher's talk was aimed at the students who cheated on the test.* **4** try: *He aimed to please his teachers.* **5** purpose: *Her aim was to do two years' work in one.* **1,3,4** *verb,* **2,5** *noun.*

ain't (ānt), **1** am not; is not. **2** are not. **3** have not; has not. Careful speakers and writers do not use *ain't.*

air (er *or* ar), **1** the mixture of gases that surrounds the earth. Air consists of nitrogen, oxygen, hydrogen, and other gases. *We breathe air.* **2** space overhead; sky: *Birds fly in the air.* **3** let fresh air in: *Open the windows and air the room.* **4** airline; airplane: *We traveled by air on our vacation.* **5** make known: *Don't air your troubles too often.* **6** a simple melody or tune. **7** way; look; manner: *an air of importance.* **8 airs,** unnatural or showy manners: *Your friends will laugh if you put on airs.* **1,2,4,6-8** *noun,* **3,5** *verb.*

in the air, going around: *Wild rumors were in the air.*

on the air, broadcasting: *Is that radio show still on the air?*

air base, headquarters and airfield for military aircraft.

air conditioner, device for the air conditioning of a building, room, car, or other place. Air conditioners usually cool the air and remove moisture and dust from it.

air conditioning, a means of regulating the temperature and humidity of air and of cleaning it.

air craft (er′kraft′ *or* ar′kraft′), **1** airplanes, airships, helicopters, or balloons. **2** any airplane, airship, helicopter, or balloon. *noun, plural* **air craft.**

air field (er′fēld′ *or* ar′fēld′), landing field of an airport. *noun.*

air force, part of the armed forces that uses aircraft.

air line (er′līn′ *or* ar′līn′), company that carries passengers and freight by aircraft from one place to another. *noun.*

air lin er (er′lī′nər *or* ar′lī′nər), a large passenger airplane. *noun.*

air mail, 1 mail sent by aircraft. **2** system of sending mail by aircraft.

air man (er′mən *or* ar′mən), **1** pilot of an aircraft. **2** an enlisted man or woman of the lowest rank in the air force. *noun, plural* **air men.**

air plane (er′plān′ *or* ar′plān′), a flying machine that has one or more planes or wings and is driven by a propeller or jet engine. *noun.*

air port (er′pôrt′ *or* ar′pôrt′), area used by aircraft to land and take off. An airport has buildings for passengers and for keeping and repairing aircraft. *noun.*

air ship (er′ship′ *or* ar′ship′), a kind of balloon that can be steered; dirigible. An airship is filled with a gas that is lighter than air. *noun.*

air tight (er′tīt′ *or* ar′tīt′), **1** so tight that no air can get in or out. **2** leaving no weak points open to attack: *She presented an airtight argument which convinced us she was right. adjective.*

air way (er′wā′ *or* ar′wā′), route for aircraft. *noun.*

air y (er′ē *or* ar′ē), **1** breezy; with air moving through it: *an airy room.* **2** gay; lighthearted: *the children's airy laughter.* **3** light as air; graceful; delicate: *She sang an airy tune. adjective,* **air i er, air i est.**

aisle (īl), **1** passage between rows of seats in a hall, theater, church, or school. **2** any long, narrow passage. *noun.*

a jar (ə jär′), slightly open: *Please leave the door ajar. adjective.*

a kim bo (ə kim′bō), with the hands on the hips and the elbows bent outward. See picture. *adjective.*

a kin (ə kin′), **1** alike; similar: *His tastes in music seem akin to mine.* **2** belonging to the same family; related: *Your cousins are akin to you. adjective.*

Al a bam a (al′ə bam′ə), one of the south central states of the United States. *noun.* [*Alabama* was named for an American Indian tribe that once lived in the area. The tribe's name came from Indian words meaning "I clear the thicket."]

a larm (ə lärm′), **1** sudden fear; excitement caused by fear of danger: *The deer darted off in alarm.* **2** make afraid; frighten: *The breaking of a branch under my foot alarmed the deer.* **3** a warning of approaching danger: *The alarm went out that a tornado was approaching.* **4** a bell or other device that makes a noise to warn or waken people. **5** a call to arms or action. See picture. 1,3-5 *noun,* 2 *verb.*

alarm clock, clock that can be set to ring or sound at a chosen time.

a las (ə las′), exclamation of sorrow, grief, regret, pity, or dread. *interjection.*

A las ka (ə las′kə), one of the Pacific states of the United States, in the northwestern part of North America. *noun.* [*Alaska* got its name from a word used by people living on nearby islands. The word meant "mainland."]

al bum (al′bəm), **1** book with blank pages for holding things like photographs, pictures, and stamps. **2** a case for a phonograph record or records. *noun.*

al co hol (al′kə hôl), a colorless liquid in wine, beer, whiskey, gin, rum, and vodka. Alcohol can make people drunk. Alcohol in different forms is used in medicines, in manufacturing, and as a fuel. *noun.*

al co hol ic (al′kə hô′lik), **1** of alcohol: *This wine has a high alcoholic content.* **2** containing alcohol: *Whiskey and gin are alcoholic liquors.* **3** person who suffers from alcoholism. 1,2 *adjective,* 3 *noun.*

al co hol ism (al′kə hô liz′əm), disease in which too much alcoholic liquor is drunk. *noun.*

al cove (al′kōv), a small room opening out of a larger room. *noun.*

al der (ôl′dər), a tree or shrub somewhat like a birch. Alders usually grow in wet land. *noun.*

a hat	i it	oi oil	ch child	a in about
ā age	ī ice	ou out	ng long	e in taken
ä far	o hot	u cup	sh she	ə = i in pencil
e let	ō open	ù put	th thin	o in lemon
ē equal	ô order	ü rule	ᴛʜ then	u in circus
ėr term			zh measure	

akimbo
She stood with
her arms **akimbo**.

alarm (definition 5)
Paul Revere gave the **alarm** to the towns near Boston.

ale (āl), a strong beer made from malt and hops. *noun.*

a lert (ə lėrt′), **1** watchful; wide-awake: *The dog was alert to every sound.* **2** lively; nimble: *A sparrow is very alert in its movements.* **3** signal warning of an attack by approaching enemy aircraft, a hurricane, or other danger. **4** make alert; warn. 1,2 *adjective,* 3 *noun,* 4 *verb.*

on the alert, watchful: *A sentry must be on the alert.*

al fal fa (al fal′fə), a plant with leaves like clover, deep roots, and bluish-purple flowers. Alfalfa is grown as food for horses and cattle. *noun.*

al gae (al′jē), group of water plants that can make their own food. Algae contain chlorophyll but lack true stems, roots, or leaves. Some algae form scum on rocks; others, such as the seaweeds, are very large. See picture. *noun plural.*

al ge bra (al′jə brə), branch of mathematics that deals with the relations between quantities. Algebra uses letters as symbols that can stand for many different numbers. *noun.*

al i bi (al′ə bī), **1** the claim that an accused person was somewhere else when a crime was committed: *The gang's alibi was that they were in another city when the bank was robbed.* **2** an excuse: *What is your alibi for failing to do your homework? noun, plural* **al i bis.**

al ien (ā′lyən), **1** foreigner. People who are not citizens of the country in which they live are aliens. **2** of another country; foreign: *French is an alien language to Americans.* **3** entirely different; not in agreement; strange: *Cruelty is alien to his nature.* 1 *noun,* 2,3 *adjective.*

a light (ə līt′), **1** get down; get off: *She alighted from the bus.* **2** come down from the air; come down from flight: *The bird alighted on our window sill. verb,* **a light ed, a light ing.**

a lign (ə līn′), bring into line; arrange in a straight line: *I aligned the sights of my rifle with the target. A mechanic aligned the front wheels of our car. verb.*

a like (ə līk′), **1** in the same way: *She and her sister think alike.* **2** like one another; similar: *The children in that family look alike.* 1 *adverb,* 2 *adjective.*

al i men tar y ca nal (al′ə men′tər ē kə nal′), the parts of the body through which food passes while it is being digested. The alimentary canal is a tube which begins at the mouth and ends where solid waste leaves the body. See picture.

al i mo ny (al′ə mō′nē), a regular sum of money paid to a person's former wife or husband after a divorce. The amount of alimony is fixed by a court. *noun.*

a live (ə līv′), **1** having life; living: *Was the snake alive or dead?* **2** active: *All winter we kept our hopes alive for a warm spring. adjective.*

alive with, full of; swarming with: *The streets were alive with people.*

all (ôl), **1** every one of: *All the children came. You all know the teacher.* **2** everyone: *All of us are going.* **3** everything: *All is well.* **4** the whole of: *The mice ate all the cheese.* **5** the whole amount: *All of the bread has been eaten.* **6** wholly; entirely: *The cake is all gone.* 1,4 *adjective,* 2,3,5 *pronoun,* 6 *adverb.*

after all, nevertheless; when everything has been considered: *It was cloudy, but we decided to have the picnic after all.*

all over, everywhere: *There were toys all over.*

at all, 1 under any conditions: *maybe he won't be able to go at all.* **2** in any way: *She was not at all upset by the change in plan.*

in all, counting every person or thing; altogether: *There were 100 people in all.*

all-a round (ôl′ə round′), able to do many things; useful in many ways: *He is an all-around football player—he runs, passes, and punts. adjective.*

algae—red algae growing on a rock surrounded by green moss

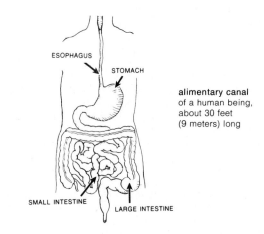

ESOPHAGUS

STOMACH

alimentary canal of a human being, about 30 feet (9 meters) long

SMALL INTESTINE

LARGE INTESTINE

alligator—about 10 feet (3 meters) long

al lege (ə lej'), **1** assert; declare: *Although he has no proof, this man alleges that the janitor stole his watch.* **2** give as a reason, excuse, or argument: *She was tardy this morning, and alleges that her bus was late. verb,* **al leged, al leg ing.**

al le giance (ə lē'jəns), **1** the loyalty owed by a citizen to his country or government: *I pledge allegiance to the flag.* **2** loyalty; faithfulness; devotion: *We owe allegiance to our friends. noun.*

al ler gic (ə lėr'jik), **1** having an allergy: *People who are allergic to poison ivy break out in a rash if they touch it.* **2** caused by an allergy: *Hay fever is an allergic reaction to a kind of pollen. adjective.*

al ler gy (al'ər jē), an unusual reaction of body tissue to certain things such as particular kinds of pollen, food, hair, or cloth. Hay fever and asthma are common signs of allergy. *noun, plural* **al ler gies.**

al ley (al'ē), **1** a narrow back street in a city or town. **2** a long, narrow lane along which the ball is rolled in bowling. **3** building having a number of lanes for bowling. *noun, plural* **al leys.**

al li ance (ə lī'əns), a union of persons, groups, or nations formed for some special purpose or benefit. Alliances may be formed between nations by treaties. *noun.*

al lied (ə līd' *or* al'īd), **1** united by agreement: *France, Great Britain, Russia, and the United States were allied nations during World War II.* **2** similar in some way; related; connected: *Painting, drawing, and sculpture are allied arts. adjective.*

al li ga tor (al'ə gā'tər), a large reptile with a rather thick skin. It is like the crocodile but has a shorter and flatter head. Alligators live in the rivers and marshes of the warm parts of America and China. See picture. *noun.* [*Alligator* comes from Spanish words meaning "the lizard."]

al lot (ə lot'), **1** divide and distribute in parts or shares: *The money from the sale of the property was allotted equally among the three owners.* **2** give to as a share; assign: *Each class was allotted a part in the school program. verb,* **al lot ted, al lot ting.**

al low (ə lou'), **1** let (someone) do something; permit: *My parents won't allow us to swim in the river.* **2** let have; give: *My parents allowed me a dollar to spend as I wish.* **3** add or subtract to make up for something: *The trip will cost only $20; but you ought to allow $5 more for extra expenses. verb.*

allow for, take into consideration: *I buy my jeans a little large to allow for shrinking.*

al low ance (ə lou'əns), **1** a sum of money given or set aside for expenses: *a child's weekly allowance of $1, a household allowance for groceries of $50 a week.* **2** amount subtracted to make up for something; discount: *The salesman offered us an allowance of $400 on our old car; so we got a $3000 car for $2600. noun.*

make allowance for, take into consideration; allow for: *We made allowance for the heavy traffic by leaving half an hour early.*

al loy (al'oi), **1** metal made by melting and mixing two or more metals. An alloy may be harder, lighter, and stronger than the metals of which it is made. Brass is an alloy of copper and zinc. **2** an inferior metal mixed with a more valuable one: *This is not pure gold; there is some alloy in it. noun.*

all right, **1** without error; correct: *The answers were all right.* **2** satisfactory: *The work was not done very well; but it was all right.* **3** yes: *"Will you come with me?" "All right."*

al lude (ə lüd'), refer indirectly; mention slightly: *Don't tell them about our plan; don't even allude to it. verb,* **al lud ed, al lud ing.**

al lu sion (ə lü'zhən), slight mention; indirect reference: *Don't make any allusion to the surprise party while he is present. noun.*

al ly (al'ī *for 1;* ə lī' *for 2*), **1** person, group, or nation united with another for some special purpose: *England and France were allies in some wars and enemies in others.* **2** combine for some special purpose; unite by agreement. Small nations sometimes ally themselves with larger ones for protection. **1** *noun, plural* **al lies;** **2** *verb,* **al lied, al ly ing.**

al ma nac (ôl'mə nak), **1** a booklike calendar that also gives information about the weather, sun, moon, stars, tides, church days, and other facts. **2** a book published every year which has tables of facts and figures and brief information on many subjects. *noun.*

al might y (ôl mī'tē), **1** possessing all power. **2 the Almighty,** God. **1** *adjective,* **2** *noun.*

al mond (ä'mənd), **1** the nut of a peachlike fruit growing in warm regions. **2** tree that the fruit grows on. *noun.*

al most (ôl'mōst), nearly: *It is almost ten o'clock. I almost missed the train. adverb.*

alms (ämz), money or gifts to help the poor: *The beggar asked for alms. noun singular or plural.*

a loft (ə lôft'), **1** far above the earth; high up. See picture. **2** high up among the sails and masts of a

a hat	**i** it	**oi** oil	**ch** child		a in about
ā age	**ī** ice	**ou** out	**ng** long		e in taken
ä far	**o** hot	**u** cup	**sh** she	**ə =**	i in pencil
e let	**ō** open	**u̇** put	**th** thin		o in lemon
ē equal	**ô** order	**ü** rule	**ŦH** then		u in circus
ėr term			**zh** measure		

aloft (definition 1)—tennis played aloft

altar (definition 1)—a Buddhist altar

ship: *The sailor went aloft to get a better view of the distant shore. adverb.*

a lo ha (ə lō′ə *or* ä lō′hä), a Hawaiian word meaning: **1** greetings; hello. **2** good-by; farewell. *noun, interjection.*

a lone (ə lōn′), **1** apart from other persons or things: *After my friends left, I was alone. One tree stood alone on the hill.* **2** without help from others: *I solved the problem alone.* **3** without anyone else; only: *She alone can do this work.* **4** without anything more: *Bread alone is not enough for lunch.* 1,3,4 *adjective,* 1,2 *adverb.*
leave alone *or* **let alone,** not bother; not meddle with: *Let her alone so she can get her work done.*

a long (ə lông′), **1** from one end to the other end of: *Trees are planted along the street.* **2** from one end to the other; lengthwise: *Cars are parked along by the stadium.* **3** forward; onward: *March along quickly.* **4** together with someone or something: *We took our dog along.* 1 *preposition,* 2-4 *adverb.*
all along, all the time: *He knew the answer all along.*
along with, in company with: *I'll go along with you.*
get along, 1 manage: *Can you get along without our help?* **2** agree: *They get along with each other.*

a long side (ə lông′sīd′), **1** at the side; side by side: *A car pulled up alongside.* **2** by the side of; side by side with: *The boat was alongside the wharf.* 1 *adverb;* 2 *preposition.*

a loof (ə lüf′), **1** away; apart: *One boy stood aloof from all the others.* **2** tending to keep to oneself; not interested; indifferent: *Her aloof manner kept her from making many friends.* 1 *adverb,* 2 *adjective.*

a loud (ə loud′), loud enough to be heard; not in a whisper: *She read the story aloud to me. adverb.*

al pha bet (al′fə bet), the letters of a language arranged in their usual order, not as they are in words. The English alphabet is a b c d e f g h i j k l m n o p q r s t u v w x y z. See picture. *noun.*
[*Alphabet* comes from the names of the first two letters of the Greek alphabet: *alpha* A and *beta* B.]

al pha bet i cal (al′fə bet′ə kəl), arranged by letters in the order of the alphabet: *Dictionary entries are listed in alphabetical order. adjective.*

al pha bet i cal ly (al′fə bet′ik lē), in the usual order of the letters of the alphabet. *adverb.*

al pha bet ize (al′fə bə tīz), arrange in the order of the letters of the alphabet: *Alphabetize the words in your spelling lesson. verb,* **al pha bet ized, al pha bet iz ing.**

al read y (ôl red′ē), before this time; by this time; even now: *You are half an hour late already. adverb.*

al so (ôl′sō), too; in addition: *I like summer but I enjoy winter also. adverb.*

al tar (ôl′tər), **1** table or stand used in religious worship in a church or temple: *The priest knelt in prayer before the altar.* See picture. **2** a raised place built of earth or stone on which to place sacrifices or burn offerings to a god. *noun.*

al ter (ôl′tər), make or become different; change: *If this coat is too large, a tailor can alter it to fit you. Since her summer on the farm, her whole outlook has altered. verb.*

al ter a tion (ôl′tə rā′shən), change: *I made some alterations in my new slacks. We put in new cabinets and made other alterations in our kitchen. noun.*

al ter nate (ôl′tər nāt *for 1-3;* ôl′tər nit *for 4-6*), **1** happen or be arranged by turns, first one and then the other. Squares and circles alternate in this row:□ ○ □ ○ □ ○ . **2** arrange by turns: *He alternated work and pleasure.* **3** take turns: *My brother and I will alternate in setting the table.* **4** first one and then the other by turns: *The United States flag has alternate stripes of red and white.* **5** every other: *Our dairy no longer delivers milk daily, but only on alternate days.* **6** substitute: *We have several alternates on our debating team.* 1-3 *verb,* **al ter nat ed, al ter nat ing;** 4,5 *adjective,* 6 *noun.*

al ter nate ly (ôl′tər nit lē), by turns. *adverb.*

alternating current, an electric current that reverses its direction at regular intervals.

alphabet on needlework done by a child in 1799

al ter na tive (ôl tėr′nə tiv), **1** choice from among two or more things: *She had the alternative of going to summer school or finding a summer job.* **2** one of the things to be chosen: *She chose the first alternative and went to summer school.* **3** giving or requiring a choice between two or more things: *I offered the alternative plans of having a picnic or taking a trip on a boat.* 1,2 *noun,* 3 *adjective.*

al though or **al tho** (ôl ŦH̄ō′), though: *Although it rained all day, they went on the hike. conjunction.*

al tim e ter (al tim′ə tər), instrument for measuring altitude. Altimeters are used in aircraft to indicate height above the earth's surface. *noun.*

al ti tude (al′tə tüd *or* al′tə tyüd), **1** height above the earth's surface: *What altitude did the airplane reach?* **2** height above sea level: *The altitude of Denver is 5300 feet.* **3** a high place: *At some altitudes snow never melts. noun.*

al to (al′tō), **1** the lowest female or boys' singing voice. **2** singer with such a voice. **3** part sung by such a voice. *noun, plural* **al tos.**

al to geth er (ôl′tə geŦH′ər), **1** completely; entirely: *The house was altogether destroyed by fire.* **2** on the whole: *Altogether, he was pleased. adverb.*

al um (al′əm), a white mineral salt used in medicine and in dyeing. Alum is sometimes used to stop the bleeding of a small cut. *noun.*

a lu mi num (ə lü′mə nəm), a very light, silver-white metal that does not tarnish easily. Aluminum is much used for making pots and pans, instruments, and aircraft parts. *noun.*

al ways (ôl′wiz), **1** at all times; every time: *Night always follows day.* **2** all the time: *Home is always a cheerful place at holiday time. adverb.*

am (am *or* əm). *The little boy said, "I am six years old. I am going to school." verb.*

a.m. or **A.M.,** before noon; in the time from midnight to noon: *School begins at 9 a.m.* [The abbreviations *a.m.* and *A.M.* stand for the Latin words *ante meridiem,* meaning "before noon."]

a mass (ə mas′), heap together; pile up; accumulate: *She invested her money wisely and amassed a fortune. verb.*

am a teur (am′ə chər *or* am′ə tər), **1** person who does something for pleasure, not for money: *Only amateurs can compete in college sports.* **2** person who does something rather poorly: *This painting is the work of an amateur; it shows very little skill.* **3** of amateurs; by amateurs: *Our school has an amateur orchestra.* 1,2 *noun,* 3 *adjective.*

a maze (ə māz′), surprise greatly; strike with sudden wonder: *She was amazed at how different the strand of hair looked under a microscope. verb,* **a mazed, a maz ing.**

a maze ment (ə māz′mənt), great surprise; sudden wonder: *I was filled with amazement when I first saw the ocean. noun.*

a maz ing (ə mā′zing), very surprising. *adjective.*

am bas sa dor (am bas′ə dər), **1** a representative of highest rank sent by one government or ruler to another: *The U.S. ambassador to France lives in Paris and speaks and acts for the government of the United States.* **2** any messenger with a special

a hat	**i** it	**oi** oil	**ch** child	⎡ a in about
ā age	**ī** ice	**ou** out	**ng** long	⎥ e in taken
ä far	**o** hot	**u** cup	**sh** she	ə = ⎨ i in pencil
e let	**ō** open	**u̇** put	**th** thin	⎥ o in lemon
ē equal	**ô** order	**ü** rule	**ŦH** then	⎣ u in circus
ėr term			**zh** measure	

errand; agent: *The famous musician was welcomed abroad as an ambassador of good will. noun.*

am ber (am′bər), **1** a hard yellow or yellowish-brown gum, used for jewelry and in making stems of pipes. Amber is the resin of fossil pine trees. **2** made of amber: *amber beads.* **3** yellow or yellowish brown: *a black cat with amber eyes.* 1 *noun,* 2,3 *adjective.*

am big u ous (am big′yü əs), having more than one possible meaning. The sentence "After John hit Dick he ran away" is ambiguous because we cannot tell which boy ran away. *adjective.*

am bi tion (am bish′ən), **1** a strong desire for fame or success; seeking after a high position or great power: *He was filled with ambition to become a concert violinist, and practiced many hours every day.* **2** thing for which one has a strong desire: *Her ambition is to be a doctor. noun.*

am bi tious (am bish′əs), **1** having ambition; full of ambition: *She was ambitious to become a senator and campaigned long and hard for votes.* **2** showing ambition: *an ambitious plan. adjective.*

am ble (am′bəl), **1** an easy, slow pace in walking. **2** walk at an easy, slow pace. 1 *noun,* 2 *verb,* **am bled, am bling.**

am bu lance (am′byə ləns), automobile, boat, or aircraft equipped to carry sick or wounded persons. *noun.* [Ambulance comes from French words meaning "a walking hospital."]

am bush (am′bu̇sh), **1** soldiers or other persons hidden so that they can make a surprise attack on an approaching enemy. **2** place where they are hidden: *The soldiers lay in ambush, waiting for the signal to open fire.* **3** a surprise attack on an approaching enemy from some hiding place. **4** attack from an ambush: *The bandits ambushed the stagecoach.* 1-3 *noun, plural* **am bush es;** 4 *verb.*

a me ba (ə mē′bə), a very simple animal made up of only one cell. Amebas are so small that they cannot be seen without a microscope. Many amebas live in water; others live as parasites in other animals. *noun.* Also spelled **amoeba.** [Ameba comes from a Greek word meaning "change." The animal was called this because its shape is always changing.]

a men (ā′men′ *or* ä′men′), so be it; may it become true. *Amen is said after a prayer, a wish, or a statement with which one agrees. interjection.*

a mend (ə mend′), **1** change: *The Constitution of the United States was amended so that women could vote.* **2** change for the better; improve: *It is time you amended your poor table manners. verb.*

a mend ment (ə mend′mənt), **1** a change: *The Constitution of the United States has over twenty amendments.* **2** a change for the better; improvement. *noun.*

a mends (ə mendz′), something given or paid to make up for a wrong or an injury done; payment for loss; compensation: *I bought my friend a new book to make amends for the one I lost.* noun singular or plural.

A mer i ca (ə mer′ə kə), **1** the United States of America. **2** North America. **3** North America and South America. noun. [The name *America* was made up by a German map maker in 1507 from the name *Americus* Vespucius. He was an Italian navigator who lived from 1451 to 1512. He claimed to have explored the Atlantic coast of South America.]

A mer i can (ə mer′ə kən), **1** of the United States; having something to do with the United States or its people; from the United States. **2** person born or living in the United States. **3** native only to North America and South America. **4** of North America and South America; having something to do with North America and South America or their people; from North America and South America. **5** person born or living in North America or South America. 1,3,4 *adjective*, 2,5 *noun*.

American Indian, one of the people who have lived in America from long before the time of the first European settlers.

am e thyst (am′ə thist), **1** a purple or violet kind of quartz, used for jewelry. **2** purple; violet. 1 *noun*, 2 *adjective*.

a mi a ble (ā′mē ə bəl), good-natured and friendly; pleasant and agreeable: *She is an amiable girl who gets along with everyone.* adjective.

a mid (ə mid′), in the middle of; among: *One small house stood amid the tall buildings.* preposition.

a mid ships (ə mid′ships), in or toward the middle of a ship. adverb.

a midst (ə midst′), amid. preposition.

a miss (ə mis′), wrong; not the way it should be; out of order: *We knew something was amiss when we saw that the window had been forced open.* adverb, adjective.

am mo ni a (ə mō′nyə), **1** a colorless gas, consisting of nitrogen and hydrogen, that has a strong smell. **2** this gas dissolved in water. Ammonia is very useful for cleaning. noun.

am mu ni tion (am′yə nish′ən), **1** bullets, shells, gunpowder, and bombs that can be exploded or fired from guns or other weapons. **2** military explosives and missiles to be used against an enemy. noun.

am ne sia (am nē′zhə), loss of memory caused by injury to the brain, or by disease or shock. noun.

a moe ba (ə mē′bə), ameba. noun.

a mong (ə mung′), **1** one of: *The United States is among the largest countries in the world.* **2** with; in the company of: *to spend time among friends.* **3** surrounded by: *There is a house among the trees.* **4** with a portion for each of: *Divide the fruit among all of us.* **5** throughout: *Talk of revolution spread among the crowd.* preposition.

a mongst (ə mungst′), among. preposition.

a mount (ə mount′), **1** total sum: *What is the*

amphibian (definitions 1, 2, and 3)

amount of the bill for the groceries? **2** quantity or number (of something): *No amount of coaxing would make the dog leave its owner.* **3** reach; add up: *The loss from the flood amounts to ten million dollars.* **4** be equal: *Keeping what belongs to another amounts to stealing.* 1,2 *noun*, 3,4 *verb*.

am pere (am′pir), a unit for measuring the strength of an electric current. Ordinary light bulbs take from $1/2$ to 1 ampere. noun. [The *ampere* was named for André M. Ampère, who lived from 1775 to 1836. He was a French scientist who studied the electric current.]

am phib i an (am fib′ē ən). See picture. **1** one of a group of cold-blooded animals having a backbone and a moist skin without scales. Their young usually have gills and live in water until they develop lungs for living on land. **2** aircraft that can take off from and land on either land or water. **3** tank, truck, or other vehicle able to travel across land or water. noun. [*Amphibian* is from a Greek word meaning "living in two ways." The animal was called this because it can live both on land and in water.]

am phib i ous (am fib′ē əs), able to live both on land and in water: *Frogs are amphibious.* adjective.

am phi the a ter (am′fə thē′ə tər), a circular or oval building with rows of seats around a central open space. Each row is higher than the one in front of it. *noun.*

am ple (am′pəl), **1** more than enough: *We had ample time to catch our train, so we stopped for a soda.* **2** enough: *My allowance is ample for carfare and lunches.* **3** large; roomy: *This house has ample closets.* *adjective,* **am pler, am plest.**

am pli fy (am′plə fī), **1** make greater; make stronger: *When sound is amplified, it can be heard a greater distance.* **2** expand; enlarge: *Please amplify your description of the accident by giving us more details.* *verb,* **am pli fied, am pli fy ing.**

am ply (am′plē), in an ample manner: *We were amply supplied with food.* *adverb.*

am pu tate (am′pyə tāt), cut off (all or part of a leg, arm, or finger). *verb,* **am pu tat ed, am pu tat ing.**

a muse (ə myüz′), **1** cause to laugh or smile: *The playful puppy running around the room amused the baby.* **2** keep pleasantly interested; cause to feel cheerful or happy; entertain. See picture. *verb,* **a mused, a mus ing.**

a muse ment (ə myüz′mənt), **1** condition of being amused: *The boy's amusement was so great that we all had to laugh with him.* **2** anything that amuses, such as an entertainment or sport: *Most outdoor sports are healthy amusements.* *noun.*

an (an *or* ən), **1** any: *Is there an apple in the box?* **2** one: *I had an egg for breakfast.* **3** every: *He earns two dollars an hour.* *adjective* or *indefinite article.*

an a con da (an′ə kon′də), a very large South American snake that crushes its prey in its coils. Anacondas live in tropical forests and rivers and are the longest snakes in America, sometimes over 30 feet (9 meters). See picture. *noun.*

a nal y sis (ə nal′ə sis), **1** separation of anything into its parts or elements to find out what it is made of. A chemical analysis of ordinary table salt shows that it is made up of two elements, sodium and chlorine. **2** an examining carefully and in detail. An analysis can be made of a book or a person's character. *noun, plural* **a nal y ses** (ə nal′ə sēz′).

an a lyze (an′l īz), **1** separate anything into its parts or elements to find out what it is made of: *The chemistry teacher analyzed water into two colorless gases, oxygen and hydrogen.* **2** examine carefully and in detail: *The reporter analyzed the results of the election.* *verb,* **an a lyzed, an a lyz ing.**

a nat o my (ə nat′ə mē), **1** science of the structure of animals and plants. Anatomy is a part of biology. **2** structure of an animal or plant: *The anatomy of an earthworm is much simpler than that of a human being.* *noun, plural* **a nat o mies.**

an ces tor (an′ses′tər), person from whom one is directly descended. Your grandfathers, your grandmothers, and so on back, are your ancestors. *noun.*

an ces tral (an ses′trəl), **1** of ancestors: *England was the ancestral home of the Pilgrims.* **2** inherited from ancestors: *Black hair is an ancestral trait in that family.* *adjective.*

an ces try (an′ses′trē), ancestors: *Many early*

a	hat	i	it	oi	oil	ch	child		a in about
ā	age	ī	ice	ou	out	ng	long		e in taken
ä	far	o	hot	u	cup	sh	she	ə =	i in pencil
e	let	ō	open	ů	put	th	thin		o in lemon
ē	equal	ô	order	ü	rule	ŦH	then		u in circus
ėr	term					zh	measure		

settlers in California had Spanish ancestry. noun.

an chor (ang′kər), **1** a heavy piece of iron or steel fastened to a chain or rope and dropped from a ship to the bottom of the water to hold the ship in place: *The anchor caught in the mud at the bottom of the lake and kept the boat from drifting.* See picture. **2** hold in place with an anchor: *Can you*

amuse (definition 2)
Playing cards **amused** royalty hundreds of years ago.

anchor (definition 1)

anaconda

anchor the boat in this storm? **3** stop or stay in place by using an anchor: *The ship anchored in the bay.* **4** hold in place; fix firmly: *The scouts anchored the tent to the ground.* **5** something that makes a person feel safe and secure: *The weekly talks with an understanding teacher were an anchor to the troubled child.* 1,5 *noun,* 2-4 *verb.*

an chor age (ang′kər ij), place to anchor. *noun.*

an cient (ān′shənt), **1** belonging to times long past: *In Egypt, we saw the ruins of an ancient temple built six thousand years ago.* **2 the ancients,** people who lived long ago, such as the ancient Greeks, Romans, and Egyptians. 1 *adjective,* 2 *noun.*

and (and *or* ənd), **1** as well as: *I play the violin and the piano.* **2** added to; with: *4 and 2 make 6. I like ham and eggs.* *conjunction.*

and i ron (and′ī′ərn), one of a pair of metal supports for wood in a fireplace. See picture. *noun.*

an ec dote (an′ik dōt), a short account of some interesting incident or event: *Many anecdotes are told about Abraham Lincoln.* *noun.*

a ne mi a (ə nē′mē ə), a weak condition caused by not enough red cells in the blood or by a loss of blood. *noun.*

an es thet ic (an′əs thet′ik), substance that causes a loss of the feeling of pain, touch, or cold. Ether is an anesthetic used by doctors so that patients will feel no pain. *noun.*

a new (ə nü′ *or* ə nyü′), again; once more: *I made so many mistakes I had to begin my work anew.* *adverb.*

an gel (ān′jəl), **1** messenger from God: *The angels told the shepherds about the birth of Christ.* See picture. **2** person who is good, kind, or very pleasant to look at. *noun.*

an gel ic (an jel′ik), like an angel; good, kind, or very pleasant to look at: *The little baby had an angelic face.* *adjective.*

an ger (ang′gər), **1** the feeling that one has toward someone or something that hurts, opposes, offends, or annoys: *In a moment of anger, I hit my friend.* **2** make angry: *The girl's disobedience angered her parents.* 1 *noun,* 2 *verb.*

an gle[1] (ang′gəl), **1** the space between two lines or surfaces that meet. **2** the figure formed by two such lines or surfaces. See picture. **3** move or bend at an angle: *The road angles to the right here.* **4** corner: *We took a picture of the northeast angle of the school.* **5** point of view: *We are treating the problem from a new angle.* 1,2,4,5 *noun,* 3 *verb,* **an gled, an gling.**

an gle[2] (ang′gəl), **1** fish with a hook and line. **2** try to get something by using tricks or schemes: *They angled for an invitation to dinner by flattering the cook.* *verb,* **an gled, an gling.**

an gler (ang′glər), person who fishes with a hook and line, especially one who does so for sport. *noun.*

an gle worm (ang′gəl wèrm′), earthworm. *noun.*

an gri ly (ang′grə lē), in an angry manner. *adverb.*

an gry (ang′grē), **1** feeling or showing anger: *My parents were very angry when I disobeyed them. My*

andirons

angel (definition 1)

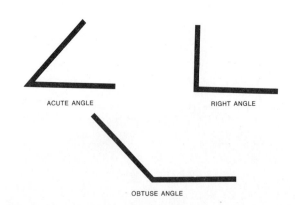
angle[1] (definition 2)—three kinds of angles

ACUTE ANGLE

RIGHT ANGLE

OBTUSE ANGLE

friend's angry words hurt my feelings. **2** stormy: *The dark clouds made the sky look angry. adjective,* **an gri er, an gri est.**

an guish (ang′gwish), very great pain or grief: *the anguish of a toothache. noun.*

an gu lar (ang′gyə lər), **1** having angles; having sharp corners: *I cut my hand on an angular piece of rock.* **2** somewhat thin and bony; not plump: *Many basketball players have tall, angular bodies. adjective.*

an i mal (an′ə məl), **1** any living thing that is not a plant. Most animals can move about, feed upon plants or other animals, and have a nervous system. A human being, a dog, a bird, a fish, a snake, a fly, and a worm are animals. **2** an animal other than a human being. *noun.*

an i mat ed (an′ə mā′tid), **1** lively; gay: *The children had an animated discussion about their trip.* **2** seeming to be alive: *an animated cartoon. adjective.*

an i mos i ty (an′ə mos′ə tē), violent hatred; active dislike; ill will: *Gossips soon earn the animosity of their neighbors. noun, plural* **an i mos i ties.**

an kle (ang′kəl), joint that connects the foot with the leg. *noun.*

an nex (ə neks′ *for 1;* an′eks *for 2*), **1** join or add (a smaller thing) to a larger thing: *The United States annexed Texas in 1845.* **2** something annexed; an added part: *We are building an annex to the school.* **1** *verb,* **2** *noun, plural* **an nex es.**

an nex a tion (an′ek sā′shən), annexing; being annexed: *The annexation of Texas enlarged the United States. noun.*

an ni hi late (ə nī′ə lāt), destroy completely; wipe out of existence: *An avalanche annihilated the village. verb,* **an ni hi lat ed, an ni hi lat ing.**

an ni ver sar y (an′ə vėr′sər ē), **1** the yearly return of a special date: *Your birthday is an anniversary you like to have remembered.* **2** celebration of the yearly return of a special date: *My parents invited their friends to their wedding anniversary. noun, plural* **an ni ver sar ies.**

an nounce (ə nouns′), **1** give public or formal notice of: *Please announce to the children that there will be no school this afternoon.* **2** make known the presence or arrival of: *The loudspeaker announced each airplane as it landed at the airport.* **3** introduce programs or read news on the radio or television. *verb,* **an nounced, an nounc ing.**

an nounce ment (ə nouns′mənt), **1** an announcing; making known: *Look in the bulletin for the announcement of the next meeting.* **2** what is announced or made known: *The principal made two announcements. noun.*

an nounc er (ə noun′sər), **1** person or thing that announces. **2** person who announces on the radio or television. *noun.*

an noy (ə noi′), make somewhat angry; disturb: *The baby is always annoying his sister by pulling her hair. verb.*

an noy ance (ə noi′əns), **1** being annoyed; feeling of dislike or trouble: *Her face showed her annoyance at the delay.* **2** something that annoys: *The heavy traffic on our street is an annoyance.*

a hat	**i** it	**oi** oil	**ch** child	⎧a in about
ā age	**ī** ice	**ou** out	**ng** long	e in taken
ä far	**o** hot	**u** cup	**sh** she	**ə** = ⎨ i in pencil
e let	**ō** open	**ù** put	**th** thin	o in lemon
ē equal	**ô** order	**ü** rule	**ᵺ** then	⎩u in circus
ėr term			**zh** measure	

3 annoying: *The teacher scolded the noisy students for their annoyance of the class. noun.*

an nu al (an′yü əl), **1** coming once a year: *Your birthday is an annual event.* **2** in a year; for a year: *For the last two years her annual salary has been $9000.* **3** living but one year or season: *Corn and beans are annual plants.* **4** plant that lives but one year or season. 1-3 *adjective,* 4 *noun.*

an nu al ly (an′yü ə lē), yearly; each year; year by year. *adverb.*

a noint (ə noint′), **1** put oil on; rub with a healing ointment; smear: *to anoint sunburned skin with lotion.* **2** put oil on (a person) as part of a ceremony: *The bishop anointed the new king. verb.*

a non y mous (ə non′ə məs), **1** by or from a person whose name is not known or given: *an anonymous phone call.* **2** having no name; of unknown name; nameless: *an anonymous author. adjective.*

an oth er (ə nuᵺ′ər), **1** one more: *Have another glass of milk. She ate a piece of candy and then asked for another.* **2** a different: *Show me another kind of hat.* **3** a different one: *I don't like this book; give me another.* 1,2 *adjective,* 1,3 *pronoun.*

an swer (an′sər), **1** speak or write in return to a question: *When I asked her a question, she answered right away.* **2** words spoken or written in return to a question: *The boy gave a quick answer.* **3** an act or movement done in return: *A nod was her only answer.* **4** act in return to a call or signal; respond: *I knocked on the door, but no one answered.* **5** solution to a problem: *What is the correct answer to this arithmetic problem?* **6** be responsible: *The bus driver must answer for the safety of the children in the bus.* **7** agree with; correspond: *The house answers to her description.* 1,4,6,7 *verb,* 2,3,5 *noun.*

ant (ant), a small insect that lives in tunnels in the ground or in wood. Ants live together in large groups called colonies. Ants, bees, and wasps belong to the same group of insects. *noun.*

an tag o nism (an tag′ə niz′əm), active opposition; hostility: *During the argument, the boy's antagonism showed plainly in his face. noun.*

an tag o nist (an tag′ə nist), person who fights, struggles, or competes against another; opponent: *The knight defeated each antagonist who came against him. noun.*

an tag o nis tic (an tag′ə nis′tik), acting against each other; opposing; conflicting: *Cats and dogs are antagonistic. adjective.*

an tag o nize (an tag′ə nīz), make an enemy of; arouse dislike in: *Her unkind remarks antagonized people who had been her friends. verb,* **an tag o nized, an tag o niz ing.**

ant arc tic (ant′ärk′tik *or* ant′är′tik), **1** at or near the South Pole; of the south polar region. **2 the Antarctic,** the south polar region. 1 *adjective,* 2 *noun.*

Ant arc ti ca (ant′ärk′tə kə *or* ant′är′tə kə), continent around the South Pole. Only two other continents, Europe and Australia, are smaller than Antarctica. It is almost totally covered by ice. *noun.*

ant eat er (ant′ē′tər), animal with a long, sticky tongue, that eats ants and termites. Anteaters have no teeth but use their very long claws to dig into ant hills. See picture. *noun.*

an te lope (an′tl ōp), **1** an animal of Africa and Asia that chews its cud and has hoofs. It is like the deer in appearance, grace, and speed but is related to goats and cows. **2** an animal like this, found on the plains of western North America; pronghorn. See picture. *noun, plural* **an te lope** or **an te lopes.**

an ten na (an ten′ə), **1** one of the long, slender feelers on the heads of insects, crabs, lobsters, and shrimps. See picture. **2** the aerial of a radio or television set. *noun, plural* **an ten nae** (an ten′ē) or **an ten nas** for 1, **an ten nas** for 2.

an them (an′thəm), **1** song of praise, devotion, or patriotism: *"The Star-Spangled Banner" is the national anthem of the United States.* **2** piece of sacred music, usually with words from some passage in the Bible. *noun.*

an ther (an′thər), the top part of the stamen of a flower. The anthers produce the pollen. See picture. *noun.*

ant hill, heap of earth piled up by ants around the entrance to their tunnels.

an thra cite (an′thrə sīt), coal that burns with very little smoke and flame; hard coal. *noun.*

an thro pol o gist (an′thrə pol′ə jist), person who is an expert in anthropology. *noun.*

an thro pol o gy (an′thrə pol′ə jē), the science that studies the origin and development of human beings. It includes the study of their customs, cultures, and beliefs. *noun.* [*Anthropology* comes from Greek words meaning "discussion of a human being."]

an ti air craft (an′tē er′kraft′ *or* an′tē ar′kraft′), used in defense against enemy aircraft. *adjective.*

an ti bi ot ic (an′ti bī ot′ik), substance produced by bacteria and fungi that destroys or weakens germs. Penicillin is an antibiotic useful in treating many infections. *noun.*

an ti bod y (an′ti bod′ē), a protein substance produced in the blood of animals and human beings. Antibodies destroy or weaken bacteria or neutralize poisons produced by bacteria. *noun, plural* **an ti bod ies.**

an tic i pate (an tis′ə pāt), **1** look forward to; expect: *We are anticipating a good time at your party.* **2** do before others do; be ahead of in doing: *The Chinese anticipated the European discovery of gunpowder.* **3** take care of ahead of time; consider in advance: *We anticipated hot weather and took our bathing suits with us.* verb, **an tic i pat ed, an tic i pat ing.**

anteater—about 6 feet (2 meters) long with the tail

antelope—about 3 feet (1 meter) high at the shoulder

antenna (definition 1)—antennae of a grasshopper

an tic i pa tion (an tis′ə pā′shən), act of anticipating; looking forward to; expectation: *In anticipation of a cold winter, the farmer cut more firewood than usual.* noun.

an tics (an′tiks), funny gestures or actions: *The antics of the clown amused us.* noun plural.

an ti dote (an′ti dōt), medicine that counteracts the harmful effects of a poison; remedy: *Milk is an antidote for some poisons.* noun.

an ti freeze (an′ti frēz′), substance added to the water in an automobile radiator, to prevent it from freezing. noun.

an tique (an tēk′), **1** of times long ago; from times long ago. See picture. **2** something made long ago: *This carved chest is a genuine antique.* 1 adjective, 2 noun.

an ti sep tic (an′tə sep′tik), substance that prevents the growth of germs that cause infection. Iodine and alcohol are antiseptics. noun.

an ti tox in (an′ti tok′sən), **1** a kind of antibody that can prevent certain diseases, cure them, or make them milder. **2** serum that contains an antitoxin. It is injected into people to protect them from a disease. noun.

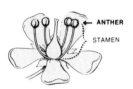

antler (definition 1)
antlers of a deer

antique (definition 1)—an antique automobile

a hat	**i** it	**oi** oil	**ch** child		a in about
ā age	**ī** ice	**ou** out	**ng** long		e in taken
ä far	**o** hot	**u** cup	**sh** she	ə =	i in pencil
e let	**ō** open	**u̇** put	**th** thin		o in lemon
ē equal	**ô** order	**ü** rule	**ᵀʜ** then		u in circus
ėr term			**zh** measure		

ant ler (ant′lər), **1** a bony, hornlike growth on the head of a male deer, elk, or moose. Antlers usually have one or more branches. They are shed once a year and grow back again during the next year. See picture. **2** branch of such a growth. noun.

an to nym (an′tə nim), word that means the opposite of another word. "Hot" is the antonym of "cold." noun.

an vil (an′vəl), an iron or steel block on which metals are hammered and shaped. Blacksmiths use anvils. noun.

anx i e ty (ang zī′ə tē), **1** uneasy thoughts or fears about what may happen; troubled, worried, or uneasy feeling: *The passengers were filled with anxiety when the airplane was caught in the storm.* **2** eager desire: *Her anxiety to succeed led her to work hard.* noun, plural **anx i e ties.**

anx ious (angk′shəs), **1** uneasy because of thoughts or fears of what may happen; troubled; worried: *I felt anxious about my final exams. The week of the flood was an anxious time for all of us.* **2** wishing very much; eager: *They were anxious to start their vacation.* adjective.

an y (en′ē), **1** one out of many: *Choose any book you like from the books on the shelf.* **2** some: *Have you any fresh fruit? We haven't any.* **3** every: *Any child knows that.* **4** at all: *Has my singing improved any?* 1-3 adjective, 2 pronoun, 4 adverb.

an y bod y (en′ē bod′ē), **1** any person; anyone: *Has anybody been here?* **2** an important person: *Everybody who's anybody stays at that hotel.* 1 pronoun, 2 noun.

an y how (en′ē hou), **1** in any case; at any rate; anyway: *I can see as well as you can, anyhow.* **2** in any way whatever: *The answer is wrong anyhow you look at it.* adverb.

an y one (en′ē wun), any person; anybody: *Can anyone go to this movie or is it just for adults?* pronoun.

an y thing (en′ē thing), **1** any thing: *Do you have anything to eat?* **2** at all: *My bike isn't anything like yours.* 1 pronoun, 2 adverb.

an y way (en′ē wā), in any case: *I am coming anyway, no matter what you say.* adverb.

an y where (en′ē hwer), in, at, or to any place: *I'll meet you anywhere you say.* adverb.

a or ta (ā ôr′tə), the main artery that carries the blood from the left side of the heart to all parts of the body except the lungs. noun.

a part (ə pärt′), **1** to pieces; in pieces; in separate parts: *She took the watch apart to see how it runs.* **2** away from each other: *Keep the dogs apart.* **3** to one side; aside: *He sets some money apart for a vacation each year.* adverb.
apart from, besides: *Apart from its cost, the plan was a good one.*

a part ment (ə pärt′mənt), room or group of rooms to live in; flat: *Our apartment is on the second floor of that building. noun.*

ap a thy (ap′ə thē), lack of interest or feeling; indifference: *Because of apathy, few people voted in the election. noun, plural* **ap a thies.**

ape (āp), **1** a large, tailless monkey with long arms. Apes can stand almost erect and walk on two feet. Chimpanzees, gorillas, orangutans, and gibbons are apes. **2** any monkey. **3** imitate; mimic: *The children aped the way the TV star talked.* **4** person who imitates or mimics. **1,2,4** *noun,* **3** *verb,* **aped, ap ing.**

ap er ture (ap′ər chər), an opening; gap; hole. A shutter regulates the size of the aperture through which light passes into a camera. *noun.*

a phid (ā′fid *or* af′id), a very small insect that lives by sucking juices from plants. *noun.*

a piece (ə pēs′), for each one; each: *These apples cost ten cents apiece. adverb.*

a pol o get ic (ə pol′ə jet′ik), making an excuse; expressing regret: *He sent me an apologetic note saying he was sorry for forgetting to come to my party. adjective.*

a pol o gize (ə pol′ə jīz), make an apology; say one is sorry; offer an excuse: *She apologized for hurting my feelings. verb,* **a pol o gized, a pol o giz ing.**

a pol o gy (ə pol′ə jē), **1** words saying one is sorry for an offense, fault, or accident; explanation asking pardon: *I made an apology to my teacher for being late.* **2** a poor substitute; makeshift: *One piece of toast is a skimpy apology for a breakfast. noun, plural* **a pol o gies.**

a pos tle *or* **A pos tle** (ə pos′əl), **1** one of the twelve special followers of Christ. He chose them to go out and spread His teachings everywhere. **2** any early Christian leader or missionary: *Saint Paul was called the "Apostle to the Gentiles." noun.*

a pos tro phe (ə pos′trə fē), sign (') used: **1** to show the omission of one or more letters in contractions, as in *isn't* for *is not, tho'* for *though.* **2** to show the possessive forms of nouns, as in *Lee's book, the lions' den.* **3** to form plurals of letters and numbers: *There are two o's in apology and four 9's in 959,990. noun.*

ap pall *or* **ap pal** (ə pôl′), fill with horror or fear; dismay; terrify: *She was appalled when she saw the river had risen to the doorstep. verb,* **ap palled, ap pall ing.**

ap pa ra tus (ap′ə rā′təs *or* ap′ə rat′əs), anything necessary to carry out a purpose or for a particular use. Tools, special instruments, and machines are apparatus. Test tubes and beakers are apparatus; so are a grocer's scales and the equipment in a gymnasium. *noun, plural* **ap pa ra tus** *or* **ap pa ra tus es.**

ap par el (ə par′əl), **1** clothing; dress: *Does this store sell children's apparel?* **2** clothe; dress up: *The horseback riders, gaily appareled, formed part of the circus parade.* **1** *noun,* **2** *verb.*

ap par ent (ə par′ənt), **1** plain to see; so plain that one cannot help seeing it: *The stain is apparent from across the room.* **2** easily understood: *It is apparent that the days become shorter in October and November.* **3** seeming; appearing to be: *The apparent size of an airplane in the sky is smaller than the airplane really is. adjective.*

ap par ent ly (ə par′ənt lē), as far as one can judge by appearances; seemingly: *Their lights are not on; apparently they are not home. adverb.*

ap pa ri tion (ap′ə rish′ən), **1** ghost: *The apparition, clothed in a white robe, glided through the wall.* **2** the appearing of something strange, remarkable, or unexpected: *I suddenly saw the apparition of a blazing star shooting across the sky. noun.*

ap peal (ə pēl′), **1** ask earnestly; ask for help or sympathy: *When the children were in trouble they appealed to their parents.* **2** an earnest request; call for help or sympathy: *an appeal to someone for forgiveness, an appeal for money for the poor.* **3** ask that a case be taken to a higher court or judge to be heard again: *When the judge ruled against them, they decided to appeal.* **4** a request to have a case heard again before a higher court or judge: *Their appeal was granted.* **5** be attractive, interesting, or enjoyable: *Blue and red appeal to me but I don't like gray or yellow.* **6** attraction or interest: *Television has a great appeal for most young people.* **1,3,5** *verb,* **2,4,6** *noun.*

ap pear (ə pir′), **1** be seen; come in sight: *One by one the stars appear.* **2** seem; look: *The apple appeared sound on the outside, but it was rotten inside.* **3** be published: *Her latest book appeared a year ago.* **4** show or present oneself in public: *The singer will appear on television today. verb.*

ap pear ance (ə pir′əns), **1** act of coming in sight: *His appearance in the doorway was welcomed with shouts.* **2** coming before the public: *The singer made her first appearance in a concert in San Francisco.* **3** the way a person or thing looks: *I knew from his appearance that he was ill. noun.*

ap pease (ə pēz′), **1** satisfy: *A good dinner will appease your hunger.* **2** make calm; quiet: *I tried to appease the crying child by giving him candy.* **3** give in to the demands of: *The girl appeased her parents and returned to finish school. verb,* **ap peased, ap peas ing.**

ap pen di ci tis (ə pen′də sī′tis), soreness and swelling of the appendix. *noun.*

ap pen dix (ə pen′diks), **1** addition at the end of a book or document. **2** a slender, closed tube growing out of the large intestine. See picture. *noun, plural* **ap pen dix es, ap pen di ces** (ə pen′də sēz′).

ap pe tite (ap′ə tīt), **1** desire for food: *Swimming seems to increase my appetite.* **2** desire: *The lively children had a great appetite for excitement and amusement. noun.*

ap pe tiz er (ap′ə tī′zər), something that arouses the appetite, usually served before a meal. Pickles and olives are appetizers. *noun.*

ap pe tiz ing (ap′ə tī′zing), arousing or exciting the appetite: *Appetizing food always smells delicious. adjective.*

ap plaud (ə plôd′), **1** show approval by clapping hands or shouting: *The audience applauds anything that pleases it in a play or concert.* **2** approve; praise: *Her parents applauded her decision to study medicine.* verb.

ap plause (ə plôz′), **1** approval shown by clapping the hands or shouting: *Applause for the singer's good performance rang out from the audience.* **2** approval; praise. noun.

ap ple (ap′əl), the firm, fleshy, somewhat round fruit of a tree widely grown in temperate regions. Apples have red, yellow, or green skin, and are eaten either raw or cooked. noun.

ap ple sauce (ap′əl sôs′), apples cut in pieces and cooked with sugar, spices, and water until soft. noun.

ap pli ance (ə plī′əns), thing like a tool or small machine used in doing something. A can opener is an appliance for opening tin cans. Vacuum cleaners, washing machines, and refrigerators are household appliances. noun.

ap pli ca ble (ap′lə kə bəl), appropriate; suitable: *The rule "Look before you leap" is almost always applicable.* adjective.

ap pli cant (ap′lə kənt), person who applies (for a job, money, position, or help). noun.

ap pli ca tion (ap′lə kā′shən), **1** putting to use; use: *The application of what you know will help you solve new problems.* **2** applying; putting on: *The painter's careless application of paint spattered the floor.* **3** thing applied: *An application of salve relieved my sunburn.* **4** a request made in person or in writing: *I put in an application for a job at the supermarket.* **5** continued effort; close attention: *Application to her work got her a promotion.* noun.

ap ply (ə plī′), **1** put on: *He applied two coats of paint to the table.* **2** use: *I know the rule but I don't know how to apply it.* **3** be useful or suitable; fit: *When does this rule apply?* **4** ask: *He is applying for a job as clerk.* **5** set to work and stick to it: *She applied herself to learning to play the piano.* verb, **ap plied, ap ply ing.**

ap point (ə point′), **1** to name for an office or position; choose: *The class president appointed five*

students to the entertainment committee. **2** decide on; set (a time or place to be somewhere or to meet someone): *He appointed the schoolhouse as the place for the meeting. We shall appoint eight o'clock as the hour to begin.* verb.

ap point ment (ə point′mənt), **1** act of naming for an office or position; choosing: *The appointment of a new Secretary of State was announced.* **2** office or position: *The lawyer was offered a high government appointment.* **3** a meeting with someone at a certain time and place; engagement: *I have an appointment to see the doctor at four o'clock.* noun.

ap praise (ə prāz′), **1** estimate the value, amount, or quality of: *An employer should be able to appraise the ability of an employee.* **2** set a price on; fix the value of: *The jeweler appraised the diamond ring at $1000.* verb, **ap praised, ap prais ing.**

ap pre ci ate (ə prē′shē āt), **1** think highly of; recognize the worth or quality of; value; enjoy: *Almost everybody appreciates good food.* **2** be thankful for: *We appreciate your help.* **3** have an opinion of the value, worth, or quality of; estimate: *Most of us appreciate the importance of exercise for good health.* **4** be aware of; recognize: *A musician is able to appreciate small differences in sounds.* verb, **ap pre ci at ed, ap pre ci at ing.**

ap pre ci a tion (ə prē′shē ā′shən), **1** valuing highly; sympathetic understanding: *She has no appreciation of modern art.* **2** appreciating; valuing: *He showed his appreciation of her help by sending a letter of thanks.* noun.

ap pre ci a tive (ə prē′shē ā′tiv), having appreciation; showing appreciation; recognizing the value: *The appreciative audience applauded the performer.* adjective.

ap pre hend (ap′ri hend′), **1** fear; dread: *I apprehended disaster as the hurricane approached.* **2** arrest; seize: *The burglars were apprehended by the police.* **3** understand: *Though I couldn't hear him, I could apprehend his meaning from his gestures.* verb.

ap pre hen sion (ap′ri hen′shən), **1** fear; dread: *The roar of the hurricane filled us with apprehension.* **2** a seizing or being seized; arrest: *The appearance of the suspect's picture in all the papers led to her apprehension.* **3** understanding: *I do not have a clear apprehension of fractions.* noun.

ap pre hen sive (ap′ri hen′siv), afraid, anxious, or worried: *I felt apprehensive before taking my first airplane trip.* adjective.

ap pren tice (ə pren′tis), **1** person who is learning a trade or an art by working with a skilled worker. In former times, apprentices worked for little or no pay. **2** bind or take as an apprentice: *Benjamin Franklin's father apprenticed him to a printer.* **1** noun, **2** verb, **ap pren ticed, ap pren tic ing.**

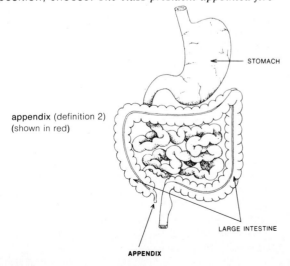

appendix (definition 2)
(shown in red)

STOMACH

LARGE INTESTINE

APPENDIX

aqueduct (definition 2)

arch¹ (definition 1)

architect
and
construction worker

ap proach (ə prōch′), **1** come near or nearer: *Walk softly as you approach the baby's crib. Winter is approaching.* **2** act of coming near or nearer: *Sunset announces the approach of night.* **3** way by which a place or person can be reached; access: *The approach to the house was a narrow path. Our best approach to the senator is through a mutual friend.* **4** method of starting work on a task or problem: *She seems to have a good approach to the problem.* **5** speak to about a plan or request: *We approached our teacher about having a class party.* 1,5 *verb,* 2-4 *noun, plural* **ap proach es.**

ap proach a ble (ə prō′chə bəl), **1** able to be approached: *The house on the mountain is approachable only on foot.* **2** easy to approach and talk to: *No matter how busy the teacher was, she was always approachable. adjective.*

ap pro pri ate (ə prō′prē it *for 1;* ə prō′prē āt *for 2,3*), **1** suitable; proper: *Plain, simple clothes are appropriate for school wear.* **2** set apart for some special use: *The state appropriated money for a new road into our town.* **3** take for oneself: *You should not appropriate other people's belongings without their permission.* 1 *adjective,* 2,3 *verb,* **ap pro pri at ed, ap pro pri at ing.**

ap pro pri a tion (ə prō′prē ā′shən), **1** sum of money appropriated: *Our town received a state appropriation of $5000 for a new playground.* **2** act of appropriating: *The appropriation of the land made it possible to have a park. noun.*

ap prov al (ə prü′vəl), **1** favorable opinion; approving; praise: *We all like others to show approval of what we do.* **2** permission; consent: *The principal gave her approval to our plan for a class picnic. noun.*

on approval, so that the customer can inspect the item and decide whether to buy or return it: *We bought the television set on approval.*

ap prove (ə prüv′), **1** think well of; be pleased with: *The teacher looked at her work and approved it.* **2** give a favorable opinion: *I'm not sure I can approve of what you propose to do.* **3** consent to: *The school board approved the budget. verb,* **ap proved, ap prov ing.**

ap prox i mate (ə prok′sə mit *for 1;* ə prok′sə māt *for 2*), **1** nearly correct: *The approximate length of this room is 12 feet; the exact length is 12 feet 3 inches.* **2** come near to; approach: *The crowd approximated a thousand people. Your account of what happened approximates the truth, but there are several small errors.* 1 *adjective,* 2 *verb,* **ap prox i mat ed, ap prox i mat ing.**

ap prox i mate ly (ə prok′sə mit lē), nearly; about: *We are approximately 200 miles from home. adverb.*

ap prox i ma tion (ə prok′sə mā′shən), **1** a nearly correct amount: *25,000 miles is an approximation of the circumference of the earth.* **2** approach: *Their story was a close approximation to the truth. noun.*

Apr., April.

a pri cot (ā′prə kot *or* ap′rə kot), **1** a round, pale, orange-colored fruit that grows on a tree. Apricots are smaller than peaches and have a smoother skin. They are good to eat. **2** pale orange-yellow. **1** *noun,* **2** *adjective.*

A pril (ā/prəl), the fourth month of the year. It has 30 days. *noun.* [*April* comes from Latin words meaning "the month of Aphrodite." She was the Greek goddess of love and beauty.]

a pron (ā/prən), garment worn over the front part of the body to cover or protect clothes: *a kitchen apron, a carpenter's apron. noun.*

apt (apt), **1** likely; inclined: *A careless person is apt to make mistakes.* **2** right for the occasion; suitable; fitting: *His apt reply to the question showed that he had understood it very well.* **3** quick to learn: *Some pupils are more apt than others. adjective.*

ap ti tude (ap/tə tüd *or* ap/tə tyüd), **1** natural tendency or talent; ability; capacity: *Edison had a remarkable aptitude for inventing.* **2** quickness to understand: *She is a pupil of great aptitude. noun.*

a quar i um (ə kwer/ē əm), **1** tank or glass bowl in which living fish, other water animals, and water plants are kept. **2** building used for showing collections of living fish, water animals, and water plants. *noun.*

a quat ic (ə kwat/ik), **1** growing or living in water: *Water lilies are aquatic plants.* **2** taking place in or on water: *Swimming and sailing are aquatic sports. adjective.*

aq ue duct (ak/wə dukt), **1** an artificial channel or large pipe for bringing water from a distance. **2** structure like a bridge that supports such a channel or pipe as it crosses a river or valley. See picture. *noun.*

Ar ab (ar/əb), **1** person born or living in Arabia. **2** member of a people living in southwestern and southern Asia and northern Africa. **3** of or having something to do with the Arabs or Arabia. **1,2** *noun,* **3** *adjective.*

A ra bi a (ə rā/bē ə), large peninsula in southwestern Asia. *noun.*

A ra bi an (ə rā/bē ən), **1** of or having something to do with Arabia or the Arabs. **2** person born or living in Arabia; Arab. **1** *adjective,* **2** *noun.*

Ar a bic (ar/ə bik), **1** language of the Arabs. **2** of the Arabs or their language. **1** *noun,* **2** *adjective.*

Arabic numerals, the figures 1, 2, 3, 4, 5, 6, 7, 8, 9, 0. They are called Arabic because they were first made known to Europeans by Arabian scholars.

ar a ble (ar/ə bəl), fit for plowing: *There is no arable land on a rocky mountain. adjective.*

a rach nid (ə rak/nid), one of a large group of animals that includes spiders, scorpions, mites, and ticks. An arachnid has eight legs but no antennae and no wings. The body is divided into only two regions. *noun.*

ar bi trar y (är/bə trer/ē), based on one's own wishes, notions, or will; not going by any rule or law: *The judge tried to be fair and did not make arbitrary decisions. adjective.*

ar bi trate (är/bə trāt), **1** give a decision in a dispute: *The teacher arbitrated between the two girls in their quarrel.* **2** settle by arbitration; submit to arbitration: *The two nations finally agreed to*

a hat	i it	oi oil	ch child	a in about
ā age	ī ice	ou out	ng long	e in taken
ä far	o hot	u cup	sh she	i in pencil
e let	ō open	u̇ put	th thin	o in lemon
ē equal	ô order	ü rule	ŦH then	u in circus
ėr term			zh measure	

(ə =)

arbitrate their dispute and war was avoided. verb, **ar bi trat ed, ar bi trat ing.**

ar bi tra tion (är/bə trā/shən), settlement of a dispute by a person or persons chosen to judge both sides: *Arbitration prevented that strike. noun.*

ar bor (är/bər), a shaded place formed by trees or shrubs or by vines growing on a lattice. *noun.*

arc (ärk), **1** any part of the circumference of a circle. See picture. **2** any part of a curved line. *noun.*

arch[1] (ärch), **1** a curved structure that bears the weight of the material above it. Arches often form the tops of doors, windows, and gateways. See picture. **2** monument forming an arch or arches. **3** bend into an arch; curve: *The wind had arched the trees over the road.* **4** the lower part of the foot which makes a curve between the heel and the toes: *Fallen arches cause flat feet.* **1,2,4** *noun, plural* **arch es;** **3** *verb.*

arch[2] (ärch), **1** playfully mischievous: *The little boy gave his mother an arch look and ran away.* **2** chief; principal; leading: *The arch villain of the story was a pirate. adjective.*

ar chae ol o gist (är/kē ol/ə jist), person who is an expert in archaeology. *noun.*

ar chae ol o gy (är/kē ol/ə jē), study of the people, customs, and life of ancient times by excavating the remains of ancient cities and classifying and studying tools, pottery, or monuments. *noun.*

arch bish op (ärch/bish/əp), bishop having the highest rank. *noun.*

arch er (är/chər), person who shoots with a bow and arrow. *noun.*

arch er y (är/chər ē), practice or sport of shooting with a bow and arrow. *noun.*

ar chi pel a go (är/kə pel/ə gō), **1** group of many islands. **2** sea having many islands in it. *noun, plural* **ar chi pel a gos** *or* **ar chi pel a goes.**

ar chi tect (är/kə tekt), person who designs buildings, and then sees that the plans are followed by the contractors and workers who actually put up the buildings. See picture. *noun.*

ar chi tec ture (är/kə tek/chər), **1** science or art of planning and designing buildings. **2** style or special manner of building: *Greek architecture made much use of columns. noun.*

arch way (ärch/wā/), **1** entrance or passageway with an arch above it. **2** arch covering a passageway. *noun.*

arc tic (ärk/tik *or* är/tik), **1** at or near the North Pole; of the north polar region: *They explored the great arctic wilderness of northern Canada.* **2 the Arctic,** the north polar region. The Arctic has an extremely cold winter. **1** *adjective,* **2** *noun.*

Arctic Ocean, ocean of the north polar region.

ar dent (ärd′nt), very enthusiastic; eager: *He is an ardent scout. adjective.*

ar dor (är′dər), great enthusiasm; eagerness: *The reporter spoke with ardor about her work. noun.*

ar du ous (är′jü əs), hard to do; requiring much effort; difficult: *an arduous lesson. adjective.*

are (är or ər). *We are ready. You are next. They are waiting.* We say: I am, you are, he is, she is, it is, we are, you are, they are. *verb.*

ar e a (er′ē ə *or* ar′ē ə), **1** amount of surface; extent: *The area of this floor is 600 square feet.* **2** range of knowledge or interest: *Our science teacher is familiar with the areas of physics and chemistry.* **3** region: *The Rocky Mountain area is the most mountainous in the United States. noun.*

area code, combination of three numbers used to dial directly by telephone from one region of the United States and Canada to another.

a re na (ə rē′nə), **1** space in which contests or shows took place: *Gladiators fought with lions in the arena at Rome.* **2** building in which indoor sports are played. **3** place of conflict: *The United Nations is an arena for world debate. noun.*

aren't (ärnt), are not.

Ar gen ti na (är′jən tē′nə), country in southern South America. *noun.*

ar gue (är′gyü), **1** discuss with someone who disagrees: *He argued with his sister about who should wash the dishes.* **2** give reasons for or against something: *The children argued about who should wash the dishes.* **3** persuade by giving reasons: *They argued me into going. verb,* **ar gued, ar gu ing.**

ar gu ment (är′gyə mənt), **1** discussion by persons who disagree; dispute: *She won the argument by producing facts to prove her point.* **2** reason or reasons offered for or against something: *Their arguments for a new school are persuasive. noun.*

ar id (ar′id), **1** having very little rainfall; dry: *Desert lands are arid.* **2** uninteresting; dull: *an arid, boring speech. adjective.*

a rise (ə rīz′), **1** rise up; get up: *The children arose from their seats to salute the flag.* **2** move upward: *Smoke arises from the chimney.* **3** come into being; come about: *A great wind arose. Accidents often arise from carelessness. verb,* **a rose, a ris en** (ə riz′n), **a ris ing.**

ar is toc ra cy (ar′ə stok′rə sē), **1** class of people having a high position in society because of birth, rank, or title. Earls, duchesses, and princes belong to the aristocracy. **2** class of people considered superior because of intelligence, culture, or wealth. **3** government in which the nobles rule. *noun, plural* **ar is toc ra cies.**

a ris to crat (ə ris′tə krat), **1** person who belongs to the aristocracy; a noble. **2** person who has the tastes, opinions, and manners of a noble. *noun.*

a ris to crat ic (ə ris′tə krat′ik), **1** belonging to the upper classes; considered superior because of birth, intelligence, culture, or wealth. **2** like an aristocrat in manners; proud. **3** having something to do with an aristocracy. *adjective.*

a rith me tic (ə rith′mə tik), branch of mathematics that deals with adding, subtracting, multiplying, and dividing numbers. *noun.*

Ar i zo na (ar′ə zō′nə), one of the southwestern states of the United States. *noun.* [*Arizona* got its name from an American Indian word meaning "place of the small spring."]

ark (ärk), **1** (in the Bible) the large boat in which Noah saved himself, his family, and a pair of each kind of animal from the Flood. **2** the chest or box in which the Hebrews kept the two stone tablets containing the Ten Commandments. *noun.*

Ar kan sas (är′kən sô), one of the south central states of the United States. *noun.* [*Arkansas* was named for an American Indian tribe that once lived in the area. This name came from an Indian word meaning "downstream people."]

arm[1] (ärm), **1** the part of the body between the shoulder and the hand. **2** something shaped or used like an arm. An armchair has two arms. An inlet is an arm of the sea. *noun.*

arm[2] (ärm), **1 arms,** weapons of any kind. Guns, swords, axes, or sticks—any of these might be arms for defense or attack. **2** supply with weapons: *During the American Revolutionary War the French helped arm the colonists.* **3** supply with any means of defense or attack: *The lawyer entered court armed with the evidence to support his case.* **4** take up weapons; prepare for war: *The soldiers armed for battle.* 1 *noun plural,* 2-4 *verb.*

ar ma da (är mä′də), **1** a large fleet of warships. **2** a large fleet of airplanes. *noun.*

ar ma dil lo (är′mə dil′ō), a small, burrowing animal that has a very hard shell. Some kinds can roll themselves up into a ball when attacked. Armadillos are found in South America and some parts of southern North America. See picture. *noun, plural* **ar ma dil los.**

ar ma ment (är′mə mənt), **1** war equipment and supplies. **2** the army, navy, and other military forces of a country. **3** the guns on a naval vessel, a tank, or an airplane. *noun.*

arm chair (ärm′cher′ *or* ärm′char′), chair with pieces at the side to support a person's arms or elbows. *noun.*

armadillo—2½ feet (76 centimeters) long with the tail

arm ful (ärm′fůl), as much as one arm can hold; as much as both arms can hold: *I carried an armful of groceries. noun, plural* **arm fuls.**

ar mi stice (är′mə stis), a stop in fighting; temporary peace; truce. *noun.*

ar mor (är′mər), **1** a covering, usually of metal or leather, worn to protect the body in fighting. See picture. **2** any kind of protective covering. The steel plates of a warship and the scales of a fish are armor. *noun.*

ar mored (är′mərd), covered or protected with armor: *an armored car. adjective.*

ar mor y (är′mər ē), **1** place where weapons are kept or manufactured. **2** a building with rooms for the militia to drill in. *noun, plural* **ar mor ies.**

arm pit (ärm′pit′), the hollow place under the arm at the shoulder. *noun.*

arms (ärmz), **1** See **arm**[2] (definition 1). **2** fighting; war: *A soldier is a man of arms.* **3** design used as a symbol of a family or government; coat of arms. *noun plural.*

ar my (är′mē), **1** a large, organized group of soldiers trained and armed for war: *American armies have fought in many lands.* **2** any group of people organized for a purpose: *The Salvation Army helps the poor.* **3** a very large number; multitude: *an army of ants. noun, plural* **ar mies.**

a ro ma (ə rō′mə), fragrance; spicy odor: *Just smell the aroma of the cake baking in the oven. noun.*

a rose (ə rōz′). See **arise.** *She arose from her chair. verb.*

a round (ə round′), **1** in a circle about: *She has traveled around the world.* **2** in a circle: *The top spun around.* **3** in circumference: *The tree measures four feet around.* **4** on all sides of: *Woods lay around the house.* **5** on the far side of; so as to round: *The store is just around the corner. I drove too fast around the curve.* **6** here and there; about: *We walked around to see the town. Don't leave your books around the house.* **7** somewhere about; near: *We waited around for an hour.* **8** through a round of time: *Summer will soon come around again.* 1,4-6 *preposition,* 2,3,6-8 *adverb.*

a rouse (ə rouz′), **1** stir to action; excite: *The mystery story aroused my imagination.* **2** awaken: *The barking dog aroused me from my sleep. verb,* **a roused, a rous ing.**

ar range (ə rānj′), **1** put in the proper order: *Please arrange the books on the library shelf. She arranged her business so that she could take a vacation in September.* **2** plan; form plans: *Can you arrange to meet me this evening?* **3** adapt; fit: *This music for the violin is also arranged for the piano. verb,* **ar ranged, ar rang ing.**

ar range ment (ə rānj′mənt), **1** a putting or a being put in proper order: *Careful arrangement of books in a library makes them easier to find.* **2** way or order in which things or persons are put: *You can make six arrangements of the letters A, B, and C.* **3** something arranged in a particular way: *a beautiful flower arrangement. This piece of music for the piano also has an arrangement for the violin.* **4** **arrangements,** plans; preparations: *All*

Courtesy of The Metropolitan Museum of Art

armor

arrangements have been made for our trip to Chicago. noun.

ar ray (ə rā/), **1** order: *The troops were formed in battle array.* **2** put in order: *The general arrayed his troops for the battle.* **3** display of persons or things: *The team had an impressive array of fine players.* **4** clothes; dress: *The royal family appeared in gorgeous array.* **5** dress in fine clothes; adorn: *The royal family was arrayed in silks and satins.* 1,3,4 *noun,* 2,5 *verb.*

ar rest (ə rest/), **1** seize by authority of the law; take to jail or court: *The police arrested the burglar.* **2** a stopping; seizing: *We saw the arrest of the burglar.* **3** stop; check: *Filling a tooth arrests decay.* **4** catch and hold: *Our attention was arrested by a strange sound.* 1,3,4 *verb,* 2 *noun.*

ar riv al (ə rī/vəl), **1** act of arriving; coming: *She is waiting for the arrival of the plane.* **2** person or thing that arrives: *We greeted the new arrivals at the door. noun.*

ar rive (ə rīv/), **1** come to a place: *We arrived in Boston a week ago.* **2** come: *Summer vacation finally arrived. verb,* **ar rived, ar riv ing.**

arrive at, come to; reach: *You should arrive at school before nine o'clock.*

ar ro gance (ar/ə gəns), too great pride; haughtiness: *He was a talented actor, but his arrogance made him unpopular. noun.*

ar ro gant (ar/ə gənt), too proud; haughty. *adjective.*

ar row (ar/ō), **1** a slender, pointed shaft or stick which is shot from a bow. **2** anything like an arrow in shape or speed. **3** a sign (→) used to show direction or position in maps, on road signs, and in writing. *noun.*

ar row head (ar/ō hed/), head or tip of an arrow. See picture. *noun.*

ar se nal (är/sə nəl), **1** a building for storing or manufacturing weapons and ammunition for an army or navy. **2** storehouse. *noun.*

ar se nic (är/sə nik), a white, tasteless powder that is a violent poison. *noun.*

ar son (är/sən), the crime of intentionally setting fire to a building or other property. *noun.*

art[1] (ärt), **1** painting, drawing, and sculpture: *I am studying art and music.* **2** paintings, sculptures, and other works of art: *We went to an exhibit at the museum of art.* See picture. **3** a branch of learning that depends more on special practice than on general principles. Writing compositions is an art; grammar is a science. The fine arts include painting, drawing, sculpture, architecture, music, and dancing. **4** set of principles or methods gained by experience: *She understands the art of making friends.* **5** some kind of skill or practical application of skill. Cooking and housekeeping are household arts. **6** trick; cunning; skillful act: *The witch's arts deceived the children. noun.*

art[2] (ärt), an old form meaning **are.** "Thou art" means "You are." *verb.*

ar ter y (är/tər ē), **1** any of the tubes that carry blood from the heart to all parts of the body. **2** a main road; important channel: *Main Street and*

Broadway are the two arteries of traffic in our city. noun, plural **ar ter ies.**

art ful (ärt/fəl), **1** slyly clever; crafty; deceitful: *A swindler uses artful tricks to get people's money away from them.* **2** skillful; clever: *Her artful handling of the situation prevented an argument. adjective.*

ar thri tis (är thrī/tis), soreness and swelling of a joint or joints of the body. *noun.*

ar thro pod (är/thrə pod), one of a large group of animals having bodies in two or three parts and jointed legs. Insects, arachnids, and crustaceans are arthropods. *noun.*

ar ti choke (är/tə chōk), the flower bud of a plant that looks somewhat like a thistle with large, prickly leaves. Artichokes are cooked and eaten as a vegetable. *noun.*

ar ti cle (är/tə kəl), **1** a written composition that is part of a magazine, newspaper, or book: *This is a good article on gardening.* **2** clause in a contract, treaty, or statute: *When the Constitution of the United States was adopted it had seven articles.* **3** a particular thing; item: *Gloves are articles of clothing.* **4** one of the words *a, an,* or *the,* as in *a book, an egg, the boy. A* and *an* are **indefinite articles;** *the* is the **definite article.** *noun.*

ar ti fice (är/tə fis), **1** a clever device; trick: *The child used every artifice to avoid going to the dentist.* **2** trickery; craft: *His conduct is free from artifice. noun.*

ar ti fi cial (är/tə fish/əl), **1** made by human skill or labor; not natural: *artificial flowers. At night, you read by artificial light.* **2** put on; pretended: *When nervous, he had an artificial laugh. adjective.*

ar til ler y (är til/ər ē), **1** cannon that are supported by wheels, wheeled vehicles, or a heavy metal base. **2** the part of an army that uses and manages cannon. *noun.*

ar ti san (är/tə zən), person skilled in a craft or trade; craftsman. Carpenters, masons, plumbers, and electricians are artisans. *noun.*

art ist (är/tist), **1** person who paints pictures. **2** person who is skilled in any of the fine arts, such as sculpture, music, or literature. **3** person who does work with skill and good taste. *noun.*

ar tis tic (är tis/tik), **1** of art or artists: *Our museum has many artistic treasures.* **2** done with skill and good taste: *That actress gave an artistic performance.* **3** having good color and design: *an artistic wallpaper.* **4** having or showing appreciation of beauty: *artistic tastes. adjective.*

as (az *or* əz), **1** to the same degree; equally: *I am as tall as you.* **2** doing the work of: *Who will act as teacher?* **3** while; when: *As they were walking, it began to rain.* **4** in the same way that: *Treat others as you wish them to treat you.* **5** for example: *Some animals, as dogs and cats, eat meat.* **6** because: *As she was a skilled worker, she received good wages.* 1,5 *adverb,* 2 *preposition,* 3,4,6 *conjunction.*

as if or **as though,** the way it would be if: *You sound as if you were angry.*

as bes tos (as bes/təs), a kind of mineral which does not burn. Asbestos separates into fibers that can be made into cloth: *Some workers wear*

a hat	**i** it	**oi** oil	**ch** child	⎧ a in about
ā age	**ī** ice	**ou** out	**ng** long	⎪ e in taken
ä far	**o** hot	**u** cup	**sh** she	**ə** = ⎨ i in pencil
e let	**ō** open	**u̇** put	**th** thin	⎪ o in lemon
ē equal	**ô** order	**ü** rule	**ᴛʜ** then	⎩ u in circus
ėr term			**zh** measure	

art¹ (definition 2)—art by a ten-year-old child

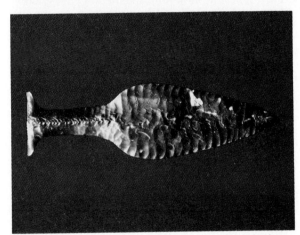

arrowhead

asbestos suits for protection from fire. noun.

as cend (ə send′), go up; rise; climb: *We watched the airplane ascend higher and higher. A small party is planning to ascend Mount Everest. verb.*

as cent (ə sent′), **1** going up; rising; climbing: *The sudden ascent of the elevator made us dizzy. The ascent of Mount Everest is difficult.* **2** place or way that slopes up: *The gradual ascent of the hill made it easy to climb. noun.*

as cer tain (as′ər tān′), find out: *The detective tried to ascertain the facts about the robbery. verb.*

ash¹ (ash), what remains of a thing after it has been thoroughly burned: *He flicked his cigarette ash into the fireplace. noun, plural* **ash es.**

ash² (ash), a kind of shade tree that has a tough wood. *noun, plural* **ash es.**

a shamed (ə shāmd′), **1** feeling shame; disturbed or uncomfortable because one has done something wrong, improper, or silly: *I was ashamed of the lies I had told.* **2** unwilling because of fear of shame: *I was ashamed to tell my parents I had failed math. adjective.*

ash es (ash′iz), what remains of a thing after it has thoroughly burned: *I removed the ashes from the fireplace. noun plural.*

a shore (ə shôr′), **1** to the shore; to land: *The ship's passengers went ashore.* **2** on the shore; on land: *The sailor had been ashore for months. adverb.*

A sia (ā′zhə), the largest continent, east of Europe and west of the Pacific Ocean. China, India, and Israel are countries in Asia. *noun.*

A sian (ā′zhən), **1** of Asia; having something to do with Asia or its people; from Asia. **2** person born or living in Asia. **1** *adjective,* **2** *noun.*

a side (ə sīd′), on one side; to one side; away: *He stepped aside to let me pass. adverb.*

ask (ask), **1** try to find out by words: *Why don't you ask? She asked about our health. Ask the way.* **2** seek the answer to: *Ask any questions you wish.* **3** put a question to: *Ask him how old he is.* **4** try to get by words: *Ask them to sing. Ask for help if you need it.* **5** invite: *I asked ten people to my party. verb.*

a skance (ə skans′), with suspicion or disapproval: *The students looked askance at the plan to have classes on Saturday. adverb.*

a skew (ə skyü′), to one side; turned or twisted the wrong way; out of the proper position: *The wind blew my hat askew. Isn't that picture askew? adverb, adjective.*

a sleep (ə slēp′), **1** not awake; sleeping: *The cat is asleep.* **2** into a condition of sleep: *The tired children fell asleep.* **3** numb: *My foot is asleep.* **1,3** *adjective,* **2** *adverb.*

as par a gus (ə spar′ə gəs), the tender, green shoots of a plant with scalelike leaves. Asparagus is eaten as a vegetable. *noun.*

as pect (as′pekt), **1** one side or part or view (of a subject): *We must consider each aspect of this plan before we decide.* **2** look; appearance: *The judge has a solemn aspect. noun.*

as pen (as′pən), a kind of poplar tree whose leaves tremble and rustle in the slightest breeze. *noun.*

as phalt (as′fôlt), **1** a dark substance much like tar, found in various parts of the world or obtained by refining petroleum. **2** a smooth, hard mixture of this substance with crushed rock or sand. Asphalt is used to pave roads. *noun.*

as pi ra tion (as′pə rā′shən), earnest desire; longing; ambition: *She has aspirations to be a doctor. noun.*

as pire (ə spīr′), have an ambition for something; desire earnestly; seek: *He aspired to be captain of the team. verb,* **as pired, as pir ing.**

as pir in (as′pər ən), drug used to relieve pain and reduce fever. *noun.*

ass (as), **1** donkey. **2** a stupid, silly, or stubborn person; fool. *noun, plural* **ass es.**

as sail (ə sāl′), attack with violence: *The soldiers assailed the enemy fort. verb.*

aster

as sail ant (ə sā′lənt), person who attacks: *The injured man did not know who his assailant was.* noun.

as sas sin (ə sas′n), murderer, especially one hired or chosen to murder by a sudden or secret attack. noun. [*Assassin* comes from an Arabic word meaning "eaters of hashish." Members of a secret group used to drug themselves with hashish before they murdered their victims.]

as sas si nate (ə sas′n āt), murder by a sudden or secret attack: *President Kennedy was assassinated in 1963.* verb, **as sas si nat ed, as sas si nat ing.**

as sas si na tion (ə sas′n ā′shən), a murdering by a sudden or secret attack. noun.

as sault (ə sôlt′), **1** a sudden, vigorous attack: *The soldiers made an assault on the enemy fort.* **2** make an assault on; attack. 1 noun, 2 verb.

as sem ble (ə sem′bəl), **1** gather together; bring together: *The principal assembled all the students in the auditorium.* **2** come together; meet: *Congress assembles in January.* **3** put together; fit together: *Will you help me assemble my model airplane?* verb, **as sem bled, as sem bling.**

as sem bly (ə sem′blē), **1** a group of people gathered together for some purpose; meeting. A reception or a ball may be called an assembly. **2** a meeting of lawmakers. The Senate and the House of Representatives are assemblies. **3** a putting together; fitting together: *In Detroit we saw the assembly of the parts which make up an automobile.* **4** the complete group of parts required to put something together: *The rear of an airplane has a tail assembly.* noun, plural **as sem blies.**

as sent (ə sent′), **1** agree; express agreement; consent: *Everyone assented to the plans for the picnic.* **2** agreement; acceptance of a proposal or statement: *She smiled her assent to the plan.* 1 verb, 2 noun.

as sert (ə sėrt′), **1** state positively; declare firmly: *She asserts that her story is absolutely true.* **2** defend or insist on (a right or claim): *Assert your independence.* verb.
assert oneself, insist on one's rights; demand recognition: *If you feel you've been treated unfairly, you should assert yourself.*

as ser tion (ə sėr′shən), **1** a very strong statement; firm declaration: *His assertion of innocence was believed by the jury.* **2** an insisting on (a right or claim): *She moved away from home as an assertion of her independence.* noun.

as sess (ə ses′), estimate the value of (property or income) for taxation; value: *The property was assessed at $10,000.* verb.

as ses sor (ə ses′ər), person who estimates the value of property or income for taxation. noun.

as set (as′et), **1** something that has value: *Ability to get along with people is an asset.* **2** **assets,** things of value or property: *Her assets include a house, a car, stocks, bonds, and jewelry.* noun.

as sign (ə sīn′), **1** give as a task to be done: *The teacher assigned the next ten problems.* **2** appoint: *We were assigned to decorate the room.* **3** fix; set: *The judge assigned a day for the trial.* verb.

as sign ment (ə sīn′mənt), **1** something assigned: *Today's assignment in arithmetic consists of ten examples.* **2** an assigning; appointment: *The soldier was informed of his assignment to a new base.* noun.

as sist (ə sist′), help: *She assisted the science teacher with the experiment.* verb.

as sist ance (ə sis′təns), help; aid: *I need your assistance.* noun.

as sist ant (ə sis′tənt), **1** helper; aid: *I was her assistant in the library.* **2** helping; assisting: *He is an assistant teacher.* 1 noun, 2 adjective.

as so ci ate (ə sō′shē āt for 1,3 and 4; ə sō′shē it for 2,5 and 6), **1** connect in thought: *We associate turkey with Thanksgiving.* **2** joined with another or others: *I am an associate editor of the school paper.* **3** join as a companion, partner, or friend: *She is associated with her brothers in business.* **4** be friendly; keep company: *He associated with interesting people.* **5** companion, partner, or friend: *She is an associate in a law firm.* **6** admitted to some, but not all, rights and privileges: *She is an associate member of the historical society.* 1,3,4 verb, **as so ci at ed, as so ci at ing;** 2,6 adjective, 5 noun.

as so ci a tion (ə sō′sē ā′shən), **1** group of people joined together for some purpose: *Will you join the young people's association at our church?* **2** an associating or being associated: *I look forward to my association with the counselors I will have at camp.* **3** companionship or friendship: *They had enjoyed a close association over many years.* **4** connection; relation: *Many people make the association of the color red with anger.* noun.

as sort ed (ə sôr′tid), **1** selected so as to be of different kinds; various: *They served assorted cakes.* **2** arranged by kinds; classified: *There were socks assorted by size on the shelf.* **3** suited to one another; matched: *They are a poorly assorted couple, always quarreling.* adjective.

as sort ment (ə sôrt′mənt), collection of various kinds: *These scarves come in an assortment of colors.* noun.

as sume (ə süm′), **1** take for granted; suppose: *He assumed that the train would be on time.* **2** take upon oneself; undertake: *The class president* assumed the leadership in planning the picnic. **3** take on; put on: *The problem has assumed a new form.* **4** pretend: *Although she was afraid, she assumed a confident manner. verb,* **as sumed, as sum ing.**

as sump tion (ə sump/shən), **1** act of assuming. **2** thing assumed: *His assumption that he would win the prize proved incorrect. noun.*

as sur ance (ə shur/əns), **1** statement intended to make a person more sure or certain: *Do I have your assurance that you will not do it again?* **2** confidence in one's own ability: *His careful preparation gave him assurance in reciting. noun.*

as sure (ə shur/), **1** tell positively: *They assured us that the plane would be on time.* **2** make sure or certain: *She assured herself that the bridge was safe before she crossed it. verb,* **as sured, as sur ing.**

as sur ed ly (ə shur/id lē), **1** surely; certainly: *I will assuredly come.* **2** confidently; boldly. *adverb.*

as ter (as/tər), a common plant having daisylike flowers with white, pink, or purple petals around a yellow center. See picture. *noun.* [*Aster* comes from a Greek word meaning "star." The plant was called this because its petals look like rays.]

a stern (ə stėrn/), **1** at or toward the rear of a ship or boat: *The captain went astern.* **2** backward: *The boat moved slowly astern.* **3** behind: *Some yachts tow small boats astern. adverb.*

as ter oid (as/tə roid/), any of about 1600 very small planets that revolve about the sun, chiefly between the orbits of Mars and Jupiter. *noun.*

asth ma (az/mə), disease that makes breathing difficult and causes coughing. *noun.*

a stir (ə stėr/), in motion; up and about: *Although it was midnight, the whole town was astir. adjective.*

as ton ish (ə ston/ish), surprise greatly; amaze: *The gift of ten dollars astonished me. verb.*

as ton ish ment (ə ston/ish mənt), great surprise; sudden wonder; amazement. *noun.*

as tound (ə stound/), shock with alarm or surprise; amaze: *She was astounded by the news that she had won the contest. verb.*

a stray (ə strā/), out of the right way; wandering. See picture. *adjective, adverb.*

a stride (ə strīd/), with one leg on each side of: *to sit astride a horse. preposition.*

as trol o gy (ə strol/ə jē), study of the stars and planets to reveal their supposed influence on persons or events, and to foretell what will happen. *noun.*

as tro naut (as/trə nôt), pilot or member of the crew of a spacecraft. *noun.* [*Astronaut* comes from Greek words meaning "star sailor."]

as tron o mer (ə stron/ə mər), person who is an expert in astronomy. *noun.*

as tro nom i cal (as/trə nom/ə kəl), **1** having something to do with astronomy: *A telescope is an astronomical instrument.* **2** enormous; very great: *an astronomical sum of money. adjective.*

as tron o my (ə stron/ə mē), science that deals with the sun, moon, planets, stars, and other heavenly bodies. *noun.*

a sun der (ə sun/dər), in pieces; into separate parts; apart. See picture. *adverb.*

a hat	**i** it	**oi** oil	**ch** child	a in about
ā age	**ī** ice	**ou** out	**ng** long	e in taken
ä far	**o** hot	**u** cup	**sh** she	ə = { i in pencil
e let	**ō** open	**u̇** put	**th** thin	o in lemon
ē equal	**ô** order	**ü** rule	**ẋH** then	u in circus
ėr term			**zh** measure	

A BULL FROM THE FIELDS WENT ASTRAY,

CHINA

WANDERING INTO A SHOP ONE FINE DAY,

WITH HOOFBEATS LIKE THUNDER KNOCKING TEACUPS ASUNDER

WHICH FRIGHTENED THE PATRONS AWAY.

a sy lum (ə sī/ləm), **1** institution for the support and care of the mentally ill, the blind, orphans, or other groups of people who are unable to care for themselves. **2** refuge; shelter. In olden times a church might be an asylum for a debtor or a criminal, since no one was allowed to drag a person from the altar. Now asylum is sometimes given by one nation to persons of another nation who are accused of political crimes. *noun.*

at (at, ət, *or* it), **1** in; on; by; near: *I will be at the store. There is someone at the front door.* **2** in the direction of; to; toward: *I aimed at the target.* **3** on or near the time of: *She goes to bed at nine o'clock.* **4** in a place or condition of: *England and France were at war.* **5** for: *We bought two books at a dollar each. preposition.*

ate (āt). See **eat.** *We ate our dinner. verb.*

ath lete (ath/lēt/), person trained in exercises of physical strength, speed, and skill. Baseball players and swimmers are athletes. *noun.*

ath let ic (ath let/ik), **1** of an athlete; like or suited to an athlete: *athletic feats.* **2** having something to do with active games and sports: *He joined an athletic association.* **3** strong and active: *She is an athletic girl. adjective.*

ath let ics (ath let/iks), sports and exercises that require physical strength and skill. Athletics include baseball and tennis. *noun plural.*

At lan tic (at lan/tik), **1** ocean east of North and South America. It extends to Europe and Africa. **2** of the Atlantic Ocean. **3** on or near the Atlantic Ocean: *New York is on the Atlantic coast of North America.* **4** of or on the Atlantic coast of the United States: *New Jersey is one of the Atlantic states.* **1** *noun,* **2-4** *adjective.*

at las (at/ləs), book of maps. A big atlas has maps of every country. *noun, plural* **at las es.** [*Atlas* comes from the name of a giant in Greek myths, who held up the sky on his shoulders. His picture often appeared in early books of maps.]

at mo sphere (at/mə sfir), **1** air that surrounds the earth. **2** mass of gases that surrounds any heavenly body: *The atmosphere of Venus is cloudy.* **3** air in any given place: *Our cellar has a damp atmosphere.* **4** mental and moral surroundings; surrounding influence: *Nuns live in a religious atmosphere. noun.*

at mo spher ic (at/mə sfir/ik), of, in, or having something to do with the atmosphere: *Atmospheric conditions often prevent observations of the stars. adjective.*

at oll (at/ol), a coral island or group of islands forming a ring around a shallow lagoon. *noun.*

at om (at/əm), **1** the smallest particle of a chemical element that can unite with other atoms without being permanently changed. An atom is made up of protons and neutrons in a central nucleus surrounded by electrons. A molecule of water consists of two atoms of hydrogen and one atom of oxygen. **2** a very small particle; tiny bit: *There is not an atom of truth in his whole story. noun.*

atom bomb, atomic bomb.

a tom ic (ə tom/ik), **1** of or having something to do

with atoms: *atomic research.* **2** using atomic energy: *an atomic submarine. adjective.*

atomic bomb, bomb in which the splitting of atomic nuclei results in an explosion of tremendous force and heat, accompanied by a blinding light.

atomic energy, energy that exists inside atoms. Some atoms can be made to release some of their energy, either slowly (in a reactor) or very suddenly (in a bomb), by the splitting or the combining of their nuclei.

a tone (ə tōn/), make up; make amends: *She atoned for her unkindness to her sister by taking her to the movies. verb,* **a toned, a ton ing.**

a top (ə top/), on the top of: *He had a hat atop his head. preposition.*

a tro cious (ə trō/shəs), **1** very wicked or cruel; very savage or brutal: *Kidnaping is an atrocious crime.* **2** very unpleasant: *The weather has been simply atrocious. adjective.*

a troc i ty (ə tros/ə tē), very great wickedness or cruelty; brutality: *Many acts of atrocity are committed in war. noun, plural* **a troc i ties.**

at tach (ə tach/), **1** fasten: *I attached a rope to my sled.* **2** add at the end: *The signers attached their names to the Constitution.* **3** bind by affection: *She is very attached to her cousin.* **4** fasten itself; belong: *The blame for this accident attaches to the driver who did not stop. verb.*

at tach ment (ə tach/mənt), **1** attaching or being attached; connection: *The attachment of a rope to the sled took less than a minute.* **2** thing attached, such as an additional device. Some sewing machines have attachments for making buttonholes. **3** means of attaching; fastening: *an attachment that holds a basket to a bicycle.* **4** affection; devotion: *The children have a great attachment to their dog. noun.*

at tack (ə tak/), **1** set upon to hurt; begin fighting against someone: *The dog attacked the cat. The enemy attacked at dawn.* **2** talk or write against: *The candidate attacked his opponent's record as mayor.* **3** go at with vigor: *attack a hard lesson. The hungry hikers attacked dinner as soon as it was ready.* **4** attacking: *The enemy attack took us by surprise.* **5** act harmfully on: *Locusts attacked the crops.* **6** a sudden occurrence of illness or discomfort: *I had an attack of flu.* **1-3,5** *verb,* **4,6** *noun.*

at tain (ə tān/), **1** arrive at: *Grandfather has attained the age of 80.* **2** gain by effort; accomplish: *She attained her goal. verb.*

at tain ment (ə tān/mənt), **1** attaining: *Her main goal was the attainment of a medical degree.* **2** accomplishment; ability: *Benjamin Franklin was a man of varied attainments; he was a diplomat, statesman, writer, and inventor. noun.*

at tempt (ə tempt/), **1** try. See picture. **2** a try; effort: *They made an attempt to climb the mountain.* **3** attack: *An assassin made an attempt upon the king's life.* **1** *verb,* **2,3** *noun.*

at tend (ə tend/), **1** be present at: *Children must attend school.* **2** give care and thought; apply oneself: *Attend to your work.* **3** go with;

accompany: *Noble ladies attended the queen.* **4** wait on; care for; tend: *Nurses attend the sick. verb.*

at tend ance (ə ten′dəns), **1** act of being present at a place; attending: *Our class had perfect attendance today.* **2** number of people present; persons attending: *The attendance at the meeting was over 200. noun.*

at tend ant (ə ten′dənt), **1** person who waits on another, such as a servant or follower. **2** waiting on another to help or serve: *An attendant nurse is at the patient's bedside.* **3** going with as a result; accompanying: *Coughing is one of the attendant discomforts of a cold.* **1** *noun,* **2,3** *adjective.*

at ten tion (ə ten′shən), **1** act or fact of attending; heed: *Pay attention to the teacher.* **2** power of attending; notice: *She called my attention to the problem.* **3** care and thought; consideration: *The children showed their grandparents much attention.* **4 attentions,** acts of courtesy or devotion: *She received many attentions, such as invitations to parties, candy, and flowers.* **5** a military attitude of readiness: *The private stood at attention during inspection. noun.*

at ten tive (ə ten′tiv), **1** paying attention; observant: *The attentive pupil is most likely to learn.*

attire (definition 1)
He wore ceremonial attire.

attempt (definition 1)
He attempted to draw a picture of himself.

a hat	i it	oi oil	ch child	a in about
ā age	ī ice	ou out	ng long	e in taken
ä far	o hot	u cup	sh she	ə = i in pencil
e let	ō open	u̇ put	th thin	o in lemon
ē equal	ô order	ü rule	ŦH then	u in circus
ėr term			zh measure	

2 courteous; polite: *Good hosts are attentive to their guests. adjective.*

at test (ə test′), give proof of; testify to: *Your good work attests the care you have taken. The handwriting expert attested to the genuineness of the signature. verb.*

at tic (at′ik), space in a house just below the roof and above the other rooms. *noun.*

at tire (ə tīr′), **1** clothing or dress. See picture. **2** clothe or dress; array: *The king was attired in a cloak trimmed with ermine.* **1** *noun,* **2** *verb,* **at tired, at tir ing.**

at ti tude (at′ə tüd *or* at′ə tyüd), **1** way of thinking, acting, or feeling: *I used to dislike that teacher but I've changed my attitude.* **2** position of the body: *He raised his fists in the attitude of a boxer ready to fight. noun.*

at tor ney (ə tėr′nē), lawyer. *noun, plural* **at tor neys.**

at tract (ə trakt′), **1** draw to itself or oneself: *The magnet attracted the iron filings.* **2** be pleasing to; win the attention and liking of: *Bright colors attract children. verb.*

at trac tion (ə trak′shən), **1** thing that delights or attracts people: *The elephants were the chief attraction at the circus.* **2** act or power of attracting: *The iron filings were drawn to the magnet by attraction. Sports have no attraction for me. noun.*

at trac tive (ə trak′tiv), **1** winning attention and liking; pleasing: *an attractive young couple.* **2** attracting: *Magnets have great attractive power. adjective.*

at trib ute (ə trib′yüt *for 1 and 2;* at′rə byüt *for 3*), **1** think of as caused by: *She attributes her good health to a proper diet.* **2** think of as belonging to or appropriate to: *We attribute courage to the lion and cunning to the fox.* **3** a quality considered as belonging to a person or thing; characteristic: *Patience is an attribute of a good teacher.* **1,2** *verb,* **at trib ut ed, at trib ut ing; 3** *noun.*

at tune (ə tün′ *or* ə tyün′), bring into agreement; adjust: *Our ears became attuned to the noise of the city. verb,* **at tuned, at tun ing.**

au burn (ô′bərn), reddish brown. *adjective.*

auc tion (ôk′shən), **1** a public sale in which each thing is sold to the person who offers the most money for it. **2** sell at an auction. **1** *noun,* **2** *verb.*

au da cious (ô dā′shəs), **1** having the courage to take risks; bold; daring: *an audacious explorer.* **2** too bold; impudent: *The audacious waiter demanded a larger tip. adjective.*

au dac i ty (ô das′ə tē), **1** boldness; reckless daring: *It took great audacity for the acrobat to walk a tightrope over Niagara Falls.* **2** rude boldness; impudence: *They had the audacity to go to the party without being invited. noun.*

austere

Grant Wood, "American Gothic," Courtesy of The Art Institute of Chicago

autograph (definition 2)
baseball player autographing a program

au di ble (ô′də bəl), loud enough to be heard; capable of being heard: *Without a microphone the speaker was barely audible. adjective.*

au di ence (ô′dē əns), **1** people gathered in a place to hear or see: *The audience at the theater enjoyed the play.* **2** any persons within hearing: *The audience of this television program consists of over ten million people.* **3** chance to be heard; hearing: *The committee will give you an audience so you may present your plan.* **4** formal interview with a person of high rank: *The ambassador was granted an audience with the queen. noun.*

au di tion (ô dish′ən), **1** a hearing to test the ability of a singer, actor, or other performer. **2** perform at or give such a hearing: *audition for a part in a play. The director auditioned ten actors.* **1** *noun,* **2** *verb.*

au di to ri um (ô′də tôr′ē əm), **1** large room for an audience in a theater, school, or the like; large hall. **2** a building especially designed for public meetings, concerts, and lectures. *noun.*

Aug., August.

au ger (ô′gər), tool for boring holes in wood. *noun.*

aug ment (ôg ment′), increase: *He augmented his income by working overtime three nights a week. verb.*

au gust (ô gust′), inspiring reverence and admiration; majestic. *adjective.*

Au gust (ô′gəst), the eighth month of the year. It has 31 days. *noun.* [*August* was named for Augustus, the first emperor of Rome. He lived from 63 B.C. to A.D. 14.]

aunt (ant), **1** sister of one's father or mother. **2** wife of one's uncle. *noun.*

aus pic es (ô′spə siz), approval or support: *The school fair was held under the auspices of the Parents' Association. noun plural.*

aus pi cious (ô spish′əs), with signs of success; favorable: *The popularity of his first book was an auspicious beginning for his career. adjective.*

aus tere (ô stir′), **1** stern; harsh: *My father was a silent, austere man, very strict with us.* See picture. **2** strict in morals: *Some of the ideas of the Puritans seem too austere to us.* **3** severely simple: *The tall, plain columns stood against the sky in austere beauty. adjective.*

Aus tral ia (ô strā′lyə), the smallest continent, located southeast of Asia between the Pacific and Indian oceans. The country of Australia covers the whole continent. *noun.*

Aus tral ian (ô strā′lyən), **1** of Australia; having something to do with Australia or its people; from Australia. **2** person born or living in Australia. **1** *adjective,* **2** *noun.*

au then tic (ô then′tik), **1** reliable: *We read an authentic account of the plane crash given by one of the survivors.* **2** genuine; real: *That is her authentic signature, not a forgery. adjective.*

au thor (ô′thər), **1** person who writes books, poems, stories, or articles; writer: *My little sister's favorite author is Dr. Seuss.* **2** person who creates or begins anything: *Are you the author of this scheme? noun.*

au thor i ta tive (ə thôr′ə tā′tiv), **1** having authority: *An authoritative source in the government stated that there would be no food shortage.* **2** commanding: *In authoritative tones the policeman shouted to us, "Keep back."* **3** that can be believed because it comes from expert knowledge: *A doctor's statement concerning the cause of an illness is considered authoritative. adjective.*

au thor i ty (ə thôr′ə tē), **1** power; control: *Parents have authority over their children.* **2** right: *The police have the authority to arrest speeding drivers.* **3** person or group that has power or right. **4** the **authorities**, the officials in control: *Who are the proper authorities to give permits to hunt or fish?* **5** source of information or advice: *A good dictionary is an authority on the meanings of words.* **6** an expert on some subject: *She is an authority on the Revolutionary War. noun, plural* **au thor i ties.**

au thor i za tion (ô′thər ə zā′shən), **1** giving legal power to: *The authorization of the police to give tickets to jaywalkers reduced the number of accidents.* **2** official permission: *I have the authorization of the owner to fish in this pond. noun.*

au tho rize (ô′thə rīz′), **1** give power or right to: *The committee authorized us to proceed with our plan.* **2** approve: *The mayor authorized the spending of money for better public transportation. verb,* **au tho rized, au tho riz ing.**

au to (ô′tō), automobile. *noun, plural* **au tos.**

au to bi og ra phy (ô′tə bī og′rə fē), story of a person's life written by that person. *noun, plural* **au to bi og ra phies.**

au to graph (ô′tə graf), **1** a person's signature: *Many people collect the autographs of celebrities.* **2** write one's name in or on. See picture. **1** *noun,* **2** *verb.*

au to mat ic (ô′tə mat′ik), **1** moving or acting by itself: *When you press a button the automatic elevator takes you to the floor you want.* **2** done without thought or attention: *Breathing and swallowing are usually automatic.* **3** gun that throws out the empty shell and reloads by itself. An automatic continues to fire until the pressure on the trigger is released. **1,2** *adjective,* **3** *noun.*

au to mat i cal ly (ô′tə mat′ik lē), in an automatic manner: *Electric refrigerators work automatically. adverb.*

au to ma tion (ô′tə mā′shən), the use of automatic controls in the operation of a machine or group of machines. In automation, machines do many of the tasks formerly performed by people. *noun.*

au to mo bile (ô′tə mə bēl′), a passenger vehicle for traveling on roads and streets. An automobile is powered by an engine that drives usually the rear wheels. *noun.* [*Automobile* comes from a Greek word meaning "self" and a Latin word meaning "movable."]

au top sy (ô′top sē), medical examination of a dead body to find the cause of death: *The autopsy showed that the patient died of a heart attack. noun, plural* **au top sies.**

au tumn (ô′təm), **1** season of the year between summer and winter; fall. **2** of, for, or coming in autumn: *autumn leaves.* **1** *noun,* **2** *adjective.*

a hat	i it	oi oil	ch child	a in about
ā age	ī ice	ou out	ng long	e in taken
ä far	o hot	u cup	sh she	ə = { i in pencil
e let	ō open	u̇ put	th thin	o in lemon
ē equal	ô order	ü rule	ŦH then	u in circus
ėr term			zh measure	

aux il iar y (ôg zil′yər ē), **1** helping; assisting: *Some sailboats have auxiliary engines.* **2** person or thing that helps; aid: *The microscope is a useful auxiliary to the human eye.* **1** *adjective,* **2** *noun, plural* **aux il iar ies.**

a vail (ə vāl′), **1** be of use or value to; help: *Money will not avail you after you are dead.* **2** help: *Matches are of no avail if they are wet.* **1** *verb,* **2** *noun.* **avail oneself of,** take advantage of; make use of: *While traveling in France, he availed himself of the opportunity to learn French.*

a vail a ble (ə vā′lə bəl), **1** able to be used: *She is not available for the job; she has other work now.* **2** able to be had or obtained: *All available tickets were sold. adjective.*

av a lanche (av′ə lanch), a large mass of snow and ice, or of dirt and rocks, rapidly sliding or falling down the side of a mountain. *noun.*

av ar ice (av′ər is), too great a desire to acquire money or property; greed for wealth. *noun.*

Ave., Avenue.

a venge (ə venj′), get revenge for: *They fought to avenge the enemy's invasion of their country. verb,* **a venged, a veng ing.**

av e nue (av′ə nü *or* av′ə nyü), **1** a wide street. **2** road or walk bordered by trees. **3** way of approach: *Hard work is one avenue to success. noun.*

av er age (av′ər ij), **1** quantity found by dividing the sum of all the quantities by the number of quantities. The average of 3 and 5 and 10 is 6 (because 3 + 5 + 10 = 18, and 18 ÷ 3 = 6). **2** find the average of: *Will you average those numbers for me?* **3** obtained by averaging: *The average temperature for the week was 82.* **4** have as an average; amount on the average to: *The cost of our lunches at school averaged three dollars a week.* **5** usual sort or amount: *The amount of rain this year has been below average.* **6** usual; ordinary: *The average person likes TV.* **1,5** *noun,* **2,4** *verb,* **av er aged, av er ag ing; 3,6** *adjective.*

a verse (ə vėrs′), opposed; unwilling: *I am averse to smoking. adjective.*

a ver sion (ə vėr′zhən), a strong dislike: *He has an aversion to tea. noun.*

a vert (ə vėrt′), **1** keep from happening; prevent; avoid: *The driver averted an accident by a quick turn of the steering wheel.* **2** turn away; turn aside: *I averted my eyes from the automobile accident. verb.*

a vi ar y (ā′vē er′ē), place where many birds, especially wild birds, are kept. *noun, plural* **a vi ar ies.**

a vi a tion (ā′vē ā′shən), the art or science of

designing, operating, and navigating aircraft, and the business of manufacturing them. *noun.* [*Aviation* comes from a Latin word meaning "bird."]

a vi a tor (ā′vē ā′tər), person who flies an aircraft; pilot. *noun.*

av id (av′id), extremely eager: *an avid desire for fame, an avid reader of detective stories. adjective.*

av o ca do (av′ə kä′dō), the fruit of a tree that grows in warm regions. Avocados are shaped like pears and have a dark-green skin and a very large seed. Their yellow-green pulp is used in salads. *noun, plural* **av o ca dos.**

av o ca tion (av′ə kā′shən), something that a person likes to do in addition to a regular job; hobby: *She is a lawyer, but writing stories is her avocation. noun.*

a void (ə void′), keep away from; keep out of the way of: *We avoided driving through large cities on our trip. verb.*

a void ance (ə void′ns), act of avoiding; keeping away from: *Her avoidance of me made me wonder if I had offended her. noun.*

a wait (ə wāt′), **1** wait for; look forward to: *We anxiously awaited the arrival of the plane.* **2** be ready for; be in store for: *Many pleasures await you on your trip. verb.*

a wake (ə wāk′), **1** wake up; arouse: *I awoke from a sound sleep. The alarm clock awoke me.* **2** roused from sleep; not asleep: *She is always awake early.* **3** alert; watchful: *We are awake to the dangers of air pollution.* 1 *verb,* **a woke** or **a waked, a wak ing;** 2,3 *adjective.*

a wak en (ə wā′kən), wake up; stir up; arouse: *The sun was shining when he awakened. I was awakened early this morning. verb.*

a ward (ə wôrd′), **1** give after careful consideration; grant: *A medal was awarded to the best speller.* **2** something given after careful consideration; prize: *My dog won the highest award.* **3** decide upon or settle by law: *The court awarded damages of $5000 to each injured person.* **4** decision by a judge: *We thought the award was fair.* 1,3 *verb,* 2,4 *noun.*

a ware (ə wer′ or ə war′), having knowledge; realizing; conscious: *I was too sleepy to be aware how cold it was. She was not aware of her danger. adjective.*

a way (ə wā′), **1** from a place; to a distance: *Stay away from the fire.* **2** at a distance; a way off: *The travelers were far away from home. His home is miles away.* **3** absent; gone: *My friend is away today.* **4** out of one's possession, notice, or use: *He gave his boat away.* **5** out of existence: *The sounds died away.* **6** in another direction; aside: *She turned her car away to avoid an accident.* **7** without stopping: *She worked away at her job.* **8** without delay; at once: *Fire away!* 1,2,4-8 *adverb,* 2,3 *adjective.*

awe (ô), **1** great fear and wonder; fear and reverence: *The sight of the great waterfall filled us with awe. The child stood in awe before the queen.* **2** cause to feel awe; fill with awe: *The majesty of the mountains awed us.* 1 *noun,* 2 *verb,* **awed, aw ing.**

aw ful (ô′fəl), **1** causing fear; dreadful; terrible: *An awful storm with thunder and lightning came up.* **2** deserving great respect and reverence: *He felt the awful power of God.* **3** filling with awe; impressive: *The mountains rose to awful heights.* **4** very bad: *I have an awful headache. adjective.*

aw ful ly (ô′flē or ô′fə lē), **1** dreadfully; terribly: *The broken leg hurt awfully.* **2** very: *I'm awfully sorry that I hurt your feelings. adverb.*

a while (ə hwīl′), for a short time: *I usually read awhile before going to bed. adverb.*

awk ward (ôk′wərd), **1** clumsy; not graceful or skillful in movement: *Seals are very awkward on land, but graceful in the water.* **2** not well suited to use: *The handle of this pitcher has an awkward shape.* **3** not easily managed: *This is an awkward corner to turn.* **4** embarrassing: *He asked me such an awkward question that I did not know what to reply. adjective.*

awl (ôl), a pointed tool used for making small holes in leather or wood. *noun.*

awn ing (ô′ning), piece of canvas, metal, wood, or plastic spread over or before a door, window, porch, deck, or patio. Awnings are used for protection from the sun or rain. *noun.*

a woke (ə wōk′). See **awake.** *I awoke them at seven. We awoke early. verb.*

a wry (ə rī′), **1** with a twist or turn to one side: *My hat was blown awry by the wind.* **2** wrong; out of order: *Our plans have gone awry. adverb.*

ax or **axe** (aks), tool with a flat, sharp blade fastened on a handle, used for chopping, splitting, and shaping wood. *noun, plural* **ax es.**

ax is (ak′sis), a straight line about which an object turns or seems to turn. The axis of the earth is an imaginary line through the North Pole and the South Pole. See picture. *noun, plural* **ax es** (ak′sēz′).

ax le (ak′səl), bar or shaft on which a wheel turns. Some axles turn with the wheel. *noun.*

aye or **ay** (ī), **1** yes: *Aye, aye, sir.* **2** an affirmative answer, vote, or voter: *The ayes won when the vote was taken.* 1 *adverb,* 2 *noun.*

a zal ea (ə zā′lyə), shrub bearing many showy flowers. *noun.* [*Azalea* is from a Greek word meaning "to dry up." The plant was called this because it was thought to grow well in dry soil.]

az ure (azh′ər), blue; blue like the sky. *adjective.*

axis

B b

a hat	i it	oi oil	ch child	⎧ a in about
ā age	ī ice	ou out	ng long	e in taken
ä far	o hot	u cup	sh she	ə = ⎨ i in pencil
e let	ō open	u̇ put	th thin	o in lemon
ē equal	ô order	ü rule	ᴛʜ then	⎩ u in circus
ėr term			zh measure	

B or **b** (bē), the second letter of the English alphabet. There are two *b*'s in *baby. noun, plural* **B's** or **b's.**

baa (bä), **1** the sound a sheep makes; bleat. **2** make this sound; bleat. 1 *noun,* 2 *verb.*

bab ble (bab′əl), **1** make sounds like a baby: *My baby brother babbles and coos in his crib.* **2** talk that cannot be understood: *A confused babble filled the room.* **3** talk foolishly: *They babbled on and on about the weather.* **4** foolish talk. **5** talk too much; tell secrets: *He babbled all about the surprise party we had planned.* **6** make a murmuring sound: *The little brook babbled away just behind our tent.* 1,3,5,6 *verb,* **bab bled, bab bling;** 2,4 *noun.*

babe (bāb), baby. *noun.*

ba boon (ba bün′), a large, fierce monkey with a doglike face. Baboons live in the rocky hills of Africa and Arabia. See picture. *noun.*

ba by (bā′bē), **1** a very young child. **2** the youngest of a family or group. **3** young; small: *The sheep gave birth to a baby lamb.* **4** of or for a baby: *baby shoes, a baby bottle.* **5** like that of a baby; childish: *baby talk.* **6** person who acts like a baby: *Don't be a baby.* **7** treat as a baby: *You are too old to be babied.* 1,2,6 *noun, plural* **ba bies;** 3-5 *adjective,* 7 *verb,* **ba bied, ba by ing.**

ba by ish (bā′bē ish), like a baby; childish. *adjective.*

ba by-sit (bā′bē sit′), take care of a child or children while the parents are away for a while. *verb,* **ba by-sat** (bā′bē sat′), **ba by-sit ting.**

ba by-sit ter (bā′bē sit′ər), person who takes care of a child or children while the parents are away for a while. *noun.*

baby teeth, the first set of teeth.

bach e lor (bach′ə lər), an unmarried man. *noun.*

back (bak), **1** the part of a person's body opposite to the face or to the front part of the body. **2** the upper part of an animal's body from the neck to the end of the backbone. **3** the backbone; spine: *She fell from the ladder and broke her back.* **4** the side of anything away from one: *I had a bruise on the back of my hand.* **5** opposite the front: *the back seat of the car.* **6** part of a chair, couch, bench, or the like, which supports the back of a person sitting down. **7** support or help: *Her friends backed her plan.* **8** move or cause to move backward: *I backed the car out of the driveway. We backed away from the dog.* **9** behind in space or time: *Please walk back three steps. Have you read the back issues of this magazine?* **10** in return: *They paid back what they borrowed.* **11** in the place from which something or someone came: *Put the books back.* 1-4,6 *noun,* 5,9 *adjective,* 7,8 *verb,* 9-11 *adverb.*

back and forth, first one way and then the other: *The dog ran back and forth across the field.*

back down, give up an attempt or claim; withdraw: *I said I would go swimming, but I backed down when I found out how cold the water was.*

back out or **back out of, 1** break a promise: *I promised to buy everyone ice cream, but I backed out when I found I had no money with me.* **2** withdraw from an undertaking: *The village backed out of building a pool when the cost got too high.*

baboon—about 3½ feet (1 meter) long with the tail

back bone (bak′bōn′), **1** the main bone along the middle of the back in human beings and other mammals, birds, reptiles, amphibians, and fishes; spine. The backbone consists of many separate bones, called vertebrae, held together by muscles and tendons. **2** the most important part. **3** strength of character: *It takes backbone to stand up for an unpopular belief. noun.*

back field (bak′fēld′), in football, the players on the team with the ball, whose positions are behind the line of scrimmage. *noun.*

back ground (bak′ground′), **1** the part of a picture or scene toward the back: *The cottage stands in the foreground with the mountains in the background.* **2** part which shows off the chief thing or person: *The curtains had blue flowers on a white background.* **3** earlier conditions or events that help to explain some later condition or event: *This book gives the background of the Revolutionary War.* **4** past experience, knowledge, and training: *His early background included living on a farm. noun.*

in the background, out of sight or not in clear view: *I stayed in the background during their argument because I didn't want to get involved.*

back pack (bak′pak′), go hiking or camping while carrying a pack containing food, clothes, and equipment on the back. *verb.*

back track (bak′trak′), go back over a course or path. *verb.*

back ward (bak′wərd), **1** with the back first: *He*

tumbled over backward. **2** toward the back: *I looked backward. She gave me a backward look.* **3** opposite to the usual way: *Can you count backward?* **4** from better to worse: *In some towns living conditions improved; in some they went backward.* **5** toward the past: *He looked backward forty years and talked about his childhood.* **6** slow in development: *Backward students need special help in school.* **7** shy; bashful: *Shake hands with her; don't be backward.* 1-5 *adverb,* 2,6,7 *adjective.*

back wards (bak/wərdz), backward (definitions 1-5). *adverb.*

back woods (bak/wŭdz/), uncleared forests or wild regions far away from towns. *noun plural.*

back yard (bak/yärd/), yard behind a house or building. *noun.*

ba con (bā/kən), salted and smoked meat from the back and sides of a pig or hog. *noun.*

bac ter i a (bak tir/ē ə), very tiny and simple plants, so small that they can usually be seen only through a microscope. Certain bacteria cause diseases such as pneumonia and typhoid fever; others do useful things, such as turning cider into vinegar. See picture. *noun plural of* **bac ter i um** (bak tir/ē əm). [*Bacteria* comes from a Greek word meaning "a little rod." Bacteria were called this because some of them are rod-shaped.]

bad (bad), **1** not good; not as it ought to be: *Reading in dim light is bad for your eyes. The repair job on our car was bad, and it soon broke down again.* **2** evil; wicked: *Murder is a bad crime.* **3** not friendly; cross; unpleasant: *a bad temper.* **4** naughty; not behaving well: *My sister was bad when she ate my candy.* **5** unfavorable: *You came at a bad time.* **6** severe: *A bad thunderstorm delayed the airplane.* **7** rotten; spoiled: *Don't use that egg; it's bad.* **8** sorry: *I feel bad about losing your baseball.* **9** sick: *Her cold made her feel bad.* **10** incorrect: *a bad guess. adjective,* **worse, worst.**

bade (bad). See **bid.** *They bade her remain. verb.*

badge (baj), something worn to show that a person belongs to a certain occupation, school, class, club, or society. *noun.*

badg er (baj/ər), **1** a hairy, gray animal that feeds at night and digs a hole to live in. See picture. **2** its fur. **3** keep on annoying or teasing: *The child badgered me with endless questions.* 1,2 *noun,* 3 *verb.*

bad ly (bad/lē), **1** in a bad manner: *She sings badly.* **2** very much: *He wants to go swimming badly. adverb.*

bad min ton (bad/min tən), game in which two or four players use light rackets to hit a small cork and plastic object back and forth over a high net. *noun.* [*Badminton* was named for an estate in England. The game came from India and was first played in England in 1873.]

bad-tem pered (bad/tem/pərd), having a bad temper; cross; irritable. *adjective.*

baf fle (baf/əl), be too hard for (a person) to understand or solve; bewilder: *This puzzle baffles me. verb,* **baf fled, baf fling.**

bag (bag), **1** container made of paper, cloth, or other soft material that can be pulled together to close at the top: *Fresh vegetables are sometimes sold in plastic bags.* **2** something like a bag in its use. A suitcase or a purse is a bag. **3** put into a bag or bags: *We bagged the cookies we had baked so we could sell them.* **4** bulge; swell: *These pants bag at the knees.* **5** kill or catch in hunting: *The hunter bagged a duck.* 1,2 *noun,* 3-5 *verb,* **bagged, bag ging.**

ba gel (bā/gəl), a hard roll made of raised dough, shaped into a ring. It is simmered in water, then baked. *noun.*

bag gage (bag/ij), the trunks, bags, or suitcases that you take with you when you travel. *noun.*

bag gy (bag/ē), hanging loosely: *The clown had baggy pants. adjective,* **bag gi er, bag gi est.**

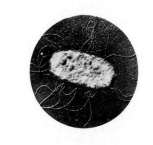

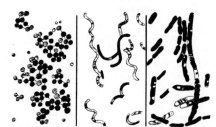

bacteria
bottom, three types of bacteria;
top, the rod type as seen through a microscope

badger (definition 1)—about 2 feet (60 centimeters) long

bag pipe (bag′pīp′), a musical instrument made of a tube to blow through, a leather bag for air, and four pipes. Bagpipes produce shrill tones and are used especially in Scotland and Ireland. See picture. *noun.*

bail[1] (bāl), **1** the money offered in order to free a person under arrest from jail until a trial is held: *They put up bail for their friend, who was accused of stealing.* **2** set (a person under arrest) free by offering this money: *They bailed out their friend.* **1** *noun,* **2** *verb.*

bail[2] (bāl), throw (water) out of a boat with a bucket, pail, or any other container: *We bailed water from our sinking rowboat. verb.*

bail out, jump from an airplane by parachute: *When the plane caught fire, the pilot bailed out.*

bait (bāt), **1** anything, especially food, used to attract fish or other animals so that they may be caught. **2** put bait on (a hook) or in (a trap): *I baited my fishhook.* **3** thing used to tempt or attract a person to do something. **4** torment or worry by unkind or annoying remarks: *A group of rowdies kept baiting the speaker.* **1,3** *noun,* **2,4** *verb.*

bake (bāk), **1** cook by the dry heat of an oven: *I baked a cake. I bake every Saturday.* **2** dry or harden by heat: *Bricks are baked in a kiln.* **3** become baked: *Cookies bake quickly. verb,* **baked, bak ing.**

bak er (bā′kər), person who makes or sells bread, pies, and cakes. *noun.*

baker's dozen, thirteen.

bak er y (bā′kər ē), store where bread, pies, and cakes are made or sold. *noun, plural* **bak er ies.**

baking powder, mixture of chemicals used instead of yeast to cause biscuits or cakes to rise.

baking soda, a white powder used in cooking and medicine.

bal ance (bal′əns), **1** instrument for weighing. See picture. **2** weigh two things against each other on scales, in one's hands, or in one's mind to see which is heavier or more important: *She balanced a trip to the mountains against a chance to go to a summer camp.* **3** condition of being equal in weight or amount: *Keep the balance between the two sides of the scale.* **4** condition of not falling over in any direction; steady position: *I lost my balance and fell off the ladder.* **5** put or keep in a steady condition or position: *Can you balance a coin on its edge?* **6** all-around development and steadiness of character: *His balance kept him from losing his temper.* **7** part that is left over; remainder: *I will be away for the balance of the week.* **1,3,4,6,7** *noun,* **2,5** *verb,* **bal anced, bal anc ing.**

in the balance, undecided: *The outcome of the game was in the balance until the last inning.*

bal co ny (bal′kə nē), **1** an outside platform enclosed by a railing, that juts out from an upper floor of a building. See picture. **2** a projecting upper floor in a theater or hall, with seats for part of the audience. *noun, plural* **bal co nies.**

bald (bôld), **1** wholly or partly without hair on the head. **2** without its natural covering: *A mountain with no trees or grass is bald.* **3** obvious; plain: *the bald truth, a bald lie. adjective.*

a hat	i it	oi oil	ch child	⎧ a in about
ā age	ī ice	ou out	ng long	⎪ e in taken
ä far	o hot	u cup	sh she	ə = ⎨ i in pencil
e let	ō open	u̇ put	th thin	⎪ o in lemon
ē equal	ô order	ü rule	ŦH then	⎩ u in circus
ėr term			zh measure	

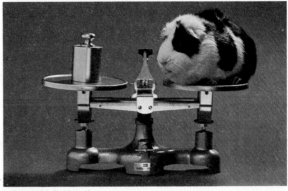

balance (definition 1)
The guinea pig is balanced by a 1000 gram weight. Therefore, the guinea pig weighs 1000 grams (about 2 pounds).

bagpipe

balcony (definition 1)

bald eagle, a large, powerful, North American eagle with white feathers on its head, neck, and tail. See picture.

bale (bāl), **1** a large bundle of material securely wrapped or bound for shipping or storage: *a bale of cotton.* **2** make into bales: *We saw a big machine bale hay.* 1 *noun,* 2 *verb,* **baled, bal ing.**

balk (bôk), **1** stop short and stubbornly refuse to go on: *My horse balked at the fence.* **2** prevent from going on; hinder: *The police balked the robber's plans. verb.*

ball¹ (bôl), **1** a round or somewhat oval object that is thrown, batted, kicked, rolled, or carried in various games. Different sizes and types of balls are used in tennis, baseball, football, and soccer. Balls may be either hollow or solid. **2** game in which some kind of ball is thrown, hit, or kicked, especially baseball. **3** anything round or roundish; something that is somewhat like a ball: *I have a ball of string. I have a blister on the ball of my foot.* **4** baseball pitched too high, too low, or not over the plate, that the batter does not strike at. **5** a round, solid object shot from a gun or cannon: *musket ball, cannon ball. noun.*

ball² (bôl), a large, formal party with dancing. *noun.*

bal lad (bal′əd), **1** a simple song. **2** poem that tells a story. Ballads are often sung. *noun.*

bal last (bal′əst), something heavy carried in a ship to steady it. *noun.*

ball bearing, 1 bearing in which the shaft turns upon a number of freely moving steel balls. Ball bearings are used to lessen friction. **2** one of these steel balls.

bal le ri na (bal′ə rē′nə), a woman ballet dancer. *noun, plural* **bal le ri nas.**

bal let (bal′ā), **1** an elaborate dance by a group on a stage. A ballet usually tells a story through the movements of the dancing and the music. **2** the dancers: *The Royal Ballet will soon perform in our city. noun.*

bal loon (bə lün′), **1** an airtight bag filled with some gas lighter than air, so that it will rise and float in the air. Some balloons have a basket or container for carrying persons or instruments high up in the air. **2** a child's toy made of thin rubber filled with air or some gas lighter than air. **3** swell out like a balloon: *The sails of the boat ballooned in the wind.* 1,2 *noun,* 3 *verb.*

bal lot (bal′ət), **1** piece of paper or other object used in voting: *Have you cast your ballot?* **2** the total number of votes cast. **3** vote or decide by using ballots: *We will now ballot for president of the club.* 1,2 *noun,* 3 *verb.*

ball-point pen (bôl′point′ pen′), pen that writes with a tiny hard ball. The ball turns inside the end of a cartridge that holds the ink.

ball room (bôl′rüm′), a large room for dancing. *noun.*

balm y (bä′mē), mild; gentle: *A balmy breeze blew across the lake.* adjective, **balm i er, balm i est.**

bal sa (bôl′sə), **1** a tropical American tree with strong wood which is very light in weight. **2** its

bald eagle—about 3 feet (1 meter) from head to tail

bamboo

banjo

wood, used in making rafts or airplane models. *noun.*

bal sam (bôl'səm), a kind of fir tree. *noun.*

bam boo (bam bü'), a woody or treelike grass with a very tall, stiff, hollow stem that has hard, thick joints. Bamboo grows in warm regions. Its stems are used for making canes, fishing poles, furniture, and even houses. See picture. *noun, plural* **bam boos.**

ban (ban), **1** forbid; prohibit: *Swimming is banned in this lake.* **2** the forbidding of an act or speech by authority: *The city has a ban on parking cars in this busy street.* **1** *verb,* **banned, ban ning; 2** *noun.*

ba nan a (bə nan'ə), a slightly curved, yellow or red tropical fruit with firm, creamy flesh. Bananas are five to eight inches long and grow in large bunches. The plant is like a tree with great long leaves. *noun.*

band[1] (band), **1** number of persons or animals joined or acting together: *A band of robbers held up the train.* **2** unite in a group: *The children banded together to buy a present for their teacher.* **3** group of musicians performing together: *The school band played several marches.* **1,3** *noun,* **2** *verb.*

band[2] (band), **1** a thin, flat strip of material for binding, trimming, or some other purpose: *The oak box was strengthened with bands of iron.* **2** put a band on: *Students of birds often band them in order to identify them later.* **3** a stripe: *The white cup has a gold band.* **4** a particular range of frequencies in radio broadcasting. **1,3,4** *noun,* **2** *verb.*

band age (ban'dij), **1** strip of cloth or other material used in binding up and dressing a wound or injury. **2** bind or dress with a bandage. **1** *noun,* **2** *verb,* **band aged, band ag ing.**

Band-Aid (band'ād'), trademark for a small bandage, used to cover minor wounds. *noun.*

ban dan na or **ban dan a** (ban dan'ə), a large, colored handkerchief. *noun.*

ban dit (ban'dit), robber or thief, especially one of a gang of outlaws. *noun.*

bang (bang), **1** a sudden, loud noise: *We heard the bang of firecrackers.* **2** make a sudden, loud noise: *The door banged as it blew shut. He banged the door.* **3** a violent, noisy blow: *She gave the drum a bang.* **4** hit with violent and noisy blows: *The baby was banging the pan with a spoon.* **1,3** *noun,* **2,4** *verb.*

bangs (bangz), fringe of hair cut short and worn over the forehead. *noun plural.*

ban ish (ban'ish), **1** force (a person) to leave a country: *The king banished some of his enemies.* **2** force to go away; drive away: *The children banished her from their game for cheating. verb.*

ban ish ment (ban'ish mənt), **1** act of banishing: *The queen ordered the banishment of her enemies.* **2** condition of being banished: *Their banishment was for twenty years. noun.*

ban is ter (ban'ə stər), handrail of a staircase and its row of supports. *noun.*

ban jo (ban'jō), a musical instrument having four or five strings, played by plucking the strings with the fingers or a pick. See picture. *noun, plural* **ban jos.**

a hat	i it	oi oil	ch child	a in about
ā age	ī ice	ou out	ng long	e in taken
ä far	o hot	u cup	sh she	ə = { i in pencil
e let	ō open	ù put	th thin	o in lemon
ē equal	ô order	ü rule	℡ then	u in circus
ėr term			zh measure	

bank[1] (bangk), **1** a long pile or heap: *a bank of snow.* **2** pile up; heap up: *Tractors banked the snow by the roadside.* **3** ground bordering a river or lake; shore: *We fished from the bank.* **4** a shallow place in a body of water; shoal: *The fishing banks of Newfoundland are famous.* **5** the sloping of an airplane to one side when turning. **6** make (an airplane) do this. **7** cover (a fire) with ashes or fresh fuel so that it will burn slowly: *The janitor banked the fire for the night.* **1,3-5** *noun,* **2,6,7** *verb.*

bank[2] (bangk), **1** place of business for keeping, lending, exchanging, and issuing money. **2** keep or put money in a bank: *We bank at the First National.* **3** any place where reserve supplies are kept: *a blood bank.* **1,3** *noun,* **2** *verb.*

bank[3] (bangk), **1** row of things: *We saw a bank of machines in the factory.* **2** row of keys on an organ or typewriter. *noun.*

bank er (bang'kər), person or company that runs a bank. *noun.*

bank ing (bang'king), business of a bank or banker. *noun.*

bank rupt (bang'krupt), **1** person who is declared by a court of law to be unable to pay his or her debts. A bankrupt's property is divided among the people who are owed money. **2** unable to pay one's debts. **3** make bankrupt: *Foolish expenditures will bankrupt him.* **1** *noun,* **2** *adjective,* **3** *verb.*

ban ner (ban'ər), **1** flag: *Banners of the world's nations fly outside the headquarters of the United Nations.* **2** piece of cloth with some design or words on it: *Our scout troop has a banner which we carry in parades.* **3** leading or outstanding: *This has been a banner year for apples.* **1,2** *noun,* **3** *adjective.*

ban quet (bang'kwit), **1** a large meal with many courses, prepared for a special occasion or for many people; feast: *a wedding banquet.* **2** a formal dinner with speeches. *noun.*

ban ter (ban'tər), **1** playful teasing; joking: *There was much banter going on at the party.* **2** tease playfully; talk in a joking way: *The two friends bantered and laughed as they walked.* **1** *noun,* **2** *verb.*

bap tism (bap'tiz əm), ceremony in which a person is dipped in water or sprinkled with water, as a sign of washing away sin and admission to the Christian church. *noun.*

bap tize (bap tīz'), **1** dip (a person) into water or sprinkle with water as a sign of washing away sin and admission into the Christian church. **2** give a first name to (a person) at baptism; christen: *She was baptized Maria. verb,* **bap tized, bap tiz ing.**

bar (bär), **1** an evenly shaped piece of some solid, longer than it is wide or thick: *a bar of soap, a chocolate bar. The United States stores its gold in the form of bars.* **2** rod or pole put across an opening to close it off: *The windows of the prison have iron*

bare (definition 5)—The dog bared its teeth.

barometer (definition 1)

BARB

barge (definition 1)

bars. *The farmer let down the pasture bars so the cows could come in.* **3** put bars across; fasten or shut off: *Bar the door.* **4** anything that blocks the way or prevents progress: *A bar of sand kept boats out of the harbor. Being shy is often a bar to making new friends.* **5** block; obstruct: *Fallen trees bar the road.* **6** keep out: *Dogs are barred from that store.* **7** band of color; stripe: *There is a blue bar of cloud across the setting sun.* **8** unit of rhythm in music. *The regular accent falls on the first note of each bar.* **9** the dividing line between two such units on a musical staff. **10** counter or place where drinks (and sometimes food) are served to customers. **11** place where a prisoner stands in a court of law. **12** the whole group of practicing lawyers: *After passing her law examinations, she was admitted to the bar.* **13** court of law: *try a case at the bar.* 1,2,4,7-13 *noun,* 3,5,6 *verb,* **barred, bar ring.**

barb (bärb), point sticking out and curving backward from the main point of an arrow or fishhook. See picture. *noun.*

bar bar i an (bär ber′ē ən *or* bär bar′ē ən), **1** person belonging to a people or to a tribe that is not civilized: *Rome was conquered by barbarians.* **2** not civilized; cruel and coarse. 1 *noun,* 2 *adjective.*

bar be cue (bär′bə kyü), **1** an outdoor meal in which meat is cooked over an open fire. **2** grill or open fireplace for cooking meat, fish, or fowl, usually over charcoal. **3** meat cooked over an open fire. **4** cook over an open fire or hot charcoal. **5** cook (meat, fish, or fowl) in a highly flavored sauce. 1-3 *noun,* 4,5 *verb,* **bar be cued, bar be cu ing.** [*Barbecue* comes from a Spanish word meaning "framework for roasting meat." The Spanish word was taken from a Central American Indian word.]

barbed (bärbd), having a barb or barbs. A fishhook is barbed. Barbed wire has sharp points every few inches. *adjective.*

bar ber (bär′bər), person whose work is cutting hair and shaving or trimming beards. *noun.* [*Barber* comes from a French word meaning "beard."]

bare (ber *or* bar), **1** without covering; not clothed; naked: *The sun burned his bare shoulders. The top of the hill was bare, but trees grew part way up its slope.* **2** empty; not furnished: *a room bare of furniture.* **3** plain; not adorned: *a bare little cabin in the woods.* **4** just enough and no more: *She earns only a bare living.* **5** make bare; uncover; reveal: *to bare one's feelings.* See picture. 1-4 *adjective,* **bar er, bar est;** 5 *verb,* **bared, bar ing.**

bare back (ber′bak′ *or* bar′bak′), without a saddle; on a horse's bare back. *adverb, adjective.*

bare foot (ber′fut′ *or* bar′fut′), wearing nothing on the feet. *adjective, adverb.*

bare foot ed (ber′fut′id *or* bar′fut′id), barefoot. *adjective, adverb.*

bare head ed (ber′hed′id *or* bar′hed′id), wearing nothing on the head: *You shouldn't be bareheaded in such cold weather. adjective.*

bare ly (ber′lē *or* bar′lē), with nothing to spare;

only just: *I barely had time to catch my bus.* adverb.

bar gain (bär′gən), **1** agreement to trade or exchange: *You can't back out on our bargain.* **2** something offered for sale cheap or bought cheap: *This hat is a bargain.* **3** try to get good terms; try to make a good deal: *I bargained with the shopkeeper and bought the book for $2 instead of $5.* 1,2 noun, 3 verb.

bargain for, be prepared for or expect: *He hadn't bargained for rain and had left his umbrella at home.*

barge (bärj), **1** a large, strongly built, flat-bottomed boat for carrying freight on rivers and canals. See picture. **2** a large boat used for excursions, pageants, and special occasions. **3** move clumsily like a barge: *He barged into the table and knocked the lamp over.* **4** push oneself rudely: *Don't barge in where you're not wanted.* 1,2 noun, 3,4 verb, **barged, barg ing.**

bar i tone (bar′ə tōn), **1** a man's singing voice between tenor and bass. **2** singer with such a voice. **3** part sung by such a voice. noun.

bark[1] (bärk), **1** the tough outside covering of the trunk and branches of trees. **2** scrape the skin from: *I fell down the steps and barked my shins.* 1 noun, 2 verb.

bark[2] (bärk), **1** the short, sharp sound that a dog makes. **2** speak gruffly or sharply: *The policeman barked out his order.* 1 noun, 2 verb.

bar ley (bär′lē), the grain of a kind of cereal grass, or the plant that it grows on. Barley grows in cool climates and is used as food for people and farm animals. noun.

bar mitz vah (bär′ mits′və), **1** ceremony or celebration held when a Jewish boy becomes thirteen years old. It signifies he has reached the age of religious responsibility. **2** the boy himself.

barn (bärn), building for storing hay and grain and for sheltering cows and horses. noun.

bar na cle (bär′nə kəl), a small, saltwater animal with a shell. It fastens itself to rocks, the timbers of wharves and docks, and the bottoms of ships. noun.

barn yard (bärn′yärd′), yard around a barn. noun.

ba rom e ter (bə rom′ə tər), **1** instrument for measuring the pressure of air. It is used to predict changes in the weather. See picture. **2** something that indicates change: *Newspapers are often called barometers of public opinion.* noun.

bar on (bar′ən), **1** nobleman of the lowest rank. **2** an English nobleman during the Middle Ages who held his lands directly from the king. noun.

bar on ess (bar′ə nis), **1** wife or widow of a baron. **2** woman whose rank is equal to that of a baron. noun, plural **bar on ess es.**

bar racks (bar′əks), a building or group of buildings for soldiers to live in, usually in a fort or camp. noun plural or singular.

bar rel (bar′əl), **1** container with a round, flat top and bottom and sides that curve out slightly. Barrels are usually made of boards held together by hoops. **2** amount that a barrel can hold: *They picked a barrel of apples.* **3** put in barrels: *We plan to barrel the cider today.* **4** a metal tube, such as

the part of a gun from which the bullet is discharged. 1,2,4 noun, 3 verb.

bar ren (bar′ən), **1** not able to bear seeds, fruit, or young: *a barren fruit tree, a barren animal.* **2** not able to produce much: *a barren desert.* adjective.

bar rette (bə ret′), pin with a clasp for holding the hair in place. noun.

bar ri cade (bar′ə kād′), a rough, hastily made barrier for defense: *The soldiers cut down trees to make a barricade across the road.* noun.

bar ri er (bar′ē ər), **1** something that stands in the way; something stopping progress or preventing approach: *The landslide created a barrier across the road. Lack of water was a barrier to settling much of New Mexico.* **2** something that separates or keeps apart: *Our argument had created a barrier between us.* noun.

bar ter (bär′tər), **1** trade by exchanging one kind of goods for other goods without using money; exchange: *The trapper bartered furs for supplies.* **2** exchanging goods: *Nations sometimes trade by barter instead of paying money for the things they need.* 1 verb, 2 noun.

base[1] (bās), **1** the part on which anything stands or rests; bottom: *This big machine has a wide steel base.* **2** starting place; headquarters: *an army base. The base for our hike was the cabin.* **3** set up and keep going; found: *Their large business was based on good service.* **4** thing or part on which something depends; basis: *This paint has an oil base.* **5** station or goal in certain games, such as baseball or hide-and-seek: *A home run doesn't count if you fail to touch a base.* **6** a chemical substance that unites with an acid to form a salt. The water solution of a base turns red litmus paper blue. 1,2,4-6 noun, 3 verb, **based, bas ing.**

base[2] (bās), **1** mean; selfish and cowardly: *To betray a friend is a base action.* **2** having little value when compared with something else; inferior: *Iron and lead are base metals; gold and silver are precious metals.* adjective, **bas er, bas est.**

base ball (bās′bôl′), **1** game played with bat and ball by two teams of nine players each, on a field with four bases. A player who touches all the bases, under the rules, scores a run. **2** ball used in this game. noun.

base man (bās′mən), a baseball player guarding first, second, or third base. noun, plural **base men.**

base ment (bās′mənt), the lowest story of a building, partly or wholly below ground. noun.

bash ful (bash′fəl), uneasy in the presence of strangers; easily embarrassed; shy: *The child was too bashful to greet us.* adjective.

ba sic (bā′sik), forming the basis; fundamental: *Addition, subtraction, multiplication, and division are the basic processes of arithmetic.* adjective.

ba si cal ly (bā′sik lē), chiefly; fundamentally. *adverb.*

ba sin (bā′sn), **1** a wide, shallow dish for holding liquids; bowl. **2** amount that a basin can hold: *They have used up a basin of water.* **3** a shallow area containing water: *Part of the harbor is a basin for yachts.* **4** all the land drained by a river and the streams that flow into it: *The Mississippi basin extends from the Appalachians to the Rockies. noun.*

ba sis (bā′sis), the main part; foundation: *The basis of their friendship was a common interest in sports. noun, plural* **ba ses** (bā′sēz′).

bask (bask), warm oneself pleasantly: *The cat basks before the fire. verb.*

bas ket (bas′kit), **1** container made of twigs, grasses, fibers, plastic, or strips of wood woven together: *a clothes basket.* **2** amount that a basket holds: *We ate a basket of peaches.* **3** anything that looks like or is shaped like a basket: *This basket for waste paper is made of metal.* **4** a metal hoop with a net open at the bottom, shaped like a basket. It is used as a goal in basketball. **5** score made in basketball. *noun.*

bas ket ball (bas′kit bôl′), **1** game played with a large, round ball between two teams of five players each. The players score points by tossing the ball through baskets 10 feet (3 meters) high at either end of the court. **2** ball used in this game. *noun.*

bass[1] (bās), **1** the lowest singing voice of a man. **2** singer with such a voice. **3** part sung by such a voice. **4** instrument playing such a part. **5** having a deep, low sound. **1-4** *noun, plural* **bass es**; **5** *adjective.*

bass[2] (bas), any of several North American freshwater or saltwater fishes used for food. *noun, plural* **bass es** or **bass.**

bas soon (bə sün′), a deep-toned wind instrument with a doubled wooden body and a curved metal mouthpiece. See picture. *noun.*

bassoon

baste (bāst), drip or pour melted fat or butter on (meat or fowl) while roasting: *Baste the turkey to keep it from drying out.* verb, **bast ed, bast ing.**

bat[1] (bat), **1** a stout wooden stick or club, used to hit the ball in baseball, cricket, and similar games. **2** hit with a bat; hit: *He bats well. I batted the balloon with my hand.* **3** a turn at batting: *Who goes to bat first?* **1,3** *noun,* **2** *verb,* **bat ted, bat ting.**

bat[2] (bat), a flying mammal with a body like that of a mouse and wings made of thin skin. Bats fly at night. Most of them eat insects but some live on fruit and a few suck the blood of other mammals. See picture. *noun.*

batch (bach), **1** quantity of bread, cookies, or rolls made at one baking. **2** quantity of anything made as one lot or set: *Our second batch of candy was better than the first.* **3** number of persons or things taken together: *She caught a fine batch of fish. noun, plural* **batch es.**

bath (bath), **1** washing of the body: *I took a hot bath.* **2** water in a tub for a bath: *Your bath is ready.* **3** tub, room, or other place for bathing: *The house had two baths. noun, plural* **baths** (ba₮HZ).

bathe (bā₮H), **1** take a bath: *I bathe before going to bed.* **2** give a bath to: *She is bathing her dog.* **3** apply water to: *Bathe your feet if they are tired.* **4** go swimming; go into a river, lake, or ocean for pleasure or to get cool. **5** cover or surround: *The valley was bathed in light. verb,* **bathed, bath ing.**

bathing suit, garment worn for swimming.

bath room (bath′rüm′), **1** a room fitted out for taking baths, usually with a sink and a toilet. **2** a room containing a toilet. *noun.*

bath tub (bath′tub′), tub to bathe in. *noun.*

bat mitz vah (bät′ mits′və), **1** ceremony or celebration held when a Jewish girl becomes thirteen years old. It signifies she has reached the age of religious responsibility. **2** the girl herself.

ba ton (ba ton′), the stick used by the leader of an orchestra, chorus, or band for beating time to the music. *noun.*

bat tal ion (bə tal′yən), any large part of an army organized to act together. Two or more companies make a battalion. *noun.*

bat ter[1] (bat′ər), strike with repeated blows so as to bruise, break, or get out of shape; pound: *The fireman battered down the door with an ax. verb.*

bat ter[2] (bat′ər), a liquid mixture of flour, milk, and eggs that becomes solid when cooked. Cakes and muffins are made from batter. *noun.*

bat ter[3] (bat′ər), player whose turn it is to bat in baseball, cricket, and similar games. *noun.*

bat tered (bat′ərd), damaged by hard use: *I found a battered old book in the office. The floor was worn and battered by many feet. adjective.*

bat ter y (bat′ər ē), **1** a single electric cell: *Most flashlights work on two batteries.* **2** set of two or more electric cells that produce electric current. Batteries provide the current that starts automobile and truck engines. **3** any set of similar or connected things: *The mayor spoke before a battery of television cameras.* **4** set of big guns for combined action in attack or defense: *Four*

bat² —wingspread about 15 inches (38 centimeters)

battle-ax

battlement—view from the battlements of a castle in Spain

a hat	i it	oi oil	ch child	a in about
ā age	ī ice	ou out	ng long	e in taken
ä far	o hot	u cup	sh she	ə = { i in pencil
e let	ō open	ù put	th thin	o in lemon
ē equal	ô order	ü rule	∓H then	u in circus
ėr term			zh measure	

batteries began firing. **5** (in baseball) the pitcher and catcher together. *noun, plural* **bat ter ies.**

bat tle (bat′l), **1** a fight between armies, air forces, or navies: *The battle for the island lasted six months.* **2** fighting or warfare: *The soldier received his wounds in battle.* **3** any fight or contest: *The candidates fought a battle of words during the campaign.* **4** take part in a battle; fight; struggle: *battle with wolves. The swimmer had to battle a strong current.* 1-3 *noun,* 4 *verb,* **bat tled, bat tling.**

bat tle-ax or **bat tle-axe** (bat′l aks′), ax with a broad blade, formerly used as a weapon in battle. See picture. *noun, plural* **bat tle-ax es.**

bat tle field (bat′l fēld′), place where a battle is fought or has been fought. *noun.*

bat tle ground (bat′l ground′), battlefield. *noun.*

bat tle ment (bat′l mənt), a low wall for defense at the top of a tower or wall, built with open places to shoot through. See picture. *noun.*

bat tle ship (bat′l ship′), a very large warship having the heaviest armor and the most powerful guns. The last battleships were built during World War II. *noun.*

bawl (bôl), **1** shout or cry out in a noisy way: *The lost calf was bawling for its mother. "Attention!" bawled the sergeant.* **2** weep loudly. *verb.*

bawl out, scold loudly: *She bawled me out for denting her bicycle.*

bay¹ (bā), part of a sea or lake extending into the land. A bay is usually smaller than a gulf and larger than a cove. *noun.*

bay² (bā), **1** a long, deep barking, especially by a large dog: *We heard the distant bay of the hounds.* **2** to bark with long, deep sounds: *Dogs sometimes bay at the moon.* **3** a stand made to face or keep off pursuers when escape is impossible: *The deer stood at bay against the hounds.* 1,3 *noun,* 2 *verb.*

bay³ (bā), **1** reddish brown. **2** a reddish-brown horse with black mane and tail. 1 *adjective,* 2 *noun.*

bay o net (bā′ə nit), **1** knife attached to the muzzle of a rifle. **2** pierce or stab with a bayonet. 1 *noun,* 2 *verb.* [*Bayonet* was named for Bayonne, a city in southern France. Bayonets were first made in this city.]

bay ou (bī′ü), a marshy, slow-moving outlet of a lake or swamp in the southern United States, especially in Louisiana. *noun.* [*Bayou* was a word used by the French in Louisiana. It came from an American Indian word meaning "creek."]

ba zaar or **ba zar** (bə zär′), **1** street or streets full of small shops and booths in Oriental countries. **2** place for the sale of many kinds of goods. **3** sale of things given for some special purpose. *noun.*

B.C., before Christ. The abbreviation B.C. is used for dates before the birth of Christ. The abbreviation A.D. is used for dates after the birth of Christ. 350 B.C. is 100 years earlier than 250 B.C. From 20 B.C. to A.D. 50 is 70 years.

be (bē). *He will be here all year. Be careful. They will be rewarded. verb,* **was** or **were, been, be ing.**

beach (bēch), **1** an almost flat shore of sand or pebbles over which water washes when high. **2** run (a boat) ashore; pull up on the shore. 1 *noun, plural* **beach es;** 2 *verb.*

bea con (bē′kən), **1** fire or light used as a signal to guide or warn. **2** a radio signal for guiding aircraft and ships through fogs and storms. **3** a tall tower for a signal; lighthouse. *noun.*

bead (bēd), **1** a small ball or bit of glass, metal, or plastic with a hole through it, so that it can be strung on a thread with others like it. **2 beads, a** a string of beads. **b** a string of beads for keeping count in saying prayers; rosary. **3** put beads on; ornament with beads. **4** any small, round object like a drop or bubble: *Beads of sweat covered his forehead.* **5** piece of metal at the front end of a gun to aim by. 1,2,4,5 *noun,* 3 *verb.*

bea gle (bē′gəl), a small hunting dog with smooth hair, short legs, and drooping ears. *noun.*

beak (bēk), **1** bill of a bird. Eagles and hawks have strong, hooked beaks that are useful in striking or tearing. **2** anything shaped like a beak, such as the projecting prow of an ancient warship or the spout of a pitcher or jug. *noun.*

beak er (bē′kər), **1** a large cup or drinking glass with a wide mouth. **2** a thin glass or metal cup used in laboratories. A beaker has a flat bottom, no handle, and a small lip for pouring. *noun.*

beam (bēm), **1** a large, long piece of timber, iron, or steel, ready for use in building. **2** the main horizontal support of a building or ship. **3** any long piece or bar: *The beam of a balance supports a pair of scales.* **4** ray of light: *a flashlight beam.* **5** send out rays of light; shine. **6** a bright look or smile. **7** look or smile brightly: *Her face beamed with delight.* **8** a radio signal directed in a straight line, used to guide aircraft or ships. **9** direct (a broadcast): *A program was beamed at Russia.* 1-4,6,8 *noun,* 5,7,9 *verb.*

bean (bēn), **1** the smooth, somewhat flat seed of a bush or vine, eaten as a vegetable. **2** the long green or yellow pod containing such seeds, also used as a vegetable. **3** any seed shaped somewhat like a bean. Coffee beans are seeds of the coffee plant. *noun.*

bean bag (bēn′bag′), a small bag partly filled with dry beans, used to toss in play. *noun.*

bean stalk (bēn′stôk′), stem of a bean plant. *noun.*

bear[1] (ber *or* bar), **1** carry or support; hold up: *The hikers were bearing heavy packs. The ice is too thin to bear your weight.* **2** put up with; endure: *He cannot bear any more pain.* **3** bring forth; produce: *This tree bears fine apples.* **4** give birth to: *She was born on May 15. Our cat will soon bear kittens. verb,* **bore, borne** or **born, bear ing.**
bear down, press down: *The lead will break if you bear down too hard on your pencil.*

bear[2] (ber *or* bar), **1** a large animal with thick,

coarse fur and a very short tail. A bear walks flat on the soles of its feet. **2** a gruff or bad-tempered person. *noun.*

beard (bird), **1** the hair growing on a man's chin and cheeks. **2** something like this. The chin tuft of a goat is a beard; so are the stiff hairs on the heads of plants like oats, barley, and wheat. *noun.*

bear ing (ber′ing *or* bar′ing), **1** way of standing, sitting, walking, or behaving; manner: *A general should have a military bearing.* **2** connection in thought or meaning; relation: *Do not ask questions that have no bearing on our discussion.* **3 bearings,** position in relation to other things; direction: *We had no compass, so we got our bearings from the stars.* **4** part of a machine on which another part moves. A bearing supports the moving part and reduces friction by turning with the motion. *noun.*

beast (bēst), **1** any four-footed animal. Lions, bears, cows, and horses are beasts. A **beast of burden** is an animal used for carrying loads. **2** a coarse, dirty, or brutal person. *noun.*

beast ly (bēst′lē), **1** like a beast; coarse, dirty, or brutal; vile. **2** unpleasant: *I have a beastly headache. adjective,* **beast li er, beast li est.**

beat (bēt), **1** strike again and again: *The baby beat the floor with the toy hammer.* **2** stroke or blow made again and again: *We heard the beat of a drum.* **3** get the better of; defeat; overcome: *Their team beat ours by a huge score.* **4** make flat: *The jeweler beat gold into thin strips with a hammer.* **5** mix by stirring rapidly with a fork, spoon, or other utensil: *I helped make the cake by beating the eggs.* **6** sound made by the regular action of the heart as it pumps blood. **7** throb: *My heart beat fast with joy.* **8** move up and down; flap: *The bird beat its wings.* **9** unit of time or accent in music: *A waltz has three beats to a measure.* **10** a regular round or route taken by a policeman or watchman. **11** tired; worn out: *I was beat after running the race.* 1,3-5,7,8 *verb,* **beat, beat en** or **beat, beat ing;** 2,6,9,10 *noun,* 11 *adjective.*

beat en (bēt′n), **1** whipped; struck: *The beaten dog ran away from its owner.* **2** much walked on or traveled: *The children had worn a beaten path across the grass.* **3** defeated; overcome: *a beaten team.* **4** shaped by blows of a hammer: *This bowl is made of beaten silver.* **5** See **beat.** *Our team was beaten in football on Saturday.* 1-4 *adjective,* 5 *verb.*

beat-up (bēt′up′), worn out from long or hard use: *a beat-up car. adjective.*

beau ti ful (byü′tə fəl), very pleasing to see or hear; delighting the mind or senses: *a beautiful park, beautiful music. adjective.*

beau ti fy (byü′tə fī), make beautiful: *Flowers beautify a room. verb,* **beau ti fied, beau ti fy ing.**

beau ty (byü′tē), **1** good looks: *The child had beauty and intelligence.* **2** quality that pleases in flowers, pictures, or music: *There is beauty in a fine painting.* **3** something or someone beautiful: *the beauties of nature. noun, plural* **beau ties.**

bea ver (bē′vər), **1** a gnawing animal with soft fur, a broad, flat tail, and webbed hind feet for swimming. Beavers live both in water and on land.

beaver (definition 1)—about 3½ feet (1 meter) long with the tail

a hat	i it	oi oil	ch child	a in about
ā age	ī ice	ou out	ng long	e in taken
ä far	o hot	u cup	sh she	ə = { i in pencil
e let	ō open	u̇ put	th thin	o in lemon
ē equal	ô order	ü rule	₮H then	u in circus
ėr term			zh measure	

They gnaw down trees and build dams and nests in streams. See picture. **2** its soft brown fur. *noun.*

be came (bi kām′). See **become.** *The seed became a plant. verb.*

be cause (bi kôz′), for the reason that; since: *Because we were late, we ran the whole way home. conjunction.*

because of, by reason of; on account of: *The game was called off because of rain.*

beck on (bek′ən), signal (to a person) by motion of the head or hand: *She beckoned me to follow her. verb.*

be come (bi kum′), **1** come to be; grow to be: *It is becoming colder. I became tired and fell asleep.* **2** look well on; suit: *That blue sweater becomes you. verb,* **be came, be come, be com ing.**

become of, happen to: *What has become of the box of candy?*

be com ing (bi kum′ing), **1** fitting; suitable: *the kindness and patience becoming to a teacher.* **2** pleasant to look at; attractive: *a very becoming new coat. adjective.*

bed (bed), **1** anything to sleep or rest on. **2** any place where people or animals sleep or rest: *The cat made its bed by the fireplace.* **3** provide with a bed; put to bed; go to bed: *She bedded the horse in the barn.* **4** a flat base on which anything rests; foundation: *The tall flagpole was set in a bed of concrete.* **5** the ground under a body of water: *The river bed was soft and muddy.* **6** piece of ground in a garden in which plants are grown: *We planted a bed of tulips.* **7** plant in a garden bed: *These tulips should be bedded in rich soil.* **8** layer; stratum: *The*

beetle—about life size

miners struck a bed of coal deep in the earth. **1,2,4-6,8** *noun,* **3,7** *verb,* **bed ded, bed ding.**

bed bug (bed′bug′), a small, flat, reddish-brown insect that sucks blood. It is found in houses, most often in beds, and its bite is painful. *noun.*

bed clothes (bed′klōz′), sheets, blankets, or quilts. *noun plural.*

bed ding (bed′ing), **1** bedclothes. **2** material for beds: *Straw is used as bedding for cows. noun.*

bed lam (bed′ləm), uproar; confusion. *noun.* [*Bedlam* was the old name for Saint Mary of Bethlehem, a hospital for insane people in London.]

be drag gled (bi drag′əld), **1** wet and hanging limp: *I tried to comb my bedraggled hair.* **2** soiled by being dragged in the dirt. *adjective.*

bed room (bed′rüm′), a room to sleep in. *noun.*

bed side (bed′sīd′), side of a bed: *The nurse sat by the patient's bedside. noun.*

bed spread (bed′spred′), cover for a bed that is spread over the blankets to make the bed look neater. *noun.*

bed stead (bed′sted′), the wooden or metal framework of a bed. *noun.*

bed time (bed′tīm′), time to go to bed: *Her regular bedtime is nine o'clock. noun.*

bee (bē), **1** insect that makes honey and wax. A bee has four wings and usually a sting. Honeybees and bumblebees live in large groups. **2** a gathering for work or amusement: *The teacher let us have a spelling bee in class today. noun.*

beech (bēch), **1** tree with smooth, gray bark and glossy leaves. It bears a sweet nut which is good to eat. **2** its wood. *noun, plural* **beech es** or **beech** for 1.

beef (bēf), **1** meat from a steer, cow, or bull. **2** steer, cow, or bull when full-grown and fattened for food. *noun.*

beef steak (bēf′stāk′), slice of beef for broiling or frying; steak. *noun.*

bee hive (bē′hīv′), **1** hive or house for bees. **2** a busy, swarming place. *noun.*

bee line (bē′līn′), the straightest way between two places, like the flight of a bee to its hive. *noun.*

been (bin). See **be.** *I have been sick. The book has been read by everyone in the class. verb.*

beer (bir), an alcoholic drink made from malted barley flavored with hops. *noun.*

bees wax (bēz′waks′), wax made by bees, from which they make their honeycomb. *noun.*

beet (bēt), the thick, fleshy root of a garden plant. Red beets are eaten as a vegetable. Sugar is made from white beets. *noun.*

bee tle (bē′tl), insect that has two hard, shiny cases that cover its wings when not flying. See picture. *noun.*

be fall (bi fôl′), **1** happen to: *They feared that harm had befallen the pilot.* **2** happen: *The knight swore to kill the dragon, no matter what befell. verb,* **be fell** (bi fel′), **be fall en** (bi fô′lən), **be fall ing.**

be fore (bi fôr′), **1** earlier than: *Come before noon.* **2** earlier: *Come at five o'clock, not before.* **3** until now; in the past: *You were never late before.* **4** in front of; ahead of: *Walk before me.* **5** in front; ahead: *The scout went before to see if the trail was safe.* **6** rather than; sooner than: *I'd starve before giving in.* 1,4,6 *preposition,* 2,3,5 *adverb.*

be fore hand (bi fôr′hand′), ahead of time: *Get everything ready beforehand. adverb, adjective.*

be friend (bi frend′), act as a friend to; help: *The children befriended the stray dog. verb.*

beg (beg), **1** ask for (food, money, or clothes) as a charity: *The old woman was so poor that she had to beg for food.* **2** ask a favor; ask earnestly or humbly: *The children begged for a ride on the pony.* **3** ask politely and courteously: *I beg your pardon. verb,* **begged, beg ging.**

be gan (bi gan′). See **begin.** *Snow began to fall. verb.*

beg gar (beg′ər), **1** person who lives by begging. **2** a very poor person. *noun.*

be gin (bi gin′), **1** do the first part; start: *When shall we begin? I began reading the book yesterday.* **2** come into being: *The club began years ago.* **3** be near; come near: *Your big brother's suit wouldn't even begin to fit you. verb,* **be gan, be gun, be gin ning.**

be gin ner (bi gin′ər), person who is doing something for the first time; person who lacks skill and experience: *You skate well for a beginner. noun.*

be gin ning (bi gin′ing), **1** a start: *to make a good beginning.* **2** time when anything begins: *December 22nd marks the beginning of winter.* **3** first part: *I enjoyed this book from beginning to end.* **4** starting point; source; origin: *The idea of the airplane had its beginning in the flight of birds. noun.*

be gone (bi gôn′), go away: *"Begone!" said the prince. The princess bade the witch begone. interjection, verb.*

be gun (bi gun′). See **begin.** *It has begun to rain. verb.*

be half (bi haf′), side, interest, or favor: *A friend will act in my behalf while I'm away. noun.*
in behalf of or **on behalf of,** in the interest of; for: *I am speaking in behalf of my friend.*

be have (bi hāv′), **1** act: *The children behaved well during the trip. The ship behaves well even in a storm.* **2** act properly; do what is right: *If you behave today, we can come here again. verb,* **be haved, be hav ing.**

be hav ior (bi hā′vyər), way of acting; conduct; actions: *Her sullen behavior showed that she was angry. The boat's behavior was perfect on the trial trip. noun.*

be head (bi hed′), cut off the head of. *verb.*

be held (bi held′). See **behold.** *The little child beheld the approaching storm with fear. verb.*

be hind (bi hīnd′), **1** at the back of: *I hid behind a bush.* **2** at the back: *The dog's tail hung down behind.* **3** supporting: *Your friends are behind you.* **4** farther back: *The rest of the hikers are still quite a way behind.* **5** later than: *The milkman is behind his usual time.* **6** not on time; late: *The class is behind in its work.* **7** less advanced than: *I am behind my class because I missed two weeks of school.* **8** in the place that has been or is being left: *When my family went to New York, I stayed behind.* 1,3,5,7 *preposition,* 2,4,6,8 *adverb.*

be hold (bi hōld′), look at; see; observe: *They wanted to behold the sunrise. Behold! the queen! verb,* **be held, be hold ing;** *interjection.*

beige (bāzh), pale brown. *adjective.*

be ing (bē′ing), **1** See **be.** *The dog is being fed.* **2** person; living creature: *a human being, beings from outer space.* **3** life; existence: *The world came into being long ago.* 1 *verb,* 2,3 *noun.*

be lat ed (bi lā′tid), happening or coming late; delayed: *Your belated letter has arrived at last. adjective.*

belch (belch), **1** allow air or gas to escape from the stomach through the throat and mouth: *If you drink pop too fast, you are apt to belch.* **2** throw out with force: *The volcano belched fire and smoke.* **3** act of belching. 1,2 *verb,* 3 *noun, plural* **belch es.**

bel fry (bel′frē), **1** tower for a bell or bells. **2** space in a tower in which a bell or bells may be hung. *noun, plural* **bel fries.**

be lief (bi lēf′), **1** what is held to be true or real; thing believed: *It was once a common belief that the earth is flat.* **2** acceptance as true or real: *His belief in ghosts makes him afraid of the dark.* **3** faith; trust: *She expressed her belief in people. noun.*

be liev a ble (bi lē′və bəl), able to be believed. *adjective.*

be lieve (bi lēv′), **1** think (something) is true or real: *Who doesn't believe that the earth is round?* **2** think (somebody) tells the truth: *I believe you.* **3** have faith; trust: *We believe in our friends.* **4** think; suppose: *I believe we are going to have a test soon. verb,* **be lieved, be liev ing.**

be lit tle (bi lit′l), make seem little; make less important: *They belittled your success because they were jealous. verb,* **be lit tled, be lit tling.**

bell (bel), **1** a hollow metal object shaped like a cup, that makes a musical sound when struck by a clapper or hammer. **2** anything that makes a ringing sound as a signal: *I heard the bell ring, and ran to open the door.* **3** stroke or sound of a bell: *Our teacher dismissed us five minutes before the bell.* **4** stroke of a bell used on shipboard to indicate a half hour of time. **5** anything shaped like a bell: *the bell of a trumpet. noun.*

bell boy (bel′boi′), person whose work is carrying baggage and doing errands for the guests of a hotel or club. *noun.*

bel lig er ent (bə lij′ər ənt), **1** at war; engaged in war; fighting: *Great Britain and Germany were belligerent powers in 1941.* **2** nation at war: *France and Germany were belligerents in World War II.* **3** fond of fighting; warlike: *a belligerent neighborhood gang.* 1,3 *adjective,* 2 *noun.*

bel low (bel/ō), **1** make a loud, deep noise; roar as a bull does. **2** a loud, deep noise; roar. **3** shout loudly, with anger, or with pain. 1,3 *verb*, 2 *noun*.

bel lows (bel/ōz), device for producing a strong current of air, used for blowing fires or sounding an organ or accordion. See picture. *noun singular or plural.*

bel ly (bel/ē), **1** the lower front part of the human body, below the chest; abdomen. It contains the stomach and intestines. **2** the under part of an animal's body. **3** stomach. **4** the bulging part of anything, or the hollow in it: *the belly of a sail. The damaged plane skidded on its belly.* **5** swell out; bulge: *The sails bellied in the wind.* 1-4 *noun, plural* **bel lies**; 4,5 *verb*, **bel lied, bel ly ing.**

be long (bi lông/), have one's or its proper place: *That book belongs on this shelf. verb.*
belong to, 1 be the property of: *Does this cap belong to you?* **2** be a part of: *That top belongs to this box.* **3** be a member of: *She belongs to the team.*

be long ings (bi lông/ingz), things that belong to a person; possessions. *noun plural.*

be lov ed (bi luv/id *or* bi luvd/), **1** dearly loved; dear. **2** person who is loved. 1 *adjective*, 2 *noun.*

be low (bi lō/), **1** in or to a lower place: *From the airplane we could see the fields below.* **2** on a lower floor or deck; downstairs: *The ship's cargo is stored below.* **3** lower than; under: *My brother's room is below mine.* **4** less than: *It is four degrees below freezing.* **5** after or later in a book or article: *See the note below.* **6** below zero: *The temperature is five below today.* 1,2,5,6 *adverb*, 3,4 *preposition.*

belt (belt), **1** strip of leather or cloth, fastened around the waist to hold in or support clothes, tools, or weapons. **2** put a belt around: *She belted her dress.* **3** fasten with a belt: *to belt on a hunting knife.* **4** beat with a belt. **5** hit suddenly and hard: *She belted the ball over the fence.* **6** any broad strip or band: *A belt of trees grew between the two fields. The cotton belt is the region where cotton is grown.* **7** an endless band that transfers motion from one wheel or pulley to another: *A belt connected to the motor moves the fan in an automobile.* See picture. 1,6,7 *noun*, 2-5 *verb.*

bench (bench), **1** a long seat, usually of wood or stone. **2** a strong, heavy table used by a carpenter, or by any person who works with tools and materials; workbench. **3** judge or group of judges sitting in a court of law: *Bring the prisoner before the bench.* **4** position as a judge: *The attorney was appointed to the bench.* **5** take (a player) out of a game. 1-4 *noun, plural* **bench es;** 5 *verb.*

bend (bend), **1** part that is not straight; curve; turn: *There is a sharp bend in the road here.* **2** make or become crooked; curve: *bend a wire. The branch began to bend as I climbed along it.* **3** turn or move in a certain direction; direct: *His steps were bent toward home now.* **4** stoop; bow: *She bent down and picked up a stone.* 1 *noun*, 2-4 *verb*, **bent, bend ing.**

be neath (bi nēth/), **1** in a lower place; below; underneath; under: *What you drop will fall upon the spot beneath. The dog sat beneath the tree.* **2** not worthy of: *Your insulting remarks are beneath*

a hat	i it	oi oil	ch child	(a in about
ā age	ī ice	ou out	ng long	e in taken
ä far	o hot	u cup	sh she	ə = { i in pencil
e let	ō open	ù put	th thin	o in lemon
ē equal	ô order	ü rule	ŦH then	(u in circus
ėr term			zh measure	

bellows

notice. 1 *adverb*, 1,2 *preposition.*

be ne dic tion (ben/ə dik/shən), **1** the asking of God's blessing at the end of a religious service. **2** blessing. *noun.* [*Benediction* comes from Latin words meaning "to speak well."]

ben e fac tor (ben/ə fak/tər), person who has given money or kindly help. *noun.*

ben e fi cial (ben/ə fish/əl), favorable; helpful; producing good: *Sunshine is beneficial to plants. adjective.*

ben e fit (ben/ə fit), **1** anything which is for the good of a person or thing; advantage: *Good roads are of great benefit to travelers.* **2** do good to; be good for: *Rest will benefit a sick person.* **3** receive good; profit: *He benefited from the medicine.* 1 *noun*, 2,3 *verb.*

be nev o lence (bə nev/ə ləns), **1** good will; kindly feeling. **2** act of kindness; something good that is done. *noun.*

be nev o lent (bə nev/ə lənt), kindly; charitable: *Giving money to help the hospital is a benevolent act. adjective.*

bent (bent), **1** See **bend.** *He bent the wire.* **2** not straight; crooked; curved: *The farmer's back was bent from years of toil.* **3** determined: *He is bent on being a doctor.* **4** a natural ability and liking: *She has a bent for mathematics.* 1 *verb*, 2,3 *adjective*, 4 *noun.*

be numb (bi num/), make numb: *My fingers were benumbed by the cold. verb.*

be queath (bi kwēŦH/), **1** give or leave by means of a will when one dies: *She bequeathed her fortune to her children.* **2** hand down; pass along: *One age bequeaths its knowledge to the next. verb.*

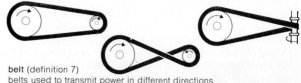
belt (definition 7)
belts used to transmit power in different directions

be ret (bə rā′), a soft, flat, round cap of wool or felt. *noun.*

ber ry (ber′ē), **1** any small, juicy fruit with many seeds. Strawberries and raspberries are berries. **2** gather or pick berries. **3** the dry seed or kernel of grain or other plants. Grains of wheat are sometimes called wheat berries. 1,3 *noun, plural* **ber ries;** 2 *verb,* **ber ried, ber ry ing.**

berth (bėrth), **1** place to sleep on a ship or a railroad sleeping car. **2** a ship's place at anchor or at a wharf. *noun.*

be seech (bi sēch′), ask earnestly; beg; implore: *I beseech you to listen to me. verb,* **be sought** or **be seeched, be seech ing.**

be set (bi set′), attack; attack from all sides: *We were beset by mosquitoes in the swamp. In the darkness he was suddenly beset by fear. verb,* **be set, be set ting.**

be side (bi sīd′), **1** by the side of; close to; near: *Grass grows beside the fence.* **2** compared with: *The wolf seems tame beside the tiger.* **3** away from: *That question is beside the point and shows that you were not listening.* **4** besides. 1-3 *preposition,* 4 *adverb.*
beside oneself, out of one's mind; crazy: *They're beside themselves with worry over their lost child.*

be sides (bi sīdz′), **1** more than that; also; moreover: *I won't go to the movies; besides, I have no money.* **2** in addition to: *Others came to the picnic besides our class.* 1 *adverb,* 2 *preposition.*

be siege (bi sēj′), **1** try for a long time to take (a place) by armed force; surround and try to capture: *For ten years the Greeks besieged Troy.* **2** crowd around: *Hundreds of admirers besieged the astronaut.* **3** overwhelm with requests or questions: *Flood victims besieged the Red Cross with calls for help. verb,* **be sieged, be sieg ing.**

be sought (bi sôt′). See **beseech.** *She besought the doctor to stop the pain. verb.*

best (best), **1** most good, excellent, or useful: *My work is good; your work is better; but her work is best. I want to be one of the best students in the class.* **2** in the most excellent way: *Who reads best?* **3** in or to the highest degree: *I like this book best.* **4** person or thing that is best: *He is the best in the class.* **5** largest: *I spent the best part of the day at school.* **6** the most that is possible: *I did my best to finish the work on time.* **7** outdo; defeat: *Our team was bested in the final game.* 1,5 *adjective, superlative of* **good;** 2,3 *adverb, superlative of* **well**[1]; 4,6 *noun,* 7 *verb.*
get the best of, defeat: *They got the best of us in the game.*
make the best of, do as well as possible with: *Try to make the best of a bad job.*

be stow (bi stō′), give (something) as a gift; give: *The millionaire bestowed a large sum of money on the university. verb.*

bet (bet), **1** a promise between two people or groups that the one that is wrong will give something of value to the one that is right: *We made a 25 cent bet on who would win the game.* **2** to promise something of value to another if you are wrong; wager: *I bet her a candy bar that my team*

bias (definition 1)—cloth cut on the bias

would win. **3** the money or thing promised: *My bet on the game was 25 cents.* **4** be very sure: *I bet you are wrong about that.* **5** thing to bet on: *Which horse is a good bet?* 1,3,5 *noun,* 2,4 *verb,* **bet** or **bet ted, bet ting.**

be tray (bi trā′), **1** give away to the enemy: *The traitor betrayed his country.* **2** be unfaithful to: *She betrayed her promise.* **3** show signs of; reveal: *The boy's wet shoes betrayed the fact that he had walked through puddles. verb.*

be tray al (bi trā′əl), act of betraying. *noun.*

bet ter (bet′ər), **1** more good, excellent, or useful than another: *She drew a better picture than her friend.* **2** in a more excellent way: *Try to read better next time.* **3** in a higher degree: *I know my old friend better than I know anyone else.* **4** person or thing that is better: *Which is the better of these two dresses?* **5** make better; improve: *We can better that work by being more careful next time.* **6** do better than: *The other team could not better our score.* **7** larger: *Four days is the better part of a week.* **8** improved in health: *The sick child is better today.* 1,7,8 *adjective, comparative of* **good;** 2,3 *adverb, comparative of* **well**[1]; 4 *noun,* 5,6 *verb.*
better off, in a better condition: *He is better off now that he has a new job.*
get the better of, be superior to; defeat: *The tortoise got the better of the hare.*
had better, ought to; should: *I had better go now.*

be tween (bi twēn′), **1** in the space or time separating two points, objects, or places: *The valley lay between two mountains. We don't go to school between Friday and Monday. The bus from Main Street to Broadway stops at every corner between.* **2** in the range of: *She earned between ten and twelve dollars.* **3** connecting; linking: *There is a good highway between Chicago and Detroit.* **4** having to do with; involving: *A war between two countries can affect the whole world.* **5** either one or the other of: *We must choose between the two books.* **6** by the joint action of: *They caught twelve fish between them.* 1-6 *preposition,* 1 *adverb.*

bev er age (bev′ər ij), liquid used or prepared for drinking. Milk, tea, coffee, beer, and wine are beverages. *noun.*

be ware (bi wer′ or bi war′), be on your guard against; be careful: *You must beware of swimming in a strong current. verb.*

be wil der (bi wil′dər), confuse completely; puzzle: *I was bewildered by the crowds. verb.*

be witch (bi wich′), **1** put under a spell; use magic on: *The wicked fairy bewitched the princess and made her fall into a long sleep.* **2** charm; delight very much: *We were bewitched by our bright little cousin. verb.*

be yond (bi yond′), **1** on or to the farther side of: *I* live beyond those trees. **2** farther on than: *I fell asleep on the bus and rode beyond my stop.* **3** farther away: *Your ball did not fall here; look beyond.* **4** later than; past: *I stayed up beyond my usual bedtime.* **5** out of the reach or understanding of: *This wilted plant is beyond help. The poem's meaning is beyond me.* **6** more than: *The price of the suit was beyond what he could pay. The trip was beyond all we had hoped.* 1,2,4-6 *preposition,* 3 *adverb.*

bi as (bī′əs), **1** a slanting line. Cloth is cut on the bias when it is cut diagonally across the weave. See picture. **2** opinion before there is a reason for it; prejudice: *An umpire should have no bias in favor of either side. noun, plural* **bi as es.**

bi ased (bī′əst), favoring one side too much; prejudiced: *a biased opinion. adjective.*

bib (bib), cloth worn under the chin by babies and small children to protect their clothing during meals. *noun.*

Bi ble (bī′bəl), **1** a book of writings containing the Old Testament and the New Testament. The Old Testament is sacred to both Jews and Christians. The New Testament is sacred to Christians. **2** book of the sacred writings of any religion. The Koran is the Bible of the Moslems. *noun.* [*Bible* is from a Greek word meaning "books." This came from another Greek word meaning "papyrus." A book or scroll was called this because it was written on papyrus brought from the ancient port of Byblos.]

bib li cal or **Bib li cal** (bib′lə kəl), of the Bible; having something to do with the Bible: *the biblical story of Adam and Eve. adjective.*

bick er (bik′ər), take part in a noisy quarrel about something unimportant; squabble: *The children bickered through the hot summer afternoon. verb.*

bi cus pid (bī kus′pid), a double-pointed tooth that tears and grinds food. Adult human beings have eight bicuspids. *noun.*

bi cy cle (bī′sik′əl), **1** a light vehicle with two wheels, one behind the other. The wheels support a metal frame on which there is a seat. The rider pushes two pedals to move the back wheel and steers with handlebars. **2** ride a bicycle. 1 *noun,* 2 *verb,* **bi cy cled, bi cy cling.**

bid (bid), **1** tell (someone) what to do or where to go; command: *We were bidden to stay in our seats until the bus stopped.* **2** say; tell: *His friends bade him good-by.* **3** offer to pay (a certain price): *She bid $5 for the table.* **4** an offer to pay a certain price: *She made a bid on the table.* **5** amount offered or stated: *My bid was $7.* **6** invite: *The king bade the nobles stay.* **7** a try; an attempt: *The senator made a bid for reelection.* 1-3,6 *verb,* **bade** or **bid, bid den** or **bid, bid ding;** 4,5,7 *noun.*

bid den (bid′n). See **bid.** *Twelve guests were bidden to the feast. verb.*

bid ding (bid′ing), **1** command; order: *The servant awaited the queen's bidding.* **2** invitation: *He joined the club at my bidding.* **3** offering of a price for something: *The bidding at the auction was slow.* **4** See **bid.** *We are bidding him good-by.* 1-3 *noun,* 4 *verb.*

a hat	i it	oi oil	ch child	(a in about
ā age	ī ice	ou out	ng long	e in taken
ä far	o hot	u cup	sh she	ə = { i in pencil
e let	ō open	u̇ put	th thin	o in lemon
ē equal	ô order	ü rule	ᴛʜ then	(u in circus
ėr term			zh measure	

bide (bīd), continue; wait; abide: *Bide here awhile. verb,* **bid ed, bid ing.**

big (big), **1** great in amount or size: *Making automobiles is a big business. Dogs are bigger than mice.* **2** grown up: *You are a big girl now.* **3** important; great: *The election of a president is big news. adjective,* **big ger, big gest.**

bike (bīk), **1** a bicycle. **2** ride a bicycle. 1 *noun,* 2 *verb,* **biked, bik ing.**

bile (bīl), a bitter, greenish-yellow liquid produced by the liver. It aids digestion in the small intestine. *noun.*

bill¹ (bil), **1** statement of money owed for work done or things supplied: *The store sent me a $35 bill for clothing I had charged.* **2** send a bill to: *The dairy bills us each month.* **3** piece of paper money: *a dollar bill.* **4** a written or printed public notice, such as an advertisement or poster. See picture. **5** announce by bills or public notice: *Many interesting television programs are billed for next week.* **6** a written or printed statement; list of items. A **bill of rights** lists all the rights belonging to the citizens of a country. **7** a proposed law presented to a lawmaking body for its approval: *The tax bill will be voted on by the Senate today.* 1,3,4,6,7 *noun,* 2,5 *verb.*

bill² (bil), **1** the horny part of the jaws of a bird; beak. **2** anything shaped like a bird's bill. *noun.*

bill board (bil′bôrd′), a large board, usually outdoors, on which to display advertisements or notices. *noun.*

bill¹ (definition 4)
They stood looking at the colorful circus bill.

"The Circus Is Coming" 1871, Charles C. Ward, The Metropolitan Museum of Art
Bequest of Susan Vanderpoel Clark, 1967

bill fold (bil′fōld′), a small, flat leather case for carrying paper money or cards in one's pocket or handbag; wallet. *noun.*

bil liards (bil′yərdz), game played with three hard balls on a special table with a raised, cushioned edge. A long stick called a cue is used in hitting the balls. *noun.*

bil lion (bil′yən), 1 (in the United States, Canada, and France) one thousand millions; 1,000,000,000. 2 (in Great Britain and Germany) one million millions; 1,000,000,000,000. *noun, adjective.*

bil low (bil′ō), 1 a great, swelling wave. 2 rise or roll in big waves: *Waves billowed toward the shore. Smoke billowed from the room.* 3 swell out; bulge: *Sheets on a line billow in the wind.* 1 *noun,* 2,3 *verb.*

bin (bin), box or enclosed place for holding or storing grain, coal, and similar things. *noun.*

bind (bīnd), 1 tie together; hold together; fasten: *She bound the package with ribbon.* 2 fasten (sheets of paper) into a cover; put a cover on (a book): *The loose pages were bound into a book.* 3 hold by a promise, duty, or law; oblige: *Parents are bound by law to send their children to school.* 4 put a bandage on: *bind up a wound.* 5 put a border or edge on to strengthen or ornament: *The collar was bound with leather. verb,* **bound, bind ing.**

bin go (bing′gō), game in which players cover numbers on their cards as the numbers are called out. The first player to cover a row of numbers in any direction wins. *noun.*

bi noc u lars (bə nok′yə lərz), a double telescope made for use with both eyes. Field glasses are binoculars. See picture. *noun plural.*

bi o de grad a ble (bī′ō di grā′də bəl), that can be removed from the environment by the action of bacteria and other living things. A biodegradable detergent does not pollute water. *adjective.*

bi og ra phy (bī og′rə fē), the written story of a person's life. *noun, plural* **bi og ra phies.**

bi ol o gist (bī ol′ə jist), person who is an expert in biology. *noun.*

bi ol o gy (bī ol′ə jē), science of living things; study of plant and animal life. Biology deals with the origin, structure, activities, and distribution of plants and animals. Botany, zoology, and ecology are branches of biology. *noun.*

bi on ic (bī on′ik), having electronic parts that replace parts of the body. *adjective.*

birch (bėrch), 1 tree with a smooth bark that peels off in thin layers. 2 its hard wood, often used in making furniture. *noun, plural* **birch es** for 1.

bird (bėrd), one of a group of warm-blooded animals that have a backbone, feathers, two legs, and wings. Birds lay eggs; most birds can fly. A **bird of prey** eats flesh. Eagles, hawks, vultures, and owls are birds of prey. *noun.*

birth (bėrth), 1 a coming into life; being born: *At birth, most babies weigh about 6 or 8 pounds.* 2 a beginning; origin: *the birth of a nation.* 3 descent; family: *a person of Spanish birth. noun.*
give birth to, bring forth; bear: *The dog gave birth to four puppies.*

birth day (bėrth′dā′), 1 day on which a person

binoculars

bison—about 5¹/₂ feet (1¹/₂ meters) at the shoulder

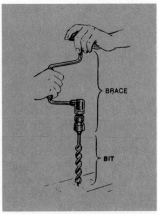
bit³ (definition 1)

was born or on which something began. **2** yearly return of this day. *noun.*

birth mark (bėrth′märk′), spot or mark on the skin that was there at birth. *noun.*

birth place (bėrth′plās′), **1** place where a person was born. **2** place of origin: *Philadelphia is the birthplace of the United States. noun.*

birth right (bėrth′rīt′), rights or privileges to which a person is entitled by birth: *Freedom of speech is a birthright in the United States. noun.*

bis cuit (bis′kit), **1** soft bread dough baked in small shapes. **2** a thin, flat, dry bread or cake; cracker. *noun, plural* **bis cuits** or **bis cuit.**

bish op (bish′əp), **1** clergyman of high rank who is the head of a church district. **2** one of the pieces in the game of chess. *noun.*

bi son (bī′sn *or* bī′zn), a wild ox of North America, which has a big, shaggy head and strong front legs; buffalo. See picture. *noun, plural* **bi son.**

bit[1] (bit), **1** small piece; small amount: *A pebble is a bit of rock.* **2** a short time: *Stay a bit.* **3** 12$\frac{1}{2}$ cents. A quarter is two bits. *noun.*
a bit, a little; slightly: *I am a bit tired.*

bit[2] (bit). See **bite.** *The strong trap bit the leg of the fox. The postman was bit by our dog. verb.*

bit[3] (bit), **1** tool for boring or drilling that fits into a handle called a brace. See picture. **2** the part of a bridle that goes in a horse's mouth. *noun.*

bite (bīt), **1** seize, cut into, or cut off with the teeth: *She bit the apple. When I'm nervous I bite my nails.* **2** a cutting or seizing with the teeth; nip: *The dog gave a bite or two at the bone.* **3** a piece bitten off; mouthful: *Eat the whole apple, not just a bite.* **4** a light meal; snack: *Have a bite with me now or you'll get hungry later.* **5** wound with teeth, fangs, or a sting: *My dog never bites. A mosquito bit me.* **6** a wound made by biting or stinging: *Mosquito bites itch.* **7** a sharp, smarting pain: *We felt the bite of the wind.* **8** cause a sharp, smarting pain to: *The icy wind bit her nose and ears.* **9** take a bait; be caught: *The fish are biting well today.* 1,5,8-9 *verb*, **bit, bit ten** or **bit, bit ing;** 2-4,6,7 *noun.*

bit ing (bī′ting), **1** sharp; cutting: *Dress warmly before you go out in that biting wind.* **2** sarcastic: *Biting remarks hurt people's feelings. adjective.*

bit ten (bit′n). See **bite.** *Finish the apple, now that you have bitten into it. verb.*

bit ter (bit′ər), **1** having a sharp, harsh, unpleasant taste: *Quinine is bitter medicine.* **2** causing pain or grief; hard to admit or bear: *a bitter defeat. The death of his father was a bitter loss.* **3** showing pain or grief: *The lost child shed bitter tears.* **4** harsh or cutting: *a bitter remark.* **5** very cold: *The bitter winter killed our apple tree. adjective.*

bi tu mi nous coal (bə tü′mə nəs kōl′), coal that burns with much smoke and a yellow flame; soft coal.

black (blak), **1** the color of coal. This sentence is printed in black. **2** having this color: *a black sweater.* **3** a black paint, dye, or pigment. **4** make black: *I blacked my shoes before going out.* **5** without any light; very dark: *The room was black as night.* **6** gloomy: *This has been a black day.*

blackbird—about 9 inches (23 centimeters) long

blacken (definition 2)
The storm clouds gathered and the sky **blackened.**

7 sullen; angry: *She gave her brother a black look.* **8** Also, **Black, a** having dark skin; Negro. **b** person who has dark skin; Negro. 1,3,8b *noun,* 2,5-8a *adjective,* 4 *verb.*

black ber ry (blak′ber′ē), a small, black or dark purple fruit of certain thorny bushes and vines. It is sweet and juicy. *noun, plural* **black ber ries.**

black bird (blak′bėrd′), any of various American birds so named because the male is mostly black. See picture. *noun.*

black board (blak′bôrd′), a smooth, hard surface, used for writing or drawing on with chalk. *noun.*

black en (blak′ən), **1** make black: *Soot blackened the snow.* **2** become black. See picture. **3** speak evil of: *blacken someone's good name with false gossip. verb.*

black mail (blak′māl′), **1** money got from a person by threatening to reveal something bad about that person. **2** get or try to get money from (someone) by threats. **3** an attempt to get money by threats. 1,3 *noun,* 2 *verb.*

black out (blak′out′), a turning off or going out of all the lights of a city or district. A blackout may be used as a protection against enemy planes at night during war, or it may happen when the power for electricity goes off. *noun.*

black smith (blak′smith′), person who makes things out of iron by heating it in a forge and hammering it into shape on an anvil. Blacksmiths can mend tools and shoe horses. *noun.*

blad der (blad′ər), a soft, thin bag in the body that stores urine from the kidneys until it is discharged by the body. *noun.*

blade (blād), **1** the cutting part of anything like a knife or sword: *A carving knife should have a very sharp blade.* **2** sword. **3** leaf of grass. **4** the flat, wide part of a leaf. **5** the flat, wide part of anything. An oar or a paddle has a blade at one end of the shaft. *noun.*

blame (blām), **1** hold responsible for something bad or wrong: *The driver blamed the fog for the accident.* **2** responsibility for something bad or wrong: *I won't take the blame for something I didn't do.* **3** find fault with: *I don't blame her for wanting a better bicycle.* 1,3 *verb,* **blamed, blam ing;** 2 *noun.*

bland (bland), mild; soothing; not irritating: *a bland manner, a bland diet of baby food. adjective.*

blank (blangk), **1** space left empty or to be filled in: *Leave a blank if you can't answer the question.* **2** not written or printed on: *blank paper.* **3** a paper with spaces to be filled in: *Fill out this application blank and return it at once.* **4** with spaces left for filling in: *Here is a blank form for you to fill in and return.* **5** an empty or vacant place: *When I read the hard questions my mind became a complete blank.* **6** empty; vacant: *There was a blank look on his face.* **7** cartridge containing gunpowder but no bullet or shot. 1,3,5,7 *noun,* 2,4,6 *adjective.*

blan ket (blang′kit), **1** a soft, heavy covering woven from wool, cotton, nylon, or other material, used to keep people or animals warm. **2** anything like a blanket: *A blanket of snow covered the ground.* **3** cover with a blanket: *The snow blanketed the ground.* 1,2 *noun,* 3 *verb.*

blare (bler *or* blar), **1** make a loud, harsh sound: *The trumpets blared.* **2** a loud, harsh sound. 1 *verb,* **blared, blar ing;** 2 *noun.*

blast (blast), **1** a strong, sudden rush of wind or air: *Last night we felt the icy blasts of winter.* **2** the blowing of a trumpet, horn, or whistle: *The warning blast of a bugle aroused the camp.* **3** sound made by blowing a trumpet, horn, or whistle. **4** blow up (rocks or earth) with dynamite or gunpowder: *The big boulders were blasted to clear the way for a new road.* **5** explosion: *We heard the blast a mile away.* **6** to ruin: *blast one's hopes.* 1-3,5 *noun,* 4,6 *verb.*

blast off, take off into flight propelled by rockets: *The spacecraft will be checked before it blasts off.*

blaze¹ (blāz), **1** bright flame or fire: *We could see the blaze of the campfire across the beach.* **2** burn with a bright flame: *A fire was blazing in the fireplace.* **3** glow of brightness; glare: *the blaze of the noon sun.* **4** show bright colors or lights: *On New Year's Eve the big house blazed with lights.* **5** bright display: *The tulips made a blaze of color.* **6** burst out in anger or excitement: *She blazed at the insult.* **7** a sudden or violent outburst: *a blaze of temper.* 1,3,5,7 *noun,* 2,4,6 *verb,* **blazed, blaz ing.**

blaze² (blāz), **1** mark made on a tree by cutting off a piece of bark, to indicate a trail or boundary in a forest. **2** mark (a tree, trail, or boundary) with a blaze or by making blazes. 1 *noun,* 2 *verb,* **blazed, blaz ing.**

bleach (blēch), **1** make white by exposing to sunlight or by using chemicals: *animal skulls bleached by the desert sun. We bleached the linen napkins in the wash.* **2** any chemical used in bleaching: *Laundries often use bleach to get dirty shirts clean.* 1 *verb,* 2 *noun, plural* **bleach es.**

bleach ers (blē′chərz), a low-priced area of seats or benches for people at a baseball game or other outdoor event. *noun.*

bleak (blēk), **1** swept by winds; bare: *The rocky peaks of high mountains are bleak.* **2** chilly; cold: *a bleak winter wind.* **3** cheerless and depressing; dismal: *A prisoner's life is bleak. adjective.*

bleat (blēt), **1** cry made by a sheep, goat, or calf. **2** a sound like this: *The victim gave a bleat of terror.* **3** make the cry of a sheep, goat, or calf. **4** make a sound like this. 1,2 *noun,* 3,4 *verb.*

bled (bled). See **bleed.** *The cut bled for ten minutes. verb.*

bleed (blēd), **1** lose blood: *The cut on your leg is bleeding.* **2** suffer wounds or death: *They fought and bled for their country.* **3** lose sap or juice from a surface that has been cut or scratched: *Trees bleed if they are pruned when the sap is rising in the spring.* **4** feel pity, sorrow, or grief: *My heart bleeds for the poor little orphan. verb,* **bled, bleed ing.**

blem ish (blem′ish), **1** something that spoils beauty; defect; flaw: *A pimple is a blemish on the skin.* **2** injure; mar: *The scandal blemished his reputation.* 1 *noun, plural* **blem ish es;** 2 *verb.*

blend (blend), **1** mix together; mix or become mixed so thoroughly that the things mixed cannot be distinguished or separated: *Blend the butter and the sugar before adding the other ingredients of the cake.* **2** shade into each other, little by little: *The colors of the rainbow blend into one another.* **3** go well together; harmonize. **4** thorough mixture made by blending: *This coffee is a blend of three varieties.* 1-3 *verb,* 4 *noun.*

bless (bles), **1** make holy or sacred: *The bishop blessed the new church.* **2** ask God's favor for: *Bless these little children.* **3** wish good to; feel grateful to: *Bless you for your kindness.* **4** make happy or fortunate: *I have always been blessed with good health.* **5** praise: *to bless the Lord. verb,* **blessed** or **blest, bless ing.**

bless ed (bles′id *or* blest), holy; sacred. *adjective.*

bless ing (bles′ing), **1** prayer asking God's favor.

2 a wish for happiness or success: *When I left home, I received my family's blessing.* 3 anything that makes one happy and contented: *A good temper is a great blessing.* noun.

blest (blest). See **bless**. *She was blest with good fortune.* verb.

blew (blü). See **blow²**. *The wind blew.* verb.

blimp (blimp), a kind of balloon that can be steered. A blimp is filled with a gas that is lighter than air. See picture. noun.

blind (blīnd), 1 not able to see: *The man with the white cane is blind.* 2 make unable to see: *The bright lights blinded me for a moment.* 3 hard to see; hidden: *a blind curve on the highway.* 4 by means of instruments instead of the eyes: *blind flying of an aircraft at night. We flew blind through the storm.* 5 without thought, judgment, or good sense: *She was in a blind fury.* 6 take away the power to understand or judge: *His strong opinions blinded him to the facts.* 7 something that keeps out light or hinders sight. A window shade or shutter is a blind. 1,3-5 adjective, 2,6 verb, 4 adverb, 7 noun.

blind fold (blīnd′fōld′), 1 cover the eyes of: *We blindfolded her.* 2 with the eyes covered: *He walked the line blindfold.* 3 thing covering the eyes. 1 verb, 2 adjective, 3 noun.

blink (blingk), 1 look with the eyes opening and shutting: *She blinked at the sudden light.* 2 open and shut the eyes; wink: *We blink every few seconds.* 3 shine with an unsteady light: *A little lantern blinked through the darkness.* verb.

bliss (blis), great happiness; perfect joy: *What bliss it is to plunge into the waves on a hot day!* noun.

bliss ful (blis′fəl), very happy; joyful. adjective.

blis ter (blis′tər), 1 a small area of skin that puffs out into a bubble. Blisters fill with a clear watery liquid from the skin underneath. They are often caused by burns or by rubbing. *My new shoes have made blisters on my heels.* 2 a bubble on the surface of a plant, on metal, on painted wood, or in glass. 3 raise a blister on: *Sunburn has blistered my back.* 4 become covered with blisters; have blisters: *People often blister when they get sunburned.* 1,2 noun, 3,4 verb.

blithe (blī∓H), happy and cheerful; gay. adjective, **blith er, blith est.**

bliz zard (bliz′ərd), a blinding snowstorm with a

blimp

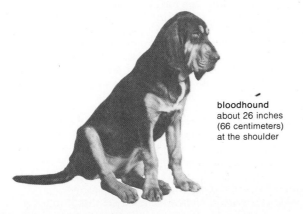

bloodhound
about 26 inches
(66 centimeters)
at the shoulder

very strong wind and very great cold. noun.

bloat (blōt), swell up; puff up: *Overeating bloated the cow's stomach.* verb.

blob (blob), a small, soft drop; sticky lump: *Blobs of wax covered the candlestick.* noun.

block (blok), 1 a solid piece of wood, stone, metal, or ice: *The Pyramids are made of blocks of stone.* 2 fill up so as to prevent passage or progress: *The country roads were blocked with snow.* 3 put things in the way of; hinder: *Mother's illness blocked my plans for her birthday party.* 4 anything or any group of persons that keeps something from being done: *A block in traffic kept our car from moving on.* 5 space in a city or town enclosed by four streets; square. 6 length of one side of a block in a city or town: *Walk one block east.* 7 number of buildings close together. 8 holder in which a pulley or pulleys are mounted. 1,4-8 noun, 2,3 verb.

block ade (blo kād′), 1 blocking of a place by an army or navy to control who or what goes into or out of it. 2 put under blockade. 3 anything that blocks up or obstructs. 4 block up; obstruct. 1,3 noun, 2,4 verb, **block ad ed, block ad ing.**

block house (blok′hous′), a small fort or building with loopholes to shoot from. noun, plural **block hous es** (blok′hou′ziz).

blond or **blonde** (blond), 1 light in color: *blond hair, blond furniture.* 2 having yellow or light-brown hair, blue or gray eyes, and a fair skin. 3 a man or boy of this sort is usually called a blond. A woman or girl of this sort is usually called a blonde. 1,2 adjective, 3 noun.

blood (blud), 1 the red liquid in the veins and arteries; the red liquid that flows from a cut. Blood is circulated by the heart. It carries oxygen and digested food to all parts of the body and carries away waste materials. 2 family; parentage; descent: *We are related by blood.* 3 temper; state of mind: *There was bad blood between them.* noun.

in cold blood, cruelly or on purpose: *The bandits shot down three men in cold blood.*

blood bank, 1 blood that is kept for use in transfusions. 2 place where such blood is kept.

blood hound (blud′hound′), a large dog with a keen sense of smell. See picture. noun.

blood pressure, pressure of the blood against the inner walls of the arteries. Blood pressure varies with physical activity, excitement, health, and age.

blood shed (blud′shed′), the shedding of blood; slaughter. *noun.*

blood stream (blud′strēm′), blood as it flows through the body. *noun.*

blood thirst y (blud′thėr′stē), eager for bloodshed; cruel and murderous: *a bloodthirsty pirate. adjective.*

blood vessel, any tube in the body through which the blood circulates. Arteries and veins are blood vessels.

blood y (blud′ē), 1 covered with blood; bleeding: *a bloody nose.* 2 accompanied by much killing: *a bloody battle. adjective,* **blood i er, blood i est.**

bloom (blüm), 1 have flowers; open into flowers; blossom: *Many plants bloom in the spring.* 2 a flower; blossom. 3 condition or time of flowering: *violets in bloom.* 4 condition or time of greatest health, vigor, or beauty: *the bloom of youth.* 5 be in the condition or time of greatest health, vigor, or beauty; flourish: *Water makes the desert bloom.* 6 coating like fine powder on some fruits and leaves. 1,5 *verb,* 2-4,6 *noun.*

blos som (blos′əm), 1 flower, especially of a plant that produces fruit: *apple blossoms.* 2 condition or time of flowering: *pear trees in blossom.* 3 have flowers; open into flowers: *Orchards blossom in spring.* 4 open out; develop: *The shy child blossomed into an outgoing teenager.* 1,2 *noun,* 3,4 *verb.*

blot (blot), 1 a spot of ink or stain of any kind. 2 make blots on; stain; spot: *My pen slipped and blotted the paper.* 3 dry (ink) with paper that soaks up ink: *I blotted my signature so the ink wouldn't smear.* 4 a blemish; disgrace: *The field of rusting cars was a blot on the landscape.* 1,4 *noun,* 2,3 *verb,* **blot ted, blot ting.**

blot out, 1 cover up entirely; hide: *He blotted out the mistake with ink.* 2 wipe out; destroy: *When the dam broke, an entire village was blotted out.*

blotch (bloch), 1 a large, irregular spot or stain. 2 place where the skin is red or broken out. *noun, plural* **blotch es.**

blot ter (blot′ər), a soft paper used to dry writing by soaking up ink. *noun.*

blouse (blous), 1 a loose upper garment worn by women and children as a part of their outer clothing. 2 a loosely fitting garment for the upper part of the body: *The sailor wore a wool blouse as part of his uniform. noun.*

blow[1] (blō), 1 a hard hit; knock; stroke: *The boxer struck his opponent a blow that knocked him down.* 2 a sudden happening that causes misfortune or loss; severe shock: *His mother's death was a great blow to him.* 3 a sudden attack: *The army struck a swift blow at the enemy. noun.*

blow[2] (blō), 1 send forth a strong current of air: *Blow on the fire or it will go out.* 2 move rapidly or with power: *The wind blew in gusts.* 3 drive or carry by a current of air: *The wind blew the curtain.*

4 force a current of air into, through, or against: *I blew on the hot coals to start the fire. She blew her nose.* 5 form or shape by air; swell with air: *blow bubbles.* 6 make a sound by a current of air or steam: *The whistle blows at noon.* 7 break by an explosion: *The dynamite blew the wall to bits.* 8 melt: *The short circuit caused the fuse to blow.* 9 gale of wind: *Last night's big blow brought down several trees.* 1-8 *verb,* **blew, blown, blow ing;** 9 *noun.*

blow up, 1 explode: *The ammunition ship blew up and sank when it hit the rocks.* 2 fill with air: *blow up a bicycle tire.* 3 become very angry: *She blew up at me for keeping her waiting for two hours.* 4 become stronger; arise: *A storm blew up suddenly.*

blow er (blō′ər), 1 person or thing that blows: *This vase was made by an expert glass blower.* 2 fan or other machine for forcing air into a building, furnace, mine, or other enclosed area. *noun.*

blown (blōn). See **blow**[2]. *My hat was blown away by the wind. verb.*

blow out (blō′out′), 1 the bursting of a tire. 2 a sudden or violent escape of air, steam, or the like. *noun.*

blow torch (blō′tôrch′), device that shoots out a very hot flame. A blowtorch is used to melt metal and burn off paint. *noun, plural* **blow torch es.**

blub ber (blub′ər), 1 fat of whales and some other sea animals. Oil obtained from whale blubber was burned in lamps. 2 weep noisily. 1 *noun,* 2 *verb.*

bludg eon (bluj′ən), 1 a short, heavy club. 2 strike with a bludgeon. 1 *noun,* 2 *verb.*

blue (blü), 1 the color of the clear sky in daylight. 2 having this color. 3 having a dull-bluish color; livid: *My hands were blue from cold.* 4 sad; discouraged: *I felt blue when I failed.* 1 *noun,* 2-4 *adjective,* **blu er, blu est.**

out of the blue, completely unexpectedly: *Her visit came out of the blue.*

blue ber ry (blü′ber′ē), a small, round, sweet, blue berry that grows on a shrub. *noun, plural* **blue ber ries.**

blue bird (blü′bėrd′), a small songbird of North America. The male usually has a bright blue back and wings and a chestnut-brown breast. See picture. *noun.*

blue grass (blü′gras′), grass with bluish-green stems. It is valuable for pasturage and hay. *noun.*

blue jay, a noisy, chattering North American bird with a crest and a blue back. See picture.

blue print (blü′print′), copy of an original drawing of a building plan or map that shows white outlines on a blue background. *noun.*

blues (blüz), 1 a slow, sad song with jazz rhythm. 2 **the blues,** low spirits: *A rainy day always gives me the blues. noun plural.*

bluff[1] (bluf), 1 a high, steep bank or cliff. 2 abrupt, frank, and hearty in manner. 1 *noun,* 2 *adjective.*

bluff[2] (bluf), 1 a pretending to be confident in order to fool or mislead others: *She acted as if she had high cards, but it was only a bluff.* 2 deceive by a show of confidence; fool: *By using logs for cannons the general bluffed the enemy.* 3 threat that

bluebird
about 7 inches (18 centimeters) long

boar (definition 2)
2½ feet (76 centimeters) high at the shoulder

blue jay—about 12 inches
(30 centimeters) long

a hat	**i** it	**oi** oil	**ch** child	**a** in about
ā age	**ī** ice	**ou** out	**ng** long	**e** in taken
ä far	**o** hot	**u** cup	**sh** she	**ə =** **i** in pencil
e let	**ō** open	** u̇** put	**th** thin	**o** in lemon
ē equal	**ô** order	**ü** rule	**ᵺ** then	**u** in circus
ėr term			**zh** measure	

cannot be carried out: *The bully's attempt to scare us is merely a bluff.* 1,3 *noun,* 2 *verb.*

blu ish (blü′ish), somewhat blue. *adjective.*

blun der (blun′dər), **1** a stupid mistake: *Misspelling the title of a book is a silly blunder to make in a book report.* **2** make a stupid mistake: *Someone blundered in sending you to the wrong address.* **3** move as if blind; stumble: *I blundered through the dark house.* 1 *noun,* 2,3 *verb.*

blun der buss (blun′dər bus), a short gun with a wide muzzle, formerly used to shoot balls or slugs a very short distance without exact aim. *noun, plural* **blun der buss es.**

blunt (blunt), **1** without a sharp edge or point; dull: *a blunt knife.* **2** make less sharp; make less keen: *a knife blunted from use. A cold blunted my sense of smell.* **3** saying what one thinks very frankly, without trying to be tactful; outspoken: *When I asked her if she liked my painting, her blunt answer was "No."* 1,3 *adjective,* 2 *verb.*

blur (blėr), **1** make less clear in form or outline: *Mist blurred the hills.* **2** dim: *Tears blurred my eyes.* **3** thing seen dimly or indistinctly: *Without my glasses on, your face is just a blur.* **4** smear; smudge: *I blurred my painting by touching it before the paint was dry. The letter had many blots and blurs.* 1,2,4 *verb,* **blurred, blur ring;** 3,4 *noun.*

blurt (blėrt), say suddenly or without thinking: *In his excitement he blurted out the secret. verb.*

blush (blush), **1** become red in the face because of shame, confusion, or excitement: *The little boy blushed when everyone laughed at his mistake.* **2** a reddening of the face caused by confusion, shame, or excitement. **3** be ashamed: *I blushed at my sister's bad table manners.* **4** rosy color: *the blush of dawn.* 1,3 *verb,* 2,4 *noun, plural* **blush es.**

blus ter (blus′tər), **1** storm noisily; blow violently: *The wind blustered around the corner of the house.* **2** stormy noise and violence: *the bluster of the wind.* **3** talk noisily and violently: *He was very excited and angry and blustered for a while.* **4** noisy and violent talk: *angry bluster.* 1,3 *verb,* 2,4 *noun.*

boar (bôr), **1** a male pig or hog. **2** a wild pig or hog. See picture. *noun.*

board (bôrd), **1** a broad, thin piece of wood for use in building: *We used boards 10 inches wide, 1 inch thick, and 3 feet long for shelves.* **2** cover with such pieces of wood: *We board up the windows of our summer cottage in the fall.* **3** a flat piece of wood or other material used for one special purpose: *an ironing board, a drawing board.* **4** table to serve food on; table. **5** meals provided for pay: *The cost of going away to college includes room and board.* **6** give or get meals, or room and meals, for pay: *You will have to board elsewhere.* **7** group of persons managing something; council: *a school*

bobcat—23 inches (58 centimeters) high at the shoulder

bolt (top, definition 1; bottom, definition 2)

bobsled

board, a board of directors. **8** get on (a ship, train, bus, or airplane): *We board the school bus at the corner.* 1,3-5,7 *noun,* 2,6,8 *verb.*

on board, on a ship, train, bus, or airplane: *When everybody was on board, the ship sailed.*

board er (bôr′dər), person who pays for meals, or for room and meals, at another's house. *noun.*

board ing house (bôr′ding hous′), house where meals, or room and meals, are provided for pay. *noun, plural* **board ing hous es** (bôr′ding hou′ziz).

boarding school, school with buildings where the pupils live during the school term.

boast (bōst), **1** speak too highly of oneself or what one owns: *He boasts about his grades in school.* **2** statement speaking too highly of oneself or what one owns; boasting words: *I don't believe her boast that she can run faster than I can.* **3** have (something) to be proud of: *Our town boasts a new high school.* 1,3 *verb,* 2 *noun.*

boast ful (bōst′fəl), fond of boasting: *It is hard to listen very long to a boastful person. adjective.*

boat (bōt), **1** a small, open vessel, such as a motorboat or a rowboat. **2** a large vessel, such as a steamship or ocean liner; ship. **3** go in a boat. 1,2 *noun,* 3 *verb.*

boat house (bōt′hous′), house or shed for sheltering a boat or boats. *noun, plural* **boat hous es** (bōt′hou′ziz).

bob[1] (bob), **1** move up and down, or to and fro, with short, quick motions: *The pigeon bobbed its head as it picked up crumbs.* **2** a short, quick motion up and down, or to and fro. 1 *verb,* **bobbed, bob bing;** 2 *noun.*

bob[2] (bob), **1** a child's or woman's haircut that is fairly short all around the head. **2** cut (hair) short. **3** a float for a fishing line. 1,3 *noun,* 2 *verb,* **bobbed, bob bing.**

bob bin (bob′ən), reel or spool for holding thread, yarn, and the like. *noun.*

bob cat (bob′kat′), a small lynx of North America. It has a reddish-brown coat with black spots. See picture. *noun.*

bob o link (bob′ə lingk), a common North American songbird that lives in fields and meadows. *noun.*

bob sled (bob′sled′), a long sled with two sets of runners. It has a steering wheel and brakes. See picture. *noun.*

bob white (bob′hwīt′), an American quail that has a grayish body with brown and white markings. Its call sounds like its name. *noun.*

bode (bōd), be a sign of: *The rumble of thunder boded rain. verb,* **bod ed, bod ing.**

bod i ly (bod′l ē), **1** of the body; in the body: *Athletes have bodily strength.* **2** in person: *Although she cannot be with us bodily, she is here in spirit.* **3** as a whole; entirely: *The audience rose bodily to cheer the performer.* 1 *adjective,* 2,3 *adverb.*

bod y (bod′ē), **1** the whole material or physical part of a person, animal, or plant: *I exercise to keep my body strong and healthy.* **2** the main part of an animal, not the head, limbs, or tail. **3** the main part of anything. **4** group of persons or things: *The*

student body of our school gathered for an assembly.
5 a dead person or animal. **6** mass: *A lake is a body of water. The moon, the sun, and the stars are heavenly bodies.* **7** thickness; density: *Pea soup has more body than chicken broth.* noun, plural **bod ies.**

bod y guard (bod′ē gärd′), person or persons who guard someone: *A bodyguard usually accompanies the President.* noun.

bog (bog), **1** soft, wet, spongy ground; marsh; swamp. **2 bog down,** sink in or get stuck so that one cannot get out without help: *I am bogged down with all this homework.* **1** noun, **2** verb, **bogged, bog ging.**

bo gey man (bō′gē man′ or bug′ē man′), a frightening imaginary creature. noun, plural **bo gey men.**

boil¹ (boil), **1** bubble up and give off steam: *Water boils when heated.* **2** cause (a liquid) to boil by heating it: *Boil some water for tea.* **3** cook by boiling: *We boil eggs four minutes.* **4** have its contents boil: *The pot is boiling.* **5** be very excited; be stirred up: *He boiled with anger.* **6** boiling condition: *heat water to a boil.* **1-5** verb, **6** noun.

boil² (boil), a painful, red swelling on the skin caused by infection. Boils have a hard core and are filled with pus. noun.

boil er (boi′lər), **1** tank for making steam to heat buildings or drive engines. **2** tank for heating and holding hot water. **3** container for heating liquids. noun.

bois ter ous (boi′stər əs), **1** noisily cheerful: *The room was filled with boisterous laughter.* **2** violent; rough: *a boisterous wind.* adjective.

bold (bōld), **1** without fear; having or showing courage; brave: *a bold knight. Climbing the steep mountain was a bold act.* **2** rude; impudent: *The bold child made faces at us as we passed.* **3** sharp and clear to the eye; striking: *The mountains stood in bold outline against the sky.* adjective.

boll (bōl), the seed pod of a plant like cotton or flax. noun.

bol ster (bōl′stər), **1** a long pillow or cushion for a couch or bed. **2** keep from falling; support; prop: *Her faith bolstered my confidence.* **1** noun, **2** verb.

bolt (bōlt), **1** rod with a head at one end and a screw thread for a nut at the other. Bolts are used to fasten things together or hold something in place. See picture. **2** a sliding fastening for a door or gate. See picture. **3** part of a lock moved by a key. **4** fasten with a bolt: *Bolt the doors.* **5** a sudden discharge of lightning. See picture. **6** a sudden start; a running away: *The rabbit saw the fox and made a bolt for safety.* **7** dash off; run away: *The horse bolted at the sight of the car.* **8** swallow (food) quickly without chewing: *The dog bolted its food.* **9** roll of cloth or wallpaper. **1-3,5,6,9** noun, **4,7,8** verb.

bolt upright, stiff and straight: *Awakened by a noise, I sat bolt upright in bed.* See picture.

bomb (bom), **1** container filled with an explosive. A bomb is set off by a fuse or by the force with which it hits something. **2** hurl bombs at; drop bombs on. **1** noun, **2** verb.

a hat	**i** it	**oi** oil	**ch** child		a in about
ā age	**ī** ice	**ou** out	**ng** long		e in taken
ä far	**o** hot	**u** cup	**sh** she	**ə =**	i in pencil
e let	**ō** open	**ù** put	**th** thin		o in lemon
ē equal	**ô** order	**ü** rule	**ŦH** then		u in circus
ėr term			**zh** measure		

bom bard (bom bärd′), **1** attack with bombs or heavy fire of shot and shell from big guns: *The artillery bombarded the enemy all day.* **2** keep attacking vigorously: *The lawyer bombarded the witness with one question after another.* verb.

bomb er (bom′ər), aircraft used to drop bombs. noun.

bond (bond), **1** anything that ties, binds, or unites: *There is a bond of affection between the two sisters.* **2 bonds,** chains; shackles: *the bonds of slavery.* **3** certificate issued by a government or private company which promises to pay back with interest the money borrowed from the buyer of the certificate: *The city issued bonds to raise money for a new park.* **4** a written agreement by which a person promises to pay money if he or she does not perform certain duties properly. noun.

bond age (bon′dij), lack of freedom; slavery. noun.

bone (bōn), **1** one of the pieces of the skeleton of an animal with a backbone: *the bones of the hand.* **2** take bones out of: *We boned the fish before eating it.* **3** the hard substance of which bones are made. **4** something like bone. Ivory is sometimes called bone. **1,3,4** noun, **2** verb, **boned, bon ing.**

bon fire (bon′fīr′), fire built outdoors: *We had to sit around the bonfire to keep warm.* noun. [*Bonfire* comes from the words *bone* and *fire.* It was called this because in the past old bones were burned to make a fire.]

EVERY LIGHTNING **BOLT** MAKES THEM SIT **BOLT** UPRIGHT!

bon net (bon′it). See picture. **1** a covering for the head usually tied under the chin with strings or ribbons, worn by women and children. **2** cap worn by men and boys in Scotland. **3** headdress of feathers worn by North American Indians. *noun.*

bo nus (bō′nəs), something extra, given in addition to what is due: *The company gave each worker a bonus of $20. noun, plural* **bo nus es.**

bon y (bō′nē), **1** of bone: *the bony structure of the skull.* **2** full of bones: *bony fish.* **3** having bones that stick out; very thin: *bony hands, an old horse with bony hips. adjective,* **bon i er, bon i est.**

boo (bü), **1** sound made to show dislike or contempt, or to frighten: *They were frightened when I jumped from behind the door and shouted, "Boo!"* **2** make such a sound; shout "boo" at: *He sang so badly that the audience booed him.* 1 *noun, plural* **boos;** 1 *interjection,* 2 *verb.*

book (bùk), **1** written or printed sheets of paper bound together between covers: *She read the first two chapters of her book.* **2** blank sheets bound together: *You can keep a record of what you spend in this book.* **3** a main division of a book: *Genesis is the first book of the Old Testament.* **4** make reservations to get tickets or to engage service: *He had booked passage by airplane from New York to London.* **5** write down an accusation against (a person) in a police record: *At the police station an officer booked the suspect.* 1-3 *noun,* 4,5 *verb.*

book case (bùk′kās′), piece of furniture with shelves for holding books. *noun.*

book keep er (bùk′kē′pər), person who keeps a record of business accounts. *noun.*

book let (bùk′lit), a little book; thin book. Booklets often have paper covers. *noun.*

book mo bile (bùk′mə bēl′), truck that serves as a traveling branch of a library. *noun.*

book worm (bùk′wėrm′), person who is very fond of reading and studying. *noun.*

boom[1] (büm), **1** a deep hollow sound like the roar of cannon or of big waves: *A bell tolled with a loud boom.* **2** make a deep hollow sound: *His voice boomed out above the rest.* **3** rapid growth: *A recent boom doubled the size of the town.* **4** grow rapidly: *Business is booming.* 1,3 *noun,* 2,4 *verb.*

boom[2] (büm), a long pole or beam. A boom is used to extend the bottom of a sail or as the lifting pole of a derrick. *noun.*

boo me rang (bü′mə rang′), a curved piece of wood, used as a weapon by the original people of Australia. Certain boomerangs can be thrown so that they return to the thrower. See picture. *noun.*

boon (bün), great benefit; blessing: *Those warm boots were a boon to me in the cold weather. noun.*

boost (büst), **1** push or shove that helps a person in rising or advancing: *a boost over the fence.* **2** lift or push from below or behind. 1 *noun,* 2 *verb.*

boost er shot (bü′stər shot′), an additional injection of a vaccine or serum to continue the effect of a previous injection.

boot (büt), **1** a leather or rubber covering for the foot and lower part of the leg. **2** a kick: *She gave the ball a boot.* **3** give a kick to. 1, 2 *noun,* 3 *verb.*

bonnet (definitions 1, 2, and 3)

boomerang—man demonstrating the use of a boomerang

booth (büth), **1** place where goods are sold or shown at a fair, market, or convention. **2** a small enclosed or partly enclosed place: *a telephone booth, a voting booth, a booth in a restaurant. noun, plural* **booths** (büŦHz *or* büths).

boo ty (bü′tē), **1** things taken from the enemy in war. **2** things taken by force; plunder: *The pirates fought over the booty.* **3** prize. *noun, plural* **boo ties.**

bor der (bôr′dər), **1** the side, edge, or boundary of anything, or the part near it: *We pitched our tent on the border of the lake.* **2** touch at the edge or boundary: *Canada borders on the United States.* **3** a strip on the edge of anything for strength or ornament: *a lace border.* **4** put a border on: *We bordered our garden with shrubs.* **1,3** *noun,* **2,4** *verb.*

bore[1] (bôr), **1** make a hole by means of a tool that keeps turning, or as a worm does in fruit: *Bore through the handle of that brush so that we can hang it up.* **2** make a hole by pushing through or digging out: *A mole has bored its way under the hedge.* **3** hole made by a revolving tool. **4** the hollow space inside a pipe, tube, or gun barrel: *He cleaned the bore of his gun.* **5** distance across the inside of a hole or tube: *The bore of this pipe is two inches.* **1,2** *verb,* **bored, bor ing; 3-5** *noun.*

bore[2] (bôr), **1** make weary by tiresome talk or by being dull: *This book bores me, so I shall not finish it.* **2** a dull, tiresome person or thing: *It is a bore to wash dishes.* **1** *verb,* **bored, bor ing; 2** *noun.*

bore[3] (bôr). See **bear**[1]. *She bore her loss bravely. verb.*

born (bôrn), **1** brought into life; brought forth: *a newly born calf.* **2** by birth; by nature: *She could swim and skate at such an early age, we believed she was a born athlete.* **3** See **bear**[1]. *He was born on December 30, 1900.* **1,2** *adjective,* **3** *verb.*

borne (bôrn). See **bear**[1]. *I have borne the pack for three miles. She has borne three children. verb.*

bor ough (bėr′ō), **1** town with certain privileges. **2** one of the five divisions of New York City. *noun.*

bor row (bor′ō), **1** get (something) from another person with the understanding that it must be returned: *I borrowed the book and promised to return it to him in a week.* **2** take and use as one's own; adopt; take: *The word for the vegetable "squash" was borrowed from the Indians. verb.*

bos om (bùz′əm), **1** the upper, front part of the human body; breast. **2** center or inmost part: *He did not mention it even in the bosom of his family.* **3** close and trusted: *Very dear friends are bosom friends.* **1,2** *noun,* **3** *adjective.*

boss (bôs), **1** person who hires workers or watches over or directs them; foreman; manager. **2** person who controls a political organization. **3** be the boss of; direct; control: *Who is bossing this job?* **1,2** *noun, plural* **boss es; 3** *verb.*

bo tan i cal (bə tan′ə kəl), having to do with the study of plants. *adjective.*

bot a nist (bot′n ist), person who is an expert in botany. *noun.*

bot a ny (bot′n ē), the science of plants; the study of plants and plant life. Botany is a branch of biology. *noun.*

a hat	i it	oi oil	ch child		a in about
ā age	ī ice	ou out	ng long		e in taken
ä far	o hot	u cup	sh she	ə =	i in pencil
e let	ō open	ù put	th thin		o in lemon
ē equal	ô order	ü rule	ŦH then		u in circus
ėr term			zh measure		

both (bōth), **1** the two; the one and the other: *Both houses are white.* **2** the two together: *Both belong to her.* **3** together; alike; equally: *He fears and hopes both at once. She is both strong and healthy.* **1** *adjective,* **2** *pronoun,* **3** *adverb, conjunction.*

both er (boŦH′ər), **1** much fuss or worry; trouble: *What a lot of bother about nothing!* **2** take trouble; concern oneself: *Don't bother to cook; we'll eat out.* **3** person or thing that causes worry, fuss, or trouble: *A door that will not shut is a bother.* **4** annoy: *Hot weather bothers me.* **1,3** *noun,* **2,4** *verb.*

bot tle (bot′l), **1** container without handles for holding liquids, usually made of glass. Most bottles have narrow necks which can be closed with caps or stoppers. **2** amount that a bottle can hold: *He can drink a whole bottle of milk at one meal.* **3** put into bottles: *Dairies bottle milk.* **1,2** *noun,* **3** *verb,* **bot tled, bot tling.**

bottle up, hold in; control: *I bottled up my anger.*

bot tom (bot′əm), **1** the lowest part: *These berries at the bottom of the basket are crushed.* **2** part on which anything rests: *The bottom of that glass is wet.* **3** ground under water: *Many wrecks lie at the bottom of the sea.* **4** the low land along a river. **5** seat: *This chair needs a new bottom.* **6** basis; foundation; origin: *We will get to the bottom of the mystery.* **7** lowest or last: *I see a robin on the bottom branch of that tree.* **1-6** *noun,* **7** *adjective.*

bot tom less (bot′əm lis), **1** without a bottom. **2** very, very deep: *a bottomless lake. adjective.*

bough (bou), one of the main branches of a tree. *noun.*

bought (bôt). See **buy.** *We bought apples at the market. I have bought two new pencils. verb.*

boul der (bōl′dər), a large rock, rounded or worn by the action of water and weather. *noun.*

boul e vard (bùl′ə värd), a broad street, often with a line of trees planted along its sides, or down the center. *noun.*

bounce (bouns), **1** spring into the air like a ball: *The baby likes to bounce up and down on the bed.* **2** cause to bounce: *Bounce the ball to me.* **3** bound; spring: *I caught the ball on the first bounce.* **1,2** *verb,* **bounced, bounc ing; 3** *noun.*

bound[1] (bound), **1** under some obligation; obliged: *I feel bound by my promise.* **2** certain; sure: *Everyone is bound to make a mistake sooner or later.* **3** See **bind.** *She bound the package with string. They have bound my hands.* **4** put in covers: *a bound book.* **1,2,4** *adjective,* **3** *verb.*

bound[2] (bound), **1** spring back; bounce: *The ball bounded from the wall.* **2** a springing back; bounce: *I caught the ball on the first bound.* **3** leap or spring lightly along; jump: *Mountain goats can bound from rock to rock.* **4** jump: *With one bound the deer went into the woods.* **1,3** *verb,* **2,4** *noun.*

box¹ (definition 4)—theater boxes

boxers (definition 1)

"Both Members of this Club," George Bellows, Courtesy of National Gallery of Art, Washington. Gift of Chester Dale

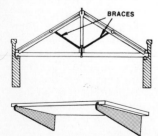

BRACES

brace (definition 1)

bracket (definition 1)
a shelf supported by brackets

bound³ (bound), **1** boundary; limiting line; limit: *the farthest bounds of the earth. Keep your hopes within bounds.* **2** form the boundary of; limit: *Canada bounds the United States on the north.* **1** *noun,* **2** *verb.*

bound⁴ (bound), on the way; going: *I am bound for home. adjective.*

bound ar y (boun′dər ē), a limiting line or thing; limit; border: *Lake Superior forms part of the boundary between Canada and the United States. noun, plural* **bound ar ies.**

bound less (bound′lis), not limited: *Outer space is boundless. She has boundless energy. adjective.*

boun ti ful (boun′tə fəl), **1** generous; giving freely: *the help of bountiful friends.* **2** more than enough; plentiful; abundant: *We put in so many plants that we have a bountiful supply of tomatoes. adjective.*

boun ty (boun′tē), **1** whatever is given freely; generous gift. **2** generosity: *the bounty of Nature.* **3** reward: *The state government used to give a bounty for killing coyotes. noun, plural* **boun ties.**

bou quet (bō kā′ *or* bü kā′), **1** bunch of flowers. **2** fragrance. *noun.*

bout (bout), **1** trial of strength; contest: *Those are the two boxers who will appear in the main bout.* **2** length of time; spell: *I have just had a long bout of illness. noun.*

bow¹ (bou), **1** bend the head or body in greeting, respect, worship, or submission: *The people bowed before the queen.* **2** a bending of the head or body in this way: *She answered his bow with a curtsy.* **3** show by bowing: *The actors bowed their thanks at the end of the play.* **4** bend: *The old man was bowed by age.* **5** submit; yield: *The boy bowed to his parents' wishes.* **1,3-5** *verb,* **2** *noun.*

bow² (bō), **1** weapon for shooting arrows. A bow usually consists of a strip of flexible wood bent by a string. **2** a slender rod with horsehairs stretched on it, for playing a violin or cello. **3** something curved; curve: *A rainbow is a bow.* **4** a knot that has loops: *The package had a bow on top. noun.*

bow³ (bou), the front part of a ship or boat. *noun.*

bow els (bou′əlz), **1** the tube in the body into which food passes from the stomach; intestines. **2** the inner part of anything: *Miners dig for coal in the bowels of the earth. noun plural.*

bow ie knife (bō′ē nīf′ *or* bü′ē nīf′), a long, single-edged hunting knife carried in a sheath. [The *bowie knife* was named for Colonel James Bowie, who lived from 1799 to 1836. He was an American pioneer who made the knife popular.]

bowl¹ (bōl), **1** a hollow, rounded dish, usually without handles: *a mixing bowl.* **2** amount that a bowl can hold: *She had a bowl of soup for lunch.* **3** the hollow, rounded part of anything: *The bowl of a pipe holds the tobacco. noun.*

bowl² (bōl), **1** a large, heavy ball used in certain games. **2** play the game of bowling. **3** roll or move along rapidly and smoothly: *Our car bowled along on the new highway.* **1** *noun,* **2,3** *verb.*

bowl over, knock over: *He nearly bowled me over.*

bow leg ged (bō′leg′id), having the legs curved outward: *a bowlegged cowboy. adjective.*

bowl ing (bō′ling), game played indoors, in which balls are rolled down an alley at bottle-shaped wooden pins. *noun.*

bow man (bō′mən), person who shoots with bow and arrows; archer. *noun, plural* **bow men.**

bow string (bō′string′), a strong cord stretched from the ends of a bow, pulled back by the archer to send the arrow forward. *noun.*

box[1] (boks), **1** container, usually with four sides, a bottom, and a lid, to pack or put things in: *We packed the boxes full of books.* **2** amount that a box can hold: *I bought a box of soap.* **3** pack in a box; put into a box: *She boxed the candy before she sold it.* **4** an enclosed space with seats: *a jury box, a theater box.* See picture. **5** the driver's seat on a coach or carriage. **6** small shelter: *a box for a sentry.* **7** (in baseball) place where the pitcher, batter, or catcher stands. 1,2,4-7 *noun, plural* **box es;** 3 *verb.*

box[2] (boks), **1** a blow with the open hand or fist: *A box on the ear hurts.* **2** strike with such a blow: *I will box your ears if you yell at me again.* **3** fight with the fists as a sport: *He had not boxed since he left school.* 1 *noun, plural* **box es;** 2,3 *verb.*

box car (boks′kär′), a railroad freight car enclosed on all sides. Most boxcars are loaded and unloaded through a sliding door on either side. *noun.*

box er (bok′sər), **1** person who fights with the fists as a sport, usually in padded gloves and according to special rules. See picture. **2** a medium-sized dog with a smooth brown coat. It is related to the bulldog and terrier. *noun.*

box ing (bok′sing), act or sport of fighting with the fists, usually while wearing padded leather gloves. *noun.*

boy (boi), **1** a male child from birth to about eighteen. **2** a male servant. *noun.*

boy cott (boi′kot), **1** join together against and agree not to buy from, sell to, or associate with (a person, business, or nation). People boycott in order to force a change or to punish. **2** act of boycotting. 1 *verb,* 2 *noun.* [*Boycott* was named for Captain Charles Boycott, who lived from 1832 to 1897. He was an English manager of estates in Ireland. His tenants and neighbors would have nothing to do with him when he refused to lower rents in hard times.]

boy hood (boi′hud), time of being a boy. *noun.*

boy ish (boi′ish), **1** of a boy. **2** like a boy. **3** like a boy's; suitable for a boy. *adjective.*

boy scout, member of the Boy Scouts.

Boy Scouts, organization for boys that seeks to develop character, citizenship, usefulness to others, and various skills.

brace (brās), **1** thing that holds parts together or in place, such as a timber used to strengthen a building or a metal frame to hold the ankle straight. See picture. **2 braces,** metal wires used to straighten crooked teeth. **3** give strength or firmness to; support: *We braced the roof with four poles.* **4** prepare (oneself): *He braced himself for the crash.* **5** give strength and energy to; refresh: *The*

a hat	**i** it	**oi** oil	**ch** child	a in about
ā age	**ī** ice	**ou** out	**ng** long	e in taken
ä far	**o** hot	**u** cup	**sh** she	ə = { i in pencil
e let	**ō** open	**u̇** put	**th** thin	o in lemon
ē equal	**ô** order	**ü** rule	**ᴛʜ** then	u in circus
ėr term			**zh** measure	

mountain air braced us after the long climb. **6** a pair; couple: *a brace of ducks.* **7** handle for a tool or drill used for boring. 1,2,6,7 *noun,* 3-5 *verb,* **braced, brac ing.**

brace let (brās′lit), band or chain worn for ornament around the wrist or arm. *noun.*

brack et (brak′it), **1** a flat piece of stone, wood, or metal projecting from a wall as a support for a shelf or a statue. See picture. **2** either of these signs [ ], used to enclose words or figures. The word histories in this dictionary are enclosed in brackets. **3** enclose within brackets: *The teacher bracketed the mistakes in my work.* 1,2 *noun,* 3 *verb.*

brag (brag), **1** boast: *They bragged about their new car.* **2** boasting talk. 1 *verb,* **bragged, brag ging;** 2 *noun.*

braid (brād), **1** band formed by weaving together three or more strands of hair, ribbon, or straw: *She wore her hair in braids.* **2** weave or twine together (three or more strands of hair, ribbon, or straw): *She can braid her own hair.* 1 *noun,* 2 *verb.*

Braille or **braille** (brāl), system of writing and printing for blind people. The letters in Braille are represented by different arrangements of raised points and are read by touching them. *noun.* [*Braille* was named for Louis Braille, who lived from 1809 to 1852. He was a French teacher of the blind, who invented this system.]

brain (brān), **1** a soft mass of nerve cells and nerve fibers enclosed in the skull or head of persons and animals. With the brain we can learn, think, and remember. **2** kill by smashing the skull of. **3 brains,** intelligence: *A dog has more brains than a worm.* 1,3 *noun,* 2 *verb.*

brain storm (brān′stôrm′), a sudden idea or inspiration: *I've had a brainstorm; to make money let's put on a play and charge admission. noun.*

brake[1] (brāk), **1** anything used to slow or stop the motion of a wheel or vehicle by pressing or scraping or by rubbing against. The brakes on a railroad train are blocks that press against the wheels. **2** slow or stop by using a brake: *The driver braked the speeding car and it slid to a stop.* 1 *noun,* 2 *verb,* **braked, brak ing.**

brake[2] (brāk), a thick growth of bushes; thicket. *noun.*

brake man (brāk′mən), member of a train crew who helps the conductor. *noun, plural* **brake men.**

bram ble (bram′bəl), shrub with slender, drooping branches covered with little thorns that prick. Blackberry and raspberry plants are brambles. *noun.*

bran (bran), the broken covering of grains like wheat and rye. When flour is made from these grains, the bran is sifted out and used in cereals and as food for farm animals. *noun.*

branch (branch), **1** part of a tree growing out from the trunk; any large, woody part of a tree above the ground except the trunk. A bough is a large branch. A twig is a very small branch. **2** division; part: *a branch of a river, a branch of a family. Biology is a branch of science.* **3** divide into branches: *The road branches at the bottom of the hill.* 1,2 *noun, plural* **branch es;** 3 *verb.*

brand (brand), **1** a certain kind, grade, or make: *Do you like this brand of flour?* **2** a name or mark that a company uses to distinguish its goods from the goods of others. **3** an iron stamp for burning a mark. **4** mark made by burning the skin with a hot iron: *The cattle on this big ranch have a brand which shows who owns them.* **5** to mark by burning the skin with a hot iron. See picture. **6** a mark of disgrace: *He could never rid himself of the brand of coward.* **7** put a mark of disgrace on: *She has been branded as a traitor.* **8** piece of wood that is burning or partly burned. 1-4,6,8 *noun,* 5,7 *verb.*

brand-new (brand′nü′ or brand′nyü′), very new; entirely new. *adjective.*

bran dy (bran′dē), a strong alcoholic drink made from wine or fermented fruit juice. *noun, plural* **bran dies.**

brass (bras), **1** a yellowish metal that is made of copper and zinc. **2** anything made of brass, such as a band instrument, an ornament, or a dish: *I polished all the brass. noun, plural* **brass es.**

brat (brat), an unpleasant child. *noun.*

brave (brāv), **1** without fear; having courage; showing courage: *The brave girl went into the burning house to save a baby.* **2** brave people: *The United States has been called "the land of the free and the home of the brave."* **3** meet without fear; defy: *The early settlers braved the hardships of life in a new land.* **4** a North American Indian warrior. 1 *adjective,* **brav er, brav est;** 2,4 *noun,* 3 *verb,* **braved, brav ing.**

brav er y (brā′vər ē), courage; being brave: *They owed their lives to the bravery of the fireman. noun, plural* **brav er ies.**

brawl (brôl), **1** noisy quarrel. **2** quarrel in a noisy way. 1 *noun,* 2 *verb.*

brawn y (brô′nē), strong; muscular: *brawny arms. adjective,* **brawn i er, brawn i est.**

bray (brā), **1** the loud, harsh cry or noise made by a donkey. **2** any loud, harsh cry or noise: *the bray of trumpets.* **3** make a loud, harsh cry or noise: *The trumpets brayed.* 1,2 *noun,* 3 *verb.*

Bra zil (brə zil′), country in central South America. *noun.*

breach (brēch), **1** an opening made by breaking down something solid; gap: *Cannon fire had made a breach in the wall of the fort.* **2** break through; make an opening in: *The wall had been breached in several places.* **3** breaking or neglect: *For me to leave now would be a breach of duty.* **4** breaking of friendly relations; quarrel: *There was never a breach between the two friends.* 1,3,4 *noun, plural* **breach es;** 2 *verb.*

bread (bred), **1** food made of flour or meal mixed with milk or water and baked. **2** food; livelihood:

brand (definition 5)—branding a calf

How will you earn your daily bread? noun.

breadth (bredth), how broad a thing is; distance across; width: *He has traveled the length and the breadth of this land. noun.*

break (brāk), **1** come apart or make come apart; smash: *The plate broke into pieces when it fell on the floor.* **2** a broken place; crack: *a break in the wall.* **3** damage: *She broke her watch by winding it too tightly.* **4** crack the bone of: *break one's arm.* **5** fail to keep: *Never break a promise.* **6** force a way: *The lion broke loose from its cage.* **7** a forcing a way out: *The prisoners made a break for freedom.* **8** come suddenly: *The storm broke within ten minutes.* **9** change suddenly: *The spell of rainy weather has broken.* **10** a sudden change: *a break in the weather.* **11** a short interruption in work or practice: *The coach told us to take a break for five minutes.* **12** make less; lessen: *The bushes broke her fall from the tree.* **13** become weak; give way; fail: *His spirit broke when he lost his job.* **14** dawn; appear: *The day is breaking.* **15** put an end to; stop: *break one's fast.* **16** train to obey; tame: *break a colt.* **17** go beyond: *The speed of the new train has broken all records.* **18** make known; reveal: *Someone must break the news of the girl's accident to her parents.* 1,3-6,8,9,12-18 *verb,* **broke, bro ken, break ing;** 2,7,10,11 *noun.*

break down, 1 go out of order; fail to work: *The car's engine broke down.* **2** become weak; fail suddenly: *Her health broke down.* **3** begin to cry: *He broke down when he heard the bad news.*

break in, 1 prepare for work or use; train: *The sales manager broke in the new salesman.* **2** enter by force: *The thieves broke in through the cellar.* **3** interrupt: *He broke in with a remark while the teacher was reading to us.*

break into, 1 enter by force: *Robbers broke into the warehouse.* **2** begin suddenly: *When the rain started, we broke into a run.* **3** interrupt: *He rudely broke into their conversation.*

break off, 1 stop suddenly: *I had to break off in the middle of my speech to clear my throat.* **2** stop being friends: *She broke off with her old classmates* *when she went away to college.*

break out, 1 start suddenly; begin: *A fire broke out in the garage.* **2** have pimples or rashes appear on the skin: *The child broke out with measles.*

break up, 1 scatter: *The fog is breaking up.* **2** put an end to; stop: *We broke up the meeting early.*

break down (brāk′doun′), **1** failure to work: *Lack of oil caused a breakdown in the motor.* **2** loss of health; collapse: *If you don't stop worrying, you will have a breakdown. noun.*

break er (brā′kər), wave that breaks into foam on the beach or on rocks. See picture. *noun.*

break fast (brek′fəst), **1** the first meal of the day. **2** eat breakfast: *I like to breakfast alone.* **1** *noun,* **2** *verb.* [*Breakfast* comes from the phrase *break (one's) fast,* meaning "to end a period of not eating."]

breast (brest), **1** the upper, front part of the body between the shoulders and the stomach; chest. **2** gland that gives milk. **3** heart or feelings: *Pity tore his breast.* **4** struggle with; face or oppose: *The swimmer breasted the waves with powerful strokes.* **1-3** *noun,* **4** *verb.*

make a clean breast of, confess completely: *When he was shown proof that he broke the window, he made a clean breast of it.*

breast bone (brest′bōn′), the thin, flat bone in the front of the chest to which the ribs are attached. *noun.*

breast plate (brest′plāt′), piece of armor worn over the chest. *noun.*

breath (breth), **1** the air drawn into and forced out of the lungs. **2** breathing: *Hold your breath a moment.* **3** moisture in the air when a person breathes out: *You can see your breath on a very cold day.* **4** ability to breathe easily: *Running so fast made me lose my breath.* **5** slight movement in the air: *Not a breath was stirring. noun.*

catch one's breath, stop for breath; rest: *After the race we sat down to catch our breath.*

under one's breath, in a whisper: *She was talking under her breath so no one could hear.*

breathe (brēŦH), **1** draw air into the lungs and force it out. You breathe through your nose or through your mouth. **2** stop for breath; stop to rest after hard work or exercise: *Let's take a minute to breathe before we begin to work again.* **3** say softly; whisper: *Don't breathe a word of this to anyone.* **4** send out; give: *Her enthusiasm breathed new life into our club. verb,* **breathed, breath ing.**

breath less (breth′lis), **1** out of breath: *Running fast made me breathless.* **2** unable to breathe freely because of fear, interest, or excitement: *The beauty of the scenery left her breathless. adjective.*

breath tak ing (breth′tā′king), thrilling; exciting: *a breathtaking ride on a runaway horse, a breathtaking sunset.* See picture. *adjective.*

bred (bred). See **breed.** *They bred cattle for market. Our parents have bred us to be honest. verb.*

breech es (brich′iz), **1** short trousers fastened below the knees. See picture. **2** trousers. *noun plural.*

breathtaking

breeches (definition 1)

breaker

breed (brēd), **1** produce young: *Rabbits breed rapidly.* **2** raise or grow: *This farmer breeds cattle for market.* **3** produce; be the cause of: *Careless driving breeds accidents.* **4** bring up; train: *The princess was born and bred to one day be queen.* **5** group of animals or plants looking much alike and having the same type of ancestors: *Terriers and spaniels are breeds of dogs.* 1-4 *verb,* **bred, breed ing;** 5 *noun.*

breed ing (brē/ding), bringing up; training; behavior; manners: *Politeness is a sign of good breeding. noun.*

breeze (brēz), **1** a light, gentle wind. **2** move easily or briskly: *She breezed through her homework.* 1 *noun,* 2 *verb,* **breezed, breez ing.**

breez y (brē/zē), **1** with light winds blowing: *It was a breezy day.* **2** lively and jolly: *We like his breezy, joking manner. adjective,* **breez i er, breez i est.**

brev i ty (brev/ə tē), shortness; briefness: *The brevity of such an exciting story disappointed the children. noun.*

brew (brü), **1** make (beer or ale) by soaking, boiling, and fermenting malt and hops. **2** make (a drink) by soaking, boiling, or mixing: *Tea is brewed in boiling water.* **3** a drink that is brewed: *The last brew of beer tasted bad.* **4** to plan; plot: *The group whispering in the corner are brewing some mischief.* **5** begin to form; gather: *Dark clouds show that a storm is brewing.* 1,2,4,5 *verb,* 3 *noun.*

bri ar (brī/ər), brier. *noun.*

bribe (brīb), **1** anything given or offered to get someone to do something wrong: *The thief offered the policemen a bribe to let him go.* **2** reward for doing something that a person does not want to do: *The stubborn child needed a bribe to go to bed.* **3** give or offer a bribe to: *A gambler bribed one of the boxers to lose the fight.* 1,2 *noun,* 3 *verb,* **bribed, brib ing.**

brib er y (brī/bər ē), **1** giving a bribe. **2** taking a bribe: *The dishonest detective was arrested for bribery. noun, plural* **brib er ies.**

brick (brik), **1** block of clay baked by sun or fire. Bricks are used to build walls or houses and pave walks. **2** bricks: *Chimneys are usually built of brick.* **3** anything shaped like a brick: *Ice cream is often sold in bricks.* **4** build or pave with bricks; cover or fill in with bricks: *brick a walk, brick up an old window.* 1-3 *noun,* 4 *verb.*

brick lay er (brik/lā/ər), person whose work is building with bricks. *noun.*

bride (brīd), woman just married or about to be married. *noun.*

bride groom (brīd/grüm/), man just married or about to be married; groom. *noun.*

brides maid (brīdz/mād/), a young woman who attends the bride at a wedding. *noun.*

bridge (brij), **1** something built over a river, road, or railroad so that people, cars, or trains can get across. **2** make a way over a river or anything that hinders: *A log bridged the brook. Politeness will bridge many difficulties.* **3** platform above the deck of a ship for the officer in command: *The captain directed the course of the ship from the bridge.* **4** the

upper, bony part of the nose. 1,3,4 *noun,* 2 *verb,* **bridged, bridg ing.**

bri dle (brī/dl), **1** the part of a harness that fits over a horse's head. The bridle holds the horse back from running away, and helps to control its actions. See picture. **2** put a bridle on: *I saddled and bridled my horse.* 1 *noun,* 2 *verb,* **bri dled, bri dling.**

brief (brēf), **1** short: *The meeting was brief. A brief shower fell in the afternoon.* **2** using few words: *She made a brief announcement. Be as brief as you can.* **3** a short statement: *The lawyer prepared a brief of the facts in the case.* **4** give detailed information to: *The forest ranger briefed the campers on fire prevention.* 1,2 *adjective,* 3 *noun,* 4 *verb.*

bri er (brī/ər), a thorny or prickly plant or bush. The blackberry plant and rosebush are often called briers. *noun.* Also spelled **briar.**

brig (brig), **1** ship with two masts and square sails. **2** prison on a warship. *noun.*

bri gade (bri gād/), **1** part of an army, usually made up of two or more regiments. **2** any group of persons organized for some purpose. A fire brigade puts out fires. *noun.*

bright (brīt), **1** giving much light; shining: *The stars are bright, but sunshine is brighter.* **2** very light or clear: *a bright day, bright yellow.* **3** clever: *a bright student.* **4** lively or cheerful: *Everybody was bright and gay at the party.* **5** favorable: *There is a bright outlook for the future.* **6** in a bright manner: *The fire shines bright.* 1-5 *adjective,* 6 *adverb.*

bright en (brīt/n), make or become bright or brighter: *The good news brightened my day. verb.*

bril liance (bril/yəns), **1** great brightness; sparkle: *the brilliance of a fine diamond.* **2** splendor: *the brilliance of the royal court.* **3** great ability: *His brilliance as a pianist was known all over the world. noun.*

bril liant (bril/yənt), **1** shining brightly; sparkling: *brilliant jewels, brilliant sunshine.* **2** splendid; magnificent: *The singer gave a brilliant performance.* **3** having great ability: *She is a brilliant musician. adjective.*

brim (brim), **1** edge of a cup or bowl: *a glass filled to the brim.* **2** edge or border of anything; rim: *the brim of a canyon.* **3** fill to the brim; be full to the brim: *The pond was brimming with water after the heavy rain.* **4** the projecting edge of something: *The hat's wide brim shaded my eyes from the sun.* 1,2,4 *noun,* 3 *verb,* **brimmed, brim ming.**

brine (brīn), very salty water. Some pickles are kept in brine. *noun.*

bring (bring), **1** come with (some thing or person) from another place: *Bring me a clean plate and take the dirty one away. The bus brought us home.* **2** cause to come: *What brings you into town today?* **3** influence; persuade: *The principal was brought to agree with us by our arguments about the program.* **4** sell for: *Tomatoes bring a high price in winter. verb,* **brought, bring ing.**

bring about, cause; cause to happen: *The flood was brought about by a heavy rain.*

bring on, cause; cause to happen: *My headache*

bridle (definition 1)

a hat	i it	oi oil	ch child		a in about
ā age	ī ice	ou out	ng long		e in taken
ä far	o hot	u cup	sh she	ə =	i in pencil
e let	ō open	ů put	th thin		o in lemon
ē equal	ô order	ü rule	ŦH then		u in circus
ėr term			zh measure		

was brought on by a cold.

bring out, 1 reveal; show: *The lawyer brought out new evidence at the trial.* **2** offer to the public: *The company is bringing out a new product.*

bring up, 1 care for in childhood: *My grandparents brought up four children.* **2** educate or train: *His good manners showed he was well brought up.* **3** suggest for action or discussion: *Please bring your plan up at the meeting.*

brink (bringk), **1** edge at the top of a steep place: *the brink of the cliff.* **2** edge: *Their business is on the brink of ruin.* noun.

brisk (brisk), **1** quick and active; lively: *a brisk walk.* **2** keen; sharp: *a brisk wind. adjective.*

bris tle (bris′əl), **1** one of the short, stiff hairs of some animals or plants. See picture. **2** stand up straight: *The dog growled and its hair bristled.* **3** have one's hair stand up straight: *The frightened kitten bristled when it saw the dog.* **4** show that one is angry and ready to fight: *The insult made him bristle.* 1 noun, 2-4 verb, **bris tled, bris tling.**

Brit ain (brit′n), England, Scotland, and Wales; Great Britain. noun.

Brit ish (brit′ish), **1** of or having something to do with Great Britain or its people. **2** people of Great Britain. 1 adjective, 2 noun plural.

brit tle (brit′l), very easily broken; breaking with a snap; apt to break: *Thin glass is brittle. adjective.*

broach (brōch), begin to talk about: *I didn't want to broach the subject because I knew it would upset them. verb.*

broad (brôd), **1** wide; large across: *Many cars can go on that broad, new road.* **2** large; not limited or narrow; of wide range: *Our teacher has had broad experience with children.* **3** including only the most important parts; general: *Give the broad outlines of today's lesson.* **4** clear; full: *The theft was made in broad daylight. adjective.*

broad cast (brôd′kast′), **1** something sent out by radio or television; radio or television program of speech, music, and the like: *The President's broadcast was televised from Washington, D.C.* **2** send out by radio or television: *Some stations broadcast twenty-four hours a day.* **3** sending out by radio or television: *a nationwide broadcast.* **4** scatter widely: *broadcast seed. Don't broadcast gossip.* 1,3 noun, 2,4 verb, **broad cast (or broad cast ed for 2), broad cast ing.**

broad en (brôd′n), make or become broad or broader; widen: *The river broadens at its mouth. Travel broadens a person's experience. verb.*

bro cade (brō kād′), an expensive cloth with raised designs on it. See picture. noun.

broc co li (brok′ə lē), vegetable with green, branching stems and flower heads. noun, plural **broc co li.**

brocade

bristle (definition 1)—The walrus has bristles.

broil (broil), **1** cook directly over heat on a rack or under heat in a pan: *We often broil steaks.* **2** be very hot: *You will broil in this hot sun. verb.*

broil er (broi′lər), **1** pan or rack for broiling. **2** a young chicken for broiling. *noun.*

broke (brōk). See **break.** *She broke her glasses. verb.*

bro ken (brō′kən), **1** See **break.** *The window was broken by a ball.* **2** separated into parts by a break; in pieces: *a broken cup.* **3** not in working condition; damaged: *a broken watch.* **4** rough; uneven: *broken ground.* **5** acted against; not kept: *a broken promise.* **6** imperfectly spoken: *The French girl speaks broken English.* **7** weakened in strength or spirit; tamed; crushed: *broken by failure.* **1** *verb,* **2-7** *adjective.*

bro ken-heart ed (brō′kən här′tid), crushed by sorrow or grief; heartbroken. *adjective.*

bron chi (brong′kī), the two large, main branches of the windpipe, one going to each lung. *noun plural* of **bron chus** (brong′kəs).

bron chi al (brong′kē əl), having to do with the bronchi or with their many branching tubes. *adjective.*

bron chi tis (brong kī′tis), soreness and swelling of the mucous membrane that lines the bronchial tubes. A cough goes with it. *noun.*

bron co (brong′kō), a wild or partly tamed horse of the western United States. See picture. *noun, plural* **bron cos.**

brooch

bronco—cowgirl riding a bronco

bronze (bronz), **1** a brown metal made of copper and tin. **2** made of this metal: *a bronze medal.* **3** dark yellowish brown. **4** make or become a dark yellowish brown: *The lifeguard was bronzed by the sun.* **1** *noun,* **2,3** *adjective,* **4** *verb,* **bronzed, bronz ing.**

brooch (brōch *or* brüch), an ornamental pin having the point fastened by a catch. Brooches are often made of gold, silver, or jewels. See picture. *noun, plural* **brooch es.**

brood (brüd), **1** the young birds hatched at one time in the nest or cared for together: *a brood of chicks.* **2** children in one family: *Our neighbors have a brood of twelve.* **3** sit on eggs in order to hatch. Hens and other birds brood till the young are hatched. **4** worry a long time about some one thing: *The boy brooded over his lost dog.* **1,2** *noun,* **3,4** *verb.*

brook (brúk), a small stream. *noun.*

broom (brüm), **1** brush with a long handle for sweeping. **2** bush with slender branches, small leaves, and yellow flowers. *noun.*

broom stick (brüm′stik′), the long handle of a broom. *noun.*

broth (brôth), a thin soup made from water in which meat or fish has been boiled. *noun, plural* **broths** (brôᵺz *or* brôths).

broth er (bruᵺ′ər), **1** son of the same parents. A boy is a brother to the other children of his parents. **2** a close friend or companion. **3** a male member of the same union, club, or religious organization. *noun.*

broth er hood (bruᵺ′ər húd), **1** bond between brothers; feeling of brother for brother: *Soldiers who are fighting together often have a strong feeling of brotherhood.* **2** persons joined as brothers; association of men with some common aim, characteristic, belief, or profession. *noun.*

broth er-in-law (bruᵺ′ər in lô′), **1** brother of one's husband or wife. **2** husband of one's sister. *noun, plural* **broth ers-in-law.**

broth er ly (bruᵺ′ər lē), of or like a brother; friendly; kindly: *brotherly teasing. The older boys gave me some brotherly advice. adjective.*

brought (brôt). See **bring.** *She brought her lunch yesterday. I was brought to school in a bus. verb.*

brow (brou), **1** part of the face above the eyes; forehead: *a wrinkled brow.* **2** arch of hair over the eye; eyebrow: *He has heavy brows over his eyes.* **3** edge of a steep place; top of a slope: *Our house is on the brow of a hill. noun.*

brown (broun), **1** the color of coffee and toast. **2** having this color: *Many people have brown hair.* **3** make or become brown: *The cook browned the onions in hot butter.* **1** *noun,* **2** *adjective,* **3** *verb.*

brown ie (brou′nē), **1** a good-natured elf or fairy, especially one supposed to help secretly at night. **2** Brownie, member of the junior division of the Girl Scouts. **3** a small, flat, sweet chocolate cake, often containing nuts. *noun.*

brown ish (brou′nish), somewhat brown. *adjective.*

brown out (broun′out′), a partial lowering of

electric power that causes lights to dim. *noun.*

browse (brouz), **1** feed on growing grass or leaves by nibbling and eating here and there; graze: *The sheep browsed in the meadow.* **2** read or look here and there, as in a book, library, or store: *She browsed through her new schoolbooks. They spent the afternoon browsing in the shops on Main Street. verb,* **browsed, brows ing.**

bruise (brüz), **1** injury to the body, caused by a fall or a blow, that does not break the skin: *The bruise turned black and blue.* **2** injury to the outside of a fruit, vegetable, or plant. **3** injure the outside of: *Rough handling bruised the apples before they could be sold.* **4** hurt; injure: *Their harsh words bruised her feelings.* **5** become bruised: *Her flesh bruises easily.* **1,2** *noun,* **3-5** *verb,* **bruised, bruis ing.**

bru nette or **bru net** (brü net′), **1** having dark-brown or black hair, brown or black eyes, and dark skin. **2** person having a dark skin, dark-brown or black hair, and brown or black eyes: *Many people of Spanish descent are brunettes; many people of Swedish descent are blonds.* **1** *adjective,* **2** *noun.*

brush¹ (brush), **1** tool for cleaning, sweeping, scrubbing, and for putting on paint. A brush is made of bristles, hair, or wire set in a stiff back or fastened to a handle. **2** clean, sweep, scrub, or paint with a brush; use a brush on: *I brushed my hair until it was shiny.* **3** a brushing; a rub with a brush: *She gave her puppy a good brush.* **4** wipe away; remove: *The child brushed the tears from his eyes.* **5** touch lightly in passing: *No harm was done—your bumper just brushed our fender.* **6** a light touch in passing: *Give the desk a brush with the cloth.* **7** short, brisk fight or quarrel: *The policemen had a brush with the rioters.* **8** the bushy tail of an animal, especially of a fox. **1,3,6-8** *noun, plural* **brush es; 2,4,5** *verb.*

brush up on or **brush up,** refresh one's knowledge of: *I brushed up on fractions before taking the arithmetic test.*

brush² (brush), **1** branches broken or cut off. **2** shrubs, bushes, and small trees growing thickly in the woods. *noun.*

Brus sels sprouts (brus′əlz sprouts′), vegetable that looks like small heads of cabbage. The heads grow together along the stalk of a garden plant.

bru tal (brü′tl), like a brute; coarse and savage; cruel: *The Vikings were brutal in battle. adjective.*

bru tal i ty (brü tal′ə tē), **1** brutal conduct; cruelty: *The brutality of the punishment shocked the onlookers.* **2** a brutal act. *noun, plural* **bru tal i ties.**

brute (brüt), **1** an animal without power to reason. **2** like an animal; without power to reason. **3** a stupid, cruel, or coarse person. **4** without feeling: *We are often powerless against the brute forces of nature.* **1,3** *noun,* **2,4** *adjective.*

bu., bushel or bushels.

bub ble (bub′əl), **1** a round, thin film of liquid enclosing air or gas. When water boils, it is full of bubbles which come to the top and break. **2** a round space filled with air in a liquid or solid. Sometimes there are bubbles in ice or in glass.

a hat	**i** it	**oi** oil	**ch** child	a in about
ā age	**ī** ice	**ou** out	**ng** long	e in taken
ä far	**o** hot	**u** cup	**sh** she	ə = i in pencil
e let	**ō** open	**ù** put	**th** thin	o in lemon
ē equal	**ô** order	**ü** rule	**∓H** then	u in circus
ėr term			**zh** measure	

3 send up or rise in bubbles; make sounds like water boiling: *Water bubbled up between the stones.* **1,2** *noun,* **3** *verb,* **bub bled, bub bling.**

buc ca neer (buk′ə nir′), pirate. *noun.*

buck (buk), **1** a male deer, goat, hare, or rabbit. **2** jump into the air with the back curved and come down with the front legs stiff: *My horse began to buck, but I managed to stay on.* **3** throw by bucking: *The cowboy was bucked by the bronco.* **4** charge against; work against: *The swimmer bucked the current with strong strokes.* **1** *noun,* **2-4** *verb.*

buck et (buk′it), **1** pail made of wood, metal, or plastic. Buckets are used for carrying such things as water, milk, or coal. **2** bucketful: *Pour in about four buckets of water. noun.*

buck et ful (buk′it fùl), amount that a bucket can hold. *noun, plural* **buck et fuls.**

buck le (buk′əl), **1** catch or clasp used to hold together the ends of a belt, strap, or ribbon. **2** fasten together with a buckle: *She buckled her belt.* **3** a metal ornament for a shoe. **4** bend; wrinkle: *The heavy snowfall caused the roof of the shed to buckle.* **5** a bend or wrinkle. **1,3,5** *noun,* **2,4** *verb,* **buck led, buck ling.**

buckle down to, work hard at: *I buckled down to my studies before the test.*

buck skin (buk′skin′), a strong, soft leather, yellowish or grayish in color, made from the skins of deer or sheep. *noun.*

buck wheat (buk′hwēt′), **1** plant with black or gray triangular seeds and fragrant white flowers. The seeds of buckwheat are fed to horses and fowls; they are also ground into flour for pancakes. **2** flour made from buckwheat. *noun.*

bud (bud), **1** a small swelling on a plant that will grow into a flower, leaf, or branch: *Buds on the trees are a sign of spring.* **2** a partly opened flower or leaf. **3** put forth buds: *The rosebush has budded.* **1,2** *noun,* **3** *verb,* **bud ded, bud ding.**

Bud dha (bü′də), founder of Buddhism. The name means "The Enlightened One." *noun.*

Bud dhism (bü′diz əm), religion based on the teachings of Buddha. *noun.*

Bud dhist (bü′dist), **1** person who believes in Buddhism. **2** of Buddha or Buddhism. **1** *noun,* **2** *adjective.*

bud ding (bud′ing), showing signs of becoming; developing: *She is a budding scientist. adjective.*

bud dy (bud′ē), a close friend; comrade; pal. *noun, plural* **bud dies.**

budge (buj), move even a little: *The stone was so heavy that we couldn't budge it. I was too tired to budge from my chair. verb,* **budged, budg ing.**

budg et (buj′it), **1** a plan that helps make the best use of money or time. Governments, companies, schools, and people make budgets. **2** make a plan for spending: *She budgeted her allowance so that she could save money for a tennis racket. Budget your time.* 1 *noun,* 2 *verb.*

buff (buf), **1** dull yellow. **2** a strong, soft, dull-yellow leather. Buff was formerly made from the skin of buffalo and is now made from the skin of oxen. **3** polish; shine: *I buffed my shoes to make them shine.* 1 *adjective,* 2 *noun,* 3 *verb.*

buf fa lo (buf′ə lō), **1** the bison of North America, a wild ox with a great shaggy head and strong front legs. Herds of buffaloes used to graze on the plains of the United States. **2** any of several kinds of oxen. The tame water buffalo is found in many parts of Asia; the wild buffalo of Africa is very fierce and dangerous. *noun, plural* **buf fa loes, buf fa los,** or **buf fa lo.**

buf fet (bu fā′), **1** a piece of dining-room furniture with a flat top for dishes and with shelves or drawers for holding silver and table linen; sideboard. **2** meal at which guests serve themselves from food laid out on a table or sideboard. *noun.*

bug (bug), **1** a crawling insect with a pointed beak for piercing and sucking. **2** any insect or other animal somewhat like a true bug. Ants, spiders, beetles, and flies are often called bugs. **3** a disease germ: *the flu bug.* **4** defect in the operation of a machine: *My car is running better now, but there are still a few bugs in it.* **5** hide a small microphone within (a room or telephone) for overhearing a conversation: *The spy bugged enemy headquarters.* 1-4 *noun,* 5 *verb,* **bugged, bug ging.**

bug gy (bug′ē), a light carriage with or without a top, pulled by one horse and having a single large seat. See picture. *noun, plural* **bug gies.**

bu gle (byü′gəl), a musical instrument like a small trumpet, made of brass or copper. Bugles are used in the army and navy to sound certain signals, including reveille and taps. *noun.*

bu gler (byü′glər), person who blows a bugle. *noun.*

build (bild), **1** make by putting materials together: *People build houses, bridges, ships, and machines. Birds build nests.* **2** produce gradually; develop: *build a business. A lawyer's case should be built on facts.* **3** form, style, or manner in which something is put together: *a person with a heavy build.* 1,2 *verb,* **built, build ing;** 3 *noun.*

build er (bil′dər), **1** person or animal that builds: *The pioneers were the builders of the West. Beavers are builders.* **2** person whose business is constructing buildings. *noun.*

build ing (bil′ding), **1** thing built. Barns, factories, stores, houses, and hotels are all buildings. **2** business, art, or process of making houses, stores, bridges, ships, and similar things. *noun.*

built (bilt). See **build.** *The bird built a nest. It was built of twigs. verb.*

built-in (bilt′in′), not movable; put in or prepared for as part of the plan of anything: *All the apartments have built-in dishwashers. adjective.*

bulb (bulb), **1** a round, underground bud from which certain plants grow. Onions, tulips, and

buggy

bullfight

bulldozer

lilies grow from bulbs. 2 any object with a rounded end or swelling part: *an electric light bulb, the bulb of a thermometer. noun.*

bulge (bulj), 1 swell outward: *His pockets bulged with candy.* 2 an outward swelling: *This can of soup has a bulge in it.* 1 *verb,* **bulged, bulg ing;** 2 *noun.*

bulk (bulk), 1 size, especially large size: *An elephant has great bulk.* 2 the largest part of: *The oceans form the bulk of the earth's surface. noun.*

in bulk, lying loose in heaps, not in packages: *Some markets sell fresh fruit in bulk.*

bulk y (bul/kē), 1 taking up much space; large: *Bulky shipments are often sent in freight cars.* 2 hard to handle; clumsy: *a bulky package of curtain rods. adjective,* **bulk i er, bulk i est.**

bull (bul), 1 the full-grown male of cattle. 2 the male of the whale, elephant, seal, and other large animals. *noun.*

bull dog (bul/dôg/), 1 a heavy, muscular dog of medium height. It has a large head, very short nose, strong jaws, and short hair. 2 like a bulldog's: *a bulldog grip.* 1 *noun,* 2 *adjective.*

bull doz er (bul/dō/zər), a powerful tractor with a wide steel blade that pushes rocks and earth, and knocks down trees. Bulldozers are used to make rough ground level and to help build roads. See picture. *noun.*

bul let (bul/it), piece of lead, steel, or other metal shaped to be fired from a pistol, rifle, or other small gun. *noun.*

bul le tin (bul/ə tən), 1 a short statement of news: *Sports bulletins and weather bulletins are published in most newspapers.* 2 a small magazine or newspaper appearing regularly: *Our club publishes a bulletin each month. noun.*

bulletin board, a special board or a part of a wall, on which notices are fastened and shown for everyone to read.

bull fight (bul/fīt/), fight between men and a bull in an arena. Bullfights are popular in Spain, Portugal, Mexico, and parts of South America. See picture. *noun.*

bull finch (bul/finch/), a European songbird with a blue and gray back and light-red breast, and a short, stout bill. *noun, plural* **bull finch es.**

bull frog (bul/frog/), a large frog that makes a loud, croaking noise. *noun.*

bull's-eye (bulz/ī/), 1 center of a target. 2 shot that hits it. *noun.*

bul ly (bul/ē), 1 person who teases, frightens, threatens, or hurts smaller or weaker people. 2 frighten into doing something by noisy talk or threats: *Stop trying to bully me into doing what you want.* 1 *noun, plural* **bul lies;** 2 *verb,* **bul lied, bul ly ing.**

bum (bum), 1 an idle person; tramp. 2 beg: *We tried to bum a ride.* 3 loaf around. 4 of poor quality; worthless. 1 *noun,* 2,3 *verb,* **bummed, bum ming;** 4 *adjective,* **bum mer, bum mest.** [*Bum* was shortened from the earlier word *bummer,* meaning "person who loafs."]

bum ble bee (bum/bəl bē/), a large bee with a thick, hairy body, usually banded with gold.

a hat	**i** it	**oi** oil	**ch** child	a in about
ā age	**ī** ice	**ou** out	**ng** long	e in taken
ä far	**o** hot	**u** cup	**sh** she	ə = i in pencil
e let	**ō** open	**ů** put	**th** thin	o in lemon
ē equal	**ô** order	**ü** rule	**ᴛʜ** then	u in circus
ėr term			**zh** measure	

Bumblebees make a loud, buzzing sound. *noun.*

bump (bump), 1 push, throw, or strike against something large or solid: *She bumped against the table.* 2 hit or come against with heavy blows: *That truck bumped our car.* 3 heavy blow or knock: *The bump knocked our car forward a few feet.* 4 move with jolts or jerks: *Our car bumped along the dirt road.* 5 swelling caused by a bump: *I had a bump on my head from getting hit by a baseball.* 6 any swelling or lump: *Avoid the bump in the road.* 1,2,4 *verb,* 3,5,6 *noun.*

bump er (bum/pər), 1 bar or bars of metal across the front and back of a car, truck, or bus that protect it from being damaged if bumped. 2 unusually large: *There was a bumper crop of wheat last year.* 1 *noun,* 2 *adjective.*

bump y (bum/pē), rough or uneven; having or causing bumps: *We drove over the bumpy road. adjective,* **bump i er, bump i est.**

bun (bun), 1 bread or cake in small shapes. Buns are often slightly sweetened and may contain spice or raisins. 2 hair coiled at the back of the head in a knot. *noun.*

bunch (bunch), 1 group of things of the same kind growing, fastened, placed, or thought of together: *a bunch of grapes, a bunch of sheep.* 2 group of people: *They are a friendly bunch.* 3 come together in one place: *The sheep were all bunched in the shed to keep warm.* 4 bring together and make into a bunch: *We have bunched the flowers for you to carry home.* 1,2 *noun, plural* **bunch es;** 3,4 *verb.*

bun dle (bun/dl), 1 number of things tied or wrapped together: *a bundle of old newspapers.* 2 parcel; package: *We sent my uncle a large bundle on his birthday.* 3 tie or wrap together; make into a bundle: *We bundled all our old newspapers for the school's paper drive.* 1,2 *noun,* 3 *verb,* **bun dled, bun dling.**

bundle up, dress warmly: *You should bundle up on cold winter mornings.*

bun ga low (bung/gə lō), a small one-story house. *noun.* [*Bungalow* comes from a Hindu word meaning "of Bengal." Bungalows were called this because such houses were common in the Bengal region of northeastern India.]

bunk (bungk), 1 a narrow bed, one of two or more stacked one above another: *I sleep in the top bunk.* 2 sleep in a bunk; occupy a bunk. 3 sleep in rough quarters: *We bunked in a barn.* 1 *noun,* 2,3 *verb.*

bun ny (bun/ē), a pet name for a rabbit. *noun, plural* **bun nies.**

bunt (bunt), 1 tap (a pitched baseball) lightly so that the ball goes only a short distance into the infield. 2 baseball hit in this way. 1 *verb,* 2 *noun.*

bun ting (bun/ting), 1 a thin cloth used for flags. 2 long pieces of cloth having the colors and designs of a flag, used to decorate buildings and streets on holidays and special occasions. *noun.*

buoy (boi), **1** a floating object anchored on the water to warn against hidden rocks or shallows or to show the safe part of a channel. **2** a life buoy. *noun.*

buoy up, 1 hold up; keep from sinking: *His life preserver buoyed him up until rescuers came.* **2** support or encourage: *Hope can buoy you up, even when something goes wrong.*

bur (bėr), **1** a prickly, clinging seedcase or flower of some plants. Burs stick to cloth and fur. **2** plant or weed that has burs. *noun.* Also spelled **burr.**

bur den (bėrd′n), **1** something carried; load (of things, care, work, duty, or sorrow): *A light burden was laid on the mule's back. Everyone in my family shares the burden of housework.* **2** a load too heavy to carry easily; heavy load: *Her debts are a burden that will bankrupt her.* **3** put a burden on; load too heavily; oppress: *The mule was burdened with heavy bags of ore. I don't want to burden you with my troubles.* **1,2** *noun,* **3** *verb.*

bur den some (bėrd′n səm), hard to bear; very heavy; wearying: *The President's many duties are burdensome. adjective.*

bur eau (byùr′ō), **1** chest of drawers for clothes. It often has a mirror. **2** office: *We asked about the airplane fares at the travel bureau.* **3** a division within a government department: *The Forest Service is a bureau of the Department of Agriculture. noun.*

bur glar (bėr′glər), person who breaks into a house or other building, usually at night, to steal. *noun.*

bur glar y (bėr′glər ē), a breaking into a house or other building, usually at night, to steal. *noun, plural* **bur glar ies.**

bur i al (ber′ē əl), **1** act of putting a dead body in a grave, in a tomb, or in the sea; burying: *The sailor was given a burial at sea.* **2** having to do with burying: *a burial service.* **1** *noun,* **2** *adjective.*

bur ied (ber′ēd). See **bury.** *The dog buried the bone. Many nuts were buried under the leaves. verb.*

bur lap (bėr′lap), a coarse fabric made from jute and hemp. Burlap is used to make sacks, curtains, wall coverings, and upholstery. *noun.*

burn (bėrn), **1** be on fire; set on fire; be or cause to be very hot: *The campfire burned all night. They burned wood in the fireplace.* **2** destroy by fire: *Please burn those old papers.* **3** injure by fire or heat: *The flame from the candle burned her finger.* **4** injury caused by fire or heat; burned place: *When I spilled the hot spaghetti sauce, it caused a bad burn on my hand.* **5** make by fire or heat: *A spark from the fireplace burned a hole in the rug. She burned designs on wood to make a picture.* **6** feel hot; give a feeling of heat to: *His forehead burns with fever.* **7** give light: *Lamps were burning in every room.* **8** use to produce heat: *Our furnace burns oil.* **1-3,5-8** *verb,* **burned** or **burnt, burn ing;** **4** *noun.*

burn er (bėr′nər), part of a lamp, stove, or furnace where the flame or heat is produced. *noun.*

burnt (bėrnt), burned. See **burn.** *I don't like burnt toast. verb.*

burp (bėrp), belch. *noun, verb.*

burr (bėr), bur. *noun.*

bur ro (bėr′ō), a small donkey used to carry loads or packs in the southwestern United States. *noun, plural* **bur ros.**

bur row (bėr′ō), **1** hole dug in the ground by an animal. Rabbits live in burrows. **2** dig a hole in the ground: *The mole quickly burrowed out of sight.* **3** dig: *Rabbits have burrowed the ground for miles around.* **4** search: *She burrowed in the library for a book about insects.* **1** *noun,* **2-4** *verb.*

burst (bėrst), **1** open or be opened suddenly: *They burst the lock. The trees had burst into bloom.* **2** fly apart suddenly with force; explode: *If you stick a pin into a balloon, it will burst.* **3** go, come, or do by force or suddenly: *Don't burst into the room without knocking.* **4** be very full: *The barns were bursting with grain.* **5** bursting; outbreak: *There was a burst of laughter when the clown fell down.* **6** sudden display of activity or energy: *In a burst of speed, he won the race at the last minute.* **1-4** *verb,* **burst, burst ing;** **5,6** *noun.*

bur y (ber′ē), **1** put (a dead body) in the earth, in a tomb, or in the sea: *The children buried the dead bird.* **2** cover up; hide: *The squirrels buried nuts under the dead leaves.* **3** put or sink (oneself) deeply; absorb: *I buried myself in an interesting book. verb,* **bur ied, bur y ing.**

bus (bus), **1** a large motor vehicle with seats inside and formerly also on the roof. Buses carry passengers from one place to another along a certain route. **2** take or go by bus: *The city bused the children to school.* **1** *noun, plural* **bus es** or **bus ses;** **2** *verb,* **bused, bus ing** or **bussed, bus sing.** [*Bus* comes from a Latin word meaning ''for everyone.'' The vehicle was called this because it was considered large enough for everyone making the trip.]

bush (bùsh), **1** a woody plant smaller than a tree, often with many separate branches starting from or near the ground. Some bushes are used as hedges; others are grown for their fruit. **2** open forest or wild land. *noun, plural* **bush es.**

beat around the bush, avoid coming straight to the point: *Tell me the truth right now; don't beat around the bush.*

bush el (bùsh′əl), **1** a unit of measure for grain, fruit, vegetables, and other dry things, equal to 4 pecks or 32 quarts. **2** container that holds a bushel. *noun.*

bush y (bùsh′ē), spreading out like a bush; growing thickly: *a bushy beard. adjective,* **bush i er, bush i est.**

bus i ly (biz′ə lē), in a busy manner; actively: *Bees were busily collecting nectar in the clover. adverb.*

busi ness (biz′nis), **1** thing that one is busy at; work; occupation: *A carpenter's business is building.* **2** matter; affair: *I am tired of the whole business.* **3** buying and selling; trade: *This hardware store does a big business in tools.* **4** a store, factory, or other commercial enterprise: *They sold the* *bakery business. noun, plural* **busi ness es** for 4.

busi ness like (biz′nis līk′), well managed; practical: *She runs her store in a businesslike manner. adjective.*

busi ness man (biz′nis man′), man who is in business or runs a business. *noun, plural* **busi ness men.**

busi ness wom an (biz′nis wum′ən), woman who is in business or runs a business. *noun, plural* **busi ness wom en.**

bus ing (bus′ing), sending students by bus from one neighborhood to another in order to achieve racial balance in schools. *noun.*

bus ses (bus′iz), a plural of **bus.** *noun.*

bust (bust), **1** statue of a person's head, shoulders, and upper part of the chest. See picture. **2** a woman's breasts. *noun.* [*Bust* comes from a Latin word meaning "a funeral monument." Roman funeral monuments were often decorated with a bust of the dead person.]

bus tle (bus′əl), **1** be noisily busy and in a hurry: *The children bustled to get ready for the party.* **2** noisy or excited activity: *There was a great bustle as the children got ready for the party.* 1 *verb,* **bus tled, bus tling;** 2 *noun.*

bus y (biz′ē), **1** having plenty to do; working; active: *The principal of our school is a busy person.* **2** full of work or activity: *Main Street is a busy place.* **3** make busy; keep busy: *The bees busied themselves at making honey.* **4** in use: *The phone was busy.* 1,2,4 *adjective,* **bus i er, bus i est;** 3 *verb,* **bus ied, bus y ing.**

bus y bod y (biz′ē bod′ē), person who meddles into the affairs of others; meddler. *noun, plural* **bus y bod ies.**

but (but), **1** on the other hand: *You may go, but you must come home at six o'clock.* **2** except: *I went swimming every day this week but Tuesday.* **3** unless; except that: *It never rains but it pours.* **4** only: *The child was but two years old. We can but try.* 1,3 *conjunction,* 2 *preposition,* 4 *adverb.*

butch er (buch′ər), **1** person who sells meat. **2** person whose work is killing animals for food. **3** kill (animals) for food. **4** kill (people, wild animals, or birds) needlessly, cruelly, or in large numbers. **5** spoil by poor work: *Don't butcher that song by singing off key.* 1,2 *noun,* 3-5 *verb.* [*Butcher* comes from an early French word meaning "person who kills and sells male goats."]

but ler (but′lər), the head male servant in a household. *noun.*

butt¹ (but), **1** the thicker end of a tool or weapon: *the butt of a gun.* **2** end that is left; stub or stump: *a cigar butt. noun.*

butt² (but), person who is a target of fun or ridicule: *to be made the butt of a joke. noun.*

butt³ (but), **1** strike or push by knocking hard with the head: *A goat butts.* **2** a push or blow with the head. 1 *verb,* 2 *noun.*

butte (byüt), a steep hill that has a flat top and stands alone. A butte is usually smaller than a mesa and not as steep. See picture. *noun.*

but ter (but′ər), **1** the solid yellowish fat separated

bust (definition 1)

butte

from cream by churning. **2** put butter on: *Please butter my bread.* **3** food like butter in looks or use: *apple butter, peanut butter.* 1,3 *noun,* 2 *verb.*

but ter cup (but′ər kup′), a common plant with bright yellow flowers shaped like cups. *noun.*

but ter fly (but′ər flī′), an insect with a slender body and two pairs of large, usually brightly colored, wings. Butterflies fly mostly in the daytime. See picture. *noun, plural* **but ter flies.**

but ter milk (but′ər milk′), the salty liquid left after butter has been churned from cream. *noun.*

but ter nut (but′ər nut′), **1** an oily kind of walnut grown in North America. Butternuts are good to eat. **2** tree that bears butternuts. *noun.*

but ter scotch (but′ər skoch′), **1** candy made from brown sugar and butter. **2** flavored with brown sugar and butter: *butterscotch pudding.* 1 *noun,* 2 *adjective.*

but tocks (but′əks), the fleshy hind part of the body where the legs join the back; rump. *noun plural.*

but ton (but′n), **1** a round, flat piece of metal, bone, glass, or plastic, fastened on garments to hold them closed or to decorate them. **2** fasten the buttons of: *Please button my shirt for me.* **3** knob or disk pushed or turned to cause something to work: *Push the button of the elevator to make it go up.* 1,3 *noun,* 2 *verb.*

but ton hole (but′n hōl′), **1** hole or slit through which a button is passed. **2** hold in conversation or force to listen, as if holding someone by the buttonhole of his coat. 1 *noun,* 2 *verb,* **but ton holed, but ton hol ing.**

but tress (but′ris), **1** a support built against a wall or building to strengthen it. **2** a support like this; prop. **3** support and strengthen: *The committee buttressed its report with facts and figures.* 1,2 *noun, plural* **but tress es;** 3 *verb.*

buy (bī), **1** get by paying a price; purchase: *You can buy a pencil for five cents.* **2** bargain: *That book was a real buy.* 1 *verb,* **bought, buy ing;** 2 *noun.*

buy er (bī′ər), person who buys. *noun.*

buzz (buz), **1** the humming sound made by flies, mosquitoes, or bees. **2** the low, confused sound of many people talking quietly: *The buzz of whispers stopped when the teacher entered the room.* **3** make a steady, humming sound; hum loudly: *The radio should be fixed; it buzzes when you turn it on.* **4** talk with enthusiasm or excitement: *The whole class buzzed with the news of the holiday.* **5** fly an airplane very fast and low over (a place or person): *The pilot buzzed the treetops.* 1,2 *noun,* 3-5 *verb.*

buz zard (buz′ərd), **1** a large, heavy, slow-moving hawk. **2** a kind of vulture. *noun.*

butterflies—about life-size

buzz er (buz′ər), an electrical device that makes a buzzing sound as a signal. *noun.*

by (bī), **1** near; beside: *The garden is by the house. Sit by me.* **2** along; over; through: *They went by the main road.* **3** through the means, use, or action of: *We traveled by airplane. The house was destroyed by fire. The story was written by our teacher's older sister.* **4** in the measure of: *They sell eggs by the dozen.* **5** as soon as; not later than: *Be here by six o'clock.* **6** during: *The sun shines by day.* **7** past: *The Pilgrims lived in days gone by. A car raced by. We ran by the cemetery.* **8** aside or away: *She puts money by every week to save for a new bicycle.* **9** according to: *They all work by the rules.* 1-7,9 *preposition,* 7,8 *adverb.*

by and by, after a while; before long; soon: *Summer vacation will come by and by.*

by gone (bī′gôn′), **1** gone by; past; former: *The ancient Romans lived in bygone days.* **2** bygones, what is gone by and past: *Let bygones be forgotten.* 1 *adjective,* 2 *noun.*

by-pass (bī′pas′), **1** road, channel, or pipe providing a secondary passage to be used instead of the main passage: *Drivers use the by-pass to avoid the city when there is a lot of traffic.* **2** go around: *The new highway by-passes the entire city.* 1 *noun, plural* **by-pass es;** 2 *verb.*

by-prod uct (bī′prod′əkt), something of value produced in making the main product or doing something else: *Kerosene is a by-product of petroleum refining. noun.*

by stand er (bī′stan′dər), person who stands near or looks on but does not take part; onlooker. *noun.*

by way (bī′wā′), a side path or road; way that is little used. *noun.*

C c

a hat	i it	oi oil	ch child	(a in about
ā age	ī ice	ou out	ng long	e in taken
ä far	o hot	u cup	sh she	ə = { i in pencil
e let	ō open	ů put	th thin	o in lemon
ē equal	ô order	ü rule	ͭͪ then	(u in circus
ėr term			zh measure	

C or **c** (sē), the third letter of the English alphabet. *noun, plural* **C's** or **c's.**

cab (kab), **1** automobile that can be hired with its driver; taxicab. **2** carriage that can be hired, pulled by one horse. **3** the covered part of a railroad engine where the engineer and fireman sit. **4** the covered part of a truck, crane, or other machine, where the driver or operator sits. *noun.*

cab bage (kab′ij), vegetable whose thick leaves are closely folded into a round head. *noun.*

cab in (kab′ən), **1** a small, roughly built house; hut: *a cabin in the woods.* **2** a private room in a ship: *The 500 passengers occupied 200 cabins.* **3** place for passengers in an aircraft. *noun.*

cab i net (kab′ə nit), **1** piece of furniture with shelves or drawers, used to hold articles such as dishes, jewels, or letters for use or display. **2** group of advisers chosen by the head of a nation to direct certain departments of the government. *noun.*

ca ble (kā′bəl), **1** a strong, thick rope, usually made of wires twisted together: *The truck towed the automobile with a cable.* **2** a protected bundle of wires which carries an electric current. Underwater cables carry telegraph messages across the ocean. See picture. **3** message sent under the ocean by cable. **4** send a message under the ocean by cable. 1-3 *noun,* 4 *verb,* **ca bled, ca bling.**

ca boose (kə büs′), a small railroad car, usually the last car of a freight train. The conductor and train crew ride and work in the caboose. *noun.*

ca ca o (kə kā′ō), the seeds of a tropical American tree. Cocoa and chocolate are made from cacao. See picture. *noun, plural* **ca ca os.**

cack le (kak′əl), **1** the shrill, broken sound that a hen makes, especially after laying an egg. **2** make this sound: *The hens started to cackle early in the morning.* 1 *noun,* 2 *verb,* **cack led, cack ling.**

cac tus (kak′təs), plant with a thick, fleshy stem that usually has spines but no leaves. Most cactuses grow in very hot, dry regions of America and often have brightly colored flowers. See picture. *noun, plural* **cac tus es, cac ti** (kak′tī).

ca det (kə det′), a person in training for service as an officer in the army, navy, or air force. *noun.*

ca fé (ka fā′), place to buy and eat a meal; restaurant. *noun, plural* **ca fés.**

caf e ter i a (kaf′ə tir′ē ə), restaurant where people wait on themselves. *noun.*

caf feine or **caf fein** (kaf′ēn′), a slightly bitter, stimulating drug found in coffee and tea. *noun.*

cage (kāj), **1** frame or place closed in with wires, strong iron bars, or wood. Birds and wild animals are kept in cages. **2** thing shaped or used like a cage. The car or closed platform of an elevator is

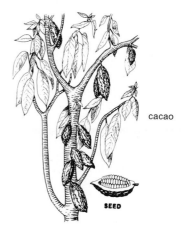

cacao

SEED

cable (definition 2)

cactus

a cage. **3** put or keep in a cage: *After the lion was caught, it was caged.* 1,2 *noun,* 3 *verb,* **caged, cag ing.**

cake (kāk), **1** a baked mixture of flour, sugar, eggs, flavoring, and other things: *I baked a chocolate cake with white frosting for my sister's birthday.* **2** a flat, thin mass of dough baked or fried; pancake. **3** a shaped mass of food or other substance: *That restaurant makes good fish cakes. I carved a cake of soap into the shape of a dog.* **4** form into a solid mass; harden: *Mud cakes as it dries.* 1-3 *noun,* 4 *verb,* **caked, cak ing.**

ca lam i ty (kə lam′ə tē), **1** a great misfortune such as a flood, a fire, the loss of one's sight or hearing, or of much money or property; disaster. **2** serious trouble; misery: *Many people still suffer from the calamity of hunger and poverty. noun, plural* **ca lam i ties.**

cal ci um (kal′sē əm), a soft, white metal. Calcium is a part of limestone, chalk, milk, bone, shells, teeth, and many other things. Calcium is needed to grow strong, healthy bones. *noun.*

cal cu late (kal′kyə lāt), **1** find out by adding, subtracting, multiplying, or dividing: *They calculated the cost of building a house.* **2** find out beforehand by any process of reasoning; estimate: *Calculate the day of the week on which New Year's Day will fall.* **3** plan or intend: *That remark was calculated to make me angry. verb,* **cal cu lat ed, cal cu lat ing.** [*Calculate* comes from a Latin word meaning "a stone used in counting."]

cal cu la tion (kal′kyə lā′shən), **1** act of adding, subtracting, multiplying, or dividing to find a result. **2** result found by calculating. **3** careful thinking; deliberate planning: *The success of the expedition was the result of much calculation. noun.*

cal cu la tor (kal′kyə lā′tər), machine that calculates, especially one that solves difficult problems. See picture. *noun.*

cal en dar (kal′ən dər), table showing the months, weeks, and days of the year. A calendar shows the day of the week on which each day of the month falls. *noun.*

calf[1] (kaf), **1** a young cow or bull. **2** a young deer, elephant, whale, or seal. **3** calfskin: *The gloves are made of calf. noun, plural* **calves** for 1 and 2.

calf[2] (kaf), the thick, fleshy part of the back of the leg below the knee. *noun, plural* **calves.**

calf skin (kaf′skin′), **1** skin of a calf. **2** leather made from it. *noun.*

cal i co (kal′ə kō), **1** a cotton cloth that usually has colored patterns printed on one side. **2** spotted in colors: *a calico cat.* 1 *noun, plural* **cal i coes** or **cal i cos;** 2 *adjective.*

Cal i for nia (kal′ə fôr′nyə), one of the Pacific states of the United States. *noun.* [*California* probably got its name from the name of an island in a Spanish adventure story written about 1500. Spanish explorers thought that Lower California was an island.]

call (kôl), **1** speak or say in a loud voice; shout or cry out: *He called from downstairs.* **2** a loud sound

calculator

camel—7½ feet (2½ meters) high at the hump

camouflage (definition 1)—The chipmunk's coloring is a natural camouflage which keeps it from being easily seen.

or shout: *I heard the swimmer's call for help.* **3** the special noise or cry an animal or bird makes: *The call of a moose came from the forest.* **4** make this noise or cry: *The crows called to each other from the trees around the meadow.* **5** give a signal to; arouse: *Call me at seven o'clock.* **6** command or ask to come: *I called my dog with a loud whistle.* **7** invitation or command: *Many people answered the mayor's call for volunteer workers in the campaign.* **8** give a name to; name: *They called the new baby "Leslie."* **9** read over aloud: *The teacher called the class roll.* **10** talk to by telephone; communicate by telephone: *I called my parents to say I would be late. Did anyone call today?* **11** talk or communication by telephone: *Were there any calls for me while I was out?* **12** make a short visit or stop: *The girl scouts called yesterday selling cookies.* **13** a short visit or stop: *The rabbi made six calls.* **14** consider; estimate: *Everyone called the party a success.* 1,4-6,8-10,12,14 *verb*, 2,3,7,11,13 *noun*.

call for, 1 go and get; stop and get: *The cab called for her at the hotel.* **2** need; require: *This recipe calls for two eggs.*

call off, 1 do away with; cancel: *We called off our trip.* **2** say or read over aloud in succession: *The teacher called off the names on the roll.*

call on or **call upon, 1** pay a short visit to: *We must call on our new neighbors.* **2** appeal to: *They called upon their friends for help.*

call up, 1 bring to mind; bring back: *The old friends called up childhood memories.* **2** telephone to: *I called her up at her office.*

on call, ready or available: *Doctors are expected to be on call day and night.*

call er (kô′lər), **1** person who makes a short visit: *The doctor said that the patient was now able to receive callers.* **2** person who calls out names or steps at a square dance. *noun.*

cal lus (kal′əs), a hard, thickened place on the skin. *noun, plural* **cal lus es.**

calm (käm), **1** quiet; still; not stormy or windy: *In fair weather, the sea is usually calm.* **2** not stirred up; peaceful: *Although she was frightened, she answered with a calm voice.* **3** quietness; stillness: *There was a sudden calm as the wind dropped.* **4** make or become calm: *The crying baby soon calmed down.* 1,2 *adjective,* 3 *noun,* 4 *verb.*

cal o rie or **cal o ry** (kal′ər ē), **1** unit for measuring the amount of heat. **2** unit of the energy supplied by food. An ounce of sugar will produce about one hundred calories. *noun, plural* **cal o ries.**

calves (kavz), more than one calf. *noun plural.*

ca lyx (kā′liks), the sepals of a flower. *noun, plural* **ca lyx es.**

came (kām). See **come.** *He came early. verb.*

cam el (kam′əl), a large, four-footed animal with a long neck and cushioned feet. It is used as a beast of burden in the deserts of northern Africa and central Asia because it can go for a long time without drinking water. The camel of northern Africa has one hump, made up mostly of stored body fat; the camel of central Asia has two

a hat	**i** it	**oi** oil	**ch** child	
ā age	**ī** ice	**ou** out	**ng** long	a in about
ä far	**o** hot	**u** cup	**sh** she	e in taken
e let	**ō** open	**u̇** put	**th** thin	ə = i in pencil
ē equal	**ô** order	**ü** rule	**ŦH** then	o in lemon
ėr term			**zh** measure	u in circus

humps. See picture. *noun.*

cam er a (kam′ər ə), instrument for taking motion pictures or photographs. A camera lens focuses light rays through the dark inside part of the camera onto film which is sensitive to light. *noun.*

cam ou flage (kam′ə fläzh), **1** a disguise or false appearance in order to conceal. See picture. **2** giving soldiers or weapons a false appearance to conceal them from the enemy. **3** give a false appearance to in order to conceal; disguise: *The hunters were camouflaged with shrubbery so that they blended with the green landscape.* 1,2 *noun,* 3 *verb,* **cam ou flaged, cam ou flag ing.**

camp (kamp), **1** group of tents, huts, or other shelters where people live for a time: *We hiked six miles before we made camp.* **2** live away from home for a time outdoors or in a tent or hut: *The scout troop camped at the foot of the mountain for two weeks.* **3** place where one lives in a tent or hut or outdoors: *Last year I spent a week at summer camp.* **4** persons living in a camp: *The camp was awakened by the bugler.* **5** live simply, as one does in a tent: *We camped in the empty house until our furniture arrived.* 1,3,4 *noun,* 2,5 *verb.*

cam paign (kam pān′), **1** a number of connected military operations in a war which are aimed at some special purpose: *The general planned a campaign to capture the enemy's most important city.* **2** a number of connected activities to do or get something: *a campaign to raise money for a new hospital.* **3** take part or serve in a campaign: *The candidates for mayor campaigned by giving speeches.* 1,2 *noun,* 3 *verb.*

camp er (kam′pər), **1** person who camps. **2** vehicle fitted out for camping. It may be pulled by an automobile, or have its own engine so that it can be driven from place to place. *noun.*

camp fire (kamp′fīr′), fire in a camp used for cooking, warmth, or social gatherings. *noun.*

cam phor (kam′fər), a white substance with a strong odor. It is used in medicine and to protect clothes from moths. *noun.*

camp site (kamp′sīt′), place where people camp. *noun.*

cam pus (kam′pəs), grounds of a college, university, or school. *noun, plural* **cam pus es.**

can[1] (kan or kən), **1** be able to: *You can run fast.* **2** know how to: *She can speak Spanish.* **3** have the right to: *Anyone can cross the street here.* **4** may: *Can I go now? verb, past tense* **could.**

can[2] (kan), **1** container of metal, usually with a cover or lid: *a trash can, a paint can, a can of peaches.* **2** amount that a can holds: *Add three cans of water to make the orange juice.* **3** put in an airtight can or jar to preserve: *We are going to can tomatoes.* 1,2 *noun,* 3 *verb,* **canned, can ning.**

Can a da (kan′ə də), country in North America, north of the United States. *noun.*

Ca na di an (kə nā′dē ən), **1** of or having something to do with Canada or its people. **2** person born or living in Canada. 1 *adjective,* 2 *noun.*

ca nal (kə nal′), **1** waterway dug across land for ships or small boats to go through or to carry water to places that need it. **2** tube in the body of an animal that carries food, liquid, or air. The food that we eat goes through the alimentary canal. *noun.*

ca nar y (kə ner′ē), **1** a small, yellow songbird. It is a kind of finch and is often kept as a pet. **2** light yellow. 1 *noun, plural* **ca nar ies;** 2 *adjective.*

can cel (kan′səl), **1** put an end to, set aside, or withdraw; do away with; stop: *She canceled her appointment with the dentist.* **2** cross out; mark, stamp, or punch so that it cannot be used again: *The post office cancels the stamp on a letter. verb.*

can cer (kan′sər), a very harmful growth in the body. Cancer tends to spread and destroy the healthy tissues and organs of the body. *noun.*

can did (kan′did), **1** frank and sincere: *Please be candid with me.* **2** not posed: *a candid photograph of children playing. adjective.*

can di date (kan′də dāt), person who seeks, or is proposed for, some office or honor: *There are three candidates for president of our club. noun.*

can died (kan′dēd), cooked in sugar; coated with sugar: *candied sweet potatoes, candied apples. adjective.*

can dle (kan′dl), stick of wax or tallow with a wick in it, burned to give light. Long ago, before there was gas or electric light, people burned candles to see by. *noun.*

can dle light (kan′dl līt′), light of a candle or candles. *noun.*

can dle stick (kan′dl stik′), holder for a candle, to make it stand up straight. *noun.*

can dy (kan′dē), **1** sugar or syrup, boiled with water and flavoring, then cooled and made into small pieces for eating. **2** piece of this: *Take a candy from the box. noun, plural* **can dies.**

cane (kān), **1** a slender stick used as an aid in walking. **2** stick used to beat with: *A blow with a cane was an old form of punishment.* **3** beat with a cane: *Some schoolmasters used to cane boys when they did not obey.* **4** a long, jointed stem, such as that of the bamboo. **5** plant having such stems. Sugar cane and bamboo are canes. 1,2,4,5 *noun,* 3 *verb,* **caned, can ing.**

ca nine tooth (kā′nīn tüth′), one of the four pointed teeth next to the incisors. [The word *canine* comes from a Latin word meaning "dog." The tooth was called this because it looks like the pointed tooth of a dog.]

canned (kand), put in a can; preserved by being put in airtight cans or jars: *canned peaches. adjective.*

can ner y (kan′ər ē), factory where food is canned. *noun, plural* **can ner ies.**

can ni bal (kan′ə bəl), **1** person who eats human

canoe
(definition 1)

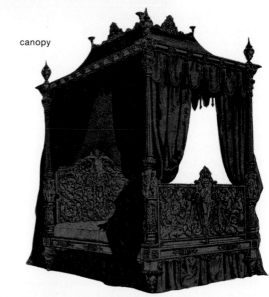

canopy

capsule
(definition 2)

flesh. **2** animal that eats others of its own kind: *Some fishes are cannibals. noun.*

can non (kan′ən), a big gun, especially one that is supported by a set of wheels, or a heavy flat base. Artillery is another word for cannons. Formerly, especially during the American Civil War, old-fashioned cannons fired solid cannonballs. *noun, plural* **can nons** or **can non.**

can non ball (kan′ən bôl′), a large, solid iron or steel ball, that used to be fired from cannons. *noun.*

can not (kan′ot or ka not′), can not. *verb.*

ca noe (kə nü′), **1** a light boat pointed at both ends and moved with a paddle. See picture. **2** paddle a canoe; go in a canoe. 1 *noun,* 2 *verb,* **ca noed, ca noe ing.**

can o py (kan′ə pē), a covering fixed over a bed, throne, or entrance, or carried on poles over a person. See picture. *noun, plural* **can o pies.**

can't (kant), can not.

can ta loupe or **can ta loup** (kan′tl ōp), a kind of muskmelon. *noun.*

can teen (kan tēn′), **1** a small container for carrying water or other drinks. **2** a store in a school, camp, or factory where food, drinks, and other articles are sold or given out. *noun.*

can ter (kan′tər), **1** gallop gently: *I cantered my horse down the road. The horse cantered across the meadow.* **2** a gentle gallop. 1 *verb,* 2 *noun.*

can vas (kan′vəs), **1** a strong cloth with a coarse weave often made of cotton. It is used to make tents, sails, raincoats, and the tops of sneakers. Artists paint on canvas. **2** made of canvas: *The boat had canvas sails.* **3** something made of canvas: *The artist painted on a large canvas.* **4** picture painted on canvas; oil painting: *The beautiful canvas was hanging in the art gallery.* 1,3,4 *noun, plural* **can vas es;** 2 *adjective.*

can yon (kan′yən), a narrow valley with high, steep sides, usually with a stream at the bottom. *noun.*

cap (kap), **1** a soft, close-fitting covering for the head, usually having little or no brim. **2** a special head covering worn to show rank or occupation: *a nurse's cap, a student's cap and gown.* **3** anything like a cap. The stopper or top of a jar, bottle, tube, or fountain pen is a cap. **4** highest part; top: *the polar cap at the North Pole.* **5** put a cap on; cover the top of: *cap a bottle. Whipped cream capped the dessert.* **6** do or follow up with something as good or better: *Each of the two clowns capped the other's last joke.* **7** a small amount of explosive in a wrapper or covering: *This toy gun uses caps.* 1-4,7 *noun,* 5,6 *verb,* **capped, cap ping.**

ca pa bil i ty (kā′pə bil′ə tē), ability to learn or do; power or fitness; capacity: *A computer has the capability of solving mathematical problems very quickly. noun, plural* **ca pa bil i ties.**

ca pa ble (kā′pə bəl), able; having fitness, power, or ability: *She was such a capable teacher that the school appointed her principal. adjective.*

capable of, having ability, power, or fitness for: *an airplane capable of going 1000 miles an hour.*

a hat	i it	oi oil	ch child	a in about
ā age	ī ice	ou out	ng long	e in taken
ä far	o hot	u cup	sh she	ə = i in pencil
e let	ō open	u̇ put	th thin	o in lemon
ē equal	ô order	ü rule	ᴛʜ then	u in circus
ėr term			zh measure	

ca pac i ty (kə pas′ə tē), **1** amount of room or space inside; largest amount that can be held by a container: *A gallon can has a capacity of 4 quarts.* **2** ability to receive and hold: *The theater has a seating capacity of 400.* **3** ability to learn or do; power or fitness: *A bright student has a capacity for learning.* **4** position: *She is here in the capacity of teacher. noun, plural* **ca pac i ties.**

cape[1] (kāp), an outer garment, or part of one, without sleeves, worn falling loosely from the shoulders and often fastened at the neck. *noun.*

cape[2] (kāp), point of land extending into the water. *noun.*

ca per (kā′pər), prank; trick. *noun.*

cap i tal (kap′ə təl), **1** city where the government of a country or state is located. Washington is the capital of the United States. Each state of the United States has a capital. **2** A, B, C, D, or any similar large letter. **3** very important; leading; chief: *The invention of the telephone was a capital advance in communication.* **4** of the best kind; excellent: *An oak tree gives capital shade.* **5** punishable by death: *Murder is a capital crime in many countries.* **6** amount of money or property that a company or a person uses in carrying on a business: *The Smith Company has a capital of $100,000.* **7** the top part of a column. 1,2,6,7 *noun,* 3-5 *adjective.*

cap i tal i za tion (kap′ə tə lə zā′shən), a writing or printing with capital letters. *noun.*

cap i tal ize (kap′ə tə līz), write or print with a capital letter: *You always capitalize the first letter of your name. verb,* **cap i tal ized, cap i tal iz ing.**

Cap i tol (kap′ə təl), **1** the building at Washington, D.C., in which Congress meets. **2** the building in which a state legislature meets. *noun.*

cap size (kap sīz′), turn bottom side up; upset; overturn: *The sailboat nearly capsized in the high wind. verb,* **cap sized, cap siz ing.**

cap sule (kap′səl), **1** a small case or covering. Medicine is often given in capsules made of gelatin. The seeds of some plants grow in capsules. **2** the enclosed front section of a rocket made to carry instruments or astronauts into space. In flight the capsule can separate from the rest of the rocket and go into orbit or be directed back to earth. See picture. *noun.*

cap tain (kap′tən), **1** head of a group; leader or chief: *the captain of a basketball team.* **2** commander of a ship. **3** an army, air force, or marine officer ranking below a major. **4** navy officer in command of a warship. **5** lead or command as captain: *She will captain the softball team next season.* 1-4 *noun,* 5 *verb.*

cap tion (kap′shən), title by a picture explaining it or at the head of a page or chapter. *noun.*

cap tive (kap′tiv), **1** person or animal captured and held unwillingly; prisoner: *The pirates took many captives during raids along the coast.* **2** made a prisoner; held against one's will: *a captive sparrow. The enemy released the captive soldiers.* **1** *noun,* **2** *adjective.*

cap tiv i ty (kap tiv′ə tē), **1** condition of being in prison. **2** condition of being held unwillingly: *Some animals cannot bear captivity, and die after a few weeks in a cage. noun, plural* **cap tiv i ties.**

cap tor (kap′tər), person who takes or holds a prisoner. *noun.*

cap ture (kap′chər), **1** make a prisoner of; take by force, skill, or trick: *We captured butterflies with a net.* **2** person or thing taken in this way: *Captain Jones's first capture was an enemy ship.* **3** a capturing or a being captured: *The capture of this ship took place on July 6.* **4** attract and hold; catch and keep: *The story of Alice in Wonderland captures the imagination.* **1,4** *verb,* **cap tured, cap tur ing;** **2,3** *noun.*

car (kär), **1** automobile. **2** any vehicle that moves on its wheels along tracks: *a subway car, a railroad car.* **3** the closed platform of an elevator, balloon, or airship for carrying passengers or cargo. *noun.*

car a mel (kar′ə məl *or* kär′məl), **1** sugar browned or burned over heat, used for coloring and flavoring food. **2** chewy candy flavored with this sugar. *noun.*

car at (kar′ət), **1** unit of weight for precious stones, equal to $1/5$ gram. **2** karat. *noun.*

car a van (kar′ə van), **1** group of merchants, pilgrims, tourists, or the like traveling together for safety through difficult or dangerous country: *A caravan of Arab merchants and camels, carrying spices and silks, moved across the desert.* **2** a closed truck or trailer, or formerly a large, covered wagon, for moving people or goods; van. *noun.*

car bo hy drate (kär′bō hī′drāt), substance made from carbon dioxide and water by green plants in sunlight. Carbohydrates are made up of carbon, hydrogen, and oxygen. Sugar and starch are carbohydrates. *noun.*

car bon (kär′bən), a very common substance that is in all plants and animals. Coal and charcoal are mostly carbon. Diamonds and graphite are pure carbon in the form of crystals. *noun.*

car bon di ox ide (kär′bən dī ok′sīd), a heavy, colorless, odorless gas, present in the atmosphere or formed when any fuel containing carbon is burned. The air that is breathed out of an animal's lungs contains carbon dioxide. Plants absorb it from the air and use it to make plant tissue. Carbon dioxide is used in soda water, in fire extinguishers, and in other ways. *noun.*

car bu re tor (kär′bə rā′tər), device for mixing air with a liquid fuel to produce an explosive mixture. A carburetor is part of the gasoline engine of an automobile. *noun.*

car cass (kär′kəs), body of a dead animal: *Steak is cut from a beef carcass. noun, plural* **car cass es.**

card (kärd), **1** a flat piece of stiff paper or thin cardboard: *The store sells post cards and birthday cards, but not report cards.* **2** one of a pack of cards used in playing games. *noun.*

card board (kärd′bôrd′), a stiff material made of layers of paper pressed together, used to make cards and boxes. *noun.*

car di nal (kärd′n əl), **1** of first importance; chief; principal: *The cardinal value of the plan is that it is simple.* **2** one of the high officials of the Roman Catholic Church, appointed by the Pope and ranking next below him. Cardinals wear red robes and red hats. **3** bright, rich red. **4** a North American songbird. The male has bright-red feathers marked with black. See picture. **1,3** *adjective,* **2,4** *noun.*

cardinal (definition 4)
9 inches (23 centimeters) long

cards (kärdz), **1** game or games played with a pack of cards. **2** playing such games: *Many of the people at the party were busy at cards. noun plural.*

care (ker *or* kar), **1** worry: *I haven't a care in the world.* **2** attention: *A pilot's work requires great care.* **3** object of worry or attention: *The sick puppy was a care to its owners.* **4** feel interest: *Musicians care about music.* **5** watchful keeping; charge: *The little girl was left in her older brother's care.* **6** food, shelter, and protection: *While you are away, we will give your pets the best of care.* **7** like; want; wish: *A cat does not care to be washed.* **1-3,5,6** *noun,* **4,7** *verb,* **cared, car ing.**

care for, 1 be fond of; like: *I don't care for her friends.* **2** want; wish: *I don't care for any dessert.* **3** take charge of: *The nurse will care for him now.*

take care, be careful: *Take care to be accurate.*

take care of, 1 take charge of; attend to: *A baby-sitter is expected to take care of children. She took care of the check for our lunch.* **2** watch over; be careful with: *Take care of your money.*

ca reer (kə rir′), **1** a general course of action or progress through life: *It is exciting to read about the careers of explorers.* **2** way of living; occupation or profession: *I plan to make law my career. noun.*

care free (ker′frē′ *or* kar′frē′), without worry; happy; gay: *The children spent a carefree summer sailing and swimming at the seashore. adjective.*

care ful (ker′fəl *or* kar′fəl), **1** thinking what one says; watching what one does; watchful; cautious: *He is careful to tell the truth at all times. Be careful with my new bicycle!* **2** showing care; done with thought or effort; exact; thorough: *Arithmetic requires careful work. adjective.*

care less (ker′lis *or* kar′lis), **1** not thinking or

watching what you say or do; not careful: *I was careless and broke the cup.* **2** done without enough thought or effort; not exact or thorough: *careless work.* **3** not caring or troubling; indifferent: *a careless attitude toward school, careless about one's appearance. adjective.*

ca ress (kə res'), **1** a touch showing affection; tender embrace or kiss. **2** touch or stroke tenderly; embrace or kiss. **1** *noun, plural* **ca ress es; 2** *verb.*

care tak er (ker'tā'kər *or* kar'tā'kər), person who takes care of another person, a place, or a thing, often for the owner or for another. *noun.*

car fare (kär'fer' *or* kär'far'), money paid for riding on a bus or subway, in a taxicab, or in other passenger vehicles. *noun.*

car go (kär'gō), load of goods carried by a ship or plane: *The freighter had docked to unload a cargo of wheat. noun, plural* **car goes** *or* **car gos.**

car load (kär'lōd'), as much as a car can hold or carry. *noun.*

car na tion (kär nā'shən), **1** a red, white, or pink flower with a spicy fragrance, grown in gardens and greenhouses. **2** rosy pink. **1** *noun,* **2** *adjective.*

car ni val (kär'nə vəl), place of amusement or a traveling show having merry-go-rounds, games, and shows. *noun.*

car niv or ous (kär niv'ər əs), meat-eating; feeding chiefly on flesh. Cats, dogs, lions, tigers, and bears are carnivorous animals. *adjective.*

car ol (kar'əl), **1** song of joy. **2** hymn of joy sung at Christmas. **3** sing joyously; sing: *The birds carol in the early morning.* **1,2** *noun,* **3** *verb.*

carp[1] (kärp), find fault; complain. *verb.*

carp[2] (kärp), a bony, freshwater fish which lives in ponds and slow streams. It feeds mostly on plants and sometimes grows quite large. *noun, plural* **carps** *or* **carp.**

car pen ter (kär'pən tər), person whose work is building and repairing the wooden parts of houses, barns, and ships. *noun.*

car pet (kär'pit), **1** a heavy, woven fabric used for covering floors and stairs. **2** anything like a carpet: *a carpet of grass.* **3** cover with a carpet: *The ground was carpeted with leaves.* **1,2** *noun,* **3** *verb.*

car pool, arrangement made by a group of persons to take turns driving themselves or others to and from a place: *The parents formed a car pool to take their children to school.*

car port (kär'pôrt'), shelter for automobiles, usually attached to a house and open on at least one side. *noun.*

car riage (kar'ij), **1** vehicle that moves on wheels. Some carriages are pulled by horses and are used to carry people. Baby carriages are small and light, and can often be folded. **2** frame on wheels that supports a gun. **3** a moving part of a machine that supports some other part: *a typewriter carriage. noun.*

car ri er (kar'ē ər), person or thing that carries something. A postman is a mail carrier. A porter is a baggage carrier. Railroads, airlines, bus systems, and truck companies are carriers. *noun.*

a hat	**i** it	**oi** oil	**ch** child	a in about
ā age	**ī** ice	**ou** out	**ng** long	e in taken
ä far	**o** hot	**u** cup	**sh** she	ə = { i in pencil
e let	**ō** open	**ů** put	**th** thin	o in lemon
ē equal	**ô** order	**ü** rule	**ŦH** then	u in circus
ėr term			**zh** measure	

car ri on (kar'ē ən), dead and decaying flesh: *Some crows feed largely on carrion. noun.*

car rot (kar'ət), the long, tapering, orange-red root of a garden plant. Carrots are eaten as a vegetable, either cooked or raw. *noun.*

car rou sel (kar'ə sel'), merry-go-round. *noun.*

car ry (kar'ē), **1** take (a thing or person) from one place to another: *Railroads carry coal from the mines to the factories. The man carried the child home. This story will carry your thoughts back to last winter.* **2** have with one: *I carry an umbrella whenever it looks like rain.* **3** hold up; support: *Rafters carry the weight of the roof.* **4** hold (one's body and head) in a certain way: *The ballet dancer carries himself gracefully.* **5** capture or win: *Our side carried the election.* **6** cover the distance: *The singer's voice carries to the last row of the theater.* **7** sing (a melody or part) with correct pitch: *The children in the chorus can all carry a tune.* **8** keep in stock: *This store carries toys and games.* **9** transfer (a number) from one place or column in the sum to the next: *A 10 in the 1's column must be carried to the 10's column. verb,* **car ried, car ry ing.**

carry away, arouse strong feeling in; influence beyond reason: *Have you ever been so carried away by a sad movie that you began to cry?*

carry on, 1 do; manage; conduct: *She carried on a successful business.* **2** keep going; not stop; continue: *We must carry on in our effort to establish world peace.* **3** behave wildly or foolishly: *The children carried on at the party.*

carry out, get done; do; complete: *They carried out the job well.*

cart (kärt), **1** a strong vehicle with two wheels, used in farming and for carrying heavy loads. Horses, donkeys, and oxen are often used to draw carts. See picture. **2** a light wagon, used to deliver

cart (definition 1)

goods. **3** a small vehicle on wheels, moved by hand: *a grocery cart.* **4** carry in a cart: *Cart away this rubbish.* 1-3 *noun,* 4 *verb.*

car ti lage (kär′tl ij), a tough, elastic substance forming parts of the skeleton of animals with a backbone; gristle. Cartilage is more flexible than bone and not as hard. The outer part of the ear is made of cartilage and skin. *noun.*

car ton (kärt′n), **1** box made of pasteboard or cardboard: *a candy carton. Pack the books in large cartons.* **2** amount that a carton holds: *The children drink a carton of milk at each meal. noun.*

car toon (kär tün′), **1** sketch or drawing which interests or amuses us by showing persons, things, or events in an exaggerated way: *Political cartoons often represent the United States as a tall man with chin whiskers, called Uncle Sam.* **2** comic strip. *noun.*

car tridge (kär′trij), **1** case made of metal, plastic, or cardboard for holding gunpowder and a bullet or shot. **2** a small container holding a roll of photographic film or ink for a pen. *noun.*

cart wheel (kärt′hwēl′), **1** wheel of a cart. **2** a sideways handspring or somersault. *noun.*

carve (kärv), **1** cut into slices or pieces: *I carved the meat at the dinner table.* **2** make by cutting; cut: *Statues are often carved from marble, stone, or wood.* **3** decorate with figures or designs cut on the surface: *a carved box. The oak chest was carved with flowers. verb,* **carved, carv ing.**

carv ing (kär′ving), **1** carved work; carved decoration: *a wood carving.* **2** See **carve.** *I am carving the meat for dinner.* 1 *noun,* 2 *verb.*

cas cade (ka skād′), a small waterfall. See picture. *noun.*

case[1] (kās), **1** any special condition of a person or thing; example; instance: *A case of chicken pox kept me away from school. The children agreed that every case of cheating should be punished.* **2** the actual condition; real situation: *She said the work was done, but that was not the case.* **3** person who is being treated by a doctor; patient: *I was the first case of poison ivy at camp.* **4** matter for a court of law to decide: *The case will be brought before the court tomorrow. noun.*

in any case, no matter what happens: *In any case, you should prepare for the worst.*

in case of, if there should be: *In case of fire walk quietly to the nearest door.*

case[2] (kās), **1** thing to hold or cover something: *a typewriter case.* **2** box: *There is a big case full of books in the hall.* **3** amount that a case can hold: *The children drank a case of ginger ale at the party.* **4** frame. A window fits in a case. *noun.*

cash (kash), **1** money in the form of coins and bills. **2** money paid at the time of buying something: *Do you want to pay cash for the clothes or charge them?* **3** give cash for: *The bank will cash your check.* **4** get cash for: *I cashed a check at the store.* 1,2 *noun,* 3,4 *verb.*

cash ew (kash′ü), the small, kidney-shaped nut of a tropical American tree. Cashews are good to eat. *noun.*

cash ier (ka shir′), person who has charge of money in a bank, or in any business. *noun.*

cash mere (kash′mir), a fine, soft wool, used in making sweaters or scarves. The finest cashmere is obtained from a breed of long-haired goats of Asia. *noun.*

cask (kask), **1** barrel. A cask may be large or small, and is usually made to hold liquids. **2** amount that a cask holds. *noun.*

cas ket (kas′kit), **1** coffin. **2** a small box or chest, often fine and beautiful, used to hold jewels and letters. *noun.*

cas se role (kas′ə rōl′), **1** a covered baking dish in which food can be both cooked and served. **2** food cooked and served in such a dish. *noun.*

cas sette (kə set′), **1** container holding plastic tape for playing or recording sound. **2** cartridge for film. *noun.*

cast (kast), **1** throw: *cast a stone, cast a fishing line. She was cast into the water when the railing of the bridge broke.* **2** throw off; let fall; shed: *The snake cast its skin.* **3** distance a thing is thrown; throw: *The fisherman made a long cast with his line.* **4** direct or turn: *She cast a glance of surprise at me.* **5** put on record: *I cast my vote for President of the United States.* **6** shape by pouring or squeezing into a mold to harden. Metal is first melted and then cast. **7** thing shaped in a mold: *The sculptor made a cast of Queen Elizabeth.* **8** mold used to shape or support: *My cousin's broken arm is in a plaster cast.* **9** select for a part in a play: *The teacher cast me in the role of Christopher Columbus.* **10** actors in a play: *The cast was listed on the program.* **11** outward form or look; appearance: *His face had a gloomy cast.* **12** a slight amount of color; tinge: *a white shirt with a pink cast.* 1,2,4-6,9 *verb,* **cast, cast ing;** 3,7,8,10-12 *noun.*

cast down, 1 turn downward; lower: *She cast down her eyes to avoid looking at me.* **2** make sad or discouraged: *He was cast down by the bad news.*

cast off, 1 let loose; set free: *cast off a boat from its moorings.* **2** abandon or discard: *She cast off her old friends when she moved.*

cast iron, a hard, brittle form of iron shaped by pouring into a mold to harden.

cas tle (kas′əl), **1** a large building or group of buildings with thick walls, towers, and other defenses against attack. Usually a water-filled ditch, or moat, surrounded the castle. See picture. **2** a large and imposing residence. **3** one of the pieces in the game of chess; rook. *noun.*

cas u al (kazh′ü əl), **1** happening by chance; not planned or expected; accidental: *Our long friendship began with a casual meeting at a party.* **2** without plan or method; careless: *I didn't read the newspaper but gave it only a casual glance.* **3** informal: *We dressed in casual clothes for the picnic. Her casual behavior was sometimes mistaken for rudeness. adjective.*

cas u al ty (kazh′ü əl tē), **1** soldier, sailor, or other member of the armed forces who has been wounded, killed, or captured: *The war produced many casualties.* **2** person injured or killed in an

cascade

a hat	i it	oi oil	ch child	(a in about
ā age	ī ice	ou out	ng long	e in taken
ä far	o hot	u cup	sh she	ə = { i in pencil
e let	ō open	u̇ put	th thin	o in lemon
ē equal	ô order	ü rule	ᴛʜ then	u in circus
ėr term			zh measure	

accident: *If drivers were more careful, there would be fewer casualties on the highways.* **3** accident, especially a fatal or serious one: *a casualty at sea.* *noun, plural* **cas u al ties.**

cat (kat), **1** a small, furry animal, often kept as a pet or for catching mice and rats. **2** any animal of the group including cats, lions, tigers, and leopards. *noun.*
let the cat out of the bag, tell a secret.
rain cats and dogs, pour down rain very hard.

cat a log (kat′l ôg), **1** a list. A library usually has a catalog of its books, arranged in alphabetical order. Some companies print catalogs showing pictures and prices of the things that they have to sell. **2** make a list of; enter in the proper place in a list: *to catalog an insect collection.* **1** *noun,* **2** *verb.*

cat a logue (kat′l ôg), catalog. *noun, verb,*
cat a logued, cat a logu ing.

cat a pult (kat′ə pult), **1** weapon used in ancient times for shooting stones or arrows. See picture. **2** slingshot. **3** device for launching an airplane from the deck of a ship. **4** throw; hurl: *He stopped his bicycle so suddenly that he was catapulted over the handlebars.* **1-3** *noun,* **4** *verb.*

cat a ract (kat′ə rakt′), **1** a large, steep waterfall. **2** a violent rush or downpour of water; flood: *Cataracts of rain flooded the streets.* **3** disease of the eye in which the lens develops a cloudy film. A cataract makes a person partly or entirely blind. *noun.*

ca tas tro phe (kə tas′trə fē), a sudden, terribly bad or horrifying thing that happens; very great misfortune. An earthquake, tornado, flood, or big fire is a catastrophe. *noun.*

cat bird (kat′bėrd′), a North American songbird with gray feathers. It can make a sound like a cat mewing. *noun.*

catch (kach), **1** take and hold (something moving); seize: *Catch the ball with both hands. The children chased the puppy and caught it. We were caught in the storm. Bright colors catch the baby's eye.* **2** take or get: *Paper catches fire easily. Put on a warm coat or you will catch cold. I caught a glimpse of my grandmother waving as her plane took off.* **3** reach or get to in time: *You have just five minutes to catch your train.* **4** see, hear, or understand: *He spoke so rapidly that I didn't catch the meaning of what he said.* **5** become hooked or fastened: *My sweater caught in the door.* **6** come upon suddenly; surprise: *Mother caught me just as I was hiding her birthday present.* **7** act as catcher in baseball: *He catches for our team.* **8** act of catching: *She made a fine catch with one hand.* **9** thing that fastens: *The catch on that door is broken.* **10** thing caught: *A dozen fish is a good catch.* **11** a hidden or tricky condition: *There is a catch to that question.* **1-7**

catapult (definition 1)—By means of ropes, ancient soldiers drew this very heavy bow. It could send an arrow a great distance.

castle (definition 1)

caterpillar—about 1 inch (2½ centimeters) long

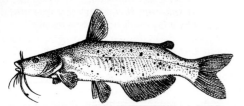

catfish—20 inches (50 centimeters) long

catkins

cattails

verb, caught, catch ing; 8-11 *noun, plural* **catch es.**

catch on, 1 get the idea; understand: *The second time the teacher explained the problem, I caught on.* **2** be widely used or accepted: *That new song caught on quickly.*

catch up with, come up even with a person or thing while going the same way; overtake: *I was late, and had to run to catch up with my friends.*

catch er (kach′ər), **1** person or thing that catches. **2** a baseball player who stands behind the batter to catch the ball thrown by the pitcher. *noun.*

catch ing (kach′ing), **1** spread by infection; contagious: *Colds are catching.* **2** likely to spread from one person to another: *Enthusiasm is catching. adjective.*

catch y (kach′ē), pleasing and easy to remember: *a catchy new song. adjective,* **catch i er, catch i est.**

cat e chism (kat′ə kiz′əm), **1** book of questions and answers about religion. **2** set of questions and answers about any subject. *noun.*

cat e go ry (kat′ə gôr′ē), group or general division in classification; class: *The characters in the story can be divided into two categories: those who are very good and those who are very bad. noun, plural* **cat e go ries.**

ca ter (kā′tər), **1** provide food and supplies, and sometimes service: *They run a restaurant and also cater for weddings and parties.* **2** provide what is needed or wanted: *The new store caters to tourists by selling souvenirs. verb.*

cat er pil lar (kat′ər pil′ər), the wormlike larva of a butterfly or a moth which has just hatched from its egg. See picture. *noun.*

cat fish (kat′fish′), a fish without scales and with long, slender growths around the mouth that look somewhat like a cat's whiskers. See picture. *noun, plural* **cat fish es** or **cat fish.**

ca the dral (kə thē′drəl), **1** the official church of a bishop. The bishop of a district or diocese has a throne in the cathedral. **2** a large or important church. *noun.*

Cath o lic (kath′ə lik), **1** of the Christian church governed by the pope; Roman Catholic. **2** member of this church. **1** *adjective,* **2** *noun.*

cat kin (kat′kən), the soft, downy or scaly, pointed flower, without petals, that grows on willow or birch trees. Pussy willows are catkins. See picture. *noun.*

cat sup (kech′əp *or* kat′səp), sauce made to use with meat or fish. Tomato catsup is made of tomatoes, onions, salt, sugar, and spices. *noun.*

cat tail (kat′tāl′), a tall marsh plant with flowers in long, round, furry, brown spikes. See picture. *noun.*

cat tle (kat′l), animals that chew their cud, have hoofs, and are raised for meat, milk, and hides; cows, bulls, and steers. *noun plural.*

cat tle man (kat′l mən), person who raises or takes care of cattle. *noun, plural* **cat tle men.**

caught (kôt). See **catch.** *I caught the ball. The mouse was caught in a trap. verb.*

cau li flow er (kô′lə flou′ər), vegetable having a

solid, white head with a few leaves around it. *noun.*

cause (kôz), **1** person, thing, or event that makes something happen: *The flood was the cause of much damage.* **2** make happen; make do; bring about: *The fire caused much damage. A loud noise caused me to jump.* **3** reason or occasion for action: *a cause for celebration. You have no cause to complain.* **4** subject or movement in which many people are interested and to which they give their support: *World peace is the cause she works for.* 1,3,4 *noun,* 2 *verb,* **caused, caus ing.**

cau tion (kô′shən), **1** great care; unwillingness to take chances: *Use caution in crossing streets.* **2** warning: *A sign with "Danger" on it is a caution.* **3** urge to be careful; warn: *My parents cautioned me against playing in the street.* 1,2 *noun,* 3 *verb.*

cau tious (kô′shəs), very careful; not taking chances: *A cautious driver never drives too fast.* *adjective.*

cav al cade (kav′əl kād′), a long, continuous line of persons riding on horses, in carriages, or in automobiles. *noun.*

cav al ry (kav′əl rē), soldiers fighting on horseback or from tanks and other armored vehicles. *noun, plural* **cav al ries.**

cave (kāv), **1** a hollow space underground, especially one with an opening in the side of a hill or mountain. **2 cave in,** fall in; sink: *The weight of the snow caused the roof of the cabin to cave in.* 1 *noun,* 2 *verb,* **caved, cav ing.**

cave man, person who lived in a cave.

cav ern (kav′ərn), a large cave. *noun.*

cav i ty (kav′ə tē), hollow place; hole. *Cavities in teeth are caused by decay. noun, plural* **cav i ties.**

caw (kô), **1** the harsh cry made by a crow or raven. **2** make this cry. 1 *noun,* 2 *verb.*

cease (sēs), stop: *The music ceased suddenly. verb,* **ceased, ceas ing.**

cease less (sēs′lis), going on all the time; never stopping; continual: *the ceaseless roar of the waterfall. adjective.*

ce dar (sē′dər), an evergreen tree with widely spreading branches. Its fragrant, durable, reddish wood is used for lining clothes closets and for making chests, pencils, and posts. *noun.*

cello

ceil ing (sē′ling), **1** the inside, top covering of a room. **2** the greatest height to which an airplane can go under certain conditions: *That plane has a ceiling of more than 100,000 feet.* **3** distance between the earth and the lowest clouds: *The weather report said that the ceiling was only 300 feet.* **4** top limit: *There is a ceiling on the amount candidates can spend for election campaigns. noun.*

cel e brate (sel′ə brāt), **1** observe (a special time or day) with the proper activities: *We celebrated my birthday with a party and cake and ice cream.* **2** perform publicly with the proper ceremonies and rites: *The priest celebrates Mass in church.* **3** have a gay time: *When the children saw the snow, they celebrated. verb,* **cel e brat ed, cel e brat ing.**

cel e brat ed (sel′ə brā′tid), famous; well-known; much talked about: *a celebrated poet. adjective.*

cel e bra tion (sel′ə brā′shən), **1** special services or activities in honor of a particular person, act, time, or day: *A Fourth of July celebration often includes a display of fireworks.* **2** act of celebrating: *celebration of a birthday. noun.*

ce leb ri ty (sə leb′rə tē), **1** famous person; person who is well known or much talked about: *I collect the autographs of celebrities.* **2** fame; being well known or much talked about: *Her celebrity as a tennis player brought her many offers to appear on television. noun, plural* **ce leb ri ties.**

cel er y (sel′ər ē), vegetable whose long, crisp stalks are whitened by keeping the stalks covered as they grow. Celery is eaten raw or cooked. *noun.*

ce les tial (sə les′chəl), of the sky; having something to do with the sky: *The sun, moon, planets, and stars are celestial bodies. adjective.*

cell (sel), **1** a small room in a prison, convent, or monastery. **2** any small, hollow place: *Bees store honey in the cells of a honeycomb.* **3** the extremely small unit of living matter of which all plants and animals are made. Most cells consist of protoplasm, have a nucleus near the center, and are enclosed by a very thin membrane. The body has blood cells, nerve cells, and muscle cells. **4** container holding materials which produce electricity by chemical action. A battery consists of one or more cells. *noun.*

cel lar (sel′ər), underground room or rooms, usually under a building and often used for storing food or fuel. *noun.*

cel lo (chel′ō), a musical instrument like a violin, but very much larger and with a lower tone; violoncello. It is held between the knees while being played. See picture. *noun, plural* **cel los.**

cel lo phane (sel′ə fān), transparent substance somewhat like paper, made from cellulose. It is used as a wrapping to keep food, candy, or tobacco fresh and clean. *noun.*

cel lu lose (sel′yə lōs), substance that forms the walls of plant cells; the woody part of trees and plants. Wood, cotton, flax, and hemp are largely cellulose. Cellulose is used to make paper, rayon, plastics, and explosives. *noun.*

Cel si us (sel′sē əs). On the Celsius **thermometer,** 0 degrees is the temperature at which water freezes, and 100 degrees is the temperature at which water boils. *adjective.* [*Celsius* was named for Anders Celsius, who lived from 1701 to 1744. He was a Swedish scientist who invented this thermometer.]

ce ment (sə ment′), **1** a fine, gray powder made by burning clay and limestone. Cement mixed with water and such materials as sand and gravel · becomes hard like stone when it dries. It is used to make concrete for sidewalks, streets, floors, and walls. Cement, sand, and water form mortar used to hold stones and bricks together in the walls of buildings. **2** any soft substance which when it hardens makes things stick together: *rubber cement.* **3** fasten together with cement: *A broken plate can be cemented.* **4** spread cement over: *to cement a sidewalk.* 1,2 *noun,* 3,4 *verb.*

cem e ter y (sem′ə ter′ē), place for burying the dead. *noun, plural* **cem e ter ies.**

cen sure (sen′shər), **1** expression of unfavorable opinion; criticism: *Censure is sometimes harder to bear than punishment.* **2** find fault with; criticize: *I was censured by the club for not paying my dues.* 1 *noun,* 2 *verb,* **cen sured, cen sur ing.**

cen sus (sen′səs), an official count of the people of a country or district. It is taken to find out the number of people, their age, sex, what they do to make a living, and many other facts about them. *noun, plural* **cen sus es.**

cent (sent), coin of the United States and Canada; penny. One hundred cents make one dollar. *noun.*

cen ten ni al (sen ten′ē əl), **1** having to do with the 100th anniversary. **2** a 100th anniversary: *The town is celebrating its centennial.* 1 *adjective,* 2 *noun.*

cen ter (sen′tər), **1** point within a circle or sphere equally distant from all points of the circumference or surface. **2** middle point, place, or part: *the center of a room.* **3** person, thing, or group that is the central point of attraction: *The Egyptian mummy was the center of the exhibit.* **4** point toward which people or things go, or from which they come; main point: *New York City is one of the centers of world trade.* **5** place in or at a center: *The bowl of fruit was centered on the table.* **6** collect at a center: *The guests centered around the table.* **7** player who has a position at the center of a team in football, basketball, hockey, and some other sports. 1-4,7 *noun,* 5,6 *verb.*

cen ti grade (sen′tə grād), divided into 100 degrees. The **centigrade thermometer** has 0 degrees for the temperature at which ice melts (or water freezes) and 100 degrees for the temperature at which water boils. *adjective.*

cen ti me ter or **cen ti me tre** (sen′tə mē′tər), a unit of length equal to $1/100$ of a meter or about $2/5$ of an inch. *noun.*

cen ti pede (sen′tə pēd′), a flat, wormlike animal with many pairs of legs. Centipedes vary in length from an inch or so to nearly a foot. The bite of some centipedes is painful. See picture. *noun.*

cen tral (sen′trəl), **1** of the center; forming the center: *The sun is central in the solar system.* **2** at the center; near the center: *The park is in the central part of the city.* **3** forming the center of an organization or system; head: *The central library sends books to its branches.* **4** equally distant from all points; easy to get to or from: *We shop at a central market.* **5** main; chief; principal: *the central idea of the story. adjective.*

Central America, part of North America between Mexico and South America.

cen tral ly (sen′trə lē), at or near the center: *The business district is centrally located. adverb.*

cen tur y (sen′chər ē), **1** each 100 years, counting from some special time, such as the birth of Christ. The first century is 1 through 100; the nineteenth century is 1801 through 1900; the twentieth century is 1901 through 2000. **2** period of 100 years. From 1824 to 1924 is a century. *noun, plural* **cen tur ies.**

ce ram ics (sə ram′iks), art of making pottery, earthenware, or porcelain. See picture. *noun.*

cer e al (sir′ē əl), **1** any grass that produces grain which is used as a food. Wheat, rice, corn, oats, and barley are cereals. **2** the grain. **3** food made from the grain. Oatmeal and corn meal are cereals. **4** of or having something to do with grain: *cereal crops, cereal products.* 1-3 *noun,* 4 *adjective.* [*Cereal* comes from a Latin word meaning "of Ceres." She was the Roman goddess of agriculture and the harvest.]

cer e mo ni al (ser′ə mō′nē əl), **1** of or having something to do with ceremony: *ceremonial costumes.* **2** very formal: *The ambassador receives guests in a ceremonial way.* **3** the formal actions proper to an occasion. Bowing the head and kneeling are ceremonials of some religions. 1,2 *adjective,* 3 *noun.*

cer e mo ni ous (ser′ə mō′nē əs), very formal; extremely polite: *a ceremonious bow. adjective.*

cer e mo ny (ser′ə mō′nē), **1** a special act or set of acts to be done on special occasions such as weddings, funerals, graduations, or holidays: *The graduation ceremony was held in the school auditorium.* **2** very polite conduct; way of conducting oneself that follows all the rules of polite social behavior: *Dinner was served with a great deal of ceremony. noun, plural* **cer e mo nies.**

cer tain (sėrt′n), **1** sure: *I am certain that these are the facts.* **2** some; particular: *Certain plants will not grow in this country.* **3** settled: *She works a certain number of hours each day.* **4** reliable: *I have certain information that school will end a day earlier this year. adjective.*

cer tain ly (sėrt′n lē), without a doubt; surely: *I will certainly be at the party. adverb.*

cer tain ty (sėrt′n tē), **1** freedom from doubt; being certain: *The man's certainty was amusing, for we could all see that he was wrong.* **2** something certain; a sure fact: *The coming of spring and summer is a certainty. noun, plural* **cer tain ties.**

cer tif i cate (sər tif′ə kit), a written or printed statement that may be used as proof of some fact. Your birth certificate gives the date and place of your birth and the names of your parents. *noun.*

cer ti fy (sėr′tə fī), **1** declare (something) true or correct by an official spoken, written, or printed statement: *This diploma certifies that you have completed high school.* **2** guarantee the quality or value of: *The fire inspector certified the school building as fireproof. verb,* **cer ti fied, cer ti fy ing.**

chafe (chāf), make sore or become sore by rubbing: *chafe one's neck. verb,* **chafed, chaf ing.**

chaff (chaf), **1** the stiff, strawlike bits around the grains of wheat, oats, or rye. Chaff is separated from grain by threshing. **2** worthless stuff. *noun.*

chain (chān), **1** row of links joined together: *The dog is fastened to a post by a chain.* **2** series of things linked together: *a chain of mountains, a chain of restaurants, a chain of events.* **3** fasten with a chain: *The dog was chained to a post.* **4** anything that binds or restrains: *the chains of duty.* **5** bind; restrain: *Work chained him to his desk.* **6** keep in prison; make a slave of. **7 chains, a** bonds; fetters: *The rebels were brought back in chains.* **b** imprisonment or bondage: *The dictator's enemies had spent years in chains.* 1,2,4,7 *noun,* 3,5,6 *verb.*

chain store, one of a group of stores owned and operated by the same company.

chair (cher *or* char), **1** seat that has a back and, sometimes, arms, usually for one person. **2** position or authority of a person who has a certain rank or dignity: *Professor Smith has the chair of astronomy at this college.* **3** chairman or chairwoman. *noun.*

chair man (cher′mən *or* char′mən), **1** person who is in charge of a meeting. **2** person at the head of a committee. *noun, plural* **chair men.**

chair per son (cher′pėr′sən *or* char′pėr′sən), **1** person who is in charge of a meeting. **2** person at the head of a committee. *noun.*

chair wom an (cher′wùm′ən *or* char′wùm′ən), **1** woman in charge of a meeting. **2** woman at the head of a committee. *noun, plural* **chair wom en.**

chal ice (chal′is), cup or goblet. See picture. *noun.*

chalk (chôk), **1** a soft, white or gray limestone, made up mostly of very small fossil seashells. Chalk is used for making lime and for writing or drawing. **2** a white or colored substance like chalk, used for writing or drawing on a blackboard or chalkboard. **3** mark, write, or draw with chalk. 1,2 *noun,* 3 *verb.*

chalk up, 1 write down; record: *You learned your lesson the hard way and you can chalk it up to experience.* **2** score: *The team chalked up 10 points.*

chalk board (chôk′bôrd′), a smooth, hard surface, used for writing or drawing on with chalk. *noun.*

chalk y (chô′kē), **1** of chalk; containing chalk. **2** like chalk; white as chalk: *The clown's face was chalky. adjective,* **chalk i er, chalk i est.**

a hat	i it	oi oil	ch child	a in about
ā age	ī ice	ou out	ng long	e in taken
ä far	o hot	u cup	sh she	ə = { i in pencil
e let	ō open	ù put	th thin	o in lemon
ē equal	ô order	ü rule	ᵫ then	u in circus
ėr term			zh measure	

centipede—1 inch (2½ centimeters) long

ceramics
This plate is an example of early American ceramics.

chalice
This chalice was used in religious ceremonies more than 1000 years ago.

chal lenge (chal′ənj), **1** invitation to a game or contest. Giving a challenge often means that one undertakes to beat everybody else. *The champions accepted our team's challenge.* **2** invite to a game or contest; dare: *They challenged our swimming team to beat their team.* **3** call to fight: *The knight challenged his rival to a duel.* **4** a call to fight: *His rival accepted the challenge.* **5** a sudden questioning or calling to answer and explain: *"Who goes there?" was the challenge of the soldier on guard.* **6** stop and question a person about an action: *When I tried to enter the building, the guard at the door challenged me.* **7** doubt; demand proof before one will accept: *The teacher challenged my statement that rice grows in Oregon.* **8** a demand for proof of the truth of a statement; a doubting or questioning of the truth of a statement: *Her challenge led me to read widely about Oregon.* **9** anything that claims or commands effort, interest, or feeling: *Fractions are a real challenge to me.* **10** claim or command effort, interest, or feeling: *Disease prevention challenges everyone.* 1,4,5,8,9 *noun,* 2,3,6,7,10 *verb,* **chal lenged, chal leng ing.**

chal leng er (chal′ən jər), person who challenges another or others. *noun.*

cham ber (chām′bər), **1** a room, especially a bedroom. **2** hall where lawmakers meet: *the council chamber.* **3** group of lawmakers: *The Congress of the United States has two chambers, the Senate and the House of Representatives.* **4** an enclosed space in the body of an animal or plant, or in some kinds of machinery. The heart has four chambers. The part of a gun that holds the charge is called the chamber. *noun.*

cha me le on (kə mē′lē ən), a small lizard that can change the color of its skin to blend with the surroundings. *noun.*

cham pi on (cham′pē ən), **1** person, animal, or thing that wins first place in a game or contest: *a swimming champion. Her steer was the champion at the county fair last year.* **2** first; ahead of all others: *a champion runner. My sister is the champion reader in our house.* 1 *noun,* 2 *adjective.*

cham pi on ship (cham′pē ən ship), position of a champion; first place: *Our school won the championship in baseball. noun.*

chance (chans), **1** favorable time; opportunity: *Now is your chance. I saw a chance to earn some money selling newspapers.* **2** possibility: *There's a good chance that you will be well enough to return to school next week. The chances are against snow in May.* **3** fate, fortune, or luck: *Chance led to the finding of gold in California.* **4** happen: *I chanced to meet an old friend today.* **5** risk: *You will be taking a chance if you try to swim that wide river.* **6** take the risk of: *Don't chance driving in this blizzard.* **7** not expected or planned; accidental: *We had a chance visit from Grandmother last week.* 1-3,5 *noun,* 4,6 *verb,* **chanced, chanc ing;** 7 *adjective.*

chan cel lor (chan′sə lər), a very high official. Chancellor is the title used for the chief official in the government of some European countries,

chandelier

for the chief judge in some courts of law, and for the president of some universities. *noun.*

chan de lier (shan′də lir′), fixture with branches for lights, usually hanging from the ceiling. See picture. *noun.*

change (chānj), **1** make different; become different: *She changed the room by painting the walls green. The wind changed from east to west.* **2** put (something) in place of another; take in place of; exchange: *You can change soiled clothes for clean ones. Can you change a dollar bill for ten dimes? She changed seats with me.* **3** passing from one form or place to a different one: *The change from flower to fruit is interesting to watch. Vacationing in the country is a pleasant change from city life.* **4** money returned to you when you have given a larger amount than the price of what you buy: *I handed the clerk a quarter for the candy bar, and he gave me five cents in change.* **5** small coins: *He always carries a pocketful of change.* **6** change one's clothes: *After swimming we went to the cabin and changed.* 1,2,6 *verb,* **changed, chang ing;** 3-5 *noun.*

change a ble (chān′jə bəl), able to change; likely to change; varying; fickle: *April weather is changeable. adjective.*

chan nel (chan′l), **1** the bed of a stream or river: *Rivers cut their own channels to the sea.* **2** body of water joining two larger bodies of water: *The English Channel lies between the North Sea and the Atlantic Ocean.* **3** the deeper part of a waterway: *There is shallow water on both sides of the channel in this river.* **4** passage for liquids; groove: *the poison channel in a snake's fangs.* **5** the means by which something moves or is carried: *The information came through secret channels.* **6** form a channel in; wear or cut into a channel: *The river had channeled its way through the rocks.* **7** a narrow band of frequencies that carries the programs of a television or radio station. 1-5,7 *noun,* 6 *verb.*

chant (chant), **1** song in which several words or syllables are sung on one tone. Chants are sometimes used in religious services. **2** sing: *chant a prayer.* 1 *noun,* 2 *verb.*

cha os (kā′os), very great confusion; complete disorder: *The tornado left the town in chaos.* See picture. *noun.*

chap[1] (chap), **1** crack open; become rough: *A person's lips or skin often chap in cold weather.* **2** make rough: *Cold weather chaps my skin. verb,* **chapped, chap ping.**

chap[2] (chap), fellow; man or boy: *Hello, old chap! noun.*

chap el (chap′əl), **1** a building for worship, not as large as a church. **2** a small place for worship in a larger building: *a hospital chapel. noun.*

chap lain (chap′lən), clergyman on duty with a family, court, regiment, warship, or the like: *a hospital chaplain, a prison chaplain. noun.*

chaps (shaps *or* chaps), strong leather trousers without a back, worn over other trousers by cowboys. See picture. *noun plural.*

chap ter (chap′tər), **1** a main division of a book, dealing with a particular part of the story or subject. **2** part; section: *The first moon flight is an interesting chapter in space travel.* **3** a local division of an organization, which holds its own meetings; branch of a club. *noun.*

char (chär), **1** burn to charcoal. **2** burn enough to blacken; scorch: *After the fire a carpenter replaced the badly charred floor. verb,* **charred, char ring.**

char ac ter (kar′ik tər), **1** all the qualities or

a hat	i it	oi oil	ch child	ə = { a in about
ā age	ī ice	ou out	ng long	e in taken
ä far	o hot	u cup	sh she	i in pencil
e let	ō open	u̇ put	th thin	o in lemon
ē equal	ô order	ü rule	ŦH then	u in circus
ėr term			zh measure	

chaps—cowboy wearing chaps

features of anything; kind; sort; nature: *The soil on the prairies is of a different character from that in the mountains.* **2** moral nature; moral strength or weakness. The special way in which you feel, think, and act, considered as good or bad, makes up your character. *She has an honest, dependable character.* **3** person or animal in a play, poem, story, or book: *My favorite character in "Charlotte's Web" is Wilbur, the pig.* **4** person who attracts attention by being different or odd: *My great-grandmother was considered a character because she smoked a corncob pipe.* **5** letter, mark, or sign used in writing or printing: *There are 52 characters in our alphabet, consisting of 26 small letters and 26 capital letters. noun.*

char ac ter is tic (kar′ik tə ris′tik), **1** marking off or distinguishing a certain person or thing from others; special: *Bananas have their own characteristic smell.* **2** a special quality or feature; whatever distinguishes one person or thing from others: *Cheerfulness is a characteristic that we admire in people. An elephant's trunk is its most noticeable characteristic.* 1 *adjective,* 2 *noun.*

char ac ter ize (kar′ik tə rīz′), **1** describe the special qualities or features of (a person or thing): *The story of "Red Riding Hood" characterizes the wolf as a cunning and savage beast.* **2** distinguish; mark out: *A camel is characterized by the humps on its back and its ability to go without water for several days. verb,* **char ac ter ized, char ac ter iz ing.**

char coal (chär′kōl′), a black, brittle form of carbon made by partly burning wood or bones in a place from which the air is shut out. Charcoal is used as fuel, in filters, and as a pencil for drawing. *noun.*

charge (chärj), **1** ask as a price; put a price of: *The grocer charged 75 cents a dozen for eggs.* **2** price; expense: *The charge for delivery is $3.* **3** put on record as a debt to be paid later: *We charged the table, so its cost will be included in our monthly bill from the department store.* **4** load or fill: *He charged the gun with powder and shot. The battery in our car was charged with electricity.* **5** amount needed to load or fill something; load. A gun is fired by exploding the charge of powder and shot. **6** give a task or duty to: *My parents charged me to take good care of the baby.* **7** task; duty: *I accepted the charge to take good care of my baby sister.* **8** care; management: *Doctors and nurses have charge of sick people.* **9** person or thing under the care of someone: *Sick people are the charges of doctors and nurses.* **10** direct: *She charged us to keep the plan secret. The judge charged the jury to come to a fair decision.* **11** order; command; direction: *a judge's charge to the jury to arrive at a verdict.* **12** accuse; blame: *The driver was charged with speeding.* **13** accusing: *He admitted the truth of the charge and paid a fine.* **14** rush at; attack: *The herd of elephants charged the hunters. The captain gave the order to charge.* **15** an attack: *The charge drove the enemy back.* 1,3,4,6,10,12,14 *verb,* **charged, charg ing;** 2,5,7-9,11,13,15 *noun.*

in charge, in command; responsible: *The mate is in charge when the captain leaves the ship.*

in charge of, having the care or management of; in command of; responsible for: *My mother is in charge of her company's art department.*

charg er (chär′jər), horse ridden in war. *noun.*

char i ot (char′ē ət), a two-wheeled carriage pulled by horses. The chariot was used in ancient times for fighting, for racing, and in processions. See picture. *noun.*

char i ta ble (char′ə tə bəl), **1** generous in giving to poor, sick, or helpless people: *He was a charitable man who used his wealth to help others.* **2** of charity; for charity: *The Salvation Army is a charitable organization.* **3** kindly in judging people and their actions: *Grandparents are usually charitable toward the mistakes of their grandchildren.* *adjective.*

char i ty (char′ə tē), **1** generous giving to the poor, or to organizations which look after the sick, the poor, and the helpless: *The charity of our citizens enabled the hospital to purchase new beds.* **2** fund or organization for helping the sick, the poor, and the helpless: *She gives money regularly to the Salvation Army and other charities.* **3** kindness in judging people's faults. *noun, plural* **char i ties.**

charm (chärm), **1** power of delighting or fascinating: *the charm of a cottage by the sea. The child's charm won our hearts.* **2** please greatly; delight: *They were charmed by the pet raccoon.* **3** a small ornament or trinket worn on a watch chain or bracelet. **4** word, verse, act, or thing supposed to have magic power to help or harm people. **5** act

on as if by magic: *Their laughter charmed away our troubles.* 1,3,4 *noun,* 2,5 *verb.*

charm ing (chär′ming), very pleasing; delightful; fascinating: *a charming flower garden. They are a charming couple.* *adjective.*

chart (chärt), **1** map. A sailor's chart shows the coasts, rocks, and shallow places of a sea. **2** sheet of information arranged in pictures, tables, or diagrams. **3** make a map or chart of: *The navigator charted the course of the ship.* 1,2 *noun,* 3 *verb.*

char ter (chär′tər), **1** a written grant of certain rights by a ruler to his or her subjects, or by a legislature to citizens or to companies formed to do special kinds of business: *The proposed new airline must obtain a government charter.* **2** give a charter to: *The government chartered the new airline.* **3** hire: *Our school chartered a bus to take the class to the zoo.* 1 *noun,* 2,3 *verb.*

chase (chās), **1** run after to catch or kill: *The cat chased the mouse.* **2** drive; drive away: *The blue jay chased the squirrel from its nest.* **3** follow; pursue: *The children chased the ball as it rolled downhill.* **4** act of running after to catch or kill: *We watched the children in their chase after butterflies.* **5** hunting as a sport; hunt: *The fox hunter was devoted to the chase.* **6** a hunted animal: *The chase escaped the hunter.* 1-3 *verb,* **chased, chas ing;** 4-6 *noun.*

chasm (kaz′əm), **1** a deep opening or crack in the earth. **2** wide difference of feeling or interests between two persons, two groups, or two parties: *The chasm between England and the American colonies grew until it finally resulted in the Revolutionary War.* *noun.*

chat (chat), **1** easy, familiar talk: *We had a pleasant chat about old times.* **2** talk in an easy, familiar way: *We sat chatting by the fire after supper.* 1 *noun,* 2 *verb,* **chat ted, chat ting.**

chat ter (chat′ər), **1** talk constantly and quickly about unimportant things: *The children chattered about the circus.* **2** constant, quick talk about unimportant things: *The pupils' chatter disturbed the classroom.* **3** make quick, indistinct sounds: *Monkeys chatter.* **4** quick, indistinct sounds: *She was awakened at dawn by the chatter of sparrows.* **5** rattle together: *Cold makes your teeth chatter.* 1,3,5 *verb,* 2,4 *noun.*

chat ty (chat′ē), fond of friendly, familiar talk. *adjective,* **chat ti er, chat ti est.**

chauf feur (shō′fər *or* shō fėr′), person whose work is driving an automobile. *noun.*

cheap (chēp), **1** costing little: *Potatoes are cheap at this time of year.* **2** costing less than it is worth: *My clothes are cheap, because I make them myself.* **3** charging low prices: *I bought the shoes at a very cheap store.* **4** easily obtained: *She thinks that the cheapest way to make friends is to give presents.* **5** common; of low value: *cheap jokes.* *adjective.*

cheap en (chēp′ən), make cheap; lower the value of. *verb.*

cheap ly (chēp′lē), at a low price; without spending much money or effort. *adverb.*

cheat (chēt), **1** deceive or trick; play or do business in a way that is not honest: *I hate to play* games with someone who cheats. **2** person who is not honest and does things to deceive and trick others. **3** fraud; trick. 1 *verb*, 2,3 *noun*.

check (chek), **1** stop suddenly: *The boys checked their steps.* **2** sudden stop: *The storm warning put a check to our plans for a picnic.* **3** hold back; control: *check one's anger.* **4** holding back; control: *It's often hard to keep a check on a quick temper.* **5** in hockey, a blocking of a player on the other team. **6** prove true or right by comparing: *Check your watch with the school clock.* **7** proving or proof by comparing: *My work will be a check on yours.* **8** mark (✓) to show that something has been looked at or compared. Often it shows that the thing looked at was found to be true or right. *I put a check beside the correct answers.* **9** write the mark (✓) next to: *The teacher corrected my spelling test and checked three wrong answers.* **10** a ticket or metal piece given in return for a coat, hat, baggage, or package to show ownership or the right to claim again later: *You will need this check to get your suitcase at the Chicago airport.* **11** get a check for; put a check on: *The hotel checked our baggage.* **12** a written order directing a bank to pay money to the person named: *My parents pay most of their bills by check.* **13** a written statement of the amount owed in a restaurant: *After we finished eating, the waiter brought the check to our table.* **14** pattern made of squares: *Do you want a check or a stripe for your new shirt?* **15** a single one of these squares: *The checks in this dress are big.* 1,3,6,9,11 *verb*, 2,4,5,7,8,10,12-15 *noun*.

check book (chek′bùk′), book of blank checks on a bank. *noun.*

check er board (chek′ər bôrd′), board marked in a pattern of 64 squares of two alternating colors, used in playing checkers or chess. *noun.*

check ers (chek′ərz), game played by two people, each with 12 flat, round pieces to move on a checkerboard. *noun.*

check up (chek′up′), **1** careful examination: *The manager gave the store a final checkup before closing for the night.* **2** thorough physical examination: *I went to the doctor for a checkup. noun.*

cheek (chēk), **1** side of the face below either eye. **2** rude talk or behavior; impudence: *They had the cheek to barge into line ahead of everyone. noun.*

cheep (chēp), **1** make a noise like a young bird; chirp; peep. **2** a young bird's cry. 1 *verb*, 2 *noun.*

cheer (chir), **1** a shout of encouragement and support or praise: *Give three cheers for the players who won the game.* **2** show praise and approval by cheers: *We all cheered loudly.* **3** urge on with cheers: *Everyone cheered our team.* **4** good spirits; hope; gladness: *The warmth of the fire and a good meal brought us cheer.* **5** give joy to; make glad; comfort: *It cheered me to have my friends visit me while I was sick.* 1,4 *noun*, 2,3,5 *verb.*

cheer up, brighten up; be or make glad; raise one's spirits: *Cheer up, perhaps we'll win next time.*

cheer ful (chir′fəl), **1** full of cheer; joyful; glad: *She is a smiling, cheerful girl.* **2** pleasant; bringing cheer: *This is a cheerful, sunny room.* **3** willing:

chariot—Roman chariot

cheetah—about 7 feet (2 meters) long with the tail

When my little brother wants to play he is not a very cheerful helper. adjective.

cheer i ly (chir′ə lē), in a cheerful or cheery manner. *adverb.*

cheer less (chir′lis), gloomy; dreary. *adjective.*

cheer y (chir′ē), cheerful; pleasant; bright; gay. *adjective,* **cheer i er, cheer i est.**

cheese (chēz), a solid food made from the curds of milk. *noun.*

chee tah (chē′tə), a flesh-eating animal that is somewhat like a leopard and is found in southern Asia and Africa. Cheetahs run very fast and can be taught to hunt deer and antelope. See picture. *noun.*

chef (shef), **1** a head cook: *the chef of a large restaurant.* **2** any cook. *noun.*

chem i cal (kem′ə kəl), **1** of chemistry: *Chemical research has made possible many new products.* **2** made by chemistry; used in chemistry: *Burning is a process of chemical change in which the oxygen of the air unites with wood or coal to give ashes, light, and heat.* **3** any substance used in chemistry. Acids, bases, and gases such as oxygen and hydrogen are chemicals. 1,2 *adjective*, 3 *noun.*

chem ist (kem′ist), person who is an expert in chemistry. See picture. *noun.*

chem is try (kem′ə strē), science that deals with the characteristics of simple substances (elements), the changes that take place when they combine to form other substances, and the laws of their behavior under various conditions. *noun.*

cher ish (cher′ish), **1** hold dear; treat with tenderness; aid or protect: *Parents cherish their children.* **2** keep in mind; cling to: *We cherished the hope of their safe return.* *verb.*

cher ry (cher′ē), **1** a small, round, juicy fruit with a stone or pit in it. Cherries grow on trees and are good to eat. **2** bright red: *cherry ribbons.* **1** *noun, plural* **cher ries; 2** *adjective.*

chess (ches), game played by two persons, each with 16 pieces. The pieces can be moved in various ways on a board having 64 squares of two alternating colors. See picture. *noun.*

chest (chest), **1** the front part of the body between the neck and the stomach. **2** large box with a lid, used for holding things: *a tool chest. noun.*

chest nut (ches′nut), **1** a sweet nut in a prickly bur. It is good to eat. **2** the tree it grows on. **3** the wood of this tree. **4** reddish brown. **1-3** *noun,* **4** *adjective.*

chew (chü), **1** crush or grind with the teeth: *We chew food.* **2** a bite. **1** *verb,* **2** *noun.*

chewing gum, gum for chewing. It is usually sweetened and flavored.

chew y (chü′ē), requiring much chewing: *chewy caramels. adjective,* **chew i er, chew i est.**

Chi ca no (chi kä′nō), an American of Mexican descent; Mexican American. *noun.*

chick (chik), **1** a young chicken. **2** a young bird. **3** child. *noun.*

chick a dee (chik′ə dē′), a small bird with black, white, and gray feathers. Its cry sounds somewhat like its name. *noun.*

chick en (chik′ən), **1** a common domestic fowl raised for food; hen or rooster. **2** a young hen or rooster. **3** any young bird. **4** the flesh of a chicken used for food: *fried chicken. noun.*

chick en pox (chik′ən poks′), a mild disease most often of children that causes a rash on the skin. You can catch chicken pox if you are around someone who has it.

chide (chīd), find fault with; blame; scold. *verb,* **chid ed** or **chid** (chid), **chid ing.**

chief (chēf), **1** head of a tribe or group; leader; person highest in rank or authority: *a chief of police.* **2** at the head; leading: *the chief engineer of a building project.* **3** most important; main: *the chief town in the county.* **1** *noun,* **2,3** *adjective.*

chief ly (chēf′lē), **1** mainly; mostly: *This juice is made chiefly of tomatoes.* **2** first of all; above all: *We visited Washington chiefly to see the Capitol and the White House. adverb.*

chief tain (chēf′tən), **1** chief of a clan or tribe: *a Scottish chieftain.* **2** head of a group; leader. *noun.*

child (chīld), **1** young boy or girl: *games for children.* **2** son or daughter: *She is our neighbor's child.* **3** baby. *noun, plural* **chil dren.**

chemist

chimpanzee—up to 4½ feet (1½ meters) tall when standing

chess

child hood (chīld/hu̇d), time during which one is a child. *noun.*

child ish (chīl/dish), **1** of or like a child: *childish games, childish chatter.* **2** not proper for a grown person; silly: *Crying for things you can't have is childish. adjective.*

chil dren (chil/drən), **1** young boys and girls. **2** sons and daughters: *Parents love their children. noun plural.*

chil i (chil/ē), a highly seasoned Mexican dish of chopped meat cooked with red peppers and, usually, beans. *noun.*

chill (chil), **1** unpleasant coldness: *There's a chill in the air today.* **2** unpleasantly cold: *A chill wind blew across the lake.* **3** make or become cold: *The icy wind chilled us to the bone. My blood chilled as I read the horror story.* **4** a sudden coldness of the body with shivering: *I had a chill yesterday and still feel ill.* 1,4 *noun,* 2 *adjective,* 3 *verb.*

chill y (chil/ē), **1** cold; unpleasantly cool: *It is a rainy, chilly day.* **2** cold in manner; unfriendly: *We gave a chilly reception to the people who came to our party uninvited. adjective,* **chill i er, chill i est.**

chime (chīm), **1** a set of bells tuned to the musical scale and played usually by hammers or simple machinery. **2** the music made by a set of tuned bells. **3** ring out musically: *The bells chimed at midnight.* 1,2 *noun,* 3 *verb,* **chimed, chim ing.**

chime in, join in a conversation, especially to express one's agreement: *I said I would like to go to a movie and my friends chimed in.*

chim ney (chim/nē), **1** an upright structure of brick or stone, connected with a fireplace or furnace, to make a draft and carry away smoke. **2** a glass tube placed around the flame of a lamp. *noun, plural* **chim neys.**

chimney sweep, person whose work is cleaning out chimneys.

chim pan zee (chim/pan zē/ *or* chim pan/zē), an African ape smaller than a gorilla. Chimpanzees are very intelligent. See picture. *noun.*

chin (chin), **1** the front of the lower jaw below the mouth. **2 chin oneself,** hang by the hands from an overhead bar and pull up until the chin is even with or above the bar. 1 *noun,* 2 *verb,* **chinned, chin ning.**

chi na (chī/nə), **1** a fine, white pottery made of clay baked by a special process, first used in China. Colored designs can be baked into china. **2** dishes, vases, or ornaments made of china. *noun.*

Chi na (chī/nə), a large country in eastern Asia. *noun.*

Chi nese (chī nēz/), **1** of or having something to do with China, its people, or their language. **2** person born or living in China. **3** language of China. 1 *adjective,* 2,3 *noun, plural* **Chi nese.**

chink (chingk), narrow opening; crack: *The chinks in the cabin let in wind and snow. noun.*

chip (chip), **1** a small, thin piece cut from wood or broken from stone or china: *They used chips of wood to light a fire.* **2** place in china or stone from which a small piece has been broken: *This plate*

has a chip on the edge. **3** cut or break off in small, thin pieces: *I chipped off the old paint. These cups chip if they are not handled carefully.* 1,2 *noun,* 3 *verb,* **chipped, chip ping.**

chip in, join with others in giving (money or help): *We all chipped in to buy our teacher a gift.*

chip munk (chip/mungk), a small, striped North American animal somewhat like a squirrel. It lives in a burrow in the ground. See picture. *noun.*

chipmunk—10 inches (25 centimeters) long with the tail

chirp (chėrp), **1** the short, sharp sound made by some small birds and insects: *the chirp of a sparrow.* **2** make a chirp: *The crickets chirped outside the house.* 1 *noun,* 2 *verb.*

chis el (chiz/əl), **1** tool with a sharp edge at the end of a strong blade. Chisels are used for shaping wood, stone, or metal. **2** cut or shape with a chisel: *The sculptor was at work chiseling a statue.* 1 *noun,* 2 *verb.*

chiv al ry (shiv/əl rē), **1** the qualities of an ideal knight in the Middle Ages; skill in fighting with arms, bravery, honor, protection of the weak, respect for women, and fairness to an enemy. **2** the rules, customs, and beliefs of knights in the Middle Ages. *noun.*

chlo rine (klôr/ēn/), a greenish-yellow, bad-smelling, poisonous gas, used as a bleach and disinfectant. Chlorine is very irritating to the nose and throat. *noun.*

chlo ro phyll (klôr/ə fil), the green coloring matter of plants. *noun.*

choc o late (chôk/lit *or* chôk/ə lit), **1** substance made by roasting and grinding cacao seeds. It has a strong, rich flavor and much value as food. **2** drink made of chocolate with hot milk or water and sugar. **3** candy made of chocolate. **4** made of or flavored with chocolate: *chocolate cake.* **5** dark brown. 1-3 *noun,* 4,5 *adjective.*

choice (chois), **1** act of choosing: *She was careful in her choice of friends.* **2** power or chance to choose: *I have my choice between a radio and a camera for my birthday.* **3** person or thing chosen: *This camera is my choice.* **4** quantity and variety to choose from: *We found a wide choice of vegetables in the market.* **5** excellent; of fine quality: *The choicest fruit had the highest price.* 1-4 *noun,* 5 *adjective,* **choic er, choic est.**

choir (kwīr), **1** group of singers who sing together in a church service. **2** part of a church set apart for the singers. **3** any group of singers. *noun.*

choke (chōk), **1** stop the breath of (an animal or person) by squeezing the throat or by blocking it up: *The smoke from the burning building almost choked the fireman.* **2** be unable to breathe: *I choked when a piece of meat stuck in my throat.* **3** act or sound of choking: *After a few chokes I got my breath.* **4** check or put out by cutting off air; smother: *A bucket of sand will choke a fire.* **5** hold; control: *She choked down her anger. He choked back a sharp remark. She choked her laughter with a cough.* **6** fill up or block: *Sand is choking the river.* 1,2,4-6 *verb,* **choked, chok ing;** 3 *noun.*

chol er a (kol'ər ə), a painful disease of the stomach and intestines that causes cramps and vomiting. *noun.*

choose (chüz), **1** pick out; select from a number: *Choose a book. She chose wisely.* **2** prefer and decide; think fit: *The cat did not choose to go out in the rain.* *verb,* **chose, cho sen, choos ing.**

chop[1] (chop), **1** cut by hitting with something sharp: *You can chop wood with an ax. I chopped down five trees.* **2** cut into small pieces: *to chop up cabbage.* **3** a cutting blow or stroke: *He felled the tree with one chop of his ax.* **4** slice of meat, especially of lamb, veal, or pork with a piece of rib. 1,2 *verb,* **chopped, chop ping;** 3,4 *noun.*

chop[2] (chop), jaw: *The cat licked the milk off its chops. noun.*

chop py (chop'ē), **1** jerky: *The speaker made nervous, choppy gestures.* **2** forming short, irregular, broken waves: *The wind made the water choppy. adjective,* **chop pi er, chop pi est.**

chop sticks (chop'stiks'), pair of small slender sticks used by Oriental people to eat solid food with. *noun plural.*

chord (kôrd), a combination of two or more notes of music sounded at the same time in harmony. *noun.*

chore (chôr), odd job; small task: *Feeding my pets is my daily chore. noun.*

cho rus (kôr'əs), **1** group of singers who sing together, such as a choir: *Our school chorus gave a concert at the town hall.* **2** song sung by many singers together. A chorus is often a part of an opera. **3** the repeated part of a song coming after each stanza: *Everybody knew the chorus by heart.* **4** sing or speak all at the same time: *The birds were chorusing around me.* **5** a saying by many at the same time: *My question was answered by a chorus of "no's."* **6** group of singers and dancers. 1-3,5,6 *noun, plural* **cho rus es;** 4 *verb.*

chose (chōz). See **choose.** *She chose the red dress. verb.*

cho sen (chō'zn), **1** See **choose.** *Have you chosen a book from the library?* **2** picked out; selected from a group: *Six chosen scouts marched in front of the parade.* 1 *verb,* 2 *adjective.*

chow der (chou'dər), a thick soup made of clams or fish with potatoes, onions, and milk. *noun.*

Christ (krīst), Jesus, the founder of the Christian religion. *noun.*

chris ten (kris'n), **1** give a first name to (a person) at baptism: *The child was christened Maria.* **2** give a name to: *The new ship was christened before it was launched.* **3** baptize as a Christian. *verb.*

chris ten ing (kris'n ing), baptism; act or ceremony of baptizing and naming. *noun.*

Chris tian (kris'chən), **1** person who believes in Christ and follows His teachings. **2** believing in or belonging to the religion of Christ: *the Christian church, Christian countries.* **3** showing a gentle, humble, helpful spirit: *Christian kindness.* **4** of Christ, His teachings, or His followers: *the Christian faith.* 1 *noun,* 2-4 *adjective.*

Chris ti an i ty (kris'chē an'ə tē), the religion based on the teachings of Christ as they appear in the Bible. *noun.*

Christ mas (kris'məs), the yearly celebration of the birth of Christ on December 25. *noun, plural* **Christ mas es.**

Christmas tree, an evergreen tree hung with decorations at Christmas time.

chrome (krōm), chromium. *noun.*

chro mi um (krō'mē əm), a grayish, hard, brittle metal that does not rust or become dull easily. Chromium is used in alloys, for making dyes and paints, and in photography. *noun.*

chron ic (kron'ik), lasting a long time: *a chronic disease. adjective.*

chron i cle (kron'ə kəl), **1** record of happenings in the order in which they happened; history; story: *Columbus kept a chronicle of his voyages.* **2** write the history of; tell the story of: *Many of the old monks chronicled the Crusades.* 1 *noun,* 2 *verb,* **chron i cled, chron i cling.**

chry san the mum (krə san'thə məm), a round flower with many petals, which blossoms in the fall. *noun.*

chub by (chub'ē), round and plump: *chubby cheeks. adjective,* **chub bi er, chub bi est.**

chuck le (chuk'əl), **1** laugh softly or quietly: *She chuckled to herself.* **2** a soft laugh; quiet laughter. 1 *verb,* **chuck led, chuck ling;** 2 *noun.*

chuck wag on (chuk' wag'ən), (in the western United States) a wagon or truck that carries food and cooking equipment for cowhands or harvest workers.

chug (chug), **1** short, loud burst of sound: *We heard the chug of a steam engine.* **2** make such sounds. 1 *noun,* 2 *verb,* **chugged, chug ging.**

chum (chum), **1** very close friend. **2** be on very friendly terms. 1 *noun,* 2 *verb,* **chummed, chum ming.**

chunk (chungk), thick piece or lump: *I ate two large chunks of candy. noun.*

chunk y (chung'kē), **1** like a chunk; short and

a hat	**i** it	**oi** oil	**ch** child	a in about
ā age	**ī** ice	**ou** out	**ng** long	e in taken
ä far	**o** hot	**u** cup	**sh** she	ə = { i in pencil
e let	**ō** open	**ů** put	**th** thin	o in lemon
ē equal	**ô** order	**ü** rule	**ŦH** then	u in circus
ėr term			**zh** measure	

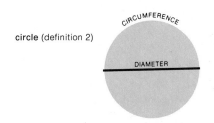

circle (definition 2)

churn (definition 1)

thick: *a chunky log.* **2** stocky: *The child had a chunky build. adjective,* **chunk i er, chunk i est.**

church (chėrch), **1** a building for public Christian worship: *The church was full on Sunday morning.* **2** public worship of God in a church: *Don't be late for church.* **3** group of persons with the same religious beliefs and under the same authority; denomination. *noun, plural* **church es.** [*Church* comes from Greek words meaning "the Lord's house."]

church yard (chėrch′yärd′), the ground around a church. A churchyard is sometimes used for a burial ground. *noun.*

churn (chėrn), **1** container or machine in which butter is made from cream by beating and shaking. See picture. **2** beat and shake (cream) in a churn. **3** move as if beaten and shaken: *The water churns in the rapids.* **1** *noun,* **2,3** *verb.*

chute (shüt), a steep slide. There are chutes for carrying mail, soiled clothes, and coal to a lower level. A toboggan slide is called a chute. *noun.*

ci der (sī′dər), juice pressed out of apples, used as a drink and in making vinegar. *noun.*

ci gar (sə gär′), tight roll of tobacco leaves for smoking. *noun.*

cig a rette (sig′ə ret′), a small roll of finely cut tobacco enclosed in a thin sheet of paper for smoking. *noun.*

cinch (sinch), **1** a strong girth for fastening a saddle or pack on a horse. **2** fasten on with a cinch; bind firmly. **1** *noun, plural* **cinch es; 2** *verb.*

cin der (sin′dər), **1** piece of wood or coal partly burned and no longer flaming. **2** burned-up wood or coal; ash. Cinders are made up of larger and coarser pieces than ashes are. *noun.*

cin e ma (sin′ə mə), **1** a motion picture. **2** a motion-picture theater. *noun.*

cin na mon (sin′ə mən), **1** spice made from the inner bark of a tree growing in the East Indies. **2** the tree itself. **3** light reddish brown: *a cinnamon bear.* **1,2** *noun,* **3** *adjective.*

cir cle (sėr′kəl), **1** a round line. Every point on a circle is the same distance from the center. **2** a figure bounded by such a line. See picture. **3** anything shaped like a circle or part of one: *a circle around the moon.* **4** ring: *We sat in a circle around the teacher.* **5** go around in a circle: *The plane circled until the fog lifted and it was able to land. We circled the town trying to find the road to your house.* **6** form a circle around; surround: *A ring of trees circled the clearing.* **7** complete series: *A year is a circle of twelve months.* **8** group of people held together by the same interests: *the family circle, a circle of friends.* **1-4,7,8** *noun,* **5,6** *verb,* **cir cled, cir cling.**

cir cuit (sėr′kit), **1** a going around; a moving around: *The earth takes a year to make its circuit of the sun.* **2** route over which a person or group makes repeated journeys at certain times: *Some judges make a circuit, stopping at certain towns along the way to hold court.* **3** the part of the country through which such journeys are made. **4** the path over which an electric current flows. *noun.*

circuit breaker, switch that automatically breaks an electric circuit when the current gets too strong.

cir cu lar (sėr′kyə lər), **1** round like a circle: *The full moon has a circular shape.* **2** moving in a circle: *A merry-go-round makes a circular trip.* **3** letter, notice, or advertisement sent to each of a number of people. **1,2** *adjective,* **3** *noun.*

cir cu late (sėr′kyə lāt), **1** go around: *A newspaper circulates among the people who read it. Water circulates in the pipes of a building. Money circulates as it goes from person to person.* **2** send around from person to person or place to place: *The children circulated the news of the holiday.* **3** flow from the heart through the arteries and veins back to the heart. *verb,* **cir cu lat ed, cir cu lat ing.**

cir cu la tion (sėr′kyə lā′shən), **1** a going around; circulating: *Open windows increase the circulation of air in a room.* **2** the flow of the blood from the heart through the arteries and veins and back to the heart. **3** a sending around of books, papers, or news from person to person or place to place. *noun.*

cir cu la to ry (sėr'kyə lə tôr'ē), having something to do with circulation. Arteries and veins are parts of the circulatory system of the human body. *adjective.*

cir cum fer ence (sər kum'fər əns), the distance around a circle: *The circumference of the earth at the equator is almost 25,000 miles. noun.*

cir cum nav i gate (sėr'kəm nav'ə gāt), sail around: *Magellan's ship circumnavigated the earth. verb,* **cir cum nav i gat ed, cir cum nav i gat ing.**

cir cum stance (sėr'kəm stans), **1** condition that accompanies an act or event: *What were the circumstances that made you change your mind?* **2** fact or event: *It was a lucky circumstance that she found her money.* **3 circumstances,** state of affairs: *A rich person is in good circumstances; a poor person is in bad circumstances. noun.*

cir cus (sėr'kəs), **1** a traveling show of acrobats, clowns, horses, riders, and wild animals. The performers who give the show and the show that they give are both called the circus. **2** a round or oval space with seats around it in rows, each row higher than the one in front of it. *noun, plural* **cir cus es.**

cit a del (sit'ə dəl), **1** fortress, especially one in a city. **2** a strongly fortified place; stronghold. *noun.*

ci ta tion (sī tā'shən), **1** honorable mention for bravery in war: *The soldier received a citation from the President.* **2** quotation. *noun.*

cite (sīt), **1** quote: *She cited the United States Constitution to prove her statement.* **2** refer to; mention; bring up as an example: *Can you cite another case like this one? verb,* **cit ed, cit ing.**

cit i zen (sit'ə zən), **1** person who by birth or choice is a member of a nation. A citizen owes loyalty to that nation and is given certain rights by it. *Many immigrants have become citizens of the United States.* **2** inhabitant of a city or town. *noun.*

cit i zen ry (sit'ə zən rē), citizens as a group. *noun, plural* **cit i zen ries.**

cit i zen ship (sit'ə zən ship), the duties, rights, and privileges of a citizen. *noun.*

cit rus (sit'rəs), any tree bearing lemons, limes, oranges, grapefruit, or similar fruits. *noun, plural* **cit rus es.**

cit y (sit'ē), **1** a large, important center of population and business activity. New York, Buenos Aires, London, Cairo, and Shanghai are major world cities. **2** the people living in a city: *The city was alarmed by the great fire.* **3** of a city. **4** in a city. **1,2** *noun, plural* **cit ies; 3,4** *adjective.*

civ ic (siv'ik), **1** of a city: *She is interested in civic affairs and will be a candidate for mayor.* **2** of citizenship. A person's civic duties include such things as obeying the laws, voting, and paying taxes. **3** of citizens. *adjective.*

civ ics (siv'iks), study of the duties, rights, and privileges of citizens. *noun.*

civ il (siv'əl), **1** of a citizen or citizens; having something to do with citizens: *civil duties.* **2** not naval, military, or connected with the church: *The accused soldier was tried in a civil rather than in a military court. The bride and groom had both a civil and a religious marriage ceremony.* **3** polite; courteous: *It was hard for me to give a civil answer to their rude question. adjective.*

ci vil ian (sə vil'yən), **1** person who is not a member of any of the armed forces. **2** of civilians; not military or naval: *Soldiers on leave usually wear civilian clothes.* **1** *noun,* **2** *adjective.*

civ i li za tion (siv'ə lə zā'shən), **1** civilized condition. **2** the ways of living of a people or nation: *There are differences between Chinese civilization and our own. noun.*

civ i lize (siv'ə līz), change from a primitive way of life. Civilized people usually have a written language and an advanced knowledge of agriculture, the sciences, and the arts. *verb,* **civ i lized, civ i liz ing.**

civil rights, the rights of every citizen of the United States, of whatever race, color, religion, or sex.

civil service, branch of government service concerned with affairs not military, naval, legislative, or judicial. It includes all civilian government workers who are appointed rather than elected. Forest rangers and postal service employees belong to the United States civil service.

civil war, war between opposing groups of citizens of one nation.

clack (klak), **1** make a short, sharp sound: *The train clacked over the rails.* **2** short, sharp sound: *We could hear the clack of typewriters in the office next to us.* **1** *verb,* **2** *noun.*

clad (klad), clothed. See **clothe.** *He was clad all in green. verb.*

claim (klām), **1** demand as one's own or one's right: *The settlers claimed the land as theirs. Does anyone claim this pencil?* **2** such a demand: *She makes a claim to the pencil.* **3** a right or title to a thing; a right to demand something: *She has a legal claim to the property. There are too many claims on my time.* **4** piece of land which someone claims: *a miner's claim.* **5** require; call for; deserve: *This homework claims all of my attention.* **6** say strongly; maintain; declare as a fact: *She claimed that her answer was correct.* **7** declaration of something as a fact: *Careful study showed that the claims that the vaccine would prevent polio were correct.* **1,5,6** *verb,* **2-4,7** *noun.*

clam (klam), **1** shellfish with a soft body and a shell in two hinged halves. Clams burrow in sand along the seashore, or at the edges of rivers and lakes. Many kinds are good to eat. **2** go out after clams; dig for clams. **1** *noun,* **2** *verb,* **clammed, clam ming.**

clam bake (klam'bāk'), picnic where clams are baked or steamed. *noun.*

clam ber (klam'bər), climb, using both hands and feet; scramble: *We clambered up the cliff. verb.*

clam my (klam'ē), cold and damp: *A frog is a clammy creature. adjective,* **clam mi er, clam mi est.**

clam or (klam′ər), **1** loud noise, especially of voices; confused shouting: *The clamor of the crowd filled the air.* **2** make a loud noise. **3** noisy demand. **4** demand or ask for noisily. 1,3 *noun,* 2,4 *verb.*

clamp (klamp), **1** brace, band, wedge, or other device for holding things tightly together: *I used a clamp to hold the arm on the chair until the glue dried.* See picture. **2** fasten together with a clamp; fix in a clamp; strengthen with clamps: *A picture frame must be clamped together while the glue is drying.* 1 *noun,* 2 *verb.*

clamp down, become more strict: *The police clamped down on speeders.*

clan (klan), group of related families that claim to be descended from a common ancestor. *noun.*

clang (klang), **1** a loud, harsh, ringing sound like metal being hit: *The clang of the fire bell aroused the town.* **2** make a loud, harsh, resounding sound: *The fire bells clanged.* **3** cause to clang: *The firemen clanged the bell on the fire truck.* 1 *noun,* 2,3 *verb.*

clank (klangk), **1** a sharp, harsh sound like the rattle of a heavy chain: *The clank of heavy machinery filled the factory.* **2** make such a sound: *The steel door clanked shut.* 1 *noun,* 2 *verb.*

clap (klap), **1** strike together loudly: *clap one's hands.* **2** applaud by striking the hands together: *When the show was over, we all clapped.* **3** a sudden noise, such as a single burst of thunder, the sound of the hands struck together, or the sound of a loud slap. **4** strike with a quick blow: *My friend clapped me on the back.* **5** a loud, quick blow; slap: *a clap on the shoulder.* 1,2,4 *verb,* **clapped, clap ping;** 3,5 *noun.*

clap per (klap′ər), the movable part inside a bell that strikes against and rings the outer part. *noun.*

clar i fy (klar′ə fī), **1** make clearer; explain: *The teacher's explanation clarified the difficult instructions.* **2** make or become clear: *The cook clarified the fat by heating it with a little water and straining it through cloth.* *verb,* **clar i fied, clar i fy ing.**

clar i net (klar′ə net′), a wooden wind instrument played by means of holes and keys. See picture. *noun.*

clar i ty (klar′ə tē), clearness: *He expresses his ideas with great clarity. noun.*

clash (klash), **1** a loud, harsh sound like that of two things running into each other, of striking metal, or of bells rung together but not in tune: *the clash of cymbals.* **2** hit with a clash: *The metal gate clashed shut.* **3** a strong disagreement; a conflict: *There were many clashes of opinion between the opposing candidates.* **4** disagree strongly; conflict; go badly together: *Your red shirt and purple pants clash with each other.* 1,3 *noun, plural* **clash es;** 2,4 *verb.*

clasp (klasp), **1** a thing to fasten two parts or pieces together. A buckle on a belt is one kind of clasp. **2** fasten together with a clasp. **3** hold closely with the arms; embrace: *She clasped the kitten tenderly.* **4** a close hold with the arms: *The hunter escaped from the bear's clasp.* **5** grip firmly

a hat	i it	oi oil	ch child	(a in about
ā age	ī ice	ou out	ng long	e in taken
ä far	o hot	u cup	sh she	ə = { i in pencil
e let	ō open	ú put	th thin	o in lemon
ē equal	ô order	ü rule	ŦH then	u in circus
ėr term			zh measure	

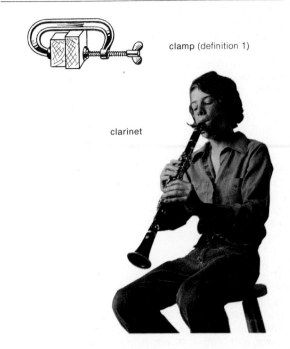

clamp (definition 1)

clarinet

with the hand; grasp: *I clasped the railing as I climbed the stairs.* **6** a firm grip with the hand: *He gave my hand a warm clasp.* 1,4,6 *noun,* 2,3,5 *verb.*

class (klas), **1** group of persons or things alike in some way; kind; sort. **2** group of pupils taught together: *an art class.* **3** meeting of such a group: *She was absent and missed a great many classes.* **4** group of pupils entering a school together and graduating in the same year: *The class of 1972 graduates in 1972.* **5** rank of society: *the upper class, the middle class, the lower class.* **6** put in a class; classify: *She is classed among the best swimmers in the school.* **7** grade or quality: *The class of work you do determines your mark in school.* 1-5,7 *noun, plural* **class es;** 6 *verb.*

clas sic (klas′ik), **1** an author or an artist of acknowledged excellence: *Shakespeare is a classic.* **2** a fine book or painting produced by such a person: *"Alice in Wonderland" is a classic.* **3** of the highest rank or quality; excellent: *a classic author.* **4** simple and fine in form: *the classic style of Bach's music.* **5** **the classics,** the literature of ancient Greece and Rome. 1,2,5 *noun,* 3,4 *adjective.*

clas si cal (klas′ə kəl), **1** of or having to do with the literature, art, and life of ancient Greece and Rome: *Classical languages include ancient Greek and the Latin of the ancient Romans.* **2** excellent; first-class. **3** simple and fine in form. **4** of high musical quality. Symphonies, concertos, and operas are considered classical music. *adjective.*

clas si fi ca tion (klas′ə fə kā′shən), arrangement in classes or groups; grouping according to some system: *The classification of books in a library helps you to find the books you want.* noun.

clas si fy (klas′ə fī), arrange in groups or classes: *In the post office mail is classified according to the places where it is to go.* verb, **clas si fied, clas si fy ing.**

class mate (klas′māt′), member of the same class in school. noun.

class room (klas′rüm′), room in which classes are held; schoolroom. noun.

clat ter (klat′ər), **1** confused noise like that of many plates being struck together: *The clatter in the school cafeteria made it hard to hear one another talk.* **2** move or fall with confused noise; make a confused noise: *The horse's hoofs clattered over the stones.* **3** noisy talk. **4** talk fast and noisily. 1,3 noun, 2,4 verb.

clause (klôz), **1** part of a sentence having a subject and a verb. In "He came before we left," "He came" is a main clause, and "before we left" is a subordinate clause that depends upon the main clause for completion of its meaning. **2** a single provision of a law, a treaty, or any other written agreement; short sentence: *There is a clause in our lease that says we may not keep a dog in this building.* noun.

claw (klô), **1** a sharp, hooked nail on a bird's or animal's foot. **2** a foot with such sharp, hooked nails. **3** the pincers of a lobster or crab. **4** anything like a claw. The part of a hammer used for pulling nails is the claw. **5** scratch, tear, seize, or pull with claws or hands: *The kitten was clawing the screen door.* 1-4 noun, 5 verb.

clay (klā), a sticky kind of earth that can be easily shaped when wet and hardens when it is dried or baked. Bricks and dishes are made from various kinds of clay. noun.

clean (klēn), **1** free from dirt or filth; not soiled or stained: *clean clothes. Soap and water make us clean.* **2** innocent; without guilt; free from wrong: *He served in politics for many years and had a clean record.* **3** having habits that keep one free of dirt: *Cats are clean animals.* **4** make free from dirt or filth: *Washing cleans clothes. Clean up the yard.* **5** make things free of dirt: *I'm going to clean this morning.* **6** clear, even, or regular: *a clean cut with no ragged edges, the clean features of a handsome face.* **7** well-shaped; trim: *an airplane with clean, sleek lines.* **8** complete; entire; total: *After he lost his job, he made a clean break with the friends he had at work.* **9** completely; entirely; totally: *The horse jumped clean over the brook.* 1-3,6-8 adjective, 4,5 verb, 9 adverb.

clean er (klē′nər), **1** person whose work is keeping buildings, windows, or other objects clean. **2** anything that removes dirt, grease, or stains. noun.

clean li ness (klen′lē nis), cleanness; being always, or nearly always, clean: *Cleanliness is good for health.* noun.

clean ly[1] (klen′lē), clean; always, or nearly always,

clipper (definition 2)

cleaver

clinch (definition 4)—boxers in a clinch

clean: *A cat is a cleanly animal.* adjective, **clean li er, clean li est.**

clean ly[2] (klēn′lē), in a clean manner: *The butcher's knife cut cleanly through the meat.* adverb.

cleanse (klenz), **1** make clean: *cleanse a wound before bandaging.* **2** make pure: *cleanse the soul.* verb, **cleansed, cleans ing.**

cleans er (klen′zər), substance that cleans. Soap and water are good cleansers. Detergents are cleansers. noun.

clear (klir), **1** clean and free from anything that makes it hard to see or understand: *A clear sky is free from clouds. The witness gave a clear account of the accident.* **2** make clean and free; get clear: *After dinner, we cleared the table.* **3** become clear: *It rained and then it cleared.* **4** pass by or over without touching: *The horse cleared the fence.* **5** in a clear manner; clearly; distinctly; entirely: *We could see* *clear to the bottom of the lake.* 1 *adjective,* 2-4 *verb,* 5 *adverb.*

clear up, explain: *She cleared up our problem by showing us what we had done wrong.*

clear ance (klir′əns), **1** act of clearing: *Clearance of the theater was quick during the fire.* **2** a clear space: *There was only a foot of clearance between the top of the truck and the roof of the tunnel. noun.*

clear ing (klir′ing), an open space of cleared land in a forest. *noun.*

cleat (klēt), **1** strip of wood or iron fastened across anything for support or for sure footing: *The gangplank had cleats to keep the passengers from slipping.* **2** piece of metal, wood, stiff leather, or plastic fastened to the sole or heel of a shoe to prevent slipping. *noun.*

cleave[1] (klēv), cut or split open: *A blow of the whale's tail caused the whaling boat to cleave in two.* *verb,* **cleft** or **cleaved** or **clove, cleft** or **cleaved** or **clo ven, cleav ing.**

cleave[2] (klēv), hold fast; cling: *cleave to an old-fashioned idea.* *verb,* **cleaved, cleav ing.**

cleav er (klē′vər), a butcher's tool with a heavy blade and a short handle, used for cutting through meat or bone. See picture. *noun.*

clef (klef), symbol in music indicating the pitch of the notes on a staff. *noun.*

cleft (kleft), **1** cut. See **cleave**[1]. *A blow of the ax cleft the log in two.* **2** split; divided: *a cleft stick.* **3** space or opening made by splitting; crack: *a cleft in the rocks.* 1 *verb,* 2 *adjective,* 3 *noun.*

clem en cy (klem′ən sē), **1** mercy: *The judge showed clemency to the prisoner.* **2** mildness: *The clemency of the weather allowed them to live outdoors. noun, plural* **clem en cies.**

clench (klench), **1** close tightly together: *to clench one's teeth, to clench one's hand, a clenched fist.* **2** grasp firmly: *I clenched her arm in terror.* **3** a firm grasp; tight grip: *I felt the clench of his hand on my arm as I began to slip.* **4** clinch (a nail or staple). 1,2,4 *verb,* 3 *noun, plural* **clench es.**

cler gy (klėr′jē), persons ordained for religious work; ministers, pastors, priests, and rabbis. *noun, plural* **cler gies.**

cler gy man (klėr′jē mən), member of the clergy; a minister, pastor, priest, or rabbi. *noun, plural* **cler gy men.**

clerk (klėrk), **1** person employed to sell goods in a store or shop. **2** person employed in an office to file records, copy letters, or keep accounts. **3** work as a clerk: *I clerk in a drugstore after school.* 1,2 *noun,* 3 *verb.*

clev er (klev′ər), **1** bright; intelligent; having a ready mind: *She is the cleverest person in our class.* **2** skillful in doing some particular thing: *My friend is clever at working with wood.* **3** showing skill or intelligence: *The magician did a clever trick. His answer to the riddle was clever. adjective.*

click (klik), **1** a short, sharp sound like that of a key turning in a lock: *I heard a click as the dime went down the coin slot.* **2** make such a sound: *The key clicked in the lock.* 1 *noun,* 2 *verb.*

cli ent (klī′ənt), **1** person for whom a lawyer,

accountant, or other professional person acts. **2** customer. *noun.*

cliff (klif), a very steep slope of rock or clay. *noun.*

cli mate (klī′mit), **1** the kind of weather a place has. Climate includes conditions of heat and cold, moisture and dryness, clearness and cloudiness, wind and calm. **2** a region with certain conditions of heat and cold, rainfall, wind, or sunlight: *We went to a warmer climate on our winter vacation. noun.*

cli max (klī′maks), the highest point of interest; the most exciting part: *A visit to the Grand Canyon was the climax of our trip. noun, plural* **cli max es.**

climb (klīm), **1** go up, especially by using the hands or feet, or both: *She climbed the stairs quickly.* **2** go in any direction, especially with the help of the hands: *climb over a fence, climb down a ladder.* **3** grow upward. A vine climbs by twining about a support of some kind. **4** act of going up: *Our climb took two hours.* **5** move upward; rise: *Smoke climbed slowly from the chimney. The price of sugar climbed last year.* **6** place to be climbed: *The path ended in a difficult climb.* 1-3,5 *verb,* 4,6 *noun.*

clime (klīm), **1** region. **2** climate. *noun.*

clinch (klinch), **1** fasten (a nail that sticks through something) firmly by bending over the point that sticks out. **2** fasten firmly; settle decisively: *A deposit of five dollars clinched the bargain.* **3** hold on to each other tightly in boxing or wrestling. **4** act of clinching. See picture. 1-3 *verb,* 4 *noun, plural* **clinch es.**

cling (kling), stick or hold fast: *A vine clings to its support. Wet clothes cling to the body. Some people cling to old-fashioned ideas.* *verb,* **clung, cling ing.**

clin ic (klin′ik), place where people can receive medical treatment, usually free or at low cost. A clinic is connected with a hospital or medical school: *an eye clinic, a dental clinic. noun.*

clink (klingk), **1** a light, sharp, ringing sound, like that of glasses hitting together. **2** make a sharp, ringing sound: *The spoon clinked in the glass.* 1 *noun,* 2 *verb.*

clip[1] (klip), **1** cut; cut short; trim with shears or scissors: *A sheep's fleece is clipped off to get wool.* **2** cut the hair or fleece of: *Our dog is clipped every summer.* **3** cut out of a newspaper or magazine: *She clipped the cartoon and passed it around the class.* **4** fast motion: *The bus passed at quite a clip.* 1-3 *verb,* **clipped, clip ping;** 4 *noun.*

clip[2] (klip), **1** hold tight; fasten: *I clipped the papers together.* **2** something used for clipping things together. A paper clip is made of a piece of bent wire. 1 *verb,* **clipped, clip ping;** 2 *noun.*

clip per (klip′ər), **1** tool for cutting: *hair clippers, a nail clipper.* **2** a fast sailing ship: *American clippers used to sail all over the world.* See picture. *noun.*

clip ping (klip′ing), piece cut out of a newspaper or magazine. *noun.*

clique (klēk), a small, exclusive group of people within a larger group. *noun.*

cloak (klōk), 1 loose outer garment with or without sleeves. 2 anything that covers or hides: *They hid their dislike of us behind a cloak of friendship.* 3 cover up; conceal: *I cloaked my fear by pretending to be unafraid.* 1,2 *noun,* 3 *verb.*

clock (klok), instrument for measuring and showing time. A clock is not made to be carried about as a watch is. *noun.* [*Clock* comes from a Latin word meaning "bell." It was called this because bells were used to mark the hours before the invention of modern clocks.]

clock wise (klok′wīz′), in the direction in which the hands of a clock move: *Turn the key clockwise to unlock the door.* *adverb, adjective.*

clock work (klok′wėrk′), machinery of a clock or like that of a clock. Toys that move are often run by clockwork. *noun.*

clod (klod), 1 lump of earth. 2 a stupid person. *noun.*

clog (klog), 1 fill up; choke up: *Grease clogged the drain.* 2 hold back; hinder: *An accident clogged traffic.* 3 shoe with a thick, wooden sole. 1,2 *verb,* **clogged, clog ging;** 3 *noun.*

clois ter (kloi′stər), 1 a covered walk along the wall of a building, with a row of pillars on the open side. A cloister is often built around the courtyard of a monastery, church, or college building. 2 convent or monastery. *noun.*

clone (klōn), 1 an animal or plant produced from one parent, often from a single cell. Parent and offspring have the same hereditary characteristics and are, therefore, exactly alike. 2 produce from a single parent. 1 *noun,* 2 *verb,* **cloned, clon ing.**

close[1] (klōz), 1 shut: *Close the door. The sleepy child's eyes are closing.* 2 bring together; come together: *The troops closed ranks.* 3 come or bring to an end: *The meeting closed with a speech by the president.* 4 end: *She spoke at the close of the meeting.* 1-3 *verb,* **closed, clos ing;** 4 *noun.*

close[2] (klōs), 1 with little space between; near together; near: *These two houses are close. That cloth has a close weave.* 2 tight; narrow: *They live in very close quarters.* 3 having little fresh air: *With the windows shut, the room was hot and close.* 4 stingy: *They were selfish and close with their money.* 5 nearly equal: *The last game was a close contest.* *adjective,* **clos er, clos est.**

close ly (klōs′lē), 1 with little difference; to a close degree; greatly: *She closely resembles her sister.* 2 snugly; tightly: *My coat fits closely.* *adverb.*

clos et (kloz′it), a small room used for storing clothes or household supplies. *noun.*

clot (klot), 1 half-solid lump: *A clot of blood formed in the cut and stopped the bleeding.* 2 form into clots: *Blood clots when it is exposed to the air.* 1 *noun,* 2 *verb,* **clot ted, clot ting.**

cloth (klôth), 1 woven or knitted material made from wool, cotton, silk, rayon, or other fiber. Cloth is used for clothing, curtains, bedding, and many other purposes. 2 piece of cloth used for a special purpose: *a cloth for the table.* *noun, plural* **cloths** (klôᴛʜz *or* klôths).

clothe (klōᴛʜ), 1 put clothes on; cover with clothes; dress: *I clothed the child warmly in a heavy sweater and pants.* 2 provide with clothes: *to clothe one's family.* 3 cover: *The sun clothes the earth with light.* *verb,* **clothed** *or* **clad, cloth ing.**

clothes (klōz), coverings for the body: *I bought a jacket, jeans, and other clothes.* *noun plural.*

clothes pin (klōz′pin′), wooden or plastic clip to hold clothes on a line. *noun.*

cloth ing (klō′ᴛʜing), clothes. *noun.*

cloud (kloud), 1 a white or gray or almost black mass in the sky, made up of tiny drops of water or ice crystals: *Sometimes when it rains, the sky is covered with dark clouds.* 2 mass of smoke or dust in the air. 3 cover with a cloud or clouds: *A mist clouded our view.* 4 grow cloudy: *eyes clouded with tears.* 5 anything like a cloud: *a cloud of birds in flight.* We may speak of a person as being under a cloud of disgrace or suspicion. 6 make dark; become gloomy: *His face clouded with anger.* 1,2,5 *noun,* 3,4,6 *verb.*

cloud burst (kloud′bėrst′), a sudden, violent rainfall. *noun.*

cloud less (kloud′lis), clear and bright; sunny: *a cloudless sky.* *adjective.*

cloud y (klou′dē), 1 covered with clouds; having clouds in it: *a cloudy sky.* 2 not clear: *a cloudy liquid.* *adjective,* **cloud i er, cloud i est.**

clout (klout), 1 a rap or knock: *She gave her brother a clout.* 2 hit: *I clouted the ball.* 1 *noun,* 2 *verb.*

clove[1] (klōv), a strong, fragrant spice, made from the dried flower buds of a tropical tree. *noun.*

clove[2] (klōv). See cleave[1]. *With one blow of the ax I clove the log in two.* *verb.*

clo ven (klō′vən), 1 cleft. See cleave[1]. 2 split; divided into two parts: *Cows have cloven hoofs.* 1 *verb,* 2 *adjective.*

clo ver (klō′vər), a plant with leaves of three small leaflets and sweet-smelling rounded heads of red, white, or purple flowers. Clover is grown as food for livestock and to make the soil richer. *noun.*

clown (kloun), 1 person who makes a business of making people laugh by tricks and jokes: *The clowns in the circus were very funny.* See picture. 2 act like a clown; play tricks and jokes; act silly. 3 person who acts like a clown; silly person. 1,3 *noun,* 2 *verb.*

club (klub), 1 a heavy stick of wood, thicker at one end, used as a weapon. 2 a stick or bat used to hit a ball in some games: *golf clubs.* 3 beat or hit with a club or something similar. 4 group of people joined together for some special purpose: *a tennis club.* 5 building or rooms used by a club. 1,2,4,5 *noun,* 3 *verb,* **clubbed, club bing.**

cluck (kluk), 1 the sound that a hen makes when calling to her chickens. 2 make such a sound. 1 *noun,* 2 *verb.*

clue (klü), fact or object which aids in solving a mystery or problem: *The police could find no*

clown

a hat	i it	oi oil	ch child	a in about
ā age	ī ice	ou out	ng long	e in taken
ä far	o hot	u cup	sh she	ə = i in pencil
e let	ō open	u̇ put	th thin	o in lemon
ē equal	ô order	ü rule	ŦH then	u in circus
ėr term			zh measure	

fingerprints or other clues to help them in solving the robbery. *noun.*

clump (klump), **1** cluster: *I hid in a clump of trees.* **2** walk with a heavy, clumsy, noisy tread: *The hiker clumped along in heavy boots.* 1 *noun,* 2 *verb.*

clum sy (klum′zē), **1** awkward in moving: *The cast on my broken leg made me clumsy.* **2** not well-shaped or well-made: *Our boat was a clumsy affair made out of scrap wood. adjective,* **clum si er, clum si est.**

clung (klung). See **cling.** *The child clung to her mother. The mud had clung to my fingers. verb.*

clus ter (klus′tər), **1** number of things of the same kind growing or grouped together: *a cluster of grapes, a little cluster of houses in the valley.* **2** be in a bunch; gather in a group: *The children clustered around their teacher.* 1 *noun,* 2 *verb.*

clutch (kluch), **1** a tight grasp: *The eagle flew away with a rabbit in the clutches of its claws.* **2** grasp tightly: *I clutched the railing to keep from falling.* **3** snatch; seize eagerly: *I clutched at a branch as I fell from the tree.* **4** a grasping claw, paw, or hand: *The fish wiggled out of the hungry bear's clutches.* **5** device in a machine for connecting or disconnecting the engine or motor that makes it go. 1,4,5 *noun, plural* **clutch es;** 2,3 *verb.*

clut ter (klut′ər), **1** litter; confusion; disorder: *It was hard to find the lost pen in the clutter of his room.* **2** to litter with things: *Her desk was cluttered with papers, strings, and trash.* 1 *noun,* 2 *verb.*

coach (kōch), **1** a large, closed carriage with seats inside and often on top. In former times, most coaches carried passengers along a regular run, stopping for meals and fresh horses. **2** a passenger car of a railroad train. **3** bus. **4** a class of passenger seating and service on a commercial aircraft at lower rates than first class. **5** person who teaches or trains an athlete, a performer, or athletic teams: *a swimming coach.* **6** train or teach: *She coaches swimmers.* 1-5 *noun, plural* **coach es;** 6 *verb.*

coach man (kōch′mən), man who drives a coach or carriage for a living. *noun, plural* **coach men.**

co ag u late (kō ag′yə lāt), change from a liquid to a thickened mass; thicken: *Cooking coagulates the whites of eggs. verb;* **co ag u lat ed, co ag u lat ing.**

coal (kōl), **1** a black mineral that is mostly carbon. Coal burns and is used as fuel. **2** piece or pieces of this mineral for burning. **3** supply or be supplied with coal: *The ship stopped just long enough to coal.* **4** piece of burning wood or coal: *The big log had burned down to a few glowing coals.* 1,2,4 *noun,* 3 *verb.*

coarse (kôrs), **1** not fine; made up of fairly large parts: *coarse sand.* **2** rough: *Burlap is a coarse cloth.* **3** common; poor; inferior: *coarse food.* **4** not

cockatoo—about 18 inches
(46 centimeters) long

coat of arms—Each colored shield is the
coat of arms of a different family.

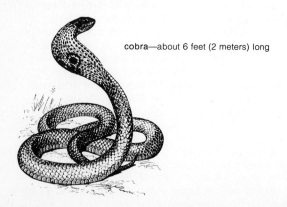

cobra—about 6 feet (2 meters) long

delicate; crude; vulgar: *coarse manners. adjective,*
coars er, coars est.

coars en (kôr′sən), make coarse; become coarse.
verb.

coast (kōst), **1** land along the sea; seashore: *Many
ships were wrecked on that rocky coast.* **2** go along
or near the shore of: *We coasted South America on
our trip last winter.* **3** slide down a hill or ride
without using effort or power: *You can coast
downhill on a sled. He shut off the engine and the car
coasted into the driveway.* **1** *noun,* **2,3** *verb.*

coast al (kō′stl), at the coast; along a coast; near
a coast: *coastal shipping. adjective.*

coast guard, 1 a group whose work is
protecting lives and property and preventing
smuggling along the coast of a country. **2** member
of any such group.

coast line (kōst′līn′), outline of a coast. *noun.*

coat (kōt), **1** outer garment of cloth or fur with
sleeves: *a winter coat. Father wears a coat and tie
to work.* **2** any outer covering: *a dog's coat of hair.*
3 thin layer: *a coat of paint.* **4** cover with a thin
layer: *The floor is coated with varnish. This pill is
coated with sugar.* **1-3** *noun,* **4** *verb.*

coat ing (kō′ting), layer of any substance spread
over a surface: *a coating of paint. noun.*

coat of arms, shield, or drawing of a shield,
with pictures and designs on it. Each knight or
lord had his own coat of arms. See picture. *plural*
coats of arms.

coax (kōks), persuade by soft words; influence by
pleasant ways: *She coaxed me into letting her use
my bike. I coaxed a smile from the baby. verb.*

cob (kob), the central part of an ear of corn, on
which the grains grow; corncob. *noun.*

co balt (kō′bôlt), a silver-white metal used in
making steel or paint. *noun.* [*Cobalt* comes from a
German word meaning "goblin." The metal was
called this because miners believed that it caused
strange or evil things to happen.]

cob bler[1] (kob′lər), person whose work is
mending shoes. *noun.*

cob bler[2] (kob′lər), a fruit pie baked in a deep
dish. *noun.*

cob ble stone (kob′əl stōn′), a rounded stone that
was formerly much used in paving. *noun.*

co bra (kō′brə), a very poisonous snake of
southern Asia and Africa. It can make its head and
neck larger so that they look like a hood. See
picture. *noun.*

cob web (kob′web′), a spider's web, or the stuff it
is made of. *noun.*

cock[1] (kok), **1** a male chicken; a rooster. **2** the
male of other birds: *a turkey cock.* **3** faucet used to
turn the flow of a liquid or gas on or off. **4** pull
back the hammer of (a gun), ready to fire: *There
was a click as the sheriff cocked his revolver.* **1-3**
noun, **4** *verb.*

cock[2] (kok), turn or stick up, especially as if to
defy: *The little bird cocked its eye at me. verb.*

cock a too (kok′ə tü′), a large, brightly colored
parrot of Australia. See picture. *noun, plural*
cock a toos.

cock le (kok′əl), **1** a small shellfish that is good to eat. **2** its heart-shaped shell. *noun.*

cock pit (kok′pit′), **1** place where the pilot sits in an airplane. **2** the small, open place in a small boat where the pilot or passengers sit. *noun.*

cock roach (kok′rōch′), a brown insect with a flattened body. It is often found in kitchens and around water pipes. Cockroaches usually come out at night to feed. *noun, plural* **cock roach es.**

cock y (kok′ē), too sure of oneself; conceited: *He is a cocky fellow. adjective,* **cock i er, cock i est.**

co co (kō′kō), coconut palm. *noun, plural* **co cos.**

co coa (kō′kō), **1** powder that tastes much like chocolate. Cocoa is made by roasting, grinding, and removing some of the fat from the seeds of the cacao tree. **2** drink made from this powder with sugar and milk or water. *noun.*

co co nut or **co coa nut** (kō′kə nut′), the large, round, brown, hard-shelled fruit of the coconut palm. Coconuts have a white lining that is good to eat and a white liquid called **coconut milk.** The white lining is cut up into shreds and used for cakes, puddings, and pies. *noun.*

coconut palm, a tall, tropical palm tree on which coconuts grow.

co coon (kə kün′), silky case spun by caterpillars to live in while they are turning into adult insects: *In the spring a moth came out of the cocoon the caterpillar had spun. noun.*

cogs on gears

coil (definition 2)
a coil of rope

cod (kod), a large fish much used for food. It is found in the cold parts of the northern Atlantic Ocean. **Cod-liver oil** is an oil taken from the livers of cod; it is rich in vitamins. *noun, plural* **cods** or **cod.**

cod dle (kod′l), **1** treat tenderly; pamper: *They coddled their sick child.* **2** cook in hot water without boiling: *coddle an egg. verb,* **cod dled, cod dling.**

code (kōd), **1** arrangement of words or figures to keep a message short or secret; system of secret writing: *The army tried to figure out the code that the enemy used to write messages.* **2** change into a code: *The spy coded a message to headquarters.* **3** a collection of the laws of a country arranged in a clear way so that they can be understood and used. **4** any set of rules: *A traffic code contains rules for driving.* **5** system of signals for sending messages. Long and short sounds and combinations of them stand for the letters of the alphabet in the code used in telegraphy. 1,3-5 *noun,* 2 *verb,* **cod ed, cod ing.**

cod fish (kod′fish′), cod. *noun, plural* **cod fish es** or **cod fish.**

codg er (koj′ər), an odd or peculiar person. *noun.*

co erce (kō ėrs′), compel; force: *The prisoner was coerced into confessing the crime. verb,* **co erced, co erc ing.**

cof fee (kô′fē), **1** a dark-brown drink made from the roasted and ground seeds of a tall, tropical shrub. **2** the seeds from which the drink is made. *noun.*

cof fer (kô′fər), box, chest, or trunk, especially one used to hold money or valuable things. *noun.*

cof fin (kô′fən), box into which a dead person is put to be buried. *noun.*

cog (kog), one of a series of teeth on the edge of a gear. See picture. *noun.*

coil (koil), **1** wind around and around into a pile, a tube, or a curl: *The snake coiled itself around the branch. The wire spring was evenly coiled.* **2** anything that is coiled. One wind or turn of a coil is a single coil. See picture. **3** wire wound round and round into a spiral for carrying electric current. 1 *verb,* 2,3 *noun.*

coin (koin), **1** piece of metal stamped by the government for use as money. Pennies, nickels, dimes, and quarters are coins. **2** metal money. A government makes coin by stamping metals. **3** make (money) by stamping metal: *The mint coins millions of nickels and dimes each year.* **4** make (metal) into money. **5** make up; invent: *We often coin new words to name new products. Alfred Nobel coined the word "dynamite."* 1,2 *noun,* 3-5 *verb.*

coin age (koi′nij), **1** the making of coins: *The United States mint is in charge of coinage.* **2** coins; metal money. **3** making up or inventing: *Travel in* outer space has led to the coinage of many new words. *noun.*

co in cide (kō′in sīd′), **1** occupy the same place in space. If these triangles △△ were placed one on top of the other, they would coincide. **2** occupy the same time: *The working hours of the two friends coincide.* **3** be just alike; correspond exactly: *Her answers are correct and coincide with the answers in the book. verb,* **co in cid ed, co in cid ing.**

co in ci dence (kō in′sə dəns), **1** the chance occurrence of two things at the same time or place in such a way as to seem remarkable or fitting: *It is a coincidence that my cousin and I were born on the same day.* **2** coinciding; occupying the same time or place: *the coincidence of two triangles or circles. noun.*

coke (kōk), the black substance that is left after coal has been heated in an oven from which most of the air has been shut out. It is used as a fuel. *noun.*

co la (kō′lə), a soft drink flavored with a nut from a tropical evergreen tree. *noun, plural* **co las.**

cold (kōld), **1** much less warm than the body: *Snow and ice are cold.* **2** less warm than it usually is: *The weather is cold for April.* **3** feeling cold or chilly: *Put on a sweater, or you will be cold.* **4** coldness; being cold: *Warm clothes protect against the cold of winter.* **5** a common sickness that causes a running at the nose and a sore throat. **6** not kind and cheerful; unfriendly: *Since our argument she has been cold to me.* 1-3,6 *adjective,* 4,5 *noun.*
catch cold, become sick with a cold.

cold-blood ed (kōld′blud′id), **1** having blood that is about the same temperature as the air or water around the animal. The blood of such animals is colder in winter than in summer. Turtles are cold-blooded; dogs are warm-blooded. **2** lacking in feeling; cruel: *a cold-blooded murderer. adjective.*

col lage (kə läzh′), picture made by pasting on a background such things as parts of photographs and newspapers, fabric, and string. *noun.* [Collage comes from a French word meaning "pasting" or "gluing."]

col lapse (kə laps′), **1** fall in; shrink together suddenly: *Sticking a pin into the balloon caused it to collapse.* **2** falling in; sudden shrinking together: *A heavy flood caused the collapse of the bridge.* **3** break down; fail suddenly: *The business collapsed because it was run poorly.* **4** breakdown; failure: *Overwork can cause the collapse of a person's health.* 1,3 *verb,* **col lapsed, col laps ing;** 2,4 *noun.*

col lar (kol′ər), **1** the part of a coat, a dress, or a shirt that makes a band around the neck. **2** a separate band of linen, lace, or other material worn around the neck: *a fur collar.* **3** a leather or metal band for the neck of a dog or other pet animal. **4** a leather roll for a horse's neck to bear the weight of the loads it pulls. **5** any of the various kinds of rings, bands, or pipes in machinery. Sometimes a collar is a short pipe connecting two other pipes. **6** seize by the collar; capture. See picture. 1-5 *noun,* 6 *verb.*

col league (kol′ēg′), associate; fellow worker: *His*

colleagues taught his classes while he was ill. *noun.*

col lect (kə lekt′), **1** bring together; come together; gather together: *We collected sticks of wood to make a fire. I collect stamps as a hobby. Dust is collecting under the bed. A crowd soon collected at the scene of the accident.* **2** ask and receive pay for (debts, bills, dues, or taxes): *My scout troop collects dues each week. verb.*

col lect ed (kə lek′tid), not confused or disturbed; calm: *Throughout all the excitement she remained cool and collected. adjective.*

col lec tion (kə lek′shən), **1** a bringing together; coming together: *The collection of these stamps took ten years.* **2** group of things gathered from many places and belonging together: *Our library has a large collection of books.* **3** money gathered from people: *A church takes up a collection to help pay its expenses.* **4** mass or heap: *a collection of dust under the bed. noun.*

col lec tor (kə lek′tər), **1** person or thing that collects: *I am a stamp collector.* **2** person hired to collect money owed: *a tax collector. noun.*

col lege (kol′ij), **1** a school beyond high school that gives degrees or diplomas: *After I finish high school, I plan to go to college to become a teacher.* **2** school for special training: *I went to business college to learn to be a bookkeeper. noun.*

col lide (kə līd′), **1** crash; hit or strike hard together: *Two ships collided in the harbor and sank.* **2** clash; conflict. *verb,* **col lid ed, col lid ing.**

col lie (kol′ē), a large, intelligent, long-haired dog. Collies are used for tending sheep and as pets. See picture. *noun.*

col li sion (kə lizh′ən), **1** crash; hitting or striking hard together: *The car was badly damaged in the collision.* **2** clash; conflict. *noun.*

co lon[1] (kō′lən), mark (:) of punctuation. Colons are used before explanations, lists, and long quotations to set them off from the rest of the sentence. An illustrative sentence in this dictionary has a colon before it. For an example see the sentence after definition 1 of **collision.** *noun.*

co lon[2] (kō′lən), the lower part of the large intestine. *noun.*

colo nel (kėr′nl), officer who commands a regiment of soldiers. *noun.*

co lo ni al (kə lō′nē əl), **1** of or having to do with a colony or colonies. **2** having something to do with the thirteen British colonies which became the United States of America. **3** person who lives in a colony. 1,2 *adjective,* 3 *noun.*

col o nist (kol′ə nist), **1** person who lives in a colony; settler: *Early colonists in New England suffered from cold and hunger.* **2** person who helps to found a colony. *noun.*

col o ni za tion (kol′ə nə zā′shən), the setting up of a colony or colonies. *noun.*

col o nize (kol′ə nīz), set up a colony or colonies in: *The English colonized New England. verb,* **col o nized, col o niz ing.**

col on nade (kol′ə nād′), a series of columns set the same distance apart. See picture. *noun.*

collar (definition 6)—She **collared** the muddy boy and tried to wash him under the pump.

collie—about 2 feet (60 centimeters) high at the shoulder

colonnade

a hat	i it	oi oil	ch child	a in about
ā age	ī ice	ou out	ng long	e in taken
ä far	o hot	u cup	sh she	ə = { i in pencil
e let	ō open	ů put	th thin	o in lemon
ē equal	ô order	ü rule	ℲH then	u in circus
ėr term			zh measure	

col o ny (kol′ə nē), **1** group of people who leave their own country and go to settle in another land, but who still remain citizens of their own country: *The Pilgrim colony came from England to America in 1620.* **2** the settlement made by such a group of people: *The Pilgrims founded a colony at Plymouth, Massachusetts.* **3 the Colonies,** the thirteen British colonies that became the United States of America; New Hampshire, Massachusetts, Rhode Island, Connecticut, New York, New Jersey, Pennsylvania, Delaware, Maryland, Virginia, North Carolina, South Carolina, and Georgia. **4** territory distant from the country that governs it: *Hong Kong is a British colony.* **5** group of people of one country or occupation living in their own part of a city: *the Chinese colony in San Francisco. There is a colony of artists in Paris.* **6** group of animals or plants of the same kind living or growing together: *We found two colonies of ants under the steps. noun, plural* **col o nies.**

col or (kul′ər), **1** red, yellow, blue, or any combination of them. Green is a combination of yellow and blue; purple is a combination of red and blue. **2** give color to; put color on; change the color of: *I colored a picture with crayons.* **3** paint; stain; dye: *The color was so thick on the canvas that it began to peel off.* **4** change to give a wrong idea: *The fisherman colored the facts to make his catch seem the biggest of all.* **5 the colors,** the flag: *Salute the colors.* 1,3,5 *noun,* 2,4 *verb.*

Col o rad o (kol′ə rad′ō *or* kol′ə rä′dō), one of the western states of the United States. *noun.* [*Colorado* was named for the Colorado River, which flows through the state. The river got its name from a Spanish word meaning "colored" or "reddish." It was called this because the water looked reddish as it flowed through the canyons of red stone.]

col ored (kul′ərd), **1** having color; not black or white: *This book has colored pictures.* **2** of the black race or any race other than white. This meaning of *colored* is often considered offensive. **3** See **color.** *He colored the sky blue.* 1,2 *adjective,* 3 *verb.*

col or ful (kul′ər fəl), interesting or exciting: *Her letters describe her colorful travels. adjective.*

col or ing (kul′ər ing), **1** way in which a person or thing is colored: *Our cat has a tan coloring.* **2** substance used to color. **3** false appearance: *Her story had the coloring of truth, but we knew we could not believe her. noun.*

col or less (kul′ər lis), **1** without color: *Water is colorless.* **2** not interesting: *a colorless person. adjective.*

co los sal (kə los′əl), huge; gigantic; vast: *We saw a colossal stone monument 50 feet high. adjective.*

colt (kōlt), a young horse, donkey, or zebra. A

male horse until it is four or five years old is a colt. *noun.*

col umn (kol′əm). See picture. **1** a slender, upright structure; a pillar. Columns are usually made of stone, wood, or metal, and used as supports or ornaments to a building. **2** anything that seems slender and upright like a column: *A column of smoke rose from the fire. You add a column of figures.* **3** line of persons or things following one behind another. **4** a narrow division of a page reading from top to bottom, kept separate by lines or by blank spaces. This page has two columns. **5** part of a newspaper used for a special subject or written by a special writer: *the sports column.* *noun.*

column (definitions 1, 2, 3, and 5)

co ma (kō′mə), a long period of deep unconsciousness. A coma may be caused by a severe head injury, paralysis, or poison. *noun.* [*Coma* comes from a Greek word meaning "deep sleep."]

comb (kōm), **1** piece of metal, rubber, plastic, or bone with teeth, used to arrange or straighten the hair or to hold it in place. **2** anything shaped or used like a comb. One kind of comb cleans and takes out the tangles in wool or flax. **3** straighten; take out tangles in; arrange with a comb: *You should comb your hair every morning.* **4** search through: *We had to comb the whole city before we found our lost dog.* **5** the red, fleshy piece on the top of the head of chickens and some other fowls. **6** honeycomb. 1,2,5,6 *noun,* 3,4 *verb.*

com bat (kəm bat′ *or* kom′bat *for 1;* kom′bat *for 2 and 3*), **1** fight against; struggle with: *The whole town turned out to combat the fire.* **2** fighting with weapons; battle: *The soldier was wounded in combat.* **3** any fight or struggle. 1 *verb,* 2,3 *noun.*

com bi na tion (kom′bə nā′shən), **1** one whole made by combining two or more different things: *The color purple is a combination of red and blue.* **2** a combining or being combined; union: *The combination of flour and water makes paste.* *noun.*

com bine (kəm bīn′ *for 1;* kom′bīn *for 2*), **1** join two or more things together; unite: *combine work and play. Our club combined the offices of secretary and treasurer. Two atoms of hydrogen combine with one of oxygen to form water.* **2** machine for harvesting and threshing grain. 1 *verb,* **com bined, com bin ing;** 2 *noun.*

com bus ti ble (kəm bus′tə bəl), capable of taking fire and burning; easy to burn: *Gasoline is highly combustible. adjective.*

com bus tion (kəm bus′chən), act or process of burning. We sometimes heat houses by the combustion of oil. *noun.*

come (kum), **1** move toward: *Come this way. One boy came toward me; the other boy went away from me.* **2** get near; reach; arrive: *The girls will come home tomorrow. The train comes at noon.* **3** take place; happen: *Snow comes in winter.* **4** be born: *She comes from a musical family.* **5** turn out to be; become: *My wish came true.* **6** be equal; amount: *The bill comes to five dollars. verb,* **came, come, com ing.**

come about, 1 take place; happen: *Many changes have come about in the past year.* **2** turn around: *The sailboat came about, heading back to the dock.*
come at, rush toward; attack.
come back, return: *Come back home.*
come down, lose position, rank, or money.
come forward, offer oneself for work or duty.
come in, 1 arrive: *When did you come in this morning?* **2** enter: *Come in, please.*
come off, 1 take place; happen: *The rocket launching comes off next week.* **2** turn out: *Our first meeting did not come off as I had expected.* **3** finish in a certain way: *Our team came off with a great victory in last week's game.*
come on, 1 find or meet by chance. **2** improve;

a hat	**i** it	**oi** oil	**ch** child	a in about
ā age	**ī** ice	**ou** out	**ng** long	e in taken
ä far	**o** hot	**u** cup	**sh** she	ə = { i in pencil
e let	**ō** open	**ù** put	**th** thin	o in lemon
ē equal	**ô** order	**ü** rule	**ŦH** then	u in circus
ėr term			**zh** measure	

progress: *My friend is coming on well and will soon leave the hospital.*

come out, 1 be revealed or shown: *The sun came out from behind the clouds.* **2** take place in the end; result: *The ball game came out in our favor.* **3** be offered to the public: *The singer's new recording will come out next fall.* **4** put in an appearance; turn out: *How many people came out to cheer the team?*

come up, arise; develop: *The question is not likely to come up.*

co me di an (kə mē′dē ən), **1** actor in comedies. **2** person who amuses others with funny talk and actions. *noun.*

com e dy (kom′ə dē), **1** an amusing play or show having a happy ending. **2** an amusing happening. *noun, plural* **com e dies.**

come ly (kum′lē), pleasant to look at; attractive: *a comely girl. adjective,* **come li er, come li est.**

com et (kom′it), a bright heavenly body with a starlike center and often with a cloudy tail of light. Comets move around the sun like planets, but in a long oval course. We can see comets only when they come close to the earth. See picture. *noun.* [*Comet* comes from Greek words meaning "long-haired star." It was called this because the tail of a comet looks like long, flowing hair.]

com fort (kum′fərt), **1** ease the grief or sorrow of. See picture. **2** anything that makes trouble or sorrow easier to bear: *Your friendship brought me comfort while I was sick.* **3** person or thing that makes life easier or takes away hardship: *The warm fire was a comfort to the cold campers.* **4** ease; freedom from hardship: *It's nice to have enough money to live in comfort.* **1** *verb,* **2-4** *noun.*

com fort a ble (kum′fər tə bəl), **1** giving comfort: *A soft, warm bed is comfortable.* **2** in comfort; free from pain or hardship: *We felt comfortable in the warm house after a cold day outdoors. adjective.*

com fort a bly (kum′fər tə blē), in a comfortable manner; easily. *adverb.*

com ic (kom′ik), **1** causing laughter or smiles; amusing; funny. **2** comedian. **3** of comedy; in comedies: *a comic actor.* **4** comic book. **5** **comics,** comic strips. **1,3** *adjective,* **2,4,5** *noun.*

com i cal (kom′ə kəl), amusing; funny: *You look comical in that battered old hat. adjective.*

comic book, magazine containing comic strips.

comic strip, group of drawings, sometimes funny, that often tell a story or an adventure.

com ing (kum′ing), **1** approach; arrival: *the coming of summer.* **2** approaching; next: *this coming spring.* **1** *noun,* **2** *adjective.*

com ma (kom′ə), a mark (,) of punctuation, usually used where a pause would be made in speaking a sentence aloud. Notice the commas after the pronunciations in this dictionary. In the sentence under definition 1 of **comfortable,** notice the comma between *soft* and *warm. noun.*

com mand (kə mand′), **1** give an order to; order; direct: *The queen commanded the admiral to set sail at once.* **2** order; direction: *The admiral obeyed the queen's command.* **3** be in authority over; have power over; be master of: *The captain commands*

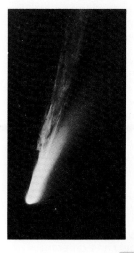

comet

comfort (definition 1)
The policeman comforted the frightened child.

his ship. **4** possession of authority; power; control: *When the fire started, she took command and led everyone to safety.* **5** the soldiers or ships or a region under a person who has the right to command them: *The captain knew every man in his command.* **6** control by position; rise high above; overlook: *The castle is built on a cliff that commands the entire valley.* **7** be able to have and use: *I cannot command such a large sum of money.* **8** ability to have and use. "She has an excellent command of English" means that she speaks it unusually well. **9** deserve and get: *Food commands a higher price when it is scarce.* **1,3,6,7,9** *verb,* **2,4,5,8** *noun.*

com mand er (kə man′dər), **1** person who commands. Anyone who controls people or supplies is the commander of them. **2** officer in the navy, ranking next below a captain. *noun.*

com mand ment (kə mand′mənt), **1** (in the Bible) one of the ten laws that God gave to Moses. "Thou shalt not kill" is one of the Ten Commandments. **2** any law or command. *noun.*

com mem o rate (kə mem′ə rāt′), preserve or honor the memory of. See picture. *verb,* **com mem o rat ed, com mem o rat ing.**

com mence (kə mens′), begin; start: *The play will commence at ten o'clock. verb,* **com menced, com menc ing.**

com mence ment (kə mens′mənt), **1** beginning; start. **2** ceremony during which colleges and schools give diplomas to persons who have completed their studies; day of graduation. *noun.*

com mend (kə mend′), praise: *The teacher commended the pupils who studied for the test. verb.*

com ment (kom′ent), **1** a note or remark that explains, praises, or finds fault with a book, a person, or a thing: *The teacher had written helpful comments on the last page of my composition.* **2** make notes or remarks (about persons or things): *Everyone commented on my new coat.* **1** *noun,* **2** *verb.*

com merce (kom′ərs), trade; buying and selling of goods in large amounts between different places. *noun.*

com mer cial (kə mėr′shəl), **1** having something to do with trade or business: *a store or other commercial establishment.* **2** supported by an advertiser: *a commercial television program.* **3** an advertising message on radio or television, broadcast between or during programs. **1,2** *adjective,* **3** *noun.*

com mis sion (kə mish′ən), **1** a written paper giving certain powers, privileges, and duties. In the army a person who is appointed to the rank of lieutenant or higher receives a commission. **2** give (a person) the right, the power, or the duty (to do something): *My parents commissioned a real estate agent to sell our house.* **3** the thing a person is trusted to do; errand: *The class gave me the commission of selecting a birthday present for our teacher.* **4** group of people appointed or elected with authority to do certain things: *The Senate appointed a commission to find out why food costs so much.* **5** doing; committing: *the commission of crimes.* **6** put into active service; make ready for use: *A new ship is commissioned when it has the officers, crew, and supplies needed for a sea trip.* **7** working order; service; use: *A flat tire put my bicycle out of commission.* **1,3-5,7** *noun,* **2,6** *verb.*

com mis sion er (kə mish′ə nər), **1** member of a commission. **2** official in charge of some department of a government: *a police commissioner, a health commissioner. noun.*

com mit (kə mit′), **1** do or perform (usually something wrong): *A person who steals commits a crime.* **2** hand over for safekeeping; deliver: *The judge committed the thief to prison.* **3** put: *I committed the poem to memory. She committed her thoughts to writing.* **4** bind or involve (oneself);

Lexington & Concord 1775 by Sandham
US Bicentennial 10 cents

commemorate—This stamp commemorates the beginning of the Revolutionary War at Lexington and Concord in 1775.

pledge: *I have committed myself now and must keep my promise. verb,* **com mit ted, com mit ting.**

com mit tee (kə mit′ē), group of persons appointed or elected to do some special thing: *Our teacher appointed a committee of five pupils to plan the class picnic. noun.*

com mod i ty (kə mod′ə tē), anything that is bought and sold: *Groceries are commodities. noun, plural* **com mod i ties.**

com mon (kom′ən), **1** belonging equally to all: *The house is the common property of the three brothers.* **2** general; of all; from all; by all: *By common consent of the class, she was chosen for president.* **3** often met with; usual; familiar: *Snow is common in cold countries.* **4** without rank; having no special position: *A private is a common soldier; a sergeant is not.* **5** coarse; vulgar: *a common person.* **6** belonging to the entire community; public: *It is in the common interest to clean up pollution.* **7** land owned or used by all the people of a village or town. **1-6** *adjective,* **7** *noun.*

in common, equally with another or others; owned, used, or done by both or all: *The two sisters have many interests in common.*

com mon ly (kom′ən lē), usually; generally: *Arithmetic is commonly taught in schools. adverb.*

com mon place (kom′ən plās′), ordinary; not new or interesting: *The plots of television movies are often commonplace. adjective.*

common sense, good sense in everyday affairs; practical intelligence: *He was not a good student, but he had a lot of common sense.*

com mon wealth (kom′ən welth′), **1** the people who make up a nation; citizens of a state. **2** nation in which the people have the right to make the laws; republic: *Brazil, Australia, the United States, and West Germany are commonwealths.* **3** any state of the United States. **4** group of nations united by some common interest: *Great Britain, Canada, Australia, and India are members of the Commonwealth of Nations. noun.*

com mo tion (kə mō′shən), violent movement; confusion; disturbance; tumult: *Their fight caused quite a commotion in the hall. noun.*

com mu ni ca ble (kə myü′nə kə bəl), able to be

transferred or passed along to others: *Scarlet fever is a communicable disease. adjective.*

com mu ni cate (kə myü′nə kāt), give or exchange information or news: *communicate by telephone. She communicated her wishes to me in a letter. verb,* **com mu ni cat ed, com mu ni cat ing.**

com mu ni ca tion (kə myü′nə kā′shən), **1** giving information or news: *People who are deaf often use sign language as a means of communication.* **2** the information or news given; letter or message which gives information or news: *Your communication came in time to change all my plans.* **3** means of going from one to the other; passage: *There is no communication between these two rooms.* **4 communications,** a system of communicating by telephone, telegraph, radio, or television: *A network of communications links all parts of the civilized world. noun.*

com mun ion (kə myü′nyən), **1** a having in common; sharing: *The partners had a communion of interests.* **2** exchange of thoughts and feelings; fellowship. **3** group of people having the same religious beliefs. **4 Communion,** a Christian church service in which bread and wine are blessed to commemorate Christ's last supper before His death. *noun.*

com mu nism (kom′yə niz′əm), system in which most or all property is owned by the state and is shared by all. *noun.*

com mu nist (kom′yə nist), person who favors or supports communism. *noun.*

com mu ni ty (kə myü′nə tē), **1** all the people living in the same place; the people of any district or town: *This lake provides water for six communities.* **2** group of people living together or sharing common interests: *a community of monks, the scientific community.* **3 the community,** the public: *To be successful a new product needs the approval of the community. noun, plural* **com mu ni ties.**

com mute (kə myüt′), **1** change (an obligation or penalty) for an easier one: *The governor commuted the prisoner's sentence of death to one of life imprisonment.* **2** travel regularly to and from work by train, bus, automobile, or other transportation. *verb,* **com mut ed, com mut ing.**

com mut er (kə myü′tər), person who travels regularly to and from work by train, bus, automobile, or other transportation. *noun.*

com pact[1] (kəm pakt′ *for 1-3;* kom′pakt *for 4,5*), **1** closely and firmly packed together: *The leaves of a cabbage are folded into a compact head.* **2** having the parts neatly or tightly arranged within a small space: *a compact portable TV.* **3** using few words; brief: *compact sentences.* **4** a small case containing face powder or rouge. **5** automobile smaller than most models. 1-3 *adjective,* 4,5 *noun.*

com pact[2] (kom′pakt), agreement: *The United Nations is a result of a compact among nearly all nations of the world. noun.*

com pan ion (kəm pan′yən), **1** one who often goes along with or accompanies another; one who shares in what another is doing. See picture.

a hat	i it	oi oil	ch child	a in about
ā age	ī ice	ou out	ng long	e in taken
ä far	o hot	u cup	sh she	ə = { i in pencil
e let	ō open	ů put	th thin	o in lemon
ē equal	ô order	ü rule	ŦH then	u in circus
ėr term			zh measure	

2 anything that matches or goes with another in kind, size, and color: *I can't find the companion to this shoe. noun.* [*Companion* comes from a Latin word meaning "one who eats bread with another."]

com pan ion a ble (kəm pan′yə nə bəl), sociable; agreeable; pleasant as a companion. *adjective.*

com pan ion ship (kəm pan′yən ship), being a companion; fellowship: *I enjoy the companionship of my friends. noun.*

com pan ion way (kəm pan′yən wā′), stairway from the deck of a ship down to the rooms or area below. *noun.*

com pa ny (kum′pə nē), **1** group of people joined together for some purpose: *a company of tourists, a company of actors. I work for a company that makes furniture.* **2** companions: *I was with talkative company last night.* **3** companionship: *Her dog provided the old woman with company during the long winters.* **4** guest or guests; visitor or visitors: *company for the weekend. Do you expect company for dinner tonight?* **5** the part of an army commanded by a captain. Two or more platoons make a company. **6** a ship's crew. *noun, plural* **com pa nies.**

keep company, stay with for companionship: *My dog kept me company while you were away.*

part company, go separate ways: *The friends parted company at the gate.*

com par a ble (kom′pər ə bəl), **1** able to be compared: *A campfire is comparable with a stove; both can cook food.* **2** fit to be compared: *A cave is not comparable to a house for comfort. adjective.*

companions (definition 1)

com par a tive (kəm par′ə tiv), **1** able to compare: *He made a comparative study of bees and wasps.* **2** measured by comparison with something else: *Screens give us comparative freedom from flies.* **3** *Fairer, faster,* and *better* are the comparatives of *fair, fast,* and *good. More quickly* is the comparative of *quickly.* See picture. **1,2** *adjective,* **3** *noun.*

com par a tive ly (kəm par′ə tiv lē), by comparison; relatively; somewhat: *Mountains are comparatively free from mosquitoes. adverb.*

com pare (kəm per′ *or* kəm par′), **1** find out or point out how persons or things are alike and how they are different: *I compared my answers with the teacher's and found I had made a mistake.* **2** liken; say (something) is like (something else): *The fins of a fish may be compared to the legs of a dog; both are used in moving.* **3** be considered like or equal: *Canned fruit cannot compare with fresh fruit. verb,* **com pared, com par ing.**

com par i son (kəm par′ə sən), **1** act of comparing; finding out the likenesses and the differences: *The teacher's comparison of the heart to a pump helped the students to understand how the heart works.* **2** likeness; similarity: *There is no comparison between these two cameras; one is much better than the other. noun.*

in comparison with, compared with: *Even a large lake is small in comparison with an ocean.*

com part ment (kəm pärt′mənt), a separate division set off by walls or partitions: *Your pencil box has several compartments for holding different things. noun.*

com pass (kum′pəs), **1** instrument for showing directions, consisting of a needle that points to the North Magnetic Pole, which is near the North Pole. See picture. **2** instrument for drawing circles and measuring distances. See picture. *noun, plural* **com pass es.**

com pas sion (kəm pash′ən), pity; feeling for another's sorrow or hardship that leads to help; sympathy: *His compassion for the orphans caused him to give a large amount of money for their support. noun.*

com pas sion ate (kəm pash′ə nit), pitying; wishing to help those that suffer. *adjective.*

com pat i ble (kəm pat′ə bəl), able to exist or get on well together; agreeing; in harmony: *Cats and birds are seldom compatible. adjective.*

com pel (kəm pel′), force: *The rain compelled us to stop our ball game. verb,* **com pelled, com pel ling.**

com pen sate (kom′pən sāt), **1** make an equal return to; give an equivalent to: *We compensated our neighbor for the window we broke by replacing it.* **2** balance by equal weight or power; make up (for): *Skill sometimes compensates for lack of strength.* **3** pay: *The company always compensated her for her extra work. verb,* **com pen sat ed, com pen sat ing.**

com pen sa tion (kom′pən sā′shən), **1** something given to make up for something else; something which makes up for something else: *He gave me a new knife as compensation for the one of mine he*

comparative (definition 3)—Shorter is the **comparative** of short. Shortest is the superlative of short.

competition (definition 2)—The racers prepared for the **competition**.

compass (definition 1)

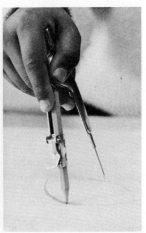

compass (definition 2)

lost. **2** pay: *The same compensation should be given to men and women for the same work. noun.*

com pete (kəm pēt′), **1** try hard to win or gain something wanted by others: *She competed against many fine athletes. It is difficult for a small grocery store to compete with a supermarket.* **2** take part (in a contest): *Will you compete in the final race? verb,* **com pet ed, com pet ing.**

com pe tent (kom′pə tənt), able; skilled: *a competent secretary. adjective.*

com pe ti tion (kom′pə tish′ən), **1** rivalry; competing; trying hard to win or gain something wanted by others: *There is competition in many games.* **2** contest. See picture. *noun.*

com pet i tive (kəm pet′ə tiv), decided by competition; using competition: *A competitive examination for the job of postal clerk will be held January 10. adjective.*

com pet i tor (kəm pet′ə tər), person who tries hard to win or gain something wanted by others; rival: *There are many competitors for the golf championship. noun.*

com pile (kəm pīl′), **1** collect and bring together in one list or account: *I compiled a list of the groceries we needed.* **2** make (a book, a report, or an article) out of various materials: *It takes many experts to compile an encyclopedia. verb,* **com piled, com pil ing.**

com pla cent (kəm plā′snt), pleased or satisfied with oneself: *The winner's complacent smile annoyed the loser. adjective.*

com plain (kəm plān′), **1** say that something is wrong; find fault: *We complained that the room was cold.* **2** talk about one's pain or troubles: *He is always complaining about his health.* **3** make an accusation or charge: *I complained to the police about the barking of my neighbor's dog. verb.*

com plaint (kəm plānt′), **1** a complaining; finding fault: *Her letter is filled with complaints about the food at camp.* **2** accusation; charge: *The judge heard the complaint and ordered an investigation.* **3** illness; disease: *A cold is a very common complaint. noun.*

com ple ment (kom′plə mənt *for 1 and 2;* kom′plə ment *for 3*), **1** something that completes or makes perfect: *The teacher considers homework a necessary complement to classroom work.* **2** number required to complete or make perfect: *The plane had its full complement of passengers; all seats were taken.* **3** supply a lack of any kind; complete: *My fishing poles complement his hooks and lines, so that together we can go fishing.* **1,2** *noun,* **3** *verb.*

com plete (kəm plēt′), **1** with all the parts; whole; entire: *We have a complete set of garden tools.* **2** make whole or perfect; make up the full number or amount of: *I completed the set of dishes by buying the cups and saucers.* **3** perfect; thorough: *a complete surprise.* **4** make perfect or thorough: *The good news completed my happiness.* **5** finished; done: *My homework is complete.* **6** finish: *She completed her homework early in the evening.* **1,3,5** *adjective,* **2,4,6** *verb,* **com plet ed, com plet ing.**

com plete ly (kəm plēt′lē), **1** entirely; wholly. **2** thoroughly; perfectly. *adverb.*

com ple tion (kəm plē′shən), **1** finishing; act of completing: *After the completion of the job, she went home.* **2** condition of being completed: *The work is near completion. noun.*

com plex (kəm pleks′), **1** made up of a number of parts: *A watch is a complex device.* **2** hard to understand: *The instructions for building the radio were so complex we could not follow them. adjective.*

com plex ion (kəm plek′shən), **1** the color, quality, and general appearance of the skin, particularly of the face. **2** general appearance; nature; character: *The complexion of the war was changed by two great victories. noun.*

com plex i ty (kəm plek′sə tē), complex quality or condition: *The complexity of the road map puzzled him. noun, plural* **com plex i ties.**

com pli cate (kom′plə kāt), **1** make hard to understand or to settle; mix up; confuse: *Too many rules complicate a game.* **2** make worse or more mixed up: *Headaches can be complicated by eye trouble. verb,* **com pli cat ed, com pli cat ing.**

com pli cat ed (kom′plə kā′tid), hard to understand: *Many airplane models have very complicated directions for their assembly. adjective.*

com pli ca tion (kom′plə kā′shən), **1** confused state of affairs that is hard to understand or settle: *Such a complication of little rules makes this game hard to learn.* **2** something that makes matters harder to untangle or settle: *Pneumonia was the complication the doctor feared most after the operation. noun.*

com pli ment (kom′plə mənt *for 1 and 3;* kom′plə ment *for 2*), **1** something good said about you; something said in praise of your work: *She received many compliments on her science project.* **2** pay a compliment to; congratulate: *The principal complimented the boy on his good grades.* **3** **compliments,** greetings: *In the box of flowers was a card saying "With the compliments of a friend."* **1,3** *noun,* **2** *verb.*

com pli men tar y (kom′plə men′tər ē), **1** expressing a compliment; praising: *a complimentary remark.* **2** given free: *Mother received two complimentary tickets to the circus. adjective.*

com ply (kəm plī′), act in agreement with a request or a command: *I will comply with the doctor's orders. verb,* **com plied, com ply ing.**

com pose (kəm pōz′), **1** make up: *The ocean is composed of salt water. Our party was composed of three grown-ups and four children.* **2** put together. To compose a story or poem is to construct it from words. To compose a piece of music is to invent the tune and write down the notes. To compose a picture is to get an artistic arrangement of the things in it. **3** make calm: *Stop crying and compose yourself. verb,* **com posed, com pos ing.**

com pos er (kəm pō′zər), **1** person who composes. **2** writer of music. *noun.*

com pos ite (kəm poz′it), made up of various parts; compound: *The photographer made a composite picture by putting together parts of several others. adjective.*

com po si tion (kom′pə zish′ən), **1** the make-up of anything; what is in it: *The composition of this candy includes sugar, chocolate, and milk.* **2** a putting together of a whole. Writing sentences, making pictures, and setting type in printing are all forms of composition. **3** thing composed. A symphony, poem, or painting is a composition. **4** short essay written as a school exercise: *I wrote a composition about my dog. noun.*

com po sure (kəm pō′zhər), calmness; quietness; self-control. *noun.*

com pound (kom′pound *for 1-3;* kom pound′ *for 4),* **1** having more than one part: *A clover leaf is a compound leaf. "Steamship" is a compound word.* **2** a mixture: *Many medicines are compounds.* **3** a substance formed by chemical combination of two or more substances: *Water is a compound of hydrogen and oxygen.* **4** mix; combine: *The druggist compounded several medicines to fill the prescription.* **1** *adjective,* **2,3** *noun,* **4** *verb.*

com pre hend (kom′pri hend′), **1** understand: *If you can use a word correctly, you comprehend it.* **2** include; contain: *His report of the accident comprehended all the facts. verb.*

com pre hen sion (kom′pri hen′shən), act or power of understanding: *Arithmetic is beyond the comprehension of a baby. noun.*

com pre hen sive (kom′pri hen′siv), including much: *The month's schoolwork ended with a comprehensive review. adjective.*

com press (kəm pres′ *for 1;* kom′pres *for 2),* **1** squeeze together; make smaller by pressure: *Cotton is compressed into bales.* **2** pad of cloth applied to a part of the body to stop bleeding or to lessen soreness and swelling: *I put a cold compress on my forehead to relieve my headache.* **1** *verb,* **2** *noun, plural* **com press es.**

com prise (kəm prīz′), consist of; include: *The United States comprises 50 states. verb,* **com prised, com pris ing.**

com pro mise (kom′prə mīz), **1** settle (a quarrel or difference of opinion) by agreeing that each side will give up part of what it demands. **2** settlement of a quarrel or a difference of opinion by a partial yielding on both sides: *They both wanted the apple; their compromise was to share it.* **3** put under suspicion: *You will compromise your good name if you go around with such a bad crowd.* **1,3** *verb,* **com pro mised, com pro mis ing;** **2** *noun.*

com pul sion (kəm pul′shən), compelling; use of force; force: *A contract signed under compulsion is not legal. noun.*

com pul sor y (kəm pul′sər ē), **1** compelled; required: *Attendance at school is compulsory for*

children over seven years old. **2** compelling; using force. *adjective.*

com pu ta tion (kom′pyə tā′shən), figuring out; calculation. Addition and subtraction are forms of computation. *noun.*

com pute (kəm pyüt′), do by arithmetic; calculate; figure out: *Mother computed the cost of our trip. verb,* **com put ed, com put ing.**

com put er (kəm pyü′tər), machine which computes, especially an electronic machine which either solves problems when given certain coded information or processes that information in some way. *noun.*

com rade (kom′rad), **1** companion and friend. **2** person who shares in what another is doing; partner; fellow worker. *noun.*

con (kon), **1** against: *The two groups argued the question pro and con.* **2** a reason against: *The pros and cons of a question are the arguments for and against it.* **1** *adverb,* **2** *noun.*

con cave (kon kāv′), hollow and curved in like the inside of a circle or sphere: *The palm of one's hand is slightly concave. adjective.*

con ceal (kən sēl′), put or keep out of sight; hide: *He concealed the ball behind his back. verb.*

con ceal ment (kən sēl′mənt), **1** hiding or keeping secret: *The witness's concealment of facts prevented a fair trial.* **2** means or place for hiding. *noun.*

con cede (kən sēd′), **1** admit; admit as true: *I conceded that I had made a mistake.* **2** allow (a person) to have; grant: *They conceded us the right to use their driveway. verb,* **con ced ed, con ced ing.**

con ceit (kən sēt′), too much pride in oneself or in one's ability to do things. See picture. *noun.*

con ceit ed (kən sē′tid), having too high an opinion of oneself; vain. *adjective.*

con ceiv a ble (kən sē′və bəl), able to be thought of; imaginable: *I looked for my lost watch in every conceivable place. adjective.*

AT SPORTS I ALWAYS EXCEL, MY MIND'S BRILLIANT AS WELL, BUT DON'T ACCUSE ME OF **CONCEIT,** BECAUSE MY PERFECTION'S COMPLETE!

con ceive (kən sēv′), **1** form in the mind; think up; imagine: *The Wright brothers conceived the design of the first successful powered airplane.* **2** have an idea or feeling; think: *Young children cannot conceive of life without automobiles and television.* *verb,* **con ceived, con ceiv ing.**

con cen trate (kon′sən trāt), **1** bring or come together in one place: *A magnifying glass can concentrate enough sunlight to scorch paper. The audience at the music festival concentrated around the stage.* **2** pay close attention: *I concentrated on my reading so that I would understand the story.* **3** make stronger. A concentrated solution of acid is one which has very much acid in it. *verb,* **con cen trat ed, con cen trat ing.**

con cen tra tion (kon′sən trā′shən), **1** concentrating: *a concentration of effort.* **2** close attention: *When he gave the problem his full concentration, he figured out the answer.* *noun.*

con cept (kon′sept), thought; general notion or idea: *I believe in the concept that a person is innocent until proven guilty.* *noun.*

con cep tion (kən sep′shən), **1** thought; notion; idea: *Her conception of the problem was different from mine.* **2** act of forming an idea or thought. *noun.*

con cern (kən sėrn′), **1** have to do with; belong to: *This letter is private and concerns nobody but me.* **2** anything that touches or has to do with one's work or one's interests: *The party decorations are my concern; you pay attention to refreshments.* **3** troubled interest; worry: *Their concern over their sick child kept them awake all night.* **4** cause to worry; trouble: *We didn't want to concern you with the bad news.* **5** a business company; firm: *We wrote to two big concerns for their catalogs.* 1,4 *verb,* 2,3,5 *noun.*

con cerned (kən sėrnd′), **1** troubled; worried; anxious: *We are quite concerned about the rising cost of food.* **2** interested: *Concerned citizens make use of their right to vote.* *adjective.*

con cern ing (kən sėr′ning), having to do with; about: *The reporter asked many questions concerning the accident.* *preposition.*

con cert (kon′sərt), a musical performance in which several musicians or singers take part: *The school orchestra gave a free concert.* *noun.*
in concert, all together; in agreement: *The class worked in concert.*

con cer to (kən cher′tō), a piece of music to be played by one or more principal instruments, such as a violin or piano, accompanied by an orchestra. *noun, plural* **con cer tos.**

con ces sion (kən sesh′ən), **1** conceding; yielding: *As a concession to my pleas, I was allowed to stay up late.* **2** anything conceded or yielded: *I have made all the concessions that I intend to make.* **3** something granted or leased by a government or other group for a special purpose: *The park has a concession that sells food and drinks.* *noun.*

conch (kongk *or* konch), **1** a shellfish with a large, spiral shell. **2** its shell. *noun, plural* **conchs** (kongks), **conch es** (kon′chiz).

a hat	**i** it	**oi** oil	**ch** child	a in about
ā age	**ī** ice	**ou** out	**ng** long	e in taken
ä far	**o** hot	**u** cup	**sh** she	ə = i in pencil
e let	**ō** open	**ů** put	**th** thin	o in lemon
ē equal	**ô** order	**ü** rule	**ŦH** then	u in circus
ėr term			**zh** measure	

con cil i ate (kən sil′ē āt), win over; soothe: *I conciliated the angry child with a candy bar.* *verb,* **con cil i at ed, con cil i at ing.**

con cise (kən sīs′), expressing much in few words; brief but full of meaning: *He gave a concise report of the meeting.* *adjective.*

con clude (kən klüd′), **1** end: *The play concluded with a happy ending and the curtain came down.* **2** reach (certain decisions or opinions) by reasoning: *From the tracks we saw, we concluded that the animal must have been a deer.* **3** settle; arrange: *The two countries concluded a trade agreement.* *verb,* **con clud ed, con clud ing.**

con clu sion (kən klü′zhən), **1** end: *the conclusion of the story.* Textbooks sometimes have conclusions summing up all the important facts in a chapter. **2** decision or opinion reached by reasoning: *She came to the conclusion that she would have to work harder to finish on time.* **3** settlement; arrangement: *the conclusion of a peace treaty between two countries.* *noun.*

con clu sive (kən klü′siv), decisive; final: *The evidence against the burglar was conclusive.* *adjective.*

con coct (kon kokt′), prepare; make up: *She concocted a drink made of grape juice and ginger ale. He concocted an excuse to explain his lateness.* *verb.*

con cord (kon′kôrd), agreement; peace; harmony: *concord between friends.* *noun.*

con crete (kon′krēt′ *or* kon krēt′), **1** real; existing as an actual object: *A painting is concrete, but its beauty is not.* **2** mixture of cement, sand or gravel, and water that hardens as it dries. Concrete is used for foundations, whole buildings, sidewalks, roads, dams, and bridges. **3** made of this mixture: *a concrete sidewalk.* 1,3 *adjective,* 2 *noun.*

con cur (kən kėr′), agree; be of the same opinion: *The judges all concurred in giving her the prize.* *verb,* **con curred, con cur ring.**

con cus sion (kən kush′ən), **1** violent shaking; shock: *The concussion caused by the explosion broke many windows.* **2** injury to the brain or spine from a blow, fall, or other shock. *noun.*

con demn (kən dem′), **1** express strong disapproval of: *We condemn cruelty to animals.* **2** pronounce guilty of crime or wrong: *The accused man was condemned by the jury.* **3** sentence; doom: *The spy was condemned to death.* **4** declare not sound or suitable for use: *This bridge was condemned because it is no longer safe.* *verb.*

con dem na tion (kon′dem nā′shən), a condemning or a being condemned: *the condemnation of an unsafe bridge, a criminal's condemnation by a jury.* *noun.*

con den sa tion (kon′den sā′shən), **1** a condensing or a being condensed: *the*

condor—4 feet (1½ meters) long;
wingspread up to 10 feet (3 meters)

cone (definitions 1, 2, and 3)

condensation of steam into water. **2** condensed mass. A cloud is a condensation of water vapor in the atmosphere. *noun.*

con dense (kən dens′), **1** make denser; become more compact: *Milk is condensed by removing much of the water from it.* **2** increase the strength of: *Light is condensed by means of lenses.* **3** change from a gas or a vapor to a liquid. If warm air touches a cold surface, it condenses into tiny drops of water. **4** say briefly; put into fewer words: *A long story can often be condensed. verb,* **con densed, con dens ing.**

con de scend (kon′di send′), come down willingly to the level of one's inferiors in rank: *The king condescended to eat with the beggars. verb.*

con di tion (kən dish′ən), **1** state in which a person or thing is: *My room is in a messy condition.* **2** good condition; good health: *People who take part in sports must keep in condition.* **3** put in good condition: *Exercise conditions your muscles.* **4** social position; rank: *They were poor people of humble condition.* **5** **conditions,** set of circumstances: *Icy roads cause bad driving conditions.* **6** thing on which something else depends; thing without which something else cannot be: *One condition of the peace treaty was the return of all prisoners.* **7** accustom: *This dog was conditioned to expect food when it heard a bell.* 1,2,4-6 *noun,* 3,7 *verb.*
on condition that, if: *I'll go on condition that you will too.*

con di tion al (kən dish′ə nəl), depending on something else: *"I will come if the sun is shining" is a conditional promise. adjective.*

con do min i um (kon′də min′ē əm), **1** an apartment house in which each apartment is owned rather than rented. **2** apartment in a building like this. *noun.*

con dor (kon′dər), large vulture with a bare neck and head. Condors live on high mountains in South America and California. See picture. *noun.*

con duct (kon′dukt *for 1;* kən dukt′ *for 2-5*), **1** way of acting; behavior thought of as good or bad: *Her conduct was rude.* **2** act in a certain way; behave: *At home he is disorderly, but in company he conducts himself well.* **3** manage; direct: *to conduct an orchestra, to conduct a business.* **4** guide or lead: *Conduct me to him.* **5** be a channel for: *Metals conduct heat and electricity.* 1 *noun.* 2-5 *verb.*

con duc tor (kən duk′tər), **1** guide or leader; person who is conducting. The conductor of an orchestra or chorus trains the performers to work together, beats time for them, and selects the music to be used. **2** person in charge of passengers on a train or a bus. The conductor collects fares. **3** thing that transmits heat, electricity, light, or sound: *Copper wire is used as a conductor of electricity. noun.*

cone (kōn). See picture. **1** a solid object that has a flat, round base and narrows to a point at the top. **2** anything shaped like a cone: *an ice-cream cone, the cone of a volcano.* **3** part that bears the seeds on pine, cedar, and other evergreen trees. *noun.*

con fed er a cy (kən fed′ər ə sē), union of

countries; group of people joined together for a special purpose. *noun, plural* **con fed er a cies.**

con fed er ate (kən fed′/ər it), **1** person or country joined with another for a special purpose; ally: *The thief and his confederates escaped to another city.* **2** joined together for a special purpose; allied. **1** *noun,* **2** *adjective.*

con fed e ra tion (kən fed′/ə rā′shən), **1** joining together in a league or alliance: *The conference devised a plan for a confederation of the colonies.* **2** league; confederacy; alliance. *noun.*

con fer (kən fėr′), **1** talk things over; consult together; exchange ideas: *My parents conferred with the teacher about my schoolwork.* **2** give; bestow: *The university conferred an honorary degree on the scientist. verb,* **con ferred, con fer ring.**

con fer ence (kon′fər əns), **1** meeting of interested persons to discuss a particular subject: *A conference was called to discuss the best way of getting a playground for the school.* **2** group of athletic teams, churches, or clubs, joined together for some special purpose. *noun.*

con fess (kən fes′), **1** acknowledge; admit; own up: *I confessed to eating all the cake. I confess you are right on one point.* **2** admit one's guilt: *The guilty person confessed.* **3** tell one's sins to a priest in order to obtain forgiveness. *verb.*

con fes sion (kən fesh′ən), **1** owning up; confessing; telling one's mistakes or sins: *The guilty person made a full confession.* **2** thing confessed. *noun.*

con fide (kən fīd′), **1** tell as a secret: *He confided his troubles to his sister.* **2** show trust by telling secrets: *She always confided in her friend.* **3** put trust: *to confide in God.* **4** give to another to be kept safe; hand over: *She confides her baby to the day nursery while she is at work. verb,* **con fid ed, con fid ing.**

con fi dence (kon′fə dəns), **1** firm belief or trust: *We have no confidence in a liar.* **2** firm belief in oneself and one's abilities: *Years of experience at his work have given him great confidence.* **3** trust that a person will not tell others what is told to him: *The secret was told to me in strict confidence.* **4** thing told as a secret: *I would never reveal a confidence. noun.*

con fi dent (kon′fə dənt), firmly believing; certain; sure: *I feel confident that our team will win. adjective.*

con fi den tial (kon′fə den′shəl), **1** spoken or written as a secret: *This story is confidential; you must never repeat it.* **2** trusted with secret matters: *a confidential secretary. adjective.*

con fine (kən fīn′ for 1; kon′fīn for 2), **1** keep in; hold in: *to be confined in prison for two years.* **2** boundary; limit: *These people have never been beyond the confines of their own valley.* **1** *verb,* **con fined, con fin ing; 2** *noun.*

con fine ment (kən fīn′mənt), confining; being confined: *confinement indoors because of a cold. noun.*

con firm (kən fėrm′), **1** prove to be true or correct; make certain: *The rumor that war had ended was

a hat	i it	oi oil	ch child	a in about
ā age	ī ice	ou out	ng long	e in taken
ä far	o hot	u cup	sh she	ə = { i in pencil
e let	ō open	ů put	th thin	o in lemon
ē equal	ô order	ü rule	ŦH then	u in circus
ėr term			zh measure	

confirmed by a news broadcast.* **2** make more certain by putting in writing, by consent, or by encouragement: *We sent a letter to confirm our telephone order. The Senate confirmed the treaty.* **3** admit to full membership in a church or synagogue after required study and preparation. *verb.*

con fir ma tion (kon′fər mā′shən), **1** making sure by more information or evidence: *I telephoned the theater for confirmation of the starting time of the movie.* **2** thing that confirms; proof: *Don't believe rumors that lack confirmation.* **3** ceremony of admitting a person to full membership in a church or synagogue after required study and preparation. *noun.*

con firmed (kən fėrmd′), **1** firmly established; proved: *a confirmed rumor.* **2** settled; habitual: *a confirmed bachelor. adjective.*

con fis cate (kon′fə skāt), **1** seize for the public treasury: *The traitor's property was confiscated.* **2** seize by authority; take and keep: *The teacher confiscated my comic book. verb,* **con fis cat ed, con fis cat ing.**

con flict (kon′flikt *for 1 and 2;* kən flikt′ *for 3),* **1** a fight or struggle, especially a long one: *The conflict between Greece and Troy lasted for ten years.* **2** active opposition of persons or ideas: *A conflict of opinion arose over what food was best for our rabbit.* **3** be opposed; clash; differ in thought and action: *The witnesses conflicted on whether the robber had light or dark hair.* **1,2** *noun,* **3** *verb.*

con form (kən fôrm′), **1** act according to law or rule; be in agreement with generally accepted standards: *Members must conform to the rules of our club.* **2** be like; make similar: *I cut the material to conform to the pattern. verb.*

con front (kən frunt′), **1** meet face to face; stand facing. **2** face boldly; oppose: *I crept downstairs with baseball bat in hand to confront the prowler.* **3** bring face to face; place before: *The teacher confronted me with my failing grade. verb.*

con fuse (kən fyüz′), **1** throw into disorder; mix up: *So many people talking at once confused me.* **2** be unable to tell apart; mistake (one thing or person for another): *People often confuse this girl with her twin sister. verb,* **con fused, con fus ing.**

con fu sion (kən fyü′zhən), **1** confused condition; disorder: *the confusion in an untidy room, the confusion in a busy street after an accident.* **2** mistaking one thing for another: *Words like "believe" and "receive" sometimes cause confusion in spelling. noun.*

con geal (kən jēl′), **1** harden or make solid by cold; freeze. **2** thicken; stiffen: *The blood around the wound had congealed. verb.*

con gest (kən jest′), **1** fill too full; overcrowd: *The

streets of this city are often congested with traffic.
2 become too full of blood or mucus. *The lungs are congested in pneumonia. verb.*

con grat u late (kən grach′ə lāt), express your pleasure at the happiness or good fortune of: *Everyone congratulated the winner of the race. verb,* **con grat u lat ed, con grat u lat ing.**

con grat u la tion (kən grach′ə lā′shən), **1** a congratulating; wishing a person joy. **2 congratulations,** expression of pleasure at another's happiness or good fortune: *Congratulations on your high grades. noun.*

con gre gate (kong′grə gāt), come together into a crowd or mass: *The scouts congregated around the campfire. verb,* **con gre gat ed, con gre gat ing.**

con gre ga tion (kong′grə gā′shən), **1** act of coming together into a crowd or mass. **2** group of people gathered together for religious worship or instruction. *noun.*

con gress (kong′gris), **1** the lawmaking body of a nation, especially of a republic. **2 Congress,** the national lawmaking body of the United States, consisting of the Senate and the House of Representatives, with members elected from every state. **3** coming together; meeting: *Doctors came from all over the world to the medical congress on heart disease. noun, plural* **con gress es.**

con gress man (kong′gris mən), member of the United States Congress, especially of the House of Representatives. *noun, plural* **con gress men.**

con gress wom an (kong′gris wùm′ən), a woman member of Congress, especially of the House of Representatives. *noun, plural* **con gress wom en.**

con gru ent (kən grü′ənt), having the same size and shape: *congruent triangles. adjective.*

con i cal (kon′ə kəl), shaped like a cone: *Volcanic mountains are conical. adjective.*

con junc tion (kən jungk′shən), **1** word that connects words, phrases, clauses, or sentences. *And, but, or, though,* and *if* are conjunctions. **2** a joining together; union; combination: *Our school, in conjunction with two other schools, will hold an art fair next week. noun.*

con nect (kə nekt′), **1** join one thing to another; fasten together; unite: *connect a hose to a faucet.* **2** think of one thing with another: *We usually connect spring with sunshine and flowers.* **3** join with others in some business or interest; have any kind of practical relation with: *This store is connected with a chain of stores. verb.*

Con nect i cut (kə net′ə kət), one of the northeastern states of the United States. *noun.* [*Connecticut* was named for the Connecticut River, which flows through the state. The river got its name from an American Indian word meaning "at the long tidal river."]

con nec tion (kə nek′shən), **1** act of connecting: *The connection of our telephone took several hours.* **2** being joined together or connected; union: *Her connection with that company lasted thirty years.* **3** thing that connects; connecting part: *The connection between the radiator and the pipe has become loose.* **4** any kind of practical relation with

another thing: *I had no connection with that prank.* **5** linking together of words or ideas in proper order: *His last remark had no connection with the earlier part of his talk.* **6** meeting of trains, ships, buses, or airplanes so that passengers can change from one to the other without delay: *The bus arrived late at the airport and we missed our airplane connection.* **7** related person; relative: *A brother-in-law is a connection by marriage. noun.*

con quer (kong′kər), overcome by force; get the better of; take in war: *conquer a bad habit. verb.*

con quer or (kong′kər ər), person who conquers. *noun.*

con quest (kon′kwest), **1** act of conquering: *the conquest of a country.* **2** thing conquered: *Troy was the Greeks' hardest conquest. noun.*

con science (kon′shəns), sense of right and wrong; ideas and feelings within you that tell you when you are doing right and warn you of what is wrong. *noun.*

con sci en tious (kon′shē en′shəs), **1** careful to do what one knows is right; controlled by conscience. **2** done with care to make it right: *Conscientious work is careful and exact. adjective.*

con scious (kon′shəs), **1** knowing; aware: *I was conscious of a sharp pain.* **2** able to feel; awake: *About five minutes after fainting he became conscious again.* **3** aware of what one is doing; done on purpose; intended: *She made a conscious effort to improve. adjective.*

con scious ness (kon′shəs nis), **1** being conscious; awareness: *The injured woman lost consciousness.* **2** all the thoughts and feelings of a person. *noun.*

con se crate (kon′sə krāt), **1** set apart as sacred; make holy: *A church is consecrated to worship.* **2** set apart for a purpose; dedicate: *A doctor's life is consecrated to keeping people well. verb,* **con se crat ed, con se crat ing.**

con sec u tive (kən sek′yə tiv), following one right after another: *Monday, Tuesday, and Wednesday are consecutive days of the week. adjective.*

con sent (kən sent′), **1** agree; give approval or permission: *My parents would not consent to my staying.* **2** agreement; permission: *We have the owner's consent to swim in this pond.* **1** *verb,* **2** *noun.*

con se quence (kon′sə kwens), **1** result: *He was always late and, as a consequence, he lost his job.* **2** importance: *This is of little consequence. noun.* **take the consequences,** accept what happens because of one's action: *She did not study for the test, so she had to take the consequences.*

con se quent (kon′sə kwent), resulting; following as an effect: *My illness and consequent absence put me behind in my schoolwork. adjective.*

con se quent ly (kon′sə kwent′lē), as a result; therefore: *He overslept and, consequently, he was late. adverb.*

con ser va tion (kon′sər vā′shən), protecting from loss or being used up; avoidance of waste; preservation: *Conservation of forests is important. noun.*

con serv a tive (kən sėr′və tiv), **1** inclined to keep

a hat	**i** it	**oi** oil	**ch** child	a in about
ā age	**ī** ice	**ou** out	**ng** long	e in taken
ä far	**o** hot	**u** cup	**sh** she **ə** =	i in pencil
e let	**ō** open	**u̇** put	**th** thin	o in lemon
ē equal	**ô** order	**ü** rule	**ᴛʜ** then	u in circus
ėr term			**zh** measure	

things as they are or were in the past: *A conservative person distrusts and opposes change and too many new ideas.* **2** person opposed to change. **3** not inclined to take risks; cautious: *This old, reliable company has conservative business methods.* 1,3 *adjective,* 2 *noun.*

con serve (kən sėrv′), keep from harm or decay; protect from loss or from being used up; preserve: *to conserve natural resources. Try to conserve your strength for the end of the race.* verb, **con served, con serv ing.**

con sid er (kən sid′ər), **1** think about in order to decide: *Before you dash off an answer, take time to consider the problem.* **2** think to be; regard as: *I consider him a very able student.* **3** allow for; take into account: *This watch runs very well, if you consider how old it is.* **4** be thoughtful of (others and their feelings): *A kind person considers the feelings of others.* verb.

con sid er a ble (kən sid′ər ə bəl), **1** worth thinking about; important: *Air pollution is a considerable problem.* **2** not a little; much: *$500 is a considerable sum of money.* adjective.

con sid er a bly (kən sid′ər ə blē), much; a good deal: *The boy was considerably older than he looked.* adverb.

con sid er ate (kən sid′ər it), thoughtful of others and their feelings: *It was considerate of you to bring me flowers.* adjective.

con sid er a tion (kən sid′ə rā′shən), **1** thinking about things in order to decide them: *Give careful consideration to these questions before answering them.* **2** something thought of as a reason: *Price and quality are two considerations in buying anything.* **3** thoughtfulness for others and their feelings: *Playing the radio loud at night shows a lack of consideration for the neighbors.* noun.

in consideration of, 1 because of: *In consideration of my bad cold, the teacher let me leave school early.* **2** in return for: *The neighbor gave the girl a dollar in consideration of her help.*

take into consideration, take into account; consider; make allowance for: *The judge took the boy's age into consideration.*

con sid er ing (kən sid′ər ing), taking into account; making allowance for: *Considering her age, the little girl reads very well.* preposition.

con sign (kən sīn′), **1** hand over; deliver: *His will consigned his property to his sister.* **2** send: *We will consign the goods to you by express.* verb.

con sist (kən sist′), be made up: *A week consists of seven days. A chair consists of a seat with a back, supported by four legs.* verb.

con sist en cy (kən sis′tən sē), **1** degree of firmness or stiffness: *Frosting for a cake must be of the right consistency to spread easily without dripping.* **2** keeping to the same principles or course: *You show no consistency if you are always changing your mind.* noun, plural **con sist en cies.**

con sist ent (kən sis′tənt), **1** thinking or acting today in agreement with what you thought yesterday; keeping to the same principles and habits. **2** harmonious; in agreement: *Driving very fast on a rainy night is not consistent with safety.* adjective.

con so la tion (kon′sə lā′shən), **1** comfort. **2** comforting person, thing, or event. noun.

con sole[1] (kən sōl′), comfort: *The policeman consoled the lost child by speaking kindly to him.* verb, **con soled, con sol ing.**

con sole[2] (kon′sōl), **1** part of an organ containing the keyboard, stops, and pedals. **2** a radio, television, or phonograph cabinet made to stand on the floor. noun.

con sol i date (kən sol′ə dāt), **1** unite; combine: *The three banks consolidated and formed a single large bank.* **2** strengthen: *The political party consolidated its power by winning many state elections.* verb, **con sol i dat ed, con sol i dat ing.**

con so nant (kon′sə nənt), **1** any letter of the alphabet that is not a vowel. *B, c, d,* and *f* are consonants. **2** sound represented by such a letter or combination of letters. The two consonants in *ship* are spelled by the letters *sh* and *p.* noun.

con sort (kon′sôrt *for 1;* kən sôrt′ *for 2*), **1** a husband or wife. **2** associate: *The politician was accused of consorting with criminals.* 1 *noun,* 2 *verb.*

con spic u ous (kən spik′yü əs), **1** easily seen: *A traffic light should be placed where it is conspicuous.* **2** remarkable; attracting notice: *conspicuous bravery.* adjective.

con spir a cy (kən spir′ə sē), secret planning with others to do something wrong or unlawful; plot: *a conspiracy to overthrow the government.* noun, plural **con spir a cies.**

con spir a tor (kən spir′ə tər), person who conspires; one who joins in a plot: *A group of conspirators planned to overthrow the dictator.* noun.

con spire (kən spīr′), **1** plan secretly with others to do something wrong or unlawful; plot: *The spies conspired to steal secret government documents.* **2** act together: *All things conspired to make her birthday a happy one.* verb, **con spired, con spir ing.**

con sta ble (kon′stə bəl *or* kun′stə bəl), police officer; policeman. noun.

con stant (kon′stənt), **1** never stopping: *Three days of constant rain made the field muddy.* **2** continually happening: *A clock makes a constant ticking sound.* **3** always the same; not changing: *If you walk due north, your direction is constant.* **4** faithful; loyal: *A constant friend helps you when you need help.* adjective.

con stant ly (kon′stənt lē), **1** always: *He is constantly late.* **2** without stopping: *If a clock is kept wound it runs constantly.* **3** often: *She has to be reminded constantly to clean her room.* adverb.

con stel la tion (kon′stə lā′shən), group of stars. The Big Dipper is the easiest constellation to locate. noun.

con ster na tion (kon/stər nā/shən), dismay; alarm: *To our consternation the child darted out in front of the speeding car. noun.*

con stit u ent (kən stich/ü ənt), **1** forming a necessary part; making up: *Flour, water, salt, and yeast are constituent parts of bread.* **2** part of a whole; necessary part: *Sugar is the main constituent of candy.* **3** voter: *Senators are eager to hear from their constituents.* 1 *adjective,* 2,3 *noun.*

con sti tute (kon/stə tüt *or* kon/stə tyüt), **1** make up; form: *Seven days constitute a week.* **2** set up; establish: *Schools are constituted by law to teach boys and girls.* **3** appoint; elect: *The group constituted one member as its leader. verb,* **con sti tut ed, con sti tut ing.**

con sti tu tion (kon/stə tü/shən *or* kon/stə tyü/shən), **1** the way in which a person or thing is organized; nature; make-up: *A person with a good constitution is strong and healthy.* **2** the fundamental principles according to which a country, a state, or a society is governed: *Many clubs have written constitutions.* **3** the Constitution, the written set of fundamental principles by which the United States is governed. *noun.*

con sti tu tion al (kon/stə tü/shə nəl *or* kon/stə tyü/shə nəl), **1** of or in the constitution of a person or thing: *A constitutional weakness makes him catch a cold easily.* **2** of or according to the constitution of a nation, state, or group: *The Supreme Court must decide whether this law is constitutional.* **3** walk taken for the health: *After Sunday dinner Grandfather always takes his constitutional.* 1,2 *adjective,* 3 *noun.*

con struct (kən strukt/), put together; fit together; build: *We constructed a raft of logs fastened with rope. verb.*

con struc tion (kən struk/shən), **1** act of constructing; building; putting together: *The construction of the bridge took nearly a month.* **2** way in which a thing is constructed: *Cracks and leaks are signs of poor construction.* **3** thing built or put together: *The dolls' house was a construction of wood and cardboard.* **4** arrangement of words in a sentence. *noun.*

con struc tive (kən struk/tiv), helpful; tending to be useful: *During the experiment the teacher gave some constructive suggestions that prevented accidents. adjective.*

con strue (kən strü/), show the meaning of; explain; interpret: *Different lawyers may construe the same law differently. verb,* **con strued, con stru ing.**

con sul (kon/səl), officer appointed by a government to live in some foreign city in order to look after its business interests and to protect its citizens who are traveling or living there. *noun.*

con sult (kən sult/), **1** seek information or advice from. You can consult persons, books, or maps to find out what you wish to know. **2** take into consideration; have regard for: *A good teacher consults the interests of the class. verb.*

con sume (kən süm/), **1** use up; spend. See picture. **2** eat or drink up: *We will each consume at least two sandwiches on our hike.* **3** destroy; burn up: *A huge fire consumed the entire forest. verb,* **con sumed, con sum ing.**

con sum er (kən sü/mər), **1** person who uses food, clothing, or anything grown or made by producers: *A low price for wheat should reduce the price of flour to the consumer.* **2** person or thing that consumes. *noun.*

con sump tion (kən sump/shən), **1** using up; use: *We took along some food for our consumption on the trip.* **2** amount used up: *In November the oil consumption of our furnace reached 200 gallons.* **3** a disease that destroys parts of the lungs; tuberculosis. *noun.*

con tact (kon/takt), **1** condition of touching; touching together: *A magnet will draw iron filings into contact with it.* **2** connection: *The control tower lost radio contact with the airplane pilot.* **3** get in touch with; make a connection with: *I've been trying to contact you for two days.* 1,2 *noun,* 3 *verb.*

contact lens, a very small, thin, plastic lens fitted on the front of the eyeball.

con ta gious (kən tā/jəs), **1** catching; spreading by contact: *Mumps is a contagious disease.* **2** easily spreading from one to another: *Yawning is often contagious. adjective.*

con tain (kən tān/), **1** have within itself; hold as contents: *My wallet contains two dollars. Books contain information.* **2** be capable of holding: *That pitcher will contain a quart of milk.* **3** be equal to: *A pound contains 16 ounces.* **4** control; hold back; restrain (one's feelings): *She could not contain her excitement over winning the contest. verb.*

con tain er (kən tā/nər), box, can, jar, or carton used to hold or contain something. A pitcher is a container. *noun.*

con tam i nate (kən tam/ə nāt), make impure by contact; defile; pollute; corrupt: *The water was contaminated by sewage. verb,* **con tam i nat ed, con tam i nat ing.**

consume (definition 1)
Rockets **consume** large quantities of fuel when they take off.

contemplation

a hat	i it	oi oil	ch child		a in about
ā age	ī ice	ou out	ng long		e in taken
ä far	o hot	u cup	sh she	ə =	i in pencil
e let	ō open	ù put	th thin		o in lemon
ē equal	ô order	ü rule	ᴛʜ then		u in circus
ėr term			zh measure		

con tem plate (kon′təm plāt), **1** look at or think about for a long time: *I will contemplate your offer. We contemplated the beautiful mountain landscape.* **2** have in mind; expect; intend: *She is contemplating a trip to Europe. verb,* **con tem plat ed, con tem plat ing.**

con tem pla tion (kon′təm plā′shən), looking at or thinking about something for a long time; deep thought. See picture. *noun.*

con tem po rar y (kən tem′pə rer′ē), **1** belonging to the same period of time: *The telephone and the phonograph were contemporary inventions.* **2** person who belongs to the same period of time: *Abraham Lincoln and Robert E. Lee were contemporaries.* **1** *adjective,* **2** *noun, plural* **con tem po rar ies.**

con tempt (kən tempt′), **1** despising; scorn; feeling that a person or act is mean and low: *to feel contempt for a cheat.* **2** condition of being despised; disgrace: *The traitor was held in contempt. noun.*

con tempt i ble (kən temp′tə bəl), deserving contempt or scorn: *a contemptible lie. adjective.*

con tend (kən tend′), **1** fight; struggle: *The first settlers in America had to contend with harsh winters, sickness, and lack of food.* **2** take part in a contest: *Five runners were contending in the first race.* **3** declare to be true; argue: *Most doctors contend that cigarette smoking is dangerous to one's health. verb.*

con tent¹ (kon′tent), **1 contents,** what is contained in anything; all things inside: *An old chair, a desk, and a bed were the only contents of the room. The contents of the box fell out in her lap.* **2** what is written in a book; what is said in a speech: *I didn't understand the content of his speech.* **3** amount contained: *Maple syrup has a high sugar content. noun.*

con tent² (kən tent′), **1** satisfy; please: *Nothing contents me when I am sick.* **2** satisfied; contented: *Will you be content to wait till tomorrow?* **3** contentment; satisfaction: *The cat lay beside the fire in sleepy content.* **1** *verb,* **2** *adjective,* **3** *noun.*

con tent ed (kən ten′tid), satisfied: *A contented person is happy with things as they are. adjective.*

con ten tion (kən ten′shən), **1** statement or point that one has argued for: *Columbus's contention that the earth was round turned out to be correct.* **2** arguing; disputing; quarreling: *There was some contention about choosing a captain for the baseball team. noun.*

con tent ment (kən tent′mənt), satisfaction; being pleased; happiness. *noun.*

con test (kon′test *for 1 and 2;* kən test′ *for 3*), **1** trial of skill to see which can win. A game or race is a contest. **2** dispute; struggle; fight: *The contest between France and England for North America ended in a victory for England.* **3** fight for; struggle for: *The soldiers contested every inch of ground.* **1,2** *noun,* **3** *verb.*

con test ant (kən tes′tənt), person who contests; person who takes part in a contest: *My sister was a contestant in the 100-yard dash. noun.*

con text (kon′tekst), part directly before and after a word or sentence that influences its meaning. You can often tell the meaning of a word from its use in context. *noun.*

con ti nent (kon′tə nənt), **1** one of the seven great masses of land on the earth. The continents are North America, South America, Europe, Africa, Asia, Australia, and Antarctica. **2 the Continent,** the mainland of Europe. *noun.*

con ti nent al (kon′tə nen′tl), of a continent; like a continent. *adjective.*

con tin u al (kən tin′yü əl), **1** never stopping: *the continual flow of the river.* **2** repeated many times; very frequent: *I can't study with these continual interruptions. adjective.*

con tin u al ly (kən tin′yü ə lē), **1** always; without stopping: *A doctor is continually on call.* **2** again and again; very frequently: *I am continually losing my gloves. adverb.*

con tin u ance (kən tin′yü əns), **1** going on; lasting: *the continuance of a friendship.* **2** remaining; stay: *The senator's continuance in office depends on the voters. noun.*

con tin u a tion (kən tin′yü ā′shən), **1** act of going on with a thing after stopping; a beginning again: *Continuation of my reading was hard after so many interruptions.* **2** anything by which a thing is continued; added part: *The continuation of the story will be seen on next week's program. noun.*

con tin ue (kən tin′yü), **1** keep up; keep on; not stop; last; cause to last: *The rain continued all day. The road continues for miles.* **2** take up; carry on: *The story will be continued next week.* **3** stay: *The*

children must continue in school till the end of June.
4 maintain; cause to stay: *The club members voted to continue the president in office for another term.* verb, **con tin ued, con tin u ing.**

con ti nu i ty (kon′tə nü′ə tē *or* kon′tə nyü′ə tē), going on without stopping; continuing without interruption: *The continuity of his story was broken when the telephone rang.* noun.

con tin u ous (kən tin′yü əs), connected; unbroken; without a stop: *a continuous sound, a continuous line of cars.* adjective.

con tor tion (kən tôr′shən), **1** twisting out of shape. **2** twisted condition: *The acrobat went through various contortions.* noun.

con tour (kon′tür), outline: *The contour of the Atlantic coast of America is very irregular.* noun.

con tra band (kon′trə band), goods brought into or taken out of a country illegally; smuggled goods: *Customs officials went through each bag looking for contraband.* noun.

con tract (kən trakt′ *for 1-4;* kon′trakt *for 5 and 6;* kon′trakt *or* kən trakt′ *for 7*), **1** draw together; make shorter: *Wrinkling your forehead contracts your brows.* **2** shrink; become shorter or smaller: *Wool fibers contract in hot water. Earthworms can contract.* **3** shorten (a word) by omitting some of the letters or sounds: *In talking we contract "do not" to "don't."* **4** bring on oneself; get; form: *Bad habits are easy to contract and hard to get rid of.* **5** agreement. In a contract two or more people agree to do or not to do certain things. **6** a written agreement that can be enforced by law. **7** make a contract: *The builder contracted to build a new house for a certain price.* 1-4,7 verb, 5,6 noun.

con trac tion (kən trak′shən), **1** contracting: *Cold causes the contraction of liquids, metals, and gases.* **2** being contracted; decrease in size or volume: *The contraction of mercury by cold makes it go down in thermometers.* **3** something contracted; a shortened form: *"Can't" is a contraction of "cannot."* noun.

con trac tor (kon′trak tər *or* kən trak′tər), person who agrees to furnish materials or to do a piece of work for a certain price: *a building contractor.* noun.

con tra dict (kon′trə dikt′), **1** say that a statement is not true; deny: *I contradicted the rumor that I was moving to another town.* **2** say the opposite of what a person has said: *It is rude to contradict a guest.* **3** be contrary to; disagree with: *Your story and her story contradict each other.* verb.

con tra dic tion (kon′trə dik′shən), **1** denying what has been said: *The expert spoke without fear of contradiction by his listeners.* **2** statement that contradicts another; denial. **3** disagreement. noun.

con tra dic tor y (kon′trə dik′tər ē), contradicting; in disagreement; saying the opposite. See picture. adjective.

con tral to (kən tral′tō), **1** the lowest singing voice of a woman. **2** singer with such a voice. **3** part sung by such a voice. noun, plural **con tral tos.**

con tra ry (kon′trer ē *for 1 and 2;* kən trer′ē *for 3*), **1** opposed; opposite; completely different: *Her*

taste in music is contrary to mine. **2** the opposite: *After promising to come early, she did the contrary and came late.* **3** opposing others; stubborn: *The contrary boy often refused to do what was suggested.* 1,3 adjective, 2 noun, plural **con tra ries.**
on the contrary, exactly opposite to what has been said: *He is not stingy; on the contrary, no one could be more generous.*

con trast (kon′trast *for 1 and 2;* kən trast′ *for 3 and 4*), **1** difference; a great difference: *There is a great contrast between life now and life years ago.* See picture. **2** person, thing, or event that shows differences when put side by side with another: *Her dark hair is in sharp contrast to her brother's light hair.* **3** compare (two things) so as to show their differences: *Contrast birds with fishes.* **4** show differences when compared or put side by side: *The black and the gold contrast well in that design.* 1,2 noun, 3,4 verb.

con trib ute (kən trib′yüt), **1** give money or help: *Will you contribute to the Red Cross? Everyone was asked to contribute suggestions for the party.* **2** write (articles or stories) for a newspaper or magazine. verb, **con trib ut ed, con trib ut ing.**
contribute to, help bring about: *A poor diet contributed to the child's bad health.*

con tri bu tion (kon′trə byü′shən), **1** act of contributing; giving money or help: *Contribution to worthy causes is one of her pet projects.* **2** money or help contributed; gift: *Our contribution to the picnic was the lemonade.* **3** something written for a newspaper or magazine. noun.

con trite (kən trīt′ *or* kon′trīt), **1** sorry for doing something wrong; repentant: *I felt contrite after losing my temper and hitting my friend.* **2** showing deep regret: *I wrote a contrite apology.* adjective.

con triv ance (kən trī′vəns), **1** thing invented; mechanical device: *A can opener is a handy contrivance.* **2** act or manner of contriving: *By careful contrivance she repaired the old clock and made it go.* **3** plan; scheme. noun.

con trive (kən trīv′), **1** invent; design: *The inventor had contrived a new engine.* **2** plan; scheme; plot: *contrive a robbery.* **3** manage: *I will contrive to be there by ten o'clock.* verb, **con trived, con triv ing.**

con trol (kən trōl′), **1** have power or authority over; direct: *The government controls the printing of money.* **2** power; authority; direction: *Children are under their parents' control.* **3** hold back; keep down: *I was so upset by the accident that I couldn't control my tears.* **4** a holding back; a keeping down; restraint; check: *to lose control of one's temper.* **5** a device on or connected to a machine: *This control starts the dishwasher.* **6** the controls, the instruments and devices by which an airplane, locomotive, or car is operated. 1,3 verb, **con trolled, con trol ling;** 2,4-6 noun.

control tower, tower at an airfield for controlling the taking off and landing of aircraft.

con tro ver sy (kon′trə vėr′sē), dispute; a long dispute; argument: *The controversy between the company and the union ended after the strike was settled.* noun, plural **con tro ver sies.**

contrast
(definition 1)

a hat	**i** it	**oi** oil	**ch** child	⎧ a in about
ā age	**ī** ice	**ou** out	**ng** long	⎪ e in taken
ä far	**o** hot	**u** cup	**sh** she	**ə** = ⎨ i in pencil
e let	**ō** open	**u̇** put	**th** thin	⎪ o in lemon
ē equal	**ô** order	**ü** rule	**ŦH** then	⎩ u in circus
ėr term			**zh** measure	

con va lesce (kon′və les′), recover health and strength after illness: *I convalesced at home for a week after my operation.* verb, **con va lesced, con va lesc ing.**

con va les cent (kon′və les′nt), **1** recovering health and strength after illness. **2** person recovering after illness. 1 *adjective*, 2 *noun.*

con vene (kən vēn′), **1** meet for some purpose; gather in one place; assemble: *Congress convenes at least once a year.* **2** call together: *Any member may convene our club in an emergency.* verb, **con vened, con ven ing.**

con ven ience (kən vē′nyəns), **1** being convenient: *The convenience of packaged goods increases their sale.* **2** comfort; advantage: *Many towns have camping places for the convenience of tourists.* **3** anything handy or easy to use; thing that saves trouble or work: *We find our folding table a great convenience. noun.*

at your convenience, when it is convenient for you: *Come by to pick me up at your convenience.*

con ven ient (kən vē′nyənt), **1** suitable; saving trouble; well arranged; easy to use: *take a convenient bus, live in a convenient house.* **2** easily done; not troublesome: *Will it be convenient for you to bring your lunch to school?* **3** within easy reach; handy: *meet at a convenient place. adjective.*

con vent (kon′vent), **1** group of nuns living together. **2** building or buildings in which they live. *noun.*

con ven tion (kən ven′shən), **1** a meeting arranged for some particular purpose: *The Democratic and Republican parties hold conventions every four years to choose candidates for President.* **2** general agreement; common consent; custom: *Convention influences how we dress.* **3** custom or practice approved by general agreement: *Using the right hand to shake hands is a convention. noun.*

con ven tion al (kən ven′shə nəl), **1** depending on conventions; customary: *"Good morning" is a conventional greeting.* See picture. **2** acting or behaving according to commonly accepted and approved ways: *The people living next door are quiet, conventional people.* **3** of the usual type or design: *conventional furniture. adjective.*

con ver sa tion (kon′vər sā′shən), friendly talk; exchange of thoughts by talking informally together. *noun.*

con verse (kən vėrs′), talk together in an informal way. verb, **con versed, con vers ing.**

con ver sion (kən vėr′zhən), **1** a turning; a change: *Heat causes the conversion of water into steam.* **2** a change from one belief to another or from lack of belief to faith. *noun.*

con vert (kən vėrt′ for 1 and 2; kon′vėrt′ for 3), **1** change; turn: *The generators at the dam convert*

contradictory—The fruit seller is making a **contradictory** statement.

conventional (definition 1)—It used to be **conventional** for everyone to do the laundry on Monday morning.

convertible (definition 2)

cooperate—They **cooperated** and got the job done quickly.

corkscrew (definition 1)

coral—The stony branches (definition 1) are formed by the flowerlike little animals (definition 2).

water power into electricity. *One last effort converted defeat into victory.* **2** cause to change from one belief to another or from lack of belief to faith: *Missionaries tried to convert the villagers.* **3** person who has been converted. 1,2 *verb,* 3 *noun.*

con vert i ble (kən vėr′tə bəl), **1** capable of being converted: *A dollar bill is convertible into ten dimes.* **2** automobile with a folding top. See picture. 1 *adjective,* 2 *noun.*

con vex (kon veks′ *or* kon′veks), curved out, like the outside of a sphere or circle: *The lens of an automobile headlight is convex on the outside.* *adjective.*

con vey (kən vā′), **1** carry: *A bus conveyed the passengers to the airport. A wire conveys an electric circuit.* **2** make known; communicate: *Do the author's words convey any meaning to you?* **3** give; make over; transfer: *They conveyed their business to their children and retired.* *verb.*

con vey ance (kən vā′əns), **1** carrying; transmission; communication: *Freighters engage in the conveyance of goods from one port to another.* **2** thing that carries people and goods; vehicle: *Trains and buses are public conveyances. noun.*

con vict (kən vikt′ *for* 1; kon′vikt *for* 2), **1** prove or declare guilty: *The jury convicted the accused woman of stealing.* **2** person serving a prison sentence for some crime. 1 *verb,* 2 *noun.*

con vic tion (kən vik′shən), **1** proving or declaring guilty: *The trial resulted in the conviction of the accused man.* **2** being proved or declared guilty: *The thief's conviction meant a year in prison.* **3** firm belief: *It is my conviction that you are right. noun.*

con vince (kən vins′), make (a person) feel sure; cause to believe; persuade firmly: *The mistakes she made convinced me that she had not studied her lesson.* *verb,* **con vinced, con vinc ing.**

con voy (kən voi′ *or* kon′voi *for* 1; kon′voi *for* 2 and 3), **1** go with in order to protect; escort: *Armed guards convoyed the gold to the bank.* **2** a convoying; protection: *The gold was moved from the truck to the bank's vault under convoy of armed guards.* **3** warships or soldiers that convoy. 1 *verb,* 2,3 *noun.*

con vulse (kən vuls′), **1** shake violently: *An earthquake convulsed the island, damaging many of the buildings.* **2** cause violent disturbance in; disturb violently: *to be convulsed with rage.* **3** throw into convulsions; shake with spasms of pain: *The sick child was convulsed before the doctor came.* **4** throw into fits of laughter; cause to shake with laughter: *The clown's funny antics convulsed the audience.* *verb,* **con vulsed, con vuls ing.**

con vul sion (kən vul′shən), **1** a violent drawing together of the muscles; fit: *We called the veterinarian when our dog had convulsions.* **2** fit of laughter. **3** violent disturbance: *An earthquake is a convulsion of the earth. noun.*

coo (kü), **1** the soft, murmuring sound made by doves or pigeons. **2** make this sound. **3** murmur softly: *to coo to a baby.* 1 *noun, plural* **coos;** 2,3 *verb.*

cook (kük), **1** prepare (food) by using heat.

Boiling, frying, broiling, roasting, and baking are forms of cooking. **2** undergo cooking; be cooked: *Let the meat cook slowly.* **3** person who cooks. 1,2 *verb*, 3 *noun*.

cook ie or **cook y** (kük′ē), a small, flat, sweet cake. *noun, plural* **cook ies.**

cook out (kük′out′), a picnic where the food is cooked outdoors on a grill. *noun.*

cool (kül), **1** somewhat cold; more cold than hot: *a cool day.* **2** allowing or giving a cool feeling: *a cool, thin shirt.* **3** not excited; calm: *Everyone kept cool when paper in the wastebasket caught fire.* **4** having little enthusiasm or interest; not cordial: *My former friend gave me a cool greeting.* **5** something cool; cool part, place, or time: *in the cool of the evening.* **6** make or become cool: *Ice cools water. The ground cools off after the sun goes down.* 1-4 *adjective*, 5 *noun*, 6 *verb*.

coon (kün), raccoon. *noun.*

coop (küp), **1** a small cage or pen for chickens, rabbits, and other small animals. **2** keep in a coop; confine in a small place: *The children were cooped indoors by the rain.* 1 *noun*, 2 *verb*.

co op e rate (kō op′ə rāt′), work together. See picture. *verb*, **co op e rat ed, co op e rat ing.**

co op e ra tion (kō op′ə rā′shən), working together; united effort or labor: *Cooperation can accomplish what no individual could do alone. noun.*

co op e ra tive (kō op′ə rā′tiv), wanting or willing to work together with others. *adjective.*

co or di nate (kō ôrd′n āt for 1; kō ôrd′n it for 2), **1** arrange in proper order; put in proper relation; adjust; harmonize: *Coordinating the movements of the arms and legs is the hardest part of learning to swim.* **2** equal in importance; of equal rank. 1 *verb*, **co or di nat ed, co or di nat ing;** 2 *adjective.*

co or di na tion (kō ôrd′n ā′shən), acting or working together in a smooth way: *good muscular coordination. noun.*

cope (kōp), to struggle and not fail; struggle with some chance of success; deal successfully: *She was busy but was still able to cope with the extra work. verb*, **coped, cop ing.**

co pi lot (kō′pī′lət), the assistant or second pilot in an aircraft. *noun.*

co pi ous (kō′pē əs), more than enough; plentiful; abundant: *a copious harvest. adjective.*

cop per (kop′ər), **1** a reddish metal, easy to work with. Copper is an excellent conductor of heat and electricity. **2** made of this metal: *a copper kettle.* **3** a coin made of copper or bronze, especially a penny. **4** reddish brown: *She had copper hair.* 1,3 *noun*, 2,4 *adjective.*

cop per head (kop′ər hed′), a poisonous snake of North America. It has a copper-colored head, and grows to be about three feet (one meter) long. *noun.*

cop ra (kō′prə), the dried meat of coconuts. *noun.*

cop y (kop′ē), **1** thing made to be just like another; thing made on the model of another. A written page, a picture, a dress, or a piece of furniture can be an exact copy of another. **2** make a copy of: *Copy this page. I copied the painting.* **3** be a copy of; follow as an example; imitate: *to copy someone's way of dressing.* **4** one of a number of books, magazines, newspapers, or pictures made at the same printing: *Please get six copies of today's newspaper.* **5** written material ready to be set in print in newspapers, magazines, or books. 1,4,5 *noun, plural* **cop ies;** 2,3 *verb*, **cop ied, cop y ing.**

co ral (kôr′əl), **1** a hard substance made up of the skeletons of tiny sea animals called polyps. Red, pink, and white coral is often used for jewelry. See picture. **2** the little sea animal which makes coral. It is mostly stomach and mouth. **3** deep pink; red. 1,2 *noun*, 3 *adjective.*

cord (kôrd), **1** thick string; very thin rope: *He tied the package with a cord.* **2** something resembling a cord. A pair of covered wires with fittings to connect an electric iron or lamp to a socket is a cord. **3** nerve, tendon, or other structure in an animal body that is something like a cord. The spinal cord is in the backbone. **4** a unit for measuring cut wood equal to 128 cubic feet. A pile of wood 4 feet wide, 4 feet high, and 8 feet long is a cord. *noun.*

cor dial (kôr′jəl), sincere; hearty; warm; friendly: *My friends gave me a cordial welcome. adjective.*

cor di al i ty (kôr′jē al′ə tē), cordial quality; cordial feeling; heartiness; warm friendliness: *The cordiality of his welcome made me feel at home. noun, plural* **cor di al i ties.**

cor du roy (kôr′də roi′), thick cotton or rayon cloth with close, raised ribs or ridges that run lengthwise along the cloth. *noun.*

core (kôr), **1** the hard, central part containing the seeds of fruits like apples and pears: *After eating the apple he threw the core away.* **2** the central or most important part: *She is honest to the core. The core of the senator's speech was that we must not waste natural resources.* **3** take out the core of: *We cored the apples.* 1,2 *noun*, 3 *verb*, **cored, cor ing.**

cork (kôrk), **1** the light, thick, outer bark of a kind of oak tree. Cork is used for bottle stoppers, floats for fishing lines, filling for some kinds of life preservers, and some floor coverings. **2** a shaped piece of cork: *the cork of a bottle.* **3** any stopper for a bottle or flask, made of glass or rubber. **4** stop up with a cork: *Fill and cork these bottles.* 1-3 *noun*, 4 *verb.*

cork screw (kôrk′skrü′), **1** tool used to pull corks out of bottles. See picture. **2** shaped like a corkscrew; spiral. 1 *noun*, 2 *adjective.*

corn (kôrn), **1** the grain of a kind of cereal grass, or the plant that it grows on. Corn grows on large ears. Corn is used as food for people and farm animals. Also called **maize** or **Indian corn.** **2** any small, hard seed or grain of wheat, barley, or oats. *noun.*

a hat	i it	oi oil	ch child	a in about
ā age	ī ice	ou out	ng long	e in taken
ä far	o hot	u cup	sh she	i in pencil
e let	ō open	ù put	th thin	o in lemon
ē equal	ô order	ü rule	ŦH then	u in circus
ėr term			zh measure	

corn bread, bread made of corn meal instead of flour.

corn cob (kôrn′kob′), the central, woody part of an ear of corn, on which the kernels grow. *noun.*

cor ne a (kôr′nē ə), the transparent outside coat of the eyeball. It covers the iris and the pupil. *noun.*

corned (kôrnd), preserved with strong salt water or dry salt: *corned beef. adjective.*

cor ner (kôr′nər), **1** place where two lines or surfaces meet; angle: *the corner of a room. I watched what she was doing out of the corner of my eye.* **2** place where two streets meet: *There is a traffic light at the corner.* **3** at a corner: *a corner house.* **4** for a corner: *a corner cupboard.* **5** secret place; place away from crowds: *The money was hidden in odd corners all over the house.* **6** region; part; place that is far away: *People have searched in all corners of the earth for gold.* **7** difficult place: *His enemies had driven him into a corner.* **8** force into an awkward or difficult position; drive into a corner: *This question cornered him. Workers at the zoo cornered the lion in the alley and returned it to its cage.* 1,2,5-7 *noun,* 3,4 *adjective,* 8 *verb.*

cor net (kôr net′), a musical wind instrument like a trumpet, usually made of brass. See picture. *noun.*

corn meal, coarsely ground dried corn.

corn stalk (kôrn′stôk′), stalk of corn. *noun.*

co rol la (kə rol′ə), the petals of a flower. *noun.*

co ro na tion (kôr′ə nā′shən), ceremony of crowning a king, queen, emperor, or empress. *noun.*

cor por al[1] (kôr′pər əl), of the body: *Spanking someone is corporal punishment. adjective.*

cor por al[2] (kôr′pər əl), the lowest ranking officer in the army. A corporal is higher than a private and lower than a sergeant. *noun.*

cor po ra tion (kôr′pə rā′shən), group of persons who obtain a charter giving them as a group certain rights and privileges. A corporation can buy and sell, own property, and manufacture and ship products as if its members were a single person. *noun.*

corps (kôr), **1** group of soldiers, trained for special military service: *the Medical Corps, the Signal Corps.* **2** group of people with special training, organized for working together: *A large hospital has a corps of nurses. noun, plural* **corps** (kôrz).

corpse (kôrps), a dead human body. *noun.*

cor pu lent (kôr′pyə lənt), fat; stout. See picture. *adjective.*

cor pus cle (kôr′pus′əl), any of the cells that form a large part of blood. Red corpuscles carry oxygen from the lungs to various parts of the body; some white corpuscles destroy disease germs. *noun.*

cor ral (kə ral′), **1** pen for horses, cattle, and other animals. **2** drive into or keep in a corral: *The cowhands corralled the herd of wild ponies.* **3** hem in; surround; capture: *The reporters corralled the mayor and began asking questions.* 1 *noun,* 2,3 *verb,* **cor ralled, cor ral ling.**

cor rect (kə rekt′), **1** free from mistakes; true; right: *She gave the correct answer.* **2** agreeing with a good standard of taste; proper: *correct manners.* **3** mark the mistakes in; change to what is right: *The teacher corrected our tests and returned them to us.* **4** adjust to agree with some standard: *correct the reading of a barometer.* **5** punish; set right by punishing; find fault with to improve: *correct a child for misbehaving.* 1,2 *adjective,* 3-5 *verb.*

cor rec tion (kə rek′shən), **1** correcting; setting right: *The correction of all my mistakes took nearly an hour.* **2** something put in place of an error or mistake: *Write in your corrections neatly.* **3** punishment. A prison is sometimes called a **house of correction.** *noun.*

cor re spond (kôr′ə spond′), **1** agree; be in harmony: *Her answers correspond with mine.* **2** be similar: *The fins of a fish correspond to the wings of a bird.* **3** exchange letters; write letters to one another: *Will you correspond with me while I am away? verb.*

cor re spond ence (kôr′ə spon′dəns), **1** agreement: *Your account of the accident has little correspondence with the story the other witness told.* **2** exchange of letters; friendly letter writing: *The boy kept up a correspondence with his friend in Europe.* **3** letters: *Bring me the correspondence concerning that order. noun.*

cor re spond ent (kôr′ə spon′dənt), **1** person who exchanges letters with another: *My cousin and I are correspondents.* **2** person employed to send news from a distant place: *There was a report on the news tonight from the correspondent in China. noun.*

cor ri dor (kôr′ə dər), long hallway; passage in a large building into which rooms open: *Our classroom is at the end of a corridor. noun.*

cor rode (kə rōd′), eat away gradually: *Moisture corrodes iron. verb,* **cor rod ed, cor rod ing.**

cor ru gate (kôr′ə gāt), bend or shape into wavy folds or ridges; wrinkle: *The carton was made of corrugated cardboard. verb,* **cor ru gat ed, cor ru gat ing.**

cor rupt (kə rupt′), **1** wicked: *The thief led a corrupt life.* **2** make evil or wicked: *Bad companions may corrupt a person.* **3** influenced by bribes; dishonest: *a corrupt judge.* **4** bribe: *That judge cannot be corrupted.* 1,3 *adjective,* 2,4 *verb.*

cor rup tion (kə rup′shən), **1** a making or being made evil or wicked. **2** evil conduct. **3** bribery; dishonesty: *The police force must be kept free from corruption. noun.*

cor sage (kôr säzh′), bouquet to be worn on the waist or shoulder of a woman's dress. *noun.*

cor set (kôr′sit), a stiff, close-fitting undergarment worn about the waist and hips to support or shape the body. *noun.*

cos met ic (koz met′ik), preparation for beautifying the skin or hair. Powder and rouge are cosmetics. *noun.*

cos mic (koz′mik), **1** having to do with the whole universe: *Cosmic forces produce stars and meteors.* **2** vast: *a cosmic explosion. adjective.*

corpulent

cost (kôst), **1** price paid: *The cost of this watch was $10.* **2** be obtained at the price of; require: *This watch costs $10. The school play cost much time and effort.* **3** loss; sacrifice: *The fox escaped the trap at the cost of a leg.* 1,3 *noun,* 2 *verb,* **cost, cost ing.**

cost ly (kôst′lē), **1** of great value: *costly jewels.* **2** costing much: *He made a costly mistake and had to do his work over. adjective,* **cost li er, cost li est.**

cos tume (kos′tüm *or* kos′tyüm), **1** dress; outer clothing; style of dress, including the way the hair is worn: *The clown wore a funny costume. The kimono is part of the national costume of Japan.* **2** dress belonging to another time or place, worn on the stage: *The actors wore colonial costumes.* **3** complete set of outer garments: *a street costume.* **4** provide a costume for; dress. 1-3 *noun,* 4 *verb,* **cos tumed, cos tum ing.**

co sy (kō′zē), cozy. *adjective,* **co si er, co si est.**

cot (kot), narrow bed, sometimes made of canvas stretched on a frame that folds together. *noun.*

cot tage (kot′ij), **1** small house. **2** house at a summer resort. *noun.*

cottage cheese, a soft, white cheese made from the curds of sour milk.

cotton (definition 2)

cot ton (kot′n), **1** soft, white fibers in a fluffy mass around the seeds of a plant, used in making fabrics or thread. **2** plant that produces these fibers. See picture. **3** thread or cloth made of cotton. **4** made of cotton: *a cotton handkerchief.* 1-3 *noun,* 4 *adjective.*

cot ton tail (kot′n tāl′), a common American wild rabbit with a fluffy, white tail. *noun.*

cot ton wood (kot′n wu̇d′), **1** a kind of American poplar tree with tufts that look like cotton on its seeds. **2** the soft wood of this tree. *noun.*

couch (kouch), **1** bed or sofa for sleep or rest. **2** any place for sleep or rest: *The deer got up from its grassy couch.* **3** put in words; express: *His thoughts were couched in beautiful language.* 1,2 *noun, plural* **couch es;** 3 *verb.*

cou gar (kü′gər), puma. *noun.*

cough (kôf), **1** force air from the lungs with sudden effort and noise. **2** act of coughing. **3** sound of coughing. **4** condition that causes repeated coughing: *I had a bad cough.* 1 *verb,* 2-4 *noun.*

could (ku̇d), **1** was able; was able to: *She could ski very well.* **2** might be able to: *Perhaps I could go with you tomorrow. verb.*

could n't (ku̇d′nt), could not.

coun cil (koun′səl), **1** group of people called together to give advice and to discuss or settle questions. **2** group of people elected by citizens to make laws for and manage a city or town. *noun.*

coun ci lor (koun′sə lər), member of a council. *noun.*

cornet

coun sel (koun′səl), **1** act of exchanging ideas; act of talking things over: *We benefited from our frequent counsel.* **2** advice: *A wise person gives good counsel.* **3** person or group that gives advice about the law; lawyer or group of lawyers: *Each side of a case in a court of law has its own counsel.* **4** give advice to; advise: *My teacher counseled me to join the school band.* **5** recommend: *He counseled acting at once. The doctor counseled operating at once.* 1-3 noun, 4,5 verb, **coun seled, coun sel ing.**

coun se lor (koun′sə lər), person who gives advice; adviser. *noun.*

count[1] (kount), **1** name numbers in order: *The child can count from one to ten.* **2** add up; find the number of: *I counted the books and found there were fifty.* **3** adding up; finding out how many: *The count showed more than 5000 votes had been cast.* **4** total number; amount: *The exact count was 5170 votes.* **5** include in the total number; take into account: *Let's not count that practice game.* **6** be included in the total number; be taken into account: *Your first race is only for practice; it won't count.* **7** have an influence; be of account or value: *Every vote counts in an election. Every penny counts.* **8** think of as; consider: *You can count yourself lucky to have good health.* **9** depend; rely: *We count on your help.* 1,2,5-9 verb, 3,4 noun.

count[2] (kount), European nobleman about equal in rank to an English earl. *noun.*

count down (kount′doun′), **1** the time just before the launching of a missile or rocket. **2** the calling out of the passing minutes or seconds of this period as they pass. *noun.*

coun te nance (koun′tə nəns), **1** expression of the face: *Her angry countenance showed how she felt.* **2** face; features: *a person with a noble countenance.* *noun.*

count er[1] (koun′tər), **1** long table in a store, restaurant, or bank on which money is counted out, and across which goods, food, or drinks are given to customers. **2** thing used for counting. Round, flat disks are often used as counters to keep score in card games. **3** an imitation coin. *noun.*

coun ter[2] (koun′tər), person or thing that counts. *noun.*

coun ter[3] (koun′tər), **1** contrary; opposed: *She acted counter to her promise.* **2** oppose: *He countered my plan with one of his own.* 1 adverb, adjective, 2 verb.

coun ter act (koun′tər akt′), act against; hinder: *A hot bath will sometimes counteract a chill.* verb.

coun ter clock wise (koun′tər klok′wīz′), in the direction opposite to that in which the hands of a clock go. See picture. *adverb, adjective.*

coun ter feit (koun′tər fit), **1** copy (money, pictures, or handwriting) in order to deceive: *They were arrested for counterfeiting ten-dollar bills.* **2** something copied and passed as genuine: *This ten-dollar bill looks genuine, but it is a counterfeit.* **3** not genuine: *a counterfeit stamp.* **4** pretend: *They counterfeited interest in order to be polite.* 1,4 verb, 2 noun, 3 adjective.

coun ter part (koun′tər pärt′), person or thing closely resembling another: *She is the counterpart of her twin sister.* noun.

coun ter sign (koun′tər sīn′), secret signal; watchword; password: *The soldier had to give the countersign before he could pass the sentry.* noun.

count ess (koun′tis), **1** wife or widow of a count or an earl. **2** woman whose rank is equal to that of a count or an earl. *noun, plural* **count ess es.**

count less (kount′lis), too many to count: *the countless stars. adjective.*

coun try (kun′trē), **1** land; region: *The country around the town was rough and hilly.* **2** all the land of a nation: *France is a country in Europe.* **3** land where a person was born or where he or she is a citizen: *The United States is my country.* **4** people of a nation: *The country rejoiced when the war ended.* **5** land outside of cities and towns: *She likes the farms and fields of the country.* **6** of the country; in the country: *He likes hearty country food and fresh country air.* 1-5 noun, plural **coun tries;** 6 adjective.

coun try man (kun′trē mən), a person of one's own country. *noun, plural* **coun try men.**

coun try side (kun′trē sīd′), rural district; country: *I saw many cows in the countryside.* noun.

coun ty (koun′tē), **1** one of the districts into which a state or country is divided for purposes of government. The county officers collect taxes, hold court, keep county roads in repair, and maintain county schools. **2** the land, the people, or the officials of a county. *noun, plural* **coun ties.**

cou ple (kup′əl), **1** two things of the same kind that go together; pair: *She bought a couple of tires for her bicycle.* **2** man and woman who are married, engaged, or partners in a dance. **3** join together: *The brakeman coupled the freight cars.* 1,2 noun, 3 verb, **cou pled, cou pling.**

cou pling (kup′ling), **1** a joining together. **2** device for joining together parts of machinery. *noun.*

cou pon (kü′pon *or* kyü′pon), part of a ticket, advertisement, or package that gives the person who holds it certain rights: *I saved coupons from boxes of cereal and got a free toy.* noun.

cour age (kėr′ij), bravery; meeting danger without fear. *noun.*

cou ra geous (kə rā′jəs), fearless; brave; full of courage. *adjective.*

cour i er (kėr′ē ər *or* kur′ē ər), messenger sent in haste. *noun.*

course (kôrs), **1** onward movement: *Our history book traces the course of human development from the cave to modern city living.* **2** direction taken: *Our course was straight to the north.* **3** line of action; way of doing: *The only sensible course was to go home.* **4** way; path; track; channel: *the winding course of a stream.* **5** number of like things arranged in some regular order: *a course of lectures.* **6** regular order: *Mother gets little rest in the course of her daily work.* **7** series of studies in a school, college, or university. A student must complete a certain course in order to graduate. **8** one of the studies in such a series: *Each course in geography lasts one year.* **9** part of a meal served

at one time: *The first course was chicken soup.*
10 place for races or games: *a golf course.* **11** run:
The blood courses through the veins. 1-10 *noun,*
11 *verb,* **coursed, cours ing.**

of course, 1 surely; certainly: *Of course you can
go!* **2** naturally; as should be expected: *She gave
me a gift, and, of course, I accepted it.*

court (kôrt), **1** space partly or wholly enclosed by
walls or buildings: *The four apartment houses were
built around a court of grass.* **2** short street. **3** place
marked off for a game: *a tennis court, a basketball
court.* **4** place where a king, queen, or other ruler
lives; royal palace. **5** household and followers of a
king, queen, or other ruler: *The court of Queen
Elizabeth I was noted for its splendor.* **6** ruler and
his or her advisers as a governing body or power:
*An order of the Court of St. James's is an order of
the British government.* **7** assembly held by a king,
queen, or other ruler: *The queen held court to hear
from her advisers.* **8** place where justice is
administered: *The prisoner was brought to court for
trial.* **9** persons who administer justice; judge or
judges: *The court found him guilty.* **10** assembly of
such persons to administer justice: *Several cases
await trial at the next court.* **11** seek the favor of; try
to please: *The nobles courted the king to get
positions of power.* **12** try to win the love of; pay
loving attention to in order to marry: *He courted
her by bringing her flowers every day.* See picture.
13 try to get; seek: *It is foolish to court danger.* 1-10
noun, 11-13 *verb.*

cour te ous (kėr'tē əs), polite: *The clerks are
courteous at this store. adjective.*

cour te sy (kėr'tə sē), **1** polite behavior;
thoughtfulness for others: *It is a sign of courtesy to
give one's seat to an old person on a bus.* **2** a
kindness; act of consideration; polite act: *Thanks
for all your courtesies. noun, plural* **cour te sies.**

court house (kôrt'hous'), **1** building in which
courts of law are held. **2** building used for the
government of a county. *noun, plural*
court hous es (kôrt'hou'ziz).

cour ti er (kôr'tē ər), person often present at a
royal court. *noun.*

court ly (kôrt'lē), having manners fit for a royal
court; polite; elegant. *adjective,* **court li er,
court li est.**

court ship (kôrt'ship), condition or time of
courting in order to marry: *Their brief courtship
was a very happy one. noun.*

court yard (kôrt'yärd'), space enclosed by walls,
in or near a large building. *noun.*

cous in (kuz'n), son or daughter of one's uncle or
aunt. First cousins have the same grandparents;
second cousins have the same great-
grandparents; and so on for third and fourth
cousins. *noun.*

cove (kōv), small bay; mouth of a creek; inlet on
the shore. *noun.*

cov er (kuv'ər), **1** put something over: *I covered the
child with a blanket.* **2** be over; spread over: *Snow
covered the ground.* **3** anything that protects or
hides: *the cover of a book. A thicket makes good

court (definition 12)

cover for animals to hide in.* **4** hide: *I tried to cover
my mistake by pretending it was a joke.* **5** go over;
travel: *The travelers covered 400 miles a day by car.*
6 include; take in: *The math review covers
everything we've studied.* 1,2,4-6 *verb,* 3 *noun.*

cover up, 1 cover completely. **2** hide; conceal.

covered wagon, wagon having a canvas cover
that can be taken off.

cov er ing (kuv'ər ing), anything that covers: *A
blanket is a bed covering. noun.*

cov et (kuv'it), desire eagerly (something that
belongs to another): *Her friends coveted her new
sled. verb.*

cow[1] (kou), **1** the full-grown female of domestic

cattle that gives milk. **2** female of the buffalo, moose, and other large animals that nurse their young: *an elephant cow.* *noun.*

cow[2] (kou), make afraid; frighten: *I was cowed by their threats and stayed out of their sight.* *verb.*

cow ard (kou′ərd), person who lacks courage or is easily made afraid; one who runs from danger. *noun.*

cow ard ice (kou′ər dis), lack of courage; being easily made afraid: *to be guilty of cowardice in the presence of danger.* *noun.*

cow ard ly (kou′ərd lē), without courage; like a coward. *adjective.*

cow bird (kou′bėrd′), a small North American blackbird that is often found with cattle. *noun.*

cow boy (kou′boi′), man whose work is looking after cattle on a ranch. *noun.*

cow catch er (kou′kach′ər), a metal frame on the front of a locomotive or streetcar to clear the tracks of anything in the way. *noun.*

cow er (kou′ər), crouch in fear or shame: *The dog cowered under the table after being scolded.* *verb.*

cow girl (kou′gėrl′), woman who works on a ranch or at rodeos. *noun.*

cow hand (kou′hand′), person who works on a cattle ranch. *noun.*

cow hide (kou′hīd′), **1** the hide of a cow. **2** leather made from it. *noun.*

cowl (koul), **1** monk's cloak with a hood. **2** the hood itself. *noun.*

cow punch er (kou′pun′chər), cowboy. *noun.*

cow slip (kou′slip), a wild plant with bright, yellow flowers that bloom in early spring. *noun.*

cox swain (kok′sən *or* kok′swān′), person who steers a boat. *noun.*

coy (koi), **1** shy; modest; bashful. **2** acting more shy than one really is. *adjective.*

coy o te (kī ō′tē *or* kī′ōt), a small wolflike animal living on the prairies of western North America. See picture. *noun, plural* **coy o tes** *or* **coy o te.**

co zi ly (kō′zə lē), in a snug and comfortable manner. *adverb.*

co zy (kō′zē), warm and comfortable; snug: *The cat lay in a cozy corner near the fireplace.* *adjective,* **co zi er, co zi est.** Also spelled **cosy.**

crab (krab), a shellfish with eight legs, two claws, and a broad, flat shell covering. Many kinds of crabs are good to eat. See picture. *noun.*

crab apple, a small, sour kind of apple used to make jelly.

crab by (krab′ē), cross, grouchy, or bad-tempered. *adjective,* **crab bi er, crab bi est.**

crack (krak), **1** split or opening made by breaking without separating into parts: *There is a crack in this cup.* **2** break without separating into parts: *You have cracked the window.* **3** a narrow opening: *I opened the door just a crack.* **4** a sudden, sharp noise like that made by loud thunder, by a whip, or by something breaking. **5** make or cause to make a sudden, sharp noise: *to crack a whip. The whip cracked.* **6** break with a sudden, sharp noise: *The tree cracked loudly and fell. We cracked the nuts.* **7** a hard, sharp blow: *The falling branch gave me a*

crane
(definition 1)

coyote—about 21 inches (53 centimeters) high at the shoulder

crab—shell about 4 inches (10 centimeters) wide

crater (definition 2)—a crater on the moon

crack on the head. **8** hit with a hard, sharp blow: *The falling branch cracked me on the head.* 1,3,4,7 *noun,* 2,5,6,8 *verb.*

crack up, 1 crash or smash: *The driver skidded off the road and cracked up his car against a tree.* **2** suffer a mental or physical collapse: *She was in danger of cracking up under the strain of overwork.*

crack er (krak′ər), a thin, crisp biscuit. *noun.*

crack le (krak′əl), **1** make slight, sharp sounds: *A fire crackled in the fireplace.* **2** a slight, sharp sound, such as paper makes when it is crushed. 1 *verb,* **crack led, crack ling;** 2 *noun.*

crack up (krak′up′), **1** a crash; smash: *a truck crackup.* **2** a mental or physical collapse. *noun.*

cra dle (krā′dl), **1** a small bed for a baby, usually mounted on rockers. **2** put or rock in a cradle; hold as in a cradle: *I cradled the baby in my arms.* **3** place where anything begins its growth: *The sea is thought to have been the cradle of life.* **4** any kind of framework looking like or used as a cradle. The framework on which a ship, boat, or aircraft rests during building or repairs is a cradle. The part of a telephone that supports the receiver is also a cradle. 1,3,4 *noun,* 2 *verb,* **cra dled, cra dling.**

craft (kraft), **1** special skill: *The carpenter shaped and fitted the wood into a cabinet with great craft.* **2** trade or art requiring skilled work: *Carpentry is a craft.* **3** skill in deceiving others; slyness; sly tricks: *By craft the gambler tricked them out of all their money.* **4** boats, ships, or aircraft: *Craft of all kinds come into New York every day. noun.*

crafts man (krafts′mən), person skilled in a craft or trade. *noun, plural* **crafts men.**

craft y (kraf′tē), skillful in deceiving others: *The crafty fox lured the rabbit from its hole. adjective,* **craft i er, craft i est.**

crag (krag), a steep, rugged rock rising above others. *noun.*

cram (kram), **1** force into; force down; stuff: *I crammed all my clothes into a suitcase.* **2** fill too full; crowd: *The hall was crammed, with many people standing.* **3** eat too fast or too much: *She had to cram down her breakfast to get to school on time.* **4** try to learn too much in a short time: *As he hasn't studied during the year, he has to cram for his final tests. verb,* **crammed, cram ming.**

cramp (kramp), **1** a sudden, painful contracting or pulling together of muscles, often from chill or strain: *The swimmer was seized with a cramp and had to be helped from the pool.* **2** confine in a small space; limit: *The closet was so small, I was cramped for space to hang my clothes.* 1 *noun,* 2 *verb.*

cran ber ry (kran′ber′ē), a firm, sour, dark-red berry that grows on low shrubs in marshes. Cranberries are used in making sauce and jelly. *noun, plural* **cran ber ries.**

crane (krān), **1** machine with a long, swinging arm, for lifting heavy objects. See picture. **2** a large wading bird with long legs, neck, and bill. **3** stretch (the neck) as a crane does, in order to see better. 1,2 *noun,* 3 *verb,* **craned, cran ing.**

cra ni um (krā′nē əm), **1** skull. **2** part of the skull enclosing the brain. *noun.*

a hat	**i** it	**oi** oil	**ch** child	a in about
ā age	**ī** ice	**ou** out	**ng** long	e in taken
ä far	**o** hot	**u** cup	**sh** she	ə = { i in pencil
e let	**ō** open	**ù** put	**th** thin	o in lemon
ē equal	**ô** order	**ü** rule	**ŦH** then	u in circus
ėr term			**zh** measure	

crank (krangk), **1** part or handle of a machine connected at right angles to another part to set it in motion: *I turned the crank of the sharpener to sharpen my pencil.* **2** work or start by means of a crank: *I cranked the eggbeater.* **3** odd person; person who has strange ideas or habits. **4** cross or ill-tempered person. 1,3,4 *noun,* 2 *verb.*

crank y (krang′kē), cross; irritable. *adjective,* **crank i er, crank i est.**

crash (krash), **1** a sudden, loud noise like many dishes falling and breaking, or like sudden, loud band music: *The lightning was followed by a crash of thunder.* **2** make a sudden, loud noise: *The thunder crashed loudly.* **3** fall, hit, or break with force and a loud noise: *The dishes crashed to the floor.* **4** falling, hitting, or breaking with force and a loud noise: *the crash of dishes on the floor.* **5** the violent striking of one solid thing against another: *There was a crash of two cars at the corner.* **6** strike violently and shatter: *The baseball crashed through the window.* **7** fall to the earth in such a way as to be damaged or wrecked: *The airplane lost power and crashed.* **8** such a fall or landing: *The skillful pilot brought down the damaged airplane without a crash.* **9** sudden ruin; severe failure in business: *Many people lost all their savings in the stock market crash.* **10** go to (a party or dance) without being invited. 1,4,5,8,9 *noun,* 2,3,6,7,10 *verb.*

crate (krāt), **1** a large frame, box, or basket made of strips of wood, for shipping glass, china, fruit, household goods, or furniture. **2** pack in a crate: *crate a mirror for moving.* 1 *noun,* 2 *verb,* **crat ed, crat ing.**

cra ter (krā′tər), **1** the opening at the top of a volcano. **2** a hole in the ground shaped like a bowl: *The meteor crashed to earth and formed a huge crater.* See picture. *noun.*

crave (krāv), **1** long for; desire very much: *The thirsty hiker craved water.* **2** ask earnestly for; beg: *He craved a favor of the king. verb,* **craved, crav ing.**

crav ing (krā′ving), longing; yearning; strong desire: *I had a craving for something sweet. noun.*

craw fish (krô′fish′), crayfish. *noun, plural* **craw fish es** or **craw fish.**

crawl (krôl), **1** move slowly, pulling the body along the ground: *Worms and snakes crawl.* **2** creep on hands and knees: *We crawled through a hole in the fence.* **3** move slowly: *The heavy traffic crawled through the narrow tunnel.* **4** slow movement: *The crawl of traffic annoyed the impatient driver.* **5** swarm with crawling things: *The ground was crawling with ants.* **6** feel creepy: *My flesh crawled at the thought of the huge black snakes.* **7** a fast way of swimming by overarm strokes and rapid kicking of the feet. 1-3,5,6 *verb,* 4,7 *noun.*

cray fish (krā′fish′), a freshwater animal looking much like a small lobster. *noun, plural* **cray fish es** or **cray fish.**

cray on (krā′on *or* krā′ən), **1** stick or pencil of chalk, charcoal, or a waxlike, colored substance, used for drawing or writing. **2** draw with crayons. **3** drawing made with crayons. 1,3 *noun,* 2 *verb.*

craze (krāz), **1** a short-lived, eager interest in doing some one thing: *The craze for flying kites was replaced by another for roller-skating.* **2** make crazy: *The broken leg nearly crazed the horse with pain.* 1 *noun,* 2 *verb,* **crazed, craz ing.**

cra zy (krā′zē), **1** having a diseased or injured mind; insane. **2** greatly distressed or shaken by strong emotion: *The parents of the kidnaped child were crazy with worry.* **3** foolish: *It was crazy to jump out of such a high tree.* **4** very enthusiastic: *crazy about horses. adjective,* **cra zi er, cra zi est.**

creak (krēk), **1** squeak loudly: *The hinges on the door creaked because they needed oiling.* **2** creaking noise: *The creak of the stairs in the old house was spooky.* 1 *verb,* 2 *noun.*

creak y (krē′kē), likely to creak; creaking: *creaky floors. adjective,* **creak i er, creak i est.**

cream (krēm), **1** the oily, yellowish part of milk. Cream rises to the top when milk as it comes from the cow is allowed to stand. Butter is made from cream. **2** form a thick layer like cream on the top. **3** a fancy sweet dessert or candy made of cream: *chocolate creams.* **4** make a smooth mixture like cream: *I creamed butter and sugar for the cake.* **5** an oily preparation put on the skin to make it smooth and soft. **6** yellowish white. **7** best part of anything: *The cream of a class is made up of the best students.* 1,3,5,7 *noun,* 2,4 *verb,* 6 *adjective.*

cream er y (krē′mər ē), **1** place where butter and cheese are made. **2** place where cream, milk, and butter are bought and sold. *noun, plural* **cream er ies.**

cream y (krē′mē), **1** like cream; smooth and soft. **2** having much cream in it: *pie with a rich, creamy filling. adjective,* **cream i er, cream i est.**

crease (krēs), **1** line or mark produced by folding; fold; ridge: *Her slacks have a sharp crease down the front.* **2** wrinkle: *The creases on his face showed that he was old.* **3** make creases in: *I creased my slacks with an iron.* 1,2 *noun,* 3 *verb,* **creased, creas ing.**

cre ate (krē āt′), **1** make a thing which has not been made before; cause to be: *Composers create music.* **2** be the cause of: *The noise created a disturbance. verb,* **cre at ed, cre at ing.**

cre a tion (krē ā′shən), **1** creating; act of making a thing which has not been made before: *The gasoline motor led to the creation of the modern automobile.* **2** all things that have been created; the world; the universe: *Let all creation praise the Lord.* **3** thing produced by intelligence or skill, usually an important or original one: *A poem is a creation of the imagination. noun.*

cre a tive (krē ā′tiv), having the power to create; inventive; productive: *creative artists. adjective.*

cre a tor (krē ā′tər), **1** person who creates. **2 the Creator,** God. *noun.*

crea ture (krē′chər), **1** any living person or animal: *We fed the lost dog because the poor creature was starving.* **2** anything created: *Ghosts are creatures of the imagination. noun.*

cred it (kred′it), **1** belief in the truth of something; faith; trust: *I put great credit in what he says.* **2** believe; have faith in; trust: *I can credit all that you are telling me.* **3** a trust in a person's ability and intention to pay: *This store will extend credit to you by opening a charge account in your name.* **4** one's reputation in money matters: *If you pay your bills on time, your credit will be good.* **5** praise; honor: *The person who does the work should get the credit.* 1,3-5 *noun,* 2 *verb.*

credit with, think that someone has: *I credit you with the ability to do well.*

do credit to, bring honor or praise to: *The winning team did credit to the school's reputation.*

on credit, on a promise to pay later: *He bought a new car on credit.*

cred it a ble (kred′ə tə bəl), bringing praise or honor: *She has a creditable record as a senator. adjective.*

credit card, a plastic card that identifies its holder, and allows that person to charge the cost of goods or services instead of paying cash.

cred i tor (kred′ə tər), person to whom money or goods are due; one to whom a debt is owed. *noun.*

creed (krēd), **1** a brief statement of the essential points of religious belief as approved by some church. **2** any statement of faith, belief, or opinion: *"Honesty is the best policy" was their creed in all their business dealings. noun.*

creek (krēk *or* krik), small stream. *noun.*

creep (krēp), **1** move slowly with the body close to the ground or floor; crawl: *The cat was creeping toward the mouse. Babies creep on their hands and knees before they begin to walk.* **2** move slowly: *The traffic crept over the narrow bridge.* **3** move in a timid or stealthy way: *They didn't see me creeping up on them. The dog crept into the room.* **4** grow along the ground or over a wall by means of clinging stems: *Ivy had crept up the wall of the old house.* **5** feel as if things were creeping over the skin: *It made my flesh creep to hear the wolves howl.* **6** creeping; slow movement. **7 the creeps,** a feeling of fear or horror, as if things were creeping over one's skin. 1-5 *verb,* **crept, creep ing;** 6,7 *noun.*

creep y (krē′pē), having a feeling of horror, as if things were creeping over one's skin; frightened: *The ghost stories made me creepy. adjective,* **creep i er, creep i est.**

crepe (krāp), a very thin pancake, usually served folded around a filling. *noun.*

crepe pa per (krāp′ pā′pər), a thin, crinkled tissue paper used for making decorations.

crept (krept). See **creep.** *The cat crept toward the mouse. We had crept up on them without their seeing us. verb.*

cres cent (kres′nt), **1** shape of the moon when it is small and thin. **2** anything that curves in a

similar way, such as a street or a row of houses.
3 shaped like the moon when it is small and thin:
a crescent pin. 1,2 *noun,* 3 *adjective.*

cress (kres), the leaves of a garden plant, used as
a garnish or in a salad. *noun, plural* **cress es.**

crest (krest), **1** tuft or comb on the head of a bird
or animal. See picture. **2** plumes, feathers, or
other decoration on the top of a helmet.
3 decoration at the top of a coat of arms. A family
crest is sometimes put on silver, dishes, or letter
paper. **4** top part: *the crest of a wave, the crest of
the hill. noun.*

crest ed (kres′tid), having a crest: *a crested bird.*
adjective.

crest fall en (krest′fô′lən), dejected; discouraged:
The students who had failed the test were crestfallen.
adjective.

cre vasse (krə vas′), deep crack or split in the ice
of a glacier, or in the ground after an earthquake.
See picture. *noun.*

crev ice (krev′is), narrow split or crack: *Tiny ferns
grew in crevices in the stone wall. noun.*

crew[1] (krü), **1** the sailors needed to do the work
on a ship, or to row a boat. **2** group of persons
working aboard an aircraft. **3** any group of people
working or acting together: *A train crew runs a
railroad train.* **4** gang; mob: *The kids in that
neighborhood are a rough crew. noun.*

crew[2] (krü), crowed. See **crow**[1]. *The cock crew at
dawn. verb.*

crib (krib), **1** small bed with high barred sides to
keep a baby from falling out. **2** rack or manger for
horses and cows to eat from. **3** building or box for
storing grain, salt, or similar things: *Rats damaged
much of the corn in the crib.* **4** use notes or helps
unfairly in doing schoolwork: *The teacher caught
two students cribbing.* 1-3 *noun,* 4 *verb,* **cribbed,
crib bing.**

crick et[1] (krik′it), a black insect related to the
grasshopper. Male crickets make a chirping noise
by rubbing their front wings together. See picture.
noun.

crick et[2] (krik′it), an English outdoor game played
by two teams of eleven players each, with ball,
bats, and wickets. *noun.*

crime (krīm), **1** very wrong deed that is against the
law: *Murder is a crime.* **2** violation of law: *Crime is
increasing in the cities.* **3** evil or wrong act: *It is a
crime to let people live without food and clothing and
do nothing to help them. noun.*

crim i nal (krim′ə nəl), **1** person who has
committed a crime: *The criminal was sentenced to
prison for theft.* **2** guilty of wrongdoing: *a criminal
person.* **3** of or having to do with crime or its
punishment: *A criminal court hears criminal cases.*
4 like crime; wrong: *It is criminal to let a dog out in
this blizzard.* 1 *noun,* 2-4 *adjective.*

crim son (krim′zən), **1** deep red. **2** turn deep red
in color: *The child's face crimsoned with
embarrassment.* 1 *adjective,* 2 *verb.*

cringe (krinj), shrink from danger or pain; crouch
in fear: *I cringed when I saw the nurse coming to
give me a shot. verb,* **cringed, cring ing.**

a hat	i it	oi oil	ch child	a in about
ā age	ī ice	ou out	ng long	e in taken
ä far	o hot	u cup	sh she	ə = i in pencil
e let	ō open	u̇ put	th thin	o in lemon
ē equal	ô order	ü rule	ᴛʜ then	u in circus
ėr term			zh measure	

crest (definition 1)—These birds have showy **crests**.

cricket[1]—about 1 inch (2½ centimeters) long

crevasse—The climbers approached a **crevasse**.

crin kle (kring′kəl), **1** wrinkle; ripple. See picture. **2** rustle: *Paper crinkles when it is crushed. verb,* **crin kled, crin kling;** *noun.*

crip ple (krip′əl), **1** person or animal that cannot use an arm or leg properly because of injury or deformity; lame person or animal: *Long John Silver was a cripple who limped on a wooden leg.* **2** make a cripple of. **3** damage; weaken: *The ship was crippled by the storm.* **1** *noun,* **2,3** *verb,* **crip pled, crip pling.**

cri sis (krī′sis), **1** point at which a change must come, either for the better or the worse: *The scandal was a crisis in the senator's career.* **2** time of difficulty and of anxious waiting: *Because of the scarcity of oil, we face an energy crisis.* **3** turning point in a disease, toward life or death: *After his fever broke, the doctor said he had passed the crisis and would recover. noun, plural* **cri ses** (krī′sēz′).

crisp (krisp), **1** hard and thin; breaking easily with a snap: *Dry toast is crisp. Fresh celery is crisp.* **2** make crisp; become crisp: *Crisp the lettuce in cold water.* **3** fresh; sharp and clear; bracing: *The fresh air was cool and crisp.* **4** short and decided; definite: *a crisp manner. "Sit down!" was her crisp command.* **1,3,4** *adjective,* **2** *verb.*

criss cross (kris′krôs′), **1** mark or cover with crossed lines: *Little cracks crisscrossed the wall.* **2** come and go across: *Buses and cars crisscross the city.* **3** made or marked with crossed lines; crossed; crossing: *Plaids have a crisscross pattern.* **4** pattern of crossed lines: *The messy paper was a crisscross of lines and scribbles.* **1,2** *verb,* **3** *adjective,* **4** *noun, plural* **criss cross es.**

crit ic (krit′ik), **1** person who makes judgments of the merits and faults of books, music, pictures, plays, or acting: *We read what the critics in the newspapers had to say about the new play.* **2** person who disapproves or finds fault: *Don't be a critic if you don't know all the facts. noun.*

crit i cal (krit′ə kəl), **1** inclined to find fault or disapprove: *Do not be so critical.* **2** coming from one who is skilled as a critic: *a critical judgment.* **3** of a crisis; being important to the outcome of a situation: *Help arrived at the critical moment.* **4** full of danger or difficulty: *The patient was in a critical condition. adjective.*

crit i cism (krit′ə siz′əm), **1** unfavorable remarks or judgments; finding fault: *I could not let their rudeness pass without criticism.* **2** making judgments; approving or disapproving. *noun.*

crit i cize (krit′ə sīz), **1** blame; find fault with: *Do not criticize her until you know all the circumstances.* **2** judge or speak as a critic: *The editor criticized the author's new novel, comparing it with his last one. verb,* **crit i cized, crit i ciz ing.**

croak (krōk), **1** the deep, hoarse sound made by a frog, a crow, or a raven. **2** make this sound. **1** *noun,* **2** *verb.*

cro chet (krō shā′), make (sweaters, lace, and other things) by looping thread or yarn into links with a single hooked needle. Crocheting is similar to knitting. *verb,* **cro cheted** (krō shād′), **cro chet ing** (krō shā′ing).

crocus

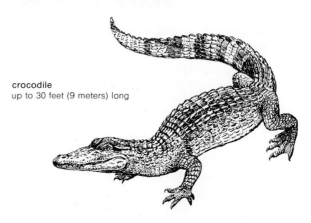
crocodile
up to 30 feet (9 meters) long

crinkle (definition 1)
Aluminum foil **crinkles** easily.

crock (krok), pot or jar made of baked clay. *noun.*

croc o dile (krok′ə dīl), a large reptile with a long body, four short legs, a thick skin, a pointed snout, and a long tail. Crocodiles live in the rivers and marshes of the warm parts of Africa, Asia, Australia, and America. See picture. *noun.*

cro cus (krō′kəs), a small plant that blooms very early in the spring and has white, yellow, or purple flowers. See picture. *noun, plural* **cro cus es.**

cro ny (krō′nē), a very close friend; chum. *noun, plural* **cro nies.**

crook (krùk), **1** make a hook or curve in; bend: *I crooked my leg around the branch to keep from falling.* **2** hooked, curved, or bent part: *the crook of the elbow. There is a crook in the stream.* **3** a shepherd's hooked staff. **4** a dishonest person; thief or swindler: *The crook stole all my money.* **1** *verb,* **2-4** *noun.*

crook ed (krùk′id), **1** not straight; bent; curved; twisted: *a crooked toe.* **2** not honest: *a crooked scheme. adjective.*

croon (krün), hum, sing, or murmur in a low tone: *I crooned a lullaby to the baby. verb.*

crop (krop), **1** plants grown or gathered by people for their use: *Wheat, corn, and cotton are three main crops of the United States.* **2** the whole amount (of wheat, corn, or the produce of any plant or tree) which is borne in one season: *The drought made the state's potato crop very small this year.* **3** cut or bite off the top of: *Sheep had cropped the grass very short.* **4** clip or cut short: *to crop a horse's tail.* **5** act or result of cropping. A short haircut is a crop. **6** a baglike swelling of a bird's food passage. In the crop food is prepared for digestion. **7** a short whip with a loop instead of a lash. **1,2,5-7** *noun,* **3,4** *verb,* **cropped, crop ping.**

crop up, turn up unexpectedly: *All sorts of difficulties cropped up.*

cro quet (krō kā′), an outdoor game played by knocking wooden balls through small wire arches with mallets. See picture. *noun.*

cross (krôs), **1** stick or post with another across it like a T or an X. **2 the Cross,** the cross on which Christ died. **3** anything shaped like this. A cross is a symbol of the Christian religion. A person who cannot write makes a cross instead of a signature. **4** draw a line across: *In writing you cross the letter "t." She crossed out the wrong word.* **5** put or lay across: *He crossed his arms.* **6** move from one side to another; go across: *He crossed the street. The bridge crosses the river.* **7** lying or going across; crossing: *I saw you standing at the intersection of the cross streets.* **8** make the sign of the cross on or over: *She crossed herself as she went into the church.* **9** act against; get in the way of; oppose: *If anyone crosses him, he gets very angry.* **10** in a bad temper: *Children are often cross when they don't feel well.* **11** trouble; burden of duty or suffering: *Most people have at least one cross to bear.* **12** mix kinds or breeds of: *A new plant is sometimes made by crossing two others.* **13** mixing or mixture of kinds or breeds: *My dog is a cross between a collie and a*

poodle. **1-3,11,13** *noun, plural* **cross es; 4-6,8,9,12** *verb,* **7,10** *adjective.*

cross bar (krôs′bär′), bar, line, or stripe going crosswise. *noun.*

cross bones (krôs′bōnz′), two bones placed crosswise, usually below a skull, to mean death: *Poisonous medicines are sometimes marked with a skull and crossbones.* See picture. *noun plural.*

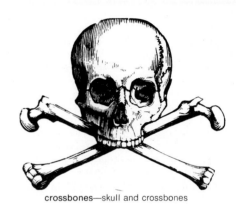

crossbones—skull and crossbones

croquet

cross bow (krôs′bō′), an old-time weapon for shooting arrows or stones, consisting of a bow fixed across a wooden stock to direct the arrows or stones. See picture. *noun.*

cross cut (krôs′kut′), cut, course, or path going across: *Take a crosscut through the fields. noun.*

cross-eyed (krôs′īd′), having both eyes turned toward the nose, and unable to focus on the same point. *adjective.*

cross ing (krô′sing), **1** place where lines or tracks cross: *"Railroad crossing! Stop! Look! Listen!"* **2** place at which a street or river may be crossed: *White lines mark the crossing. noun.*

cross piece (krôs′pēs′), piece of wood or metal that is placed across something. *noun.*

cross road (krôs′rōd′), **1** road that crosses another. **2 crossroads,** place where roads cross: *At the crossroads we stopped and read the signs. noun.*

cross section, 1 act of cutting anything across: *I sliced the tomatoes by making a series of cross sections.* **2** piece cut in this way. See picture. **3** sample; small selection of people, animals, or things with the same qualities as the entire group.

cross walk (krôs′wôk′), area marked with lines, used by pedestrians in crossing a street. *noun.*

cross ways (krôs′wāz′), crosswise. *adverb.*

cross wise (krôs′wīz′), **1** across: *The tree fell crosswise over the stream.* **2** in the form of a cross: *The streets come together crosswise at the intersection. adverb.*

cross word puz zle (krôs′werd′ puz′əl), puzzle with sets of numbered squares to be filled in with words, one letter to each square, so that the words may be read both across and down. Synonyms, definitions, or other clues are given with numbers corresponding to the numbers in the squares.

crotch (kroch), forked piece or part: *The nest was in the crotch of a tree. noun, plural* **crotch es.**

crouch (krouch), **1** stoop low with bent legs as though ready to spring: *The cat crouched in the corner, waiting for the mouse to come out of its hole.* **2** shrink down in fear: *The family crouched in the basement waiting for the tornado to pass.* **3** a crouching. **4** crouching position. **1,2** *verb,* **3,4** *noun, plural* **crouch es.**

croup (krüp), a children's disease of the throat and windpipe that causes a cough and difficult breathing. *noun.*

crow[1] (krō), **1** the loud cry of a rooster. **2** make this cry: *The cock crowed as the sun rose.* **3** a happy sound made by a baby. **4** make this sound. **5** boast; show one's happiness and pride: *The winning team crowed over its victory.* **1,3** *noun,* **2,4,5** *verb,* **crowed** (or **crew** for **2**), **crowed, crow ing.**

crow[2] (krō), a large, glossy, black bird with a harsh cry. *noun.*
eat crow, be forced to do something very disagreeable.

crow bar (krō′bär′), bar of iron or steel used to lift things or pry them apart. *noun.*

crowd (kroud), **1** large number of people together:

crossbow—soldiers using crossbows

cross sections (definition 2)

A crowd gathered at the scene of the fire. **2** people in general: *Advertisements seek to appeal to the crowd.* **3** set; group: *Our crowd wasn't invited to the party.* **4** collect in large numbers: *The children crowded around the edge of the swimming pool to hear the instructor.* **5** fill; fill too full: *Christmas shoppers crowded the store.* **6** push; shove: *The big man crowded the child out of his way.* **7** press forward; force one's way: *She crowded into the subway car.* 1-3 *noun,* 4-7 *verb.*

crown (kroun), **1** a head covering of precious metal and jewels, worn by a king or queen. **2** the **Crown,** royal power; supreme governing power in a country ruled by a king or queen: *The Crown granted lands in colonial America to William Penn.* **3** make king or queen: *The prince was crowned in London.* **4** of a crown; having to do with a crown: *crown jewels.* **5** wreath for the head: *The winner of the race received a crown.* **6** honor; reward: *Her hard work was crowned with success.* **7** head: *Jack fell down and broke his crown.* **8** top; highest part: *the crown of a hat, the crown of a mountain.* **9** be on top of; cover the highest part of: *A fort crowns the hill.* **10** part of a tooth which appears beyond the gum, or an artificial substitute for it. **11** put an artificial crown on (a tooth). **12** British coin worth 5 shillings or 25 new pence. 1,2,5,7,8,10,12 *noun,* 3,6,9,11 *verb,* 4 *adjective.*

crow's-nest (krōz′nest′), platform for the lookout, near the top of a ship's mast. *noun.*

cru cial (krü′shəl), very important; critical; decisive: *This was the crucial game that would decide the championship. adjective.*

cru ci fix (krü′sə fiks), cross with the figure of Christ crucified on it. *noun, plural* **cru ci fix es.**

cru ci fix ion (krü′sə fik′shən), **1** crucifying. **2** the **Crucifixion,** the putting to death of Christ on the Cross. *noun.*

cru ci fy (krü′sə fī), **1** put to death by nailing or binding the hands and feet to a cross. **2** treat severely; torture. *verb,* **cru ci fied, cru ci fy ing.**

crude (krüd), **1** in a natural or raw state. Crude oil is oil as it is pumped from the wells before it is refined and prepared for use. **2** rough; coarse: *a crude chair made out of a box.* **3** lacking finish, grace, taste, or refinement: *the crude manners of a rude person. adjective,* **crud er, crud est.**

cru el (krü′əl), **1** ready to give pain to others or to delight in their suffering; hardhearted: *Kicking a dog is cruel.* **2** showing a cruel nature: *cruel acts.* **3** causing pain or suffering: *a cruel war. adjective.*

cru el ty (krü′əl tē), **1** readiness to give pain to others or to delight in their suffering; having a cruel nature. **2** cruel act or acts: *an organization that seeks to prevent cruelty to animals. noun, plural* **cru el ties.**

cru et (krü′it), glass bottle to hold vinegar, oil, or other liquid for the table. See picture. *noun.*

cruise (krüz), **1** sail about from place to place: *We cruised to Bermuda on our vacation. Freighters and tankers cruise the oceans of the world.* **2** voyage for pleasure with no special destination in view: *We went for a cruise on the Great Lakes last summer.*

a hat	**i** it	**oi** oil	**ch** child	a in about
ā age	**ī** ice	**ou** out	**ng** long	e in taken
ä far	**o** hot	**u** cup	**sh** she	ə = i in pencil
e let	**ō** open	**u̇** put	**th** thin	o in lemon
ē equal	**ô** order	**ü** rule	**ᴛʜ** then	u in circus
ėr term			**zh** measure	

3 travel or journey from place to place: *The taxicab cruised the city streets in search of passengers.* 1,3 *verb,* **cruised, cruis ing;** 2 *noun.*

cruis er (krü′zər), warship with less armor and more speed than a battleship. *noun.*

crul ler (krul′ər), piece of rich, sweet dough fried brown in deep fat. The dough is usually shaped in twists and cut in short pieces. *noun.*

crumb (krum), **1** very small piece of bread or cake broken from a larger piece: *I fed crumbs to the birds.* **2** break into crumbs. **3** little bit: *a crumb of comfort.* 1,3 *noun,* 2 *verb.*

crum ble (krum′bəl), **1** break into small pieces or crumbs: *Do not crumble your bread on the table.* **2** fall to pieces; decay: *The old wall was crumbling away at the edges. verb,* **crum bled, crum bling.**

crum ple (krum′pəl), **1** crush together; wrinkle: *She crumpled the paper into a ball.* **2** fall down: *He crumpled to the floor in a faint. verb,* **crum pled, crum pling.**

crunch (krunch), **1** crush noisily with the teeth: *She crunched a carrot.* **2** make such a sound: *The hard snow crunched under our feet.* **3** act or sound of crunching. 1,2 *verb,* 3 *noun, plural* **crunch es.**

cru sade (krü sād′), **1** any one of the Christian military expeditions between the years 1096 and 1272 to recover the Holy Land from the Moslems. **2** vigorous movement against a public evil or in favor of some new idea: *Everyone was asked to join the crusade against cancer.* **3** take part in a crusade. 1,2 *noun,* 3 *verb,* **cru sad ed, cru sad ing.**

cru sad er (krü sā′dər), person who takes part in a crusade. *noun.*

crush (krush), **1** squeeze together violently so as to break or bruise: *The car door slammed and crushed her fingers.* **2** wrinkle or crease by wear or rough handling: *My suitcase was so full that my*

cruet

clothes were crushed. **3** break into fine pieces by grinding, pounding, or pressing: *The ore is crushed between steel rollers.* **4** violent pressure like grinding or pounding: *He pushed his way through the crush of the crowd.* **5** mass of people crowded close together: *There was a crush at the narrow exits after the football game.* **6** subdue; conquer: *The revolt was crushed.* **7** a sudden, strong liking for a person: *I once had a crush on my third-grade teacher.* 1-3,6 *verb,* 4,5,7 *noun, plural* **crush es.**

crust (krust), **1** the hard outside part of bread. **2** piece of the crust; any hard, dry piece of bread. **3** rich dough rolled out thin and baked for pies. **4** any hard outside covering: *The crust of the snow was thick enough to walk on.* **5** the solid outside part of the earth. **6** cover with a crust; form into a crust; become covered with a crust: *By the next day the snow had crusted over.* 1-5 *noun,* 6 *verb.*

crus ta cean (krus/tā/shən), any of a group of animals with hard shells that live mostly in water. Crabs, lobsters, and shrimps are crustaceans. *noun.*

crutch (kruch), **1** a support to help a lame or injured person walk. It is a stick with a padded crosspiece at the top that fits under a person's arm and supports part of the weight in walking. **2** a support; prop; anything like a crutch in shape or use: *She has to learn to make her own decisions and not to lean on her friend as a crutch. noun, plural* **crutch es.**

cry (krī), **1** call loudly: *The drowning man cried, "Help!"* **2** loud call; shout: *a cry of rage. We heard his cry for help.* **3** shed tears: *My little sister cried when she broke her favorite toy.* **4** time of shedding tears; fit of weeping: *Sometimes you feel much better after a good cry.* **5** noise or call of an animal: *the cry of the wolf.* **6** make such a noise: *The crows cried to one another from the treetops.* **7** call to action; slogan: *"Forward" was the army's cry as it attacked.* **8** offer for sale by calling out: *Peddlers cry their wares in the street to sell them.* **9** call that means things are for sale: *We felt hungry as soon as we heard the cry of the hot-dog man at the ball game.* 1,3,6,8 *verb,* **cried, cry ing;** 2,4,5,7,9 *noun, plural* **cries.**

crys tal (kris/tl), **1** a clear, transparent mineral that looks like ice. It is a kind of quartz. **2** piece of crystal cut into form for use or ornament. Crystals may be hung around lights or worn as beads. **3** clear and transparent like crystal: *crystal water.* **4** very transparent glass from which drinking glasses, vases, and other things are made: *They have a collection of fine crystal.* **5** made of crystal: *crystal beads, crystal water goblets.* **6** the transparent glass or plastic over the face of a watch. **7** one of the regularly shaped pieces with angles and flat surfaces into which many substances solidify. Snow is water vapor that has frozen into crystals. 1,2,4,6,7 *noun,* 3,5 *adjective.*

crys tal line (kris/tl ən), **1** made of crystals: *Sugar and salt are crystalline.* **2** clear and transparent like crystal: *A crystalline sheet of ice covered the pond. adjective.*

crys tal lize (kris/tl īz), **1** form into crystals. Water vapor crystallizes to form snow. **2** form into definite shape: *After much thought her vague ideas crystallized into a clear plan. verb,* **crys tal lized, crys tal liz ing.**

cub (kub), a young bear, fox, or lion. *noun.*

cube (kyüb), **1** a solid object with 6 square sides. See picture. **2** anything shaped like a cube: *ice cubes, a cube of sugar.* **3** make or form into the shape of a cube: *The beets were cubed instead of sliced.* 1,2 *noun,* 3 *verb,* **cubed, cub ing.**

cu bic (kyü/bik), **1** shaped like a cube: *The block of ice had a cubic form.* **2** having length, width, and thickness. A cubic foot is the volume of a cube whose edges are each one foot long. *adjective.*

cub scout, member of the junior division of the Boy Scouts.

cuck oo (kü/kü), bird whose call sounds much like its name. The European cuckoo lays its eggs in the nests of other birds instead of hatching them itself. The American cuckoo builds its own nest and has a call less like the name. *noun, plural* **cuck oos.**

cu cum ber (kyü/kum bər), a long, green vegetable with firm flesh inside. Cucumbers grow on vines and are eaten usually in thin slices as a salad, or used to make pickles. *noun.*

cud (kud), mouthful of food brought back from the first stomach of cattle or related animals for a slow second chewing in the mouth. *noun.*

cud dle (kud/l), **1** hold close and lovingly in one's arms or lap: *I cuddled the kitten.* **2** lie close and comfortably; curl up: *The two puppies cuddled together in front of the fire. verb,* **cud dled, cud dling.**

cudg el (kuj/əl), **1** a short, thick stick used as a weapon; club. **2** beat with a cudgel. 1 *noun,* 2 *verb.*

cue[1] (kyü), **1** the last words of an actor's speech in a play which serve as the signal for another actor to come on the stage or to speak. **2** signal like this to a singer or musician. **3** hint as to what should be done: *Take your cue from me at the party about when it is time to leave. noun.*

cue[2] (kyü), a long stick used for striking the ball in the game of billiards or pool. *noun.*

cuff[1] (kuf), **1** band of some material worn around the wrist. **2** the turned-up fold around the bottom of a sleeve or of a leg of a pair of trousers. *noun.*

cuff[2] (kuf), **1** hit with the hand; slap. **2** a hit with the hand; slap. 1 *verb,* 2 *noun.*

cull (kul), pick out; select: *We culled the berries, discarding the bad ones. verb.*

cul prit (kul/prit), **1** offender; person guilty of a fault or crime: *The culprit who broke the window should pay for it.* **2** prisoner in court accused of a crime. *noun.*

cul ti vate (kul/tə vāt), **1** prepare and use (land) to raise crops by plowing it, planting seeds, and taking care of the growing plants. **2** help (plants) grow by labor and care. **3** loosen the ground around (growing plants) to kill weeds. **4** improve; develop: *cultivate one's mind, cultivate good manners.* **5** give time, thought, and effort to: *She*

cultivated people who could help her. verb,
cul ti vat ed, cul ti vat ing.

cul ti va tion (kul′tə vā′shən), **1** preparing land
and growing crops by plowing, planting, and
necessary care: *Better cultivation of soil will result
in better crops.* **2** giving time and thought to
improving and developing (the body, mind, or
manners). **3** culture; result of improvement or
growth through education and experience. *noun.*

cul ti va tor (kul′tə vā′tər), **1** person or thing that
cultivates. **2** tool or machine used to loosen the
ground and destroy weeds. A cultivator is pulled
or pushed between rows of growing plants. *noun.*

cul tur al (kul′chər əl), **1** having to do with
culture: *Literature, art, and music are cultural
studies.* **2** having to do with a culture: *a cultural
trait, cultural ties between countries.* adjective.

cul ture (kul′chər), **1** fineness of feelings,
thoughts, tastes, or manners; the result of good
education and surroundings: *A person of culture
appreciates art, music, and literature.* **2** the customs,
arts, and conveniences of a nation or people at a
certain time: *She spoke on the culture of the ancient
Egyptians.* **3** training of the mind or of the body.
4 preparation of land and producing of crops;
cultivation. **5** growth of bacteria in a special
medium for scientific use. *noun.*

cul tured (kul′chərd), cultivated; refined. *adjective.*

cul vert (kul′vərt), a small drain for water
crossing under a road or railroad. *noun.*

cum ber some (kum′bər səm), hard to manage;
clumsy; burdensome; troublesome: *The armor
worn by knights was often so cumbersome they had
to be helped onto their horses.* adjective.

cun ning (kun′ing), **1** clever in deceiving; sly: *The
cunning fox outwitted the dogs and got away.*
2 skillful or sly ways of getting what one needs or
wants, or of escaping one's enemies: *The fox has
a great deal of cunning.* **3** skillful; clever in doing:
*With cunning hand the sculptor shaped the little
statue.* **4** skill; cleverness: *The old sculptor's hand
never lost its cunning.* 1,3 *adjective,* 2,4 *noun.*

cup (kup), **1** a hollow, rounded dish to drink from.
Most cups have handles. **2** as much as a cup
holds: *She drank a cup of milk.* **3** a unit of measure
used in cooking equal to 8 fluid ounces. One half
cup is equal to 8 tablespoons. **4** anything shaped
like a cup. The petals of some flowers form a cup.
5 shape like a cup: *He cupped his hands to catch
the ball.* 1-4 *noun,* 5 *verb,* **cupped, cup ping.**

cup board (kub′ərd), closet or cabinet with
shelves for dishes and food supplies. See picture.
noun.

cup cake (kup′kāk′), a small cake baked in a pan
shaped like a cup. *noun.*

cup ful (kup′fül), as much as a cup can hold.
noun, plural **cup fuls.**

Cu pid (kyü′pid), **1** the Roman god of love, son of
Venus. Cupid is usually represented as a winged
boy with bow and arrows. **2 cupid,** a winged baby
used as a symbol of love: *cupids on a valentine.*
See picture. *noun.*

cur (kėr), a dog of mixed breed; mongrel. *noun.*

cube (definition 1)

cupboard

cupids
(definition 2)

cur ate (kyȯr′it), an assistant clergyman; helper of a pastor, rector, or vicar. *noun.*

curb (kėrb), **1** a raised border of concrete or stone along the edge of a pavement or sidewalk: *The driver parked the car close to the curb.* **2** hold in check; restrain: *I curbed my hunger by eating a piece of cheese.* **3** check; restraint: *Put a curb on your temper.* **4** chain or strap fastened to a horse's bit and passing under its lower jaw. When the reins are pulled tight, the curb checks the horse. 1,3,4 *noun,* 2 *verb.*

curd (kėrd), the thick part of milk that separates from the watery part when the milk sours. Cheese is made from curds. *noun.*

cur dle (kėr′dl), **1** form into curds: *Milk curdles when it is kept too long in a warm place.* **2** thicken. *verb,* **cur dled, cur dling.**

cure (kyȯr), **1** bring back to health; make well: *The medicine cured the sick child.* **2** get rid of: *cure a cold. Only great determination can cure a bad habit like smoking.* **3** remedy; something that removes or relieves disease or any bad condition: *a cure for a cold.* **4** preserve (bacon or other meat) by drying or salting. 1,2,4 *verb,* **cured, cur ing;** 3 *noun.*

cur few (kėr′fyü), **1** rule requiring certain persons to be off the streets or at home before a fixed time: *There is a 10 p.m. curfew for children in our city.* **2** the ringing of a bell at a fixed time in the evening as a signal. **3** time when a curfew begins: *You'll get into trouble if you stay out after the curfew. noun.* [*Curfew* comes from old French words meaning "to cover the fire." In the Middle Ages the ringing of a bell was the signal to put out the fires in the camp or in the town.]

cur i os i ty (kyȯr′ē os′ə tē), **1** eager desire to know: *Curiosity got the better of me, and I opened the unmarked box.* **2** a strange, rare object: *One of his curiosities was a cane made of the horn of a deer. noun, plural* **cur i os i ties.**

cur i ous (kyȯr′ē əs), **1** eager to know: *Small children are very curious, and they ask many questions.* **2** strange; odd; unusual: *I found a curious old box in the attic. adjective.*

curl (kėrl), **1** twist into rings: *curl someone's hair. The baby's hair curls naturally.* **2** curve or twist out of shape: *Paper curls as it burns.* **3** rise in rings: *Smoke curled slowly from the fire.* **4** a curled lock of hair. **5** anything curled or bent into a curve: *Curls of smoke rose from the fire.* 1-3 *verb,* 4,5 *noun.*

curl up, draw up one's legs: *I curled up on the sofa.*

curl y (kėr′lē), **1** curling; wavy: *curly hair.* **2** having curls or curly hair: *a curly head. adjective,* **curl i er, curl i est.**

cur rant (kėr′ənt), **1** a small raisin without seeds made from certain sorts of small, sweet grapes. Currants are used in puddings, cakes, and buns. **2** a small and sour red, black, or white berry, which grows on a bush and is used for jelly and preserves. *noun.*

cur ren cy (kėr′ən sē), **1** money in actual use in a country: *Coins and paper money are currency in the United States.* **2** circulation; passing from person to person: *People who spread a rumor give it currency.* **3** general use or acceptance; common occurrence: *Words such as "couldst" and "thou" have little currency now. noun, plural* **cur ren cies.**

cur rent (kėr′ənt), **1** flow; stream. Running water or moving air makes a current. *The current swept the stick down the river. The draft created a current of cold air over my feet.* **2** flow of electricity through a wire. Metals are good conductors of electric current. **3** course or movement (of events or of opinions): *Newspapers influence the current of public opinion.* **4** of the present time. The current issue of a magazine is the latest one published. *We discuss current events in our history class.* **5** in general use: *Long ago the belief was current that the earth was flat.* **6** passing from person to person: *A rumor is current that school will close tomorrow.* 1-3 *noun,* 4-6 *adjective.*

cur rent ly (kėr′ənt lē), **1** at the present time; now: *The flu is currently going around school and many people are absent.* **2** generally; commonly: *a currently held belief among scientists. adverb.*

cur ry[1] (kėr′ē), rub and clean (a horse) with a brush or currycomb. *verb,* **cur ried, cur ry ing.**

cur ry[2] (kėr′ē), **1** a peppery sauce or powder. Curry is a popular seasoning in India. **2** food flavored with it. *noun, plural* **cur ries.**

cur ry comb (kėr′ē kōm′), brush with metal teeth for rubbing and cleaning a horse. *noun.*

curse (kėrs), **1** ask God to bring evil or harm on: *The witch cursed everyone she hated.* **2** the words that a person says when asking God to curse someone or something: *to utter a curse against an enemy.* **3** bring evil or harm on; trouble greatly; torment: *He was cursed with a bad temper. She was cursed with bad luck.* **4** trouble; harm: *My quick temper is a curse to me.* **5** swear; say bad words. **6** words used in swearing: *Their talk was full of curses.* 1,3,5 *verb,* **cursed, curs ing;** 2,4,6 *noun.*

curt (kėrt), short; short and rude; abrupt: *The impatient clerk gave a curt reply. adjective.*

cur tail (kėr′tāl′), cut short; stop part of; reduce: *My parents curtailed my allowance. verb.*

cur tain (kėrt′n), **1** cloth hung at windows or in doors for protection or ornament. **2** a hanging screen which separates the stage of a theater from the part where the audience sits. **3** provide with a curtain; hide by a curtain: *The children took two sheets and curtained off a space in the corner.* 1,2 *noun,* 3 *verb.*

curt sy (kėrt′sē), **1** bow of respect or greeting by women and girls, made by bending the knees and lowering the body slightly. See picture. **2** make a curtsy: *The actress curtsied when the audience applauded.* 1 *noun, plural* **curt sies;** 2 *verb,* **curt sied, curt sy ing.**

cur va ture (kėr′və chər), curving. *noun.*

curve (kėrv), **1** line that has no straight part. A circle is a closed curve. **2** bend in a road: *The automobile had to slow down to go around the curves.* **3** bend so as to form a line that has no straight part: *The highway curved to the right in a sharp turn.* 1,2 *noun,* 3 *verb,* **curved, curv ing.**

curtsy
(definition 1)

a hat	i it	oi oil	ch child	(a in about
ā age	ī ice	ou out	ng long	e in taken
ä far	o hot	u cup	sh she	ə = { i in pencil
e let	ō open	u̇ put	th thin	o in lemon
ē equal	ô order	ü rule	ŦH then	u in circus
ėr term			zh measure	

cush ion (ku̇sh/ən), **1** soft pillow or pad used to sit, lie, or kneel on: *I rested my head by laying it on a cushion.* **2** anything that makes a soft place: *a cushion of moss.* **3** supply with a cushion: *cushion a chair.* **4** soften or ease the effects of: *Nothing could cushion the shock of my friend's death.* 1,2 *noun,* 3,4 *verb.*

cus tard (kus/tərd), a baked, boiled, or frozen mixture of eggs, milk, and sugar. Custard is used as a dessert or as a food for sick persons. *noun.*

cus to di an (ku stō/dē ən), **1** person in charge; keeper; guardian: *He is the custodian of the library's collection of rare books.* **2** janitor: *a school custodian. noun.*

cus to dy (kus/tə dē), keeping; care: *Parents have the custody of their young children. noun.*
in custody, in prison or in the care of the police: *The person accused of the robbery is now in custody.*

cus tom (kus/təm), **1** any usual action: *It was her custom to rise early.* **2** a long-established habit that has almost the force of law: *The social customs of many countries differ from ours.* **3** for a special order: *Custom clothes are made specially according to the order of one individual.* **4 customs, a** taxes paid to the government on things brought in from a foreign country: *I paid $4 in customs on the $100 Swiss watch.* **b** office at a seaport, airport, or border-crossing point where imported goods are checked. 1,2,4 *noun,* 3 *adjective.*

cus tom ar y (kus/tə mer/ē), usual: *My customary bedtime is ten o'clock. adjective.*

cus tom er (kus/tə mər), person who buys, especially a regular shopper at a particular store. *noun.*

cut (kut). See picture. **1** divide, separate, open, or remove with something sharp: *The butcher cut the meat with a knife. We cut a branch from the tree. I used the scissors to cut my nails.* **2** pierce or wound with something sharp: *She cut her finger on the broken glass.* **3** opening made by a knife or sharp-edged tool: *I put a bandage on my leg to cover the cut.* **4** place that has been made by cutting: *The train went through a deep cut in the side of the mountain.* **5** piece that has been cut off or cut out: *A leg of lamb is a tasty cut of meat.* **6** make by cutting: *He cut a hole through the wall with an ax.* **7** way in which a thing is cut; style; fashion: *the narrow, close-fitting cut of his coat.* **8** have (teeth) grow through the gums. **9** make less; reduce; decrease: *We must cut our expenses to save money.* **10** a making less; reduction; decrease: *The store tried to get more business by making a cut in prices.* **11** go by a short cut; go: *Let's cut through the woods and get ahead of them.* **12** cross; divide by crossing: *A brook cuts through that field.* **13** hit or strike sharply: *The cold wind cut me to the bone.*

cut (definitions 3, 5, 10, and 11)

cutter (definition 3)

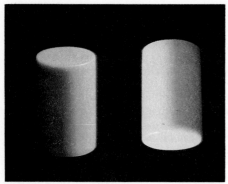

cylinders (definition 1)

cymbals

14 an action or speech that hurts the feelings. **15** act as if one does not know (a person): *After our fight, she cut me whenever we met.* **16** stay away from on purpose: *The principal called my parents when I cut two classes.* **17** share: *Each partner has a cut of the profits.* 1,2,6,8,9,11-13,15,16 *verb,* **cut, cut ting;** 3-5,7,10,14,17 *noun.*

cute (kyüt), **1** pretty and dear: *a cute baby.* **2** clever; shrewd: *a cute trick. adjective,* **cut er, cut est.**

cu ti cle (kyü′tə kəl), outer skin. The cuticle about the fingernails tends to become hard. *noun.*

cut lass (kut′ləs), a short, heavy, slightly curved sword. *noun, plural* **cut lass es.**

cut out (kut′out′), shape or design to be cut out. Some books for children have cutouts. *noun.*

cut ter (kut′ər), **1** person who cuts: *A garment cutter cuts out pieces of fabric to be made into clothes.* **2** tool or machine for cutting: *The blade of a meat cutter is very sharp.* **3** a small sleigh. See picture. **4** a small, armed ship of the coast guard, used to patrol coastal waters. **5** boat belonging to a ship, used to carry people and supplies to and from the ship. *noun.*

cut ting (kut′ing), **1** a small shoot cut from a plant to grow a new plant. **2** a newspaper clipping. **3** that cuts: *Shears and scissors are cutting implements.* **4** hurting the feelings: *He was offended by her cutting remark.* 1,2 *noun,* 3,4 *adjective.*

cut worm (kut′wėrm′), caterpillar that cuts off the stalks of young plants. *noun.*

cy cle (sī′kəl), **1** any period of time or complete process of growth or action which repeats itself in the same order. The seasons of the year—spring, summer, autumn, and winter—make a cycle. **2** complete set or series: *a cycle of songs.* **3** all the stories or legends told about a certain hero or event: *There is a cycle of stories about the adventures of King Arthur and his knights.* **4** a long period of time. **5** ride a bicycle, tricycle, or motorcycle. 1-4 *noun,* 5 *verb,* **cy cled, cy cling.**

cy clone (sī′klōn), **1** a very violent windstorm. **2** storm moving around and toward a calm center of low pressure, which also moves. *noun.*

cyl in der (sil′ən dər), **1** a hollow or solid object shaped like a round pole or tube. Tin cans and rollers are cylinders. See picture. **2** the part of an automobile engine that contains the piston. *noun.*

cy lin dri cal (sə lin′drə kəl), shaped like a cylinder. Cans of fruit, candles, and water pipes are usually cylindrical. *adjective.*

cym bal (sim′bəl), one of a pair of brass plates used as a musical instrument. When cymbals are struck together, they make a loud, ringing sound. See picture. *noun.*

cy press (sī′prəs), **1** an evergreen tree with hard wood and dark leaves. **2** the wood of this tree. Cypress is much used for boards and shingles and for doors. *noun, plural* **cy press es.**

czar (zär), emperor. When Russia had an emperor, his title was czar. *noun.*

cza ri na (zä rē′nə), wife of a czar; Russian ruler. *noun.*

D d

a hat	**i** it	**oi** oil	**ch** child		a in about
ā age	**ī** ice	**ou** out	**ng** long		e in taken
ä far	**o** hot	**u** cup	**sh** she	**ə =**	i in pencil
e let	**ō** open	**u̇** put	**th** thin		o in lemon
ē equal	**ô** order	**ü** rule	**ŦH** then		u in circus
ėr term			**zh** measure		

D or **d** (dē), the fourth letter of the English alphabet. There are two *d*'s in *dead. noun, plural* **D's** or **d's.**

dab (dab), **1** touch lightly; tap: *I dabbed my lips with a napkin.* **2** a pat or tap: *The cat made a dab at the butterfly.* **3** a small, soft or moist mass: *dabs of butter.* **4** a little bit: *Put a dab of paint on this spot you missed.* 1 *verb,* **dabbed, dab bing;** 2-4 *noun.*

dab ble (dab′əl), **1** dip in and out of water; splash: *We sat and dabbled our feet in the pool.* **2** work at a little: *He dabbled at painting but soon gave it up. verb,* **dab bled, dab bling.**

dachs hund (däks′hunt′), a small dog with a long body and very short legs. *noun.* [*Dachshund* comes from German words meaning "badger dog." The breed was called this because it was developed for hunting badgers.]

dad (dad), father. *noun.*

dad dy (dad′ē), father. *noun, plural* **dad dies.**

dad dy-long legs (dad′ē lông′legz′), animal that looks much like a spider, but does not bite. It has a small body and long, thin legs. *noun, plural* **dad dy-long legs.**

daf fo dil (daf′ə dil), plant with long, slender leaves and yellow flowers that bloom in the spring. Daffodils grow from bulbs. *noun.*

dag ger (dag′ər), a small weapon with a short, pointed blade, used for stabbing. *noun.*

dai ly (dā′lē), **1** done, happening, or appearing every day: *a daily visit. She reads a daily paper to keep up with the news.* **2** every day; day by day: *The bus runs daily.* **3** newspaper printed every day, or every day but Sunday. 1 *adjective,* 2 *adverb,* 3 *noun, plural* **dai lies.**

dain ti ly (dān′tl ē), in a dainty way. *adverb.*

dain ty (dān′tē), **1** fresh, delicate, and pretty: *The violet is a dainty spring flower.* **2** delicate in tastes and feeling: *A person who is dainty about eating never spills or takes big bites.* **3** good to eat; delicious: *The royal cook prepared many dainty dishes.* **4** something very good to eat: *Candy and nuts are dainties.* 1-3 *adjective,* **dain ti er, dain ti est;** 4 *noun, plural* **dain ties.**

dair y (der′ē), **1** farm where milk and cream are produced and butter and cheese made. **2** store or company that sells milk, cream, butter, and cheese. **3** room or building where milk and cream are kept and made into butter and cheese. *noun, plural* **dair ies.**

da is (dā′is), a raised platform at one end of a hall or large room. A throne, seats of honor, or a desk may be set on a dais. *noun, plural* **da is es.**

dai sy (dā′zē), a wild flower having white, pink, or yellow petals around a yellow center. See picture. *noun, plural* **dai sies.** [*Daisy* comes from earlier English words meaning "day's eye." The flower

daisy

dally (definition 2)
He **dallied** along the way and was late for school.

was called this because its petals open in the morning and close in the evening.]

dale (dāl), valley. *noun.*

dal ly (dal′ē), **1** talk, act, or think about without being serious; trifle: *For over a month she dallied with the idea of buying a new car.* **2** linger idly; loiter. See picture. **3** waste (time): *He dallied the afternoon away looking out the window and daydreaming. verb,* **dal lied, dal ly ing.**

Dal ma tian (dal mā′shən), a large, short-haired dog, usually white with black spots. *noun.*

dam (dam), **1** wall built to hold back the water of a stream, creek, or river. See picture. **2** put up a dam; block up with a dam: *Beavers had dammed the stream.* **1** *noun,* **2** *verb,* **dammed, dam ming.**

dam age (dam′ij), **1** harm or injury that lessens value or usefulness: *The accident did some damage to the car.* **2** harm or injure so as to lessen value or usefulness; hurt: *I damaged my sweater when I fell.* **1** *noun,* **2** *verb,* **dam aged, dam ag ing.**

dame (dām), **1 Dame,** title for a woman raised to the same rank as a knight because of great achievement or service: *Dame Edith Evans.* **2** a slang term for a woman. *noun.*

damn (dam), **1** declare (something) to be bad; condemn: *Several people who reviewed the new book damned it.* **2** doom to hell. **3** swear or swear at by saying "damn"; curse. **4** a saying of "damn"; a curse. **1-3** *verb,* **4** *noun.*

damp (damp), **1** slightly wet; moist: *This house is damp in rainy weather.* **2** moisture: *When it's foggy you can feel the damp in the air.* **3** dull; check; put out: *Weariness damped the traveler's enthusiasm.* **4** any poisonous or explosive gas that collects in mines. **1** *adjective,* **2,4** *noun,* **3** *verb.*

damp en (dam′pən), **1** make damp; become damp: *He sprinkled water over the clothes to dampen them before ironing.* **2** cast a chill over; depress; discourage: *The sad news dampened our spirits.* *verb.*

dam sel (dam′zəl), maiden; young girl. *noun.*

dance (dans), **1** move in time with music: *She can dance very well.* **2** movement in time with music. **3** some special group of steps: *The waltz is a well-known dance.* **4** party where people dance: *My older brother is going to the high-school dance.* **5** one round of dancing: *May I have the next dance?* **6** piece of music for dancing. **7** jump up and down; move in a lively way: *See that boat dancing on the water.* **1,7** *verb,* **danced, danc ing; 2-6** *noun.*

danc er (dan′sər), person who dances. *noun.*

dan de li on (dan′dl ī′ən), plant that grows as a weed. It has deeply notched leaves and bright-yellow flowers. *noun.* [*Dandelion* comes from French words meaning "lion's tooth." The plant was called this because it has toothed leaves.]

dan druff (dan′drəf), small, whitish scales of dead skin that flake off the scalp. *noun.*

dan dy (dan′dē), **1** man very careful of his dress and appearance. **2** an excellent or first-rate thing: *That new bike is a dandy.* **3** excellent; first-rate: *I got a dandy new bike.* **1,2** *noun, plural* **dan dies;** **3** *adjective,* **dan di er, dan di est.**

dan ger (dān′jər), **1** chance of harm; nearness to harm; risk; peril: *The trip through the jungle was full of danger.* **2** thing that may cause harm: *Hidden rocks are a danger to ships. noun.*

dan ger ous (dān′jər əs), likely to cause harm; not safe; risky: *Shooting off firecrackers can be dangerous. adjective.*

dan gle (dang′gəl), **1** hang and swing loosely. See picture. **2** hold or carry (a thing) so that it swings loosely: *The cat played with the string I dangled in front of it.* verb, **dan gled, dan gling.**

dap ple (dap′əl), marked with spots; spotted: *a dapple horse. adjective.*

dare (der *or* dar), **1** be bold; be bold enough: *The children dared to explore the haunted house.* **2** have courage to try; be bold enough for; not be afraid of: *The pioneers dared the dangers of a strange land.* **3** challenge: *I dare you to jump the puddle.* **4** a challenge: *I took his dare to jump.* **1-3** *verb,* **dared, dar ing; 4** *noun.*

dar ing (der′ing *or* dar′ing), **1** boldness; courage to take risks: *The lifeguard's daring saved a swimmer's life.* **2** bold; fearless: *Saving the swimmer was a daring act.* **1** *noun,* **2** *adjective.*

dark (därk), **1** without light: *A night without a moon is dark.* **2** nearly black in color: *She has dark-brown eyes.* **3** gloomy: *Rain and clouds make a dark day.* **4** darkness: *Do not be afraid of the dark.* **1-3** *adjective,* **4** *noun.*

in the dark, in ignorance: *He said nothing, leaving me in the dark about his plans.*

dark en (där′kən), make dark or darker; become dark or darker: *We darkened the room by drawing the shades. verb.*

dark ness (därk′nis), quality or state of being dark: *It was hard to see anything in the darkness of the closet. noun.*

dar ling (där′ling), **1** person very dear to another; person much loved: *The baby is the family darling.* **2** very dear; much loved: *"My darling daughter,"* her letter began. **3** pleasing or attractive: *What a darling little puppy!* **1** *noun,* **2,3** *adjective.*

darn (därn), mend by making rows of stitches back and forth across a hole or torn place. *verb.*

dart (därt), **1** a slender, pointed weapon, usually thrown by hand. **2 darts,** an indoor game in which darts are thrown at a target. **3** throw suddenly and quickly: *The Eskimos darted spears at the seal.* **4** a sudden, swift movement. **5** move suddenly and swiftly: *The deer saw us and darted away.* **6** send suddenly: *The girl darted an angry glance at her younger sister.* **1,2,4** *noun,* **3,5,6** *verb.*

dash (dash), **1** throw: *In a fit of anger he dashed his ruler against the door.* **2** splash: *The car sped by and dashed muddy water all over me.* **3** a splash: *She was sprayed by a dash of salt water.* **4** to rush: *They dashed by in a hurry.* **5** a rush: *She made a dash for safety.* **6** throw and break; smash: *I was so angry I dashed the glass to bits on the tile floor.* **7** ruin: *Our hopes were dashed by the bad news.* **8** small amount: *Put in just a dash of pepper.* **9** a short race: *the fifty-yard dash.* **10** energy; spirit; liveliness: *The winning team played with dash against the losers.* **11** mark (—) used in writing or printing. A dash shows that there is a break in thought, or that letters or words have been left out. **1,2,4,6,7** *verb,* **3,5,8-11** *noun.*

dash board (dash′bôrd′), panel with instruments and gauges in front of the driver in an automobile or aircraft. *noun.*

dash ing (dash′ing), **1** full of energy and spirit; lively: *a dashing young man.* **2** showy: *The band members wore bright, dashing uniforms. adjective.*

dam (definition 1)

a hat	**i** it	**oi** oil	**ch** child	⎧ a in about
ā age	**ī** ice	**ou** out	**ng** long	⎪ e in taken
ä far	**o** hot	**u** cup	**sh** she	ə = ⎨ i in pencil
e let	**ō** open	**u̇** put	**th** thin	⎪ o in lemon
ē equal	**ô** order	**ü** rule	**ᴛH** then	⎩ u in circus
ėr term			**zh** measure	

da ta (dā′tə *or* dat′ə), facts; facts known or granted; information: *Names, ages, and other data about the class are written in the teacher's book.* noun plural.

date¹ (dāt), **1** time when something happens or happened: *July 4, 1776, is the date of the signing of the Declaration of Independence.* **2** statement of time: *There is a date stamped on every piece of United States money.* **3** mark the time of; put a date on: *Please date your letter.* **4** find out the date of; give a date to: *The scientist was unable to date the fossil.* **5** period of time: *At that date there were no airplanes.* **6** belong to a certain period of time; have its origin: *The oldest house in town dates from the 1780's.* **7** appointment for a certain time: *Don't forget to keep your Monday morning date with the dentist.* 1,2,5,7 *noun,* 3,4,6 *verb,* **dat ed, dat ing.**
out of date, old-fashioned: *I refused to wear the suit because it was out of date.*
up to date, 1 in fashion; modern: *Their clothes are always up to date.* **2** up to the present time: *The teacher entered our latest grades on our report cards to bring them up to date.*

date² (dāt), the sweet fruit of a kind of palm tree. *noun.*

daub (dôb), **1** cover with plaster, clay, mud, or any soft material that will stick: *She filled the cracks in the wall by daubing them with cement.* **2** anything daubed on: *Just a few daubs of glue will mend the broken plate.* **3** apply (something) without skill: *I wore a clown costume and daubed paint on my face.* 1,3 *verb,* 2 *noun.*

daugh ter (dô′tər), female child. A girl is the daughter of her father and mother. *noun.*

daugh ter-in-law (dô′tər in lô′), wife of one's son. *noun, plural* **daugh ters-in-law.**

daunt (dônt), frighten; discourage: *Rain did not daunt the campers.* verb.

daunt less (dônt′lis), brave; not to be frightened or discouraged: *She is a dauntless explorer.* adjective.

daw dle (dô′dl), waste time; be idle; loiter: *Don't dawdle so long over your work.* verb, **daw dled, daw dling.**

dawn (dôn), **1** beginning of day; the first light in the east. See picture. **2** beginning: *Dinosaurs roamed the earth before the dawn of human life.* **3** grow bright or clear: *It was dawning when I awoke.* **4** grow clear to the eye or mind: *When the dog kept barking, it dawned on me that it wanted to go out.* **5** begin; appear: *Day dawns in the east.* 1,2 *noun,* 3-5 *verb.*

day (dā), **1** time of light between sunrise and sunset: *Days are longer in summer than in winter.* **2** the 24 hours of day and night. **3** hours for work; working day: *An eight-hour day is common.* **4** time;

dangle (definition 1)
The mountain climber **dangled** from a rope.

dawn (definition 1)

period: *the present day, in days of old.* **5** game, battle, or contest: *The debate was over; our side won the day.* noun.

day break (dā′brāk′), dawn; time when it first begins to get light in the morning. *noun.*

day dream (dā′drēm′), **1** dreamy thinking about pleasant things. **2** think about pleasant things in a dreamy way. 1 *noun,* 2 *verb.*

day light (dā′līt′), **1** light of day: *It is easier to read by daylight than by lamplight.* **2** daytime. **3** dawn; daybreak: *He was up at daylight. noun.*

day time (dā′tīm′), time when it is day and not night: *The baby sleeps even in the daytime. noun.*

daze (dāz), **1** confuse; bewilder: *A blow on the head dazed him so that he could not find his way home.* **2** a dazed condition: *She was in a daze after falling from her horse and could not understand what was happening.* 1 *verb,* **dazed, daz ing;** 2 *noun.*

daz zle (daz′əl), **1** hurt (the eyes) with too bright light, or quick-moving lights: *To look straight at the sun dazzles the eyes.* **2** overcome the sight or the mind of with anything very bright or splendid: *We were dazzled by the richness of the palace. verb,* **daz zled, daz zling.**

dazzling—At night, the bright lights of the city street were dazzling.

daz zling (daz′ling), brilliant or splendid: *The magician gave us a dazzling display of skill.* See picture. *adjective.*

dea con (dē′kən), **1** officer of a church who helps the minister in church duties not connected with preaching. **2** member of the clergy next below a priest in rank. *noun.*

dead (ded), **1** not alive; no longer living: *The flowers in my garden are dead.* **2 the dead,** person or persons not living any more: *We remember the dead of our wars on Memorial Day.* **3** without life: *Stone and water are dead matter.* **4** dull; quiet; not active: *This beach is crowded now, but in the winter it's dead.* **5** without force, power, spirit, feeling, or activity: *The car won't start because the battery is dead.* **6** very tired; exhausted: *I was dead when I finished the six-mile hike.* **7** sure: *a dead shot with a*

rifle. **8** complete: *There was dead silence in the library.* **9** directly; straight: *Walk dead ahead two miles.* **10** time when there is the least life stirring: *The plane landed in the dead of night.* 1,3-8 *adjective,* 2,10 *noun,* 9 *adverb.*

dead en (ded′n), make dull or weak; lessen the force of: *Some medicines deaden pain. Thick walls deaden the noises from the street. The force of the wind was deadened by the row of trees. verb.*

dead line (ded′līn′), the latest possible time to do something: *The teacher made Friday afternoon the deadline for handing in all book reports. noun.*

dead ly (ded′lē), **1** causing death; likely to cause death; fatal: *a deadly disease, deadly toadstools.* **2** like that of death: *deadly paleness.* **3** filled with hatred: *deadly enemies.* **4** extremely: *"Washing dishes is deadly dull," she said.* 1-3 *adjective,* **dead li er, dead li est;** 4 *adverb.*

deaf (def), **1** not able to hear: *A deaf person can learn to read people's lips.* **2** not able to hear well. **3** not willing to hear: *My parents were deaf to my requests for a bigger allowance. adjective.*

deaf en (def′ən), **1** make deaf: *A hard blow on the ear can deafen someone for life.* **2** stun with noise: *A sudden explosion deafened us for a moment. verb.*

deal (dēl), **1** have to do: *Arithmetic deals with numbers.* **2** act; behave: *Deal kindly with them so you don't hurt their feelings.* **3** carry on business; buy and sell: *This garage deals in gasoline, oil, and tires.* **4** bargain: *He got a good deal on a television set.* **5** give: *One fighter dealt the other a hard blow.* **6** give out among several; distribute: *The Red Cross dealt out food to the victims of the flood. It's my turn to deal the cards.* **7** arrangement; plan: *I have a deal to trade some old books with her.* 1-3,5,6 *verb,* **dealt, deal ing;** 4,7 *noun.*

a good deal or **a great deal,** a large part, portion, or amount: *A great deal of her money goes for rent.*

deal er (dē′lər), **1** person who makes a living by buying and selling: *a used-car dealer.* **2** person who deals out the cards in a card game. *noun.*

deal ing (dē′ling), **1** way of doing business: *The grocer is respected for his honest dealing.* **2** way of acting; behavior toward others: *The judge is known for her fair dealing. noun.*

dealt (delt). See **deal.** *The principal's talk dealt with fire drills. The cards have been dealt. verb.*

dear (dir), **1** much loved; precious: *His sister was very dear to him.* **2** darling; dear one: *"Come, my dear," said her grandfather.* **3** much valued; highly respected. *Dear Sir* or *Dear Madam* is a polite way to begin a letter. **4** costing much; high in price: *Fresh strawberries are dear in winter.* **5** very much; much: *That mistake will cost you dear.* **6** exclamation of surprise or trouble: *Oh, dear! I lost my pencil.* 1,3,4 *adjective,* 2 *noun,* 5 *adverb,* 6 *interjection.*

dear ly (dir′lē), **1** very much: *We love our parents dearly.* **2** at a high price: *He bought his new car quite dearly. adverb.*

death (deth), **1** dying; the ending of life in people, animals, or plants: *The old man's death was calm and peaceful.* **2** any ending that is like dying: *the*

debris—The tornado left the yard full of **debris.**

death of an empire, the death of one's hopes. **3** being dead: *In death his heart was still. noun.*

death less (deth′lis), living forever; immortal; eternal. *adjective.*

de bate (di bāt′), **1** consider; discuss; talk about reasons for and against: *I am debating buying a camera.* **2** discussion of reasons for and against: *There has been much debate about building a new school.* **3** a public argument for and against a question in a meeting: *We heard a debate over the radio.* **4** argue about (a question or topic) in a public meeting: *The two candidates debated building a new expressway.* 1,4 *verb,* **de bat ed, de bat ing;** 2,3 *noun.*

de bris (də brē′), scattered fragments; ruins; rubbish. See picture. *noun.*

debt (det), **1** something owed to another: *Having borrowed money a few times, he had debts to pay back to several people.* **2** condition of owing: *She is in debt to the bank for her new car. noun.*

debt or (det′ər), person who owes something to another: *If I borrow a dollar from you, I am your debtor. noun.*

Dec., December.

dec ade (dek′ād), ten years. From 1900 to 1910 was a decade. Two decades ago means twenty years ago. *noun.*

de cal (dē′kal *or* di kal′), design or picture that will stick fast when it is put on glass, wood, plastic, or metal. *noun.*

de cay (di kā′), **1** become rotten; rot: *The old apples got moldy and decayed. Your teeth may decay if you eat too many sweets.* **2** rotting: *The decay in the tree trunk proceeded so rapidly the tree fell over in a year.* **3** grow less in power, strength, wealth, or beauty: *Many nations have grown great and then decayed.* **4** growing less in power, strength, wealth, or beauty: *The decay of an old person's health may be very slow.* 1,3 *verb,* 2,4 *noun.*

de cease (di sēs′), **1** death: *the decease of a famous painter.* **2** die: *deceasing without leaving an heir.* 1 *noun,* 2 *verb,* **de ceased, de ceas ing.**

de ceased (di sēst′), dead: *a deceased writer. adjective.*

de ceit (di sēt′), **1** deceiving; lying; cheating;

making a person believe as true something that is false: *A dishonest person is often guilty of deceit.* **2** dishonest trick; a lie spoken or acted. **3** quality that makes a person tell lies or cheat: *The dishonest trader was full of deceit. noun.*

de ceit ful (di sēt′fəl), **1** ready or willing to deceive or lie: *a deceitful person.* **2** meant to deceive; deceiving; misleading: *She told a deceitful story to avoid punishment. adjective.*

de ceive (di sēv′), **1** make (a person) believe as true something that is false; mislead: *The magician deceived her audience into thinking she had really pulled a rabbit from a hat.* **2** lie; use deceit. *verb,* **de ceived, de ceiv ing.**

De cem ber (di sem′bər), the 12th and last month of the year. It has 31 days. *noun.* [*December* came from a Latin word meaning "ten." In the ancient Roman calendar December was the tenth month of the year.]

de cen cy (dē′sn sē), **1** being decent; proper behavior: *Common decency requires that you pay for the window you broke.* **2** something decent or proper: *Courtesy and kindness are two of the decencies of life. noun, plural* **de cen cies.**

de cent (dē′snt), **1** respectable; modest; proper and right: *It is not decent to make fun of a crippled person.* **2** good enough; not wonderful and not very bad: *I get decent marks at school.* **3** not severe; rather kind: *The teacher was very decent to excuse my absence yesterday. adjective.*

de cep tion (di sep′shən), **1** deceiving: *The twins' deception in exchanging places fooled everybody.* **2** being deceived: *The deception of the magician's audience was complete.* **3** trick meant to deceive; fraud; sham: *The scheme is all a deception. noun.*

de cep tive (di sep′tiv), **1** deceiving or misleading: *Travelers on the desert are often fooled by the deceptive appearance of trees and water.* **2** meant to deceive: *The deceptive friendliness of the fox fooled the rabbit. adjective.*

de cide (di sīd′), **1** settle: *Let us decide the question by tossing a penny.* **2** give judgment: *Our teacher decided in favor of a trip to the zoo.* **3** resolve; make up one's mind: *She decided to be a scientist. verb,* **de cid ed, de cid ing.**

de cid ed (di sī′did), **1** definite; unquestionable: *There was a decided change in the temperature.* **2** firm; determined: *She studied hard because she had a decided wish to go to college. adjective.*

de cid ed ly (di sī′did lē), clearly; definitely; without question: *Her work is decidedly better than his. It was a decidedly warm morning. adverb.*

dec i mal (des′ə məl), **1** a fraction like .04 or ⁴/₁₀₀, .2 or ²/₁₀. **2** a number like 75.24, 3.062, .7, or .091. **3** of tens; counting by tens: *United States money has a decimal system.* 1,2 *noun,* 3 *adjective.*

decoration—man wearing seven decorations

decoy (definition 2)—a handmade wooden decoy

deface—Many people had **defaced** the wall with their scribbling.

decimal point, period placed before a fraction given in decimal figures, as in 2.03 or .623.

dec i me ter (des′ə mē′tər), a unit of length equal to ¹/₁₀ of a meter or about 4 inches. *noun.*

de ci pher (di sī′fər), **1** make out the meaning of (bad writing, an unknown language, or anything puzzling): *We just couldn't decipher the mystery.* **2** change (something in code) into ordinary language; interpret (secret writing) by using a key: *The spy deciphered the secret message. verb.*

de ci sion (di sizh′ən), **1** deciding; judgment; making up one's mind: *I have not yet come to a decision about buying a coat.* **2** firmness and determination: *She is a woman of decision who makes up her mind what to do and then does it. noun.*

de ci sive (di sī′siv), **1** having or giving a clear result; settling something beyond question: *The team won by 20 points, which was a decisive victory.* **2** having or showing decision: *When I asked for a decisive answer, he said flatly, "No." adjective.*

deck (dek), **1** one of the floors or platforms extending from side to side and often from end to end of a ship. The upper, main, middle, and lower decks of a ship are somewhat like the stories of a house. Often the upper deck has no roof over it. **2** a pack of playing cards: *He shuffled the deck and dealt the cards.* **3** cover; dress or adorn; decorate; trim: *Deck the halls with holly.* 1,2 *noun,* 3 *verb.*

dec la ra tion (dek′lə rā′shən), **1** declaring: *The judges' declaration that we had won the contest pleased us.* **2** thing declared; public statement: *The royal declaration was announced in every city and town. noun.*

Declaration of Independence, statement made on July 4, 1776, declaring that the Colonies were independent of Great Britain.

de clare (di kler′ *or* di klar′), **1** say; make known: *Congress has the power to declare war. Travelers returning to the United States must declare the things which they bought abroad.* **2** say openly or strongly: *I declared that I would never do anything so foolish again. verb,* **de clared, de clar ing.**

de cline (di klīn′), **1** turn away from doing; refuse (to do something): *They declined to do as they were told.* **2** refuse politely: *I declined her offer of help.* **3** grow less in power, strength, wealth, or beauty; grow worse; decay: *Great nations have risen and declined. A person's strength declines in old age.* **4** growing worse: *Lack of money for books and equipment led to a decline in the condition of the school.* **5** falling to a lower level; sinking: *a decline in prices, the decline of the sun to the horizon.* **6** bend or slope down: *The hill declines to a fertile valley.* 1-3,6 *verb,* **de clined, de clin ing;** 4,5 *noun.*

de code (dē kōd′), translate (secret writing) from code into ordinary language. *verb,* **de cod ed, de cod ing.**

de com pose (dē′kəm pōz′), decay; rot: *The old fruits and vegetables decomposed quickly in the heat. verb,* **de com posed, de com pos ing.**

dec o rate (dek′ə rāt′), **1** make beautiful; trim; adorn: *We decorated the Christmas tree.* **2** paint or paper (a room): *The old rooms looked like new after they had been decorated.* **3** give a badge, ribbon, or medal to: *The general decorated the soldier for his brave act.* verb, **dec o rat ed, dec o rat ing.**

dec o ra tion (dek/ə rā/shən), **1** thing used to decorate; ornament: *We put pictures and other decorations up in the classroom.* **2** badge, ribbon, or medal given as an honor. See picture. **3** decorating: *Decoration of the room took most of the day before the spring festival.* noun.

dec o ra tive (dek/ə rā/tiv), decorating; ornamental; helping to make beautiful: *The paper chains gave a decorative effect to the room.* adjective.

dec o ra tor (dek/ə rā/tər), person who decorates. An **interior decorator** plans the woodwork, wallpaper, and furnishings for a house. noun.

de coy (di koi/ for 1 and 4, dē/koi or di koi/ for 2, 3, and 5), **1** lead (wild birds or animals) into a trap or near the hunter: *I decoyed the rats with cheese.* **2** an artificial bird used to lure birds into a trap or near the hunter. See picture. **3** bird or other animal trained to lure others of its kind into a trap. **4** lead or tempt into danger by trickery; entice. **5** any person or thing used to lead or tempt into danger; lure. 1, 4 verb, 2, 3, 5 noun.

de crease (di krēs/ for 1 and 2; dē/krēs for 3 and 4), **1** grow or become less: *Hunger decreases as one eats.* **2** make less: *Decrease the dose of medicine as you feel better.* **3** growing less: *Toward night there was a decrease of heat.* **4** amount by which a thing becomes less or is made less: *The decrease in heat was 10 degrees.* 1, 2 verb, **de creased, de creas ing;** 3, 4 noun.

de cree (di krē/), **1** something ordered or settled by authority; official decision; law: *The new state holiday was declared by a decree of the Governor.* **2** order or settle by authority: *The city government decreed that all dogs must be licensed.* 1 noun, 2 verb, **de creed, de cree ing.**

ded i cate (ded/ə kāt), **1** set apart for a purpose: *The doctor dedicated her life to serving the poor. The library was dedicated to the memory of a great writer.* **2** address (a book or other work) to a friend or patron as a mark of affection, respect, or gratitude. verb, **ded i cat ed, ded i cat ing.**

ded i ca tion (ded/ə kā/shən), setting apart for a purpose; being set apart for a purpose: *the dedication of a park.* noun.

de duct (di dukt/), take away; subtract: *When I broke the window, my parents deducted its cost from my allowance.* verb.

de duc tion (di duk/shən), **1** act of taking away; subtraction: *No deduction in pay is made for absence due to illness.* **2** amount deducted: *There was a deduction of $20 from the price of the chair because it was damaged.* noun.

deed (dēd), **1** something done; an act; an action: *To feed the hungry is a good deed. Deeds, not words, are needed.* **2** a written or printed agreement. The buyer of land receives a deed to the property from the former owner. noun.

deep (dēp), **1** going a long way down from the top or surface: *The ocean is deep here. They dug a deep*

well to get pure water. **2** far down; far on: *They dug deep before they found water.* **3** going a long way back from the front: *The lot on which the house stands is 100 feet deep.* **4** low in pitch: *the low tones of Father's deep voice.* **5** hard to understand; needing much time for thought: *It takes a lot of study to understand a deep subject.* **6** strong; great; intense; extreme: *She fell into a deep sleep after the game. Deep feeling is hard to put into words.* **7** rich and dark in color: *The deep red roses are beautiful.* **8 the deep,** the sea: *Frightened sailors thought they saw monsters from the deep.* 1, 3-7 adjective, 2 adverb, 8 noun.

deep en (dē/pən), **1** make deeper: *We deepened the hole.* **2** become deeper: *The water deepened as the tide came in.* verb.

deer (dir), a swift, graceful animal that has hoofs and chews the cud. The male deer has antlers which are shed and grow again every year. noun, plural **deer.** [*Deer* comes from an earlier English word meaning "a wild animal."]

deer skin (dir/skin/), **1** skin of a deer. **2** leather made from it. **3** clothing made of this leather. noun.

de face (di fās/), spoil the appearance of; mar. See picture. verb, **de faced, de fac ing.**

de feat (di fēt/), **1** overcome; win a victory over: *to defeat the enemy in battle, to defeat another school in basketball.* **2** cause to fail; make useless: *to defeat someone's plans.* **3** defeating: *The crowd cheered their team's defeat of the visiting team.* **4** being defeated: *We were unhappy about our team's defeat.* 1, 2 verb, 3, 4 noun.

de fect (dē/fekt or di fekt/), **1** fault; blemish; imperfection: *The cloth had holes and other defects.* **2** lack of something needed for completeness; falling short: *A defect in his sense of right and wrong made him steal.* noun.

de fec tive (di fek/tiv), not complete; not perfect; faulty: *This pump is defective and will not work.* adjective.

de fend (di fend/), **1** keep safe; guard from attack or harm; protect: *The soldiers defended the fort.* **2** act, speak, or write in favor of: *The newspapers defended the governor's action. Lawyers are hired to defend people who are charged with crimes.* verb.

de fense (di fens/), **1** any thing or act that defends, guards, or protects: *A wall around a city was a defense against enemies. A warm coat is a defense against cold weather.* **2** defending: *The army, navy, and air force are responsible for the defense of the country.* **3** a defending team or force: *Our football team has a good defense.* noun.

de fense less (di fens/lis), having no defense; helpless against attack; not protected: *a defenseless village, a defenseless child.* adjective.

de fen sive (di fen′siv), of or for defense; intended to defend: *defensive armor, a defensive attitude. adjective.*

on the defensive, ready to defend, apologize, or explain: *The losing player was on the defensive.*

de fer[1] (di fėr′), put off; delay: *The test was deferred because so many students were sick. verb,* **de ferred, de fer ring.**

de fer[2] (di fėr′), yield in judgment or opinion: *The children deferred to their parents' wishes. verb,* **de ferred, de fer ring.**

def er ence (def′ər əns), respect for the judgment, opinion, or wishes of another: *People often show deference to others who are older and wiser. noun.*

de fi ance (di fī′əns), defying; standing up against authority and refusing to recognize or obey it: *Robin Hood shouted his defiance at the sheriff. noun.*

in defiance of, without regard for; in spite of: *We played football all day in defiance of the rain.*

de fi ant (di fī′ənt), showing defiance; openly resisting; disobedient: *She told us in a defiant manner that she was against our plans. adjective.*

de fi cien cy (di fish′ən sē), 1 lack or absence of something needed: *A deficiency of calcium in your diet can cause soft bones and teeth.* 2 amount by which a thing falls short or is too small: *If a bill to be paid is $10 and you have only $6, the deficiency is $4. noun, plural* **de fi cien cies.**

de fi cient (di fish′ənt), 1 not complete: *The child's knowledge of arithmetic is deficient.* 2 not enough; lacking: *a diet deficient in calcium and iron. adjective.*

de file (di fīl′), 1 make dirty, bad-smelling, or in any way disgusting. 2 destroy the pureness or cleanness of (anything sacred): *The barbarians defiled the church by using it as a stable. verb,* **de filed, de fil ing.**

de fine (di fīn′), 1 make clear the meaning of; explain: *A dictionary defines words.* 2 make clear; make distinct: *The shadow defined the shape of the building.* 3 settle the limits of: *The boundary between the United States and Canada is defined by treaty. verb,* **de fined, de fin ing.**

def i nite (def′ə nit), clear; exact; not vague: *Say "Yes" or "No," or give me some definite answer. adjective.*

def i nite ly (def′ə nit lē), 1 in a definite manner: *Say definitely what you have in mind.* 2 certainly: *Will you go? Definitely. adverb.*

def i ni tion (def′ə nish′ən), 1 explaining the nature of a thing; making clear the meaning of a word. 2 statement in which the nature of a thing is explained or the meaning of a word is made clear. One definition of "home" is "the place where a person or family lives." *noun.*

de form (di fôrm′), 1 spoil the form or shape of: *Shoes that are too tight may deform the feet.* 2 make ugly: *Great pain deformed the patient's face. verb.*

de form i ty (di fôr′mə tē), 1 part of the body that is not properly formed, such as a hump on the back. 2 condition of being improperly formed: *Doctors can now cure many deformities. noun, plural* **de form i ties.**

de frost (di frôst′), 1 remove frost or ice from: *We defrosted the refrigerator.* 2 thaw out: *Cooking defrosts frozen foods. verb.*

deft (deft), quick and skillful in action: *The fingers of a violinist must be deft. adjective.*

de fy (di fī′), 1 set oneself openly against (authority); resist boldly: *The American Colonies defied many British laws.* 2 withstand; resist: *This strong fort defies capture.* 3 challenge (a person) to do or prove something: *We defy you to show that our game is not fair. verb,* **de fied, de fy ing.**

de grade (di grād′), 1 reduce to a lower rank, often as a punishment; take away a position or an honor from: *The corporal was degraded to private for disobeying orders.* 2 make worse; lower: *The students degraded themselves by cheating on the test. verb,* **de grad ed, de grad ing.**

de gree (di grē′), 1 a step in a scale; stage in a process: *By degrees I became better at swimming.* 2 amount; extent: *To what degree are you interested in reading?* 3 unit for measuring temperature: *The freezing point of water is 32 degrees (32°) Fahrenheit.* 4 a unit for measuring an angle or a part of a circle. There are 90 degrees in a right angle and 360 degrees in the circumference of a circle. See picture. 5 rank: *The prince and princess were persons of high degree.* 6 rank or title given by a college or university to a student who graduates or to a famous person as an honor. *noun.*

de i ty (dē′ə tē), 1 god or goddess: *Juno was the queen of the ancient Roman deities.* 2 **the Deity,** God. *noun, plural* **de i ties.**

de ject ed (di jek′tid), sad; discouraged. See picture. *adjective.*

Del a ware (del′ə wer *or* del′ə war), one of the eastern states of the United States. *noun.* [*Delaware* was named for the Delaware River. The river was named for Baron De La Warr, who lived from 1577 to 1618. He was the first governor of the colony of Virginia.]

de lay (di lā′), 1 put off till a later time: *We will delay the party for a week and hold it next Saturday.* 2 putting off till a later time: *The delay upset our plans.* 3 make late; keep waiting; hinder the progress of: *The accident delayed the train for two hours.* 4 go slowly; stop along the way: *Do not delay on this errand.* 5 stopping along the way: *We were so late that we could afford no further delay.* 1,3,4 *verb,* 2,5 *noun.*

del e gate (del′ə git *or* del′ə gāt *for* 1; del′ə gāt *for* 2), 1 person given power or authority to act for others; a representative: *Our club sent two delegates to the meeting.* 2 appoint or send (a person) as a representative: *Her team delegated her to buy the new baseball bat.* 1 *noun,* 2 *verb,* **del e gat ed, del e gat ing.**

del e ga tion (del′ə gā′shən), 1 delegating. 2 group of delegates: *Each club sent a delegation to the meeting. noun.*

de lib er ate (di lib′ər it *for* 1-3; di lib′ə rāt′ *for* 4 and 5), 1 intended; done on purpose; thought over beforehand: *Their excuse was a deliberate lie.* 2 slow and careful in deciding what to do: *Deliberate*

delicate (definition 2)—A spider web is very delicate.

a hat	**i** it	**oi** oil	**ch** child	a in about
ā age	**ī** ice	**ou** out	**ng** long	e in taken
ä far	**o** hot	**u** cup	**sh** she	ə = i in pencil
e let	**ō** open	**ù** put	**th** thin	o in lemon
ē equal	**ô** order	**ü** rule	**ŦH** then	u in circus
ėr term			**zh** measure	

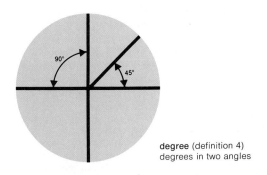

degree (definition 4)
degrees in two angles

dejected—The people waiting in the employment office looked tired and dejected.

persons do not make up their minds quickly. **3** slow; not hurried: *The old man walked with deliberate steps.* **4** think over carefully; consider: *I am deliberating where to put up my new picture.* **5** talk over reasons for and against; debate: *Congress deliberated the question of raising taxes.* 1-3 *adjective*, 4,5 *verb*, **de lib er at ed, de lib er at ing.**

de lib er ate ly (di lib′ər it lē), **1** on purpose. **2** slowly. *adverb.*

de lib e ra tion (di lib′ə rā′shən), **1** careful thought: *After long deliberation, he decided not to go.* **2** talking about reasons for or against an action: *the deliberations of Congress over raising taxes.* **3** slowness and care: *She drove the car over the icy bridge with great deliberation. noun.*

del i ca cy (del′ə kə sē), **1** fineness of weave, quality, or make: *the delicacy of lace, the delicacy of a flower.* **2** fineness of feeling for small differences: *The pianist had great delicacy of touch.* **3** need of care, skill, or tact: *His refusal required delicacy; he did not wish to hurt his friend's feelings.* **4** thought for the feelings of others. **5** weakness; being easily hurt or made ill: *The parents often worried about their child's delicacy.* **6** a choice kind of food. Nuts and candy are delicacies. *noun*, *plural* **del i ca cies.**

del i cate (del′ə kit), **1** pleasing to the taste; mild or soft: *delicate foods, delicate colors.* **2** of fine weave, quality, or make; thin; easily torn. See picture. **3** requiring care, skill, or tact: *a delicate situation.* **4** very quickly responding to slight changes of condition: *delicate instruments, a delicate sense of touch.* **5** easily hurt or made ill: *a weak and delicate child. adjective.*

del i ca tes sen (del′ə kə tes′n), store that sells prepared foods, such as cooked meats, smoked fish, cheese, salads, and sandwiches. *noun.*

de li cious (di lish′əs), very pleasing or satisfying; delightful, especially to the taste or smell: *a delicious cake. adjective.*

de light (di līt′), **1** great pleasure; joy: *We took great delight in our toys.* **2** something which gives great pleasure: *Swimming is her delight.* **3** please greatly: *The circus delighted the children.* **4** have great pleasure: *Children delight in surprises.* 1,2 *noun*, 3,4 *verb.*

de light ful (di līt′fəl), giving joy; very pleasing: *a delightful visit from an old friend. adjective.*

de lir i ous (di lir′ē əs), **1** out of one's senses for a short time; wandering in mind; raving: *The patient with the high fever was delirious.* **2** wildly excited: *The students were delirious with joy when their team won the tournament. adjective.*

de lir i um (di lir′ē əm), **1** a sickness of the mind that may come during fevers, insanity, or drunkenness, and lasts only a short time. People in delirium are often restless and excited. They sometimes talk wildly and see or hear things that aren't there. **2** wild excitement. *noun.*

de liv er (di liv′ər), **1** carry and give out; distribute: *deliver mail.* **2** give up; hand over: *The defeated army delivered the fort to the enemy.* **3** give forth in words: *She delivered a talk on her travels in Africa. The jury delivered its verdict.* **4** strike; throw: *The boxer delivered a blow.* **5** set free; rescue; save: *A passing ship delivered the shipwrecked passengers from a certain death at sea.* **6** help a woman give birth to a child. *verb.*

de liv er ance (di liv′ər əns), rescue; release; freedom: *The shipwrecked passengers rejoiced at their deliverance. noun.*

de liv er y (di liv′ər ē), **1** carrying and giving out letters or goods: *There is one delivery of mail a day in our city.* **2** giving up; handing over: *The captive was released upon the delivery of the ransom.* **3** manner of speaking; way of giving a speech or lecture: *The speaker had an excellent delivery.* **4** act or way of striking or throwing: *That pitcher has a fast delivery.* **5** giving birth to a child. *noun, plural* **de liv er ies.**

dell (del), a small, sheltered glen or valley, usually with trees in it. *noun.*

del ta (del′tə), deposit of earth and sand that collects at the mouth of some rivers and is usually three-sided. *noun.* [*Delta* is the name of the fourth letter of the Greek alphabet. It is a three-sided figure written like this: Δ.]

de lude (di lüd′), mislead; deceive: *He deluded me into thinking he was on my side. verb,* **de lud ed, de lud ing.**

del uge (del′yüj), **1** a great flood. See picture. **2** heavy fall of rain: *We were caught in a deluge.* **3** to flood; overflow: *Water deluged our cellar when the big pipe broke.* **4** overwhelm: *The singer was deluged with requests for her autograph.* **5** any overwhelming rush: *The post office has a deluge of mail just before Christmas.* **1,2,5** *noun,* **3,4** *verb,* **del uged, del ug ing.**

de lu sion (di lü′zhən), false belief or opinion: *She was under the delusion that she could pass any test without studying for it. noun.*

delve (delv), search carefully for information: *The scholar delved in many libraries for facts to support her theory. verb,* **delved, delv ing.**

de mand (di mand′), **1** ask for as a right: *The prisoner demanded a trial.* **2** ask for with authority: *The teacher demanded the name of the student who rang the fire alarm.* **3** call for; require; need: *Training a puppy demands patience.* **4** claim: *Parents have many demands upon their time.* **5** desire and ability to buy: *Because of the large crop, the supply of apples is greater than the demand this year.* **1-3** *verb,* **4,5** *noun.*

de mer it (di mer′it), **1** fault or defect. **2** a mark against a person's record for bad behavior or poor work. *noun.*

de moc ra cy (di mok′rə sē), **1** government that is run by the people who live under it. In a democracy either the people rule through

meetings that all may attend, such as a town meeting in New England, or they elect representatives to take care of the business of government. **2** country or town in which the government is a democracy. **3** treating other people as one's equals: *The teacher's democracy made him liked by all his pupils. noun, plural* **de moc ra cies.**

dem o crat (dem′ə krat), **1** person who believes that a government should be run by the people who live under it. **2** person who treats other people as equals. **3 Democrat,** member of the Democratic Party. *noun.*

dem o crat ic (dem′ə krat′ik), **1** of a democracy; like a democracy. **2** treating other people as one's equals: *The queen's democratic ways made her dear to her people.* **3 Democratic,** of the Democratic Party. *adjective.*

Democratic Party, one of the two main political parties in the United States.

de mol ish (di mol′ish), pull or tear down; destroy. See picture. *verb.*

de mon (dē′mən), **1** devil; evil spirit; fiend. **2** person with great energy: *My music teacher is a demon for practicing. noun.*

dem on strate (dem′ən strāt), **1** show clearly; prove: *Can you demonstrate that the earth is round?* **2** teach by carrying out experiments, or by showing and explaining samples or specimens: *If you will come with me to the laboratory, I will demonstrate the process to you.* **3** show, advertise, or make publicly known, by carrying out a process in public: *The saleswoman played a record to demonstrate the stereo to us.* **4** show (feeling) openly: *I hugged the puppy to demonstrate that I liked it.* **5** take part in a parade or meeting to protest or to make demands: *An angry crowd demonstrated in front of the mayor's office for more police protection. verb,* **dem on strat ed, dem on strat ing.**

dem on stra tion (dem′ən strā′shən), **1** clear proof: *The ease with which he solved the hard problem was a demonstration of his ability in arithmetic.* **2** teaching by carrying out experiments or by showing and explaining samples or specimens: *A compass was used in a demonstration of the earth's magnetism.* **3** showing some new product or process in a public place: *the demonstration of a new vacuum cleaner.* **4** open show or expression of feeling: *I greeted the friend I had not seen in years with a demonstration of joy.* **5** parade or meeting to protest or make demands. See picture. *noun.*

dem on stra tor (dem′ən strā′tər), **1** person or thing that demonstrates. **2** person who takes part in a parade or meeting to protest or make demands. *noun.*

de mote (di mōt′), put back to a lower grade; reduce in rank: *The student who had trouble with fourth grade was demoted to third grade. verb,* **de mot ed, de mot ing.**

de mure (di myür′), **1** seeming more modest and proper than one really is: *the demure smile of a*

flirt. **2** serious; thoughtful; sober. *adjective,*
de mur er, de mur est.

den (den), **1** a wild animal's home: *The bear's den was in a cave.* **2** place where thieves or the like have their headquarters. **3** a small, dirty room. **4** one's private room for reading and work, usually small and cozy. *noun.*

de ni al (di nī′əl), **1** saying that something is not true: *a denial of the existence of ghosts.* **2** saying that one does not hold or accept a belief: *Galileo was forced to make a public denial of his belief that the earth goes around the sun.* **3** refusing: *Their quick denial of our request was very rude. noun.*

den im (den′əm), **1** a heavy, coarse cotton cloth used for jeans, skirts, and other clothing. **2 denims,** pants made of this cloth. *noun.*

de nom i na tion (di nom′ə nā′shən), **1** name for a group or class of things; name. **2** a religious group or sect: *Methodists and Baptists are two large Protestant denominations.* **3** class or kinds of units: *Changing ⁵/₁₂, ¹/₃, and ¹/₆ to the same denomination gives ⁵/₁₂, ⁴/₁₂, and ²/₁₂. noun.*

de nom i na tor (di nom′ə nā′tər), the number below the line in a fraction: *In ³/₄, 4 is the denominator, and 3 is the numerator. noun.*

de note (di nōt′), **1** indicate; be the sign of: *A fever usually denotes sickness.* **2** mean: *The word "stool" denotes a small chair without a back. verb,*
de not ed, de not ing.

de nounce (di nouns′), **1** speak against; express strong disapproval of; condemn: *The mayor denounced crime in the streets.* **2** report as bad; give information against; accuse: *The police arrested the person who had been denounced as a spy. verb,*
de nounced, de nounc ing.

dense (dens), **1** closely packed together; thick: *a dense forest, a dense fog.* **2** stupid: *The dense looks of the students showed that they did not understand. adjective,* **dens er, dens est.**

den si ty (den′sə tē), **1** closeness; compactness; thickness: *The density of the forest prevented us from seeing more than a little way ahead.* **2** the amount of matter in a unit of volume: *The density of lead is greater than the density of wood.* **3** stupidity. *noun, plural* **den si ties.**

dent (dent), **1** a hollow made by a blow or pressure: *When my bicycle fell over, it put a dent in the fender.* **2** make a dent in: *The movers dented the top of the table when they banged it against the doorknob.* **3** become dented: *Soft wood dents easily.* **1** *noun,* **2,3** *verb.*

den tal (den′tl), **1** of or for the teeth: *dental care.* **2** of or for a dentist's work: *a dental drill. adjective.*

den tine (den′tēn′), hard, bony material beneath the enamel of a tooth. It forms the main part of a tooth. *noun.*

den tist (den′tist), doctor whose work is the care of teeth. A dentist fills cavities in teeth, cleans, straightens, or extracts them, and supplies artificial teeth. *noun.*

de ny (di nī′), **1** say (something) is not true: *The prisoners denied the charges against them. She denied that the old house was haunted.* **2** refuse: *I could not*

a hat	i it	oi oil	ch child	a in about
ā age	ī ice	ou out	ng long	e in taken
ä far	o hot	u cup	sh she	ə = i in pencil
e let	ō open	ù put	th thin	o in lemon
ē equal	ô order	ü rule	ŦH then	u in circus
ėr term			zh measure	

deluge (definition 1)

demolish—The old building was being **demolished** to make room for a new one.

demonstration (definition 5)
a civil rights demonstration in Washington

deny the stray cat some milk. **3** disown; refuse to acknowledge: *They denied their debts and refused to pay their bills.* verb, **de nied, de ny ing.**

de part (di pärt′), **1** go away; leave: *The train departs at 6:15.* **2** turn away; change: *He became very sloppy, departing from his usual neat ways.* **3** die. *verb.*

de part ment (di pärt′mənt), a separate part of some whole; special branch; division: *the toy department of a store. Our city government has a fire department and a police department.* noun.

department store, store that sells many different kinds of articles in separate departments under one management.

de par ture (di pär′chər), **1** act of going away; act of leaving: *His departure was very sudden.* **2** turning away; change: *a departure from our old custom.* **3** starting on a new course of action or thought: *Attending this dancing class will be a new departure for me, for I have never done anything like it.* noun.

de pend (di pend′), **1** be controlled by something else; be a result of: *The success of our picnic will depend on the weather.* **2** have as a support; get help from: *Children depend on their parents for food and clothing.* **3** rely; trust: *I depend on my alarm clock to wake me in time for school.* verb.

de pend ence (di pen′dəns), **1** fact or condition of being dependent: *We learned about the dependence of crops on good weather.* **2** trusting or relying on another for support or help: *I am going to work so that I can end my dependence on my parents.* **3** trust; reliance: *I do not put much dependence on the buses because they are always late.* noun.

de pend ent (di pen′dənt), **1** trusting to or depending on another person or thing for support or help: *A child is dependent on its parents.* **2** person who is supported by another. **3** depending; possible if something else takes place: *Good crops are dependent on the right amount of sunshine and rainfall.* 1,3 *adjective,* 2 *noun.*

de pict (di pikt′), represent by drawing, painting, or describing; portray: *The artist tried to depict the splendor of the sunset.* verb.

de plore (di plôr′), be very sorry about; express great sorrow for: *We deplore the accident.* verb, **de plored, de plor ing.**

de port ment (di pôrt′mənt), behavior; conduct; way a person acts. *noun.*

de pos it (di poz′it), **1** put down; lay down; leave lying: *She deposited her bundles on the table. The flood deposited a layer of mud in the streets.* **2** material laid down or left lying by natural means: *There is often a deposit of sand and mud at the mouth of a river.* **3** put in a place to be kept safe: *Deposit your money in the bank.* **4** something put in a certain place to be kept safe: *Money put in the bank is a deposit.* **5** pay as a pledge for carrying out a promise to do something or to pay more later: *If you will deposit $5, the store will reserve the coat for you until you pay the rest.* **6** money paid as a pledge to do something or to pay more later: *I put down a $25 deposit on the coat, and I will pay the remaining $50 next month.*

derrick (definition 1)

7 mass of some mineral in rock or in the ground: *deposits of coal.* 1,3,5 *verb,* 2,4,6,7 *noun.*

de pos i tor (di poz′ə tər), person who deposits: *Depositors in savings banks may receive interest on the money deposited.* noun.

de pot (dē′pō *for 1;* dep′ō *for 2 and 3*), **1** a railroad or bus station. **2** storehouse. **3** place where military supplies are stored. *noun.*

de press (di pres′), **1** make sad or gloomy: *Rainy weather always depresses me.* **2** press down; lower: *When you play the piano, you depress the keys.* **3** make less active; weaken: *Some medicines depress the action of the heart.* verb.

de pres sant (di pres′nt), a drug that slows down the activity of the body. *noun.*

de pres sion (di presh′ən), **1** a pressing down; lowering or sinking: *A rapid depression of the mercury in a barometer usually indicates the approach of a storm.* **2** low place; hollow: *Rain formed puddles in the depressions in the ground.* **3** low spirits; sadness: *Failure usually brings on a feeling of depression.* **4** lowering of activity; dullness of trade: *Many people lose their jobs during a business depression.* noun.

de prive (di prīv′), **1** take away from by force: *People who capture wild animals deprive them of their freedom.* **2** keep from having or doing: *The children were deprived of supper. His troubles deprived him of sleep.* verb, **de prived, de priv ing.**

depth (depth), **1** distance from the top to the bottom: *The depth of the lake was so great we could not see the bottom.* **2** distance from front to back: *The depth of our playground is 250 feet.* **3** the deepest or most central part of anything: *in the depths of the earth, in the depths of one's heart, in the depth of winter.* **4** deep quality; deepness: *They admired their teacher's depth of understanding.* noun.

dep u ty (dep′yə tē), person appointed to do the work or take the place of another: *The sheriff*

appointed deputies to help him enforce the law. **noun,**
plural dep u ties.

der by (dėr′bē), **1** an important horse race or
other competition. **2** a stiff hat with a rounded
crown and narrow brim. *noun, plural* **der bies.**

de rive (di rīv′), get; receive; obtain: *She derives*
much pleasure from reading adventure stories. The
word "December" is derived from the Latin word
"decem," which means "ten." verb, **de rived,**
de riv ing.

de rog a to ry (di rog′ə tôr′ē), unfavorable: *We*
don't like to hear derogatory remarks about our
school. adjective.

der rick (der′ik), **1** machine for lifting and moving
heavy objects. A derrick has a long arm that
swings at an angle from the base of an upright
post or frame. See picture. **2** a towerlike
framework over an oil well that holds the drilling
and hoisting machinery. *noun.*

de scend (di send′), **1** go or come down from a
higher to a lower place: *I descended the stairs to*
the basement. The river descends from the mountains
to the sea. **2** go from earlier to later time: *That*
superstition is descended from the Middle Ages. **3** be
handed down from parent to child: *This land has*
descended from my grandfather to my mother and
now to me. **4** make a sudden attack: *The wolves*
descended on the sheep and killed them. verb.

de scend ant (di sen′dənt), **1** person born of a
certain family or group: *a descendant of the*
Pilgrims. **2** offspring; child, grandchild,
great-grandchild, and so on. You are a direct
descendant of your parents, grandparents, and
great-grandparents. *noun.*

de scent (di sent′), **1** coming or going down from
a higher to a lower place: *The descent of the*
balloon was more rapid than its rise had been.
2 downward slope: *We climbed down a steep*
descent. **3** handing down from parent to child: *We*
can trace the descent of blond hair in this family
through five generations. **4** family line; ancestors:
We can trace my descent back to a family in
England. **5** sudden attack: *The descent of the*
bandits on the village was unexpected. noun.

de scribe (di skrīb′), **1** tell in words how a person
looks, feels, or acts, or how a place, a thing, or an
event looks; tell or write about: *The reporter*
described the accident in detail. **2** trace or form;
draw the outline of: *The spinning top described a*
figure 8. verb, **de scribed, de scrib ing.**

de scrip tion (di skrip′shən), **1** telling in words
how a person, place, thing, or event looks or
behaves; describing. **2** composition or account
that describes or gives a picture in words: *The*
vivid description of the hotel fire made me feel as if I
had seen it. **3** kind; sort: *I saw no dog of any*
description today. noun.

de scrip tive (di skrip′tiv), describing; using
description: *A descriptive booklet tells about the*
places to be seen on the trip. adjective.

de seg re gate (dē seg′rə gāt), bring about
desegregation. *verb,* **de seg re gat ed,**
de seg re gat ing.

de seg re ga tion (dē seg′rə gā′shən), doing away
with the practice of providing separate schools,
eating places or recreation areas, and separate
seating in theaters and transportation vehicles for
blacks and whites. *noun.*

des ert[1] (dez′ərt), **1** region without water and
trees. It is usually sandy. There is a great desert in
the northern part of Africa. **2** not inhabited
or cultivated; wild: *They were shipwrecked on a desert*
island. **1** *noun,* **2** *adjective.*

de sert[2] (di zėrt′), forsake; go away and leave a
person or a place, especially one that should not
be left: *A husband should not desert his wife and*
children. A soldier who deserts is punished. The
deserted house fell into ruins. verb.

de sert[3] (di zėrt′), what one deserves; suitable
reward or punishment: *The reckless driver got his*
just deserts; he was fined and his driver's license was
suspended. noun.

de sert er (di zėr′tər), **1** person who deserts.
2 soldier or sailor who runs away from duty. *noun.*

de serve (di zėrv′), have a right to; have a claim
to; be worthy of: *A hard worker deserves good pay.*
A naughty child deserves punishment. verb,
de served, de serv ing.

de sign (di zīn′), **1** a drawing, plan, or sketch made
to serve as a pattern from which to work: *The*
design showed how to build the machine.
2 arrangement of details, form, and color in
painting, weaving, or building. See picture.
3 make a first sketch of; plan out; arrange form
and color of: *We designed a tree house.* **4** plan in
mind to be carried out; purpose: *My sister's design*

design (definition 2)—a colorful Indian design

is to be a lawyer. **5** set apart; intend; plan: *The nursery was designed for the baby's use.* 1,2,4 *noun,* 3,5 *verb.*

des ig nate (dezʹig nāt), **1** mark out; point out; show: *Red lines designate main roads on this map.* **2** select; appoint: *She has been designated by the mayor as superintendent of schools. verb,* **des ig nat ed, des ig nat ing.**

de sign ing (di zīʹning), scheming; plotting. *adjective.*

de sir a bil i ty (di zīʹrə bilʹə tē), desirable quality; condition to be wished for: *Nobody doubts the desirability of good health. noun.*

de sir a ble (di zīʹrə bəl), worth wishing for; worth having; pleasing; good: *Main Street is a very desirable location for a department store. adjective.*

de sire (di zīrʹ), **1** wish: *My desire is to travel.* **2** wish earnestly for: *The people in the warring nations desired peace.* **3** ask for: *The principal desires your presence in his office.* **4** a long, earnest wish. **5** thing wished for: *Her greatest desire was a bicycle.* 1,4,5 *noun,* 2,3 *verb,* **de sired, de sir ing.**

de sist (di zistʹ), stop; cease: *Desist at once! verb.*

desk (desk), piece of furniture with a flat or sloping top on which to write or to rest books for reading. *noun.*

des o late (desʹə lit *for 1,2, and 4;* desʹə lāt *for 3 and 5*), **1** not producing anything; barren. See picture. **2** not lived in; deserted: *a desolate house.* **3** make unfit to live in: *The tornado desolated the whole town.* **4** unhappy; forlorn: *The lost child looked desolate.* **5** make unhappy: *We are desolated to hear that you are going away.* 1,2,4 *adjective,* 3,5 *verb,* **des o lat ed, des o lat ing.**

des o la tion (desʹə lāʹshən), **1** making desolate: *The people mourned the desolation of their town by a tornado.* **2** ruined, lonely, or deserted condition: *After the fire the forest was in desolation.* **3** a desolate place. **4** sadness; lonely sorrow: *A person feels desolation at the loss of loved ones. noun.*

de spair (di sperʹ *or* di sparʹ), **1** loss of hope; being without hope; a dreadful feeling that nothing good can happen to you: *Despair seized us as we felt the boat sinking.* **2** person or thing that causes loss of hope: *The students who never did homework were the despair of the teacher.* **3** lose hope; be without hope: *The doctors despaired of saving the patient's life.* 1,2 *noun,* 3 *verb.*

des per ate (desʹpər it), **1** not caring what happens because hope is gone: *Suicide is a desperate act.* **2** ready to run any risk: *a desperate robber.* **3** having little chance for hope or cure; very dangerous: *a desperate illness. adjective.*

des pe ra tion (desʹpə rāʹshən), a hopeless and reckless feeling; readiness to try anything: *In desperation he jumped out the window when he saw the stairs were on fire. noun.*

de spise (di spīzʹ), look down upon; scorn; think of as beneath your notice, or as too mean or low for you to do: *I despise baseball but I love basketball. verb,* **de spised, de spis ing.**

de spite (di spītʹ), in spite of: *We went for a walk despite the rain. preposition.*

de spond ent (di sponʹdənt), having lost heart, courage, or hope; discouraged; dejected. *adjective.*

des pot (desʹpət), **1** ruler who has unlimited power over others. Despots are sometimes cruel and unjust. **2** person who does just as he or she likes; tyrant. *noun.*

des sert (di zẻrtʹ), course of pie, cake, ice cream, cheese, fruit, or the like served at the end of a meal. *noun.*

des ti na tion (desʹtə nāʹshən), place to which a person or thing is going or is being sent. *noun.*

des tine (desʹtən), **1** intend; set apart for a special purpose or use: *The thoroughbred was destined from birth to be a race horse.* **2** cause by fate: *My letter was destined never to reach him. verb,* **des tined, des tin ing.**

destined for, intended to go to; bound for: *The ships were destined for England.*

desolate (definition 1)
The pioneers named this **desolate** land Death Valley.

des ti ny (desʹtə nē), **1** what becomes of a person or thing in the end; one's lot or fortune: *It was young Washington's destiny to become the first President of the United States.* **2** fate; what is determined beforehand to happen: *She felt that destiny had been unkind to make her poor. noun, plural* **des ti nies.**

des ti tute (desʹtə tüt *or* desʹtə tyüt), lacking necessary things such as food, clothing, and shelter: *A destitute family needs help from charity. adjective.*

destitute of, having no; empty of: *A bald head is destitute of hair.*

de stroy (di stroiʹ), **1** break to pieces; spoil; ruin; make useless: *A tornado destroyed the farmhouse.* **2** put an end to; do away with: *A heavy rain destroyed all hope of a picnic.* **3** kill: *Fire destroys many trees every year. verb.*

de stroy er (di stroiʹər), **1** person or thing that destroys. **2** small, fast warship with guns, torpedoes, and other weapons. See picture. *noun.*

de struc tion (di struk′shən), **1** destroying: *A bulldozer was used in the destruction of the old barn.* **2** ruin: *The storm left destruction behind it.* *noun.*

de struc tive (di struk′tiv), **1** destroying; causing destruction: *Fires and earthquakes are destructive.* **2** not helpful; damaging: *Destructive criticism shows things to be wrong, but does not show how to correct them.* *adjective.*

de tach (di tach′), **1** unfasten; loosen and remove; separate: *I detached a key from the chain.* **2** to send away on special duty: *One squad of soldiers was detached to guard the road.* *verb.*

de tach ment (di tach′mənt), **1** separation. **2** lack of interest: *He watched the dull motion picture with detachment.* **3** troops or ships sent away on some special duty. *noun.*

de tail (di tāl′ or dē′tāl), **1** small or unimportant part: *Her report was complete; it did not leave out a single detail.* **2** dealing with small things one by one: *I do not enjoy the details of housekeeping.* **3** tell fully; tell even the small and unimportant parts: *Our neighbors detailed to us all the things they had done on their vacation.* **4** a small group sent on some special duty: *A detail of six scouts was sent out to find firewood.* **5** send on special duty: *Several police officers were detailed to direct traffic after the big game.* **1,2,4** *noun,* **3,5** *verb.*

de tain (di tān′), **1** keep from going ahead; hold back; delay: *The heavy traffic detained us for almost an hour.* **2** keep from going away; hold as a prisoner: *Police detained the suspected thief for questioning.* *verb.*

de tect (di tekt′), find out; make out; discover; catch: *Could you detect any odor in the room? She was detected hiding presents in the closet.* *verb.*

de tec tive (di tek′tiv), **1** member of a police force or other person whose work is finding information secretly and solving crimes. **2** having something to do with detectives and their work: *She likes reading detective stories.* **1** *noun,* **2** *adjective.*

destroyer (definition 2)

a hat	i it	oi oil	ch child		a in about
ā age	ī ice	ou out	ng long		e in taken
ä far	o hot	u cup	sh she	ə =	i in pencil
e let	ō open	ù put	th thin		o in lemon
ē equal	ô order	ü rule	ŦH then		u in circus
ėr term			zh measure		

de ter (di tėr′), discourage; keep back; hinder: *The barking dog deterred me from crossing the neighbor's yard.* *verb,* **de terred, de ter ring.**

de ter gent (di tėr′jənt), substance used for cleansing. Many detergents are chemical compounds that act like soap. *noun.*

de ter mi na tion (di tėr′mə nā′shən), **1** great firmness in carrying out a purpose: *The boy's determination was not weakened by the difficulties he met.* **2** deciding; settling beforehand: *The determination of what things we needed to take on our camping trip took a long time.* *noun.*

de ter mine (di tėr′mən), **1** make up one's mind very firmly: *He determined to become the best scout in his troop.* **2** find out exactly: *The pilot determined how far she was from the airport.* **3** be the deciding fact in reaching a certain result; settle: *The number of answers you get right determines your mark on this test. Tomorrow's weather will determine whether we go to the beach or stay home.* **4** fix or settle beforehand; decide: *Can we now determine the date for our party? verb,* **de ter mined, de ter min ing.**

de ter mined (di tėr′mənd), **1** with one's mind firmly made up: *He was determined to go in spite of the storm.* **2** firm; resolute: *Her determined look showed that she had made up her mind.* *adjective.*

de test (di test′), dislike very much; hate: *Many people detest snakes.* *verb.*

de test a ble (di tes′tə bəl), deserving to be detested; hateful: *Murder is a detestable crime.* *adjective.*

de throne (di thrōn′), put off a throne; remove from ruling power: *The rebels dethroned the weak king.* *verb,* **de throned, de thron ing.**

de tour (dē′tùr), **1** road that is used when the main or direct road cannot be traveled. **2** a roundabout way: *He took several detours before getting the right answer.* **3** use a detour: *We detoured around the bridge that had been washed out.* **1,2** *noun,* **3** *verb.*

de tract (di trakt′), take away a part; remove some of the quality or worth: *The ugly frame detracts from the beauty of the picture.* *verb.*

dev as tate (dev′ə stāt), destroy; ravage; lay waste; make unfit to live in: *A long war devastated the country.* *verb,* **dev as tat ed, dev as tat ing.**

de vel op (di vel′əp), **1** grow; bring or come into being or activity: *Plants develop from seeds. The seeds develop into plants. Scientists have developed many new drugs to fight disease. He developed an interest in collecting stamps. Swimming will develop many different muscles.* **2** work out in greater and greater detail: *Gradually we developed our plans for the club.* **3** treat (a photographic film or plate) with chemicals to bring out the picture. *verb.*

diagonal (definition 2)

A ——————————————— B

diameter
(definition 1)

dew (definition 1)—In the morning there was **dew** everywhere.

de vel op ment (di vel′əp mənt), **1** process of developing; growth: *The doctor followed the child's development closely.* **2** outcome; result; new event: *A newspaper gives news about the latest developments in the elections.* **3** working out in greater and greater detail: *The development of plans for a flight to the moon took many years.* noun.

de vice (di vīs′), **1** something invented, devised, or fitted for a particular use or special purpose. A can opener is a device. *Our gas stove has a device for lighting it automatically.* **2** plan, scheme, or trick: *In order to stay outside she used the device of pretending not to hear her mother calling her.* noun.
leave to one's own devices, leave to do as one thinks best: *The teacher left us to our own devices in choosing the books for our reports.*

dev il (dev′əl), **1 the Devil,** the evil spirit, the enemy of goodness, or Satan. **2** any evil spirit. **3** a wicked or cruel person. **4** a very clever, energetic, or reckless person: *a mischievous devil.* **5** bother; tease; torment: *My friends deviled me all day because I wore socks that didn't match.* 1-4 *noun,* 5 *verb,* **dev iled, dev il ing.**

dev iled (dev′əld), prepared with seasonings, such as salt, pepper, and spices: *deviled eggs.* adjective.

de vise (di vīz′), think out; plan; contrive; invent: *The kids are trying to devise a scheme of earning money during vacation.* verb, **de vised, de vis ing.**

de vote (di vōt′), give up (oneself, one's money, time, or efforts) to some person, purpose, or service: *She devoted herself to her studies. He is devoting his efforts to cleaning up our lakes and rivers.* verb, **de vot ed, de vot ing.**

de vot ed (di vō′tid), very loyal; faithful: *Dogs are often devoted companions.* adjective.

de vo tion (di vō′shən), **1** deep, steady affection; loyalty: *the devotion of parents to their children.* **2** giving up or being given up to some person, purpose, or service: *Her devotion to the Girl Scouts made her attend every meeting.* **3** devotions, worship, prayers, or praying. noun.

de vour (di vour′), **1** eat (said of animals): *The lion devoured the sheep.* **2** eat like an animal; eat very hungrily: *The hungry girl devoured her dinner.* **3** consume; destroy: *The raging fire devoured the forest.* **4** take in with eyes or ears in a hungry, greedy way: *He devoured the new book about airplanes.* verb.

de vout (di vout′), **1** religious; active in worship and prayer: *a devout Moslem, a devout Christian.* **2** earnest; sincere; hearty: *You have my devout wishes for a safe trip.* adjective.

dew (dü *or* dyü), **1** moisture from the air that condenses and collects in small drops on cool surfaces during the night. See picture. **2** something fresh or refreshing like dew: *the dew of youth, the dew of sleep.* noun.

dew drop (dü′drop′ *or* dyü′drop′), drop of dew. noun.

dex ter i ty (dek ster′ə tē), skill in using the hands, body, or mind: *A good surgeon works with dexterity.* noun.

di a be tes (dī/ə bē/tis), disease in which a person's system cannot properly absorb normal amounts of sugar and starch. *noun.*

di a crit i cal mark (dī/ə krit/ə kəl märk/), mark like ·· ^ - ′ put over or under a letter to indicate pronunciation or accent. See the diacritical marks in the short key in the upper right corner of this page.

di ag nose (dī/əg nōs/), find out the nature of by an examination: *The doctor diagnosed the disease as measles. verb,* **di ag nosed, di ag nos ing.**

di ag no sis (dī/əg nō/sis), finding out what disease a person or animal has by examination and careful study of the symptoms: *The doctor used X rays and blood samples in her diagnosis. noun, plural* **di ag no ses** (dī/əg nō/sēz/).

di ag o nal (dī ag/ə nəl), **1** a straight line that cuts across in a slanting direction, often from corner to corner. **2** taking the direction of a diagonal; slanting: *diagonal stripes in cloth.* See picture. **1** *noun,* **2** *adjective.*

di ag o nal ly (dī ag/ə nəl ē), in a diagonal direction. *adverb.*

di a gram (dī/ə gram), **1** drawing or sketch showing important parts of a thing. A diagram may be an outline, a plan, a drawing, a figure, a chart, or a combination of any of these, made to show clearly what a thing is or how it works. A plan of a house or a steamship is a diagram. **2** put on paper or on a blackboard in the form of a drawing or sketch; make a diagram of: *Our teacher diagramed how we should leave the building during a fire drill.* **1** *noun,* **2** *verb.*

di al (dī/əl), **1** plate or disk with numbers, letters, or marks on it and a moving pointer that shows how much there is of something. The face of a clock or of a compass is a dial. A dial may show the amount of water in a tank or the amount of steam pressure in a boiler. **2** plate or disk of a radio or television set with numbers and letters on it for tuning in to a radio or television station. **3** tune in by using a radio or television dial: *He dialed his favorite station.* **4** the round, movable part of a telephone used in making telephone calls. **5** call by means of a telephone dial: *She dialed the wrong number.* **1,2,4** *noun,* **3,5** *verb.*

di a lect (dī/ə lekt), a form of speech spoken in a certain district or by a certain group of people: *The Scottish dialect of English has many words and pronunciations that Americans do not use. A dialect of French is spoken in southern Louisiana by descendants of French Canadians. noun.*

di a logue (dī/ə lôg), **1** conversation: *Two actors had a dialogue in the middle of the stage.* **2** conversation written out: *That book has a good plot and much clever dialogue. noun.*

di am e ter (dī am/ə tər), **1** a straight line that goes from one side through the center of a circle or sphere to the other side. See picture. **2** length of such a line: *The diameter of the earth is about 8000 miles. The tree trunk was almost 2 feet in diameter. noun.*

dia mond (dī/mənd), **1** a colorless or tinted precious stone, formed of pure carbon in crystals. Diamond is the hardest substance known. **2** figure shaped like this ◇. **3** the space inside the lines that connect the bases in baseball. *noun.*

di a per (dī/ə pər), piece of cloth or other soft material folded and used as underpants for a baby. *noun.*

di a phragm (dī/ə fram), **1** a layer of muscles and tendons separating the cavity of the chest from the cavity of the abdomen. **2** a thin dividing layer. *noun.*

di ar y (dī/ər ē), **1** account, written down each day, of what has happened to one, or what one has done or thought, during that day. **2** book for keeping such a daily account. It has a blank space for each day of the year. *noun, plural* **di ar ies.**

dice (dīs), **1** small cubes with a different number of spots (one to six) on each side. Dice are used in playing some games. **2** cut into small cubes: *Carrots are sometimes diced before being cooked.* **1** *noun plural of* **die²; 2** *verb,* **diced, dic ing.**

dic tate (dik/tāt), **1** say or read (something) aloud for another person to write down: *The teacher dictated a list of books to the students.* **2** speak with authority; make others do what one says: *Big nations sometimes dictate to little ones. No one shall dictate to me.* **3** command or order that is to be carried out or obeyed: *The people followed the dictates of their leaders.* **1,2** *verb,* **dic tat ed, dic tat ing; 3** *noun.*

dic ta tion (dik tā/shən), **1** saying or reading words aloud to another person who writes them down: *The pupils wrote down the spelling words at the teacher's dictation.* **2** words said or read aloud in this way: *The secretary took the dictation in shorthand and typed it out later.* **3** giving orders; making rules: *I am tired of obeying the constant dictation of my older sisters and brothers. noun.*

dic ta tor (dik/tā tər), person who rules, using complete authority: *The dictator seized control of the government and took complete power over the people of the country. noun.*

dic ta tor ship (dik/tā tər ship), **1** position or rank of a dictator. **2** country ruled by a dictator. **3** power to give orders that must be obeyed. *noun.*

dic tion ar y (dik/shə ner/ē), book that explains the words of a language, or some special kind of words. It is arranged alphabetically. You can use this dictionary to find out the meaning, pronunciation, or spelling of a word. *noun, plural* **dic tion ar ies.**

did (did). See **do.** *Did he go to school yesterday? Yes, he did. verb.*

did n't (did/nt), did not.

die¹ (dī), **1** stop living; become dead: *The flowers in the garden died from frost.* **2** lose force or strength;

a hat	i it	oi oil	ch child	(a in about
ā age	ī ice	ou out	ng long	e in taken
ä far	o hot	u cup	sh she	ə = i in pencil
e let	ō open	ů put	th thin	o in lemon
ē equal	ô order	ü rule	₮H then	(u in circus
ėr term			zh measure	

come to an end: *The music died away. The motor sputtered and died.* **3** want very much: *I was dying for an ice-cream cone. verb,* **died, dy ing.**

die² (dī), **1** a carved metal block or plate. Different kinds of dies are used for coining money, for raising letters up from the surface of paper, and for giving a certain shape to articles made by forging and cutting. **2** a small cube used in games. See **dice.** *noun, plural* **dies** for 1, **dice** for 2.

die sel en gine (dē′zəl en′jən), engine that burns oil with heat from compressed air. [The *diesel engine* was named for Rudolf Diesel, who lived from 1858 to 1913. He was a German engineer who invented it.]

di et (dī′ət), **1** the usual kind of food and drink: *My diet is made up of meat, fish, vegetables, fruits, water, and milk. Grass is a large part of a cow's diet.* **2** any special selection of food eaten in sickness, or to make oneself fat or thin: *While I was sick I was on a liquid diet.* **3** eat special food as a part of a doctor's treatment, or in order to gain or lose weight. **1,2** *noun,* **3** *verb.*

di e ti tian (dī′ə tish′ən), person trained to plan meals that have the right amount of various kinds of food. Many hospitals and schools employ dietitians. *noun.*

dif fer (dif′ər), **1** be unlike; be different: *My answer to the problem differed from hers.* **2** hold or express a different opinion; disagree: *The two of us differ about how we should spend the money. verb.*

dif fer ence (dif′ər əns), **1** being different: *the difference of night and day.* **2** amount or manner of being different; way in which people or things are different: *The only difference between the twins is that John weighs five pounds more than Bob.* **3** what is left after subtracting one number from another: *The difference between 6 and 15 is 9.* **4** dispute: *We had a difference over a name for the puppy. noun.*

make a difference, be important; matter: *Painting the house will really make a difference in the way it looks.*

dif fer ent (dif′ər ənt), **1** not alike; not like: *People have different names. A boat is different from an automobile.* **2** not the same; separate; distinct: *She won three different swimming contests.* **3** not like others or most others; unusual: *That story was really different; I've never read one like it. adjective.*

dif fi cult (dif′ə kult), **1** hard to do or understand: *Arithmetic is difficult for some pupils.* **2** hard to manage; hard to please: *My cousins are difficult and always want things their own way. adjective.*

dif fi cul ty (dif′ə kul′tē), **1** condition of being difficult; degree to which something is difficult: *The difficulty of the job kept us from finishing it on time.* **2** hard work; much effort: *I finished the long arithmetic problem with difficulty.* **3** something which stands in the way of getting things done; thing that is hard to do or understand: *Lack of time and lack of money were two difficulties we had to overcome.* **4** trouble: *Some children have difficulty learning how to spell. noun, plural* **dif fi cul ties.**

dig (dig), **1** use hands, shovel, spade, claws, or

snout in making a hole or in turning over the ground: *Dogs bury bones and dig for them later.* **2** make by digging: *dig a well, dig a cellar.* **3** make a way by digging: *They dug a tunnel through a mountain.* **4** get by digging: *dig potatoes, dig clams.* **5** make a thrust or stab into; prod: *The cat dug its claws into my hand.* **6** a thrust or poke: *I gave my friend a dig in the ribs.* **7** work or study hard. **1-5,7** *verb,* **dug, dig ging;** **6** *noun.*

di gest (də jest′ for 1 and 2; dī′jest for 3), **1** change (food) in the stomach and intestines, so that the body can use it: *We digest our food slowly. Our food digests.* **2** think over (something) until you understand it clearly, or until it becomes a part of your own thought: *It often takes a long time to digest new ideas.* **3** a brief statement of what is in a longer book or article; summary. **1,2** *verb,* **3** *noun.*

di ges tion (də jes′chən), **1** the digesting of food: *Proper digestion is necessary for good health.* **2** ability to digest food: *A person's digestion can be affected by illness. noun.*

di ges tive (də jes′tiv), having something to do with digestion: *Saliva is one of the digestive juices. adjective.*

dig it (dij′it), **1** any of the figures 0, 1, 2, 3, 4, 5, 6, 7, 8, 9. Sometimes 0 is not called a digit. **2** finger or toe. *noun.*

dig ni fied (dig′nə fīd), having dignity; noble; stately: *The queen has a dignified manner. adjective.*

dig ni fy (dig′nə fī), give dignity to; make noble, worthwhile, or worthy: *The low farmhouse was dignified by the great elms around it. verb,* **dig ni fied, dig ni fy ing.**

dig ni tar y (dig′nə ter′ē), person who has a position of honor. A bishop is a church dignitary. *noun, plural* **dig ni tar ies.**

dig ni ty (dig′nə tē), **1** proud and self-respecting character or manner; stately appearance: *the dignity of a cathedral.* **2** quality of character or ability that wins the respect and high opinion of others: *A judge should maintain the dignity of his or her position.* **3** high office, rank, or title; position of honor: *the dignity of the presidency.* **4** worth; nobleness: *Honest work has dignity. noun, plural* **dig ni ties.**

dike (dīk), a bank of earth or a dam built as a defense against flooding by a river or the sea. *noun.* Also spelled **dyke.**

di lap i dat ed (də lap′ə dā′tid), falling to pieces; partly ruined or decayed through neglect. See picture. *adjective.*

di late (dī lāt′), make or become larger or wider: *The pupil of the eye dilates when the light gets dim. verb,* **di lat ed, di lat ing.**

dil i gence (dil′ə jəns), working hard; careful effort; ability to work steadily: *The student's diligence was rewarded with high marks. noun.*

dil i gent (dil′ə jənt), hard-working; industrious; not lazy: *The diligent student kept on working until he had finished his homework. adjective.*

dil ly dal ly (dil′ē dal′ē), loiter; waste time; trifle. *verb,* **dil ly dal lied, dil ly dal ly ing.**

di lute (də lüt′), **1** make weaker or thinner by

diminutive—The **diminutive** child was no larger than a butterfly.

dilapidated—an old, dilapidated house

dimple
(definition 1)

a hat	**i** it	**oi** oil	**ch** child	a in about
ā age	**ī** ice	**ou** out	**ng** long	e in taken
ä far	**o** hot	**u** cup	**sh** she	ə = { i in pencil
e let	**ō** open	**u̇** put	**th** thin	o in lemon
ē equal	**ô** order	**ü** rule	**ᴛʜ** then	u in circus
ėr term			**zh** measure	

adding water or some other liquid: *I diluted the concentrated orange juice with several cups of water.* **2** weakened or thinned by water or some other liquid. 1 *verb,* **di lut ed, di lut ing;** 2 *adjective.*

dim (dim), **1** not bright; not clear; not distinct: *dim light. With the shades drawn, the room was dim.* **2** not clearly seen, heard, or understood: *We could see only the dim outline of the mountain in the distance.* **3** not seeing, hearing, or understanding clearly: *My eyesight is getting dimmer.* **4** make or become dim: *She dimmed the car's headlights as the other car approached.* 1-3 *adjective,* **dim mer, dim mest;** 4 *verb,* **dimmed, dim ming.**

dime (dīm), coin of the United States and Canada equal to 10 cents. Ten dimes make one dollar. *noun.*

di men sion (də men′shən), **1** measurement of length, width, or thickness: *I need wallpaper for a room of the following dimensions: 16 feet long, 12 feet wide, and 8 feet high.* **2 dimensions,** size or extent: *Building a park in the slum area was a project of large dimensions. noun.*

di min ish (də min′ish), make or become smaller in size, amount, or importance: *A sound diminishes as you get farther and farther away from it. verb.*

di min u tive (də min′yə tiv), small; tiny. See picture. *adjective.*

dim mer (dim′ər), device that dims an electric light. *noun.*

dim ple (dim′pəl), **1** small hollow place, usually in the cheek or chin. See picture. **2** form dimples: *He dimples whenever he smiles.* 1 *noun,* 2 *verb,* **dim pled, dim pling.**

din (din), **1** a loud, confused noise that lasts: *The din of the cheering crowd was deafening.* **2** make a din. **3** say (one thing) over and over: *Our boss is always dinning into our ears the importance of hard work.* 1 *noun,* 2,3 *verb,* **dinned, din ning.**

dine (dīn), **1** eat dinner: *We dine at six o'clock.* **2** give dinner to; give a dinner for: *The principal dined the new teachers. verb,* **dined, din ing.**

din er (dī′nər), **1** person who is eating dinner. **2** railroad car in which meals are served. **3** a small eating place, that often looks like a railroad car. *noun.*

di nette (dī net′), a small dining room. *noun.*

din ghy (ding′ē), a small rowboat. *noun, plural* **din ghies.**

din gy (din′jē), dirty-looking; lacking brightness or freshness; dull: *Dingy curtains covered the windows of the dusty old room. adjective,* **din gi er, din gi est.**

dining room, room in which dinner and other meals are served.

din ner (din′ər), **1** the main meal of the day: *In the city we have dinner at night, but in the country we* *have dinner at noon.* **2** a formal meal in honor of some person or occasion: *The city officials gave the mayor a dinner to celebrate his reelection. noun.*

di no saur (dī′nə sôr), one of a group of extinct reptiles that lived many millions of years ago. Some dinosaurs were bigger than elephants. Some were smaller than cats. See picture. *nouh.* [*Dinosaur* comes from Greek words meaning "terrible lizard."]

di o cese (dī′ə sis), the church district over which a bishop has authority. *noun.*

dip (dip), **1** put under water or any liquid and lift quickly out again: *He dipped his hand into the pool to see how cold the water was.* **2** go under water and come quickly out again: *She dipped a few times in the ocean to cool herself off.* **3** a dipping of any kind, especially a plunge into and out of water: *She felt cool after a dip in the ocean.* **4** liquid in which to dip something for washing or cleaning: *The sheep were driven through a dip to disinfect their coats.* **5** make (a candle) by putting a wick into hot tallow or wax. 1,2,5 *verb,* **dipped, dip ping;** 3,4 *noun.*

diph ther i a (dif thir′ē ə), an often fatal disease of the throat that attacks children especially. Unless you have been inoculated against diphtheria, you can catch the disease if you are around someone who has it. *noun.*

diph thong (dif′thông), a vowel sound made up of two vowel sounds pronounced in one syllable, such as *oi* in *noise* or *ou* in *out. noun.*

di plo ma (də plō′mə), a written or printed paper, given by a school or college, which says that a person has completed a certain course of study, or has been graduated after a certain amount of work. *noun.*

dip lo mat (dip′lə mat), **1** person whose work is to handle the relations of his or her country with other nations. **2** person who is skillful in dealing with people. *noun.*

dip lo mat ic (dip′lə mat′ik), **1** having to do with the management of relations between nations: *Ambassadors are members of the diplomatic service.* **2** skillful in dealing with people; tactful: *I gave a diplomatic answer to avoid hurting my friend's feelings. adjective.*

dip per (dip′ər), **1** a long-handled cup or larger container for lifting water or liquids. **2** The **Big Dipper** and **Little Dipper** are two groups of stars in the northern sky somewhat resembling the shape of a dipper. *noun.*

dire (dīr), dreadful; causing great fear or suffering: *We fear the dire results of an atomic war. adjective.*

di rect (də rekt′), **1** manage or guide; control: *The teacher directs the work of the pupils.* **2** order; command: *The policeman directed the traffic to stop.* **3** tell or show the way: *We turned left where the signpost directed.* **4** point or aim: *The fireman directed his hose at the flames. We should direct our effort to a useful end.* **5** straight; without a stop or turn: *The freeway crosses the county in almost a direct line.* **6** in an unbroken line: *They are direct descendants of the founder of this town.* **7** truthful;

frank; plain: *She gave direct answers to all the questions.* **8** directly: *This airplane goes to Los Angeles direct, without stopping between here and there.* 1-4 *verb,* 5-7 *adjective,* 8 *adverb.*

direct current, electric current that flows in one direction. The current from all batteries is direct current.

di rec tion (də rek′shən), **1** guiding; managing; control: *The school is under the direction of the principal.* **2** order; command. **3** knowing or telling what to do, how to do, or where to go; instruction: *He needs directions to the lake.* **4** course taken by a moving body, such as a ball or a bullet. **5** any way in which one may face or point. North, south, east, and west are directions. *Our school is in one direction and the post office is in another.* **6** course along which something moves; way of moving; tendency: *The town shows improvement in many directions. noun.*

di rect ly (də rekt′lē), **1** in a direct line or manner; straight: *This road runs directly into the center of town.* **2** exactly; absolutely: *directly opposite.* **3** immediately; at once: *Come home directly. adverb.*

di rec tor (də rek′tər), manager; person who directs. A person who directs the performance of a play, a motion picture, or a show on television or radio is called a director. *noun.*

di rec tor y (də rek′tər ē), list of names and addresses. A telephone book is a directory with telephone numbers. *noun, plural* **di rec tor ies.**

dir i gi ble (dir′ə jə bəl), a kind of balloon that can be steered. A dirigible has a rigid inner framework and is filled with a gas that is lighter than air. See picture. *noun.*

dirt (dėrt), **1** mud, dust, earth, or anything like them. Dirt soils skin, clothing, houses, or furniture. **2** loose earth or soil. *noun.*

dirt i ness (dėr′tē nis), dirty condition. *noun.*

dirt y (dėr′tē), **1** not clean; soiled by mud, dust, earth, or anything like them: *Children playing in the mud get dirty.* **2** not clean or pure in language or action. **3** not clear or pure in color: *a dirty red.* **4** make dirty; soil: *You will dirty your new clothes if you play outside on the muddy ground.* 1-3 *adjective,* **dirt i er, dirt i est;** 4 *verb,* **dirt ied, dirt y ing.**

dis-, prefix meaning: **1** not; opposite of; lack of: *Dishonest* means *not* honest, or the *opposite of* honest. *Discomfort* means the *lack of* comfort. **2** do the opposite of: *Disconnect* means *do the opposite of* connect.

dis a bil i ty (dis′ə bil′ə tē), **1** lack of ability or power: *The player's disability was due to illness.* **2** something that disables: *Deafness is a disability for a musician. noun, plural* **dis a bil i ties.**

dis a ble (dis ā′bəl), make unable; cripple: *A sprained wrist disabled the tennis player for three weeks. verb,* **dis a bled, dis a bling.**

dis ad van tage (dis′əd van′tij), **1** lack of advantage; unfavorable condition: *Her shyness was a disadvantage in company.* **2** loss; injury: *The candidate's enemies spread rumors to his disadvantage. noun.*

dis a gree (dis′ə grē′), **1** fail to agree; be different:

Your account of the accident disagrees with hers.
2 have unlike opinions; differ: *Doctors sometimes disagree about the proper method of treating a patient.* **3** quarrel; dispute: *The two neighbors never spoke to each other again after they disagreed about their boundary line.* **4** have a bad effect; be harmful: *I can't eat strawberries because they disagree with me.* verb, **dis a greed, dis a gree ing.**

dis a gree a ble (dis′ə grē′ə bəl), **1** not to one's liking; not pleasant: *A headache is disagreeable.* **2** not friendly; bad-tempered; cross: *People often become disagreeable when they are tired.* adjective.

dis a gree ment (dis′ə grē′mənt), **1** failure to agree; difference of opinion: *The disagreement that existed among members of the town council caused a postponement of the meeting.* **2** quarrel; dispute: *Their disagreement led to blows.* **3** difference; unlikeness: *There is a disagreement between her account of the accident and mine.* noun.

dis ap pear (dis′ə pir′), **1** pass from sight: *The little dog disappeared around the corner.* **2** pass from existence; stop being: *When spring comes, the snow disappears.* verb.

dis ap pear ance (dis′ə pir′əns), act of disappearing: *The disappearance of the airplane brought about a search of the area.* noun.

dis ap point (dis′ə point′), **1** fail to satisfy one's desire, wish, or hope; leave wanting something: *The circus disappointed him, for there was no elephant.* **2** fail to keep a promise to: *You said you would help; do not disappoint me.* verb.

dis ap point ment (dis′ə point′mənt), **1** being disappointed; the feeling you have when you do not get what you expected or hoped for: *When she did not get a new bicycle, her disappointment was very great.* **2** person or thing that causes disappointment: *The movie was a disappointment to me because it wasn't exciting.* noun.

dis ap prov al (dis′ə prü′vəl), having an opinion or feeling against; expressing an opinion against; dislike: *Hisses from the audience showed its disapproval of the speaker's remarks.* noun.

dis ap prove (dis′ə prüv′), consider not good or not suitable; have or express an opinion against: *Parents often disapprove of rough games in the house.* verb, **dis ap proved, dis ap prov ing.**

dis arm (dis ärm′), **1** take weapons away from: *The police captured the bandits and disarmed them.* **2** stop having an army or navy; reduce the size of an army or navy: *The nations agreed to disarm.* **3** remove anger or suspicion; make friendly: *The little boy's smile could always disarm those who were about to scold him.* **4** make harmless: *The soldiers disarmed the bomb by removing the fuse.* verb.

dis ar range (dis′ə rānj′), disturb the arrangement of; put out of order: *The wind disarranged my hair.* verb, **dis ar ranged, dis ar rang ing.**

dis as ter (də zas′tər), event that causes much suffering or loss; great misfortune. A flood, fire, shipwreck, earthquake, or great loss of money is a disaster. See picture. noun.

dis as trous (də zas′trəs), bringing disaster;

a hat	i it	oi oil	ch child	ə = { a in about
ā age	ī ice	ou out	ng long	e in taken
ä far	o hot	u cup	sh she	i in pencil
e let	ō open	u̇ put	th thin	o in lemon
ē equal	ô order	ü rule	ŦH then	u in circus
ėr term			zh measure	

disaster

dirigible

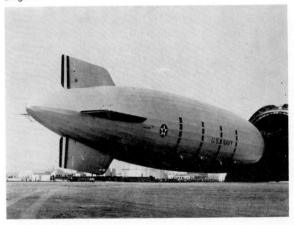

dinosaur

causing much suffering or loss: *A disastrous hurricane struck the city. adjective.*

dis band (dis band′), break up; dismiss: *When peace is declared, armies are disbanded. verb.*

dis be lief (dis′bi lēf′), lack of belief; refusal to believe: *When we heard the shocking rumor, we immediately expressed disbelief. noun.*

disc (disk), disk. *noun.*

dis card (dis kärd′), 1 throw aside; give up as useless or worn out: *You can discard clothes, ways of doing things, or beliefs.* 2 thing or things thrown aside as useless or not wanted: *That worn-out old book is a discard from the library.* 1 *verb,* 2 *noun.*

dis charge (dis chärj′), 1 unload (cargo or passengers) from ship, train, bus, or airplane: *The ship discharged its passengers at the dock.* 2 unloading: *The discharge of this cargo will not take long.* 3 fire off; shoot: *The policeman discharged his gun at the fleeing robbers.* 4 firing off a gun or a blast: *The discharge of dynamite could be heard for three miles.* 5 release; let go; dismiss: *discharge a patient from a hospital, discharge a lazy worker.* 6 release; letting go; dismissing: *I expect my discharge from the hospital in a few days.* 7 give off; let out: *The infection discharged pus.* 8 giving off; letting out: *Lightning is a discharge of electricity from thunderclouds.* 9 thing given off or let out: *the watery discharge from an eye.* 10 perform; carry out: *She discharged all the errands she had been given.* 11 performing; carrying out: *The discharge of public duties is part of the mayor's job.* 12 pay (a debt). 1,3,5,7,10,12 *verb,* **dis charged,** **dis charg ing;** 2,4,6,8,9,11 *noun.*

dis ci ple (də sī′pəl), 1 believer in the thought and teaching of any leader; follower. 2 (in the Bible) one of the followers of Jesus. *noun.*

dis ci pline (dis′ə plin), 1 training; especially training of the mind or character: *Children who have had no discipline are often hard to teach.* 2 trained condition of order and obedience; order kept among school pupils, soldiers, or members of any group: *When the fire broke out, the pupils showed good discipline.* 3 train; bring to a condition of order and obedience; bring under control: *An officer must know how to discipline men.* 4 punishment: *A little discipline would do them good.* 5 punish: *They have never disciplined their children unfairly.* 1,2,4 *noun,* 3,5 *verb,* **dis ci plined,** **dis ci plin ing.**

dis claim (dis klām′), refuse to recognize as one's own; deny connection with: *The motorist disclaimed responsibility for the accident. verb.*

dis close (dis klōz′), 1 uncover: *She opened the box and disclosed a turtle.* 2 make known: *This letter discloses a secret. verb,* **dis closed,** **dis clos ing.**

dis col or (dis kul′ər), 1 change or spoil the color of; stain: *Smoke had discolored the building.* 2 become changed in color: *Many materials fade and discolor if exposed to bright sunshine. verb.*

dis com fort (dis kum′fərt), 1 uneasiness; lack of comfort: *Embarrassing questions cause discomfort.* 2 thing that causes discomfort: *Mud and cold were the discomforts the campers minded most. noun.*

dis con nect (dis′kə nekt′), separate; unfasten; undo or break the connection of: *I disconnected the electric fan by pulling out the plug. verb.*

dis con tent (dis′kən tent′), uneasy feeling; dissatisfaction; dislike of what one has and a desire for something different: *Low pay and long hours of work caused discontent among the factory workers. noun.*

dis con tent ed (dis′kən ten′tid), not contented; not satisfied; displeased and restless; disliking what one has and wanting something different: *The discontented workers went on strike. adjective.*

dis con tin ue (dis′kən tin′yü), stop; give up; put an end or stop to: *The 10 o'clock bus to Boston has been discontinued. After we learned how to print, the teacher discontinued our printing lessons. verb,* **dis con tin ued,** **dis con tin u ing.**

dis cord (dis′kôrd), 1 difference of opinion; disputing: *Constant argument caused angry discord that spoiled the meeting.* 2 (in music) a lack of harmony in notes sounded at the same time. 3 harsh, clashing sounds. *noun.*

dis count (dis′kount), 1 take off a certain amount from a price: *The store discounts all clothes ten per cent.* 2 the amount taken off from a price: *We bought the new TV set on sale at a 20 per cent discount.* 3 believe only part of; allow for exaggeration in: *You must discount some of what he tells you, because he likes to make up stories.* 1,3 *verb,* 2 *noun.*

dis cour age (dis kėr′ij), 1 take away the courage of; destroy the hopes of: *Failing again and again discourages anyone.* 2 try to prevent by disapproving; frown upon: *All her friends discouraged her from such a dangerous swim.* 3 frown on; make seem not worth while: *The chill of coming winter soon discouraged our picnics. verb,* **dis cour aged,** **dis cour ag ing.**

dis cour age ment (dis kėr′ij mənt), 1 condition of being or feeling discouraged. 2 something that discourages. 3 act of discouraging. *noun.*

dis course (dis′kôrs for 1 and 2; dis kôrs′ for 3), 1 long written or spoken discussion of some subject: *Sermons and lectures are discourses.* 2 talk; conversation. 3 to talk; converse. 1,2 *noun,* 3 *verb,* **dis coursed,** **dis cours ing.**

dis cour te ous (dis kėr′tē əs), not courteous; not polite; rude. *adjective.*

dis cour te sy (dis kėr′tə sē), lack of courtesy; impoliteness; rudeness. *noun, plural* **dis cour te sies.**

dis cov er (dis kuv′ər), find out; see or learn of for the first time: *Madame Curie discovered the element radium in 1898. I discovered their secret. verb.*

dis cov er y (dis kuv′ər ē), 1 finding out; seeing or learning of something for the first time: *Balboa's discovery of the Pacific Ocean occurred in 1513.* 2 thing found out: *One of Benjamin Franklin's discoveries was that lightning is electricity. noun, plural* **dis cov er ies.**

dis cred it (dis kred′it), 1 cast doubt on; destroy belief, faith, or trust in: *The lawyer discredited the witnesses by proving that they both had lied.* 2 loss of belief, faith, or trust; doubt: *This newspaper story throws discredit on your account of the trip.* **3** refuse to believe: *We discredit her because she has lied so often.* **4** do harm to the good name or standing of; give a bad reputation to: *His cheating during tests discredited him among his classmates.* **5** loss of good name or standing: *The player who took a bribe brought discredit upon the team.* 1,3,4 *verb,* 2,5 *noun.*

dis creet (dis krēt′), very careful in speech and action; showing good judgment: *A discreet person does not spread gossip. "Perhaps" is a discreet answer. adjective.*

dis cre tion (dis kresh′ən), **1** good judgment; care in speech and action; caution: *She rushed across the street in front of a car, but I showed more discretion.* **2** freedom to judge or choose: *It is within the principal's discretion to punish a pupil. noun.*

dis crim i nate (dis krim′ə nāt), **1** make or see a difference between; distinguish: *People who are color-blind usually cannot discriminate between red and green.* **2** show an unfair difference in treatment: *It is wrong to discriminate against people because of their race, religion, nationality, or sex. verb,* **dis crim i nat ed, dis crim i nat ing.**

dis crim i na tion (dis krim′ə nā′shən), **1** making or recognizing differences and distinctions: *Do not buy clothes without discrimination.* **2** ability to discriminate accurately between things that are very much alike; good judgment: *He lacked discrimination in his choice of friends.* **3** making a difference in favor of or against: *Racial or religious discrimination in hiring employees is against the law. noun.*

dis cuss (dis kus′), talk over; consider from various points of view: *The class discussed several problems. Congress is discussing taxes. verb.*

dis cus sion (dis kush′ən), talk; talk about the reasons for and against; discussing things: *After hours of discussion, we came to a decision. noun.*

dis dain (dis dān′), **1** consider to be lower; look down on; scorn: *Now that they live in a new neighborhood, they disdain their old friends.* **2** a feeling that someone or something is beneath oneself: *The older students tended to treat the younger ones with disdain, and wouldn't have much to do with them.* 1 *verb,* 2 *noun.*

dis dain ful (dis dān′fəl), proud and scornful. See picture. *adjective.*

dis ease (də zēz′), **1** sickness; illness; condition in which an organ, system, or part does not work properly: *People, animals, and plants can all suffer from disease. Cleanliness helps prevent disease.* **2** any particular illness: *Measles and chicken pox are two diseases of children. noun.*

dis eased (də zēzd′), having a disease: *A diseased lung may be removed by an operation. adjective.*

dis fa vor (dis fā′vər), **1** dislike; disapproval: *The workers looked with disfavor on any attempt to lower their wages.* **2** condition of having lost favor or trust: *The government was in disfavor with the people. noun.*

a hat	i it	oi oil	ch child	a in about
ā age	ī ice	ou out	ng long	e in taken
ä far	o hot	u cup	sh she	ə = { i in pencil
e let	ō open	u̇ put	th thin	o in lemon
ē equal	ô order	ü rule	�H then	u in circus
ėr term			zh measure	

dis fig ure (dis fig′yər), spoil the appearance of; hurt the beauty of: *A scar may disfigure a person's face. verb,* **dis fig ured, dis fig ur ing.**

dis grace (dis grās′), **1** loss of honor or respect; shame: *The disgrace of being sent to prison was hard for them to bear.* **2** loss of favor or trust: *The king's former adviser is now in disgrace.* **3** cause disgrace to; bring shame upon: *The traitor disgraced his family and friends.* **4** person or thing that causes dishonor or shame: *The slums in many cities are a disgrace.* 1,2,4 *noun,* 3 *verb,* **dis graced, dis grac ing.**

dis grace ful (dis grās′fəl), shameful; causing dishonor or loss of respect: *Their rude behavior was disgraceful. adjective.*

dis guise (dis gīz′), **1** hide what one is by looking like someone else: *On Halloween I disguised myself as a ghost.* **2** the use of a changed or unusual dress and appearance in order not to be known: *Detectives sometimes depend on disguise.* **3** clothes or actions used to hide or deceive: *Glasses and a wig formed the spy's disguise.* **4** hide what (a thing) really is; make (a thing) seem like something else: *The pirates disguised their ship as a trading vessel. She disguised her handwriting by writing with her left hand.* 1,4 *verb,* **dis guised, dis guis ing;** 2,3 *noun.*

dis gust (dis gust′), **1** strong dislike; sickening dislike: *We feel disgust for bad odors or tastes.* **2** cause a feeling of disgust in: *The smell of rotten eggs disgusts many people.* 1 *noun,* 2 *verb.*

dish (dish), **1** anything to serve food in. Plates, platters, bowls, cups, and saucers are all dishes. **2** amount served in a dish: *I ate two dishes of ice*

disdainful
She gave the children a **disdainful** look.

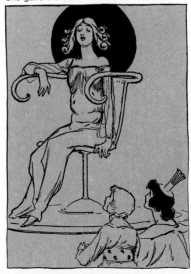

cream. **3** food served: *Sliced peaches with cream is the dish I like best.* **4** put (food) into a dish for serving at the table: *You may dish up the dinner now.* 1-3 *noun,* 4 *verb.*

dis heart en (dis härt′n), discourage; depress: *Long illness is disheartening. verb.*

dis hon est (dis on′ist), **1** not fair play: *Lying, cheating, and stealing are dishonest.* **2** not honest; ready to cheat: *A person who lies or steals is dishonest. adjective.*

dis hon es ty (dis on′ə stē), **1** lack of honesty: *People who lie or cheat can't be trusted because of their dishonesty.* **2** dishonest act. *noun, plural* **dis hon es ties.**

dis hon or (dis on′ər), **1** disgrace; shame; loss of reputation or standing: *Treason brought dishonor to a proud family.* **2** person or thing that causes dishonor: *The team's poor sportsmanship was a dishonor to the school.* **3** bring reproach or shame upon: *The player who cheated dishonored the entire team.* 1,2 *noun,* 3 *verb.*

dis hon or a ble (dis on′ər ə bəl), without honor; disgraceful; shameful. *adjective.*

dish wash er (dish′wosh′ər), machine for washing dishes, pots, and glasses. *noun.*

dis in fect (dis′in fekt′), destroy the disease germs in: *The dentist disinfected his instruments. verb.*

dis in fect ant (dis′in fek′tənt), substance used to destroy disease germs. Alcohol and iodine are disinfectants. *noun.*

dis in te grate (dis in′tə grāt), break up; separate into small parts or bits: *The old papers had disintegrated into a pile of fragments and dust. verb,* **dis in te grat ed, dis in te grat ing.**

dis in ter est ed (dis in′tər ə stid), free from selfish motives; impartial; fair: *An umpire makes disinterested decisions. adjective.*

disk (disk), **1** a flat, thin, round object shaped like a coin. **2** a round, flat surface, or a surface that seems so. **3** a phonograph record. *noun.* Also spelled **disc.**

disk jockey, announcer for a radio program that consists chiefly of recorded popular music.

dis like (dis līk′), **1** not like; object to; have a feeling against: *He dislikes studying and would rather play football.* **2** a feeling of not liking; a feeling against: *I have a dislike of rain and fog.* 1 *verb,* **dis liked, dis lik ing;** 2 *noun.*

dis lo cate (dis′lō kāt), put out of joint: *He dislocated his shoulder when he fell. verb,* **dis lo cat ed, dis lo cat ing.**

dis lodge (dis loj′), drive or force out of a place or position: *She used a crowbar to dislodge a heavy stone from the wall. verb,* **dis lodged, dis lodg ing.**

dis loy al (dis loi′əl), not loyal; faithless: *a disloyal friend, a disloyal act. adjective.*

dis loy al ty (dis loi′əl tē), unfaithfulness. *noun, plural* **dis loy al ties.**

dis mal (diz′məl), **1** dark; gloomy. See picture. **2** dreary; miserable: *Sickness or bad luck often makes a person feel dismal. adjective.*

dis man tle (dis man′tl), **1** remove furniture or equipment from: *They dismantled the gym before*

dismal (definition 1)—It was a **dismal** afternoon.

display (definition 1) The children **displayed** their drawings.

LAST BUS FOR SUNSET BEACH! ROOM FOR TWO MORE PEOPLE!

ORDERLY

DISORDERLY

painting it. **2** pull down; take apart: *We had to dismantle the bookcases in order to move them. verb,* **dis man tled, dis man tling.**

dis may (dis mā′), **1** sudden loss of courage because of fear or danger; great worry: *They were filled with dismay when they saw the rattlesnake.* **2** trouble greatly; make afraid: *The thought that she might fail the test dismayed her.* **1** *noun,* **2** *verb.*

dis miss (dis mis′), **1** send away; allow to go: *At noon the teacher dismissed the class for lunch.* **2** remove from office or service; not allow to keep a job: *We dismissed the painters because their work was so poor.* **3** put out of mind; stop thinking about: *Dismiss your troubles. verb.*

dis miss al (dis mis′əl), **1** act of dismissing: *The dismissal of those five workers caused a strike.* **2** condition or fact of being dismissed: *The company refused to announce the reason for the workers' dismissal. noun.*

dis mount (dis mount′), **1** get off a horse or bicycle: *She dismounted and led her horse across the stream.* **2** take (a thing) from its setting or support: *The cannons were dismounted for shipping to another fort. verb.*

dis o be di ence (dis′ə bē′dē əns), refusal to obey; failure to obey: *The children were punished for disobedience. noun.*

dis o be di ent (dis′ə bē′dē ənt), failing to follow orders or rules; refusing to obey: *The disobedient child would not go to bed on time. adjective.*

dis o bey (dis′ə bā′), refuse to obey; fail to obey: *The student who disobeyed the teacher was punished. verb.*

dis or der (dis ôr′dər), **1** lack of order; confusion: *The room was in disorder after the birthday party.* **2** disturb the regular order or working of; throw into confusion: *A series of accidents disordered the shop.* **3** public disturbance; riot: *The police needed help from the army to end the disorder in the streets.* **4** sickness; disease: *Eating the wrong food can cause a stomach disorder.* **1,3,4** *noun,* **2** *verb.*

dis or der ly (dis ôr′dər lē), **1** not orderly; untidy; confused: *I can never find anything in this disorderly closet.* **2** causing disorder; making a disturbance; breaking rules; unruly: *The disorderly crowd pushed and shoved to get on the bus.* See picture. *adjective.*

dis or gan ize (dis ôr′gə nīz), throw into confusion or disorder: *Heavy snowstorms delayed all flights and disorganized the airline schedule. verb,* **dis or gan ized, dis or gan iz ing.**

dis own (dis ōn′), refuse to recognize as one's own; cast off: *They disowned their daughter. verb.*

dis patch (dis pach′), **1** send off to some place or for some purpose: *The captain dispatched a boat to bring a doctor on board ship.* **2** a sending off: *Please hurry the dispatch of this telegram.* **3** a written message, such as special news or government business: *The correspondent rushed dispatches to her newspaper in New York about the fire in Paris.* **4** get (something) done promptly: *The teacher dispatched the roll call and began the lesson.* **5** promptness in doing anything; speed: *This boy*

a hat	i it	oi oil	ch child	(a in about
ā age	ī ice	ou out	ng long	e in taken
ä far	o hot	u cup	sh she	ə = { i in pencil
e let	ō open	u̇ put	th thin	o in lemon
ē equal	ô order	ü rule	ᵺ then	(u in circus
ėr term			zh measure	

works with neatness and dispatch. **1,4** *verb,* **2,3,5** *noun, plural* **dis patch es.**

dis pel (dis pel′), make go away; drive away and scatter: *Talking with the pilot helped dispel my fear of flying. verb,* **dis pelled, dis pel ling.**

dis pense (dis pens′), **1** give out; distribute: *The Red Cross dispensed food and clothing to the flood victims.* **2** carry out; put in force; apply: *Judges and courts of law dispense justice.* **3** prepare and give out: *Druggists must dispense medicine with the greatest care. verb,* **dis pensed, dis pens ing.**
dispense with, do without: *I shall dispense with these crutches as soon as my leg heals.*

dis perse (dis pėrs′), spread in different directions; scatter: *The police dispersed the onlookers. The crowd dispersed when it began raining. verb,* **dis persed, dis pers ing.**

dis place (dis plās′), **1** take the place of; put something else in the place of: *The automobile has displaced the horse and buggy.* **2** put out of place; move from its usual place or position: *Please do not displace any of my tools. verb,* **dis placed, dis plac ing.**

dis play (dis plā′), **1** show: *The lecturer displayed her good nature by patiently answering all our questions.* See picture. **2** showing: *a display of bad temper.* **3** show in a special way, so as to attract attention: *The stores are displaying the new spring clothes in their windows.* **4** a showing off: *Their fondness for display led them to buy flashy cars.* **5** a planned showing of a thing, for some special purpose. **1,3** *verb,* **2,4,5** *noun.*

dis please (dis plēz′), offend; annoy; not please: *You displease your parents when you don't obey them. verb,* **dis pleased, dis pleas ing.**

dis pleas ure (dis plezh′ər), annoyance; dislike; slight anger; dissatisfaction. *noun.*

dis pos a ble (dis pō′zə bəl), able to be disposed of or thrown away after use: *disposable diapers. adjective.*

dis pos al (dis pō′zəl), **1** act of getting rid (of something): *The city takes care of the disposal of garbage.* **2** dealing with; settling: *His disposal of the difficulty pleased everybody. noun.*
at one's disposal, ready for one's use or service at any time: *I will put my room at your disposal.*

dis pose (dis pōz′), **1** put in a certain order or position; arrange: *The flags were disposed in a straight line for the parade.* **2** make ready or willing; influence: *The good pay disposed him to take the new job. verb,* **dis posed, dis pos ing.**
dispose of, 1 get rid of: *Dispose of that rubbish.* **2** give away or sell: *The owner disposed of her house for $35,000.* **3** arrange; settle: *The committee disposed of all its business in an hour.*

dis po si tion (dis′pə zish′ən), **1** one's natural way of acting toward others: *His cheerful disposition made him popular.* **2** tendency; inclination: *A quarrelsome person has a disposition to start trouble.* **3** putting in a certain order; arrangement: *The teacher changed the disposition of desks in the classroom.* *noun.*

dis prove (dis prüv´), prove false or incorrect: *She disproved my claim that I had less candy by weighing both boxes.* *verb,* **dis proved, dis prov ing.**

dis pute (dis pyüt´), **1** give reasons or facts for or against something; argue; debate; discuss: *The lawmakers disputed over the need for new taxes.* **2** argument; debate: *There is a dispute over where to build the new school.* **3** quarrel: *They disputed over the last piece of cake.* **4** a quarrel because of a difference of opinion: *The dispute between the two neighbors ended their friendship.* **5** disagree with (a statement); say that (it) is false or doubtful: *The insurance company disputed his claim for damages to his car.* **6** fight for; fight over: *The soldiers disputed every inch of ground when the enemy attacked.* **7** try to win: *Our team disputed the victory up to the last minute of play.* **1,3,5-7** *verb,* **dis put ed, dis put ing; 2,4** *noun.*

dis qual i fy (dis kwol´ə fī), **1** make unable to do something: *Her broken leg disqualified her from all sports.* **2** declare unfit or unable to do something: *Students with low grades were disqualified from acting in the school play.* *verb,* **dis qual i fied, dis qual i fy ing.**

dis re gard (dis´ri gärd´), **1** pay no attention to; take no notice of: *Disregarding the cold weather, we played outside all day.* **2** neglect; lack of attention: *They failed the test because of their disregard for studying.* **1** *verb,* **2** *noun.*

dis re pair (dis´ri per´ or dis´ri par´), bad condition: *The house was in disrepair.* *noun.*

dis rep u ta ble (dis rep´yə tə bəl), **1** having a bad reputation: *a disreputable dance hall.* **2** not respectable: *a disreputable old hat.* *adjective.*

dis re spect (dis´ri spekt´), rudeness; lack of respect: *I meant no disrespect by my hasty remark.* *noun.*

dis re spect ful (dis´ri spekt´fəl), rude; impolite: *Making fun of your elders is disrespectful.* *adjective.*

dis rupt (dis rupt´), break up; split: *A quarrel over money disrupted their friendship.* *verb.*

dis sat is fac tion (dis´sat i sfak´shən), discontent; displeasure: *Low pay caused dissatisfaction among the workers.* *noun.*

dis sat is fied (dis sat´i sfīd), discontented; displeased: *When we do not get what we want, we are dissatisfied.* *adjective.*

dis sect (di sekt´), cut apart (an animal or plant) so as to examine or study the structure. *verb.*

dis sen sion (di sen´shən), disputing; quarreling; hard feeling caused by a difference in opinion: *The club broke up because of dissension among its members.* *noun.*

dis sent (di sent´), **1** disagree; think differently; express a different opinion from others: *Two of the judges dissented from the decision of the other three.* **2** disagreement; difference of opinion: *Dissent among the members broke up the club.* **1** *verb,* **2** *noun.*

dis sim i lar (di sim´ə lər), unlike; different. *adjective.*

dis si pate (dis´ə pāt), **1** scatter; spread in different directions: *The fog is beginning to dissipate.* **2** spend foolishly; waste on things of little value: *People who inherit money sometimes dissipate it carelessly.* *verb,* **dis si pat ed, dis si pat ing.**

dis solve (di zolv´), **1** make liquid; become liquid, especially by putting or being put into a liquid: *You can dissolve sugar in water.* **2** break up; end: *They dissolved the partnership over a quarrel.* *verb,* **dis solved, dis solv ing.**

dis suade (di swād´), persuade not to do something: *I dissuaded her from quitting the swimming team.* *verb,* **dis suad ed, dis suad ing.**

dis tance (dis´təns), **1** space in between: *The distance from the farm to the town is five miles.* **2** place far away: *She saw a light in the distance.* *noun.*

at a distance, a long way: *The farm is at a distance from the railroad.*

keep at a distance, refuse to be friendly or familiar with; treat coldly: *The teacher kept the students at a distance.*

dis tant (dis´tənt), **1** far away in space: *The sun is distant from the earth.* **2** away: *The town is three miles distant.* **3** far apart in time, relationship, or likeness; not close: *We plan a trip to Europe in the distant future.* **4** not friendly: *She gave him only a distant nod.* *adjective.*

dis taste (dis tāst´), dislike: *His distaste for carrots showed clearly on his face.* *noun.*

dis taste ful (dis tāst´fəl), unpleasant; disagreeable; offensive: *a distasteful medicine, a distasteful task.* *adjective.*

dis tem per (dis tem´pər), disease of dogs and other animals that causes a cough, fever, and weakness. *noun.*

dis till (dis til´), make (a liquid) pure by heating it and turning it into a vapor and then cooling it into liquid form again: *distilled water. Gasoline is distilled from crude oil. Alcoholic liquor is distilled from mash made from grain.* *verb.*

dis tinct (dis tingkt´), **1** separate; not the same: *She asked me about it three distinct times.* **2** different in quality or kind: *Mice are distinct from rats.* **3** clear; easily seen, heard, or understood: *Large, distinct print is easy to read.* **4** unmistakable; definite: *A tall player has a distinct advantage in basketball.* *adjective.*

dis tinc tion (dis tingk´shən), **1** making a difference: *They treated all their children alike without distinction.* **2** difference: *The distinction between hot and cold is easily noticed.* **3** mark or sign of honor: *The lifeguard received a medal as a distinction for bravery.* **4** honor: *The judge served on the court for many years with distinction.* **5** excellence; superiority: *Presidents should be people of great distinction.* *noun.*

dis tinc tive (dis tingk´tiv), distinguishing from

others; special; characteristic: *The police wear a distinctive uniform. adjective.*

dis tin guish (dis ting′gwish), **1** see the differences in; tell apart: *Can you distinguish cotton cloth from wool?* **2** see or hear clearly; make out plainly: *On a clear, bright day you can distinguish things far away.* **3** make different; be a special quality or feature of: *A trunk distinguishes the elephant.* **4** make famous or well known: *He distinguished himself by winning three prizes. verb.*

dis tin guished (dis ting′gwisht), famous; well-known: *a distinguished artist. adjective.*

dis tort (dis tôrt′), **1** pull or twist out of shape; make crooked or ugly. See picture. **2** change from the truth: *The driver distorted the facts of the accident to escape blame. verb.*

dis tract (dis trakt′), **1** draw away (the mind or attention): *Noise distracts my attention from study.* **2** confuse; disturb: *Several people talking at once distract a listener. verb.*

dis tress (dis tres′), **1** great pain or sorrow; anxiety; trouble: *The lost kitten caused us much distress.* **2** cause pain or sorrow to; make unhappy: *Your tears distress me.* **3** misfortune; dangerous condition; difficult situation: *A burning or sinking ship is in distress.* **1,3** *noun,* **2** *verb.*

dis trib ute (dis trib′yüt), **1** give some to each; deal out: *I distributed the candy among my friends.* **2** spread; scatter: *A painter should distribute the paint evenly over the wall.* **3** divide into parts: *The children were distributed into three groups for the trip to the museum.* **4** arrange; put each in its place: *A mail clerk distributes mail when he puts each letter into the proper bag. verb,* **dis trib ut ed, dis trib ut ing.**

dis tri bu tion (dis′trə byü′shən), **1** act of distributing: *After the contest the distribution of prizes to the winners took place.* **2** way of being distributed: *If some get more than others, there is an uneven distribution.* **3** thing distributed. *noun.*

dis trict (dis′trikt), **1** part of a larger area; region: *The leading farming district of the United States is in the Middle West.* **2** part of a country, a state, or a city, marked off for a special purpose, such as providing schools, electing certain government officers, or supporting a church: *a school district. noun.*

dis trust (dis trust′), **1** have no confidence in; not trust; not depend on; doubt: *Everyone should distrust shaky ladders.* **2** lack of trust; lack of belief in the goodness of: *I could not explain my distrust of the stranger.* **1** *verb,* **2** *noun.*

dis turb (dis tėrb′), **1** destroy the peace, quiet, or rest of: *Heavy truck traffic disturbed the neighborhood.* **2** break in upon with noise; bother: *Please do not disturb her while she's studying.* **3** put out of order: *Someone has disturbed my books; I can't find the one I want.* **4** make uneasy; trouble: *He was disturbed to hear of his friend's illness. verb.*

dis turb ance (dis tėr′bəns), **1** a disturbing or being disturbed. **2** thing that disturbs. **3** confusion; disorder: *The police were called to quiet the disturbance at the street corner. noun.*

a hat	i it	oi oil	ch child	(a in about
ā age	ī ice	ou out	ng long	e in taken
ä far	o hot	u cup	sh she	ə = i in pencil
e let	ō open	u put	th thin	o in lemon
ē equal	ô order	ü rule	ŦH then	(u in circus
ėr term			zh measure	

distort (definition 1)
The girl's nose is distorted.

ditch (dich), a long, narrow place dug in the earth. Ditches are usually used to carry off water. *noun, plural* **ditch es.**

dive (dīv), **1** plunge headfirst into water. **2** act of diving: *We applauded his graceful dive.* See picture. **3** plunge (the body, the hand, or the mind) suddenly into anything: *She dived into her pockets and brought out a dollar.* **4** plunge downward at a steep angle: *The hawk dived straight at the field mouse.* **5** a downward plunge at a steep angle: *The submarine made a dive toward the bottom.* 1,3,4 *verb,* **dived** or **dove, dived, div ing;** 2,5 *noun.*

div er (dī′vər), **1** one that dives. **2** person whose occupation is to work under water. **3** a diving bird, such as a penguin. *noun.*

di verse (də vėrs′), different; completely unlike: *A great many diverse opinions were expressed at the meeting. adjective.*

di ver sion (də vėr′zhən), **1** a turning aside: *A magician's talk creates a diversion of our attention so that we do not see how the tricks are done.* **2** relief from work or care; amusement; entertainment; pastime: *Watching TV is a popular diversion. noun.*

di ver si ty (də vėr′sə tē), **1** complete difference; unlikeness: *The quiet student and the active athlete were close friends in spite of the diversity of their dispositions.* **2** variety: *The diversity of food on the table made it hard for us to choose. noun, plural* **di ver si ties.**

di vert (də vėrt′), **1** turn aside: *A ditch diverted water from the stream into the fields. The siren of the fire engine diverted the audience's attention from the play.* **2** amuse; entertain: *We were diverted by the clown's tricks. verb.*

di vide (də vīd′), **1** separate into parts: *A brook divides the field. The road divides and forms two roads.* **2** separate into equal parts: *When you divide 8 by 2, you get 4.* **3** give some of to each; share: *We divided the candy.* **4** separate in feeling or opinion; disagree: *The school divided on the choice of a motto.* **5** ridge of land between the regions drained by two different river systems: *The Rocky Mountains form part of the Continental Divide.* 1-4 *verb,* **di vid ed, di vid ing;** 5 *noun.*

div i dend (div′ə dend), **1** number to be divided by another: *In 728 ÷ 16, 728 is the dividend.* **2** money earned as profit by a company and divided among the owners of the company. *noun.*

di vine (də vīn′), **1** of God or a god: *The Bible describes the creation of the world as a divine act.* **2** by or from God: *The king believed that his power to rule was a divine right.* **3** to or for God; sacred; holy: *divine worship.* **4** like God or a god; heavenly. **5** excellent; unusually good or great: *Oh, what a divine vacation we had!* **6** find out or foretell by inspiration, by magic, or by guessing; predict. 1-5 *adjective,* 6 *verb,* **di vined, di vin ing.**

di vin i ty (də vin′ə tē), **1** a divine being; god or goddess. **2** divine nature or quality. *noun, plural* **di vin i ties.**

di vis i ble (də viz′ə bəl), capable of being divided: *In arithmetic 12 is divisible by 4. adjective.*

di vi sion (də vizh′ən), **1** dividing; being divided.

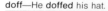
dive (definition 2)

dodo
about 4 feet (1 meter) long

doff—He doffed his hat.

2 giving some to each; sharing: *The making of automobiles in large numbers is made possible by a division of labor, in which each worker has a certain part of the work to do.* **3** process of dividing one number by another: *26 ÷ 2 = 13 is a simple division.* **4** thing that divides. A boundary or a partition is a division. **5** one of the parts into which a thing is divided; group; section. Two or more regiments make a division of the army. **6** difference of opinion, thought, or feeling; disagreement. *noun.*

di vi sor (də vī′zər), number by which another is divided: *In 728 ÷ 16, 16 is the divisor. noun.*

di vorce (də vôrs′), **1** the legal ending of a marriage. **2** end legally a marriage between: *The judge divorced Mr. and Mrs. Jones.* **3** separate from by divorce: *She divorced her husband.* **4** separate: *In sports, exercise and play are not divorced.* **5** separation: *In this country there is a complete divorce of government and religion.* 1,5 *noun,* 2-4 *verb,* **di vorced, di vorc ing.**

di vulge (də vulj′), tell; reveal; make known: *The traitor divulged secret plans to the enemy. verb,* **di vulged, di vulg ing.**

diz zi ness (diz′ē nis), dizzy condition. *noun.*

diz zy (diz′ē), **1** likely to fall, stagger, or spin around; not steady: *When you spin round and round, and stop suddenly, you feel dizzy.* **2** confused; bewildered: *The noise and crowds of the city streets made the little boy dizzy.* **3** likely to make dizzy; causing dizziness: *The airplane climbed to a dizzy height. adjective,* **diz zi er, diz zi est.**

do (dü), **1** carry through to an end any action or piece of work; carry out; perform: *Do your work well.* **2** take care of: *Who does the dishes at your house?* **3** act; behave: *You did very well today.* **4** be satisfactory: *That hat will do.* **5** Do is used: **a** to ask questions: *Do you like milk?* **b** to make what one says stronger: *I do want to go. Do come, please.* **c** to stand for another word already used: *My dog goes where I do. Her brother walks just as she does.* **d** in expressions that contain *not: People talk; animals do not. verb,* **did, done, do ing.**

do up, wrap up: *Please do up this package for me.*

doc ile (dos′əl), easily managed; obedient: *Persons who are just starting to ride should use a docile horse. adjective.*

dock[1] (dok), **1** platform built on the shore or out from the shore; wharf; pier. Ships load and unload beside a dock. **2** platform for loading and unloading trucks or boxcars. **3** bring (a ship) to dock: *The crew docked the ship and began to unload it.* 1,2 *noun,* 3 *verb.*

dock[2] (dok), **1** cut off a part of: *The company docks the workers' wages if they come to work late.* **2** cut short; cut off the end of. Dogs' tails are sometimes docked. *verb.*

dock[3] (dok), place where an accused person stands in a court of law to be tried. *noun.*

doc tor (dok′tər), **1** person who knows how to treat diseases; physician; surgeon. A doctor must have a license to practice medicine. **2** treat disease in: *My mother doctored me when I had a*

a hat	**i** it	**oi** oil	**ch** child		a in about
ā age	**ī** ice	**ou** out	**ng** long		e in taken
ä far	**o** hot	**u** cup	**sh** she	**ə =**	i in pencil
e let	**ō** open	**u̇** put	**th** thin		o in lemon
ē equal	**ô** order	**ü** rule	**ᴛʜ** then		u in circus
ėr term			**zh** measure		

cold. **3** dentist. 1,3 *noun,* 2 *verb.*

doc trine (dok′trən), **1** what is taught as the belief of a church, a nation, or a group of persons; belief: *Christian doctrine.* **2** what is taught; teachings. *noun.*

doc u ment (dok′yə mənt), something written or printed that gives information and can be used as proof of some fact; any object used as evidence. Letters, maps, and pictures are documents. *noun.*

dodge (doj), **1** move or jump quickly to one side: *As I looked, he dodged behind a bush.* **2** move quickly in order to get away from (a person, a blow, or something thrown): *She dodged the ball as it came flying at her.* **3** a sudden movement to one side. **4** get away from by some trick: *She dodged our question by changing the subject.* **5** a trick to cheat: *They used a clever dodge to see the show without buying a ticket.* 1,2,4 *verb,* **dodged, dodg ing;** 3,5 *noun.*

do do (dō′dō), a large clumsy bird not able to fly. Dodos are now extinct. See picture. *noun, plural* **do dos** or **do does.**

doe (dō), a female deer, goat, rabbit, or hare. *noun.*

does (duz). See do. *She does all her work. Does he sing well? verb.*

does n't (duz′nt), does not.

doff (dof), take off; remove. See picture. *verb..* [*Doff* was shortened from the words *do off.*]

dog (dôg), **1** a four-legged animal used as a pet, for hunting, and for guarding property. **2** hunt or follow like a dog: *The police dogged the suspected thief until they caught him.* 1 *noun,* 2 *verb,* **dogged, dog ging.**

go to the dogs, be ruined; go to ruin.

dog ged (dô′gid), stubborn; not giving up: *Her dogged determination helped her win the race. adjective.*

do gie (dō′gē), calf without a mother, on the range or in a herd. *noun.*

dog wood (dôg′wud′), tree with tiny springtime flowers surrounded by large white or pinkish leaves. The tree bears red berries in the fall. *noun.*

doi ly (doi′lē), a small piece of linen, lace, paper, or plastic used under plates, other dishes, or vases. *noun, plural* **doi lies.**

do ings (dü′ingz), things done; actions. *noun plural.*

dol drums (dol′drəmz), gloomy feeling; low spirits: *They have been in the doldrums since their bicycles were stolen. noun plural.*

dole (dōl), **1** portion of money, food, or clothing given in charity. **2** a small portion. **3** give in small portions: *The teacher doled out a dab of paste to each student.* 1,2 *noun,* 3 *verb,* **doled, dol ing.**

doll (dol), a child's toy made to look like a baby, a child, or a grown person. *noun.*

dol lar (dol′ər), **1** unit of money in the United States and Canada equal to 100 cents. $1.00 means one dollar. **2** a coin or a paper bill equal to 100 cents. *noun.*

dol phin (dol′fən), a sea mammal much like a small whale. It has a snout like a beak and remarkable intelligence. See picture. *noun.*

dolt (dōlt), a dull, stupid person. *noun.*

do main (dō mān′), **1** lands under the control of one ruler or government. **2** field of thought and action: *the domain of science, the domain of religion. noun.*

dome (dōm), **1** a large, rounded roof on a circular or many-sided base. See picture. **2** thing shaped like a dome: *the rounded dome of a hill. noun.*

do mes tic (də mes′tik), **1** of the home, the household, or family affairs: *domestic duties.* **2** servant in a household. A butler or a maid is a domestic. **3** not wild; tame. Horses, dogs, cats, cows, and pigs are domestic animals. **4** of one's own country; not foreign: *Most newspapers publish both domestic and foreign news.* **1,3,4** *adjective,* **2** *noun.*

do mes ti cate (də mes′tə kāt), tame; change (animals and plants) from a wild to a tame state. See picture. *verb,* **do mes ti cat ed, do mes ti cat ing.**

dom i nant (dom′ə nənt), **1** ruling; governing; controlling; most influential: *The principal was the dominant person at the meeting. Football is the dominant sport in the fall.* **2** rising high above its surroundings; occupying a commanding position: *A dominant cliff rose at the bend of the river. adjective.*

dom i nate (dom′ə nāt), **1** control or rule by strength or power: *She was very outspoken and tended to dominate our club meetings.* **2** rise high above; hold a commanding position over: *The mountain dominates the city and its harbor. verb,* **dom i nat ed, dom i nat ing.**

dom i na tion (dom′ə nā′shən), control; rule; dominating: *British domination of the seas lasted over 200 years. noun.*

dom i neer ing (dom′ə nir′ing), inclined to dominate; arrogant; overbearing: *A bully has a domineering attitude. adjective.*

do min ion (də min′yən), **1** rule; control: *The ancient Romans had dominion over a large part of the world.* **2** lands under the control of one ruler or government. *noun.*

dom i no (dom′ə nō), one of a set of small pieces of bone or wood marked with spots. **Dominoes** is the game played with them. *noun, plural* **dom i noes** or **dom i nos.**

don (don), put on (clothing): *The knight donned his armor. verb,* **donned, don ning.** [*Don* was shortened from the words *do on.*]

do nate (dō′nāt), give; contribute: *I donated ten dollars to charity. verb,* **do nat ed, do nat ing.**

do na tion (dō nā′shən), **1** gift; contribution: *a donation to charity.* **2** act of giving. *noun.*

done (dun), **1** finished; completed; ended: *She is done with her homework.* **2** cooked: *The steak was*

domesticate—The children **domesticated** the wild deer.

dolphin—about 10 feet long (3 meters)

dory

a hat	i it	oi oil	ch child		a in about
ā age	ī ice	ou out	ng long		e in taken
ä far	o hot	u cup	sh she	ə =	i in pencil
e let	ō open	u̇ put	th thin		o in lemon
ē equal	ô order	ü rule	ᴛʜ then		u in circus
ėr term			zh measure		

dome (definition 1)—dome of the United States Capitol

dormer
(definition 2)

dormouse
about 5 inches
(13 centimeters)
long with the tail

done just right. **3** See **do.** *Have you done all your chores?* 1,2 *adjective,* 3 *verb.*

don key (dong′kē), **1** animal with hoofs that is somewhat like a small horse but with longer ears, a shorter mane, and a tuft of hair at the end of its tail. **2** a stubborn person; silly or stupid person. *noun, plural* **don keys.**

do nor (dō′nər), person who gives; giver. *noun.*

don't (dōnt), do not.

doom (düm), **1** fate. **2** terrible fate; ruin; death: *As the ship sank, the voyagers faced their doom.* **3** sentence to an unhappy or terrible fate: *The prisoner was doomed to death.* **4** judgment; sentence: *The judge pronounced the prisoner's doom.* **5** make a bad or unwelcome outcome certain: *The weather doomed our hopes of a picnic.* 1,2,4 *noun,* 3,5 *verb.*

door (dôr), **1** a movable part to close an opening in a wall of a building. A door turns on hinges or slides open and shut. **2** doorway: *He walked into the room through the door. noun.*

door bell (dôr′bel′), bell to be rung as a signal that someone wishes to have the door opened. *noun.*

door knob (dôr′nob′), handle on a door. *noun.*

door step (dôr′step′), step leading from an outside door to the ground. *noun.*

door way (dôr′wā′), opening in a wall where a door is. *noun.*

dope (dōp), **1** a narcotic drug, such as opium. **2** a very stupid person. **3** a thick varnish or similar liquid applied to a fabric to strengthen or waterproof it. *noun.*

dor mant (dôr′mənt), **1** sleeping; still and quiet as if sleeping: *Bears and other animals that hibernate are dormant during the winter.* **2** not active: *Many volcanoes are dormant. The artist's talent for painting was dormant until her teacher discovered it. adjective.*

dor mer (dôr′mər), **1** an upright window that sticks out from a sloping roof. **2** part of a roof that sticks out and has such a window. See picture. *noun.*

dor mi to ry (dôr′mə tôr′ē), a building with many rooms for sleeping in. Many colleges have dormitories for students whose homes are somewhere else. *noun, plural* **dor mi to ries.**

dor mouse (dôr′mous′), a small animal somewhat like a mouse and somewhat like a squirrel. It sleeps during cold weather. See picture. *noun, plural* **dor mice** (dôr′mīs′).

do ry (dôr′ē), rowboat with a narrow, flat bottom and high sides, often used in fishing. See picture. *noun, plural* **do ries.**

dose (dōs), **1** amount of a medicine to be taken at one time: *a dose of cough medicine.* **2** give medicine

to: *The doctor dosed the sick child with penicillin.*
1 *noun,* 2 *verb,* **dosed, dos ing.**

dot (dot), **1** a tiny, round mark; point: *Put a dot over each i.* **2** a small spot: *a blue necktie with white dots.* **3** mark with a dot or dots: *Dot your i's and j's.* **4** be here and there in: *Trees dotted the lawn.* 1,2 *noun,* 3,4 *verb,* **dot ted, dot ting.**

dote (dōt). **dote on,** be foolishly fond of; be too fond of: *Parents sometimes dote on their youngest children, giving them too many presents. verb,* **dot ed, dot ing.**

dou ble (dub′əl), **1** twice as much, as large, or as strong: *They were given double pay for working on Sunday.* **2** twice: *He was paid double by mistake.* **3** number or amount that is twice as much: *Four is the double of two.* **4** make or become twice as much or twice as many: *They doubled their money in ten years by investing it wisely.* **5** made of two like parts; in a pair: *double doors.* **6** having two meanings or characters. The spelling *b-e-a-r* has a double meaning: *carry* and *a certain animal.* **7** two (of everything) instead of one: *The blow on the head made him see double.* **8** person or thing just like another: *Her twin sister is her double.* **9** fold over: *She doubled the slice of bread to make a sandwich.* **10** close tightly together; clench: *They doubled their fists and began to fight.* **11** bend or turn sharply backward: *The fox doubled on its track and escaped the dogs.* **12** hit by which a batter gets to second base in baseball. **13** make such a hit in baseball. 1,5,6 *adjective,* 2,7 *adverb,* 3,8,12 *noun,* 4,9-11,13 *verb,* **dou bled, dou bling.**

dou ble-cross (dub′əl krôs′), promise to do one thing and then do another. *verb.*

dou ble head er (dub′əl hed′ər), two games played one after another on the same day. *noun.*

double play, in baseball, a play in which two runners are put out.

dou bloon (du blün′), a former Spanish gold coin. Its value varied from about $5 to about $16. *noun.*

dou bly (dub′lē), in a double manner, amount, or degree: *Doubly careful means twice as careful. adverb.*

doubt (dout), **1** not believe; not be sure; feel uncertain: *She doubted if we would arrive on time.* **2** difficulty in believing: *Our faith helped overcome our doubt.* **3** an uncertain state of mind: *We were in doubt as to the right road.* 1 *verb,* 2,3 *noun.*
no doubt, certainly: *No doubt we will win.*

doubt ful (dout′fəl), full of doubt; not sure; not certain: *We are doubtful about the weather for tomorrow. adjective.*

doubt less (dout′lis), without doubt; surely. *adverb.*

dough (dō), a soft, thick mixture of flour, liquid, and other things from which bread, biscuits, cake, and pie crust are made. *noun.*

dough nut (dō′nut′), a small cake of sweetened dough cooked in deep fat. A doughnut is usually made in the shape of a ring. *noun.*

douse (dous), **1** plunge into water or any other liquid. **2** throw water over; drench: *She quickly doused the flames. verb,* **doused, dous ing.**

dove[1] (duv), bird with a thick body and short legs; pigeon. The dove is often a symbol of peace. See picture. *noun.*

dove[2] (dōv), dived. See **dive.** *The diver dove deep into the water after the sunken treasure. verb.*

down[1] (doun), **1** to a lower place; in a lower place: *They ran down from the top of the hill.* **2** from an earlier time to a later time: *The story has come down through many years.* **3** down along: *You can ride down a hill, sail down a river, or walk down a street.* **4** put down: *He was downed in a fight. She downed the medicine with one swallow.* **5** in cash when bought: *You can pay $10 down and the rest later. We made a down payment on a new car.* **6** in football, a play that begins when the center passes the ball to a back. 1,2,5 *adverb,* 3 *preposition,* 4 *verb,* 5 *adjective,* 6 *noun.*

down[2] (doun), **1** soft feathers: *the down of a young bird.* **2** soft hair or fluff: *The down on a boy's chin develops into a beard. noun.*

down cast (doun′kast′). See picture. **1** turned downward. **2** dejected; sad; discouraged: *After all our plans failed, we felt very downcast. adjective.*

down fall (doun′fôl′), **1** bringing to ruin; sudden overthrow: *the downfall of an empire. Pride caused their downfall.* **2** a heavy fall of rain or snow. *noun.*

down heart ed (doun′här′tid), discouraged; dejected; depressed. *adjective.*

down hill (doun′hil′), **1** down the slope of a hill; downward: *I ran downhill.* **2** going or sloping downward: *a downhill race.* 1 *adverb,* 2 *adjective.*

down pour (doun′pôr′), a heavy rainfall. *noun.*

down right (doun′rīt′), **1** thorough; complete: *a downright fool, a downright lie.* **2** thoroughly; completely: *They were downright rude to me.* **3** plain; positive: *His downright answer left no doubt as to what he thought.* 1,3 *adjective,* 2 *adverb.*

down stairs (doun′sterz′ or doun′starz′), **1** down the stairs: *I hurried downstairs.* **2** on or to a lower floor: *Look downstairs for my glasses. The downstairs rooms are dark.* **3** lower floor or floors: *She lived in the downstairs of the house.* 1,2 *adverb,* 2 *adjective,* 3 *noun.*

down stream (doun′strēm′), with the current of a stream; down a stream: *It is easy to swim or row downstream. adverb, adjective.*

down town (doun′toun′), to or in the main part or business part of a town or city: *My parents went downtown shopping. adverb, adjective.*

down ward (doun′wərd), **1** toward a lower place or condition: *The downward trip on the elevator was very slow.* **2** toward a later time: *There has been great progress in science from the 1900's downward. adverb, adjective.*

down wards (doun′wərdz), downward. *adverb.*

down y (dou′nē), **1** of soft feathers, hair, or fluff: *a downy pillow.* **2** covered with soft feathers or hair: *a downy chick.* **3** soft and fluffy: *A kitten's fur is downy. adjective,* **down i er, down i est.**

dow ry (dou′rē), money or property that a woman brings to her husband when she marries him. *noun, plural* **dow ries.**

doz., dozen.

doze (dōz), **1** sleep lightly; be half asleep: *The old cat dozed by the fire.* **2** light sleep; nap. 1 *verb,* **dozed, doz ing;** 2 *noun.*

doz en (duz′n), 12; group of 12: *We had to have dozens of chairs for the party. We will need three dozen eggs and a dozen rolls.* noun, *plural* **doz ens** or (*after a number*) **doz en.**

Dr., Doctor: *Dr. W. H. Smith.*

drab (drab), **1** dull; not attractive: *The smoky mining town was full of drab houses.* **2** dull brownish-gray. *adjective,* **drab ber, drab best.**

draft (draft), **1** current of air: *I caught cold from sitting in a draft.* **2** device for controlling a current of air: *Opening the draft of the furnace causes the fire to burn faster.* **3** plan; sketch: *Before starting to build, we had the architect make a draft of how the finished house should look.* **4** make a plan or sketch of. **5** rough copy: *She made two different drafts of her book report before she handed it in in final form.* **6** write out a rough copy of: *Three members of the club drafted a set of rules to be discussed and voted on.* **7** selection of persons for some special purpose. Men needed as soldiers are supplied to the army by draft. **8** persons selected for special service. **9** select for some special purpose: *If no one volunteers, I will draft someone for the job.* **10** act of pulling loads. **11** for pulling loads. A draft horse is used for pulling wagons and plows. **12** depth of water a ship needs for floating, or the depth it sinks into the water. A ship's draft is greater when it is loaded than when it is empty. **13** amount taken at one drink. **14** note to a bank, ordering that a certain sum of money be paid to the person named. 1-3,5,7,8,10,12-14 *noun,* 4,6,9 *verb,* 11 *adjective.* Also spelled **draught.**

drag (drag), **1** pull or move along heavily or slowly; pull or draw along the ground: *A team of horses dragged the big log out of the forest.* **2** go too slowly: *Time drags when you are bored.* **3** pull a net, hook, or harrow over or along for some purpose: *The fishermen dragged the lake for fish.* **4** anything that holds back; obstruction; hindrance: *If you don't practice, you'll be a drag on the team.* 1-3 *verb,* **dragged, drag ging;** 4 *noun.*

drag net (drag′net′), **1** net pulled over the bottom of a river, pond, or lake, or along the ground. Dragnets are used to catch fish and small birds. **2** means of catching or gathering in: *All kinds of criminals were caught in the police dragnet.* noun.

drag on (drag′ən), (in old stories) a huge, fierce animal supposed to look like a winged snake with scales and claws, which often breathed out fire and smoke. *noun.*

drag on fly (drag′ən flī′), a large, harmless insect with a long, slender body and two pairs of wings. It flies about very rapidly to catch flies, mosquitoes, and other insects. See picture. *noun, plural* **drag on flies.**

dra goon (drə gün′), soldier trained to fight either on foot or on horseback. *noun.*

drain (drān), **1** draw off or flow off slowly: *The water drains into the river.* **2** draw water or other liquid from; empty or dry by draining: *The farmers*

dove[1]—about 13 inches (33 centimeters) long

downcast

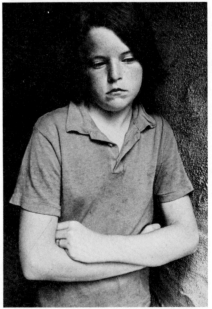

dragonfly—about life-size

drained the swamps to get more land for crops. Set the dishes here to drain. **3** channel or pipe for carrying off water or waste of any kind. **4** take away from slowly; use up little by little: *The war drained the country of its people and money.* **5** slow taking away; using up little by little: *Working or playing too hard is a drain on your strength.* 1,2,4 *verb*, 3,5 *noun*.

drain age (drā′nij), draining; drawing off water: *The drainage of swamps improved the land near the river. noun.*

drake (drāk), a male duck. *noun.*

dra ma (drä′mə *or* dram′ə), **1** play such as one sees in a theater; story written to be acted out by actors on the stage. **2** art of writing and producing plays: *He is studying drama.* **3** part of real life that seems to have been planned like a story: *The history of America is a great and thrilling drama. noun.*

dra mat ic (drə mat′ik), **1** of drama; having to do with plays: *a dramatic actor.* **2** exciting; full of action or feeling: *The runner scored a dramatic win in a close race. adjective.*

dra mat i cal ly (drə mat′ik lē), in a dramatic manner. *adverb.*

dram a tist (dram′ə tist), writer of plays. *noun.*

dram a ti za tion (dram′ə tə zā′shən), **1** act of dramatizing. **2** what is dramatized: *That play is a dramatization of the life of Joan of Arc. noun.*

dram a tize (dram′ə tīz), **1** arrange or present in the form of a play: *The children dramatized the story of Rip Van Winkle.* **2** make seem exciting and thrilling: *The speaker dramatized her story with her hands and voice. verb,* **dram a tized, dram a tiz ing.**

drank (drangk). See **drink.** *I drank four glasses of milk yesterday. verb.*

drape (drāp), **1** cover or hang with cloth falling loosely in folds, especially as a decoration: *The buildings were draped with red, white, and blue bunting.* **2** arrange to hang loosely in folds: *I draped the cape around my shoulders.* **3** cloth hung in folds; draperies: *There are drapes on the large windows in the living room.* 1,2 *verb,* **draped, drap ing;** 3 *noun.*

dra per y (drā′pər ē), **1** window curtains arranged in folds: *The draperies in the living room are bright red.* **2** cloths or fabrics hung in loose folds for decoration. *noun, plural* **dra per ies.**

dras tic (dras′tik), acting with force or violence; extreme: *The police took drastic measures to put a stop to the wave of robberies. adjective.*

draught (draft), draft. *noun, verb, adjective.*

draw (drô), **1** pull; drag; haul: *The horses draw the wagon.* **2** pull out; pull up; cause to come out; take out; get: *Draw a pail of water from this well. She drew ten dollars from the bank. Until you hear both sides of the argument, draw no conclusions.* **3** act of pulling out or taking out: *She was a good marksman and was very quick on the draw.* **4** move: *The car drew near.* **5** attract: *A parade always draws crowds.* **6** make a picture or likeness of anything with pen, pencil, or chalk: *Draw a circle.* **7** make a

current of air to carry off smoke: *The chimney does not draw well.* **8** breathe in; inhale: *Draw a deep breath.* **9** tie. A game is a draw when neither side wins. **10** make longer; stretch: *draw out a rubber band.* **11** sink to a depth of; need for floating: *A ship draws more water when it is loaded than when it is empty.* **12** a kind of valley: *The rancher found the strayed cattle grazing in a draw.* 1,2,4-8,10,11 *verb,* **drew, drawn, draw ing;** 3,9,12 *noun.*

draw up, 1 arrange in order: *The marchers were drawn up in formation for the parade.* **2** write out in proper form: *Our family lawyer drew up my parents' wills.* **3** stop: *A car drew up in front of the house.*

draw back (drô′bak′), disadvantage; anything which makes a situation or experience less complete or satisfying: *Our trip was interesting, but the rainy weather was a drawback. noun.*

draw bridge (drô′brij′), bridge that can be entirely or partly lifted, lowered, or moved to one side. In old castles drawbridges were lifted to keep out enemies. A drawbridge over a river is lifted to let boats pass. *noun.*

drawer (drôr), box with handles built to slide in and out of a table, desk, or bureau: *He kept his shirts in the dresser drawer. noun.*

draw ing (drô′ing), **1** picture, sketch, plan, or design done with pen, pencil, or crayon. **2** the making of such a sketch, plan, or design; representing objects by lines. *noun.*

drawl (drôl), **1** talk in a slow way, drawing out the vowels. **2** the speech of a person that drawls. 1 *verb,* 2 *noun.*

drawn (drôn). See **draw.** *That old horse has drawn many loads. verb.*

dread (dred), **1** fear greatly (what is to come); dislike to experience: *I dreaded my visits to the dentist. Cats dread water.* **2** fear, especially fear of something that will happen, or may happen. **3** dreaded; dreadful: *The dread day of the trial was approaching.* 1 *verb,* 2 *noun,* 3 *adjective.*

dread ful (dred′fəl), **1** causing dread; terrible; fearful: *The fairy tale was about a dreadful dragon.* **2** very bad; very unpleasant: *I have a dreadful cold. adjective.*

dream (drēm), **1** something thought, felt, or seen during sleep: *I had a bad dream last night.* **2** something unreal like a dream; daydream: *Sometimes I sit at my desk and have dreams about faraway places.* **3** think, feel, hear, or see during sleep; have dreams: *The little boy dreamed that he was flying.* **4** form fancies; imagine: *For years they dreamed of fame and riches.* **5** think of (something) as possible; imagine: *The day was so bright that we never dreamed it would rain.* 1,2 *noun,* 3-5 *verb,* **dreamed** *or* **dreamt, dream ing.**

dream er (drē′mər), **1** person who has dreams. **2** person whose ideas do not fit real conditions. *noun.*

dreamt (dremt), dreamed. See **dream.** *verb.*

dream y (drē′mē), **1** full of dreams: *a dreamy sleep.* **2** like a dream; vague; dim: *a dreamy recollection.* **3** fond of daydreaming; fanciful; not practical: *a dreamy person. adjective,* **dream i er, dream i est.**

drear y (drir′ē), dull; without cheer; gloomy: *A cold, rainy day is dreary. adjective,* **drear i er, drear i est.**

dredge (drej), **1** machine with a scoop or series of buckets for cleaning out or deepening a harbor or channel. **2** clean out or deepen with a dredge. **3** machine with a net used for gathering oysters from the bottom of a river or the sea. **4** bring up or gather with a dredge. 1,3 *noun,* 2,4 *verb,* **dredged, dredg ing.**

dregs (dregz), **1** small bits that settle to the bottom of a liquid: *After pouring the tea I rinsed the dregs out of the teapot.* **2** the least desirable part: *The murderer came from the dregs of the population. noun plural.*

drench (drench), wet thoroughly; soak: *A heavy rain drenched the campers. verb.*

driftwood

dress (dres), **1** an outer garment worn by women and girls. **2** clothes; clothing: *neat dress.* **3** put clothes on: *Please dress the baby.* **4** wear clothes properly and attractively: *Some people don't know how to dress.* **5** make ready for use: *The butcher dressed the chicken by pulling out the feathers, cutting off the head and feet, and taking out the insides.* **6** care for. To dress hair is to comb and brush it. To dress a cut or sore is to treat it with medicine and bandages. **7** form in a straight line: *The captain ordered the soldiers to dress their ranks.* 1,2 *noun, plural* **dress es;** 3-7 *verb,* **dressed, dress ing.**

dress er (dres′ər), piece of furniture with drawers for clothes and usually a mirror; bureau. *noun.*

dress ing (dres′ing), **1** medicine and bandage, put on a wound or sore. **2** mixture of bread crumbs and seasoning used to stuff chickens or turkeys. **3** sauce for salads, fish, meat, or other foods. *noun.*

dress mak er (dres′mā′kər), person whose work is making women's or children's clothing. *noun.*

drew (drü). See **draw.** *She drew a picture. verb.*

drib ble (drib′əl), **1** flow or let flow in drops or small amounts; trickle: *That faucet dribbles.* **2** drip from the mouth: *Babies dribble on their bibs.* **3** a dropping; dripping; trickle: *There's a dribble of milk running down your chin.* **4** move (a ball) along by bouncing it or giving it short kicks: *dribble a basketball, dribble a soccer ball.* 1,2,4 *verb,* **drib bled, drib bling;** 3 *noun.*

dried (drīd). See **dry.** *I dried my hands. verb.*

dri er (drī′ər), **1** more dry: *This towel is drier than that one.* **2** thing or person that dries. **3** dryer. 1 *adjective, comparative of* **dry;** 2,3 *noun.*

dries (drīz). See **dry.** *Dad dries the dishes. verb.*

dri est (drī′ist), most dry: *Which is the driest towel? adjective, superlative of* **dry.**

drift (drift), **1** carry or be carried along by currents of air or water: *The breeze was drifting the rowboat toward the shore. A raft drifts if it is not steered.* **2** go along without knowing or caring where one is going: *Some people have a purpose in life, but others just drift.* **3** movement caused by currents of air or water: *the drift of an iceberg.* **4** direction of such movement: *The drift of the Gulf Stream is to the north.* **5** meaning; direction of thought: *Please explain that again; I did not quite get the drift of your words.* **6** heap or be heaped up by the wind: *The wind is so strong it's drifting the snow.* **7** snow or sand heaped up by the wind: *After the heavy snow there were deep drifts in the yard.* 1,2,6 *verb,* 3-5,7 *noun.*

drift wood (drift′wùd′), wood carried along by water; wood washed ashore from the water. See picture. *noun.*

drill (dril), **1** tool or machine for boring holes. See picture. **2** bore (a hole) with a drill; use a drill. **3** teach by having the learner do a thing over and over: *The sergeant drilled the new soldiers.* **4** teaching or training by having the learners do a thing over and over for practice: *The teacher gave the class plenty of drill in arithmetic.* 1,4 *noun,* 2,3 *verb.*

drill (definition 1)

a hat | i it | oi oil | ch child | a in about
ā age | ī ice | ou out | ng long | e in taken
ä far | o hot | u cup | sh she | ə = i in pencil
e let | ō open | ủ put | th thin | o in lemon
ē equal | ô order | ü rule | ŦH then | u in circus
ėr term | | | zh measure |

drink (dringk), **1** swallow anything liquid, such as water or milk: *A person must drink water to stay alive.* **2** liquid swallowed or to be swallowed: *Water is a good drink to quench one's thirst.* **3** portion of a liquid: *Please give me a drink of milk.* **4** suck up; absorb: *The dry soil drank up the rain.* **5** alcoholic liquor. **6** drink alcoholic liquor. 1,4,6 *verb*, **drank, drunk, drink ing;** 2,3,5 *noun.*

drink in, take in with eagerness and pleasure: *Our ears drank in the music.*

drip (drip), **1** fall or let fall in drops: *Rain drips from an umbrella.* **2** falling in drops. **3** be so wet that drops fall: *My forehead was dripping with sweat.* 1,3 *verb*, **dripped, drip ping;** 2 *noun.*

drive (drīv), **1** make go: *Drive the dog away. Drive the nails into the board. The wind drives the windmill. The noise of the drums almost drove me mad.* **2** make go where one wishes; control the movement of: *drive a team of horses. Can you drive a car?* **3** go or carry in an automobile or carriage: *We want to drive through the mountains on the way home. She drove us to the station.* **4** trip in an automobile or carriage: *On Sunday we took a drive in the country.* **5** road: *He built a drive from the street to his house.* **6** force; urge on: *Hunger drove them to steal.* **7** a strong force; push; pressure: *She has a drive to succeed.* **8** bring about or obtain by cleverness or force: *He drove a good bargain at the store.* **9** special effort: *The town had a drive to get money for charity.* **10** work hard or compel to work hard: *The workers said their boss drove them too hard.* 1-3,6,8,10 *verb*, **drove, driv en, driv ing;** 4,5,7,9 *noun.*

drive-in (drīv′in′), **1** arranged and equipped so that customers may drive in and be served or entertained while staying in their cars: *a drive-in theater, a drive-in bank.* **2** place arranged and equipped this way. 1 *adjective*, 2 *noun.*

driv en (driv′ən). See **drive.** *Mom has just driven to work. verb.*

driv er (drī′vər), **1** person who drives, especially a person who drives an automobile. **2** person who makes people who are lower in rank work very hard. *noun.*

drive way (drīv′wā′), road to drive on, often leading from a house or garage to the road. *noun.*

driz zle (driz′əl), **1** rain gently, in very small drops like mist. **2** very small drops of rain like mist. 1 *verb*, **driz zled, driz zling;** 2 *noun.*

droll (drōl), odd and amusing; laughable: *We smiled at the monkey's droll tricks. adjective.*

drom e dar y (drom′ə der′ē), a swift camel with one hump, used for riding in Arabia and northern Africa. See picture. *noun, plural* **drom e dar ies.**

drone (drōn), **1** male bee that fertilizes the queen. Drones have no stings, and do no work. **2** make a deep, continuous humming sound: *Bees droned among the flowers.* **3** a deep, continuous humming sound: *the drone of mosquitoes, the drone of a far-off car.* **4** talk or say with the same dull voice: *Several people in the audience fell asleep as the speaker droned on.* **5** person not willing to work; loafer. 1,3,5 *noun*, 2,4 *verb*, **droned, dron ing.**

drool (drül), let saliva run from the mouth as a baby does. *verb.*

droop (drüp), **1** hang down; bend down: *These flowers will soon droop if they are not put in water.* **2** hanging down; bending position: *The droop of the branches brought them within our reach.* **3** become weak and discouraged; lose strength and energy: *The hikers were drooping by the end of the walk in the hot sun.* 1,3 *verb*, 2 *noun.*

drop (drop), **1** a small amount of liquid in a round shape: *a drop of rain, a drop of blood.* **2** a very small amount of liquid: *Take a few drops of this medicine.* **3** **drops,** liquid medicine given in drops: *eye drops, nose drops.* **4** fall or let fall in very small amounts. **5** a sudden fall: *a drop in temperature, a drop in prices.* **6** the distance down; a sudden fall in level; length of a fall: *From the top of the cliff to the water is a drop of 200 feet.* **7** take a sudden fall: *The acrobat dropped from the high rope into the net below.* **8** fall or let fall: *It was so quiet you could hear a pin drop. Did you drop this package?* **9** cause to fall: *He dropped his attacker with a single punch.* **10** fall dead, wounded, or tired out: *After working all day I was ready to drop.* **11** cause to fall wounded or dead; shoot down: *The hunter dropped the deer with a single shot.* **12** go lower; sink: *His voice dropped to a whisper.* **13** make lower: *Drop your voice.* **14** let go; dismiss: *Members who do not pay their dues will be dropped from the club.* **15** leave out; omit: *Drop the "e" in "drive" before adding "ing."* **16** stop; end: *The matter is not important; let it drop.* **17** send: *Drop me a note from camp.* **18** let out from an automobile, ship, or carriage: *Drop me at the corner of Main Street.* 1-3,5,6 *noun*, 4,7-18 *verb*, **dropped, drop ping.**

drop in, visit informally: *Drop in and see me.*

drop out (drop′out′), student who leaves school or college before completing a course or a term. *noun.*

drop per (drop′ər), a small glass tube with an opening at one end. It is used to put drops of liquid into the eyes, nose, or throat. *noun.*

drought (drout), **1** a long period of dry weather; continued lack of rain. See picture. **2** lack of water; dryness. *noun.*

drouth (drouth), drought. *noun.*

drove[1] (drōv). See **drive.** *We drove two hundred miles today. verb.*

drove[2] (drōv), **1** group of cattle, sheep, or hogs moving or driven along together; herd; flock: *The rancher sent a drove of cattle to market.* **2** many people moving along together; crowd: *A drove of people came out of the theater. noun.*

drown (droun), **1** die under water or other liquid because of lack of air to breathe: *We almost drowned when our boat overturned.* **2** kill by keeping under water or other liquid: *The flood drowned many cattle in the lowlands.* **3** be stronger than; keep from being heard: *The boat's whistle drowned out what she was trying to tell us. verb.*

drowse (drouz), be half asleep: *She drowsed, but did not quite fall asleep. verb*, **drowsed, drows ing.**

drow sy (drou′zē), **1** sleepy; half asleep. **2** making

a hat	i it	oi oil	ch child	a in about
ā age	ī ice	ou out	ng long	e in taken
ä far	o hot	u cup	sh she	ə = { i in pencil
e let	ō open	u̇ put	th thin	o in lemon
ē equal	ô order	ü rule	ŦH then	u in circus
ėr term			zh measure	

drum (definition 1)—This drum was used in the Civil War.

drought (definition 1)

dromedary
7½ feet (2½ meters) high at the hump

one sleepy: *It was a warm, quiet, drowsy afternoon.* *adjective,* **drow si er, drow si est.**

drudge (druj), **1** person who does hard, tiresome, or disagreeable work. **2** do hard, tiresome, or disagreeable work. 1 *noun,* 2 *verb,* **drudged, drudg ing.**

drudg er y (druj′ər ē), work that is hard, without interest, or disagreeable: *I think that washing dishes is drudgery. noun, plural* **drudg er ies.**

drug (drug), **1** a substance used to treat, prevent, or cure disease. Penicillin and aspirin are drugs. **2** a substance taken for its effect and not for medical reasons. Such drugs speed up or slow down the activity of the body or affect the senses. Marijuana is a drug. **3** give drugs to, often drugs that are harmful or cause sleep: *The spy drugged the guard and then stole the secret code.* **4** mix harmful drugs with (food or drink): *The spy drugged the guard's coffee.* **5** make (a person) dull or sleepy in a way that is not natural: *The wine had drugged them.* 1,2 *noun,* 3-5 *verb,* **drugged, drug ging.**

drug gist (drug′ist), person who is skilled at preparing the medicine that a doctor has told a patient to take. *noun.*

drug store (drug′stôr′), store that sells drugs and other medicines and often such things as soft drinks, cosmetics, and magazines. *noun.*

drum (drum), **1** a musical instrument that makes a sound when it is beaten. A drum is hollow with a cover stretched tight over the ends. See picture. **2** sound made by beating a drum. **3** any sound like this: *I heard the drum of rain on the roof.* **4** beat or play the drum: *I drum in the school band.* **5** beat, tap, or strike again and again: *Stop drumming on the table with your fingers.* **6** teach or drive into one's head by repeating over and over: *Arithmetic had to be drummed into me because I couldn't understand it.* **7** container or other thing shaped somewhat like a drum: *an oil drum.* 1-3,7 *noun,* 4-6 *verb,* **drummed, drum ming.**

drum mer (drum′ər), person who plays a drum. *noun.*

drum stick (drum′stik′), **1** stick for beating a drum. **2** the lower half of the leg of a cooked chicken or turkey. *noun.*

drunk (drungk), **1** affected by alcoholic drink. People who are drunk lose control over their mental powers. **2** person who is drunk. **3** See **drink.** *He has drunk several glasses of milk already.* 1 *adjective,* 2 *noun,* 3 *verb.*

drunk ard (drung′kərd), person who is often drunk; person who drinks too much alcoholic liquor. *noun.*

drunk en (drung′kən), **1** drunk. **2** caused by being drunk: *drunken words. adjective.*

dubious (definition 1)—She was **dubious** about the way she looked in the new hat.

duck¹ (definition 1)—a wild duck

dumbbell—The strong man lifted a large **dumbbell**.

dry (drī), **1** not wet; not moist: *Dust is dry. This bread is dry.* **2** make or become dry: *We washed and dried the dishes after dinner. Clothes dry in the sun.* **3** having little or no rain: *Arizona has a dry climate.* **4** empty of water or other liquid: *I can't write with a dry pen. The kettle has boiled dry.* **5** thirsty; wanting a drink: *I am dry after that hike.* **6** not under, in, or on water: *He was glad to be on dry land and away from the swamp.* **7** quietly humorous in a sharp, biting way: *a dry wit, a dry remark.* **8** not interesting; dull: *A book full of facts and figures is dry.* **9** without butter: *dry toast.* 1,3-9 *adjective,* **dri er, dri est;** 2 *verb,* **dried, dry ing.**

dry cell, a cell in which a mixture of chemicals produces electric current. This mixture is a paste made with gelatin or sawdust so that it cannot spill.

dry-clean (drī′klēn′), clean (clothes) with a chemical cleaning fluid instead of water. *verb.*

dry er (drī′ər), machine that removes water by heat or air: *a clothes dryer, a hair dryer. noun.* Also spelled **drier.**

dry goods, cloth, ribbons, laces, and the like.

dry ly (drī′lē), in a dry manner: *He spoke little and dryly. adverb.*

du al (dü′əl *or* dyü′əl), **1** consisting of two parts; double; twofold: *The automobile had dual controls, one set for the learner and one for the teacher.* **2** of two; showing two. *adjective.*

dub (dub), **1** give a name or nickname to; call: *We dubbed our new sailboat "Sea Breeze."* **2** make (a person) a knight by touching the shoulder lightly with a sword. *verb,* **dubbed, dub bing.**

du bi ous (dü′bē əs *or* dyü′bē əs), **1** doubtful; uncertain. See picture. **2** of questionable character; probably bad: *The police are investigating the swindler's dubious schemes for making money. adjective.*

duch ess (duch′is), **1** wife or widow of a duke. **2** woman whose rank is equal to that of a duke. *noun, plural* **duch ess es.**

duck¹ (duk), **1** a wild or tame swimming bird with a flat bill, short neck, short legs, and webbed feet. See picture. **2** a female duck. The male is called a drake. **3** the flesh of a duck used for food: *roast duck. noun.*

duck² (duk), **1** plunge or dip under water and come up quickly, as a duck does. **2** a sudden plunge or dip under water and out again. **3** lower the head or bend the body quickly to keep from being hit or seen: *She ducked to avoid a low branch.* **4** a sudden lowering of the head or bending of the body to keep from being hit or seen. 1,3 *verb,* 2,4 *noun.*

duck ling (duk′ling), a young duck. *noun.*

duct (dukt), **1** tube, pipe, or channel for carrying liquid or air. **2** tube in the body for carrying a bodily fluid: *tear ducts. noun.*

due (dü *or* dyü), **1** owed as a debt; owing; to be paid as a right: *The money due her for her work was paid today. Respect is due to older people.* **2** a person's right; what is owed to a person: *Courtesy is his due while he is your guest.* **3** proper; rightful;

fitting: *You will receive a due reward for your good work.* **4** as much as needed; enough: *Use due care in crossing streets.* **5 dues,** amount of money it costs to be a member of a club; fee or tax for some purpose: *Members who do not pay dues will be suspended from the club.* **6** looked for; expected; promised to come or to do: *The train is due at noon. Your report is due tomorrow.* **7** straight; exactly; directly: *The ship sailed due west.* 1,3,4,6 *adjective,* 2,5 *noun,* 7 *adverb.*

due to, 1 caused by: *The accident was due to the driver's carelessness.* **2** because of: *The game was called off due to rain.*

du el (dü′əl *or* dyü′əl), **1** a formal fight to settle a quarrel. Duels are fought with pistols or swords between two persons in the presence of two others called seconds. **2** any fight or contest between two opponents: *The lawyers fought a duel of wits in the court of law.* **3** fight a duel. 1,2 *noun,* 3 *verb.*

du et (dü et′ *or* dyü et′), **1** piece of music for two voices or instruments. **2** two singers or players performing together. *noun.*

dug (dug). See **dig**. *The dog dug a hole in the ground. The potatoes have all been dug. verb.*

dug out (dug′out′), **1** a rough shelter or dwelling formed by digging into the side of a hill or trench. During war, soldiers use dugouts for protection against bullets and bombs. **2** a small shelter at the side of a baseball field, used by players not on the field. **3** boat made by hollowing out a large log. *noun.*

duke (dük *or* dyük), nobleman ranking just below a prince. *noun.*

dull (dul), **1** not sharp or pointed: *It is hard to cut with a dull knife.* **2** not bright or clear: *dull eyes, a dull color, a dull day.* **3** slow in understanding; stupid: *a dull mind. A dull person often fails to get the meaning of a joke.* **4** not felt sharply: *the dull pain of a bruise.* **5** not interesting; tiresome; boring: *a dull book.* **6** not active: *The fur coat business is usually dull in summer.* **7** make or become dull: *Chopping wood dulled the blade of the ax. This cheap knife dulls easily.* 1-6 *adjective,* 7 *verb.*

dul ly (dul′ē), in a dull manner. *adverb.*

du ly (dü′lē *or* dyü′lē), properly; as due; in a proper way; rightly; suitably: *The documents were duly signed before a lawyer. adverb.*

dumb (dum), **1** not able to speak: *Even intelligent animals are dumb.* **2** unwilling to speak; silent; not speaking. **3** slow in understanding; stupid; dull. *adjective.*

dumb bell (dum′bel′), short bar of wood or iron with large, heavy, round ends. It is lifted or swung around to exercise the muscles of the arms or back. See picture. *noun.*

dum my (dum′ē), **1** a life-size figure of a person, used to display clothing in store windows, to shoot at in rifle practice, to tackle in football, or in other ways. **2** a stupid person with no more sense than such a figure. **3** made to resemble the real thing; imitation: *We had a sword fight with dummy*

swords made of wood. 1,2 *noun, plural* **dum mies;** 3 *adjective.*

dump (dump), **1** empty out; throw down: *The truck dumped the coal on the sidewalk.* **2** place for throwing rubbish: *Garbage is taken to the city dump.* **3** a dirty, shabby, or untidy place. **4** place for storing military supplies: *an ammunition dump.* 1 *verb,* 2-4 *noun.*

dunce (duns), person who is stupid or slow to learn. *noun.* [*Dunce* was named for John Duns Scotus, a religious scholar who lived in England in the 1200's. Those who were against his teachings made fun of his followers and called them *Dunses* or *Dunces.*]

dunes

dune (dün *or* dyün), a mound or ridge of loose sand heaped up by the wind. See picture. *noun.*

dun ga ree (dung′gə rē′), **1** a coarse cotton cloth, used for work clothes. **2 dungarees,** trousers or clothing made of this cloth. *noun.*

dun geon (dun′jən), a dark underground room or cell to keep prisoners in. *noun.*

dupe (düp *or* dyüp), **1** person easily deceived or tricked. **2** deceive; trick: *The dishonest merchant tried to dupe us.* 1 *noun,* 2 *verb,* **duped, dup ing.**

du pli cate (dü′plə kit *or* dyü′plə kit *for 1,2, and 4;* dü′plə kāt *or* dyü′plə kāt *for 3*), **1** exactly like something else: *We have duplicate keys for the front door.* **2** one of two things exactly alike; exact copy: *He mailed the letter, but kept a duplicate.* **3** make an exact copy of; repeat exactly: *Duplicate the picture so that we may both have copies of it.* **4** having two corresponding parts; double: *A* *human being has duplicate lungs but only one heart.* 1,4 *adjective,* 2 *noun,* 3 *verb,* **du pli cat ed, du pli cat ing.**

du pli ca tion (dü′plə kā′shən *or* dyü′plə kā′shən), **1** duplicating or being duplicated: *Duplication of effort is a waste of time.* **2** a duplicate copy: *Her answers were a duplication of her sister's. noun.*

dur a ble (dúr′ə bəl *or* dyúr′ə bəl), **1** able to withstand wear or decay: *Work clothes are made of durable fabric.* **2** lasting a long time: *Another war destroyed all hopes of a durable peace between the two nations. adjective.*

du ra tion (dù rā′shən *or* dyù rā′shən), length of time; time during which anything continues: *The storm was sudden and of short duration. noun.*

dur ing (dúr′ing *or* dyúr′ing), **1** through the whole time of: *We played during the afternoon.* **2** at some time in; in the course of: *Come sometime during the day. preposition.*

dusk (dusk), **1** the time just before dark: *We saw the evening star at dusk.* **2** shade; gloom: *the dusk of a forest.* **3** dusky. 1,2 *noun,* 3 *adjective.*

dusk y (dus′kē), **1** somewhat dark; dark-colored. **2** dim; obscure: *the dusky light of the late afternoon. adjective,* **dusk i er, dusk i est.**

dust (dust), **1** fine, dry earth: *Dust lay thick on the road.* **2** any fine powder: *The old papers had turned to dust.* **3** get dust off; brush or wipe the dust from: *I dusted the furniture.* **4** sprinkle (with dust or powder): *The cook dusted the cake with sugar.* 1,2 *noun,* 3,4 *verb.*

dust pan (dust′pan′), a wide, flat pan with a handle, onto which dust can be swept from the floor. *noun.*

dust y (dus′tē), **1** covered with dust; filled with dust: *He found some dusty old books in the attic.* **2** like dust; dry and powdery: *dusty chalk.* **3** having the color of dust: *a dusty brown. adjective,* **dust i er, dust i est.**

Dutch (duch), **1** of or having something to do with the Netherlands, its people, or their language. **2** people of the Netherlands. **3** their language. 1 *adjective,* 2 *noun plural,* 3 *noun singular.*

du ti ful (dü′tə fəl *or* dyü′tə fəl), doing your duty; obedient: *They are dutiful children, always helping their parents with the housework. adjective.*

du ty (dü′tē *or* dyü′tē), **1** the thing that is right to do; what a person ought to do: *It is your duty to obey the laws.* **2** obligation: *A sense of duty sometimes makes people do what they think is right even when they don't want to do it.* **3** things that one must do in one's work: *Her duties at the post office are to sort and to weigh packages.* **4** a tax on taking articles out of, or bringing them into, a country. *noun, plural* **du ties.**

on duty, working at one's job or position.

dwarf (dwôrf), **1** person, animal, or plant much smaller than the usual size for its kind. **2** (in fairy tales) an ugly little man with magic power. **3** smaller than the usual size for its kind. **4** keep from growing large. See picture. **5** cause to seem small by contrast or by distance: *That tall building dwarfs all those around it.* 1,2 *noun, plural* **dwarfs, dwarves** (dwôrvz); 3 *adjective,* 4,5 *verb.*

dwell (dwel), live; make one's home: *They dwell in the country but work in the city. verb,* **dwelt** *or* **dwelled, dwell ing.**

dwell on, think, speak, or write about for a long time: *My mind dwelt on my pleasant day in the country.*

dwell er (dwel′ər), person who dwells or lives: *A city dweller lives in a city. noun.*

dwell ing (dwel′ing), house; place in which one lives. *noun.*

dwelt (dwelt). See **dwell.** *We dwelt there for a long time. We have dwelt in the country for years. verb.*

dwin dle (dwin′dl), become smaller and smaller; shrink: *During the storm the trapper's supply of food dwindled day by day. verb,* **dwin dled, dwin dling.**

dye (dī), **1** substance that can be mixed with water and used to color cloth, hair, and other things. **2** a color produced by such a substance: *A good dye will not fade.* **3** color or stain: *I dyed my shirt red. The spilled grape juice dyed the tablecloth purple.* 1,2 *noun,* 3 *verb,* **dyed, dye ing.**

dy ing (dī′ing), **1** about to die; ceasing to live: *a dying old woman.* **2** coming to an end: *the dying year.* **3** of death; at death: *dying words.* **4** See **die[1].** *The storm is dying down.* 1-3 *adjective,* 4 *verb.*

dyke (dīk), dike. *noun.*

dy nam ic (dī nam′ik), active; forceful. *adjective.*

dy na mite (dī′nə mīt), **1** a powerful explosive most commonly used in blasting rocks. **2** blow up with dynamite. 1 *noun,* 2 *verb,* **dy na mit ed, dy na mit ing.** [*Dynamite* was made up from a Greek word meaning "force" by Alfred Nobel, a Swedish chemist who lived from 1833 to 1896. He invented the explosive.]

dy na mo (dī′nə mō), machine that makes electricity; generator. *noun, plural* **dy na mos.**

dy nas ty (dī′nə stē), series of rulers who belong to the same family. *noun, plural* **dy nas ties.**

dwarf (definition 4)—This tree has been **dwarfed.**

E e

a hat	i it	oi oil	ch child		a in about
ā age	ī ice	ou out	ng long		e in taken
ä far	o hot	u cup	sh she	ə =	i in pencil
e let	ō open	u̇ put	th thin		o in lemon
ē equal	ô order	ü rule	ŦH then		u in circus
ėr term			zh measure		

E or **e** (ē), the fifth letter of the English alphabet. There are two *e*'s in *see. noun, plural* **E's** or **e's.**

E or **E.,** **1** east. **2** eastern.

each (ēch), **1** every one of: *Each child has a name. Each of the students has a pencil.* **2** for each: *These pencils are five cents each.* **1** *adjective, pronoun,* **2** *adverb.*

each other, each one the other one. *They struck each other* means "each one of them struck the other one."

ea ger (ē′gər), wanting very much: *The child is eager to have the candy. adjective.*

ea gle (ē′gəl), a large bird that can see far and has powerful wings. The bald eagle is the symbol of the United States. *noun.*

ear[1] (ir), **1** the part of the body by which people and animals hear. **2** something shaped somewhat like the outer part of an ear. **3** sense of hearing. **4** ability to hear small differences in sounds: *She has a good ear for music.* **5** attention: *Please give ear to my request. noun.*

prick up one's ears, 1 point the ears upward: *The dog pricked up its ears at the sudden noise.* **2** give sudden attention: *I pricked up my ears when I heard my name mentioned.*

ear[2] (ir), the part of certain plants that contains the grains. The grains of corn, wheat, oats, barley, and rye are formed on ears. *noun.*

ear ache (ir′āk′), pain in the ear. *noun.*

ear drum (ir′drum′), a thin, skinlike layer that stretches across the middle ear. It vibrates when sound waves strike it. *noun.*

earl (ėrl), a British nobleman ranking below a marquess and above a viscount. *noun.*

ear ly (ėr′lē), **1** in the beginning; in the first part: *The sun is not hot early in the day.* **2** before the usual time: *We have an early dinner today. Please come early. adverb, adjective,* **ear li er, ear li est.**

ear muffs (ir′mufs′), pair of coverings worn over the ears in cold weather to keep them warm. *noun plural.*

earn (ėrn), **1** get in return for work or service; be paid: *She earns $175 a week.* **2** do enough work for; do good enough work for; deserve: *He is paid more than he really earns.* **3** win; bring or get as deserved: *Her hard work earned her the respect of her teachers. verb.*

ear nest (ėr′nist), strong and firm in purpose; eager and serious: *The earnest pupil tried very hard to do his best. adjective.*

in earnest, determined or sincere; serious: *She is in earnest about becoming a famous painter.*

earn ings (ėr′ningz), money earned; wages; profits. *noun plural.*

ear phone (ir′fōn′), receiver for a telephone, telegraph, radio, or television set that is fastened or placed over the ear. *noun.*

ear ring (ir′ring′), ornament for the ear. *noun.*

ear shot (ir′shot′), distance a sound can be heard; range of hearing: *We shouted, but he was out of earshot and could not hear our voices. noun.*

earth (ėrth), **1** the planet on which we live. **2** ground: *The earth in his garden is good soil. noun.*

earth en (ėr′thən), **1** made of baked clay: *an earthen jug.* **2** made of earth. *adjective.*

earth en ware (ėr′thən wer′ *or* ėr′thən war′), dishes or containers made of baked clay. Pottery or crockery is earthenware. See picture. *noun.*

earth ly (ėrth′lē), **1** having to do with the earth, not with heaven. **2** possible: *That junk is of no earthly use. adjective.*

earth quake (ėrth′kwāk′), a shaking or sliding of the ground, caused by the sudden movement of rock far beneath the earth's surface. See picture. *noun.*

earthenware

earthquake—houses damaged by the San Francisco earthquake in 1906

earth worm (ėrth/wėrm/), a reddish-brown or grayish worm that lives in the soil; angleworm. Earthworms help loosen the soil. *noun.*

ease (ēz), **1** freedom from pain or trouble; comfort: *When school is out, I am going to live a life of ease for a whole week.* **2** make free from pain or trouble: *Her kind words eased my worried mind.* **3** very little need to try hard: *You can do this lesson with ease.* **4** make less; lighten: *Some medicines ease pain.* **5** make easy; loosen: *The belt is too tight; ease it a little.* **6** move slowly and carefully: *He eased the big box through the narrow door.* 1,3 *noun,* 2,4-6 *verb,* **eased, eas ing.**

ea sel (ē/zəl), stand for a picture or blackboard. *noun.* [*Easel* comes from a Dutch word meaning "donkey." It was called this because it has legs and serves as a support.]

eas i ly (ē/zə lē), **1** in an easy manner. **2** without trying hard; with little effort: *The simple tasks were quickly and easily done.* **3** without pain or trouble; comfortably: *A few hours after the operation, the patient was resting easily.* **4** by far; without question: *He is easily the best player on the field.* **5** very likely: *She is a good writer who works hard and may easily become famous.* *adverb.*

east (ēst), **1** direction of the sunrise. **2** toward the east; farther toward the east: *Walk east to find the road.* **3** coming from the east: *an east wind.* **4** in the east: *the east wing of a house.* **5** the part of any country toward the east. **6 the East, a** the eastern part of the United States. **b** the countries in Asia: *China and Japan are in the East.* 1,5,6 *noun,* 3,4 *adjective,* 2 *adverb.*

east of, further east than: *Ohio is east of Indiana.*

Eas ter (ē/stər), the yearly Christian celebration of Christ's rising from the dead. Easter comes between March 22 and April 25. *noun.* [*Easter* was named for an ancient goddess of the dawn. Her feast was celebrated in the spring.]

east er ly (ē/stər lē), **1** toward the east. **2** from the east: *an easterly wind. adjective, adverb.*

east ern (ē/stərn), **1** toward the east: *an eastern trip.* **2** from the east: *eastern tourists.* **3** of the east; in the east: *eastern schools.* **4 Eastern, a** of or in the eastern part of the United States. **b** of or in the countries in Asia. *adjective.*

east ward (ēst/wərd), toward the east; east: *to walk eastward, an eastward slope. adverb, adjective.*

east wards (ēst/wərdz), eastward. *adverb.*

eas y (ē/zē), **1** not hard to do or get: *easy work quickly done.* **2** free from pain, trouble, or worry: *The wealthy family led an easy life.* **3** giving comfort or rest: *an easy chair.* **4** not strict or harsh: *We bought our new car on easy terms of payment.* **5** smooth and pleasant; not awkward: *Our hosts had easy manners. She has an easy way of speaking to everyone. adjective,* **eas i er, eas i est.**

eas y go ing (ē/zē gō/ing), taking matters easily; not worrying: *The new teacher is pleasantly easygoing and relaxed with the class. adjective.*

eat (ēt), **1** chew and swallow (food): *Cows eat grass and grain.* **2** have a meal: *Where shall we eat?* **3** destroy as if by eating: *The flames ate up the wood. This acid eats metal. verb,* **ate, eat en, eat ing.**

eat en (ēt/n). See **eat.** *Have you eaten your dinner? verb.*

eaves (ēvz), the lower edge of a roof that stands out a little from the side of a building. See picture. *noun plural.*

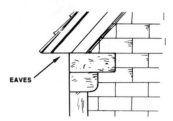

EAVES

eaves drop per (ēvz/drop/ər), person who listens secretly to other people talking among themselves. *noun.*

ebb (eb), **1** flowing of the tide away from the shore; fall of the tide. **2** flow out; fall: *We waded farther out as the tide ebbed.* **3** growing less or weaker; decline: *Our hopes were at an ebb.* **4** grow less or weaker; decline: *His courage began to ebb as he neared the haunted house.* 1,3 *noun,* 2,4 *verb.*

eb on y (eb/ə nē), a hard, black wood, used for the black keys of a piano, for the backs of brushes, and for ornamental woodwork. *noun, plural* **eb on ies.**

ec cen tric (ek sen/trik), **1** out of the ordinary; not usual; peculiar; odd: *People stared at the artist's eccentric clothes.* **2** person who behaves in an unusual manner. 1 *adjective,* 2 *noun.*

ech o (ek/ō), **1** a repeated sound. You hear an echo when a sound you make bounces back from a distant hill or wall so that you hear it again. **2** be heard again: *The gunshot echoed through the valley.* **3** say or do always what another says or does: *They never think for themselves; they just echo what their friends say.* 1 *noun, plural* **ech oes;** 2,3 *verb.*

e clipse (i klips/), **1** the blocking of light from one heavenly body by another heavenly body. An eclipse of the sun occurs when the moon passes between the sun and the earth. An eclipse of the moon occurs when the moon enters the earth's shadow. **2** cut off or dim the light from; darken. **3** do much better than; surpass: *Several of my friends eclipse me at sports.* 1 *noun,* 2,3 *verb,* **e clipsed, e clips ing.**

e col o gy (ē kol/ə jē), the science that deals with the relation of living things to their environment and to each other. Ecology is a branch of biology. *noun.*

e co nom ic (ē/kə nom/ik *or* ek/ə nom/ik), having to do with economics. *adjective.*

e co nom i cal (ē/kə nom/ə kəl *or* ek/ə nom/ə kəl), avoiding waste; thrifty; saving. *adjective.*

e co nom ics (ē kə nom/iks *or* ek/ə nom/iks), science of how people produce wealth, how they distribute it among themselves, and how they use it. *noun.*

e con o mize (i kon′ə mīz), **1** use little of; use to the best advantage: *If you can economize your time, you will get more done in less time.* **2** cut down expenses: *We must economize or we will go into debt.* verb, **e con o mized, e con o miz ing.**

e con o my (i kon′ə mē), making the most of what one has; thrift; the use of something without any waste: *Because of our economy in buying food and clothes, we were able to save enough money for our vacation.* noun, plural **e con o mies.**

ec sta sy (ek′stə sē), condition of very great joy; thrilling or overwhelming delight; rapture: *The little girl was speechless with ecstasy over her birthday present.* noun, plural **ec sta sies.**

ed dy (ed′ē), **1** a small whirlpool or whirlwind; water, air, or smoke whirling around. **2** whirl: *The water eddied out of the sink.* **1** noun, plural **ed dies;** **2** verb, **ed died, ed dy ing.**

edge (ej), **1** line or place where something ends; part farthest from the middle; side: *This page has four edges.* **2** the thin side that cuts: *The knife had a very sharp edge.* **3** put an edge on; form an edge on: *The gardener edged the path with white stones.* **4** move sideways: *She edged her way through the crowd.* **5** move little by little: *The dog edged nearer to the fire.* **1,2** noun, **3-5** verb, **edged, edg ing.**

edge ways (ej′wāz′), with the edge forward; in the direction of the edge. adverb.

edge wise (ej′wīz′), edgeways. adverb.

ed i ble (ed′ə bəl), fit to eat. adjective.

ed it (ed′it), **1** prepare (another person's writings) for publication: *The teacher is editing famous*

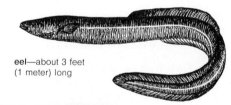

eel—about 3 feet (1 meter) long

eerie—an eerie face

speeches for use in schoolbooks. **2** have charge of (a newspaper or magazine) and decide what shall be printed in it: *Two girls were chosen to edit the school paper.* verb.

e di tion (i dish′ən), **1** all the copies of a book, newspaper, or magazine printed just alike and at or near the same time: *The second edition of the book had many corrections for the errors in the first edition.* **2** form in which a book is printed: *This edition of "Alice in Wonderland" has large print and pictures.* noun.

ed i tor (ed′ə tər), **1** person who edits: *He is the editor of our school paper.* **2** person who writes editorials. noun.

ed i to ri al (ed′ə tôr′ē əl), **1** article in a newspaper or magazine giving the editor's or publisher's opinion on some subject. **2** of an editor: *editorial work.* **1** noun, **2** adjective.

ed u cate (ej′ə kāt), **1** teach; train: *The job of teachers is to educate the young.* **2** send to school: *My brother is being educated in the East and returns home only for vacations.* verb, **ed u cat ed, ed u cat ing.**

ed u ca tion (ej′ə kā′shən), **1** training: *In the United States, public schools offer an education to all children.* **2** knowledge and abilities gained through training: *A person with education knows how to speak, write, and read well.* noun. [Education comes from a Latin word meaning "a bringing up" or "a leading out."]

ed u ca tion al (ej′ə kā′shə nəl), **1** having something to do with education: *The teachers in our school belong to the state educational associations.* **2** giving education: *Our science class saw an educational motion picture about wild animals.* adjective.

eel (ēl), a long, slippery fish shaped like a snake. See picture. noun, plural **eels** or **eel.**

eer ie or **eer y** (ir′ē), strange; weird; causing fear. See picture. adjective, **eer i er, eer i est.**

ef face (ə fās′), rub out; blot out; do away with; destroy; wipe out: *The writing on many old monuments has been effaced by time.* verb, **ef faced, ef fac ing.**

ef fect (ə fekt′), **1** something made to happen by a person or thing; result: *The effect of the gale was to overturn several boats.* **2** bring about; make happen: *Florence Nightingale effected many changes in nursing.* **3** power to produce results; force; influence: *The medicine had an immediate effect.* **4** effects, goods; belongings: *We lost all of our personal effects in the fire.* **1,3,4** noun, **2** verb.

for effect, for show; to impress others: *He said that only for effect; he really didn't mean it.*

take effect, operate; become active: *That pill takes effect as soon as you swallow it.*

ef fec tive (ə fek′tiv), **1** able to cause something: *She is a principal who really knows how to make effective rules.* **2** able to cause some desired result: *Several new drugs are effective in treating serious diseases.* **3** in operation; active: *A law passed by Congress becomes effective as soon as the President signs it. adjective.*

ef fi cien cy (ə fish′ən sē), ability to do things without waste of time or energy: *The carpenter worked with great efficiency. noun, plural* **ef fi cien cies.**

ef fi cient (ə fish′ənt), able to produce the effect wanted without waste of time or energy; capable: *An efficient worker deserves good pay. adjective.*

ef fort (ef′ərt), **1** use of energy and strength to do something; trying hard: *Climbing a steep hill takes effort.* **2** hard try; strong attempt: *She did not win, but at least she made an effort.* **3** result of effort; thing done with effort: *Works of art are artistic efforts. noun.*

egg[1] (eg), **1** the round or oval object which is laid by the female of birds, insects, many reptiles and fish, and other types of animals. Young animals hatch from these eggs. **2** the contents of an egg, especially a hen's egg, used as food: *I like two boiled eggs for breakfast.* **3** egg cell. *noun.*

egg[2] (eg), urge: *We egged the team on to victory. verb.*

egg cell, cell in a female for producing young. After an egg cell combines with a sperm cell, a new organism starts to grow.

egg plant (eg′plant′), a large, egg-shaped, purple fruit that is eaten as a vegetable. *noun.*

egg roll, a small tube of egg dough, filled with a mixture of minced vegetables and roast pork, and fried.

egg shell (eg′shel′), shell covering an egg. *noun.*

E gypt (ē′jipt), country in northeastern Africa. The Nile River flows through Egypt. *noun.*

E gyp tian (i jip′shən), **1** of or having something to do with Egypt or its people. **2** person born or living in Egypt. **3** language of the ancient Egyptians. 1 *adjective,* 2,3 *noun.*

eight (āt), one more than seven; 8. Four and four make eight. *noun, adjective.*

eight een (ā′tēn′), eight more than ten; 18. *noun, adjective.*

eight eenth (ā′tēnth′), **1** next after the 17th. **2** one of 18 equal parts. *adjective, noun.*

eighth (ātth), **1** next after the seventh. **2** one of eight equal parts. *adjective, noun.*

eight i eth (ā′tē ith), **1** next after the 79th. **2** one of 80 equal parts. *adjective, noun.*

eight y (ā′tē), eight times ten; 80. *noun, plural* **eight ies;** *adjective.*

ei ther (ē′ᴛʜər *or* ī′ᴛʜər), **1** one or the other of two: *You may read either book. Either come in or go out.* **2** each of two: *There are fields of corn on either side of the river.* **3** any more than another; also; likewise: *If you do not go, I shall not go either.* 1 *adjective, pronoun, conjunction,* 2 *adjective,* 3 *adverb.*

e ject (i jekt′), throw out; turn out; drive out: *The volcano ejected lava and ashes. verb.*

e lab or ate (i lab′ər it *for 1;* i lab′ə rāt′ *for 2*), **1** worked out with great care; having many details; complicated: *The scientists made elaborate plans for sending a spaceship to Mars.* See picture. **2** work out with great care; add details to: *The author spent weeks elaborating her plans for a new book.* 1 *adjective,* 2 *verb,* **e lab or at ed, e lab or at ing.**

e lapse (i laps′), pass; slip away; glide by: *Hours elapsed while he slept. verb,* **e lapsed, e laps ing.**

e las tic (i las′tik), **1** able to spring back to its original shape, after being pressed together or stretched out: *Rubber bands, sponges, and steel springs are elastic.* **2** getting back to normal easily or quickly: *His elastic spirits never let him be discouraged for long.* **3** tape or cloth woven partly of rubber. 1,2 *adjective,* 3 *noun.*

e las tic i ty (i las tis′ə tē), elastic quality: *Rubber has great elasticity. noun.*

e late (i lāt′), raise the spirits of; make joyful or proud: *Her success in the contest elated her. verb,* **e lat ed, e lat ing.**

e la tion (i lā′shən), high spirits; joy or pride: *He was filled with elation at winning the first prize. noun.*

el bow (el′bō), **1** joint between the upper and lower arm. **2** any bend or corner having the same shape as a bent arm. A sharp turn in a road or a river may be called an elbow. **3** push with the elbow: *Don't elbow me off the sidewalk.* 1,2 *noun,* 3 *verb.*

eld er (el′dər), **1** older: *my elder brother.* **2** an older person: *I took the advice of my elders.* **3** an officer in some Christian churches. 1 *adjective,* 2,3 *noun.*

eld er ly (el′dər lē), somewhat old. *adjective.*

eld est (el′dist), oldest. *adjective.*

e lect (i lekt′), **1** choose by voting: *Americans elect a President every four years.* **2** choose: *She elected to study chemistry. verb.*

e lec tion (i lek′shən), **1** choosing by vote: *In our city we have an election for mayor every two years.* **2** choice. *noun.*

e lec tric (i lek′trik), **1** of electricity; having something to do with electricity: *an electric light, an electric current.* **2** charged with electricity: *an electric battery.* **3** run by electricity: *an electric stove.* **4** exciting; thrilling: *an electric feeling. adjective.*

e lec tri cal (i lek′trə kəl), electric. *adjective.*

e lec tri cian (i lek′trish′ən), person who repairs or installs electric wiring, lights, or motors. *noun.*

e lec tric i ty (i lek′tris′ə tē), **1** form of energy which can produce light, heat, motion, and magnetism: *Electricity makes light bulbs shine, radios and televisions play, cars start, and subways run.* **2** electric current: *Most refrigerators are run by electricity. noun.* [*Electricity* comes from a Greek word meaning "amber." It was called this because amber becomes charged with electricity when it is rubbed.]

e lec tri fy (i lek′trə fī), **1** charge with electricity. **2** equip for the use of electric power: *Some railroads once run by steam are now electrified.* **3** excite; thrill: *She electrified us with ghost stories. verb,* **e lec tri fied, e lec tri fy ing.**

e lec tro mag net (i lek/trō mag/nit), piece of iron that becomes a strong magnet when an electric current is passing through wire coiled around it. *noun.*

e lec tron (i lek/tron), a tiny particle having one unit of negative electricity. All atoms are made up of electrons and protons. *noun.*

e lec tron ic (i lek/tron/ik), of or having to do with electrons or electronics. *adjective.*

e lec tron ics (i lek/tron/iks), branch of physics that deals with electrons in motion. Electronics has made possible the development of television, radio, radar, and computers. *noun.*

el e gance (el/ə gəns), good taste; grace and beauty that is combined with dignity: *The king and queen always dressed with elegance. noun.*

el e gant (el/ə gənt), showing good taste; graceful; beautiful: *The palace had elegant furnishings. adjective.*

el e ment (el/ə mənt), **1** one of over 100 simple substances from which all other things are made up. An element cannot be separated into simpler parts by chemical means. Gold, iron, oxygen, carbon, and tin are elements. **2** one of the parts of which anything is made up: *Honesty and kindness are elements of a good life.* **3** simple or necessary part: *We learn the elements of arithmetic before the seventh grade.* **4 the elements,** the forces of the air, especially in bad weather: *The raging storm seemed to be a war of the elements. noun.*

el e men tar y (el/ə men/tər ē), introductory; dealing with the simpler parts: *We learned addition and subtraction in elementary arithmetic. adjective.*

elementary school, 1 school of six grades for pupils from about six to twelve years of age, followed by junior high school. **2** school of eight grades for pupils from about six to fourteen years, followed by a four-year high school.

el e phant (el/ə fənt), the largest land animal now living. It has a long snout called a trunk. Ivory comes from its tusks. See picture. *noun, plural* **el e phants** or **el e phant.** [*Elephant* comes from a Greek word meaning "ivory." The animal was called this because its tusks are made of ivory.]

el e vate (el/ə vāt), raise; lift up: *She spoke from an elevated platform. I tried to elevate my mind by studying hard. verb,* **el e vat ed, el e vat ing.**

el e va tion (el/ə vā/shən), **1** a raised place; high place: *A hill is an elevation.* **2** height above the earth's surface: *The airplane flew at an elevation of 20,000 feet.* **3** height above sea level: *The elevation of that city is 5300 feet.* **4** elevating or being elevated: *The elevation of a clerk to store manager surprised us. noun.*

el e va tor (el/ə vā/tər), **1** something which raises or lifts up. **2** a moving platform or cage to carry people and things up and down in a building or mine. **3** building for storing grain. See picture. **4** a movable, flat piece on the tail of an airplane to cause it to go up or down. *noun.*

e lev en (i lev/ən), **1** one more than ten; 11. **2** team of eleven football or cricket players. **1,2** *noun,* **1** *adjective.*

a hat	**i** it	**oi** oil	**ch** child	(a in about
ā age	**ī** ice	**ou** out	**ng** long	e in taken
ä far	**o** hot	**u** cup	**sh** she	ə = { i in pencil
e let	**ō** open	**ù** put	**th** thin	o in lemon
ē equal	**ô** order	**ü** rule	**ŦH** then	(u in circus
ėr term			**zh** measure	

elephant—11 feet (3½ meters) high at the shoulder; body 8 feet (2½ meters) long

elevator (definition 3)

elaborate (definition 1) a plate with an elaborate design

e lev enth (i lev′ənth), **1** next after the tenth. **2** one of 11 equal parts. *adjective, noun.*

elf (elf), (in stories) a tiny being that is full of mischief; fairy. *noun, plural* **elves.**

el i gi ble (el′ə jə bəl), fit to be chosen; desirable; qualified: *Pupils must pass in all subjects to be eligible for the team. adjective.*

e lim i nate (i lim′ə nāt), **1** remove; get rid of: *Bridges over railroad tracks eliminate danger in crossing.* **2** leave out; omit: *The architect eliminated the cost of furniture in figuring the cost of the house. verb,* **e lim i nat ed, e lim i nat ing.**

elk (elk), **1** a large deer of Europe and Asia. It has antlers like a moose. **2** a large red deer of North America. See picture. *noun, plural* **elks** or **elk.**

el lipse (i lips′), a figure shaped like an oval with both ends alike. See picture. *noun.*

elm (elm), **1** a tall, graceful shade tree. **2** its hard, heavy wood. *noun.*

e lon gate (i lông′gāt), make or become longer; lengthen; extend; stretch. See picture. *verb,* **e lon gat ed, e lon gat ing.**

e lope (i lōp′), run away to get married. *verb,* **e loped, e lop ing.**

el o quence (el′ə kwəns), **1** flow of speech that has grace and force: *The jury was moved by the eloquence of the lawyer's words.* **2** power to win by speaking; art of speaking so as to stir the feelings. *noun.*

el o quent (el′ə kwənt), **1** having the power of expressing one's feelings or thoughts with grace and force: *an eloquent speaker.* **2** very expressive: *eloquent eyes. adjective.*

else (els), **1** other; different; instead: *Will somebody else speak? What else could I say?* **2** in addition, more; besides: *The Browns are here; do you expect anyone else?* **3** differently: *How else can it be done?* **4** otherwise; if not, or: *Hurry, else you will be late.* **1,2** *adjective,* **3,4** *adverb.*

else where (els′hwer *or* els′hwar), somewhere else; in or to some other place. *adverb.*

e lude (i lüd′), avoid or escape by quickness or cleverness; slip away from: *The sly fox eluded the dogs. verb,* **e lud ed, e lud ing.**

e lu sive (i lü′siv), **1** hard to describe or understand: *I had an idea that was too elusive to be put in words.* **2** tending to elude or escape: *The elusive fox got away. adjective.*

elves (elvz), more than one elf; fairies. *noun plural.*

e man ci pate (i man′sə pāt), set free from slavery of any kind; release: *Women have been emancipated from many old restrictions. verb,* **e man ci pat ed, e man ci pat ing.**

em balm (em bäm′), treat (a dead body) with chemicals to keep it from decaying. *verb.*

em bank ment (em bangk′mənt), a raised bank of earth or stones, used to hold back water or support a roadway. *noun.*

em bark (em bärk′), **1** go on board ship: *Many people embark for Europe at New York harbor.* **2** set out; start: *After leaving college, the young woman embarked upon a business career. verb.*

em bar rass (em bar′əs), **1** make uneasy and

elongate—The cake Alice ate elongated her like a telescope.

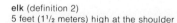

ellipse—three ellipses

elk (definition 2)
5 feet (1½ meters) high at the shoulder

ashamed; make self-conscious: *She embarrassed me by asking me if I really liked her.* **2** burden with debt: *The company was financially embarrassed and could not pay its employees last week.* verb.

em bar rass ment (em bar′əs mənt), **1** uneasiness; shame: *I blushed in embarrassment at my stupid mistake.* **2** thing that embarrasses: *Forgetting the name of an old friend is a great embarrassment.* noun.

em bas sy (em′bə sē), **1** ambassador and his or her staff of assistants. **2** residence and offices of an ambassador in a foreign country. *noun, plural* **em bas sies.**

em bed (em bed′), fix or enclose in a surrounding substance: *Precious stones are often found embedded in rock.* verb, **em bed ded, em bed ding.**

em ber (em′bər), **1** piece of wood or coal still glowing in the ashes of a fire. **2 embers,** ashes in which there is still some fire: *He stirred the embers to make them blaze up again.* noun.

em bez zle (em bez′əl), steal (money entrusted to one's care): *The cashier embezzled $50,000 from the bank and left the country.* verb, **em bez zled, em bez zling.**

em bit ter (em bit′ər), make bitter: *They were embittered by the loss of all their money.* verb.

em blem (em′bləm), symbol; sign that stands for

embroidery

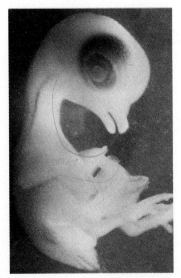

embryo of a chicken

an idea; token: *The dove is an emblem of peace. The white flag is the emblem of surrender.* noun.

em bod y (em bod′ē), put into a form that can be seen: *A building embodies the idea of the architect.* verb, **em bod ied, em bod y ing.**

em boss (em bôs′), decorate with a design or pattern that stands out from the surface: *Our coins are embossed with letters and figures.* verb.

em brace (em brās′), **1** fold in the arms to show love or friendship; hold in the arms; hug: *I embraced my old friend.* **2** a hug: *My old friend gave me a fond embrace.* **3** take up; accept: *He eagerly embraced the offer of a trip to Europe.* **4** include; contain: *The cat family embraces cats, lions, tigers, and similar animals.* **5** surround; enclose: *Vines embraced the hut.* 1,3-5 *verb,* **em braced,** **em brac ing;** 2 *noun.*

em broi der (em broi′dər), **1** decorate (cloth or leather) with a pattern of stitches: *I embroidered the shirt with a colorful design.* **2** add imaginary details to; exaggerate: *They didn't exactly lie, but they did embroider their story.* verb.

em broi der y (em broi′dər ē), ornamental designs sewn in cloth or leather with a needle. See picture. *noun, plural* **em broi der ies.**

em bry o (em′brē ō), animal or plant in the earlier stages of its development, before birth, hatching, or sprouting. *The plant contained within a seed is an embryo. A chicken within an egg is an embryo.* See picture. *noun, plural* **em bry os.**

em er ald (em′ər əld), **1** a bright-green precious stone or jewel. **2** bright green. 1 *noun,* 2 *adjective.*

e merge (i mėrj′), come out; come up; come into view: *The sun emerged from behind a cloud. Many facts emerged as a result of a second investigation.* verb, **e merged, e merg ing.**

e mer gen cy (i mėr′jən sē), **1** a sudden need for immediate action: *I keep a box of tools in my car for use in an emergency.* **2** for a time of sudden need: *When the brakes failed, the driver pulled on the emergency brake and stopped the car. The surgeon performed an emergency operation.* 1 *noun, plural* **e mer gen cies;** 2 *adjective.*

em er y (em′ər ē), a hard, dark mineral which is used for grinding, smoothing, and polishing metals or stones. *noun.*

em i grant (em′ə grənt), person who leaves his or her own country to settle in another: *My grandparents were emigrants from Japan.* noun.

em i grate (em′ə grāt), leave one's own country to settle in another: *My grandparents emigrated from Ireland to come to the United States.* verb, **em i grat ed, em i grat ing.**

em i gra tion (em′ə grā′shən), leaving one's own country to settle in another: *There has been much emigration from Italy to the United States.* noun.

em i nence (em′ə nəns), rank or position above all or most others; greatness; fame: *The surgeon's eminence was due to his superior skill.* noun.

em i nent (em′ə nənt), above all others in rank; famous; distinguished: *an eminent poet.* adjective.

em is sar y (em′ə ser′ē), person sent on a mission or errand. noun, plural **em is sar ies.**

e mit (i mit′), send out; give off: *The sun emits light and heat. Volcanoes emit lava. The trapped lion emitted roars of rage.* verb, **e mit ted, e mit ting.**

e mo tion (i mō′shən), a strong feeling of any kind. Joy, grief, fear, hate, love, anger, and excitement are emotions. noun.

e mo tion al (i mō′shə nəl), 1 of the emotions: *A person who is always afraid may be suffering from a serious emotional disorder.* 2 appealing to the emotions: *The speaker made an emotional plea for money to help crippled children.* 3 easily excited: *Emotional people are likely to cry if they hear sad music or read sad stories.* adjective.

em per or (em′pər ər), 1 man who is the ruler of an empire. 2 ruler who has the title of "emperor." Japan has an emperor. noun.

em pha sis (em′fə sis), 1 stress; importance: *That school puts emphasis on arithmetic and reading.* 2 special force of voice put on particular words or syllables: *In reading, our teacher puts emphasis upon the most important words.* noun, plural **em pha ses** (em′fə sēz′).

em pha size (em′fə sīz), 1 give special force to; stress; make important: *He emphasized her name by saying it very loudly.* 2 call attention to: *The large number of automobile accidents emphasizes the need for careful driving.* verb, **em pha sized, em pha siz ing.**

em phat ic (em fat′ik), 1 said or done with force; meant to stand out; clear; positive: *Her answer was an emphatic "No!"* 2 very noticeable; striking: *The club made an emphatic success of its party.* adjective.

em phat i cal ly (em fat′ik lē), in an emphatic manner. adverb.

em pire (em′pīr), 1 group of nations or states under one ruler or government. 2 country that has an emperor or empress. 3 power; rule: *India was once under the empire of Great Britain.* noun.

em ploy (em ploi′), 1 give work and pay to: *That big factory employs many workers.* 2 service for pay; employment: *There are many workers in the employ of that big factory.* 3 use: *You employ a knife, fork, and spoon in eating.* 4 keep busy: *She employed herself in reading.* 1,3,4 verb, 2 noun.

em ploy ee (em ploi′ē), person who works for some person or firm for pay. noun.

em ploy er (em ploi′ər), person or firm that employs one or more persons. noun.

em ploy ment (em ploi′mənt), 1 work; job: *She had no difficulty finding employment. His employment was sorting mail.* 2 employing or being employed: *A large office requires the employment of many people.* 3 use: *The painter was clever in his employment of brushes and colors.* noun.

em pow er (em pou′ər), give power or authority to: *The secretary was empowered to sign certain contracts.* verb.

em press (em′pris), 1 wife of an emperor. 2 woman who is the ruler of an empire. noun, plural **em press es.**

emp ti ness (emp′tē nis), being empty; lack of contents. noun.

emp ty (emp′tē), 1 with nothing in it: *The birds had gone, and their nest was left empty.* 2 pour out or take out all that is in (a thing): *He emptied his glass quickly.* 3 flow out: *The Mississippi River empties into the Gulf of Mexico.* 4 not real; without meaning: *An empty promise is one that you do not plan to keep.* 1,4 adjective, **emp ti er, emp ti est;** 2,3 verb, **emp tied, emp ty ing.**

em u la tion (em′yə lā′shən), imitation in order to equal or excel; desire to equal or excel: *Emulation of the lives of great people influences many ambitious young persons.* noun.

e mul sion (i mul′shən), mixture of liquids that do not dissolve in each other. In an emulsion one of the liquids contains tiny drops of the other evenly distributed throughout. noun.

en a ble (en ā′bəl), make able; give ability, power, or means to: *Airplanes enable people to travel great distances rapidly.* verb, **en a bled, en a bling.**

en act (en akt′), 1 make into law: *Congress enacted a bill to restrict the sale of guns.* 2 act out; play: *He enacted the part of Long John Silver very well.* verb.

e nam el (i nam′əl), 1 a glasslike substance melted and then cooled to make a smooth, hard surface. Different colors of enamel are used to cover or decorate metal or pottery. See picture. 2 paint used to make a smooth, hard, glossy surface. 3 the smooth, hard, glossy outer layer that covers and protects a tooth. 4 cover or decorate with enamel. 1-3 noun, 4 verb.

en camp (en kamp′), make camp; live in tents for a time: *It took the scouts an hour to encamp.* verb.

en camp ment (en kamp′mənt), 1 forming a camp. 2 place where a camp is; camp. See picture. noun.

en chant (en chant′), 1 use magic on; put under a spell: *The witch had enchanted the princess.* 2 delight greatly; charm: *The music enchanted us all.* verb. [*Enchant* comes from a Latin word meaning "to chant or sing words having magic power."]

en chant ment (en chant′mənt), 1 the use of magic spells; spell or charm: *In "The Wizard of Oz" Dorothy finds herself at home again by the enchantment of the Good Witch.* 2 something that delights or charms: *We felt the enchantment of the moonlight on the lake.* noun.

en cir cle (en sėr′kəl), 1 form a circle around; surround: *Trees encircled the pond.* 2 go in a circle around: *The moon encircles the earth.* verb, **en cir cled, en cir cling.**

en close (en klōz′), 1 shut in on all sides; surround: *The little park was enclosed by tall apartment buildings.* 2 put a wall or fence around: *We are going to enclose our backyard to keep dogs out.* 3 put in an envelope along with a letter: *He*

a hat	i it	oi oil	ch child	a in about
ā age	ī ice	ou out	ng long	e in taken
ä far	o hot	u cup	sh she	ə = { i in pencil
e let	ō open	u̇ put	th thin	o in lemon
ē equal	ô order	ü rule	ŦH then	u in circus
ėr term			zh measure	

encumber—A soldier should not be **encumbered** with too much equipment.

enamel (definition 1)
a pin made of enamel

encampment (definition 2)—an encampment of British soldiers in India a hundred years ago

enclosed a check when he mailed his order. verb,
en closed, en clos ing. Also spelled **inclose.**

en clo sure (en klō′zhər), **1** an enclosed place: *A pen is an enclosure for animals.* **2** thing that encloses: *A wall or fence is an enclosure.* **3** thing enclosed: *The envelope contained a letter and $5 as an enclosure.* **4** enclosing or being enclosed. *noun.* Also spelled **inclosure.**

en com pass (en kum′pəs), go or reach all the way around; encircle: *The atmosphere encompasses the earth. verb.*

en core (äng′kôr), **1** once more; again: *The audience liked the song so much they shouted, "Encore! Encore!"* **2** an additional song or piece of music given in answer to the applause of the audience. **1** *interjection,* **2** *noun.*

en coun ter (en koun′tər), **1** meet unexpectedly: *What if we should encounter a bear?* **2** unexpected meeting: *A fortunate encounter brought the two friends together after a long separation.* **3** be faced with: *She encountered many difficulties before the job was done.* **4** meet as an enemy: *He encountered the strange knight in hand-to-hand conflict.* **5** a meeting of enemies; fight; battle: *The two armies had a desperate encounter.* **1,3,4** *verb,* **2,5** *noun.*

en cour age (en kėr′ij), **1** give hope, courage, or confidence to; urge on: *The cheers of the crowd encouraged the players to try to win.* **2** give help to; be favorable to: *Sunlight encourages the growth of green plants. verb,* **en cour aged, en cour ag ing.**

en cour age ment (en kėr′ij mənt), **1** urging on toward success. **2** something that gives hope, courage, or confidence. *noun.*

en croach (en krōch′), **1** go beyond proper or usual limits: *The sea encroached upon the shore and covered the beach.* **2** trespass upon the property or rights of another; intrude: *The cattle from the next farm have been encroaching on our land. verb.*

en crust (en krust′), cover with a crust or hard coating: *The inside of the kettle was encrusted with rust. verb.*

en cum ber (en kum′bər), to burden; hold back; hinder. See picture. *verb.*

en cy clo pe di a (en sī′klə pē′dē ə), book or set of books giving information on all branches of knowledge, with its articles arranged alphabetically. *noun.*

end (end), **1** last part: *He read to the end of the book.* **2** part where a thing begins or where it stops: *Every stick has two ends. Drive to the end of this road.* **3** bring or come to its last part; finish: *Let us end this fight.* **4** purpose; what is aimed at in doing something: *She had this end in mind—to do her work without a mistake.* **5** result; outcome: *It is hard to tell what the end will be.* **6** a football player at either end of the line. **1,2,4-6** *noun,* **3** *verb.*

en dan ger (en dān′jər), cause danger to: *Fire endangered the hotel's guests.* See picture. *verb.*

en dan gered (en dān′jərd), liable to become extinct: *an endangered species. adjective.*

en dear (en dir′), make dear: *Their kindness endeared them to me. verb.*

en deav or (en dev′ər), 1 try hard; make an effort; strive: *A runner endeavors to win a race.* 2 an effort; an attempt: *With each endeavor she did better.* 1 *verb,* 2 *noun.*

end ing (en′ding), end; last part: *The story has a sad ending. noun.*

end less (end′lis), 1 having no end; never stopping; lasting or going on forever: *the endless rotation of the earth around the sun.* 2 seeming to have no end: *Doing housework is an endless task.* 3 joined in a circle; without ends: *The chain that turns the back wheel of a bicycle is an endless chain. adjective.*

en dorse (en dôrs′), 1 write one's name on the back of (a check, note, or other document): *He had to endorse the check before the bank would cash it.* 2 approve; support: *They endorsed the plan for a school playground. verb,* **en dorsed, en dors ing.**

en dow (en dou′), 1 give money or property to provide an income for: *Rich people sometimes endow the college they have attended.* 2 give from birth: *Nature endowed him with good looks. verb.*

en dow ment (en dou′mənt), 1 money or property given to a person or institution to provide an income: *This college has a large endowment.* 2 gift; talent: *A good sense of rhythm is a natural endowment. noun.*

en dur ance (en dur′əns *or* en dyur′əns), 1 power to last and to withstand hard wear: *A runner must have great endurance to run 30 miles in a day.* 2 power to stand something without giving out; power to put up with something: *Her endurance of pain is remarkable. noun.*

en dure (en dur′ *or* en dyur′), 1 last; keep on: *Metal and stone endure for a long time.* 2 put up with; bear; stand: *The pioneers endured many hardships. verb,* **en dured, en dur ing.**

end ways (end′wāz′), 1 on end. 2 with the end forward. 3 lengthwise. 4 end to end. *adverb.*

en e my (en′ə mē), 1 person or group that hates or tries to harm another. Two countries fighting against each other are enemies. 2 anything that will harm: *Frost is an enemy of flowers. noun, plural* **en e mies.**

en er get ic (en′ər jet′ik), full of energy; active; eager to work; full of force: *Cool autumn days make us feel energetic. adjective.*

en er get i cal ly (en′ər jet′ik lē), with energy; vigorously. *adverb.*

en er gy (en′ər jē), 1 vigor; will to work: *I was so full of energy that I could not keep still.* 2 power to work or act; force: *All our energies were used in keeping the fire from spreading.* 3 the capacity for doing work, such as lifting or moving an object. Light, heat, and electricity are different forms of energy. Atomic energy is the energy released by atoms when they are split. *noun, plural* **en er gies.**

en fold (en fōld′), 1 fold in; wrap up: *I enfolded myself in a warm blanket.* 2 embrace; clasp: *The little boy enfolded the puppy in his arms. verb.*

en force (en fôrs′), force obedience to; cause to be carried out: *The police will enforce the laws of the city. verb,* **en forced, en forc ing.**

en force ment (en fôrs′mənt), enforcing: *Strict enforcement of the laws against speeding will reduce automobile accidents. noun.*

en gage (en gāj′), 1 keep oneself busy; be active; take part: *They engaged in conversation.* 2 keep busy; occupy: *Work engages much of his time.* 3 take for use or work; hire: *We engaged two rooms in the hotel.* 4 promise or pledge to marry: *He is engaged to my sister. My sister and he are engaged.* 5 attract: *Bright objects engage a baby's attention.* 6 promise; bind oneself; pledge: *He engaged himself as an apprentice to a printer.* 7 fit into; lock together. The teeth in one gear engage with those in another. See picture. 8 start a battle against; attack: *Our soldiers engaged the enemy. verb,* **en gaged, en gag ing.**

en gaged (en gājd′), 1 pledged to marry: *The engaged girl wore a diamond ring.* 2 busy; occupied: *Engaged in conversation, they did not see us. adjective.*

en gage ment (en gāj′mənt), 1 promise; pledge: *She tries to fulfill all of her engagements.* 2 promise to marry: *Their parents announced the young couple's engagement.* 3 meeting with someone at a certain time; an appointment: *He made a point of being punctual in all his engagements.* 4 period of being hired; time of use or work: *The actor had an engagement of three weeks in a play.* 5 battle. *noun.*

en gag ing (en gā′jing), attractive; pleasing: *an engaging smile. adjective.*

en gine (en′jən), 1 machine that has various parts which work together to make something move or run. Cars and airplanes have engines. 2 machine that pulls a railroad train. *noun.*

en gi neer (en′jə nir′), 1 person who takes care of or runs engines. 2 person who is an expert in engineering. 3 guide; manage with skill: *She engineered the whole job from start to finish.* 1,2 *noun,* 3 *verb.*

en gi neer ing (en′jə nir′ing), science of planning and building engines, machines, roads, bridges, canals, and the like. *noun.*

Eng land (ing′glənd), the largest division of Great Britain, in the southern part. *noun.*

Eng lish (ing′glish), 1 of or having something to do with England, its people, or their language. 2 people of England. 3 language of England. English is spoken also in Ireland, Scotland, Canada, the United States, and many other places. 1 *adjective,* 2 *noun plural,* 3 *noun singular.*

English horn, a wooden musical instrument resembling an oboe, but larger and having a lower tone.

English sparrow, a small, brownish-gray bird, now very common in America.

en grave (en grāv′), 1 carve in; carve in an artistic way: *The jeweler engraved the boy's initials on the*

endanger
The whooping crane is **endangered** and may become extinct. Less than 100 are still alive.

engage (definition 7)
gears engaged   gears not engaged

engross—The men were **engrossed** in watching the contest.

"Nearing the Issue at the Cockpit," Horace Bonham. In the collection of The Corcoran Gallery of Art

a hat	i it	oi oil	ch child		a in about
ā age	ī ice	ou out	ng long		e in taken
ä far	o hot	u cup	sh she	ə =	i in pencil
e let	ō open	u̇ put	th thin		o in lemon
ē equal	ô order	ü rule	ŦH then		u in circus
ėr term			zh measure		

back of the watch. **2** cut (a picture, design, or map) in lines on wood, stone, metal, or glass plates for printing. **3** fix firmly: *My childhood home is engraved on my memory.* verb, **en graved, en grav ing.**

en grav ing (en grā′ving), **1** art or act of a person who engraves. **2** picture made from an engraved plate; print. *noun.*

en gross (en grōs′), occupy wholly; fill the mind of. See picture. *verb.*

en gulf (en gulf′), swallow up; overwhelm: *A wave engulfed the small boat.* verb.

en hance (en hans′), add to; make greater: *Health enhances beauty. The growth of a city often enhances the value of land close to it.* verb, **en hanced, en hanc ing.**

en joy (en joi′), **1** have or use with joy; be happy with; take pleasure in: *The children enjoyed their visit to the museum.* **2** have as an advantage or benefit: *He enjoys good health.* verb.
    enjoy oneself, be happy; have a good time: *Enjoy yourself at the party.*

en joy a ble (en joi′ə bəl), giving joy; pleasant. *adjective.*

en joy ment (en joi′mənt), **1** pleasure; joy; delight. **2** a having as an advantage or benefit: *She has the enjoyment of good health.* noun.

en large (en lärj′), **1** make larger: *The factory was enlarged to make room for more machinery.* **2** grow larger: *The balloon enlarged as we pumped air into it.* verb, **en larged, en larg ing.**

en large ment (en lärj′mənt), **1** making larger. **2** an addition that makes something else larger. **3** photograph or other thing that has been made larger. *noun.*

en light en (en līt′n), make clear; give truth and knowledge to; inform; instruct: *She found the lesson very enlightening.* verb.

en list (en list′), **1** join the army, navy, or some other branch of the armed forces: *He enlisted in the navy.* **2** get to join some branch of the armed forces: *Many men were enlisted during the war.* **3** get to join in some cause or undertaking: *We enlisted her help in building our new club house.* verb.

en liv en (en lī′vən), make lively, active, gay, or cheerful: *Spring enlivens all nature. Bright curtains enliven a dull room.* verb.

en mi ty (en′mə tē), the feeling that enemies have for each other; hatred. *noun, plural* **en mi ties.**

e nor mous (i nôr′məs), very, very large; huge: *Long ago enormous animals lived on the earth.* adjective.

e nough (i nuf′), **1** as many as needed: *Are there enough seats for all?* **2** as much as needed: *Has he had enough to eat?* **3** sufficiently; until no more is needed or wanted: *Have you played enough?* **1** adjective, **2** noun, **3** adverb.

en rage (en rāj′), make very angry; make furious; madden: *The dog was enraged by the teasing.* verb, **en raged, en rag ing.**

en rich (en rich′), make rich or richer: *An education enriches your mind. Adding vitamins or minerals to food enriches it. Fertilizer enriches the soil.* verb.

en roll or **en rol** (en rōl′), 1 write in a list: *The secretary enrolled our names.* 2 have one's name written in a list. 3 make a member: *He enrolled his son in a music school.* 4 become a member: *Her mother enrolled in a boating class.* verb, **en rolled, en roll ing.**

en roll ment or **en rol ment** (en rōl′mənt), 1 enrolling: *Enrollment took place in the fall.* 2 number enrolled: *The school has an enrollment of 200 students.* noun.

en route (än rüt′), on the way: *We shall stop at Philadelphia en route from New York to Washington.*

en sign (en′sīn or en′sən for 1; en′sən for 2), 1 flag or banner: *The ensign of the United States is the Stars and Stripes.* 2 officer in the navy ranking next below a lieutenant, junior grade. noun.

en slave (en slāv′), make a slave of; take away freedom from. verb, **en slaved, en slav ing.**

en sure (en shùr′), 1 make sure or certain: *Careful planning and hard work ensured the success of the party.* 2 make sure of getting; secure: *A letter of introduction will ensure you an interview.* 3 make safe; protect: *Proper clothing ensured us against suffering from the cold.* verb, **en sured, en sur ing.**

en tan gle (en tang′gəl), 1 get twisted up and caught. See picture. 2 involve; get into difficulty: *Do not entangle us in your schemes.* verb, **en tan gled, en tan gling.**

en tan gle ment (en tang′gəl mənt), 1 entangling or being entangled: *The new nation kept out of entanglements with other countries.* 2 thing that entangles; snare; something hard to get out of or to get through: *The trenches were protected by barbed wire entanglements.* noun.

en ter (en′tər), 1 go into; come into: *He entered the house.* 2 go in; come in: *Let them enter.* 3 join; become a part or member of: *She entered the contest.* 4 cause to join or enter; enroll: *Parents*

entangle (definition 1)—The fishing net is entangled.

enter their children in school. 5 begin; start: *After years of training, the doctor entered the practice of medicine.* 6 write or print in a book or list: *Words are entered alphabetically in a dictionary.* 7 make a record of: *The teller entered the deposit in my bank book.* verb.

en ter prise (en′tər prīz), 1 an important, difficult, or dangerous undertaking: *A trip into space is a daring enterprise.* 2 any undertaking; project: *She has two enterprises—raising hamsters and collecting coins.* 3 readiness to start projects: *The American pioneers were people of great enterprise.* noun.

en ter pris ing (en′tər prī′zing), likely to start projects; ready to face difficulties: *an enterprising young businessman.* adjective.

en ter tain (en′tər tān′), 1 keep pleasantly interested; please or amuse: *The circus entertained the children.* 2 have as a guest: *She entertained ten people at dinner.* 3 have guests; provide entertainment for guests: *He entertains a great deal.* 4 take into the mind; consider: *I refuse to entertain such a foolish idea.* verb.

en ter tain er (en′tər tā′nər), 1 person who entertains. 2 singer, musician, or actor who performs in public. noun.

en ter tain ing (en′tər tā′ning), interesting; pleasing or amusing. adjective.

en ter tain ment (en′tər tān′mənt), 1 something that interests, pleases, or amuses, such as a show or a circus. 2 act of entertaining: *We devoted ourselves to the entertainment of our guests.* 3 condition of being entertained: *I played the piano for their entertainment.* noun.

en thrall or **en thral** (en thrôl′), enchant; fascinate; charm: *The pilot enthralled her audience with stories about stunt flying.* verb, **en thralled, en thrall ing.**

en thuse (en thüz′), 1 show enthusiasm: *She enthused over the idea of going on a picnic.* 2 fill with enthusiasm: *The plan for a trip out West enthused the family.* verb, **en thused, en thus ing.**

en thu si asm (en thü′zē az′əm), eager interest; zeal: *Going swimming aroused our enthusiasm.* noun.

en thu si ast (en thü′zē ast), person who is filled with enthusiasm: *a baseball enthusiast.* noun.

en thu si as tic (en thü′zē as′tik), full of enthusiasm; eagerly interested: *My little brother is enthusiastic about going to kindergarten.* adjective.

en thu si as ti cal ly (en thü′zē as′tik lē), with enthusiasm. adverb.

en tice (en tīs′), attract; lead into something by raising hopes or desires; tempt: *The smell of food enticed the hungry children into the house.* verb, **en ticed, en tic ing.**

en tire (en tīr′), whole; complete; having all the parts: *The entire class behaved very well on the trip.* adjective.

en tire ly (en tīr′lē), wholly; completely; fully: *He is entirely wrong.* adverb.

en tire ty (en tīr′tē), completeness; the whole. noun, plural **en tire ties.**

in its entirety, wholly; completely: *He enjoyed the concert in its entirety.*

en ti tle (en tī/tl), **1** give a claim or right: *The one who wins is entitled to first prize.* **2** give the title of; name: *I entitled my theme "Looking for Treasure."* *verb,* **en ti tled, en ti tling.**

en trance[1] (en/trəns), **1** act of entering: *The actor's entrance was greeted with applause.* **2** place by which to enter; door or passageway: *The entrance to the hotel was blocked with baggage.* **3** right to enter; permission to enter: *Entrance to the exhibit is on weekdays only.* *noun.*

en trance[2] (en trans/), delight; fill with joy: *From the first note the singer's voice entranced the audience.* *verb,* **en tranced, en tranc ing.**

en treat (en trēt/), keep asking earnestly; beg and pray: *I entreated my parents to send me to summer camp. The prisoners entreated their captors to let them go.* *verb.*

en treat y (en trē/tē), earnest request: *My parents gave in to my entreaties.* *noun, plural* **en treat ies.**

en trust (en trust/), **1** trust; charge with a trust: *We entrusted the class treasurer with all the money for bus fares on our class trip.* **2** give the care of; hand over for safekeeping: *While traveling, they entrusted their child to her grandparents.* *verb.*

en try (en/trē), **1** act of entering: *His sudden entry startled me.* **2** place by which to enter; way to enter. An entrance hall is an entry. **3** thing written or printed in a book or list. Each word explained in a dictionary is an entry or **entry word.** **4** person or thing that takes part in a contest: *The car race had nine entries.* *noun, plural* **en tries.**

en twine (en twīn/), twine together or twine around. *verb,* **en twined, en twin ing.**

e nu me rate (i nü/mə rāt/ *or* i nyü/mə rāt/), **1** name one by one; list: *He enumerated the capitals of the 50 states.* **2** find the number of; count. *verb,* **e nu me rat ed, e nu me rat ing.**

e nun ci ate (i nun/sē āt), speak or pronounce words: *Radio and television announcers must enunciate very clearly.* *verb,* **e nun ci at ed, e nun ci at ing.**

e nun ci a tion (i nun/sē ā/shən), manner of pronouncing words. *noun.*

en vel op (en vel/əp), wrap, cover, or hide: *The baby was so enveloped in blankets that we could hardly see her face. Fog enveloped the village.* *verb.*

en ve lope (en/və lōp), **1** a paper cover in which a letter or anything flat can be mailed. It can usually be folded over and sealed by wetting a gummed edge. **2** wrapper; covering. *noun.*

en vi a ble (en/vē ə bəl), to be envied; desirable: *She has an enviable school record.* *adjective.*

en vi ous (en/vē əs), feeling or showing discontent or ill will because you wish to have something someone else has: *The weak are often envious of the strong.* *adjective.*

en vi ron ment (en vī/rən mənt), all the surrounding things, conditions, and influences that have to do with the growth of living things: *A child's character is greatly influenced by the environment at home. A plant will often grow differently in a different environment.* *noun.*

en vi ron men tal (en vī/rən men/tl), having to do with environment: *the environmental sciences.* *adjective.*

en voy (en/voi), **1** messenger. **2** diplomat next below an ambassador in rank. *noun.*

en vy (en/vē), **1** discontent or ill will at another's good fortune because you wish it had been yours; dislike for a person who has what you want: *All of us were filled with envy when we saw her new bicycle.* **2** object of such feeling; person or thing envied: *Their new car was the envy of the neighborhood.* **3** feel envy toward: *Some people envy the rich.* **4** feel envy because of: *He envied his friend's success.* 1,2 *noun, plural* **en vies;** 3,4 *verb,* **en vied, en vy ing.**

ep i dem ic (ep/ə dem/ik), rapid spreading of a disease so that many people have it at the same time: *All the schools in the city were closed during the epidemic of measles.* *noun.*

ep i sode (ep/ə sōd), a single happening or group of happenings in real life or a story: *Being elected class president was an important episode in her life at school.* *noun.*

ep och (ep/ək), **1** period of time; era: *There were few peaceful epochs in the history of our country.* **2** period of time in which striking things happened: *The years of the Civil War were an epoch in the United States.* *noun.*

e qual (ē/kwəl), **1** the same in amount, size, number, value, or rank: *Ten dimes are equal to one dollar. All persons are considered equal before the law.* **2** be the same as: *Four times five equals twenty.* **3** person or thing that is equal: *In spelling she had no equal.* **4** make or do something equal to: *Our team equaled the other team's score, and the game ended in a tie.* 1 *adjective,* 2,4 *verb,* 3 *noun.*
equal to, strong enough for: *One horse is not equal to pulling a load of five tons.*

e qual i ty (i kwol/ə tē), exact likeness in amount, size, number, value, or rank. *noun, plural* **e qual i ties.**

e qual ize (ē/kwə līz), make equal. *verb,* **e qual ized, e qual iz ing.**

e qual ly (ē/kwə lē), in equal shares; in an equal manner; to an equal degree: *Divide the pie equally. My sister and brother are equally talented.* *adverb.*

e qua tion (i kwā/zhən), statement that two quantities are equal. EXAMPLE: $4 + 5 = 9.$ *noun.*

e qua tor (i kwā/tər), an imaginary circle around the middle of the earth, halfway between the North Pole and the South Pole. The United States is north of the equator; Australia is south of it. *noun.*

e qua to ri al (ē/kwə tôr/ē əl), **1** of or near the equator: *Ecuador is an equatorial country.* **2** like conditions at or near the equator: *The weather this week was hot and humid; it was almost equatorial.* *adjective.*

a hat	**i** it	**oi** oil	**ch** child	a in about
ā age	**ī** ice	**ou** out	**ng** long	e in taken
ä far	**o** hot	**u** cup	**sh** she	ə = { i in pencil
e let	**ō** open	**ù** put	**th** thin	o in lemon
ē equal	**ô** order	**ü** rule	**ŦH** then	u in circus
ėr term			**zh** measure	

equilibrium—The bareback rider maintained her **equilibrium** while standing on the horse's back.

e qui lib ri um (ē′kwə lib′rē əm), balance: *Scales are in equilibrium when the weights on each side are equal.* See picture. *noun.*

e qui nox (ē′kwə noks), either of the two times in the year when the center of the sun crosses the equator and day and night are of equal length in all parts of the earth. It occurs about March 21 and September 22. *noun, plural* **e qui nox es.**

e quip (i kwip′), fit out; provide; supply with all that is needed: *The scouts equipped themselves with canteens and food for the hike. Is the ship fully equipped for its voyage? verb,* **e quipped, e quip ping.**

e quip ment (i kwip′mənt), **1** fitting out; providing: *The equipment of the expedition took six months.* **2** outfit; what one is equipped with; supplies: *We keep our camping equipment in order. noun.*

eq ui ta ble (ek′wə tə bəl), fair; just: *It is equitable to pay a person good wages for work well done. adjective.*

eq ui ty (ek′wə tē), fairness; justice: *The judge was noted for the equity of her decisions. noun, plural* **eq ui ties.**

e quiv a lent (i kwiv′ə lənt), **1** equal: *Nodding your head is equivalent to saying yes.* **2** something equivalent: *Five pennies are the equivalent of a nickel.* **1** *adjective,* **2** *noun.*

-er¹, suffix meaning person or thing that _____s: Follow*er* means a *person or thing that* follows.

-er², suffix meaning more: Soft*er* means *more* soft. Slow*er* means *more slow.*

er a (ir′ə), **1** an age in history; historical period: *The years from 1817 to 1824 in United States history are often called the Era of Good Feeling.* **2** period of time starting from some important or significant happening or date: *We live in the 20th century of the Christian era. noun.*

e rad i cate (i rad′ə kāt), get rid of entirely; destroy completely: *Yellow fever has been eradicated in the United States but it still exists in some other countries. verb,* **e rad i cat ed, e rad i cat ing.**

e rase (i rās′), rub out; wipe out: *He erased the wrong answer and wrote in the right one. verb,* **e rased, e ras ing.**

e ras er (i rā′sər), something used to erase marks made with pencil, ink, or chalk: *My pencil is equipped with an eraser made of rubber. noun.*

ere (er *or* ar), an old word meaning before: *He will come ere long. preposition, conjunction.*

e rect (i rekt′), **1** straight up; not tipping; not bending: *A telephone pole stands erect.* **2** put straight up; set upright: *They erected a television antenna on the roof.* **3** put up; build: *That house was erected forty years ago.* **1** *adjective,* **2,3** *verb.*

e rec tion (i rek′shən), setting up; raising: *The erection of the tent took only a few minutes. noun.*

er mine (ėr′mən), **1** weasel that is brown in summer, but white in winter, except for a black tip on its tail. See picture. **2** its soft, white fur, used on the robes of English judges and for coats and trimming. *noun, plural* **er mines** *or* **er mine.**

e rode (i rōd′), eat out; eat away; wear away: *Acid erodes metal. Running water erodes soil and rock. verb,* **e rod ed, e rod ing.**

e ro sion (i rō′zhən), eating away; being worn away little by little: *In geography, we study the erosion of the earth by wind and water.* See picture. *noun.*

err (ėr *or* er), **1** go wrong; make a mistake: *Everyone errs at some time or other.* **2** do wrong; sin: *To err is human; to forgive, divine. verb.*

er rand (er′ənd), **1** trip to do something: *She has gone on an errand to the store.* **2** what one is sent to do: *I did ten errands in one trip. noun.*

er rat ic (ə rat′ik), **1** uncertain; irregular: *An erratic clock is not dependable.* **2** unusual; odd: *erratic ideas. adjective.*

er ro ne ous (ə rō′nē əs), mistaken; incorrect; wrong: *Years ago many people held the erroneous belief that the earth was flat. adjective.*

er ror (er′ər), **1** mistake; something done that is wrong; something that is not the way it ought to be: *I failed my test because of errors in spelling.* **2** in baseball, a fielder's mistake that either allows a batter to reach first, or a runner to advance one or more bases. *noun.*

e rupt (i rupt′), burst forth: *Lava and ashes erupted from the volcano.* See picture. *verb.*

e rup tion (i rup′shən), **1** bursting forth: *an eruption of lava.* **2** red spots on the skin; rash: *In measles, there is an eruption on the body. noun.*

es ca la tor (es′kə lā′tər), a moving stairway: *The store had both an elevator and an escalator. noun.*

erupt—a volcano erupting

ermine (definition 1)—11 inches (28 centimeters) long with the tail

erosion—The shape of this rock was caused by erosion.

a hat	i it	oi oil	ch child		a in about
ā age	ī ice	ou out	ng long		e in taken
ä far	o hot	u cup	sh she	ə =	i in pencil
e let	ō open	u̇ put	th thin		o in lemon
ē equal	ô order	ü rule	ᴛʜ then		u in circus
ėr term			zh measure		

es cape (e skāp′), **1** get free; get out and away: *The bird escaped from its cage.* **2** keep free or safe from: *We all escaped the measles.* **3** act of escaping: *Their escape was aided by the thick fog.* **4** way of escaping: *There was no escape from the trap.* 1,2 *verb,* **es caped, es cap ing;** 3,4 *noun.*

es cort (es′kôrt *for 1-3;* e skôrt′ *for 4*), **1** one or more persons going with other persons, or with valuable goods, to see that they keep safe, or to honor them: *An escort of several city officials accompanied the famous visitor.* **2** one or more ships or airplanes serving as a guard: *During World War II destroyers often served as escorts to tankers.* **3** man who goes on a date with a woman: *Her escort to the party was a tall young man.* **4** go with to keep safe or to honor: *Warships escorted the steamer. I enjoyed escorting my cousin to the movies.* 1-3 *noun,* 4 *verb.*

Es ki mo (es′kə mō), **1** member of a people living in the arctic regions of North America and northeastern Asia. **2** language of the Eskimos. **3** of or having to do with the Eskimos or their language. 1,2 *noun, plural* **Es ki mos** *or* **Es ki mo** *for* 1; 3 *adjective.*

e soph a gus (ē sof′ə gəs), passage for food from the mouth to the stomach. *noun.*

es pe cial (e spesh′əl), special; more than others: *Your birthday is an especial day for you. adjective.*

es pe cial ly (e spesh′ə lē), more than others; particularly; principally; chiefly: *This book is especially designed for students. adverb.*

es pi o nage (es′pē ə nij), spying; the use of spies. Nations use espionage to find out other countries' secrets. *noun.*

es say (es′ā), a short composition on a particular subject. *noun.*

es sence (es′ns), that which makes a thing what it is; necessary part or parts: *Being thoughtful of others is the essence of politeness. noun.*

es sen tial (ə sen′shəl), **1** needed to make a thing what it is; necessary; very important: *Good food is essential to good health.* **2** an absolutely necessary element or quality: *Learn the essentials first; then learn the details.* 1 *adjective,* 2 *noun.*

es sen tial ly (ə sen′shə lē), in essence; in essentials; in an essential manner. *adverb.*

-est, suffix meaning most: *Warmest means most warm. Slowest means most slow.*

es tab lish (e stab′lish), **1** set up and keep going for a long time: *to establish a government, to establish a business. The English established colonies in America.* **2** settle in a position; set up in business: *A new doctor has established himself on this street.* **3** show beyond dispute; prove: *I established my innocence by showing that I was at school when the cookies were stolen. verb.*

estate (definition 1)—an English estate of the 1600's

etching (definition 1)

everglade

es tab lish ment (e stab′lish mənt), **1** establishing: *The establishment of the business took several years.* **2** something established. A household, a large store, a church, or an army is called an establishment. *noun.*

es tate (e stāt′), **1** a large piece of land. See picture. **2** that which a person owns: *When the rich woman died, she left an estate of two million dollars.* Land and buildings are called real estate. *noun.*

es teem (e stēm′), **1** think highly of: *We esteem courage.* **2** a very favorable opinion; high regard: *Courage is held in esteem.* **1** *verb,* **2** *noun.*

es ti mate (es′tə mit *for 1;* es′tə māt *for 2*), **1** judgment or opinion about how much, how many, or how good: *Her estimate of the length of the fish was 15 inches.* **2** form a judgment or an opinion: *We estimated it would take four hours to weed the garden.* **1** *noun,* **2** *verb,* **es ti mat ed, es ti mat ing.**

es ti ma tion (es′tə mā′shən), **1** opinion; judgment: *In my estimation, your plan will not work.* **2** esteem; respect: *The doctor was held in high estimation by the community. noun.*

etc., et cetera. *Etc.* is usually read "and so forth." The definition of *etching* below uses *etc.* after the words *metal* and *glass.* This means that *etching* can be done on other items similar to metal and glass.

et cet er a (et set′ər ə), and so forth; and so on; and the rest; and the like. [*Et cetera* is a Latin phrase meaning "and the others."]

etch (ech), **1** engrave (a design) on a metal plate by acid that eats lines into it. Filled with ink, the lines of the design will reproduce a copy on paper. **2** use this method of producing designs and pictures. *verb.*

etch ing (ech′ing), **1** picture or design printed from an etched plate. See picture. **2** process of engraving a drawing or design on metal, glass, etc., by means of acid. *noun.*

e ter nal (i tėr′nl), **1** without beginning or ending; lasting throughout all time. **2** always and forever the same: *the eternal truths.* **3** seeming to go on forever: *When will we have an end to this eternal noise? adjective.*

e ter ni ty (i tėr′nə tē), **1** all time; all the past and all the future. **2** period of time that seems endless: *I waited in the dentist's office for an eternity. noun, plural* **e ter ni ties.**

-eth, suffix meaning: number _____ in order or position in a series. Sixti*eth* means *number* sixty *in order or position in a series.* The suffix *-th* is used to form numbers like *sixth.*

e ther (ē′thər), liquid that causes one to become unconscious when its fumes are inhaled. It is sometimes used in operations so that a person won't feel pain. *noun.*

e ther e al (i thir′ē əl), **1** light; airy; delicate. **2** not of the earth; heavenly: *An angel is an ethereal messenger. adjective.*

eth nic (eth′nik), of or having to do with a group of people who have the same race, nationality, or culture. *adjective.*

et i quette (et′ə ket), the usual rules for behavior

in society: *Etiquette requires that we eat peas with a fork, not a knife.* noun.

eu ca lyp tus (yü′kə lip′təs), a very tall tree that grows mainly in Australia. It is valued for its timber and for a medicinal oil made from its leaves. *noun, plural* **eu ca lyp tus es.**

Eur ope (yùr′əp), continent west of Asia and east of the Atlantic Ocean. Only one other continent, Australia, is smaller than Europe. France, Sweden, and Greece are countries in Europe. *noun.*

Eur o pe an (yùr′ə pē′ən), **1** of Europe; having something to do with Europe or its people; from Europe. **2** person born or living in Europe. Frenchmen, Germans, and Spaniards are Europeans. 1 *adjective,* 2 *noun.*

e vac u ate (i vak′yü āt), **1** leave empty; withdraw from: *People quickly evacuated the burning building.* **2** make empty: *to evacuate the stomach.* verb, **e vac u at ed, e vac u at ing.**

e vade (i vād′), get away from by trickery; avoid by cleverness: *The thief evaded the police and escaped. When my parents asked who broke the lamp, I tried to evade the question by saying, "I wonder who!"* verb, **e vad ed, e vad ing.**

e val u ate (i val′yü āt), find out the value or the amount of: *An expert will evaluate the old furniture you wish to sell.* verb, **e val u at ed, e val u at ing.**

e vap o rate (i vap′ə rāt′), **1** turn into vapor: *Boiling water evaporates rapidly.* **2** remove water from: *Heat is used to evaporate milk.* **3** vanish; disappear: *My good resolutions evaporated soon after New Year.* verb, **e vap o rat ed, e vap o rat ing.**

e vap o ra tion (i vap′ə rā′shən), evaporating: *Wet clothes on a line become dry by evaporation of the water in them.* noun.

eve (ēv), **1** evening or day before some holiday or special day: *Christmas Eve.* **2** time just before: *Everything was still on the eve of the tornado.* **3** evening. noun.

e ven (ē′vən), **1** level; flat; smooth: *The country is even, with no high hills.* **2** at the same level: *The snow was even with the window.* **3** keeping about the same; regular; uniform: *The car goes with an even motion. This child has an even temper.* **4** equal; no more or less than: *They divided the money in even shares.* **5** make equal or level: *She evened the edges by trimming them.* **6** able to be divided by 2 without a remainder: *2, 4, 6, 8, and 10 are even numbers.* **7** neither more nor less; exact: *Twelve apples make an even dozen.* **8** just: *She left even as you came.* **9** indeed: *He is ready, even eager, to go.* **10** though one would not expect it; as one would not expect: *Even young children can use this device. Even the weather service was surprised by the snowstorm.* **11** still; yet: *You can read even better if you try.* 1-4,6,7 *adjective,* 5 *verb,* 8-11 *adverb.*
even if, although: *I will come, even if it rains.*

eve ning (ēv′ning), the time between sunset and bedtime: *We spent the evening watching TV.* noun.

e vent (i vent′), **1** happening; important happening: *The discovery of America was a great event.* **2** item or contest in a program of sports:

a hat	i it	oi oil	ch child	a in about
ā age	ī ice	ou out	ng long	e in taken
ä far	o hot	u cup	sh she	ə = i in pencil
e let	ō open	ů put	th thin	o in lemon
ē equal	ô order	ü rule	ᴛʜ then	u in circus
ėr term			zh measure	

Running a mile was the last event. noun.
in the event of, in the case of: *In the event of rain, the party will be held indoors.*

e vent ful (i vent′fəl), full of events; having many unusual events: *The class spent an eventful day touring the new zoo.* adjective.

e ven tu al (i ven′chü əl), coming in the end: *After several failures, his eventual success surprised us.* adjective.

e ven tu al ly (i ven′chü ə lē), finally; in the end: *We searched a long time for the key but eventually we found it.* adverb.

ev er (ev′ər), **1** at any time: *Is she ever at home?* **2** at all times; always: *She is ever ready to accept a new challenge.* **3** by any chance; at all: *What did you ever do to make him so angry?* adverb.
ever so, very: *The ocean is ever so deep.*

ev er glade (ev′ər glād), a large swamp or marsh. See picture. noun.

ev er green (ev′ər grēn′), **1** having green leaves all the year. **2** an evergreen plant. Pine, spruce, cedar, ivy, and rhododendrons are evergreens. **3** evergreens, evergreen twigs or branches used for decoration, especially at Christmas. 1 *adjective,* 2,3 *noun.*

ev er last ing (ev′ər las′ting), **1** lasting forever; never stopping: *the everlasting beauty of nature.* **2** lasting too long; tiresome: *Their everlasting complaints annoyed me.* adjective.

ev er more (ev′ər môr′), always; forever: *I shall evermore remember this narrow escape from death.* adverb.

eve ry (ev′rē), each one of the entire number of: *Read every word on the page. Every student must have a book.* adjective.
every now and then, from time to time: *Every now and then we have a frost that ruins the crop.*
every other, every second: *Every other day it's my turn to do the dishes.*

eve ry bod y (ev′rə bud′ē *or* ev′rē bod′ē), every person: *Everybody likes the new principal.* pronoun.

eve ry day (ev′rē dā′), **1** of every day; daily: *Accidents are everyday occurrences.* **2** for every ordinary day; not for Sundays or holidays: *She wears everyday clothes to work.* **3** usual; not exciting: *He had only an everyday story to tell.* adjective.

eve ry one (ev′rē wun *or* ev′rē wən), each one; everybody: *Everyone in the class is here.* pronoun.

eve ry thing (ev′rē thing), **1** every thing; all things: *She did everything she could to help her friend.* **2** something extremely important: *This news means everything to us.* 1 *pronoun,* 2 *noun.*

eve ry where (ev′rē hwer *or* ev′rē hwar), in every place; in all places or lands: *A smile is understood everywhere.* adverb.

ev i dence (ev′ə dəns), **1** facts; proof; anything that shows or makes clear: *The jam on his face was evidence that he had been in the kitchen.* **2** make easy to see or understand; show clearly: *Their smiles evidenced their obvious pleasure.* **1** *noun,* **2** *verb,* **ev i denced, ev i denc ing.**

in evidence, easily seen or noticed: *The damage caused by the flood was much in evidence.*

ev i dent (ev′ə dənt), easy to see or understand; clear; plain: *It was evident that the shattered vase could never be repaired. adjective.*

e vil (ē′vəl), **1** bad; wrong; causing harm: *an evil life, an evil character, an evil plan.* **2** something bad; evil quality or act: *Their thoughts were full of evil.* **3** thing causing harm: *Crime and poverty are some of the evils of society.* **1** *adjective,* **2,3** *noun.*

ev o lu tion (ev′ə lü′shən), gradual development: *the evolution of the flower from the bud, the evolution of one kind of animal or plant from a simpler kind. noun.*

e volve (i volv′), unfold; develop gradually: *Buds evolve into flowers. The modern automobile evolved from the horse and buggy. She evolved a plan for earning money during her summer vacation. verb,* **e volved, e volv ing.**

ewe (yü), a female sheep. *noun.*

ex act (eg zakt′), **1** without any mistake; correct; accurate: *an exact measurement, the exact amount, an exact thinker.* **2** demand and get: *If you do the work, you can exact payment for it.* **1** *adjective,* **2** *verb.*

ex act ing (eg zak′ting), **1** requiring much; hard to please: *An exacting teacher will not permit careless work.* **2** needing hard work, care, or attention: *Flying an airplane is exacting work. adjective.*

ex act ly (eg zakt′lē), **1** without any error; precisely. **2** just so; quite right. *adverb.*

ex ag ge rate (eg zaj′ə rāt′), make too large; say or think something is greater than it is; go beyond the truth: *The little boy exaggerated when he said there were a million cats in the backyard. verb,* **ex ag ge rat ed, ex ag ge rat ing.**

ex ag ge ra tion (eg zaj′ə rā′shən), statement that goes beyond the truth: *It is an exaggeration to say that you would rather die than touch a snake. noun.*

ex alt (eg zôlt′), **1** make high in rank, honor, or power: *The queen exalted the landowner to the rank of earl.* **2** fill with pride or joy or noble feeling: *They were exalted by success. verb.*

ex am i na tion (eg zam′ə nā′shən), **1** examining: *The doctor made a careful examination of my eyes.* **2** test: *an examination in arithmetic. noun.*

ex am ine (eg zam′ən), **1** look at closely and carefully: *The doctor examined the wound.* **2** test; test the knowledge or ability of; ask questions of: *The lawyer examined the witness. verb,* **ex am ined, ex am in ing.**

ex am ple (eg zam′pəl), **1** sample; one thing taken to show what the others are like: *New York is an example of a busy city.* **2** model; pattern: *Children often follow the example set by their parents.* **3** problem in arithmetic: *She wrote the example on the blackboard.* **4** warning to others: *The principal made an example of the students who were tardy by making them come to school early for a week. noun.*

set an example, give, show, or be a model of conduct.

ex as pe rate (eg zas′pə rāt′), irritate very much; annoy greatly; make angry: *The pupils' constant noise exasperated the teacher. verb,* **ex as pe rat ed, ex as pe rat ing.**

ex as pe ra tion (eg zas′pə rā′shən), extreme annoyance; anger; irritation. *noun.*

ex ca vate (ek′skə vāt), **1** make hollow; hollow out: *The tunnel was made by excavating the side of a mountain.* **2** make by digging; dig: *The builders excavated a basement for the new house.* **3** dig out; scoop out: *Big machines excavated the dirt and loaded it into trucks.* **4** uncover by digging: *They excavated an ancient buried city. verb,* **ex ca vat ed, ex ca vat ing.**

ex ca va tion (ek′skə vā′shən), **1** digging out; digging: *The excavation for the basement of our new house took three days.* **2** hole made by digging: *The excavation for the new building was fifty feet across. noun.*

ex ceed (ek sēd′), **1** be more or greater than: *The sum of 5 and 7 exceeds 10. Lifting that heavy trunk exceeds my strength.* **2** do more than; go beyond: *Drivers should not exceed the speed limit. verb.*

ex ceed ing (ek sē′ding), very great; unusual: *She is a girl of exceeding talent. adjective.*

ex ceed ing ly (ek sē′ding lē), very greatly; more than others; very: *Yesterday was an exceedingly hot day. adverb.*

ex cel (ek sel′), **1** be better than; do better than: *He excelled his class in spelling.* **2** be better than others; do better than others: *She excels in arithmetic. verb,* **ex celled, ex cel ling.**

ex cel lence (ek′sə ləns), very high quality; being better than others: *His teacher praised him for the excellence of his report. noun.*

Ex cel len cy (ek′sə lən sē), title of honor used in speaking to or of a prime minister, governor, bishop, or other high official: *Your Excellency, His Excellency, Her Excellency. noun, plural* **Ex cel len cies.**

ex cel lent (ek′sə lənt), very, very good; better than others: *Excellent work deserves high praise. adjective.*

ex cept (ek sept′), **1** leaving out; other than: *He works every day except Sunday.* **2** leave out: *Those who passed the first test were excepted from the second.* **3** only; but: *I would have had a perfect score except I missed the last question.* **1** *preposition,* **2** *verb,* **3** *conjunction.*

ex cept ing (ek sep′ting), leaving out; except; but: *School is open every day excepting Saturday and Sunday. preposition.*

ex cep tion (ek sep′shən), **1** leaving out: *I like all my studies with the exception of arithmetic.* **2** person or thing left out: *She praised the pictures, with two exceptions.* **3** thing that is different from the rule: *He comes on time every day; today is an exception. noun.*

take exception, 1 object: *Several teachers and*

students took exception to the plan of having classes on Saturdays. **2** be offended: *I took exception to their rude remarks.*

ex cep tion al (ek sep′shə nəl), unusual; out of the ordinary: *This warm weather is exceptional for January. She is an exceptional student. adjective.*

ex cess (ek ses′ *for 1 and 2;* ek′ses *for 3*), **1** part that is too much: *Pour off the excess. We had an excess of snow last month.* **2** amount by which one thing is greater than another: *The excess of 7 over 5 is 2.* **3** extra: *Passengers must pay for excess baggage taken on an airplane.* 1,2 *noun, plural* **ex cess es;** 3 *adjective.*

ex ces sive (ek ses′iv), too much; too great; extreme: *Some teen-agers spend an excessive amount of time on the phone. See picture. adjective.*

ex change (eks chānj′), **1** give for something else; change: *I will exchange two dimes for twenty pennies.* **2** give and take (things of the same kind): *exchange letters. They exchanged blows.* **3** giving and taking: *Ten pennies for a dime is a fair exchange. During the truce there was an exchange of prisoners.* **4** place where people trade. Stocks are bought, sold, and traded in a stock exchange. **5** a central station or office. A telephone exchange handles telephone calls. 1,2 *verb,* **ex changed, ex chang ing;** 3-5 *noun.*

ex cit a ble (ek sī′tə bəl), easily excited. *adjective.*

ex cite (ek sīt′), **1** stir up the feelings of: *The news of war excited everybody.* **2** bring out; arouse: *Plans for a field trip excited the students' interest.* **3** stir to action: *Do not excite the dog; keep away from it. verb,* **ex·cit ed, ex cit ing.**

ex cit ed (ek sī′tid), stirred up; aroused: *The excited mob rushed into the mayor's office. adjective.*

ex cite ment (ek sīt′mənt), **1** excited condition: *The baby's first step caused great excitement in the family.* **2** something that excites: *The circus was an excitement to all of us. noun.*

ex cit ing (ek sī′ting), causing excitement; arousing; stirring: *an exciting story about pirates. adjective.*

ex claim (ek sklām′), cry out; speak suddenly in surprise or strong feeling: *"Here you are at last!" I exclaimed. verb.*

ex cla ma tion (ek′sklə mā′shən), something said suddenly as the result of feeling. *Oh! Hurrah! Well! Look!* and *Listen!* are common exclamations. *See picture. noun.*

exclamation mark or **exclamation point,** mark (!) used after a word or sentence to show that it was exclaimed. EXAMPLE: *Hurrah! We are going to the circus.*

ex clam a to ry (ek sklam′ə tôr′ē), using, containing, or expressing exclamation. *adjective.*

ex clude (ek sklüd′), shut out; keep out: *Curtains exclude light. Government rules exclude immigrants who have certain diseases. verb,* **ex clud ed, ex clud ing.**

ex clu sion (ek sklü′zhən), **1** excluding: *Swimmers asked for the exclusion of boats from one side of the lake.* **2** being excluded: *Their exclusion from the meeting hurt their feelings. noun.*

a hat	**i** it	**oi** oil	**ch** child	a in about
ā age	**ī** ice	**ou** out	**ng** long	e in taken
ä far	**o** hot	**u** cup	**sh** she	**ə** = i in pencil
e let	**ō** open	** u̇** put	**th** thin	o in lemon
ē equal	**ô** order	**ü** rule	**ᴛʜ** then	u in circus
ėr term			**zh** measure	

DO YOU THINK I HAVE AN EXCESSIVE AMOUNT OF HAIR?

exclamations

ex clu sive (ek sklü′siv), **1** shutting out all others. "Tree" and "animal" are exclusive terms; a thing cannot be both a tree and an animal. **2** shutting out all or most others: *She gave her exclusive attention to the teacher's instructions.* **3** single; sole; not divided or shared with others: *Inventors have an exclusive right for a certain number of years to make what they have invented and patented.* **4** very particular about choosing friends, members, and so on: *It is hard to get admitted to an exclusive club.* *adjective.*

exclusive of, leaving out; not counting: *There are 26 days in that month, exclusive of Sundays.*

ex clu sive ly (ek sklü′siv lē), with the exclusion of all others; only: *She is interested exclusively in sports. adverb.*

ex cur sion (ek skėr′zhən), **1** trip taken for interest or pleasure, often by a number of people together: *Our club went on an excursion to the mountains.* **2** round trip to a place of interest at fares lower than usual, by train, bus, or ship. *noun.*

ex cuse (ek skyüz′ *for 1,3-5;* ek skyüs′ *for 2 and 6*), **1** offer an apology for; try to remove the blame of: *She excused her lateness by blaming traffic.* **2** reason, real or pretended, that is given; explanation: *He had many excuses for coming late.* **3** be a reason or explanation for: *Sickness excuses absence from school.* **4** pardon; forgive: *Excuse me; I have to go now. Will you excuse my carelessness in spilling the milk?* **5** free from duty; let off: *Those who passed the first test will be excused from the second one.* **6** act of excusing. 1,3-5 *verb,* **ex cused, ex cus ing;** 2,6 *noun.*

excuse oneself, ask to be pardoned: *He excused himself for bumping into me.*

ex e cute (ek′sə kyüt), **1** carry out; do: *The magician executed a difficult trick.* **2** put into effect; enforce: *Congress makes the laws; the President executes them.* **3** put to death according to law: *The murderer was executed.* **4** make according to a plan or design: *The same artist executed that painting and that statue. verb,* **ex e cut ed, ex e cut ing.**

ex e cu tion (ek′sə kyü′shən), **1** carrying out; doing: *She was prompt in the execution of her duties.* **2** a putting into effect. **3** way of carrying out or doing; skill. **4** a putting to death according to law. **5** a making according to a plan or design. *noun.*

ex e cu tion er (ek′sə kyü′shə nər), person who puts criminals to death according to law. *noun.*

ex ec u tive (eg zek′yə tiv), **1** having to do with management: *An executive job is a job at managing something. The President is the executive head of the nation.* **2** person who manages things and who decides or helps decide on what should be done: *The president of a business is an executive.* **3** person, group, or branch of government that has the duty and power of putting laws into effect: *The highest executive of a state is the governor.* 1 *adjective,* 2,3 *noun.*

ex em pli fy (eg zem′plə fī), show by example; be an example of: *The lifeguard exemplified courage. verb,* **ex em pli fied, ex em pli fy ing.**

exercise (definitions 1, 2, 3, 4, and 5)

ex empt (eg zempt′), **1** make free (from a duty, obligation, or rule); release: *Students who get very high marks will be exempted from the final examinations.* **2** freed from a duty, obligation, or rule: *School property is exempt from all taxes.* 1 *verb,* 2 *adjective.*

ex er cise (ek′sər sīz). See picture. **1** use; practice: *Exercise of the body is good for the health.* **2** make use of: *It is wise to exercise caution in crossing the street.* **3** something that gives practice: *I perform physical exercises each day to strengthen my body. Study the lesson, and then do the exercises at the end.* **4** take exercise; go through exercises: *I exercise for ten minutes each morning.* **5 exercises,** ceremony or program: *She gave the farewell address at the graduation exercises.* 1,3,5 *noun,* 2,4 *verb,* **ex er cised, ex er cis ing.**

ex ert (eg zėrt´), use; put into use; use fully: *A gymnast must exert both strength and skill. A ruler exerts authority.* verb.

exert oneself, make an effort; try hard; strive: *You will really have to exert yourself to make up the work you missed.*

ex er tion (eg zėr´shən), **1** effort: *Our exertions kept the fire from spreading.* **2** use; active use; putting into action: *exertion of the mind, exertion of authority.* noun.

ex hale (eks hāl´), **1** breathe out: *We exhale air from our lungs.* **2** give off (air, vapor, smoke, or odor). verb, **ex haled, ex hal ing.**

ex haust (eg zôst´), **1** empty completely: *exhaust an oil well.* **2** use up: *exhaust the supply of water, exhaust one's strength.* **3** tire out: *The long, hard climb up the hill exhausted us.* **4** escape of used steam or gasoline from an engine. **5** pipe through which used steam or gasoline escapes from an engine. **6** the used steam or gasoline that escapes: *The exhaust from an automobile engine is poisonous.* 1-3 verb, 4-6 noun.

ex haust ed (eg zô´stid), **1** used up: *The teacher's patience was exhausted by the students' jabbering.* **2** worn out; very tired: *The exhausted hikers stopped to rest after their long walk.* adjective.

ex haus tion (eg zôs´chən), **1** act of exhausting. **2** condition of being exhausted; great tiredness: *The hikers were suffering from extreme exhaustion.* noun.

ex hib it (eg zib´it), **1** show: *Both of their children exhibit a talent for music. He exhibits interest whenever you talk about dogs.* **2** show publicly; put on display: *She hopes to exhibit her paintings in New York.* **3** thing or things shown publicly. See picture. 1,2 verb, 3 noun.

ex hi bi tion (ek´sə bish´ən), **1** showing: *I never saw such an exhibition of bad manners before.* **2** a public show: *The art school holds an exhibition of paintings every year.* **3** thing or things shown publicly; exhibit. noun.

ex hil a rate (eg zil´ə rāt´), cheer; make merry; make lively: *The joy of the holiday season exhilarates us all. We enjoy an exhilarating swim.* verb, **ex hil a rat ed, ex hil a rat ing.**

ex ile (eg´zīl or ek´sīl), **1** make (a person) go from home or country, often by law as a punishment; banish: *The traitors were exiled from their country for life.* **2** person who is banished: *She has been an exile for ten years.* **3** banishment: *He was sent into exile for life.* 1 verb, **ex iled, ex il ing;** 2,3 noun.

ex ist (eg zist´), **1** be: *The world has existed a long time.* **2** be real: *Do elves exist or not?* **3** live: *A person cannot exist without air.* **4** occur: *Cases exist of persons who cannot smell anything.* verb.

ex ist ence (eg zis´təns), **1** being: *When we are born, we come into existence.* **2** being real: *Most people do not now believe in the existence of ghosts.* **3** life: *Drivers of racing cars lead a dangerous existence.* noun.

ex it (eg´zit or ek´sit), **1** way out: *The theater had six exits.* **2** act of going out: *When the cat came in, the mice made a hasty exit.* **3** act of leaving the stage: *The actor made a graceful exit.* noun.

ex or bi tant (eg zôr´bə tənt), very excessive; much too high: *One dollar is an exorbitant price for a pack of gum.* adjective.

ex ot ic (eg zot´ik), foreign; strange. See picture. adjective.

ex pand (ek spand´), spread out; open out; unfold; swell; make or grow larger: *A balloon expands when it is blown up. A bird expands its wings before flying. Our country has expanded many times. You can expand a short speech into a long one.* verb.

a hat	**i** it	**oi** oil	**ch** child	a in about
ā age	**ī** ice	**ou** out	**ng** long	e in taken
ä far	**o** hot	**u** cup	**sh** she	ə = i in pencil
e let	**ō** open	**ù** put	**th** thin	o in lemon
ē equal	**ô** order	**ü** rule	**ŦH** then	u in circus
ėr term			**zh** measure	

exotic—Have you ever seen such an **exotic** fish?

exhibit (definition 3)
a museum exhibit of the first giraffes brought to England

ex panse (ek spans′), an open or unbroken stretch; wide, spreading surface: *The Pacific Ocean is a vast expanse of water.* noun.

ex pan sion (ek span′shən), **1** expanding: *Heat causes the expansion of liquids, metals, and gases.* **2** being expanded; increase in size or volume: *The expansion of the factory made room for more machines.* noun.

ex pect (ek spekt′), **1** look for; think something will probably come or happen: *We expect hot days in summer.* **2** think; suppose; guess: *I expect you're right about that.* verb.

ex pect ant (ek spek′tənt), expecting; looking for; thinking something will come or happen: *She opened her package with an expectant smile.* adjective.

ex pec ta tion (ek′spek tā′shən), **1** expecting or being expected; anticipation: *the expectation of a good harvest.* **2** something expected. **3** good reason for expecting something; prospect: *He has expectations of money from a rich aunt.* noun.

ex pe di ent (ek spē′dē ənt), **1** useful; helping to bring about some result: *It is expedient to be friendly and pleasant if you want to have friends.* **2** way of getting something: *Having no ladder or rope, the prisoner tied sheets together and escaped by this expedient.* 1 adjective, 2 noun.

ex pe di tion (ek′spə dish′ən), **1** journey for a special purpose, such as exploration or scientific study. **2** the people that make such a journey: *The expedition climbed the mountain peak.* See picture. **3** prompt action; speed: *They completed their work with expedition.* noun.

ex pel (ek spel′), **1** drive out with much force: *When we exhale, we expel air from our lungs.* **2** put out; dismiss: *A pupil who cheats or steals may be expelled from school.* verb, **ex pelled, ex pel ling.**

ex pend (ek spend′), spend; use up: *He expended thought, work, and money on his project.* verb.

ex pend i ture (ek spen′də chùr), **1** spending; using up: *Building a sailboat requires the expenditure of much money, time, and effort.* **2** amount of money, time, or effort spent; expense: *Her expenditures for Christmas presents were $1.05 and 14 hours of work.* noun.

ex pense (ek spens′), **1** cost; charge: *The expense of the trip was small. The class traveled to the zoo at the school's expense. We had many a laugh at their expense.* **2** expending; paying out money: *Supporting a child at college puts parents to quite a bit of expense.* **3** cause of spending: *Running an automobile is an expense.* noun.

ex pen sive (ek spen′siv), costly; high-priced: *He had a very expensive pen which cost $10.* adjective.

ex per i ence (ek spir′ē əns), **1** what happens to a person: *We had several pleasant experiences on our trip. People learn by experience.* **2** practice; knowledge gained by doing or seeing things: *Have you had any experience in this kind of work?* **3** feel; have happen to one: *experience great pain.* 1,2 noun, 3 verb, **ex per i enced, ex per i enc ing.**

ex per i enced (ek spir′ē ənst), **1** taught by experience: *The job calls for a person experienced in*

explore (definition 2)—The boys **explored** the cave.

experimental (definition 3)—This is an experimental model of a car with three wheels.

expedition (definition 2)

teaching children. **2** skillful or wise because of experience: *an experienced teacher, an experienced nurse. adjective.*

ex per i ment (ek sper′ə ment *for 1*; ek sper′ə mənt *for 2*), **1** try in order to find out; make trials or tests: *Babies experiment with their hands. The painter is experimenting with different paints to get the color he wants.* **2** trial or test to find out something: *a cooking experiment. Scientists test out theories by experiment.* **1** *verb,* **2** *noun.*

ex per i men tal (ek sper′ə men′tl), **1** based on experiments: *Chemistry is an experimental science.* **2** used for experiments: *A new variety of wheat was developed at the experimental farm.* **3** for testing or trying out. See picture. *adjective.*

ex per i men ta tion (ek sper′ə men tā′shən), experimenting: *Cures for disease are often found by experimentation on animals. noun.*

ex pert (ek′spėrt′ *for 1*; ek spėrt′ *or* ek′spėrt′ *for 2*), **1** person who has much skill or who knows a great deal about some special thing: *She is an expert at fishing.* **2** having much skill; knowing a great deal about some special thing: *an expert painter.* **1** *noun,* **2** *adjective.*

ex pi ra tion (ek′spə rā′shən), **1** coming to an end: *We shall move at the expiration of our lease.* **2** breathing out: *The expiration of used air from the lungs is a part of breathing. noun.*

ex pire (ek spīr′), **1** come to an end: *You must obtain a new automobile license when your old one expires.* **2** die. **3** breathe out: *Used air is expired from the lungs. verb,* **ex pired, ex pir ing.**

ex plain (ek splān′), **1** make plain or clear; tell the meaning of; tell how to do: *The teacher explained multiplication to the class.* **2** give reasons for; state the cause of: *Can somebody explain her absence? verb.*

ex pla na tion (ek′splə nā′shən), **1** explaining; clearing up a difficulty or mistake: *He did not understand the teacher's explanation of multiplication.* **2** something that explains: *This diagram is a good explanation of how an automobile engine works. noun.*

ex plan a to ry (ek splan′ə tôr′ē), able to explain; helping to make clear: *Read the explanatory part of the lesson before you try to do the problems. adjective.*

ex plic it (ek splis′it), clearly expressed; distinctly stated; definite: *She gave such explicit directions that everyone understood them. adjective.*

ex plode (ek splōd′), **1** blow up; burst with a loud noise: *The building was destroyed when the defective boiler exploded.* **2** cause to explode: *Some people explode firecrackers on the Fourth of July.* **3** burst forth noisily: *The speaker's mistake was so funny the audience exploded with laughter. verb,* **ex plod ed, ex plod ing.**

ex ploit (ek′sploit *for 1*; ek sploit′ *for 2 and 3*), **1** bold, unusual act; daring deed: *This book tells about the exploits of Robin Hood.* **2** make use of; turn to practical account: *A mine is exploited for its minerals.* **3** make unfair use of; use selfishly for one's own advantage: *Nations used to exploit their*

a hat	i it	oi oil	ch child	a in about
ā age	ī ice	ou out	ng long	e in taken
ä far	o hot	u cup	sh she	ə = i in pencil
e let	ō open	ů put	th thin	o in lemon
ē equal	ô order	ü rule	ŦH then	u in circus
ėr term			zh measure	

colonies, taking as much wealth out of them as they could. **1** *noun,* **2,3** *verb.*

ex plo ra tion (ek′splə rā′shən), **1** traveling in little-known lands, seas, or in outer space for the purpose of discovery. **2** going over carefully; looking into closely; examining. *noun.*

ex plore (ek splôr′), **1** travel over little-known lands, seas, or in outer space for the purpose of discovery: *Some day people may explore Mars and Venus.* **2** go over carefully; examine: *to explore a subject thoroughly.* See picture. *verb,* **ex plored, ex plor ing.**

ex plor er (ek splôr′ər), person who explores. *noun.*

ex plo sion (ek splō′zhən), **1** blowing up; bursting with a loud noise: *The explosion of the bomb shook the whole neighborhood.* **2** a loud noise caused by this: *People five miles away heard the explosion.* **3** a noisy bursting forth; outbreak: *explosions of anger.* **4** a sudden or rapid increase or growth: *The explosion of the world's population has created a shortage of food in many countries. noun.*

ex plo sive (ek splō′siv), **1** of or for explosion; tending to explode: *Gunpowder is explosive.* **2** explosive substance: *Explosives are used in making fireworks.* **3** tending to burst forth noisily: *an explosive temper, explosive laughter.* **1,3** *adjective,* **2** *noun.*

ex port (ek spôrt′ *or* ek′spôrt *for 1*; ek′spôrt *for 2 and 3*), **1** send (goods) out of one country for sale and use in another: *The United States exports automobiles.* **2** thing exported: *Cotton is an important export of the United States.* **3** act or fact of exporting: *the export of wool from Great Britain.* **1** *verb,* **2,3** *noun.*

ex pose (ek spōz′), **1** lay open; uncover; leave without protection: *While we fished, we were exposed to the hot sun. The whole class has been exposed to the flu.* **2** put in plain sight; display: *Goods are exposed for sale in a store.* **3** make known; reveal: *They exposed the plot to the police.* **4** allow light to reach and act on (a photographic film or plate). *verb,* **ex posed, ex pos ing.**

ex po si tion (ek′spə zish′ən), **1** public show or exhibition. A world's fair is an exposition. **2** explanation. *noun.*

ex po sure (ek spō′zhər), **1** exposing; laying open; making known: *The exposure of the real criminal cleared the innocent suspect. Movie stars have a great deal of public exposure.* **2** being exposed: *Exposure to the rain has spoiled this machinery.* **3** position in relation to the sun and wind. A house with a southern exposure is open to sun and wind from the south. **4** time taken to get an image on a photographic film. **5** part of a photographic film used for one picture. *noun.*

ex press (ek spres′), **1** put into words: *Try to express your idea clearly.* **2** show by look, voice, or action: *A smile expresses joy.* **3** clear and definite: *It was his express wish that we should go without him.* **4** special; particular: *She came for the express purpose of seeing you.* **5** a quick or direct means of sending. Packages and money can be sent by express in trains or airplanes. **6** send by some quick means: *express a package.* **7** by express; directly: *Please send this package express to Boston.* **8** quick: *an express train.* **9** train, bus, or elevator that goes direct from one point to another without making intermediate stops. **10** for fast traveling: *an express highway.* 1,2,6 *verb,* 3,4,8,10 *adjective,* 5,9 *noun, plural* **ex press es** for 9; 7 *adverb.*

express oneself, say what one thinks: *You must be able to express yourself clearly to become a good public speaker.*

ex pres sion (ek spresh′ən), **1** putting into words: *the expression of an idea.* **2** word or group of words used as a unit: *"Wise guy" is a slang expression.* **3** showing by look, voice, or action: *A sigh is often an expression of sadness.* **4** look that shows feeling: *The winners all had happy expressions on their faces.* **5** bringing out the meaning or beauty of something read, spoken, sung, or played: *Try to read with more expression. noun.*

ex pres sive (ek spres′iv), **1** expressing: *"Alas!" is a word expressive of sadness.* **2** having much feeling or meaning: *"The cat's skin hung on its bones" is a more expressive sentence than "The cat was very thin." adjective.*

ex press ly (ek spres′lē), **1** plainly; definitely: *The package is not for you; you are expressly forbidden to touch it.* **2** specially; on purpose: *You ought to talk to her, since she came expressly to see you. adverb.*

ex press way (ek spres′wā′), highway built for motor-vehicle travel at high speeds. *noun.*

ex pul sion (ek spul′shən), **1** forcing out: *Expulsion of used air from the lungs is part of breathing.* **2** being forced out: *Expulsion from school is a punishment for bad behavior. noun.*

ex qui site (ek′skwi zit), **1** very lovely; delicate; beautifully made: *The violet is an exquisite flower.* **2** sharp; intense: *A toothache causes exquisite pain.* **3** of highest excellence; most admirable: *They have exquisite taste and manners. adjective.*

ex tend (ek stend′), **1** stretch out: *extend your hand, an extended visit, a road that extends to New York.* **2** give; grant: *This organization extends help to poor people. verb.*

ex ten sion (ek sten′shən), **1** stretching out: *the extension of a road.* **2** addition: *The new extension to our school will make room for more students.* **3** telephone connected with the main telephone or with a switchboard but in a different location. *noun.*

ex ten sive (ek sten′siv), far-reaching; large: *extensive changes, an extensive park. adjective.*

ex tent (ek stent′), **1** size, space, length, amount, or degree to which a thing extends: *Railroads carry people and goods through the whole extent of the country. The extent of a judge's power is limited by law.* **2** something extended; extended space: *a vast extent of prairie. noun.*

ex ter i or (ek stir′ē ər), **1** outside; outward appearance: *I saw only the exterior of the house, not the interior. Some people have a harsh exterior but a kind heart.* **2** outer: *The skin of an apple is its exterior covering.* **3** coming from outside; happening outside: *Exterior influences caused me to change my mind.* 1 *noun,* 2,3 *adjective.*

ex ter mi nate (ek stėr′mə nāt), destroy completely: *This poison will exterminate rats. verb,* **ex ter mi nat ed, ex ter mi nat ing.**

ex ter nal (ek stėr′nl), **1** on the outside; outer: *An ear of corn has an external husk.* **2** outside part. 1 *adjective,* 2 *noun.*

ex tinct (ek stingkt′), **1** no longer existing: *The dinosaur is an extinct animal.* **2** not active; gone out: *an extinct volcano. adjective.*

ex tinc tion (ek stingk′shən), **1** extinguishing: *The sudden extinction of the lights left us in total darkness.* **2** bringing to an end; wiping out; destruction: *Physicians are working for the extinction of diseases. noun.*

ex tin guish (ek sting′gwish), **1** put out: *Water extinguished the fire.* **2** wipe out; destroy; bring to an end: *One failure after another extinguished their hopes. verb.*

ex tra (ek′strə), **1** beyond what is usual, expected, or needed: *extra pay, extra fine quality, extra fare.* **2** something extra; anything beyond what is usual, expected, or needed: *Their parents bought an expensive new car that had many extras.* **3** special edition of a newspaper: *The paper published an extra to announce the end of the war.* 1 *adjective,* 2,3 *noun.*

ex tract (ek strakt′ *for 1;* ek′strakt *for 2*), **1** draw out, usually with some effort; take out: *extract oil from olives or iron from the earth, extract a tooth, extract a confession.* **2** something drawn out or taken out: *He read several extracts from the poem. Vanilla extract is made from vanilla beans.* 1 *verb,* 2 *noun.*

ex traor di nar i ly (ek strôr′də ner′ə lē), most unusually. *adverb.*

ex traor di nar y (ek strôr′də ner′ē), beyond what is ordinary; very unusual; remarkable; special: *Eight feet is an extraordinary height for a person. adjective.*

ex trav a gance (ek strav′ə gəns), **1** careless and lavish spending; waste: *Their extravagance kept them always in debt.* **2** going beyond the bounds of reason: *I knew that the story was not true because of its extravagance. noun.*

ex trav a gant (ek strav′ə gənt), **1** spending carelessly and lavishly; wasteful: *An extravagant person has extravagant tastes and habits.* **2** beyond the bounds of reason: *A dinner for four people at $75 is extravagant. To call a poodle "the sweetest thing alive" is extravagant. adjective.*

ex treme (ek strēm′), **1** much more than usual; very great; very strong: *She drove with extreme caution during the snowstorm.* **2** at the very end; the farthest possible; last: *The extreme north stops at* the North Pole. **3** something extreme: *Love and hate are two extremes of feeling.* 1,2 *adjective,* **ex trem er, ex trem est; 3** *noun.*

go to extremes, do or say too much: *A person who owns twenty cats is going to extremes.*

ex treme ly (ek strēm′lē), much more than usual; very: *It is extremely cold in the Arctic. adverb.*

ex trem i ty (ek strem′ə tē), **1** the very end; the tip: *Florida is at the southeastern extremity of the United States.* **2 extremities,** the hands and feet. **3** very great danger or need: *People on a sinking ship are in extremity.* **4** extreme degree: *Joy is the extremity of happiness.* **5** an extreme action: *The police were forced to the extremity of closing several downtown streets to control the mob. noun, plural* **ex trem i ties.**

ex tri cate (ek′strə kāt), release; set free from entanglements, difficulties, or embarrassing situations. See picture. *verb,* **ex tri cat ed, ex tri cat ing.**

ex ult (eg zult′), be very glad; rejoice greatly: *The winners exulted in their victory. verb.*

ex ult ant (eg zult′nt), exulting; rejoicing greatly; triumphant: *The students gave an exultant shout when the teacher told them there would be no classes on Monday. adjective.*

ex ul ta tion (eg′zul tā′shən), great joy; triumph: *There was exultation over our team's overwhelming victory. noun.*

eye (ī), **1** the part of the body by which people and animals see. **2** the colored part of the eye; iris: *She has brown eyes.* **3** region surrounding the eye: *The blow gave him a black eye.* **4** ability to see small differences in things: *An artist should have an eye for color.* **5** look; glance: *I cast an eye over the books and quickly found one I liked.* **6** watch; observe. See picture. **7** way of thinking; view; opinion: *Stealing is a crime in the eye of the law.* **8** something like an eye or that suggests an eye. The little spots on potatoes, the hole in a needle, and the loop into which a hook fastens are all called eyes. 1-5,7,8 *noun,* 6 *verb,* **eyed, ey ing** or **eye ing.**

catch one's eye, attract one's attention: *A bright red flower caught my eye.*

keep an eye on, look after; watch carefully: *Keep an eye on the baby.*

see eye to eye, agree entirely: *My parents and I do not see eye to eye on my weekly allowance.*

eye ball (ī′bôl′), the eye without the surrounding lids and bony socket. *noun.*

eye brow (ī′brou′), **1** hair that grows along the bony ridge just above the eye. **2** the bony ridge above the eye. *noun.*

eye glass (ī′glas′), **1** lens to aid poor vision. **2 eyeglasses,** pair of glass lenses to help vision; glasses. *noun, plural* **eye glass es.**

eye lash (ī′lash′), **1** one of the hairs on the edge of the eyelid. **2** fringe of such hairs. *noun, plural* **eye lash es.**

eye let (ī′lit), **1** a small, round hole for a lace or cord to go through. **2** metal ring around such a hole to strengthen it. *noun.*

a hat	i it	oi oil	ch child	a in about
ā age	ī ice	ou out	ng long	e in taken
ä far	o hot	u cup	sh she	ə = i in pencil
e let	ō open	u̇ put	th thin	o in lemon
ē equal	ô order	ü rule	ŦH then	u in circus
ėr term			zh measure	

extricate—She rushed to **extricate** him from his perilous situation.

eye (definition 6)—The man **eyed** the fish and the fish **eyed** the man.

eye lid (ī′lid′), the movable cover of skin, upper or lower, by means of which we can shut and open our eyes. *noun.*

eye piece (ī′pēs′), lens or set of lenses in a telescope or microscope, that is nearest the eye of the user. *noun.*

eye sight (ī′sīt′), **1** power of seeing; sight: *A hawk has keen eyesight.* **2** range of vision; view: *The water was within eyesight. noun.*

eye tooth (ī′tüth′), an upper canine tooth. *noun, plural* **eye teeth.**

F f

F or f (ef), the sixth letter of the English alphabet. There are two f's in *offer. noun, plural* **F's** or **f's.**

fa ble (fā′bəl), **1** story that is made up to teach a lesson. Fables are often about animals who can talk, such as *The Hare and the Tortoise.* **2** story that is not true. *noun.*

fab ric (fab′rik), woven or knitted material; cloth. Velvet, canvas, linen, and flannel are fabrics. *noun.*

fab u lous (fab′yə ləs), too extraordinary to seem possible; beyond belief; amazing: *Ten dollars is a fabulous price for a pencil. adjective.*

face (fās), **1** the front part of the head. Your eyes, nose, and mouth are parts of your face. **2** look; expression: *His face was sad.* **3** ugly or funny look made by twisting the face. See picture. **4** the front part; the right side; surface: *The face of a clock or watch has numbers on it.* **5** outward appearance: *The tall buildings changed the face of the city.* **6** have the front toward: *The house faces the street. The picture faces page 60 in my book.* **7** meet bravely or boldly: *face a challenge.* **8** self-respect; personal importance: *lose face.* **9** cover with a different material: *That wooden house is being faced with brick.* 1-5,8 *noun,* 6,7,9 *verb,* **faced, fac ing.**
in the face of, 1 in the presence of: *No one wanted to surrender even in the face of invasion.* **2** in spite of: *She said she was right in the face of facts that proved she was wrong.*

fac et (fas′it), one of the small, polished surfaces of a cut gem. *noun.*

fa cial (fā′shəl), **1** of the face. **2** for the face. *adjective.*

fa cil i tate (fə sil′ə tāt), make easy; lessen the labor of; help forward; assist: *A good vacuum cleaner facilitates housework. verb,* **fa cil i tat ed, fa cil i tat ing.**

fa cil i ty (fə sil′ə tē), **1** ease; absence of difficulty: *The twins ran and dodged with such facility that no one could catch them.* **2** power to do anything easily and quickly; skill in using the hands or mind: *She has the facility to become a fine composer.* **3 facilities,** aid; service. *noun, plural* **fa cil i ties.**

fact (fakt), **1** thing known to be true; thing known to have happened: *It is a fact that the Pilgrims sailed to America on the Mayflower in 1620.* **2** what is true; truth: *The fact is, I did not want to go to the dance.* **3** thing said or supposed to be true or to have really happened: *We doubted his facts. noun.*

fac tor (fak′tər), **1** any one of the causes that helps bring about a result; one element in a situation: *The low price was a factor in my decision to buy this car.* **2** any of the numbers that produce a given number when multiplied together: *2 and 5 are factors of 10. noun.*

face (definition 3)—Everyone in the class is making **faces.**

fad

fac tor y (fak′tər ē), building or group of buildings where things are made with machines, or by hand. A factory usually has machines in it. *noun, plural* **fac tor ies.**

fac tu al (fak′chü əl), concerned with fact; consisting of facts: *I kept a factual account of our trip in my diary. adjective.*

fac ul ty (fak′əl tē), **1** power to do some special thing, especially a power of the mind: *the faculty of hearing. She has a great faculty for arithmetic.* **2** the teachers of a school, college, or university. *noun, plural* **fac ul ties.**

fad (fad), something everybody is very much interested in for a short time; fashion or craze. See picture. *noun.*

fade (fād), **1** become less bright; lose color: *My blue jeans faded after they were washed several times.* **2** lose freshness or strength; wither: *The flowers in our garden faded at the end of the summer.* **3** die away; disappear little by little: *The sound of the train faded after it went by. verb,* **fad ed, fad ing.**

Fahr en heit (far′ən hīt). On the **Fahrenheit thermometer**, 32 degrees is the temperature at which water freezes, and 212 degrees is the temperature at which water boils. *adjective.* [*Fahrenheit* was named for Gabriel D. Fahrenheit, who lived from 1686 to 1736. He was a German physicist who invented the mercury thermometer.]

fail (fāl), **1** not succeed; come to nothing; not be able to do: *He tried hard to learn to sing, but he failed.* **2** not do; neglect: *She failed to follow our advice.* **3** be of no use to when needed: *When I needed their help, they failed me.* **4** be missing; be not enough: *The wind failed us, so that we could not sail home.* **5** lose strength; grow weak; die away: *The patient's heart was failing.* **6** be unable to pay what one owes: *The company lost all its money and failed in business. verb.*
without fail, surely: *You must do your homework without fail.*

fail ing (fā′ling), **1** failure. **2** fault; weakness; defect: *We all have our failings; none of us is perfect. noun.*

fail ure (fā′lyər), **1** failing; lack of success: *failure in one's work.* **2** a not doing; neglecting: *Failure to follow directions may cause errors.* **3** falling short: *failure of crops.* **4** losing strength; becoming weak: *failure of eyesight.* **5** being unable to pay what one owes. **6** person or thing that has failed: *The picnic was a failure because it rained. noun.*

faint (fānt), **1** not clear or plain; dim: *faint colors.* **2** weak; feeble: *a faint voice.* **3** a state in which for a short time a person lies as though asleep. When you are in a faint, you don't know what is going on around you. **4** fall into a faint. **5** ready to faint; dizzy and weak: *I felt faint.* **1,2,5** *adjective,* **3** *noun,* **4** *verb.*

fair[1] (fer *or* far), **1** honest; just; giving the same treatment to all: *a fair judge. Try to be fair, even to people you dislike.* **2** according to the rules: *fair play.* **3** not good and not bad; average: *There is a fair crop of wheat this year.* **4** light; not dark: *A blond person has fair hair and skin.* **5** clear; sunny; not cloudy or stormy: *fair weather.* **6** beautiful: *a fair lady.* **7** in a just manner; honestly: *The tennis champion was known for playing fair.* **1-6** *adjective,* **7** *adverb.*

fair[2] (fer *or* far), **1** a showing of farm products and goods of a certain region: *Prizes were given for the best livestock at the county fair.* **2** a gathering of buyers and sellers, often held at the same time and place every year: *a trade fair, an art fair.* **3** sale of articles: *Our church held a fair to raise money for charity. noun.*

fair ground (fer′ground′ *or* far′ground′), place outdoors where fairs are held. *noun.*

fair ly (fer′lē *or* far′lē), **1** in a fair manner; justly: *All contestants will be treated fairly.* **2** not extremely; to a moderate degree; rather; somewhat: *She is a fairly good pupil, about average. adverb.*

fair y (fer′ē *or* far′ē), **1** (in stories) a tiny being, very lovely and delicate, who could help or harm human beings. **2** of fairies. **3** like a fairy; lovely;

a hat	**i** it	**oi** oil	**ch** child	a in about
ā age	**ī** ice	**ou** out	**ng** long	e in taken
ä far	**o** hot	**u** cup	**sh** she	ə = i in pencil
e let	**ō** open	**u̇** put	**th** thin	o in lemon
ē equal	**ô** order	**ü** rule	**ŦH** then	u in circus
ėr term			**zh** measure	

delicate. **1** *noun, plural* **fair ies; 2,3** *adjective.*

fair y land (fer′ē land′ *or* far′ē land′), **1** place where the fairies are supposed to live. **2** an enchanting and pleasant place. *noun.*

fairy tale, 1 story about fairies. **2** something said that is not true; lie.

faith (fāth), **1** belief without proof; trust; confidence: *We have faith in our friends.* **2** belief in God or in God's promises. **3** what a person believes. **4** religion: *the Jewish faith, the Christian faith.* **5** being loyal. *noun.*
in good faith, honestly; sincerely.

faith ful (fāth′fəl), **1** worthy of trust; loyal: *A faithful friend will keep your secret. Several workers were given awards for long and faithful service.* **2** true to fact; accurate: *The witness gave a faithful account of what happened. adjective.*

faith less (fāth′lis), not true to duty or to one's promises; not loyal: *a faithless traitor. adjective.*

fake (fāk), **1** make something false appear real in order to deceive; counterfeit: *fake someone else's signature. They faked the picture by pasting two photographs together.* **2** pretend: *I wasn't really crying; I was only faking.* **3** fraud: *The diamond ring was a fake.* **4** not real; false: *a fake fur, fake money.* **1,2** *verb,* **faked, fak ing; 3** *noun,* **4** *adjective.*

fal con (fôl′kən *or* fal′kən), **1** hawk trained to hunt and kill birds and small game. In the Middle Ages, hunting with falcons was a popular sport. See picture. **2** a swift-flying hawk having a short, curved bill and long claws and wings. *noun.*

falcon (definition 1)—Falcons are trained to perch on a glove or cover around the hand.

fall (fôl). See picture. **1** drop or come down from a higher place: *Snow is falling fast. Her hat fell off. Leaves fall from the trees. The light falls on my book.* **2** dropping from a higher place: *a fall from a horse.* **3** amount that comes down: *a heavy fall of snow.* **4** distance anything drops or comes down: *The fall of the river here is two feet.* **5 falls,** waterfall: *Niagara Falls. We enjoyed visiting the falls.* **6** come down suddenly from a standing position: *A baby who is learning to walk often falls.* **7** coming down suddenly from a standing position: *The child had a bad fall.* **8** do wrong; become bad or worse: *In the Bible, Adam was tempted by Eve and he fell.* **9** becoming bad or worse; ruin; destruction: *Adam's fall.* **10** lose position, power, or dignity; be taken by any evil: *The ruler fell from the people's favor. The city has fallen into the power of its enemies.* **11** drop wounded or dead; be killed: *fall in battle.* **12** pass into some condition or position: *He fell sick. The baby fell asleep. The boy and girl fell in love.* **13** come by chance or luck: *Our choice fell on her.* **14** happen; take place: *This year my birthday falls on a Monday.* **15** become lower or less: *Prices are falling. The water in the river has fallen two feet.* **16** becoming lower or less: *a fall in prices.* **17** season of the year between summer and winter; autumn. **18** look sad or disappointed: *His face fell at the news.* 1,6,8,10-15,18 *verb,* **fell, fall en, fall ing;** 2-5,7,9,16,17 *noun.*

fall back on, turn to (someone or something) when other things fail.

fall in, 1 take a place in line: *"Fall in!" said the officer to the soldiers.* **2** meet: *On our trip we fell in with some interesting people.* **3** agree: *They fell in with our plans.*

fall off, drop; become less: *The profits of her business fell off last month.*

fall on or **fall upon,** attack: *The invading army fell on the city during the night.*

fall out, 1 leave a place in line: *"Fall out!" said the officer to the soldiers.* **2** quarrel; stop being friends: *She fell out with most of her friends.*

fall through, fail: *Their plans fell through.*

fall en (fô′lən), **1** See **fall.** *Much rain has fallen.* **2** dropped: *feet with fallen arches.* **3** down on the ground; down flat: *a fallen tree.* **4** overthrown; ruined: *a fallen fortress.* **5** dead: *fallen heroes.* 1 *verb,* 2-5 *adjective.*

fall out (fôl′out′), radioactive particles or dust that fall to the earth after a nuclear explosion. *noun.*

fal low (fal′ō), **1** plowed but not seeded for a season or more; uncultivated: *The north forty acres lay fallow last spring.* **2** land plowed but not seeded for a season or more. 1 *adjective,* 2 *noun.*

false (fôls), **1** not true; not correct; wrong: *false statements.* A **false note** is wrong in pitch. A **false step** is a stumble or a mistake. **2** lying: *a false witness.* **3** not loyal; deceitful: *a false friend.* **4** used to deceive: *false weights, false signals.* A ship sails under **false colors** when it raises the flag of another country than its own. **5** not real; artificial: *false teeth.* **6** based on wrong notions: *False pride*

fall (definitions 1, 5, and 17)

kept him from accepting help from his friends when he needed it. adjective, **fals er, fals est.**

play one false, deceive, cheat, trick, or betray one: *My memory played me false; I called her by the wrong name.*

false hood (fôls′hud), **1** a false statement; a lie. **2** being false. **3** something false. *noun.*

fal ter (fôl′tər), **1** not go straight on; hesitate; waver; lose courage: *I faltered for a moment before making my decision.* **2** become unsteady in movement; stumble; totter: *I faltered up the rocky path in the dark.* **3** speak in hesitating and broken words: *Greatly embarrassed, he faltered out his thanks. verb.*

fame (fām), having much said or written about one; being very well known: *the hero's fame. noun.*

famed (fāmd), famous; well-known. *adjective.*

fa mil iar (fə mil′yər), **1** well-known; common: *a familiar face. A knife is a familiar tool. French was as familiar to him as English.* **2** well acquainted: *She is familiar with French and English.* **3** close; personal; intimate: *Those familiar friends know each other very well.* **4** too friendly; forward: *His manner is too familiar. adjective.*

fa mil iar i ty (fə mil′yar′ə tē), **1** close acquaintance: *The Indian scout's familiarity with the hilly country was a great help to the explorers.* **2** thing done or said in a familiar way: *I dislike such familiarities as the use of my nickname by people I have just met.* **3** freedom of behavior suitable only to friends; lack of formality or ceremony. *noun, plural* **fa mil iar i ties.**

fam i ly (fam′ə lē), **1** father, mother, and their children: *Our town has about a thousand families.* **2** children of a father and mother; offspring: *They are raising a family.* **3** group of people living in the same house. **4** all of a person's relatives: *a family reunion.* **5** group of related people; tribe; race. **6** group of related animals or plants. Lions, tigers, and leopards belong to the cat family. **7** any group of related or similar things. *noun, plural* **fam i lies.**

fam ine (fam′ən), **1** lack of food in a place; a time of starving: *Many people died during the famine in India.* **2** starvation: *Many people died of famine.* **3** a very great lack of anything: *a coal famine. noun.*

fam ish (fam′ish), be very hungry; starve: *She was famished after not eating for ten hours. verb.*

fa mous (fā′məs), very well known; noted: *The famous singer was greeted by a large crowd. adjective.*

fan[1] (fan), **1** instrument or device with which to stir the air in order to cool a room or one's face, or to blow dust away. **2** stir (the air); blow on; stir up: *Fan the fire to make it burn faster.* **3** use a fan on: *She fanned herself.* **4** anything that is flat and spread out like an open fan: *The peacock spread out its tail into a beautiful fan.* **1,4** *noun,* **2,3** *verb,* **fanned, fan ning.**

fan[2] (fan), person extremely interested in some sport, the movies, the radio, or television: *A baseball fan would hate to miss the championship game. noun.* [*Fan*[2] was shortened from the English word *fanatic.*]

fa nat ic (fə nat′ik), **1** person who is carried away beyond reason by his feelings or beliefs: *My friend is a fanatic about fresh air and refuses to stay in a room with closed windows.* **2** enthusiastic or zealous beyond reason: *a fanatic follower of some leader or belief.* **1** *noun,* **2** *adjective.*

fan ci ful (fan′sə fəl), **1** showing fancy; quaint; odd; fantastic: *Fanciful decorations are made up, not patterned after something.* **2** led by fancy; using fancies: *Hans Christian Andersen was a fanciful writer.* **3** suggested by fancy; imaginary; unreal. See picture. *adjective.*

fan cy (fan′sē), **1** picture to oneself; imagine: *Can you fancy yourself on the moon?* **2** power to imagine: *Fairies are creatures of fancy.* **3** idea; notion; something imagined or thought of: *He had*

a hat	i it	oi oil	ch child	a in about
ā age	ī ice	ou out	ng long	e in taken
ä far	o hot	u cup	sh she	ə = i in pencil
e let	ō open	ů put	th thin	o in lemon
ē equal	ô order	ü rule	ᴛʜ then	u in circus
ėr term			zh measure	

a sudden fancy to drive instead of going by plane. **4** liking: *They took a great fancy to each other.* **5** like; be fond of: *She fancies bright colors, but he prefers pastels.* **6** not plain or simple; decorated: *fancy needlework, a fancy dinner for guests.* **7** requiring much skill: *fancy skating.* **8** of high quality or an unusual kind: *The shop offered a wide choice of fancy fruits for sale.* **9** much too high: *She paid a fancy price for that car.* **1,5** *verb,* **fan cied, fan cy ing; 2-4** *noun, plural* **fan cies; 6-9** *adjective,* **fan ci er, fan ci est.**

fang (fang), a long, pointed tooth of a dog, wolf, or snake. *noun.*

fan tas tic (fan tas′tik), very odd; due to fancy; unreal; strange and wild in shape or manner: *The firelight cast weird, fantastic shadows on the walls. adjective.*

fan ta sy (fan′tə sē), **1** play of the mind; product of the imagination. Fairy tales are fantasies. **2** picture existing only in the mind: *I have a fantasy in which I walk about in a lovely garden.* **3** a wild, strange fancy: *This tale of talking horses is merely fantasy. noun, plural* **fan ta sies.**

far (fär), **1** a long way; a long way off: *She studied far into the night.* **2** not near; distant: *They live in a far country. The moon is far from the earth.* **3** more distant: *We live on the far side of the hill.* **4** much: *It is far better to go by train.* **1,4** *adverb,* **far ther, far thest** or **fur ther, fur thest; 2,3** *adjective,* **far ther, far thest** or **fur ther, fur thest.**

by far, very much: *This is by far the best restaurant in town.*

far a way (fär′ə wā′), **1** distant; far away: *He read*

fanciful (definition 3)
I read a fanciful story about a rose and a butterfly.

of faraway places in geography books. **2** dreamy: *A faraway look in her eyes showed that she was thinking of something else. adjective.*

fare (fer *or* far), **1** the money that a person pays to ride in a bus, taxi, subway, airplane, train, or ship. **2** passenger on a train, taxi, bus, ship, or aircraft. **3** food: *delicious fare.* **4** do; get on: *He is faring well in school.* 1-3 *noun,* 4 *verb,* **fared, far ing.**

Far East, China, Japan, and other parts of eastern Asia.

fare well (fer′wel′ *or* far′wel′), **1** good luck; good-by. **2** good wishes at parting. **3** parting; last: *a farewell kiss. The singer gave a farewell performance.* 1,2 *noun, interjection,* 3 *adjective.*

farm (färm), **1** piece of land which a person uses to raise crops or animals. **2** raise crops or animals either to eat or to sell: *Her parents farm for a living.* **3** cultivate (land): *They farm fifty acres.* 1 *noun,* 2,3 *verb.*
farm out, let for hire: *He farms out the right to pick berries on his land.*

farm er (fär′mər), person who raises crops or animals on a farm. *noun.*

farm house (färm′hous′), house to live in on a farm. *noun, plural* **farm hous es** (farm′hou′ziz).

farm ing (fär′ming), business of raising crops or animals on a farm; agriculture. *noun.*

farm yard (färm′yärd′), the yard connected with the farm buildings or enclosed by them. *noun.*

far-off (fär′ôf′), distant; far away. *adjective.*

far-reach ing (fär′rē′ching), having a wide influence or effect; extending far: *The use of atomic energy has far-reaching effects. adjective.*

far sight ed (fär′sī′tid), seeing distant things more clearly than near ones. Some farsighted people wear glasses to read. *adjective.*

far ther (fär′ᴛнər), **1** more distant: *Three miles is farther than two.* **2** to a greater distance: *We walked farther than we meant to.* **3** to a more advanced point: *She has looked into the problem farther than anyone else.* 1 *adjective, comparative of* **far;** 2,3 *adverb, comparative of* **far.**

far thest (fär′ᴛнist), **1** most distant: *Ours is the house farthest down the road.* **2** to or at the greatest distance: *He hit the ball farthest.* **3** most: *Their ideas were the farthest advanced at that time.* 1 *adjective, superlative of* **far;** 2,3 *adverb, superlative of* **far.**

fas ci nate (fas′n āt), **1** charm: *The designs and colors in African art fascinated her.* **2** hold motionless by strange power or by terror: *Snakes are said to fascinate small birds. verb,* **fas ci nat ed, fas ci nat ing.**

fas ci na tion (fas′n ā′shən), **1** fascinating. **2** very strong attraction; charm. *noun.*

fash ion (fash′ən), **1** way a thing is shaped or made or done: *He walks in a peculiar fashion.* **2** current custom in dress, manners, or speech; style: *the latest fashion in shoes.* **3** make, shape, or form. See picture. 1,2 *noun,* 3 *verb.*

fash ion a ble (fash′ə nə bəl), following the fashion; in fashion; stylish. See picture. *adjective.*

fast[1] (fast), **1** quick; rapid; swift: *She is a fast runner.* **2** quickly; rapidly; swiftly: *Airplanes go fast.*

3 showing a time ahead of the real time: *That clock is fast.* **4** firm; secure; tight: *a fast hold on a rope.* **5** firmly: *He held fast as the sled went on down the hill.* **6** loyal; faithful: *They have been fast friends for years.* **7** that will not fade easily: *cloth dyed with fast color.* **8** thoroughly: *The baby is fast asleep.* 1,3,4,6,7 *adjective,* 2,5,8 *adverb.*

fast[2] (fast), **1** go without food; eat little or nothing; go without certain kinds of food. **2** act of fasting. **3** day or time of fasting. 1 *verb,* 2,3 *noun.*

fas ten (fas′n), **1** tie, lock, or make hold together in any way: *fasten a door, fasten a seat belt.* **2** fix; direct: *The dog fastened its eyes on me. verb.*

fas ten er (fas′n ər), **1** person who fastens. **2** attachment or device used to fasten a door or garment. A zipper is a fastener. *noun.*

fas ten ing (fas′n ing), thing used to fasten something. Locks, bolts, clasps, hooks, and buttons are all fastenings. *noun.*

fast-food (fast′füd′), serving food that is prepared quickly, such as hamburgers, pizza, or fried chicken: *fast-food restaurants. adjective.*

fas tid i ous (fa stid′ē əs), hard to please: *a fastidious dresser. adjective.*

fat (fat), **1** a white or yellow oily substance formed in the body of animals. Fat is also found in plants, especially in some seeds. **2** having much of this: *fat meat.* **3** having much flesh; well fed: *a fat baby, a fat pig.* **4** plentiful; full of good things: *That fat job pays well.* 1 *noun,* 2-4 *adjective,* **fat ter, fat test.**
live off the fat of the land, have the best of everything: *The rich family lived off the fat of the land.*

fa tal (fā′tl), **1** causing death: *Careless drivers cause many fatal accidents.* **2** causing destruction or ruin: *The loss of all our money was fatal to our plans.* **3** important; fateful: *At last the fatal day for the contest arrived. adjective.*

fate (fāt), **1** power that is supposed to decide and control what is to happen in the future. Fate is thought to be beyond anyone's control: *Many people don't believe in fate.* **2** what happens to a person or group; one's fortune: *History shows the fate of many nations. noun.*

fat ed (fā′tid), controlled by fate: *The fortuneteller told me I was fated to become famous. adjective.*

fate ful (fāt′fəl), **1** controlled by fate. **2** determining what is to happen; important; decisive: *a fateful battle.* **3** causing death, destruction, or ruin; disastrous: *a fateful poison. adjective.*

fa ther (fä′ᴛнər), **1** a male parent. **2** man who did important work as a maker or leader: *Washington is called the father of his country.* **3** be the cause of; originate: *Edison fathered many inventions.* **4** priest. **5 Father,** God. 1,2,4,5 *noun,* 3 *verb.*

fa ther hood (fä′ᴛнər hùd), condition of being a father. *noun.*

fa ther-in-law (fä′ᴛнər in lô′), father of one's husband or wife. *noun, plural* **fa thers-in-law.**

fa ther land (fä′ᴛнər land′), one's native country; land of one's ancestors. *noun.*

fa ther less (fä′ᴛнər lis), having no father: *a fatherless child. adjective.*

a hat	i it	oi oil	ch child	a in about
ā age	ī ice	ou out	ng long	e in taken
ä far	o hot	u cup	sh she	ə = i in pencil
e let	ō open	u̇ put	th thin	o in lemon
ē equal	ô order	ü rule	ŦH then	u in circus
ėr term			zh measure	

fashionable—a fashionable young woman around 1900

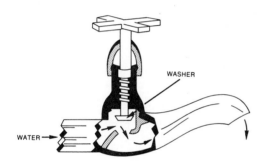

faucet—the inside of a faucet when the water is turned on. To stop the flow of water, the handle is turned until the round washer covers the circular hole.

fashion (definition 3)
The girls and boys fashioned puppets from paper bags.

fa ther ly (fä′ŦHər lē), of or like a father; kindly: *a fatherly person, a fatherly smile. adjective.*

fath om (faŦH′əm), **1** a unit of length equal to 6 feet. It is used in measuring the depth of water and the length of the ropes and cables on ships. **2** find the depth of. **3** get to the bottom of; understand: *I can't fathom what you mean.* **1** *noun,* **2,3** *verb.*

fa tigue (fə tēg′), **1** a tired feeling caused by hard work or effort: *I felt extreme fatigue after studying for three hours.* **2** make weary or tired. **1** *noun,* **2** *verb,* **fa tigued, fa ti guing.**

fat ten (fat′n), **1** make fat: *fatten pigs for market.* **2** become fat: *The pigs fattened on corn. verb.*

fat ty (fat′ē), **1** of fat; containing fat. **2** like fat; oily; greasy. *adjective,* **fat ti er, fat ti est.**

fau cet (fô′sit), device for turning on or off a flow of liquid from a pipe or a container holding it; tap. See picture. *noun.*

fault (fôlt), **1** something that is not as it should be: *Her dog has two faults; it eats too much, and it howls at night.* **2** mistake; error: *a fault in the answer to an arithmetic problem.* **3** cause for blame; responsibility: *Whose fault was it? noun.*
find fault, find mistakes; complain: *Why do you find fault so much?*
find fault with, object to or criticize: *My teacher is always finding fault with my homework.*

fault less (fôlt′lis), without a single fault or defect; perfect. *adjective.*

fault y (fôl′tē), having faults; imperfect; defective: *The leak in the faucet was caused by a faulty valve. adjective,* **fault i er, fault i est.**

faun (fôn), a minor god in Roman myths that lived in fields and woods and helped farmers and shepherds. A faun was supposed to look like a man, but to have the ears, horns, tail, and legs of a goat. *noun.*

fa vor (fā′vər), **1** act of kindness: *Will you do me a favor?* **2** show kindness to; oblige: *Favor us with a song.* **3** liking; approval: *to look with favor on a plan.* **4** like; approve: *We favor his plan.* **5** more than fair treatment: *He divided the candy among the children without favor to any one.* **6** give more than is fair to: *The teacher favors you.* **7** aid; help: *A sunny day favored the success of our picnic.* **8** a small gift given to every guest at a party or dinner: *Paper hats were used as favors at the birthday party.* **9** look like: *That girl favors her mother a great deal.* **1,3,5,8** *noun,* **2,4,6,7,9** *verb.*
in favor of, 1 on the side of: *He argued in favor of her plan.* **2** to the advantage of: *The referee's decision was in favor of the other team.*
in one's favor, for one; to one's benefit: *Her basket scored points in our favor.*

fa vor a ble (fā′vər ə bəl), **1** favoring; approving:

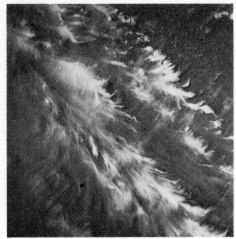

feathery clouds

fencing

"Yes" is a favorable answer to a request. **2** being to one's advantage; helping: *A favorable wind made the boat go faster. adjective.*

fa vor a bly (fā′vər ə blē), with consent or approval; kindly. *adverb.*

fa vor ite (fā′vər it), **1** liked better than others: *What is your favorite flower?* **2** the one liked better than others; person or thing liked very much: *He is a favorite with everybody.* 1 *adjective,* 2 *noun.*

fawn[1] (fôn), **1** deer less than a year old. **2** light, yellowish brown. 1 *noun,* 2 *adjective.*

fawn[2] (fôn), **1** try to get favor or notice by slavish acts: *Many flattering relatives fawned on the rich old man.* **2** show fondness by crouching, wagging the tail, and licking the hand as a dog does. *verb.*

fear (fir), **1** a feeling that danger or evil is near: *I have a fear of high places.* **2** be afraid of: *Our cat fears big dogs. Our baby brother fears loud noises.* **3** feel fear; have an uneasy feeling or idea: *I fear that my friends are in danger. I fear that I am late.* 1 *noun,* 2,3 *verb.*

fear ful (fir′fəl), **1** causing fear; terrible; dreadful: *a fearful dragon.* **2** feeling fear; frightened: *The child was fearful of the dark.* **3** showing fear: *We heard a fearful cry. adjective.*

fear less (fir′lis), afraid of nothing; brave. *adjective.*

feast (fēst), **1** a rich meal prepared for some special occasion and for a number of guests; banquet: *We went to the wedding feast.* **2** eat a rich meal; have a feast: *They feasted on goose.* **3** provide a rich meal for: *The queen feasted her followers.* **4** take delight in; delight: *We feasted our eyes on the sunset.* **5** festival or celebration: *Easter is an important Christian feast; Passover is an important Jewish feast.* 1,5 *noun,* 2-4 *verb.*

feat (fēt), great deed; act showing great skill, strength, or daring. See picture. *noun.*

feath er (feᴛʜ′ər), **1** one of the light, thin growths that cover a bird's skin. Because feathers are soft and light, they are used to fill pillows. **2** supply or cover with feathers. 1 *noun,* 2 *verb.*

feath er y (feᴛʜ′ər ē), **1** having or covered with feathers. **2** like feathers. See picture. *adjective.*

fea ture (fē′chər), **1** part of the face. The eyes, nose, mouth, chin, and forehead are features. **2** a distinct part or quality; thing that stands out and attracts attention: *Your plan for the picnic has many good features and some bad ones. The main features of southern California are the climate and the scenery.* **3** the main film shown on a motion-picture program: *After the previews, we settled back in our seats for the feature. noun.*

Feb., February.

Feb ru ar y (feb′rü er′ē), the second month of the year. It has 28 days except in leap years, when it has 29. *noun.* [*February* comes from the name of a Roman feast celebrated on February 15.]

fed (fed). See **feed.** *We fed the birds yesterday. Have they been fed today? verb.*

fed up, bored, impatient, or disgusted with something.

fed er al (fed′ər əl), **1** formed by an agreement of

feat—Twelve people riding on one bicycle is quite a feat.

states: *Switzerland and the United States both became nations by federal union.* **2** of the central government of the United States, not of any state or city alone: *Coining money is a federal power.* *adjective.*

fed e ra tion (fed′ə rā′shən), league; union by agreement, often a union of states or nations: *Each member of the federation controls its own affairs. noun.*

fee (fē), money asked for or paid for some service or privilege; charge: *an admission fee. Doctors and lawyers receive fees for their services. noun.*

fee ble (fē′bəl), weak: *An old or sick person is often feeble. A feeble attempt is liable to fail. adjective,* **fee bler, fee blest.**

feed (fēd), **1** give food to: *We feed a baby who cannot feed himself.* **2** give as food: *Feed this grain to the chickens.* **3** eat: *We put cows to feed in the pasture.* **4** food for animals: *Give the chickens their feed.* **5** supply with material: *Feed the fire.* **1-3,5** *verb,* **fed, feed ing; 4** *noun.*

feed er (fē′dər), device for supplying food for an animal: *The bird feeder in our yard is filled with seed. noun.*

feel (fēl), **1** touch: *Feel this cloth.* **2** way something seems to the touch; feeling: *I like the feel of silk. Wet soap has a greasy feel.* **3** try to find or make (one's way) by touch: *He felt his way across the room when the lights went out.* **4** find out by touching: *Feel how cold my hands are.* **5** be aware of: *He felt the cool breeze. She felt the heat.* **6** be; have the feeling of being: *She feels glad. He feels angry. We felt hot. She felt sure.* **7** seem; give the feeling of being: *The air feels cold.* **8** have in one's mind; experience: *They feel pity. I felt pain. He felt fear of the thunder.* **9** have a feeling: *I felt for the poor, lonesome dog. Try to feel more kindly toward her. I feel that he will come.* **1,3-9** *verb,* **felt, feel ing; 2** *noun.*

feel er (fē′lər), **1** a special part of an animal's body for touching. The long feelers on the heads of insects help them find their way. **2** suggestion, remark, hint, or question made to find out what others are thinking or planning. *noun.*

feel ing (fē′ling), **1** sense of touch. By feeling we tell what is hard from what is soft. **2** sensation; condition of being aware: *She had no feeling in her leg.* **3** emotion. Joy, sorrow, fear, and anger are feelings. *The loss of the ball game stirred up much feeling.* **4** **feelings,** tender or sensitive side of one's nature: *You hurt my feelings when you yelled at me.* **5** opinion: *I have no feeling about the plan, one way or the other. noun.*

feet (fēt), more than one foot: *A dog has four feet. I am five feet tall. noun plural.*

feign (fān), pretend: *Some animals feign death when in danger. She isn't sick; she is only feigning. verb.*

feint (fānt), **1** pretense: *He made a feint of being absorbed in his lessons, but really he was listening to the radio.* **2** movement made with the purpose of deceiving; pretended attack or blow: *The fighter made a feint at his opponent with his right hand and struck with his left.* **3** make a feint: *The fighter*

a hat	i it	oi oil	ch child	a in about
ā age	ī ice	ou out	ng long	e in taken
ä far	o hot	u cup	sh she	ə = { i in pencil
e let	ō open	u̇ put	th thin	o in lemon
ē equal	ô order	ü rule	ŦH then	u in circus
ėr term			zh measure	

feinted with his right hand and struck with his left. **1,2** *noun,* **3** *verb.*

fell[1] (fel). See **fall.** *Snow fell last night. verb.*

fell[2] (fel), **1** cause to fall; knock down: *A blow on the head felled her to the ground.* **2** cut down (a tree): *They had to fell many trees to clear the land. verb.*

fel low (fel′ō), **1** a male person; man or boy. **2** person; anybody; one: *What can a fellow do?* **3** companion; one of the same class; equal: *He was cut off from his fellows.* **4** being in the same or a like condition: *fellow citizens, fellow sufferers, fellow workers.* **1-3** *noun,* **4** *adjective.*

fel low ship (fel′ō ship), **1** companionship; friendliness. **2** being one of a group; membership; sharing: *I have enjoyed fellowship in this club. noun.*

felt[1] (felt). See **feel.** *I felt the cat's soft fur. It was felt that the picnic should be postponed. verb.*

felt[2] (felt), **1** cloth that is not woven, but is made by rolling and pressing together wool, hair, or fur. **2** made of felt: *a felt hat.* **1** *noun,* **2** *adjective.*

fe male (fē′māl), **1** woman or girl. **2** of or having to do with women or girls. **3** belonging to the sex that can give birth to young or lay eggs. Mares, cows, and hens are female animals. **4** animal belonging to this sex. **1,4** *noun,* **2,3** *adjective.*

fem i nine (fem′ə nən), **1** of women or girls. **2** like a woman; womanly. *adjective.*

fence (fens), **1** railing or wall put around a yard, garden, field, or farm to show where it ends or to keep people or animals out or in. Most fences are made of wood, wire, or metal. A stone fence is a wall. A fence of growing bushes is a hedge. **2** put a fence around. **3** fight with long slender swords or foils. **4** person who buys and sells stolen goods. **1,4** *noun,* **2,3** *verb,* **fenced, fenc ing.**

fenc er (fen′sər), person who knows how to fight with a sword or foil. *noun.*

fenc ing (fen′sing), art or sport of fighting with swords or foils. See picture. *noun.*

fend er (fen′dər), **1** metal frame over the wheel of a car, truck, or bicycle. The fender protects the wheel and reduces splashing in wet weather. **2** bar, frame, or screen in front of a fireplace to keep hot coals and sparks from flying into the room. *noun.*

fer ment (fər ment′ *for 1;* fėr′ment *for 2*), **1** undergo or produce a gradual chemical change in which sugar changes to alcohol and gives off bubbles of carbon dioxide. Vinegar is formed when cider ferments. **2** tumult; excitement: *The school was in a ferment.* **1** *verb,* **2** *noun.*

fern (fėrn), kind of plant that has roots, stems, and feathery leaves, but no flowers. The tiny seeds (called spores) grow in the little brown dots on the backs of the leaves. *noun.*

ferocious

fe ro cious (fə rō′shəs), fierce; savage; very cruel: *I was frightened when I saw the ferocious-looking statue.* See picture. *adjective.*

fe roc i ty (fə ros′ə tē), fierceness; savage behavior; great cruelty: *The wolves fought with bloodthirsty ferocity. noun.*

fer ret (fer′it), **1** a white or yellowish-white European polecat which people use for killing rats and driving rabbits from their holes. **2** hunt with ferrets. **3** hunt; search: *It took the detectives over a year to ferret out the criminal.* 1 *noun,* 2,3 *verb.*

Fer ris wheel (fer′is hwēl′), a large revolving wheel with hanging seats, used in carnivals, amusement parks, and fairs. See picture.

fer ry (fer′ē), **1** carry (people, vehicles, and goods) across a river or narrow stretch of water. **2** boat that makes the trip; ferryboat. **3** place where boats carry people and goods across a river or narrow stretch of water. **4** go across in a ferryboat. **5** carry back and forth in an airplane. 1,4,5 *verb,* **fer ried, fer ry ing;** 2,3 *noun, plural* **fer ries.**

fer ry boat (fer′ē bōt′), boat that carries people, vehicles, and goods across a river or narrow stretch of water. *noun.*

fer tile (fer′tl), **1** able to bear seeds, fruit, or young: *a fertile animal or plant.* **2** able to develop into a new individual; fertilized: *Chicks hatch from fertile eggs.* **3** able to produce much; producing crops easily: *Fertile soil yields good crops.* **4** producing ideas; creative: *a fertile mind. adjective.*

fer til i ty (fər til′ə tē), **1** bearing, or abundant bearing, of seeds, fruits, crops, or young. **2** power to produce. *Fertility of the mind means power to produce many ideas. noun.*

fer ti lize (fer′tl īz), **1** make fertile. **2** make (a thing) start to grow. **3** make (the soil) produce more by putting manure or other fertilizer into or on the soil. *verb,* **fer ti lized, fer ti liz ing.**

fer ti liz er (fer′tl ī′zər), manure or other substance put into or on the soil to make it produce more. *noun.*

fer vent (fer′vənt), showing great emotion; very earnest: *She made a fervent plea for food and medicine for the earthquake victims. adjective.*

fer vor (fer′vər), great emotion; enthusiasm; earnestness: *The patriot spoke with such fervor that his voice trembled. noun.*

fes ti val (fes′tə vəl), **1** day or special time of rejoicing or feasting, often in memory of some great happening: *Christmas is a Christian festival; Hanukkah is a Jewish festival.* **2** celebration; entertainment: *a summer music festival. noun.*

fes tive (fes′tiv), of or suitable for a feast or holiday; gay; merry. See picture. *adjective.*

fes tiv i ty (fe stiv′ə tē), rejoicing and feasting; merry party: *The wedding festivities were very gay. noun, plural* **fes tiv i ties.**

fetch (fech), **1** go and get; bring: *Please fetch me my glasses.* **2** be sold for: *These eggs will fetch a good price. verb.*

fet ter (fet′ər), **1** chain or shackle for the feet: *Fetters prevented the prisoner's escape.* **2** bind with fetters; chain the feet of. 1 *noun,* 2 *verb.*

feud (fyüd), **1** a long and deadly quarrel between families. Feuds are often passed down from generation to generation. **2** bitter hatred between two persons or groups. *noun.*

fe ver (fē′vər), **1** body temperature that is greater than usual. A sick person may have a fever. **2** any sickness that heats the body and makes the heart beat fast: *typhoid fever.* **3** an excited, restless condition: *When gold was discovered the miners were in a fever of excitement. noun.*

fe ver ish (fē′vər ish), **1** having fever. **2** having some fever but not much. **3** excited; restless: *He packed his bags in feverish haste. adjective.*

few (fyü), **1** not many: *Few people came to the meeting because of the storm.* **2** a small number: *Winter in New England has not many warm days, only a few.* 1 *adjective,* 2 *noun.*

fez (fez), a felt cap, usually red and ornamented

with a long black tassel. *noun, plural* **fez zes.**

fib (fib), **1** a lie about some small matter. **2** tell such a lie. **1** *noun,* **2** *verb,* **fibbed, fib bing.**

fi ber (fī′bər), **1** thread; threadlike part. A muscle is made up of many fibers. **2** substance made up of threads or threadlike parts: *Hemp fiber can be spun or woven.* **3** any part of food that cannot be digested and so speeds the movement of food and waste products through the intestines. The cellulose in vegetables is fiber. **4** character; nature: *A person of strong moral fiber can resist temptation. noun.*

fick le (fik′əl), changing; not constant; likely to change without reason: *a fickle friend. adjective.*

fic tion (fik′shən), **1** story that is not fact. Short stories and novels are fiction. "Robinson Crusoe" is fiction. **2** something made up: *She exaggerates her experiences so much that it is hard to separate fact from fiction. noun.*

fid dle (fid′l), **1** violin. **2** play on a violin. **1** *noun,* **2** *verb,* **fid dled, fid dling.**

fidg et (fij′it), move about restlessly: *Children sometimes fidget if they have to sit still too long. verb.*

field (fēld), **1** land with few or no trees; open country: *They drove through the woods until they came to a field covered with wild flowers.* **2** piece of land used for crops or for pasture. **3** piece of land used for some special purpose: *a baseball field.* **4** battlefield: *the field of Gettysburg.* **5** land yielding some product: *the coal fields of Pennsylvania.* **6** flat space; broad surface: *A field of ice surrounds the North Pole.* **7** range of interest; area of activity: *the field of art.* **8** (in baseball) to stop or catch (a batted ball) and throw it in. **1-7** *noun,* **8** *verb.*

field day, day for athletic contests and outdoor sports.

field er (fēl′dər), a baseball player who is stationed around or outside the diamond to stop the ball and throw it in. *noun.*

field glasses or **field glass,** small binoculars for use outdoors.

field trip, trip away from school to give students the opportunity to see things closely and at first hand: *The class went on a field trip to the zoo to observe animals they had read about.*

fiend (fēnd), **1** devil; evil spirit. **2** a very wicked or cruel person. *noun.*

fiend ish (fēn′dish), very cruel or wicked: *the fiendish laughter of a wicked witch. adjective.*

fierce (firs), **1** savage; wild: *A wounded lion can be fierce.* **2** very great or strong; intense: *fierce anger, a fierce wind. adjective,* **fierc er, fierc est.**

fie ry (fī′rē), **1** containing fire; burning; flaming: *a fiery furnace.* **2** like fire; very hot; glowing: *a fiery red, fiery heat.* **3** full of feeling or spirit: *a fiery speech.* **4** easily aroused or excited: *a fiery temper. adjective,* **fie ri er, fie ri est.**

fi es ta (fē es′tə), **1** a religious festival. **2** holiday; festivity. *noun.*

fife (fīf), a small, shrill musical instrument like a flute, played by blowing. Fifes are used with drums to make music for marching. See picture. *noun.*

festive—A wedding is a **festive** occasion.

Ferris wheel—The first Ferris wheel was built for the Chicago world's fair in 1893.

fife—The soldiers marched to the sound of **fife** and drum.

fif teen (fif′tēn′), five more than ten; 15. *noun, adjective.*

fif teenth (fif′tēnth′), **1** next after the 14th. **2** one of 15 equal parts. *adjective, noun.*

fifth (fifth), **1** next after the fourth. **2** one of five equal parts. *adjective, noun.*

fif ti eth (fif′tē ith), **1** next after the 49th. **2** one of 50 equal parts. *adjective, noun.*

fif ty (fif′tē), five times ten; 50. *noun, plural* **fif ties;** *adjective.*

fig (fig), a small, soft, sweet fruit of a tree that grows in warm regions. Figs are sometimes eaten fresh or canned, but usually are dried like dates and raisins. *noun.*

fight (fīt), **1** a violent struggle; combat; contest: *A fight ends when one side gives up.* **2** an angry dispute; quarrel: *Their fights were always over money.* **3** take part in a fight: *When people fight they hit one another. Soldiers fight by shooting with guns. Countries fight with armies.* **4** take part in a fight against; struggle against: *fight disease, fight one's fear of the dark.* **5** carry on (a fight or conflict): *fight a duel.* **6** get or make by fighting: *She had to fight her way through the crowd.* **7** power or will to fight: *There was not much fight left in the losing team.* 1,2,7 *noun,* 3-6 *verb,* **fought, fight ing.**

fight er (fī′tər), **1** a person that fights. **2** a professional boxer. *noun.*

fig ur a tive (fig′yər ə tiv), using words out of their ordinary meaning. Much poetry is figurative. *adjective.*

fig ure (fig′yər), **1** symbol for a number. 1, 2, 3, 4, etc., are figures. **2** use numbers to find out the answer to some problem. **3** figures, arithmetic: *She is very good at figures.* **4** price: *The house was sold at a very high figure.* **5** Squares, triangles, cubes, and other shapes are called figures. **6** form or shape: *I could see the figure of a woman against the window.* **7** person; character: *The governor is a well-known figure throughout the state.* **8** stand out; appear: *The names of great leaders figure in the story of human progress.* **9** picture; drawing; diagram; illustration: *This book has many figures to help explain words.* **10** design or pattern: *the figures in the wallpaper.* 1,3-7,9,10 *noun,* 2,8 *verb,* **fig ured, fig ur ing.**

figure out, think out; understand: *Even the repairman couldn't figure out what had gone wrong with the washer.*

fig ure head (fig′yər hed′), **1** person who is head in name only, without real authority. **2** figure placed for ornament on the bow of a ship. See picture. *noun.*

figure of speech, expression in which words are used out of their ordinary meaning to add beauty or force. When we say someone has "the eye of an eagle," we are using a figure of speech.

fil a ment (fil′ə mənt), a very fine thread; very slender part that is like a thread. The wire that gives off light in an electric light bulb is a filament. The slender stem of the stamen of a flower is a filament. *noun.*

file[1] (fīl), **1** container, drawer, or folder for keeping memorandums, letters, or other papers in order. **2** set of papers kept in order: *a file of receipts.* **3** put away in order: *Please file those letters.* **4** row of persons or things one behind another: *a file of soldiers marching in time, ships sailing in file.* **5** march or move in a file: *The pupils filed out of the room during the fire drill.* 1,2,4 *noun,* 3,5 *verb,* **filed, fil ing.** [An earlier English meaning of *file*[1] was "a string or wire on which papers are hung." It was taken from a Latin word meaning "thread."]

file[2] (fīl), **1** a steel tool with many small ridges or teeth on it. Its rough surface is used to smooth rough materials or wear away hard substances. **2** smooth or wear away with a file. 1 *noun,* 2 *verb,* **filed, fil ing.**

fi let (fi lā′ *or* fil′ā), slice of fish or meat without bones or fat; fillet. *noun.*

fil ings (fī′lingz), small pieces of iron or wood which have been removed by a file. *noun plural.*

figurehead (definition 2)

fingerprint (definition 1)—the eight basic kinds of fingerprints. Almost all fingerprints can be classified by using these patterns.

PLAIN ARCH · LOOP · PLAIN WHORL · DOUBLE LOOP

TENTED ARCH · LOOP · CENTRAL POCKET LOOP · ACCIDENTAL

fill (fil), **1** make full; put into until there is room for nothing more: *Fill this bottle with water. We filled the pots with soil before planting the seeds.* **2** become full: *The well filled with water.* **3** take up all the space in; spread throughout: *The crowd filled the hall. Smoke filled the room.* **4** all that is needed or wanted: *There is plenty of food, so eat your fill.* **5** supply with all that is needed or wanted for: *The druggist filled the doctor's prescription.* **6** stop up or close by putting something in: *The dentist filled my tooth.* **7** hold and do the duties of (a position or office): *We need someone to fill the office of vice-president.* **8** something that fills. Earth or rock used to make uneven land level is called fill. 1-3,5-7 *verb,* 4,8 *noun.*

fil let (fi lā′ *or* fil′ā), **1** slice of meat or fish without bones or fat. **2** cut (fish or meat) into fillets. 1 *noun,* 2 *verb.*

fill ing (fil′ing), thing put in to fill something: *a filling in a tooth. noun.*

fil ly (fil′ē), a young female horse or donkey. A mare until it is four or five years old is a filly. *noun, plural* **fil lies.**

film (film), **1** a very thin surface or coating, often of liquid: *Oil on water will spread and make a film.* **2** cover or become covered with a film: *Her eyes filmed over with tears.* **3** roll or sheet of thin material covered with a coating that is changed by light, used to take photographs: *He bought two rolls of film for his camera.* **4** motion picture: *We saw a film about animals.* **5** make a motion picture of: *They filmed "The Wizard of Oz."* **6** photograph or be photographed for motion pictures: *They filmed the scene three times.* 1,3,4 *noun,* 2,5,6 *verb.*

fil ter (fil′tər), **1** device for passing water or other liquids, or air, through felt, paper, sand, or charcoal, in order to remove impurities. **2** material through which the liquid or air passes in a filter. **3** pass or flow very slowly: *Water filters through the sandy soil and into the well.* **4** put through a filter: *We filter this water for drinking.* **5** act as a filter for: *The charcoal filtered the water.* **6** remove by a filter: *Filter the dirt out of the water.* 1,2 *noun,* 3-6 *verb.*

filth (filth), foul, disgusting dirt: *The alley was filled with garbage and filth. noun.*

filth y (fil′thē), very dirty; foul. *adjective,* **filth i er, filth i est.**

fin (fin), **1** one of the movable winglike or fanlike parts of a fish's body. By moving its fins a fish can swim and balance itself in the water. The large fins of a flying fish unfold like a fan and can carry it a little way through the air. **2** thing shaped or used like a fin. Some aircraft have fins to help balance them when they move. *noun.*

fi nal (fi′nl), **1** at the end; coming last: *The book was interesting from the first to the final chapter.* **2** deciding completely; settling the question: *The one with the highest authority makes the final decisions.* **3** finals, the last or deciding set in a series of games or examinations. 1,2 *adjective,* 3 *noun.*

fi na le (fə nä′lē), the last part of a piece of music or a play. *noun.*

fi nal ly (fi′nl ē), **1** at the end; at last: *The lost dog finally came home.* **2** in such a way as to decide or settle the question: *They must tackle the issue finally. adverb.*

fi nance (fə nans′ *or* fi′nans), **1** money matters: *A successful banker must have skill in finance.* **2** finances, money matters; funds; revenues: *New taxes were needed to increase the nation's finances.* **3** provide money for: *A part-time job helped finance her college education.* 1,2 *noun,* 3 *verb.*

fi nan cial (fə nan′shəl *or* fi nan′shəl), having to do with money matters: *My financial affairs are in good order. adjective.*

fin an cier (fin′ən sir′ *or* fi′nən sir′), person occupied or skilled in money matters. Bankers are financiers. *noun.*

finch (finch), a small songbird with a bill shaped like a cone. Sparrows, cardinals, and canaries are finches. *noun, plural* **finch es.**

find (fīnd), **1** meet with; come upon: *I found a dime on the sidewalk. They find friends everywhere.* **2** look for and get: *Please find my hat for me.* **3** learn; discover: *We found that he could not swim.* **4** get; get the use of: *Can you find time to do this?* **5** reach; arrive at: *The arrow found its mark.* **6** decide and declare: *The jury found the woman guilty.* **7** something found. 1-6 *verb,* **found, find ing;** 7 *noun.*

find out, learn about; come to know; discover.

find ing (fīn′ding), **1** discovery. **2** thing found. *noun.*

fine[1] (fīn), **1** very good; excellent: *Everyone praised his fine singing. She is a fine student.* **2** very small or thin: *Thread is finer than rope. Sand is finer than gravel.* **3** sharp: *a tool with a fine edge.* **4** delicate: *fine linen.* **5** elegant; refined: *fine manners.* **6** very well; excellently: *I'm doing fine.* 1-5 *adjective,* **fin er, fin est;** 6 *adverb.*

fine[2] (fīn), **1** sum of money paid as a punishment for breaking a law or regulation. **2** make pay such a sum: *The judge fined the driver twenty dollars for speeding.* 1 *noun,* 2 *verb,* **fined, fin ing.**

fin er y (fī′nər ē), showy clothes or ornaments. *noun, plural* **fin er ies.**

fin ger (fing′gər), **1** one of the five end parts of the hand, especially the four besides the thumb. **2** anything shaped or used like a finger. **3** touch or handle with the fingers; use the fingers on: *to finger the keyboard of a piano.* 1,2 *noun,* 3 *verb.*

fin ger nail (fing′gər nāl′), hard layer of horn at the end of a finger. *noun.*

fin ger print (fing′gər print′), **1** a mark made by the fleshy tip of a finger. Your fingerprints can be used to identify you because no two fingers have the same pattern of lines on them. See picture. **2** take the fingerprints of. 1 *noun,* 2 *verb.*

fin ish (fin′ish), **1** complete; bring to an end; reach the end of: *finish one's dinner, finish painting a picture.* **2** end: *a fight to the finish.* **3** use up completely: *finish a bottle of milk.* **4** way in which the surface is prepared: *a smooth finish on furniture.* **5** prepare the surface of in some way: *finish metal with a dull surface.* 1,3,5 *verb,* 2,4 *noun, plural* **fin ish es.**

fiord (fyôrd), a long, narrow bay bordered by steep cliffs. See picture. *noun.*

fir (fėr), an evergreen tree somewhat like a spruce. Small firs are often used for Christmas trees. The needles of fir trees have a pleasant smell. *noun.*

fire (fīr), **1** flame, heat, and light caused by something burning. **2** something burning. **3** destruction by burning: *A cigarette thrown into the woods in dry weather may start a fire.* **4** make burn; set on fire. **5** heat of feeling; readiness to act; excitement: *Their hearts were full of patriotic fire.* **6** arouse; excite; inflame: *Stories of adventure fire the imagination.* **7** the shooting or discharge of guns: *rifle fire.* **8** discharge: *A policewoman must know how to fire a gun correctly.* **9** dismiss from a job: *The manager fired two sales clerks last week.* 1-3,5,7 *noun,* 4,6,8,9 *verb,* **fired, fir ing.**
catch fire, begin to burn.
on fire, 1 burning. **2** excited.
open fire, begin shooting.
under fire, 1 exposed to shooting from the enemy's guns: *Soldiers are under fire in a battle.* **2** attacked; blamed.

fire arm (fīr′ärm′), gun, pistol, or other weapon to shoot with. A firearm usually can be carried and used by one person. *noun.*

fire crack er (fīr′krak′ər), a paper roll containing gunpowder and a fuse. Firecrackers explode with a loud noise. *noun.*

fire engine, truck with a machine for throwing water to put out fires; fire truck.

fire escape, stairway or ladder used when a building is on fire.

fire ex tin guish er (fīr′ ek sting′gwish ər), container filled with chemicals which are sprayed on a fire to put it out.

fire fight er (fīr′fī′tər), person whose work is putting out fires. *noun.*

fire fly (fīr′flī′), a small insect that gives off flashes of light when it flies at night. See picture. *noun, plural* **fire flies.**

fire house (fīr′hous′), building where fire engines are kept, and where firemen are on duty. *noun, plural* **fire hous es** (fīr′hou′ziz).

fire light (fīr′līt′), light from a fire. *noun.*

fire man (fīr′mən), **1** person whose work is putting out fires. **2** person who looks after fires in engines or furnaces. *noun, plural* **fire men.**

fire place (fīr′plās′), place built to hold a fire. An indoor fireplace is usually made of brick or stone, with a chimney leading up from it through the roof. *noun.*

fire proof (fīr′prüf′), **1** that will not burn, or will not burn easily: *A building made entirely of steel and concrete is fireproof.* **2** make so that it will not

fiord

firefly—about two times life size

burn, or not burn easily: *fireproof a theater curtain.* 1 *adjective,* 2 *verb.*

fire side (fīr′sīd′), **1** space around a fireplace or hearth. **2** home; hearth: *The weary travelers longed to be back at their own fireside. noun.*

fire truck, fire engine.

fire wood (fīr′wüd′), wood to make a fire. *noun.*

fire works (fīr′wėrks′), firecrackers, skyrockets, and other things that make a loud noise or a beautiful fiery display at night. *noun plural.*

firm¹ (fėrm), **1** not yielding when pressed: *firm flesh, firm ground.* **2** solid; fixed in place; not easily shaken or moved: *a tree firm in the earth.* **3** not easily changed; determined; positive: *a firm voice, a firm character, a firm belief. adjective.*

firm² (fėrm), company of two or more persons in business together. *noun.*

first (fėrst), **1** coming before all others: *He is first in his class.* **2** before all others; before anything else: *We eat first and then feed the cat.* **3** person, thing, or place that is first: *We were the first to get here.* **4** the beginning: *At first I did not like school.*

5 for the first time: *When we first met, we were both in grade school.* **6** rather; sooner: *I won't give up; I will die first.* **1** *adjective,* **2,5,6** *adverb,* **3,4** *noun.*

first aid, emergency treatment given to an injured or sick person before a doctor sees the person.

first-class (ferst/klas/), **1** of the highest class or best quality; excellent: *a first-class teacher.* **2** by the best and most expensive passenger seating and service offered by ship, airplane, or train: *We could not afford to travel first-class.* **1** *adjective,* **2** *adverb.*

first hand (ferst/hand/), direct; from the original source: *firsthand information. adjective, adverb.*

first-rate (ferst/rat/), **1** of the highest class; excellent; very good: *a first-rate summer.* **2** well: *She did first-rate on the test.* **1** *adjective,* **2** *adverb.*

fish (fish), **1** one of a group of cold-blooded animals with a long backbone that live in water and have gills instead of lungs for breathing. Fish are usually covered with scales and have fins for swimming. Some fishes lay eggs in the water; others produce living young. **2** flesh of fish used for food. **3** catch fish; try to catch fish. **4** try for something as if with a hook: *The boy fished with a stick for his watch, which had fallen through a grating.* **5** search: *I fished in my pocket for a dime.* **6** find and pull: *She fished the map from the drawer.* **7** try to get by means of cunning: *to fish for compliments.* **1,2** *noun, plural* **fish es** or **fish;** **3-7** *verb.*

fish er man (fish/ər mən), person who fishes, especially one who makes a living by catching fish. *noun, plural* **fish er men.**

fish er y (fish/ər ē), **1** place for catching fish. **2** place for breeding fish. *noun, plural* **fish er ies.**

fish hook (fish/hůk/), hook used for catching fish. *noun.*

fish line (fish/lin/), cord used with a fishhook for catching fish. *noun.*

fish y (fish/ē), **1** like a fish in smell, taste, or shape. **2** doubtful; unlikely: *That story sounds fishy; I don't believe it. adjective,* **fish i er, fish i est.**

fis sion (fish/ən), the splitting apart of atomic nuclei to produce tremendous amounts of energy. *noun.*

fist (fist), a tightly closed hand: *He shook his fist at me. noun.*

fit¹ (fit), **1** having the necessary qualities; suitable: *Grass is a fit food for cows, not for people.* **2** right; proper: *It is fit that we give thanks.* **3** healthy and strong: *Proper exercise and good food help to keep us fit.* **4** be right, proper, or suitable to: *The role of the queen's friend fits you perfectly.* **5** make right, proper, or suitable; suit: *She fitted the words to the music.* **6** have the right size or shape; have the right size or shape for: *Does this glove fit?* **7** make the right size or shape; adjust: *I had my new jacket fitted at the store.* **8** way that something fits: *The coat was not a very good fit; it was too tight.* **9** supply with everything needed; equip: *fit a store with counters, fit out a room.* **1-3** *adjective,* **fit ter, fit test;** **4-7,9** *verb,* **fit ted, fit ting;** **8** *noun.*

a hat	i it	oi oil	ch child	a in about
ā age	ī ice	ou out	ng long	e in taken
ä far	o hot	u cup	sh she	ə = i in pencil
e let	ō open	ů put	th thin	o in lemon
ē equal	ô order	ü rule	ŦH then	u in circus
ėr term			zh measure	

fit² (fit), **1** a sudden, sharp attack of disease. **2** any sudden, sharp attack: *In a fit of anger, I smashed the dish.* **3** a short period of doing some one thing: *a fit of coughing, a fit of laughing. noun.*

by fits and starts, starting, stopping, beginning again, and so on; irregularly: *He does his homework by fits and starts instead of steadily.*

fit ful (fit/fəl), irregular; going on and then stopping for a while: *I had a fitful sleep during the storm, waking up every few minutes. adjective.*

fit ting (fit/ing), right; proper; suitable. *adjective.*

five (fīv), one more than four; 5. *noun, adjective.*

fix (fiks), **1** make firm: *I fixed the post in the ground. He fixed the spelling lesson in his mind.* **2** set; put or place definitely: *She fixed the price at two dollars. It was not possible to fix the blame for the accident on either driver.* **3** direct or hold steadily: *We fixed our eyes on the blackboard.* **4** make ready; prepare: *We fixed our own breakfast this morning.* **5** mend; repair: *fix a watch.* **6** pay someone money in advance to arrange the result of: *fix a jury, fix a race.* **7** position hard to get out of: *Whoever took my bicycle is going to be in a fix.* **1-6** *verb,* **7** *noun, plural* **fix es.**

fix ture (fiks/chər), thing put in place to stay: *light fixtures. noun.*

fizz (fiz), **1** make a hissing sound. **2** hissing sound; bubbling: *the fizz of soda water.* **1** *verb,* **2** *noun, plural* **fizz es.**

flag¹ (flag), **1** piece of cloth, usually with square corners, on which is the picture or pattern that stands for some country: *the flag of the United States, the British flag.* Flags are hung on poles over buildings, ships, army camps, and similar places. **2** cloth or banner, such as is used for a signal: *a red flag showing danger, the white flag of truce.* **3** signal or stop (a person, train, bus, ship, or airplane) by waving a flag: *The train was flagged at the bridge.* **1,2** *noun,* **3** *verb,* **flagged, flag ging.**

flag² (flag), get tired; grow weak; droop: *My horse was flagging, but I urged him on. verb,* **flagged, flag ging.**

flag pole (flag/pōl/), pole from which a flag is flown. *noun.*

flail (flāl), a tool for threshing grain by hand. A flail consists of a wooden handle with a short, heavy stick fastened by a strip of leather. *noun.*

flair (fler *or* flar), natural talent: *The poet had a flair for making clever rhymes. noun.*

flake (flāk), **1** a flat, thin piece, usually not very large: *a flake of snow, flakes of rust, corn flakes.* **2** come off in flakes; separate into flakes: *Spots showed where the paint had flaked off.* **1** *noun,* **2** *verb,* **flaked, flak ing.**

flame (flām), **1** one of the glowing tongues of light that rise or shoot up when a fire blazes up: *a*

candle's flame, the flames of a burning house.
2 blaze; rise up in flames. **3** burning with flames;
blaze: *The dying fire suddenly burst into flame.*
4 shine brightly; flash: *Her eyes flamed with rage.*
5 something like flame. 1,3,5 *noun,* 2,4 *verb,*
flamed, flam ing.

fla min go (flə ming′gō), a tropical wading bird
with very long legs and neck, and feathers that
vary from pink to scarlet. See picture. *noun, plural*
fla min gos or **fla min goes.**

flam ma ble (flam′ə bəl), easily set on fire;
inflammable. *adjective.*

flank (flangk), **1** side of an animal or a person
between the ribs and the hip. **2** be at the side of:
A garage flanked the house. **3** the far right or the far
left side of an army, fort, or fleet. **4** get around the
far right or the far left side of (an enemy's army).
5 attack from or on the side. 1,3 *noun,* 2,4,5 *verb.*

flan nel (flan′l), **1** a soft, warm, woolen or cotton
cloth. **2** made of flannel. 1 *noun,* 2 *adjective.*

flap (flap), **1** swing or sway about loosely and with
some noise: *The sails flapped in the wind.* **2** move
(wings or arms) up and down: *The goose flapped
its wings but could not rise from the ground.* **3** fly by
flapping the wings: *The bird flapped away.* **4** a
flapping motion; flapping noise: *the flap of
banners, the flap of a bird's wing.* **5** strike noisily
with something broad and flat: *The clown's big
shoes flapped along the ground.* **6** piece hanging or
fastened at one edge only: *a coat with flaps on the
pockets.* 1-3,5 *verb,* **flapped, flap ping;** 4,6 *noun.*

flap jack (flap′jak′), pancake. *noun.*

flare (fler *or* flar), **1** flame up briefly or unsteadily,
sometimes with smoke: *A gust of wind made the
torches flare.* **2** blaze; bright, brief, unsteady flame:
The flare of a match showed us his face. **3** a dazzling
light that burns for a short time, used for
signaling or lighting up a battlefield: *The Coast
Guard vessel responded to the flare sent up from the
lifeboat.* **4** a sudden outburst: *a flare of anger.*
5 spread out in the shape of a bell: *These pants
flare at the bottom.* **6** spreading out into a bell
shape: *the flare of a skirt.* 1,5 *verb,* **flared, flar ing;**
2-4,6 *noun.*

flare up, burst into sudden anger or violence.

flash (flash), **1** a sudden, brief light or flame: *a
flash of lightning.* **2** give out such a light or flame:
The lighthouse flashes signals twice a minute. **3** come
suddenly; pass quickly: *A train flashed by. A
thought flashed across my mind.* **4** a sudden, short
feeling or display: *a flash of hope.* **5** a very short
time: *It all happened in a flash.* **6** give out or send
out like a flash: *Her eyes flashed defiance.* 1,4,5
noun, plural **flash es;** 2,3,6 *verb.*

flash light (flash′līt′), a portable electric light,
operated by batteries. *noun.*

flash y (flash′ē), **1** dazzling or sparkling; brilliant
for a short time: *The dancers' performance yesterday
was flashy, but today's show was not at all exciting.*
2 showy; gaudy: *flashy jackets. adjective,* **flash i er,
flash i est.**

flask (flask), a glass or metal bottle, especially
one with a narrow neck. *noun.*

flamingo—about 4¹/₂ feet (1¹/₂ meters) tall
from head to toe

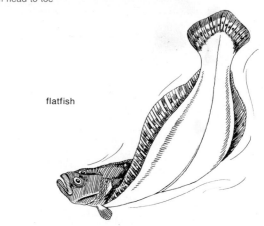

flatfish

flexible—His arms and legs were as
flexible as rubber.

flat[1] (flat), **1** smooth and level; even: *flat land.*
2 horizontal; at full length: *The storm left the trees flat on the ground.* **3** the flat part: *The flat of one's hand is the palm.* **4** land that is smooth and level: *There were flats on both sides of the river.* **5** not very deep or thick: *A plate is flat.* **6** with little air in it: *A nail or sharp stone can cause a flat tire.* **7** tire with little air in it: *Our car got a flat when we drove over a nail.* **8** positive; not to be changed: *A flat refusal is complete. We paid a flat rate with no extra charges.* **9** without much life, interest, or flavor; dull: *a flat voice. Without seasoning many foods would taste flat.* **10** below the true pitch in music: *The singer's high notes were flat. Try not to sing flat.* **11** tone one-half step below natural pitch: *music written in B flat.* **12** sign in music (♭) that shows this. **13** in a flat manner: *He fell flat on the floor.* 1,2,5,6,8,9,10 *adjective,* **flat ter, flat test;** 3,4,7,11,12 *noun,* 10,13 *adverb.*

flat[2] (flat), apartment or set of rooms on one floor. *noun.*

flat boat (flat′bōt′), a large boat with a flat bottom, used especially for floating goods down a river or canal. *noun.*

flat car (flat′kär′), a railroad car without a roof or sides, used for hauling freight. *noun.*

flat fish (flat′fish′), any of a group of fishes having a flat body and swimming on one side. Halibut, flounder, and sole are flatfishes. See picture. *noun, plural* **flat fish es** *or* **flat fish.**

flat ten (flat′n), make flat; become flat: *Use a rolling pin to flatten the pie dough. verb.*

flat ter (flat′ər), **1** praise too much or beyond the truth: *Were you only flattering me when you said I sang well, or did you mean it?* **2** show as more beautiful or better looking than what is true: *This picture flatters me.* **3** try to win over or please by praising words or actions: *to flatter someone with lots of attention and many gifts. verb.*

flat ter y (flat′ər ē), **1** act of flattering. **2** words of praise, usually untrue or exaggerated: *Some people use flattery to get favors. noun, plural* **flat ter ies.**

flaunt (flônt), show off: *They flaunted their expensive toys in front of their classmates. verb.*

fla vor (flā′vər), **1** taste: *Chocolate and vanilla have different flavors.* **2** give added taste to; season: *We use salt, pepper, and spices to flavor food.* **3** a special quality: *Stories about ships and sailors have a flavor of the sea.* 1,3 *noun,* 2 *verb.*

fla vor ing (flā′vər ing), something used to give a particular taste to food or drink: *chocolate flavoring. noun.*

flaw (flô), a slight defect; blemish; fault: *a flaw in a mirror. Her quick temper is a flaw in her character. noun.*

flaw less (flô′lis), without a flaw; perfect. *adjective.*

flax (flaks), **1** a slender, upright plant with narrow leaves and blue flowers. Linseed oil is made from its seeds and linen from its stems. **2** the threadlike parts into which the stems of this plant separate. Flax is spun into thread and woven into linen cloth. *noun.*

a hat	i it	oi oil	ch child	a in about
ā age	ī ice	ou out	ng long	e in taken
ä far	o hot	u cup	sh she	ə = i in pencil
e let	ō open	u̇ put	th thin	o in lemon
ē equal	ô order	ü rule	ŦH then	u in circus
ėr term			zh measure	

flax en (flak′sən), **1** made of flax. **2** like flax; pale yellow: *Flaxen hair is very light. adjective.*

flea (flē), a small, jumping insect without wings. Fleas live in the fur of dogs, cats, and other animals or under the clothing of human beings, and feed on their blood. *noun.*

fleck (flek), **1** a small spot or patch; speck: *Freckles are brown flecks on the skin.* **2** mark with spots of color or light: *The bird's breast is flecked with brown.* 1 *noun,* 2 *verb.*

fled (fled). See **flee.** *The enemy fled when we attacked. The prisoner has fled. verb.*

fledg ling (flej′ling), **1** a young bird just able to fly. **2** a young, inexperienced person. *noun.*

flee (flē), **1** run away: *The robbers tried to flee, but they were caught.* **2** go quickly; move swiftly: *The clouds are fleeing before the wind. verb,* **fled, flee ing.**

fleece (flēs), **1** wool that covers a sheep. The coat of wool cut off or shorn from one sheep is called a fleece. **2** cut the fleece from. **3** rob of money or belongings; cheat: *The gamblers fleeced him of all his money.* 1 *noun,* 2,3 *verb,* **fleeced, fleec ing.**

fleec y (flē′sē), like a fleece; soft and white: *fleecy clouds. adjective,* **fleec i er, fleec i est.**

fleet[1] (flēt), **1** group of ships under one command: *the United States fleet.* **2** group of ships sailing together: *a fleet of fishing boats.* **3** group of airplanes, automobiles, or the like, moving or working together: *A fleet of trucks carried the lumber. noun.*

fleet[2] (flēt), swiftly moving; rapid: *a fleet horse. adjective.*

fleet ing (flē′ting), passing swiftly; soon gone: *a fleeting smile. adjective.*

flesh (flesh), **1** the soft substance of the body that covers the bones and is covered by skin. Flesh is made up mostly of muscles and fat. **2** meat. **3** the soft part of fruits or vegetables; the part of fruits that can be eaten: *The flesh of apples is white. noun.*

flesh and blood, family; relatives by birth.

in the flesh, really present, not merely thought of; in person.

flesh y (flesh′ē), having much flesh; plump; fat. *adjective,* **flesh i er, flesh i est.**

flew (flü). See **fly**[2]. *The bird flew away. verb.*

flex (fleks), bend: *She flexed her stiff arm slowly. verb.*

flex i ble (flek′sə bəl), able to be bent without breaking; not stiff; easily bent in all directions. Leather, rubber, and wire are flexible. See picture. *adjective.*

flick (flik), **1** a sudden light blow or movement: *The flick of a whip. She threw the dart with a flick of the wrist.* **2** strike lightly with a quick blow: *He*

flicked the dust from his shoes with a handkerchief.
3 make a sudden blow with: *The children flicked wet towels at each other.* **1** *noun,* **2,3** *verb.*

flick er[1] (flik′ər), **1** shine or burn with a wavering, unsteady light: *The firelight flickered on the walls.* **2** a wavering, unsteady light or flame: *the flicker of an oil lamp.* **3** move lightly and quickly in and out, or back and forth: *We heard the birds flicker among the leaves.* **4** a quick, light movement: *the flicker of an eyelash.* **1,3** *verb,* **2,4** *noun.*

flick er[2] (flik′ər), a large, common woodpecker of North America, with yellow markings on the wings and tail. See picture. *noun.*

flied (flīd). See **fly**[2] (definition 10). *The batter flied to center field. verb.*

fli er (flī′ər), **1** person or thing that flies, such as a bird or insect: *That eagle is a high flier.* **2** pilot of an airplane; aviator. *noun.* Also spelled **flyer.**

flies[1] (flīz), more than one fly: *There are many flies on the window. noun plural.*

flies[2] (flīz). See **fly**[2]. *A bird flies. He flies an airplane. verb.*

flight[1] (flīt), **1** act or manner of flying: *the flight of a bird through the air.* **2** distance a bird, bullet, or airplane can fly. **3** group of things flying through the air together: *a flight of pigeons.* **4** trip in an aircraft. **5** airplane that makes a scheduled trip: *She took the three o'clock flight to Boston.* **6** soaring above or beyond the ordinary: *a flight of the imagination.* **7** set of stairs from one landing or one story of a building to the next. *noun.*

flight[2] (flīt), running away; escape: *The flight of the prisoners was discovered. noun.*

flim sy (flim′zē), light and thin; slight; frail; without strength; easily broken: *I accidentally tore the flimsy paper. Their excuse was so flimsy that no one believed it.* *adjective,* **flim si er, flim si est.**

flinch (flinch), **1** draw back from difficulty, danger, or pain; shrink: *She flinched when she touched the hot radiator.* **2** act of drawing back. **1** *verb,* **2** *noun.*

fling (fling), **1** throw; throw with force: *fling a stone.* **2** a throw. **3** rush; dash: *In a rage the child flung out of the room.* **4** move violently; plunge; kick: *The excited horse flung about in its stall.* **5** time of doing as one pleases: *He had his fling when he was young.* **6** a lively Scottish dance. **1,3,4** *verb,* **flung, fling ing;** **2,5,6** *noun.*

flint (flint), a very hard stone, which makes a spark when struck against steel. *noun.*

flint lock (flint′lok′), **1** gunlock in which a piece of flint striking against steel makes sparks that explode the gunpowder. **2** old-fashioned gun with such a gunlock. *noun.*

flip (flip), **1** toss or move by the snap of a finger and thumb: *He flipped a coin on the counter.* **2** move with a jerk or toss: *flip the pages of a book. The branch flipped back and scratched her face.* **3** snap; tap; sudden jerk: *The cat gave the kitten a flip on the ear. The winner was picked by the flip of a coin.* **1,2** *verb,* **flipped, flip ping;** **3** *noun.*

flip pant (flip′ənt), too free in speech or action; not properly serious or respectful: *His flippant answer to my serious question annoyed me. adjective.*

flicker[2]—about 12 inches (30 centimeters) long

flourish (definition 4)

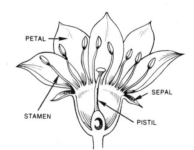

PETAL

SEPAL

STAMEN

PISTIL

flower (definition 1)
parts of a flower

float (definition 5)—The king of the parade rode by on a **float.**

flip per (flip′ər), a broad, flat limb used for swimming. Seals have flippers. *noun.*

flirt (flėrt), **1** play at making love; make love without meaning it. **2** person who makes love without meaning it. **1** *verb,* **2** *noun.*

flit (flit), **1** fly lightly and quickly; flutter: *Birds flitted from tree to tree.* **2** pass lightly and quickly: *Many thoughts flitted through my mind as I sat daydreaming.* *verb,* **flit ted, flit ting.**

float (flōt), **1** stay on top of or be held up by air, water, or other liquid. A cork will float, but a stone sinks. **2** anything that stays up or holds up something else in water. A raft is a float. A cork on a fishline is a float. **3** move with a moving liquid; drift: *The boat floated out to sea.* **4** rest or move in a liquid or in the air: *Clouds floated in the sky.* **5** a low, flat car that carries an exhibit in a parade. See picture. **1,3,4** *verb,* **2,5** *noun.*

flock (flok), **1** group of animals of one kind keeping, feeding, or herded together: *a flock of sheep, a flock of geese, a flock of birds.* **2** a large number; crowd: *Visitors came in flocks to the zoo to see the new gorilla.* **3** go in a flock; keep in groups: *Sheep usually flock together.* **4** people of the same church group. **5** come crowding; crowd: *The children flocked around the ice-cream stand.* **1,2,4** *noun,* **3,5** *verb.*

floe (flō), a field or sheet of floating ice. *noun.*

flog (flog), beat or whip hard. *verb,* **flogged, flog ging.**

flood (flud), **1** fill to overflowing: *A wave flooded the holes I had dug in the sand.* **2** flow over: *The river flooded our fields.* **3** a great flow of water over what is usually dry land: *The heavy rains caused a serious flood near the river.* **4** the Flood, (in the Bible) the water that covered the earth in the time of Noah. **5** a great outpouring of anything: *a flood of words.* **6** fill, cover, or overcome like a flood: *a room flooded with light.* **1,2,6** *verb,* **3-5** *noun.*

flood light (flud′līt′), lamp that gives a broad beam of light. *noun.*

floor (flôr), **1** the part of a room to walk on: *The floor of this room is made of wood.* **2** put a floor in or on: *The carpenter will floor this room with oak.* **3** a flat surface at the bottom: *They dropped their net to the floor of the ocean.* **4** story of a building: *They live on the fourth floor.* **5** right to speak: *"You may have the floor," said the chairman.* **6** knock down: *The boxer floored his opponent with one blow.* **7** confuse; puzzle: *The last question on the test completely floored us.* **1,3-5** *noun,* **2,6,7** *verb.*

flop (flop), **1** move loosely or heavily; flap around clumsily: *The fish flopped helplessly on the deck.* **2** fall, drop, throw, or move heavily or clumsily: *The tired girl flopped down into a chair.* **3** flopping: *I threw myself on the bed with a flop.* **4** a dull, heavy sound made by flopping. **5** failure: *The party was a flop.* **6** fail: *Their first business venture flopped.* **1,2,6** *verb,* **flopped, flop ping; 3-5** *noun.*

flo ral (flôr′əl), of flowers: *floral designs.* *adjective.*

Flo ri da (flôr′ə də), one of the southeastern states of the United States. *noun.* [*Florida* comes from a Spanish word meaning "full of flowers."

a hat	i it	oi oil	ch child	⎧ a in about
ā age	ī ice	ou out	ng long	e in taken
ä far	o hot	u cup	sh she	ə = ⎨ i in pencil
e let	ō open	ů put	th thin	o in lemon
ē equal	ô order	ü rule	₮H then	⎩ u in circus
ėr term			zh measure	

The state was named this by Ponce de León, because when he discovered it the land was full of flowers.]

flo rist (flôr′ist), person who raises or sells flowers. *noun.*

floss (flôs), **1** a shiny, silk or cotton thread that has not been twisted. Floss is used for embroidery. Dental floss is used for cleaning between the teeth. **2** use dental floss, or use dental floss on: *I flossed my teeth this morning.* **1** *noun,* **2** *verb.*

floun der[1] (floun′dər), **1** struggle without making much progress; plunge about: *After the blizzard, we found cattle floundering in snowdrifts.* **2** be clumsy or confused and make mistakes: *The children were bothered when the audience laughed, and floundered through the rest of their song.* *verb.*

floun der[2] (floun′dər), flatfish that lives in salt water and is much used for food. *noun, plural* **floun ders** or **floun der.**

flour (flour), **1** the fine powder or meal made by grinding and sifting wheat or other grain, potatoes, soybeans, and so on. **2** cover or sprinkle with flour. **1** *noun,* **2** *verb.*

flour ish (flėr′ish), **1** grow or develop with vigor; do well; thrive: *Your radishes are flourishing. Their newspaper business grew and flourished.* **2** wave in the air: *She flourished the letter at us.* **3** waving about: *He removed his hat with a flourish.* **4** an extra ornament or curve in handwriting: *John Hancock's signature has several flourishes.* See picture. **5** a showy trill or passage in music: *a flourish of trumpets.* **6** a showy display: *The agent showed us about the house with much flourish.* **1,2** *verb,* **3-6** *noun, plural* **flour ish es.**

flout (flout), treat with contempt or scorn; mock; scoff at: *You are foolish to flout good advice.* *verb.*

flow (flō), **1** run like water; move in a current or stream: *Blood flows through our bodies.* **2** current; stream: *There is a constant flow of water from the spring.* **3** pour; move steadily: *The crowd flowed out of the town hall and down the main street.* **4** glide; move easily: *a flowing movement in a dance.* **5** any smooth, steady movement: *a rapid flow of speech.* **6** hang loose and waving: *flowing robes, a flowing tie.* **7** pouring out: *a flow of blood.* **8** rate of movement of a liquid: *a flow of two feet per second.* **9** rise of the tide. **1,3,4,6** *verb,* **2,5,7-9** *noun.*

flow er (flou′ər), **1** blossom; part of a plant or tree that produces the seed. Flowers are often beautifully colored or shaped. See picture. **2** plant grown for its blossoms. **3** have flowers; produce flowers; bloom. **4** the finest part: *the flower of the country's youth.* **5** time when a thing is at its best: *a man in the flower of life.* **6** be at its best. **1,2,4,5** *noun,* **3,6** *verb.*

flow er y (flou′ər ē), **1** having many flowers. **2** full of fine words and fanciful expressions: *a flowery speech.* adjective, **flow er i er, flow er i est.**

flown (flōn). See **fly²**. *The bird has flown. The flag is flown on all national holidays.* verb.

flu (flü), a disease much like a very bad cold. It is caused by a virus. noun.

flue (flü), tube, pipe, or other enclosed passage for smoke or hot air. A chimney has a flue. noun.

fluff (fluf), **1** soft, light, downy particles, such as hair, tiny feathers, or bits of wool. **2** a soft, light, downy mass: *The kitten looked like a fluff of fur.* **3** puff out into a soft, light mass. 1,2 *noun,* 3 *verb.*

fluff y (fluf′ē), **1** soft and light: *a fluffy scarf. Whipped cream is fluffy.* **2** covered with soft, light feathers or hair: *fluffy baby chicks.* adjective, **fluff i er, fluff i est.**

flu id (flü′id), **1** any liquid or gas; something that will flow. Water, mercury, air, and oxygen are fluids. **2** like a liquid or a gas; flowing: *We poured the fluid mass of hot fudge into a pan to harden into candy.* 1 *noun,* 2 *adjective.*

fluid ounce, a unit for measuring liquids. There are 16 fluid ounces in 1 pint.

flung (flung). See **fling**. *I flung my coat on the chair. The paper was flung into the fire.* verb.

flu o rine (flü′ə rēn′), a pale-yellow, bad-smelling, poisonous gas that occurs only in combination with other substances. It is used in small amounts in water to prevent tooth decay. noun.

flur ry (flėr′ē), **1** a sudden gust: *A flurry of wind upset the small sailboat.* **2** a light fall of rain or snow: *snow flurries.* **3** a sudden commotion: *a flurry of alarm.* **4** fluster; excite; agitate: *Noise in the audience flurried the actor so that he forgot his lines.* 1-3 *noun,* plural **flur ries;** 4 *verb,* **flur ried, flur ry ing.**

flush (flush), **1** blush; glow: *Her face flushed when they laughed at her.* **2** a rosy glow or blush: *the flush of sunrise. A sudden flush showed his embarrassment.* **3** rush suddenly: *I felt the blood flush to my cheeks.* **4** a sudden rush; rapid flow. **5** send a sudden rush of water over or through to clean or empty: *flush a toilet. The city streets were flushed to clean them.* **6** excite: *The team was flushed with its first victory.* **7** an excited feeling: *the flush of success.* **8** freshness: *the first flush of youth.* **9** even; level: *Make that shelf just flush with this one.* 1,3,5,6 *verb,* 2,4,7,8 *noun,* plural **flush es;** 9 *adjective.*

flus ter (flus′tər), **1** make nervous and excited; confuse: *The honking of horns flustered the driver, and he stalled his automobile.* **2** nervous excitement; confusion. 1 *verb,* 2 *noun.*

flute (flüt), **1** a long, slender, pipelike musical instrument. A flute is played by blowing across a hole near one end. Different notes are made by covering different holes along its length with the fingers or with keys. See picture. **2** play on a flute. **3** sing or whistle so as to sound like a flute. 1 *noun,* 2,3 *verb,* **flut ed, flut ing.**

flut ist (flü′tist), person who plays a flute. noun.

flut ter (flut′ər), **1** wave back and forth quickly and lightly: *The flag fluttered in the breeze.* **2** flap

flute (definition 1)

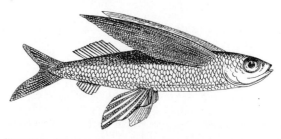

flying fish—from 8 to 18 inches (20 to 45 centimeters) long

the wings; flap: *The chickens fluttered excitedly when they saw the dog.* **3** come or go with a trembling or wavy motion: *The falling leaves fluttered to the ground.* **4** move restlessly: *They fluttered about, making preparations for the party.* **5** beat a little faster than usual: *My heart fluttered when I rose to give my speech.* **6** fluttering: *the flutter of curtains in a breeze.* **7** excitement: *The appearance of the queen caused a great flutter in the crowd.* 1-5 *verb*, 6,7 *noun.*

fly¹ (flī), **1** any of a large group of insects that have two wings, including houseflies, mosquitoes, and gnats. There are many different kinds of flies. **2** fishhook with feathers, silk, or tinsel on it to make it look like a fly. See picture. *noun, plural* **flies.**

fly² (flī), **1** move through the air with wings: *These birds fly long distances.* **2** float or wave in the air: *Our flag flies every day.* **3** cause to float or wave in the air: *The children are flying kites.* **4** travel in an aircraft: *He flew to Hawaii for a vacation.* **5** pilot (an aircraft): *My cousin flies for an airline. He flies planes for a living.* **6** carry by aircraft: *The government flew food and other supplies to the flooded city.* **7** rush; move swiftly: *She flew to my assistance.* **8** flap to cover buttons or a zipper on clothing. **9** baseball hit high in the air with a bat. **10** bat a baseball high in the air. 1-7,10 *verb*, **flew, flown, fly ing** for 1-7, **flied, fly ing** for 10; 8,9 *noun, plural* **flies.**

fly catch er (flī′kach′ər), bird that catches insects while flying. *noun.*

fly er (flī′ər), flier. *noun.*

fly ing (flī′ing), **1** able to fly; moving through the air. **2** floating or waving in the air. **3** swift. *adjective.*

flying fish, a tropical sea fish that has fins like wings and can leap through the air. See picture.

flying saucer, an unidentified disklike object, reported in the sky over many different parts of the world, especially since about 1947. See picture.

fly wheel (flī′hwēl′), a heavy wheel attached to a machine to keep it and its parts moving at an even speed. *noun.*

foal (fōl), a young horse or donkey; colt or filly. See picture. *noun.*

foam (fōm), **1** mass of very small bubbles. **2** form or gather foam: *The soda foamed over the glass.* **3** break into foam: *The stream foams over the rocks.* 1 *noun*, 2,3 *verb.*

foam rubber, a soft, spongy rubber used for mattresses, pillows, and cushions.

fo cus (fō′kəs), **1** point at which rays of light or heat meet after being reflected from a mirror or bent by a lens. See picture. **2** bring (rays of light or heat) to a focus: *The lens focused the sun's rays on a piece of paper and burned a hole in it.* **3** distance from a lens or mirror to the point where rays from it meet: *A near-sighted eye has a shorter focus than a normal eye.* **4** adjust (a lens or the eye) to make a clear image: *A near-sighted person cannot focus accurately on distant objects.*

a hat	i it	oi oil	ch child	⎧ a in about
ā age	ī ice	ou out	ng long	⎪ e in taken
ä far	o hot	u cup	sh she	ə = ⎨ i in pencil
e let	ō open	u̇ put	th thin	⎪ o in lemon
ē equal	ô order	ü rule	ŦH then	⎩ u in circus
ėr term			zh measure	

fly¹ (definition 2)—The shape and movement of these flies in the water attract fish.

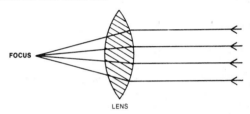

FOCUS

LENS

focus (definition 1)—Rays of light are brought to a focus by the lens.

foal—a foal beside its mother

5 make (an image) clear by adjusting a lens or the eye. **6** a central point of attraction, attention, or activity: *The baby was the focus of attention.* 1,3,6 *noun*, 2,4,5 *verb.*

fod der (fod′ər), coarse food for horses, cattle, and sheep. Hay and cornstalks are fodder. *noun.*

foe (fō), enemy. *noun.*

fog (fog), **1** cloud of fine drops of water just above the earth's surface; thick mist. **2** cover with fog. **3** make misty or cloudy: *Something fogged six of our photographs.* 1 *noun*, 2,3 *verb*, **fogged, fog ging.**

fog gy (fog/ē), **1** having much fog; misty. **2** not clear; dim; blurred: *Their ideas are confused and rather foggy.* adjective, **fog gi er, fog gi est.**

fog horn (fog/hôrn/), horn that warns ships in foggy weather. noun.

foil[1] (foil), outwit; prevent from carrying out (plans): *Quick thinking by the bank clerk foiled the robbers, and they were captured.* verb. [An earlier English meaning of *foil*[1] was "tread under foot" or "trample." It was taken from an old French word meaning "trample."]

foil[2] (foil), metal beaten, hammered, or rolled into a very thin sheet: *Candy is sometimes wrapped in foil to keep it fresh.* noun. [*Foil*[2] comes from a Latin word meaning "leaf."]

foil[3] (foil), long, narrow sword with a knob or button on the point to prevent injury, used in fencing. noun.

fold[1] (fōld), **1** bend or double over on itself: *to fold a letter.* **2** mark or line made by folding. **3** bend till close to the body: *She folded her arms. A bird folds its wings.* **4** put the arms around and hold tenderly: *He folded the crying child to him.* 1,3,4 verb, 2 noun.

fold[2] (fōld), pen to keep sheep in. noun.

fold er (fōl/dər), **1** holder for papers made by folding a piece of stiff paper once. **2** pamphlet made of one or more folded sheets. noun.

fo li age (fō/lē ij), leaves of a plant. noun.

folk (fōk), **1** people: *Most city folk know very little about farming.* **2** tribe; nation. **3** **folks, a** people: *Most folks enjoy eating.* **b** relatives: *Her folks are very nice.* noun, plural **folk** or **folks.**

folk dance, 1 dance originating and handed down among the common people. **2** music for it.

folk lore (fōk/lôr/), beliefs, stories, legends, and customs of a people or tribe. noun.

folk song, song originating and handed down among the common people.

folk tale, story or legend originating and handed down among the common people.

fol low (fol/ō), **1** go or come after: *Sheep follow a leader. Night follows day. You lead and we'll follow.* **2** result from; result: *Floods followed the heavy rain.* **3** go along: *Follow this road to the corner.* **4** use; obey; act according to; take as a guide: *Follow her advice.* **5** keep the eyes on: *I could not follow that bird's flight.* **6** keep the mind on: *to follow an argument.* **7** take as one's work: *to follow the profession of lawyer.* verb.

follow up, act upon with energy: *She followed up the suggestion for a field trip by making all the arrangements.*

fol low er (fol/ō ər), **1** person or thing that follows. **2** person who follows the ideas or beliefs of another: *Christians are followers of Christ.* noun.

fol low ing (fol/ō ing), **1** group of followers. **2** that follows; next after: *If that was Sunday, then the following day must have been Monday.* 1 noun, 2 adjective.

fol ly (fol/ē), **1** being foolish; lack of sense; unwise conduct: *It was folly to eat too much on the picnic.* **2** foolish act, practice, or idea; something silly. noun, plural **fol lies.**

fond (fond), loving; liking: *a fond look, fond of children.* adjective.

fon dle (fon/dl), pet; caress: *They fondled all the animals in the pet store.* verb, **fon dled, fon dling.**

font (font), **1** basin holding water for baptism. **2** basin for holy water. **3** fountain; source. noun.

food (füd), **1** anything that plants, animals, or people eat or drink that makes them live and grow. **2** what is eaten: *Give them food and drink.* **3** anything that causes growth: *Books are food for the mind.* noun.

fool (fül), **1** person without sense; person who acts unwisely. **2** clown formerly kept by a king or nobleman to amuse people. **3** act like a fool for fun; play; joke: *I was only fooling.* **4** make a fool of; deceive; trick: *You can't fool me.* 1,2 noun, 3,4 verb. [*Fool* comes from a Latin word meaning "an empty-headed person" or "a puffed-up person."]

fool har dy (fül/här/dē), foolishly bold; rash: *The man made a foolhardy attempt to go over Niagara Falls in a barrel.* adjective, **fool har di er, fool har di est.**

fool ish (fü/lish), without sense; unwise. adjective.

fool proof (fül/prüf/), so safe or simple that even a fool can use or do it: *a foolproof device, a foolproof scheme.* adjective.

foot (füt), **1** the end part of a leg; part that a person, animal, or thing stands on. **2** part opposite the head of something: *the foot of a bed.* **3** the lowest part; the bottom; base: *the foot of a column, the foot of a hill, the foot of a page.* **4** a unit of length; 12 inches. 3 feet equal 1 yard. **5** pay: *My parents footed the bill for the dinner.* 1-4 noun, plural **feet;** 5 verb.

put one's foot down, make up one's mind and act firmly: *If you don't go to bed right now, I'll have to put my foot down.*

foot ball (füt/bôl/), **1** game played with a leather ball which is to be kicked or carried past the goal line at either end of the field. **2** ball used in this game. noun.

foot hill (füt/hil/), a low hill at the base of a mountain or mountain range. noun.

foot hold (füt/hōld/), **1** place to put a foot; support for the feet: *I climbed the steep cliff by getting footholds in cracks in the rocks.* **2** firm footing or position: *It is hard to break a habit after it has a foothold.* noun.

foot ing (füt/ing), **1** a firm placing or position of the feet: *She lost her footing and fell on the ice.* **2** place or support for the feet: *The steep cliff gave us no footing.* **3** a secure position: *The new business has gained a footing in the community and is doing well.* **4** condition; position; relationship: *The United States and Canada are on a friendly footing.* noun.

foot man (füt/mən), a male servant who answers the bell, waits on table, and opens doors. Footmen usually wear a kind of uniform. noun, plural **foot men.**

foot note (füt/nōt/), note at the bottom of a page about something on the page. noun.

foot path (füt/path/), path for people on foot only. noun, plural **foot paths** (füt/paŦHz/ or füt/paths/).

foot print (fùt/print/), mark made by a foot. *noun.*

foot sore (fùt/sôr/), having sore feet from much walking: *The hike left us footsore and hungry.* *adjective.*

foot step (fùt/step/), **1** a person's step. **2** distance covered in one step. **3** sound of steps coming or going. **4** mark made by a foot; footprint. *noun.*
follow in someone's footsteps, do as another has done.

foot stool (fùt/stül/), a low stool on which to place the feet when seated. *noun.*

for (fôr *or* fər), **1** in place of: *We used boxes for chairs.* **2** in support of: *He stands for honest government.* **3** in return; in consideration of: *These apples are eight for a dollar. We thanked him for his kindness.* **4** with the object or purpose of: *He went for a walk.* **5** in order to become, have, keep, or get to: *He ran for his life. She is hunting for her cat. They left for New York yesterday.* **6** meant to belong to or be used with; suited to: *a box for gloves, books for children.* **7** with a feeling toward: *We longed for home. She has an eye for beauty.* **8** with regard or respect to: *It is warm for April. Eating too much is bad for one's health.* **9** because of; by reason of: *They were punished for stealing. A party was given for her.* **10** because: *We can't go, for it is raining.* **11** as far as: *We walked for a mile.* **12** as long as: *We worked for an hour.* **13** as being: *They know it for a fact.* **14** to the amount of: *a check for $20.* 1-9,11-14 *preposition,* 10 *conjunction.*

fo rage (fôr/ij), **1** hay, grain, or other food for horses, cattle, or other domestic animals. **2** hunt or search for food: *Rabbits forage in our garden.* **3** get by hunting or searching about. **4** hunt; search about: *We foraged for old lumber to build a tree house.* 1 *noun,* 2-4 *verb,* **fo raged, fo rag ing.**

fo ray (fôr/ā), a raid for plunder: *Bandits made forays on the villages and took away cattle. noun.*

for bade or **for bad** (fər bad/). See **forbid.** *My parents forbade me to stay out past ten o'clock. verb.*

for bear (fôr ber/ *or* fôr bar/), **1** hold back; keep from doing, saying, or using: *I forbore telling her the truth because I knew it would upset her.* **2** be patient; control oneself. *verb,* **for bore, for borne, for bear ing.**

for bear ance (fôr ber/əns *or* fôr bar/əns), patience; self-control. *noun.*

for bid (fər bid/), not allow; say one must not do; make a rule against: *The teacher forbade us to leave our seats. If my parents had known that I was going, they would have forbidden it. verb,* **for bade** or **for bad, for bid den** or **for bid, for bid ding.**

for bid den (fər bid/n), **1** not allowed; against the law or the rules: *Eve ate the forbidden fruit.* **2** See **forbid.** *My parents have forbidden me to swim in that river.* 1 *adjective,* 2 *verb.*

for bid ding (fər bid/ing), causing fear or dislike; looking dangerous or unpleasant: *The coast was rocky and forbidding. adjective.*

for bore (fôr bôr/). See **forbear.** *He forbore from showing his anger. verb.*

for borne (fôr bôrn/). See **forbear.** *We have forborne from vengeance. verb.*

a hat	i it	oi oil	ch child	ə = { a in about
ā age	ī ice	ou out	ng long	e in taken
ä far	o hot	u cup	sh she	i in pencil
e let	ō open	ù put	th thin	o in lemon
ē equal	ô order	ü rule	ᴛʜ then	u in circus
ėr term			zh measure	

force (fôrs), **1** power; strength: *The speeding car struck the tree with great force.* **2** strength used against a person or thing; violence: *The robber had to use force to get into the house.* **3** make act against one's will: *Give it to me at once, or I will force you to.* **4** get or take by strength or violence: *He forced his way in.* **5** break open; break through: *force a door.* **6** make by an unusual or unnatural effort: *The unhappy child forced a smile.* **7** hurry the growth or blossoming of: *We forced apple blossoms by cutting branches and placing them in water in our warm living room.* **8** group of people who work together: *our office force, the police force.* **9** **forces,** all of the armed services: *United States forces captured the island during World War II.* **10** any cause that produces, changes, or stops the motion of a body: *the force of gravitation.* 1,2,8-10 *noun,* 3-7 *verb,* **forced, forc ing.**
in force, 1 in use: *The old rules are still in force.* **2** in large numbers; strongly: *an attack in force.*

forced (fôrst), **1** made or driven by force: *The work of slaves was forced labor.* **2** done by unusual effort: *The soldiers made a forced march of three days.* **3** not natural; strained: *She hid her dislike with a forced smile. adjective.*

force ful (fôrs/fəl), having much force; effective; vigorous; strong: *a forceful manner. adjective.*

for ceps (fôr/seps), small pincers or tongs used by surgeons or dentists, for seizing and holding. *Dentists use forceps for pulling teeth. noun, plural* **for ceps.**

for ci ble (fôr/sə bəl), made or done by force; using force: *a forcible entrance into a house. adjective.*

for ci bly (fôr/sə blē), in a forcible manner. *adverb.*

ford (fôrd), **1** place where a river, stream, or other body of water is not too deep to cross by walking through the water. **2** cross (a river, stream, or other body of water) by walking or driving through the water. See picture. 1 *noun,* 2 *verb.*

ford (definition 2)—He forded the river in a wagon.

fore (fôr), **1** at the front; toward the beginning or front; forward: *The fore wall of a house faces the street.* **2** the front part. **1** *adjective,* **2** *noun.*

fore-, prefix meaning: **1** front: *Forefoot means a front foot.* **2** before; beforehand: *Foresee means to see beforehand.*

fore arm (fôr′ärm′), the part of the arm between the elbow and the wrist. *noun.*

fore cast (fôr′kast′), **1** predict; tell what is coming: *Cooler weather is forecast for tomorrow.* **2** prediction; a statement of what is coming: *What is the forecast for the weather for today?* **1** *verb,* **fore cast** or **fore cast ed, fore cast ing;** **2** *noun.*

fore fa ther (fôr′fä′ŦHər), ancestor. *noun.*

fore fin ger (fôr′fing′gər), finger next to the thumb; index finger. *noun.*

fore foot (fôr′fut′), one of the front feet of an animal having four or more feet. *noun, plural* **fore feet.**

fore go ing (fôr′gō′ing), preceding; going before: *Read again the foregoing pages. adjective.*

fore gone (fôr′gôn), known or decided beforehand: *It was a foregone conclusion that the popular mayor would run for reelection. adjective.*

fore ground (fôr′ground′), part of a picture or scene nearest the observer; part toward the front: *The cottage stands in the foreground with the mountains in the background. noun.*

fore head (fôr′id *or* fôr′hed′), part of the face above the eyes. *noun.*

fo reign (fôr′ən), **1** outside one's own country: *She has traveled much in foreign countries.* **2** coming from outside one's own country: *a foreign ship, a foreign language, foreign money.* **3** having to do with other countries: *foreign trade.* **4** not belonging: *Sitting still all day is foreign to a healthy child's nature. adjective.*

fo reign er (fôr′ə nər), person from another country; outsider. *noun.*

fore leg (fôr′leg′), one of the front legs of an animal having four or more legs. *noun.*

fore man (fôr′mən), **1** person in charge of a group of workers; person in charge of the work in some part of a factory. **2** person at the head of a jury. *noun, plural* **fore men.**

fore most (fôr′mōst), **1** first: *I stumbled and fell head foremost.* **2** chief; leading: *Einstein was regarded as one of the foremost scientists of this century.* **1,2,** *adjective,* **1** *adverb.*

fore noon (fôr′nün′), time between early morning and noon; part of the day from sunrise to noon. *noun.*

fore saw (fôr sô′). See **foresee.** *We foresaw that we would be late and called to tell our friends. verb.*

fore see (fôr sē′), see or know beforehand: *She could foresee that the job would take all day, so she canceled her plans for the afternoon. verb,* **fore saw, fore seen, fore see ing.**

fore seen (fôr sēn′). See **foresee.** *Nobody could have foreseen how cold it would be. verb.*

fore sight (fôr′sīt′), **1** power to see or know beforehand what is likely to happen: *No one had enough foresight to predict the winner.* **2** careful

thought for the future; prudence: *A spendthrift does not use foresight. noun.*

fo rest (fôr′ist), **1** thick woods; woodland, often covering many miles. **2** of the forest: *Help prevent forest fires.* **3** to plant with forest trees. **1** *noun,* **2** *adjective,* **3** *verb.*

fo rest ed (fôr′ə stid), covered with trees; thickly wooded. *adjective.*

fo rest er (fôr′ə stər), person in charge of a forest to guard against fires or look after timber. *noun.*

fo rest ry (fôr′ə strē), science of planting and taking care of forests. *noun.*

fore tell (fôr tel′), tell beforehand; predict; prophesy: *Who can foretell what the future will be? verb,* **fore told, fore tell ing.**

fore told (fôr tōld′). See **foretell.** *The weather bureau foretold the cold wave. verb.*

for ev er (fər ev′ər), **1** for ever; without ever coming to an end: *Nobody lives forever.* **2** always; all the time: *Some children in my class are forever talking. adverb.*

for feit (fôr′fit), **1** lose or have to give up by one's own act, neglect, or fault: *Careless drivers sometimes forfeit their lives.* **2** thing lost or given up because of some act, neglect, or fault: *the forfeit of a game.* **1** *verb,* **2** *noun.*

for gave (fər gāv′). See **forgive.** *She forgave my mistake. verb.*

forge¹ (fôrj), **1** kind of small hearth or fireplace where metal is heated very hot and then hammered into shape. See picture. **2** a blacksmith's shop. **3** heat (metal) very hot and then hammer into shape: *The blacksmith forged a bar of iron into a big hook.* **4** place where iron or other metal is melted and refined. **5** make; shape; form. **6** make or write (something false) to deceive; sign falsely: *forge a letter of recommendation. You can be sent to jail for forging checks.* **1,2,4** *noun,* **3,5,6** *verb,* **forged, forg ing.**

forge² (fôrj), move forward slowly but steadily: *One runner forged ahead of the others and won the race. verb,* **forged, forg ing.**

for get (fər get′), **1** let go out of the mind; fail to remember: *I forgot my lines in the play.* **2** fail to think of; fail to do, take, or notice: *I forgot to call the dentist. He had forgotten his umbrella. verb,* **for got, for got ten** or **for got, for get ting.**

for get ful (fər get′fəl), apt to forget; having a poor memory: *Old people sometimes become forgetful. adjective.*

for get-me-not (fər get′mē not′), plant with clusters of small blue or white flowers. *noun.*

for give (fər giv′), pardon; excuse; give up the wish to punish: *She forgave me for breaking her tennis racket. Please forgive my mistake. verb,* **for gave, for giv en, for giv ing.**

for giv en (fər giv′ən). See **forgive.** *Your mistakes are forgiven, but be more careful. verb.*

for give ness (fər giv′nis), **1** act of forgiving; pardon. **2** willingness to forgive. *noun.*

for go (fôr gō′), do without; give up: *She decided to forgo the movies and do her lessons. verb,* **for went, for gone, for go ing.**

forlorn

forge¹ (definition 1)—a forge in a blacksmith's shop a hundred years ago

a hat	i it	oi oil	ch child	⎧ a in about
ā age	ī ice	ou out	ng long	e in taken
ä far	o hot	u cup	sh she	ə = ⎨ i in pencil
e let	ō open	u̇ put	th thin	o in lemon
ē equal	ô order	ü rule	₮H then	⎩ u in circus
ėr term			zh measure	

for gone (fôr gôn′). See **forgo**. *verb.*

for got (fər got′). See **forget**. *He was so busy that he forgot to eat his lunch. verb.*

for got ten (fər got′n). See **forget**. *I have forgotten many of the details of my summer vacation. verb.*

fork (fôrk), **1** handle with two or more long points, with which to lift food. **2** a much larger kind with which to lift hay; pitchfork. **3** lift, throw, or dig with a fork: *fork hay into a wagon.* **4** anything shaped like a fork; any branching: *the fork of a tree, the fork of a road.* **5** one of the branches into which anything is divided: *Take the right-hand fork.* **6** have forks; divide into forks: *There is a garage where the road forks.* 1,2,4,5 *noun,* 3,6 *verb.*

for lorn (fôr lôrn′), left alone; neglected; miserable; hopeless: *He felt forlorn because he wasn't included in the group.* See picture. *adjective.*

form (fôrm), **1** shape: *Circles are simple forms.* **2** to shape; make: *Bakers form dough into loaves.* **3** take shape: *Clouds form in the sky.* **4** become: *Water forms ice when it freezes.* **5** make up: *Parents and children form a family.* **6** develop: *She formed the good habit of doing her homework before watching television.* **7** kind; sort: *Ice, snow, and steam are forms of water.* **8** manner; method: *He is a fast runner, but his form in running is bad.* **9** formality; ceremony; set way of behaving according to custom or rule: *He said "Good morning" as a matter of form, although he hardly noticed me.* **10** piece of printed paper with blank spaces to be filled in: *We filled out a form to get a license for our dog.* **11** arrangement: *In what form was the list of words?* **12** mold; pattern: *Ice cream is often made in forms.* **13** any of the ways in which a word is spelled or pronounced to show its different meanings. *Toys* is the plural form of *toy.* 1,7-13 *noun,* 2-6 *verb.*

for mal (fôr′məl), **1** stiff; not familiar and homelike: *a formal greeting. A judge has a formal manner in a court of law.* **2** according to set customs or rules: *The new ambassador paid a formal call on the President.* **3** done with the proper forms; clear and definite: *A written contract is a formal agreement to do something.* **4** a dance, party, or other social affair at which women often wear long, fancy dresses and men wear elegant suits. 1-3 *adjective,* 4 *noun.*

for mal i ty (fôr mal′ə tē), **1** an outward form; ceremony; something required by custom: *At a wedding there are many formalities.* **2** attention to forms and customs: *The queen received her visitors with much formality.* **3** stiffness of manner, behavior, or arrangement: *The formality of the party made me uneasy. noun, plural* **for mal i ties.**

for ma tion (fôr mā′shən), **1** the forming, making, or shaping (of something): *Heat causes the formation of steam from water.* **2** way in which something is arranged; arrangement; order: *The band marched in perfect parade formation. Football players line up in various formations for their plays.* **3** thing formed: *Clouds are formations of tiny drops of water in the sky. noun.*

for mer (fôr′mər), **1** the first of two: *When she had a choice between a telescope and a camera, she chose the former because of her interest in astronomy.* **2** earlier; past; long past: *In former times, cooking was done in fireplaces instead of stoves. adjective.*

for mer ly (fôr′mər lē), in time past; some time ago: *Our teacher formerly taught elsewhere. adverb.*

for mi da ble (fôr′mə də bəl), hard to overcome; hard to deal with; to be dreaded: *A long examination is more formidable than a short test. adjective.*

for mu la (fôr′myə lə), **1** recipe or prescription: *a baby's formula.* **2** a combination of symbols used in chemistry to show the composition of a compound: *The formula for water is* H_2O. **3** a combination of symbols used in mathematics to state a rule or principle. *noun.*

for mu late (fôr′myə lāt), state definitely or exactly: *Our country formulates its laws according to its constitution. verb,* **for mu lat ed, for mu lat ing.**

for sake (fôr sāk′), give up; leave; leave alone: *He ran away, forsaking his home and friends. verb,* **for sook, for sak en, for sak ing.**

for sak en (fôr sā′kən), **1** See **forsake.** *She has forsaken her old friends.* **2** deserted; abandoned; forlorn: *We found an old, forsaken graveyard out in the country.* **1** *verb,* **2** *adjective.*

for sook (fôr sůk′). See **forsake.** *He forsook his family. verb.*

for syth i a (fôr sith′ē ə), shrub having many bell-shaped, yellow flowers in early spring before its leaves come out. *noun.* [*Forsythia* was named for William Forsyth, an English botanist who lived from 1737 to 1804.]

fort (fôrt), a strong building or place that can be defended against an enemy. *noun.*

forth (fôrth), **1** forward: *From this day forth I'll try to do better.* **2** out; into view: *The sun came forth from behind the clouds. adverb.*

and so forth, and so on; and the like: *We ate cake, candy, nuts, and so forth.*

forth com ing (fôrth′kum′ing), **1** about to appear; approaching: *The forthcoming week will be busy.* **2** coming forth; ready when wanted: *I needed help, but none was forthcoming. adjective.*

for ti eth (fôr′tē ith), **1** next after the 39th. **2** one of 40 equal parts. *adjective, noun.*

for ti fi ca tion (fôr′tə fə kā′shən), **1** making strong; adding strength to: *The general was responsible for the fortification of the town.* **2** wall or fort built to make a place strong. **3** place made strong by building walls and forts. *noun.*

for ti fy (fôr′tə fī), **1** build forts or walls to protect a place against attack; strengthen against attack. **2** give support to; strengthen: *They fortified each other against the coming ordeal.* **3** enrich with vitamins and minerals: *fortify bread. verb,* **for ti fied, for ti fy ing.**

for ti tude (fôr′tə tüd *or* fôr′tə tyüd), courage in facing pain, danger, or trouble. *noun.*

fort night (fôrt′nīt), two weeks. *noun.*

for tress (fôr′tris), place built with walls and defenses; large fort or fortification. *noun, plural* **for tress es.**

for tu nate (fôr′chə nit), **1** having good luck; lucky: *You are fortunate in having such a fine family.* **2** bringing good luck; having favorable results: *a fortunate occurrence. adjective.*

for tune (fôr′chən), **1** a great deal of money or property; riches; wealth: *The family made a fortune in oil.* **2** luck; chance; what happens: *Fortune was against us and we lost.* **3** good luck; success; prosperity. **4** what is going to happen to a person; fate: *Gypsies often claim that they can tell people's fortunes. noun.*

for tune tell er (fôr′chən tel′ər), person who claims to be able to tell what is going to happen to people. *noun.*

for ty (fôr′tē), four times ten; 40. *noun, plural* **for ties;** *adjective.*

fo rum (fôr′əm), **1** the public square of an ancient Roman city, where business was done and courts and public assemblies were held. **2** assembly for the discussion of questions of public interest: *An open forum was held last Tuesday evening. noun.*

for ward (fôr′wərd), **1** onward; ahead: *Forward, march! From this time forward we shall be friends.* **2** to the front: *to come forward. Our cabin is in the forward part of the ship.* **3** advanced: *A child of four years who can read is forward for his age.* **4** into consideration; out: *In her talk she brought forward several new ideas.* **5** help on: *She did everything she could to forward her friend's plan.* **6** send on farther: *Please forward my mail to my new address.* **7** ready; eager: *He knew his lesson and was forward with his answers.* **8** too sure of oneself; bold: *Don't be so forward as to interrupt the speaker.* **9** player in basketball, soccer, and some other games who plays in the front line. **1,2,4** *adverb,* **2,3,7,8** *adjective,* **5,6** *verb,* **9** *noun.*

for wards (fôr′wərdz), forward. *adverb.*

for went (fôr went′). See **forgo.** *verb.*

fos sil (fos′əl), **1** the hardened remains or traces of an animal or plant of a former age. Fossils of ferns are sometimes found in coal. See picture. **2** forming a fossil: *the fossil remains of a dinosaur.* **3** belonging to the outworn past: *fossil ideas.* **1** *noun,* **2,3** *adjective.*

fos ter (fô′stər), **1** help the growth or development of; encourage: *Our city fosters libraries and parks.* **2** care for fondly; cherish. **3** bring up; help to grow; make grow. **4** in the same family, but not related by birth. A **foster child** is a child brought up by a person not his or her parent. A **foster father, foster mother,** and **foster parent** are persons who bring up the child of another. **1-3** *verb,* **4** *adjective.*

fought (fôt). See **fight.** *They fought for their rights. A battle was fought there. verb.*

foul (foul), **1** very dirty; nasty; smelly: *foul air.* **2** make dirty; become dirty; soil: *Oil fouled the harbor.* **3** very wicked; vile: *Murder is a foul crime.* **4** unfair; against the rules. **5** (in football, basketball, and other sports) an unfair play; thing done against the rules. **6** baseball hit so that it falls outside the base lines. **7** get tangled up with: *The rope they threw fouled our anchor chain.* **8** clog up: *Grease has fouled this drain.* **9** unfavorable; stormy: *Foul weather delayed us.* **1,3,4,9** *adjective,* **2,7,8** *verb,* **5,6** *noun.*

found[1] (found). See **find.** *We found the treasure. The lost child was found. verb.*

found[2] (found), establish: *The Pilgrims founded a colony at Plymouth. verb.*

foun da tion (foun dā′shən), **1** part on which other parts rest or depend; base: *The foundation of a house is built first.* **2** basis: *This report has no foundation in fact.* **3** founding; establishing: *The foundation of the United States began in 1776. noun.*

found er[1] (foun′dər), **1** fill with water and sink: *A ship foundered in the storm.* **2** fall down; stumble; break down: *Cattle foundered in the swamp. The business foundered and finally closed. verb.*

found er² (foun′dər), person who founds or establishes something. *noun.*

found ling (found′ling), baby or little child found deserted. *noun.*

found ry (foun′drē), place where metal is melted and molded; place where things are made of melted metal. *noun, plural* **found ries.**

foun tain (foun′tən), **1** water flowing or rising into the air in a spray. See picture. **2** pipes through which the water is forced and the basin built to receive it. **3** spring of water. **4** place to get a drink: *a drinking fountain.* **5** source: *My friend is a fountain of information about football. noun.*

fountain pen, pen for writing that gives a steady supply of ink from a rubber or plastic tube.

four (fôr), one more than three; 4. *noun, adjective.*

four fold (fôr′fōld′), **1** four times as much or as many. **2** having four parts. 1,2 *adjective,* 1 *adverb.*

four-foot ed (fôr′fut′id), having four feet: *A dog is a four-footed animal. adjective.*

four score (fôr′skôr′), four times twenty; 80. *adjective, noun.*

four teen (fôr′tēn′), four more than ten; 14. *noun, adjective.*

four teenth (fôr′tēnth′), **1** next after the 13th. **2** one of 14 equal parts. *adjective, noun.*

fourth (fôrth), **1** next after the third. **2** quarter; one of four equal parts. *adjective, noun.*

Fourth of July, holiday in honor of the adoption of the Declaration of Independence on July 4, 1776.

fowl (foul), **1** any of several kinds of large birds used for food. Chickens, ducks, and turkeys are fowls. **2** flesh of these birds used for food. **3** wild fowl. *noun, plural* **fowls** or **fowl.**

fox (foks), **1** a wild animal somewhat like a dog. In many stories the fox gets the better of other animals by its cleverness. **2** its fur. **3** a clever or crafty person. *noun, plural* **fox es.**

fox hound (foks′hound′), hound with a keen sense of smell, trained to hunt foxes. *noun.*

fox y (fok′sē), crafty; like a fox. *adjective,* **fox i er, fox i est.**

fra cas (frā′kəs), disorderly noise; a noisy quarrel or fight. See picture. *noun, plural* **fra cas es.**

frac tion (frak′shən), **1** one or more of the equal parts of a whole. ¹/₂, ¹/₃, and ³/₄ are fractions; so are ⁴/₃ and ¹⁰/₆. **2** a very small part; not all of a thing: *I had time to do only a fraction of my homework. noun.*

frac ture (frak′chər), **1** breaking of a bone or cartilage. **2** breaking or a being broken: *a fracture of the ice.* **3** result of breaking: *The fracture in the foundation is widening.* **4** break; crack: *I fell from the tree and fractured my arm.* 1-3 *noun,* 4 *verb,* **frac tured, frac tur ing.**

frag ile (fraj′əl), easily broken; delicate; frail: *Be careful; that thin glass is fragile. adjective.*

frag ment (frag′mənt), part broken off; piece of something broken: *After I broke the vase, I tried to glue the fragments back together. noun.*

fra grance (frā′grəns), sweet smell; pleasing odor: *the fragrance of flowers or of perfume. noun.*

a hat	i it	oi oil	ch child	a in about
ā age	ī ice	ou out	ng long	e in taken
ä far	o hot	u cup	sh she	ə = i in pencil
e let	ō open	u put	th thin	o in lemon
ē equal	ô order	ü rule	ᴛʜ then	u in circus
ėr term			zh measure	

fountain (definitions 1 and 2)

fracas—Their argument ended in a fracas.

fossil (definition 1)—fossils of leaves

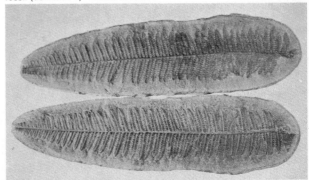

fra grant (frā′grənt), sweet-smelling: *This rose is fragrant. adjective.*

frail (frāl), **1** slender and not very strong; weak: *a frail and sickly child.* **2** easily broken or giving way: *Be careful; those little branches are a very frail support. adjective.*

frail ty (frāl′tē), **1** weakness: *a sick person's physical frailty, frailty of character.* **2** fault caused by weakness: *No one is perfect; we all have our frailties. noun, plural* **frail ties.**

frame (frām), **1** support over which something is stretched or built: *the frame of a house.* See picture. **2** body: *a person of small frame.* **3** make; put together; plan: *frame an answer to a difficult question.* **4** border in which a thing is set: *a picture frame.* **5** put a border around: *frame a picture.* **6** make seem guilty by some false arrangement: *frame an innocent person.* 1,2,4 *noun,* 3,5,6 *verb,* **framed, fram ing.**

frame of mind, way one is thinking or feeling; disposition; mood.

frame work (frām′wėrk′), **1** support or skeleton; stiff part which gives shape to a thing: *The bridge had a steel framework.* **2** way in which a thing is put together; structure; system: *the framework of government. noun.*

franc (frangk), unit of money in France, Belgium, Switzerland, and some other countries. *noun.*

France (frans), country in western Europe. *noun.*

frank (frangk), free in expressing one's real thoughts, opinions, and feelings; open; not hiding one's mind; not afraid to say what one thinks: *She was frank in telling me that she did not like my new hat. adjective.*

frank furt er (frangk′fər tər), a reddish sausage made of beef and pork, or of beef alone. Frankfurters on buns are called hot dogs. *noun.* [*Frankfurter* comes from a German word meaning "of Frankfurt" or "from Frankfurt." This type of sausage is a specialty of Frankfurt, a city in West Germany.]

fran tic (fran′tik), very much excited; wild with rage, fear, pain, or grief: *The trapped animal made frantic efforts to escape. adjective.*

fran ti cal ly (fran′tik lē), in a frantic manner; with wild excitement. *adverb.*

fra ter nal (frə tėr′nl), brotherly. *adjective.*

fra ter ni ty (frə tėr′nə tē), **1** group of men or boys joined together for fellowship or for some other purpose. There are student fraternities in many American colleges. **2** group having the same interests or kind of work: *the engineering fraternity.* **3** brotherhood. *noun, plural* **fra ter ni ties.**

fraud (frôd), **1** dishonest dealing; cheating; trickery: *obtain a prize by fraud.* **2** dishonest act or statement; something which is not what it seems to be. **3** person who is not what he or she pretends to be. *noun.*

fraught (frôt), loaded; filled: *The attempt to climb Mount Everest was fraught with danger. adjective.*

fray[1] (frā), separate into threads; make or become ragged or worn along the edge: *Long wear had frayed the collar of his old shirt. verb.*

fray[2] (frā), fight; noisy quarrel. *noun.*

freak (frēk), **1** something very queer or unusual: *A green leaf growing in the middle of a rose would be called a freak of nature.* **2** animal, plant, or person that has developed in an abnormal way: *A circus often has a sideshow of freaks.* See picture. *noun.*

freck le (frek′əl), one of the small, light-brown spots that some people have on the skin. *noun.*

free (frē), **1** not under another's control; not a slave: *a free man, a free people, a free nation.* **2** loose; not fastened or shut up: *They set free the bear cub caught in the trap.* **3** not held back from acting or thinking as one pleases: *She was free to do as she liked.* **4** make free; let loose; let go: *We freed the bird from the cage. She freed her foot from a tangled vine.* **5** clear: *The judge freed her of all charges.* **6** without anything to pay: *These tickets are free. We were admitted to the play free.* 1-3,6 *adjective,* **fre er, fre est;** 4,5 *verb,* **freed, free ing;** 6 *adverb.*

free from or **free of,** without: *free from fear, air free of dust.*

free dom (frē′dəm), **1** being free. **2** liberty; power to do, say, or think as one pleases. **3** free use: *We gave our guest the freedom of the house.* **4** too great liberty: *I dislike his freedom of manner.* **5** ease of movement or action: *A fine athlete performs with freedom. noun.*

free hand (frē′hand′), done by hand without using instruments or measurements: *freehand drawing. adjective.*

free man (frē′mən), person not a slave or a serf. *noun, plural* **free men.**

free way (frē′wā′), highway for fast traveling on which no tolls are charged. *noun.*

freeze (frēz), **1** harden by cold; turn into a solid. **2** make or become very cold: *The north wind froze the spectators. We froze at the football game.* **3** kill or injure by frost; be killed or injured by frost: *This cold weather will freeze the flowers. The flowers froze last night.* **4** cover or become covered with ice; clog with ice: *The snow and hail will freeze the pond. The pipes froze.* **5** fix or become fixed to something by freezing: *The cold weather froze the milk bottles to the porch. His fingers froze to the tray of ice cubes.* **6** a freezing or a being frozen. **7** make or become stiff and unfriendly: *The reporter's questions froze her so that she wouldn't answer. The shy boy froze up when I tried to be friendly.* **8** chill or be chilled with fear: *The howling of the wolves froze him with terror. She froze at the sight of the ghostly hand in the dimly lit room.* **9** become motionless: *The baby rabbit froze with fear at the strange sound.* **10** fix at a definite amount: *freeze prices, freeze rents.* 1-5,7-10 *verb,* **froze, fro zen, freez ing;** 6 *noun.*

freeze-dry (frēz′drī′), dry (food) by freezing and evaporating the liquid content in a vacuum. Freeze-dried food keeps well without being refrigerated. *verb,* **freeze-dried, freeze-dry ing.**

freez er (frē′zər), **1** machine to freeze ice cream. **2** a refrigerator cabinet for freezing foods or storing frozen food. *noun.*

a hat	i it	oi oil	ch child	a in about
ā age	ī ice	ou out	ng long	e in taken
ä far	o hot	u cup	sh she	ə = i in pencil
e let	ō open	ů put	th thin	o in lemon
ē equal	ô order	ü rule	ŦH then	u in circus
ėr term			zh measure	

freak (definition 2)—This monstrous squash is a freak.

frame (definition 1)—the frame of a skyscraper

freight (frāt), **1** goods that a train, truck, ship, or aircraft carries. **2** the carrying of goods on a train, ship, aircraft, or truck: *He sent the box by freight.* **3** train or ship for carrying goods. *noun.*

freight er (frā′tər), ship or aircraft that carries mainly freight. *noun.*

French (french), **1** of or having something to do with France, its people, or their language. **2** people of France. **3** language of France. 1 *adjective,* 2 *noun plural,* 3 *noun singular.*

French fries, potatoes cut into thin strips and fried in deep fat until crisp on the outside.

French horn, a brass wind instrument that has a mellow tone.

fren zied (fren′zēd), frantic; wild; very much excited. *adjective.*

fren zy (fren′zē), **1** near madness; frantic condition: *They were in a frenzy after hearing that their child was missing.* **2** a very great excitement: *The crowd was in a frenzy after the home team scored the winning goal. noun, plural* **fren zies.**

fre quen cy (frē′kwən sē), **1** rate of occurrence: *The flashes of light came with a frequency of three per minute.* **2** frequent occurrence: *The frequency of their visits annoyed us. noun, plural* **fre quen cies.**

fre quent (frē′kwənt *for 1;* fri kwent′ *for 2),* **1** happening often, near together, or every little while: *In my part of the country, storms are frequent in March.* **2** be often in; go to often: *Frogs frequent ponds, streams, and marshes.* 1 *adjective,* 2 *verb.*

fre quent ly (frē′kwənt lē), often. *adverb.*

fresh[1] (fresh), **1** newly made, grown, or gathered: *fresh footprints, fresh coffee, fresh flowers.* **2** new; recent: *Is there any fresh news from home?* **3** another: *After her failure she made a fresh start.* **4** not salty: *Rivers are usually fresh water.* **5** not spoiled; not stale: *Is this milk fresh?* **6** not artificially preserved: *Fresh foods often have better flavor than canned foods.* **7** not tired out; vigorous; lively: *Fresh horses pulled the stagecoach the last part of the trip.* **8** cool; refreshing: *a fresh breeze. adjective.*

fresh[2] (fresh), rude; too bold; disrespectful. *adjective.*

fresh en (fresh′ən), make or become fresh: *The rest freshened me. verb.*

fresh man (fresh′mən), student in the first year of high school or college. *noun, plural* **fresh men.**

fresh ness (fresh′nis), fresh condition; being fresh. *noun.*

fresh wa ter (fresh′wô′tər), of or living in water that is not salty: *The catfish is a freshwater fish. adjective.*

fret (fret), be or cause to be cross, discontented, or worried: *Don't fret over your mistakes. The baby frets in hot weather. verb,* **fret ted, fret ting.**

frigate—an American frigate firing its guns in battle

fronds of a fern

fret ful (fret′fəl), cross, discontented, or worried; ready to fret: *My baby brother is fretful because he is cutting his teeth. adjective.*

fri ar (frī′ər), man who belongs to one of certain religious brotherhoods of the Roman Catholic Church. *noun.*

fric tion (frik′shən), **1** a rubbing of one thing against another, such as skates on ice, hand against hand, or a brush on shoes: *Matches are lighted by friction.* **2** resistance to motion of surfaces that touch: *Oil reduces friction. A sled moves more easily on smooth ice than on rough ground because there is less friction.* **3** conflict of differing ideas or opinions; disagreement; clash: *Constant friction between the two nations brought them dangerously close to war. noun.*

Fri day (frī′dē), the sixth day of the week; the day after Thursday. *noun.* [*Friday* is from an earlier English word meaning "Frig's day." Frig is a name of the goddess of love.]

fried (frīd), **1** cooked in hot fat: *fried eggs.* **2** See **fry.** *I fried the ham. The potatoes had been fried.* **1** *adjective,* **2** *verb.*

friend (frend), **1** person who knows and likes another. **2** person who favors and supports: *He was a generous friend of the art museum.* **3** person

who belongs to the same side or group: *Are you friend or enemy? noun.*

friend less (frend′lis), without friends. *adjective.*

friend li ness (frend′lē nis), friendly feeling or behavior. *noun.*

friend ly (frend′lē), **1** like a friend; kind: *a friendly teacher.* **2** like a friend's: *a friendly greeting.* **3** on good terms: *friendly relations between countries.* **4** wanting to be a friend: *a friendly dog. adjective,* **friend li er, friend li est.**

friend ship (frend′ship), **1** condition of being friends. **2** liking between friends. **3** friendly feeling or behavior; friendliness. *noun.*

frieze (frēz), band of decoration around a room, building, or mantel. *noun.*

frig ate (frig′it), fast, three-masted sailing warship of medium size. Frigates were much used from 1750 to 1850. See picture. *noun.*

fright (frīt), **1** sudden fear; sudden terror: *The howl filled me with fright.* **2** person or thing that is ugly, shocking, or ridiculous: *When I put on the wig, they laughed and said I looked like a fright. noun.*

fright en (frīt′n), **1** fill with fright; make afraid; scare: *Thunder frightened the puppy.* **2** drive or force by terrifying: *The sudden noise frightened the deer away. verb.*

fright ful (frīt′fəl), **1** able to frighten; dreadful: *a frightful explosion.* **2** ugly; shocking: *the frightful destruction caused by a fire. adjective.*

frig id (frij′id), **1** very cold: *a frigid climate.* **2** cold in feeling or manner; stiff; chilling: *a frigid stare. adjective.*

Frigid Zone, either of two regions within the polar circles.

frill (fril), **1** ruffle. **2** thing added merely for show; useless ornament. *noun.*

fringe (frinj), **1** border or trimming made of threads or cords, either loose or tied together in small bunches. **2** anything like this; border: *A fringe of hair hung over her forehead.* **3** make a fringe for. **4** be a fringe for: *Bushes fringed the road.* **1,2** *noun,* **3,4** *verb,* **fringed, fring ing.**

Fris bee (friz′bē), trademark for a saucer-shaped disk of colored plastic for tossing back and forth in play. *noun.*

frisk (frisk), run and jump about playfully; dance and skip joyously: *Our lively puppy frisks all over the house. verb.*

frisk y (fris′kē), playful; lively. *adjective,* **frisk i er, frisk i est.**

friv o lous (friv′ə ləs), **1** lacking in seriousness or sense; silly: *Frivolous behavior is out of place in a courtroom.* **2** of little worth or importance: *Don't waste time on frivolous matters. adjective.*

fro (frō). **to and fro,** first one way and then back again; back and forth: *rock to and fro. adverb.*

frock (frok), **1** a woman's or girl's dress; gown. **2** robe worn by a clergyman. *noun.*

frog (frog), a small, leaping animal with webbed feet that lives in or near water. Frogs hatch from eggs as tadpoles and live in the water until they grow legs. Some frogs live in trees. *noun.*

frog man (frog′man′), person trained and

equipped for underwater operations of various kinds. *noun, plural* **frog men.**

frol ic (frol′ik), **1** a joyous game or party; play; fun. **2** play about joyously; have fun together: *The children frolicked with the puppy.* **1** *noun,* **2** *verb,* **frol icked, frol ick ing.**

from (from, frum, *or* frəm), **1** out of: *a train from New York. Steel is made from iron.* **2** out of the possession of: *Take the book from her.* **3** beginning with: *A week from today is a holiday.* **4** because of: *I am suffering from a cold.* **5** as distinguished from: *Anyone can tell apples from oranges.* **6** off: *He took a book from the table. preposition.*

frond (frond), leaf of a fern or palm. See picture. *noun.*

front (frunt), **1** part that faces forward; forward part: *the front of a car, the front of a coat.* **2** the first part; beginning: *There is an introduction in the front of this book.* **3** place where fighting is going on. **4** land facing a street or a body of water: *We have a house on the lake front.* **5** on or in the front; at the front: *a front room.* **6** have the front toward; face: *My house fronts the park.* **7** the dividing surface between two air masses: *A cold front is moving toward this area from Canada.* **1-4,7** *noun,* **5** *adjective,* **6** *verb.*

fron tier (frun tir′), **1** the last edge of settled country, where the wilds begin. **2** part of one country that touches the edge of another; boundary line between two countries. **3** an uncertain or undeveloped region: *explore the frontiers of science. noun.*

fron tiers man (frun tirz′mən), man who lives on the frontier. *noun, plural* **fron tiers men.**

frost (frôst), **1** a freezing condition; very cold weather; temperature below the point at which water freezes: *Frost came early last winter.* **2** moisture frozen on or in a surface; feathery crystals of ice formed when water vapor in the air condenses at a temperature below freezing: *On cold fall mornings, there is frost on the grass.* **3** cover with frost. **4** cover with anything that suggests frost: *The cook frosted the cake with icing.* **1,2** *noun,* **3,4** *verb.*

frost bite (frôst′bīt′), injury to a part of the body caused by freezing. *noun.*

frost bit ten (frôst′bit′n), injured by freezing: *My ears were frostbitten. adjective.*

frost ing (frô′sting), **1** mixture of sugar and some liquid, with flavoring, to cover cake; icing. **2** a dull finish on glass or metal. *noun.*

frost y (frô′stē), **1** cold enough for frost: *a frosty morning.* **2** covered with frost: *The glass is frosty.* **3** cold and unfriendly; with no warmth of feeling: *a frosty manner. adjective,* **frost i er, frost i est.**

froth (frôth), **1** foam: *the froth on a chocolate soda.* **2** give out froth; foam. **3** something light and trifling; unimportant talk. **1,3** *noun,* **2** *verb.*

frown (froun), **1** wrinkling of the forehead to show disapproval or anger. **2** wrinkle the forehead to show disapproval or anger; look displeased or angry: *My teacher frowned when I came in late.* **3** look with disapproval: *The principal frowned on*

a hat	i it	oi oil	ch child		a in about
ā age	ī ice	ou out	ng long		e in taken
ä far	o hot	u cup	sh she	ə =	i in pencil
e let	ō open	u̇ put	th thin		o in lemon
ē equal	ô order	ü rule	ᵀH then		u in circus
ėr term			zh measure		

our plan for a picnic just before examinations. **1** *noun,* **2,3** *verb.*

froze (frōz). See **freeze.** *The water in the pond froze last week. verb.*

fro zen (frō′zn), **1** hardened with cold; turned into ice: *a river frozen over, frozen sherbet.* **2** very cold: *My hands are frozen; I need some gloves.* **3** preserved by being subjected to low temperatures: *frozen foods.* **4** killed or injured by frost: *frozen flowers.* **5** covered or clogged with ice: *frozen water pipes.* **6** cold and unfeeling: *a frozen heart, a frozen stare.* **7** too frightened or stiff to move: *frozen to the spot in horror.* **8** See **freeze.** *The water has frozen to ice.* **1-7** *adjective,* **8** *verb.*

fru gal (frü′gəl), **1** without waste; not wasteful; saving; using things well: *A frugal person always shops for bargains.* **2** costing little; barely enough: *He ate a frugal supper of bread and milk. adjective.*

fruit (früt), **1** a juicy or fleshy product of a tree, bush, shrub, or vine which is usually sweet and good to eat. Apples, oranges, bananas, and berries are fruit. **2** part of the plant in which the seeds are. Pea pods, acorns, and grains of wheat are fruits. **3** a useful product of plant growth: *The fruits of the earth are used mostly for food.* **4** result of anything: *This invention was the fruit of much effort.* **5** produce fruit: *The apple tree didn't fruit this year.* **1-4** *noun,* **5** *verb.*

fruit ful (früt′fəl), **1** producing much fruit. **2** producing much of anything: *a fruitful mind.* **3** having good results; bringing benefit or profit: *Our plan was fruitful. adjective.*

fruit less (früt′lis), **1** having no results; useless; unsuccessful: *Our search was fruitless; we could not find the lost book.* **2** producing no fruit: *fruitless soil. adjective.*

fruit y (frü′tē), tasting or smelling like fruit: *the fruity odor of jam. adjective,* **fruit i er, fruit i est.**

frus trate (frus′trāt), defeat; make useless or worthless; block: *Heavy rain frustrated our plans for a picnic. verb,* **frus trat ed, frus trat ing.**

fry (frī), **1** cook in hot fat: *We fried the potatoes in a deep pan.* **2** something fried. **1** *verb,* **fried, fry ing;** **2** *noun, plural* **fries.**

ft., 1 foot or feet. **2** fort.

fudge (fuj), soft candy made of sugar, milk, chocolate, and butter. *noun.*

fu el (fyü′əl), **1** anything that can be burned to make a useful fire. Coal, wood, and oil are fuels. **2** anything that keeps up or increases a feeling: *Insults will only add fuel to an argument. noun.*

fu gi tive (fyü′jə tiv), **1** person who is running away or has run away: *The robber became a fugitive from justice.* **2** running away; having run away: *a fugitive slave.* **3** lasting only a very short time; passing swiftly. **1** *noun,* **2,3** *adjective.*

-ful, suffix meaning: **1** full of _____: Cheer*ful* means *full of* cheer. **2** showing _____: Care*ful* means *showing* care. **3** enough to fill a _____: Cup*ful* means *enough to fill a* cup.

ful crum (ful′krəm), support on which a lever turns or is supported in moving or lifting something. See picture. *noun.*

ful fill or **ful fil** (fül fil′), **1** carry out (a promise or prophecy). **2** perform or do (a duty or command): *She fulfilled all the teacher's requests.* **3** satisfy (a requirement or condition): *This diet will fulfill your needs in food.* **4** bring to an end; finish or complete: *fulfill a contract.* verb, **ful filled, ful fill ing.**

ful fill ment or **ful fil ment** (fül fil′mənt), fulfilling; completion; accomplishment. *noun.*

full (fül), **1** able to hold no more. Anything is full when it holds all that it is intended to hold. *This suitcase is full.* **2** complete; entire: *a full supply of clothes.* **3** completely: *Fill the pail full.* **4** completeness; greatest degree: *We discussed the matter to the full.* **5** plump; round; well filled out: *a full face.* **6** having wide folds or much cloth: *a full skirt.* **7** directly: *The ball hit me full in the face.* 1,2,5,6 *adjective,* 3,7 *adverb,* 4 *noun.*

full of, filled with: *The child's room is full of toys.*

full-grown (fül′grōn′), fully grown. *adjective.*

ful ly (fül′ē), **1** completely; entirely: *I am fully satisfied.* **2** abundantly: *The gymnasium was fully equipped with ropes and rings.* **3** quite: *He could not fully describe what he had seen. adverb.*

fum ble (fum′bəl), **1** grope awkwardly: *I fumbled in the darkness for the doorknob.* **2** handle awkwardly; let drop instead of catching and holding: *The quarterback fumbled the ball, and the other team recovered it.* **3** an awkward attempt to find or handle something. 1,2 *verb,* **fum bled, fum bling;** 3 *noun.*

fume (fyüm), **1** vapor, gas, or smoke, especially if harmful or strong: *The fumes from the automobile exhaust nearly choked me.* **2** give off vapor, gas, or smoke: *The candle fumed, sputtered, and went out.* **3** let off one's rage in angry complaints: *She fumed about the slowness of the train.* 1 *noun,* 2,3 *verb,* **fumed, fum ing.**

fu mi gate (fyü′mə gāt), disinfect with fumes; expose to fumes: *They fumigated the building to kill the cockroaches.* verb, **fu mi gat ed, fu mi gat ing.**

fun (fun), playfulness; merry play; amusement; joking: *They had a lot of fun at the party. noun.*

make fun of or **poke fun at,** laugh at; ridicule.

func tion (fungk′shən), **1** proper work; purpose; use: *The function of the stomach is to digest food.* **2** work; act: *One of the older students can function as teacher. This old fountain pen does not function very well.* **3** a formal public or social gathering for some purpose: *The hotel ballroom is often used for weddings and other functions.* 1,3 *noun,* 2 *verb.*

fund (fund), **1** sum of money set aside for a special purpose: *Our school has a fund of $2000 to buy books with.* **2 funds, a** money ready to use: *We took $10 from the club's funds to buy a flag.* **b** money: *I used up my allowance and was low on*

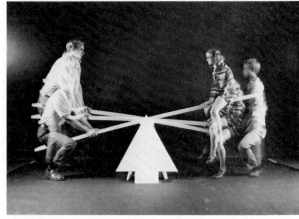

fulcrum—The seesaw moves on a fulcrum.

fungus on a tree trunk

furrow (definition 1)

funds. **3** stock or store ready for use: *There is a fund of information in our new library. noun.*

fun da men tal (fun′də men′tl), forming a basis; essential: *Reading is a fundamental skill. adjective.*

fu ner al (fyü′nər əl), **1** ceremonies held at the burial of a dead person. A funeral usually includes a religious service and taking the body to the place where it is buried or burned. **2** of a funeral; suitable for a funeral: *The funeral march was very slow.* **1** *noun,* **2** *adjective.*

fun gi (fun′jī), more than one fungus. *noun plural.*

fun gus (fung′gəs), plant without flowers, leaves, or green coloring matter. Mushrooms, toadstools, molds, and mildews are fungi. See picture. *noun, plural* **fun gi** *or* **fun gus es.**

fun nel (fun′l), **1** a tapering tube with a wide mouth shaped like a cone. A funnel is used to pour liquid, powder, or grain into a small opening without spilling. **2** smokestack or chimney on a steamship or steam engine. *noun.*

fun nies (fun′ēz), comic strips. *noun plural.*

fun ny (fun′ē), **1** causing laughter: *The clown's funny jokes kept us laughing.* **2** strange; queer; odd: *It's funny that they are so late. adjective,* **fun ni er, fun ni est.**

fur (fėr), **1** the soft hair covering the skin of many animals. **2** skin with such hair on it. Fur is used to make, cover, trim, or line clothing. *noun.*

fur i ous (fyùr′ē əs), **1** full of wild, fierce anger: *The owner of the house was furious when she learned of the broken window.* **2** raging; violent: *A hurricane is a furious storm. adjective.*

furl (fėrl), roll up; fold up: *furl a sail, furl a flag. The birds furled their wings. verb.*

fur long (fėr′lông), a unit for measuring length or distance. It is equal to ¹/₈ of a mile or 220 yards. *noun.*

fur lough (fėr′lō), leave of absence: *The soldier has two weeks' furlough. noun.*

fur nace (fėr′nis), an enclosed chamber or box to make a very hot fire in. Furnaces are used to heat buildings, melt metals, and make glass. *noun.*

fur nish (fėr′nish), **1** supply; provide: *furnish an army with blankets. The sun furnishes heat.* **2** supply (a room, house, or office) with furniture or equipment: *furnish a bedroom. verb.*

fur nish ings (fėr′ni shingz), furniture or equipment for a room or a house. *noun plural.*

fur ni ture (fėr′nə chər), movable articles needed in a room or house. Beds, chairs, tables, and desks are furniture. *noun.*

fur row (fėr′ō), **1** a long, narrow groove or track cut in the earth by a plow. See picture. **2** cut furrows in. **3** wrinkle: *a furrow in one's brow.* **4** make wrinkles in: *The old woman's face was furrowed with age.* **1,3** *noun,* **2,4** *verb.*

fur ry (fėr′ē), **1** of fur; consisting of fur. **2** covered with fur. **3** soft like fur. *adjective,* **fur ri er, fur ri est.**

fur ther (fėr′℻ər), **1** more distant: *on the further side.* **2** to a more advanced point: *Inquire further into the matter.* **3** more: *Do you need further help?* **4** help forward: *Let us further the cause of peace.*

a hat	i it	oi oil	ch child	a in about
ā age	ī ice	ou out	ng long	e in taken
ä far	o hot	u cup	sh she	ə = { i in pencil
e let	ō open	u̇ put	th thin	o in lemon
ē equal	ô order	ü rule	℻ then	u in circus
ėr term			zh measure	

5 also; in addition: *My parents told me to clean my room and said further that I must wash the dishes.* **1,3** *adjective, comparative of* **far;** **4** *verb,* **2,5** *adverb, comparative of* **far.**

fur ther more (fėr′℻ər môr), moreover; also; besides. *adverb.*

fur ther most (fėr′℻ər mōst), furthest. *adjective.*

fur thest (fėr′℻ist), **1** most distant. **2** most. **1** *adjective, superlative of* **far;** **2** *adverb, superlative of* **far.**

fur tive (fėr′tiv), **1** done by stealth; secret: *a furtive glance into the forbidden room.* **2** sly: *The thief had a furtive manner. adjective.*

fur y (fyùr′ē), **1** rage; storm of anger. **2** violence; fierceness: *the fury of a hurricane.* **3** a raging or violent person. *noun, plural* **fur ies.**

fuse[1] (fyüz), a slow-burning wick or other device used to set off a shell, bomb, or blast of gunpowder. *noun.*

fuse[2] (fyüz), **1** a wire or strip of metal in an electric circuit that melts and breaks the circuit if the current becomes dangerously strong. **2** melt; join together by melting: *Copper and zinc are fused to make brass.* **3** blend; unite: *The intense heat fused the rocks together.* **1** *noun,* **2,3** *verb,* **fused, fus ing.**

fu se lage (fyü′sə läzh *or* fyü′sə lij), body of an airplane to which the wings and tail are fastened. The fuselage holds the passengers and cargo. *noun.*

fu sion (fyü′zhən), **1** fusing; melting; melting together: *Bronze is made by the fusion of copper and tin.* **2** the combining of atomic nuclei to produce tremendous amounts of energy. *noun.*

fuss (fus), **1** much bother about small matters; useless talk and worry; attention given to something not worth it. **2** make a fuss: *She fussed about with her work in a nervous manner.* **1** *noun, plural* **fuss es;** **2** *verb.*

fuss y (fus′ē), **1** hard to please; never satisfied: *A sick person is likely to be fussy about food.* **2** elaborately made: *a fussy blouse with many bows and much lace. adjective,* **fuss i er, fuss i est.**

fu tile (fyü′tl), useless; not successful: *He fell down after making futile attempts to keep his balance. adjective.*

fu ture (fyü′chər), **1** time to come; what is to come: *You cannot change the past, but you can do better in the future.* **2** coming; that will be: *We hope your future years will all be happy.* **3** expressing something expected to happen or exist in time to come: *the future tense of a verb.* **1** *noun,* **2,3** *adjective.*

fuzz (fuz), fine down; loose, light fibers or hairs: *Caterpillars and peaches are covered with fuzz. noun.*

fuzz y (fuz′ē), **1** of fuzz. **2** like fuzz. **3** covered with fuzz. *adjective,* **fuzz i er, fuzz i est.**

G g

G or **g** (jē), the seventh letter of the English alphabet. There are two *g*'s in *egg. noun, plural* **G's** or **g's.**

gab ble (gab/əl), talk rapidly with little or no meaning. *verb,* **gab bled, gab bling.**

ga ble (gā/bəl), end of a roof having a ridge, with the three-cornered piece of wall that it covers. See picture. *noun.*

gable—You can see three gables on this house.

gadg et (gaj/it), a small mechanical device or contrivance: *A can opener is a kitchen gadget. noun.*

gag (gag), **1** something put in a person's mouth to keep him or her from talking or crying out. **2** stop up the mouth of with a gag: *The robbers tied the watchman's arms and gagged him.* **3** strain in an effort to vomit: *I gagged on the bad-tasting medicine.* **4** joke: *The clown's gags made us laugh.* 1,4 *noun,* 2,3 *verb,* **gagged, gag ging.**

gai e ty (gā/ə tē), **1** being happy and full of fun; cheerful liveliness; being gay: *Their gaiety helped to make the party a success.* **2** a bright appearance: *gaiety of dress. noun.*

gai ly (gā/lē), **1** in a happy way; merrily; happily; in a gay manner. **2** brightly: *They were gaily dressed in colorful costumes. adverb.*

gain (gān), **1** come to have; get; obtain; win: *gain possession of land. She gained recognition as an author.* **2** what one gains; increase, addition, or advantage: *a gain in weight. The company had a gain of ten per cent over last year's earnings.* **3 gains,** profits; earnings; winnings. **4** get as an increase, addition, or advantage; profit: *The car gained speed. What will you gain by worrying?* **5** make progress: *The sick child is gaining and will soon be well.* **6** arrive at: *The swimmer gained the shore.* 1,4-6 *verb,* 2,3 *noun.*

gain on, come closer to; catch up with: *One boat is gaining on another.*

gait (gāt), the kind of steps used in going along; manner of walking: *a springy gait. A gallop is one of the gaits of a horse. noun.*

gal., gallon or gallons.

ga la (gā/lə), festive: *Thanksgiving is a gala day for our family. adjective.*

gal ax y (gal/ək sē), group of billions of stars forming one system. The earth and sun are part of one galaxy. Many galaxies outside our own can be seen with a telescope. See picture. *noun, plural* **gal ax ies.**

gale (gāl), **1** a very strong wind. **2** a noisy outburst: *gales of laughter. noun.*

gall[1] (gôl), **1** a bitter liquid made in the liver; bile. **2** anything very bitter. *noun.*

gall[2] (gôl), annoy; irritate: *The child was galled by being scolded so much. verb.*

gal lant (gal/ənt), noble in spirit or in conduct; brave: *King Arthur was a gallant knight. adjective.*

gal lant ry (gal/ən trē), bravery; dashing courage. *noun.*

gal le on (gal/ē ən), a large, high ship of former times, usually with several decks. See picture. *noun.*

gal ler y (gal/ər ē), **1** hall or long narrow passage. **2** the highest balcony of a theater. **3** people who sit there. **4** building or room used to show collections of pictures and statues. *noun, plural* **gal ler ies.**

gal ley (gal/ē), **1** a long, narrow ship of former times having oars and sails. Galleys were often rowed by slaves or convicts. See picture. **2** kitchen of a ship or airplane. *noun, plural* **gal leys.**

gal lon (gal/ən), a unit for measuring liquids equal to 4 quarts: *Our car holds 16 gallons of gasoline. noun.*

gal lop (gal/əp), **1** the fastest gait of a horse or other four-footed animal. In a gallop, all four feet are off the ground together at each leap. **2** ride at a gallop: *The hunters galloped after the hounds.* **3** go or cause to go at a gallop: *The wild horse galloped off. We galloped our horses down the road.* **4** go very fast; hurry: *gallop through a book.* 1 *noun,* 2-4 *verb.*

gal lows (gal/ōz), **1** a wooden frame made of a crossbar on two upright posts, used for hanging criminals. **2** punishment by hanging: *The judge sentenced the murderer to the gallows. noun, plural* **gal lows es** or **gal lows.**

ga losh es (gə losh/iz), rubber or plastic overshoes covering the ankles, worn in wet or snowy weather. *noun plural.*

gam ble (gam/bəl), **1** play games of chance for money: *gamble at cards.* **2** take great risks in business; take a risk: *She gambled in the stock market and made a fortune.* **3** risk (money or other things of value): *The firefighters gambled their lives to rescue the child from the burning building.* **4** a risky act or undertaking: *Putting money into a new business is often a gamble.* 1-3 *verb,* **gam bled, gam bling;** 4 *noun.*

gam bler (gam/blər), **1** person who gambles a great deal. **2** person whose occupation is gambling. *noun.*

galaxy

galleon

galley
(definition 1)

gape (definition 3)
the gaping mouth
of a hippopotamus

a hat	i it	oi oil	ch child	a in about
ā age	ī ice	ou out	ng long	e in taken
ä far	o hot	u cup	sh she	ə = i in pencil
e let	ō open	ů put	th thin	o in lemon
ē equal	ô order	ü rule	ŦH then	u in circus
ėr term			zh measure	

gam bol (gam′bəl), run and jump about in play; frolic: *Lambs gamboled in the meadow. verb.*

game (gām), **1** way of playing; something done for fun: *Tag is a game that we enjoy.* **2** contest with certain rules, in which one person or side tries to win: *a football game, a game of checkers.* **3** things needed for a game: *This store sells many kinds of games.* **4** scheme; plan: *They tried to trick us, but we saw through their game.* **5** wild animals, birds, or fish hunted or caught for sport or for food. **6** flesh of wild animals or birds when used for food. **7** having to do with wild animals, hunting, or fishing: *Game laws protect wildlife.* **8** brave; plucky: *The losing team put up a game fight.* **9** having spirit enough: *The explorer was game for any adventure.* 1-6 *noun,* 7-9 *adjective,* **gam er, gam est.**

gan der (gan′dər), a male goose. *noun.*

gang (gang), **1** group of people acting or going around together: *a gang of criminals.* **2** group of people working together under one foreman: *A gang of workers were repairing the road.* **3** form a gang: *The girls ganged together to build a tree house.* 1,2 *noun,* 3 *verb.*

gang plank (gang′plangk′), a movable bridge used in getting on and off a ship. *noun.*

gang ster (gang′stər), member of a gang of criminals. *noun.*

gang way (gang′wā′), **1** a passageway, especially on a ship. **2** gangplank. **3** Get out of the way! 1,2 *noun,* 3 *interjection.*

gap (gap), **1** a broken place; opening: *The cows got out of the field through a gap in the fence.* **2** unfilled space; blank: *The record is not complete; there are several gaps in it.* **3** pass through mountains. *noun.*

gape (gāp), **1** open wide: *A deep hole in the earth gaped before us.* **2** a wide opening. **3** open the mouth wide; yawn. See picture. **4** act of opening the mouth wide; yawning. **5** stare with the mouth open: *The crowd gaped at the tightrope walkers.* 1,3,5 *verb,* **gaped, gap ing;** 2,4 *noun.*

ga rage (gə räzh′), **1** place where automobiles are kept. **2** shop for repairing automobiles. *noun.*

garage sale, sale of used furniture, clothing, tools, or household goods, held in the seller's garage, yard, or basement.

garb (gärb), **1** the way one is dressed; clothing: *military garb, royal garb, splendid garb.* **2** clothe: *The doctor was garbed in white.* 1 *noun,* 2 *verb.*

gar bage (gär′bij), scraps of food to be thrown away from a kitchen, dining room, or store. *noun.*

gar den (gärd′n), **1** piece of ground used for growing vegetables, flowers, or fruits. **2** take care of a garden: *I garden as a hobby.* 1 *noun,* 2 *verb.*

gar den er (gärd′nər), **1** person hired to take care of a garden or lawn. **2** person who makes a garden or works in a garden. *noun.*

garter snake—20 to 30 inches
(50 to 75 centimeters) long

gargoyle

gazelle—about 2 feet (60 centimeters) high at the shoulder

gar de nia (gär dē′nyə), a sweet-smelling, white flower with smooth, waxlike petals. *noun.* [The *gardenia* was named for Dr. Alexander Garden. He was an American botanist who lived from 1730 to 1791.]

gar gle (gär′gəl), **1** wash (the throat or mouth) with a liquid which is kept moving by the outgoing breath: *I gargled with hot salt water to relieve my sore throat.* **2** liquid used for gargling. 1 *verb*, **gar gled, gar gling;** 2 *noun.*

gar goyle (gär′goil), spout which sticks out from the gutter of a building and ends in a grotesque figure. It carries off rain water. See picture. *noun.*

gar land (gär′lənd), **1** wreath of flowers or leaves. **2** decorate with garlands. 1 *noun*, 2 *verb.*

gar lic (gär′lik), plant like an onion, used in cooking. Its flavor is stronger than that of an onion. *noun.*

gar ment (gär′mənt), any article of clothing. *noun.*

gar ner (gär′nər), gather and store away: *Wheat is cut and garnered at harvest time. verb.*

gar net (gär′nit), **1** a deep-red stone, used as a gem. **2** deep red. 1 *noun*, 2 *adjective.*

gar nish (gär′nish), **1** something laid on or around a dish as a decoration: *The turkey was served with a garnish of cranberries and parsley.* **2** decorate (food). 1 *noun, plural* **gar nish es;** 2 *verb.*

gar ret (gar′it), space in a house just below a sloping roof; attic. *noun.*

gar ri son (gar′ə sən), **1** the soldiers stationed in a fort or town to defend it. **2** place that has a garrison. **3** station soldiers in (a fort or town) to defend it. **4** occupy (a fort or town) as a garrison. 1,2 *noun*, 3,4 *verb.*

gar ter (gär′tər), band or strap to hold up a stocking or sock. It is usually elastic. *noun.*

garter snake, a harmless snake, brown or green with long yellow stripes. See picture.

gas (gas), **1** substance that is not a solid or a liquid; substance that has no shape or size of its own and can expand without limit. Oxygen and hydrogen are gases at ordinary temperatures. **2** any mixture of gases that can be burned. Gas is used for cooking and heating. **3** a substance in the form of a gas that poisons, suffocates, or stuns. **4** kill or injure by poisonous gas. **5** gasoline. 1-3,5 *noun, plural* **gas es;** 4 *verb*, **gassed, gas sing.**

gas e ous (gas′ē əs), in the form of or like gas: *Steam is water in a gaseous condition. adjective.*

gash (gash), **1** a long, deep cut or wound. **2** make a long, deep cut or wound in. 1 *noun, plural* **gash es;** 2 *verb.*

gas mask, a tight covering that fits over the mouth and nose to prevent breathing poisonous gas or smoke.

gas o hol (gas′ə hôl), a motor fuel made of ninety percent gasoline and ten percent alcohol. *noun.*

gas o line or **gas o lene** (gas′ə lēn′ or gas′ə lēn′), a colorless liquid made from petroleum. It evaporates and burns very easily. Gasoline is used to run automobiles. *noun.*

gasp (gasp), **1** try hard to get one's breath with open mouth. A person gasps when out of breath or surprised. **2** a trying hard to get one's breath with open mouth. **3** utter with gasps: *"Help! Help!" gasped the drowning man.* 1,3 *verb,* 2 *noun.*

gate (gāt), **1** door in a wall or fence: *Someone left the gate open and the dog got out of the yard.* **2** opening in a wall or fence where a door is. **3** door or valve to stop or control the flow of water in a pipe, dam, canal, or lock. *noun.*

gate way (gāt′wā′), **1** opening in a wall or fence where a gate is. **2** way to go in or out; way to get to something: *A good education can be a gateway to success. noun.*

gath er (gaŦH′ər), **1** collect; bring into one place: *He gathered his books and papers and started to school.* **2** come together: *A crowd gathered to hear the speech.* **3** pick; glean or pluck: *gather crops.* **4** put together in the mind: *I gather from the excitement that something important has happened.* **5** pull together in folds: *The dressmaker gathered the skirt at the waist. She gathered her brows into a frown.* **6** one of the little folds between the stitches when cloth is gathered. 1-5 *verb,* 6 *noun.*

gath er ing (gaŦH′ər ing), assembly; meeting: *We had a large family gathering at our house on Thanksgiving. noun.*

gaud y (gô′dē), too bright and gay to be in good taste; cheap and showy: *gaudy jewelry. adjective,* **gaud i er, gaud i est.**

gauge (gāj), **1** a standard measure; measure. There are gauges of the capacity of a barrel, the thickness of sheet iron, the diameter of a shotgun bore, wire, etc. **2** instrument for measuring. A steam gauge measures the pressure of steam. **3** measure accurately. **4** estimate; judge: *It's hard to gauge the educational value of television.* **5** distance between the rails of a railroad. 1,2,5 *noun,* 3,4 *verb,* **gauged, gaug ing.**

gaunt (gônt), **1** very thin and bony; with hollow eyes and a starved look: *Hunger had made him gaunt.* **2** looking bare and gloomy; desolate. *adjective.*

gaunt let (gônt′lit), **1** an iron glove which was part of a knight's armor. **2** a stout, heavy glove with a deep, flaring cuff. *noun.*

throw down the gauntlet, give a challenge.

gauze (gôz), a very thin, light cloth, easily seen through. Gauze is often used for bandages. *noun.*

gave (gāv). See **give.** *She gave me some of her candy. verb.*

gav el (gav′əl), a small mallet used by a presiding officer to signal for attention or order: *The chairman rapped on the table twice with his gavel. noun.*

gay (gā), **1** happy and full of fun; merry: *The children were cheerful and gay on the day of the first snowfall.* **2** bright-colored: *a gay dress. adjective.*

gaze (gāz), **1** look long and steadily: *For hours we sat gazing at the stars.* **2** a long, steady look. 1 *verb,* **gazed, gaz ing;** 2 *noun.*

ga zelle (gə zel′), a small, graceful, deerlike animal with large, soft eyes. See picture. *noun, plural* **ga zelles** or **ga zelle.**

ga zette (gə zet′), newspaper. *noun.*

a hat	**i** it	**oi** oil	**ch** child	⎧ a in about
ā age	**ī** ice	**ou** out	**ng** long	⎪ e in taken
ä far	**o** hot	**u** cup	**sh** she	ə = ⎨ i in pencil
e let	**ō** open	**u̇** put	**th** thin	⎪ o in lemon
ē equal	**ô** order	**ü** rule	**ŦH** then	⎩ u in circus
ėr term			**zh** measure	

gear (gir), **1** wheel having teeth that fit into teeth in another wheel; wheels turning one another by teeth. If the wheels are of different sizes they will turn at different speeds. See picture. **2** equipment that is needed, such as harness, tools, clothing, or household goods: *Fishing gear includes a line, a pole, and hooks.* **3** make fit; adjust; adapt: *industry geared to the needs of war.* 1,2 *noun,* 3 *verb.*

in gear, connected with the motor.

out of gear, not connected with the motor.

gears (definition 1)

gear shift (gir′shift′), device for connecting a motor to any of several sets of gears. *noun.*

geese (gēs), more than one goose. *noun plural.*

Gei ger count er (gī′gər koun′tər), device which detects and measures radioactivity. [The *Geiger counter* was named for Hans Geiger, who lived from 1882 to 1947. He was a German scientist who helped to develop it.]

gel a tin (jel′ə tən), substance like glue or jelly obtained by boiling the bones, hoofs, and other waste parts of animals. Gelatin is used in making glue and jellied desserts. *noun.*

gem (jem), **1** a precious stone, especially when cut or polished for ornament; jewel. Diamonds and rubies are gems. **2** person or thing that is very beautiful or precious: *The gem of her collection was a rare Italian stamp. noun.*

gen er al (jen′ər əl), **1** of all; for all; from all: *A government takes care of the general welfare of its citizens.* **2** widespread; not limited to a few; for many; from many: *There is a general interest in television.* **3** not detailed: *The teacher gave us only general instructions.* **4** not special: *a general store, a general magazine. A general reader reads different kinds of books.* **5** chief: *The Attorney General is the head of the legal department of the government.* **6** a high officer in command of many soldiers in an army. 1-5 *adjective,* 6 *noun.*

in general, usually; commonly: *She is friendly with me in general, but she was particularly friendly today.*

gen er al ize (jen′ər ə līz), make into a general rule; conclude from particular facts: *If you know that cats, lions, leopards, and tigers eat meat, you can generalize that the cat family eats meat. verb,* **gen er al ized, gen er al iz ing.**

gen er al ly (jen′ər ə lē), **1** in most cases; usually: *They are generally on time.* **2** for the most part; widely: *It was once generally believed that the earth is flat.* **3** in a general way: *Generally speaking, we had a nice trip. adverb.*

gen e rate (jen′ə rāt′), produce; cause to be: *Heating water can generate steam. The steam can generate electricity by turning an electric generator. verb,* **gen e rat ed, gen e rat ing.**

gen e ra tion (jen′ə rā′shən), **1** the people born in the same period. Your parents and their friends belong to one generation; you and your friends belong to the next generation. **2** about thirty years, or the time from the birth of one generation to the birth of the next generation. **3** one step in the descent of a family: *The picture showed four generations—great-grandmother, grandmother, mother, and baby.* **4** act or process of producing: *Steam and water power are used for the generation of electricity. noun.*

gen e ra tor (jen′ə rā′tər), a machine for producing electricity. Generators change mechanical energy into electric energy. *noun.*

ge ner ic (jə ner′ik), not sold under a trademark or brand name: *generic drugs, generic canned goods. adjective.*

gen e ros i ty (jen′ə ros′ə tē), **1** being generous; unselfishness; willingness to share with others: *That wealthy family is known for its generosity.* **2** generous behavior; generous act. *noun, plural* **gen e ros i ties.**

gen er ous (jen′ər əs), **1** willing to share with others; unselfish: *Our teacher is always generous with his time.* **2** noble and forgiving; not mean: *She was generous in accepting their apology.* **3** large; plentiful: *A quarter of a pie is a generous piece. adjective.*

gen ial (jē′nyəl), smiling and pleasant; cheerful and friendly; kindly: *She was glad to see us again and gave us a genial welcome. adjective.*

ge nie (jē′nē), a powerful spirit: *When Aladdin rubbed his lamp, the genie came and did what Aladdin asked. noun.*

gen ius (jē′nyəs), **1** very great natural power of mind: *Important discoveries are usually made by men and women of genius.* **2** person having such power: *Benjamin Franklin was a genius.* **3** great natural ability: *Beethoven played the piano well, but he had a genius for composing music. noun.*

gen tile or **Gen tile** (jen′tīl), **1** person who is not a Jew. **2** not Jewish. **1** *noun,* **2** *adjective.*

gen til i ty (jen til′ə tē), good manners; refinement: *Her gentility was evident by the gracious way in which she greeted us. noun.*

gen tle (jen′tl), **1** mild; not severe, rough, or violent: *a gentle tap.* **2** soft; low: *a gentle sound.* **3** moderate: *gentle heat, a gentle slope.* **4** kindly; friendly: *a gentle disposition.* **5** easy to manage: *a gentle dog.* **6** having or showing good manners; refined; polite. *adjective,* **gen tler, gen tlest.**

gen tle man (jen′tl mən), **1** man of good family and social position. **2** a well-bred man. **3** a polite term for any man: *"Gentlemen" is often used in speaking or writing to a group of men. noun, plural* **gen tle men.**

gen tle man ly (jen′tl mən lē), like a gentleman; well-bred; polite. *adjective.*

gen tle wom an (jen′tl wüm′ən), **1** woman of good family and social position. **2** a well-bred woman. **3** a woman attendant of a lady of rank. *noun, plural* **gen tle wom en.**

gent ly (jent′lē), **1** in a gentle way; tenderly; softly: *Handle the baby gently.* **2** gradually: *a gently sloping hillside. adverb.*

gen u ine (jen′yü ən), **1** real; true: *genuine leather, a genuine diamond. The table is genuine mahogany, not wood stained to look like it.* **2** frank; free from pretense; sincere: *genuine sorrow. adjective.*

ge o graph ic (jē′ə graf′ik), geographical. *adjective.*

ge o graph i cal (jē′ə graf′ə kəl), of geography; having something to do with geography. *adjective.*

ge og ra phy (jē og′rə fē), **1** study of the earth's surface, climate, continents, countries, peoples, industries, and products. **2** the surface features of a place, region, or country. *noun, plural* **ge og ra phies.**

ge o log i cal (jē′ə loj′ə kəl), of geology; having something to do with geology. *adjective.*

ge ol o gist (jē ol′ə jist), person who is an expert in geology. *noun.*

ge ol o gy (jē ol′ə jē), science that deals with the earth's crust, the layers of which it is composed, and their history. *noun, plural* **ge ol o gies.**

ge o met ric (jē′ə met′rik), made up of straight lines, circles, and other simple shapes; regular and evenly balanced. See picture. *adjective.*

ge om e try (jē om′ə trē), branch of mathematics that measures and compares points, lines, angles, surfaces, and solids. *noun.*

Geor gia (jôr′jə), one of the southeastern states of the United States. [*Georgia* was named in 1732 for George II, king of England, who lived from 1683 to 1760.]

ge ra ni um (jə rā′nē əm), plant with showy flowers of red, pink, or white, often grown in pots for window plants. *noun.* [*Geranium* comes from a Greek word meaning "crane." The plant was called this because its seed pod looks something like a crane's bill.]

ger bil (jėr′bəl), an animal somewhat like a mouse with long hind legs. Gerbils are used for scientific experiments and are kept as pets. See picture. *noun.*

germ (jėrm), **1** a simple animal or plant, too small to be seen without a microscope. Some germs cause disease. **2** the earliest form of a living thing; seed or bud. **3** the beginning of anything: *His tale gave me the germ of an idea for a book. noun.*

Ger man (jėr′mən), **1** of or having something to do with Germany, its people, or their language. **2** person born or living in Germany. **3** language of Germany. **1** *adjective,* **2,3** *noun.*

German shepherd, a large, strong, intelligent dog often trained to work with soldiers and police or to guide blind persons.

Ger ma ny (jėr′mə nē), former country in central Europe. Since 1949 Germany has been divided into West Germany and East Germany. *noun.*

ger mi nate (jėr′mə nāt), start growing or developing; sprout: *Seeds germinate in the spring. Warmth and moisture germinate seeds. verb,* **ger mi nat ed, ger mi nat ing.**

ges ture (jes′chər), **1** movement of the hands, arms, or any part of the body, used instead of words or with words to help express an idea or feeling: *Speakers often make gestures with their hands to stress something they are saying.* **2** any action for effect or to impress others: *Her refusal was merely a gesture; she really wanted to go.* **3** make gestures; use gestures. 1,2 *noun,* 3 *verb,* **ges tured, ges tur ing.**

get (get), **1** come to have; obtain; receive: *I got a present.* **2** reach; arrive: *I got home early last night.* **3** catch; get hold of: *I got the cat by one leg.* **4** cause to be or do: *Get the windows open.* **5** become: *It is getting colder.* **6** persuade; influence: *Try to get them to come, too. verb,* **got, got** or **got ten, get ting.**

get along, 1 be friendly: *to get along with others.* **2** manage: *I got along without their help.*

get away, 1 go away: *Let's get away from here.* **2** escape: *The prisoner got away.*

get away with, take or do something and escape safely: *Don't let them get away with such lies.*

get in, 1 go in: *I had hoped to get in without being seen.* **2** put in: *They kept talking, and I couldn't get in a word.* **3** arrive: *Our train should get in at 9 p.m.*

get off, 1 come down from or out of: *We got off our horses.* **2** take off: *Get your coat off.* **3** escape punishment: *If you disobey again, you will not get off so easily.* **4** start: *The horses in the race got off well.*

get on, 1 go up on or into: *We got on a train.* **2** put on: *Get on your rubbers; we have to go out in the rain.* **3** advance: *get on in years.* **4** succeed: *How are you getting on in your new job?* **5** agree: *The roommates get on with each other very well.*

get out, 1 go out: *Let's get out of here!* **2** become known: *The secret got out.*

get over, recover from: *I finally got over my cold.*

get to, be allowed to: *I got to stay up late last night.*

get together, 1 come together; meet: *Let's get together next week.* **2** come to an agreement: *The jury was unable to get together.*

get up, 1 arise: *She got up at six o'clock.* **2** stand up: *I fell on the ice and couldn't get up.*

gey ser (gī′zər), a spring that sends up fountains or jets of hot water or steam. See picture. *noun.*

Gha na (gä′nə), country in western Africa. *noun.*

ghast ly (gast′lē), **1** horrible: *The destruction caused by the forest fire was a ghastly sight.* **2** like a dead person or ghost; deathly pale: *The sick man looked ghastly.* **3** very bad: *a ghastly failure. adjective,* **ghast li er, ghast li est.**

ghet to (get′ō), part of a city where any racial group or nationality lives. *noun.*

ghost (gōst), spirit of one who is dead appearing

a hat	i it	oi oil	ch child	(a in about
ā age	ī ice	ou out	ng long	e in taken
ä far	o hot	u cup	sh she	ə = { i in pencil
e let	ō open	ů put	th thin	o in lemon
ē equal	ô order	ü rule	ᴛʜ then	(u in circus
ėr term			zh measure	

geyser—a geyser in Yellowstone National Park

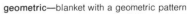

geometric—blanket with a geometric pattern

gerbil—about 8 inches (20 centimeters) long with the tail

to the living: *The ghost of the murdered servant was said to haunt the house.* noun.

ghost ly (gōst′lē), like a ghost; pale, dim, and shadowy: *A ghostly form walked across the stage.* adjective, **ghost li er, ghost li est.**

gi ant (jī′ənt), **1** an imaginary being like a huge man. **2** person of great size or very great power. **3** huge: *a giant potato.* 1,2 noun, 3 adjective.

gib bon (gib′ən), a small ape of southeastern Asia that has very long arms. Gibbons live in trees. See picture. noun.

gibe (jīb), **1** speak in a sneering way; jeer; scoff; sneer: *They gibed at my efforts to paint a picture.* **2** a jeer; taunt; sneer: *Their gibes hurt my feelings.* 1 verb, **gibed, gib ing;** 2 noun.

gid dy (gid′ē), **1** dizzy; having a whirling in the head: *giddy from riding the merry-go-round.* **2** making dizzy: *a giddy ride on the merry-go-round.* **3** never serious; living for the pleasure of the moment; in a whirl: *That giddy crowd thinks only of parties.* adjective, **gid di er, gid di est.**

gift (gift), **1** something given; present: *a birthday gift.* **2** giving: *The land came to her by gift from an aunt.* **3** natural talent; special ability: *A great artist must have a gift for painting.* noun.

gift ed (gif′tid), very able; having special ability: *a gifted musician.* adjective.

gi gan tic (jī gan′tik), big like a giant; huge: *An elephant is a gigantic animal.* adjective.

gig gle (gig′əl), **1** laugh in a silly or undignified way. **2** a silly or undignified laugh. 1 verb, **gig gled, gig gling;** 2 noun.

gild (gild), **1** cover with a thin layer of gold. **2** make (something) look bright and pleasing. verb, **gild ed** or **gilt, gild ing.**

gill (gil), part of the body of a fish, tadpole, or crab by which it breathes in water. noun.

gilt (gilt), **1** gilded. **2** material with which a thing is gilded: *The gilt is coming off from this frame.* **3** See **gild.** 1 adjective, 2 noun, 3 verb.

gin[1] (jin), a strong alcoholic drink, made from grain and usually flavored with juniper berries. noun.

gin[2] (jin), machine for separating cotton from its seeds. noun.

gin ger (jin′jər), spice made from the root of a tropical plant. The root is often preserved in syrup or candied. noun.

ginger ale, a bubbling drink flavored with ginger. It contains no alcohol.

gin ger bread (jin′jər bred′), kind of cake flavored with ginger. Gingerbread is often made in fancy shapes. noun.

gin ger ly (jin′jər lē), **1** with extreme care or caution: *to walk gingerly across the ice.* **2** extremely cautious or careful: *to take gingerly steps.* 1 adverb, 2 adjective.

ging ham (ging′əm), a cotton cloth made from colored threads. The patterns are usually in stripes, plaids, and checks. noun.

gip sy (jip′sē), gypsy. noun, plural **gip sies;** adjective.

gi raffe (jə raf′), a large African animal that chews its cud and has hoofs, a very long neck and long legs, and a spotted skin. Giraffes are the tallest living animals. noun.

gird er (gėr′dər), a main supporting beam. The weight of a floor is usually supported by girders. A tall building or big bridge often has steel girders for its frame. noun.

gir dle (gėr′dl), **1** belt, sash, or cord, worn around the waist. **2** anything that surrounds: *a girdle of trees around a pond.* **3** a light corset worn about the hips or waist. noun.

girl (gėrl), **1** a female child from birth to about eighteen. **2** a female servant. noun.

girl hood (gėrl′hud), time of being a girl. noun.

girl ish (gėr′lish), **1** of a girl. **2** like a girl. **3** like a girl's; suitable for a girl. adjective.

girl scout, member of the Girl Scouts.

Girl Scouts, organization for girls that seeks to develop character, citizenship, usefulness to others, and various skills.

girth (gėrth), **1** the measure around anything: *a man of large girth, the girth of a tree.* **2** strap or band that keeps the saddle in place on a horse. noun.

give (giv), **1** hand over as a present; make a gift of: *My parents gave me ice skates for my birthday.* **2** hand over: *Give me that pencil.* **3** pay: *She gave three dollars for the wagon.* **4** let have; cause to have: *She gave us permission to go. Don't give the teacher any trouble.* **5** cause by some action of the body: *Some boys give hard blows, even in play.* **6** offer; present: *This newspaper gives a full story of the game.* **7** put forth; utter: *He gave a cry of pain.* **8** supply; produce: *Lamps give light.* **9** yield to force: *The lock gave under hard pushing.* **10** yielding to force. 1-9 verb, **gave, giv en, giv ing;** 10 noun.

give away, 1 give as a present: *She gave away her best toy.* **2** present (a bride) to a bridegroom: *The bride was given away by her father.* **3** cause to be known; reveal; betray: *The spy gave away secrets to the enemy.*

give in, stop fighting and admit defeat: *Stubborn people will not give in easily even when they are proved wrong.*

give out, 1 send out; put forth: *The bomb fell, giving out a huge flash of fire.* **2** distribute: *The supplies will be given out tomorrow.* **3** make known: *Who has given out this information?* **4** become used up or worn out: *My strength gave out after the long climb.*

give up, 1 hand over; surrender: *When the troops saw that they were surrounded, they gave up.* **2** stop having or doing: *We gave up the search when it got dark.* **3** stop trying: *Don't give up so soon; try again and maybe you will succeed this time.*

giv en (giv′ən), **1** stated: *You must finish the test in a given time.* **2** inclined; disposed: *given to boasting.* **3** See **give.** *That book was given to me.* 1,2 adjective, 3 verb.

giv er (giv′ər), person who gives. noun.

giz zard (giz′ərd), a bird's second stomach, where the food from the first stomach is ground up. noun.

gibbon—about 3 feet
(1 meter) tall

a hat	**i** it	**oi** oil	**ch** child		a in about	
ā age	**ī** ice	**ou** out	**ng** long		e in taken	
ä far	**o** hot	**u** cup	**sh** she	**ə** =	i in pencil	
e let	**ō** open	**ù** put	**th** thin		o in lemon	
ē equal	**ô** order	**ü** rule	**ŦH** then		u in circus	
ėr term			**zh** measure			

glam our (glam′ər), glamor. *noun.*

glance (glans), **1** a quick look: *She gave the pictures only a glance.* **2** look quickly: *I glanced out of the window.* **3** hit and go off at a slant: *I dropped the cup and it glanced off the edge of the table.* 1 *noun,* 2,3 *verb,* **glanced, glanc ing.**

gland (gland), organ in the body which makes and gives out some substance. Glands make the liquid that keeps the mouth wet. A cow has glands which make milk. The liver, the kidneys, and the pancreas are glands. *noun.*

glare (gler *or* glar), **1** a strong, unpleasant light; light that shines so brightly that it hurts the eyes. **2** shine strongly or unpleasantly; shine so brightly as to hurt the eyes. **3** a fierce, angry stare. **4** stare fiercely and with anger. 1,3 *noun,* 2,4 *verb,* **glared, glar ing.**

glar ing (gler′ing *or* glar′ing), **1** shining so brightly that it hurts the eyes. **2** staring fiercely and angrily. **3** too bright and showy: *glaring colors.* **4** very easily seen: *The student made a glaring error in spelling. adjective.*

glass (glas), **1** a hard substance that breaks easily and can usually be seen through. Windows are made of glass. **2** something to drink from made of glass: *He filled the glass with water.* **3** amount a glass can hold: *Drink a glass of water.* **4** mirror: *Look at yourself in the glass.* **5 glasses,** pair of glass lenses to help vision. **6** lens, telescope, or other thing made of glass. **7** made of glass: *a glass dish.* **8** cover or protect with glass. 1-6 *noun, plural* **glass es;** 7 *adjective,* 8 *verb.*

glass y (glas′ē), **1** like glass; smooth; easily seen through. **2** having a fixed, stupid stare: *The dazed man's eyes were glassy. adjective,* **glass i er, glass i est.**

glaze (glāz), **1** put glass in; cover with glass. Pieces of glass cut to the right size are used to glaze windows and picture frames. **2** a smooth, glassy surface or glossy coating: *the glaze on a china cup. A glaze of ice on the walk is dangerous.* **3** become glossy or glassy: *The patient's eyes were glazed with fever.* 1,3 *verb,* **glazed, glaz ing;** 2 *noun.*

gleam (glēm), **1** a flash or beam of light: *We saw the gleam of headlights through the rain.* **2** send forth a gleam; shine: *A candle gleamed in the dark.* **3** short appearance: *The rain brought a gleam of hope to the farmers during the drought.* 1,3 *noun,* 2 *verb.*

glean (glēn), **1** gather stalks of grain left on the field by reapers. **2** gather little by little: *The spy gleaned information by listening to the soldiers' talk. verb.*

glee (glē), lively joy; great delight: *The children laughed with glee at the clown's antics. noun.*

glee club, group organized for singing songs.

glacier—a glacier in the state of Washington

gla cial (glā′shəl), icy; of ice; having much ice; having many glaciers: *During the glacial period, much of the Northern Hemisphere was covered with great ice sheets. adjective.*

gla cier (glā′shər), a large mass of ice formed from the snow on high ground and moving very slowly down a mountain or along a valley. See picture. *noun.*

glad (glad), **1** happy; pleased: *She is glad to see us.* **2** bringing joy; pleasant: *glad news.* **3** willing; ready: *I will be glad to go if you need me. adjective,* **glad der, glad dest.**

glad den (glad′n), make glad; become glad: *We were gladdened by the good news. verb.*

glade (glād), a little open space in a wood or forest. *noun.*

glad i a tor (glad′ē ā′tər), slave, captive, or paid fighter who fought at the public shows in the arenas in ancient Rome. *noun.*

glad i o lus (glad′ē ō′ləs), plant with spikes of large, handsome flowers in various colors. *noun, plural* **glad i o li** (glad′ē ō′lē), **glad i o lus es.**

glam or (glam′ər), fascination; charm; attractiveness: *the glamor of circus life. noun.* Also spelled **glamour.**

glam or ous (glam′ər əs), fascinating; charming: *a glamorous job in a foreign city. adjective.*

glee ful (glē′fəl), merry and gay; joyous. See picture. *adjective.*

glen (glen), a small, narrow valley. *noun.*

glide (glīd), 1 move along smoothly, evenly, and easily: *Birds, ships, dancers, and skaters glide.* See picture. 2 a smooth, even, easy movement. 3 come down slowly at a slant without using a motor. An airplane can glide about a mile for every thousand feet that it is above the ground. 1,3 *verb,* **glid ed, glid ing;** 2 *noun.*

glid er (glī′dər), airplane without a motor. Rising air currents keep a glider up in the air. *noun.*

glim mer (glim′ər), 1 a faint, unsteady light. 2 shine with a faint, unsteady light: *The candle glimmered and went out.* 3 a vague idea; dim notion; faint glimpse: *A few clouds gave a glimmer of hope that rain might come.* 1,3 *noun,* 2 *verb.*

glimpse (glimps), 1 a very brief view; short look: *I caught a glimpse of the falls as our train went by.* 2 catch a brief view of: *I glimpsed the falls as our train went by.* 1 *noun,* 2 *verb,* **glimpsed, glimps ing.**

glint (glint), 1 gleam; flash: *The glint in her eye showed that she was angry.* 2 to gleam; flash. 1 *noun,* 2 *verb.*

glis ten (glis′n), sparkle; glitter; shine. *verb, noun.*

glit ter (glit′ər), 1 shine with a bright, sparkling light: *The jewels and new coins glittered.* 2 a bright, sparkling light: *The glitter of the harsh lights hurt my eyes.* 3 be bright and showy. 4 brightness; showiness. 1,3 *verb,* 2,4 *noun.*

gloat (glōt), gaze or think about intently and with satisfaction: *She gloated over her success. The miser gloated over his gold. verb.*

glob al (glō′bəl), 1 spread throughout the world: *the threat of global war.* 2 shaped like a globe: *a global map. adjective.*

globe (glōb), 1 anything round like a ball. 2 the earth; world. 3 sphere with a map of the earth or the sky on it. *noun.*

gloom (glüm), 1 darkness; deep shadow; dim light. 2 dark thoughts and feelings; low spirits; sadness. *noun.*

gloom i ly (glü′mə lē), in a gloomy manner. *adverb.*

gloom y (glü′mē), 1 dark; dim: *a gloomy winter day.* 2 in low spirits; sad; melancholy: *a gloomy mood.* 3 dismal; causing gloom; discouraging: *There were gloomy predictions of a major earthquake. adjective,* **gloom i er, gloom i est.**

glo ri fy (glôr′ə fī), 1 give glory to; make glorious: *glorify a hero or a saint.* 2 worship; praise: *hymns glorifying God.* 3 make more beautiful or splendid: *The sunset glorified the valley. verb,* **glo ri fied, glo ri fy ing.**

glo ri ous (glôr′ē əs), 1 having or deserving glory. 2 giving glory: *Our team won a glorious victory.* 3 magnificent; splendid: *The children had a glorious time at the fair. adjective.*

glo ry (glôr′ē), 1 great praise and honor; fame: *His heroic act won him glory.* 2 something that brings praise and honor: *America's great men and women are her glory.* 3 be proud; rejoice: *The teacher*

gloried in her class's achievements. 4 brightness; splendor: *the glory of the royal palace.* 5 condition of magnificence, splendor, or greatest prosperity: *The British empire reached its greatest glory in the 1800's, during the reign of Queen Victoria.* 1,2,4,5 *noun, plural* **glo ries;** 3 *verb,* **glo ried, glo ry ing.**

gloss (glôs), a smooth, shiny surface on anything: *Varnished furniture has a gloss. noun.*

gloss over, make (something) seem right even though it is really wrong: *They tried to gloss over their mistakes.*

glos sar y (glos′ər ē), list of hard words with explanations: *Some schoolbooks have glossaries at the end. noun, plural* **glos sar ies.**

gloss y (glô′sē), smooth and shiny. *adjective,* **gloss i er, gloss i est.**

glove (gluv), 1 a covering for the hand, usually with separate places for each of the four fingers and the thumb. 2 cover with a glove. 1 *noun,* 2 *verb,* **gloved, glov ing.**

glow (glō), 1 shine because of heat; be red-hot or white-hot: *Embers still glowed in the fireplace after the fire had died down.* 2 the shine from something that is red-hot or white-hot: *the glow of molten steel.* 3 a similar shine without heat: *the glow of gold.* 4 give off light without heat: *Some clocks glow in the dark.* 5 a bright, warm color: *the glow of sunset.* 6 the warm feeling or color of the body: *the glow of health on her cheeks.* 7 show a warm color; look warm: *His cheeks glowed as he jogged.* 8 an eager look on the face: *a glow of excitement.* 9 look eager: *Their eyes glowed at the thought of a trip.* 1,4,7,9 *verb,* 2,3,5,6,8 *noun.*

glow er (glou′ər), stare angrily; scowl fiercely: *The fighters glowered at each other. verb.*

glow worm (glō′wėrm′), any insect larva or insect which glows in the dark. Fireflies develop from some glowworms. *noun.*

glue (glü), 1 substance used to stick things together. Glue is often made by boiling the hoofs, skins, and bones of animals in water. 2 any similar sticky substance. Glues are stronger than pastes. 3 stick together with glue. 4 fasten tightly: *Her hands were glued to the steering wheel as she drove down the dangerous mountain road.* 1,2 *noun,* 3,4 *verb,* **glued, glu ing.**

glum (glum), gloomy; dismal; sullen: *I felt very glum when my friend moved away. adjective,* **glum mer, glum mest.**

glut ton (glut′n), a greedy eater; person who eats too much. *noun.*

gnarl (närl), knot in wood; hard, rough lump: *Wood with gnarls is hard to cut. noun.*

gnarled (närld), containing gnarls; knotted; twisted; rugged: *The farmer's gnarled hands grasped the plow firmly. adjective.*

gnash (nash), strike or grind (the teeth) together; grind together: *The angry animals gnashed their teeth. verb.*

gnat (nat), a small, two-winged fly somewhat like a mosquito. Most gnats make bites that itch. *noun.*

gnaw (nô), bite at and wear away: *A mouse has gnawed right through the cover of this box. verb.*

gnome (nōm), dwarf supposed to live in the earth and to guard treasures of precious metals and stones. *noun.*

go (gō), **1** move along: *Cars go on the road.* **2** move away; leave: *Don't go yet.* **3** be in motion; act; work; run: *Make the washing machine go.* **4** get to be; become: *go mad.* **5** be habitually; be: *go hungry for a week.* **6** proceed; advance: *go to New York.* **7** take part in the activity of: *go skiing, go swimming.* **8** put oneself: *Don't go to any trouble for me.* **9** extend; reach: *Does your memory go back that far?* **10** pass: *Summer had gone. Vacation goes quickly.* **11** be given: *First prize goes to you.* **12** have its place; belong: *This book goes on the top shelf.* **13** make a certain sound: *The cork went "pop!"* *verb,* **went, gone, go ing.**

go by, 1 pass: *We went by that store often.* **2** be guided by; follow: *Go by what she says.* **3** be known by: *He goes by the name of Smith.*

go off, 1 leave; depart: *My sister has gone off to college.* **2** be fired; explode: *The pistol went off unexpectedly.* **3** start to ring; sound: *I was already awake when the alarm went off.*

go on, 1 go ahead; continue: *After a pause he went on reading.* **2** happen: *What goes on here?*

go out, 1 go to a party or show: *We had a very good time when we went out Saturday night.* **2** stop burning: *Don't let the candle go out.*

go up, 1 ascend; rise: *The thermometer is going up.* **2** increase: *The price of milk has gone up.*

goad (gōd), **1** stick for driving cattle that has a point on the end. **2** anything that drives or urges one on. **3** drive or urge on; act as a goad to: *Hunger goaded her to steal food.* **1,2** *noun,* **3** *verb.*

goal (gōl), **1** place where a race ends. **2** place which players try to reach in certain games. **3** points won by reaching this place. **4** something desired: *The goal of her ambition was to be a scientist. noun.*

goal ie (gō′lē), goalkeeper. *noun.*

goal keep er (gōl′kē′pər), player who tries to keep the puck from crossing the goal in hockey. *noun.*

goat (gōt), an animal with horns, a beard, and hoofs that chews its cud. Goats are stronger, less timid, and more active than sheep. They are raised for their milk and their hides. *noun, plural* **goats** or **goat.**

get one's goat, make a person angry or annoyed; tease a person.

goat skin (gōt′skin′), **1** skin of a goat. **2** leather made from it. *noun.*

gob ble[1] (gob′əl), eat fast and greedily. *verb,* **gob bled, gob bling.**

gob ble[2] (gob′əl), **1** the noise a turkey makes. **2** make this noise or one like it. **1** *noun,* **2** *verb,* **gob bled, gob bling.**

gob bler (gob′lər), a male turkey. *noun.*

gob let (gob′lit), a drinking glass that stands high above its base on a stem, and has no handle. See picture. *noun.*

gob lin (gob′lən), a mischievous spirit or elf in the form of an ugly-looking dwarf. *noun.*

a hat	i it	oi oil	ch child	a in about
ā age	ī ice	ou out	ng long	e in taken
ä far	o hot	u cup	sh she	ə = i in pencil
e let	ō open	u̇ put	th thin	o in lemon
ē equal	ô order	ü rule	ŦH then	u in circus
ėr term			zh measure	

glide (definition 1)
The skater **glided** across the ice.

goblet

gleeful

god (god), **1** a being thought to have powers beyond those of human beings and considered worthy of worship. **2** likeness or image; idol. **3** person or thing greatly respected or thought of as very important: *Wealth and power are his gods.* *noun.*

God (god), the maker and ruler of the world. *noun.*

god dess (god′is), a female god. *noun, plural* **god dess es.**

god fa ther (god′fä′ᴦʜər), man who sponsors a child when it is baptized. The godfather promises to help the child to be a good Christian. *noun.*

god ly (god′lē), obeying, loving, and fearing God; religious; pious. *adjective,* **god li er, god li est.**

god moth er (god′muᴦʜ′ər), woman who sponsors a child when it is baptized. The godmother promises to help the child to be a good Christian. *noun.*

goes (gōz). See **go.** *He goes to school. verb.*

gog gles (gog′əlz), large, close-fitting eyeglasses to protect the eyes from light or dust. *noun plural.*

go ing (gō′ing), **1** leaving: *His going was very sudden.* **2** moving; in action; working; running: *Set the clock going.* **3** condition of the ground or road for walking or riding: *The going is bad through this muddy road.* **4** that goes; that can or will go: *That new business is a going concern.* 1,3 *noun,* 2,4 *adjective.*

be going to, will; be about to: *Is it going to rain?*

gold (gōld), **1** a heavy, bright-yellow, precious metal. Gold is used in making coins, watches, and rings. **2** made of this metal: *a gold watch.* **3** money in large sums; wealth; riches. **4** bright yellow. 1,3 *noun,* 2,4 *adjective.*

gold en (gōl′dən), **1** made of or containing gold. See picture. **2** shining like gold; bright-yellow: *golden hair.* **3** very good; extremely favorable, valuable, or important: *a golden opportunity.* **4** very happy; flourishing: *a golden age. adjective.*

gold en rod (gōl′dən rod′), plant with tall stalks of small yellow flowers. It blooms in the autumn. *noun.*

gold finch (gōld′finch′), a small yellow songbird marked with black. *noun, plural* **gold finch es.**

gold fish (gōld′fish′), a small fish, usually of a reddish or golden color, kept in garden pools or in glass bowls indoors. *noun, plural* **gold fish es** or **gold fish.**

gold smith (gōld′smith′), person who makes articles of gold. *noun.*

golf (golf), **1** an outdoor game played by hitting a small, hard ball with one of a set of clubs. The player tries to drive the ball into a series of holes with as few strokes as possible. **2** play this game. 1 *noun,* 2 *verb.*

gon do la (gon′dl ə), **1** a long, narrow boat with a high peak at each end, used on the canals of Venice. See picture. **2** car that hangs under a dirigible and holds the motors, passengers, and instruments. *noun.*

gone (gôn), **1** moved away; left: *The students are gone on their vacation.* **2** dead: *Great-grandmother is gone now.* **3** used up; consumed: *Is all the candy*

gorilla—up to 6 feet (2 meters) tall when standing

gondola (definition 1)

golden (definition 1)—a golden mask.

gone? **4** See **go.** *She has gone to the movies.* 1-3 *adjective,* 4 *verb.*

gong (gông), piece of metal shaped like a bowl or a saucer which makes a loud noise when struck. A gong is a kind of bell. *noun.*

good (gùd), **1** having high quality; well done: *The teacher said my report was good.* **2** right; as it ought to be: *good health, good weather.* **3** behaving well; that does what is right: *a good boy.* **4** kind; friendly: *Say a good word for me.* **5** desirable: *a good book for children.* **6** reliable; dependable: *She showed good judgment.* **7** real; genuine: *It is not always easy to tell counterfeit money from good money.* **8** pleasant: *Have a good time.* **9** beneficial; useful: *drugs good for a fever.* **10** benefit: *What good will it do?* **11** satisfying: *a good meal.* **12** that which is good: *find the good in people.* 1-9,11 *adjective,* **bet ter, best;** 10,12 *noun.*

as good as, almost; practically: *The battle was as good as won.*

for good, forever; finally; permanently: *They have moved out for good.*

make good, 1 make up for; pay for: *The boys made good the damage they had done.* **2** succeed: *He made good in business.*

good-by (gùd′bī′), farewell: *We said "Good-by" and went home. interjection, noun, plural* **good-bys.** [*Good-by* was shortened from the phrase *God be with you.*]

good-bye (gùd′bī′), good-by. *interjection, noun, plural* **good-byes.**

Good Friday, the Friday before Easter.

good-heart ed (gùd′här′tid), kind and generous. *adjective.*

good-look ing (gùd′lùk′ing), having a pleasing appearance; handsome. *adjective.*

good ly (gùd′lē), **1** good-looking: *a goodly youth.* **2** considerable; rather large: *a goodly quantity. adjective,* **good li er, good li est.**

good-na tured (gùd′nā′chərd), pleasant; kindly; obliging; cheerful. *adjective.*

good ness (gùd′nis), being good; kindness. *noun.*

goods (gùdz), **1** belongings; personal property: *When we moved we shipped our household goods in a van.* **2** thing or things for sale; wares. *noun plural.*

good-sized (gùd′sīzd′), somewhat large. *adjective.*

good-tem pered (gùd′tem′pərd), easy to get along with; cheerful; agreeable. *adjective.*

good will, 1 kindly feeling; friendly attitude. **2** the good reputation a business has with its customers.

goose (güs), **1** a tame or wild bird like a duck, but larger and with a longer neck. A goose has webbed feet. **2** a female goose. The male is called a gander. **3** flesh of a goose used for food. **4** a silly person. *noun, plural* **geese.**

cook one's goose, do damage to a person; ruin a person's plans or chances.

goose ber ry (güs′ber′ē), **1** a small, sour berry somewhat like a currant but larger. Gooseberries are used to make pies, tarts, or jam. **2** the thorny bush that it grows on. *noun, plural* **goose ber ries.**

go pher (gō′fər), a ratlike animal of North America

a hat	i it	oi oil	ch child	
ā age	ī ice	ou out	ng long	a in about
ä far	o hot	u cup	sh she	e in taken
e let	ō open	ù put	th thin	ə = { i in pencil
ē equal	ô order	ü rule	ᴛʜ then	o in lemon
ėr term			zh measure	u in circus

with large cheek pouches. Gophers dig holes in the ground. *noun.*

gore[1] (gôr), blood that is spilled; thick blood: *The battlefield was covered with gore. noun.*

gore[2] (gôr), wound with a horn or tusk: *The angry bull gored the farmer. verb,* **gored, gor ing.**

gorge (gôrj), **1** a deep, narrow valley, usually steep and rocky. **2** eat greedily until full; stuff with food: *She gorged herself with cake at the party.* 1 *noun,* 2 *verb,* **gorged, gorg ing.**

gor geous (gôr′jəs), richly colored; splendid: *The peacock spread its gorgeous tail. adjective.*

go ril la (gə ril′ə), the largest and most powerful ape. It is found in the forests of central Africa. See picture. *noun.*

gor y (gôr′ē), bloody. *adjective,* **gor i er, gor i est.**

gos ling (goz′ling), a young goose. *noun.*

gos pel (gos′pəl), **1** the teachings of Jesus and the Apostles. **2** the absolute truth: *They took the doctor's words as gospel. noun.* [*Gospel* comes from an earlier English word meaning "good news."]

gos sa mer (gos′ə mər), **1** film or thread of cobweb. **2** any very thin, light cloth or substance. **3** very light and thin. See picture. 1,2 *noun,* 3 *adjective.*

gossamer (definition 3)—the gossamer wings of an insect

gos sip (gos′ip), **1** idle talk, not always true, about other people and their affairs. **2** repeat what one knows or hears about other people and their affairs. **3** person who gossips a good deal. 1,3 *noun,* 2 *verb.*

got (got). See **get.** *We got the letter yesterday. We had got tired of waiting for it. verb.*

got ten (got′n), got. See **get.** *It has gotten to be quite late. verb.*

gouge (gouj), **1** chisel with a curved blade. Gouges are used for cutting round grooves or holes in wood. **2** cut with a gouge; dig out. **3** groove or hole made by gouging. 1,3 *noun,* 2 *verb,* **gouged, goug ing.**

gourd (gôrd), **1** the fruit of certain vines whose hard, dried shell is used for cups, bottles, bowls, and other utensils. See picture. **2** the vine it grows on. *noun.*

gov ern (guv′ərn), **1** rule; control; manage: *govern a nation.* **2** determine or guide: *What reasons governed your decision? verb.*

gov ern ess (guv′ər nis), woman who teaches and trains children in their home. *noun.*

gov ern ment (guv′ərn mənt), **1** the ruling of a country, state, district, or city: *local government.* **2** person or persons ruling a country, state, district, or city at any time: *The government of the United States consists of the President and the cabinet, the Congress, and the Supreme Court.* **3** system of ruling: *The United States has a democratic form of government.* **4** rule; control. *noun.*

gov er nor (guv′ər nər), **1** official elected as the executive head of a state of the United States. The governor of a state carries out the laws made by the state legislature. **2** ruler of a province, colony, city, or fort. **3** device arranged to keep a machine going at an even speed. *noun.*

gown (goun), **1** a woman's dress. **2** a loose outer piece of clothing worn by graduating college students, judges, and others; robe. **3** nightgown. *noun.*

grab (grab), **1** seize suddenly; snatch: *The dog grabbed the meat and ran.* **2** a snatching; sudden seizing: *I made a grab at the butterfly.* **1** *verb,* **grabbed, grab bing;** **2** *noun.*

grace (grās), **1** beauty of form or movement: *The ballet dancer danced with much grace.* **2** pleasing or agreeable quality: *They had all the social graces of a good host and hostess.* **3** the favor and love of God. **4** a short prayer of thanks given before or after a meal. **5** **Grace,** title of a duke, duchess, or archbishop: *May I assist Your Grace?* **6** give grace or honor to: *The queen graced the ball with her presence.* **1-5** *noun,* **6** *verb,* **graced, grac ing.**
in one's good graces, favored or liked by: *I wonder if I am in the teacher's good graces.*
with good grace, pleasantly; willingly: *He obeyed the order with good grace.*

grace ful (grās′fəl), **1** beautiful in form or movement: *a graceful dancer.* **2** pleasing; agreeable: *a graceful speech of thanks. adjective.*

gra cious (grā′shəs), pleasant and kindly; courteous: *We were greeted in such a gracious manner that we immediately felt at ease. adjective.*

grack le (grak′əl), a large blackbird with shiny, black feathers. *noun.*

grade (grād), **1** class in school: *the fifth grade.* **2** **the grades,** elementary school. **3** degree in rank, quality, or value: *The best grade of milk is grade A.* **4** group of persons or things having the same rank, quality, or value. **5** sort; place according to class: *These apples are graded by size.* **6** number or letter that shows how well one has done; mark: *My grade in English is B.* **7** give a mark or grade to: *The teacher graded the papers.* **8** slope of a road or railroad track: *a steep grade.* **9** make more nearly

level: *The road up that steep hill was graded.* **1-4,6,8** *noun,* **5,7,9** *verb,* **grad ed, grad ing.**

grade school, elementary school; grammar school.

grad u al (graj′ü əl), by degrees too small to be separately noticed; little by little: *This low hill has a gradual slope. adjective.*

grad u ate (graj′ü āt *for 1 and 3;* graj′ü it *for 2*), **1** finish the course of a school or college and be given a diploma or paper saying so. **2** person who has graduated and has a diploma. **3** mark out in equal spaces for measuring: *My ruler is graduated in inches.* **1,3** *verb,* **grad u at ed, grad u at ing;** **2** *noun.*

grad u a tion (graj′ü ā′shən), **1** a graduating from a school or college. **2** ceremony of graduating; graduating exercises. *noun.*

graft (graft), **1** put (a shoot or bud from one tree or plant) into a slit in another tree or plant, so it will grow there as a part of it. See picture. **2** shoot or bud used in grafting. A graft from a fine apple tree may be put on a worthless one to improve it. **1** *verb,* **2** *noun.* [*Graft* comes from a Greek word meaning "a pointed instrument for writing." A graft was called this because it looks something like this instrument.]

grain (grān), **1** the seed of wheat, oats, corn, and other cereal grasses. **2** one of the tiny bits of which sand, sugar, or salt is made up. **3** the smallest possible amount; tiniest bit: *There isn't a grain of truth in their story.* **4** the little lines and markings in wood or marble; arrangement of the particles of anything: *That mahogany table has a fine grain. noun.*
with a grain of salt, with a little doubt: *The story must be taken with a grain of salt.*

gram (gram), unit of weight in the metric system. Twenty-eight grams weigh about one ounce. *noun.*

gram mar (gram′ər), **1** study of the forms and uses of words in sentences. **2** rules about the use of words. **3** use of words according to these rules: *My English teacher's grammar is excellent. noun.*

grammar school, elementary school.

gram mat i cal (grə mat′ə kəl), **1** according to the correct use of words: *Our French teacher speaks grammatical English but has a French accent.* **2** of grammar: *"Between you and I" is a grammatical mistake; "between you and me" is correct. adjective.*

gran ar y (gran′ər ē *or* grā′nər ē), place or building where grain is stored. *noun, plural* **gran ar ies.**

grand (grand), **1** large and of fine appearance: *grand mountains.* **2** of very high or noble quality; dignified: *a very grand palace, grand music, a grand old man.* **3** highest or very high in rank; chief: *a grand duchess.* **4** great; important; main: *the grand staircase.* **5** complete; comprehensive: *the grand total.* **6** very satisfactory: *a grand time. adjective.*

grand child (grand′child′), child of one's son or daughter. *noun, plural* **grand chil dren** (grand′chil′drən).

grand daugh ter (grand′dô′tər), daughter of one's son or daughter. *noun.*

gran deur (gran/jər), greatness; majesty; nobility; splendor: *the grandeur of Niagara Falls.* noun.

grand fa ther (grand/fä/ŦHər), father of one's father or mother. noun.

grand ma (grand/mä/), grandmother. noun.

grand moth er (grand/muŦH/ər), mother of one's mother or father. noun.

grand pa (grand/pä/), grandfather. noun.

grand par ent (grand/per/ənt *or* grand/par/ənt), grandfather or grandmother. noun.

grand son (grand/sun/), son of one's son or daughter. noun.

grand stand (grand/stand/), the main seating place for people at an athletic field, race track, or parade. noun.

gran ite (gran/it), a very hard rock, much used for buildings and monuments. Granite is made of grains of other rocks and is usually gray. noun.

gran ny (gran/ē), grandmother. noun, *plural* **gran nies.**

gra no la (grə nō/lə), a dry breakfast cereal of rolled oats, flavored with other things such as honey, chopped dried fruit, and nuts. noun.

grant (grant), **1** allow; give what is asked: *grant a request.* **2** admit; accept without proof: *I grant that you are right so far.* **3** give. **4** gift, especially land or rights given by the government. 1-3 *verb,* 4 *noun.*
take for granted, 1 regard as proved or agreed to: *We take for granted the existence of atoms.* **2** accept as probable: *We took for granted that the sailor could swim.*

grape (grāp), a small, round fruit, red, purple, or pale-green, that grows in bunches on a vine. Grapes are eaten raw or made into raisins or wine. noun.

grape fruit (grāp/früt/), the pale-yellow, juicy fruit of a tree grown in warm climates. Grapefruits are like oranges, but are larger and sourer. noun.

grape vine (grāp/vīn/), vine that grapes grow on. noun.

graph (graf), line or diagram showing how one quantity depends on or changes with another. You could draw a graph to show how your weight has changed each year with your change in age. See picture. noun.

graph ic (graf/ik), **1** lifelike; vivid: *Your graphic description of the English countryside made me feel as though I had been there myself.* **2** shown by a graph: *The school board kept a graphic record of school attendance for a month.* **3** of or about drawing, painting, engraving, or etching: *The school had courses in the graphic arts. adjective.*

graph ite (graf/īt), a soft, black form of carbon used for lead in pencils and for greasing machinery. noun. [*Graphite* comes from a Greek word meaning "to write." Graphite was called this because it is used in pencils.]

grap ple (grap/əl), **1** seize and hold fast; grip or hold firmly. **2** struggle; fight: *grapple with a problem. The wrestlers grappled in the center of the ring. verb,* **grap pled, grap pling.**

grasp (grasp), **1** seize and hold fast by closing the fingers around: *I grasped the sleeve of her coat as I*

gourds (definition 1)

graft (definition 1)—three types. The pieces are tied or taped together.

graph—This bar graph shows how long certain animals usually live.

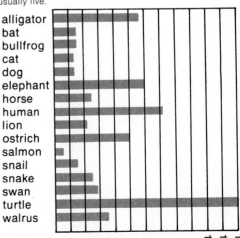

fell. **2** seizing and holding tightly; clasp of the hand. **3** power of seizing and holding; reach: *Success is within his grasp.* **4** control; possession: *The people regained power from the grasp of the dictator.* **5** understand: *He grasped my meaning at once.* **6** understanding: *She has a good grasp of arithmetic.* 1,5 *verb,* 2-4,6 *noun.*

grasp at, 1 try to take hold of; try to grasp. **2** accept eagerly: *She grasped at the opportunity.*

grass (gras), **1** plants with green blades that cover fields, lawns, and pastures. Horses, cows, and sheep eat grass. **2** plant that has jointed stems and long, narrow leaves. Wheat, corn, and sugar cane are grasses. **3** land covered with grass; pasture. *noun, plural* **grass es.**

grass hop per (gras/hop/ər), insect with wings and strong hind legs for jumping. *noun.*

grass land (gras/land/), land with grass on it, used for pasture. *noun.*

grass y (gras/ē), **1** covered with grass; having much grass. **2** of grass. **3** like grass. *adjective,* **grass i er, grass i est.**

grate[1] (grāt), **1** framework of iron bars to hold burning fuel in a furnace or fireplace. **2** framework of bars over a window or opening; grating. *noun.*

grate[2] (grāt), **1** have an annoying or unpleasant effect: *Rude manners and loud voices grate on me.* **2** make a harsh, jarring noise by rubbing: *The door grated on its old, rusty hinges.* **3** wear down or grind off in small pieces: *The cook grated the cheese before melting it. verb,* **grat ed, grat ing.**

grate ful (grāt/fəl), feeling kindly because of a favor received; thankful: *I am grateful for your help. adjective.*

grat i fi ca tion (grat/ə fə kā/shən), **1** gratifying; satisfaction: *The gratification of a person's every wish is not always possible.* **2** something that pleases or satisfies: *Your faith in my ability is a gratification to me. noun.*

grat i fy (grat/ə fī), **1** please; give pleasure to: *Praise gratifies most people.* **2** give satisfaction to: *The afternoon snack gratified my hunger until dinner. verb,* **grat i fied, grat i fy ing.**

gra ting[1] (grā/ting), grate; framework of parallel or crossed bars. Windows in a prison, bank, or ticket office often have gratings over them. *noun.*

gra ting[2] (grā/ting), **1** irritating; unpleasant. **2** harsh or jarring in sound. *adjective.*

grat i tude (grat/ə tüd *or* grat/ə tyüd), kindly feeling because of a favor received; desire to do a favor in return; thankfulness. *noun.*

grave[1] (grāv), **1** hole dug in the ground where a dead body is to be buried. **2** any place of burial: *a watery grave.* **3** death. *noun.*

grave[2] (grāv), **1** important; weighty: *a grave decision.* **2** serious; threatening; critical: *a grave illness, grave news.* **3** sober; dignified; solemn: *a grave face, grave music. adjective,* **grav er, grav est.**

grav el (grav/əl), **1** pebbles and pieces of rock that are larger than particles of sand. Gravel is much used for roads and walks. **2** lay or cover with gravel. 1 *noun,* 2 *verb.*

grave yard (grāv/yärd/), cemetery. *noun.*

grav i tate (grav/ə tāt/), move or tend to move toward a body by the force of gravity: *The planets gravitate toward the sun. verb,* **grav i tat ed, grav i tat ing.**

grav i ta tion (grav/ə tā/shən), the force or pull that makes all objects in the universe tend to move toward one another. Gravitation keeps the planets in their orbits around the sun. *noun.*

grav i ty (grav/ə tē), **1** the natural force that causes objects to move or tend to move toward the center of the earth. Gravity causes objects to have weight. **2** the natural force that makes objects move or tend to move toward each other; gravitation. **3** heaviness; weight: *I balanced the long pole at its center of gravity.* **4** seriousness: *The gravity of the child playing nurse was amusing in one so small.* **5** importance: *The gravity of the situation was greatly increased by threats of war. noun, plural* **grav i ties.**

gra vy (grā/vē), **1** juice that comes out of meat in cooking. **2** sauce for meat, potatoes, or other food, made from this juice. *noun, plural* **gra vies.**

gray (grā), **1** color that is a mixture of black and white. **2** having this color: *gray hair.* **3** make or become gray: *Her hair is graying fast.* **4** dark; gloomy; dismal: *a gray, rainy day.* 1 *noun,* 2,4 *adjective,* 3 *verb.* Also spelled **grey.**

gray ish (grā/ish), somewhat gray. *adjective.*

graze[1] (grāz), **1** feed on growing grass: *Cattle were grazing in the field.* **2** put (cattle, sheep, or other farm animals) to feed on growing grass or a pasture: *The farmer grazed his sheep. verb,* **grazed, graz ing.**

graze[2] (grāz), **1** touch lightly in passing; rub lightly against: *The car grazed the garage door.* **2** scrape the skin from: *She grazed her knee when she fell.* **3** a grazing. 1,2 *verb,* **grazed, graz ing;** 3 *noun.*

grease (grēs), **1** soft, melted animal fat. **2** any thick, oily substance. **3** rub grease on: *grease a cake pan.* **4** put grease or oil in or on: *Please grease my car.* 1,2 *noun,* 3,4 *verb,* **greased, greas ing.**

greas y (grē/sē), **1** having grease on it. **2** containing much grease; oily: *Greasy food is hard to digest.* **3** like grease; smooth; slippery. *adjective,* **greas i er, greas i est.**

great (grāt), **1** big; large: *a great house, a great crowd.* **2** much; more than is usual: *great pain, great kindness.* **3** important; high in rank; remarkable; famous: *a great singer, a great event, a great picture. adjective.*

Great Britain, England, Scotland, and Wales. Great Britain is the largest island of Europe.

great coat (grāt/kōt/), a heavy overcoat. *noun.*

great-grand child (grāt/grand/child/), child of one's grandchild. *noun, plural* **great-grand chil dren** (grāt/grand/chil/dren).

great-grand fa ther (grāt/grand/fä/ŦHər), father of one's grandparent. *noun.*

great-grand moth er (grāt/grand/muŦH/ər), mother of a grandparent. *noun.*

great ly (grāt/lē), **1** in a great manner: *Solomon ruled greatly and wisely.* **2** much: *greatly feared. adverb.*

great ness (grāt′nis), **1** being great; bigness. **2** high place or power. **3** great mind or character. *noun.*

Greece (grēs), country in southeastern Europe. *noun.*

greed (grēd), wanting more than one's share; greedy behavior; greedy desire: *a miser's greed for money. noun.*

greed i ly (grē′dl ē), in a greedy manner. *adverb.*

greed y (grē′dē), **1** wanting to get more than one's share; wanting to get a great deal: *The dictator was greedy for power and money. The lonely child was greedy for affection.* **2** wanting to eat a great deal in a hurry. *adjective,* **greed i er, greed i est.**

Greek (grēk), **1** of or having something to do with Greece, its people, or their language. **2** person born or living in Greece. **3** language of Greece. **1** *adjective,* **2,3** *noun.*

greyhound
about 28 inches
(70 centimeters)
at the shoulder

green (grēn), **1** the color of most growing plants, grass, and the leaves of trees in summer. **2** having this color: *green paint.* **3** covered with growing plants, grass, or leaves: *green fields.* **4** not ripe; not fully grown: *Most green fruit is not good to eat.* **5** not dried, cured, seasoned, or otherwise prepared for use: *green tobacco, green wood.* **6** not trained; without experience: *Several of the players were green when the season started.* **7** ground covered with grass: *the village green.* **8 greens, a** green leaves and branches used for decoration. **b** leaves and stems of plants used for food: *beet greens.* **1,7,8** *noun,* **2-6** *adjective.*

green er y (grē′nər ē), green plants, grass, or leaves. *noun.*

green house (grēn′hous′), building with a glass roof and glass sides kept warm for growing plants; hothouse. *noun, plural* **green hous es** (grēn′hou′ziz).

green ish (grē′nish), somewhat green. *adjective.*

green thumb, a remarkable ability to grow flowers and vegetables: *You certainly must have a green thumb to have such a beautiful garden.*

green wood (grēn′wùd′), forest in spring and summer when the trees are green with leaves. *noun.*

greet (grēt), **1** speak or write to in a friendly, polite way; address in welcome; hail: *She greeted us with a friendly "Hello."* **2** respond to: *His speech was greeted with cheers.* **3** meet; present itself to: *When*

a hat	i it	oi oil	ch child		a in about
ā age	ī ice	ou out	ng long		e in taken
ä far	o hot	u cup	sh she	ə =	i in pencil
e let	ō open	ù put	th thin		o in lemon
ē equal	ô order	ü rule	ŦH then		u in circus
ėr term			zh measure		

we opened the door, an icy wind greeted us. verb.

greet ing (grē′ting), **1** act or words of a person who greets somebody; welcome. **2 greetings,** friendly wishes on a special occasion. *noun.*

gre nade (grə nād′), a small bomb which is thrown by hand or fired from a rifle. *noun.* [*Grenade* comes from Latin words meaning "seedy apple" or "pomegranate." A grenade was called this because it is filled with sharp bits of metal and resembles a pomegranate filled with seeds.]

grew (grü). See **grow.** *It grew colder as the sun went down. verb.*

grey (grā), gray. *noun, adjective, verb.*

grey hound (grā′hound′), a tall, slender hunting dog with a long nose. Greyhounds can run very fast. See picture. *noun.*

grid (grid), a pattern of evenly spaced vertical and horizontal lines. Grids are used on maps to locate places, and in mathematics to locate pairs of numbers. *noun.*

grid dle (grid′l), a heavy, flat plate, usually of metal, on which to cook pancakes, bacon, and similar foods. *noun.*

grid i ron (grid′ī′ərn), **1** grill for broiling. **2** a football field. *noun.*

grief (grēf), great sadness caused by trouble or loss; heavy sorrow. *noun.*

come to grief, have trouble; fail.

griev ance (grē′vəns), a real or imagined wrong; reason for being annoyed or angry: *Report any grievances you have to your supervisor. noun.*

grieve (grēv), **1** feel grief; be very sad: *The children grieved over their kitten's death.* **2** cause to feel grief; make sad: *The news of your illness grieved us. verb,* **grieved, griev ing.**

griev ous (grē′vəs), **1** hard to bear; causing great pain or suffering; severe: *grievous cruelty.* **2** outrageous: *Wasting food when people were starving was a grievous wrong.* **3** causing grief: *a grievous loss.* **4** full of grief; showing grief: *a grievous cry. adjective.*

grill (gril), **1** utensil with parallel bars for cooking directly over a fire. It is used to hold meat, fish, or fowl. **2** cook on a grill; broil. **3** dish of broiled meat or fish. **4** dining room in a hotel or restaurant that specializes in serving broiled meat or fish. **5** question severely and persistently: *The detectives grilled several suspects concerning the crime.* **1,3,4** *noun,* **2,5** *verb.*

grim (grim), **1** stern; harsh; fierce; without mercy: *grim, stormy weather.* **2** not yielding; not relenting: *grim resolve.* **3** looking stern, fierce, or harsh: *My parents were grim when they heard about the six broken windows.* **4** horrible; frightful; ghastly: *As we walked past the cemetery, she made grim jokes about death and ghosts. adjective,* **grim mer, grim mest.**

grimace

grizzly bear—up to about 5 feet
(1½ meters) high at the shoulder

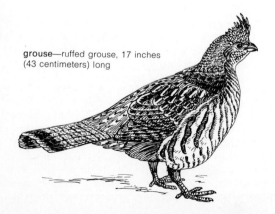

grouse—ruffed grouse, 17 inches
(43 centimeters) long

gri mace (grə mās′ *or* grim′is), **1** twisting of the face; ugly or funny smile: *a grimace caused by pain.* See picture. **2** make faces: *The clown grimaced at the children.* 1 *noun,* 2 *verb,* **gri maced, gri mac ing.**

grime (grīm), dirt rubbed deeply and firmly into a surface: *Soap and water removed only a little of the grime on the coal miner's hands. noun.*

grim y (grī′mē), covered with grime; very dirty: *grimy hands. adjective,* **grim i er, grim i est.**

grin (grin), **1** smile broadly. **2** a broad smile. **3** draw back the lips and show the teeth in anger, pain, or scorn: *The wolf grinned in an ugly way.* 1,3 *verb,* **grinned, grin ning;** 2 *noun.*

grind (grīnd), **1** crush into bits or powder: *That mill grinds corn into meal and wheat into flour.* **2** sharpen, smooth, or wear by rubbing on something rough: *grind an ax on a grindstone.* **3** rub harshly together: *grind one's teeth.* **4** work by turning a handle: *grind a pepper mill.* **5** long, hard work or study: *To some of the students, science was a grind.* 1-4 *verb,* **ground, grind ing;** 5 *noun.*

grind stone (grīnd′stōn′), a flat, round stone set in a frame and turned by hand, foot, or a motor. It is used to sharpen tools, such as axes and knives, or to smooth and polish things. *noun.*

grip (grip), **1** seizing and holding tight; tight grasp; firm hold. **2** seize and hold tight; take a firm hold on: *The dog gripped the stick.* **3** part to take hold of; handle. **4** a certain way of gripping the hand as a sign of belonging to some secret society. **5** a small suitcase or handbag. **6** firm control: *in the grip of poverty.* **7** understanding: *He has a grip of the subject.* 1,3-7 *noun,* 2 *verb,* **gripped, grip ping.**

grist (grist), **1** grain to be ground. **2** grain that has been ground; meal or flour. *noun.*

gris tle (gris′əl), a tough, elastic tissue, such as is found in meat; cartilage. *noun.*

grit (grit), **1** very fine bits of gravel or sand. **2** pluck; endurance; courage. **3** grind; make a grating sound by holding closed and rubbing: *She gritted her teeth and plunged into the cold water.* 1,2 *noun,* 3 *verb,* **grit ted, grit ting.**

grits (grits), coarsely ground corn, oats, or wheat with the outer covering removed. Grits are eaten boiled. *noun plural.*

griz zled (griz′əld), grayish; gray: *a grizzled beard. adjective.*

griz zly (griz′lē), **1** grayish. **2** grizzly bear. 1 *adjective,* **griz zli er, griz zli est;** 2 *noun, plural* **griz zlies.**

grizzly bear, a large, fierce, brownish-gray bear of western North America. See picture.

groan (grōn), **1** sound made down in the throat that expresses grief, pain, or disapproval; deep, short moan: *When I tried to wake her, she rolled over and with a groan went back to sleep.* **2** give a groan or groans: *The movers groaned as they lifted the piano.* 1 *noun,* 2 *verb.*

gro cer (grō′sər), person who sells food and household supplies. *noun.*

gro cer y (grō′sər ē), **1** store that sells food and household supplies. **2 groceries,** articles of food and household supplies sold by a grocer. *noun,* *plural* **gro cer ies.**

grog gy (grog′ē), not steady; shaky; dazed: *A blow on the head made me groggy. adjective.*

groom (grüm), **1** person whose work is taking care of horses. **2** feed, rub down, brush, and generally take care of (horses). **3** take care of the appearance of; make neat and tidy. **4** bridegroom. **1,4** *noun,* **2,3** *verb.*

groove (grüv), **1** a long, narrow channel or furrow, especially one cut by a tool: *My desk has a groove for pencils.* **2** any similar channel; rut: *grooves in a dirt road.* **3** make a groove in: *The counter of the sink is grooved so that the water will run off.* **4** a fixed way of doing things: *It's hard to get out of a groove.* **1,2,4** *noun,* **3** *verb,* **grooved, groov ing.**

grope (grōp), **1** feel about with the hands: *He groped for a flashlight when the lights went out.* **2** search blindly and uncertainly: *The detectives groped for some clue to the mysterious crime.* **3** find by feeling about with the hands; feel (one's way) slowly: *I groped my way across the dark room. verb,* **groped, grop ing.**

gross (grōs), **1** with nothing taken out; total; whole; entire. Gross receipts are all the money taken in before costs are deducted. **2** the total amount. **3** twelve dozen; 144. **4** very easily seen; glaring: *gross errors in adding.* **5** coarse; vulgar: *gross manners, gross language.* **6** too big and fat; fed too much. **1,4-6** *adjective,* **2,3** *noun, plural* **gross es** for 2, **gross** for 3.

gro tesque (grō tesk′), odd or unnatural in shape, appearance, or manner; fantastic; odd: *The book had pictures of hideous dragons and other grotesque monsters. adjective.*

grouch (grouch), a sulky person. *noun, plural* **grouch es.**

grouch y (grou′chē), tending to grumble or complain; surly; ill-tempered. *adjective,* **grouch i er, grouch i est.**

ground[1] (ground), **1** the surface of the earth; soil: *A heavy blanket of snow covered the ground.* **2** any piece of land or region used for some purpose: *hunting grounds, a parade ground.* **3** **grounds,** **a** land, lawns, and gardens around a house or school. **b** small bits that sink to the bottom of a drink such as coffee or tea; dregs; sediment. **4** of or on the surface of the earth: *All the classrooms at our school are on the ground floor.* **5** in baseball, hit a ball that rolls or bounces along the ground. **6** run aground; hit the bottom or shore: *The boat grounded in shallow water.* **7** reason; foundation for what is said, thought, or done: *What are your grounds for that statement?* **8** fix firmly; establish: *This class is well grounded in arithmetic. His beliefs are grounded on facts.* **9** connect (an electric wire) with the earth. **10** keep (a pilot or an aircraft) from flying: *The pilot was grounded by injury.* **1-3,7** *noun,* **4** *adjective,* **5,6,8-10** *verb.*

lose ground, 1 retreat; yield: *We lost ground because of the storm.* **2** become less common or widespread: *Superstition is losing ground as people become more educated.*

a hat	i it	oi oil	ch child	⎧ a in about
ā age	ī ice	ou out	ng long	e in taken
ä far	o hot	u cup	sh she	ə = ⎨ i in pencil
e let	ō open	ú put	th thin	o in lemon
ē equal	ô order	ü rule	ŦH then	⎩ u in circus
ėr term			zh measure	

ground[2] (ground). See **grind.** *The miller ground the corn into meal. The wheat was ground to make flour. verb.*

ground hog (ground′hôg′), woodchuck. Groundhogs grow fat in summer and sleep all winter. **Groundhog Day,** February 2, is the day when the groundhog is believed to come out of its hole. If the sun is shining and it sees its shadow, it goes back in the hole and winter lasts for six more weeks. *noun.*

group (grüp), **1** number of persons or things together: *A group of children were playing tag.* **2** number of persons or things belonging or classed together: *Wheat, rye, and oats belong to the grain group.* **3** form into a group: *The children grouped themselves in front of the steps.* **4** put in a group; arrange in groups: *Group the numbers to form three columns.* **1,2** *noun,* **3,4** *verb.*

grouse (grous), a brown bird with feathered legs that is hunted for food. See picture. *noun, plural* **grouse.**

grove (grōv), group of trees standing together. An orange grove is an orchard of orange trees. *noun.*

grov el (gruv′əl), lie face downward; crawl at someone's feet; humble oneself: *The dog groveled before its owner when it was punished. verb.*

grow (grō), **1** become bigger; increase: *Plants grow from seeds. Her business has grown fast.* **2** live and become big: *Few trees grow in the desert.* **3** cause to grow; raise: *We grow cotton in the southern part of the United States.* **4** become: *It grew cold. verb,* **grew, grown, grow ing.**

grow up, become full-grown; become an adult: *What will you be when you grow up?*

growl (groul), **1** make a deep, low, angry sound: *The dog growled at the stranger.* **2** sound like that made by a fierce dog; deep, warning snarl. **3** grumble; complain: *The sailors growled about the poor food.* **1,3** *verb,* **2** *noun.*

grown (grōn), **1** arrived at full growth. A grown man is an adult. **2** See **grow.** *The corn has grown very tall.* **1** *adjective,* **2** *verb.*

grown-up (grōn′up′), **1** arrived at full growth; adult: *a grown-up person, grown-up manners.* **2** an adult: *The children conducted themselves like grown-ups.* **1** *adjective,* **2** *noun.*

growth (grōth), **1** process of growing; development. **2** amount grown; increase; progress: *one year's growth.* **3** what has grown or is growing: *A thick growth of bushes covered the ground. noun.*

grub (grub), **1** a soft, thick, wormlike larva of an insect such as a beetle that has just hatched from its egg. **2** dig; dig up; root out of the ground: *Pigs grub for roots.* **3** toil. **4** food. **1,4** *noun,* **2,3** *verb,* **grubbed, grub bing.**

grudge (gruj), **1** ill will; sullen feeling against; dislike of long standing: *Our neighbors have had a grudge against us since we asked them to keep their dog out of our yard.* **2** allow unwillingly; envy the possession of: *He grudged me my little prize even though he had won a better prize himself.* **3** give or let have unwillingly: *My boss grudged me even a small raise in pay.* **1** *noun,* **2,3** *verb,* **grudged, grudg ing.**

gru el (grü′əl), a nearly liquid food made by boiling oatmeal or other cereal in water or milk. *noun.*

grue some (grü′səm), horrible; causing fear or horror: *a gruesome crime. adjective.*

gruff (gruf), **1** deep and harsh: *a gruff voice.* **2** rough; rude; unfriendly; bad-tempered: *a gruff manner. adjective.*

grum ble (grum′bəl), **1** complain in a rather sullen way; mutter in discontent; find fault: *The students are always grumbling about the cafeteria's food.* **2** mutter of discontent; bad-tempered complaint. **3** make a low, heavy sound like far-off thunder. **1,3** *verb,* **grum bled, grum bling;** **2** *noun.*

grump y (grum′pē), bad-tempered; grouchy: *I went to bed late last night and woke up this morning feeling grumpy. adjective,* **grump i er, grump i est.**

grunt (grunt), **1** the deep, hoarse sound that a hog makes. **2** sound like this: *She lifted the heavy box with a grunt.* **3** make this sound: *She grunted as she lifted the heavy box.* **4** say with this sound: *to grunt an apology.* **1,2** *noun,* **3,4** *verb.*

guar an tee (gar′ən tē′), **1** promise to pay or do something if another fails to do it; pledge to replace goods if they are not as represented: *We have a one-year guarantee on our new car.* **2** stand back of; give a guarantee for: *This company guarantees its clocks for a year.* **3** undertake to secure for another: *The landlady will guarantee us possession of the house by May.* **4** make secure; protect: *Our home insurance guarantees us against loss in case of fire or theft.* **5** pledge (to do something); promise that (something) has been or will be: *The store guaranteed to deliver my purchase by Friday. Wealth does not guarantee happiness.* **1** *noun,* **2-5** *verb,* **guar an teed, guar an tee ing.**

guard (gärd), **1** watch over; take care of; keep safe; defend: *The dog guarded the child day and night.* **2** keep from escaping; check; hold back: *Guard the prisoners. Guard your tongue.* **3** person or group that protects or watches. A soldier or group of soldiers protecting a person or place is a guard. **4** take precautions: *Guard against cavities by brushing your teeth regularly.* **5** anything that gives protection; arrangement to give safety: *A helmet is a guard against head injuries.* **6** careful watch: *The shepherd kept guard over his sheep.* **7** player at either side of the center in football. **8** either of two basketball players who usually play near the center of the court on offense. **1,2,4** *verb,* **3,5-8** *noun.*

on guard, ready to defend or protect; watchful: *A sentry should always be on guard.*

guard i an (gär′dē ən), **1** person who takes care of another or of some special thing. **2** person appointed by law to take care of the affairs of someone who is young or who cannot take care of his or her own affairs. *noun.*

guess (ges), **1** form an opinion when one does not know exactly: *Do you know this or are you just guessing?* **2** opinion formed without really knowing: *My guess is that it will rain tomorrow.* **3** get right by guessing: *Can you guess the answer to that riddle?* **4** think; believe; suppose: *I guess you are right.* **1,3,4** *verb,* **2** *noun, plural* **guess es.**

guest (gest), **1** person who is received and entertained at another's house or table; visitor. **2** person who is staying at a hotel or motel. *noun.*

guid ance (gīd′ns), guiding; direction; leadership: *Under her mother's guidance, she learned how to swim. noun.*

guide (gīd), **1** show the way; lead; direct: *The scout guided us through the wilderness. The counselor guided him in the choice of a career.* **2** person or thing that shows the way: *Tourists sometimes hire guides.* **1** *verb,* **guid ed, guid ing;** **2** *noun.*

guided missile, missile that can be guided in flight to its target by means of radio signals from the ground or by automatic devices inside the missile which direct its course.

guide word, word put at the top of a page as a guide to the contents of the page. The guide words for this page are *grudge* and *guillotine.*

gull—about 23 inches (58 centimeters) long

guild (gild), **1** society for mutual aid or for some common purpose: *The author is a member of the Writers Guild.* **2** In the Middle Ages, a guild was a union of the people in one trade to keep standards high, and to look out for the interests of their trade. *noun.*

guile (gīl), crafty deceit; cunning; crafty behavior; sly tricks: *By guile the fox got the cheese from the crow. noun.*

guil lo tine (gil′ə tēn′), machine for cutting off people's heads by a heavy blade that slides up and down in grooves made in two posts. See picture. *noun.* [The *guillotine* was named for Joseph Guillotin, who lived from 1738 to 1814. He was a French doctor who suggested the use of this machine as a faster, more merciful way to execute criminals. It was first used in 1792 during the French Revolution.]

guilt (gilt), fact or condition of having done wrong; being guilty; being to blame: *The evidence proved their guilt.* noun.

guilt y (gil′tē), **1** having done wrong; deserving to be blamed and punished: *The jury found her guilty of theft.* **2** knowing or showing that one has done wrong: *a guilty conscience, a guilty look.* adjective, **guilt i er, guilt i est.**

guin ea fowl (gin′ē foul′), fowl somewhat like a pheasant, having dark-gray feathers with small, white spots. Guinea fowls are raised like chickens and used for food.

guin ea hen (gin′ē hen′), **1** guinea fowl. **2** a female guinea fowl.

guin ea pig (gin′ē pig′), a burrowing animal with short ears and no tail. Guinea pigs are kept as pets and used in scientific experiments. See picture.

guise (gīz), **1** style of dress; garb: *The spy in the guise of a monk was not recognized by the enemy.* **2** appearance: *That theory is nothing but an old idea in a new guise.* **3** pretended appearance: *Under the guise of friendship they plotted treachery.* noun.

gui tar (gə tär′), a musical instrument having six strings, played with the fingers or with a pick. See picture. noun.

gulch (gulch), a very deep, narrow valley with steep sides. noun, plural **gulch es.**

gulf (gulf), **1** a large part of an ocean or sea that extends into surrounding land: *The Gulf of Mexico is between Florida and Mexico.* **2** a very deep break or cut in the earth: *The earthquake made a gulf in the earth.* **3** wide separation: *The quarrel left a gulf between the old friends.* noun.

gull (gul), a graceful gray-and-white bird living on or near large bodies of water. A gull has long wings, webbed feet, and a thick, strong beak. See picture. noun.

gul li ble (gul′ə bəl), easily deceived or cheated. adjective.

gul ly (gul′ē), a narrow gorge; little steep valley; ditch made by heavy rains or running water. noun, plural **gul lies.**

gulp (gulp), **1** swallow eagerly or greedily: *The hungry girl gulped down the bowl of soup.* **2** act of swallowing: *He ate the cookie in one gulp.* **3** amount swallowed at one time; mouthful: *She took a gulp of milk.* **4** keep in; choke back; repress: *The disappointed child gulped down a sob and tried to smile.* **5** gasp; choke: *The spray of cold water made me gulp.* **1,4,5** verb, **2,3** noun.

gum¹ (gum), **1** the sticky juice of certain trees which is used to make mucilage, candy, and medicine. **2** tree that yields gum. **3** gum prepared for chewing. **4** stick together with gum. **5** make or become sticky: *The pages were all gummed with candy.* **1-3** noun, **4,5** verb, **gummed, gum ming.**

gum² (gum), the flesh around the teeth. noun.

gum bo (gum′bō), soup thickened with okra pods. noun, plural **gum bos.** [*Gumbo* comes from a Bantu word, possibly a word meaning "okra."]

gum drop (gum′drop′), a stiff, jellylike piece of candy. noun.

a hat	**i** it	**oi** oil	**ch** child	a in about
ā age	**ī** ice	**ou** out	**ng** long	e in taken
ä far	**o** hot	**u** cup	**sh** she	ə = i in pencil
e let	**ō** open	** u̇** put	**th** thin	o in lemon
ē equal	**ô** order	**ü** rule	**ᴛʜ** then	u in circus
ėr term			**zh** measure	

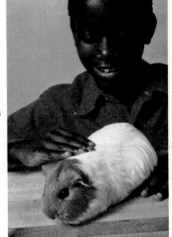
guinea pig—about 6 inches (15 centimeters) long

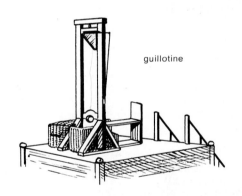
guillotine

guitar

gun (gun), **1** weapon with a metal tube for shooting bullets or shells. Cannons, rifles, pistols, and revolvers are guns. **2** anything resembling a gun in use or shape: *a spray gun.* **3** shooting of a gun as a signal or salute: *The President got a salute of 21 guns.* **4** shoot with a gun; hunt with a gun: *They went gunning for rabbits.* 1-3 *noun,* 4 *verb,* **gunned, gun ning.**

gun boat (gun′bōt′), a small warship that can be used in shallow water. *noun.*

gun man (gun′mən), man who uses a gun to rob or kill. *noun, plural* **gun men.**

gun ner (gun′ər), **1** man trained to fire artillery; soldier who handles and fires cannon. **2** a naval officer in charge of a ship's guns. *noun.*

gun pow der (gun′pou′dər), powder that explodes when touched with fire. Gunpowder is used in guns, blasting, and fireworks. *noun.*

gun shot (gun′shot′), **1** shot fired from a gun. **2** the shooting of a gun: *We heard gunshots.* **3** distance that a gun will shoot: *The deer was within gunshot. noun.*

gun wale (gun′l), the upper edge of a ship's or boat's side. *noun.*

gup py (gup′ē), a very small, brightly colored fish of tropical fresh water, often kept in aquariums. The female gives birth to live young instead of laying eggs. *noun, plural* **gup pies.** [*Guppy* was named for Robert Guppy. He was a British minister of the West Indies, who sent samples of this fish to London in the 1800's.]

gur gle (gėr′gəl), **1** flow or run with a bubbling sound: *Water gurgles when it is poured out of a bottle or flows over stones.* **2** a bubbling sound. **3** make a bubbling sound: *The baby gurgled happily.* 1,3 *verb,* **gur gled, gur gling;** 2 *noun.*

gush (gush), **1** rush out suddenly; pour out: *Oil gushed from the new well.* **2** rush of water or other liquid from an enclosed space: *If you get a deep cut, there usually is a gush of blood.* **3** talk in a way that shows too much silly feeling. 1,3 *verb,* 2 *noun.*

gush er (gush′ər), an oil well that gives oil in great quantities without pumping. *noun.*

gust (gust), **1** a sudden, violent rush of wind: *A gust upset the small sailboat.* **2** outburst of anger or other feeling: *gusts of laughter. noun.*

gut (gut), **1** the whole alimentary canal or its lower portion; intestine. **2** string made from the intestines of animals. Gut is used for violin strings and for tennis rackets. *noun.*

gut ter (gut′ər), **1** channel or ditch along the side of a street or road to carry off water; low part of a street beside the sidewalk. **2** channel or trough along the lower edge of a roof to carry off rain water. **3** flow or melt in streams: *The candle guttered so that a pool of wax formed on the table.* 1,2 *noun,* 3 *verb.*

guy[1] (gī), rope, chain, or wire attached to something to steady it. *noun.*

guy[2] (gī), a man or boy; fellow. *noun.* [*Guy* was named for Guy Fawkes, the leader of a plot to blow up the British king and parliament in 1605. He lived from 1570 to1606.]

gym (jim), **1** gymnasium. **2** physical education. *noun.*

gym na si um (jim nā′zē əm), room or building fitted up for physical exercises or training and for indoor athletic sports. *noun, plural* **gym na si ums, gym na si a** (jim nā′zē ə). [*Gymnasium* comes from a Greek word meaning "naked," because Greek athletes were usually naked when they exercised.]

gym nas tics (jim nas′tiks), exercises for developing the muscles, such as are done in a gymnasium. See picture. *noun plural.*

gyp sy (jip′sē), **1** Also, **Gypsy.** person belonging to a wandering group of people having dark skin and black hair, who came from India long ago. **2** of the gypsies: *gypsy music.* 1 *noun, plural* **gyp sies;** 2 *adjective.* Also spelled **gipsy.** [*Gypsy* was shortened from the name *Egyptian.* Gypsies were called this because they were supposed to have come from Egypt.]

gy rate (jī′rāt), go in a circle or spiral; whirl; rotate: *A spinning top gyrates. verb,* **gy rat ed, gy rat ing.**

gy ro scope (jī′rə skōp), instrument consisting of a wheel mounted so that its axis can turn freely in one or more directions. A spinning gyroscope tends to resist any change in the direction of its axis, no matter which way its base is turned. Gyroscopes are used to keep ships and airplanes steady. See picture. *noun.*

gyroscope

gymnastics

H h

H or **h** (āch), the eighth letter of the English alphabet. There are two *h*'s in *high*. *noun, plural* **H's** or **h's.**

ha (hä), **1** a cry of surprise, joy, or triumph: *"Ha! I've caught you!" cried the giant to Jack.* **2** sound of a laugh: *"Ha! ha! ha!" laughed the boys. interjection.*

hab it (hab′it), **1** custom; practice. Doing a thing over and over again makes it a habit. *Form the habit of brushing your teeth after every meal.* **2** the clothing worn by members of some religious orders. Monks and nuns often wear habits. *noun.*

hab i tat (hab′ə tat), place where an animal or plant naturally lives or grows: *The jungle is the habitat of monkeys. noun.*

hab i ta tion (hab′ə tā′shən), **1** place or building to live in. **2** living in: *A barn is not fit for human habitation. noun.*

ha bit u al (hə bich′ü əl), **1** done by habit: *a habitual smile. Habitual courtesy is always being polite to others.* **2** regular; steady: *A habitual reader reads a great deal.* **3** usual; customary: *The ice-cream man stood at his habitual corner. adjective.*

ha ci en da (hä′sē en′də), a ranch or country house in Mexico or the southwestern United States. *noun.*

hack (hak), **1** cut roughly: *She hacked the meat into jagged pieces.* **2** a rough cut. **3** give short, dry coughs. **1,3** *verb,* **2** *noun.*

had (had). See **have.** *She had a party. A fine time was had by all who came. verb.*

had dock (had′ək), a food fish of the northern Atlantic, somewhat like a cod, but smaller. *noun, plural* **had docks** or **had dock.**

had n't (had′nt), had not.

hag (hag), **1** a very ugly old woman. **2** witch. *noun.*

hag gard (hag′ərd), looking worn from pain, fatigue, worry, or hunger; worn by care. See picture. *adjective.*

hai ku (hī′kü), a poem of three lines and containing only 17 syllables. *noun, plural* **hai ku.**

hail[1] (hāl), **1** small, roundish pieces of ice coming down from the clouds in a shower; frozen rain: *Hail fell with such violence that it broke windows.* **2** fall in hail: *Sometimes it hails during a summer thunderstorm.* **3** shower like hail: *A hail of bullets met the soldiers.* **4** pour down in a shower like hail: *The angry crowd hailed insults at the speaker.* **1,3** *noun,* **2,4** *verb.*

hail[2] (hāl), **1** greet; cheer; shout in welcome to: *The crowd hailed the winner.* **2** shout of welcome; greeting; cheer. **3** greetings! welcome!: *Hail to the winner!* **4** call out or signal to: *I hailed a taxi to take me to the airport.* **1,4** *verb,* **2** *noun,* **3** *interjection.*

hail from, come from: *She hails from Boston.*

hail stone (hāl′stōn′), a frozen drop of rain.

Hailstones are usually very small, but sometimes they are as big as marbles. *noun.*

hair (her *or* har), **1** a fine threadlike growth from the skin of people and animals. **2** mass of such growths: *I combed my hair.* **3** a fine growth from the outer layer of plants. *noun.*

hair cut (her′kut′ *or* har′kut′), act or manner of cutting the hair. *noun.*

hair do (her′dü′ *or* har′dü′), way of arranging the hair. *noun, plural* **hair dos.**

hair less (her′lis *or* har′lis), without hair. *adjective.*

hair y (her′ē *or* har′ē), covered with hair; having much hair: *hairy hands, a plant with hairy leaves. adjective,* **hair i er, hair i est.**

hale (hāl), strong and well; healthy: *Grandpa is still hale and hearty at seventy. adjective,* **hal er, hal est.**

half (haf), **1** one of two equal parts: *A half of 4 is 2. Two halves make a whole.* **2** being one of two equal parts: *a half pound, a half hour.* **3** to a half of the full amount or degree: *a glass half full of milk.* **4** one of the two equal periods of play in certain games, such as football, basketball, or soccer. **5** partly; not completely: *I was only half awake when the phone rang. The potatoes were half cooked.* **1,4** *noun, plural* **halves;** **2** *adjective,* **3,5** *adverb.*

not half bad, fairly good.

half back (haf′bak′), a football player who runs with the ball, blocks for another runner, or tries to catch a pass. *noun.*

half brother, brother related through one parent only.

haggard—Poverty, pain, and worry made the woman look **haggard.**

---

half heart ed (haf′här′tid), lacking courage, interest, or enthusiasm. *adjective.*

half-mast (haf′mast′), position halfway or part way down from the top of a mast or staff. A flag is lowered to half-mast as a mark of respect for someone who has died or as a signal of distress. *noun.*

half sister, sister related through one parent only.

half way (haf′wā′), **1** half the way: *The rope reached only halfway around the tree.* **2** one half: *The lesson is halfway finished.* **3** midway: *Chicago was the halfway point in our trip from New York to Denver.* **4** not going far enough; incomplete: *Fires cannot be prevented by halfway measures.* 1,2 *adverb,* 3,4 *adjective.*

meet halfway, do one's share to agree or be friendly with.

hal i but (hal′ə bət), a very large flatfish, much used for food. Halibuts sometimes weigh several hundred pounds. *noun, plural* **hal i buts** or **hal i but.**

hall (hôl), **1** way for going through a building: *A hall ran the length of the upper floor of the house.* **2** passage or room at the entrance of a building: *Leave your umbrella in the hall.* **3** a large room for holding meetings, parties, or banquets: *No hall in town was large enough for the crowd gathered to hear the famous singer.* **4** building for public business or meetings: *The mayor's office is in the town hall.* **5** building of a school or college in which students live or classes are held. **6** house of an English lord, squire, or owner of an estate. *noun.*

hal low (hal′ō), make holy or sacred: *"Hallowed be Thy name."* *verb.*

Hal low een or **Hal low e'en** (hal′ō ēn′), the evening of October 31. *noun.*

hall way (hôl′wā′), **1** hall. **2** passageway or room at the entrance of a building. *noun.*

ha lo (hā′lō), **1** ring of light around the sun, moon, or other shining body. **2** a golden circle or disk of light represented about the head of a saint or angel in pictures or statues. See picture. *noun, plural* **ha los** or **ha loes.**

halt[1] (hôlt), **1** stop for a time: *The hikers halted and rested from their climb. The store halted deliveries during the strike.* **2** a stop for a time: *When there is a strike all work comes to a halt.* 1 *verb,* 2 *noun.*

halt[2] (hôlt), hesitate: *Shyness made the child speak in a halting manner. verb.*

hal ter (hôl′tər), **1** rope or strap for leading or tying an animal. See picture. **2** a backless blouse which fastens behind the neck and across the back, worn by women and girls. *noun.*

halve (hav), **1** divide into two equal parts; share equally: *He and I agreed to halve expenses on our trip.* **2** reduce to half: *The new machine will halve the time and cost of doing the work by hand. verb,* **halved, halv ing.**

halves (havz), more than one half. Two halves make one whole. *noun plural.*

ham (ham), **1** meat from the upper part of a hog's hind leg, usually salted and smoked. **2** the back of

halo (definition 2)

halter (definition 1)

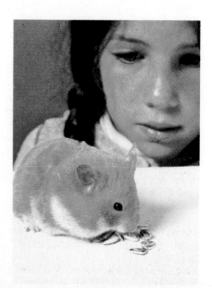
hamster
about 5 inches
(13 centimeters) long

the thigh; the thigh and buttock. **3** an amateur radio operator. *noun.*

ham burg er (ham′bėr′gər), **1** ground beef, usually shaped into round flat cakes and fried or broiled. **2** sandwich made with hamburger, usually in a roll or bun. *noun.* [*Hamburger* comes from a German word meaning "of Hamburg." Hamburg is a city in West Germany.]

ham let (ham′lit), a small village; little group of houses in the country. *noun.*

ham mer (ham′ər), **1** tool with a metal head and a handle, used to drive nails and to beat metal into shape. **2** something shaped or used like a hammer. The hammer of a gun explodes the charge. **3** drive, hit, or work with a hammer. **4** beat into shape with a hammer: *The silver was hammered into bowls.* **5** fasten by using a hammer. **6** hit again and again: *The teacher hammered on the desk with a ruler to get the class to quiet down.* **7** force by many efforts: *to hammer common sense into someone's head.* 1,2 *noun,* 3-7 *verb.*

ham mock (ham′ək), a hanging bed or couch made of canvas or netted cord. *noun.*

ham per¹ (ham′pər), get in the way of; hold back; hinder: *Wet wood hampered our efforts to start the campfire. verb.*

ham per² (ham′pər), a large basket with a cover: *a picnic hamper, a laundry hamper. noun.*

ham ster (ham′stər), animal somewhat like a mouse, but larger. Hamsters have a short tail and large cheek pouches. They are often kept as pets. See picture. *noun.*

hand (hand), **1** the end part of the arm, which takes and holds objects. Each hand has four fingers and a thumb. **2** thing like a hand: *the hands of a clock or watch.* **3** a hired worker who uses his or her hands: *a factory hand.* **4** give with the hand; pass: *Please hand me a spoon.* **5** help with the hand: *I handed the old woman into the bus.* **6 hands,** possession; control: *This property is no longer in my hands.* **7** part or share in doing something: *She had no hand in the matter.* **8** side: *There was a small table at my left hand.* **9** style of handwriting: *He writes in a clear hand.* **10** skill; ability: *The artist's work showed a master's hand.* **11** round of applause or clapping: *The crowd gave the winner a big hand.* **12** promise of marriage: *He asked the king for his daughter's hand.* **13** the breadth of a hand; 4 inches: *This horse is 18 hands high.* **14** the cards held by a player in one round of a card game. **15** a single round in a card game. **16** of, for, by, or in the hand: *a hand mirror, hand weaving, a hand pump.* 1-3,6-15 *noun,* 4,5 *verb,* 16 *adjective.*

at second hand, from the knowledge or experience of another: *The story he heard at second hand proved to be untrue.*

hand down, pass along: *Great-grandmother's ring is handed down to the oldest child in the family.*

hand to hand, close together: *The soldiers fought hand to hand.*

lend a hand, help: *I asked my friend to lend me a hand with my homework.*

a hat	**i** it	**oi** oil	**ch** child	a in about
ā age	**ī** ice	**ou** out	**ng** long	e in taken
ä far	**o** hot	**u** cup	**sh** she	**ə** = { i in pencil
e let	**ō** open	**ú** put	**th** thin	o in lemon
ē equal	**ô** order	**ü** rule	**ŦH** then	u in circus
ėr term			**zh** measure	

on hand, 1 within reach; near: *Try to be on hand when I need you.* **2** ready: *We have bandages on hand in case of an accident.*

on the other hand, from the opposite point of view: *On the other hand, it costs too much money.*

play into the hands of, act so as to give the advantage to: *If we delay the attack, we will play into the hands of the enemy.*

hand bag (hand′bag′), **1** a woman's small bag for money, keys, and cosmetics; purse. **2** a small bag to hold clothes and other things. *noun.*

hand ball (hand′bôl′), **1** game played by hitting a small, hard ball against a wall with the hand. **2** ball used in this game. *noun.*

hand book (hand′bùk′), a small book of information or directions: *a handbook on birds, a handbook on automobile repairs. noun.*

hand cuff (hand′kuf′), **1** one of two steel rings joined by a short chain and fastened around the wrists of a prisoner. **2** put handcuffs on. 1 *noun,* 2 *verb.*

hand ful (hand′fùl), **1** as much or as many as the hand can hold: *a handful of candy.* **2** a small number or quantity: *Only a handful of football fans sat watching the game. noun, plural* **hand fuls.**

hand i cap (han′dē kap′), **1** something that puts a person at a disadvantage; hindrance: *A sore throat was a handicap to the singer.* **2** put at a disadvantage; hinder: *The swimmer was handicapped by a sore arm.* **3** race, contest, or game in which better contestants are given special disadvantages and others are given special advantages, so that all have an equal chance to win. **4** the advantage or disadvantage given in such a race, contest, or game: *A runner with a handicap of 5 yards in a 100-yard dash must run either 95 yards or 105 yards.* **5** give a handicap to. 1,3,4 *noun,* 2,5 *verb,* **hand i capped, hand i cap ping.** [*Handicap,* from the words *hand in cap,* was an old betting game. Money was put inside a cap or hat held by an umpire. He decided on the odds needed to give everyone an equal chance to win.]

hand i capped (han′dē kapt′), **1** having a physical or mental disability. **2 the handicapped,** people with physical or mental disabilities. 1 *adjective,* 2 *noun.*

hand i craft (han′dē kraft′), **1** skill with the hands. **2** trade or art requiring skill with the hands: *Weaving baskets from rushes is a handicraft. noun.*

hand ker chief (hang′kər chif), a square of cloth used for wiping the nose, face, or hands. *noun.*

han dle (han′dl), **1** part of a thing made to be held or grasped by the hand. Spoons, pitchers, hammers, and pails have handles. **2** touch, feel, or use with the hand: *I handled the old book carefully* *to avoid tearing the pages.* **3** manage; direct: *The rider handled the horse well.* **4** behave or act when handled: *This car handles easily.* **5** treat; deal with: *The teacher handled discipline problems with ease.* **6** deal in; trade in: *That store handles meat and groceries.* 1 *noun,* 2-6 *verb,* **han dled, han dling.**

han dle bar (han′dl bär′), the curved bar on a bicycle or motorcycle that the rider holds and steers by. *noun.*

hand made (hand′mād′), made by hand, not by machine: *handmade pottery. adjective.*

hand out (hand′out′), portion of food, clothing, or money handed out: *The beggar asked for a handout. noun.*

hand rail (hand′rāl′), railing used as a guard or support on a stairway or platform. *noun.*

hand shake (hand′shāk′), act of clasping and shaking of each other's hands in friendship, agreement, or greeting. *noun.*

hand some (han′səm), **1** good-looking; pleasing in appearance. We usually say that a man is handsome, but that a woman is pretty or beautiful. **2** fairly large; considerable: *A thousand dollars is a handsome sum of money.* **3** generous: *They gave the school a handsome gift of two hundred dollars. adjective,* **hand som er, hand som est.**

hand spring (hand′spring′), somersault made by springing onto the hands, flipping the body over backwards, and landing on the feet. See picture. *noun.*

hand writ ing (hand′rī′ting), **1** writing by hand; writing with pen or pencil. **2** manner or style of writing: *He recognized his mother's handwriting on the envelope. noun.*

hand y (han′dē), **1** easy to reach or use; saving work; useful: *There were handy shelves near the kitchen sink.* **2** skillful with the hands: *He is handy with tools. adjective,* **hand i er, hand i est.**

hang (hang), **1** fasten or be fastened to something above: *Hang your cap on the hook. The swing hangs from a tree.* **2** fasten or be fastened so as to leave swinging freely: *hang a door on its hinges.* **3** put to death by hanging with a rope around the neck. **4** droop; bend down: *She hung her head in shame.* **5** cover or decorate with things that are fastened to something above: *The walls were hung with pictures.* **6** depend: *His future hangs on your decision.* **7** way in which a thing hangs: *There's something wrong with the hang of this coat.* **8** way of using or doing: *Riding a bicycle is easy after you get the hang of it.* **9** idea; meaning: *After studying an hour I finally got the hang of the lesson.* 1-6 *verb,* **hung** (or, usually, **hanged** for 3), **hang ing;** 7-9 *noun.*

hang on, 1 hold tight: *Hang on to my hand going down these steep stairs.* **2** be unwilling to let go, stop, or leave: *The dying man hung on to life for a few days.*

hang ar (hang′ər), shed for airplanes or airships. *noun.*

hang er (hang′ər), thing on which something else is hung: *a coat hanger. noun.*

hang ing (hang′ing), **1** death by hanging with a rope around the neck. **2** thing that hangs from a window, wall, or bed: *a wall hanging.* **3** that hangs: *a hanging basket of flowers.* 1,2 *noun,* 3 *adjective.*

hang man (hang′mən), man who puts condemned criminals to death by hanging them. *noun, plural* **hang men.**

hang nail (hang′nāl′), bit of skin that hangs partly loose near a fingernail. *noun.*

Ha nuk kah (hä′nə kə), a yearly Jewish festival that lasts eight days. It celebrates the recapture of the holy Jewish Temple many centuries ago. *noun.*

hap haz ard (hap′haz′ərd), **1** random; not planned: *Haphazard answers are usually wrong.* **2** by chance; at random: *Papers were scattered haphazard on the desk.* 1 *adjective,* 2 *adverb.*

hap pen (hap′ən), **1** take place; occur: *Nothing interesting happens here.* **2** be or take place by chance: *Accidents will happen.* **3** have the fortune; chance: *I happened to find my old diary yesterday.* **4** be done: *Something has happened to this lock; the key won't turn. verb.*

happen on, 1 meet: *The two friends happened on each other by chance.* **2** find: *She happened on a dime while looking for her ball.*

hap pen ing (hap′ə ning), something that happens; event: *The evening newscast reviewed the happenings of the day. noun.*

hap pi ly (hap′ə lē), **1** in a happy manner; with pleasure, joy, and gladness: *They lived happily forever after.* **2** by luck; with good fortune: *Happily, I saved you from falling. adverb.*

hap pi ness (hap′ē nis), being happy; gladness. *noun.*

hap py (hap′ē), **1** feeling as you do when you are well and are having a good time; glad; pleased; contented: *She is happy in her work.* **2** showing that one is glad: *a happy smile, a happy look.* **3** lucky: *By a happy chance, I found the lost money. adjective,* **hap pi er, hap pi est.**

hap py-go-luck y (hap′ē gō luk′ē), trusting to luck; carefree; easygoing: *The happy-go-lucky student was not interested in getting high marks. adjective.*

har ass (har′əs *or* hə ras′), **1** trouble by repeated attacks: *Pirates harassed the villages along the coast.* **2** disturb; worry: *The heat and the flies harassed us on the journey. verb.*

har bor (här′bər), **1** place of shelter for ships. **2** any place of shelter: *The child fled to the harbor of her father's arms.* **3** give shelter to: *The dog's shaggy hair harbors fleas.* **4** have and keep in the mind: *It's never good to harbor a grudge.* 1,2 *noun,* 3,4 *verb.*

hard (härd), **1** like steel, glass, and rock; not soft; not yielding to touch: *hard wood.* **2** firm; solid: *a hard knot.* **3** firmly; solidly: *Don't hold my hand so hard.* **4** not yielding to influence; stern: *a hard master.* **5** needing much ability, effort, or time: *a hard job, a hard lesson, a hard person to get along with.* **6** with effort: *I worked hard on this project.* **7** with vigor or violence: *It is raining hard.* **8** vigorous: *a hard run.* **9** severe; causing much pain, trouble, or care: *We had a hard winter last* *year. When my parents were out of work, we had a hard time.* **10** severely; badly: *It will go hard with you if you are lying.* **11** not pleasant; harsh; ugly: *a hard laugh, a hard face.* **12** containing mineral salts that keep soap from forming suds: *hard water.* 1,2,4,5,8,9,11,12 *adjective.* 3,6,7,10 *adverb.*

hard of hearing, somewhat deaf.

hard-boiled (härd′boild′), **1** boiled until hard: *hard-boiled eggs.* **2** not easily moved by the feelings; tough; rough. *adjective.*

hard coal, coal that burns with very little smoke or flame; anthracite.

hard en (härd′n), make hard; become hard: *Don't harden your heart to the needs of the poor. When the candy cooled, it hardened. verb.*

hard head ed (härd′hed′id), **1** not easily excited or deceived; practical; shrewd. **2** stubborn; obstinate. *adjective.*

hard heart ed (härd′här′tid), without pity; cruel; unfeeling. *adjective.*

hard ly (härd′lē), **1** only just; not quite; barely: *We hardly had time to eat breakfast. I am hardly strong enough to lift this heavy box.* **2** probably not: *They will hardly come in all this rain. adverb.*

hard ship (härd′ship), something hard to bear; hard condition of living: *Hunger, cold, and sickness were among the hardships of pioneer life. noun.*

hard ware (härd′wer′ *or* härd′war′), articles made from metal. Locks, hinges, nails, screws, or knives are hardware. *noun.*

hard wood (härd′wud′), hard, compact wood. Oak, cherry, maple, ebony, and mahogany are hardwoods. *noun.*

har dy (här′dē), able to bear hard treatment; strong; robust: *Cold weather does not kill hardy plants. adjective,* **har di er, har di est.**

hare (her *or* har), animal with long ears, a divided upper lip, a short tail, and long hind legs. A hare is very much like a rabbit, but larger. *noun, plural* **hares** *or* **hare.**

harm (härm), **1** something that causes pain or loss; injury; damage: *He slipped and fell down but suffered no harm.* **2** evil; wrong: *It was an accident; she meant no harm.* **3** damage; injure; hurt: *Do not pick or harm the flowers in the park.* 1,2 *noun,* 3 *verb.*

harm ful (härm′fəl), causing harm; injurious; hurtful: *harmful germs. adjective.*

harm less (härm′lis), causing no harm; not harmful: *It's only a harmless spider. adjective.*

har mon i ca (här mon′ə kə), a small musical instrument with metal reeds which is played by the mouth. See picture. *noun.*

har mo ni ous (här mō′nē əs), **1** agreeing in feelings, ideas, or actions; getting on well together: *The children played together in a harmonious group.* **2** going well together: *A beautiful picture has harmonious colors.* **3** sweet-sounding; musical: *the harmonious sounds of a chorus. adjective.*

har mo nize (här′mə nīz), **1** bring into harmony; make harmonious: *We harmonized the two plans by using parts of each one.* **2** be in harmony: *The colors*

used in the room harmonized to give a pleasing effect. **3** add tones to (a melody) to make chords in music. *verb,* **har mo nized, har mo niz ing.**

har mo ny (här′mə nē), **1** getting on well together. See picture. **2** going well together: *In a beautiful*

harmony (definition 1)
They all lived together in perfect **harmony.**

handspring

harmonica

landscape there is harmony of the different colors.
3 the sounding together of musical tones in a chord. **4** sweet or musical sound. *noun, plural* **har mo nies.**

har ness (här′nis), **1** leather straps, bands, and other pieces for a horse, which connect it to a carriage, wagon, or plow, or are used in riding. Reins, collar, and bridle are parts of a horse's harness. **2** put harness on: *Harness the horse.* **3** control and put to work: *We have harnessed these streams by building dams and putting in machinery for the water to turn. noun, plural* **har ness es.**

harp (härp), a large stringed musical instrument played with the fingers. See picture. *noun.*

harp ist (här′pist), person who plays a harp. *noun.*

har poon (här pün′), **1** spear with a rope tied to it. It is used for catching whales and other sea animals. See picture. **2** strike, catch, or kill with a harpoon. **1** *noun,* **2** *verb.*

har row (har′ō), **1** a heavy farm instrument with iron teeth or upright disks. Harrows break up plowed ground into finer pieces and cover seeds with earth. **2** draw a harrow over. **3** cause pain or torment to; distress: *to be harrowed with grief.* **1** *noun,* **2,3** *verb.*

harsh (härsh), **1** rough to the touch, taste, eye, or ear: *a harsh voice, a harsh climate.* **2** cruel; unfeeling; severe: *a harsh judge. adjective.*

hart (härt), a male deer, especially the male red deer after its fifth year. *noun, plural* **harts** or **hart.**

har vest (här′vist), **1** reaping and gathering in of grain and other food crops. **2** time or season of the harvest, usually in the late summer or early autumn. **3** gather in and bring home for use: *harvest wheat.* **4** one season's yield of any natural product; crop: *The oyster harvest was small this year.* **5** result; consequences: *She is reaping the harvest of her hard work.* **1,2,4,5** *noun,* **3** *verb.*

har vest er (här′və stər), **1** person who works in a harvest field; reaper. **2** machine for harvesting crops, especially grain. *noun.*

harvest moon, the full moon at harvest time or about September 23.

has (haz). See **have.** *Who has my book? He has been to Europe. verb.*

hash (hash), **1** mixture of cooked meat, potatoes, and other vegetables, chopped into small pieces and fried or baked. **2** chop into small pieces. **3** mixture. **1,3** *noun,* **2** *verb.*

has n't (haz′nt), has not.

haste (hāst), **1** trying to be quick; hurry: *All my haste was of no use; I missed the bus anyway.* **2** quickness without thought or care; rashness: *Haste makes waste. noun.*
make haste, hurry; be quick: *Make haste or you will miss your train.*

has ten (hā′sn), **1** hurry; cause to be quick; speed: *Sunshine and rest hastened my recovery from illness.* **2** be quick; go fast: *She hastened to explain that she had not meant to be rude. verb.*

hast i ly (hā′stl ē), **1** in a hurried way; quickly and not very carefully. **2** rashly. **3** in a quick-tempered way. *adverb.*

harp

harpoon (definition 1)

I HATE TO SEE THE OLD PLACE GO. IT'S ONE OF MY FAVORITE HAUNTS.

hast y (hā′stē), **1** quick; hurried: *He gave his watch a hasty glance and ran for the train.* **2** rash; not well thought out: *A hasty decision may cause unhappiness.* **3** easily angered; quick-tempered: *She is sometimes hasty with people who ask her personal questions. adjective,* **hast i er, hast i est.**

hat (hat), covering for the head when outdoors. A hat usually has a crown and a brim. *noun.*

hatch[1] (hach), **1** bring forth (young) from an egg or eggs: *A hen hatches chickens.* **2** keep (an egg or eggs) warm until the young come out: *The heat of the sun hatches turtles' eggs.* **3** come out from the egg: *Three of the chickens hatched today.* **4** the brood hatched: *There are twelve chickens in this hatch.* **5** plan secretly; plot: *The spies hatched a scheme to steal government secrets.* 1-3,5 *verb,* 4 *noun, plural* **hatch es.**

hatch[2] (hach), **1** opening in a ship's deck or in the floor or roof of a building. A ship's cargo is loaded through the hatch. **2** trap door covering such an opening. *noun, plural* **hatch es.**

hatch et (hach′it), a small ax with a handle about a foot long, for use with one hand. *noun.*

hate (hāt), **1** dislike very much: *Cats usually hate dogs.* **2** very strong dislike: *feel hate toward one's enemies, have a hate for war.* 1 *verb,* **hat ed, hat ing;** 2 *noun.*

hate ful (hāt′fəl), **1** causing hate: *hateful behavior.* **2** feeling hate; showing hate: *a hateful comment. adjective.*

ha tred (hā′trid), very strong dislike; hate. *noun.*

haugh ty (hô′tē), **1** too proud of oneself and too scornful of others: *A haughty person is often unpopular.* **2** showing too great pride of oneself and scorn for others: *haughty words. adjective,* **haugh ti er, haugh ti est.**

haul (hôl), **1** pull or drag with force: *The logs were loaded on wagons and hauled to the mill by horses.* **2** transport; carry: *Trucks, trains, and ships haul freight.* **3** act of hauling; hard pull. **4** load hauled: *Powerful trucks are used for these heavy hauls.* **5** distance that a load is hauled: *Long hauls cost more than short ones.* **6** amount won or taken at one time; catch: *The fishing boats made a good haul and came back fully loaded.* 1,2 *verb,* 3-6 *noun.*

haunch (hônch), **1** the part of the body around the hips: *The dog sat on its haunches.* **2** the leg and loin of an animal, used for food: *a haunch of venison. noun, plural* **haunch es.**

haunt (hônt), **1** go often to; visit frequently: *People say ghosts haunt that old house.* **2** place visited often. See picture. **3** be often with; come often to: *That song I heard this morning has haunted me all day. Memories of his youth haunted the old man.* 1,3 *verb,* 2 *noun.*

haunt ed (hôn′tid), visited by ghosts: *a haunted house. adjective.*

have (hav), **1** hold in one's hand; hold in one's keeping; hold in one's possession: *I have a stick in my hand. They have a big house and farm. A house has windows. She has no news of her brother.* **2** be forced; be compelled: *All animals have to sleep. He will have to go now because his work begins.* **3** cause

a hat	i it	oi oil	ch child	⎧ a in about
ā age	ī ice	ou out	ng long	⎪ e in taken
ä far	o hot	u cup	sh she	ə = ⎨ i in pencil
e let	ō open	ù put	th thin	⎪ o in lemon
ē equal	ô order	ü rule	ᴛʜ then	⎩ u in circus
ėr term			zh measure	

(somebody to do something or something to be done): *Please have the store deliver the suit. She will have the car washed.* **4** get: *You need to have a rest.* **5** take; accept: *Will you have a cup of tea?* **6** allow; permit: *She won't have any noise while she is reading.* **7** hold in the mind: *have an idea.* **8** give birth to: *She had a girl.* **9** be the parent or parents of: *They have three children.* **10** *Have* is used with words like *asked, been, broken, done,* or *called* to express completed action. *They have eaten. She had gone before. I have called him. They will have left by Sunday. verb,* **has, had, hav ing.**

have to do with, relate to; deal with: *Botany has to do with the study of plants.*

ha ven (hā′vən), **1** harbor, especially one for shelter from a storm. **2** place of shelter and safety: *To the weary hikers, the cabin was a welcome haven from the storm. noun.*

have n't (hav′ənt), have not.

hav er sack (hav′ər sak), bag used by soldiers and hikers for carrying food when on a march or hike. *noun.*

hav oc (hav′ək), very great destruction or injury: *Tornadoes, severe earthquakes, and plagues create widespread havoc. noun.*

Ha wai i (hə wī′ē), state of the United States in the northern Pacific, consisting of the Hawaiian Islands. *noun.* [*Hawaii* comes from the Hawaiian name of the largest island in the group. According to legend, the original Polynesian settlers of Hawaii named it for their homeland.]

Ha wai ian (hə wī′yən), **1** of or having something to do with Hawaii or its people. **2** person born or living in Hawaii. **3** the original language of Hawaii. 1 *adjective,* 2,3 *noun.*

Hawaiian Islands, group of islands in the northern Pacific.

hawk[1] (hôk), **1** bird of prey with a strong, hooked beak, and large curved claws. Long ago hawks were trained to hunt and kill other birds. See picture. **2** hunt with trained hawks. 1 *noun,* 2 *verb.*

hawk[1] (definition 1)—about 2 feet (60 centimeters) long

hazardous—Building a skyscraper is **hazardous** work.

hawk² (hôk), carry about and offer for sale by shouting: *Peddlers hawked their wares in the street.* *verb.*

haw thorn (hô′thôrn), shrub or small tree with many thorns and clusters of fragrant white, red, or pink flowers and small, red berries. *noun.*

hay (hā), **1** grass, alfalfa, or clover cut and dried as food for cattle and horses. **2** cut and dry grass, alfalfa, or clover for hay: *They are haying in the east field.* **1** *noun,* **2** *verb.*

hay fever, allergy caused by the pollen of ragweed and other plants. Hay fever often causes sneezing, a running nose, and itching nose and eyes.

hay field (hā′fēld′), field in which grass, alfalfa, or clover is grown for hay. *noun.*

hay loft (hā′lôft′), place in a stable or barn where hay is stored. *noun.*

hay mow (hā′mou′), place in a barn for storing hay. *noun.*

hay stack (hā′stak′), a large pile of hay outdoors. *noun.*

haz ard (haz′ərd), **1** risk; danger: *Mountain climbing is full of hazards.* **2** take a chance with; risk: *I won't even hazard a guess.* **1** *noun,* **2** *verb.*

haz ard ous (haz′ər dəs), dangerous; risky. See picture. *adjective.*

haze (hāz), **1** a small amount of mist or smoke in the air: *A thin haze veiled the distant hills.* **2** a vague condition of the mind; slight confusion: *Everything happened so fast that my mind is in a haze.* *noun.*

ha zel (hā′zəl), **1** shrub or small tree whose light-brown nuts are good to eat. **2** light brown. **1** *noun,* **2** *adjective.*

ha zy (hā′zē), **1** misty; smoky; dim: *a hazy sky.* **2** not distinct; obscure: *She was not there so she has only a hazy idea of what happened.* *adjective,* **ha zi er, ha zi est.**

H-bomb (āch′bom′), hydrogen bomb. *noun.*

he (hē), **1** boy, man, or male animal spoken about: *He works hard, but his work pays him well.* **2** a male: *Is your dog a he or a she?* **3** anyone: *He who hesitates is lost.* **1,3** *pronoun, plural* **they;** **2** *noun.*

head (hed), **1** the top part of the human body or the front part of most animal bodies where the eyes, ears, nose, mouth, and brain are. **2** the top part of anything: *the head of a pin, the head of a page.* **3** the front part of anything: *the head of a parade, the head of a street.* **4** at the front or top: *the head group of a parade.* **5** be at the front or the top of: *head a parade.* **6** coming from in front: *a head wind.* **7** move toward; face toward: *Our ship headed south.* **8** the chief person; leader: *A principal is the head of a school.* **9** chief; leading: *the head clerk in a store.* **10** be the head or chief of; lead: *Who will head the team?* **11** one or ones; an individual. Ten cows are ten head of cattle. **12** anything rounded like a head: *a head of cabbage.* **13** the striking or cutting part of a tool or implement: *You hit the nail with the head of a hammer.* **14** mind; understanding; intelligence: *He has a good head for figures.* **15** topic: *I arranged my book report under four main heads.* **16** crisis; conclusion: *Her refusal to do the job brought matters to a head.* **17** pressure: *a head of steam.* **18** source: *the head of a brook.* **19** **heads,** the top side of a coin. **1-3,8,11-19** *noun, plural* **heads** for **1-3,8,12-19,** **head** for **11; 4,6,9** *adjective,* **5,7,10** *verb.*

head off, get in front of; check: *She tried to head off the runaway horse.*

out of one's head, crazy.

over one's head, too hard for one to understand: *Chemistry is way over my head.*

head ache (hed′āk′), pain in the head. *noun.*

head band (hed′band′), band worn around the head. *noun.*

head dress (hed′dres′), covering or decoration for the head. See picture. *noun, plural* **head dress es.**

head first (hed′fėrst′), **1** with the head first. **2** hastily; rashly. *adverb.*

head ing (hed′ing), title of a page, chapter, or topic. *noun.*

head land (hed′lənd), cape; point of land jutting out into water. *noun.*

head less (hed′lis), **1** having no head. See picture. **2** without a leader. **3** foolish; stupid. *adjective.*

head light (hed′līt′), a bright light at the front of an automobile, train, or truck. *noun.*

head line (hed′līn′), words printed in heavy type at the top of a newspaper article telling what it is about. *noun.*

head long (hed′lông), **1** with the head first. See picture. **2** with great haste and force: *rush headlong into the crowd.* **3** in too great a rush; without stopping to think: *The boy ran headlong across the busy street.* *adverb, adjective.*

head-on (hed′on′), with the head or front first: *a head-on collision. adjective, adverb.*

head quar ters (hed′kwôr′tərz), **1** place from which the chief or commanding officer of an army or police force sends out orders. **2** the main office; the center of operations or of authority: *The headquarters of the American Red Cross is in Washington. noun plural or singular.*

a hat	i it	oi oil	ch child	⎧ a in about
ā age	ī ice	ou out	ng long	e in taken
ä far	o hot	u cup	sh she	ə = ⎨ i in pencil
e let	ō open	u̇ put	th thin	o in lemon
ē equal	ô order	ü rule	ŦH then	⎩ u in circus
ėr term			zh measure	

headlong—The enraged elephant ran **headlong** into a tree.

headdress—Africans wearing native headdresses

headless—This headless doll in a swing belonged to a Greek child more than 3500 years ago.

head strong (hed′strông′), rashly or foolishly determined to have one's own way; hard to control or manage: *a headstrong child. adjective.*

head wa ters (hed′wô′tərz), the sources or upper parts of a river. *noun plural.*

head way (hed′wā′), **1** motion forward: *The ship could make no headway against the strong wind and tide.* **2** progress with work or other activity: *Science has made much headway in fighting disease. noun.*

heal (hēl), make or become well; return to health; cure: *The cut healed in a few days. verb.*

health (helth), **1** being well or not sick; freedom from illness of any kind: *Rest, sleep, exercise, and cleanliness are important to your health.* **2** condition of the body or mind: *be in excellent health. noun.*

health food, food grown without chemicals or prepared without preservatives, chosen for its value as nourishment and believed to be good for one's health.

health ful (helth′fəl), giving health; good for the health: *a healthful diet, healthful exercise. adjective.*

health y (hel′thē), **1** having good health: *a healthy baby.* **2** giving health; good for the health: *healthy exercise. adjective,* **health i er, health i est.**

heap (hēp), **1** pile of many things thrown or lying together: *a heap of stones.* **2** form into a heap; gather in heaps: *I heaped the dirty clothes beside the washing machine.* **3** a large amount: *a heap of trouble.* **4** give generously or in large amounts: *to heap praise on someone.* **5** fill full or more than full: *heap a plate with food.* **1,3** *noun,* **2,4,5** *verb.*

hear (hir), **1** take in a sound or sounds through the ear: *We couldn't hear in the back row. I can hear my watch tick.* **2** listen: *The town crier shouted "Hear ye!"* **3** listen to: *You must hear what he has to say.* **4** receive information: *Have you heard from your sister in Los Angeles? verb,* **heard, hear ing.**

heard (hėrd). See **hear.** *I heard the noise. The gun was heard a mile away. verb.*

hear ing (hir′ing), **1** power to hear; sense by which sound is perceived: *The doctor tested my hearing.* **2** act or process of perceiving sound, of listening, or of receiving information: *Hearing the good news made us happy.* **3** chance to be heard: *The judge gave both sides a hearing.* **4** distance that a sound can be heard: *I must stay within hearing of the telephone. noun.*

hear say (hir′sā′), common talk; gossip. *noun.*

heart (härt), **1** the part of the body that pumps the blood. **2** the part that feels, loves, hates, and desires: *a heavy heart, a kind heart. She knew in her heart that she was wrong.* **3** love; affection: *give one's heart to someone.* **4** kindness; sympathy: *Have you no heart?* **5** courage; enthusiasm: *The losing team still had plenty of heart.* **6** middle; center: *in the heart of the forest.* **7** the main part; most important part: *the very heart of the matter.* **8** figure shaped somewhat like this: ♥: *The valentine was covered with hearts.* noun.

at heart, in one's deepest thoughts or feelings: *He is kind at heart, though he appears to be gruff.*

by heart, by memory: *I learned the poem by heart.*

take heart, be encouraged: *I'm sure that we'll find them, so take heart.*

heart bro ken (härt′brō′kən), crushed by sorrow or grief. *adjective.*

heart en (härt′n), cheer; cheer up; encourage: *This good news will hearten you.* verb.

heart felt (härt′felt′), sincere; genuine: *heartfelt sympathy.* adjective.

hearth (härth), **1** the stone or brick floor of a fireplace. **2** fireside; home: *The soldiers longed to be at their own hearths.* noun.

heart i ly (här′tl ē), **1** with sincere feeling; warmly: *She welcomed her cousins heartily.* **2** with courage, spirit, or enthusiasm; vigorously: *set to work heartily.* **3** with a good appetite: *eat heartily.* **4** very; completely: *She is heartily tired of doing all the work herself.* adverb.

heart i ness (här′tē nis), **1** sincere feeling. **2** vigor. noun.

heart less (härt′lis), without kindness or sympathy; unfeeling; cruel. *adjective.*

heart y (här′tē), **1** warm and friendly; full of feeling; sincere: *We gave our old friends a hearty welcome.* **2** strong and well; vigorous: *Hearty pioneers moved westward.* **3** with plenty to eat; nourishing: *A hearty meal satisfied her appetite.* adjective, **heart i er, heart i est.**

heat (hēt), **1** condition of being hot; hotness; warmth: *the heat of a fire.* **2** make or become warm or hot: *The stove heats the room. The soup is heating slowly.* **3** hot weather: *the heat of summer.* **4** the hottest point; most violent stage; excitement: *In the heat of the argument we all lost our tempers.* **5** one trial in a race: *I won the first heat, but lost the final race.* 1,3-5 *noun,* 2 *verb.*

heat er (hē′tər), thing that gives heat or warmth, such as a stove, furnace, or radiator. *noun.*

heath (hēth), **1** open wasteland with heather or low bushes growing on it; moor. A heath has few or no trees. **2** a low bush growing on such land. Heather is one kind of heath. *noun.*

hea then (hē′ŦHən), **1** person who does not believe in the God of the Bible; person who is not a Christian, Jew, or Moslem. **2** people who are heathens. **3** of or having to do with heathens. 1,2 *noun, plural* **hea thens** or **hea then;** 3 *adjective.*

heath er (heŦH′ər), a low shrub which covers wastelands in Scotland and England. *noun.*

heave (hēv), **1** lift with force or effort: *She heaved the heavy box onto the truck.* **2** lift and throw: *The sailors heaved the anchor overboard.* **3** pull with force or effort; haul: *They heaved on the rope.* **4** give (a sigh or groan) with a deep, heavy breath. **5** rise and fall alternately: *The waves heaved in the storm.* **6** rise; swell; bulge: *The ground heaved from the earthquake.* **7** heaving; throw: *With a mighty heave my friends and I pushed the boat into the*

water. 1-6 *verb,* **heaved, heav ing;** 7 *noun.*

heav en (hev′ən), **1** (in Christian and some other religious use) place where God and the angels live. **2 Heaven,** God; Providence: *It was the will of Heaven.* **3** place or condition of greatest happiness. **4 heavens,** upper air in which clouds float, winds blow, and birds fly; sky: *Millions of stars were shining in the heavens.* noun.

heav en ly (hev′ən lē), **1** of or in heaven: *heavenly angels, heavenly Father.* **2** like heaven; suitable for heaven; very happy, beautiful, or excellent: *a heavenly spot, heavenly peace.* **3** of or in the heavens: *The sun, the moon, and the stars are heavenly bodies.* adjective.

heav i ly (hev′ə lē), in a heavy way or manner. *adverb.*

heav i ness (hev′ē nis), **1** being heavy; great weight. **2** sadness: *a heaviness in one's heart.* noun.

heav y (hev′ē), **1** hard to lift or carry; having much weight: *Iron is heavy and feathers are light.* **2** of more than usual weight for its kind: *heavy silk, heavy bread.* **3** large; greater than usual: *a heavy rain, a heavy crop, a heavy meal, a heavy vote, a heavy sea, a heavy sleep.* **4** hard to bear or endure: *Their troubles became heavier.* **5** hard to digest: *heavy food.* **6** weighted down; laden: *air heavy with moisture, eyes heavy with sleep, a heavy heart full of sorrow.* adjective, **heav i er, heav i est.**

He brew (hē′brü), **1** Jew; descendant of one of the desert tribes led by Moses that settled in Palestine. **2** Jewish. **3** the ancient language of the Jews, in which the Old Testament was recorded. Citizens of Israel speak a modern form of Hebrew. 1,3 *noun,* 2 *adjective.*

hec tic (hek′tik), very exciting: *The children had a hectic time getting to school the morning after the big snowstorm.* adjective.

he'd (hēd), **1** he had. **2** he would.

hedge (hej), **1** a thick row of bushes or small trees planted as a fence. **2** put a hedge around: *hedge a garden.* **3** avoid giving a direct answer; evade questions. 1 *noun,* 2,3 *verb,* **hedged, hedg ing.**

hedge in, hem in; surround on all sides: *The town was hedged in by mountains and a dense forest.*

hedge hog (hej′hog′), **1** a small animal of Europe, Asia, and Africa, with spines on its back. When attacked, hedgehogs roll up into a bristling ball. See picture. **2** porcupine of North America. *noun.*

heed (hēd), **1** give careful attention to; take notice of: *Now heed what I say.* **2** careful attention; notice: *Pay heed to her instructions.* 1 *verb,* 2 *noun.*

heed less (hēd′lis), careless; thoughtless. *adjective.*

heel[1] (hēl), **1** the back part of the foot, below the ankle. **2** the part of a stocking or shoe that covers the heel. **3** the part of a shoe or boot that is under the heel or raises the heel: *The heels on these shoes are too high.* **4** anything shaped, used, or placed at an end like a heel, such as an end crust of bread, the rind of cheese, the rear end of a ship's keel, or the lower end of a mast. *noun.*

heel[2] (hēl), lean over to one side: *The sailboat heeled as it turned.* verb.

hedgehog (definition 1)
about 9 inches (23 centimeters) long

helicopter

helmets
above, astronaut's helmet;
right, ancient iron helmet

a hat	i it	oi oil	ch child	a in about
ā age	ī ice	ou out	ng long	e in taken
ä far	o hot	u cup	sh she	ə = i in pencil
e let	ō open	ù put	th thin	o in lemon
ē equal	ô order	ü rule	∓H then	u in circus
ėr term			zh measure	

heif er (hef′ər), a young cow that has not had a calf. *noun.*

height (hīt), **1** how tall a person is; how high anything is; how far up a thing goes: *the height of a mountain. Seven feet is an unusual height for a man.* **2** a fairly great distance up: *rising at a height above the valley.* **3** a high point or place; hill: *on the mountain heights.* **4** the highest part; top. **5** the highest point; greatest degree: *Fast driving on icy roads is the height of folly. noun.*

height en (hīt′n), **1** make or become higher. **2** make or become stronger or greater; increase: *The wind whistling in the trees outside heightened the suspense of the ghost story. verb.*

heir (er *or* ar), person who has the right to somebody's property or title after the death of its owner. *noun.*

heir ess (er′is *or* ar′is), **1** heir who is a woman or girl. **2** woman or girl inheriting great wealth. *noun, plural* **heir ess es.**

heir loom (er′lüm′ *or* ar′lüm′), possession handed down from generation to generation: *This old clock is a family heirloom. noun.*

held (held). See **hold**[1]. *He held the kitten gently. The swing is held by strong ropes. verb.*

hel i cop ter (hel′ə kop′tər), aircraft without wings that is lifted from the ground and kept in the air by horizontal propellers. See picture. *noun.* [*Helicopter* comes from Greek words meaning "wing moving in a spiral."]

hel i port (hel′ə pôrt′), airport for helicopters. Heliports may be built on the tops of buildings. *noun.*

he li um (hē′lē əm), a very light gas that will not burn, much used in balloons and dirigibles. *noun.*

hell (hel), **1** (in Christian and some other religious use) the place where wicked persons are punished after death. **2** any very bad place or condition. *noun.*

he'll (hēl), **1** he will. **2** he shall.

hel lo (he lō′ *or* hə lō′), **1** call of greeting or surprise. We usually say "hello" when we call or answer a call on the telephone. *"Hello, Mother!" the boy said.* **2** a call or shout: *The girl gave a loud hello to let us know where she was.* **1** *interjection,* **2** *noun, plural* **hel los.**

helm (helm), **1** handle or wheel by which a ship is steered. **2** position of control or guidance: *Upon the President's death, the Vice-President took the nation's helm. noun.*

hel met (hel′mit), covering to protect the head. Knights wore helmets as part of their armor. Soldiers wear steel helmets; firemen often wear leather helmets. See picture. *noun.*

help (help), **1** give or do what is needed or useful: *My father helped me with my homework. Help me put* my coat on. **2** act of helping; aid: *I need some help with my work. The dying woman was beyond help.* **3** person or thing that helps: *A sewing machine is a help in making clothes. The storekeeper treats his help well.* **4** make better: *This medicine will help your cough.* **5** means of making better: *The medicine was a help.* **6** avoid; keep from: *I can't help yawning.* 1,4,6 *verb,* 2,3,5 *noun.*

help oneself to, take for or serve oneself: *Help yourself to the milk.*

help ful (help/fəl), giving help; useful. *adjective.*

help ing (hel/ping), portion of food served to a person at one time. *noun.*

help less (help/lis), **1** not able to help oneself: *A little baby is helpless.* **2** without help or protection: *Though he was alone and helpless, he managed to keep the boat from sinking until help arrived.* *adjective.*

hem (hem), **1** border or edge on a garment; edge made by folding over the cloth and sewing it down. **2** fold over and sew down the edge of (cloth): *to hem a skirt.* 1 *noun,* 2 *verb,* **hemmed, hem ming.**

hem in, hem around, or **hem about,** close in or surround, and not let out.

hem i sphere (hem/ə sfir), **1** half of a sphere or globe. **2** half of the earth's surface. North and South America are in the Western Hemisphere; Europe, Asia, and Africa are in the Eastern Hemisphere. All the countries north of the equator are in the Northern Hemisphere; those south of the equator are in the Southern Hemisphere. *noun.*

hem lock (hem/lok), **1** a poisonous plant with spotted stems, finely divided leaves, and small white flowers. **2** poison made from hemlock. **3** an evergreen tree with flat needles, small cones, and reddish bark. Bark from hemlocks is used in tanning. **4** its wood. *noun.*

hemp (hemp), a tall plant of Asia whose tough fibers are made into heavy string, rope, and coarse cloth. *noun.*

hen (hen), **1** a full-grown female chicken. **2** female of other birds: *a hen sparrow. noun.*

hence (hens), **1** therefore: *The king died, and hence his son became king.* **2** from now: *Come back a week hence.* **3** from here: *"Go hence, I pray thee." adverb.*

hence forth (hens/fôrth/), from this time on. *adverb.*

her (hėr), **1** *She* and *her* mean the girl or woman or female animal spoken about. *She is not here. Have you seen her? Find her.* **2** of her; belonging to her; done by her: *She has left her book. The cat won't let you touch her kittens. She has finished her work.* 1 *pronoun,* 2 *adjective.*

her ald (her/əld), **1** person who carries messages and makes announcements: *The king sent a herald to the duke.* **2** bring news of; announce: *The first robin heralded the coming of spring. The newspapers heralded the signing of a peace treaty.* See picture. **3** one that goes before or is sent before and shows something more is coming: *Dawn is the herald of day.* 1,3 *noun,* 2 *verb.*

herb (ėrb *or* hėrb), **1** plant whose leaves and stems are used for medicine and seasoning. Sage, mint, and lavender are herbs. **2** any flowering plant whose stem lives only one season and does not become woody as the stems of trees and shrubs do. Corn, wheat, lettuce, tulips, and peonies are herbs. *noun.*

Her cu les (hėr/kyə lēz/), hero of Greek and Roman mythology famous for his great strength. *noun.*

herd (hėrd), **1** group of animals of one kind, especially large animals, keeping, feeding, or moving together: *a herd of cows, a herd of horses, a herd of elephants.* **2** a large number of people. **3** join together; flock together: *Several people herded under an awning to get out of the rain.* **4** form into a flock, herd, or group: *The farmer herded the cows over to the barn door.* **5** tend or take care of (cattle or sheep). 1,2 *noun,* 3-5 *verb.*

herds man (hėrdz/mən), person who tends a herd. *noun, plural* **herds men.**

here (hir), **1** in this place; at this place: *We live here in the summer. We will stop here.* **2** to this place: *Bring the children here for their lesson.* **3** this place: *Where do we go from here?* **4** now; at this time: *Here the speaker paused.* **5** an answer showing that one is present when roll is called. **6** exclamation used to call attention to a person or thing: *"Here! take away the dishes."* 1,2,4 *adverb,* 3 *noun,* 5,6 *interjection.*

here af ter (hir af/tər), **1** after this; after now; in the future. **2** the life or time after death. 1 *adverb,* 2 *noun.*

here by (hir bī/), by this; by this means: *The license said, "You are hereby given the right to hunt and fish in Dover County." adverb.*

he red i tar y (hə red/ə ter/ē), **1** coming by inheritance: *"Prince" is a hereditary title.* **2** holding a position by inheritance: *The queen of England is a hereditary ruler.* **3** caused by heredity: *Color blindness is hereditary.* **4** coming from one's parents: *a hereditary belief. adjective.*

he red i ty (hə red/ə tē), **1** the passing of physical or mental characteristics from one generation of plants and animals to the next. **2** the characteristics of body and mind that have come to a child from its parents. *noun, plural* **he red i ties.**

here's (hirz), here is.

her e sy (her/ə sē), **1** belief different from the accepted belief of a church or some other group. **2** holding of such a belief. *noun, plural* **her e sies.**

her e tic (her/ə tik), person who holds a belief that is different from the accepted belief of a church or some other group. *noun.*

here to fore (hir/tə fôr/), before this time; until now. *adverb.*

her it age (her/ə tij), what is handed down from one generation to the next; inheritance: *The heritage of freedom is precious to Americans. noun.*

her mit (hėr/mit), person who goes away from others and lives alone. A hermit often lives a religious life. *noun.*

her o (hir′ō), **1** person admired for bravery, great deeds, or noble qualities. **2** the most important male person in a story, play, or poem. *noun, plural* **her oes.**

he ro ic (hi rō′ik), **1** like a hero; very brave; great; noble: *The lifeguard made a heroic rescue.* **2** of or about heroes: *a heroic poem.* **3** unusually daring or bold: *Only heroic measures could save the town from the flood. adjective.*

her o ine (her′ō ən), **1** a girl or woman admired for her bravery, great deeds, or noble qualities. **2** the most important female person in a story, play, or poem. *noun.*

her o ism (her′ō iz′əm), **1** great bravery; daring courage. **2** a very brave act; doing something noble at great cost to oneself. *noun.*

her on (her′ən), a wading bird with a long neck, a long bill, and long legs. See picture. *noun.*

a hat	i it	oi oil	ch child	⌈a in about
ā age	ī ice	ou out	ng long	e in taken
ä far	o hot	u cup	sh she	ə = ⟨ i in pencil
e let	ō open	u̇ put	th thin	o in lemon
ē equal	ô order	ü rule	ᴛʜ then	⌊u in circus
ėr term			zh measure	

herald (definition 2) The trumpets **heralded** the arrival of the king and queen.

heron—about 4 feet (1 meter) tall

her ring (her′ing), a small food fish of the northern Atlantic Ocean. The grown fish are eaten fresh, salted, or smoked, and the young are canned as sardines. *noun, plural* **her rings** or **her ring.**

hers (hėrz), the one or ones belonging to her: *This money is hers. Your answers are wrong; hers are right. pronoun.*

her self (hər self′), **1** *Herself* is used to make a statement stronger. *She herself did it. She herself brought the book.* **2** *Herself* is used instead of *she* or *her* in cases like: *She hurt herself. She did it by herself.* **3** her real or true self: *She is so tired that she's not herself. pronoun.*

he's (hēz), **1** he is. **2** he has.

hes i tant (hez′ə tənt), hesitating; doubtful; undecided: *I was hesitant about accepting the invitation. adjective.*

hes i tate (hez′ə tāt), **1** hold back; feel doubtful; be undecided; show that one has not yet made up one's mind: *I hesitated about taking his side until I knew the whole story.* **2** feel that perhaps one shouldn't; not wish to: *I hesitated to ask you; you were so busy.* **3** stop for an instant; pause: *She hesitated before asking the question.* **4** speak with short stops or pauses; stammer. *verb,* **hes i tat ed, hes i tat ing.**

hes i ta tion (hez′ə tā′shən), **1** act of hesitating; doubt. **2** a slight stopping: *a hesitation in one's speech. noun.*

hew (hyü), **1** cut; chop: *I hewed down the tree.* **2** cut into shape; form by cutting with an ax: *They hewed the logs into beams. verb,* **hewed, hewed** or **hewn** (hyün), **hew ing.**

hey (hā), sound made to attract attention, express surprise or other feeling, or ask a question: *"Hey! stop!" "Hey? what did you say?" interjection.*

hi (hī), a call of greeting; hello. *interjection.*

hi ber nate (hī′bər nāt), spend the winter in sleep, as bears, woodchucks, and some other wild animals do. *verb,* **hi ber nat ed, hi ber nat ing.**

hi ber na tion (hī′bər nā′shən), hibernating. *noun.*

hic cup (hik′up), **1** a sudden, uncontrollable intake of breath with a muffled clicking sound. **2 hiccups,** condition of having one hiccup after another. **3** have the hiccups. **1,2** *noun,* **3** *verb,* **hic cupped, hic cup ping.**

hick or y (hik′ər ē), **1** a North American tree whose nuts are good to eat. **2** its tough, hard wood. *noun, plural* **hick or ies.**

hid (hid). See **hide**[1]. *The dog hid the bone. The money was hid in a safe place. verb.*

hid den (hid′n), **1** put or kept out of sight; secret; not clear: *The story is about hidden treasure.* **2** See **hide**[1]. *The moon was hidden behind a dark cloud.* **1** *adjective,* **2** *verb.*

hideous
The actor was made up as a **hideous** mummy.

hippopotamus—about 13 feet (4 meters) long

hieroglyphic (definition 1)
Egyptian hieroglyphics

A KINGLY

GIFT OF AN

OFFERING TABLE

TO

RA-HORUS

THE GREAT

GOD

LORD OF

HEAVEN

hide¹ (hīd), **1** put out of sight; keep out of sight: *Hide it where no one else can find it.* **2** shut off from sight; be in front of: *Clouds hide the sun.* **3** keep secret: *I hid my joy.* **4** hide oneself: *I'll hide, and you find me. verb,* **hid, hid den** or **hid, hid ing.**

hide² (hīd), an animal's skin, either raw or tanned. *noun.*

hide-and-seek (hīd′n sēk′), a children's game in which one player tries to find the other players who have hidden. *noun.*

hid e ous (hid′ē əs), very ugly; frightful; horrible. See picture. *adjective.*

hi er o glyph ic (hī′ər ə glif′ik), **1** picture, character, or symbol standing for a word, idea, or sound. The ancient Egyptians used hieroglyphics instead of an alphabet like ours. See picture. **2 hieroglyphics,** writing that uses hieroglyphics. *noun.* [*Hieroglyphic* is from a Greek word meaning "written in sacred pictures or symbols."]

high (hī), **1** tall: *a high building. The mountain is over 20,000 feet high.* **2** up above the ground: *a high leap, an airplane high in the air.* **3** up above others: *She is a high government official.* **4** greater, stronger, or better than others; great: *a high price, a high wind.* **5** most important; chief; main: *the high altar.* **6** shrill; sharp: *a high voice.* **7** at or to a high point, place, rank, amount, degree, price, or pitch: *The price of gas has gone too high.* **8** a high point, level, or position: *Food prices reached a new high last month.* **9** arrangement of gears to give the greatest speed. 1-6 *adjective,* 7 *adverb,* 8,9 *noun.*

high and dry, 1 up out of water: *The boat ran ashore, high and dry.* **2** alone; without help.

high jump, contest to determine how high each contestant can jump over a raised crossbar.

high land (hī′lənd), **1** country or region that is higher and hillier than the neighboring country. **2 Highlands,** a hilly region in northern and western Scotland. *noun.*

high ly (hī′lē), **1** in a high degree; very; very much: *highly amusing, highly recommended.* **2** very favorably: *He spoke highly of his best friend.* **3** at a high price: *highly paid. adverb.*

High ness (hī′nis), title of honor given to members of royal families: *The Prince of Wales is addressed as "Your Highness." noun.*

high-rise (hī′rīz′), **1** having many stories; very tall. **2** a building having many stories. 1 *adjective,* 2 *noun.*

high school, school attended after elementary school or junior high school.

high seas, the open ocean. The high seas are outside the authority of any country.

high spirits, cheerfulness; gaiety.

high-strung (hī′strung′), very sensitive; very nervous. *adjective.*

high tide, the time when the ocean comes up highest on the shore.

high way (hī′wā′), a main public road. *noun.*

high way man (hī′wā′mən), man who robs travelers on the public road. *noun, plural* **high way men.**

hi jack (hī′jak′), rob or take by force. *verb.*

hike (hīk), **1** take a long walk; tramp; march. **2** a long walk; tramp or march: *It was a four-mile hike through the forest to the camp.* 1 *verb,* **hiked, hik ing;** 2 *noun.*

hi lar i ous (hə ler′ē əs *or* hə lar′ē əs), very merry; very funny; noisy and cheerful: *a hilarious party.* *adjective.*

hi lar i ty (hə lar′ə tē), loud laughter; noisy cheerfulness. *noun.*

hill (hil), **1** a raised part of the earth's surface, not so big as a mountain. **2** a little heap or pile: *Ants and moles make hills. The soil put over and around the roots of a plant is a hill.* **3** plant with a little heap of soil over and around its roots: *a hill of corn. noun.*

hill side (hil′sīd′), side of a hill. *noun.*

hill top (hil′top′), top of a hill. *noun.*

hill y (hil′ē), having many hills: *hilly country.* *adjective,* **hill i er, hill i est.**

hilt (hilt), handle of a sword or dagger. *noun.*

him (him), *He* and *him* mean the boy or man or male animal spoken about. *Take him home. Give him a drink. Go to him. pronoun.*

him self (him self′), **1** *Himself* is used to make a statement stronger. *He himself did it. Did you see Roy himself?* **2** *Himself* is used instead of *he* or *him* in cases like: *He cut himself. He asked himself what he really wanted. He kept the toy for himself. He cared more for himself than for anybody else.* **3** his real or true self: *He feels like himself again.* *pronoun.*

hind (hīnd), back; rear: *hind legs. adjective.*

hin der (hin′dər), keep back; hold back; get in the way of; make hard to do: *Deep mud hindered travel. verb.*

hin drance (hin′drəns), **1** person or thing that hinders; obstacle: *Heavy clothes are a hindrance to swimming. Noise was a hindrance to our studying.* **2** act of hindering. *noun.*

Hin du (hin′dü), **1** native or inhabitant of India. **2** having to do with the Hindus, their language, or their religion. **3** person who believes in Hinduism. 1,3 *noun, plural* **Hin dus;** 2 *adjective.*

Hin du ism (hin′dü iz′əm), religion and social system of the Hindus. *noun.*

hinge (hinj), **1** joint on which a door, gate, cover, or lid moves back and forth. **2** furnish with hinges; attach by hinges: *The lid is hinged to the box.* **3** depend: *The success of the picnic hinges on the kind of weather we will have.* 1 *noun,* 2,3 *verb,* **hinged, hing ing.**

hint (hint), **1** a slight sign; indirect suggestion: *A small black cloud gave a hint of a coming storm.* **2** suggest slightly; show in an indirect way: *She hinted that she was tired by yawning several times.* 1 *noun,* 2 *verb.*

hip (hip), **1** the part that sticks out on each side of the body below a person's waist where the leg joins the body. **2** a similar part in animals, where the hind leg joins the body. *noun.*

hip po pot a mus (hip′ə pot′ə məs), a huge, thick-skinned, almost hairless animal found in and near the rivers of Africa. It often weighs as much

a hat	i it	oi oil	ch child	a in about
ā age	ī ice	ou out	ng long	e in taken
ä far	o hot	u cup	sh she	ə = i in pencil
e let	ō open	u̇ put	th thin	o in lemon
ē equal	ô order	ü rule	ᴛʜ then	u in circus
ėr term			zh measure	

as four tons. Hippopotamuses feed on plants and can stay under water for a long time. See picture. *noun, plural* **hip po pot a mus es, hip po pot a mi** (hip′ə pot′ə mī). [*Hippopotamus* is from a Greek word meaning "river horse."]

hire (hīr), **1** pay for the use of (a thing) or the work or services of (a person): *She hired a car and a driver. The storekeeper hired me to deliver groceries.* **2** payment for the use of a thing or the work or services of a person: *Are these boats for hire?* 1 *verb,* **hired, hir ing;** 2 *noun.*

his (hiz), **1** of him; belonging to him: *His name is Bill. This is his book.* **2** the one or ones belonging to him: *My books are new; his are old.* 1 *adjective,* 2 *pronoun.*

hiss (his), **1** make a sound like *ss,* or like a drop of water on a hot stove: *Air or steam rushing out of a small opening hisses. Geese and snakes hiss.* **2** a sound like *ss: Hisses were heard from many who disliked what the speaker was saying.* **3** show disapproval of by hissing: *The audience hissed the dull play.* 1,3 *verb,* 2 *noun, plural* **hiss es.**

his to ri an (hi stôr′ē ən), person who writes about history. *noun.*

his to ric (hi stôr′ik), famous or important in history: *Plymouth Rock and Bunker Hill are historic spots. adjective.*

his to ri cal (hi stôr′ə kəl), **1** of history; having something to do with history: *historical documents.* **2** according to history; based on history: *a historical novel.* **3** known to be real or true; in history, not in legend: *It is a historical fact that in 1920 women in the United States were granted the right to vote.* **4** famous in history: *a historical town. adjective.*

his tor y (his′tər ē), **1** story or record of important past events that happened to a person or nation: *the history of the United States.* **2** all past events: *People should learn from the lessons of history.* **3** statement of what has happened. *noun, plural* **his tor ies.**

hit (hit), **1** come against with force; give a blow to; strike: *He hit the ball with a bat. The ball hit against the window. She hit out at the fly buzzing around her head.* **2** blow; stroke: *I drove the stake into the ground with one hit.* **3** come upon; meet with; find: *We hit the right road in the dark. We hit upon a plan for making money.* **4** have a painful effect on; influence in a bad way: *They were hard hit by the failure of their business.* **5** a successful attempt or performance: *The new play is the hit of the season.* **6** a successful hitting of the baseball so that the batter gets at least to first base. 1,3,4 *verb,* **hit, hit ting;** 2,5,6 *noun.*

hit it off, agree; get along well together: *The two friends hit it off from the start.*

hitch (hich), **1** fasten with a hook, ring, rope, or strap: *She hitched her horse to a post.* **2** a fastening; catch: *Our car has a hitch for pulling a trailer.* **3** kind of knot used to fasten a rope to a post or to some other object for a short time. See picture. **4** move or pull with a jerk: *He hitched his chair nearer to the fire.* **5** a short, sudden pull or jerk: *He gave his pants a hitch.* **6** obstacle; stopping: *A hitch in their plans made them miss the train.* 1,4 *verb,* 2,3,5,6 *noun, plural* **hitch es.**

hitch hike (hich′hīk′), travel by walking and getting free rides from passing automobiles or trucks. *verb,* **hitch hiked, hitch hik ing.**

hith er (hiᴛʜ′ər), here; to this place: *Come hither, child. adverb.*

hither and thither, here and there.

hith er to (hiᴛʜ′ər tü′), up to this time; until now: *a fact hitherto unknown. adverb.*

hit ter (hit′ər), person or thing that hits. *noun.*

hive (hīv), **1** house or box for bees to live in. **2** a large number of bees living together: *The whole hive was busy.* **3** a busy place full of people or animals. *noun.*

hives (hīvz), condition in which the skin itches and shows raised patches of red. *noun.*

ho (hō), **1** exclamation of surprise, joy, or scornful laughter. **2** exclamation to get attention: *Ho! Listen to this! interjection.*

hoard (hôrd), **1** save and store away: *The squirrel hoarded nuts for the winter. A miser hoards money.* **2** what is saved and stored away; things stored: *The squirrel kept its hoard of nuts in a tree.* 1 *verb,* 2 *noun.*

hoarse (hôrs), **1** sounding rough and deep: *the hoarse sound of the bullfrog.* **2** having a rough voice: *A bad cold can make you hoarse. adjective,* **hoars er, hoars est.**

hoax (hōks), a mischievous trick, especially a made-up story passed off as true: *The report of an attack on the earth from Mars was a hoax. noun, plural* **hoax es.**

hob ble (hob′əl), **1** walk awkwardly; limp: *The hiker hobbled along with a sprained ankle.* **2** a limping walk. **3** tie the legs of (a horse) together: *He hobbled his horse at night so that it would not wander away.* **4** rope or strap used to hobble an animal. 1,3 *verb,* **hob bled, hob bling;** 2,4 *noun.*

hob by (hob′ē), something a person likes to do as a pastime: *Our teacher's hobby is gardening. noun, plural* **hob bies.** [The earliest meaning of *hobby* was "a small horse" or "a pony." Later, the word was used to mean "a toy horse" or "a hobbyhorse." Still later, it came to mean "any favorite pastime."]

hob by horse (hob′ē hôrs′), stick with a horse's head, used as a child's plaything. See picture. *noun.*

hob gob lin (hob′gob′lən), **1** goblin; elf. **2** ghost. *noun.*

ho bo (hō′bō), person who wanders about and lives by begging or doing odd jobs; tramp. *noun, plural* **ho bos** or **ho boes.**

hock ey (hok′ē), game played by two teams on ice or on a field. The players hit a rubber disk or a ball with curved sticks to drive it across a goal. *noun.*

hodge podge (hoj′poj′), a disorderly mixture; mess; jumble. *noun.*

hoe (hō), **1** tool with a thin blade set across the end of a long handle, used for loosening soil or cutting small weeds. **2** loosen, dig, or cut with a hoe. 1 *noun,* 2 *verb,* **hoed, hoe ing.**

hog (hog), **1** pig. **2** a full-grown pig, raised for food. **3** a selfish, greedy, or dirty person. *noun.*

ho gan (hō′gän′), dwelling used by the Navaho Indians of North America. Hogans are built with logs and covered with earth. See picture. *noun.*

hog gish (hog′ish), **1** like a hog; greedy; very selfish. **2** dirty; filthy. *adjective.*

hoist (hoist), **1** raise on high; lift up, often with ropes and pulleys: *hoist a flag, hoist sails, hoist blocks of stone in building.* **2** hoisting; lift: *She gave me a hoist up the wall.* **3** elevator. 1 *verb,* 2,3 *noun.*

hold[1] (hōld), **1** grasp and keep: *Please hold my hat. Hold my watch while I play this game.* **2** grasp or grip: *Take a good hold of this rope.* **3** thing to hold by: *The face of the cliff had enough holds for a good climber.* **4** keep in some place or position: *Hold the dish level. Hold the paper steady while you draw.* **5** not break, loosen, or give way: *The dike held during the flood.* **6** keep from acting; keep back: *Hold your breath.* **7** keep: *The soldiers held the fort against the enemy.* **8** keep in; contain: *How much water will this cup hold? This theater holds five hundred people.* **9** have: *Shall we hold a meeting of the club? We hold some property in the city. She has held the office of mayor for four years. I hold a high opinion of them.* **10** consider; think: *People once held that the world was flat.* **11** be faithful: *I held to my promise.* **12** be true: *Will this rule hold in all cases?* 1,4-12 *verb,* **held, hold ing;** 2,3 *noun.*

hold on, 1 keep one's hold: *Are you holding on to the railing?* **2** keep on; continue: *The team held on until there was no chance of winning.* **3** stop! *Hold on! Wait until I get my coat.*

hold out, continue; last: *The food will only hold out two days more.*

hold over, keep for future action; postpone: *The bill has been held over until next year.*

hold up, 1 keep from falling; support: *The roof is held up by pillars.* **2** show; display: *He held up the sign so we could all see it.* **3** continue; last; endure: *If this wind holds up, we can go sailing.* **4** stop: *We will hold up our answer to your proposal until we know the cost.* **5** stop by force and rob: *Bandits held up the stagecoach.*

lay hold of, seize; grasp.

hold[2] (hōld), the part inside of a ship or airplane where the cargo is carried. *noun.*

hold er (hōl′dər), **1** person who holds something. An owner or possessor of property is a holder. **2** thing to hold something else with. Pads of cloth are used as holders for lifting hot dishes. *noun.*

hold ing (hōl′ding), land; piece of land: *The government has vast holdings in the West that are used as national parks. noun.*

hold up (hōld′up′), **1** act of stopping by force and robbing. **2** stopping. *noun.*

hole (hōl), **1** an open place: *a hole in a stocking.* **2** a hollow place in something solid: *a hole in the road. Swiss cheese has holes in it. Rabbits dig holes in the ground to live in.* **3** a small, dark, dirty place. **4** a small, round, hollow place on a golf course, into which a golf ball is hit. **5** one of the divisions of a golf course. A regular golf course has 18 holes. *noun.*

hole up, go or put in a hole: *In November the badgers all hole up for the winter.*

hol i day (hol′ə dā), **1** day when one does not work; a day for pleasure and enjoyment: *The Fourth of July is a holiday for everyone.* **2 holidays,** vacation: *We will spend our holidays in the mountains. noun.* [*Holiday* comes from earlier English words meaning "holy day" or "time of a religious festival."]

ho li ness (hō′lē nis), **1** being holy or sacred. **2 Holiness,** title used in speaking to or of the pope: *The pope is addressed as "Your Holiness" and spoken of as "His Holiness." noun.*

hol low (hol′ō), **1** having nothing, or only air, inside; empty; with a hole inside; not solid: *A tube or pipe is hollow. Most rubber balls are hollow.* **2** shaped like a bowl or cup: *a hollow dish for soup.* **3** a hollow place; hole: *a hollow in the road.* **4** bend or dig out to a hollow shape: *She hollowed a whistle out of the piece of wood.* **5** valley: *Sleepy Hollow.* **6** as if coming from something hollow; deep and dull: *the hollow boom of a foghorn. The barrel gave out a hollow sound when I hit it.* **7** deep and sunken: *A starving person has hollow eyes and cheeks.* **8** not real or sincere; false: *hollow promises, hollow joys.* **1,2,6-8** *adjective,* **3,5** *noun,* **4** *verb.*

hol ly (hol′ē), **1** an evergreen tree or shrub with shiny, sharp-pointed green leaves and bright-red berries. **2** its leaves and berries, often used as Christmas decorations. *noun, plural* **hol lies.**

hol ly hock (hol′ē hok), a tall plant with clusters of large, showy flowers of various colors. *noun.*

hol ster (hōl′stər), a leather case for a pistol, attached to a person's belt. A holster for a rifle is attached to a saddle. *noun.*

ho ly (hō′lē), **1** given or belonging to God; set apart for God's service; coming from God; sacred: *the Holy Bible, holy sacraments.* **2** like a saint; spiritually perfect; very good; pure in heart: *a holy man.* **3** worthy of reverence: *Jerusalem is a holy city to Jews, Christians, and Moslems. adjective,* **ho li er, ho li est.**

hom age (hom′ij), **1** respect; reverence; honor: *Everyone paid homage to the great leader.* **2** a pledge of loyalty and service by a vassal to a lord in the Middle Ages. *noun.*

home (hōm), **1** place where a person or family lives; one's own house: *Her home is at 25 South Street.* **2** place where a person was born or brought up; one's own town or country: *His home is Virginia.* **3** place where a thing is specially common: *Alaska is the home of the fur seal.* **4** place where people who are homeless, poor, old, sick,

a hat	i it	oi oil	ch child	⎧ a in about
ā age	ī ice	ou out	ng long	e in taken
ä far	o hot	u cup	sh she	ə = ⎨ i in pencil
e let	ō open	u̇ put	th thin	o in lemon
ē equal	ô order	ü rule	ᴛʜ then	⎩ u in circus
ėr term			zh measure	

hobbyhorse

hitch (definition 3)

hogan

or blind may live: *a nursing home, a home for the aged.* **5** having something to do with one's home or country: *Write me all the home events.* **6** at or to one's home or country: *I want to go home.* **7** goal in many games. **8** to the place where it belongs; to the thing aimed at: *The spear struck home.* **9** to the center; deep in: *drive a nail home.* 1-4,7 *noun,* 5 *adjective,* 6,8,9 *adverb.*

home land (hōm′land′), country that is one's home; native land. *noun.*

home less (hōm′lis), without a home: *a stray, homeless dog. adjective.*

home like (hōm′līk′), like home; friendly; familiar; comfortable. *adjective.*

home ly (hōm′lē), **1** ugly; plain; not good-looking: *a homely face.* **2** suited to home life; simple; everyday: *homely pleasures, homely food. adjective,* **home li er, home li est.**

home made (hōm′mād′), made at home: *homemade bread. adjective.*

home mak er (hōm′mā′kər), person who manages a home and its affairs. *noun.*

home sick (hōm′sik′), overcome by sadness because home is far away; ill with longing for home. *adjective.*

home spun (hōm′spun′), **1** spun or made at home. **2** cloth made of yarn spun at home. **3** plain; simple: *homespun manners.* 1,3 *adjective,* 2 *noun.*

home stead (hōm′sted′), **1** house with its land and other buildings; farm with its buildings. **2** public land granted to a settler under certain conditions by the United States government. *noun.*

home ward (hōm′wərd), toward home: *We turned homeward. The ship is on its homeward course. adverb, adjective.*

home wards (hōm′wərdz), homeward. *adverb.*

home work (hōm′wėrk′), **1** work done at home. **2** lesson to be studied or prepared outside the classroom. *noun.*

hom i ny (hom′ə nē), corn hulled and used whole or coarsely ground. Hominy is eaten boiled. *noun.*

hom o graph (hom′ə graf), word having the same spelling as another word, but a different history and meaning. *Bass* (bas), meaning "a kind of fish," and *bass* (bās), meaning "a male singing voice," are homographs. *noun.*

hom o nym (hom′ə nim), word having the same sound, or the same spelling, or both, as another word. Homonyms have different histories and meanings. *Mail,* meaning "letters," *mail,* meaning "armor," and *male,* meaning "masculine," are homonyms. *noun.*

hom o phone (hom′ə fōn), word having the same sound as another, but a different history and meaning. *Ate* and *eight* are homophones. *noun.*

hon est (on′ist), **1** fair and upright; truthful; not lying, cheating, or stealing: *They are honest people.* **2** obtained by fair means; without lying, cheating, or stealing: *They made an honest profit. He lived an honest life.* **3** not hiding one's real nature; frank; open: *She has an honest face.* **4** not mixed with something of less value; genuine; pure: *Stores should sell honest goods. adjective.*

hon es ty (on′ə stē), honest behavior; honest nature; honest quality: *She shows honesty in all her business affairs. noun.*

hon ey (hun′ē), **1** a thick, sweet, yellow liquid, good to eat, that bees make out of the drops they collect from flowers. **2** something sweet like honey; sweetness. **3** darling; dear. *noun, plural* **hon eys.**

hon ey bee (hun′ē bē′), bee that makes honey. See picture. *noun.*

hon ey comb (hun′ē kōm′), **1** structure of wax made up of rows of six-sided cells. It is made by honeybees to store honey, pollen, and their eggs. See picture. **2** anything like this. **3** like a honeycomb: *a honeycomb pattern in knitting.* **4** make or pierce with many holes or openings: *The old castle was honeycombed with passages.* 1,2 *noun,* 3 *adjective,* 4 *verb.*

hon ey moon (hun′ē mün′), **1** holiday spent together by a newly married couple. **2** spend or have a honeymoon. 1 *noun,* 2 *verb.*

hon ey suck le (hun′ē suk′əl), a climbing shrub with fragrant white, yellow, or red flowers. *noun.*

honk (hongk), **1** the cry of a wild goose. **2** a sound like the cry of a wild goose: *the honk of an automobile horn.* **3** make such a sound: *We honked as we drove past our friends' house.* 1,2 *noun,* 3 *verb.*

hon or (on′ər), **1** credit for acting well; glory or fame; good name: *It was greatly to her honor to be given the scholarship.* **2** honors, special mention given to a student by a school for having done work much above the average. **3** source of credit; person or thing that reflects honor: *It is an honor to be chosen class president.* **4** a sense of what is right or proper; nobility of mind. **5** great respect; high regard: *He was held in honor by all who knew him.* **6** Honor, title of respect used in speaking to a judge, mayor, governor, senator, or similar public official. **7** act that shows respect or high regard: *funeral honors, military honors.* **8** respect highly; think highly of. **9** show respect to: *We honor our country's dead soldiers every year on Memorial Day.* 1-7 *noun,* 8,9 *verb.*

hon or a ble (on′ər ə bəl), **1** having or showing a sense of what is right and proper; honest; upright: *It is not honorable to lie or cheat.* **2** bringing honor or honors to somebody: *honorable wounds.* **3** noble; worthy of honor: *an honorable name, perform honorable deeds.* **4** having a title, rank, or position of honor: *of honorable rank. adjective.*

hon or ar y (on′ə rer′ē), **1** given or done as an honor: *The university awarded honorary degrees to three prominent scientists.* **2** as an honor only; without pay or regular duties: *That association has an honorary secretary as well as a regular paid secretary. adjective.*

hood (hùd), **1** a soft covering for the head and neck, either separate or as part of a coat: *My raincoat has a hood.* **2** anything like a hood in shape or use. **3** a metal covering over the engine of an automobile. **4** cover with a hood. 1-3 *noun,* 4 *verb.*

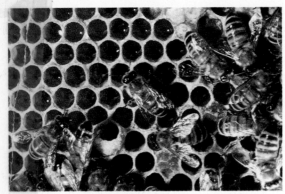

honeybees and honeycomb (definition 1)

hooked
A parrot has
a hooked beak.

a hat	i it	oi oil	ch child	a in about
ā age	ī ice	ou out	ng long	e in taken
ä far	o hot	u cup	sh she	ə = i in pencil
e let	ō open	u̇ put	th thin	o in lemon
ē equal	ô order	ü rule	ŦH then	u in circus
ėr term			zh measure	

a barrel. **2** fasten together with hoops. **3** a large wooden, iron, or plastic ring used as a toy, especially for rolling along the ground by a child. **4** a circular frame formerly used to hold out a woman's skirt. 1,2,4 *noun,* 3 *verb.*

hoot (hüt), **1** sound that an owl makes. **2** make this sound or one like it. **3** shout to show disapproval or scorn. **4** make such a shout. **5** show disapproval of, or scorn for, by hooting: *The audience hooted the speaker's plan.* **6** force or drive by hooting: *The plan was so foolish that the audience hooted the speaker off the platform.* 1,3 *noun,* 2,4-6 *verb.*

hooves (hüvz), more than one hoof. *noun plural.*

hop¹ (hop), **1** spring, or move by springing, on one foot: *How far can you hop on your right foot?* **2** spring, or move by springing, with both or all feet at once: *Many birds hop. A kangaroo hops.* **3** jump over: *hop a ditch.* **4** hopping; spring. 1-3 *verb,* **hopped, hop ping;** 4 *noun.*

hop² (hop), **1** vine having flower clusters that look like small, yellow pine cones. **2 hops,** the dried ripe flower clusters of the hop vine, used to flavor beer and other malt drinks. *noun.*

hope (hōp), **1** a feeling that what you desire will happen: *Her encouragement gave me hope.* **2** wish and expect: *I hope to do well in school this year.* **3** thing hoped for. **4** cause of hope: *You are our only hope for winning the race.* 1,3,4 *noun,* 2 *verb,* **hoped, hop ing.**

hope ful (hōp′fəl), **1** feeling or showing hope; expecting to receive what one wants. **2** causing hope; giving hope; likely to succeed. *adjective.*

hope less (hōp′lis), **1** feeling no hope: *Our attempts to get help failed so often that we became hopeless.* **2** giving no hope: *a hopeless illness. adjective.*

hop per (hop′ər), **1** grasshopper or other hopping insect. **2** container to hold something and feed it into another part. A hopper is usually larger at the top than at the bottom. *noun.*

hop scotch (hop′skoch′), a children's game in which the players hop over the lines of a figure drawn on the ground. *noun.*

horde (hôrd), multitude; crowd; swarm: *hordes of grasshoppers. noun.*

ho ri zon (hə rī′zn), **1** line where earth and sky seem to meet. You cannot see beyond the horizon. **2** limit of one's thinking, experience, interest, or outlook. *noun.*

ho ri zon tal (hôr′ə zon′tl), **1** parallel to the horizon; at right angles to a vertical line. **2** flat; level. *adjective.*

hor mone (hôr′mōn), substance formed in certain glands, which enters the bloodstream and affects or controls the activity of some organ or tissue. *noun.*

hood ed (hud′id), **1** having a hood. **2** shaped like a hood. *adjective.*

hood lum (hud′ləm), **1** criminal or gangster. **2** a young rowdy. *noun.*

hoof (huf), **1** a hard, horny covering on the feet of horses, cattle, sheep, pigs, and some other animals. **2** the whole foot of such animals. *noun, plural* **hoofs** or **hooves.**

hoofed (huft), having hoofs. *adjective.*

hook (huk), **1** piece of metal, wood, or other stiff material, curved or having a sharp angle, for catching hold of something or for hanging things on. **2** fasten with hooks: *Will you hook my dress for me?* **3** catch or take hold of with a hook. **4** a curved piece of wire, usually with a barb at the end, for catching fish. **5** catch (fish) with a hook. **6** anything curved or bent like a hook. **7** a sharp bend: *a hook in a river.* 1,4,6,7 *noun,* 2,3,5 *verb.*
by hook or by crook, in any way at all; by fair means or foul.

hooked (hukt), curved or bent like a hook. See picture. *adjective.*

hoop (hup *or* hüp), **1** ring or flat band in the form of a circle: *a hoop for holding together the staves of*

horror (definition 1)—a mask with a look of horror

horn (definition 5)—a man pouring gunpowder from a horn into a rifle during the Revolutionary War

horned toad—about 4 inches (10 centimeters) long

horn (hôrn), **1** a hard, hollow growth on the heads of cattle, sheep, goats, and some other animals that is usually curved and pointed. **2** one of a pair of solid, branching growths on the head of a deer, elk, or moose; antler. **3** anything that sticks up on the head of an animal: *a snail's horns, an insect's horns.* **4** the substance or material of horns. A person's fingernails, the beaks of birds, the hoofs of horses, and tortoise shells are all made of horn. **5** container made by hollowing out a horn. It was used to drink out of or to carry gunpowder in. See picture. **6** a musical instrument sounded by blowing into the smaller end. It was once made of horn, but now it is made of brass or other metal. **7** device sounded as a warning signal: *an automobile horn.* **8** anything that sticks out like a horn or is shaped like a horn: *a saddle horn, the horn of a bay. noun.*

horned (hôrnd), having a horn, horns, or hornlike growths. *adjective.*

horned toad, a small lizard with a broad, flat body, short tail, and many hornlike spines. See picture.

hor net (hôr′nit), a large wasp that can give a very painful sting. *noun.*

horn y (hôr′nē), **1** made of horn or a substance like it. **2** hard like horn: *A farmer's hands are horny from work. adjective,* **horn i er, horn i est.**

ho ro scope (hôr′ə skōp), **1** diagram used in telling fortunes by the planets and the stars. **2** fortune told by using such a diagram. *noun.*

hor ri ble (hôr′ə bəl), **1** causing horror; frightful; shocking: *a horrible crime, a horrible disease.* **2** extremely unpleasant: *a horrible smell. adjective.*

hor rid (hôr′id), **1** causing great fear; frightful. **2** very unpleasant: *a horrid day. adjective.*

hor ri fy (hôr′ə fī), **1** cause to feel horror. **2** shock very much: *We were horrified by the wreck. verb,* **hor ri fied, hor ri fy ing.**

hor ror (hôr′ər), **1** a shivering, shaking terror. See picture. **2** very strong dislike: *I have a horror of guns.* **3** thing that causes great fear. *noun.*

horse (hôrs), **1** a four-legged animal with hoofs and flowing mane and tail. Horses have been used from very early times to pull loads and carry riders. **2** a supporting frame with legs: *Five boards laid on two horses made our picnic table.* **3 horse around,** fool around; get into mischief. 1,2 *noun,* 3 *verb,* **horsed, hors ing.**

horse of a different color, something different.

horse back (hôrs′bak′), **1** the back of a horse. **2** on the back of a horse: *to ride horseback.* 1 *noun,* 2 *adverb.*

horse fly (hôrs′flī′), a large fly that bites animals, especially horses. *noun, plural* **horse flies.**

horse hair (hôrs′her′ or hôrs′har′), **1** hair from the mane or tail of a horse. **2** made of horsehair; stuffed with horsehair. 1 *noun,* 2 *adjective.*

horse man (hôrs′mən), **1** man who rides on horseback. **2** man who is skilled in riding or managing horses. *noun, plural* **horse men.**

horse play (hôrs′plā′), rough, boisterous fun. *noun.*

horse pow er (hôrs/pou/ər), measure of the power of an engine. One horsepower is the power to lift 550 pounds one foot in one second. *noun.*

horse shoe (hôrs/shü/), **1** a metal plate shaped like a U, nailed to a horse's hoof to protect it. **2** thing shaped like a horseshoe. *noun.*

horse wom an (hôrs/wüm/ən), **1** woman who rides on horseback. **2** woman who is skilled in riding or managing horses. *noun, plural* **horse wom en.**

hose (hōz), **1** tube of rubber or something else that will bend, for carrying any liquid for short distances. A hose is used in pumping gasoline into automobiles. **2** stockings. *noun, plural* **hos es** for 1, **hose** for 2.

ho sier y (hō/zhər ē), stockings. *noun.*

hos pi ta ble (hos/pi tə bəl *or* ho spit/ə bəl), **1** giving or liking to give a welcome, food and shelter, and friendly treatment to guests or strangers: *a hospitable family, a hospitable reception.* **2** willing and ready to entertain: *a person hospitable to new ideas. adjective.*

hos pi ta bly (hos/pi tə blē *or* ho spit/ə blē), in a hospitable manner. *adverb.*

hos pi tal (hos/pi təl), place for the care of the sick or injured. *noun.* [Earlier meanings of *hospital* were "hostel" or "hotel," operated by a "host." *Hospital, hostel,* and *hotel* all come from a Latin word meaning "host[1]."]

hos pi tal i ty (hos/pə tal/ə tē), friendly reception; generous treatment of guests or strangers. *noun, plural* **hos pi tal i ties.**

hos pi tal ize (hos/pi tə līz), put in a hospital for treatment. *verb,* **hos pi tal ized, hos pi tal iz ing.**

host[1] (hōst), person who receives another person as a guest. *noun.*

host[2] (hōst), a large number: *As it grew dark, a few stars appeared, then a host. noun.*

hos tage (hos/tij), **1** person given up to another or held by an enemy as a pledge: *The hostage will be kept safe and will be returned when our enemies' promises have been carried out.* **2** pledge; security. *noun.*

hos tel (hos/tl), a lodging place, especially a supervised lodging place for young people on bicycle or motorcycle trips or hikes; inn. *noun.*

host ess (hō/stis), **1** woman who receives another person as her guest. **2** woman employed in a restaurant or on an airplane to welcome and serve people. *noun, plural* **host ess es.**

hos tile (hos/tl), **1** of an enemy or enemies: *the hostile army.* **2** opposed; unfriendly; unfavorable: *a hostile look. adjective.*

hos til i ty (ho stil/ə tē), **1** the feeling that an enemy has; being an enemy; unfriendliness: *They showed signs of hostility toward our plan.* **2** hostilities, acts of war; warfare; fighting: *The peace treaty brought hostilities to an end. noun, plural* **hos til i ties.**

hos tler (os/lər *or* hos/lər), person who takes care of horses at an inn or stable. *noun.*

hot (hot), **1** much warmer than the body; having much heat: *That fire is hot. The sun is hot today.*

a hat	i it	oi oil	ch child	(a in about
ā age	ī ice	ou out	ng long	e in taken
ä far	o hot	u cup	sh she	ə = i in pencil
e let	ō open	ů put	th thin	o in lemon
ē equal	ô order	ü rule	₮H then	u in circus
ėr term			zh measure	

That long run has made me hot. **2** having a sharp, burning taste: *Pepper and mustard are hot.* **3** fiery: *a hot temper, hot with rage.* **4** new; fresh: *a hot scent, a hot trail.* **5** following closely: *We were in hot pursuit of the runaway horse. adjective,* **hot ter, hot test.**

hot dog, 1 sandwich made with a hot frankfurter enclosed in a bun. **2** frankfurter.

ho tel (hō tel/), house or large building that supplies rooms and food for pay to travelers and others. *noun.*

hot house (hot/hous/), building with a glass roof and sides, kept warm for growing plants; greenhouse. *noun, plural* **hot hous es** (hot/hou/ziz).

hound (hound), **1** dog of any of various breeds, most of which hunt by scent and have large, drooping ears and short hair. **2** any dog. **3** urge on: *The children hounded their parents to buy a color TV.* **1,2** *noun,* **3** *verb.*

hour (our), **1** one of the 12 equal periods of time between noon and midnight, or between midnight and noon. 60 minutes make an hour. 24 hours make a day. **2** the time of day: *This clock strikes the hours and the half hours.* **3** the time for anything: *Our breakfast hour is at eight.* **4 hours,** time for work or study: *What are the hours in this office? Our school hours are 9 to 12 and 1 to 4. noun.*

hour glass (our/glas/), device for measuring time, made up of two glass bulbs connected by a narrow neck. It takes an hour for sand in the top bulb to pass through the neck to the bottom bulb. See picture. *noun, plural* **hour glass es.**

hourglass

hour ly (our/lē), **1** done, happening, or counted every hour: *There are hourly reports of the news and weather on this radio station.* **2** every hour: *Give two doses of the medicine hourly.* **3** coming very often; frequent: *hourly messages.* **4** very often; frequently: *Messages were coming from the front hourly.* **1,3** *adjective,* **2,4** *adverb.*

house (hous *for 1-4, 6-8;* houz *for 5*), **1** building in which people live. **2** people living in a house; household. **3** family with its ancestors and descendants, especially a noble family: *He was a prince of the house of David.* **4** building for any purpose: *an engine house.* **5** take or put into a house; shelter: *Where can we house all these children?* **6** place of business or a business firm: *a publishing house.* **7** assembly for making laws. In the United States, the House of Representatives is the lower house of Congress; the Senate is the upper house. **8** audience: *The singer sang to a large house.* 1-4,6-8 *noun, plural* **hous es** (hou′ziz); 5 *verb,* **housed, hous ing.**

house boat (hous′bōt′), boat that can be used as a place to live in. *noun.*

house fly (hous′flī′), a two-winged fly that lives around and in houses, feeding on food, garbage, and filth. *noun, plural* **house flies.**

house hold (hous′hōld), **1** all the people living in a house; family; family and servants. **2** a home and its affairs. **3** of a household; having to do with a household; domestic: *household expenses, household chores.* 1,2 *noun,* 3 *adjective.*

house keep er (hous′kē′pər), woman who is hired to manage a home and its affairs and to do the housework. *noun.*

house keep ing (hous′kē′ping), management of a home and its affairs; doing the housework. *noun.*

house wife (hous′wīf′), woman who manages a home and its affairs for her family. *noun, plural* **house wives** (hous′wīvz′).

house work (hous′wėrk′), work to be done in housekeeping, such as washing, ironing, cleaning, or cooking. *noun.*

hous ing (hou′zing), **1** sheltering; providing shelter. **2** houses: *There is not enough housing in that city for the number of people living there. noun.*

hov el (huv′əl), house that is small, crude, and unpleasant to live in. *noun.*

hov er (huv′ər), **1** stay in or near one place in the air: *The two birds hovered over their nest.* **2** stay in or near one place; wait nearby: *The dogs hovered around the kitchen door at mealtime.* **3** be in an uncertain condition; waver: *The patient hovered between life and death. verb.*

how (hou), **1** in what way; by what means: *How can it be done? How did it happen? I wonder how you get there.* **2** to what degree or amount: *How tall is she? How hot is it? How much shall I bring you? How long will it take you to do this?* **3** in what state or condition: *How is your health? Tell me how she is. How do I look?* **4** for what reason; why: *How is it you are late?* 1-4 *adverb,* 1,3 *conjunction.*

how ev er (hou ev′ər), **1** nevertheless; yet; in spite of that: *We were very late for dinner; however, there was plenty left for us.* **2** to whatever degree or amount; no matter how: *I'll come however busy I am.* **3** in whatever way; by whatever means: *However did you get so dirty?* 1 *conjunction,* 2,3 *adverb.*

howl (houl), **1** give a long, loud, mournful cry: *Our*

dog often howls at night. The winter winds howled around our cabin.* **2** a long, loud, mournful cry: *the howl of a wolf.* **3** give a long, loud cry of pain or rage. **4** a loud cry of pain or rage. **5** a yell or shout: *We heard howls of laughter.* **6** yell or shout: *It was so funny that we howled with laughter.* **7** force or drive by howling: *The angry mob howled the speaker off the platform.* 1,3,6,7 *verb,* 2,4,5 *noun.*

hr., hour or hours.

hub (hub), **1** the central part of a wheel. **2** center of interest, importance, or activity: *London is the hub of English life. noun.*

hub bub (hub′ub), loud, confused noise; uproar: *There was a hubbub in the crowded street. noun.*

huck le ber ry (huk′əl ber′ē), a small berry that grows on a shrub. Huckleberries are like blueberries, but are darker in color. *noun, plural* **huck le ber ries.**

hud dle (hud′l), **1** crowd close: *The sheep huddled together in a corner.* **2** put close together: *She huddled all four boys into one bed.* **3** a grouping of football players to discuss the next play and to receive signals. 1,2 *verb,* **hud dled, hud dling;** 3 *noun.*

hue (hyü), color; shade; tint: *all the hues of the rainbow, silk of a pinkish hue. noun.*

huff (huf), **1** fit of anger: *We had a heated argument, and she left in a huff.* **2** puff; blow: *I huffed and puffed up the stairs with the heavy package.* 1 *noun,* 2 *verb.*

hug (hug), **1** put the arms around and hold close: *The girl hugged her new puppy.* **2** a tight clasp with the arms: *She gave the puppy a hug.* **3** keep close to: *The boat hugged the shore.* 1,3 *verb,* **hugged, hug ging;** 2 *noun.*

huge (hyüj), very, very large: *A whale or an elephant is a huge animal. adjective,* **hug er, hug est.**

hulk (hulk), **1** body of an old or worn-out ship. **2** a big, clumsy ship. **3** a big, clumsy person or thing: *That hulk of a ladder is hard to manage; we need a smaller and lighter one. noun.*

hulk ing (hul′king), big and clumsy: *a large, hulking boy. adjective.*

hull (hul), **1** body or frame of a ship. Masts, sails, and rigging are not part of the hull. **2** the outer covering of a seed. **3** calyx of some fruits. We call the green leaves at the stem of a strawberry its hull. **4** remove the hull or hulls from. 1-3 *noun,* 4 *verb.*

hum (hum), **1** make a continuous, murmuring sound like that of a bee or of a spinning top: *The sewing machine hums busily.* **2** a continuous, murmuring sound: *the hum of bees, the hum of the city streets.* **3** sing with closed lips, not sounding words: *She was humming a tune.* **4** put or bring by humming: *Father hummed the baby to sleep.* **5** be busy and active: *Things really hummed at campaign headquarters just before the election.* 1,3-5 *verb,* **hummed, hum ming;** 2 *noun.*

hu man (hyü′mən), **1** of persons; that people have: *Kindness is a human trait. To know what will happen in the future is beyond human power.* **2** of or having the form or qualities of people: *Men, women, and children are human beings. Those monkeys seem almost human.* **3** person; human being. 1,2 *adjective,* 3 *noun.* [*Human* comes from a Latin word meaning "of man" or "of human beings."]

hu mane (hyü mān′), kind; not cruel or brutal: *I believe in the humane treatment of animals.* adjective.

hu man i ty (hyü man′ə tē), **1** people: *All humanity will be helped by advances in medical science.* **2** the nature of human beings: *Humanity is a mixture of good and bad qualities.* **3** kindness: *Treat animals with humanity.* noun, plural **hu man i ties.**

hum ble (hum′bəl), **1** low in position or condition; not important; not grand: *He has a humble job with very low wages. They lived in a humble cottage of one room.* **2** modest; not proud: *a humble opinion, to be humble in spite of success.* **3** make humble; make lower in position, condition, or pride: *to be humbled by defeat.* 1,2 *adjective,* **hum bler, hum blest;** 3 *verb,* **hum bled, hum bling.**

hum bly (hum′blē), in a humble manner. adverb.

hum bug (hum′bug′), **1** person who pretends to be what he is not; cheat; sham. **2** nonsense or pretense: *There's no humbug about him; he speaks his mind straight out.* **3** cheat; deceive with a sham: *I won't be humbugged into buying something I don't want.* 1,2 *noun,* 3 *verb,* **hum bugged, hum bug ging.**

hu mid (hyü′mid), moist; damp: *We found that the air was very humid near the sea.* adjective.

hu mid i ty (hyü mid′ə tē), **1** moistness; dampness: *The humidity today is worse than the heat.* **2** amount of moisture in the air: *On a hot, sultry day the humidity is high.* noun.

hu mil i ate (hyü mil′ē āt), lower the pride, dignity, or self-respect of: *We felt humiliated by our failure. They humiliated me by criticizing me in front of my friends.* verb, **hu mil i at ed, hu mil i at ing.**

hu mil i a tion (hyü mil′ē ā′shən), a lowering of pride, dignity, or self-respect. noun.

hu mil i ty (hyü mil′ə tē), humbleness of mind; lack of pride; meekness. noun, plural **hu mil i ties.**

hum ming bird (hum′ing bėrd′), a very small, brightly colored American bird with a long, narrow bill and narrow wings that move so rapidly they make a humming sound in the air. See picture. noun.

hummingbird—about 4 inches (10 centimeters) long

hu mor (hyü′mər), **1** funny or amusing quality: *I see no humor in your tricks.* **2** ability to see or show the funny or amusing side of things: *Her sense of humor enabled her to joke about her problems.* **3** state of mind; mood; temper: *Is the teacher in a good humor this morning? I feel in the humor for working.* **4** give in to the fancies and whims of (a person); agree with: *to humor a sick child.* 1-3 *noun,* 4 *verb.*

out of humor, cross; in a bad mood.

hu mor ist (hyü′mər ist), a humorous talker; writer of jokes and funny stories. noun.

hu mor ous (hyü′mər əs), full of humor; funny; amusing: *We all laughed at the humorous story.* adjective.

hump (hump), **1** a rounded lump that sticks out: *Some camels have two humps on their backs.* **2** raise or bend up into a lump: *The cat humped its back when it saw the dog.* **3** mound. 1,3 *noun,* 2 *verb.*

hump backed (hump′bakt′), hunchbacked. adjective.

hu mus (hyü′məs), soil made from dead leaves and other vegetable matter, containing valuable plant foods. noun.

hunch (hunch), **1** a hump. **2** to hump: *hunch one's shoulders.* **3** draw, bend, or form into a hump: *He sat hunched up with his chin on his knees.* **4** feeling or suspicion that you don't know the reason for: *I had a hunch it would rain, so I took my umbrella.* 1,4 *noun,* plural **hunch es;** 2,3 *verb.*

hunch back (hunch′bak′), person whose back has a hump on it. noun.

hunch backed (hunch′bakt′), having a hump on the back. adjective.

hun dred (hun′drəd), ten times ten; 100. There are one hundred cents in a dollar. noun, adjective.

hun dredth (hun′drədth), **1** next after the 99th. **2** one of 100 equal parts. adjective, noun.

hung (hung). See **hang.** *He hung up his cap. Your dress has hung here all day.* verb.

hun ger (hung′gər), **1** pains in the stomach caused by having had nothing to eat. **2** desire or need for food: *I ate an apple to satisfy my hunger.* **3** feel hunger; be hungry. **4** strong desire: *The bright boy had a hunger for knowledge.* **5** have a strong desire: *to hunger for affection, to hunger for friends.* 1,2,4 *noun,* 3,5 *verb.*

hun gri ly (hung′grə lē), in a hungry manner. adverb.

hun gry (hung′grē), **1** feeling a desire or need for food: *I missed breakfast and was hungry all morning.* **2** showing hunger: *The stray cat had a hungry look.* **3** eager: *A person who longs to read and study is hungry for knowledge.* adjective, **hun gri er, hun gri est.**

hunk (hungk), a big lump or piece. noun.

hunt (hunt), **1** chase (game and other wild animals) for food or for fun. **2** act of hunting: *The hunt drew many spectators.* **3** search; seek; look: *hunt for a lost book.* **4** a search; attempt to find something: *The hunt for the lost child continued until she was found.* 1,3 *verb,* 2,4 *noun.*

hunt er (hun′tər), **1** person who hunts. **2** horse or dog trained for hunting. *noun.*

hunts man (hunts′mən), **1** hunter. **2** manager of a hunt. *noun, plural* **hunts men.**

hur dle (hėr′dl), **1** barrier for people or horses to jump over in a race. **2** **hurdles,** race in which the runners jump over hurdles. See picture. **3** jump over: *The horse hurdled both the fence and the ditch.* **4** obstacle or difficulty. **5** overcome (an obstacle or difficulty). 1,2,4 *noun,* 3,5 *verb,* **hur dled, hur dling.**

hurdle (definition 2)—The hurdles is one event in track-and-field competition.

hurl (hėrl), throw with much force; fling: *hurl a spear, hurl rocks. verb.*

hur rah (hə rä′), **1** shout of joy or approval: *Give a hurrah for the team!* **2** shout hurrahs; cheer: *We hurrahed as the congresswoman rode by in the parade.* 1 *interjection, noun,* 2 *verb.*

hur ray (hə rā′), hurrah. *interjection, noun, verb.*

hur ri cane (hėr′ə kān), storm with violent wind and, usually, very heavy rain. The wind in a hurricane blows at more than 75 miles per hour. *noun.*

hur ried (hėr′ēd), done or made in a hurry; hasty: *a hurried escape, a hurried reply. adjective.*

hur ry (hėr′ē), **1** move, drive, carry, or send quickly: *They hurried the sick child to the doctor.* **2** move or act with more than an easy or natural speed: *If you hurry, your work may be poor. She hurried to get to work on time.* **3** a hurried movement or action: *In his hurry he dropped the bag of groceries.* **4** eagerness to have quickly or do quickly: *She was in a hurry to meet her friends.* **5** urge to act soon or too soon: *The salesman hurried the customer to make a choice.* **6** urge to great speed or to too great speed: *Don't hurry the driver.* 1,2,5,6 *verb,* **hur ried, hur ry ing;** 3,4 *noun.*

hurt (hėrt), **1** cause pain or injury to: *The stone hurt my foot.* **2** a cut, bruise, or fracture; any wound or injury: *A scratch is not a serious hurt.* **3** suffer pain: *My hand hurts.* **4** have a bad effect on; do damage or harm to: *Large price increases can hurt sales. Did I hurt your feelings?* 1,3,4 *verb,* **hurt, hurt ing;** 2 *noun.*

hurt ful (hėrt′fəl), causing hurt, harm, or damage: *a mean and hurtful remark. adjective.*

hus band (huz′bənd), **1** man who has a wife; married man. **2** manage carefully; be saving of: *She carefully husbanded the money she inherited.* 1 *noun,* 2 *verb.* [*Husband* comes from an old Norse word meaning "one who dwells in a house" or "master of a house."]

hush (hush), **1** stop making a noise; make or become silent or quiet: *The wind has hushed. Hush your dog.* **2** stopping of noise; stillness. **3** stop the noise! be silent! 1 *verb,* 2 *noun,* 3 *interjection.*

husk (husk), **1** the dry outer covering of certain seeds or fruits. An ear of corn has a husk. **2** the dry or worthless outer covering of anything. **3** remove the husk from: *Husk the corn before cooking it.* 1,2 *noun,* 3 *verb.*

husk i ness (hus′kē nis), **1** hoarseness or roughness of voice. **2** being big and strong. *noun.*

husk y[1] (hus′kē), **1** big and strong: *a husky young man.* **2** dry in the throat; hoarse; rough of voice: *A cold can cause a husky cough. adjective,* **husk i er, husk i est.**

hus ky[2] or **Hus ky** (hus′kē), a strong, broad-chested dog, used in arctic regions for pulling sleds. See picture. *noun.*

hus tle (hus′əl), **1** hurry: *Mother hustled the baby to bed.* **2** rush roughly; push one's way: *hustle along through the crowd.* **3** push or shove roughly: *Guards hustled the demonstrators away from the mayor's office.* **4** go or work quickly or with energy: *He had to hustle to earn enough money to support his large family.* **5** hustling: *It was done with much hustle and bustle. It was a hustle to get the dishes washed by seven o'clock.* 1-4 *verb,* **hus tled, hus tling;** 5 *noun.*

hut (hut), a small, roughly made cabin: *The children built a hut in the woods. noun.*

hutch (huch), a box or pen for small animals. Rabbits are kept in hutches. *noun, plural* **hutch es.**

hy a cinth (hī′ə sinth), a spring plant that grows from a bulb and has a spike of small, fragrant, bell-shaped flowers. *noun.*

hy brid (hī′brid), **1** offspring of two animals or plants of different races, varieties, or species. The loganberry is a hybrid because it is a cross between a raspberry and a blackberry. **2** bred from two different races, varieties, or species: *A mule is a hybrid animal.* **3** thing of mixed origin: *A word formed of parts from different languages is a hybrid.* **4** of mixed origin. 1,3 *noun,* 2,4 *adjective.*

hy drant (hī′drənt), a large, upright pipe with a valve for drawing water directly from a water main; hose connection. Hydrants are used to get water to put out fires and to wash the streets. *noun.*

a hat	i it	oi oil	ch child	a in about
ā age	ī ice	ou out	ng long	e in taken
ä far	o hot	u cup	sh she	ə = i in pencil
e let	ō open	u̇ put	th thin	o in lemon
ē equal	ô order	ü rule	ŦH then	u in circus
ėr term			zh measure	

hyena—about 2 feet (60 centimeters) high at the shoulder

husky²—about 23 inches (58 centimeters) high at the shoulder

hy dro e lec tric (hī′drō i lek′trik), developing electricity from water power. *adjective.*

hy dro gen (hī′drə jən), a colorless gas that burns easily. Hydrogen weighs less than any other known substance. It combines with oxygen to form water. *noun.*

hydrogen bomb, bomb in which the combining of atomic nuclei results in an explosion of tremendous force; H-bomb. It is many times more powerful than the atomic bomb.

hy dro pho bi a (hī′drə fō′bē ə), the disease a mad dog has; rabies. If bitten by a mad dog, a person may get the disease. *noun.* [*Hydrophobia* comes from a Greek word meaning "fear or dislike of water." The disease was called this because a person or an animal who has it is not able to swallow water.]

hy e na (hī ē′nə), a wild animal of Africa and Asia, much like a large dog in shape and size. Hyenas have a call that sounds like hysterical laughter. See picture. *noun.*

hy giene (hī′jēn′), rules of health; science of keeping well. *noun.*

hymn (him), **1** song in praise or honor of God. **2** any song of praise. *noun.*

hym nal (him′nəl), book of hymns. *noun.*

hy phen (hī′fən), mark (-) used to join the parts of a compound word, or the parts of a word divided at the end of a line. *noun.*

hy phen ate (hī′fə nāt), join by a hyphen; write or print with a hyphen. *verb,* **hy phen at ed, hy phen at ing.**

hyp no tism (hip′nə tiz′əm), hypnotizing; putting into a sleeplike state. *noun.*

hyp no tist (hip′nə tist), person who hypnotizes. *noun.*

hyp no tize (hip′nə tīz), put (a person) into a state similar to sleep, but more active. A hypnotized person tends to follow the spoken suggestions of the hypnotist and may feel no pain or other kinds of stimulation. See picture. *verb,* **hyp no tized, hyp no tiz ing.**

hy poc ri sy (hi pok′rə sē), **1** pretending to be very good or religious. **2** pretending to be what one is not; pretense. *noun, plural* **hy poc ri sies.**

hyp o crite (hip′ə krit), **1** person who pretends to be very good or religious. **2** person who is not sincere; pretender. *noun.*

hys ter i a (hi stir′ē ə *or* hi ster′ē ə), **1** a mental illness caused by worry or anxiety. Its signs may include blindness, paralysis, or stomach upsets. **2** unchecked excitement or emotion. *noun.*

hys ter i cal (hi ster′ə kəl), **1** unnaturally excited: *hysterical weeping.* **2** showing extreme lack of control; suffering from hysteria: *The hysterical child was unable to stop crying. adjective.*

I i

iceberg—The part of an iceberg under water is about eight times bigger than the part above water.

iceboat

icebreaker—an icebreaker in the Arctic Ocean

I[1] or **i** (ī), the ninth letter of the English alphabet. There are two *i*'s in *Indian. noun, plural* **I's** or **i's**.

I[2] (ī), the person who is speaking or writing: *John said, "I am ten years old." I like my dog, and he likes me. pronoun, plural* **we**.

-ible, suffix meaning that can be _____ed: A divis*ible* fraction means a fraction *that can be* divid*ed*.

ice (īs), **1** water made solid by cold; frozen water. **2** of ice; having something to do with ice: *an ice pack, ice cubes.* **3** make cool with ice; put ice in or around: *We iced the fruit punch for the party.* **4** a frozen dessert, usually one made of sweetened fruit juice. **5** cover (cake) with icing. 1,4 *noun,* 2 *adjective,* 3,5 *verb,* **iced, ic ing**.

ice berg (īs/berg/), a large mass of ice floating in the sea. A ship may be wrecked on an iceberg. See picture. *noun.*

ice boat (īs/bōt/), a triangular frame on runners, fitted with sails or an engine for sailing on ice. See picture. *noun.*

ice bound (īs/bound/), held fast by ice; frozen in: *an icebound boat. adjective.*

ice box (īs/boks/), **1** refrigerator. **2** box in which food is kept cool with ice. *noun, plural* **ice box es**.

ice break er (īs/brā/kər), a strong boat used to break a channel through ice. See picture. *noun.*

ice cap (īs/kap/), a permanent covering of ice over an area, sloping down on all sides from a high center. *noun.*

ice cream, a smooth, frozen dessert made of cream or milk, sweetened and flavored.

i ci cle (ī/si kəl), a pointed, hanging stick of ice formed by the freezing of dripping water. *noun.*

i ci ly (ī/sə lē), very coldly. *adverb.*

ic ing (ī/sing), mixture of sugar with egg whites or other things, used to cover cakes; frosting. *noun.*

i cy (ī/sē), **1** like ice; very cold: *icy fingers.* **2** covered with ice; slippery: *The car skidded on the icy street.* **3** of ice: *an icy snowball.* **4** without warm feeling; cold and unfriendly: *She gave me an icy stare. adjective,* **i ci er, i ci est**.

I'd (īd), **1** I should. **2** I would. **3** I had.

I da ho (ī/də hō), one of the western states of the United States. *noun.* [*Idaho* may have come from the Kiowa Apache name for the Comanche Indians.]

i de a (ī dē/ə), **1** belief, plan, or picture in the mind: *Swimming is her idea of fun.* **2** thought; fancy; opinion: *I had no idea that the job would be so hard. noun.*

i de al (ī dē/əl), **1** a perfect type; model to be imitated: *Her mother is her ideal. Religion holds up high ideals for us to follow.* **2** perfect; just as one would wish: *A warm, sunny day is ideal for a picnic.* 1 *noun,* 2 *adjective.*

i den ti cal (ī den/tə kəl), **1** the same: *Both events happened on the identical day.* **2** exactly alike. See picture. *adjective.*

i den ti fi ca tion (ī den/tə fə kā/shən), **1** an identifying or a being identified. **2** something used to identify a person or thing: *She offered her driver's license as identification. noun.*

identical (definition 2)—The two girls were wearing identical clothing.

idol (definition 1)

igloo—an igloo in northern Canada

a hat	i it	oi oil	ch child	a in about
ā age	ī ice	ou out	ng long	e in taken
ä far	o hot	u cup	sh she	ə = { i in pencil
e let	ō open	u̇ put	th thin	o in lemon
ē equal	ô order	ü rule	ŦH then	u in circus
ėr term			zh measure	

i den ti fy (ī den′tə fī), **1** recognize as being a particular person or thing; prove to be the same: *He identified the wallet as his by telling what it looked like and what was in it.* **2** make the same; treat as the same: *A good king identifies his people's well-being with his own. verb,* **i den ti fied, i den ti fy ing.**

i den ti ty (ī den′tə tē), **1** individuality; who a person is; what a thing is: *The writer concealed his identity by signing his stories with a made-up name.* **2** exact likeness: *The identity of the two crimes led the police to think that the same person committed them. noun, plural* **i den ti ties.**

id i om (id′ē əm), phrase or expression whose meaning cannot be understood from the ordinary meanings of the words in it. "Hold one's tongue" is an English idiom meaning "keep still." *noun.*

id i ot (id′ē ət), **1** a word once used to mean a person born with very little mental ability. Idiots never learn to read or count and can do only very simple tasks. **2** a very stupid or foolish person: *What an idiot I was to forget my keys! noun.*

id i ot ic (id′ē ot′ik), very stupid or foolish. *adjective.*

i dle (ī′dl), **1** doing nothing; not busy; not working: *the idle hours of a holiday. Give me some help; don't just stand there idle.* **2** lazy; not willing to do things: *Some idle students do very little schoolwork.* **3** useless; worthless: *to waste time in idle pleasure.* **4** without any good reason or cause: *Stop worrying about idle rumors.* **5** do nothing; fail to work: *Instead of doing their homework they idled all weekend.* **6** spend or waste (time): *It's pleasant to idle away hours lying in a hammock.* **7** run slowly without transmitting power. A motor idles when it is out of gear and running slowly. 1-4 *adjective,* **i dler, i dlest;** 5-7 *verb,* **i dled, i dling.**

i dler (ī′dlər), a lazy person. *noun.*

i dly (ī′dlē), in an idle manner; doing nothing: *He spent the afternoon idly on the beach. adverb.*

i dol (ī′dl), **1** thing, usually an image, that is worshiped as a god. See picture. **2** person or thing that is loved very, very much: *The famous singer was an idol of the audience. noun.*

i dol ize (ī′dl īz), **1** love or admire very, very much: *Some baseball fans idolize their favorite players.* **2** worship as an idol; make an idol of: *The Bible tells how Moses destroyed the golden calf that the people idolized. verb,* **i dol ized, i dol iz ing.**

if (if), **1** supposing that; on condition that; in case: *Come if you can. If it rains tomorrow, we shall stay at home.* **2** whether: *I wonder if he will go? conjunction.*

ig loo (ig′lü), an Eskimo hut that is shaped like a dome, often built of blocks of hard snow. See picture. *noun, plural* **ig loos.**

ig ne ous (ig′nē əs), formed by the cooling and hardening of melted rock material. Lava and granite are igneous rocks. *adjective.*

ig nite (ig nīt′), **1** set on fire: *He ignited the match by scratching it on the box.* **2** take fire; begin to burn: *Gasoline ignites easily. verb,* **ig nit ed, ig nit ing.**

ig ni tion (ig nish′ən), **1** setting on fire. **2** catching on fire. **3** (in a gasoline engine) the switch and apparatus controlling the sparks that set the gasoline vapor on fire. *noun.*

ig no ble (ig nō′bəl), without honor; disgraceful; base: *To betray a friend is ignoble. adjective.*

ig nor ance (ig′nər əns), lack of knowledge; being ignorant. *noun.*

ig nor ant (ig′nər ənt), knowing little or nothing. A person who has not had much chance to learn may be ignorant but not stupid. *People who live in the city are often ignorant of farm life. adjective.*

ig nore (ig nôr′), pay no attention to; disregard: *The driver ignored the traffic light and almost hit another car. verb,* **ig nored, ig nor ing.**

i gua na (i gwä′nə), a large lizard with a row of spines along its back. It is found in tropical America. See picture. *noun.*

ill (il), **1** sick; having some disease; not well: *ill with a fever.* **2** sickness; disease: *All the ills she has had this year have left her very weak.* **3** bad; evil; harmful: *an ill wind, do a person an ill turn.* **4** badly; harmfully: *Strength is ill used in harming people's property.* **5** an evil; harm: *Poverty is an ill.* **1,3** *adjective,* **worse, worst; 2,5** *noun,* **4** *adverb.*

I'll (īl), **1** I shall. **2** I will.

il le gal (i lē′gəl), not lawful; against the law; forbidden by law. *adjective.*

il leg i ble (i lej′ə bəl), not plain enough; very hard to read: *The ink had faded so that many words were illegible. adjective.*

Il li nois (il′ə noi′ *or* il′ə noiz′), one of the north central states of the United States. *noun.* [*Illinois got its name from the way French explorers wrote the name of the Indians living in the area. The Indian name meant "men."*]

il lit er ate (i lit′ər it), **1** not knowing how to read and write: *People who have never gone to school are usually illiterate.* **2** person who does not know how to read and write. **3** showing a lack of education: *illiterate writing.* **1,3** *adjective,* **2** *noun.*

ill-na tured (il′nā′chərd), cross; disagreeable. *adjective.*

ill ness (il′nis), sickness; disease; an abnormal, unhealthy condition: *Scarlet fever is a serious illness. noun, plural* **ill ness es.**

il log i cal (i loj′ə kəl), **1** not logical: *Your illogical behavior makes it hard to guess what you will do next.* **2** not reasonable: *Many children have an illogical fear of the dark. adjective.*

ill-tem pered (il′tem′pərd), having or showing a bad temper; cross. *adjective.*

ill-treat (il′trēt′), treat cruelly; treat badly; do harm to; abuse. *verb.*

il lu mi nate (i lü′mə nāt), **1** light up; make bright: *The big searchlight illuminates a spot a mile away.* **2** make clear; explain: *Our teacher could illuminate almost any subject we studied. verb,* **il lu mi nat ed, il lu mi nat ing.**

il lu mi na tion (i lü′mə nā′shən), **1** lighting up; making bright. **2** amount of light; light. **3** making clear; explanation. *noun.*

il lu sion (i lü′zhən), **1** appearance or feeling that misleads because it is not real; thing that deceives by giving a false idea: *The long, straight highway gave the illusion of becoming narrower in the distance.* **2** a false idea or belief: *Many people have the illusion that wealth is the chief cause of happiness. noun.*

il lus trate (il′ə strāt *or* i lus′trāt), **1** make clear or explain by stories, examples, or comparisons: *The way that a pump works is used to illustrate how the heart sends blood around the body.* **2** provide with pictures, diagrams, or maps that explain or decorate: *This book is well illustrated. verb,* **il lus trat ed, il lus trat ing.**

il lus tra tion (il′ə strā′shən), **1** picture, diagram, or map used to explain or decorate something. **2** story, example, or comparison used to make clear or explain something: *The teacher cut an apple into four equal parts as an illustration of what one fourth means.* **3** act or process of illustrating: *Her illustration of how to build a bookcase taught us a lot. noun.*

il lus tra tive (i lus′trə tiv), illustrating; used to illustrate; helping to explain: *A good teacher uses many illustrative examples to explain ideas that are hard to understand. adjective.*

il lus tra tor (il′ə strā′tər), **1** artist who makes pictures to be used as illustrations. **2** person or thing that illustrates. *noun.*

il lus tri ous (i lus′trē əs), very famous; great; outstanding: *Washington and Lincoln are illustrious Americans. adjective.*

ill will, dislike; spite; unkind or unfriendly feeling: *She bears ill will toward the people who cheated her.*

I'm (īm), I am.

im-, prefix meaning "not." *Impossible means not possible. Impatient means not patient.*

im age (im′ij), **1** likeness or copy: *You will see your image in this mirror. She is almost the exact image of her mother.* **2** statue; likeness made of stone, wood, or some other material: *The shelf was full of little images of all sorts of animals.* **3** picture in the mind: *I can shut my eyes and see images of things and persons. noun.*

i mag i na ble (i maj′ə nə bəl), that can be imagined; possible: *We had the best time imaginable at the party. adjective.*

i mag i nar y (i maj′ə ner′ē), existing only in the imagination; not real: *The equator is an imaginary circle around the earth. adjective.*

i mag i na tion (i maj′ə nā′shən), **1** imagining; power of forming pictures in the mind of things not present to the senses. A poet, artist, or inventor must have imagination to create new things or ideas or to combine old ones in new forms. **2** creation of the mind; fancy: *Is it my* *imagination, or did I just see a mouse? noun.*

i mag i na tive (i maj′ə nə tiv), **1** showing imagination: *Fairy tales are imaginative.* See picture. **2** having a good imagination; able to imagine well: *The imaginative child made up stories about life on other planets.* **3** of imagination. *adjective.*

i mag ine (i maj′ən), form a picture of in the mind; have an idea: *The girl likes to imagine herself a doctor. We can hardly imagine life without electricity.* *verb,* **i mag ined, i mag in ing.**

im be cile (im′bə səl), **1** person born with very little mental ability. Imbeciles usually cannot learn to read but can do simple tasks. **2** very stupid; having little mental ability. **1** *noun,* **2** *adjective.*

im i tate (im′ə tāt), **1** try to be like; follow the example of: *The little boy imitates his older brother.* **2** copy; make or do something like: *A parrot imitates the sounds it hears.* **3** act like: *He amused the class by imitating a duck, a monkey, and a bear.* **4** be like; look like: *Wood is sometimes painted to imitate stone. verb,* **im i tat ed, im i tat ing.**

im i ta tion (im′ə tā′shən), **1** imitating: *We learn many things by imitation.* **2** copy: *Give as good an imitation as you can of a rooster crowing.* **3** not real: *You can buy imitation pearls in many jewelry stores.* **1,2** *noun,* **3** *adjective.*

im mac u late (i mak′yə lit), **1** without a spot or stain; absolutely clean: *The newly washed shirts were immaculate.* **2** pure; without sin. *adjective.*

im ma ture (im′ə chùr′, im′ə tùr′, or im′ə tyùr′), not mature; not ripe; not full-grown. *adjective.*

im meas ur a ble (i mezh′ər ə bəl), too big to be measured; very great: *the immeasurable ocean.* *adjective.*

im me di ate (i mē′dē it), **1** coming at once; without delay: *Please send an immediate reply.* **2** closest; nearest: *Your immediate neighbors live next door.* **3** close; near: *I expect an answer today, tomorrow, or in the immediate future.* **4** having to do with the present: *What are your immediate plans?* *adjective.*

im me di ate ly (i mē′dē it lē), **1** at once; without delay: *I answered his letter immediately.* **2** next; with nothing between. *adverb.*

im mense (i mens′), very big; huge; vast: *An ocean is an immense body of water.* See picture. *adjective.*

im mense ly (i mens′lē), very greatly: *We enjoyed the party immensely.* *adverb.*

im men si ty (i men′sə tē), very great size; boundless extent; vastness: *the ocean's immensity.* *noun, plural* **im men si ties.**

im merse (i mèrs′), **1** dip or lower into a liquid until covered by it: *He immersed his aching feet in a bucket of hot water.* **2** baptize by dipping (a person) completely under water. **3** involve deeply; absorb: *The young pianist immersed herself in practice seven days a week. verb,* **im mersed, im mers ing.**

im mi grant (im′ə grənt), person who comes into a foreign country or region to live: *Canada has many immigrants from Europe. noun.*

im mi grate (im′ə grāt), come into a foreign country or region to live there. *verb,* **im mi grat ed, im mi grat ing.**

a hat	i it	oi oil	ch child	a in about
ā age	ī ice	ou out	ng long	e in taken
ä far	o hot	u cup	sh she	ə = { i in pencil
e let	ō open	ù put	th thin	o in lemon
ē equal	ô order	ü rule	ŦH then	u in circus
ėr term			zh measure	

imaginative (definition 1)—I read an **imaginative** story about a boy no bigger than a mouse.

immense—People look tiny beside this **immense** machine.

iguana—about 5 feet (1¹/₂ meters) long

im mi gra tion (im′ə grā′shən), coming into a foreign country or region to live: *There has been immigration to America from all the countries of Europe.* noun.

im mi nent (im′ə nənt), likely to happen soon; about to occur: *The black clouds, thunder, and lightning show that a storm is imminent.* adjective.

im mo ral (i môr′əl), morally wrong; wicked: *Lying and stealing are immoral.* adjective.

im mor tal (i môr′tl), living forever; never dying: *A truly great artist gains immortal fame.* adjective.

im mor tal i ty (im′ôr tal′ə tē), 1 endless life; living forever. 2 fame that lasts forever. noun.

im mov a ble (i mü′və bəl), 1 too big or too heavy to be moved; firmly fixed: *immovable mountains.* 2 firm; steadfast: *Most people who lived 600 years ago were immovable in their belief that the earth was flat.* adjective.

im mune (i myün′), 1 protected from disease; having immunity: *Vaccination makes a person practically immune to polio. Some persons are immune to poison ivy.* 2 free; exempt: *Nobody is immune from criticism.* adjective.

im mu ni ty (i myü′nə tē), 1 resistance to disease or poison: *One attack of measles usually gives a person immunity to that disease.* 2 freedom: *The law gives schools and churches immunity from taxation.* noun, plural **im mu ni ties.**

im mu nize (im′yə nīz), protect from disease or poison; give immunity to: *Vaccination immunizes you against smallpox.* verb, **im mu nized, im mu niz ing.**

imp (imp), 1 a young or small devil or demon. 2 a mischievous child. noun.

im pact (im′pakt), striking of one thing against another; collision: *The impact of the heavy stone against the windowpane shattered the glass.* noun.

im pair (im per′ or im par′), make worse; damage; harm; weaken: *Poor food impaired his health.* verb.

im part (im pärt′), 1 give a share in; give: *impart happiness to one's friends. The new furniture imparted an air of newness to the old house.* 2 tell; communicate: *She imparted a love of learning to her students.* verb.

im par tial (im pär′shəl), fair; just; showing no more favor to one side than to the other: *A judge should be impartial.* adjective.

im pass a ble (im pas′ə bəl), so that one cannot go through or across: *Snow and ice made the road impassable.* adjective.

im pas sioned (im pash′ənd), full of strong feeling; emotional: *She gave an impassioned speech in favor of equal rights for all people.* adjective.

im pas sive (im pas′iv), 1 without feeling or emotion; unmoved: *Her face was impassive when we told her the bad news.* 2 not feeling pain or injury; insensible: *The wounded man lay as impassive as if he were dead.* adjective.

im pa tience (im pā′shəns), 1 lack of patience; being impatient. 2 uneasiness and eagerness; restlessness. noun.

im pa tient (im pā′shənt), 1 not patient; not willing to bear delay, opposition, pain, or bother:

He is impatient with his little brother. 2 uneasy and eager; restless: *The horses are impatient to start in the race.* 3 showing lack of patience: *an impatient answer.* adjective.

im peach (im pēch′), 1 accuse (a public officer) of wrong conduct during office before a competent tribunal: *The judge was impeached for taking a bribe.* 2 cast doubt on; call in question: *impeach a person's honor.* verb.

im pede (im pēd′), hinder; obstruct: *The deep snow impeded travel.* verb, **im ped ed, im ped ing.**

im ped i ment (im ped′ə mənt), 1 hindrance; obstacle. 2 defect in speech: *Stuttering is a speech impediment.* noun.

im pel (im pel′), drive; force; cause: *The cold impelled her to go indoors.* verb, **im pelled, im pel ling.**

im pen e tra ble (im pen′ə trə bəl), 1 not able to be entered, pierced, or passed: *The thorny branches made a thick, impenetrable hedge.* 2 not able to be seen into or understood: *His sudden disappearance was hidden in an impenetrable mystery.* adjective.

im per a tive (im per′ə tiv), not to be avoided; urgent; necessary: *It is imperative that this very sick child should stay in bed.* adjective.

im per cep ti ble (im′pər sep′tə bəl), that cannot be perceived or felt; very slight; gradual: *The road took an imperceptible rise over the low hill.* adjective.

im per fect (im pėr′fikt), 1 not perfect; having some defect or fault: *A crack in the cup made it imperfect.* 2 not complete; lacking some part. adjective.

im per fec tion (im′pər fek′shən), 1 lack of perfection; imperfect condition or character. 2 fault; defect. noun.

im pe ri al (im pir′ē əl), 1 of or having something to do with an empire or its ruler: *the imperial palace.* 2 having to do with the rule or authority of one country over other countries and colonies: *England had imperial power over many other countries.* adjective.

im per il (im per′əl), put in danger: *Children who play with matches imperil their lives.* verb.

im pe ri ous (im pir′ē əs), 1 haughty; arrogant; overbearing: *The nobles treated the common people in an imperious way, looking down on them and ordering them around.* 2 not to be avoided; urgent; necessary: *They worked to satisfy the imperious demands of hunger.* adjective.

im per son al (im pėr′sə nəl), referring to all or any persons, not to any special one: *The teacher's criticism of the class was impersonal.* adjective.

im per ti nence (im pėrt′n əns), 1 rudeness; disrespectful and impudent behavior. 2 an impertinent act or speech. noun.

im per ti nent (im pėrt′n ənt), rude; disrespectful; impudent: *Talking back to older people is impertinent.* adjective.

im pet u ous (im pech′ü əs), 1 acting hastily, rashly, or with sudden feeling: *Children are more impetuous than adults.* 2 moving with great force or speed: *The dam broke and an impetuous torrent of* *water swept away the whole town. adjective.*

im ple ment (im′plə mənt), a useful piece of equipment; tool; instrument; utensil. Plows and threshing machines are farm implements. A broom, a pail, a shovel, and an ax are implements. *noun.*

im plore (im plôr′), **1** beg earnestly for: *The prisoner implored pardon.* **2** beg (a person to do something): *I implored my parents to let me go on the trip. verb,* **im plored, im plor ing.**

im ply (im plī′), mean (a thing) without saying it outright; express in an indirect way; suggest: *The teacher's smile implied that we were forgiven. verb,* **im plied, im ply ing.**

im po lite (im′pə līt′), not polite; having or showing bad manners; rude. *adjective.*

im port (im pôrt′ *for 1 and 3;* im′pôrt *for 2,4, and 5*), **1** bring in from a foreign country for sale or use: *The United States imports coffee from Brazil.* **2** article brought into a country: *Rubber is a useful import.* **3** mean; be a sign of: *Tell me what your remark imports.* **4** meaning: *Explain the import of your remark.* **5** importance: *matters of great import.* **1,3** *verb,* **2,4,5** *noun.*

im por tance (im pôrt′ns), being important; consequence; value: *Anybody can see the importance of good health. noun.*

im por tant (im pôrt′nt), meaning much; having value or influence: *important business, an important occasion. Our mayor is an important person in our town. adjective.*

im por ta tion (im′pôr tā′shən), **1** bringing in merchandise from foreign countries. **2** something brought in: *This piece of pottery is an importation from Mexico. noun.*

im pose (im pōz′), put (a burden, tax, or punishment) on: *The judge imposed fines on each guilty person. verb,* **im posed, im pos ing.** **impose on** or **impose upon,** take advantage of; use selfishly: *Do not let the children impose on you.*

im pos ing (im pō′zing), impressive because of size, appearance, or dignity: *The Capitol at Washington, D.C., is an imposing building. adjective.*

im pos si bil i ty (im pos′ə bil′ə tē), **1** being impossible: *We all realize the impossibility of living long without food.* **2** something impossible: *Holding your breath for an hour is an impossibility. noun, plural* **im pos si bil i ties.**

im pos si ble (im pos′ə bəl), **1** that cannot be or happen: *It is impossible for two and two to make six.* **2** not possible to use; not to be done: *They proposed an impossible plan.* **3** very hard to endure: *Spending the entire summer indoors would be impossible. adjective.*

im pos si bly (im pos′ə blē), in an impossible manner. *adverb.*

im pos tor (im pos′tər), person who pretends to be someone else in order to deceive or cheat others. *noun.*

im prac ti ca ble (im prak′tə kə bəl), not working well in practice: *impracticable suggestions. adjective.*

im prac ti cal (im prak′tə kəl), not practical; not useful. *adjective.*

a hat	i it	oi oil	ch child	a in about
ā age	ī ice	ou out	ng long	e in taken
ä far	o hot	u cup	sh she	ə = i in pencil
e let	ō open	u̇ put	th thin	o in lemon
ē equal	ô order	ü rule	ŦH then	u in circus
ėr term			zh measure	

im press (im pres′ *for 1-4;* im′pres *for 5*), **1** have a strong effect on the mind or feelings of: *The movie about the pioneers impressed us with their courage.* **2** fix in the mind: *I repeated the words to impress them in my memory.* **3** make marks on by pressing or stamping: *We can impress wax with a seal.* **4** imprint; stamp. **5** act of impressing. **1-4** *verb,* **5** *noun.*

im pres sion (im presh′ən), **1** effect produced on a person: *The giraffe in the zoo made a great impression on the child.* **2** idea; notion: *I have a vague impression that I left the front door unlocked.* **3** something made by pressure, such as a mark, stamp, or print: *A deer had left impressions of its hoofs in the soft dirt. noun.*

im pres sive (im pres′iv), able to impress the mind, feelings, or conscience: *an impressive sermon, an impressive storm, an impressive ceremony. adjective.*

im print (im′print *for 1 and 2;* im print′ *for 3 and 4*), **1** mark made by pressure; print: *Your foot made an imprint in the sand.* **2** impression; mark: *Pain left its imprint on her face.* **3** put by pressing: *He imprinted a kiss on his grandmother's cheek.* **4** fix firmly in the mind: *His boyhood home was imprinted in his memory.* **1,2** *noun,* **3,4** *verb.*

im pris on (im priz′n), **1** put in prison; keep in prison. **2** confine closely; restrain. *verb.*

im pris on ment (im priz′n mənt), **1** putting or keeping in prison: *We read about the imprisonment of the convicted criminal.* **2** being put or kept in prison: *His imprisonment lasted a year. noun.*

im prob a ble (im prob′ə bəl), not probable; not likely to happen; not likely to be true: *They told an improbable story of seeing a ghost. adjective.*

im prop er (im prop′ər), **1** wrong; not correct: *to make an improper turn into a one-way street.* **2** not suitable: *A damp basement is an improper place for storing books.* **3** showing bad judgment; not decent: *improper behavior. It is improper for you to read another person's diary. adjective.*

improper fraction, fraction equal to or greater than 1. $^3/_2$, $^5/_3$, $^7/_4$, $^{21}/_{12}$, and $^8/_8$ are improper fractions.

im prove (im prüv′), **1** make better: *You could improve your writing if you tried.* **2** become better: *His health is improving.* **3** use well; make good use of: *We had two hours to wait and improved the time by seeing the city. verb,* **im proved, im prov ing.**

im prove ment (im prüv′mənt), **1** making better; becoming better: *Her schoolwork shows much improvement since last term.* **2** change or addition that adds value: *The improvements in our house were costly.* **3** person or thing that is better than a previous one; gain; advance: *Color television is an improvement over black-and-white television. noun.*

im pro vise (im′prə vīz), **1** make up (music or poetry) on the spur of the moment; sing, recite, or speak without preparation: *We improvised a play for our parents.* **2** prepare or provide offhand: *The children improvised a tent out of blankets and poles.* *verb,* **im pro vised, im pro vis ing.**

im pru dent (im prüd′nt), not wise or prudent; rash: *It is imprudent to rush into something without thinking what may happen.* *adjective.*

im pu dence (im′pyə dəns), shameless boldness; very rude and disrespectful behavior. *noun.*

im pu dent (im′pyə dənt), shamelessly bold; very rude and disrespectful: *The impudent child made faces at us.* *adjective.*

im pulse (im′puls), **1** a sudden, driving force or influence; thrust; push: *the impulse of hunger, the impulse of curiosity.* **2** a sudden inclination or tendency to act: *I had a strong impulse to write one of the friends I met at camp.* *noun.*

im pul sive (im pul′siv), acting upon impulse; easily moved: *The impulsive girl spent all her savings on records.* *adjective.*

im pure (im pyùr′), **1** not pure; dirty: *The air in cities is often impure.* **2** mixed with something of lower value: *The salt we use is slightly impure.* **3** bad; corrupt: *impure talk.* *adjective.*

im pur i ty (im pyùr′ə tē), **1** lack of purity; being impure. **2** impure thing or element; thing that makes something else impure: *Filtering the water removed some of its impurities.* *noun, plural* **im pur i ties.**

in (in), **1** within; not outside: *in the box. We live in the city.* **2** during: *It rained in the afternoon.* **3** at the end of; after: *I'll be ready in an hour.* **4** into: *Go in the house.* **5** from among; out of: *one in a hundred.* **6** because of; for: *The party is in honor of his birthday.* **7** in or into some place; on the inside: *Come in. Lock the dog in. A sheepskin coat has the woolly side in.* **1-6** *preposition,* **7** *adverb.*

ins and outs, 1 turns and twists: *She knows the ins and outs of the road because she has traveled it so often.* **2** different parts; details: *The manager knows the ins and outs of the business better than the owner.*

in., inch or inches.

in-, prefix meaning: **1** not. *Incorrect means not correct.* **2** lack of. *Injustice means the lack of justice.*

in a bil i ty (in′ə bil′ə tē), lack of ability, means, or power; being unable. *noun.*

in ac ces si ble (in′ək ses′ə bəl), **1** hard to get at; hard to reach or enter: *A house on top of a steep hill is inaccessible.* **2** not able to be reached or entered at all. *adjective.*

in ac cur a cy (in ak′yər ə sē), **1** lack of accuracy: *Our arithmetic teacher showed us how to avoid inaccuracy when we subtract numbers.* **2** error; mistake: *There are a few inaccuracies in your multiplication answers.* *noun, plural* **in ac cur a cies.**

in ac cur ate (in ak′yər it), not accurate; not exact; containing mistakes. *adjective.*

in ac tive (in ak′tiv), not active; idle; sluggish: *Bears are inactive during the winter.* *adjective.*

incline (definition 5)
The street had a steep **incline**.

Inca—These are the ruins of a mountain city built by the Incas hundreds of years ago.

in ad e quate (in ad′ə kwit), not enough; not so much as is required; not adequate: *Inadequate food will cause weakness and sometimes headaches.* adjective.

in ad vis a ble (in′əd vī′zə bəl), unwise; not sensible; not advisable. adjective.

in ap pro pri ate (in′ə prō′prē it), not appropriate; not suitable; not fitting. adjective.

in as much as (in′əz much′ az′), because: *I stayed indoors today, inasmuch as it was raining.*

in at ten tive (in′ə ten′tiv), not attentive; negligent; careless. adjective.

in au gu rate (in ô′gyə rāt′), 1 install in office with a ceremony: *A President of the United States is inaugurated every four years.* 2 make a formal beginning of; begin: *The invention of the airplane inaugurated a new era in transportation.* 3 open for public use with a ceremony or celebration: *The new city hall was inaugurated with a parade and speeches.* verb, **in au gu rat ed, in au gu rat ing.**

in au gu ra tion (in ô′gyə rā′shən), 1 act or ceremony of installing a person in office: *The inauguration of a President of the United States takes place on January 20.* 2 formal beginning; beginning. 3 opening for public use with a ceremony or celebration. noun.

in born (in′bôrn′), born in a person: *an inborn sense of rhythm, an inborn talent for drawing.* adjective.

In ca (ing′kə), member of a highly civilized South American people who ruled a large empire before it was conquered by the Spanish in the 1500's. See picture. noun, plural **In cas** or **In ca.**

in ca pa ble (in kā′pə bəl), having very little ability; not capable; not efficient: *An employer cannot afford to hire incapable workers.* adjective.

incapable of, without the ability, power, or fitness for: *The beginner was incapable of playing difficult piano music.*

in cense[1] (in′sens), 1 substance giving off a sweet smell when burned. 2 the perfume or smoke from it. 3 any sweet smell: *the incense of flowers.* noun.

in cense[2] (in sens′), make very angry: *Cruelty incenses kind people.* verb, **in censed, in cens ing.**

in cen tive (in sen′tiv), thing that urges a person on; cause of action or effort; motive; stimulus: *The fun of playing the game was a greater incentive than the prize.* noun.

in ces sant (in ses′nt), never stopping; continual: *The roar of Niagara Falls is incessant. The incessant noise from the factory kept me awake all night.* adjective.

inch (inch), 1 a unit of length, ¹/₁₂ of a foot. An inch of rainfall is the amount of water that would cover a surface to the depth of one inch. 2 move slowly or little by little: *The worm inched along.* 1 noun, plural **inch es;** 2 verb.

by inches, by degrees or gradually.

in ci dent (in′sə dənt), 1 happening; event: *I saw a funny incident on the playground today.* 2 a less important happening that helps or adds to something else: *She told us all of the main facts of her trip and a few of the amusing incidents.* 3 liable

to happen; belonging: *Hardships were incident to the lives of the pioneers.* 1,2 noun, 3 adjective.

in ci den tal (in′sə den′tl), 1 happening or likely to happen in connection with something else more important: *Certain discomforts are incidental to camping out.* 2 occurring by chance: *an incidental meeting of an old friend on the street.* 3 something incidental: *On our trip, we spent $58 for meals, room, and transportation and $5 for incidentals, such as candy, magazines, and stamps.* 1,2 adjective, 3 noun.

in ci den tal ly (in′sə den′tl ē), as an incident along with something else; by the way: *Incidentally, are you coming to the meeting tonight?* adverb.

in cin e ra tor (in sin′ə rā′tər), furnace for burning trash. noun.

in ci sor (in sī′zər), tooth having a sharp edge for cutting; one of the front teeth. Human beings have eight incisors. noun.

in cite (in sīt′), urge on; stir up; rouse: *Their leaders incited the workers to strike.* verb, **in cit ed, in cit ing.**

in clem ent (in klem′ənt), rough; stormy: *Inclement weather is common in winter.* adjective.

in cli na tion (in′klə nā′shən), 1 tendency: *He has an inclination to become overweight.* 2 preference; liking: *an inclination for sports.* 3 a leaning; bending; bowing: *A nod is an inclination of the head.* 4 slope; slant: *That high roof has a sharp inclination.* noun.

in cline (in klīn′ for 1-3 and 6; in′klīn or in klīn′ for 4 and 5), 1 be favorable; be willing; tend: *Dogs incline to eat meat as a food.* 2 make willing; influence: *I hope my arguments will incline you to change your mind.* 3 to slope; slant. 4 a slope; slant. 5 a sloping surface. The side of a hill is an incline. See picture. 6 lean; bend; bow: *She inclined her head toward the sound.* 1-3,6 verb, **in clined, in clin ing;** 4,5 noun.

in clined (in klīnd′), 1 favorable; willing; tending: *I am inclined to agree with you.* 2 sloping; slanting. adjective.

in close (in klōz′), enclose. verb, **in closed, in clos ing.**

in clo sure (in klō′zhər), enclosure. noun.

in clude (in klüd′), 1 contain: *Their farm includes 160 acres.* 2 put in a total, a class, or the like; reckon in a count: *The price includes the land, house, and furniture.* verb, **in clud ed, in clud ing.**

in clu sion (in klü′zhən), 1 including; being included. 2 thing included. noun.

in clu sive (in klü′siv), including; taking in; counting in: *"Read pages 10 to 20 inclusive" means "Begin with page 10 and read through to the very end of page 20."* adjective.

a hat	i it	oi oil	ch child		ə = {	a in about
ā age	ī ice	ou out	ng long			e in taken
ä far	o hot	u cup	sh she			i in pencil
e let	ō open	u̇ put	th thin			o in lemon
ē equal	ô order	ü rule	ŦH then			u in circus
ėr term			zh measure			

in come (in'kum'), what comes in from property, business, or work; money that comes in; receipts; returns: *A person's yearly income is all the money that person gets in a year.* noun.

income tax, government tax on a person's income above a certain amount.

in com pa ra ble (in kom'pər ə bəl), without an equal; matchless: *incomparable beauty.* adjective.

in com pe tent (in kom'pə tənt), **1** not competent; without ability or qualifications. **2** person who is without ability. 1 *adjective,* 2 *noun.*

in com plete (in'kəm plēt'), not complete; lacking some part; unfinished. *adjective.*

in com pre hen si ble (in'kom pri hen'sə bəl), impossible to understand. *adjective.*

in con sid er ate (in'kən sid'ər it), not thoughtful of others and their feelings; thoughtless. *adjective.*

in con sist ent (in'kən sis'tənt), **1** not consistent; not in agreement: *Your failure to arrive on time is inconsistent with your usual promptness.* **2** not keeping to the same principles or habits; changeable: *An inconsistent person says one thing today and the opposite tomorrow.* adjective.

in con spic u ous (in'kən spik'yü əs), not easily seen; not attracting very much attention: *They live in a small, inconspicuous gray house.* adjective.

in con ven ience (in'kən vē'nyəns), **1** trouble; bother; lack of convenience or ease. **2** cause of trouble, difficulty, or bother. **3** cause trouble, difficulty, or bother to: *Will it inconvenience you to carry this package for me?* 1,2 *noun,* 3 *verb,* **in con ven ienced, in con ven ienc ing.**

in con ven ient (in'kən vē'nyənt), not convenient; troublesome; causing bother, difficulty, or discomfort: *Shelves that are too high to reach easily are inconvenient.* adjective.

in cor po rate (in kôr'pə rāt'), **1** make (something) a part of something else; join or combine (something) with something else: *We will incorporate your suggestion in this new plan.* **2** form into a corporation: *When the business became large, the owners incorporated it.* verb, **in cor po rat ed, in cor po rat ing.**

in cor rect (in'kə rekt'), **1** not correct; wrong; faulty: *The newspaper gave an incorrect account of the accident.* **2** not agreeing with a good standard of taste; not proper. *adjective.*

in crease (in krēs' for 1 and 2; in'krēs for 3 and 4), **1** make greater, more numerous, or more powerful: *The driver increased the speed of the car.* **2** become greater; grow in numbers: *My weight has increased by five pounds. These flowers increase every year.* **3** gain in size or numbers; growth: *There has been a great increase in student enrollment during the past year.* **4** addition; amount added; result of increasing. 1,2 *verb,* **in creased, in creas ing;** 3,4 *noun.*

on the increase, increasing: *The movement of people from the cities to the suburbs is on the increase.*

in creas ing ly (in krē'sing lē), more and more: *As we traveled south, the weather became increasingly warm.* adverb.

in cred i ble (in kred'ə bəl), seeming too extraordinary to be possible; beyond belief: *The racing car rounded the curve with incredible speed. Some old superstitions seem incredible to educated people.* See picture. *adjective.*

in cred i bly (in kred'ə blē), beyond belief; so as to be incredible: *an incredibly swift flight.* adverb.

in cur (in ker'), run or fall into (something unpleasant); bring (blame, punishment, or danger) on oneself: *The explorers incurred great danger when they tried to cross the rapids.* verb, **in curred, in cur ring.**

in cur a ble (in kyur'ə bəl), **1** that cannot be cured: *an incurable invalid, an incurable disease.* **2** person having an incurable disease: *That building is a home for incurables.* 1 *adjective,* 2 *noun.*

in debt ed (in det'id), owing money or gratitude; in debt; obliged: *We are indebted to science for many of our comforts.* adjective.

in deed (in dēd'), **1** in fact; in truth; really; surely: *She is hungry; indeed, she is almost starving. War is indeed terrible.* **2** expression of surprise or contempt: *Indeed! I never would have thought it.* 1 *adverb,* 2 *interjection.*

in def i nite (in def'ə nit), **1** not clearly defined; not precise; vague: *"Maybe" is a very indefinite answer.* **2** not limited: *We have an indefinite time to finish this work.* adjective.

in del i ble (in del'ə bəl), **1** that cannot be erased or removed; permanent: *indelible ink. His experiences in India left an indelible impression on his memory.* **2** making an indelible mark: *The papers were graded with an indelible pencil.* adjective.

in dent (in dent'), **1** make notches in (an edge, line, or border): *an indented coastline. The mountains indent the horizon.* **2** begin (a line) farther from the edge than the other lines: *The first line of a paragraph is usually indented.* verb.

in de pend ence (in'di pen'dəns), freedom from the control, support, influence, or help of others: *The American colonies won independence from England.* noun.

in de pend ent (in'di pen'dənt), **1** thinking or acting for oneself; not influenced by others: *an independent voter, an independent thinker.* **2** guiding, ruling, or governing oneself; not under another's rule: *The United States is an independent country.* **3** needing, wishing, or getting no help from others: *independent work, independent thinking.* **4** not depending on others for support: *Now that I have a good job, I can be completely independent.* **5** person who votes without regard to party. 1-4 *adjective,* 5 *noun.*

in de scrib a ble (in'di skrī'bə bəl), that cannot be described; beyond description: *a scene of indescribable beauty.* adjective.

in dex (in'deks), **1** list of what is in a book, telling on what pages to find each thing. An index is usually put at the end of the book and arranged in alphabetical order. **2** provide with an index. **3** thing that points out or shows; sign: *One's face is often an index of one's mood.* 1,3 *noun, plural* **in dex es** or **in di ces;** 2 *verb.*

indignant—He was very **indignant** when I told him I didn't like his hair.

INCREDIBLE!

a hat	i it	oi oil	ch child	a in about
ā age	ī ice	ou out	ng long	e in taken
ä far	o hot	u cup	sh she	ə = i in pencil
e let	ō open	u̇ put	th thin	o in lemon
ē equal	ô order	ü rule	ŦH then	u in circus
ėr term			zh measure	

index finger, finger next to the thumb; forefinger.

In di a (in′dē ə), country in southern Asia. *noun.*

In di an (in′dē ən), **1** one of the people who have lived in America from long before the time of the first European settlers; American Indian. **2** of or having something to do with American Indians. **3** of or having something to do with India or its people. **4** person born or living in India. 1,4 *noun,* 2,3 *adjective.*

In di an a (in′dē an′ə), one of the north central states of the United States. *noun.* [*Indiana* may have come from a modern Latin word meaning "American Indian."]

Indian corn, plant whose grain grows on large ears. Also called **corn** or **maize.**

Indian Ocean, ocean south of Asia, east of Africa, and west of Australia.

Indian summer, time of mild, dry, hazy weather in late autumn.

in di cate (in′də kāt), **1** point out; point to; show; make known: *The arrow on a sign indicates the way to go. A dog indicates its feelings by growling, whining, barking, or wagging its tail.* **2** be a sign of: *Fever indicates illness.* verb, **in di cat ed, in di cat ing.**

in di ca tion (in′də kā′shən), **1** act of indicating: *We use different words for the indication of different meanings.* **2** thing that indicates; sign: *There was no indication that the house was occupied.* noun.

in di ca tor (in′də kā′tər), **1** person or thing that indicates. **2** pointer on a dial that shows the amount of heat, pressure, or speed. **3** a measuring or recording instrument. *noun.*

in di ces (in′də sēz′), indexes. *noun plural.*

in dif fer ence (in dif′ər əns), **1** not caring; lack of interest or attention: *The child's indifference to food worried its parents.* **2** lack of importance: *It is a matter of indifference to me whether we take a bus or the subway. noun.*

in dif fer ent (in dif′ər ənt), **1** not caring one way or the other: *I was indifferent to their insults. I enjoyed the trip but she was indifferent.* **2** unimportant; not mattering much: *We can go whenever you please; the time for starting is indifferent to me.* **3** neither good nor bad; just fair: *an indifferent player. adjective.*

in dif fer ent ly (in dif′ər ənt lē), **1** with indifference. **2** neither very well nor very badly. **3** poorly; badly. *adverb.*

in dig e nous (in dij′ə nəs), native; originating in the region or country where found: *Lions are indigenous to Africa. adjective.*

in di gest i ble (in′də jes′tə bəl), that cannot be digested; hard to digest. *adjective.*

in di ges tion (in′də jes′chən), difficulty in digesting food: *Several of us ate too much at the picnic, and we have been suffering from indigestion as a result. noun.*

in dig nant (in dig′nənt), angry at something unworthy, unfair, or mean. See picture. *adjective.*

in dig na tion (in′dig nā′shən), anger at something unworthy, unfair, or mean; anger mixed with scorn: *Cruelty to animals aroused his indignation. noun.*

in dig ni ty (in dig′nə tē), injury to one's dignity; insult: *He felt that his aunt's use of baby talk was an indignity. noun, plural* **in dig ni ties.**

in di go (in′də gō), **1** a blue dye that can be obtained from various plants. It is now usually made artificially. **2** plant from which indigo is obtained. **3** deep violet-blue. 1,2 *noun, plural* **in di gos** or **in di goes;** 3 *adjective.* [*Indigo* comes from Greek words meaning "Indian dye." The dye was called this because the indigo plant grew in warm climates, including that of India.]

inedible—He tried to eat his shoe but found it **inedible**.

indiscreet

infancy (definition 2)—air travel in its infancy.

in di rect (in′də rekt′), **1** not straightforward and to the point: *She would not say yes or no, but gave an indirect answer to my question.* **2** not directly connected: *Happiness is an indirect result of doing one's work well.* **3** not direct; not straight: *We walk to town by a road that is indirect, but very pleasant.* *adjective.*

in dis creet (in′dis krēt′), not discreet; not wise and judicious: *It is often indiscreet to tell your secrets.* See picture. *adjective.*

in dis pen sa ble (in′dis pen′sə bəl), absolutely necessary: *Air is indispensable to life. adjective.*

in dis posed (in′dis pōzd′), **1** slightly ill: *I have been indisposed with a cold.* **2** unwilling. *adjective.*

in dis tinct (in′dis tingkt′), not distinct; not clear to the eye, ear, or mind; confused: *I have an indistinct memory of the accident. We could hear an indistinct roar from the distant ocean. adjective.*

in di vid u al (in′də vij′ü əl), **1** person: *He is the tallest individual in his family.* **2** a single person, animal, or thing: *We saw a herd of giraffes containing 30 individuals.* **3** single; separate; for one only: *Benches are for several people; chairs are individual seats. Washbowls are for general use; toothbrushes are for individual use.* **4** belonging to or marking off one person or thing specially: *I can always identify her drawings because of their individual style.* **1,2** *noun,* **3,4** *adjective.* [*Individual* comes from a Latin word meaning "that cannot be divided" or "indivisible."]

in di vid u al i ty (in′də vij′ü al′ə tē), **1** the character or sum of the qualities which distinguish one person or thing from another: *Each human being begins in infancy to build an individuality of his or her own.* **2** being individual; existence as an individual. *noun, plural* **in di vid u al i ties.**

in di vid u al ly (in′də vij′ü ə lē), **1** personally; one at a time; as individuals: *Sometimes our teacher helps us individually.* **2** each from the others: *People differ individually. adverb.*

in di vis i ble (in′də viz′ ə bəl), that cannot be divided: *"One nation under God, indivisible, with liberty and justice for all." adjective.*

in do lence (in′dl əns), laziness; dislike of work; idleness. *noun.*

in do lent (in′dl ənt), disliking work; lazy. *adjective.*

in dom i ta ble (in dom′ə tə bəl), not able to be discouraged, beaten, or defeated: *The team's indomitable spirit helped them win a very close game. adjective.*

in door (in′dôr′), done or used in a house or building: *indoor tennis. adjective.*

in doors (in′dôrz′), in or into a house or building: *Go indoors. adverb.*

in dorse (in dôrs′), endorse. *verb,* **in dorsed, in dors ing.**

in duce (in düs′ *or* in dyüs′), **1** lead on; influence; persuade: *Advertisements induce people to buy.* **2** cause; bring about: *The doctor says that this medicine will induce sleep. verb,* **in duced, in duc ing.**

in duce ment (in düs′mənt *or* in dyüs′mənt),

something that influences or persuades: *A new bicycle for the winner was an inducement to try hard to win the contest. noun.*

in duct (in dukt′), **1** put formally in possession of (an office): *He was inducted into the office of governor.* **2** bring in; introduce (into a place, seat, or position). **3** take into the armed services. *verb.*

in dulge (in dulj′), **1** give way to one's pleasure; give oneself up to; allow oneself something desired: *A smoker indulges in tobacco.* **2** give in to the wishes or whims of; humor: *We often indulge a sick person. verb,* **in dulged, in dulg ing.**

in dul gence (in dul′jəns), **1** indulging: *Friends often treat each other with indulgence.* **2** thing indulged in: *Luxuries are indulgences.* **3** favor; privilege: *The student kept seeking indulgence from the teacher. noun.*

in dul gent (in dul′jənt), **1** giving in to another's wishes or whims; too kind or agreeable: *Their indulgent parents gave them everything they wanted.* **2** making allowances; not critical: *Our indulgent teacher praised every poem we wrote. adjective.*

in dus tri al (in dus′trē əl), of industry; having something to do with industry: *Industrial workers work at trades or in factories. An industrial school teaches trades. adjective.*

in dus tri al i za tion (in dus′trē ə lə zā′shən), development of large industries in a country. *noun.*

in dus tri al ize (in dus′trē ə līz), make industrial; develop large industries in (a country). *verb,* **in dus tri al ized, in dus tri al iz ing.**

in dus tri ous (in dus′trē əs), working hard and steadily: *An industrious student usually has good grades. adjective.*

in dus try (in′də strē), **1** any branch of business, trade, or manufacture: *the automobile industry. Industries dealing with steel, copper, coal, and oil employ millions of people.* **2** steady effort; hard work: *She became a lawyer with much industry. noun, plural* **in dus tries.**

in ed i ble (in ed′ə bəl), not fit to eat. See picture. *adjective.*

in ef fec tive (in′ə fek′tiv), not producing the desired effect; of little use: *An ineffective medicine fails to cure a disease or relieve pain. adjective.*

in ef fi cien cy (in′ə fish′ən sē), inability to get things done. *noun.*

in ef fi cient (in′ə fish′ənt), **1** not efficient; not able to produce an effect without waste of time or energy: *A machine that uses too much fuel is inefficient.* **2** not able to get things done; incapable: *The inefficient inspector examined only a few new refrigerators. adjective.*

in e qual i ty (in′i kwol′ə tē), lack of equality; being unequal in amount, size, value, or rank: *There is a great inequality between the salaries of a bank president and a bank clerk. noun, plural* **in e qual i ties.**

in ert (in ėrt′), **1** lifeless; having no power to move or act: *A stone is an inert lump of matter.* **2** inactive; slow; sluggish: *He felt sleepy and inert. adjective.*

in ev i ta ble (in ev′ə tə bəl), not to be avoided;

a hat	i it	oi oil	ch child		a in about
ā age	ī ice	ou out	ng long		e in taken
ä far	o hot	u cup	sh she	ə =	i in pencil
e let	ō open	ů put	th thin		o in lemon
ē equal	ô order	ü rule	ᵀᴴ then		u in circus
ėr term			zh measure		

sure to happen; certain to come: *Death is an inevitable occurrence; it comes to everyone. adjective.*

in ex act (in′ig zakt′), not exact; with errors or mistakes; not just right. *adjective.*

in ex cus a ble (in′ik skyü′zə bəl), not able to be pardoned or excused: *an inexcusable insult, an inexcusable mistake. adjective.*

in ex haust i ble (in′ig zô′stə bəl), **1** unable to be used up; very abundant: *The wealth of our country seems inexhaustible to many people abroad.* **2** tireless: *The new president is a man of inexhaustible energy. adjective.*

in ex pen sive (in′ik spen′siv), not expensive; cheap; low-priced. *adjective.*

in ex per i ence (in′ik spir′ē əns), lack of experience; lack of practice; lack of skill or wisdom gained by experience. *noun.*

in ex per i enced (in′ik spir′ē ənst), not experienced; without practice; lacking the skill and wisdom gained by experience. *adjective.*

in fal li ble (in fal′ə bəl), **1** free from error; that cannot be mistaken: *an infallible rule.* **2** absolutely reliable; sure: *infallible obedience. adjective.*

in fa mous (in′fə məs), **1** very wicked; so bad as to deserve public disgrace: *To betray your country is infamous.* **2** having a very bad reputation: *A traitor's name is infamous. adjective.*

in fa my (in′fə mē), **1** a very bad reputation; public disgrace: *Traitors are held in infamy.* **2** extreme wickedness. *noun, plural* **in fa mies.**

in fan cy (in′fən sē), **1** babyhood; early childhood. **2** an early stage of anything: *Space travel is still in its infancy.* See picture. *noun, plural* **in fan cies.**

in fant (in′fənt), **1** baby; very young child. **2** of or for an infant: *an infant dress, infant food.* **3** in an early stage; just beginning to develop: *an infant industry.* **1** *noun,* **2,3** *adjective.*

in fan tile (in′fən tīl), **1** of an infant or infants; having to do with infants: *Measles and chicken pox are infantile diseases.* **2** like an infant; childish: *She was upset by her friend's infantile show of temper. adjective.*

infantile paralysis, disease that causes paralysis of various muscles; polio.

in fan try (in′fən trē), soldiers trained, equipped, and organized to fight on foot. *noun, plural* **in fan tries.** [*Infantry* is from an Italian word meaning "an infant" or "a youth." Infantry was called this because in the Middle Ages the knights on horseback were attended by boys who followed them on foot.]

in fect (in fekt′), **1** cause disease in by bringing into contact with germs or viruses: *Dirt can infect an open cut. If you have a bad cold, you may infect the people around you.* **2** influence in a bad way: *A noisy student may infect the behavior of a whole* *class.* **3** influence by spreading from one to another: *The manager's good humor infected many who worked with her. verb.*

in fec tion (in fek′shən), **1** causing of disease in people, animals, and plants by bringing into contact with germs or viruses. Air, water, clothing, and insects may all be means of infection. **2** disease that can spread from one person to another: *Measles is an infection. noun.*

in fec tious (in fek′shəs), **1** spread by infection: *Measles is an infectious disease.* **2** causing infection. **3** apt to spread from one to another: *He has a jolly, infectious laugh. adjective.*

in fer (in fėr′), **1** find out by reasoning; conclude: *I inferred from the smoke that something was burning.* **2** indicate; imply: *Ragged clothing infers poverty. verb,* **in ferred, in fer ring.**

in fer ence (in′fər əns), **1** process of inferring: *What happened is only a matter of inference; no one saw the accident.* **2** that which is inferred; conclusion: *What inference do you draw from smelling smoke? noun.*

in fer i or (in fir′ē ər), **1** low in quality; below the average: *an inferior mind, an inferior grade of coffee.* **2** lower in quality; not so good; worse: *My grades are inferior this year. This cloth is inferior to real silk.* **3** lower in position or rank: *A lieutenant is inferior to a captain.* **4** person who is lower in rank or station: *A good leader gets on well with inferiors.* 1-3 *adjective,* 4 *noun.*

in fer i or i ty (in fir′ē ôr′ə tē), inferior nature or condition; quality of being inferior. *noun.*

in fer nal (in fėr′nl), **1** of the lower world; of hell. **2** fit to have come from hell: *The heartless conqueror showed infernal cruelty. adjective.*

in fest (in fest′), trouble or disturb frequently or in large numbers: *Mosquitoes infest swamps. The mountains were infested with robbers. verb.*

in fi del (in′fə dəl), **1** person who does not believe in religion. **2** person who does not accept a particular faith. During the Crusades, Moslems called Christians infidels. **3** person who does not accept Christianity. *noun.*

in field (in′fēld′), **1** the part of a baseball field roughly bounded by the bases. **2** first, second, and third basemen and shortstop of a baseball team. *noun.*

in field er (in′fēl′dər), a baseball player who plays in the infield. *noun.*

in fi nite (in′fə nit), **1** without limits or bounds; endless: *the infinite reaches of outer space.* **2** very, very great: *Working a jigsaw puzzle sometimes takes infinite patience. adjective.*

in firm (in fėrm′), weak; feeble: *The patient was old and infirm. adjective.*

in fir mi ty (in fėr′mə tē), **1** weakness; feebleness. **2** sickness; illness: *the infirmities of age. noun, plural* **in fir mi ties.**

in flame (in flām′), **1** excite; make more violent: *The stirring speech inflamed the crowd.* **2** make unnaturally hot, red, sore, or swollen: *The thick smoke inflamed our eyes. verb,* **in flamed, in flam ing.**

inflammable (definition 1)—Inflammable has the same meaning as flammable.

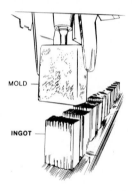

ingenuity—With ingenuity you can make a dragon puppet from an egg carton.

in flam ma ble (in flam′ə bəl), **1** easily set on fire: *Paper is inflammable.* See picture. **2** easily excited or aroused; excitable: *He had an inflammable temper. adjective.*

in flam ma tion (in′flə mā′shən), **1** a diseased condition of some part of the body, marked by heat, redness, swelling, and pain: *A boil is an inflammation of the skin.* **2** inflaming; being inflamed. *noun.*

in flate (in flāt′), **1** force air or gas into (a balloon, tire, or some other hollow thing) causing it to swell. **2** swell or puff out: *After their victory the team was inflated with pride.* **3** increase (prices or currency) beyond the normal amount. *verb,* **in flat ed, in flat ing.**

in fla tion (in flā′shən), **1** swelling, especially with air or gas. **2** a swollen state; too great expansion. **3** a sharp and sudden rise in prices often resulting from too great an increase in paper money or bank credit. *noun.*

in flex i ble (in flek′sə bəl), **1** firm; unyielding: *Our teacher's decision was inflexible, and we could not talk her into changing it.* **2** stiff; rigid: *an inflexible rod. adjective.*

in flict (in flikt′), **1** give or cause (a stroke, blow, or wound): *A knife can inflict a bad wound on a person.* **2** impose (suffering, punishment, or something unwelcome): *Only cruel people like to inflict pain. Some unpleasant neighbors came over and inflicted themselves on us all day. verb.*

in flu ence (in′flü əns), **1** power of acting on others and having an effect without using force: *Use your influence to persuade your friends to join our club.* **2** person or thing that has power: *Her thoughtfulness for others made the president of our class a good influence throughout the school.* **3** have such power or influence on: *The moon influences the tides. What we read influences our thinking.* **4** use influence on: *We tried to influence the teacher by offering him our suggestions.* **1,2** *noun,* **3,4** *verb,* **in flu enced, in flu enc ing.**

in flu en tial (in′flü en′shəl), **1** having influence: *Influential friends helped him to get a good job.* **2** using influence; producing results. *adjective.*

in form (in fôrm′), **1** tell; supply with knowledge, facts, or news: *Her letter informed us of when she expected to arrive. Please inform your students of the changes in today's schedule.* **2** tell tales about; accuse: *The criminal who was caught informed against the others who helped rob the bank. verb.*

in for mal (in fôr′məl), not formal; without ceremony: *an informal party. adjective.*

in for ma tion (in′fər mā′shən), **1** knowledge given or received of some fact or circumstance; news: *We have just received information of the astronauts' safe landing.* **2** things known; facts: *A dictionary contains much information about words.* **3** informing: *A guidebook is for the information of travelers. noun.*

in fre quent (in frē′kwənt), not frequent; occurring seldom or far apart; rare. *adjective.*

in fringe (in frinj′), **1** violate: *A false label infringes the food and drug law.* **2** go beyond the proper or usual limits; trespass: *Do not infringe upon the rights of others. verb,* **in fringed, in fring ing.**

in fur i ate (in fyur′ē āt), fill with wild, fierce anger; make furious; enrage: *Their insults infuriated us. verb,* **in fur i at ed, in fur i at ing.**

in gen ious (in jē′nyəs), **1** clever; skillful in making; good at inventing: *The ingenious girls made a trap door for their tree house.* **2** cleverly planned and made: *This trap made of an old tin can and some wire is an ingenious device. adjective.*

in ge nu i ty (in′jə nü′ə tē *or* in′jə nyü′ə tē), skill in planning or inventing; cleverness. See picture. *noun.*

in gen u ous (in jen′yü əs), frank and open; sincere: *He gave an ingenuous account of his acts, concealing nothing. adjective.*

in got (ing′gət), mass of gold, silver, or steel cast in a mold. See picture. *noun.*

in gra ti ate (in grā′shē āt), bring (oneself) into favor: *He tried to ingratiate himself with the teacher by cleaning the blackboards. verb,* **in gra ti at ed, in gra ti at ing.**

in grat i tude (in grat′ə tüd *or* in grat′ə tyüd), lack of thankfulness; being ungrateful. *noun.*

in gre di ent (in grē′dē ənt), one of the parts of a mixture: *The ingredients of a cake usually include eggs, sugar, flour, and flavoring. noun.*

in hab it (in hab′it), live in (a place, region, house, cave, or tree). *verb.*

in hab it ant (in hab′ə tənt), person or animal that lives in a place: *Our town has ten thousand inhabitants. noun.*

in hale (in hāl′), draw into the lungs; breathe in (air, vapor, smoke, or odor). *verb,* **in haled, in hal ing.**

in her ent (in hir′ənt), existing; belonging to a person or thing as a quality: *Her inherent curiosity about nature led her to study plants. adjective.*

in her it (in her′it), **1** get or have after someone dies; receive as an heir: *After Grandfather's death, Mother inherited all his property.* **2** get (characteristics) from one's parents or ancestors: *She inherits her blue eyes from her father.* **3** receive (anything) from one who came before: *I inherited this old pen from the person who used to have my desk. verb.*

in her it ance (in her′ə təns), **1** inheriting: *He received his house by inheritance from an aunt.* **2** anything inherited: *The house was his inheritance. noun.*

in hos pit a ble (in′ho spit′ə bəl *or* in hos′pi tə bəl), not hospitable; not making visitors comfortable: *Our inhospitable neighbor never offers visitors any refreshments. noun.*

in hu man (in hyü′mən), without kindness, mercy, or tenderness; cruel; brutal. *adjective.*

a hat	i it	oi oil	ch child	a in about
ā age	ī ice	ou out	ng long	e in taken
ä far	o hot	u cup	sh she	ə = i in pencil
e let	ō open	ů put	th thin	o in lemon
ē equal	ô order	ü rule	ŦH then	u in circus
ėr term			zh measure	

in iq ui ty (in ik′wə tē), **1** very great injustice; wickedness. **2** a wicked and unjust act: *Taking children from their parents and selling them was one of the iniquities of slavery. noun, plural* **in iq ui ties.**

i ni tial (i nish′əl), **1** occurring at the beginning; first; earliest: *His initial effort at skating was a failure.* **2** the first letter of a word: *The initials U.S. stand for United States.* **3** mark or sign with initials: *Lee Ann Wong initialed the note L.A.W.* **1** *adjective,* **2** *noun,* **3** *verb.*

i ni ti ate (i nish′ē āt), **1** be the first one to start; set going; begin: *This year we shall initiate a series of free concerts.* **2** admit (a person) with ceremonies into a group or society: *The old members initiated the new members.* **3** introduce into the knowledge of some art or subject: *The teacher initiated the class into the wonders of science by telling a few interesting things about the earth and stars. verb,* **i ni ti at ed, i ni ti at ing.**

i ni ti a tion (i nish′ē ā′shən), **1** act or process of being the first one to start something; beginning. **2** formal admission into a group or society. **3** ceremonies by which one is admitted to a group or society: *A great many members of the club showed up for the initiation. noun.*

i ni ti a tive (i nish′ē ə tiv), **1** active part in taking the first steps in any undertaking; lead: *She likes to take the initiative in planning class projects.* **2** readiness and ability to be the one to start a thing: *A good leader must have initiative. noun.*

in ject (in jekt′), **1** force (liquid or medicine) into the body: *The doctor injected penicillin into my arm.* **2** throw in: *While she and I were talking he injected a remark into the conversation. verb.*

in jec tion (in jek′shən), **1** act or process of injecting: *Those drugs are given by injection as well as through the mouth.* **2** liquid injected: *A drug is often given as an injection. noun.*

in junc tion (in jungk′shən), command; order: *He obeyed his mother's injunction to come home. noun.*

in jure (in′jər), do damage to; harm; hurt: *Do not break or injure the bushes in the park. The misunderstanding injured their friendship. verb,* **in jured, in jur ing.**

in jur i ous (in jùr′ē əs), causing injury; harmful: *Hail is injurious to crops. adjective.*

in jur y (in′jər ē), harm; hurt; damage: *She escaped from the train wreck without injury. The accident will be an injury to the reputation of the railroad. noun, plural* **in jur ies.**

in jus tice (in jus′tis), **1** lack of justice. **2** an unjust act: *It is an injustice to send an innocent person to jail. noun.*

ink (ingk), **1** a colored or black liquid used for writing or printing. **2** put ink on; stain with ink. **1** *noun,* **2** *verb.*

in kling (ing′kling), hint; a slight suggestion; a vague notion: *Will you give me some inkling of what's going on? noun.*

ink well (ingk′wel′), container used to hold ink on a desk or table. *noun.*

ink y (ing′kē), **1** like ink; dark; black. **2** covered or stained with ink. *adjective,* **ink i er, ink i est.**

in laid (in′lād′), **1** set in the surface as a decoration or design. See picture. **2** decorated with a design or material set in the surface: *The wooden box had an inlaid top of silver. adjective.*

in land (in′lənd), **1** away from the coast or the border; situated in the interior: *Illinois is an inland state.* **2** interior of a country; land away from the border or the coast. **3** in or toward the interior: *He traveled inland from New York to Chicago.* **1** *adjective,* **2** *noun,* **3** *adverb.*

in let (in′let), **1** a narrow strip of water running from a larger body of water into the land or between islands: *The fishing village was on a small inlet of the sea.* **2** entrance. *noun.*

in mate (in′māt), person confined in a prison, asylum, or hospital. *noun.*

in most (in′mōst), **1** farthest in; deepest within: *We went to the inmost depths of the mine.* **2** most secret: *Her inmost desire was to be a trial lawyer. adjective.*

inn (in), **1** place where travelers and others can get meals and a room to sleep in. Hotels have largely taken the place of the old inns. **2** restaurant or tavern. *noun.*

in ner (in′ər), **1** farther in; inside: *A closet is usually an inner room.* **2** more private; more secret: *He kept his inner thoughts to himself. adjective.*

inner ear, the part of the ear that is deepest inside the head. It contains the organs that change sound into nerve messages that go to the brain.

in ner most (in′ər mōst), farthest in; inmost: *the innermost parts of a machine. adjective.*

in ning (in′ing), **1** division of a baseball game during which each team has a turn at bat. **2** the turn that one team in baseball has to play and score before three outs are made. *noun.*

inn keep er (in′kē′pər), person who owns, manages, or keeps an inn. *noun.*

in no cence (in′ə səns), **1** freedom from sin, wrong, or guilt: *The innocence of an accused person is accepted unless a judge or a jury finds that person guilty.* **2** simplicity; lack of cunning: *the innocence of a little child. noun.*

in no cent (in′ə sənt), **1** doing no wrong or evil; free from sin or wrong; not guilty: *In the United States a person is innocent until proved guilty.* **2** having and showing the simple and trusting nature of a child. **3** doing no harm: *innocent amusements.* **4** an innocent person. **1-3** *adjective,* **4** *noun.*

in no va tion (in′ə vā′shən), **1** change made in the established way of doing things: *The new principal made many innovations.* **2** making changes; bringing in new things or new ways of doing things: *Many people are opposed to innovation. noun.*

in nu mer a ble (i nü′mər ə bəl *or* i nyü′mər ə bəl), too many to count; very, very many: *innumerable stars. adjective.*

in oc u late (in ok′yə lāt), give to a person or animal a preparation made from killed or weakened germs or viruses that cause a certain disease. The body then builds up protection

against the disease. *verb*, **in oc u lat ed,
in oc u lat ing.**

in oc u la tion (in ok′yə lā′shən), act or process of
inoculating; the causing of a mild form of a
disease to keep a person or animal from getting
the regular disease. *noun.*

in of fen sive (in′ə fen′siv), not offensive;
harmless; not arousing objections: *"Please try to
be more quiet" is an inoffensive way of telling people
to stop their noise. adjective.*

in quire (in kwīr′), **1** try to find out by questions;
ask: *The detective went from house to house,
inquiring if anyone had seen anything suspicious.*
2 make a search for information, knowledge, or
truth: *The man read many old documents while
inquiring into the history of the town. verb,*
in quired, in quir ing.

in quir y (in kwī′rē *or* in′kwər ē), **1** act of
inquiring; asking. **2** a search for truth, information,
or knowledge. **3** question: *The guide answered all
our inquiries. noun, plural* **in quir ies.**

in quis i tive (in kwiz′ə tiv), **1** curious; asking
many questions: *Children are usually inquisitive.*
2 too curious; prying into other people's affairs:
*Our neighbors are very inquisitive about what we do.
adjective.*

in road (in′rōd′), raid; attack: *The costs of college
made inroads upon her savings. noun.*

in sane (in sān′), **1** not sane; crazy. **2** for insane
people: *an insane asylum.* **3** extremely foolish:
*Nobody paid any attention to their insane plan for
crossing the ocean in a rowboat. adjective.*

in san i ty (in san′ə tē), **1** condition of being
insane; madness; mental illness: *The lawyer
claimed that the prisoner had murdered the guard
during a fit of temporary insanity.* **2** extreme folly: *It
is insanity to drive a car without any brakes. noun,
plural* **in san i ties.**

in sa tia ble (in sā′shə bəl), that cannot be
satisfied; very greedy: *The boy had an insatiable
appetite for candy. adjective.*

in scribe (in skrīb′), write, engrave, or mark: *The
ring was inscribed with her name. How shall we
inscribe the watch? Please inscribe my initials on it.
verb,* **in scribed, in scrib ing.**

in scrip tion (in skrip′shən), something inscribed:
the inscription on a tombstone. See picture. *noun.*

in sect (in′sekt), **1** any of a group of small animals
without a backbone, with the body divided into
three parts. Insects have three pairs of legs and
usually two pairs of wings. Flies, mosquitoes,
gnats, and bees are insects. See picture. **2** any
similar small animal with its body divided into
several parts, with several pairs of legs. Spiders
and centipedes are often called insects. *noun.*
[*Insect* comes from Latin words meaning "animal
cut into sections." An insect's body is divided into
three sections.]

in sec ti cide (in sek′tə sīd), substance for killing
insects. *noun.*

in se cure (in′si kyùr′), **1** unsafe: *a region where life
is insecure.* **2** likely to give way; not firm: *an
insecure support, an insecure lock. adjective.*

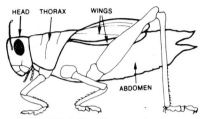
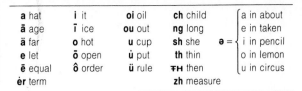

insect (definition 1)—a grasshopper

inscription

inlaid
(definition 1)
This wooden box
has an **inlaid**
design of ivory.

in sen si ble (in sen′sə bəl), **1** not sensitive; not able to feel or observe: *She appeared to be insensible to cold.* **2** not aware; indifferent: *The swimmers were insensible to the dangers of the high waves.* **3** not able to feel anything; unconscious: *The man hit by a truck was insensible for four hours.* *adjective.*

in sen si tive (in sen′sə tiv), not sensitive; without feeling: *an insensitive area of the skin. They were insensitive to the needs of others. adjective.*

in sep ar a ble (in sep′ər ə bəl), not able to be separated: *inseparable companions. adjective.*

in sert (in sėrt′ for 1; in′sėrt for 2), **1** put in; set in: *She inserted the key into the lock. He inserted a letter into the misspelled word.* **2** something put in or set in: *The book contained an insert of several pages of pictures.* **1** *verb,* **2** *noun.*

in ser tion (in sėr′shən), **1** act of inserting: *The insertion of one word can change the meaning of a whole sentence.* **2** something inserted. *noun.*

in side (in′sīd′ for 1-3 and 6; in′sīd′ for 4 and 5), **1** the part within; inner surface: *The inside of the box was lined with colored paper.* **2** the contents: *The inside of the book was more interesting than the cover.* **3** being on the inside: *an inside seat.* **4** within; in the inner part: *Please step inside.* **5** in: *The nut is inside the shell.* **6** secret; done or known by those inside: *The police thought that the theft was an inside job and suspected the clerk.* **1,2** *noun,* **3,6** *adjective,* **4** *adverb,* **5** *preposition.*

in sight (in′sīt′), **1** viewing of the inside with understanding: *Take the machine apart and get an insight into how it works.* **2** wisdom and understanding in dealing with people or with facts: *We study science to gain insight into the world we live in. noun.*

in sig ni a (in sig′nē ə), medals, badges, or other distinguishing marks of a position or of some honor: *The crown and scepter are insignia of royalty.* See picture. *noun plural.*

in sig nif i cant (in′sig nif′ə kənt), **1** having little use or importance: *A tenth of a cent is an insignificant amount of money.* **2** having little meaning: *insignificant chatter. adjective.*

in sin cere (in′sin sir′), not sincere; deceitful. *adjective.*

in sin u ate (in sin′yü āt), **1** hint; suggest in an indirect way: *To say "That worker can't do the job; it takes skill" is to insinuate that the worker is not skilled.* **2** push in or get in by an indirect, twisting way: *The spy insinuated himself into the confidence of important army officers. verb,* **in sin u at ed, in sin u at ing.**

in sist (in sist′), keep firmly to some demand, some statement, or some position: *He insists that he had a right to use his brother's tools. She insists that we should all learn to ski. verb.*

in sist ence (in sis′təns), act of insisting: *At the teacher's insistence the class became quiet. noun.*

in sist ent (in sis′tənt), **1** insisting; continuing to make a strong, firm demand or statement: *In spite of the rain she was insistent on going out.* **2** compelling attention or notice; pressing; urgent:

We heard insistent calls of "Help! Help!" adjective.

in so lence (in′sə ləns), bold rudeness; insulting behavior or speech. *noun.*

in so lent (in′sə lənt), boldly rude; insulting: *They were insolent to walk away while you were talking to them. adjective.*

in sol u ble (in sol′yə bəl), **1** not able to be dissolved: *A diamond is insoluble.* **2** not able to be solved: *The detective finally gave up, declaring the mystery insoluble. adjective.*

in spect (in spekt′), **1** look over carefully; examine. See picture. **2** examine formally or officially: *Government officials inspect factories and mines to make sure that they are safe for workers. verb.*

in spec tion (in spek′shən), **1** inspecting; examination: *An inspection of the roof showed no leaks.* **2** a formal or official examination: *The soldiers lined up for their daily inspection by their officers. noun.*

in spec tor (in spek′tər), **1** person who inspects. **2** officer appointed to inspect: *a milk inspector.* **3** a police officer ranking next below a superintendent. *noun.*

in spi ra tion (in′spə rā′shən), **1** influence of thought and strong feelings on actions, especially on good actions: *Some people get inspiration from sermons, some from nature.* **2** any influence that arouses effort to do well: *The teacher was an inspiration to his students.* **3** idea that is inspired; sudden brilliant idea. *noun.*

in spire (in spīr′), **1** fill with a thought or feeling; influence: *A chance to try again inspired us with hope.* **2** cause (thought or feeling): *The leader's courage inspired confidence in others.* **3** put thought, feeling, life, or force into: *The speaker inspired the crowd. The coach inspired the team with a desire to win.* **4** suggest; cause to be told or written: *Helen Keller's life story inspired a movie. verb,* **in spired, in spir ing.**

in stall (in stôl′), **1** place (a person) in office with ceremonies: *The new judge was installed without delay.* **2** put in a place; settle: *The cat installed itself in a chair near the fireplace.* **3** put in place for use: *The new owner of the house had a telephone installed. verb.*

in stall ment or **in stal ment** (in stôl′mənt), **1** part of a sum of money or a debt that is to be paid at stated times: *The table cost $100; we paid in two installments of $50 each.* **2** one of several parts issued at different times: *The serial story appeared in six installments. noun.*

in stance (in′stəns), **1** example; case: *The pilot is an instance of a woman who carried out her childhood dreams of flying.* **2** stage or step in an action; occasion: *I went in the first instance because I was asked to go. noun.*

in stant (in′stənt), **1** a particular moment: *Stop talking this instant!* **2** moment of time: *He paused for an instant.* **3** without delay; immediate: *The medicine gave instant relief from pain.* **4** prepared beforehand and requiring little or no cooking, mixing, or additional ingredients: *instant coffee, instant pudding.* **1,2** *noun,* **3,4** *adjective.*

in stan ta ne ous (in′stən tā′nē əs), coming or done in an instant; happening or made in an instant: *A flash of lightning is instantaneous.* *adjective.*

in stant ly (in′stənt lē), at once. *adverb.*

in stead (in sted′), in another's place; as a substitute: *She stayed home, and her sister went riding instead. adverb.*

instead of, rather than; in place of; as a substitute for: *Instead of studying, I watched television.*

in step (in′step), **1** the upper part of the foot between the toes and the ankle. See picture. **2** the part of a shoe or stocking over the instep. See picture. *noun.*

in still (in stil′), put in little by little: *Reading good books instills a love for really fine literature. verb.*

in stinct (in′stingkt), **1** a way of acting that is born in a person or animal without being learned: *Birds do not learn to build nests but build them by instinct.* **2** a natural tendency or ability; talent: *Even as a child the artist had an instinct for drawing. noun.*

in stinc tive (in stingk′tiv), born in an animal or person, not learned: *The spinning of webs is instinctive in spiders. adjective.*

in sti tute (in′stə tüt *or* in′stə tyüt), **1** organization for some special purpose. An art institute teaches or displays art. A technical school is often called an institute. **2** building used by such an organization: *We spent the afternoon in the Art Institute.* **3** set up; establish; begin: *The Pilgrims instituted Thanksgiving Day. After the accident the police instituted an inquiry into its causes.* 1,2 *noun,* 3 *verb,* **in sti tut ed, in sti tut ing.**

in sti tu tion (in′stə tü′shən *or* in′stə tyü′shən), **1** something established, such as a society, club, or any organization. A church, school, college, hospital, asylum, or prison is an institution. **2** building used for the work of an institution. **3** an established law or custom: *Marriage is an institution among most of the world's people.* **4** beginning; starting; providing for: *We need the institution of hot lunches at school. noun.*

in struct (in strukt′), **1** show how to do; teach; train; educate: *We have one teacher who instructs us in reading, English, and science.* **2** give directions or orders to; direct: *The owner of the house instructed the agent to sell it.* **3** inform; tell: *My lawyer instructs me that the contract will be signed Monday. verb.*

in struc tion (in struk′shən), **1** teaching; education; knowledge. **2** instructions, directions or orders: *The teacher's instructions were clearly understood. noun.*

in struc tive (in struk′tiv), useful for instruction; giving information; instructing: *A trip around the world is an instructive experience. adjective.*

in struc tor (in struk′tər), teacher. *noun.*

in stru ment (in′strə mənt), **1** thing used to do something; tool; mechanical device: *A forceps and a drill are two instruments used by dentists.* **2** device for producing musical sounds: *wind instruments, stringed instruments. A violin, cello, and piano were*

inspect (definition 1)—After this engine is tested and inspected it will be used in a spacecraft.

insignia—The eagle, shield, and anchors are **insignia** of the United States Navy.

INSTEP

the instruments in the trio. **3** thing with or by which something is done; person made use of by another; means: *The young king's wicked uncle used his influence as an instrument to gain power. noun.*

in stru men tal (in′strə men′tl), **1** acting or serving as a means; useful; helpful: *A friend was instrumental in getting me a job.* **2** played on or written for musical instruments: *An orchestra provided instrumental music to accompany the singing. adjective.*

in suf fer a ble (in suf′ər ə bəl), unbearable: *insufferable rudeness. The heat of the desert at noon was insufferable. adjective.*

in suf fi cient (in′sə fish′ənt), not enough; less than is needed: *The police had insufficient evidence to arrest the thief. adjective.*

in su late (in′sə lāt), **1** keep from losing or transferring electricity, heat, or sound, especially by covering, packing, or surrounding with a material that does not conduct electricity, heat, or sound: *Telephone wires are often insulated by a covering of rubber.* **2** set apart; separate from other things: *The English Channel insulates Great Britain from France and Belgium. verb,* **in su lat ed, in su lat ing.**

in su la tion (in′sə lā′shən), **1** insulating: *The electrician checked the insulation of the wiring.* **2** being insulated: *The insulation of the outer walls helps keep our house warm in the winter.* **3** material used in insulating: *Asbestos is often used as an insulation against fire. noun.*

in su la tor (in′sə lā′tər), that which insulates; something that prevents the passage of electricity or heat: *Glass is an effective insulator.* See picture. *noun.*

in sult (in sult′ *for 1;* in′sult *for 2*), **1** say or do something very scornful, rude, or harsh to: *She insulted me by calling me a liar.* **2** an insulting speech or action: *It is an insult to call someone stupid.* **1** *verb,* **2** *noun.*

in sur ance (in shùr′əns), **1** insuring of property, person, or life. Fire insurance, burglary insurance, accident insurance, life insurance, and health insurance are some of the many kinds. **2** business of insuring property or life. **3** amount of money for which a person or thing is insured: *He has $10,000 life insurance, which his wife will receive if he dies first. noun.*

in sure (in shùr′), **1** arrange for money payment in case of loss, accident, or death: *An insurance company will insure your house against fire.* **2** make safe against loss by paying money to an insurance company: *She insured her car against accident, theft, and fire. verb,* **in sured, in sur ing.**

in sur gent (in sėr′jənt), **1** person who rises in revolt; rebel: *The insurgents captured the town.* **2** rising in revolt: *The insurgent peasants burned the landowners' homes.* **1** *noun,* **2** *adjective.*

in sur rec tion (in′sə rek′shən), rising against established authority; revolt; rebellion. *noun.*

in tact (in takt′), untouched; uninjured; whole; with no part missing: *My lost wallet was returned to me intact. adjective.*

in take (in′tāk′), **1** place where water, air, or gas enters a channel, pipe, or other narrow opening. **2** act or process of taking in. **3** amount or thing taken in: *The intake through the pipe was 5000 gallons a day. noun.*

in te grate (in′tə grāt), **1** make into a whole; complete. **2** put or bring together (parts) into a whole: *The committee will try to integrate the different ideas into one uniform plan.* **3** make (schools, parks, and other public facilities) available to people of all races on an equal basis: *integrate a neighborhood. verb,* **in te grat ed, in te grat ing.**

in teg ri ty (in teg′rə tē), honesty; sincerity; uprightness: *I respect a person of integrity. noun.*

in tel lect (in′tə lekt), **1** power of knowing; understanding. Our actions are influenced by our intellect, will, and feelings. **2** intelligence; high mental ability: *Isaac Newton was a man of intellect.* **3** person of high mental ability: *He was one of the great intellects of his time. noun.*

in tel lec tu al (in′tə lek′chü əl), **1** needing or using intelligence: *Teaching is an intellectual occupation.* **2** of the intellect: *Thinking is an intellectual process.* **3** possessing or showing intelligence: *an intellectual book, an intellectual face.* **4** person who is well informed and intelligent. 1-3 *adjective,* 4 *noun.*

in tel li gence (in tel′ə jəns), **1** ability to learn and know; understanding; mind: *A dog has more intelligence than a worm. Intelligence tests are given in many schools.* **2** knowledge; news; information: *The spy gave the general secret intelligence of the plans of the enemy. noun.*

in tel li gent (in tel′ə jənt), having or showing understanding; able to learn and know; quick at learning: *Elephants are intelligent animals. adjective.*

in tel li gi ble (in tel′ə jə bəl), able to be understood; clear. *adjective.*

in tem per ance (in tem′pər əns), **1** lack of moderation or self-control; excess: *His intemperance in eating caused him to become very fat.* **2** too much drinking of intoxicating liquor. *noun.*

in tem per ate (in tem′pər it), **1** not moderate; lacking in self-control; excessive: *intemperate anger.* **2** drinking too much intoxicating liquor. **3** not temperate; severe: *an intemperate winter. adjective.*

in tend (in tend′), have in mind as a purpose; mean; plan: *We intend to go home soon. They intend that their children shall go to college. That gift was intended for you. verb.*

in tense (in tens′), **1** very much; very great; very strong: *intense happiness, intense light. Intense heat melts iron. A bad burn causes intense pain.* **2** having or showing strong feeling. An intense person is one who feels things very deeply and is likely to be extreme in action. *adjective.*

in ten si fy (in ten′sə fī), make or become more intense: *The blowing snow intensified the danger of driving on the icy highway. verb,* **in ten si fied, in ten si fy ing.**

insulator—The glass insulators keep the electricity that goes through the wires from passing into the wooden pole.

intent (definition 3)—She is intent on making an artistic arrangement of flowers.

a hat	i it	oi oil	ch child	⎧ a in about
ā age	ī ice	ou out	ng long	e in taken
ä far	o hot	u cup	sh she	ə = ⎨ i in pencil
e let	ō open	u̇ put	th thin	o in lemon
ē equal	ô order	ü rule	ᴛʜ then	⎩ u in circus
ėr term			zh measure	

in ten si ty (in ten′sə tē), **1** quality of being intense; great strength: *the intensity of sunlight.* **2** extreme degree; great vigor; violence: *intensity of thought, intensity of feeling.* **3** amount or degree of strength of electricity, heat, light, or sound per unit of area or volume. *noun, plural* **in ten si ties.**

in ten sive (in ten′siv), deep and thorough: *New laws were passed following an intensive study of the causes of pollution. adjective.*

in tent (in tent′), **1** purpose; intention: *I'm sorry I hurt you; that wasn't my intent.* **2** meaning: *What is the intent of that remark?* **3** very attentive; having the eyes or thoughts earnestly fixed on something; earnest: *A stare is an intent look.* See picture. **4** much interested: *She is intent on finishing the job today.* **1,2** *noun,* **3,4** *adjective.*
to all intents and purposes, in almost every way; almost; practically.

in ten tion (in ten′shən), purpose; design: *Our intention is to travel next summer. noun.*

in ten tion al (in ten′shə nəl), done on purpose; meant; planned; intended: *The kick she gave me under the table was intentional; it was a signal to be quiet. adjective.*

in ten tion al ly (in ten′shə nə lē), with intention; on purpose. *adverb.*

in ter cede (in′tər sēd′), plead for another; ask a favor from one person for another: *He did not dare ask the teacher himself, so I interceded for him. verb,* **in ter ced ed, in ter ced ing.**

in ter cept (in′tər sept′), **1** take or seize on the way from one place to another: *intercept a letter, intercept a messenger, intercept a pass in a football game.* **2** check; stop: *The police intercepted the flight of the escaped criminal. verb.*

in ter ces sion (in′tər sesh′ən), interceding; pleading for another: *The girl's intercession for her brother won their parents' consent to his request. noun.*

in ter change (in′tər chānj′ *for 1 and 3;* in′tər chānj′ *for 2, 4, and 5),* **1** put each of (two persons or things) in the place of the other: *If you interchange those two pictures, they'll look better.* **2** putting each of two or more persons or things in the other's place: *The word "team" may be turned into "meat" by the interchange of the end letters.* **3** make an exchange: *We interchanged our ideas and opinions before making a decision.* **4** giving and taking; exchange. **5** point at which a highway, especially an express highway, connects with another road without the streams of traffic interfering with each other. **1,3** *verb,* **in ter changed, in ter chang ing; 2,4,5** *noun.*

in ter change a ble (in′tər chān′jə bəl), **1** capable of being used in place of each other: *interchangeable parts.* **2** able to change places. *adjective.*

in ter com (in′tər kom′), any apparatus, usually using microphones and loudspeakers, with which members of an office staff or the crew of an airplane, tank, or ship can talk to each other. *noun.*

in ter course (in′tər kôrs), communication; dealings between people; exchange of thoughts, services, and feelings: *Airplanes, good roads, and telephones make intercourse with different parts of the country far easier than it was 50 years ago. noun.*

in ter est (in′tər ist), **1** a feeling of wanting to know, see, do, own, or share in: *He has an interest in reading and in collecting stamps.* **2** power of arousing such a feeling: *A dull book lacks interest.* **3** arouse such a feeling in; make curious and hold the attention of: *A good mystery interests most people.* **4** a share in property and actions: *She bought a half interest in the business.* **5** cause (a person) to take a share or part in something;

interlock
The two girls have their arms interlocked.

interference (definition 2)—Player 63 ran interference for number 40.

interlace (definition 1)

arouse the concern, curiosity, or attention of: *The salesman tried to interest us in buying a car.* **6** thing in which a person has a share or part. Any business, activity, or pastime can be an interest. **7** group of people concerned in one sort of thing: *the business interests of the town.* **8** advantage; profit; benefit: *The parents look after the interests of the family.* **9** money paid for the use of money. If you borrow money from a bank, you must pay interest on the loan. 1,2,4,6-9 *noun,* 3,5 *verb.*

in ter est ed (in′tər ə stid), **1** feeling or showing interest: *an interested spectator.* **2** having an interest or share. *adjective.*

in ter est ing (in′tər ə sting), arousing interest; holding one's attention: *Stories about travel and adventure are interesting for children. adjective.*

in ter fere (in′tər fir′), **1** clash; come into opposition with: *I will come Saturday if nothing interferes.* **2** mix in the affairs of others; meddle: *That neighbor is always interfering in other people's affairs. Don't interfere with your sister when she's busy. verb,* **in ter fered, in ter fer ing.**

in ter fer ence (in′tər fir′əns), **1** act or fact of interfering: *Your interference spoiled our fun.* **2** (in football) the protecting of the player who has the ball. See picture. *noun.*

in ter i or (in tir′ē ər), **1** inside; inner surface or part: *The interior of the house was beautifully decorated.* **2** inner; on the inside. **3** part of a region or country away from the coast or border: *There are deserts in the interior of Asia.* **4** away from the coast or border. **5** affairs within a country. In the United States, the Department of the Interior is responsible for managing federal land and the nation's natural resources. 1,3,5 *noun,* 2,4 *adjective.*

in ter jec tion (in′tər jek′shən), **1** exclamation regarded as a part of speech. *Oh! ah! alas!* and *hurrah!* are interjections. **2** remark; exclamation. *noun.*

in ter lace (in′tər lās′), **1** arrange (threads, strips, or branches) so that they go over and under each other: *Baskets are made by interlacing reeds or fibers.* See picture. **2** cross each other over and under; mingle together: *The branches of the trees interlaced above the path. verb,* **in ter laced, in ter lac ing.**

in ter lock (in′tər lok′), lock or join with one another: *The different pieces of a jigsaw puzzle interlock.* See picture. *verb.*

in ter lude (in′tər lüd), anything that is thought of as filling the time between two things: *There was an interlude of sunshine between two showers. noun.*

in ter me di ate (in′tər mē′dē it), **1** being or occurring between; middle: *Classes are offered in beginning, intermediate, and advanced French. Gray is intermediate between black and white.* **2** something in between. 1 *adjective,* 2 *noun.*

in ter mi na ble (in tėr′mə nə bəl), **1** never stopping; endless. **2** so long as to seem endless; very long and tiring. *adjective.*

in ter min gle (in′tər ming′gəl), mix together; mingle: *intermingle several styles of furniture in a* *room. verb,* **in ter min gled, in ter min gling.**

in ter mis sion (in′tər mish′ən), **1** time between periods of activity; pause: *The band played from eight to twelve with a short intermission at ten.* **2** stopping for a time; interruption: *The rain continued all day without intermission. noun.*

in ter mit tent (in′tər mit′nt), stopping and beginning again: *The pilot watched for an intermittent red light, flashing on and off every 15 seconds. adjective.*

in ter nal (in tėr′nl), **1** inner; on the inside: *An accident often causes internal injuries as well as cuts and bruises.* **2** having something to do with affairs within a country; domestic: *internal politics. Internal revenue is money from taxes on business and income in a country. adjective.*

in ter nal ly (in tėr′nl ē), **1** inside. **2** inside the body: *This ointment must not be taken internally. adverb.*

in ter na tion al (in′tər nash′ə nəl), **1** between or among nations: *A treaty is an international agreement.* **2** having something to do with the relations between nations: *international law. adjective.*

in ter plan e tar y (in′tər plan′ə ter′ē), situated or taking place between planets; in the region of the planets: *interplanetary gases, interplanetary travel. adjective.*

in ter pose (in′tər pōz′), **1** put or come between other things: *A cloud interposed and hid the sun.* **2** put in: *I'd like to interpose an objection at this point.* **3** interfere in order to help: *Mother interposed in the dispute between my brothers. verb,* **in ter posed, in ter pos ing.**

in ter pret (in tėr′prit), **1** explain the meaning of: *interpret a hard passage in a book, interpret a dream.* **2** bring out the meaning of: *The actress interpreted the part of the queen with great skill.* **3** understand: *We interpret your silence as consent.* **4** serve as an interpreter; translate. *verb.*

in ter pre ta tion (in tėr′prə tā′shən), **1** interpreting; explanation: *People often give different interpretations to the same facts.* **2** bringing out the meaning: *The musician's interpretation of the music was different from any I've heard before. noun.*

in ter pret er (in tėr′prə tər), **1** person who interprets. **2** person whose business is translating from a foreign language. *noun.*

in ter ro gate (in ter′ə gāt), ask questions of; examine by questions: *The lawyers interrogated the witness. verb,* **in ter ro gat ed, in ter ro gat ing.**

in ter ro ga tion (in ter′ə gā′shən), **1** questioning. **2** question. *noun.*

interrogation mark or **interrogation point,** question mark (?).

in ter rog a tive (in′tə rog′ə tiv), **1** asking a question; having the form of a question: *an interrogative sentence, an interrogative tone of voice.* **2** word used in asking a question. *Who, why,* and *what* are interrogatives. **1** *adjective,* **2** *noun.*

in ter rupt (in′tə rupt′), **1** break in upon (talk, work, rest, or a person speaking); hinder; stop: *A*

a hat	**i** it	**oi** oil	**ch** child		a in about
ā age	**ī** ice	**ou** out	**ng** long		e in taken
ä far	**o** hot	**u** cup	**sh** she	**ə** =	i in pencil
e let	**ō** open	**ů** put	**th** thin		o in lemon
ē equal	**ô** order	**ü** rule	**ᴛʜ** then		u in circus
ėr term			**zh** measure		

fire drill interrupted the lesson. **2** break in: *It is not polite to interrupt when someone is talking. verb.*

in ter rup tion (in′tə rup′shən), **1** interrupting; breaking in on. **2** being interrupted; break; stopping: *The rain continued without interruption all day. noun.*

in ter sect (in′tər sekt′), **1** cut or divide by passing through or crossing: *A path intersects the field.* **2** cross each other: *Streets usually intersect at right angles. verb.*

in ter sec tion (in′tər sek′shən), **1** intersecting: *Bridges are used to avoid the intersection of a railroad and a highway.* **2** place where one thing crosses another. *noun.*

in ter sperse (in′tər spėrs′), **1** vary with something put here and there: *The grass is interspersed with beds of flowers.* **2** scatter here and there among other things: *Bushes were interspersed among the trees. verb,* **in ter spersed, in ter spers ing.**

in ter state (in′tər stāt′), between persons or organizations in different states; between states: *The federal government regulates interstate commerce. adjective.*

in ter twine (in′tər twīn′), twine one with another: *The vines intertwined on the wall. verb,* **in ter twined, in ter twin ing.**

in ter val (in′tər vəl), time or space between: *an interval of fifteen minutes for recess, an interval of quiet in a busy day. noun.*

at intervals, 1 now and then: *There was a drizzling rain falling at intervals.* **2** here and there: *Villages are located at intervals along the river.*

in ter vene (in′tər vēn′), **1** come between; be between: *A week intervenes between Christmas and New Year's Day.* **2** come in to help settle a dispute: *The President was asked to intervene in the coal strike. verb,* **in ter vened, in ter ven ing.**

in ter ven tion (in′tər ven′shən), **1** intervening: *The strike was settled by the intervention of the President.* **2** interference by one nation in the affairs of another; interference. *noun.*

in ter view (in′tər vyü), **1** a meeting, generally of persons face to face, to talk over something special: *My parents had an interview with the teacher about my work.* **2** visit and talk with: *Reporters from the newspaper interviewed the important visitors.* **1** *noun,* **2** *verb.*

in ter wo ven (in′tər wō′vən), **1** woven together. **2** mixed together; mingled. *adjective.*

in tes tine (in tes′tən), part of the alimentary canal that extends below the stomach. Food from the stomach passes into the intestine where digestion is completed and water is absorbed. In adult human beings, the **small intestine** is about twenty feet long; the **large intestine** is about five feet long. *noun.*

in ti ma cy (in′tə mə sē), close acquaintance; closeness. *noun, plural* **in ti ma cies.**

in ti mate¹ (in′tə mit), **1** very familiar; known very well; closely acquainted: *Although the governor knew many people, he had few intimate friends.* **2** a close friend. **3** far within; inmost: *a person's intimate thoughts.* **1,3** *adjective,* **2** *noun.*

in ti mate² (in′tə māt), **1** hint; suggest: *Her smile intimated that she was pleased.* **2** make known. *verb,* **in ti mat ed, in ti mat ing.**

in ti ma tion (in′tə mā′shən), **1** hint; suggestion: *A frown is often an intimation of disapproval.* **2** announcement. *noun.*

in tim i date (in tim′ə dāt), frighten; make afraid; influence by fear: *to intimidate someone with threats. verb,* **in tim i dat ed, in tim i dat ing.**

in to (in′tü), **1** to the inside of; toward and inside: *Come into the house. We drove into the city. I will look into the matter.* **2** to the condition of; to the form of: *Divide the apple into three parts. Cold weather turns water into ice. preposition.*

in tol er a ble (in tol′ər ə bəl), unbearable; too hard to be endured: *The pain of the toothache was intolerable. adjective.*

in tol er ant (in tol′ər ənt), not tolerant; not willing to let others do and think as they choose. *adjective.*

intolerant of, not able to endure; unwilling to endure: *intolerant of cold.*

in tox i cate (in tok′sə kāt), **1** make drunk: *Too much wine intoxicates people.* **2** excite greatly: *The joy of victory intoxicated the team. verb,* **in tox i cat ed, in tox i cat ing.** [*Intoxicate* comes from a Latin word of the Middle Ages meaning "dipped in poison."]

in tox i ca tion (in tok′sə kā′shən), **1** an intoxicated condition; drunkenness. **2** great excitement. **3** (in medicine) poisoning. *noun.*

in trep id (in trep′id), fearless; dauntless; very brave: *an intrepid mountain climber. adjective.*

in tri cate (in′trə kit), **1** with many twists and turns; perplexing; entangled; complicated: *An intricate knot is very hard to tie or untie. A mystery story usually has a very intricate plot.* See picture. **2** very hard to understand: *The directions for building the model plane were so intricate that I made several mistakes. adjective.*

in trigue (in trēg′), **1** secret scheming and plotting; crafty dealings: *The royal palace was filled with intrigue.* **2** a crafty plot; secret scheme: *The king's younger brother took part in the intrigue to make himself king.* **3** form and carry out plots; plan in a secret or underhand way: *He pretended to be loyal while he intrigued against the king.* **4** excite the curiosity and interest of: *The book's unusual title intrigued me.* **1,2** *noun,* **3,4** *verb,* **in trigued, in tri guing.**

in tro duce (in′trə düs′ *or* in′trə dyüs′), **1** bring in: *She introduced a story into the conversation.* **2** put in; insert: *The doctor introduced a long tube into the sick man's throat so he could breathe.* **3** bring into use, notice, or knowledge: *introduce a new food, introduce a reform. Television and space travel are introducing many new words into our language.* **4** make known; bring into acquaintance with: *Mrs. Brown, may I introduce Mr. Smith? The principal introduced the speaker to the students. I introduced my visiting cousin to our city by showing her the sights.* **5** bring forward: *introduce a question for debate.* **6** begin: *He introduced his speech by telling a joke. verb,* **in tro duced, in tro duc ing.**

in tro duc tion (in′trə duk′shən), **1** introducing: *The introduction of steel made tall buildings easier to build.* **2** being introduced: *She was pleased by her introduction to so many new people.* **3** beginning of a speech, a piece of music, or a book. **4** thing made known; thing brought into use: *Television is a later introduction than radio. noun.*

in tro duc tor y (in′trə duk′tə rē), used to introduce; serving as an introduction; preliminary: *The speaker began her talk with a few introductory remarks about her subject. adjective.*

in trude (in trüd′), **1** force oneself in; come unasked and unwanted: *Do not intrude upon the privacy of your neighbors.* **2** give unasked and unwanted; force in: *Do not intrude your opinions upon others. verb,* **in trud ed, in trud ing.**

in trud er (in trü′dər), one that intrudes. *noun.*

in tru sion (in trü′zhən), act of intruding; coming unasked and unwanted: *Excuse my intrusion; I didn't know that you were busy. noun.*

in un date (in′un dāt), overflow; flood: *Heavy rains caused the river to rise and inundate the valley.* See picture. *verb,* **in un dat ed, in un dat ing.**

in vade (in vād′), **1** enter with force or as an enemy; attack: *Soldiers invaded the country to conquer it. Grasshoppers invaded the fields and ate the crops.* **2** enter as if to take possession: *Tourists invaded the city. Night invades the sky.* **3** interfere with; break in on; violate: *The law punishes people who invade the rights of others. verb,* **in vad ed, in vad ing.**

in vad er (in vā′dər), person or thing that invades. *noun.*

in va lid¹ (in′və lid), **1** a sick, weak person not able to get about and do things. **2** not well; weak and sick. **3** for the use of invalids: *an invalid chair.* **1** *noun,* **2,3** *adjective.*

in val id² (in val′id), not valid; without force; without value: *Unless a check is signed, it is invalid. adjective.*

in val u a ble (in val′yü ə bəl), priceless; very precious; valuable beyond measure: *Good health is an invaluable blessing. adjective.*

in var i a ble (in ver′ē ə bəl *or* in var′ē ə bəl), always the same; not changing: *After dinner it was her invariable habit to take a walk. adjective.*

in var i a bly (in ver′ē ə blē *or* in var′ē ə blē), without change; without exception: *Spring invariably follows winter. adverb.*

in va sion (in vā′zhən), act or fact of invading; entering by force or as an enemy; attack. *noun.*

in vent (in vent′), **1** make or think out (something new): *Alexander Graham Bell invented the telephone.* **2** make up: *Since they had no good reason for being late, they invented an excuse. verb.*

month. 1,2 *noun, plural* **in ven to ries**; 3 *verb,* **in ven to ried, in ven to ry ing.**

in vert (in vėrt′), **1** turn upside down: *Remove the cake from the pan by inverting it onto a rack.* **2** turn the other way; change to the opposite; reverse in position, direction, or order: *If you invert "I can," you have "Can I?" verb.*

in ver te brate (in vėr′tə brit), **1** without a backbone. **2** an animal without a backbone. Worms and insects are invertebrates; fishes, amphibians, reptiles, birds, and mammals are vertebrates. 1 *adjective,* 2 *noun.*

in vest (in vest′), **1** use money to buy something which will produce a profit or an income or both: *If I had any money, I would invest it in land.* **2** spend or put in (time or energy): *Much time and energy have been invested in the cancer crusade.* **3** give power, authority, or right to: *I invested my lawyer with the power to act for me. verb.*

in ves ti gate (in ves′tə gāt), search into; examine closely: *The detectives investigated the crime to find out who committed it. Scientists investigate nature to learn more about it. verb,* **in ves ti gat ed, in ves ti gat ing.**

in ves ti ga tion (in ves′tə gā′shən), a careful search; detailed or careful examination: *An investigation of the accident by the police put the blame on the drivers of both cars. noun.*

in ves ti ga tor (in ves′tə gā′tər), person who investigates. *noun.*

in vest ment (in vest′mənt), **1** investing; laying out of money: *Getting an education is a wise investment of time and money.* **2** amount of money invested: *His investments amount to thousands of dollars.* **3** something bought which is expected to yield money as interest or profit or both: *She has a good income from wise investments. noun.*

in ves tor (in ves′tər), person who invests money. *noun.*

in vig o rate (in vig′ə rāt′), give vigor to; fill with life and energy: *Exercise invigorates the body. verb,* **in vig o rat ed, in vig o rat ing.**

in vin ci ble (in vin′sə bəl), not to be overcome; unconquerable: *The champion team seemed invincible. adjective.*

in vis i ble (in viz′ə bəl), not visible; not capable of being seen: *Thought is invisible. Germs are invisible to the naked eye. adjective.*

in vi ta tion (in′və tā′shən), **1** a polite request to come to some place or to do something. Formal invitations are written or printed. *The children received invitations to the party.* **2** act of inviting. *noun.*

in vite (in vīt′), **1** ask (someone) politely to come to some place or to do something: *I invited some friends to a party.* **2** make a polite request for: *She*

intricate (definition 1)—**Intricate** knots were used in making this belt.

in ven tion (in ven′shən), **1** making something new: *the invention of gunpowder.* **2** thing invented: *Television is a modern invention.* **3** power of inventing: *An author must have invention to think up new ideas for stories.* **4** a made-up story; false statement: *That rumor is only an invention. noun.*

in ven tive (in ven′tiv), good at inventing: *An inventive person thinks up ways to save time, money, and work. adjective.*

in ven tor (in ven′tər), person who invents. *noun.*

in ven to ry (in′vən tôr′ē), **1** a complete and detailed list of articles. An inventory of property or goods tells how many there are of each article and what they are worth. **2** all the articles listed or to be listed; stock: *The store is having a sale to reduce its inventory.* **3** make a detailed list of; enter in a list: *Some stores inventory their stock once a*

isthmus

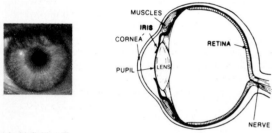

iris (definition 2)
This is a diagram of a person's eye. The iris controls the amount of light that enters the eye by making the pupil larger or smaller.

MUSCLES
IRIS
CORNEA
PUPIL
LENS
RETINA
NERVE

irrigate—This pipeline is used to irrigate crops.

invited our opinion of her story. **3** give a chance for; tend to cause: *New Year's Day invites good resolutions. Carelessness invites trouble.* **4** attract; tempt: *The cool water invited us to swim. verb,* **in vit ed, in vit ing.**

in vit ing (in vī′ting), attractive; tempting: *The cool water looks inviting. adjective.*

in vo ca tion (in′və kā′shən), calling upon in prayer; appealing for help or protection: *A religious service often begins with an invocation to God. noun.*

in voke (in vōk′), **1** call on in prayer; appeal to for help or protection: *The Pilgrims invoked God's help in their undertaking.* **2** ask earnestly for: *The condemned criminal invoked the judge's mercy.* **3** call forth by magic: *Aladdin invoked the powerful genie of the magic lamp. verb,* **in voked, in vok ing.**

in vol un tar i ly (in vol′ən ter′ə lē), without intention; against one's will. *adverb.*

in vol un tar y (in vol′ən ter′ē), **1** not voluntary; not done of one's own free will; unwilling: *Taking gym was involuntary on my part; the school requires it.* **2** not intended; not done on purpose: *An accident is involuntary.* **3** not controlled by the will: *Breathing is mainly involuntary. adjective.*

in volve (in volv′), **1** have as a necessary part; take in; include: *Housework involves cooking, washing dishes, sweeping, and cleaning.* **2** bring (into difficulty or danger): *One foolish mistake can involve you in a good deal of trouble.* **3** entangle; complicate: *Long, involved sentences are hard to understand.* **4** take up the attention of; occupy: *She was involved in working out a puzzle. verb,* **in volved, in volv ing.**

in ward (in′wərd), **1** toward the inside: *a passage leading inward.* **2** placed within; internal: *the inward parts of the body.* **3** into the mind or soul: *Turn your thoughts inward.* **4** in the mind or soul: *inward peace.* **1,3** *adverb,* **2,4** *adjective.*

in ward ly (in′wərd lē), **1** on the inside; within: *The patient was bleeding inwardly.* **2** toward the inside. **3** in the mind or soul. **4** not aloud or openly. *adverb.*

i o dine (ī′ə dīn), **1** substance used in medicine, in photography, and in making dyes. **2** a brown liquid containing iodine, put on wounds to kill disease germs and prevent infection. *noun.*

I o wa (ī′ə wə), one of the midwestern states of the United States. *noun.* [*Iowa* was named for an American Indian tribe, the Iowa. The name of the tribe came from a Dakota Indian word meaning "sleepy ones." Enemies of the Iowa Indians gave them this name to make fun of them.]

i rate (ī′rāt *or* ī rāt′), angry; enraged. *adjective.*

ire (īr), anger; wrath. *noun.*

Ire land (īr′lənd), a large island west of England. *noun.*

i ris (ī′ris), **1** plant with large, showy flowers, and leaves shaped like swords. **2** the colored part of the eye around the pupil. See picture. *noun, plural* **i ris es.**

I rish (ī′rish), **1** of or having something to do with Ireland or its people. **2** people of Ireland. **3** a language of Ireland. **1** *adjective*, **2** *noun plural*, **3** *noun singular*.

irk some (ėrk′səm), tiresome; tedious: *Washing dishes all day would be an irksome task. adjective.*

i ron (ī′ərn), **1** the commonest and most useful metal, from which tools and machinery are made. Steel is made from iron. **2** made of iron: *an iron fence.* **3** something made of iron: *a branding iron.* **4** like iron; hard; strong: *an iron will.* **5 irons,** chains or bands of iron; handcuffs; shackles. **6** implement with a flat surface which is heated and used to press clothing. **7** press with a heated iron. **8** golf club with an iron or steel head. 1,3,5,6,8 *noun,* 2,4 *adjective,* 7 *verb.*

ironing board, a padded flat surface covered with a smooth cloth, on which clothes are ironed. Most ironing boards have folding legs.

i ro ny (ī′rə nē), **1** way of speaking or writing in which the ordinary meaning of the words is the opposite of the thought in the speaker's mind: *The tallest person was called "Shorty" in irony.* **2** event or outcome which is the opposite of what would naturally be expected: *By the irony of fate the farmers had rain when they needed sun, and sun when they needed rain. noun, plural* **i ro nies.**

Ir o quois (ir′ə kwoi), member of a powerful confederacy of American Indian tribes. They lived mostly in what is now New York State. *noun, plural* **Ir o quois.**

ir reg u lar (i reg′yə lər), **1** not regular; not according to rule; out of the usual order or natural way: *irregular breathing. It would be quite irregular for a child of ten to drive a car.* **2** not even; not smooth; not straight: *New England has a very irregular coastline. adjective.*

ir reg u lar i ty (i reg′yə lar′ə tē), **1** lack of regularity; being irregular. **2** something irregular. *noun, plural* **ir reg u lar i ties.**

ir re sist i ble (ir′i zis′tə bəl), that cannot be resisted; too great to be withstood; overwhelming: *I had an irresistible desire for some ice cream. adjective.*

ir res o lute (i rez′ə lüt), not resolute; unable to make up one's mind; not sure of what one wants; hesitating: *Irresolute persons make poor leaders. adjective.*

ir re spon si ble (ir′i spon′sə bəl), untrustworthy; unreliable. *adjective.*

ir rev er ent (i rev′ər ənt), not reverent; disrespectful. *adjective.*

ir ri gate (ir′ə gāt), supply (land) with water by using ditches or by sprinkling: *After a desert is irrigated, crops will grow there.* See picture. *verb,* **ir ri gat ed, ir ri gat ing.**

ir ri ga tion (ir′ə gā′shən), supplying land with water; irrigating: *Irrigation is needed to make crops grow in dry regions. noun.*

ir ri ta ble (ir′ə tə bəl), **1** easily made angry; impatient: *When the rain spoiled her plans, she was irritable for the rest of the day.* **2** more sensitive than is natural or normal: *A baby's skin is often quite irritable. adjective.*

ir ri tate (ir′ə tāt), **1** arouse to impatience or anger; annoy; vex: *Their constant interruptions irritated me. Flies irritate horses.* **2** make (a part of the body) more sensitive than is natural or normal: *Sunburn irritates the skin. verb,* **ir ri tat ed, ir ri tat ing.**

ir ri ta tion (ir′ə tā′shən), **1** annoyance; vexation. **2** irritating; being irritated: *Irritation of the nose can make you sneeze. noun.*

is (iz). *The earth is round. He is at school. Flour is sold by the pound. verb.*

-ish, suffix meaning: **1** somewhat _____: Sweet*ish* means *somewhat* sweet. **2** like a _____: Child*ish* means *like a* child. **3** like that of a _____: Girl*ish* means *like that of a* girl.

Is lam (is′ləm), the Moslem religion, based on the teachings of Mohammed as they appear in the Koran. *noun.*

is land (ī′lənd), **1** body of land surrounded by water: *Hawaii is made up of a group of islands.* **2** something that suggests a piece of land surrounded by water. Platforms in the middle of crowded streets are called **safety islands.** *noun.*

is land er (ī′lən dər), person born or living on an island. *noun.*

isle (īl), **1** a small island. **2** island. *noun.*

is let (ī′lit), a little island. *noun.*

is n't (iz′nt), is not.

i so late (ī′sə lāt), set apart; separate from others: *People with contagious diseases should be isolated. verb,* **i so lat ed, i so lat ing.**

i so la tion (ī′sə lā′shən), **1** setting apart. **2** being set apart. *noun.*

Is ra el (iz′rē əl), **1** country in southwestern Asia, including the major part of Palestine. **2** ancient Jewish kingdom in northern Palestine. *noun.*

Is rae li (iz rā′lē), **1** of or having something to do with the country of Israel or its people. **2** person born or living in the country of Israel. 1 *adjective,* 2 *noun, plural* **Is rae lis.**

is sue (ish′ü), **1** send out; put forth: *This magazine is issued every week.* **2** something sent out: *The last issue of our weekly paper consisted of 1000 copies.* **3** sending out; putting forth: *The government controls the issue of stamps.* **4** come out; go out; proceed: *Smoke issues from the chimney.* **5** point to be debated; problem: *The voters had four issues to settle.* 1,4 *verb,* **is sued, is su ing;** 2,3,5 *noun.*

at issue, in question: *The matter at issue was where to have the party.*

take issue, disagree: *I must take issue with you on that point.*

isth mus (is′məs), a narrow strip of land, with water on both sides of it, connecting two larger bodies of land: *The Isthmus of Panama connects North America and South America.* See picture. *noun, plural* **isth mus es.**

a hat	i it	oi oil	ch child	a in about
ā age	ī ice	ou out	ng long	e in taken
ä far	o hot	u cup	sh she	ə = { i in pencil
e let	ō open	u̇ put	th thin	o in lemon
ē equal	ô order	ü rule	ᴛʜ then	u in circus
ėr term			zh measure	

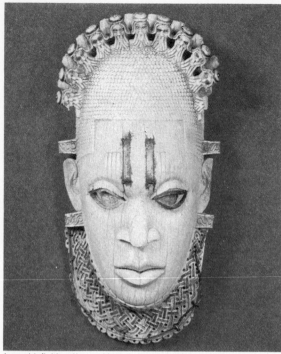

ivory (definition 1)—an African mask made from ivory

ivy (definition 1)—two kinds of ivy.

it (it), **1** the thing, part, animal, or person spoken about: *Here is your paper; read it. Look at it carefully. He said, "It is I. What is it you want?" It snows in winter. It is now my turn.* **2** in games, the player who must catch, find, or guess: *If I tag you, you're it.* 1 *pronoun, plural* **they;** 2 *noun.*

I tal ian (i tal′yən), **1** of or having something to do with Italy, its people, or their language. **2** person born or living in Italy. **3** language of Italy. 1 *adjective,* 2,3 *noun.*

i tal ic (i tal′ik), of or in type whose letters slant to the right. *These words are in italic type. adjective.* [*Italic* comes from a Latin word meaning "Italian" or "of Italy." Italic type was called this because it was introduced by an Italian printer from Venice in 1501.]

i tal i cize (i tal′ə sīz), **1** print in type in which the letters slope to the right. Example: *This sentence is italicized.* **2** underline (written words) with a single line. *We italicize expressions which we wish to distinguish or emphasize. verb,* **i tal i cized, i tal i ciz ing.**

It a ly (it′l ē), country in southern Europe. *noun.*

itch (ich), **1** a prickling feeling in the skin that makes one want to scratch. **2** disease causing this feeling. **3** cause this feeling: *My mosquito bites itch.* **4** feel this way in the skin: *My nose itches.* **5** a restless, uneasy feeling, longing, or desire for anything: *She had an itch to travel.* **6** be restless with any desire: *I itched to find out their secret.* 1,2,5 *noun, plural* **itch es;** 3,4,6 *verb.*

i tem (ī′təm), **1** a separate thing or article: *The list had twelve items on it.* **2** piece of news: *There were several interesting items in yesterday's newspaper. noun.*

i tem ize (ī′tə mīz), give each item of; list by items: *The storekeeper itemized the bill to show the price of each article. verb,* **i tem ized, i tem iz ing.**

it'll (it′l), **1** it will. **2** it shall.

its (its), of it; belonging to it: *The dog wagged its tail. adjective.*

it's (its), **1** it is. **2** it has.

it self (it self′), **1** form of *it* used to make a statement stronger: *The land itself is worth the money, without the house.* **2** form used instead of *it, him,* or *her* in cases like: *The horse tripped and hurt itself. pronoun.*

-ity, suffix meaning state or condition of being _____: *Timidity* means the *state of being timid.* The form *-ty* is often used instead of *-ity,* as in *safety.*

I've (īv), I have.

i vor y (ī′vər ē), **1** a hard, white substance making up the tusks of elephants or walruses. Ivory is used for piano keys, knife handles, and ornaments. See picture. **2** substance like ivory. **3** made of ivory. **4** of or like ivory. **5** creamy white. 1,2 *noun, plural* **i vor ies;** 3,4,5 *adjective.*

i vy (ī′vē), **1** a climbing plant with smooth, shiny evergreen leaves. See picture. **2** any of various other climbing plants, as poison ivy. *noun, plural* **i vies.**

J j

a hat	i it	oi oil	ch child	⎧ a in about
ā age	ī ice	ou out	ng long	⎪ e in taken
ä far	o hot	u cup	sh she	ə = ⎨ i in pencil
e let	ō open	ù put	th thin	⎪ o in lemon
ē equal	ô order	ü rule	ŦH then	⎩ u in circus
ėr term			zh measure	

J or j (jā), the tenth letter of the English alphabet. Few English words have two *j*'s. *noun, plural* **J's** or **j's.**

jab (jab), **1** thrust with something pointed; poke: *He jabbed his fork into the potato.* **2** a thrust with something pointed; poke: *She gave him a jab with her elbow.* **1** *verb,* **jabbed, jab bing; 2** *noun.*

jab ber (jab′ər), **1** talk very fast in a confused way; chatter. **2** very fast, confused talk; chatter. **1** *verb,* **2** *noun.*

jack (jak), **1** tool or machine for lifting or pushing up heavy weights a short distance. See picture. **2** lift with a jack: *She jacked up the car to change the flat tire.* **3** a playing card with the picture of a servant or soldier on it. It is above a ten and below a queen. **4** piece of metal tossed up and caught, used in the game of jacks. **5 jacks,** a child's game in which pieces of metal are tossed up and caught or picked up in various ways. Each player bounces the ball and picks up the jacks in between bounces. **6** a ship's flag, smaller than usual, especially one used to show nationality or as a signal. The **Union Jack** is the British naval flag. **7** man or fellow. A **jack of all trades** is a person who can do many different kinds of work fairly well. **1,3-7** *noun,* **2** *verb.* [*Jack* comes from the common first name Jack. It was first applied to any common person. Then it came to be used for any commonly found animal, machine, and so on.]

jack al (jak′əl), a wild animal of Africa and Asia somewhat like a dog and about as big as a fox. Jackals will often follow a lion or a leopard and eat what is left of the prey it kills. See picture. *noun.*

jack et (jak′it), **1** a short coat. **2** an outer covering: *a book jacket. noun.*

jack (definition 1)—He raised the car off the ground with a jack to change the flat tire.

jackal—about 15 inches (38 centimeters) high at the shoulder

jack-in-the-box (jak′in ŦHə boks′), a toy figure that springs up from a box when the lid is opened. *noun, plural* **jack-in-the-box es.**

jack knife (jak′nīf′), a large, strong pocketknife. *noun, plural* **jack knives** (jak′nīvz′).

jack-o'-lan tern (jak′ə lan′tərn), pumpkin hollowed out and cut to look like a face, used as a lantern at Halloween. *noun.*

jack pot (jak′pot′), **1** the total amount bet in a game. **2** the big prize of a game. *noun.*
hit the jackpot, 1 get the big prize. **2** have a stroke of very good luck.

jack rabbit, a large hare of western North America, having very long legs and ears.

jade (jād), a hard stone used for jewelry and ornaments. Most jade is green. *noun.*

jad ed (jā′did), worn out; tired; weary: *a jaded horse, a jaded look. adjective.*

jag ged (jag′id), with sharp points sticking out: *We cut our bare feet on the jagged rocks. adjective.*

jag uar (jag′wär), a fierce animal much like a leopard, but more heavily built. It lives in forests in tropical America. See picture. *noun.*

jaguar—about 7 feet (2 meters) long with the tail.

jail (jāl), **1** prison, especially one for persons awaiting trial or being punished for some small offense. **2** put in jail; keep in jail: *The police arrested and jailed the suspected thief.* **1** *noun,* **2** *verb.*

jail er or **jail or** (jā′lər), keeper of a jail. *noun.*

jam[1] (jam), **1** press or squeeze tightly between two surfaces: *The ship was jammed between two rocks.* **2** bruise or crush by squeezing: *I jammed my fingers in the door.* **3** press or squeeze (things or people) tightly together: *A crowd jammed into the bus.* **4** mass of people or things crowded together so that they cannot move freely: *She was delayed by the traffic jam.* **5** fill or block up (the way) by crowding: *The river was jammed with logs.* **6** stick or catch so that it cannot be worked: *The window has jammed; I cannot open it.* **7** push or thrust (a thing) hard (into a place): *I tried to jam one more book into the bookcase.* **8** difficulty or tight spot: *I was in a jam.* **1-3,5-7** *verb,* **jammed, jam ming; 4,8** *noun.*

jam[2] (jam), fruit boiled with sugar until thick: *raspberry jam, plum jam. noun.*

jam bo ree (jam′bə rē′), **1** a large rally or gathering of Boy Scouts or Girl Scouts. **2** a noisy party. *noun.*

Jan., January.

jan gle (jang′gəl), **1** sound harshly: *The pots and pans jangled in the kitchen.* **2** cause to sound harshly: *The children jangled cowbells.* **3** a harsh sound: *the jangle of the telephone.* **1,2** *verb,* **jan gled, jan gling; 3** *noun.*

jan i tor (jan′ə tər), person hired to take care of a building or offices. *noun.* [An earlier meaning of *janitor* was "a person who guards a door." It was taken from a Latin word meaning "door."]

Jan u ar y (jan′yü er′ē), the first month of the year. It has 31 days. *noun.* [*January* comes from Janus, the ancient Roman god of gates and doors and of beginnings and endings. He was shown with two faces, one looking forward and one looking backward.]

Ja pan (jə pan′), country made up of several islands in the Pacific, along the eastern coast of Asia. *noun.*

Jap a nese (jap′ə nēz′), **1** of or having something to do with Japan, its people, or their language. **2** person born or living in Japan. **3** language of Japan. **1** *adjective,* **2,3** *noun, plural* **Jap a nese.**

jar[1] (jär), **1** a deep container made of glass, earthenware, or stone, with a wide mouth. **2** amount that a jar can hold: *They ate a jar of peanut butter. noun.*

jar[2] (jär), **1** shake; rattle: *Your heavy footsteps jar my table.* **2** a shake; rattle. **3** make a harsh, grating noise. **4** a harsh, grating noise. **5** have a harsh, unpleasant effect on: *The children's screams jarred my nerves.* **6** a slight shock to the ears, nerves, or feelings. **7** clash; quarrel: *We did not get on well together; our opinions always jarred.* **8** a clash; quarrel. **1,3,5,7** *verb,* **jarred, jar ring; 2,4,6,8** *noun.*

jas per (jas′pər), a colored quartz, usually red or brown. *noun.*

jaunt (jônt), a short journey or excursion, especially for pleasure. *noun.*

jaun ty (jôn′tē), **1** easy and lively; carefree: *The happy boy walked with jaunty steps.* **2** smart; stylish: *a jaunty new hat for Easter wear. adjective,* **jaun ti er, jaun ti est.**

jave lin (jav′lən), a light spear thrown by hand. *noun.*

jaw (jô), **1** the lower part of the face. **2** the upper or lower bone or set of bones that together form the framework of the mouth. The lower jaw is movable. **3 jaws,** parts in a tool or machine that bite or grasp. *noun.*

jay (jā), **1** a noisy North American bird with a crest and blue feathers; blue jay. **2** a noisy European bird with a crest. *noun.*

jay walk (jā′wôk′), walk across a street without paying attention to traffic rules. *verb.*

jay walk er (jā′wô′kər), person who walks across a street without paying attention to traffic rules. *noun.*

jazz (jaz), **1** a kind of music in which the accents fall at unusual places: *Jazz was first played in New Orleans.* **2** of or like jazz: *a jazz band, jazz records.* **1** *noun,* **2** *adjective.* [*Jazz* is a word of American Negro origin.]

jeal ous (jel′əs), **1** fearful that somebody you love may love someone else better, or may prefer someone else to you: *The child was jealous when anyone paid attention to the new baby.* **2** envious; full of envy: *He is jealous of his brother's good grades.* **3** watchful in keeping or guarding something: *Our city is jealous of its rights within the state.* **4** close; watchful; suspicious: *The dog was such a jealous guardian of the little girl that he would not let her cross the street. adjective.*

jeal ous y (jel′ə sē), dislike or fear of rivals; envy. *noun, plural* **jeal ous ies.**

jean (jēn), **1** a stout, heavy cotton cloth used for overalls. **2 jeans,** overalls or trousers made of this cloth: *The cowgirl wore faded jeans. noun.* [*Jean* comes from an earlier English word meaning "of Genoa," a city in Italy. The cloth was called this because it was first made in Genoa.]

jeep (jēp), a small but powerful automobile, used for many purposes by soldiers, farmers, and builders. *noun.* [*Jeep* probably comes from a fast way of pronouncing *G.P.,* the abbreviation for General Purpose Car. That was the name by which this type of automobile was known in the United States Army during World War II.]

jeer (jir), **1** make fun in a rude or unkind way; scoff: *Do not jeer at the mistakes or misfortunes of others.* **2** a mocking or insulting remark. **1** *verb,* **2** *noun.*

Je ho vah (ji hō′və), one of the names of God in the Old Testament. *noun.*

jel ly (jel′ē), **1** a food, soft when hot, but somewhat firm and partly transparent when cold. Jelly can be made by boiling fruit juice and sugar together, or by cooking bones and meat juice, or by using some stiffening preparation like gelatin. **2** substance that resembles jelly. **3** become jelly;

jester
The joker on a playing card is a jester.

a hat	**i** it	**oi** oil	**ch** child	⎧ a in about
ā age	**ī** ice	**ou** out	**ng** long	e in taken
ä far	**o** hot	**u** cup	**sh** she	**ə** = ⎨ i in pencil
e let	**ō** open	**ù** put	**th** thin	o in lemon
ē equal	**ô** order	**ü** rule	**ŦH** then	⎩ u in circus
ėr term			**zh** measure	

turn into jelly: *Some soup jellies when chilled in the refrigerator.* 1,2 *noun, plural* **jel lies;** 3 *verb,* **jel lied, jel ly ing.** [*Jelly* comes from a Latin word meaning "frozen" or "stiffened." Jelly was called this because it is liquid that has become stiff.]

jel ly fish (jel′ē fish′), a sea animal like a lump of jelly. Most jellyfish have long, trailing tentacles that can sometimes sting. See picture. *noun, plural* **jel ly fish es** or **jel ly fish.**

jeop ar dy (jep′ər dē), danger; risk: *Many lives were in jeopardy during the forest fire. noun.*

jerk (jėrk), **1** a sudden, sharp pull, twist, or start: *The old car started with a jerk.* **2** pull or twist of the muscles that one cannot control; twitch. **3** pull or twist suddenly: *If the water is unexpectedly hot, you jerk your hand out.* **4** move with a jerk: *The old wagon jerked along.* 1,2 *noun,* 3,4 *verb.*

jer kin (jėr′kən), a short coat or jacket without sleeves. Men wore tight leather jerkins in the 1500's and 1600's. See picture. *noun.*

jerk y[1] (jėr′kē), with sudden starts and stops; with jerks. *adjective,* **jerk i er, jerk i est.**

jerk y[2] (jėr′kē), strips of dried meat, usually beef. *noun.*

jer sey (jėr′zē), **1** a close-fitting sweater that is pulled on over the head. **2** a knitted cloth made by a machine. *noun, plural* **jer seys.** [*Jersey* was named for the British island of *Jersey.* The cloth was called this because it had been made there for a long time.]

jest (jest), **1** a joke. **2** to joke. **3** poke fun; make fun: *They jested at my idea until I proved it would work.* **4** act of poking fun at. **5** thing to be laughed at. 1,4,5 *noun,* 2,3 *verb.*

in jest, in fun; not seriously: *Her words were spoken in jest.*

jest er (jes′tər), person who jests. In the Middle Ages, kings and queens often had jesters to amuse them with tricks, antics, and jokes. See picture. *noun.*

Je sus (jē′zəs), founder of the Christian religion. The name means "God is salvation." *noun.*

jet[1] (jet), **1** stream of water, steam, gas, or any liquid, sent with force, especially from a small opening: *A fountain sends up a jet of water.* **2** spout or nozzle for sending out a jet. **3** shoot forth in a jet or forceful stream; gush out: *Water jetted from the broken pipe.* **4** jet plane. 1,2,4 *noun,* 3 *verb,* **jet ted, jet ting.**

jet[2] (jet), **1** a hard, black kind of coal, glossy when polished, used for making beads, buttons, and ornaments. **2** deep, shining black: *jet hair.* 1 *noun,* 2 *adjective.*

jet engine, engine driven by a jet of air or gas.

jet plane, airplane that is driven by a jet of air or gas.

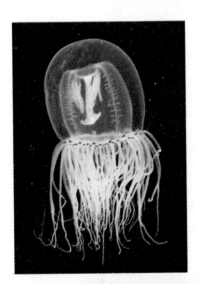

jellyfish

jerkin

jet-pro pelled (jet′prə peld′), driven in one direction by means of a jet of air or gas that is forced in the opposite direction. *adjective.*

jet propulsion, propulsion in one direction by a jet of air or gas that is forced in the opposite direction.

jet ty (jet′ē), **1** structure of stones or timbers projecting out from the shore to break the force of the current or waves; breakwater. **2** a landing place; pier. *noun, plural* **jet ties.**

Jew (jü), **1** person descended from the people led by Moses, who settled in Palestine and now live in Israel and many other countries. **2** person whose religion is Judaism. *noun.*

jew el (jü′əl), **1** a precious stone; gem. Jewels are used in the moving parts of watches, as well as worn in pins and other ornaments. **2** a valuable ornament to be worn, set with precious stones: *The queen wore the crown jewels at the ceremony.* **3** person or thing that is very precious. **4** set or adorn with jewels or with things like jewels. See picture. 1-3 *noun,* 4 *verb.*

jew el er (jü′ə lər), person who makes, sells, or repairs jewels and watches. *noun.*

jew el ry (jü′əl rē), **1** jewels: *Mother keeps her jewelry in a small locked box.* **2** ring, bracelet, or other ornament to be worn, usually set with imitation gems and made of silver- or gold-colored metal. *noun.*

Jew ish (jü′ish), of the Jews or their religion: *the Jewish faith. adjective.*

jib (jib), a triangular sail in front of the foremast. *noun.*

jif fy (jif′ē), moment; a very short time: *I was on my bike in a jiffy, pedaling down the drive. noun, plural* **jif fies.**

jig (jig), **1** a lively dance. **2** music for it. **3** dance a jig. 1,2 *noun,* 3 *verb,* **jigged, jig ging.**

jewel (definition 4)
The queen's gown was **jeweled** with pearls and priceless gems.

jig gle (jig′əl), **1** shake or jerk slightly: *Don't jiggle the desk when I'm trying to write.* **2** a slight shake; light jerk. 1 *verb,* **jig gled, jig gling;** 2 *noun.*

jig saw (jig′sô′), a narrow saw mounted in a frame and worked with an up-and-down motion, used to cut curves. *noun.*

jigsaw puzzle, picture cut into irregular pieces that can be fitted together again.

jin gle (jing′gəl), **1** a sound like that of little bells, or of coins or keys striking together. **2** make such a sound: *The sleigh bells jingle as we ride.* **3** cause (something) to jingle: *jingle one's money.* **4** verse or music that repeats similar sounds in a catchy way. "Higgledy, piggledy, my black hen" is a jingle. 1,4 *noun,* 2,3 *verb,* **jin gled, jin gling.**

jinx (jingks), person or thing that brings bad luck. *noun, plural* **jinx es.**

jit ters (jit′ərz), extreme nervousness. *noun plural.*

jit ter y (jit′ər ē), nervous. *adjective.*

job (job), **1** piece of work: *He had the job of painting the boat.* **2** work done for pay; employment: *Her sister is hunting for a job.* **3** anything a person has to do: *Washing the dishes is his job this week, not mine. noun.*

jock ey (jok′ē), person who rides horses in races as a job, *noun, plural* **jock eys.**

jog (jog), **1** shake with a push or jerk: *He jogged my elbow to get my attention.* **2** a shake, push, or nudge. **3** stir up (your own or another person's memory): *He tied a string around his finger to jog his memory.* **4** hint or reminder: *give one's memory a jog.* **5** move up or down with a jerk or a shaking motion: *The rider jogged up and down on the horse's back.* **6** walk or trot slowly: *My mother goes jogging every day.* **7** a slow walk or trot. 1,3,5,6 *verb,* **jogged, jog ging;** 2,4,7 *noun.*

jog gle (jog′əl), shake slightly. *verb,* **jog gled, jog gling.**

join (join), **1** bring or put together; connect, fasten, or clasp together: *join hands, join an island to the mainland by a bridge.* **2** unite with; come together with: *Join us as soon as you can. The stream joins the river just below the mill.* **3** make or become one; combine; unite: *join in marriage. The two clubs joined forces during the campaign.* **4** take part with others: *join in a song.* **5** become a member of: *She joined a tennis club. My uncle has joined the army. verb.*

joint (joint), **1** the place at which two things or parts are joined together. A pocketknife has a joint to fold the blade inside the handle. **2** the way parts are joined: *The square ends of the wood made a perfect joint.* **3** connect by a joint or joints. **4** the place in an animal skeleton where two bones join. There is usually motion at a joint. **5** one of the parts of which a jointed thing is made up: *the middle joint of the finger.* **6** shared or done by two or more persons: *By our joint efforts we managed to push the car back on the road.* **7** sharing: *My sister and I are joint owners of this dog.* 1,2,4,5 *noun,* 3 *verb,* 6,7 *adjective.*

out of joint, moved out of place at the joint: *The fall put his shoulder out of joint.*

joust (definition 2)—knights jousting

a hat	**i** it	**oi** oil	**ch** child	⎧ a in about
ā age	**ī** ice	**ou** out	**ng** long	e in taken
ä far	**o** hot	**u** cup	**sh** she	ə = ⎨ i in pencil
e let	**ō** open	**u̇** put	**th** thin	o in lemon
ē equal	**ô** order	**ü** rule	**ᴛʜ** then	⎩ u in circus
ėr term			**zh** measure	

joint ly (joint′lē), together; as partners: *The two girls owned the boat jointly. adverb.*

joke (jōk), **1** something said or done to make somebody laugh; something funny: *Looking for the hat that was on my head was a good joke on me.* **2** make jokes; say or do something as a joke. **3** person or thing laughed at. 1,3 *noun,* 2 *verb,* **joked, jok ing.**

jok er (jō′kər), **1** person who jokes. **2** an extra playing card used in some games. *noun.*

jol ly (jol′ē), **1** merry; very cheerful; full of fun. **2** extremely; very: *a jolly good time.* 1 *adjective,* **jol li er, jol li est;** 2 *adverb.*

jolt (jōlt), **1** shake up; jar: *The wagon jolted us when it went over the rocks.* **2** jar; jerk: *He put his brakes on suddenly, and the car stopped with a jolt.* **3** a sudden surprise or shock: *News of the plane crash gave them a jolt.* **4** move with a shock or jerk: *The car jolted across the rough ground.* 1,4 *verb,* 2,3 *noun.*

jon quil (jong′kwəl), plant with yellow or white flowers that is much like a daffodil. Jonquils grow from bulbs. *noun.*

jos tle (jos′əl), **1** strike, push, or crowd against; elbow roughly: *We were jostled by the big crowd at the entrance to the circus.* **2** a jostling; push; knock. 1 *verb,* **jos tled, jos tling;** 2 *noun.*

jot (jot), **1** write briefly or in haste: *The clerk jotted down the order.* **2** a little bit; very small amount: *I do not care a jot.* 1 *verb,* **jot ted, jot ting;** 2 *noun.*

jounce (jouns), bounce; bump; jolt: *The old car jounced along the rough road. verb,* **jounced, jounc ing.**

jour nal (jėr′nl), **1** a daily record. A diary is a journal of what a person does, thinks, and feels. A ship's log is a journal of what happens on a ship. **2** newspaper or magazine. **3** a book in which each item of business is written down: *The storekeeper kept a journal of his accounts. noun.*

jour nal ism (jėr′nl iz′əm), occupation of writing for, editing, or conducting a newspaper. *noun.*

jour nal ist (jėr′nl ist), person engaged in newspaper work. Reporters are journalists. *noun.*

jour ney (jėr′nē), **1** traveling from one place to another; trip: *a journey around the world.* **2** travel; take a trip: *She journeyed to Europe last summer.* 1 *noun, plural* **jour neys;** 2 *verb.* [*Journey* is from an old French word meaning "a day's work or travel."]

jour ney man (jėr′nē mən), worker who knows a trade. *noun, plural* **jour ney men.**

joust (joust *or* just), **1** combat between two knights on horseback, armed with lances. See picture. **2** fight with lances on horseback. Knights used to joust with each other for sport. 1 *noun,* 2 *verb.*

jo vi al (jō′vē əl), good-hearted and full of fun; good-humored and merry: *Santa Claus is pictured as a jovial old fellow. adjective.* [*Jovial* comes from a Latin word of the Middle Ages meaning "born under the influence of the planet Jupiter." It was thought that people born under the influence of this planet were happy and cheerful.]

jowl (joul), fold of flesh hanging from the jaw. *noun.*

joy (joi), **1** happiness; glad feeling; glad behavior: *She jumped for joy when she saw the circus.* **2** something that causes gladness or happiness: *On a hot day, a cool swim is a joy. noun.*

joy ful (joi′fəl), **1** glad; happy: *a joyful heart.* **2** causing joy: *joyful news.* **3** showing joy: *a joyful look. adjective.*

joy ous (joi′əs), joyful; glad; gay: *a joyous song. adjective.*

joy ride, ride in an automobile for pleasure, especially when the car is driven recklessly or without the owner's permission.

jr. *or* **Jr.,** Junior.

ju bi lant (jü′bə lənt), showing joy; rejoicing: *She was jubilant when her team won the game. adjective.*

ju bi lee (jü′bə lē), **1** an anniversary thought of as a time of rejoicing. A 50th anniversary is called a golden jubilee. **2** celebration; time of rejoicing or great joy: *We had a jubilee when the war ended. noun.*

Ju da ism (jü′dē iz′əm), religion of the Jews, based on the teachings of the Old Testament. *noun.*

judge (juj), **1** a public official appointed or elected to hear and decide cases in a court of law. **2** act as a judge; hear and decide (cases) in a court of law. **3** person chosen to settle a dispute or to decide who wins a race or contest. **4** settle a dispute; decide who wins a race or contest. **5** person who can decide how good a thing is: *a good judge of character, a judge of dogs in a dog show.* **6** form an opinion or estimate about: *judge the merits of a book.* **7** criticize; blame: *You had*

jumbo

Jupiter (definition 2)

junk²

little cause to judge him so harshly. 1,3,5 *noun,* 2,4,6,7 *verb,* **judged, judg ing.**

judg ment (juj′mənt), **1** opinion; estimate: *In my judgment she is a better student than her sister.* **2** power to judge well; good sense: *Since she has judgment in such matters, we will ask her.* **3** act of judging, especially a decision made by a judge in a court of law. **4** decision made by anybody who judges. **5** criticism; condemnation: *pass judgment on one's neighbors. noun.*

ju di cial (jü dish′əl), **1** of judges; having something to do with a court of law or the administration of justice: *a judicial decision.* **2** of or suited to a judge: *A judicial mind considers both sides fairly before making a decision. adjective.*

ju di cious (jü dish′əs), wise; sensible; having, using, or showing good judgment: *Judicious parents encourage their children to make decisions. adjective.*

ju do (jü′dō), a Japanese way of wrestling or of fighting without weapons. In judo you use the strength and weight of your opponent to your advantage; jujitsu. *noun.*

jug (jug), container for holding liquids. A jug usually has a spout or a narrow neck and a handle. *noun.*

jug gle (jug′əl), **1** do tricks that require skill of hand or eye: *He juggled with knives by balancing them on his nose.* **2** do tricks with: *She can juggle three balls, keeping them all in the air at once.* **3** change by trickery: *The dishonest cashier juggled the store's accounts to hide his thefts. verb,* **jug gled, jug gling.**

jug gler (jug′lər), person who juggles. *noun.*

jug u lar (jug′yə lər), of the neck or throat. The **jugular veins** are in the neck. *adjective.*

juice (jüs), **1** the liquid part of fruits, vegetables, and meats: *lemon juice.* **2** liquid in the body. The juices of the stomach help to digest food. *noun.*

juic y (jü′sē), full of juice; having much juice: *a juicy orange. adjective,* **juic i er, juic i est.**

ju jit su (jü jit′sü), judo. *noun.*

Ju ly (jù lī′), the seventh month of the year. It has 31 days. *noun.* [*July* was named in honor of the Roman leader Julius Caesar, because he was born in this month.]

jum ble (jum′bəl), **1** mix or confuse: *She jumbled up everything in her drawer while hunting for her white gloves.* **2** muddle; mixed-up mess; state of confusion. 1 *verb,* **jum bled, jum bling;** 2 *noun.*

jum bo (jum′bō), very big: *a jumbo ice-cream cone. adjective.* [*Jumbo* comes from the name of Jumbo, a very large elephant exhibited by P. T. Barnum, an American showman. See picture.]

jump (jump), **1** spring from the ground; leap; bound: *How high can you jump? How far can you jump? Jump across the puddle.* **2** a spring from the ground; leap; bound: *The horse made a fine jump.* **3** leap over: *jump a stream. The speeding car jumped the curb and crashed.* **4** cause to jump: *jump a horse over a fence, jump a child up and down.* **5** distance jumped: *a ten-foot jump.* **6** give a sudden start or jerk: *We often jump when a sudden sight, noise, or* *touch startles us.* **7** a sudden, nervous start or jerk: *He gave a jump at the noise of the gun.* **8** rise suddenly: *The price of orange juice jumped when the orange crop was ruined.* **9** a sudden rise: *a jump in the cost of living.* 1,3,4,6,8 *verb,* 2,5,7,9 *noun.*

jump at, accept eagerly and quickly: *jump at a chance, jump at an offer.*

jump er¹ (jum′pər), person or thing that jumps. *noun.*

jump er² (jum′pər), **1** a sleeveless dress to wear over a blouse. **2** a loose jacket. Jumpers are worn by workers to protect their clothes. *noun.*

jump y (jum′pē), nervous; easily excited or frightened: *I felt jumpy after watching the scary TV show. adjective,* **jump i er, jump i est.**

junc tion (jungk′shən), **1** joining or being joined: *The junction of the two rivers results in a large flow of water downstream.* **2** place of joining or meeting. A railroad junction is a place where railroad lines meet or cross. *noun.*

June (jün), the sixth month of the year. It has 30 days. *noun.* [*June* was named for Juno, the Roman goddess who was queen of the gods.]

jun gle (jung′gəl), wild land thickly overgrown with bushes, vines, and trees. Jungles are hot and humid regions with many kinds of plants and wild animals. *noun.*

jun ior (jü′nyər), **1** the younger (used of a son having the same name as his father): *Juan Roca, Junior, is the son of Juan Roca, Senior.* **2** a younger person: *She is her sister's junior by two years.* **3** of or for younger people: *They are playing in the junior chess tournament.* **4** of lower position; of less standing than some others: *a junior officer.* **5** person of lower position, rank, or standing. **6** student in the third year of high school or college. **7** of or having something to do with these students: *the junior class.* 1,3,4,7 *adjective,* 2,5,6 *noun.*

junior high school, school consisting of grades 7, 8, and sometimes 9, attended after an elementary school of six grades. It is followed by high school.

ju ni per (jü′nə pər), an evergreen shrub or tree with brown or bluish berrylike cones. *noun.*

junk¹ (jungk), trash; old paper, metal, and other rubbish. *noun.*

junk² (jungk), a Chinese sailing ship. See picture. *noun.*

junk food, food that contains calories but has little other value.

Ju pi ter (jü′pə tər), **1** the chief god of the ancient Romans. The Greeks called him Zeus. **2** the largest planet. See picture. *noun.*

jur or (jür′ər), member of a jury. *noun.*

jur y (jür′ē), **1** group of persons sworn to give a true answer to the question put before it in a court of law, that is, "Is the prisoner guilty or not?" **2** any group of persons chosen to give a judgment or to decide who is the winner: *The jury of teachers gave her poem the first prize. noun, plural* **jur ies.**

just (just), **1** only; merely: *He went just because his*

a hat	i it	oi oil	ch child	⎧ a in about
ā age	ī ice	ou out	ng long	⎪ e in taken
ä far	o hot	u cup	sh she	ə = ⎨ i in pencil
e let	ō open	u̇ put	th thin	⎪ o in lemon
ē equal	ô order	ü rule	ŦH then	⎩ u in circus
ėr term			zh measure	

friend was going. **2** barely: *I just caught the train.* **3** quite; truly; positively: *The weather is just glorious.* **4** exactly: *That is just a pound.* **5** nearly; almost exactly: *See the picture just above.* **6** a very little while ago: *He just left me.* **7** right; fair: *a just reward, a just opinion, a just price.* **8** good; righteous: *a just person.* 1-6 *adverb,* 7,8 *adjective.*

jus tice (jus′tis), **1** just conduct; fair dealing: *Judges should have a sense of justice.* **2** fairness; rightness; being just: *the justice of a claim. She never doubted the justice of her cause.* **3** a judge. The Supreme Court has nine justices. **4** administration of law; trial and judgment by process of law: *a court of justice. noun.*

jus ti fi a ble (jus′tə fī′ə bəl), capable of being justified; proper: *a justifiable act. adjective.*

jus ti fi ca tion (jus′tə fə kā′shən), **1** justifying. **2** being justified. **3** fact or circumstance that justifies; good reason or excuse: *What is your justification for being so late? noun.*

jus ti fy (jus′tə fī), **1** give a good reason for: *The fine quality of this cloth justifies its high cost.* **2** show to be just or right: *Can you justify your act?* **3** clear of blame or guilt: *The court ruled that he was justified in hitting the man in self-defense. verb,* **jus ti fied, jus ti fy ing.**

jut (jut), stick out; project; stand out: *The pier jutted out from the shore into the water. verb,* **jut ted, jut ting.**

jute (jüt), a strong fiber used for making coarse fabrics or rope. Jute is obtained from two tropical plants. See picture. *noun.*

ju ve nile (jü′və nəl *or* jü′və nīl), **1** young; youthful. **2** a young person. **3** of or for boys and girls: *juvenile books.* 1,3 *adjective,* 2 *noun.*

jute—farmers in South Asia carrying bundles of jute to market

K k

K or **k** (kā), the 11th letter of the English alphabet. There are two *k*'s in *kick. noun, plural* **K's** or **k's.**

ka lei do scope (kə lī/də skōp), tube containing bits of colored glass and two mirrors. As it is turned, it reflects continually changing patterns. *noun.* [*Kaleidoscope* comes from Greek words meaning "to look at a pretty shape."]

kan ga roo (kang/gə rü/), animal that lives in Australia. It has small forelegs and very strong hind legs, which give it great leaping power. The female kangaroo has a pouch in front in which she carries her young. See picture. *noun, plural* **kan ga roos** or **kan ga roo.**

Kan sas (kan/zəs), one of the midwestern states of the United States. *noun.* [*Kansas* was named for an American Indian tribe that once lived in the area. The name may have come from a native word of the Sioux Indians, meaning "people of the south wind."]

ka o lin (kā/ə lən), a fine white clay, used in making porcelain. *noun.* [*Kaolin* was named for Kao-ling, a hill in southeast China. The clay was called this because it was first dug there.]

kar at (kar/ət), one 24th part gold. A ring of 18 karats is 18 parts gold and 6 parts alloy. Also spelled **carat.** *noun.*

ka ty did (kā/tē did/), a large green insect somewhat like a grasshopper. The male makes a shrill noise that sounds like its name by rubbing its wings together. See picture. *noun.*

kay ak (kī/ak), an Eskimo canoe made of skins stretched over a light frame of wood or bone with an opening in the middle for a person. See picture. *noun.*

keel (kēl), **1** the main timber or steel piece that extends the whole length of the bottom of a ship or boat. The whole ship is built up on the keel. **2** part in an aircraft resembling a ship's keel. *noun.*
keel over, 1 upset; turn upside down: *The sailboat keeled over in the storm.* **2** fall over suddenly: *He keeled over in a faint.*

keen (kēn), **1** so shaped as to cut well: *a keen blade.* **2** sharp; cutting: *a keen wind, keen pain, keen wit.* **3** able to do its work quickly and exactly: *She has a keen mind.* **4** full of enthusiasm; eager: *He is keen about sailing. adjective.*

keep (kēp), **1** have for a long time or forever: *You may keep this book.* **2** have and not let go: *Can you keep a secret?* **3** have and take care of: *She keeps chickens on her farm.* **4** take care of and protect: *The bank keeps money for people.* **5** have; hold: *Keep this in mind.* **6** hold back; prevent: *Keep the baby from crying.* **7** maintain in good condition; preserve: *A refrigerator keeps food fresh.* **8** stay in good condition: *Milk does not keep long in hot weather.* **9** continue; stay the same: *Keep along this*

kangaroos—about 8 feet (2½ meters) long, including the tail

katydids—about 2 inches (5 centimeters) long

kayak

road. **10** cause to continue; cause to stay the same: *The blanket keeps the baby warm. Keep the fire burning.* **11** do the right thing with; observe: *keep Thanksgiving as a holiday.* **12** be faithful to: *keep a promise.* **13** food and a place to sleep: *Part of her earnings pays for her keep.* **14** the strongest part of a castle or fort; stronghold. 1-12 *verb,* **kept, keep ing;** 13,14 *noun.*

keep on, continue; go on: *The children kept on swimming in spite of the rain.*

keep up with, go or move as fast as: *You walk so fast that I cannot keep up with you.*

keep er (kē′pər), person who watches, guards, or takes care of persons or things: *the keeper of an inn. noun.*

keep ing (kē′ping), **1** care; charge: *The two older children were left in their grandparents' keeping.* **2** celebration; observance: *The keeping of Thanksgiving Day is an old American custom.* **3** agreement; harmony: *Don't trust him; his actions are not in keeping with his promises. noun.*

keep sake (kēp′sāk′), thing kept in memory of the giver: *Before my friend moved away, she gave me her picture as a keepsake. noun.*

keg (keg), a small barrel: *a keg of beer. noun.*

kelp (kelp), **1** a large, tough, brown seaweed. **2** ashes of seaweed used as a source of iodine. *noun.*

ken nel (ken′l), **1** house for a dog. **2** place where dogs are bred or cared for. *noun.*

Ken tuck y (kən tuk′ē), one of the south central states of the United States. *noun.* [*Kentucky* may have come from a Cherokee Indian word meaning "meadow land."]

Ken ya (ken′yə *or* kē′nyə), country in eastern Africa. *noun.*

kept (kept). See **keep.** *He kept the book I gave him. The milk was kept cool. verb.*

ker chief (kėr′chif), **1** piece of cloth worn over the head or around the neck. **2** handkerchief. *noun.* [*Kerchief* is from old French words meaning "to cover the head."]

ker nel (kėr′nl), **1** the softer part inside the hard shell of a nut or inside the stone of a fruit. **2** grain or seed like that of wheat or corn. **3** the central or important part of anything. *noun.*

ker o sene (ker′ə sēn′), a thin oil made from petroleum, used in lamps and stoves, and as fuel for some engines. *noun.*

ketch (kech), a small, strongly built sailing ship with two masts, and with its sails set lengthwise. *noun, plural* **ketch es.**

ketch up (kech′əp), catsup. *noun.*

ket tle (ket′l), **1** any metal container for boiling liquids or cooking fruit and vegetables. **2** a metal container with a handle and spout for heating water; teakettle. *noun.*

ket tle drum (ket′l drum′), drum consisting of a hollow hemisphere of brass or copper with a top of parchment. See picture. *noun.*

key¹ (kē), **1** a small metal instrument for fastening and unfastening the lock of a door, a padlock, or any other thing. **2** anything shaped or used like it:

a roller-skate key. **3** answer to a puzzle or problem; guide to a solution: *key to a crossword puzzle, key to a mystery story.* **4** sheet or book of answers: *a key to a test.* **5** a systematic explanation of abbreviations or symbols, used in a dictionary or map. *There is a pronunciation key in this dictionary.* **6** place that commands or gives control of a sea or a district because of its position: *Gibraltar is the key to the Mediterranean.* **7** controlling; very important: *the key industries of a nation.* **8** an important or essential person or thing: *A common interest in music is the key to their friendship.* **9** one of a set of parts pressed in playing a piano, and in operating a typewriter or other instruments: *Don't hit the keys so hard.* **10** scale or system of notes in music related to one another in a special way and based on a particular note: *a song written in the key of C.* **11** tone of voice; style of thought or expression: *The poet wrote in a sorrowful key.* **12** regulate the pitch of; tune: *key a musical instrument in preparation for a concert.* 1-6,8-11 *noun, plural* **keys;** 7 *adjective,* 12 *verb.*

key up, excite; make nervous: *The actors were keyed up before opening night.*

key² (kē), a low island or reef. There are keys south of Florida. *noun, plural* **keys.**

key board (kē′bôrd′), the set of keys in a piano, organ, or typewriter. *noun.*

key hole (kē′hōl′), opening in a lock through which a key is inserted. *noun.*

key stone (kē′stōn′), **1** the middle stone at the top of an arch, holding the other stones or pieces in place. **2** part on which other related parts depend. *noun.*

kettledrums

khak i (kak′ē *or* kä′kē), **1** dull yellowish brown. **2** a heavy cloth of this color, much used for soldiers' uniforms. **3 khakis,** a uniform made of this cloth: *Khakis will be worn in the parade.* **1** *adjective,* **2,3** *noun, plural* **khak is.**

kick (kik), **1** strike out with the foot: *This horse kicks when anyone comes near it.* **2** strike with the foot: *The horse kicked the boy.* **3** move (a thing) by kicking: *kick a ball along the ground, kick off one's shoes, kick up dust.* **4** blow with the foot: *The horse's kick knocked me down.* **5** the backward spring of a gun when it is fired. **6** spring back; recoil: *This shotgun kicks.* **7** grumble; find fault. **8** complaint; objection. **9** thrill; excitement: *The children got a kick out of going to the circus.* **1-3,6,7** *verb,* **4,5,8,9** *noun.*

kick ball (kik′bôl′), a game that is similar to baseball. The ball is rolled instead of thrown, and kicked instead of hit. *noun.*

kick off (kik′ôf′), kick that puts a football in play at the beginning of each half and after a score has been made. *noun.*

kid[1] (kid), **1** a young goat. **2** leather made from the skin of a young goat, used for gloves and shoes. **3** child. *noun.*

kid[2] (kid), tease playfully; talk in a joking way: *Those two love to kid one another.* *verb,* **kid ded, kid ding.**

kid nap (kid′nap), steal (a child); carry off (anyone) by force: *Kidnaping a child is a terrible crime.* *verb,* **kid naped, kid nap ing,** *or* **kid napped, kid nap ping.**

kid ney (kid′nē), **1** one of the pair of organs in the body that separate waste matter and water from the blood and pass them off through the bladder in liquid form. **2** kidney or kidneys of an animal, cooked for food. *noun, plural* **kid neys.**

kill (kil), **1** put to death: *The blow from the ax killed him.* **2** cause the death of: *A bolt of lightning killed the tree.* **3** act of killing. **4** animal killed. **5** put an end to; get rid of: *kill odors, kill faith.* **6** use up (time), especially in some idle or useless manner: *We killed an hour at the zoo.* **1,2,5,6** *verb,* **3,4** *noun.*

kill deer (kil′dir′), bird which has two black bands across its breast and a loud, shrill cry. It is the commonest plover of North America. *noun, plural* **kill deers** *or* **kill deer.**

kill er (kil′ər), person, animal, or thing that kills. *noun.*

kill joy (kil′joi′), person who spoils other people's fun. *noun.*

kiln (kil *or* kiln), furnace or oven for burning, baking, or drying something. Limestone is burned in a kiln to make lime. Bricks are baked in a kiln. *noun.*

ki lo (kē′lō *or* kil′ō), **1** kilogram. **2** kilometer. *noun, plural* **ki los.**

kil o gram (kil′ə gram′), the basic unit of weight in the metric system. It is equal to 1000 grams or $2\frac{1}{5}$ pounds. *noun.*

ki lom e ter (kə lom′ə tər *or* kil′ə mē′tər), a unit for measuring length or distance. It is equal to 1000 meters or about $\frac{3}{5}$ of a mile. *noun.*

kilt

kimono (definition 1)

kitten
an ocelot kitten

kil o watt (kil/ə wot/), a unit for measuring electric power equal to 1000 watts. *noun.*

kilt (kilt), a pleated skirt, reaching to the knees, worn by men in parts of Scotland. See picture. *noun.*

ki mo no (kə mō/nə), **1** a loose outer garment held in place by a sash, worn by both men and women in Japan. See picture. **2** a woman's loose dressing gown. *noun, plural* **ki mo nos.**

kin (kin), **1** family or relatives; kindred: *All our kin came to the family reunion.* **2** family relationship: *What kin is she to you?* **3** related: *Your cousin is also kin to me.* **1,2** *noun,* **3** *adjective.*

next of kin, nearest living relative.

kind¹ (kīnd), **1** friendly; doing good rather than harm: *A kind person tries to help others. Sharing your lunch was a kind thing to do.* **2** gentle: *Be kind to animals. adjective.*

kind² (kīnd), **1** sort; type: *I like many kinds of food. A kilt is a kind of skirt.* **2** natural group: *The wolf hunted in a pack with others of its kind. noun.*

of a kind, of the same sort: *The cakes were all of a kind—chocolate.*

kin der gar ten (kin/dər gärt/n), school for children from about 4 to 6 years old that educates them by games, toys, and pleasant activities. *noun.* [*Kindergarten* comes from a German word meaning "children's garden."]

kind heart ed (kīnd/här/tid), having or showing a kind heart; kindly; sympathetic. *adjective.*

kin dle (kin/dl), **1** set on fire; light: *I used a match to kindle the wood.* **2** catch fire; begin to burn: *This damp wood will never kindle.* **3** stir up; arouse: *The unfairness of the punishment kindled my anger. verb,* **kin dled, kin dling.**

kind li ness (kīnd/lē nis), **1** kindly feeling or quality. **2** a kindly act. *noun, plural* **kind li ness es.**

kin dling (kind/ling), small pieces of wood for starting a fire. *noun.*

kind ly (kīnd/lē), **1** kind; friendly: *kindly faces.* **2** in a kind or friendly way: *We thank you kindly for your help.* **3** pleasant; agreeable: *a kindly shower.* **4** with pleasure: *The cat took kindly to its warm bed.* **1,3** *adjective,* **kind li er, kind li est;** **2,4** *adverb.*

kind ness (kīnd/nis), **1** kind nature; being kind: *We admire his kindness.* **2** kind treatment: *Thank you for your kindness.* **3** a kind act: *They showed me many kindnesses. noun, plural* **kind ness es.**

kin dred (kin/drid), **1** like; similar; connected: *We are studying about dew, frost, and kindred facts of nature.* **2** related: *kindred tribes.* **3** a person's family or relatives. **1,2** *adjective,* **3** *noun.*

king (king), **1** man who rules a country and its people. **2** person who has great power in industry, business, or sports; very important person. **3** something or someone best in its class: *The lion is the king of the beasts.* **4** a playing card with the picture of a king on it. It is above a queen and, usually, below an ace. **5** an important piece in the game of chess or checkers. *noun.*

king dom (king/dəm), **1** country that is governed by a king or a queen; land or territory ruled by one king. **2** realm, domain, or province: *The mind is the kingdom of thought.* **3** one of the three divisions of the natural world; the animal kingdom, the vegetable kingdom, or the mineral kingdom. *noun.*

king fish er (king/fish/ər), a bright-colored bird with a large head and a strong beak. Kingfishers eat fish and insects. *noun.*

king ly (king/lē), **1** of a king or kings; of royal rank. **2** fit for a king: *a kingly crown.* **3** like a king; royal; noble: *kingly pride. adjective,* **king li er, king li est.**

king-size (king/sīz/), large or long for its kind: *a king-size package. adjective.*

kink (kingk), **1** twist or curl in thread, rope, or hair. **2** form a kink; make kinks in: *The rope kinked as she rolled it up.* **3** pain or stiffness in a muscle; cramp: *a kink in the back, a kink in the leg.* **4** odd idea. **1,3,4** *noun,* **2** *verb.*

kin ship (kin/ship), being kin; family relationship: *His kinship with the owner of the factory helped him to get a job. noun.*

kins man (kinz/mən), a male relative. Your brothers and uncles are your kinsmen. *noun, plural* **kins men.**

kins wo man (kinz/wùm/ən), a female relative. Your sisters and aunts are your kinswomen. *noun, plural* **kins wom en.**

kiss (kis), **1** to touch with the lips as a sign of love, greeting, or respect. **2** a touch with the lips as a sign of love, greeting, or respect. **3** put, bring, or take by kissing: *kiss away tears.* **4** kind of candy: *chocolate kisses.* **1,3** *verb,* **2,4** *noun, plural* **kiss es.**

kit (kit), **1** the parts of anything to be put together by the buyer: *a model airplane kit.* **2** a person's equipment packed for traveling: *a soldier's kit.* **3** outfit of tools or supplies: *a first-aid kit. noun.*

kitch en (kich/ən), room where food is cooked. *noun.*

kitch en ette (kich/ə net/), **1** a very small kitchen. **2** part of a room fitted up as a kitchen. *noun.*

kite (kīt), **1** a light wooden frame covered with paper, cloth, or plastic. Kites are flown in the air on the end of a long string. **2** hawk with long, pointed wings and often a long, forked tail. *noun.*

kith (kith), friends; acquaintances. *noun.*

kith and kin, friends and relatives.

kit ten (kit/n), a young cat. See picture. *noun.*

kit ty (kit/ē), a pet name for a cat or kitten. *noun, plural* **kit ties.**

Klee nex (klē/neks), trademark for a paper tissue used as a handkerchief. *noun.*

knack (nak), special skill; power to do something easily: *That clown has the knack of making very funny faces. noun.*

knap sack (nap/sak/), a leather or canvas bag for clothes or equipment carried on the back. *noun.*

knave (nāv), a tricky or dishonest man; rascal. *noun.*

knead (nēd), **1** press or mix together (dough or clay) into a soft mass. Kneading may be done with the hands or by machine. *The baker was kneading dough to make pastry.* **2** make or shape by kneading. **3** press and squeeze with the hands; massage: *Kneading the muscles in a stiff shoulder will take away the stiffness. verb.*

knee (nē), **1** the joint between the thigh and the lower leg. **2** anything like a bent knee in shape or position. *noun.*

knee cap (nē′kap′), the flat, movable bone at the front of the knee. *noun.*

kneel (nēl), go down on one's knee or knees; rest on one's knees: *to kneel in prayer. I knelt down to pull a weed from the garden. verb,* **knelt** or **kneeled, kneel ing.**

knell (nel), **1** sound of a bell rung slowly after a death or at a funeral. **2** ring slowly. **3** something regarded as a sign of death or as telling of a death: *Their refusal rang the knell of our hopes.* **4** give a warning sound. 1,3 *noun,* 2,4 *verb.*

knelt (nelt). See **kneel.** *They knelt and prayed. verb.*

knew (nü *or* nyü). See **know.** *She knew the right answer. verb.*

knick ers (nik′ərz), short, loose trousers gathered in at, or just below, the knee. *noun plural.*

knick knack (nik′nak′), a pleasing trifle; ornament; trinket. *noun.*

knife (nīf), **1** a thin, flat metal blade fastened in a handle so that it can be used to cut or spread. A table knife is stiff, with no joint; a pocketknife has a joint so that the sharp edge can be folded inside the handle. **2** a sharp blade forming part of a tool or machine: *The knives of a lawn mower cut grass.* **3** cut or stab with a knife. 1,2 *noun, plural* **knives;** 3 *verb,* **knifed, knif ing.**

knight (nīt), **1** (in the Middle Ages) a man raised to an honorable military rank and pledged to do good deeds. After serving as a page and squire, a man was made a knight by the king or a lord. See picture. **2** (in modern times) a man raised to an honorable rank because of great achievement or service. A man named John Smith becomes Sir John Smith, or Sir John, as a knight. **3** raise to the rank of knight: *He was knighted by the queen.* **4** one of the pieces in the game of chess. 1,2,4 *noun,* 3 *verb.*

knight hood (nīt′hùd), **1** rank of a knight. **2** character or qualities of a knight. **3** knights as a group: *All the knighthood of France came to the aid of the king. noun.*

knit (nit), **1** make (cloth or an article of clothing) by looping yarn or thread together with long needles, or by machinery which forms loops instead of weaving: *to knit a pair of socks.* **2** join closely and firmly together: *The players were all knit into a team that played together smoothly.* **3** grow together: *The doctor fixed his arm so that the broken bone would knit.* **4** draw (the brows) together in wrinkles: *She knits her brows when she frowns. verb,* **knit** or **knit ted, knit ting.**

knight (definition 1)

knot (definition 1)—an overhand knot

knocker

knives (nīvz), more than one knife. *noun plural.*

knob (nob), **1** a rounded lump. **2** handle on a door or drawer: *the knob on the dial of a television set.* *noun.*

knock (nok), **1** give a hard blow or blows to with the fist, knuckles, or anything hard; hit: *The ball knocked me on the head.* **2** a hit: *That knock on my head really hurt.* **3** hit and cause to fall: *The speeding car knocked over a sign.* **4** hit with a noise: *She knocked on the door.* **5** a hit with a noise. **6** make a noise, especially a rattling or pounding noise: *The engine is knocking.* **7** act of knocking. **8** sound of knocking: *I did not hear the knock on the door.* **9** sound caused by loose parts or improper burning of fuel: *a knock in an engine.* 1,3,4,6 *verb,* 2,5,7-9 *noun.*

knock down, take apart: *We knocked the bookcases down and packed them in the car.*

knock out, hit so hard as to make helpless or unconscious: *She was knocked out by a blow on the head.*

knock together, make or put together hastily: *The children knocked together a sort of raft out of old boards.*

knock er (nok′ər), a hinged knob, ring, or the like, fastened on a door for use in knocking. A knocker is used as a signal that someone wishes to have the door opened. See picture. *noun.*

knock-kneed (nok′nēd′), having legs bent inward at the knees. *adjective.*

knock out (nok′out′), a blow that makes an opponent helpless or unconscious: *The boxer won the fight by a knockout. noun.*

knoll (nōl), a small rounded hill; mound. *noun.*

knot (not), **1** a fastening made by tying or twining together pieces of one or more ropes, strings, or cords: *a square knot, a slip knot.* See picture. **2** tie in a knot. **3** tangle: *My thread has knotted.* **4** a tangle: *comb out the knots in one's hair.* **5** group; cluster: *A knot of students stood talking outside the classroom.* **6** the hard mass formed in a tree where a branch grows out, or a section of this mass, seen as a hard, round place in a board. **7** any hard mass or lump: *a knot in a muscle, a hand covered with knots.* **8** joint where leaves grow out on the stem of a plant. **9** a unit of speed used on ships and airplanes, equal to 6076 feet per hour: *The ship's speed is 20 knots.* **10** difficulty or problem: *There are a few knots in your scheme.* **11** unite closely in a way that is hard to undo. 1,4-10 *noun,* 2,3,11 *verb,* **knot ted, knot ting.**

knot hole (not′hōl′), hole in a board formed by a knot falling out. *noun.*

knot ty (not′ē), **1** full of knots: *knotty wood.* **2** difficult; puzzling: *a knotty problem. adjective,* **knot ti er, knot ti est.**

know (nō), **1** have the facts of; be skilled in: *She knows arithmetic. The teacher really knew his subject.* **2** have the facts and be sure that they are true: *We know that 2 and 2 are 4. She was there at the time; she will know.* **3** have knowledge. **4** be acquainted with: *I know her very well, but I don't know her*

sister. **5** tell apart from others: *You will know his house by the red roof. verb,* **knew, known, know ing.**

know-how (nō′hou′), ability to do something. *noun.*

know ing (nō′ing), **1** having knowledge. **2** clever; shrewd. **3** suggesting shrewd or secret understanding: *His only answer was a knowing look. adjective.*

know ing ly (nō′ing lē), **1** in a knowing way. **2** to one's own knowledge; on purpose: *I would not knowingly hurt anyone. adverb.*

knowl edge (nol′ij), **1** what one knows: *a gardener's knowledge of flowers.* **2** all that is known or can be learned: *Science is a part of knowledge.* **3** fact of knowing: *The knowledge of our victory caused great joy.* **4** act of knowing; familiarity with a thing, person, or subject: *a knowledge of the surrounding countryside. noun.*

known (nōn). **1** See **know.** *George Washington is known as the father of his country.* **2** familiar to all; generally recognized; well-known: *a known fact, a person of known ability.* 1 *verb,* 2 *adjective.*

knuck le (nuk′əl), **1** joint in a finger, especially one of the joints between a finger and the rest of the hand. **2** knee of an animal used as meat: *boiled pigs' knuckles.* **3 knuckle down,** work hard: *knuckle down to a job.* **4 knuckle under,** submit: *She would not knuckle under to their demands.* 1,2 *noun,* 3,4 *verb,* **knuck led, knuck ling.**

ko a la (kō ä′lə), a gray, furry animal of Australia that looks somewhat like a small bear, and carries its young in a pouch. Koalas live in trees. See picture. *noun.*

Ko ran (kô rän′), the sacred book of the Moslems. *noun.*

ko sher (kō′shər), right or clean according to Jewish law: *kosher meat. adjective.*

koala—about 2 feet (60 centimeters) long

L l

L or **l** (el), the 12th letter of the English alphabet. There are two *l*'s in *ball*. *noun, plural* **L's** or **l's**.

lab (lab), laboratory. *noun.*

la bel (lā′bəl), **1** slip of paper or other material attached to anything and marked to show what or whose it is, or where it is to go: *I read the label on the box.* **2** put or write a label on: *The bottle is labeled "Poison."* **3** put in a class; call; name: *They labeled the boastful student a liar.* **1** *noun,* **2,3** *verb.*

la bor (lā′bər), **1** work; toil: *The carpenter was well paid for his labor.* **2** workers as a group: *Labor favors safe working conditions.* **3** do work; work hard; toil: *I labored all day at the factory.* **4** move slowly and heavily: *The ship labored in the heavy seas. The old car labored as it climbed the steep hill.* **1,2** *noun,* **3,4** *verb.*

lab o ra to ry (lab′rə tôr′ē), place where scientific work is done: *a chemical laboratory. noun, plural* **lab o ra to ries.**

Labor Day, the first Monday in September. Labor Day is a legal holiday throughout the United States in honor of labor and laborers.

la bored (lā′bərd), done with much effort; forced: *labored breathing. The student who was always late made up labored excuses. adjective.*

la bor er (lā′bər ər), **1** person who does work that requires strength rather than skill and training. **2** worker. *noun.*

la bo ri ous (lə bôr′ē əs), needing or taking much effort; requiring hard work: *Climbing a mountain is laborious. adjective.*

labor union, group of workers joined together to protect and promote their interests.

lace (lās), **1** an open weaving or net of fine thread in an ornamental pattern. See picture. **2** trim with lace: *a velvet cloak laced with gold.* **3** cord, string, or leather strip for pulling or holding together: *These shoes need new laces.* **4** put laces through; pull or hold together with a lace or laces: *Lace up your shoes.* **1,3** *noun,* **2,4** *verb,* **laced, lac ing.**

lac e rate (las′ə rāt′), tear roughly; mangle: *The hawk's talons lacerated the field mouse. verb,* **lac e rat ed, lac e rat ing.**

lack (lak), **1** have no; be without: *Some guinea pigs lack tails.* **2** being without: *Lack of fire made him cold.* **3** have not enough: *This book lacks excitement.* **4** not having enough: *Lack of rest made them tired.* **1,3** *verb,* **2,4** *noun.*

lack ing (lak′ing), **1** not having enough: *A weak person is lacking in strength.* **2** without; not having: *Lacking butter, we ate jam on our bread.* **3** absent; not here: *Water is lacking because the pipe is broken.* **1,3** *adjective,* **2** *preposition.*

lac quer (lak′ər), **1** varnish used to give a coating or a shiny appearance to metals, wood, or paper. **2** coat with lacquer. **1** *noun,* **2** *verb.*

la crosse (lə krôs′), game played with a ball and loosely-strung rackets by two sides of ten players each. The players try to send the ball into a goal. See picture. *noun.*

lac y (lā′sē), **1** of lace. **2** like lace: *the lacy leaves of a fern. adjective,* **lac i er, lac i est.**

lad (lad), boy; young man. *noun.*

lad der (lad′ər), **1** set of rungs or steps fastened into two long pieces of wood, metal, or rope, for use in climbing up and down. **2** means of climbing higher: *Hard work is often a ladder to success. noun.*

lad en (lād′n), loaded; burdened: *a ship laden with goods. The camels were laden with bundles of silk. adjective, verb.*

la dle (lā′dl), **1** a large, cup-shaped spoon with a long handle, for dipping out liquids. **2** dip: *I ladled out the soup.* **1** *noun,* **2** *verb,* **la dled, la dling.**

la dy (lā′dē), **1** woman of good family and social position: *a lady by birth.* **2** a well-bred woman. **3** a polite term for any woman. "Ladies" is often used in speaking or writing to a group of women. **4 Lady,** title used in writing or speaking about women of certain high ranks in Great Britain: *Lord and Lady Grey attended the Queen's reception. noun, plural* **la dies.** [*Lady* is from an earlier English word originally meaning "one who kneads a loaf of bread" or "mistress of the house."]

la dy bird (lā′dē bėrd′), ladybug. *noun.*

la dy bug (lā′dē bug′), a small, round, reddish beetle with black spots. It eats certain insects that are harmful to plants. See picture. *noun.*

la dy-in-wait ing (lā′dē in wā′ting), lady who accompanies or serves a queen or princess. *noun, plural* **la dies-in-wait ing.**

lag (lag), **1** move too slowly; fall behind: *They lagged because they were tired.* **2** falling behind: *There was a lag in forwarding mail to us after we moved.* **1** *verb,* **lagged, lag ging;** **2** *noun.*

la goon (lə gün′), **1** pond or small lake connected with a larger body of water. **2** shallow water separated from the sea by low ridges of sand. **3** water within a ring-shaped island made up of coral. *noun.*

laid (lād). See **lay**[1]. *He laid down the heavy bundle. Those eggs were laid this morning. verb.*

lain (lān). See **lie**[2]. *The snow has lain on the ground a week. verb.*

lair (ler *or* lar), den or resting place of a wild animal. *noun.*

lake (lāk), body of water entirely or nearly surrounded by land. A lake is larger than a pond. *noun.*

lamb (lam), **1** a young sheep. **2** meat from a lamb: *roast lamb.* **3** a young or dear person. *noun.*

lame (lām), **1** not able to walk properly; having a hurt leg or foot; crippled: *He limps because he has been lame since birth.* **2** stiff and sore: *My arm is lame from playing ball.* **3** make lame; cripple: *The accident lamed her for life.* **4** poor; not very good: *Stopping to play is a lame excuse for being late to school.* **1,2,4** *adjective,* **lam er, lam est;** **3** *verb,* **lamed, lam ing.**

la ment (lə ment′), **1** sorrow for; mourn: *We lament* *the dead.* **2** cry; weep; sorrow: *Why do they lament so? verb.*

lamp (lamp), thing that gives light. Oil lamps hold oil and a wick by which the oil is burned. A gas or electric light, especially when covered with a glass globe or other shade, is called a lamp. *noun.*

lance (lans), **1** a long wooden spear with a sharp iron or steel head: *The knights carried lances.* **2** pierce with a lance: *lance a fish.* **3** cut open with a surgeon's knife: *The dentist lanced the gum where a new tooth had difficulty in coming through.* **1** *noun,* **2,3** *verb,* **lanced, lanc ing.**

land (land), **1** the solid part of the earth's surface: *After many weeks at sea, the sailors sighted land.* **2** come to land; bring to land: *The ship landed at the pier. The pilot landed the airplane in a field.* **3** come down from the air; come to rest: *The seaplane landed in the harbor. The eagle landed on a rock.* **4** put on land; set ashore: *The ship landed its passengers.* **5** go on shore from a ship or boat: *The passengers landed.* **6** ground; soil: *This is good land for a garden.* **7** country; region: *Switzerland is a mountainous land.* **8** people of a country; nation: *She collected folk songs from all the land.* **9** arrive: *The thief landed in jail.* **10** catch; get: *land a job.* **1,6-8** *noun,* **2-5,9,10** *verb.*

land ing (lan′ding), **1** coming to land: *the landing of the Pilgrims at Plymouth. There are many millions of takeoffs and landings at the nation's airports each year.* **2** place where persons or goods are landed from a ship or helicopter. A wharf, dock, or pier is a landing for boats. **3** platform between flights of stairs. *noun.*

landing field, field large enough and smooth enough for airplanes to land on and take off from.

land la dy (land′lā′dē), **1** woman who owns buildings or lands that she rents to others. **2** woman who runs an inn or boarding house. *noun, plural* **land la dies.**

land lord (land′lôrd′), **1** man who owns buildings or lands that he rents to others. **2** person who runs an inn or boarding house. *noun.*

land mark (land′märk′), **1** something familiar or easily seen, used as a guide: *The traveler did not lose her way in the forest because the rangers' high tower served as a landmark.* **2** any important fact or event; any happening that stands out above others: *The inventions of the printing press, telephone, telegraph, radio, and television are landmarks in the history of communication. noun.*

land own er (land′ō′nər), person who owns land. *noun.*

land scape (land′skāp), **1** land scene; view of scenery on land: *The two hills with the valley formed a beautiful landscape.* **2** picture showing such a view. **3** make (land) more pleasant to look at by arranging trees, shrubs, or flowers: *This park is landscaped.* **1,2** *noun,* **3** *verb,* **land scaped, land scap ing.**

land slide (land′slīd′), **1** a sliding down of a mass of soil or rock on a steep slope. **2** the mass that slides down. **3** an overwhelming number of votes for one political party or candidate. *noun.*

a hat	**i** it	**oi** oil	**ch** child	a in about
ā age	**ī** ice	**ou** out	**ng** long	e in taken
ä far	**o** hot	**u** cup	**sh** she	**ə** = i in pencil
e let	**ō** open	**ù** put	**th** thin	o in lemon
ē equal	**ô** order	**ü** rule	**ŦH** then	u in circus
ėr term			**zh** measure	

lacrosse

ladybug—about two times life-size

lace (definition 1)

lane (lān), **1** path between hedges, walls, or fences. **2** a narrow country road or city street: *A carriage drove down the muddy lane.* **3** any narrow way: *The bride and groom walked down a lane formed by two lines of wedding guests.* **4** course or route used by cars, ships, or aircraft going in the same direction. **5** bowling alley. *noun.*

lan guage (lang′gwij), **1** human speech, spoken or written: *Civilization would be impossible without language.* **2** the speech of one nation, tribe, or other large group of people: *the French language.* **3** form, style, or kind of language: *bad language, poetic language, the language of chemistry.* **4** wording; words: *The lawyer explained to us very carefully the language of the contract.* **5** the expression of thoughts and feelings otherwise than by words: *sign language. noun.* [*Language* comes from a Latin word meaning "tongue."]

lank (langk), **1** long and thin; slender; lean: *a lank teen-ager, lank grasses.* **2** straight and flat; not curly or wavy: *lank locks of hair. adjective.*

lan tern (lan′tərn), case to protect a light from wind or rain. A lantern has sides of glass, paper, or some other material through which light can shine. See picture. *noun.*

lap[1] (lap), the front part from the waist to the knees of a person sitting down, with the clothing that covers it: *I held the baby on my lap. noun.*

lap[2] (lap), **1** lie together, one partly over or beside another: *The shingles lapped over each other.* **2** part that laps over. **3** wind or wrap around; fold over or about something: *Lap this edge over that.* **4** one time around a racetrack: *Who won the first lap of the race?* 1,3 *verb,* **lapped, lap ping;** 2,4 *noun.*

lap[3] (lap), **1** drink by lifting up with the tongue; lick: *Cats and dogs lap up water.* **2** move or beat gently with a lapping sound; splash gently: *Little waves lapped against the boat.* **3** act of lapping: *With one lap of the tongue the bear finished the honey.* **4** sound of lapping: *The lap of waves against a boat put me to sleep.* 1,2 *verb,* **lapped, lap ping;** 3,4 *noun.*

la pel (lə pel′), either of the two front parts of a coat folded back just below the collar. *noun.*

lapse (laps), **1** a slight mistake or error: *a lapse of the tongue because of carelessness, a lapse of memory.* **2** make a slight mistake or error. **3** slipping by; passing away: *A minute is a short lapse of time.* **4** slip by; pass away: *Our interest in the dull story soon lapsed.* **5** slipping back; sinking down: *War is a lapse into savage ways.* **6** slip back; sink down: *The abandoned house lapsed into ruin.* **7** the ending of a right or privilege because not renewed or not used. **8** end in this way: *My driver's license lapsed when I failed to renew it.* 1,3,5,7 *noun,* 2,4,6,8 *verb,* **lapsed, laps ing.**

lar board (lär′bərd), **1** the left or port side of a ship. **2** on the left side of a ship. 1 *noun,* 2 *adjective.*

lar ce ny (lär′sə nē), theft. *noun, plural* **lar ce nies.**

larch (lärch), **1** tree with small cones and needles that fall off in the autumn. **2** its strong, tough wood. *noun, plural* **larch es.**

lasso (definition 2)—cowboys lassoing a steer

lantern

larva of a butterfly

lard (lärd), **1** the fat of pigs or hogs, melted down for use in cooking: *The cook uses lard in making pies.* **2** put lard on or in; grease: *Lard the pan well.* **1** *noun,* **2** *verb.*

lar der (lär′dər), **1** pantry; place where food is kept. **2** stock of food: *The hunter's larder included flour, bacon, and deer meat. noun.*

large (lärj), **1** of more than the usual size, amount, or number; big: *America is a large country. Ten thousand dollars is a large sum of money. Large crowds come to see our team play.* **2** having much scope or range; broad: *The leader of a nation should be a person of large experience. adjective,* **larg er, larg est.**

at large, 1 free: *Is the escaped prisoner still at large?* **2** in general: *The people at large want peace.*

large intestine, the lower part of the intestine. It removes water from the waste material that has not been digested by the small intestine.

large ly (lärj′lē), much; to a great extent: *A desert consists largely of sand. adverb.*

lar i at (lar′ē ət), a long rope with a noose at the end, used for catching horses and cattle; lasso. *noun.* [*Lariat* comes from Spanish words meaning "the rope."]

lark[1] (lärk), **1** a small songbird of Europe, Asia, America, and northern Africa that sings while soaring in the air. The skylark is one kind of lark. **2** the meadowlark. *noun.*

lark[2] (lärk), something that is good fun; joke: *We went wading just for a lark. noun.*

lark spur (lärk′spér′), plant with tall spikes of blue, pink, or white flowers. *noun.*

lar va (lär′və), the early form of an insect from the time it leaves the egg until it becomes a pupa. A caterpillar is the larva of a butterfly or moth. A grub is the larva of a beetle. Maggots are the larvae of flies. The silkworm is a larva. See picture. *noun, plural* **lar vae** (lär′vē). [*Larva* comes from a Latin word meaning "a mask." This stage of an insect's life was thought to hide, or mask, its later form.]

lar ynx (lar′ingks), the upper end of the windpipe, where the vocal cords are. *noun, plural* **la ryn ges** (lə rin′jēz), **lar ynx es.**

la ser (lā′zər), a device that makes a very narrow and very strong beam of light. Laser beams are used to cut or melt hard materials, remove diseased body tissues, and send television signals. *noun.*

lash[1] (lash), **1** the part of a whip that is not the handle: *The leather lash cut the side of the ox.* **2** stroke or blow with a whip: *The ox was cut by a lash of the whip.* **3** strike with a whip: *The driver of the team lashed her horses on.* **4** beat back and forth: *The lion lashed its tail. The wind lashes the sails.* **5** a sudden, swift movement: *the lash of an animal's tail.* **6** scold; hurt severely with words: *In a speech the mayor lashed the people who cheated on their taxes.* **7** hit: *The wild horse lashed out at the cowboy with its hoofs.* **8** one of the hairs on the edge of the eyelid; eyelash. **1,2,5,8** *noun, plural* **lash es; 3,4,6,7** *verb.*

lash[2] (lash), tie or fasten with a rope: *We lashed logs together to make a raft. verb.*

lass (las), girl; young woman. *noun, plural* **lass es.**

las sie (las′ē), girl. *noun.*

las so (las′ō), **1** a long rope with a noose at the end, used for catching horses and cattle; lariat. **2** catch with a lasso. See picture. **1** *noun, plural* **las sos** or **las soes; 2** *verb.*

last[1] (last), **1** coming after all others: *Z is the last letter; A is the first.* **2** after all others: *She came last in the line.* **3** latest: *When did you see him last? I saw him last week.* **4** most unlikely: *Fighting is the last thing I would do.* **5** end: *Be faithful to the last.* **1,3,4** *adjective,* **2,3** *adverb,* **5** *noun.*

at last, finally: *At last the baby fell asleep.*

last[2] (last), **1** hold out; continue: *How long will our money last? The storm lasted three days.* **2** continue in good condition: *I hope these shoes last. verb.*

last ing (las′ting), that lasts; that will last; that will last a long time: *Their thrilling experiences during the long voyage had a lasting effect on them. adjective.*

latch (lach), **1** a catch for fastening a door, gate, or window, often one not needing a key. It consists of a movable piece of metal or wood that fits into a notch or opening. **2** fasten with a latch: *Latch the door.* **1** *noun, plural* **latch es; 2** *verb.*

late (lāt), **1** after the usual or proper time: *We had a late supper because we came home late.* **2** near the end: *It was late in the evening.* **3** not long past; recent: *The late storm did much harm.* **4** recently dead: *The late Mary Lee was a good citizen.* **5** gone out of office: *The late president is still working actively.* **1-5** *adjective,* **lat er** or **lat ter, lat est** or **last; 1,2** *adverb,* **lat er, lat est** or **last.**

of late, lately; a short time ago; recently: *I haven't seen them of late.*

late ly (lāt′lē), a little while ago; not long ago; of late: *He has not been looking well lately. adverb.*

la tent (lāt′nt), present but not active; hidden: *The power of a grain of wheat to grow into a plant remains latent if it is not planted. adjective.*

lat er al (lat′ər əl), of the side; at the side; from the side; toward the side: *A lateral fin of a fish grows from its side. adjective.*

lath (lath), a thin, narrow strip of wood, used with others like it to form a support for plaster or to make a lattice. *noun, plural* **laths** (la₮нz).

lathe (lā₮н), machine for holding articles of wood or metal, and turning them rapidly against a cutting tool which shapes them. *noun.*

lath er (la₮н′ər), **1** foam made from soap and water. **2** put lather on: *He lathers his face before shaving.* **3** form a lather: *This soap lathers well.* **4** foam formed in sweating: *the lather on a horse after a race.* **5** become covered with such foam:

The horse lathered from its hard gallop. 1,4 *noun,* 2,3,5 *verb.*

Lat in (lat′n), **1** language of the ancient Romans. **2** of Latin; in Latin: *Latin poetry, Latin grammar, a Latin scholar.* **3** of the peoples (Italians, French, Spanish, and Portuguese) whose languages have come from Latin. 1 *noun,* 2,3 *adjective.*

lat i tude (lat′ə tüd *or* lat′ə tyüd), **1** distance north or south of the equator, measured in degrees. A degree of latitude is about 69 miles (111 kilometers). See picture. **2** place or region having a certain latitude: *Polar bears live in the cold latitudes.* **3** room to act; freedom from narrow rules: *You are allowed much latitude in spending your allowance. noun.*

lat ter (lat′ər), **1** the second of two: *Canada and the United States are in North America; the former lies north of the latter.* **2** more recent; later; toward the end: *Friday comes in the latter part of the week. adjective.*

lat tice (lat′is), **1** wooden or metal strips crossed with open spaces between them. **2** form into a lattice: *The cook latticed strips of dough across the pie.* **3** furnish with a lattice: *The windows are latticed with iron bars.* 1 *noun,* 2,3 *verb,* **lat ticed, lat tic ing.**

laud (lôd), praise highly: *Our teacher lauded our efforts to raise money for the new library. verb.*

laugh (laf), **1** make the sounds and movements that show one is happy or amused: *We all laughed at the clown's funny tricks.* **2** sound made when a person laughs: *She gave a hearty laugh at the joke.* **3** drive, put, or bring by laughing: *The children laughed their tears away.* 1,3 *verb,* 2 *noun.*

laugh at, make fun of: *They laughed at their friend for believing that a ghost was in the empty house.*

laugh a ble (laf′ə bəl), amusing; funny: *a laughable mistake. adjective.*

laugh ter (laf′tər), **1** sound of laughing: *Laughter filled the room.* **2** action of laughing: *The clown's antics brought forth laughter from the children. noun.*

launch[1] (lônch), **1** cause to slide into the water; set afloat: *The new ship was launched from the supports on which it was built.* **2** push out or put forth into the air: *The satellite was launched in a rocket.* **3** act of launching a rocket, missile, aircraft, or ship: *The launch of the first space vehicle was a historic event.* **4** start; set going; set out: *Our friends launched us in business by lending us money.* **5** send out; throw: *We used a slingshot to launch pebbles into the air. One team launched a wild challenge at the other team.* 1,2,4,5 *verb,* 3 *noun,* *plural* **launch es.**

launch[2] (lônch), **1** a small, more or less open motorboat for pleasure trips. **2** the largest boat carried by a warship. *noun, plural* **launch es.**

launching pad, surface or platform from which a rocket or missile is shot into the air. See picture.

laun der (lôn′dər), wash and iron clothes. *verb.*

laun dress (lôn′dris), woman whose work is washing and ironing clothes. *noun, plural* **laun dress es.**

launching pad

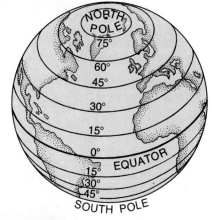

latitude (definition 1)
circles of latitude

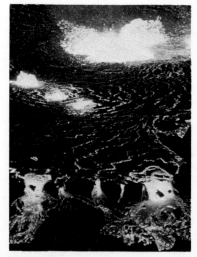

lava
(definition 1)

laun dry (lôn′drē), **1** room or building where clothes are washed and ironed. **2** clothes washed or to be washed. *noun, plural* **laun dries.**

lau rel (lôr′əl), **1** a small evergreen tree with smooth, shiny leaves. See picture. **2** any tree or shrub like this. The mountain laurel has pale-pink clusters of flowers. **3 laurels, a** high honor; fame. **b** victory. *noun.*

la va (lä′və), **1** hot, melted rock flowing from a volcano. See picture. **2** rock formed by the cooling of this melted rock. Some lavas are hard and glassy; others are light and porous. *noun.*

lav a to ry (lav′ə tôr′ē), **1** bowl or basin to wash one's hands and face in. **2** bathroom; toilet. *noun, plural* **lav a to ries.**

lav en der (lav′ən dər), **1** pale purple. **2** a small shrub with spikes of fragrant, pale-purple flowers, yielding an oil much used in perfumes. **3** its dried flowers, leaves, and stalks, used to perfume or preserve linens or clothes. **1** *adjective,* **2,3** *noun.*

lav ish (lav′ish), **1** very free in giving or spending; extravagant: *A very rich person can be lavish with money.* **2** very abundant; too abundant; more than is needed: *a lavish helping of ice cream.* **3** give or spend very freely or too freely: *We lavished kindness on our sick friend.* **1,2** *adjective,* **3** *verb.*

law (lô), **1** rule made by a country or state for all the people who live there: *Good citizens obey the laws. There is a law against spitting in trains.* **2** system of rules formed to protect society: *English law is not like French law.* **3** the study of such a system of rules; profession of a lawyer: *This student is planning a career in law.* **4** any rule that must be obeyed: *The laws of a game must be obeyed by all players.* **5** any rule or principle: *Scientists study the laws of nature. noun.*

law ful (lô′fəl), according to law; done as the law directs; allowed by law; rightful: *a lawful trial, lawful arrests. adjective.*

law less (lô′lis), **1** paying no attention to the law; breaking the law: *A criminal leads a lawless life.* **2** having no laws: *In pioneer days much of the West was lawless. adjective.*

law mak er (lô′mā′kər), person who helps make the laws of a country: *Senators are lawmakers. noun.*

law mak ing (lô′mā′king), **1** having the duty and power of making laws; legislative: *Congress is a lawmaking body.* **2** making laws; legislation. **1** *adjective,* **2** *noun.*

lawn (lôn), piece of land covered with grass kept closely cut, especially near or around a house. *noun.* [An earlier spelling of *lawn* was *laund.* This came from an old French word meaning "a wooded ground" or "a wasteland."]

lawn mow er, machine with revolving blades for cutting the grass on a lawn.

law suit (lô′süt′), case in a court of law started by one person to claim something from another; application to a court for justice. *noun.*

law yer (lô′yər), person who knows the laws and gives advice about matters of law or acts for another person in court. *noun.*

a hat	i it	oi oil	ch child	(a in about
ā age	ī ice	ou out	ng long	e in taken
ä far	o hot	u cup	sh she	ə = { i in pencil
e let	ō open	u̇ put	th thin	o in lemon
ē equal	ô order	ü rule	ŦH then	(u in circus
ėr term			zh measure	

laurel (definition 1)
a branch of laurel with blossoms

lax (laks), **1** loose; slack; not firm: *The package was tied so loosely that the cord was lax.* **2** not strict; careless: *Don't become lax about the schedule you set for studying.* **3** not exact; vague. *adjective.*

lay[1] (lā), **1** put down: *Lay your hat on the table.* **2** beat down: *A storm laid the crops low. A shower has laid the dust.* **3** place in a lying-down position: *Lay the baby down gently.* **4** place or set: *Lay your hand on your heart. The British laid a tax on tea.* **5** put: *Lay aside that book for me. The horse laid its ears back.* **6** put in place: *lay bricks. They laid the carpet on the floor.* **7** put into a certain state or condition: *lay a wound open.* **8** put down as a bet; offer as a bet: *I lay $5 he will not come.* **9** make quiet or make disappear: *lay a ghost.* **10** give forth (an egg or eggs): *Birds, fish, and reptiles lay eggs. All the hens were laying well. verb,* **laid, lay ing.**

lay about, hit out on all sides: *I laid about with a rolled newspaper at the swarm of mosquitoes.*

lay aside, lay away, or **lay by,** save: *I laid away a dollar a week toward purchasing a new bicycle.*

lay off, 1 put out of work: *During the slack season many workers were laid off.* **2** mark off: *The coach laid off the boundaries of the tennis court.* **3** stop teasing or interfering with: *Lay off me! I'm trying to study.*

lay of the land, the nature of the place; the position of hills, water, or woods: *She learned the lay of the land while on a nature hike.*

lay up, 1 put away for future use: *After the sailing season was over we laid our boat up for the winter.* **2** cause to stay in bed because of illness: *I was laid up with a bad cold last week.*

lay[2] (lā). See **lie**[2]. *I lay down for a rest. verb.*

lay er (lā′ər), **1** one thickness or fold: *the layer of clothing next to the skin. A layer cake is made of two or more layers put together.* **2** person or thing that lays: *That hen is a champion layer. noun.*

lay man (lā′mən), person outside of any particular profession: *It is hard for most laymen to understand doctors' prescriptions. noun, plural* **lay men.**

la zi ly (lā′zə lē), in a lazy manner. *adverb.*

la zi ness (lā′zē nis), dislike of work; unwillingness to work or be active. *noun.*

la zy (lā′zē), **1** not willing to work or be active: *He lost his job because he was lazy.* **2** moving slowly; not very active: *A lazy stream winds through the meadows. adjective,* **la zi er, la zi est.**

lb., pound. *plural* **lb.** or **lbs.** [The abbreviation *lb.* stands for the Latin word *libra.* This was the name of the ancient Roman pound and originally meant "a weight" or "a balance."]

lead[1] (lēd), **1** show the way by going along with or in front of: *She led the horses to water.* **2** be first among: *She leads the team in points.* **3** be a way or road: *Hard work leads to success.* **4** pass or spend (time) in some special way: *He leads a quiet life in the country.* **5** go first; begin a game: *You may lead this time.* **6** direct: *A general leads an army. She leads the community orchestra. I led the singing.* **7** place of leader; place in front: *He always takes the lead when we plan to do anything.* **8** right to go or begin first: *It is your lead this time.* **9** amount that one is ahead: *He had a lead of 3 yards in the race.* **10** a guiding indication; clue: *The librarian gave me several good leads for finding the book I wanted.* **1-6** *verb,* **led, lead ing; 7-10** *noun.*

lead[2] (led), **1** a heavy, easily melted, bluish-gray metal, used to make pipe. **2** made of lead: *a lead pipe.* **3** something made of lead. **4** bullets: *a hail of lead.* **5** a long thin piece of graphite used in pencils. **6** weight on a line used to find out the depth of water. **1,3-6** *noun,* **2** *adjective.*

lead en (led′n), **1** made of lead: *a leaden coffin.* **2** heavy; hard to lift or move: *leaden arms tired from working.* **3** bluish gray: *Do you suppose those leaden clouds may mean snow? adjective.*

lead er (lē′dər), person who leads, or is well fitted to lead: *a band leader. She is a born leader. noun.*

lead er ship (lē′dər ship), **1** being a leader. **2** ability to lead: *Leadership is an asset to an officer.* **3** direction: *Our group needs some leadership. noun.*

leaf (lēf), **1** one of the thin, flat, green parts of a tree or other plant that grow on the stem or grow up from the roots. **2** put forth leaves: *The trees along the river leaf earlier than those on the hill.* **3** petal of a flower: *a rose leaf.* **4** a thin sheet or piece: *a leaf of a book, gold leaf.* **5** turn the pages: *to leaf through a book.* **6** a flat movable piece in the top of a table: *We put two extra leaves in the table for the party.* **1,3,4,6** *noun, plural* **leaves; 2,5** *verb.*

leaf less (lēf′lis), having no leaves. *adjective.*

leaf let (lēf′lit), **1** a small flat or folded sheet of paper with printing on it: *advertising leaflets.* **2** a small or young leaf. *noun.*

leaf y (lē′fē), having many leaves; covered with leaves. *adjective,* **leaf i er, leaf i est.**

league[1] (lēg), **1** union of persons, parties, or nations formed to help one another. **2** unite in a league; form a union. **3** association of sports clubs or teams: *a baseball league.* **1,3** *noun,* **2** *verb,* **leagued, lea guing.**

league[2] (lēg), an old unit for measuring length or distance, usually about 3 miles. *noun.*

leak (lēk), **1** hole or crack not meant to be there that lets something in or out: *a leak in a paper bag that lets the sugar run out, a leak in the roof.* **2** go in or out through a hole or crack, or in ways suggesting a hole or crack: *Spies leaked into the city. The gas leaked out. The news leaked out.* **3** let something in or out which is meant to stay where it is: *My boat leaks and lets water in. That pipe leaks gas.* **1** *noun,* **2,3** *verb.*

leak age (lē′kij), **1** leaking; entrance or escape by a leak. **2** that which leaks in or out. **3** amount of leaking: *a leakage of a pailful an hour. noun.*

leak y (lē′kē), having a leak or leaks; leaking. *adjective,* **leak i er, leak i est.**

lean[1] (lēn), **1** stand slanting, not upright; bend: *The small tree leans over in the wind.* **2** rest sloping or slanting: *Lean against me.* **3** set or put in a leaning position: *Lean the ladder against the wall.* **4** depend: *lean on a friend's advice.* **5** be inclined; tend: *lean toward mercy, lean to a different explanation of the accident. verb.*

lean[2] (lēn), **1** not fat; thin: *a lean and hungry stray dog.* **2** meat having little fat. **3** producing little; scant: *a lean harvest, a lean year for business.* **1,3** *adjective,* **2** *noun.*

leap (lēp), **1** a jump or spring. **2** to jump. See picture. **3** jump over: *She leaped the wall.* **1** *noun,* **2,3** *verb,* **leaped** or **leapt, leap ing.**

leap frog (lēp′frog′), game in which one player leaps over another who is bending over. *noun.*

leapt (lept or lēpt), leaped. See **leap.** *verb.*

leap year, year having 366 days. The extra day is February 29.

learn (lėrn), **1** gain knowledge or skill: *Some children learn slowly.* **2** memorize: *learn a poem by heart.* **3** find out; come to know: *He learned that* $\frac{1}{4} + \frac{1}{4} = \frac{1}{2}$. **4** find out about; gain knowledge of: *She is learning history and geography.* **5** become able by study or practice: *In school we learn to read. verb,* **learned** or **learnt, learn ing.**

learn ed (lėr′nid), showing or requiring knowledge; scholarly: *a learned professor. adjective.*

learn ing (lėr′ning), possession of knowledge gained by study; scholarship: *men and women of great learning. noun.*

learnt (lėrnt), learned. See **learn.** *verb.*

lease (lēs), **1** right to use property for a certain length of time by paying rent for it. **2** a written statement saying for how long a certain property is rented and how much money shall be paid for it. **3** rent: *We have leased an apartment for one year.* **1,2** *noun,* **3** *verb,* **leased, leas ing.**

leash (lēsh), **1** strap or chain for holding an animal in check: *He led the dog on a leash.* **2** hold in with a leash; control: *She leashed her anger and did not* *say a harsh word.* 1 *noun, plural* **leash es;** 2 *verb.*

hold in leash, control: *Hold your anger in leash.*

least (lēst), **1** less than any other; smallest: *Ten cents is a little money; five cents is less; one cent is least.* **2** smallest amount; smallest thing: *The least you can do is to thank him.* **3** to the smallest extent or degree: *She liked that book least of all.* 1 *adjective,* 2 *noun,* 3 *adverb.*

at least, 1 at the lowest estimate; not less than: *You should brush your teeth at least once a day.* **2** at any rate; in any case: *Even if you don't want to go swimming, at least you can come with me.*

leath er (leᴛʜ′ər), **1** material made from the skins of animals by removing the hair and then tanning them: *Shoes are made of leather.* **2** made of leather: *leather gloves.* 1 *noun,* 2 *adjective.*

leath er y (leᴛʜ′ər ē), like leather; tough: *a leathery face. adjective.*

leave[1] (lēv), **1** go away: *We leave tonight.* **2** go away from: *They left the room. He has left his home and friends and gone to sea.* **3** stop living in, belonging to, or working at or for: *leave the country, leave one's job.* **4** go without taking; let stay behind: *leave a book on the table.* **5** let stay (in a certain condition): *He left the good-by unsaid. I was left alone as before. The story left him unmoved.* **6** let alone: *Then the potatoes must be left to boil for half an hour.* **7** give (to family, friends, charity) when one dies: *She left a large fortune to her children.* **8** give or hand over (to someone else) to do: *I left the driving to my sister.* **9** not attend to: *I shall leave my homework till tomorrow. verb,* **left, leav ing.**

leave off, stop: *Continue the story from where I left off.*

leave out, not say, do, or put in: *She left out two words when she read the sentence.*

leave[2] (lēv), **1** consent; permission: *Have I your leave to go?* **2** permission to be absent from duty. A **leave of absence** is an official permission to stay away from one's work, school, or military duty. **3** length of time for which one has leave of

leap (definition 2)
He **leaped** high to block his opponent.

absence: *Our annual leave is thirty days. noun.*

take leave of, say good-by to: *She took leave of her family before she went back to college.*

leaves (lēvz), more than one leaf: *oak leaves. noun plural.*

lec ture (lek′chər), **1** speech; planned talk on a chosen subject; such a talk written down or printed. **2** give a lecture: *The professor lectured on American history.* **3** scolding: *My parents give me a lecture when I come home late.* **4** scold. 1,3 *noun,* 2,4 *verb,* **lec tured, lec tur ing.**

lec tur er (lek′chər ər), person who lectures. *noun.*

led (led). See **lead**[1]. *She led her younger brother across the street. We were led through the cave by a guide. verb.*

ledge (lej), **1** a narrow shelf: *a window ledge.* **2** shelf or ridge of rock. *noun.*

lee (lē), **1** side or part sheltered from the wind: *The wind was so fierce that we ran to the lee of the house.* **2** sheltered from the wind: *the lee side of a ship.* 1 *noun,* 2 *adjective.*

leech (lēch), **1** worm living in ponds and streams that sucks the blood of animals. Doctors used to use leeches to suck blood from sick people. **2** person who is always trying to get money and favors from others, without doing anything to earn them. *noun, plural* **leech es.**

leek (lēk), vegetable somewhat like a long, thick, green onion. *noun.*

leer (lir), **1** a sly, nasty look to the side; evil glance. **2** give a sly, evil glance. 1 *noun,* 2 *verb.*

lee ward (lē′wərd *or* lü′ərd), **1** on the side away from the wind. **2** the side away from the wind. **3** in the direction toward which the wind is blowing. 1,3 *adjective, adverb,* 2 *noun.*

left[1] (left), **1** belonging to the side of the less-used hand (in most people); having something to do with the side of anything that is turned west when the main side is turned north: *I sprained my left ankle. A person has a right hand and a left hand.* **2** on this side when viewed from in front: *Take a left turn at the next light.* **3** on or to the left side: *Turn left.* **4** the left side or hand: *He sat at my left.* 1,2 *adjective,* 3 *adverb,* 4 *noun.*

left[2] (left). See **leave**[1]. *He left his hat in the hall. Milk is left at our door. She left at four o'clock. verb.*

left-hand (left′hand′), **1** on or to the left. **2** of, for, or with the left hand. *adjective.*

left-hand ed (left′han′did), **1** using the left hand more easily and readily than the right. **2** done with the left hand. **3** made to be used with the left hand. *adjective.*

left o ver (left′ō′vər), **1** thing that is left. Scraps of food from a meal are leftovers. **2** that is left; remaining: *I made some sandwiches with the leftover meat.* 1 *noun,* 2 *adjective.*

leg (leg), **1** one of the parts of the body on which people and animals stand and move about. Spiders have eight legs. **2** part of a garment that covers a leg: *I fell and tore my pants' leg.* **3** anything shaped or used like a leg; any support that is much longer than it is wide: *a table leg.* **4** one of the parts or stages of any course: *the last leg of a trip.* noun.

leg a cy (leg′ə sē), **1** money or other property left to a person by the will of someone who has died. **2** something that has been handed down from an ancestor. *noun, plural* **leg a cies.**

le gal (lē′gəl), **1** of law: *legal knowledge.* **2** of lawyers: *legal advice.* **3** according to law; lawful: *Hunting is legal only during certain seasons.* adjective.

leg end (lej′ənd), **1** story coming down from the past, which many people have believed: *The stories about Robin Hood are legends, not history.* **2** such stories as a group. **3** what is written on a coin or medal: *Read the legend on a five-cent piece.* **4** words accompanying a picture, diagram, or map: *The legend underneath the picture tells us that the woman is Queen Elizabeth I. noun.*

leg end ar y (lej′ən der′ē), of a legend or legends: *Robin Hood is a legendary person.* See picture. adjective.

leg gings (leg′ingz), extra outer coverings of cloth or leather for the legs, for use out of doors. *noun plural.*

leg i ble (lej′ə bəl), easy to read; plain and clear: *Her handwriting is quite large and legible.* adjective.

le gion (lē′jən), **1** division in the ancient Roman army containing several thousand foot soldiers and several hundred horsemen. **2** a large group of soldiers; army. **3** a great many; very large number: *Legions of grasshoppers destroyed the crops. noun.*

leg is late (lej′ə slāt), make laws: *Congress legislates for the United States.* verb, **leg is lat ed, leg is lat ing.**

leg is la tion (lej′ə slā′shən), **1** making laws: *Congress has the power of legislation.* **2** the laws made: *Important legislation is reported in today's newspaper. noun.*

leg is la tive (lej′ə slā′tiv), **1** having to do with making laws: *legislative reforms.* **2** having the duty and power of making laws: *Congress is a legislative body.* **3** ordered by law; made to be as it is by law: *a legislative decree.* adjective.

leg is la tor (lej′ə slā′tər), person who makes laws; member of a group that makes laws. Senators and Representatives are legislators. *noun.*

leg is la ture (lej′ə slā′chər), group of persons that has the duty and power of making laws for a state or country. Each state of the United States has a legislature. *noun.*

le git i mate (lə jit′ə mit), rightful; lawful; allowed: *Sickness is a legitimate reason for a child's absence from school.* adjective.

lei sure (lē′zhər), **1** time free from required work in which you may rest, amuse yourself, and do the things you like to do: *She's been too busy to have much leisure.* **2** free; not busy: *leisure hours.* **1** *noun,* **2** *adjective.*

lei sure ly (lē′zhər lē), without hurry; taking plenty of time: *a leisurely person, to stroll leisurely through the park.* adjective, adverb.

lem on (lem′ən), **1** the sour, light-yellow, juicy fruit of a tree grown in warm climates. The juice of lemons is much used for flavoring and for making lemonade. **2** pale yellow. **3** flavored with lemon. **1** *noun,* **2,3** *adjective.*

lem on ade (lem′ə nād′), drink made of lemon juice, sugar, and water. *noun.*

lend (lend), **1** let another have or use for a time: *Will you lend me your bicycle for an hour?* **2** make a loan or loans: *Banks lend money and charge interest.* **3** give; give for a time; add: *The lovely old furniture lent charm to the room. The Red Cross lends aid in time of disaster.* verb, **lent, lend ing.**

length (lengkth *or* length), **1** how long a thing is; what a thing measures from end to end; longest way a thing can be measured: *the length of your arm, eight inches in length.* **2** how long something lasts or goes on: *the length of a visit, the length of a book.* **3** distance: *The length of this race is one mile.* **4** a long stretch or extent: *Quite a length of hair hung down in a braid.* **5** something of a given length: *a length of rope, a dress length of silk.* noun.
at length, 1 at last: *At length, after many delays, the meeting started.* **2** with all the details; in full: *They told of their adventures at length.*
keep at arm's length, discourage from becoming friendly: *Some people can keep others at arm's length without seeming aloof.*

length en (lengk′thən *or* leng′thən), **1** make longer: *A tailor can lengthen trousers.* **2** become or grow longer: *Your legs have lengthened a great deal since you were five years old.* verb.

length ways (lengkth′wāz′ *or* length′wāz′) lengthwise. adverb, adjective.

length wise (lengkth′wīz′ *or* length′wīz′), in the direction of the length: *She cut the cloth lengthwise.* adverb, adjective.

length y (lengk′thē *or* leng′thē), long; too long: *His directions were so lengthy that everybody lost interest.* adjective, **length i er, length i est.**

len ient (lē′nyənt), mild; gentle; merciful: *a lenient judge, a lenient punishment.* adjective.

lens (lenz), **1** a curved piece of glass, or something like glass, that will bring closer together or send wider apart the rays of light passing through it. The lenses of a telescope make things look larger and nearer. **2** part of the eye that directs light rays upon the retina. *noun, plural* **lens es.** [*Lens* comes from a Latin word meaning "lentil." It was called this because of its shape.]

lent (lent). See **lend.** *I lent you my pencil. He had lent me his knife.* verb.

Lent (lent), the forty weekdays before Easter, observed in many Christian churches as a time for fasting and repenting of sins. *noun.*

len til (len′tl), vegetable much like a bean. Lentils are cooked like peas and are often eaten in soup. *noun.*

legendary—The **legendary** Pied Piper rid the town of its rats.

leopard—about 8 feet (2½ meters) long with the tail

leop ard (lep′ərd), a fierce animal of Africa and Asia, having a dull-yellowish fur spotted with black. Some leopards are black and may be called panthers. See picture. *noun.*

le o tard (lē′ə tärd), a tight-fitting one-piece garment, with or without sleeves. Dancers and gymnasts wear leotards. *noun.*

lep er (lep′ər), person who has leprosy. *noun.*

lep ro sy (lep′rə sē), an infectious disease that causes lumps, spots, and open sores. Leprosy attacks the skin and nerves and weakens muscles. *noun.*

less (les), **1** smaller: *of less width, less importance.* **2** not so much; not so much of: *have less rain, put on less butter, eat less meat.* **3** a smaller amount or quantity: *could do no less, weigh less than before, refuse to take less than $5.* **4** to a smaller extent or degree; not so; not so well: *less bright, less important, less known, less talked of.* **5** with (something) taken away; without: *five less two, a coat less one sleeve.* 1,2 *adjective,* 3 *noun,* 4 *adverb,* 5 *preposition.*

-less, suffix meaning: **1** without a _____; that has no _____: Home*less* means *without a home.* **2** that does not _____: A tire*less* worker means a worker that does *not* tire. **3** that cannot be _____ed: Count*less* stars means stars *that cannot be* count*ed.*

less en (les′n), **1** grow less: *The fever lessened during the night.* **2** make less. *verb.*

less er (les′ər), **1** less; smaller. **2** the less important of two. *adjective.*

les son (les′n), **1** something to be learned or taught; something that has been learned or taught: *Children study many different lessons in school.* **2** unit of teaching or learning; what is to be studied or taught at one time: *Tomorrow we study the tenth lesson.* **3** selection from the Bible, read as part of a church service. *noun.*

lest (lest), **1** for fear that: *Be careful lest you fall from that tree.* **2** that (after words meaning fear or danger): *I was afraid lest they should come too late to save us. conjunction.*

let (let), **1** allow; permit: *Let the dog have a bone. They let the visitor on board the ship.* **2** rent; hire out: *That woman lets rooms to students.* **3** *Let* is used in giving suggestions and commands: *"Let's go fishing" means "I suggest that we go fishing." Let all members do their duty.* **4** suppose: *Let the two lines be parallel. verb,* **let, let ting.**

let down, 1 lower: *We let the box down from the roof.* **2** slow up: *As their interest in the work wore off, they began to let down.* **3** disappoint: *Don't let us down today; we're counting on you to win.*

let in, admit; permit to enter: *Let in some fresh air.*

let off, permit to go free: *I was let off with a warning to do better in the future.*

let out, 1 permit to go out: *They let me out of the hospital too soon.* **2** make larger: *Let out the hem on this skirt.* **3** dismiss or be dismissed: *Our school lets out at three o'clock.*

let up, stop; pause: *They never let up in the fight.*

let down (let′doun′), **1** slowing up. **2** disappointment: *Losing the contest was a big letdown for him. noun.*

let's (lets), let us.

let ter (let′ər), **1** mark or sign that stands for any one of the sounds that make up words. There are 26 letters in our alphabet. **2** mark with letters: *Please letter a new sign.* **3** a written or printed message: *He told me about his vacation in a letter.* 1,3 *noun,* 2 *verb.*

to the letter, very exactly; just as one has been told: *I carried out your orders to the letter.*

letter carrier, person who collects and delivers mail.

let ter ing (let′ər ing), **1** letters drawn, painted, or stamped. **2** act of making letters. *noun.*

let ter-per fect (let′ər pėr′fikt), knowing one's part or lesson perfectly: *I practiced my part in the play until I was letter-perfect. adjective.*

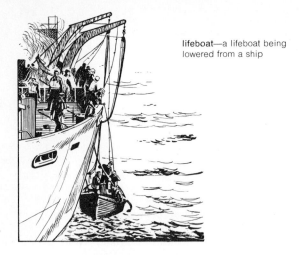

lifeboat—a lifeboat being lowered from a ship

level (definition 4)

BE AN ACHIEVER
TRY A **LEVER**
SHOW YOU'RE CLEVER
USE A **LEVER**
SAY IT EITHER WAY
BOTH ARE OK!

let tuce (let′is), the large, crisp leaves of a garden plant, used in a salad. *noun.*

let up (let′up′), a stop or pause. *noun.*

lev ee (lev′ē), **1** bank built to keep a river from overflowing: *There are levees in many places along the lower Mississippi River.* **2** a landing place for boats. *noun.*

lev el (lev′əl), **1** flat; even; having the same height everywhere: *a level floor.* **2** of equal height or importance: *The table is level with the sill of the window.* **3** something that is level. **4** instrument for showing whether a surface is level. See picture. **5** make level; put on the same level: *The builder leveled the ground with a bulldozer.* **6** raise and hold level for shooting; aim: *She leveled her rifle at the target.* **7** height: *The flood rose to a level of 60 feet.* 1,2 *adjective,* 3,4,7 *noun,* 5,6 *verb.*

lev er (lev′ər *or* lē′vər), **1** bar for raising or moving a weight at one end by pushing down at the other end. It must be supported at any point in between. See picture. **2** any bar working on an axis or support: *the brake lever of an automobile. noun.*

lev y (lev′ē), **1** order to be paid: *The government levies taxes to pay its expenses.* **2** money collected by authority or force. **3** collect (men) for an army: *Troops are levied in time of war.* **4** men collected for an army. 1,3 *verb,* **lev ied, lev y ing;** 2,4 *noun,* *plural* **lev ies.**

li a ble (lī′ə bəl), **1** likely; unpleasantly likely: *That glass is liable to break. You are liable to slip on ice.* **2** in danger of having or doing: *We are all liable to diseases.* **3** responsible; bound by law to pay: *The Postal Service is not liable for damage to a parcel unless it is insured. adjective.*

li ar (lī′ər), person who tells lies; person who says what is not true. *noun.*

lib er al (lib′ər əl), **1** generous: *A liberal giver gives much.* **2** plentiful; abundant: *There was a liberal supply of food at the party.* **3** tolerant; not narrow in one's ideas: *a liberal thinker.* **4** person favorable to progress and reforms. 1-3 *adjective,* 4 *noun.*

lib e ral i ty (lib′ə ral′ə tē), **1** generosity; generous act or behavior. **2** tolerant nature; being broad-minded. *noun, plural* **lib e ral i ties.**

lib e rate (lib′ə rāt′), set free: *In 1865 the United States liberated all slaves. verb,* **lib e rat ed, lib e rat ing.**

lib er ty (lib′ər tē), **1** freedom: *In 1865 the United States granted liberty to all slaves. The American colonies won their liberty.* **2** right or power to do as one pleases; power or opportunity to do something: *liberty of speech.* **3** permission granted to a sailor to go ashore. **4** too great freedom: *She took liberties with the facts to make the story more interesting. noun, plural* **lib er ties.**
at liberty, 1 free: *The escaped lion is still at liberty.* **2** allowed; permitted: *You are at liberty to make any choice you please.* **3** not busy: *The doctor will see us as soon as she is at liberty.*

li brar i an (lī brer′ē ən), **1** person in charge of a library. **2** person trained for work in a library. *noun.*

li brar y (lī′brer′ē), **1** a collection of books: *Those* *two girls have libraries all their own.* **2** room or building where a collection of books is kept: *He goes to the public library to borrow and return books every Saturday. noun, plural* **li brar ies.**

lice (līs), more than one louse. *noun plural.*

li cense (lī′sns), **1** permission given by law to do something: *A license to drive an automobile is issued by the state.* **2** paper, card, or plate showing such permission: *The policeman asked the reckless driver for his license.* **3** permit by law: *A doctor is licensed to practice medicine.* **4** being allowed to do something: *The farm family gave us license to fish in their brook.* **5** too much liberty of action; lack of proper control; abuse of freedom. 1,2,4,5 *noun,* 3 *verb,* **li censed, li cens ing.**

li chen (lī′kən), a plant without flowers that looks somewhat like moss. It grows in patches on rocks, trees, and other surfaces. Lichens are gray, yellow, brown, black, or greenish in color. See picture. *noun.*

lick (lik), **1** pass the tongue over: *lick a stamp.* **2** lap up with the tongue: *The cat licked the milk.* **3** stroke of the tongue over something: *She gave the ice-cream cone a big lick.* **4** pass about or play over like a tongue: *The flames were licking the roof of the burning house.* **5** place where natural salt is found and where animals go to lick it up. **6** blow: *I lost the fight, but I got in a few good licks.* **7** beat or thrash. **8** defeat in a fight; conquer. **9** small quantity: *They didn't do a lick of work.* 1,2,4,7,8 *verb,* 3,5,6,9 *noun.*

lic or ice (lik′ər is), a black, sweet-tasting substance obtained from the dried root of a plant. Licorice is used in medicine and candy. *noun.*

lid (lid), **1** a movable cover; top: *the lid of a box, a jar lid.* **2** eyelid. *noun.*

lie¹ (lī), **1** something said that is not true; something that is not true said to deceive: *I went to school today; saying I didn't is a lie.* **2** speak falsely; tell a lie: *He says that he has never lied, but I think he is lying when he says it.* 1 *noun,* 2 *verb,* **lied, ly ing.**

lie² (lī), **1** have one's body in a flat position along the ground or other surface: *lie on the grass, lie in bed.* **2** rest (on a surface): *The book was lying on the table.* **3** be kept or stay in a given state: *lie idle, lie hidden, lie unused.* **4** be; be placed: *a lake that lies to the south of us, a road that lies among trees, a ship lying offshore at anchor.* **5** exist; be found to be: *The cure for ignorance lies in education. verb,* **lay, lain, ly ing.**

lieu ten ant (lü ten′ənt), **1** person who acts in the place of someone higher in authority: *The scoutmaster used the two boys as his lieutenants.* **2** an army, air force, or marine officer ranking next below a captain. **3** officer in the navy ranking much below a captain. In the navy the order is captain, commander, lieutenant commander, lieutenant, lieutenant junior grade, ensign. *noun.*

life (līf), **1** living; being alive. People, animals, and plants have life; rocks and metals do not. Life is shown by growing and reproducing. **2** time of being alive: *During her life she was an outstanding*

lichen on a tree trunk

doctor. **3** a living being; person: *Five lives were lost.* **4** living beings: *The desert island had almost no animal or vegetable life.* **5** way of living: *a country life, a dull life.* **6** account of a person's life: *Several lives of Lincoln have been written.* **7** spirit; vigor: *Put more life into your work.* **8** period of being in power or able to operate: *The life of that government was very short. noun, plural* **lives.**

life belt, a life preserver in the form of a belt.

life boat (līf′bōt′), a strong boat specially built for saving lives at sea or along a coast. See picture. *noun.*

life buoy, a cork or plastic ring, belt, or vest used as a life preserver; buoy.

life guard (līf′gärd′), person employed on a bathing beach or at a swimming pool to help in case of accident or danger to bathers. *noun.*

life less (līf′lis), **1** without life: *a lifeless planet.* **2** dead: *The lifeless body floated ashore.* **3** dull: *a lifeless party. adjective.*

life like (līf′līk′), like life; looking as if alive; like the real thing: *a lifelike portrait. adjective.*

life long (līf′lông′), lasting all one's life: *a lifelong friendship. adjective.*

life preserver, a wide belt, ring, or vest made of plastic or cork, used to keep a person afloat in the water.

life sav ing (līf′sā′ving), **1** saving people's lives; keeping people from drowning. **2** designed or used to save people's lives. 1 *noun,* 2 *adjective.*

life-size (līf′sīz′), the same size as the living thing: *a life-size statue. adjective.*

life time (līf′tīm′), time of being alive; period during which a life lasts: *My grandparents have seen many changes in their lifetime. noun.*

lift (lift), **1** raise; raise up higher; raise into the air; take up; pick up: *Please help me lift this heavy box.*

2 rise and go; go away: *The fog lifted at dawn.* **3** go up; be raised: *Mother's spirits lifted when she received the promotion.* **4** an elevating influence or result; a raising of the spirits: *Mother's promotion gave her a big lift.* **5** act of lifting: *the lift of a helping hand.* **6** distance through which a thing is lifted. **7** a helping hand: *Give me a lift with this job.* **8** ride in a vehicle given to a traveler on foot; free ride: *Can you give me a lift home?* 1-3 *verb,* 4-8 *noun.*

lift off (lift′ôf′), the firing or launching of a rocket. *noun.*

lig a ment (lig′ə mənt), band of strong tissue that connects bones or holds organs of the body in place. *noun.*

light[1] (līt), **1** that by which we see: *The sun gives light to the earth.* **2** thing that gives light. The sun, a lamp, or a lighthouse is called a light. **3** supply of light: *A tall building cuts off our light.* **4** give light to; fill with light: *The room is lighted by six windows.* **5** bright; clear: *It was a moonlit night as light as day.* **6** brightness; clearness: *a strong or dim light.* **7** a bright part: *light and shade in a painting.* **8** make bright or clear: *Her face was lighted by a smile.* **9** become light: *The sky lights up at dawn.* **10** daytime: *The baker gets up before light.* **11** pale in color; approaching white: *light hair, light blue.* **12** set fire to: *I lighted the candles.* **13** take fire: *Matches light when you scratch them.* **14** knowledge; information: *We need more light on this subject.* **15** open view: *The reporter brought to light bribery in the city government.* **16** aspect in which a thing is viewed: *The principal put the matter in the right light.* 1-3,6,7,10,14-16 *noun,* 4,8,9,12,13 *verb,* **light ed** or **lit, light ing;** 5,11 *adjective.*

light[2] (līt), **1** easy to carry; not heavy: *a light load.* **2** having little weight for its size: *Feathers are light.* **3** having less than usual weight: *light summer clothing.* **4** less than usual in amount or force: *a light sleep, a light rain, a light meal.* **5** easy to bear or do: *light punishment, a light task.* **6** not looking heavy; graceful; delicate: *a light bridge, light carving.* **7** moving easily: *a light step.* **8** cheerfully careless; gay: *a light laugh.* **9** not serious enough: *a light mind, light of purpose.* **10** not important: *light losses.* **11** sandy: *a light soil.* **12** lightly armed or equipped: *light infantry. adjective.*

light[3] (līt), **1** come down to the ground; alight: *She lighted from her horse.* **2** come down from flight: *A bird lighted on the branch.* **3** come by chance: *My eyes lighted upon a coin in the road. verb,* **light ed** or **lit, light ing.**

light out, leave suddenly; go away quickly.

light en[1] (līt′n), brighten; become brighter: *The sky lightens before the dawn. Her face lightened. verb.*

light en[2] (līt′n), **1** reduce the load of; make or become lighter: *Your help lightened our work.* **2** make or become more cheerful: *The good news lightened our hearts. verb.*

light-head ed (līt′hed′id), **1** dizzy; giddy; out of one's head: *The fever made me feel light-headed.* **2** silly; thoughtless: *That light-headed crowd thinks of nothing but parties and games. adjective.*

light heart ed (līt′här′tid), without worry; carefree; cheerful; gay. *adjective.*

light house (līt′hous′), tower or framework with a bright light that shines far over the water. It is often located at a dangerous place to warn and guide ships. See picture. *noun, plural* **light hous es** (līt′hou′ziz).

light ning (līt′ning), flash of electricity in the sky. The sound that it makes is thunder. *noun.*

lightning bug, firefly.

lightning rod, a metal rod fixed on a building or ship to conduct lightning into the earth or water.

light weight (līt′wāt′), not heavy; light in weight: *We packed the food in lightweight containers. adjective.*

lik a ble (lī′kə bəl), having qualities that win good will or friendship; pleasing; popular: *a very likable person. adjective.*

like[1] (līk), **1** much the same as; similar: *Our house is like theirs. I never saw anything like it.* **2** such as one would expect of: *Isn't it just like them to be late?* **3** in the right condition for: *I feel like working.* **4** giving promise of: *It looks like rain.* **5** person or thing like another; equal: *We shall not see his like again.* **6** likely. 1-4 *preposition,* 1,6 *adjective,* 5 *noun.*

and the like, and other like things: *At the zoo we saw elephants, tigers, lions, and the like.*

like[2] (līk), **1** be pleased with; be satisfied with: *Cats like milk.* **2** **likes,** liking; preference: *You know all my likes and dislikes.* 1 *verb,* **liked, lik ing;** 2 *noun.*

-like, suffix meaning: like; similar to: *Daisylike means like a daisy.* See picture.

like li hood (līk′lē hůd), probability: *Is there any great likelihood of rain today? noun.*

like ly (līk′lē), **1** probable: *One likely result of this heavy rain is the rising of the river.* **2** probably: *I shall very likely be at home all day.* **3** to be expected: *It is likely to be hot in August.* **4** promising; suitable: *Is this a likely place to fish?* 1,3,4 *adjective,* **like li er, like li est;** 2 *adverb.*

lik en (lī′kən), compare; represent as like. *verb.*

like ness (līk′nis), **1** resembling; being alike: *The boy's likeness to his father was striking.* **2** something that is like; picture: *This photograph is a good likeness of you.* **3** appearance; shape: *That cloud has the likeness of a dog. noun, plural* **like ness es.**

like wise (līk′wīz′), **1** the same: *See what I do. Now you do likewise.* **2** also; moreover; too: *I must go home now, and you likewise. adverb.*

lik ing (lī′king), preference; fondness; kindly feeling: *a liking for apples, a liking for children. noun.*

li lac (lī′lək), **1** shrub with clusters of tiny, fragrant, pale pinkish-purple or white flowers. **2** pale pinkish purple. 1 *noun,* 2 *adjective.* [Lilac comes from an Arabic word meaning "bluish in color." The flowers of some varieties of lilac are bluish.]

lilt (lilt), **1** sing or play (a tune) in a light, tripping manner. **2** a lively song or tune with a swing. **3** a lively, springing movement: *She walks with a lilt.* 1 *verb,* 2,3 *noun.*

lil y (lil′ē), **1** a plant with tall, slender stems and large, showy, bell-shaped flowers. The flowers are

-like—birdlike, piglike, elephantlike,
rabbitlike, monkeylike

LIMERICK

There was an old man from the Rhine
Who was asked at what hour he'd dine.
  He replied, "At eleven,
  At three, five, and seven,
And perhaps at a quarter to nine."

lighthouse

a hat	i it	oi oil	ch child	a in about
ā age	ī ice	ou out	ng long	e in taken
ä far	o hot	u cup	sh she	ə = { i in pencil
e let	ō open	ù put	th thin	o in lemon
ē equal	ô order	ü rule	ᴛʜ then	u in circus
ėr term			zh measure	

often divided into six parts. Lilies grow from bulbs. **2** flower of any lily plant. The white lily is a symbol of purity. **3** like a white lily; pure and lovely. 1,2 *noun, plural* **lil ies; 3** *adjective.*

lily of the valley, plant having tiny, sweet-smelling, bell-shaped white flowers arranged up and down a single flower stem. *plural* **lilies of the valley.**

li ma bean (lī′mə bēn′), a broad, flat, pale-green bean, used as a vegetable.

limb (lim), **1** leg, arm, or wing. **2** a large branch: *They sawed the dead limb off the tree. noun.*

lim ber (lim′bər), **1** bending easily; flexible: *A piano player should have limber fingers. Willow is a limber wood.* **2** make or become limber: *He is stiff when he begins to skate, but limbers up quickly.* **1** *adjective,* **2** *verb.*

lime¹ (līm), a white substance obtained by burning limestone, shells, or bones. Lime is used in making mortar and on fields to improve the soil. *noun.*

lime² (līm), the light-green, juicy fruit of a tree grown in warm climates. Limes are like lemons, but are smaller and sourer. The juice of limes is used for flavoring. *noun.*

lim er ick (lim′ər ik), kind of humorous verse of five lines. See picture. *noun.*

lime stone (līm′stōn′), rock used for building and for making lime. Marble is a kind of limestone. *noun.*

lim it (lim′it), **1** the farthest edge or boundary; where something ends or must end: *Keep within the limits of the school grounds. I have reached the limit of my patience.* **2** set a limit to; restrict: *We must limit the expense to $10.* **1** *noun,* **2** *verb.*

lim it ed (lim′ə tid), **1** kept within limits; restricted: *limited space, a limited number of seats.* **2** traveling fast and making only a few stops: *a limited train or bus. adjective.*

limp¹ (limp), **1** a lame step or walk. **2** walk with a limp: *After my fall, I limped for a few days.* **1** *noun,* **2** *verb.*

limp² (limp), not at all stiff; ready to bend or droop: *Spaghetti gets limp when you cook it. adjective.*

lin den (lin′dən), a shade tree with heart-shaped leaves and clusters of small, sweet-smelling yellowish flowers. *noun.*

line¹ (līn), **1** piece of rope, cord, or wire: *a telegraph line.* **2** cord for measuring or making level. A plumb line has a plumb at the end of a line and is used to find the depth of water or to see if a wall is vertical. **3** a long narrow mark: *Draw two lines here.* **4** anything that is like a long narrow mark: *the lines in your face.* **5** mark with lines: *Please line your paper with a pencil and ruler.*

6 cover with lines: *a face lined with age.* **7** a straight line: *The lower edges of the two pictures are about on a line.* **8** edge or boundary: *the line between Texas and Mexico.* **9** row of persons or things: *a line of chairs.* **10** arrange in line: *Line your shoes along the edge of the shelf.* **11** form a line along: *Cars lined the road for a mile.* **12** row of words on a page or in a newspaper column: *a column of 40 lines.* **13** a short letter; note: *Drop me a line.* **14** a connected series of persons or things following one another in time: *trace back one's family line.* **15** course, track, or direction: *the line of march of an army, a railroad line.* **16** a certain way of doing: *Please proceed on these lines till further notice.* **17** branch of business; kind of activity: *This is not my line.* **18** kind or brand of goods: *This store carries the best line of shoes in town.* **19** (in mathematics) the path traced by a moving point. Lines have length but no thickness. **20** lines, words that an actor speaks in a play: *forget one's lines.* **21** in football: **a** line of scrimmage. **b** players along the line of scrimmage at the start of a play. 1-4,7-9,12-21 *noun,* 5,6,10,11 *verb,* **lined, lin ing.**
all along the line, at every point: *This car has given us trouble all along the line.*
bring into line, cause to agree or conform: *bring a theory in line with the facts.*
in line, in agreement: *This plan is in line with their thinking.*
line up, form a line; form into a line: *Cars were lined up along the road for a mile.*
line² (līn), **1** put a layer of paper, cloth, or felt inside of (a dress, hat, box, or bag). **2** serve as a lining for: *This piece of silk would line your coat very nicely. verb,* **lined, lin ing.**
lin e age (lin/ē ij), **1** descent in a direct line from an ancestor. **2** family; race. *noun.*
lin e ar (lin/ē ər), **1** made of lines; making use of lines: *linear designs.* **2** of length: *An inch is a linear measure. adjective.*
lin en (lin/ən), **1** cloth or thread made from flax **2** articles made of linen or some substitute. Tablecloths, napkins, sheets, towels, and shirts are all called linen. **3** made of linen. 1,2 *noun,* 3 *adjective.*
lin er¹ (lī/nər), ship or airplane belonging to a transportation system. *noun.*
lin er² (lī/nər), thing that lines or serves as a lining: *I put a fresh liner in the bottom of my desk drawer. noun.*
lin ger (ling/gər), stay on; go slowly, as if unwilling to leave: *She lingered after the others had left. verb.*
lin ing (lī/ning), **1** layer of material covering the inner surface of something: *the lining of a coat.* **2** See **line². 1** *noun,* 2 *verb.*
link (lingk), **1** any ring or loop of a chain. **2** anything that joins as a link joins: *a link in a chain of evidence, a cuff link.* **3** join as a link does; unite or connect: *Don't try to link me with this scheme.* 1,2 *noun,* 3 *verb.*
links (lingks), golf course. *noun plural.*
li no le um (lə nō/lē əm), a floor covering made by

putting a hard surface of ground cork mixed with linseed oil on a canvas back. *noun.*
lin seed oil (lin/sēd/ oil/), a yellowish oil obtained by pressing the seed of flax. It is used in making paints and printing inks.
lint (lint), **1** the soft down or fleecy material obtained by scraping linen. Formerly, lint was put on wounds to keep out air and dirt. **2** tiny bits of thread. *noun.*
lin tel (lin/tl), a horizontal beam or stone above a door or window to support the structure above it. *noun.*
li on (lī/ən), **1** a large, strong animal of Africa and southern Asia that has a dull-yellowish coat. The male has a full, flowing mane of coarse hair. See picture. **2** person who is very brave and strong. *noun.*
li on ess (lī/ə nis), a female lion. *noun, plural* **li on ess es.**
lip (lip), **1** either one of the two fleshy, movable edges of the mouth. **2** the folding or bent-out edge of any opening: *the lip of a pitcher. noun.*
lip stick (lip/stik/), a small stick of a waxlike substance, used for coloring the lips. *noun.*
liq ue fy (lik/wə fī), make liquid; become liquid: *Liquefied air is extremely cold. verb,* **liq ue fied, liq ue fy ing.**
liq uid (lik/wid), **1** any substance that is not a solid or a gas; substance that flows freely like water. **2** in the form of a liquid; melted: *liquid soap, butter heated until it is liquid.* **3** clear and bright like water. **4** clear and smooth-flowing in sound: *the liquid notes of a bird.* 1 *noun,* 2-4 *adjective.*
liq uor (lik/ər), **1** an alcoholic drink, such as brandy or whiskey. **2** any liquid, especially a liquid in which food is packaged, canned, or cooked: *Pickles are put up in a salty liquor. noun.*
lisp (lisp), **1** say the sound of *th* as in *thin* and *then* instead of *s* or *z* in speaking: *A person who lisps might say, "Thing a thong" for "Sing a song."* **2** act of saying a *th* sound for *s* and *z: I used to speak with a lisp.* 1 *verb,* 2 *noun.*
list¹ (list), **1** series of names, numbers, words, or phrases: *a shopping list.* **2** make a list of; enter in a list: *A dictionary lists words in alphabetical order.* 1 *noun,* 2 *verb.*
list² (list), **1** tipping of a ship to one side; a tilt. **2** tip to one side; tilt: *The sinking ship was listing so that water lapped its decks.* 1 *noun,* 2 *verb.*
lis ten (lis/n), try to hear; attend with the ears so as to hear: *We listened for the sound of their car. I like to listen to music. verb.*
listen in, 1 listen to others talking on a telephone: *I listened in on the extension to hear what they were saying.* **2** listen to the radio: *Listen in next week for the exciting conclusion of our story.*
list less (list/lis), seeming too tired to care about anything; not interested in things; not caring to be active: *a dull and listless mood. adjective.*
lit¹ (lit), lighted. See **light¹.** *Have you lit the candles? verb.*
lit² (lit), lighted. See **light³.** *Two birds lit on my window sill. verb.*

lion (definition 1)—about 3 feet (1 meter) high at the shoulder

a hat	i it	oi oil	ch child		a in about
ā age	ī ice	ou out	ng long		e in taken
ä far	o hot	u cup	sh she	ə =	i in pencil
e let	ō open	ů put	th thin		o in lemon
ē equal	ô order	ü rule	ŦH then		u in circus
ėr term			zh measure		

lit mus pa per (lit′məs pā′pər), paper treated with a blue dye. Blue litmus paper will turn red if put into an acid. Red litmus paper will turn blue if put into a base.

lit ter (lit′ər), **1** little bits left about in disorder; things scattered about: *We picked up the litter.* **2** scatter things about; leave odds and ends lying around; make untidy: *You have littered the room with your papers.* **3** the young animals produced at one time: *a litter of puppies.* **4** straw or hay used as bedding for animals. **5** stretcher for carrying a sick or wounded person. **6** framework to be carried on men's shoulders, or by beasts of burden, with a couch usually enclosed by curtains. See picture. **1,3-6** *noun,* **2** *verb.*

lit ter bug (lit′ər bug′), person who throws trash along a highway or sidewalk, or in a park. *noun.*

lit tle (lit′l), **1** not big or large; small. A grain of sand or the head of a pin is little. **2** short; not long in time or in distance: *Wait a little while and I'll go a little way with you.* **3** not much: *A very sick child has little strength and can eat only a little food.* **4** a small amount: *I wasn't hungry so I ate only a little.* **5** a short time or distance: *Move a little to the left. After a little you will feel better.* **6** to a small extent: *The teacher read from an interesting book that was little known to us.* **7** not at all: *Little do they know our plans.* **1-3** *adjective,* **less** or **less er, least,** or **lit tler, lit tlest; 4,5** *noun,* **6,7** *adverb,* **less, least. not a little,** much: *We were not a little upset by the accident.*

Little League, a group of baseball teams organized for children from eight to twelve years of age.

live¹ (liv), **1** have life; be alive; exist: *All creatures have an equal right to live.* **2** remain alive: *We could not live long without water.* **3** keep up life: *Most people live by working.* **4** feed: *Lions live upon other animals.* **5** dwell: *live in the country. Who lives in this house?* **6** pass life: *live well.* *verb.* **lived, liv ing.**

live² (līv), **1** having life; alive: *a live dog.* **2** burning or glowing: *live coals.* **3** full of energy or activity: *a live person.* **4** carrying an electric current: *a live wire.* **5** loaded: *a live cartridge.* **6** not recorded on tape or film: *a live television show.* *adjective.*

live li hood (līv′lē hůd), means of living; support: *write for a livelihood, farm for a livelihood. noun.*

live li ness (līv′lē nis), vigor; activity; gaiety. *noun.*

live long (liv′lông′), the whole length of; whole; entire: *We were busy the livelong day. adjective.*

live ly (līv′lē), **1** full of life and spirit; active: *A good night's sleep made us all lively again.* **2** exciting: *We had a lively time during the hurricane.* **3** bright; vivid: *lively colors.* **4** cheerful; gay: *a lively conversation.* **5** in a lively manner. **1-4** *adjective,* **live li er, live li est; 5** *adverb.*

litter (definition 6)

li ter (lē′tər), the basic unit for measuring liquid and dry matter in the metric system. It is equal to about a quart of liquid and to about ⁹/₁₀ of a quart of dry things. *noun.* [*Liter* comes from a Latin word of the Middle Ages meaning "a liquid measure."]

lit er al ly (lit′ər ə lē), **1** word for word; without exaggeration; without imagination: *Write the story literally as it happened.* **2** actually: *The earthquake literally destroyed hundreds of homes. adverb.*

lit e rar y (lit′ə rer′ē), having to do with literature. *adjective.*

lit er ate (lit′ər it), able to read and write. *adjective.*

lit er a ture (lit′ər ə chůr *or* lit′ər ə chər), **1** writings of a period or of a country, especially those kept alive by their beauty of style or thought: *Shakespeare is a great name in English literature.* **2** all the books and articles on a subject: *the literature of stamp collecting. noun.*

lithe (līŦH), bending easily; supple: *An athlete should be lithe of body. adjective.*

liv er (liv′ər), **1** the large, reddish-brown organ in people and animals that makes bile and helps the body absorb food. **2** liver of an animal used as food. *noun.*

liv er y (liv′ər ē), **1** any uniform provided for servants, or adopted by a group or profession: *A nurse's livery is often white.* **2** the feeding and care of horses for pay. **3** the hiring out of horses and carriages. **4** stable where horses are taken care of for pay or hired out. *noun, plural* **liv er ies.**

lives (līvz), more than one life. *noun plural.*

live stock (līv′stok′), farm animals. Cows, horses, sheep, and pigs are livestock. *noun.*

liv id (liv′id), **1** having a dull bluish or grayish color, as from a bruise. **2** very pale: *livid with rage. adjective.*

liv ing (liv′ing), **1** having life; being alive: *a living plant.* **2** condition of being alive: *The young people were filled with the joy of living.* **3** means of keeping alive; livelihood: *She earns her living as a reporter.* **4** manner of life: *We enjoy country living.* **5** full of life; vigorous; strong; active: *a living faith.* **6** in actual existence; still in use; alive: *living languages.* **7** true to life; vivid: *a picture which is the living image of a person.* **8** of life; for living in: *the poor living conditions in the slums.* **9** sufficient to live on: *a living wage.* **10** See live¹. **1,5-9** *adjective,* **2-4** *noun,* **10** *verb.*

living room, room for general family use.

liz ard (liz′ərd), a reptile somewhat like a snake, but with four legs and a thicker body. See picture. *noun.*

llama—about 4 feet (1 meter) high at the shoulder

lla ma (lä′mə), a South American animal somewhat like a camel, but smaller and without a hump. Llamas have woolly hair and are used as beasts of burden. See picture. *noun, plural* **lla mas** or **lla ma.**

lo (lō), look! see! behold! *interjection.*

load (lōd), **1** what one is carrying; burden: *The cart has a load of hay. That's a load off my mind.* **2** amount that usually is carried: *four loads of sand.* **3** put in or put on whatever is to be carried: *load a ship. He loaded the camera with film.* **4** one charge of powder and shot for a gun. **5** put a charge in (a gun): *The pioneer loaded his musket with powder and shot.* **1,2,4** *noun,* **3,5** *verb.*

loaf¹ (lōf), **1** bread baked as one piece. **2** anything like a loaf in shape. Meat loaf is meat chopped and mixed with other things and then baked. *noun, plural* **loaves.**

loaf² (lōf), spend time idly; do nothing: *I can loaf all day Saturday. verb.*

loam (lōm), rich, fertile earth; earth in which decaying leaves are mixed with clay and sand. *noun.*

loan (lōn), **1** letting another have and use for a time; lending: *She asked for a loan of his pen.* **2** anything that is lent, especially money: *He asked his brother for a small loan.* **3** make a loan; lend: *Her friend loaned her the money.* **1,2** *noun,* **3** *verb.*

loath (lōth), unwilling: *The little boy was loath to leave his father. adjective.* Also spelled **loth.**

loathe (lō⊤H), feel strong dislike and disgust for; abhor; hate: *We loathe rotten food or a nasty smell. verb,* **loathed, loath ing.**

loath ing (lō′⊤Hing), strong dislike and disgust; intense aversion. *noun.*

loath some (lō⊤H′səm), disgusting; making one feel sick: *a loathsome odor. adjective.*

loaves (lōvz), more than one loaf. *noun plural.*

lob by (lob′ē), **1** entrance hall; passageway: *the lobby of a theater. A hotel lobby usually has chairs and couches to sit on.* **2** person or persons that try to influence members of a lawmaking body. **3** try to influence the members of a lawmaking body: *The conservation group lobbied to outlaw the use of certain traps by hunters.* **1,2** *noun, plural* **lob bies;** **3** *verb,* **lob bied, lob by ing.**

lob ster (lob′stər), a shellfish having five pairs of legs, with large claws on the front pair. Lobsters are used for food. Their shells turn a bright red when boiled. See picture. *noun.*

lo cal (lō′kəl), **1** of a place; having something to do with a certain place or places: *the local doctor, local news.* **2** of just one part of the body: *a local pain, local disease, local application of a remedy.* **3** making all, or almost all, stops: *a local train. adjective.*

lo cal i ty (lō kal′ə tē), place; region; one place and the places near it: *She knows many people in the locality of Boston. noun, plural* **lo cal i ties.**

lo cate (lō′kāt), **1** establish in a place: *They have located their new store on Second Avenue.* **2** establish oneself in a place: *Early settlers located where there was water.* **3** find out the exact position of: *We followed the stream until we located its source.* **4** state or show the position of: *Can you locate Africa on the globe? verb,* **lo cat ed, lo cat ing.**

be located, lie or be situated: *The capital is located on a river.*

lo ca tion (lō kā′shən), **1** locating: *The scouts argued about the location of the camp.* **2** being located. **3** position or place: *The camp was in a bad location as there was no water near it.* **4** lot; plot of ground marked out by boundaries: *a mining location. noun.*

lock¹ (lok), **1** means of fastening (doors, boxes, windows, and similar things), usually needing a key of special shape to open it: *Our front door has a lock.* **2** fasten with a lock: *Lock and bar the door.* **3** shut (something in or out or up): *We lock up jewels in a safe.* **4** hold fast: *The ship was locked in ice. The secret will be locked in my heart forever.* **5** join, fit, jam, or link together: *The girls locked arms and walked down the street together.* **6** part of a canal or dock in which the level of the water can be changed by letting water in or out, to raise or lower ships. See picture. **7** part of a gun by means of which it is fired. 1,6,7 *noun*, 2-5 *verb*.

lock² (lok), **1** curl of hair. **2** portion of hair, wool, or flax. **3 locks,** the hair of the head: *The child has curly locks. noun.*

lock er (lok′ər), chest, small closet, or cupboard that can be locked. *noun.*

lock et (lok′it), a little ornamental case for holding a picture of someone or a lock of hair. A locket is usually worn around the neck on a chain or necklace. *noun.*

lock jaw (lok′jô′), form of tetanus in which the jaws become firmly closed. *noun.*

lock smith (lok′smith′), person who makes or repairs locks and keys. *noun.*

lo co mo tion (lō′kə mō′shən), act or power of moving from place to place. Walking, swimming, and flying are common forms of locomotion. *noun.*

lo co mo tive (lō′kə mō′tiv), engine that moves from place to place on its own power, used to pull railroad trains. *noun.* [The original meaning of *locomotive* was "able to move from place to place." It came from Latin words meaning "moving from a place."]

lo cust (lō′kəst), **1** a grasshopper that travels with others in great swarms, destroying the crops. **2** tree with small, rounded leaflets and clusters of sweet-smelling white flowers. *noun.*

lode (lōd), vein of metal ore: *The miners struck a rich lode of copper. noun.*

lodge (loj), **1** live in a place for a time: *We lodged in motels on our trip.* **2** supply with a place to sleep or live in for a time: *Can you lodge us for the weekend?* **3** place to live in; house, especially a small or temporary house: *My aunt and uncle rent a lodge in the mountains for the summer.* **4** live in a rented room in another's house: *We are merely lodging at present.* **5** get caught or stay in a place without falling or going farther: *My kite lodged in the branches of a big tree.* **6** put or send into a particular place: *The archer lodged an arrow in the trunk of the tree.* **7** put before some authority: *We lodged a complaint with the police.* **8** branch of a secret society. **9** place where it meets. 1,2,4-7 *verb,* **lodged, lodg ing;** 3,8,9 *noun.*

lodg er (loj′ər), person who lives in a rented room in another's house. *noun.*

lodg ing (loj′ing), **1** place where one is living only for a time: *a lodging for the night.* **2 lodgings,** a rented room or rooms in a house, not in a hotel. *noun.*

a hat	i it	oi oil	ch child	
ā age	ī ice	ou out	ng long	ə = a in about
ä far	o hot	u cup	sh she	e in taken
e let	ō open	u put	th thin	i in pencil
ē equal	ô order	ü rule	₮H then	o in lemon
ėr term			zh measure	u in circus

lizard—about 1 foot (30 centimeters) long

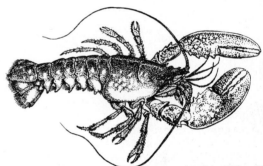

lobster—1 to 2 feet (30 to 60 centimeters) long with the claws

lock¹ (definition 6)—This ship is going through one of the locks in the Panama canal.

loft (lôft), **1** space just below the roof in a cabin; attic. **2** room under the roof of a barn: *This loft is full of hay.* **3** balcony in a church or hall: *a choir loft.* **4** an upper floor of a business building or warehouse. *noun.*

loft y (lôf′tē), **1** very high: *lofty mountains.* **2** exalted; dignified; grand: *lofty aims.* **3** proud; haughty: *He had a lofty contempt for others.* *adjective,* **loft i er, loft i est.**

log (lôg), **1** length of wood just as it comes from the tree. **2** made of logs: *a log house.* **3** cut down trees, cut them into logs, and get them out of the forest. **4** the daily record of a ship's voyage. **5** enter in a ship's log. **6** record of an airplane trip, or the performance of an engine. **7** float for measuring the speed of a ship. 1,4,6,7 *noun,* 2 *adjective,* 3,5 *verb,* **logged, log ging.**

lo gan ber ry (lō′gən ber′ē), a large, purplish-red fruit, a cross between a raspberry and a blackberry. *noun, plural* **lo gan ber ries.** [*Loganberry* was formed by combining the name of James H. Logan, who lived from 1841 to 1928, with the word *berry.* He was an American judge who first grew this fruit in 1881.]

log ging (lô′ging), work of cutting down trees, sawing them into logs, and moving the logs out from the forest. *noun.*

log ic (loj′ik), **1** science of proof and of reasoning. **2** reasoning; use of argument. **3** reason; sound sense: *There was much logic in what the speaker said. noun.*

log i cal (loj′ə kəl), **1** having something to do with logic: *logical reasoning.* **2** reasonable: *An upset stomach is a logical result of overeating.* **3** reasoning correctly: *a clear and logical mind. adjective.*

loin (loin), **1** part of the body of an animal or human being between the ribs and the hip. The loins are on both sides of the backbone and nearer to it than the flanks. **2** piece of meat from this part of an animal: *a loin of pork. noun.*

loi ter (loi′tər), **1** linger idly; stop and play along the way: *She loitered along the street, looking into all the store windows.* **2** spend (time) idly: *loiter the hours away. verb.*

loll (lol), **1** recline or lean in a lazy manner: *loll on a sofa.* **2** hang loosely or droop: *A dog's tongue lolls out in hot weather.* **3** allow to hang or droop: *The dog lolled out its tongue. verb.*

lol li pop (lol′ē pop), piece of hard candy, usually on the end of a small stick. *noun.*

lone (lōn), **1** without others; alone; single: *The lone traveler was glad to reach home.* **2** lonesome; lonely: *They lived a lone life after their children grew up and moved away. adjective.*

lone li ness (lōn′lē nis), being lonely; solitude. *noun.*

lone ly (lōn′lē), **1** feeling oneself alone and longing for company or friends: *He was lonely while his brother was away.* **2** without many people: *a lonely road.* **3** alone: *a lonely tree. adjective,* **lone li er, lone li est.**

lone some (lōn′səm), **1** feeling lonely: *I was lonesome while you were away.* **2** making one feel lonely: *a lonesome journey. adjective,* **lone som er, lone som est.**

long[1] (lông), **1** that measures much from end to end: *An inch is short; a mile is long. A year is a long time. I read a long story.* **2** in length: *My table is three feet long.* **3** having a long, narrow shape: *a long board.* **4** a long time: *Summer will come before long.* **5** for a long time: *I can't stay long.* **6** for its whole length: *all summer long, all day long.* **7** A **long vowel** is a vowel like *a* in *late, e* in *be,* or *o* in *note.* 1-3,7 *adjective,* **long er** (lông′gər), **long est** (lông′gist); 4 *noun,* 5,6 *adverb.*

long[2] (lông), wish very much; desire greatly: *I longed for my family. She longed to see her good friend. verb.*

long hand (lông′hand′), ordinary writing, not shorthand or typewriting. *noun.*

long horn (lông′hôrn′), one of a breed of cattle with very long horns, formerly common in southwestern United States. *noun.*

long ing (lông′ing), **1** strong desire: *a longing for home.* **2** having or showing strong desire: *a child's longing look at a window full of toys.* 1 *noun,* 2 *adjective.*

lon gi tude (lon′jə tüd *or* lon′jə tyüd), distance east or west on the earth's surface, measured in degrees from a certain meridian. See picture. *noun.*

lon gi tu di nal (lon′jə tüd′n əl *or* lon′jə tyüd′n əl), **1** of length; in length: *longitudinal measurements.* **2** running lengthwise: *The flag of the United States has longitudinal stripes. adjective.*

look (luk), **1** see; try to see; turn the eyes: *Look at the pictures.* **2** look hard; stare: *look questioningly.* **3** search: *I looked through the drawer to see if I could find my keys.* **4** glance; seeing: *He took a quick look at the magazine.* **5** face: *My bedroom looks upon the garden.* **6** seem; appear: *She looks pale.* **7** appearance: *A deserted house has a desolate look.* **8** looks, personal appearance: *a movie star's good looks.* 1-3,5,6 *verb,* 4,7,8 *noun.*

look after, attend to; take care of: *Will you look after my bird while I'm away?*

look at, pay attention to; examine: *You must look at all the facts.*

look down on, despise: *The miser looked down on all beggars.*

look for, expect: *We'll look for you tonight.*

look forward to, expect with pleasure: *The children are looking forward to the picnic.*

look in, make a short visit: *Look in this afternoon.*

look into, examine: investigate: *The president of our club is looking into the problem.*

look on, 1 watch without taking part: *The teacher conducted the experiment while we looked on.* **2** regard; consider: *I look on her as a very able person.*

look out, be careful; watch out: *Look out for cars as you cross the street.*

look over, examine; inspect: *I looked over my report for spelling errors.*

look to, 1 attend to; take care of: *The treasurer has to look to paying the bills of our club.* **2** turn to for help: *When I'm in trouble I look to my parents.*

look up, 1 find: *He looked up the unfamiliar word in a dictionary.* **2** call on; visit: *Look me up when you come to town.* **3** get better; improve: *Things are looking up for me since I got the new job.*

look up to, respect: *The students looked up to their teacher.*

looking glass, mirror.

look out (lùk′out′), **1** a sharp watch for someone to come or for something to happen: *Keep a good lookout for Mother.* **2** place from which to watch. A crow's-nest is a lookout. **3** person who has the duty of watching: *The lookout cried, "Land Ho!"* *noun.*

loom¹ (lüm), machine for weaving cloth. *noun.*

loom² (lüm), appear dimly or vaguely; appear as large or dangerous: *A large iceberg loomed through the thick gray fog.* *verb.*

loon (lün), a large diving bird with webbed feet that eats fish. Loons have a loud, wild cry. See picture. *noun.*

loop (lüp), **1** the part of a curved string, ribbon, bent wire, or cord that crosses itself. See picture. **2** thing, bend, course, or motion shaped like this. In writing, *b* and *g* and *h* and *l* have loops. *The road makes a wide loop around the lake.* **3** fastening or ornament formed of cord bent and crossed. **4** make a loop of. **5** make loops in. **6** fasten with a loop: *I looped the sail to the mast with a rope.* **7** form a loop or loops. 1-3 *noun,* 4-7 *verb.*

loop hole (lüp′hōl′), **1** a small opening in a wall for looking through, for letting in air, or for firing through at an enemy outside. **2** means of escape: *The clever lawyer found a loophole in the law to save his client.* *noun.*

loose (lüs), **1** not fastened: *a loose thread.* **2** not tight: *loose clothing.* **3** not firmly set or fastened in: *a loose tooth.* **4** not bound together: *loose papers.* **5** free; not shut in or up: *The dog has been loose all night.* **6** not pressed close together: *loose earth, cloth with a loose weave.* **7** not strict, close, or exact: *a loose account of the accident.* **8** careless about morals or conduct: *a loose character.* **9** set free; let go: *He loosed my arm from his grip.* **10** make loose; untie; unfasten: *loose a knot.* 1-8 *adjective,* **loos er, loos est;** 9,10 *verb,* **loosed, loos ing.**

loose-leaf (lüs′lēf′), having pages or sheets that can be taken out and replaced: *a loose-leaf notebook. adjective.*

loos en (lü′sn), **1** make loose or looser; untie; unfasten: *After our feast we had to loosen our belts.* **2** become loose or looser: *My clothes loosened as I lost weight. verb.*

loot (lüt), **1** rob; plunder: *The burglar looted the jewelry store.* **2** things taken by force; booty; spoils: *loot taken by soldiers from a captured town.* 1 *verb,* 2 *noun.*

lop (lop), **1** cut; cut off. **2** cut branches or twigs from. *verb,* **lopped, lop ping.**

lope (lōp), **1** run with a long, easy stride: *The horse loped along the trail in an easy gallop.* **2** a long, easy stride. 1 *verb,* **loped, lop ing;** 2 *noun.*

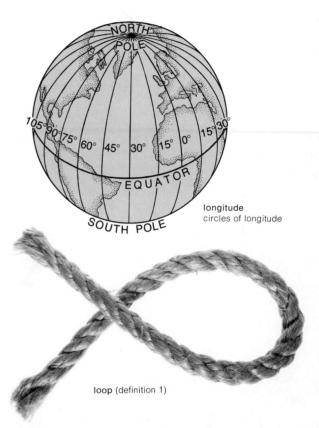

longitude
circles of longitude

loop (definition 1)

loon—about 30 inches (75 centimeters) long

lop sid ed (lop′sī′did), larger or heavier on one side than the other; leaning to one side. *adjective.*

lord (lôrd), **1** owner, ruler, or master; person who has the power. **2** rule proudly or absolutely. **3 Lord, a** God. **b** Christ: *the year of our Lord.* **4** (in Great Britain) a man of any of certain high ranks. **5 Lord,** title used in writing or speaking about men of certain high ranks in Great Britain: *Lord and Lady Grey attended the reception.* 1,3-5 *noun,* 2 *verb.* [*Lord* is from an earlier English word originally meaning "one who guards the loaf of bread" or "master of the house."]

lord it over, boss: *She was the oldest and lorded it over the rest of us.*

lord ly (lôrd′lē), **1** like a lord; suitable for a lord; grand; magnificent. **2** haughty; insolent; scornful: *His lordly airs annoyed his country cousins.* *adjective,* **lord li er, lord li est.**

lore (lôr), **1** facts and stories about a certain subject: *fairy lore, bird lore, Greek lore.* **2** learning; knowledge. *noun.*

lose (lüz), **1** not have any longer; have taken away from one by accident, carelessness, parting, or death: *lose a finger, lose a friend, lose one's life.* **2** be unable to find: *lose a book.* **3** fail to keep: *lose patience, lose your temper.* **4** miss; fail to get, catch, see, or hear: *lose a train, lose a few words of what was said.* **5** fail to win: *lose the prize.* **6** be defeated: *Our team lost.* **7** bring to destruction; ruin: *The ship and its crew were lost.* **8** waste; spend or let go by without any result: *lose time waiting, lose a chance.* **9** be or become worse off in money or in numbers: *The gambler lost heavily at poker.* **10** cause to lose: *That one mistake lost me my job.* *verb,* **lost, los ing.**

los er (lü′zər), **1** person who loses something. **2** person who is beaten in a game or battle. *noun.*

loss (lôs), **1** losing or having lost something: *The loss of health is serious, but the loss of a pencil is not.* **2** person or thing lost: *Her house was a complete loss to the fire.* **3** value of the thing lost: *The loss from the fire was $10,000.* **4** defeat: *Our team had two losses and one tie out of ten games played. noun, plural* **loss es.**

at a loss, puzzled; not sure: *The embarrassed child was at a loss as to how to act.*

lost (lôst), **1** See **lose.** *I lost my new pencil. My ruler is lost, too.* **2** no longer possessed or kept: *lost friendships.* **3** missing; no longer to be found: *lost books.* **4** not won: *a lost battle, a lost prize.* **5** hopeless: *a lost cause.* **6** not used to good purpose; wasted: *lost time.* **7** destroyed; ruined: *a lost soul.* 1 *verb,* 2-7 *adjective.*

lost in, so busy with something that one fails to notice anything else: *He was lost in a book and failed to hear us come in.*

lot (lot), **1** one of a set of objects, such as bits of paper or wood used to decide something by chance: *We drew lots to see who should be captain.* **2** such a method of deciding: *It was settled by lot.* **3** choice made in this way: *The lot fell to me.* **4** what one gets by lot; one's share. **5** one's fate or fortune: *It was her lot later to become a chemist.*

low tide
He dug clams
at low tide.

louse (definition 1)
line shows actual length

ludicrous—A dog with
an umbrella
is ludicrous.

lubricate—Dorothy lubricated the Tin Man's rusty joints.

6 plot of ground: *Our house is between two empty lots.* 7 portion or part: *I divided the fruit into four lots.* 8 number of persons or things considered as a group; collection: *This lot of pears is better than the last.* 9 a great many; much: *a lot of books, lots of money.* 10 a great deal; much: *I feel a lot better. The sky is lots bluer today.* 1-9 *noun,* 10 *adverb.*

loth (lōth), loath. *adjective.*

lo tion (lō′shən), liquid containing medicine. Lotions are applied to the skin to relieve pain, to heal, to cleanse, or to benefit the skin. *noun.*

lot ter y (lot′ər ē), scheme for distributing prizes by lot or chance. In a lottery a large number of tickets are sold, some of which draw prizes. *noun, plural* **lot ter ies.**

loud (loud), 1 not quiet or soft; making a great sound: *a loud voice. The door slammed with a loud noise.* 2 noisy: *loud music.* 3 in a loud manner: *We called loud and long for our dog.* 4 showy in dress or manner: *loud clothes.* 1,2,4 *adjective,* 3 *adverb.*

loud speak er (loud′spē′kər), device for making sounds louder, especially in a radio or phonograph. *noun.*

Lou i si an a (lü ē′zē an′ə), one of the south central states of the United States. *noun.* [*Louisiana* was named for Louis XIV, king of France. He lived from 1638 to 1715.]

lounge (lounj), 1 stand, stroll, sit, or lie at ease in a lazy way: *He lounged in an old chair.* 2 a comfortable and informal room in which one can lounge and be at ease: *a theater lounge.* 3 couch or sofa. 1 *verb,* **lounged, loung ing;** 2,3 *noun.*

louse (lous), 1 a small, wingless insect that infests the hair or skin of people and animals, biting and sucking blood. See picture. 2 any of various other insects that infest animals or plants. We spray plants to kill the lice. *noun, plural* **lice.**

lov a ble (luv′ə bəl), worthy of being loved; endearing: *She was a most lovable person, always kind and thoughtful. adjective.*

love (luv), 1 a fond, deep, tender feeling: *love for one's family, love for a sweetheart.* 2 have such a feeling for: *I love my parents. I love my country.* 3 person who is loved; sweetheart. 4 a strong liking: *a love of books.* 5 like very much; take great pleasure in: *He loves music.* 1,3,4 *noun,* 2,5 *verb,* **loved, lov ing.**
make love, caress or kiss as lovers do; pay loving attention; woo.

love li ness (luv′lē nis), beauty. *noun.*

love ly (luv′lē), 1 beautiful in mind or character; beautiful; lovable: *They are the loveliest children we know.* 2 very pleasing; delightful: *We had a lovely holiday. adjective,* **love li er, love li est.**

lov er (luv′ər), 1 person who is in love with another. 2 person having a strong liking: *a lover of books. noun.*

lov ing (luv′ing), feeling or showing love; affectionate; fond. *adjective.*

low[1] (lō), 1 not high or tall: *low walls. This footstool is very low.* 2 in a low place; near the ground: *a low shelf, a low jump.* 3 below others; inferior: *a low grade of margarine, to rise from a low position*

a hat	i it	oi oil	ch child	ə = { a in about
ā age	ī ice	ou out	ng long	e in taken
ä far	o hot	u cup	sh she	i in pencil
e let	ō open	ů put	th thin	o in lemon
ē equal	ô order	ü rule	ŦH then	u in circus
ėr term			zh measure	

as clerk to president of a company. 4 small; less than usual: *a low price, low temperature, low speed.* 5 nearly used up: *Our supply of coal is very low.* 6 unfavorable; poor: *I have a low opinion of their work.* 7 mean; coarse; vulgar. 8 feeble; weak: *a low state of health.* 9 not high in the musical scale: *a low note.* 10 not loud; soft: *a low whisper.* 11 at or to a low point, place, rank, amount, degree, price, or pitch: *The sun sank low. Supplies are running low.* 1-10 *adjective,* 11 *adverb.*

low[2] (lō), 1 make the sound of a cow; moo. 2 sound a cow makes; mooing. 1 *verb,* 2 *noun.*

low er (lō′ər), 1 let down or haul down: *We lower the flag at night.* 2 make lower: *lower the volume of the radio.* 3 sink or become lower: *The sun lowered slowly.* 4 more low: *Prices were lower last year than this.* 1-3 *verb,* 4 *adjective, adverb.*

low land (lō′lənd), land that is lower and flatter than the neighboring country. *noun.*

low ly (lō′lē), 1 low in rank, station, position, or development: *a lowly clerk, a lowly job.* 2 humble; meek; modest in feeling, behavior, or condition: *He had a lowly opinion of himself.* 3 humbly; meekly. 1,2 *adjective,* **low li er, low li est;** 3 *adverb.*

low spirits, sadness; depression.

low tide, time when the ocean is lowest on the shore. See picture.

loy al (loi′əl), 1 true and faithful to love, promise, or duty: *a loyal worker.* 2 faithful to one's king, queen, government, or country: *a loyal citizen. adjective.*

loy al ty (loi′əl tē), loyal feeling or behavior; faithfulness. *noun, plural* **loy al ties.**

lu bri cant (lü′brə kənt), oil or grease for putting on parts of machines that move against one another, to make them smooth and slippery so that they will work easily. *noun.*

lu bri cate (lü′brə kāt), make machinery smooth, slippery, and easy to work by putting on oil or grease. See picture. *verb,* **lu bri cat ed, lu bri cat ing.**

lu cid (lü′sid), 1 easy to follow or understand; clear: *A good explanation is lucid.* 2 sane: *An insane person sometimes has lucid intervals. adjective.*

luck (luk), 1 that which seems to happen or come to one by chance; fortune; chance: *Luck favored me, and I won.* 2 good luck: *She gave me a penny for luck. noun.*

luck i ly (luk′ə lē), by good luck; fortunately. *adverb.*

luck less (luk′lis), having or bringing bad luck; unlucky. *adjective.*

luck y (luk′ē), having or bringing good luck: *This is a lucky day. adjective,* **luck i er, luck i est.**

lu di crous (lü′də krəs), absurd but amusing; ridiculous. See picture. *adjective.*

lug (lug), pull along or carry with effort; drag: *We lugged the rug to the yard to clean it.* verb, **lugged, lug ging.**

lug gage (lug′ij), suitcases or handbags that a traveler carries on a trip; baggage. *noun.*

luke warm (lük′wôrm′), 1 neither hot nor cold. 2 showing little enthusiasm; half-hearted: *a lukewarm greeting. adjective.*

lull (lul), 1 soothe; cause to sleep: *The soft music lulled me to sleep.* 2 make or become calm or more nearly calm; quiet: *Their confidence lulled my fears. The wind lulled.* 3 period of less noise or violence; brief calm: *a lull in a storm.* 1,2 *verb,* 3 *noun.*

lul la by (lul′ə bī), a soft song to lull a baby to sleep. *noun, plural* **lul la bies.**

lum ber[1] (lum′bər), 1 timber that has been roughly cut into boards or planks, and prepared for use. 2 cut and prepare lumber. 1 *noun,* 2 *verb.*

lum ber[2] (lum′bər), move along heavily and noisily; roll along with difficulty: *The old stagecoach lumbered down the road. verb.*

lum ber jack (lum′bər jak′), person whose work is cutting down trees and getting out the logs. *noun.*

lum ber man (lum′bər mən), 1 lumberjack. 2 person whose work is buying and selling timber or lumber. *noun, plural* **lum ber men.**

lu mi nous (lü′mə nəs), 1 shining by its own light: *The sun and stars are luminous bodies.* 2 full of light; bright: *a luminous sunset.* 3 clear; easily understood. *adjective.*

lump (lump), 1 a small, solid mass of no particular shape: *a lump of coal.* 2 swelling; bump: *There is a lump on my head where I bumped it.* 3 form into a lump or lumps: *The gravy lumped because we cooked it too fast.* 4 in lumps; in a lump: *lump sugar.* 5 put together: *We will lump all our expenses.* 6 including a number of items: *I was given a lump sum of money for all my living expenses.* 1,2 *noun,* 3,5 *verb,* 4,6 *adjective.*

lu nar (lü′nər), 1 of the moon: *a lunar eclipse.* 2 like the moon. *adjective.*

lunar month, the interval between one new moon and the next, about 29½ days.

lu na tic (lü′nə tik), 1 an insane person. 2 insane.

3 for insane people: *a lunatic asylum.* 4 extremely foolish: *a lunatic search for buried treasure.* 1 *noun,* 2-4 *adjective.*

lunch (lunch), 1 a light meal between breakfast and dinner: *We usually have lunch at noon.* 2 a light meal. 3 eat lunch: *We lunched in the park.* 1,2 *noun, plural* **lunch es;** 3 *verb.*

lunch eon (lun′chən), 1 lunch. 2 a formal lunch. *noun.*

lung (lung), either one of a pair of organs found in the chest of those animals with a backbone that breathe air. The lungs absorb oxygen from the air and give the blood the oxygen it needs. See picture. *noun.*

lunge (lunj), 1 any sudden forward movement; thrust. 2 move suddenly forward; thrust: *The dog lunged at the stranger.* 1 *noun,* 2 *verb* **lunged, lung ing.**

lurch (lėrch), 1 a sudden leaning or roll to one side, like that of a ship, a car, or a staggering person: *The car gave a lurch and upset.* 2 make a lurch; stagger: *The wounded animal lurched forward.* 1 *noun, plural* **lurch es;** 2 *verb.*

lure (lùr), 1 power of attracting or fascinating; charm; attraction: *Many people feel the lure of the sea.* 2 lead away or into something by arousing desire; attract; tempt: *Bees are lured by the scent of flowers.* 3 decoy; bait: *I used a shiny lure to catch the fish.* 4 attract with a bait: *We lured the fox into a trap.* 1,3 *noun,* 2,4 *verb,* **lured, lur ing.**

lur id (lùr′id), 1 lighted up with a red or fiery glare: *The sky was lurid with the flames of the burning city.* 2 terrible; sensational; startling: *a lurid crime. adjective.*

lurk (lėrk), stay about without arousing attention; wait out of sight; be hidden: *A tiger was lurking in the jungle outside the village. verb.*

lus cious (lush′əs), 1 delicious; richly sweet: *a luscious peach.* 2 very pleasing to taste, smell, hear, see, or feel: *a luscious garden. adjective.*

lush (lush), 1 tender and juicy; growing thick and green: *Lush grass grows along the river banks.* 2 having abundant growth; covered with growing things. *adjective.*

lus ter (lus′tər), 1 a bright shine on the surface: *the luster of pearls.* 2 brightness: *the luster in the eyes of a happy child. noun.*

lust i ly (lus′tə lē), vigorously; heartily. *adverb.*

lus trous (lus′trəs), having luster; shining; glossy: *lustrous satin. adjective.*

lust y (lus′tē), strong and healthy; full of vigor: *a lusty athlete. adjective,* **lust i er, lust i est.**

lute (lüt), a stringed musical instrument of former times. It is like a large mandolin and is played by plucking the strings. See picture. *noun.*

lux ur i ant (lug zhùr′ē ənt), 1 growing thick and green: *luxuriant jungle growth.* 2 producing abundantly: *rich, luxuriant soil.* 3 rich in ornament. *adjective.*

lux ur i ous (lug zhùr′ē əs), 1 fond of luxury; tending toward luxury: *a luxurious taste for fine food.* 2 giving luxury; very comfortable and beautiful: *Some theaters are luxurious. adjective.*

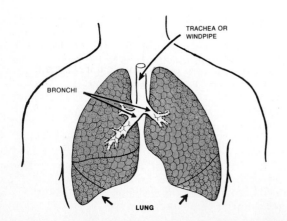

TRACHEA OR WINDPIPE

BRONCHI

LUNG

lyre

lynx—about 3 feet (1 meter)
long with the tail

lute

a hat	i it	oi oil	ch child	a in about
ā age	ī ice	ou out	ng long	e in taken
ä far	o hot	u cup	sh she	ə = { i in pencil
e let	ō open	u̇ put	th thin	o in lemon
ē equal	ô order	ü rule	₮H then	u in circus
ėr term			zh measure	

lux ur y (luk′shər ē), **1** comforts and beauties of life beyond what are really necessary: *Even very poor people today live in what would have been considered luxury 1000 years ago.* **2** use of the best and most costly food, clothes, houses, furniture, and amusements: *The movie star soon became accustomed to luxury.* **3** thing that one enjoys, usually something choice and costly: *They save some money for luxuries such as fine paintings.* **4** thing pleasant but not necessary: *Candy is a luxury. noun, plural* **lux ur ies.**

-ly[1], suffix meaning: in a _____ way or manner: Cheerful*ly* means *in a* cheerful *way.* Soft*ly* means *in a* soft *manner.*

-ly[2], suffix meaning: **1** like a _____: Ghost*ly* means *like a* ghost. **2** like that of a _____: Brother*ly* means *like that of a* brother. **3** of each or every _____; that happens or appears every _____: A month*ly* visit is a visit *that happens every* month. A dai*ly* newspaper is a newspaper *that appears every* day.

lye (lī), a strong solution used in making soap and in cleaning. *noun.*

ly ing[1] (lī′ing), **1** telling a lie; habit of telling lies. **2** false; not truthful. **3** See **lie**[1]. *I was not lying; I told the truth.* **1** *noun,* **2** *adjective,* **3** *verb.*

ly ing[2] (lī′ing). See **lie**[2]. *I was lying on the ground. verb.*

lymph (limf), a nearly colorless liquid in the tissues of the body, somewhat like blood without the red corpuscles. Lymph bathes and nourishes the tissues. *noun.*

lymphatic vessel, tube or canal through which lymph is carried to different parts of the body.

lynch (linch), put (an accused person) to death without a lawful trial: *An angry mob may lynch an innocent person. verb.* [*Lynch* was probably named for Charles Lynch, who lived from 1736 to 1796. He was a planter of Virginia who was supposed to have organized a group of neighbors to judge and punish people without a lawful trial.]

lynx (lingks), wild animal of the northern United States and Canada, somewhat like a cat but larger, that has a short tail and rather long legs. See picture. *noun, plural* **lynx es** or **lynx.**

lyre (līr), ancient stringed musical instrument somewhat like a small harp. See picture. *noun.*

lyr ic (lir′ik), **1** a short poem expressing personal emotion. A love poem and a hymn might both be lyrics. **2** having something to do with such poems: *a lyric poet.* **3** of, expressed in, or suitable for song. **4 lyrics,** the words for a song. **1,4** *noun,* **2,3** *adjective.*

lyr i cal (lir′ə kəl), **1** emotional; poetic: *She became almost lyrical when she described the scenery.* **2** lyric (definitions 2 and 3). *adjective.*

M m

M or **m** (em), the 13th letter of the English alphabet. M comes after j, k, l in the alphabet. There are three *m*'s in *mammoth. noun, plural* **M's** or **m's.**

ma'am (mam), madam. *noun.*

mac a ro ni (mak′ə rō′nē), flour paste that has been dried, usually in the form of long, hollow tubes, to be cooked for food. *noun, plural* **mac a ro nis** or **mac a ro nies.**

mac a roon (mak′ə rün′), a small, very sweet cookie made of whites of eggs, sugar, and ground almonds or coconut. *noun.*

ma chine (mə shēn′), **1** arrangement of fixed and moving parts for doing work, each part having some special job to do: *Sewing machines and washing machines make housework easier.* **2** device for applying power or changing its direction. Levers and pulleys are simple machines. *noun.*

machine gun, gun that can keep up a rapid fire of bullets.

ma chin er y (mə shē′nər ē), **1** machines: *A factory contains much machinery.* **2** the parts or works of a machine: *The machinery of a typewriter should be kept clean.* **3** any combination of persons or things by which something is kept going or something is done: *Police officers, judges, courts, and prisons are the machinery of the law. noun, plural* **ma chin er ies.**

machine shop, workshop where people make or repair machines or parts of machines.

machine tool, a tool or machine worked by power and used to shape metal. An electric drill and a lathe are machine tools.

ma chin ist (mə shē′nist), a skilled worker with machine tools. *noun.*

mack er el (mak′ər əl), a saltwater fish of the North Atlantic, much used for food. *noun, plural* **mack er el** or **mack er els.**

mack i naw (mak′ə nô), **1** kind of short coat made of heavy woolen cloth. **2** kind of thick woolen blanket, often with bars of color, used in the northern and western United States and in Canada by Indians and lumbermen. *noun.*

mack in tosh (mak′ən tosh), a waterproof coat; raincoat. *noun, plural* **mack in tosh es.** [*Mackintosh* was named for Charles Macintosh, who lived from 1766 to 1843. He was the Scottish inventor of the process of waterproofing.]

ma cron (mā′kron), a short, straight, horizontal line (-) placed over a vowel to show that it is pronounced in a certain way. EXAMPLES: cāme, bē. *noun.*

mad (mad), **1** out of one's mind; crazy; insane: *Her wild yells made me wonder if she were mad.* **2** very angry: *The insult made me mad.* **3** much excited; wild: *The dog made mad efforts to catch up with the* automobile. **4** foolish; unwise: *a mad undertaking.* **5** blindly and unreasonably fond: *My friend is mad about swimming.* **6** having rabies. A mad dog often foams at the mouth and may bite people. *adjective,* **mad der, mad dest.**

like mad, furiously; very hard or fast: *I ran like mad to catch the train.*

mad am (mad′əm), a polite title used in writing or speaking to any woman: *Good day, madam. noun.*

mad cap (mad′kap′), wild; hasty. *adjective.*

mad den (mad′n), make very angry or excited; irritate greatly: *The crowd was maddened by the umpire's decision. verb.*

made (mād), **1** See make. *The cook made the cake. It was made of flour, milk, butter, eggs, and sugar.* **2** built; constructed; formed: *a strongly made swing.* **1** *verb,* **2** *adjective.*

mad e moi selle (mad′ə mə zel′), a French word meaning Miss. *noun.*

made-up (mād′up′), **1** not real; imaginary: *a made-up story.* **2** having on rouge, powder, or other cosmetics: *made-up lips. adjective.*

mad house (mad′hous′), **1** asylum for insane people. **2** place of uproar and confusion: *The arena was a madhouse after the team won the game. noun, plural* **mad hous es** (mad′hou′ziz).

mad man (mad′man′), an insane man; person who is crazy: *The explosion was probably the act of a madman. noun, plural* **mad men.**

mad ness (mad′nis), **1** being crazy; loss of one's mind. **2** great rage; fury: *In his madness he kicked the fence post.* **3** folly: *It would be madness to try to sail a boat in this storm. noun.*

mag a zine (mag′ə zēn′), **1** publication appearing regularly, containing stories and articles by various writers. Most magazines are published either weekly or monthly. **2** room in a fort or warship for storing gunpowder and other dangerous substances that might explode. **3** building for storing gunpowder, guns, food, or other supplies. **4** place for cartridges in a repeating rifle or revolver. **5** place for holding a roll or reel of film in a camera or projector. *noun.*

mag got (mag′ət), the legless, wormlike larva of a young fly that was just hatched from its egg. *noun.*

mag ic (maj′ik), **1** the pretended art of making things happen by secret charms and sayings: *The fairy's magic changed the brothers into swans.* **2** done by magic or as if by magic: *A magic palace stood in place of their hut.* **3** something that produces results as if by magic: *The magic of the music charmed the listeners.* **1,3** *noun,* **2** *adjective.*

mag i cal (maj′ə kəl), done by magic or as if by magic: *The waving of the magician's wand produced a magical effect. adjective.*

ma gi cian (mə jish′ən), **1** person who can use magic: *The wicked magician cast a spell over the princess.* **2** person who entertains by magic tricks: *The magician pulled—not one, but three rabbits out of his hat! noun.*

Magic Marker, trademark for a marking and drawing pen with a broad felt tip.

mag is trate (maj′ə strāt), **1** officer of the

government who has power to apply the law and put it in force. The President is the chief magistrate of the United States. **2** judge. *noun.*

mag nate (mag′nāt), an important, powerful, or prominent person. *noun.*

mag ne sia (mag nē′zhə), a white, tasteless powder used as a medicine. *noun.*

mag ne si um (mag nē′zhē əm), a light, silver-white metal that burns with a dazzling white light. *noun.*

mag net (mag′nit), **1** stone or piece of iron or steel that attracts or draws to it bits of iron or steel. See picture. **2** anything that attracts: *The rabbits in our backyard were a magnet that attracted all the children in the neighborhood. noun.* [*Magnet* comes from Greek words meaning "stone from Magnesia," a region in ancient Greece.]

mag net ic (mag net′ik), **1** having the properties of a magnet: *the magnetic needle of a compass.* **2** having something to do with magnetism: *a magnetic circuit.* **3** very attractive: *I like her because she has a magnetic personality. adjective.*

magnetic field, space around a magnet in which its power of attraction is effective.

magnetic pole, 1 one of the two poles of a magnet. **2 Magnetic Pole,** one of the two poles of the earth toward which a compass needle points: *The North Magnetic Pole is south of the geographic North Pole.* See picture.

mag net ism (mag′nə tiz′əm), **1** the properties or qualities of a magnet; the showing of magnetic properties: *the magnetism of iron and steel.* **2** power to attract or charm: *A person with magnetism has many friends and admirers. noun.*

mag net ize (mag′nə tīz), **1** give the properties or qualities of a magnet to: *You can magnetize a needle by rubbing it with a magnet.* **2** attract or influence (a person): *Her stirring speech magnetized the audience. verb,* **mag net ized, mag net iz ing.**

mag nif i cence (mag nif′ə səns), richness of material, color, and ornament; grand beauty; splendor: *We were dazzled by the magnificence of mountain scenery. noun.*

mag nif i cent (mag nif′ə sənt), richly colored or decorated; grand; stately; splendid: *a magnificent palace, a magnificent view of the mountains.* See picture. *adjective.*

mag ni fy (mag′nə fī), **1** cause to look larger than the real size: *A microscope magnifies bacteria so that they can be seen and studied.* **2** make too much of; go beyond the truth in telling: *Was the fish really that big, or are you magnifying its size? verb,* **mag ni fied, mag ni fy ing.**

magnifying glass, lens or combination of lenses that causes things to look larger than they really are.

mag ni tude (mag′nə tüd *or* mag′nə tyüd), **1** greatness of size: *the height, strength, and magnitude of a building.* **2** importance: *The war brought problems of very great magnitude to many nations. noun.*

mag nol ia (mag nō′lyə), a North American tree with large white, pink, or purplish flowers. There

a hat	**i** it	**oi** oil	**ch** child	a in about
ā age	**ī** ice	**ou** out	**ng** long	e in taken
ä far	**o** hot	**u** cup	**sh** she	ə = i in pencil
e let	**ō** open	**u̇** put	**th** thin	o in lemon
ē equal	**ô** order	**ü** rule	**ŦH** then	u in circus
ėr term			**zh** measure	

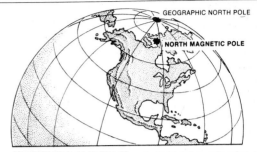
GEOGRAPHIC NORTH POLE
NORTH MAGNETIC POLE

Magnetic Pole (definition 2)

magnificent
She wore a
magnificent costume.

magnet (definition 1)

are several kinds. *noun.* [*Magnolia* was named for Pierre Magnol, who lived from 1638 to 1715. He was a French botanist.]

mag pie (mag/pī), **1** a noisy, black-and-white bird with a long tail and short wings. **2** person who chatters. *noun.*

ma hog a ny (mə hog/ə nē), **1** tree that grows in tropical America. **2** its dark reddish-brown wood. Because mahogany takes a very high polish, it is much used in making furniture. **3** dark reddish brown. 1,2 *noun, plural* **ma hog a nies;** 3 *adjective.*

maid (mād), **1** a young unmarried woman; girl. **2** an unmarried woman. **3** a woman servant. *noun.*

maid en (mād/n), **1** a young unmarried woman; maid; girl. **2** of a maiden: *maiden grace.* **3** unmarried: *a maiden aunt.* **4** first: *a ship's maiden voyage.* 1 *noun,* 2-4 *adjective.*

maid en hood (mād/n hùd), condition or time of being a girl. *noun.*

maid of honor, 1 woman who is the chief attendant of the bride at a wedding. **2** an unmarried lady who attends a queen or a princess.

mail[1] (māl), **1** letters, postcards, papers, and parcels to be sent by post. **2** system by which such mail is sent: *You can pay most bills by mail.* **3** all that comes by one post or delivery: *My mail is full of advertisements.* **4** send by mail; put in a mailbox: *Should I mail that letter for you?* 1-3 *noun,* 4 *verb.*

mail[2] (māl), armor made of metal rings, small loops of chain linked together, or plates, for protecting the body against the enemy's arrows or spears. See picture. *noun.*

mail box (māl/boks/), **1** a public box from which mail is collected. **2** a private box to which mail is delivered. *noun, plural* **mail box es.**

mail carrier, person who carries or delivers mail; postman.

mail man (māl/man/), mail carrier. *noun, plural* **mail men.**

maim (mām), cut off or make useless a part of the body, such as an arm, leg, finger, toe, or eye; injure seriously; cripple: *Two toes of his left foot were maimed by the power lawn mower. verb.*

main (mān), **1** most important; largest: *the main dish at dinner, the main street of a town.* **2** a large pipe which carries water, gas, sewage, or electricity to or from smaller branches: *When the water main broke, our cellar was flooded.* **3** the open sea; ocean: *Our daring fleet shall sail the main.* 1 *adjective,* 2,3 *noun.*

with might and main, with all one's force: *They argued with might and main.*

Maine (mān), one of the northeastern states of the United States. *noun.* [*Maine* probably comes from the English phrase *the maine,* that is, the mainland. Explorers who found many islands off the coast may have used the term to refer to the mainland.]

main land (mān/land/), the main part of a continent or country, apart from outlying islands and peninsulas. *noun.*

main ly (mān/lē), for the most part; chiefly; mostly: *He is interested mainly in art. adverb.*

main mast (mān/mast/ *or* mān/məst), the principal mast of a ship. See picture. *noun.*

main sail (mān/sāl/ *or* mān/səl), the largest sail of a ship. *noun.*

main spring (mān/spring/), **1** the principal spring in a clock or watch that you wind. **2** the main cause, motive, or influence. *noun.*

main stay (mān/stā/), **1** rope or wire supporting the mainmast. **2** main support: *Loyal friends are a person's mainstay in time of trouble. noun.*

main tain (mān tān/), **1** keep; keep up; carry on: *One must maintain a footing in a tug-of-war.* **2** uphold; support: *maintain an opinion. She maintains her family.* **3** keep in good repair: *The company employs people to maintain the machinery.* **4** declare to be true: *He maintains that he was innocent. verb.*

main te nance (mān/tə nəns), **1** maintaining: *Maintenance of quiet is necessary in a hospital.* **2** being maintained; support: *A government collects taxes to pay for its maintenance.* **3** keeping in good repair: *A state devotes much time to the maintenance of roads.* **4** enough to support life; means of living: *Their small farm provides only a maintenance. noun.*

maize (māz), plant whose grain grows on large ears. Also called **corn** or **Indian corn.** *noun.*

ma jes tic (mə jes/tik), grand; noble; dignified; stately. *adjective.*

ma jes ti cal ly (mə jes/tik lē), grandly; in a majestic manner. *adverb.*

maj es ty (maj/ə stē), **1** stately appearance; royal dignity; nobility: *the majesty of the starry heavens.* **2** **Majesty,** title used in speaking to or of a king, queen, emperor, or the like: *Your Majesty, His Majesty, Her Majesty. noun, plural* **maj es ties.**

ma jor (mā/jər), **1** larger; greater: *The major part of a little baby's life is spent in sleeping.* **2** an army, air force, or marine officer ranking next above a captain. 1 *adjective,* 2 *noun.*

ma jor i ty (mə jôr/ə tē), **1** the larger number; greater part; more than half: *A majority of the children chose red covers for the books they had made.* **2** the number by which the votes on one side are more than those on the other: *He had 18 votes, and she had 12; so he had a majority of 6.* **3** the legal age for voting; usual legal age for managing one's property. Because of different state laws, in some states of the United States a person reaches his or her majority at the age of 18; in other states the age is 21. *noun, plural* **ma jor i ties.**

make (māk), **1** bring into being; put together; build; form; shape: *make a new dress, make a fire, make jelly.* **2** way in which a thing is made; style; build; character: *Do you like the make of that coat?* **3** kind; brand: *What make of car is this?* **4** have the qualities needed for: *Wood makes a good fire.* **5** cause; bring about: *make trouble, make a noise, make peace.* **6** force to: *We made him go home.* **7** cause to be or become: *make a room warm, make a fool of oneself.* **8** become; turn out to be: *He will*

mail² used in the 1400's

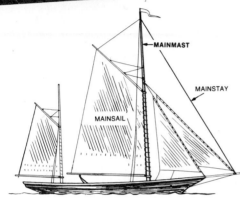

MAINMAST

MAINSTAY

MAINSAIL

a hat	i it	oi oil	ch child		a in about
ā age	ī ice	ou out	ng long		e in taken
ä far	o hot	u cup	sh she	ə =	i in pencil
e let	ō open	ù put	th thin		o in lemon
ē equal	ô order	ü rule	₮H then		u in circus
ėr term			zh measure		

make a good lawyer. **9** put into condition for use;
arrange: *I make my own bed.* **10** get; obtain; earn:
make good marks, make one's living. **11** do; perform:
make a speech, make an attempt, make a mistake.
12 amount to; add up to; count as: *2 and 3 make
5.* **13** think of as; figure to be: *I make the distance
across the room 15 feet.* **14** reach; arrive at: *Will the
ship make harbor?* **15** cause the success of: *One
successful book made the young author.* 1,4-15 *verb,*
made, mak ing; 2,3 *noun.*

make away with, 1 kill. **2** steal: *The treasurer made
away with the club's funds.*

make believe, pretend: *The girl liked to make
believe she was an airplane pilot.*

make fast, attach firmly: *Make the boat fast.*

make off with, steal; take without permission:
They made off with some apples.

make out, 1 write out: *She made out a shopping
list.* **2** show to be; try to prove: *They are trying to
make me out to be selfish.* **3** understand: *The boy
had a hard time making out the problem.* **4** see with
difficulty: *I can barely make out what these letters
are.* **5** get along; manage: *We must try to make out
with what we have.*

make over, alter; make different: *I had to make
over my costume because it was too big.*

make up, 1 put together: *make up cloth into a
shirt.* **2** invent: *make up a story.* **3** settle (a dispute);
reconcile: *make up one's differences.* **4** give or do in
place of: *I took a shortcut to make up for lost time.*
5 become friends again after a quarrel: *There we
were, quarreling and making up by turns.* **6** put
rouge, powder, or other cosmetics on the face.
7 compose; consist of; form: *Children made up the
audience.* **8** decide: *Make up your mind.*

make-be lieve (māk′bi lēv′), **1** pretending: *Fairies
live in the land of make-believe.* **2** pretended: *Some
children have make-believe playmates.* 1 *noun,*
2 *adjective.*

mak er (mā′kər), person or thing that makes.
noun.

make shift (māk′shift′), something made to use
for a time instead of the right thing: *When the
electric lights went out, we used candles as a
makeshift. noun.*

make-up (māk′up′), **1** way in which a thing is
made up or put together. **2** nature; disposition:
People of a nervous make-up are excitable.
3 cosmetics an actor uses in order to look the
part. See picture. **4** lipstick, powder, rouge, etc.,
put on the face; cosmetics. *noun.*

mal a dy (mal′ə dē), **1** sickness; illness; disease:
Cancer and malaria are serious maladies. **2** any
unwholesome condition: *Poverty and slums are
social maladies. noun, plural* **mal a dies.**

ma lar i a (mə ler′ē ə *or* mə lar′ē ə), disease that

make-up (definition 3)
The actor carefully put on his **make-up.**
The actor's **make-up** made him look frightening.

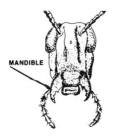

mandible (definition 1)—mandibles of a grasshopper

mango—The boy is picking a mango.

mammoth (definition 1)
about 10 feet (3 meters) high at the shoulder

causes chills, fever, and sweating. Malaria is transmitted by the bite of certain mosquitoes which have bitten infected persons. *noun.* [*Malaria* comes from Italian words meaning "bad air." It was thought that the disease was caused by harmful air coming from swamps.]

male (māl), **1** man or boy. **2** of or having to do with men or boys. **3** belonging to the sex that can fertilize eggs and be the father of young. Bucks, bulls, and roosters are male animals. **4** animal belonging to this sex. 1,4 *noun,* 2,3 *adjective.*

mal ice (mal′is), active ill will; a wish to hurt or make suffer; spite: *Lincoln asked the people to act "with malice toward none, with charity for all."* *noun.*

ma li cious (mə lish′əs), showing ill will; wishing to hurt or make suffer; spiteful: *I think that story is nothing more than malicious gossip. adjective.*

ma lign (mə līn′), **1** speak evil of; slander: *You malign an honest person when you call that person a liar.* **2** evil; injurious: *Gambling often has a malign influence.* **3** hateful; malicious. 1 *verb,* 2,3 *adjective.*

ma lig nant (mə lig′nənt), **1** very evil; very hateful; very malicious. **2** very harmful; causing death: *A cancer is a malignant growth. adjective.*

mal lard (mal′ərd), a wild duck of Europe, northern Asia, and North America. The male has a greenish-black head and a white band around its neck. *noun, plural* **mal lards** or **mal lard.**

mal le a ble (mal′ē ə bəl), **1** able to be hammered or pressed into various shapes without being broken. Gold, silver, copper, and tin are malleable; they can be beaten into thin sheets. **2** adaptable; yielding: *A malleable person can adjust to changed plans. adjective.*

mal let (mal′it), a wooden hammer. Specially shaped mallets are used to play croquet and polo. *noun.*

mal nu tri tion (mal′nü trish′ən *or* mal′nyü trish′ən), a poorly nourished condition: *People suffer from malnutrition because of eating the wrong kinds of food as well as from lack of food. noun.*

malt (môlt), **1** grain, usually barley, soaked in water until it sprouts and tastes sweet. Malt is used in making beer and ale. **2** prepare with malt. 1 *noun,* 2 *verb.*

mal ted milk (môl′tid milk′), drink prepared by mixing a powder made of dried milk, malted barley, and wheat flour with milk, flavoring, and often ice cream.

mal treat (mal trēt′), treat roughly or cruelly; abuse: *There are laws against maltreating animals. verb.*

ma ma or **mam ma** (mä′mə), mother. *noun.*

mam mal (mam′əl), one of a group of warm-blooded animals with a backbone. Mammals feed their young with milk from the mother's breasts. Human beings, cattle, dogs, cats, and whales are all mammals. *noun.*

mam moth (mam′əth), **1** a large elephant with a hairy skin and long curved tusks. The last mammoth died thousands of years ago. See picture. **2** huge; gigantic: *Digging the Panama Canal was a mammoth undertaking.* **1** *noun,* **2** *adjective.*

man (man), **1** an adult male person. When a boy grows up, he becomes a man. **2** human being; person. **3** the human race: *Man has existed for thousands of years.* **4** a male follower, servant, or employee: *Robin Hood and his merry men.* **5** husband: *man and wife.* **6** one of the pieces that is moved about on a board in such games as chess and checkers. **7** supply with a crew: *We can man ten ships.* **8** serve or operate: *Man the guns.* **1-6** *noun, plural* **men;** **7,8** *verb,* **manned, man ning.**

man age (man′ij), **1** control; conduct; handle; direct: *Good riders manage their horses well. They hired someone to manage the business.* **2** succeed in doing something: *I shall manage to keep warm with this blanket.* **3** get along: *We managed on very little money.* *verb,* **man aged, man ag ing.**

man age ment (man′ij mənt), **1** control; handling; direction: *Bad management caused the bank's failure.* **2** persons that manage a business or an institution: *The management of the store decided to increase the size of the parking lot.* *noun.*

man ag er (man′ə jər), person who manages: *She is the manager of the department store.* *noun.*

man date (man′dāt), **1** a command or official order. **2** a direction or authority given to a government by the votes of the people in an election: *The governor said she had a mandate to increase taxes.* *noun.*

man di ble (man′də bəl), **1** one of a pair of mouth parts in insects for seizing and biting. See picture. **2** either part of a bird's beak. **3** a jaw, most often the lower jaw. *noun.*

man do lin (man′də lin′), a musical instrument with a pear-shaped body and four to six pairs of metal strings. *noun.*

mane (mān), the long, heavy hair on the back of or around the neck of a horse or a lion. *noun.*

ma neu ver (mə nü′vər), **1** a planned movement of troops or warships: *Every year the army and navy held maneuvers for practice.* **2** perform maneuvers; cause troops to perform maneuvers. **3** a skillful plan or movement; clever trick: *When we refused to use his idea, he tried to force it on us by a series of maneuvers.* **4** plan skillfully; use clever tricks; scheme: *Scheming people always maneuver to get what they want.* **5** force by skillful plans; get by clever tricks: *She maneuvered her lazy sister out of bed.* **6** move or manipulate skillfully: *She maneuvered the car through the heavy traffic with ease.* **1,3** *noun,* **2,4-6** *verb.*

man ga nese (mang′gə nēz′), a hard, brittle, grayish-white metal. Manganese is used chiefly in making alloys of steel. *noun.*

man ger (mān′jər), box or trough in which hay or other food can be placed for horses or cows to eat. *noun.*

man gle (mang′gəl), **1** cut or tear roughly: *The two cats bit and clawed until both were much mangled.* **2** do or play badly; ruin: *The child mangled the*

a hat	i it	oi oil	ch child		a in about
ā age	ī ice	ou out	ng long		e in taken
ä far	o hot	u cup	sh she	ə =	i in pencil
e let	ō open	u̇ put	th thin		o in lemon
ē equal	ô order	ü rule	ŦH then		u in circus
ėr term			zh measure		

music because it was too difficult for her to play. *verb,* **man gled, man gling.**

man go (mang′gō), the slightly sour, juicy, oval fruit of a tropical tree. Mangoes have a thick, yellowish-red rind, and are eaten ripe or are pickled for eating when green. See picture. *noun, plural* **man goes** or **man gos.**

man hood (man′hu̇d), **1** condition or time of being a man: *The boy was about to enter manhood.* **2** character or qualities of a man. **3** men as a group: *the manhood of the United States.* *noun.*

ma ni a (mā′nē ə), **1** a mental illness during which a person becomes greatly excited, very active, and sometimes violent. **2** unusual fondness; craze: *She has a mania for collecting shells.* *noun.*

man i cure (man′ə kyu̇r), **1** care for (the hands and fingernails). **2** the care of the hands and fingernails. **1** *verb,* **man i cured, man i cur ing;** **2** *noun.*

man i fes ta tion (man′ə fə stā′shən), showing; act that shows or proves: *Entering the burning building was a manifestation of courage.* *noun.*

man i fold (man′ə fōld), **1** of many kinds; many and various: *manifold duties.* **2** having many parts or forms: *a manifold way to control prices.* *adjective.*

ma nip u late (mə nip′yə lāt), **1** handle or treat, especially with skill: *The driver of an automobile manipulates the steering wheel and pedals.* **2** manage by clever use of influence, especially unfair influence: *He manipulated the class so that he was elected president instead of his more qualified opponent.* **3** treat dishonestly; change for one's own purpose or advantage: *The two dishonest partners concealed their theft from the others by manipulating the company's records.* *verb,* **ma nip u lat ed, ma nip u lat ing.**

man kind (man′kīnd′ *for 1;* man′kīnd′ *for 2),* **1** the human race; all human beings. **2** men as a group: *Mankind and womankind both like praise.* *noun.*

man li ness (man′lē nis), manly quality; manly behavior. *noun.*

man ly (man′lē), **1** having qualities that are by tradition admired in a man: *a manly show of strength and courage.* **2** suitable for a man; masculine: *Boxing is a manly sport.* *adjective,* **man li er, man li est.**

man-made (man′mād′), made by people; not natural; artificial: *a man-made satellite.* *adjective.*

man ner (man′ər), **1** way of doing, being done, or happening: *The manner of their meeting makes a good story.* **2** way of acting or behaving; style; fashion: *She has a kind manner.* **3 manners,** polite ways of behaving: *People with manners say "Please" and "Thank you."* **4** kind or kinds: *We saw all manner of birds in the forest.* *noun.*

man ner ly (man′ər lē), having or showing good manners; polite. *adjective.*

man-of-war (man′əv wôr′), warship. *noun, plural* **men-of-war.**

man or (man′ər), **1** (in the Middle Ages) a large estate, part of which was set aside for the lord and the rest divided among his peasants, who paid the owner rent in goods, services, or money. If the lord sold his manor, the peasants or serfs were sold with it. **2** a large estate. *noun.*

man serv ant (man′sėr′vənt), a male servant. *noun, plural* **men serv ants.**

man sion (man′shən), a large house; stately residence. *noun.*

man slaugh ter (man′slô′tər), **1** the killing of a human being. **2** (in law) the accidental killing of a human being: *The charge against the prisoner was changed from murder to manslaughter. noun.*

man tel (man′tl), shelf above a fireplace. *noun.*

man tel piece (man′tl pēs′), mantel. *noun.*

man tle (man′tl), **1** a loose cloak without sleeves. **2** anything that covers like a mantle: *The ground had a mantle of snow. noun.*

man u al (man′yü əl), **1** of the hands; done with the hands: *manual labor.* **2** a small book that helps its readers to understand and use something; handbook. A cookbook is a manual. **1** *adjective,* **2** *noun.*

manual training, training in work done with the hands; practice in various arts and crafts, especially in making things out of wood.

man u fac ture (man′yə fak′chər), **1** make by hand or machine. A big factory manufactures goods in large quantities by using machines and dividing the work up among many people. **2** making of articles by hand or by machine, especially in large quantities. **3** make into something useful: *manufacture steel into rails.* **4** invent; make up: *Tardy students sometimes manufacture excuses.* **1,3,4** *verb,* **man u fac tured, man u fac tur ing; 2** *noun.*

man u fac tur er (man′yə fak′chər ər), person or company whose business is manufacturing; owner of a factory. *noun.*

ma nure (mə nùr′ *or* mə nyùr′), substance put in or on the soil to make it rich: *Dung from a stable is a kind of manure. noun.*

man u script (man′yə skript), book or paper written by hand or with a typewriter. Before printing was invented, all books and papers were manuscripts written by hand. *noun.*

man y (men′ē), **1** consisting of a great number: *many years ago. There are many children in the city.* **2** a great number: *Do you know many of them?* **3** a large number of people or things: *There were many at the dance.* **1** *adjective,* **more, most; 2,3** *noun, pronoun.*

how many, what number of: *How many days are there in March?*

map (map), **1** a drawing of the earth's surface or of part of it, showing countries, cities, rivers, seas, lakes, and mountains. **2** a drawing of the sky or of part of it, showing the positions of the stars and the planets. **3** make a map of; show on a map. **4** plan; arrange in detail: *Each Monday we map out the week's work.* **1,2** *noun,* **3,4** *verb,* **mapped, map ping.**

ma ple (mā′pəl), **1** tree grown for shade, ornament, its wood, or its sap. There are many kinds of maples. **2** its hard, light-colored wood. *noun.*

mar (mär), spoil the beauty of; damage; injure: *Weeds mar a garden. The nails in my shoes marred the floor. verb,* **marred, mar ring.**

Mar., March.

mar a thon (mar′ə thon), **1** a foot race of 26 miles, 385 yards (about 42 kilometers). **2** any long race or contest. *noun.* [Our word *marathon* was named for Marathon, a plain in Greece. The news of a Greek military victory in 490 B.C. was carried by a runner all the way from Marathon to the city of Athens, about 25 miles away.]

mar ble (mär′bəl), **1** a hard limestone, white or colored, that can take a beautiful polish. Marble is much used for statues and in buildings. **2** made of marble. **3** like marble; hard; unfeeling: *a marble heart.* **4** a small, usually colored glass ball, used in children's games. **5 marbles,** a children's game played with small, usually colored glass balls. Players take turns shooting a marble with a flick of the thumb to knock other marbles out of a ring. **1,4,5** *noun,* **2,3** *adjective.*

march (märch), **1** walk as soldiers do, in time and with steps of the same length: *The members of the band marched in the parade to the beat of the drums.* **2** act of marching: *The news of the enemy's march made whole villages flee.* **3** music meant for marching: *She enjoys playing marches on the piano.* **4** distance marched: *The camp is a day's march away.* **5** a long, hard walk. **6** walk or go steadily: *He marched to the front of the room and began his speech.* **7** cause to march or go: *The teacher marched the children out to the playground.* **8** progress: *History records the march of events.* **1,6,7** *verb,* **2-5,8** *noun, plural* **march es.**

steal a march, gain an advantage without being noticed.

March (märch), the third month of the year. It has 31 days. *noun.* [*March* comes from Latin words meaning "month of Mars," the Roman god of war.]

mare (mer *or* mar), a female horse or donkey. *noun.*

mar gar ine (mär′jər ən *or* mär′jə rēn′), substitute for butter, made from cottonseed oil, soybean oil, or other vegetable oils; oleomargarine. *noun.*

mar gin (mär′jən), **1** edge; border: *the margin of the lake.* **2** the blank space around a page that has no writing or printing on it: *Do not write in the margin.* **3** an extra amount; amount beyond what is necessary; difference: *We allow a margin of 15 minutes in catching a train. noun.*

mar i gold (mar′ə gōld), plant with yellow, orange, brownish, or red flowers. See picture. *noun.*

mar i jua na (mar′ə wä′nə), the dried leaves and flowers of the hemp plant. Marijuana is a drug which is sometimes smoked for its effect. *noun.*

ma rine (mə rēn′), **1** of the sea; found in the sea; produced by the sea: *Seals are marine animals.* **2** of shipping; of the navy; for use at sea: *marine law, marine power, marine supplies.* **3** shipping; fleet: *our merchant marine.* **4** soldier formerly serving only at sea, now also serving on land and in the air. 1,2 *adjective,* 3,4 *noun.*

mar i ner (mar′ə nər), one who navigates a ship; sailor; seaman. *noun.*

mar i o nette (mar′ē ə net′), doll or puppet moved by strings or by the hands, often on a little stage. See picture. *noun.*

mar i time (mar′ə tīm), **1** of the sea; having something to do with shipping and sailing: *Ships and sailors are governed by maritime law.* **2** on the sea; living on or near the sea: *Maritime people engage in boating and fishing. adjective.*

mark[1] (märk), **1** trace or impression made by some object on another. A line, dot, stain, or scar is a mark. **2** line or dot to show position: *This mark shows how far you jumped.* **3** the line where a race starts: *On the mark; get set; go.* **4** sign; something that shows what or whose a thing is: *Saying "Thank you" is a mark of good manners.* **5** a written or printed stroke or sign: *punctuation marks. She took up her pen and made a few marks on the paper.* **6** grade; letter or number to show how well one has done: *My mark in arithmetic was B.* **7** give grades to; rate: *The teacher marked our examination papers.* **8** cross or sign made by a person who cannot write, instead of signing his or her name: *Make your mark here.* **9** make a mark on or put one's name on to show whose a thing is. **10** make a mark on by stamping, cutting, or writing: *Be careful not to mark the table.* **11** put in a pin or make a line to show where a place is: *Mark all the large cities on this map.* **12** show clearly: *A tall pine marks the beginning of the trail. A frown marked her displeasure.* **13** target; something to be aimed at: *The empty can was an easy mark.* **14** standard; what is usual or proper or expected: *A tired person does not feel up to the mark.* **15** see; notice; give attention to: *Mark how carefully he moves. Mark my words; her plan will not fail.* 1-6,8,13,14 *noun,* 7,9-12,15 *verb.*

beside the mark, not hitting the thing aimed at: *The bullet went beside the mark.*

make one's mark, succeed; become well known: *That girl is a hard worker; she'll make her mark.*

mark off or **mark out,** make lines to show the position of or to separate: *We marked out a tennis court. The hedge marks off one yard from another.*

mark up, damage; spoil the appearance of: *Don't mark up the desks.*

mark[2] (märk), unit of money in East Germany and West Germany. *noun.*

marked (märkt), **1** having a mark or marks on it. **2** very noticeable; very plain: *There are marked differences between apples and oranges. adjective.*

mark er (mär′kər), person or thing that marks, especially one who keeps the score in a game. *noun.*

a hat	i it	oi oil	ch child	a in about
ā age	ī ice	ou out	ng long	e in taken
ä far	o hot	u cup	sh she	ə = i in pencil
e let	ō open	ů put	th thin	o in lemon
ē equal	ô order	ü rule	ŦH then	u in circus
ėr term			zh measure	

marigold

marionette

mar ket (mär′kit), **1** a meeting of people for buying and selling. **2** the people at such a meeting: *Excitement stirred the market.* **3** an open space or covered building where food, cattle, or other things are shown for sale. **4** sell: *The farmer cannot market all of his wheat.* **5** store for the sale of food: *a meat market.* **6** chance to buy or sell: *There is always a market for wheat.* **7** the demand (for something); price offered: *a rising market for automobiles. The drought created a high market for corn.* **8** region in which goods may be sold: *South America is a market for American automobiles.* 1-3,5-8 *noun,* 4 *verb.*

mar ket place (mär′kət plās′), place where a market is held. *noun.*

mark ing (mär′king), **1** mark or marks. **2** arrangement of marks. *noun.*

marks man (märks′mən), person who shoots well. *noun, plural* **marks men.**

mar ma lade (mär′mə lād), preserve similar to jam, made of oranges or of other fruit. The peel is usually sliced up and boiled with the fruit. *noun.*

ma roon[1] (mə rün′), very dark brownish red. *adjective.*

ma roon[2] (mə rün′), **1** put (a person) ashore in a desolate place and leave him: *Pirates used to maroon people on desert islands.* **2** leave in a lonely, helpless position: *During the storm we were marooned in a cabin miles from town. verb.*

mar quis (mär′kwis *or* mär kē′), nobleman ranking below a duke and above an earl or count. *noun, plural* **mar quis es, mar quis** (mär kē′).

mar quise (mär kēz′), **1** wife or widow of a marquis. **2** woman whose rank is equal to that of a marquis. *noun.*

mar riage (mar′ij), **1** living together as husband and wife; married life: *We wished the bride and groom a happy marriage.* **2** the ceremony of being married; wedding. *noun.*

mar ried (mar′ēd), **1** living together as husband and wife: *a married couple.* **2** having a husband or wife: *a married man.* **3** of husband and wife: *Married life has many rewards. adjective.*

mar row (mar′ō), **1** the soft substance that fills the hollow central part of most bones. **2** the inmost or important part: *The icy wind chilled me to the marrow. noun.*

mar ry (mar′ē), **1** join as husband and wife: *The minister married them.* **2** take as husband or wife: *He plans to marry her soon.* **3** become married: *She married late in life.* **4** give in marriage: *They have married off all of their children. verb,* **mar ried, mar ry ing.**

Mars (märz), **1** the Roman god of war. **2** the planet nearest the earth. It is the fourth in distance from the sun. See picture. *noun.*

marsh (märsh), low land covered at times by water; soft, wet land; swamp. *noun, plural* **marsh es.**

mar shal (mär′shəl), **1** officer of various kinds, especially a police officer. A United States marshal is an officer of a federal court whose duties are like those of a sheriff. **2** a high officer in an army. A Marshal of France is a general of the highest rank in the French Army. **3** person who arranges the order of march in a parade. **4** arrange in proper order: *She took great care in marshaling her facts for the debate.* **5** person in charge of events or ceremonies. 1-3,5 *noun,* 4 *verb.*

marsh mal low (märsh′mal′ō *or* märsh′mel′ō), a soft, white, spongy candy, covered with powdered sugar. *noun.*

marsh y (mär′shē), soft and wet like a marsh: *a marshy field. adjective,* **marsh i er, marsh i est.**

mart (märt), market; center of trade: *New York and London are two great marts of the world. noun.*

mar tial (mär′shəl), **1** of war; suitable for war: *martial music.* **2** fond of fighting; warlike: *a martial nation. adjective.* [*Martial* comes from a Latin word meaning "of Mars," the Roman god of war.]

mar tin (märt′n), a large swallow with a short beak and a forked tail. *noun.*

mar tyr (mär′tər), **1** person who is put to death or is made to suffer greatly because of his or her religion or other beliefs. Many of the early Christians were martyrs. **2** put (a person) to death or torture because of his or her religion or other beliefs. **3** person who suffers greatly. **4** cause to suffer greatly; torture. 1,3 *noun,* 2,4 *verb.*

mar vel (mär′vəl), **1** something wonderful; astonishing thing: *The airplane is one of the marvels of science.* **2** be filled with wonder; be astonished: *I marvel at your boldness. She marveled at the beautiful sunset.* 1 *noun,* 2 *verb.*

mar vel ous (mär′və ləs), **1** causing wonder; extraordinary. **2** improbable: *I like the marvelous adventures of Dorothy in Oz.* **3** excellent; splendid; fine: *a marvelous time. adjective.*

Mar y land (mer′ə lənd), one of the southeastern states of the United States. *noun.* [Charles I, king of England, named *Maryland* in 1632 in honor of his queen, Henrietta Maria, who lived from 1609 to 1669.]

Mars (definition 2)—The pictures below were taken at two different seasons. The polar icecap is brighter and larger in the picture at the left.

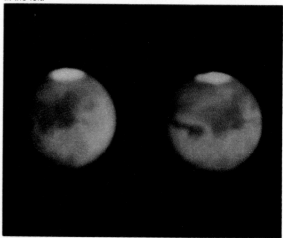

mas cot (mas′kot), animal, person, or thing supposed to bring good luck: *The children kept the stray dog as a mascot. noun.*

mas cu line (mas′kyə lin), **1** of men or boys. **2** like a man; manly. *adjective.*

mash (mash), **1** a soft mixture; a soft mass. **2** beat into a soft mass; crush to a uniform mass: *I'll mash the potatoes.* **3** a warm mixture of bran or meal and water for horses and other animals. 1,3 *noun, plural* **mash es;** 2 *verb.*

mask (mask), **1** a covering to hide or protect the face: *The burglar wore a mask.* See picture. **2** cover (the face) with a mask. **3** a clay, wax, or plaster likeness of a person's face. **4** disguise: *Their dislike for each other was hidden under a mask of friendship.* **5** hide or disguise: *A smile masked his disappointment.* 1,3,4 *noun,* 2,5 *verb.*

ma son (mā′sn), person who builds with stone or brick. *noun.*

ma son ry (mā′sn rē), **1** wall, foundation, or part of a building built by a mason. **2** the trade or skill of a mason. *noun, plural* **ma son ries.**

masque (mask), **1** an amateur dramatic entertainment, with fine costumes and scenery. Masques were much given in England in the 1500's and 1600's at court and at the homes of nobles. **2** masquerade. *noun.*

mas que rade (mas′kə rād′), **1** disguise oneself; go about under false pretenses: *The king masqueraded as a beggar to find out if his people really liked him.* **2** party or dance at which masks and fancy costumes are worn. **3** take part in a masquerade. **4** disguise; false pretense. 1,3 *verb,* **mas que rad ed, mas que rad ing;** 2,4 *noun.*

mass[1] (mas), **1** lump: *a mass of dough.* **2** a large quantity together: *a mass of flowers.* **3** gather together in quantity; form or collect into a mass: *Mass the peonies behind the roses. Many people massed in the square.* **4** majority; greater part: *The great mass of the world's population wants to live in peace.* **5** of or by many people: *a mass protest.* **6** on a large scale: *mass buying.* **7** bulk or size: *the sheer mass of an iceberg.* **8** the quantity of matter anything contains: *The mass of a piece of lead is not changed by melting it.* 1,2,4,7,8 *noun, plural* **mass es;** 3 *verb,* 5,6 *adjective.*

Mass or **mass**[2] (mas), the main service of worship in the Roman Catholic Church and in some other churches. The Mass consists of many prayers and ceremonies. *noun, plural* **Mass es** or **mass es.**

Mas sa chu setts (mas′ə chü′sits), one of the northeastern states of the United States. *noun.* [*Massachusetts* got its name from Massachusetts Bay, which was named for an American Indian tribe, the Massachuset. This name probably meant "at the big hills," that is, the Blue Hills south of Boston.]

mas sa cre (mas′ə kər), **1** a savage killing of many people or animals. **2** kill (many people or animals) needlessly or cruelly: *Big-game hunters massacred thousands of African wild animals.* 1 *noun,* 2 *verb,* **mas sa cred, mas sa cring.**

mask (definition 1)
a tribal mask

mas sage (mə säzh′), **1** rubbing and kneading the muscles and joints to make them work better and to increase the circulation of the blood: *A thorough massage feels good when you are tired.* **2** give a massage to: *Let me massage your back for you.* 1 *noun,* 2 *verb,* **mas saged, mas sag ing.**

mas sive (mas′iv), big and heavy; large and solid: *a massive wrestler. adjective.*

mast (mast), **1** a long pole of wood or steel set upright on a ship to support the sails and rigging. **2** any tall, upright pole: *the mast of a derrick. noun.* **before the mast,** serving as a common sailor, because such sailors used to sleep in the forward part of the ship.

mas ter (mas′tər), **1** person who has power or authority over others, such as the head of a household, a school, or a ship; one in control; owner, employer, or director. **2** a male teacher, especially in private schools: *The master taught his pupils how to read.* **3** title of respect for a boy: *First prize goes to Master Henry Adams.* **4** an expert, such as a great artist or skilled workman. **5** picture by a great artist: *an old master.* **6** of a master; by a master. **7** main; controlling: *a master plan, a master switch.* **8** become the master of; conquer; control: *She learned to master her temper.* **9** learn; become skillful at: *He has mastered riding his bicycle.* 1-5 *noun,* 6,7 *adjective,* 8,9 *verb.*

mas ter ful (mas′tər fəl), **1** fond of power or authority; domineering: *The masterful woman became a leader of her community.* **2** expert; skillful; masterly: *a masterful performance. adjective.*

mas ter ly (mas′tər lē), expert; skillful: *a masterly painter, a masterly book. adjective.*

mas ter piece (mas′tər pēs′), **1** anything done or made with wonderful skill; perfect piece of art or workmanship. **2** a person's greatest piece of work. *noun.*

mas ter y (mas′tər ē), **1** power such as a master has; rule; control. **2** the upper hand; victory: *The two teams vied for mastery.* **3** very great skill or knowledge: *The biologist showed a mastery of her field. noun, plural* **mas ter ies.**

mast head (mast′hed′), top of a ship's mast. A crow's-nest near the masthead of the lower mast is used as a lookout. *noun.*

mat (mat), **1** piece of fabric made of woven rushes, straw, rope, or fiber, used for floor covering or for wiping mud from the shoes. A mat is like a small rug. **2** piece of material to put under a dish, vase, or lamp. A mat is put under a hot dish when it is brought to the table. **3** anything growing thickly packed or tangled together: *a mat of weeds.* **4** pack or tangle together like a mat: *The swimmer's wet hair was matted.* 1-3 *noun,* 4 *verb,* **mat ted, mat ting.**

mat a dor (mat′ə dôr), the chief performer in a bullfight. The matador kills the bull with a sword. *noun.*

match[1] (mach), **1** a short, slender piece of wood or pasteboard tipped with a mixture that takes fire when rubbed on a rough or specially prepared surface. **2** wick or cord prepared to burn at a uniform rate, for firing guns and cannon. *noun, plural* **match es.**

match[2] (mach), **1** an equal; person or thing equal to another or much like another: *A child is not a match for an adult.* **2** be equal to in a contest: *No one could match the skill of the unknown archer.* **3** two persons or things that are alike or go well together: *Those two horses make a good match.* **4** be alike; go well together: *The rugs and the wallpaper match.* **5** find the equal of or one exactly like: *Until I can match this wool, I won't be able to finish knitting the sweater.* **6** game; contest: *a boxing match, a tennis match.* **7** try (one's skill or strength against); oppose: *She matched her skill against mine.* **8** marriage: *In former times, parents often arranged matches for their children.* **9** person considered as a possible husband or wife: *That young man is a good match.* 1,3,6,8,9 *noun, plural* **match es;** 2,4,5,7 *verb.*

match less (mach′lis), so great or wonderful that it cannot be equaled: *Pioneer women had matchless courage. adjective.*

mate (māt), **1** one of a pair: *The eagle mourned its dead mate. Where is the mate to this glove?* **2** join in a pair: *Birds mate in the spring.* **3** husband or wife. **4** marry. **5** officer of a ship next below the captain. **6** assistant: *cook's mate.* **7** companion or fellow worker: *Hand me a hammer, mate.* 1,3,5-7 *noun,* 2,4 *verb,* **mat ed, mat ing.**

ma ter i al (mə tir′ē əl), **1** what a thing is made from or done with: *dress material, building materials, writing materials, the material of which history is made.* **2** of matter or things; physical: *the material world.* **3** of the body: *Food and shelter are material comforts.* **4** that matters; important: *Hard work was a material factor in his success.* 1 *noun,* 2-4 *adjective.*

ma ter i al ize (mə tir′ē ə līz), **1** become an actual fact; be realized: *Our plans for the party did not materialize.* **2** appear or cause to appear in material or bodily form: *A spirit materialized from the smoke of the magician's fire. verb,* **ma ter i al ized, ma ter i al iz ing.**

ma ter i al ly (mə tir′ē ə lē), **1** with regard to material things; physically: *She improved materially and morally.* **2** considerably; greatly: *The tide helped the progress of the boat materially. adverb.*

ma ter nal (mə tėr′nl), **1** of or like a mother; motherly: *maternal kindness.* **2** related on the mother's side of the family: *Everyone has two paternal grandparents and two maternal grandparents. adjective.*

math (math), mathematics. *noun.*

math e mat i cal (math′ə mat′ə kəl), **1** of mathematics; having something to do with mathematics: *Mathematical problems are not always easy.* **2** exact; accurate: *mathematical measurements. adjective.*

math e ma ti cian (math′ə mə tish′ən), person who is an expert in mathematics. *noun.*

math e mat ics (math′ə mat′iks), science that deals with the measurement and relationships of quantities. Arithmetic is one part of mathematics. *noun.*

mat i nee (mat′n ā′), a dramatic or musical performance held in the afternoon. *noun.*

mat ri mo ny (mat′rə mō′nē), marriage. *noun, plural* **ma tri mo nies.**

ma tron (mā′trən), **1** wife or widow, especially an older married woman. **2** woman who manages the household matters of a school, hospital, dormitory, or other institution. A police matron has charge of the women in a jail. *noun.*

mat ter (mat′ər), **1** what things are made of; material; substance. Matter occupies space, has weight, and can exist as a solid, liquid, or gas. **2** affair: *business matters, a matter of life and death.* **3** what is written in a book; what is said in a speech: *There was very little matter of interest in her speech.* **4** an instance or case; thing: *a matter of fact, a matter of record, a matter of business.* **5** things written or printed: *reading matter.* **6** amount; quantity: *a matter of two days, a matter of twenty miles.* **7** importance: *Let it go since it is of no matter.* **8** be important: *Nothing seems to matter when you are very sick.* 1-7 *noun,* 8 *verb.*

as a matter of course, as something to be expected: *He accepted his daily chores as a matter of course.*

as a matter of fact, in truth; in reality; actually: *As a matter of fact I was not present yesterday.*

for that matter, so far as that is concerned: *For that matter, we did not know what we were doing.*

no matter, regardless of: *No matter how long it takes, I'm going to finish this project.*

What is the matter? What is the trouble? *What is the matter with the child?*

mat ter-of-fact (mat′ər əv fakt′), sticking to facts; not imaginative or fanciful. *adjective.*

mat tress (mat′ris), covering of strong cloth filled with hair, cotton, straw, or some other material. It is used on a bed or as a bed: *Many mattresses have springs inside. noun, plural* **mat tress es.**

ma ture (mə chúr′, mə tùr′, *or* mə tyùr′), **1** ripe; full-grown: *Grain is harvested when it is mature.* **2** ripen; come to full growth: *These apples are maturing fast.* **1** *adjective,* **2** *verb,* **ma tured, ma tur ing.**

ma tur i ty (mə chúr′ə tē, mə tùr′ə tē, *or* mə tyùr′ə tē), **1** ripeness; full development: *She had reached maturity by the time she was twenty.* **2** being completed or ready: *When their plans reached maturity, they were able to begin. noun.*

maul (môl), **1** a very heavy hammer or mallet. **2** beat and pull about; handle roughly: *The lion mauled its keeper badly.* **1** *noun,* **2** *verb.*

max im (mak′səm), rule of conduct; proverb: *"A stitch in time saves nine" and "Look before you leap" are maxims.* See picture. *noun.*

max i mum (mak′sə məm), **1** the largest or highest amount; greatest possible amount: *Sixteen miles in a day was the maximum that any of our club walked last summer.* **2** largest; highest; greatest possible: *The maximum score on this test is 100.* **1** *noun,* **2** *adjective.*

may (mā), **1** be permitted or allowed to: *May I have an apple? May I go now?* **2** be possible that it will: *It may rain tomorrow. The train may be late.* **3** it is hoped that: *May you have a pleasant trip. verb, past tense* **might.**

May (mā), the fifth month of the year. It has 31 days. *noun.* [*May* comes from Latin words meaning "month of Maia." Maia was a Roman goddess and wife of Vulcan, the Roman god of fire.]

may be (mā′bē), possibly; perhaps: *Maybe you'll have better luck next time. adverb.*

may on naise (mā′ə nāz′), a salad dressing made of egg yolks, vegetable oil, vinegar or lemon juice, and seasoning, beaten together until thick. *noun.*

may or (mā′ər), person at the head of a city or town government. *noun.*

maze (māz), **1** network of paths through which it is hard to find one's way: *A guide led us through the maze of caves.* See picture. **2** confusion; muddle: *I couldn't find what I wanted in the maze of papers on the desk. noun.*

M.D., Doctor of Medicine.

me (mē). *I* and *me* mean the person speaking. *She said, "Give the dog to me. I like it and it likes me." pronoun.*

mead ow (med′ō), piece of grassy land, especially one used for growing hay or as a pasture for grazing animals. *noun.*

mead ow lark (med′ō lärk′), bird of North America about as big as a robin, having a thick body, short tail, and a yellow breast marked with black. See picture. *noun.*

mea ger (mē′gər), **1** poor; scanty: *a meager meal.* **2** thin; lean: *a meager face. adjective.*

a hat	i it	oi oil	ch child	a in about
ā age	ī ice	ou out	ng long	e in taken
ä far	o hot	u cup	sh she	ə = i in pencil
e let	ō open	ù put	th thin	o in lemon
ē equal	ô order	ü rule	ᵺH then	u in circus
ėr term			zh measure	

LOST TIME IS NEVER FOUND AGAIN.

maxim

meadowlark—about 10 inches (25 centimeters) long

maze (definition 1)

meal[1] (mēl), **1** breakfast, lunch, dinner, or supper. **2** the food eaten or served at any one time: *We enjoyed each meal at the hotel.* noun.

meal[2] (mēl), **1** grain ground up: *corn meal.* **2** anything ground to a powder. noun.

meal time (mēl′tīm′), the usual time for eating a meal. noun.

meal y (mē′lē), dry and powdery: *mealy potatoes.* adjective, **meal i er, meal i est.**

mean[1] (mēn), **1** have as its thought; intend to say: *Can you make out what this sentence means?* **2** intend; have as a purpose; have in mind: *Do you think they mean to come? I mean to have the chops for dinner.* **3** be important or valuable: *Good friends mean a lot to a person.* verb, **meant, mean ing.**

mean[2] (mēn), **1** not noble; petty; unkind: *It is mean to spread gossip about your friends.* **2** low in quality or grade; poor: *"He is no mean scholar" means "he is a good scholar."* **3** low in social position or rank; humble: *A peasant is of mean birth; a king is of noble birth.* **4** of poor appearance; shabby: *The poor family lived in a mean hut.* **5** stingy; selfish: *A miser is mean about money.* **6** hard to manage; troublesome; bad-tempered: *a mean horse.* adjective.

mean[3] (mēn), **1** halfway between two extremes; average: *The mean number between 3 and 9 is 6.* **2** condition, quality, or course of action halfway between two opposites: *Eight hours is a happy mean between too much sleep and too little.* **3 means, a** what something is done by or the way something is brought about: *We won the game by fair means.* **b** wealth: *a man of means.* **1** adjective, **2,3** noun.

by all means, certainly; in any possible way; at any cost: *By all means stop in to see us.*

by means of, by the use of; through; with: *I found my dog by means of a notice in the paper.*

by no means, certainly not; in no way; not at all: *I shall by no means miss the chance to see her while she is in town.*

me an der (mē an′dər), **1** follow a winding course: *A brook meanders through the meadow.* **2** wander aimlessly: *We were meandering through the park.* **3** an aimless wandering. **1,2** verb, **3** noun. [*Meander* comes from a Greek word meaning "any winding course or pattern." This was named for the Maiandros, a winding river in southwestern Asia.]

mean ing (mē′ning), that which is meant or intended: *The meaning of that sentence is clear.* noun.

meant (ment). See **mean**[1]. *He explained what he meant. That sign was meant as a warning.* verb.

mean time (mēn′tīm′), **1** time between. **2** in the time between. **3** at the same time. **1** noun, **2,3** adverb.

mean while (mēn′hwīl′), meantime. noun, adverb.

mea sles (mē′zəlz), **1** a disease most often of children that causes a bad cold, fever, and a breaking out of small red spots on the skin. Unless you are vaccinated against measles, you can catch the disease if you are around someone who has it. **2 German measles,** a disease like

medal—a medal won in the Olympic games

measles but milder. It also causes a breaking out of small red spots on the skin. noun singular or plural.

meas ure (mezh′ər), **1** find the size or amount of (anything); find how long, wide, deep, large, or much (a thing) is: *We measured the room and found it was 20 feet long and 15 feet wide. We measured the pail by finding out how many quarts of water it would hold.* **2** mark off or out (in inches, feet, quarts, or some other unit): *Measure off 2 yards of this silk. Measure out a bushel of potatoes.* **3** compare with a standard or with some other person or thing by estimating, judging, or acting: *I'll measure my swimming ability with yours by racing you across the pool.* **4** be of a certain size or amount: *Buy some paper that measures 8 by 10 inches.* **5** find out size or amount: *Can she measure accurately?* **6** size or amount: *His waist measure is 30 inches.* **7** something with which to measure. A foot rule, a yardstick, and a quart dipper are common measures. **8** a unit or standard of measure, such as an inch, mile, acre, peck, quart, or gallon. **9** system of measurement: *liquid measure, dry measure, square measure.* **10** quantity, degree, or proportion: *Carelessness is in large measure responsible for many accidents.* **11** particular movement or arrangement in poetry or music: *the measure in which a poem or song is written.* **12** bar of music. See picture. **13** action meant as means to an end: *What measures shall we take to solve this problem?* **14** a proposed law; a law: *This measure has passed the Senate.* **1-5** verb, **meas ured, meas ur ing; 6-14** noun.

measure up to, meet the standard of: *The movie did not measure up to my expectations.*

meas ure ment (mezh′ər mənt), **1** way of measuring; way of finding the size, quantity, or amount: *Clocks give us a measurement of time.* **2** measuring; find the size, quantity, or amount: *The measurement of length by a yardstick is easy.* **3** size, quantity, or amount found by measuring:

The measurements of the room are 10 by 15 feet.
4 system of measuring or of measures: *Metric measurement is used in most countries.* noun.

meat (mēt), **1** animal flesh used for food. Fish and poultry are not usually called meat. **2** food of any kind: *meat and drink.* **3** part of anything that can be eaten: *The meat of the walnut is tasty.* **4** the essential part or parts: *the meat of an argument, the meat of a book.* noun.

me chan ic (mə kan′ik), person skilled at working with tools, especially someone who makes, uses, and repairs machines: *an automobile mechanic.* noun.

me chan i cal (mə kan′ə kəl), **1** having something to do with machinery: *She is good at solving mechanical problems.* **2** made or worked by machinery. **3** without expression: *The performance was very mechanical.* adjective.

me chan ics (mə kan′iks), **1** branch of physics dealing with the action of forces on solids, liquids, and gases at rest or in motion. **2** knowledge dealing with machinery. **3** technique: *The mechanics of playing the piano are easy for some people to acquire.* noun.

mech a nism (mek′ə niz′əm), **1** machine or its working parts: *the mechanism of a watch.* **2** system of parts working together as the parts of a machine do: *The bones and muscles are parts of the mechanism of the body.* noun.

mech a nize (mek′ə nīz), **1** make mechanical. **2** do by machinery, rather than by hand: *Much housework can be mechanized.* verb, **mech a nized, mech a niz ing.**

med al (med′l), piece of metal like a coin, with a figure or inscription stamped on it: *She received the gold medal for winning the race.* See picture. noun.

me dal lion (mə dal′yən), **1** a large medal. **2** design or ornament shaped like a medal. A design on a book or a pattern in lace may be called a medallion. noun.

med dle (med′l), busy oneself with or in other people's things or affairs without being asked or needed: *Don't meddle with my books or my toys. That busybody has been meddling in my business.* verb, **med dled, med dling.**

med dler (med′lər), person who interferes or meddles. noun.

med dle some (med′l səm), meddling; interfering; likely to meddle in other people's affairs. See picture. adjective.

me di a (mē′dē ə), more than one medium: *Newspapers, magazines, billboards, television, and radio are important media for advertising.* See definitions 3 and 4 of **medium.** noun plural.

me di ate (mē′dē āt), come in to help settle a dispute; act in order to bring about an agreement between persons or sides: *mediate in a quarrel, mediate between a company and its striking employees.* verb, **me di at ed, me di at ing.**

med i cal (med′ə kəl), having to do with healing or with the science and art of medicine: *medical advice, medical schools, medical supplies.* adjective.

a hat	i it	oi oil	ch child	a in about
ā age	ī ice	ou out	ng long	e in taken
ä far	o hot	u cup	sh she	ə = { i in pencil
e let	ō open	u̇ put	th thin	o in lemon
ē equal	ô order	ü rule	ŦH then	u in circus
ėr term			zh measure	

me dic i nal (mə dis′n əl), having value as medicine; healing; helping; relieving. adjective.

med i cine (med′ə sən), **1** substance, such as a drug, used to treat, prevent, or cure disease: *While I was sick I had to take my medicine three times a day.* **2** science of treating, preventing, or curing disease and improving health: *You must study medicine for several years before you can become a doctor.* noun.

medicine man, person considered by North American Indians to have close contact with the world of spirits. One of the tasks of medicine men was to cure sickness, which was thought to be caused by an evil spirit within the body. plural, **medicine men.**

me di e val (mē′dē ē′vəl), belonging to the Middle Ages (the years from about A.D. 500 to about 1450). adjective.

me di o cre (mē′dē ō′kər), of average or lower than average quality; neither good nor bad; ordinary: *a mediocre cake, a mediocre student.* adjective.

med i tate (med′ə tāt), **1** think quietly; reflect, especially on sacred or solemn things. **2** think about; consider; plan: *We meditated acting on her suggestion. verb,* **med i tat ed, med i tat ing.**

med i ta tion (med′ə tā′shən), quiet thought. *noun.*

Med i ter ra ne an Sea (med′ə tə rā′nē ən sē′), large sea bordered by Europe, Asia, and Africa.

me di um (mē′dē əm), **1** having a middle position, quality, or condition: *Eggs can be cooked hard, soft, or medium. He is of medium height.* **2** that which is in the middle; neither one extreme nor the other; middle condition: *a happy medium between city and country life.* **3** substance or agent through which anything acts; means: *Television and radio are media of communication. Money is a medium of exchange. Copper wire is a medium for conducting electricity.* **4** substance in which something can live; environment: *Water is the only medium in which fish can live.* **5** person through whom messages from the spirits of the dead are supposedly sent to the living. 1 *adjective,* 2-5 *noun, plural* **me di ums** or **me di a** for 3 and 4.

med ley (med′lē), **1** mixture of things that ordinarily do not belong together. **2** piece of music made up of parts from other pieces. *noun, plural* **med leys.**

meek (mēk), **1** not easily angered; mild; patient. **2** giving up too easily; not strong enough to resist; too shy or humble: *Don't be meek about asking for the job. adjective.*

meet[1] (mēt), **1** come face to face with (something or someone coming from the other direction): *Our car met another car on a narrow road.* **2** come together; join: *Two roads met near the bridge. Sword met sword in battle.* **3** keep an appointment with: *Meet me at one o'clock.* **4** be introduced to: *Have you met my sister?* **5** receive and welcome on arrival: *I must go to the station to meet my mother.* **6** be seen or heard by: *There is more to this matter than meets the eye.* **7** fulfill; put an end to; satisfy: *The campers took along enough food to meet their needs for a week.* **8** pay: *He did not have enough money to meet his bills.* **9** fight with; oppose: *meet an enemy in battle.* **10** meeting; gathering: *an athletic meet.* 1-9 *verb,* **met, meet ing;** 10 *noun.*

meet with, 1 come across: *We met with bad weather.* **2** have; get: *The plan met with approval.*

meet[2] (mēt), suitable; proper; fitting: *It is meet that you should help your friends. adjective.*

meet ing (mē′ting), **1** coming together. **2** coming together or assembly of persons for worship: *a Quaker meeting, a prayer meeting.* **3** any coming together or assembly: *Our club held a meeting.* **4** place where things meet: *a meeting of roads. noun.*

meg a phone (meg′ə fōn), a large horn used to increase the sound of the voice: *The cheerleader yelled through a megaphone.* See picture. *noun.*

mel an chol y (mel′ən kol′ē), **1** sadness; low spirits; tendency to be sad. **2** sad; gloomy. See picture. **3** causing sadness: *a melancholy scene.* 1 *noun,* 2,3 *adjective.*

megaphone

menorah

melancholy (definition 2)—The soldier became **melancholy** at the thought of being so far from home.

"At the Front," George C. Lambdin.
Courtesy of The Detroit Institute of Art

mel low (mel′ō), **1** ripe, soft, and with a good flavor; sweet and juicy: *a mellow apple.* **2** soft and rich: *a violin with a mellow tone, velvet with a mellow color.* **3** softened and made wise by age and experience. **4** make mellow; become mellow: *The apples mellowed after we picked them.* 1-3 *adjective,* 4 *verb.*

me lo di ous (mə lō′dē əs), **1** sweet-sounding; pleasing to the ear; musical: *a melodious voice.* **2** producing melody. *adjective.*

mel o dy (mel′ə dē), **1** sweet music; any sweet sound. **2** a succession of single tones in music; tune. Music has melody, harmony, and rhythm. **3** the main tune in harmony; the air. *noun, plural* **mel o dies.**

mel on (mel′ən), a large, juicy fruit of a vine much like the pumpkin, squash, and cucumber. Watermelons and muskmelons are different kinds. *noun.* [*Melon* comes from Greek words meaning "apple" and "gourd" or "ripe fruit." Melons were thought to look like apples.]

melt (melt), **1** turn into a liquid by applying heat. Ice becomes water when it melts. **2** dissolve: *Sugar melts in water.* **3** disappear gradually: *The clouds melted away, and the sun came out.* **4** change very gradually: *In the rainbow, the green melts into blue, the blue into violet.* **5** soften: *Their kindness melted her heart. verb.*

mem ber (mem′bər), **1** person, animal, or thing belonging to a group: *Every member of the family was home for the holidays. The club has one hundred members.* **2** part of a plant, animal, or human body, especially a leg, arm, or wing. *noun.*

mem ber ship (mem′bər ship), **1** being a member: *Do you enjoy your membership in the Boy Scouts?* **2** members: *All of the club's membership was present. noun.*

mem brane (mem′brān), **1** a thin, soft sheet or layer of animal tissue, lining or covering some part of the body. **2** a similar layer of vegetable tissue. *noun.*

mem o (mem′ō), memorandum. *noun, plural* **mem os.**

mem or a ble (mem′ər ə bəl), worth remembering; not to be forgotten; notable: *The play "Peter Pan" has many memorable scenes. adjective.*

mem o ran dum (mem′ə ran′dəm), **1** a short written statement for future use; note to aid one's memory: *Make a memorandum of what we will need to take on the trip.* **2** an informal letter, note, or report. *noun.*

me mo ri al (mə môr′ē əl), **1** something that is a reminder of some event or person, such as a statue, an arch or column, a book, or a holiday. **2** helping one remember. 1 *noun,* 2 *adjective.*

Memorial Day, a holiday for remembering and honoring members of the United States armed services who have died. In most states, it is usually celebrated on the last Monday in May.

mem o rize (mem′ə rīz′), commit to memory; learn by heart: *We have all memorized the alphabet. verb,* **mem o rized, mem o riz ing.**

mem or y (mem′ər ē), **1** ability to remember or keep in the mind: *She has a good memory so she will recall when that happened.* **2** act of remembering: *My memory of the trip is still fresh.* **3** person, thing, or event that is remembered: *I was so young when we moved that our old house is only a vague memory.* **4** all that a person remembers. **5** length of past time that is remembered: *This is the hottest summer within my memory. noun, plural* **mem or ies.**

in memory of, to help in remembering; as a reminder of: *I send you this card in memory of our happy summer together.*

men (men), **1** more than one man. **2** human beings; persons in general: *"All men are created equal." Men and animals have some things in common. noun plural.*

men ace (men′is), **1** threat: *In dry weather forest fires are a great menace.* **2** threaten: *Floods menaced the valley towns with destruction.* 1 *noun,* 2 *verb,* **men aced, men ac ing.**

me nag er ie (mə naj′ər ē), **1** collection of wild animals kept in cages for exhibition. **2** place where such animals are kept. *noun.*

mend (mend), **1** put in good condition again; repair: *mend a road, mend a broken doll, mend clothing.* **2** set right; improve: *to mend one's manners.* **3** place that has been mended: *The mend in your shirt scarcely shows.* **4** get better from an illness or injury; get back one's health: *My sprained ankle has mended.* 1,2,4 *verb,* 3 *noun.*

on the mend, getting better: *My health is on the mend.*

me ni al (mē′nē əl), belonging to or suited to a servant; low; mean: *Cinderella had to do menial tasks. adjective.*

me no rah (mə nôr′ə), candlestick with eight branches used during the Jewish festival of Hanukkah. See picture. *noun.*

-ment, suffix meaning: **1** act of _____ing: *Enjoyment* means the *act of* enjoy*ing.* **2** condition of being _____ed: *Amazement* means the *condition of being* amazed. **3** product or result of _____ing: *Measurement* means the *result of* measur*ing.* **4** thing that _____s: *Inducement* means a *thing that* induces.

men tal (men′tl), **1** of the mind: *a mental test, mental illness.* **2** for the mind; done by the mind: *mental arithmetic.* **3** for people having a disease of the mind: *a mental hospital. adjective.*

men tal ly (men′tl ē), with the mind; in the mind: *Grandmother is still strong physically and mentally. adverb.*

men tion (men′shən), **1** speak about: *I mentioned your idea to the group that is planning the picnic.* **2** a short statement: *There was mention of our school party in the newspaper.* 1 *verb,* 2 *noun.*

a hat	i it	oi oil	ch child		a in about
ā age	ī ice	ou out	ng long		e in taken
ä far	o hot	u cup	sh she	ə =	i in pencil
e let	ō open	u̇ put	th thin		o in lemon
ē equal	ô order	ü rule	ŦH then		u in circus
ėr term			zh measure		

men u (men′yü), list of the food served at a meal. *noun.*

me ow (mē ou′), **1** sound made by a cat or kitten. **2** make this sound. 1 *noun,* 2 *verb.*

mer ce nar y (mėr′sə ner′ē), **1** working for money only; acting with money as the motive. **2** soldier serving for pay in a foreign army. 1 *adjective,* 2 *noun, plural* **mer ce nar ies.**

mer chan dise (mėr′chən dīz), goods for sale; articles bought and sold. *noun.*

mer chant (mėr′chənt), **1** person who buys and sells: *Some merchants do most of their business with foreign countries.* **2** storekeeper. **3** trading; having something to do with trade: *merchant ships.* 1,2 *noun,* 3 *adjective.*

merchant marine, ships used in commerce.

mer ci ful (mėr′si fəl), having mercy; showing or feeling mercy; full of mercy. *adjective.*

mer ci less (mėr′si lis), without pity; having no mercy; showing no mercy: *merciless cruelty. adjective.*

mer cur y (mėr′kyər ē), a heavy, silver-white metal that is liquid at ordinary temperatures. Mercury is used in thermometers. *noun.*

Mer cur y (mėr′kyər ē), **1** the Roman god who served as messenger for the other gods. **2** the smallest planet and the one nearest the sun. *noun.*

mer cy (mėr′sē), **1** more kindness than justice requires; kindness beyond what can be claimed or expected: *The judge showed mercy to the young offender.* **2** something to be thankful for; a blessing: *It's a mercy you weren't hurt in the accident. noun, plural* **mer cies.**

at the mercy of, in the power of.

mere (mir), nothing else than; only: *The cut was the merest scratch. The mere sight of a dog makes me afraid. adjective, superlative* **mer est.**

mere ly (mir′lē), simply; only; and nothing more; and that is all. *adverb.*

merge (mėrj), **1** swallow up; absorb; combine and absorb; combine: *The big company merged various small businesses.* **2** become swallowed up or absorbed in something else: *The twilight merged into darkness. verb,* **merged, merg ing.**

me rid i an (mə rid′ē ən), circle passing through any place on the earth's surface and through the North and South Poles. All the places on the same meridian have the same longitude. See picture. *noun.*

me ri no (mə rē′nō), **1** kind of sheep with long, fine wool. **2** wool of this sheep. **3** a soft woolen yarn made from it. **4** a thin, soft woolen cloth made from this yarn or some substitute. *noun, plural* **me ri nos.**

mer it (mer′it), **1** goodness; worth; value; that which deserves reward or praise: *You will be marked according to the merit of your work.* **2** deserve: *Your excellent work merits praise.* **3 merits,** real facts or qualities, whether good or bad: *The judge will consider the case on its merits.* 1,3 *noun,* 2 *verb.*

mer maid (mėr′mād′), (in stories) a creature of the sea, with the head and body of a woman and the tail of a fish. *noun.*

mer ri ly (mer′ə lē), in a merry manner; laughing and gay. *adverb.*

mer ri ment (mer′ē mənt), laughter and gaiety; fun; mirth; merry enjoyment. *noun.*

mer ry (mer′ē), **1** full of fun; loving fun; laughing and gay: *a merry laugh.* **2** gay; joyful: *a merry holiday. adjective,* **mer ri er, mer ri est.**

mer ry-go-round (mer′ē gō round′), set of animals and seats on a platform that goes round and round by machinery. Children ride on them for fun. *noun.*

mer ry mak ing (mer′ē mā′king), **1** laughter and gaiety; fun. **2** gay festival; merry entertainment. **3** gay and full of fun; having a merry time. 1,2 *noun,* 3 *adjective.*

me sa (mā′sə), a high, steep hill that has a flat top and stands alone. A mesa is usually larger and steeper than a butte. *noun.* [*Mesa* comes from a Latin word meaning "table."]

mesh (mesh), **1** one of the open spaces of a net, sieve, or screen: *This net has half-inch meshes.* **2 meshes, a** net; network: *A fish was entangled in the meshes.* **b** snares: *entangled in the meshes of a plot.* **3** catch or be caught in a net. **4** engage or become engaged. The teeth of a small gear mesh with the teeth of a larger one. 1,2 *noun, plural* **mesh es;** 3,4 *verb.*

in mesh, in gear; fitted together.

me squite (me skēt′), a tree or shrub common in the southwestern United States and Mexico. Mesquite often grows in dense clumps or thickets and bears pods that are used as food for cattle. *noun.*

mess (mes), **1** a dirty or untidy mass or group of things; dirty or untidy condition: *Please clean up the mess in your room.* **2** make dirty or untidy: *She messed up her book by scribbling in it.* **3** confusion; difficulty: *The business's affairs are in a mess.* **4** make a failure of; spoil: *He messed up his chances of winning the race.* **5** an unpleasant or unsuccessful affair or state of affairs: *I made a mess of the test.* **6** group of people who take meals together regularly, especially such a group in the army or navy. **7** meal of such a group: *The officers are at mess now.* **8** portion of food, especially soft food: *a mess of oatmeal, a mess of fish.* 1,3,5-8 *noun, plural* **mess es;** 2,4 *verb.*

mess about or **mess around,** busy oneself without seeming to accomplish anything: *On my vacation I read and messed about with my flowers.*

mes sage (mes′ij), **1** words sent from one person to another: *a radio message, a message of welcome.* **2** an official speech or writing: *the President's message to Congress.* **3** lesson or moral contained in a story, play, or speech. *noun.*

mes sen ger (mes′n jər), person who carries a message or goes on an errand. *noun.*

mess y (mes′ē), in a mess; like a mess; untidy. *adjective,* **mess i er, mess i est.**

met (met). See **meet**[1]. *My father met us this morning at ten o'clock. We were met at the gate by our three dogs. verb.*

a hat	**i** it	**oi** oil	**ch** child	⌈a in about
ā age	**ī** ice	**ou** out	**ng** long	e in taken
ä far	**o** hot	**u** cup	**sh** she	ə = ⟨ i in pencil
e let	**ō** open	**u̇** put	**th** thin	o in lemon
ē equal	**ô** order	**ü** rule	**ᴛʜ** then	⌊u in circus
ėr term			**zh** measure	

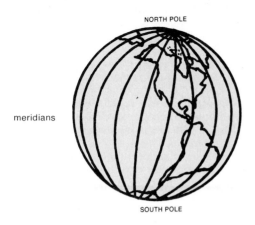

meridians

NORTH POLE

SOUTH POLE

me tab o lism (mə tab′ə liz′əm), a process by which all living things turn food into energy and living tissue. Growth and action depend on metabolism. *noun.*

met al (met′l), **1** substance such as iron, gold, silver, copper, lead, and tin. Aluminum, steel, and brass are also metals. **2** made of a metal, or a mixture of metals. **3** material; substance: *The teacher was a person of stern metal.* 1,3 *noun,* 2 *adjective.*

me tal lic (mə tal′ik), **1** of or containing metal: *a metallic substance.* **2** like metal: *This drapery fabric has a metallic gleam. adjective.*

met a mor pho sis (met′ə môr′fə sis), change of form. Tadpoles become frogs by metamorphosis; they lose their tails and grow legs. See picture. *noun.*

mete (mēt), give to each person a proper share or what is due that person; distribute: *mete out praise, mete out punishment. verb,* **met ed, met ing.**

me te or (mē′tē ər), mass of stone or metal that comes toward the earth from outer space with enormous speed; shooting star. Meteors become so hot from rushing through the air that they glow and often burn up. *noun.*

me te or ic (mē′tē ôr′ik), **1** of meteors: *meteoric dust, a meteoric shower.* **2** flashing like a meteor; swift; brilliant and soon ended: *The singer had a meteoric rise to fame. adjective.*

me te o rite (mē′tē ə rīt′), mass of stone or metal that has reached the earth from outer space. See picture. *noun.*

me ter[1] (mē′tər), **1** the basic unit of length in the metric system. It is equal to about 39$\frac{1}{3}$ inches. **2** any kind of poetic rhythm; the arrangement of beats or accents in a line of poetry: *The meter of "Jack and Jill went up the hill" is not the meter of "One, two, buckle my shoe."* **3** the arrangement of beats in music: *Three-fourths meter is waltz time. noun.* Also spelled **metre.**

me ter[2] (mē tər), something that measures, or measures and records: *a gas meter, a water meter. noun.*

meth od (meth′əd), **1** way of doing something: *a method of teaching music. Roasting is one method of cooking meat.* **2** order or system in getting things done or in thinking: *If you used more method, you wouldn't waste so much time. noun.*

me thod i cal (mə thod′ə kəl), **1** done according to a method; orderly: *a methodical check of one's work.* **2** acting according to a method: *A scientist is usually a methodical person. adjective.*

me tre (mē′tər), meter[1]. *noun.*

met ric (met′rik), of the meter or the metric system: *metric measurements, metric weights. adjective.*

meteorite

metamorphosis—Caterpillars become butterflies by metamorphosis.

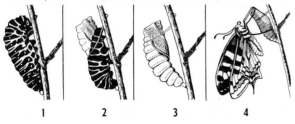

1   2   3   4

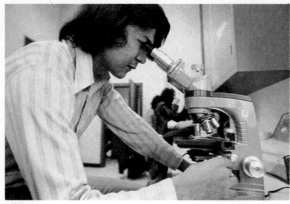

microscope

metric system, system of measures and weights which counts by tens. Its basic unit of length is the meter, its basic unit of weight is the kilogram, and its basic unit of capacity is the liter. See pictures.

met ro nome (met′rə nōm), a clocklike device that can be adjusted to tick at different speeds. People practicing music sometimes use a metronome to help them keep time. *noun.*

me trop o lis (mə trop′ə lis), **1** the most important city of a country or region: *New York is the metropolis of the United States.* **2** a large city; important center: *Chicago is a busy metropolis. noun, plural* **me trop o lis es.**

met ro pol i tan (met′rə pol′ə tən), of a large city; belonging to large cities: *metropolitan newspapers.* A **metropolitan area** is the area or region including a large city and its suburbs. *adjective.*

met tle (met′l), disposition; spirit; courage. *noun.*
on one's mettle, ready to do one's best.

mew (myü), **1** sound made by a cat or kitten. **2** make this sound; say meow: *Our kitten mews when it gets hungry.* 1 *noun,* 2 *verb.*

Mex i can (mek′sə kən), **1** of or having something to do with Mexico or its people. **2** person born or living in Mexico. 1 *adjective,* 2 *noun.*

Mex i co (mek′sə kō), country in North America, just south of the United States. *noun.*

mi., mile or miles.

mi ca (mī′kə), mineral that divides into thin, partly transparent layers. Mica is used as an insulator, especially in small electrical appliances such as toasters. *noun.*

mice (mīs), more than one mouse. *noun plural.*

Mich i gan (mish′ə gən), one of the north central states of the United States. *noun.* [*Michigan* got its name from Lake Michigan. This name came from an American Indian word meaning "the big lake."]

mi crobe (mī′krōb), a living organism of very small size; germ. Some microbes cause diseases. *noun.*

mi cro phone (mī′krə fōn), instrument for magnifying small sounds or for transmitting sounds. Microphones change sound waves into an electric current. Radio and television stations use microphones for broadcasting. *noun.*

mi cro scope (mī′krə skōp), instrument with a lens or combination of lenses for making small things look larger. Bacteria, blood cells, and other objects not visible to the naked eye are clearly visible through a microscope. See picture. *noun.*

mi cro scop ic (mī′krə skop′ik), **1** not able to be seen without using a microscope; tiny: *microscopic germs.* **2** like a microscope; suggesting a microscope: *a microscopic eye for mistakes.* **3** of a microscope; with a microscope: *She made a microscopic examination of a fly's wing. adjective.*

mid (mid), middle. *adjective.*

mid day (mid′dā′), middle of the day; noon. *noun.*

mid dle (mid′l), **1** point or part that is the same distance from each end or side; center: *the middle of the road.* **2** halfway between; in the center; at the same distance from either end or side: *the middle house in the row.* **3** in between; medium: *a man of middle size.* 1 *noun,* 2,3 *adjective.*

mid dle-aged (mid′l ājd′), neither young nor old; from about 40 to about 65 years of age. *adjective.*

Middle Ages, period in European history between ancient and modern times, from about A.D. 500 to about 1450.

middle class, class of people between the very wealthy class and the class of unskilled laborers and unemployed people. The middle class includes businessmen, professional people, office workers, and many skilled workers.

middle ear, a hollow space between the eardrum and the inner ear. In human beings it contains three small bones which pass on sound waves from the eardrum to the inner ear.

Middle East, region from the eastern Mediterranean to Iran.

Middle West, part of the United States west of the Appalachian Mountains, east of the Rocky Mountains, and north of the Ohio River and the southern boundaries of Missouri and Kansas; Midwest.

mid dy (mid′ē), **1** nickname for a midshipman. **2** a loose blouse similar to those worn by sailors. *noun, plural* **mid dies.**

mid get (mij′it), person very much smaller than normal; tiny person. *noun.*

mid land (mid′lənd), **1** the middle part of a country; the interior. **2** in or of the midland. 1 *noun,* 2 *adjective.*

mid night (mid′nīt′), **1** twelve o'clock at night; the middle of the night. **2** of or like midnight. 1 *noun,* 2 *adjective.*

mid ship man (mid′ship′mən), student at the United States Naval Academy at Annapolis. *noun, plural* **mid ship men.**

midst[1] (midst), middle. *noun.*
in our midst, among us: *a traitor in our midst.*
in the midst of, 1 among; surrounded by: *in the midst of a forest. I saw a frog in the midst of the water lilies.* **2** during: *I had to leave school in the midst of the afternoon.*

midst[2] or **'midst** (midst), amidst. *preposition.*

metric system

length

millimeter
(1/1000 of a meter)

A dime is about as <u>thick</u> as a millimeter.

centimeter
(1/100 of a meter)

This insect is about one centimeter long.

decimeter
(1/10 of a meter)

This crayon is about one decimeter long.

meter

A guitar is about one meter tall.

kilometer
(1000 meters)

This bridge is about one kilometer long.

weight

gram

This paper clip weighs about one gram.

kilogram (1000 grams)
A roller skate weighs about one kilogram.

capacity

milliliter (1/1000 of a liter)
A dropper holds about one milliliter.

liter
One liter is a little more than a quart.

mid stream (mid′strēm′), the middle of a stream. *noun.*

mid sum mer (mid′sum′ər), **1** the middle of summer. **2** the time around June 21. **3** in the middle of summer. 1,2 *noun,* 3 *adjective.*

mid way (mid′wā′), **1** halfway; in the middle: *midway between these trees and the lake, a midway position.* **2** place for games, rides, and other amusements at a fair. 1 *adverb, adjective,* 2 *noun.*

Mid west (mid′west′), Middle West. *noun.*

mid west ern (mid′wes′tərn), of the Middle West. *adjective.*

mid win ter (mid′win′tər), **1** the middle of winter. **2** the time around December 21. **3** in the middle of winter. 1,2 *noun,* 3 *adjective.*

mien (mēn), manner of holding the head and body; way of acting and looking: *She has the mien of an athlete. noun.*

might[1] (mīt). See **may**[1]. *Mother said that we might play in the barn. He might have done it when you were not looking. verb.*

might[2] (mīt), great power; strength: *Work with all your might. noun.*

might i ly (mī′tə lē), **1** in a mighty manner; powerfully; vigorously: *We freed the car from the snowbank by pushing mightily.* **2** very much; greatly: *We were mightily pleased at winning. adverb.*

might y (mī′tē), **1** showing strength or power; powerful; strong: *a mighty ruler, mighty force.* **2** very great: *a mighty famine.* **3** very: *a mighty long time.* 1,2 *adjective,* **might i er, might i est;** 3 *adverb.*

mi grant (mī′grənt), **1** migrating; roving: *a migrant worker.* **2** person, animal, bird, or plant that migrates. 1 *adjective,* 2 *noun.*

mi grate (mī′grāt), **1** move from one place to settle in another: *Pioneers from New England migrated to all parts of the United States.* **2** go from one region to another with the change in the seasons: *Most birds migrate to warmer countries in the winter. verb,* **mi grat ed, mi grat ing.**

mi gra tion (mī grā′shən), **1** moving from one place to another. **2** number of people or animals migrating together. *noun.*

mild (mīld), **1** gentle; kind: *He has a mild disposition.* **2** calm; warm; temperate; not harsh or severe: *a mild climate, a mild winter.* **3** soft or sweet to the senses; not sharp, sour, bitter, or strong in taste: *mild cheese, a mild cigar. adjective.*

mil dew (mil′dü *or* mil′dyü), **1** kind of fungus that appears on plants or on paper, clothes, or leather during damp weather: *Mildew killed the rosebuds in our garden.* **2** become covered with mildew: *A pile of damp clothes in the closet mildewed.* 1 *noun,* 2 *verb.*

mile (mīl), **1** a unit for measuring length or distance. It is equal to 5280 feet. **2 nautical mile,** a unit for measuring length or distance. It is equal to about 6080 feet. *noun.*

mile age (mī′lij), miles covered or traveled: *Our car's mileage last year was 10,000 miles. noun.*

mile stone (mīl′stōn′), **1** stone set up on a road to show the distance in miles to a certain place. **2** an

important event: *The invention of printing was a milestone in progress. noun.*

mil i tant (mil′ə tənt), **1** fighting; warlike: *a militant group. She has a militant attitude.* **2** a militant person. 1 *adjective,* 2 *noun.*

mil i tar y (mil′ə ter′ē), **1** of soldiers or war: *military training, military history.* **2** done by soldiers: *military maneuvers.* **3** fit for soldiers: *military discipline.* **4** suitable for war; warlike: *military valor.* **5 the military,** the army; soldiers: *an officer of the military.* 1-4 *adjective,* 5 *noun.*

mi li tia (mə lish′ə), army of citizens who are not regular soldiers but who are trained for war or any other emergency. Every state has a militia called the National Guard. *noun.*

milk (milk), **1** the white liquid from cows, which we drink and use in cooking. **2** a similar liquid produced by the adult females of many other animals as food for their young ones. **3** the white juice of a plant, tree, or nut: *coconut milk.* **4** draw milk from (a cow or goat). 1-3 *noun,* 4 *verb.*

milk maid (milk′mād′), woman who milks cows. *noun.*

milk man (milk′man′), person who sells milk or delivers it to customers. *noun, plural* **milk men.**

milk shake, a drink prepared by shaking or beating together milk, flavoring, and ice cream.

milk weed (milk′wēd′), a plant with white juice that looks like milk and seed pods containing long, silky hairs. *noun.*

milk y (mil′kē), **1** like milk; white as milk. **2** of milk; containing milk. *adjective,* **milk i er, milk i est.**

Milky Way, a broad band of faint light that stretches across the sky at night. It is made up of countless stars, too far away to be seen separately without a telescope.

mill (mil), **1** machine for grinding grain into flour or meal. **2** building containing such a machine. **3** grind (grain) into flour or meal. **4** any machine for crushing or grinding: *a coffee mill.* **5** grind very fine. **6** building where manufacturing is done: *Cotton cloth is made in a cotton mill.* **7** move about in a circle in a confused way: *The frightened cattle began to mill around.* 1,2,4,6 *noun,* 3,5,7 *verb.*

mill er (mil′ər), **1** person who owns or runs a mill, especially a flour mill. **2** moth whose wings look as if they were powdered with flour. *noun.*

mil let (mil′it), the very small grain of a kind of cereal grass or the plant that it grows on. Millet is grown for food in Europe, Asia, and Africa and for hay in the United States. *noun.*

mil li li ter (mil′ə lē′tər), a unit for measuring liquid and dry matter equal to $1/1000$ of a liter. *noun.*

mil li me ter (mil′ə mē′tər), a unit of length equal to $1/1000$ of a meter or about $1/25$ of an inch. A dime is about as thick as a millimeter. *noun.*

mil lion (mil′yən), one thousand thousands; 1,000,000. *noun, adjective.*

mil lion aire (mil′yə ner′ *or* mil′yə nar′), **1** person who has a million or more dollars, pounds, francs, or the like. **2** a very wealthy person. *noun.*

mil lionth (mil′yənth), **1** next after the 999,999th. **2** one of a million equal parts. *adjective, noun.*

mill stone (mil′stōn′), **1** either of a pair of round flat stones for grinding corn, wheat, or other grain. **2** heavy burden. *noun.*

mill wheel, wheel that is turned by water and supplies power for a mill. See picture.

mim e o graph (mim′ē ə graf), **1** a machine for making copies of written or typewritten material by means of stencils. **2** make (copies) with such a machine. 1 *noun,* 2 *verb.*

mim ic (mim′ik), **1** make fun of by imitating: *The children began to mimic the babysitter's English accent.* **2** person or thing that imitates. **3** copy closely; imitate: *A parrot can mimic voices.* **4** resemble closely in form or color. See picture. **5** not real, but imitated or pretended for some purpose: *Two instructors staged a mimic rescue of a drowning victim in swimming class.* 1,3,4 *verb,* **mim icked, mim ick ing;** 2 *noun,* 5 *adjective.*

min., minute or minutes.

min a ret (min′ə ret′), a slender, high tower attached to a Moslem mosque with one or more projecting balconies. From these balconies the people are called to prayer. See picture. *noun.*

mince (mins), **1** chop up into very small pieces. **2** put on fine airs in speaking or walking. **3** walk with little short steps. *verb,* **minced, minc ing.**

mince meat (mins′mēt′), mixture of chopped apples, suet, raisins, currants, spices, and sometimes meat. Mincemeat is used as a pie filling. *noun.*

mind (mīnd), **1** part of a person that knows and thinks and feels and wishes and chooses. **2** intelligence; mental ability; intellect: *a person with a good mind.* **3** person who has intelligence. **4** reason; sanity: *be out of one's mind.* **5** what one thinks or feels: *Speak your mind freely.* **6** memory: *Keep the rules in mind.* **7** notice; observe: *Now mind, these are not my ideas.* **8** be careful concerning: *Mind the step.* **9** take care: *Mind that you come on time.* **10** attend to; take care of: *Please mind the baby.* **11** obey: *Mind your father and mother.* **12** feel bad about; object to: *Would you mind if I went to the party without you? Some people don't mind cold weather.* 1-6 *noun,* 7-12 *verb.*

have a mind to, intend to; think of doing: *I have a mind to go swimming.*

make up one's mind, decide: *I made up my mind to study harder and get better grades.*

on one's mind, in one's mind; in one's thoughts: *With all this work I must do, I've got a lot on my mind.*

put in mind, remind: *Your joke puts me in mind of a joke I heard yesterday.*

set one's mind on, want very much: *I set my mind on owning a horse.*

to one's mind, to one's way of thinking; in one's opinion: *To my mind, this plan has a few flaws.*

mind ful (mīnd′fəl), **1** having in mind; thinking; being aware: *Mindful of your advice, I went slowly.* **2** taking thought; careful: *We had to be mindful of every step we took on the slippery sidewalk. adjective.*

a hat	i it	oi oil	ch child	a in about
ā age	ī ice	ou out	ng long	e in taken
ä far	o hot	u cup	sh she	ə = i in pencil
e let	ō open	u̇ put	th thin	o in lemon
ē equal	ô order	ü rule	ᴛʜ then	u in circus
ėr term			zh measure	

mill wheel

minaret
mosque with
four minarets

mimic (definition 4)—This insect **mimics** a twig.

mine[1] (mīn), the one or ones belonging to me: *This book is mine. Your shoes are black; mine are brown.* pronoun.

mine[2] (mīn), **1** a large hole or space dug in the earth to get out ores, precious stones, coal, salt, or anything valuable: *a coal mine, a gold mine.* **2** dig a mine; make a hole or space underground. **3** dig into for coal, gold, or other mineral: *mine the earth.* **4** get from a mine: *mine coal, mine gold.* **5** a rich or plentiful source: *The book proved to be a mine of information about radio.* **6** an underground passage in which gunpowder is placed to blow up an enemy's forts. **7** make underground passages below. **8** a small bomb placed in or under water, or buried just beneath the ground, to explode and destroy enemy shipping, troops, or equipment. **9** lay mines under: *mine the mouth of a harbor.* 1,5,6,8 *noun*, 2-4,7,9 *verb*, **mined, min ing.**

min er (mī′nər), person who works in a mine. *noun.*

min er al (min′ər əl), **1** substance obtained by mining or digging in the earth. Coal, gold, and mica are minerals. **2** any substance that is neither plant nor animal. Salt and sand are minerals. **3** containing minerals: *mineral water.* 1,2 *noun*, 3 *adjective.*

min e ral o gy (min′ə rol′ə jē), science of minerals. *noun.*

min gle (ming′gəl), **1** mix: *Two rivers that join mingle their waters.* **2** associate: *I tried to mingle with everyone at the party.* *verb*, **min gled, min gling.**

min i a ture (min′ē ə chùr), **1** anything copied on a small scale: *In the museum there is a miniature of the ship "Mayflower."* **2** done or made on a very small scale; tiny: *miniature cars, miniature furniture for a doll's house.* **3** a very small painting, usually a portrait. 1,3 *noun*, 2 *adjective.*

min i mum (min′ə məm), **1** the least possible amount; lowest amount: *Each of the children had to drink some milk at breakfast; half a glass was the minimum.* **2** least possible; lowest: *Eighteen is the minimum age for voting in the United States. The workers wanted a minimum wage of four dollars an hour.* 1 *noun*, 2 *adjective.*

min ing (mī′ning), **1** working mines for ores, coal, or other mineral. **2** laying explosive mines. *noun.*

min ion (min′yən), servant or follower willing to carry out all orders. *noun.*

min is ter (min′ə stər), **1** clergyman serving a church; spiritual guide; pastor. **2** act as a servant or nurse; be of service or aid; be helpful: *to minister to a sick person's needs.* **3** person who is given charge of a department of the government: *the Minister of Finance.* **4** person sent to a foreign country to represent his or her own government: *the United States Minister to Switzerland.* 1,3,4 *noun*, 2 *verb*. [*Minister* comes from a Latin word meaning "servant."]

min is try (min′ə strē), **1** the office, duties, or time of service of a minister. **2** ministers of a church. **3** ministers of a government. **4** ministering or serving. *noun, plural* **min is tries.**

miscellaneous—He made a collage of **miscellaneous** objects.

mink (mingk), **1** animal like a weasel that lives in water part of the time. **2** its valuable brown fur. *noun.*

Min ne so ta (min′ə sō′tə), one of the midwestern states of the United States. *noun.* [*Minnesota* was named for the Minnesota River. This name came from American Indian words meaning "sky-colored water."]

min now (min′ō), **1** a very small freshwater fish. **2** any fish when it is very small. *noun.*

mi nor (mī′nər), **1** smaller; lesser; less important: *Correct the important errors in your paper before you bother with the minor ones.* **2** person under the legal age of responsibility (18 or 21 years). **1** *adjective,* **2** *noun.*

mi nor i ty (mə nôr′ə tē), the smaller number or part; less than half: *A minority of the children wanted a party, but the majority chose a picnic.* *noun,* plural **mi nor i ties.**

min strel (min′strəl), **1** singer or musician in the Middle Ages who entertained in the household of a lord or went about singing or reciting poems, often of his own making. **2** member of a company of performers with blackened faces who played music, sang songs, and told jokes. *noun.*

mint[1] (mint), **1** a sweet-smelling plant used for flavoring. Peppermint and spearmint are kinds of mint. **2** piece of candy flavored with mint. *noun.*

mint[2] (mint), **1** place where money is coined by public authority. **2** coin (money). **3** a large amount: *A million dollars is a mint of money.* **1,3** *noun,* **2** *verb.*

min u end (min′yü end), number from which another is to be subtracted: *In 100 − 23 = 77, the minuend is 100. noun.*

min u et (min′yü et′), **1** a slow, stately dance. **2** music for it. *noun.*

mi nus (mī′nəs), **1** less; decreased by: *12 minus 3 leaves 9.* **2** lacking: *a book minus its cover.* **3** less than: *A mark of B minus is not so high as a mark of B.* **4** the sign (−) meaning that the quantity following it is to be subtracted. **1,2** *preposition,* **3** *adjective,* **4** *noun,* plural **mi nus es.**

min ute[1] (min′it), **1** one of the 60 equal periods of time that make up an hour; 60 seconds. **2** a short time; an instant: *I'll be there in a minute.* **3** an exact point of time: *The minute you see them, call me.* **4** one sixtieth of a degree. 10°10′ means ten degrees and ten minutes. **5 minutes,** an official written account of what happened at a meeting. *noun.*

mi nute[2] (mī nüt′ or mī nyüt′), **1** very small; tiny: *a minute speck of dust.* **2** going into small details: *minute instructions. adjective.*

min ute hand (min′it hand′), hand on a clock or watch that indicates minutes. It moves around the whole dial once in an hour.

min ute man (min′it man′), member of the American militia just before and during the Revolutionary War. The minutemen kept themselves ready for military service at a minute's notice. *noun,* plural **min ute men.**

mir a cle (mir′ə kəl), **1** a wonderful happening that

a hat	**i** it	**oi** oil	**ch** child		a in about
ā age	**ī** ice	**ou** out	**ng** long		e in taken
ä far	**o** hot	**u** cup	**sh** she	ə =	i in pencil
e let	**ō** open	**u̇** put	**th** thin		o in lemon
ē equal	**ô** order	**ü** rule	**ŦH** then		u in circus
ėr term			**zh** measure		

is beyond the known laws of nature: *It would be a miracle if the sun should stand still in the heavens for an hour.* **2** something marvelous; wonder: *It was a miracle you weren't hurt in that accident.* **3** a remarkable example: *The teacher was a miracle of patience to put up with the children's racket. noun.*

mi rac u lous (mə rak′yə ləs), **1** going against the known laws of nature: *The miraculous fountain of youth was supposed to make old people young again.* **2** wonderful; marvelous: *miraculous good fortune. adjective.*

mi rage (mə räzh′), an illusion, usually in the desert, at sea, or on a paved road, in which some distant scene appears to be much closer than it actually is. *noun.*

mire (mīr), **1** soft, deep mud; slush. **2** get stuck in mire: *He mired his car and had to go for help.* **1** *noun,* **2** *verb,* **mired, mir ing.**

mir ror (mir′ər), **1** glass in which you can see yourself; looking glass; surface that reflects light. **2** reflect as a mirror does: *The still water mirrored the trees along the bank.* **3** whatever reflects or gives a true description: *This book is a mirror of the life of the pioneers.* **1,3** *noun,* **2** *verb.*

mirth (mėrth), merry fun; laughter: *The people at the party were full of mirth. noun.*

mirth ful (mėrth′fəl), merry; jolly. *adjective.*

mis-, prefix meaning: **1** bad or wrong: *Misbehavior* means *bad* behavior. The *misuse* of a word means the *wrong* use of a word. **2** badly or wrongly: *Misbehave* means to behave *badly.* To *miscount* means to count *wrongly.*

mis be have (mis′bi hāv′), behave badly. *verb,* **mis be haved, mis be hav ing.**

mis be hav ior (mis′bi hā′vyər), bad behavior. *noun.*

mis cel la ne ous (mis′ə lā′nē əs), not all of one kind or nature. See picture. *adjective.*

mis chief (mis′chif), **1** conduct that causes harm or trouble, often without meaning it: *Playing with matches is mischief that may cause a fire.* **2** harm; injury, usually done by some person: *Why are you angry? He did you no mischief.* **3** person who does harm, often just in fun: *Where have you hidden my glasses, you little mischief?* **4** merry teasing: *Her eyes were full of mischief. noun.*

mis chie vous (mis′chə vəs), **1** full of mischief; naughty: *mischievous behavior.* **2** harmful: *mischievous gossip.* **3** full of pranks and teasing fun: *mischievous children. adjective.*

mis con duct (mis kon′dukt for 1 and 3; mis′kən dukt′ for 2 and 4), **1** bad behavior: *The misconduct of the children resulted in their being punished.* **2** behave badly. **3** bad management: *The misconduct of that business nearly ruined it.* **4** manage badly. **1,3** *noun,* **2,4** *verb.*

mis count (mis kount′ *for 1;* mis′kount′ *for 2*),
1 count wrongly or incorrectly. **2** a wrong or
incorrect count. 1 *verb,* 2 *noun.*

mis deed (mis dēd′), a bad act; wicked deed.
noun.

mis di rect (mis′də rekt′), direct wrongly; give
wrong directions to. *verb.*

mi ser (mī′zər), person who loves money for its
own sake; one who lives poorly in order to save
money and keep it. A miser dislikes to spend
money for anything, except to gain more money.
noun.

mis er a ble (miz′ər ə bəl), **1** very unhappy: *A sick
child is often miserable.* **2** causing trouble or
unhappiness: *I have a miserable cold.* **3** poor;
mean; wretched: *The ragged child lived in miserable
surroundings. adjective.*

mis er y (miz′ər ē), **1** a miserable, unhappy state of
mind: *Think of the misery of having no home or
friends.* **2** poor, mean, miserable circumstances:
They lived in the misery of the slums. noun, plural
mis er ies.

mis fit (mis′fit′), **1** person who does not fit in a
job or a group. **2** a bad fit: *Do not buy shoes that
are misfits. noun.*

mis for tune (mis fôr′chən), bad luck: *She had the
misfortune to break her arm. noun.*

mis giv ing (mis giv′ing), feeling of doubt,
suspicion, or anxiety: *We started off through the
storm with some misgivings. noun.*

mis guid ed (mis gī′did), led into mistakes or
wrongdoing; misled: *The misguided student let
others copy his homework. adjective.*

mis hap (mis′hap), an unlucky accident. See
picture. *noun.*

mis judge (mis juj′), **1** judge wrongly: *The archer
misjudged the distance to the target, and his arrow
fell short.* **2** judge unjustly: *The teacher soon
discovered that she had misjudged the girl's
character. verb,* **mis judged, mis judg ing.**

mis laid (mis lād′). See **mislay.** *She mislaid her
books. I have mislaid my pen. verb.*

mis lay (mis lā′), put in a place and then forget
where it is: *I am always mislaying my gloves. verb,*
mis laid, mis lay ing.

mis lead (mis lēd′), **1** cause to go in the wrong
direction: *Our guide misled us, and we got lost.*
2 cause to do wrong: *Bad companions can mislead
a person.* **3** lead to think what is not so; deceive:
*Some advertisements are so exaggerated that they
mislead people. verb,* **mis led, mis lead ing.**

mis lead ing (mis lē′ding), **1** causing wrong
conclusions: *The detectives found that the false clue
was misleading.* **2** causing mistakes or wrongdoing:
Bad advice can be misleading. adjective.

mis led (mis led′). See **mislead.** *We were misled on
our hike by a careless guide. verb.*

mis man age (mis man′ij), manage badly: *If you
mismanage the business, you will lose money. verb,*
mis man aged, mis man ag ing.

mis man age ment (mis man′ij mənt), bad
management. *noun.*

mis place (mis plās′), **1** put in a place and then

forget where it is. **2** put in the wrong place. **3** give
(your love or trust) to the wrong person: *I
misplaced my trust by confiding in a person who
couldn't keep a secret. verb,* **mis placed,
mis plac ing.**

mis print (mis′print′ *for 1;* mis print′ *for 2*),
1 mistake in printing. **2** print wrongly. 1 *noun,*
2 *verb.*

mis pro nounce (mis′prə nouns′), pronounce
incorrectly: *Many people mispronounce the word
"mischievous." verb,* **mis pro nounced,
mis pro nounc ing.**

mis read (mis rēd′), **1** read incorrectly: *I misread
the sign and missed the turn.* **2** misunderstand;
interpret incorrectly: *You misread my joke if you
think it was meant as an insult. verb,* **mis read**
(mis red′), **mis read ing.**

mis rule (mis rül′), **1** bad or unwise rule. **2** rule
badly. 1 *noun,* 2 *verb,* **mis ruled, mis rul ing.**

miss (mis), **1** fail to hit: *I swung at the ball and
missed.* **2** failure to hit or reach: *make more misses
than hits.* **3** fail to find, get, or meet: *I set out to
meet my father, but in the dark I missed him.* **4** let
slip by; not seize: *I missed the chance of a ride to
town.* **5** fail to catch: *miss the train.* **6** leave out:
miss a word in reading. **7** fail to do or answer
correctly: *I missed three words in today's spelling
lesson.* **8** fail to hear or understand: *What did you
say? I missed a word or two.* **9** fail to keep, do, or
be present at: *I missed my music lesson today.*
10 notice the absence of; feel keenly the absence
of: *I didn't miss my money till I got home. I missed
you while you were away.* 1,3-10 *verb,* 2 *noun, plural*
miss es.

Miss (mis), **1** title put in front of a girl's or
unmarried woman's name: *Miss Brown, the Misses
Brown, the Miss Browns.* **2 miss,** a girl or young
woman. *noun, plural* **Miss es.**

mis shap en (mis shā′pən), badly shaped;
deformed: *This fork got bent and is misshapen.
adjective.*

mis sile (mis′əl), **1** object that is thrown, hurled, or
shot, such as a stone, a bullet, an arrow, or a
lance. **2** rocket used in warfare. Missiles can be
launched from land, air, or sea. *noun.*

miss ing (mis′ing), **1** lacking or wanting: *It was a
good cake but something was missing.* **2** lost; gone;
out of its usual place: *The missing ring was found
under the dresser. One of the books was missing.*
3 absent: *Four children were missing from class
today. adjective.*

mis sion (mish′ən), **1** sending or being sent on
some special work; errand: *He was sent on a
mission to a foreign government.* **2** persons sent out
on some special business: *She was one of a
mission sent by our government to France.*
3 business on which a mission is sent: *The
diplomats successfully carried out the mission on
which they were sent by their government.* **4** station
or headquarters of a religious group: *a mission in
the slums.* **5** one's business or purpose in life;
one's calling: *It seemed to be her mission to help
improve living conditions in the city. noun.*

mishap

mistletoe

misty (definition 1)—It was a **misty** day.

a hat	i it	oi oil	ch child	a in about
ā age	ī ice	ou out	ng long	e in taken
ä far	o hot	u cup	sh she	ə = i in pencil
e let	ō open	u̇ put	th thin	o in lemon
ē equal	ô order	ü rule	ᴛʜ then	u in circus
ėr term			zh measure	

wasted: *a misspent fortune, a misspent life.* adjective.

mist (mist), **1** cloud of very fine drops of water in the air; fog. **2** come down in mist; rain in very fine drops: *It is misting.* **3** anything that dims, blurs, or obscures: *She did not cry, but a mist came over her eyes. A mist of prejudice spoiled his judgment.* **4** become covered with a mist: *The windows are misting.* **5** cover with a mist; put a mist before; make dim: *Tears misted his eyes.* 1,3 *noun,* 2,4,5 *verb.*

mis take (mə stāk′), **1** error; blunder; misunderstanding of a thing's meaning: *I used your towel by mistake.* **2** misunderstand (what is seen or heard). **3** take wrongly; take (to be some other person or thing): *I mistook that stick for a snake.* 1 *noun,* 2,3 *verb,* **mis took, mis tak en, mis tak ing.**

mis tak en (mə stā′kən), **1** wrong in opinion; having made a mistake: *I saw I was mistaken and admitted my error.* **2** wrong; wrongly judged; misplaced: *It was a mistaken kindness to give that boy more candy; it will make him sick.* **3** See **mistake.** *She was mistaken for the queen.* 1,2 *adjective,* 3 *verb.*

mis tak en ly (mə stā′kən lē), by mistake; wrongly. *adverb.*

Mis ter (mis′tər), **1** Mr., a title put before a man's name or the name of his office: *Mr. Smith, Mr. President.* **2** sir: *Mister, can you help me? noun.*

mis tle toe (mis′əl tō), plant with white berries, that grows as a parasite on trees. It is used as a Christmas decoration. See picture. *noun.*

mis took (mis tu̇k′). See **mistake.** *I mistook you for your sister yesterday. verb.*

mis treat (mis trēt′), treat badly. *verb.*

mis tress (mis′tris), **1** woman who is at the head of a household. **2** woman or country who is in control or can rule: *England was sometimes called mistress of the seas.* **3** woman who has a thorough knowledge or mastery: *She is a complete mistress of the art of cooking.* **4** woman teaching in a school, or at the head of a school, or giving lessons in a special subject: *the dancing mistress.* **5 Mistress,** in former times, Mrs., Madam, or Miss. *noun, plural* **mis tress es.**

mis trust (mis trust′), **1** feel no confidence in; doubt: *I mistrusted my ability to learn to swim.* **2** lack of trust or confidence; suspicion: *He looked with mistrust at the stranger.* 1 *verb,* 2 *noun.*

mist y (mis′tē), **1** covered with mist: *misty hills.* See picture. **2** not clearly seen or outlined. **3** as if seen through a mist; vague; indistinct: *a misty notion. adjective,* **mist i er, mist i est.**

mis un der stand (mis′un′dər stand′), **1** understand wrongly. **2** give the wrong meaning to. *verb,* **mis un der stood, mis un der stand ing.**

mis sion ar y (mish′ə ner′ē), **1** person who goes on the work of a religious mission: *Missionaries helped start churches, schools, and hospitals in many places.* **2** of religious missions or missionaries: *missionary enthusiasm.* 1 *noun, plural* **mis sion ar ies;** 2 *adjective.*

Mis sis sip pi (mis′ə sip′ē), one of the south central states of the United States. *noun.* [*Mississippi* got its name from the Mississippi River. This name came from an American Indian word meaning "the big river."]

Mis sour i (mə zu̇r′ē *or* mə zu̇r′ə), one of the midwestern states of the United States. *noun.* [*Missouri* got its name from the Missouri River. The river was named for an American Indian tribe, the Missouri, who lived near the mouth of the river. The name probably meant "people of the big canoes."]

mis spell (mis spel′), spell incorrectly. *verb,* **mis spelled** or **mis spelt** (mis spelt′), **mis spell ing.**

mis spent (mis spent′), spent foolishly or wrongly;

mis un der stand ing (mis′un/dər stan′ding),
1 wrong understanding; failure to understand;
mistake as to meaning. **2** disagreement: *After their
misunderstanding they scarcely spoke to each other.*
noun.

mis un der stood (mis′un/dər stüd′). See
misunderstand. *She misunderstood what the
teacher said and so did the wrong homework. verb.*

mis use (mis yüz′ *for 1 and 2;* mis yüs′ *for 3*),
1 use for the wrong purpose: *He misuses his knife
at the table by lifting food with it.* **2** treat badly: *The
children misused their dog by trying to ride on its
back.* **3** wrong use: *I notice a misuse of the word
"who" in your letter.* 1,2 *verb,* **mis used, mis us ing;**
3 *noun.*

mite[1] (mīt), a tiny animal that is related to the
spider and has eight legs. It lives in foods, on
plants, or on other animals. See picture. *noun.*

mite[2] (mīt), **1** anything very small; little bit: *I can't
eat even a mite of supper.* **2** a very small child: *What
a mite your baby brother is! noun.*

mitt (mit), **1** glove with a big pad over the palm
and fingers, used by baseball players: *a catcher's
mitt.* **2** mitten. *noun.*

mit ten (mit′n), kind of winter glove, covering the
four fingers together and the thumb separately.
noun.

mix (miks), **1** put together; stir well together: *We*

mite[1]
15 times actual size

moccasin (definition 2)
about 4 feet (1 meter) long

mix butter, sugar, milk, and flour for a cake.
2 prepare by putting different things together: *mix
a cake.* **3** join: *mix business and pleasure.* **4** be
mixed: *Oil and water will not mix.* **5** get along
together; make friends easily: *She likes people and
mixes well in almost any group.* **6** preparation that is
already mixed: *a cake mix.* 1-5 *verb,* **mixed** or **mixt**
(mikst), **mix ing;** 6 *noun, plural* **mix es.**

mix up, confuse: *I was so mixed up that I did very
badly on the test.*

mixed (mikst), **1** formed of different kinds: *mixed
candies, mixed emotions.* **2** of or for both men and
women: *a mixed chorus. adjective.*

mixed   number, a whole number and a fraction,
such as $3\frac{5}{8}$ and $28\frac{3}{4}$.

mix ture (miks′chər), **1** mixing: *The mixture of the
paints took almost ten minutes.* **2** mixed condition:
*At the end of the movie I felt a mixture of relief and
disappointment.* **3** something that has been mixed:
Orange is a mixture of yellow and red. noun.

mix-up (miks′up′), confusion; mess: *Our books
arrived late because of a mix-up in the orders. noun.*

mo., month or months.

moan (mōn), **1** a long, low sound of suffering.
2 any similar sound: *the moan of the winter wind.*
3 make moans: *The sick man moaned in his sleep.*
4 grieve for. **5** complain about: *They were always
moaning about their bad luck.* 1,2 *noun,* 3-5 *verb.*

moat (mōt), **1** a deep, wide ditch, usually filled
with water, dug around a castle or town as a
protection against enemies. **2** a similar ditch used
to separate animals in zoos. *noun.*

mob (mob), **1** a lawless crowd, easily moved to act
without thinking. **2** a large number of people;
crowd. **3** crowd around, especially in curiosity or
anger: *The eager children mobbed the ice-cream
truck the moment it appeared.* **4** attack with violence
as a mob does. **5** the common mass of people.
1,2,5 *noun,* 3,4 *verb,* **mobbed, mob bing.**

mo bile (mō′bəl *for 1 and 2;* mō′bēl *for 3*),
1 movable; easy to move: *Several mobile
classrooms were brought to the crowded school.*
2 moving easily; changing easily: *A mobile mind is
one that is easily moved by ideas or feelings.*
3 decorations hanging from fine wires or threads
and balanced to move in a slight breeze. 1,2
adjective, 3 *noun.*

moc ca sin (mok′ə sən), **1** a soft leather shoe
without a heel. Moccasins were first made by
North American Indians out of deerskin. **2** a
poisonous snake found in the southern part of the
United States. See picture. *noun.*

mock (mok), **1** laugh at; make fun of. **2** make fun
of by copying or imitating: *My friends mocked the
way I hobbled around on my sore foot.* **3** imitate;
copy: *Catbirds mock the songs of other birds.* **4** not
real; imitation: *a mock battle, mock modesty.* 1-3
verb, 4 *adjective.*

mock er y (mok′ər ē), **1** making fun; ridicule: *Their
mockery of my new hat hurt my feelings.* **2** a bad
copy or imitation: *Their pretended sorrow was but a
mockery of real grief. noun, plural* **mock er ies.**

mock ing bird (mok′ing bėrd′), a grayish

songbird that imitates the calls of other birds. *noun.*

mode (mōd), **1** manner or way in which a thing is done: *Riding on a donkey is a slow mode of travel.* **2** style, fashion, or custom that is current; way most people are behaving, talking, or dressing. *noun.*

mod el (mod′l), **1** a copy, especially a small copy: *a model of a ship, a model of an island, a model of a microscope.* **2** figure in clay or wax that is to be copied in marble, bronze, or other material: *a model for a statue.* **3** make, shape, or fashion; design or plan: *Model a horse in clay.* **4** way in which a thing is made; style: *Our television set is a new model.* **5** thing or person to be copied or imitated: *Your mother is a fine person; make her your model.* **6** follow as a model: *Model yourself on your father.* **7** just right or perfect, especially in conduct: *a model child.* **8** person who poses for artists and photographers. **9** person employed by a clothing store to wear clothes that are for sale, so that customers can see how they look. **1,2,4,5,8,9** *noun,* **3,6** *verb,* **7** *adjective.*

mod er ate (mod′ər it *for 1-3;* mod′ə rāt′ *for 4*), **1** kept or keeping within proper bounds; not extreme: *moderate expenses, moderate styles.* **2** calm; not violent: *moderate in speech or opinion.* **3** fair; medium; not very large or good: *make a moderate profit.* **4** make less violent; become less extreme or violent: *The wind is moderating.* **1-3** *adjective,* **4** *verb,* **mod er at ed, mod er at ing.**

mod e ra tion (mod′ə rā′shən), **1** act of moderating or of moving away from an extreme: *We all welcomed the moderation of the uncomfortably hot weather.* **2** a reasonable amount or degree: *It is all right to eat candy in moderation.* *noun.*

mod ern (mod′ərn), **1** of the present time; of times not long past: *Color television is a modern invention.* **2** up-to-date; not old-fashioned: *modern views. adjective.*

mod est (mod′ist), **1** not thinking too highly of oneself; not vain; humble: *In spite of many honors, the scientist remained a modest person.* **2** bashful; not bold; shy; held back by a sense of what is fit and proper: *a modest child.* **3** not displaying or calling attention to one's body. **4** not too great; not asking too much: *a modest request.* **5** quiet; not gaudy; humble in appearance: *a modest little house. adjective.*

mod est y (mod′ə stē), **1** not thinking too highly of oneself; being humble. **2** being shy or bashful. **3** not displaying or calling attention to one's body. *noun, plural* **mod est ies.**

mod i fi ca tion (mod′ə fə kā′shən), **1** partial alteration or change: *With these modifications your composition will do for the school paper.* **2** modifying or being modified; toning down: *A modification of the workers' demands helped settle the long strike.* **3** a modified form; variety: *This new car is a modification of last year's model. noun.*

mod i fy (mod′ə fī), **1** change somewhat: *modify the design of an automobile.* **2** make less; tone down; make less severe or strong: *The workers modified their demands.* **3** limit the meaning of: *In "red rose," red modifies rose. verb,* **mod i fied, mod i fy ing.**

Mo ham med (mō ham′id), founder of Islam, the religion of the Moslems. *noun.*

Mo ham med an (mō ham′ə dən), Moslem. *adjective, noun.*

moist (moist), slightly wet; damp. *adjective.*

mois ten (mois′n), make moist; become moist: *His eyes moistened with tears. verb.*

mois ture (mois′chər), slight wetness; water or other liquid spread in very small drops in the air or on a surface. Dew is moisture that collects at night on the grass. *noun.*

mo lar (mō′lər), tooth with a broad surface for grinding; one of the back teeth. Adult human beings have twelve molars. *noun.*

mo las ses (mə las′iz), a sweet, brown syrup. Molasses is obtained in the process of making sugar from sugar cane. *noun.* [*Molasses* comes from a Latin word meaning "honey."]

mold[1] (mōld), **1** a hollow shape in which anything is formed or cast, such as the mold into which melted metal is poured to harden into shape, or the mold in which jelly is left to stiffen. **2** shape or form which is given by a mold: *The molds of ice cream were turkeys and pumpkins.* **3** make or form into shape: *mold dough into loaves to be baked. Children mold figures out of clay. Her character was molded by the trials she went through.* **1,2** *noun,* **3** *verb.* Also spelled **mould.**

mold[2] (mōld), **1** a woolly or furry growth, often greenish in color, that appears on food and other animal or vegetable substances when they are left too long in a warm, moist place. Mold is a fungus. **2** become covered with mold. **1** *noun,* **2** *verb.* Also spelled **mould.**

mold er (mōl′dər), crumble away; break up gradually into dust. *verb.* Also spelled **moulder.**

mold ing (mōl′ding), **1** act of shaping: *the molding of dishes from clay.* **2** something molded. **3** strip, usually of wood, around the upper walls of a room, used to support pictures, to cover electric wires, or for decoration. *noun.*

mold y (mōl′dē), **1** covered with a fuzzy growth of mold: *a moldy crust of bread, moldy cheese.* **2** musty; stale: *a moldy smell. adjective,* **mold i er, mold i est.** Also spelled **mouldy.**

mole[1] (mōl), spot on the skin, usually brown. *noun.*

mole[2] (mōl), a small animal that lives underground most of the time. Moles have velvety fur and very small eyes that cannot see well. *noun.*

mol e cule (mol′ə kyül), **1** the smallest particle into which a substance can be divided without chemical change. **2** a very small particle. *noun.*

a hat	i it	oi oil	ch child	a in about
ā age	ī ice	ou out	ng long	e in taken
ä far	o hot	u cup	sh she	ə = i in pencil
e let	ō open	ù put	th thin	o in lemon
ē equal	ô order	ü rule	ŦH then	u in circus
ėr term			zh measure	

mo lest (mə lest/), meddle with and injure; interfere with and trouble; disturb: *It is cruel to molest animals.* verb.

mol lusk (mol/əsk), animal with a soft body, usually protected with a shell. Snails, oysters, and clams are mollusks. See picture. noun.

molt (mōlt), shed the feathers, skin, hair, or shell before a new growth. Birds, snakes, and insects molt. verb.

mol ten (mōlt/n), 1 melted. 2 made by melting and casting: *a molten image.* adjective.

mom (mom), mother. noun.

mo ment (mō/mənt), 1 a very short space of time; instant: *In a moment the house was in flames.* 2 a particular point of time: *I started the very moment I got your message.* 3 importance: *Congress is busy on a matter of moment.* noun.

mo men tar i ly (mō/mən ter/ə lē), 1 for a moment: *She hesitated momentarily.* 2 at every moment; from moment to moment: *The danger was increasing momentarily.* 3 at any moment: *We were expecting our visitors momentarily.* adverb.

mo men tar y (mō/mən ter/ē), lasting only a moment: *momentary hesitation.* adjective.

mo men tous (mō men/təs), very important: *Choosing between peace and war is a momentous decision.* adjective.

mo men tum (mō men/təm), force with which an object moves: *A falling object gains momentum as it falls. The momentum of the racing cars carried them far beyond the finish line.* noun.

mon arch (mon/ərk), 1 king, queen, emperor, or other ruler. 2 a large, orange-and-black butterfly. noun.

mon ar chy (mon/ər kē), 1 government by a monarch. 2 nation governed by a monarch. noun, plural **mon ar chies.**

mon as ter y (mon/ə ster/ē), building where monks live by themselves. noun, plural **mon as ter ies.**

Mon day (mun/dē), the second day of the week; the day after Sunday. noun. [*Monday* comes from an earlier English word meaning "the moon's day." It was called this because it follows Sunday, that is, the sun's day.]

mon ey (mun/ē), 1 coins of gold, silver, or other metal, or paper bills which represent these metals: *I have five dollars in Canadian money.* 2 wealth: *He is a man of money.* noun, plural **mon eys** or **mon ies.**

make money, 1 get money: *She made money in the stock market.* 2 become rich: *My ambition is to make money and retire young.*

mon goose (mong/güs), a slender animal of Africa and Asia, like a ferret. It is used for destroying rats and is noted for its ability to kill poisonous snakes without being harmed. See picture. noun, plural **mon goos es.**

mon grel (mung/grəl or mong/grəl), animal or plant of mixed breed, especially a dog. noun.

mon i tor (mon/ə tər), 1 pupil in school with special duties, such as helping to keep order and taking attendance. 2 receiver or other device that is used to check or control something: *Most banks have TV monitors to observe customers and prevent holdups.* 3 check or control something by a receiver or other device: *Police monitor traffic by using cars equipped with radar.* 1,2 noun, 3 verb.

monk (mungk), man who gives up everything else for religion and enters a monastery to live. noun.

mon key (mung/kē), 1 animal of the group most like human beings. Monkeys are very intelligent animals. 2 one of the smaller animals in this group, not a chimpanzee, gorilla, or other large ape. It usually has a long tail. 3 person, especially a child, who is full of mischief. 4 play; fool; trifle: *Don't monkey with the television.* 1-3 noun, plural **mon keys;** 4 verb.

make a monkey out of, make a fool of.

monkey wrench, wrench with a movable jaw that can be adjusted to fit different sizes of nuts.

mon o cle (mon/ə kəl), eyeglass for one eye. noun.

mon o gram (mon/ə gram), a person's initials combined in one design. Monograms are used on note paper, table linen, clothing, and jewelry. noun.

mon o logue (mon/l ôg), 1 a long speech by one person in a group. 2 entertainment by a single speaker. 3 play for a single actor. 4 part of a play in which a single actor speaks alone. noun.

mon o plane (mon/ə plān), airplane with only one pair of wings. Most modern airplanes are monoplanes. noun.

mo nop o lize (mə nop/ə līz), 1 have or get exclusive possession or control of: *One company in the country monopolized the production of copper wire.* 2 occupy wholly; keep entirely to oneself: *Don't monopolize your teacher's time.* verb, **mo nop o lized, mo nop o liz ing.**

mo nop o ly (mə nop/ə lē), 1 the exclusive control of a commodity or service: *The only milk company in our town has a monopoly on milk delivery.* 2 a company with such exclusive control. 3 the exclusive possession or control of something: *a monopoly on another person's time.* noun, plural **mo nop o lies.**

mon o rail (mon/ə rāl), 1 a railroad track having only a single rail rather than two parallel rails. 2 railroad with cars that run on a track having a single rail. See picture. noun.

mon o syl la ble (mon/ə sil/ə bəl), word of one syllable. *Yes* and *no* are monosyllables. noun.

mon o tone (mon/ə tōn), sameness of tone, of style of writing, or of color: *Don't read in a monotone; use expression.* noun.

mo not o nous (mə not/n əs), 1 continuing in the same tone: *She spoke in a monotonous voice.* 2 not varying; without change: *monotonous food.* 3 wearying because of its sameness: *Sorting mail is monotonous work.* adjective.

mo not o ny (mə not/n ē), 1 sameness of tone or pitch: *The monotony of the man's voice was irritating.* 2 lack of variety; wearisome sameness: *the monotony of the desert.* noun.

mon soon (mon sün/), 1 a seasonal wind of the Indian Ocean and southern Asia. It blows from the

mollusk—a snail about 2 inches (5 centimeters) long

a hat	i it	oi oil	ch child	a in about
ā age	ī ice	ou out	ng long	e in taken
ä far	o hot	u cup	sh she	ə = i in pencil
e let	ō open	u̇ put	th thin	o in lemon
ē equal	ô order	ü rule	ᵀHthen	u in circus
ėr term			zh measure	

monorail (definition 2)

mongoose—about 2 feet (60 centimeters) long with the tail

monster (definition 3)

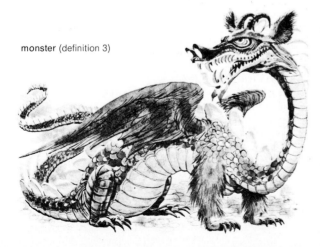

southwest from April to October and from the northeast during the rest of the year. **2** season during which this wind blows from the southwest, usually accompanied by heavy rains. *noun.*

mon ster (mon′stər), **1** any animal or plant that is very unlike those usually found in nature. A cow with two heads is a monster. **2** an imaginary creature having parts of different animals: *Mermaids and centaurs are monsters.* **3** an imaginary animal of strange and horrible appearance. See picture. **4** a huge creature or thing. **5** person too wicked to be considered human: *a horrible crime committed by a monster of cruelty. noun.*

mon strous (mon′strəs), **1** huge; enormous. **2** wrongly formed or shaped; like a monster. **3** so wrong or absurd as to be almost unheard of. **4** shocking; horrible; dreadful. *adjective.*

Mon tan a (mon tan′ə), one of the western states of the United States. *noun.* [*Montana* is from a Spanish word meaning "region having many mountains."]

month (munth), one of the twelve periods of time into which a year is divided. April, June, September, and November have 30 days; February has 28 days except in leap years; all the other months have 31 days. *noun.*

month ly (munth′lē), **1** of a month; for a month; lasting a month: *a monthly supply, a monthly salary.* **2** done, happening, or paid once a month: *a monthly meeting, a monthly examination.* **3** once a month; every month: *Some magazines come monthly.* **4** magazine published once a month. 1,2 *adjective,* 3 *adverb,* 4 *noun, plural* **month lies.**

mon u ment (mon′yə mənt), **1** something set up to keep a person or an event from being forgotten; anything that keeps alive the memory of a person or an event. A monument may be a building, pillar, arch, statue, tomb, or stone. **2** a permanent or prominent instance: *The Hoover Dam is a monument of engineering. noun.*

mon u men tal (mon′yə men′tl), **1** of a monument: *monumental decorations.* **2** serving as a monument: *a monumental chapel.* **3** like a monument: *a monumental mountain peak.* **4** weighty and lasting; important: *The Constitution of the United States is a monumental document.* **5** very great: *monumental ignorance. adjective.*

moo (mü), **1** the sound made by a cow. **2** make this sound. 1 *noun, plural* **moos;** 2 *verb.*

mood (müd), state of mind or feeling: *I am in the mood to play now; I don't want to study. noun.*

mood y (mü′dē), **1** likely to have changes of mood. **2** often having gloomy moods: *She has been moody ever since she lost her job.* **3** sunk in sadness; gloomy; sullen: *He sat in moody silence. adjective,* **mood i er, mood i est.**

moon (definition 1)

moon (mün), **1** a heavenly body that revolves around the earth once in about 29¹/₂ days. The moon shines in the sky at night and looks bright because it reflects the sun's light. See picture. **2** the American Indian month of about 29¹/₂ days. **3** moonlight. **4** anything round like the moon. **5** satellite of any planet: *the moons of Jupiter. noun.*

moon beam (mün′bēm′), ray of moonlight. *noun.*

moon light (mün′līt′), **1** light of the moon. **2** having the light of the moon: *a moonlight night.* **1** *noun,* **2** *adjective.*

moon lit (mün′lit′), lighted by the moon. *adjective.*

moor¹ (mur), put or keep (a ship) in place by means of ropes or chains fastened to the shore or to anchors. *verb.*

moor² (mur), open wasteland, especially if heather grows on it. *noun.*

Moor (mur), person born or living in northwestern Africa. The Moors are Moslems who speak Arabic. In the A.D. 700's the Moors invaded and conquered Spain. They were finally driven out in 1492. *noun.*

moor ings (mur′ingz), **1** ropes, cables, or anchors by which a ship is fastened. **2** place where a ship is moored. *noun plural.*

moose (müs), animal somewhat like a large deer, living in Canada and the northern part of the United States. The male has a large head and broad antlers. See picture. *noun, plural* **moose.** [*Moose* comes from a North American Indian word meaning "he strips off the bark." The moose was called this because it strips off and eats the bark of trees.]

mop (mop), **1** bundle of coarse yarn, rags, cloth, or a sponge, fastened at the end of a stick, for cleaning floors, dishes, and other things. **2** wash or wipe up; clean with a mop: *mop the floor.* **3** wipe tears or sweat from: *She mopped her brow with a handkerchief.* **4** a thick head of hair like a mop. **1,4** *noun,* **2,3** *verb,* **mopped, mop ping.**

mope (mōp), be dull, silent, and sad. *verb,* **moped, mop ing.**

mo ral (môr′əl), **1** good in character or conduct; virtuous according to civilized standards of right and wrong; right; just: *a moral act, a moral person.*

2 morals, character or behavior in matters of right and wrong: *a person of excellent morals.* **3** capable of understanding right and wrong: *A little baby is not a moral being.* **4** having to do with character or with the difference between right and wrong: *Whether finding should be keeping is a moral question.* **5** lesson, inner meaning, or teaching of a fable, a story, or an event: *The moral of the story was "Look before you leap."* **6** teaching a good lesson; having a good influence. **1,3,4,6** *adjective,* **2,5** *noun.*

mo rale (mə ral′), moral or mental condition in regard to courage, confidence, or enthusiasm: *The morale of the team was low after its defeat. noun.*

mo ral i ty (mə ral′ə tē), **1** the right or wrong of an action: *They spent the evening arguing about the morality of war.* **2** doing right; virtue: *They have high standards of morality.* **3** system of morals; set of rules or principles of conduct. *noun, plural* **mo ral i ties.**

mo ral ly (môr′ə lē), **1** in a moral manner: *to behave morally.* **2** in morals; as to morals: *The king was a good man morally but was too easily swayed by his crafty advisers.* **3** from a moral point of view: *What they did was morally wrong. adverb.*

mo rass (mə ras′), piece of low, soft, wet ground; swamp. *noun, plural* **mo rass es.**

mor bid (môr′bid), unhealthy; not wholesome: *morbid ideas, a morbid book. adjective.*

more (môr), **1** greater in amount, degree, or number: *more humid, more people. A foot is more than an inch.* **2** a greater or additional amount, degree, or number: *Tell me more about your camping trip. Seven people will not be enough for a softball team; we will need more.* **3** in a higher degree; to a greater extent: *A burn hurts more than a scratch does.* **4** in addition; farther: *Take one step more.* **5** further; additional: *This plant needs more sun.* **6** *More* helps to make the comparative form of most adverbs, and of most adjectives longer than one syllable: *more easily, more truly, more careful. "More common" means "commoner."* **1,5** *adjective, comparative of* **much** *and* **many;** **2** *noun,* **3,4,6** *adverb, comparative of* **much.**

more or less, 1 somewhat: *Most people are more or less selfish.* **2** about; approximately: *The distance is fifty miles, more or less.*

more o ver (môr ō′vər), also; besides: *I don't want to go skating and, moreover, the ice is too thin. adverb.*

morn (môrn), morning. *noun.*

morn ing (môr′ning), the early part of the day, ending at noon. *noun.*

morn ing-glo ry (môr′ning glôr′ē), a climbing vine that has heart-shaped leaves and funnel-shaped flowers of blue, lavender, pink, or white. *noun, plural* **morn ing-glo ries.**

Mo roc co (mə rok′ō), country in northern Africa. *noun.*

mo ron (môr′on), **1** person born with little mental ability. Morons can usually learn to read and to work at simple jobs. **2** a very stupid or foolish person. *noun.* [*Moron* comes from a Greek word meaning "foolish" or "dull."]

mo rose (mə rōs'), gloomy; sullen. *adjective.*

mor row (môr'ō), **1** the following day or time. **2** "Good morrow" is an old way of saying "Good morning." *noun.*

mor sel (môr'səl), **1** a small bite; mouthful. **2** piece; fragment. *noun.*

mor tal (môr'tl), **1** sure to die sometime: *all mortal creatures.* **2** being that is sure to die sometime. All living creatures are mortals. **3** of human beings; of mortals: *Mortal flesh has many pains and diseases.* **4** human being: *No mortal could have survived the fire.* **5** causing death: *a mortal wound, a mortal illness.* **6** to the death: *a mortal enemy, a mortal battle.* **7** very great; deadly: *mortal terror.* **8** causing death of the soul, according to the Roman Catholic Church: *Murder is a mortal sin.* 1,3,5-8 *adjective,* 2,4 *noun.*

mor tal ly (môr'tl ē), **1** so as to cause death: *mortally wounded.* **2** very greatly; bitterly: *mortally offended. adverb.*

mor tar (môr'tər), **1** mixture of lime, cement, sand, and water for holding bricks or stones together. **2** a very short cannon for shooting shells or fireworks high into the air. **3** bowl of porcelain, glass, or other very hard material, in which substances may be pounded to a powder with a pestle. *noun.*

mor ti fi ca tion (môr'tə fə kā'shən), humiliation; cause of shame or humiliation: *Imagine their mortification at having lost $100! noun.*

mor ti fy (môr'tə fī), wound (a person's feelings); make (a person) feel humbled or ashamed: *They mortified their parents with their bad behavior. verb,* **mor ti fied, mor ti fy ing.**

mo sa ic (mō zā'ik), **1** small pieces of stone, glass, or wood of different colors inlaid to form a picture or design. **2** such a picture or design. Mosaics are used in the floors, walls, or ceilings of some fine buildings. See picture. **3** anything like a mosaic. *noun.*

Mos lem (moz'ləm), **1** follower of Mohammed; believer in the religion founded by him. **2** of Mohammed or the religion founded by him. 1 *noun, plural* **Mos lems** *or* **Mos lem;** 2 *adjective.* Also spelled **Muslim.**

mosque (mosk), a Moslem place of worship. See picture. *noun.*

mo squi to (mə skē'tō), a small, slender insect with two wings. The female bites and sucks blood, causing itching. There are many kinds of mosquitoes; one kind transmits malaria; another transmits yellow fever. *noun, plural* **mo squi toes** *or* **mo squi tos.**

moss (môs), very small, soft, green plants that grow close together like a carpet on the ground, on rocks, or on trees. *noun, plural* **moss es.**

moss y (mô'sē), **1** covered with moss: *a mossy bank.* **2** like moss: *mossy green. adjective,* **moss i er, moss i est.**

most (mōst), **1** greatest in amount, degree, or number: *The winner gets the most money.* **2** the

a hat	**i** it	**oi** oil	**ch** child	a in about
ā age	**ī** ice	**ou** out	**ng** long	e in taken
ä far	**o** hot	**u** cup	**sh** she	ə = i in pencil
e let	**ō** open	**u̇** put	**th** thin	o in lemon
ē equal	**ô** order	**ü** rule	**ŦH** then	u in circus
ėr term			**zh** measure	

moose—about 6 feet (2 meters) high at the shoulder

mosque

mosaic (definition 2)

greatest amount, degree, or number: *We did most of the work around the house. Who gave the most?* **3** in the highest degree; to the greatest extent: *This tooth hurts most. They were most kind to me.* **4** almost all: *Most people like ice cream.* **5** Most helps to make the superlative form of most adverbs, and of most adjectives longer than one syllable: *most easily, most truly, most careful.* "*Most common*" means "*commonest.*" 1,4 *adjective, superlative of* **much** *and* **many;** 2 *noun,* 3,5 *adverb, superlative of* **much.**

at most, not more than: *Within an hour at most I will tell you.*

for the most part, mainly; usually: *The attempts were for the most part unsuccessful.*

most ly (mōst′lē), almost all; for the most part; mainly; chiefly: *The work is mostly done. adverb.*

mo tel (mō tel′), a roadside hotel or a group of furnished cottages or cabins providing overnight lodging for motorists. *noun.* [*Motel* was formed by blending the words *motor* and *hotel.*]

moth (môth), a winged insect very much like a butterfly, but flying mostly at night. One kind lays eggs in cloth and fur, and its larvae eat holes in the material. Some larvae, such as the silkworm, are useful to people. See picture. *noun, plural* **moths** (môᴛʜz *or* môths).

moth ball (môth′bôl′), a small ball of camphor, used to keep moths away from wool, silk, fur, and other types of clothing. *noun.*

moth er (muᴛʜ′ər), **1** a female parent. **2** take care of: *She mothers her baby sister.* **3** cause or source of anything: *Necessity is the mother of invention.* **4** head of a large community of religious women. **5** native: *one's mother country. English is our mother tongue.* 1,3,4 *noun,* 2 *verb,* 5 *adjective.*

moth er hood (muᴛʜ′ər hùd), condition of being a mother. *noun.*

moth er-in-law (muᴛʜ′ər in lô′), mother of one's husband or wife. *noun, plural* **moth ers-in-law.**

moth er less (muᴛʜ′ər lis), having no mother: *a motherless child. adjective.*

moth er ly (muᴛʜ′ər lē), of or like a mother; kindly: *a motherly person, a motherly smile. adjective.*

moth er-of-pearl (muᴛʜ′ər əv pėrl′), the hard, smooth, shiny lining of the shell of the pearl oyster and certain other shells. It changes colors as the light changes. It is used to make buttons and ornaments. *noun.*

mo tion (mō′shən), **1** movement; moving; change of position or place. Anything is in motion which is not at rest. *Can you feel the motion of the ship?* **2** make a movement, as of the hand or head, to show one's meaning: *She motioned to show us the way.* **3** show (a person) what to do by such a motion: *He motioned me out.* **4** a formal suggestion made in a meeting, to be voted on: *I made a motion to adjourn.* 1,4 *noun,* 2,3 *verb.*

mo tion less (mō′shən lis), not moving. *adjective.*

motion picture, series of pictures projected on a screen in such rapid succession that the viewer gets the impression that the persons and things

pictured are moving; moving picture; movie.

mo tive (mō′tiv), thought or feeling that makes one act: *My motive in going was a wish to travel. noun.*

mot ley (mot′lē), **1** made up of different things: *a motley collection of butterflies, shells, and stamps.* **2** of different colors like a clown's suit. **3** suit of more than one color worn by clowns: *At the party he wore motley.* 1,2 *adjective,* 3 *noun, plural* **mot leys.**

mo tor (mō′tər), **1** engine that makes a machine go: *an electric motor, a gasoline motor.* **2** run by a motor: *a motor vehicle.* **3** having to do with or by means of automobiles: *a motor tour.* **4** travel by automobile. **5** causing or having to do with motion. *Motor nerves arouse muscles to action.* 1 *noun,* 2,3,5 *adjective,* 4 *verb.*

moth—This kind of moth has a wingspread of 5 inches (13 centimeters).

mouse—about 6 inches (15 centimeters) long with the tail

mountain goat—3 feet (1 meter) high at the shoulder

mo tor boat (mō′tər bōt′), boat that is propelled by a motor. *noun.*

mo tor car (mō′tər kär′), automobile. *noun.*

mo tor cy cle (mō′tər sī′kəl), vehicle like a bicycle run by a motor. *noun.*

mo tor ist (mō′tər ist), person who drives or travels in an automobile. *noun.*

mot tled (mot′ld), spotted or streaked with different colors. *adjective.*

mot to (mot′ō), **1** a brief sentence adopted as a rule of conduct: *"Think before you speak" is a good motto.* **2** sentence, word, or phrase written or engraved on some object. *noun, plural* **mot toes** or **mot tos.**

mould (mōld), mold. *noun, verb.*

mould er (mōl′dər), molder. *verb.*

mould y (mōl′dē), moldy. *adjective,* **mould i er, mould i est.**

mound (mound), **1** bank or heap of earth or stones. **2** the slightly elevated ground from which a baseball pitcher pitches. *noun.*

mount[1] (mount), **1** go up: *mount a hill, mount a ladder.* **2** get up on: *mount a horse, mount a platform.* **3** get on a horse: *The riders mounted quickly.* **4** put on a horse; supply with a horse: *Some police officers in this city are mounted.* **5** horse for riding: *The riding instructor had an excellent mount.* **6** rise; increase; rise in amount: *The cost of living mounts steadily.* **7** put in proper position or order for use: *mount specimens on slides.* **8** have or carry (guns) as a fortress or ship does: *The ship mounts eight guns.* **9** fix in a setting, backing, or support: *mount a picture on cardboard.* **10** setting; backing; support: *the mount for a picture.* 1-4,6-9 *verb,* 5,10 *noun.*

mount[2] (mount), mountain; high hill. *Mount* is often used before the names of mountains. *Mount Rainier. noun.*

moun tain (moun′tən), **1** a very high hill. **2** of or having something to do with mountains: *mountain air, mountain plants.* **3** a very large heap or pile of anything: *a mountain of rubbish. She overcame a mountain of difficulties.* 1,3 *noun,* 2 *adjective.*

moun tain eer (moun′tə nir′), **1** person who lives in the mountains. **2** person skilled in mountain climbing. *noun.*

mountain goat, a white, goatlike antelope of the Rocky Mountains. See picture.

mountain lion, a wild North American animal somewhat like a cat but larger. Other common names for it are cougar and puma.

moun tain ous (moun′tə nəs), **1** covered with mountain ranges: *mountainous country.* **2** huge: *a mountainous wave. adjective.*

mountain range, row of mountains; large group of mountains.

moun tain side (moun′tən sīd′), slope of a mountain below the top. *noun.*

mourn (môrn), **1** grieve. **2** feel or show sorrow over: *They mourned their lost dog. verb.*

mourn ful (môrn′fəl), full of grief; sad; sorrowful: *a mournful voice. adjective.*

mourn ing (môr′ning), **1** wearing of black or

a hat	i it	oi oil	ch child	a in about
ā age	ī ice	ou out	ng long	e in taken
ä far	o hot	u cup	sh she	ə = i in pencil
e let	ō open	u̇ put	th thin	o in lemon
ē equal	ô order	ü rule	ŦH then	u in circus
ėr term			zh measure	

some other color to show sorrow for a person's death. **2** draping of buildings or the flying of flags at half-mast as an outward sign of sorrow for death. **3** clothes or decorations to show sorrow for death. **4** of mourning; used in mourning. 1-3 *noun,* 4 *adjective.*

mouse (mous), a small, gnawing animal with soft fur, a pointed snout, and a long, thin tail. The gray mouse is usually found in houses. Field mice live in fields and meadows and eat grain and other seeds. See picture. *noun, plural* **mice.**

mous tache (mus′tash), mustache. *noun.*

mouth (mouth *for 1 and 2;* mouŦH *for 3 and 4*), **1** opening through which a person or animal takes in food; space containing the tongue and teeth. **2** opening suggesting a mouth: *the mouth of a cave, the mouth of a river, the mouth of a bottle.* **3** utter (words) in an affected, pompous way: *I dislike actors who mouth their speeches.* **4** seize or rub with the mouth. 1,2 *noun, plural* **mouths** (mouŦHz); 3,4 *verb.*

mouth ful (mouth′fůl), **1** the amount the mouth can easily hold. **2** what is taken into the mouth at one time. **3** a small amount. *noun, plural* **mouth fuls.**

mouth organ, harmonica.

mouth piece (mouth′pēs′), **1** the part of a musical instrument, telephone, or pipe that is placed in, against, or near a person's mouth. **2** person or newspaper that speaks for others. *noun.*

mov a ble (mü′və bəl), **1** able to be moved: *Our fingers are movable.* **2** able to be carried from place to place as personal belongings can. **3** changing from one date to another in different years: *Easter is a movable holy day. adjective.* Also spelled **moveable.**

move (müv), **1** change the place or position of: *Do not move your hand. Move your chair to the table.* **2** change place or position: *The child moved in his sleep.* **3** change one's place of living: *We move to the country next week.* **4** put or keep in motion; shake; stir: *The wind moves the leaves.* **5** make progress; go: *The train moved slowly.* **6** do something about (some matter); act: *Congress sometimes moves slowly.* **7** action taken to bring about some result: *Our next move was to earn some money.* **8** cause to do something: *What moved you to get up so early this morning?* **9** arouse to laughter or some feeling: *The sad story moved us to tears.* **10** (in games) change to a different square according to rules: *move a pawn in chess.* **11** moving a piece in chess and other games: *That was a good move.* **12** a player's turn to move in a game: *It is your move now.* **13** (in a meeting) to bring forward or propose: *Madam Chairman, I* move that the report of the treasurer be adopted. 1-6,8-10,13 *verb*, **moved, mov ing; 7,11,12** *noun*.

move in, move oneself, one's family, or one's belongings into a new place to live: *The new couple is moving in next week.*

on the move, moving about: *Dolphins are always on the move.*

move a ble (mü′və bəl), movable. *adjective.*

move ment (müv′mənt), **1** moving: *We run by movements of the legs.* **2** change in the placing of troops or ships. **3** the moving parts of a machine; special group of connected parts that move together. The movement of a watch consists of many little wheels. See picture. **4** the efforts and results of a group of people working together to reach a common goal: *The civil rights movement was responsible for many new laws.* noun.

mov er (mü′vər), person or thing that moves. *noun.*

mov ie (mü′vē), **1** motion picture. **2 the movies,** a showing of motion pictures: *to go to the movies.* *noun.*

mov ing (mü′ving), **1** able to move: *a moving car.* **2** causing action: *He was the moving spirit in planning for the party.* **3** touching; pathetic: *a moving story.* **4** See **move.** 1-3 *adjective,* 4 *verb.*

moving picture, motion picture.

mow[1] (mō), **1** cut down with a machine or a scythe: *mow grass. I was mowing yesterday.* **2** cut down the grass or grain from: *mow a field.* **3** destroy at a sweep or in large numbers, as if by mowing: *The enemy fire mowed down a platoon of soldiers.* *verb,* **mowed, mowed or mown, mow ing.**

mow[2] (mou), **1** place in the barn where hay or grain is piled or stored. **2** pile or stack of hay or grain in a barn. *noun.*

mow er (mō′ər), person or thing that mows: *a lawn mower. noun.*

mown (mōn), mowed. See **mow**[1]. *New-mown hay is hay that has just been cut. verb.*

Mr. or Mr (mis′tər), title put in front of a man's name or the name of his position: *Mr. Jackson, Mr. Speaker.*

Mrs. or Mrs (mis′iz), title put in front of a married woman's name: *Mrs. Jackson.*

Ms. (miz), title put in front of a woman's name: *Ms. Jane Smith.*

Mt., mount or mountain: *Mt. Whitney.* plural **Mts.**

much (much), **1** in great amount or degree: *much rain, much pleasure, not much money.* **2** a great amount: *I did not hear much of the talk. Too much of this cake will make you sick.* **3** to a high degree; greatly: *I was much pleased with the toy.* **4** nearly; about: *This is much the same as the others.* 1 *adjective,* **more, most;** 2 *noun,* 3,4 *adverb,* **more, most.**

make much of, pay much attention to or do much for: *The students made much of the winning team.*

not much of a, not a very good: *Fifty dollars a week is not much of a wage.*

too much for, more than a match for: *My*

arguments were too much for them, and they admitted I was right.

mu ci lage (myü′sə lij), a sticky, gummy substance used to make things stick together. *noun.*

muck (muk), dirt; filth. *noun.*

mu cous mem brane (myü′kəs mem′brān), lining of the nose, throat, and other passages and cavities of the body that are open to the air.

mu cus (myü′kəs), a slimy substance that moistens and protects the linings of the body. A cold in the head causes a discharge of mucus. *noun.*

mud (mud), earth so wet that it is soft and sticky: *mud on the ground after rain. noun.*

mud dle (mud′l), **1** mix up; get (things) into a mess: *Somebody really muddled that job.* **2** think or act in a confused, blundering way: *muddle over a problem, muddle through a difficulty.* **3** make confused or stupid: *The more you talk, the more you muddle me.* **4** mess; disorder; confusion: *After the party the room was in a muddle.* 1-3 *verb,* **mud dled, mud dling;** 4 *noun.*

mud dy (mud′ē), **1** of or like mud: *muddy footprints on the floor.* **2** having much mud; covered with mud: *a muddy road.* **3** clouded with mud; dull; not pure: *muddy water, a muddy color.* **4** confused; not clear: *muddy thinking.* **5** make muddy; become muddy. 1-4 *adjective,* **mud di er, mud di est;** 5 *verb,* **mud died, mud dy ing.**

muff (muf), **1** covering of fur or other material for keeping both hands warm. One hand is put in at each end. See picture. **2** fail to catch (a ball) when it comes into one's hands. **3** a clumsy failure to catch a ball that comes into one's hands: *The catcher's muff allowed the runner to score.* **4** handle awkwardly. 1,3 *noun,* 2,4 *verb.*

muf fin (muf′ən), a small, round cake made of wheat flour, corn meal, or the like, often without sugar. Muffins are eaten with butter, and usually served hot. *noun.*

muf fle (muf′əl), **1** wrap or cover up in order to keep warm and dry: *I muffled my throat in a warm scarf.* **2** wrap in something in order to soften or stop the sound: *A bell can be muffled with cloth.* **3** dull or deaden (a sound). *verb,* **muf fled, muf fling.**

muf fler (muf′lər), **1** wrap or scarf worn around the neck for warmth. **2** anything used to deaden sound. An automobile muffler attached to the exhaust pipe deadens the sound of the engine's exhaust. *noun.*

mug (mug), **1** a heavy china or metal drinking cup with a handle. **2** amount a mug holds: *drink a mug of milk. noun.*

mug gy (mug′ē), warm and humid: *The weather was muggy. adjective,* **mug gi er, mug gi est.**

mul ber ry (mul′ber′ē), **1** tree with small, berrylike fruit that can be eaten. The leaves of one kind of mulberry are used for feeding silkworms. **2** its sweet, usually dark purple fruit. **3** dark purplish red. 1,2 *noun, plural* **mul ber ries;** 3 *adjective.*

mulch (mulch), **1** straw, leaves, or loose earth spread on the ground around trees or plants.

Mulch is used to protect the roots from cold or heat, to prevent evaporation of moisture from the soil, or to keep the fruit clean. As mulch decays it makes the soil richer. **2** cover with straw or leaves. **1** *noun,* plural **mulch es; 2** *verb.*

mule (myül), **1** animal which is half donkey and half horse. It has the form and size of a horse, but the large ears, small hoofs, and tufted tail of a donkey. See picture. **2** a stubborn person. *noun.*

mul ish (myü′lish), like a mule; stubborn; obstinate. *adjective.*

mul let (mul′it), fish that lives close to the shore in warm waters and is good to eat. There are red mullets and gray mullets. *noun,* plural **mul lets** or **mul let.**

mul ti ple (mul′tə pəl), **1** of, having, or involving many parts, elements, or relations: *a person of multiple interests.* **2** number that can be divided by another number a certain number of times without a remainder: *12 is a multiple of 3.* **1** *adjective,* **2** *noun.*

mul ti pli cand (mul′tə plə kand′), number to be multiplied by another: *In 497 multiplied by 5, the multiplicand is 497. noun.*

mul ti pli ca tion (mul′tə plə kā′shən), **1** multiplying; being multiplied. **2** process of multiplying one number by another: *12 times 3 = 36 is a simple multiplication. noun.*

mul ti pli er (mul′tə plī′ər), number by which another number is to be multiplied: *In 83 multiplied by 5, 5 is the multiplier. noun.*

mul ti ply (mul′tə plī), **1** add a number a given number of times: *To multiply 6 by 3 means to add 6 three times, making 18.* **2** increase in number: *As we climbed up the mountain the dangers and difficulties multiplied. verb,* **mul ti plied, mul ti ply ing.**

mul ti tude (mul′tə tüd *or* mul′tə tyüd), a great many; crowd: *a multitude of difficulties, a multitude of enemies. noun.*

mum (mum), silent; saying nothing: *Keep mum about this; tell no one. adjective.*

mum ble (mum′bəl), **1** speak indistinctly, often with the lips partly closed. **2** act or fact of mumbling; indistinct speech: *There was a mumble of protest from the team against the umpire's decision.* **1** *verb,* **mum bled, mum bling; 2** *noun.*

mum my (mum′ē), a dead body preserved from decay. Egyptian mummies have lasted more than 3000 years. *noun,* plural **mum mies.**

mumps (mumps), a disease most often of children that causes swelling of the neck and face and makes it hard to swallow. Unless you are vaccinated against mumps, you can catch the disease if you are around someone who has it. *noun.*

munch (munch), chew vigorously and steadily; chew noisily: *The horse munched its oats. verb.*

mu nic i pal (myü nis′ə pəl), **1** of or having something to do with the affairs of a city or town: *The state police assisted the municipal police.* **2** run by a city or town. *adjective.*

mu ni tion (myü nish′ən), **1** munitions, material used in war. Munitions are military supplies such

a hat	i it	oi oil	ch child	a in about
ā age	ī ice	ou out	ng long	e in taken
ä far	o hot	u cup	sh she	ə = i in pencil
e let	ō open	u̇ put	th thin	o in lemon
ē equal	ô order	ü rule	₮H then	u in circus
ėr term			zh measure	

muff (definition 1) The older child is holding a muff.

movement (definition 3)

mule (definition 1)—about 4½ feet (1½ meters) high at the shoulder

as guns, powder, or bombs. **2** having something to do with military supplies: *A munition plant is a factory for making munitions.* **1** *noun,* **2** *adjective.*

mur al (myur′əl), picture painted on a wall. See picture. *noun.*

mur der (mėr′dər), **1** the unlawful killing of a human being when it is planned beforehand. **2** instance of such a crime: *The detective solved the murder.* **3** kill a human being intentionally: *Cain murdered his brother.* **4** do something very badly; spoil or ruin: *The singer really murdered that song.* **1,2** *noun,* **3,4** *verb.*

mur der er (mėr′dər ər), person who murders somebody. *noun.*

mur der ous (mėr′dər əs), **1** able to kill: *The villain aimed a murderous blow at the hero's back.* **2** ready to murder: *a murderous villain.* **3** causing murder: *a murderous hate. adjective.*

murk (mėrk), darkness; gloom: *A light flashed through the murk of the night. noun.*

murk y (mėr′kē), dark; gloomy: *a murky prison, a murky day. adjective,* **murk i er, murk i est.**

mur mur (mėr′mər), **1** a soft, low, indistinct sound that rises and falls a little and goes on without breaks: *the murmur of a stream.* **2** make a soft, low, indistinct sound. **3** a softly spoken word or speech. **4** say in a murmur: *The shy boy murmured his thanks.* **1,3** *noun,* **2,4** *verb.*

mus cle (mus′əl), **1** the tissue in the bodies of people and animals that can be tightened or loosened to make the body move. **2** a special bundle of such tissue which moves some particular bone or part: *You can feel the muscles in your arm.* **3** strength. *noun.* [*Muscle* comes from a Latin word meaning "a little mouse." It was called this because the shape and rippling movements of some muscles, as in the arm, suggest the shape and movements of a little mouse.]

mus cu lar (mus′kyə lər), **1** of the muscles; influencing the muscles: *a muscular strain.* **2** having well-developed muscles; strong: *a muscular arm. adjective.*

muse (myüz), think in a dreamy way; think: *She spent the whole afternoon in musing. verb,* **mused, mus ing.**

mu se um (myü zē′əm), building or rooms in which a collection of objects illustrating science, ancient life, art, or other subjects is kept and displayed. *noun.*

mush (mush), **1** corn meal boiled in water or milk. **2** a soft, thick mass: *After the heavy rain the old dirt road turned to mush. noun, plural* **mush es.**

mush room (mush′rüm), **1** a small fungus shaped like an umbrella, that grows very fast. Some mushrooms are good to eat; some are poisonous. **2** of or like a mushroom. **3** grow rapidly: *Her business mushroomed when she opened the new store.* **1** *noun,* **2** *adjective,* **3** *verb.*

mu sic (myü′zik), **1** art of making sounds that are beautiful, and putting them together into beautiful arrangements. **2** beautiful, pleasing, or interesting arrangements of sounds. **3** written or printed signs for tones: *Can you read music?* **4** any pleasant

mural—The building was decorated with murals.

sound: *the music of a bubbling brook. We were made drowsy by the music of the wind blowing through the trees. noun.*

face the music, meet trouble boldly or bravely.

set to music, provide (the words of a song) with music.

mu si cal (myü′zə kəl), **1** of music: *a musical instrument, a musical composer.* **2** sounding beautiful or pleasing; like music: *a musical voice.* **3** set to music or accompanied by music: *a musical performance.* **4** fond of music: *a musical family.* **5** skilled in music: *His playing shows that he is very musical. adjective.*

musical instrument, piano, violin, or other instrument for producing music.

mu si cal ly (myü′zik lē), **1** in a musical manner. **2** in music: *She is well educated musically. adverb.*

music box, box or case containing a device that produces music mechanically.

mu si cian (myü zish′ən), **1** person skilled in music. **2** person who sings or plays on a musical instrument, especially as a profession or business: *An orchestra is composed of many musicians. noun.*

musk (musk), **1** substance with a strong and lasting odor, used in making perfumes. Musk is found in a special gland in one kind of deer. **2** odor of musk. *noun.*

mus ket (mus′kit), kind of old gun. Soldiers used muskets before rifles were invented. *noun.*

mus ket eer (mus′kə tir′), soldier armed with a musket. *noun.*

musk mel on (musk′mel′ən), a small, juicy melon with orange pulp and a hard rind. *noun.*

musk ox, an animal of Greenland and northern North America that chews its cud and has hoofs, a shaggy coat, and a strong smell like musk. It looks like a sheep in some ways and like an ox in others.

musk rat (musk′rat′), **1** a water animal of North America somewhat like a rat, but larger. **2** its dark-brown fur. Muskrat is valuable for garments. *noun, plural* **musk rats** or **musk rat.**

Mus lim (muz′ləm), Moslem. *noun, adjective.*

mus lin (muz′lən), **1** a thin, fine cotton cloth, used for dresses and curtains. **2** a heavier cotton cloth, used for sheets and undergarments. **3** made of muslin: *white muslin curtains.* 1,2 *noun,* 3 *adjective.*

muss (mus), **1** put into disorder; rumple: *The children's clothes were mussed.* **2** disorder; mess: *Straighten up your room; it's in a dreadful muss.* 1 *verb,* 2 *noun.*

mus sel (mus′əl), water animal that has two hinged parts to its shell. Mussels look like clams and are found in both fresh and salt water. *noun.*

must (must), **1** be obliged to; be forced to: *You must eat to live.* **2** ought to; should: *I must keep my promise. You must read this story.* **3** be certain to be or do: *You must be joking. I must seem very rude.* *verb, past tense* **must.**

mus tache (mus′tash), **1** hair growing on a man's upper lip. **2** hairs or bristles growing near the mouth of an animal. *noun.*

mus tang (mus′tang), a small wild or half-wild horse of the North American plains. *noun.*

mus tard (mus′tərd), a yellow powder or paste with a sharp, hot taste, made from the seeds of a plant. Mustard is used as a seasoning. *noun.*

mus ter (mus′tər), **1** assemble; gather together; collect. **2** assembly; collection. **3** summon: *muster up courage.* **4** bringing together of men or troops for review or service: *There was a muster of all the guards.* 1,3 *verb,* 2,4 *noun.*

must n't (mus′nt), must not: *The owner of this property says we mustn't skate here.*

mus ty (mus′tē), having a smell or taste suggesting mold or damp; moldy: *a musty room, musty crackers. adjective,* **mus ti er, mus ti est.**

mute (myüt), **1** silent; not making any sound: *The child stood mute with embarrassment.* **2** dumb; unable to speak. **3** person who cannot speak. **4** clip or pad put on a musical instrument to soften the sound. **5** put such a device on a musical instrument: *She muted the strings of her violin.* 1,2 *adjective,* 3,4 *noun,* 5 *verb,* **mut ed, mut ing.**

mu ti late (myü′tl āt), cut, tear, or break off a part of; injure badly by cutting, tearing, or breaking off some part: *The book was badly mutilated by someone who had torn some pages and written on others. verb,* **mu ti lat ed, mu ti lat ing.**

mu ti neer (myüt′n ir′), person who takes part in a mutiny. *noun.*

mu ti nous (myüt′n əs), rebellious: *a mutinous look, a mutinous crew. adjective.*

mu ti ny (myüt′n ē), **1** open rebellion against lawful authority, especially by sailors or soldiers against their officers. **2** take part in a mutiny; rebel. 1 *noun, plural* **mu ti nies;** 2 *verb,* **mu ti nied, mu ti ny ing.**

mut ter (mut′ər), **1** speak or utter (words) low and indistinctly, with lips partly closed. **2** complain; grumble: *The shoppers muttered about the high price of meat.* **3** a low, indistinct sound: *We heard a mutter of discontent.* 1,2 *verb,* 3 *noun.*

mut ton (mut′n), meat from a sheep: *We had roast mutton for dinner. noun.*

mu tu al (myü′chü əl), **1** done, said, or felt by each toward the other; given and received: *mutual*

a hat	**i** it	**oi** oil	**ch** child		⎧ a in about
ā age	**ī** ice	**ou** out	**ng** long		e in taken
ä far	**o** hot	**u** cup	**sh** she	**ə** = ⎨ i in pencil
e let	**ō** open	**u̇** put	**th** thin		o in lemon
ē equal	**ô** order	**ü** rule	**ᴛʜ** then		⎩ u in circus
ėr term			**zh** measure		

promises, mutual dislike: A family has mutual affection when each person likes the others and is liked by them. **2** each to the other: *mutual enemies.* **3** belonging to each of several: *We are happy to have him as our mutual friend. adjective.*

mu tu al ly (myü′chü ə lē), each toward the other: *Those three girls have been mutually friendly for years. adverb.*

muz zle (muz′əl), **1** the part of an animal's head that extends forward and contains the nose, mouth, and jaws. Dogs and horses have muzzles. **2** cover or cage of straps or wires to put over an animal's head to keep it from biting or eating. **3** put such a muzzle on. **4** compel (a person) to keep silent about something: *Fear that he might betray his friends muzzled him.* **5** the open front end of a gun or pistol. 1,2,5 *noun,* 3,4 *verb,* **muz zled, muz zling.**

my (mī), of me; belonging to me: *I learned my lesson. My house is around the corner. adjective.*

myr i ad (mir′ē əd), a very great number: *There are myriads of stars. noun.*

myr tle (mėr′tl), **1** an evergreen shrub of the southern part of Europe, with shiny leaves and fragrant white flowers. **2** a low, creeping evergreen vine found in Canada and the United States, with blue flowers. *noun.*

my self (mī self′), **1** *Myself* is used with *I* or *me* to make a statement stronger. *I did it myself.* **2** *Myself* is used instead of *I* or *me* in cases like: *I can cook for myself. I hurt myself.* **3** my real self: *I am not myself today. pronoun, plural* **our selves.**

mys ter i ous (mi stir′ē əs), **1** secret; hidden; hard to explain or understand: *Electricity is mysterious.* **2** suggesting mystery: *a mysterious look. adjective.*

mys ter y (mis′tər ē), **1** a secret; something that is hidden or unknown. **2** secrecy; obscurity. **3** something that is not explained or understood: *the mystery of the migration of birds. noun, plural* **mys ter ies.**

mys ti fy (mis′tə fī), bewilder purposely; puzzle; perplex: *The magician's tricks mystified the audience. verb,* **mys ti fied, mys ti fy ing.**

myth (mith), **1** legend or story, usually one that attempts to account for something in nature: *The story of Proserpina is a famous myth that explains summer and winter.* **2** any invented story. **3** a made-up person or thing: *Her trip to Europe was a myth invented to impress the other girls. noun.*

myth i cal (mith′ə kəl), **1** of a myth; like a myth; in myths: *mythical monsters, mythical places.* **2** not real; made-up: *Their wealth is merely mythical. adjective.*

my thol o gy (mi thol′ə jē), **1** myths: *Greek mythology.* **2** study of myths. *noun, plural* **my thol o gies.**

N n

N or **n** (en), the 14th letter of the English alphabet. There are two *n*'s in *nine*. *noun, plural* **N's** or **n's**.

N or **N.,** **1** north. **2** northern.

nag[1] (nag), scold; annoy; find fault with all the time: *I will clean up my room if you will stop nagging me. When he was sick he nagged at everybody. verb,* **nagged, nag ging.**

nag[2] (nag), **1** horse. **2** an old or inferior horse. *noun.*

nail (nāl), **1** a slender piece of metal having a point at one end and usually a flat or rounded head at the other end. Nails are hammered into or through pieces of wood to hold them together. **2** fasten with a nail or nails. **3** hold or keep fixed; make secure: *Our company nailed a large contract this week.* **4** catch; seize. **5** the hard layer of horn at the end of a finger or toe. **1,5** *noun,* **2-4** *verb.*

na ked (nā′kid), **1** bare; with no clothes on: *When you are barefoot you have naked feet.* **2** not covered: *naked fields.* The **naked truth** is the plain truth without ornament. The **naked eye** is the bare eye not helped by any glass, telescope, or microscope. *adjective.*

name (nām), **1** word or words by which a person, animal, place, or thing is spoken of or to: *Our cat's name is Mitten. My mother's name is Mary. "The Corn State" is a name for Iowa.* **2** give a name to: *to name a newborn baby.* **3** call by name; mention by name: *Three persons were named in the report.* **4** give the right name for: *Can you name these flowers?* **5** reputation: *She made a name for herself as a writer.* **6** mention; speak of; state: *She named several reasons.* **7** nominate; appoint: *He was named captain of the team.* **8** choose; settle on: *The class named the day for its party.* **1,5** *noun,* **2-4,6-8** *verb,* **named, nam ing.**

call names, call bad names; swear at; curse: *You can call me names, but I won't change my mind.*

in the name of, 1 for the sake of: *In the name of decency, you should offer to pay for the window you broke.* **2** acting for: *I ordered the supplies in the name of my boss.*

name less (nām′lis), **1** having no name: *a nameless stranger.* **2** not marked with a name: *a nameless grave.* **3** that cannot be named or described: *a strange, nameless longing.* **4** not named; unknown: *a book by a nameless writer. adjective.*

name ly (nām′lē), that is to say: *We visited two cities—namely, New York and Chicago. adverb.*

name sake (nām′sāk′), one having the same name as another, especially one named after another: *My sister, Florence, is the namesake of Florence Nightingale. noun.*

nap[1] (nap), **1** a short sleep: *The baby takes a nap after lunch.* **2** take a short sleep: *Grandfather naps in his armchair.* **3** be off guard; be unprepared: *The test caught me napping.* **1** *noun,* **2,3** *verb,* **napped, nap ping.**

nap[2] (nap), the soft, short, woolly threads or hairs on the surface of cloth: *the nap on velvet. noun.*

nape (nāp), the back of the neck. See picture. *noun.*

naph tha (naf′thə *or* nap′thə), liquid made from petroleum or coal tar used as fuel and to take spots from clothing. *noun.*

nap kin (nap′kin), **1** piece of cloth or paper used at meals for protecting the clothing or for wiping the lips or fingers. **2** any similar piece, such as a small towel. *noun.*

nar cis sus (när sis′əs), a spring plant with yellow or white flowers. It grows from a bulb. Jonquils and daffodils are narcissuses. *noun, plural* **nar cis sus es** or **nar cis sus.**

nar cot ic (när kot′ik), any drug that causes sleep and dulls pain. Opium is a narcotic. *noun.*

nar rate (nar′āt), tell the story of. *verb,* **nar rat ed, nar rat ing.**

nar ra tive (nar′ə tiv), **1** story; tale: *Her trip through Asia made an interesting narrative.* **2** the telling of stories. **3** that narrates: *"Hiawatha" is a narrative poem.* **1,2** *noun,* **3** *adjective.*

nar ra tor (nar′ā tər), person who tells a story. *noun.*

nar row (nar′ō), **1** not wide; having little width; less wide than usual for its kind: *A path a foot wide is narrow.* **2 narrows,** the narrow part of a river, strait, sound, valley, or pass. **3** limited; small: *He had only a narrow circle of friends.* **4** become smaller in width or extent; make or become narrow: *The road narrows here.* **5** close; with a small margin: *a narrow escape.* **6** lacking breadth of view or sympathy; prejudiced: *a narrow mind.* **1,3,5,6** *adjective,* **2** *noun,* **4** *verb.*

na sal (nā′zəl), **1** of, in, or from the nose: *nasal bones, a nasal discharge.* **2** spoken through the nose. M, n, and ng are nasal sounds. **3** a nasal sound. **1,2** *adjective,* **3** *noun.*

nas ti ly (nas′tl ē), in a nasty manner. *adverb.*

na stur tium (nə stėr′shəm), plant with yellow, orange, and red flowers, and rather sharp-tasting seeds and leaves. *noun.*

nas ty (nas′tē), **1** mean; cruel; hateful: *Several nasty people threw rocks at the birds on the lake.* **2** very unpleasant: *The nasty weather ruined our plans for a picnic.* **3** dirty; filthy: *Dead fish and garbage littered the surface of the nasty creek.* **4** rather serious; bad: *a nasty cut on the hand. adjective,* **nas ti er, nas ti est.**

na tion (nā′shən), **1** country; group of people occupying the same region, united under the same government, and usually speaking the same language: *The United States, Great Britain, and France are nations.* **2** a people, race, or tribe; those having the same descent, language, and history: *the Scottish nation. noun.*

na tion al (nash′ə nəl), **1** of a nation; belonging to a whole nation: *national laws.* **2** citizen of a nation: *Many nationals of Canada visit the United States.* **1** *adjective,* **2** *noun.*

na tion al i ty (nash/ə nal/ə tē), **1** nation: *Several nationalities are represented in the line of ancestors of most Americans.* **2** condition of belonging to a nation. Citizens of the same country have the same nationality. *noun, plural* **na tion al i ties.**

na tion al ly (nash/ə nə lē), **1** in a national manner; as a nation. **2** throughout the nation: *The President's speech was broadcast nationally. adverb.*

national park, land kept by the national government for people to enjoy because of its beautiful scenery or historical interest.

na tion wide (nā/shən wīd/), extending throughout the nation: *a nationwide election. adjective.*

na tive (nā/tiv), **1** person born in a certain place or country. The natives are the people living in a place, not visitors or foreigners. **2** born in a certain place or country: *People born in New York are native sons and daughters of New York.* **3** belonging to one because of one's birth: *The United States is my native land.* **4** belonging to one because of one's nation or ancestors: *French is his native language.* **5** natural; born in a person: *native ability.* **6** one of the people originally living in a place or country and found there by explorers or settlers. **7** of these people: *native customs, native tribes.* **8** animal or plant that originated in a place. **9** originating, grown, or produced in a certain place: *Tobacco is native to America.* **1,6,8** *noun,* **2-5,7,9** *adjective.*

Native American, one of the people who have lived in America from long before the time of the first European settlers; American Indian.

na tiv i ty (nə tiv/ə tē), **1** birth. **2 the Nativity,** birth of Christ. *noun, plural* **na tiv i ties.**

nat ur al (nach/ər əl), **1** produced by nature; coming in the ordinary course of events: *natural feelings and actions, a natural death.* **2** not man-made or artificial: *Coal and oil are natural products.* See picture. **3** belonging to the nature one is born with: *It is natural for ducks to swim.* **4** in accordance with the facts of some special case: *a natural conclusion.* **5** like nature; true to life: *The picture looked natural.* **6** of or about nature: *the natural sciences.* **7** (in music) not changed in pitch by a sharp or a flat. **8** person who is especially suited for something because of inborn talent or ability: *He is a natural on the saxophone.* **1-7** *adjective,* **8** *noun.*

natural gas, a gas formed naturally in the earth. Natural gas is used for cooking and heating.

nat ur al ist (nach/ər ə list), person who makes a study of animals or plants. *noun.*

nat ur al ize (nach/ər ə līz), admit (a foreigner) to citizenship. After living in the United States for a certain number of years, an immigrant can be naturalized if he or she passes a test. *verb,* **nat ur al ized, nat ur al iz ing.**

nat ur al ly (nach/ər ə lē), **1** in a natural way: *Speak naturally; don't try to imitate someone else.* **2** by nature: *a naturally obedient child.* **3** as might be expected; of course: *She offered me some candy; naturally, I took it. adverb.*

a hat	i it	oi oil	ch child	⌠a in about
ā age	ī ice	ou out	ng long	e in taken
ä far	o hot	u cup	sh she	ə = ⟨ i in pencil
e let	ō open	ů put	th thin	o in lemon
ē equal	ô order	ü rule	₮H then	⌊u in circus
ėr term			zh measure	

natural (definition 2)—a natural bridge made of rock

nape—The cat carried the kitten by the **nape** of the neck.

natural resources, materials supplied by nature that are useful or necessary for life. Minerals and forests are natural resources.

na ture (nā/chər), **1** the world; all things except those made by man: *the wonders of nature.* **2** the basic characteristic born in a person or animal and always present in a thing: *It is the nature of birds to fly.* **3** life without artificial things: *Wild animals live in a state of nature.* **4** what a person or thing really is; quality; character: *It is against her nature to be unkind.* **5** sort; kind: *books of a scientific nature. noun.*

nature study, study of animals, plants, and other things and events in nature.

naught (nôt), **1** nothing. **2** zero; 0. *noun.* Also spelled **nought.**

naugh ti ness (nô′tē nis), bad behavior; disobedience; mischief. *noun.*

naugh ty (nô′tē), bad; not behaving well: *The naughty child hit his baby brother. adjective,* **naugh ti er, naugh ti est.**

nau se a (nô′zē ə *or* nô′shə), the feeling that one is about to vomit. *noun.*

nau ti cal (nô′tə kəl), having something to do with ships, sailors, or navigation. *adjective.*

Nav a ho (nav′ə hō), Navajo. *noun, plural* **Nav a hos** or **Nav a hoes.**

Nav a jo (nav′ə hō), member of a tribe of American Indians living mainly in New Mexico, Arizona, and Utah. *noun, plural* **Nav a jos** or **Nav a joes.**

na val (nā′vəl), **1** of or for warships or the navy: *naval supplies, a naval officer.* **2** having a navy: *a naval power. adjective.*

nav i ga ble (nav′ə gə bəl), able to be traveled on by ships: *The Mississippi is a navigable river. adjective.*

nav i gate (nav′ə gāt), **1** sail, manage, or steer (a ship, aircraft, or rocket): *She navigated the sailboat through the choppy waters.* **2** sail on or over (a sea or river). **3** sail the seas. **4** manage a ship or aircraft: *Sailors of ancient times navigated by the stars. verb,* **nav i gat ed, nav i gat ing.**

nav i ga tion (nav′ə gā′shən), **1** navigating. **2** art or science of figuring out the position and course of a ship, aircraft, or rocket. *noun.*

nav i ga tor (nav′ə gā′tər), **1** person who sails the seas: *The navigator set out on his long voyage.* **2** person who has charge of the navigating of a ship or aircraft; person who is skilled in navigating. **3** explorer of the seas: *Columbus was a great navigator. noun.*

na vy (nā′vē), a large, organized group of officers and sailors trained and equipped for war, and the ships of war on which they serve. *noun, plural* **na vies.**

navy blue, a dark blue.

nay (nā), **1** no. **2** not only that, but also: *We are willing—nay, eager—to go.* **3** vote or voter against something. **1,2** *adverb,* **3** *noun.*

NE or **N.E., 1** northeast. **2** northeastern.

near (nir), **1** close; not far; to or at a short distance: *They searched far and near. The holiday season is drawing near.* **2** close by; not distant: *The post office is quite near.* **3** close to: *Our house is near the river.* **4** approach; come or draw close to: *The train slowed down as it neared the station.* **5** close in feeling or relationship: *near and dear friends, a near relative.* **6** almost; nearly: *The war lasted near a year.* **7** short; direct: *Take the nearest route.* **1,6** *adverb,* **2,5,7** *adjective,* **3** *preposition,* **4** *verb.*

near at hand, 1 within easy reach: *The telephone was near at hand in case of emergency.* **2** not far in the future: *Summer is near at hand.*

near by (nir′bī′), near; close at hand: *a nearby house. They went nearby to visit friends. adjective, adverb.*

neglect (definition 5)—Her room showed weeks of **neglect.**

neckerchief

negative (definition 7)

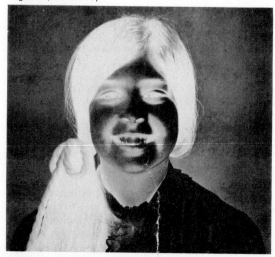

near ly (nir′lē), **1** almost: *It is nearly bedtime.* **2** closely: *It will cost more than we can afford, as nearly as I can figure it.* adverb.

near sight ed (nir′sī′tid), not able to see far; seeing things clearly at a short distance only. Nearsighted people usually wear glasses. *adjective.*

neat (nēt), **1** clean and in order: *a neat desk, a neat room, a neat suit.* **2** able and willing to keep things in order: *a neat child.* **3** well-formed; in proportion: *a neat design.* **4** skillful; clever: *a neat trick.* *adjective.*

Ne bras ka (nə bras′kə), one of the midwestern states of the United States. *noun.* [Nebraska comes from American Indian words meaning "flat river." This was originally the Indian name for the Platte River, which flows through the state.]

nec es sar i ly (nes′ə ser′ə lē), **1** because of necessity: *Leaves are not necessarily green.* **2** as a necessary result: *War necessarily causes misery and waste.* adverb.

nec es sar y (nes′ə ser′ē), **1** needed; having to be done: *Was it necessary to fix the car engine? She flies when it is necessary to save time.* **2** that must be: *Death is a necessary end.* **3** thing impossible to do without: *Food, clothing, and shelter are necessaries of life.* **1,2** *adjective,* **3** *noun, plural* **nec es sar ies.**

ne ces si tate (nə ses′ə tāt), make necessary: *Her injured leg necessitated an operation.* verb, **ne ces si tat ed, ne ces si tat ing.**

ne ces si ty (nə ses′ə tē), **1** need; something that has to be: *We understand the necessity of eating.* **2** thing which cannot be done without; necessary thing: *Food and water are necessities.* **3** that which forces one to act in a certain way: *Necessity often drives people to do disagreeable things.* **4** need; poverty: *This poor family is in great necessity.* noun, *plural* **ne ces si ties.**

neck (nek), **1** part of the body that connects the head with the shoulders. **2** part of a garment that fits the neck: *the neck of a shirt.* **3** any narrow part like a neck: *a neck of land.* noun.

neck and neck, equal or even in a race or contest.

neck er chief (nek′ər chif), cloth worn around the neck. See picture. *noun.*

neck lace (nek′lis), string of jewels, gold, silver, or beads worn around the neck as an ornament. *noun.*

neck tie (nek′tī′), a narrow band or a tie worn around the neck, under the collar of a shirt, and tied in front. *noun.*

nec tar (nek′tər), **1** (in ancient Greek stories) the drink of the gods. **2** a sweet liquid found in many flowers. Bees gather nectar and make it into honey. *noun.*

need (nēd), **1** be in want of; ought to have; be unable to do without: *I need a new hat. Plants need water.* **2** thing wanted or lacking; that for which a want is felt: *In the jungle their need was fresh water.* **3** want; lack: *Your handwriting shows a need of practice.* **4** time of need; condition of need: *When I lacked money, my uncle was a friend in need.* **5** lack of money; being poor: *This family's need was so great the children did not have shoes.* **6** must; should; have to; ought to: *He need not go. Need she go?* **7** something that has to be: *There is no need to hurry.* **1,6** *verb,* **2-5,7** *noun.*

have need to, must, should, have to, or ought to: *I have need to go to town.*

if need be, if it has to be.

need ful (nēd′fəl), needed; necessary: *a needful change.* adjective.

nee dle (nē′dl), **1** a very slender tool, sharp at one end, and with a hole or eye to pass a thread through, used in sewing. **2** a slender rod used in knitting. **3** rod with a hook at one end used in crocheting. **4** a thin steel pointer on a compass or on electrical machinery. **5** a very slender steel tube with a sharp point at one end. It is used for injecting liquid below the skin. *The doctor stuck the needle into my arm.* **6** the needle-shaped leaf of a fir tree or pine tree. **7** object resembling a needle in sharpness: *needles of broken glass.* **8** vex by sharp remarks. **1-7** *noun,* **8** *verb,* **nee dled, nee dling.**

need less (nēd′lis), not needed; unnecessary: *It is silly to take a needless risk.* adjective.

nee dle work (nē′dl wėrk′), work done with a needle; sewing; embroidery. *noun.*

need n't (nēd′nt), need not.

need y (nē′dē), very poor; not having enough to live on: *a needy family.* adjective, **need i er, need i est.**

ne'er (ner), never. adverb.

neg a tive (neg′ə tiv), **1** saying no: *A shake of the head is negative.* **2** word or statement that says no or denies: *"I won't" is a negative.* **3** the side that says no or denies in an argument. **4** not positive: *Negative suggestions are not helpful.* **5** minus; counting down from zero: *Three below zero is a negative quantity.* **6** of or having something to do with the kind of electricity produced on rubber when it is rubbed with silk. **7** a photographic image in which the lights and shadows are reversed. Prints are made from it. See picture. **8** showing the absence of a particular disease, condition, or germ. **1,4-6,8** *adjective,* **2,3,7** *noun.*

ne glect (ni glekt′), **1** give too little care or attention to: *Don't neglect your health.* **2** leave undone; not attend to: *I neglected my gardening and some of the roses died.* **3** omit; fail: *She neglected to tell us what happened.* **4** act or fact of neglecting: *His neglect of the truth was astonishing.* **5** want of attention to what should be done: *The car has been ruined by neglect.* See picture. **6** being neglected: *The children suffered from neglect.* **1-3** *verb,* **4-6** *noun.*

a hat	i it	oi oil	ch child	(a in about
ā age	ī ice	ou out	ng long	e in taken
ä far	o hot	u cup	sh she	ə = i in pencil
e let	ō open	u̇ put	th thin	o in lemon
ē equal	ô order	ü rule	ᴛʜ then	u in circus
ėr term			zh measure	

neon—The red, yellow, orange, and green lights in the flower shop sign are all filled with neon.

neg li gence (neg′lə jəns), **1** neglect; lack of proper care or attention: *Negligence was the cause of the accident.* **2** careless conduct; indifference. *noun.*

neg li gent (neg′lə jənt), **1** showing neglect. **2** careless; indifferent. *adjective.*

ne go ti ate (ni gō′shē āt), **1** talk over and arrange terms: *Both countries are negotiating for an end to the war.* **2** arrange for: *They finally negotiated a peace treaty. verb,* **ne go ti at ed, ne go ti at ing.**

Ne gro (nē′grō), **1** member of the so-called black race. The chief peoples of Africa south of the Sahara are Negroes. **2** person having black ancestry. Millions of Negroes live in America. **3** of or having something to do with Negroes. 1,2 *noun, plural* **Ne groes;** 3 *adjective.*

neigh (nā), **1** sound that a horse makes. **2** make such a sound. 1 *noun,* 2 *verb.*

neigh bor (nā′bər), **1** someone who lives in the next house or nearby. **2** person or thing that is near or next to another: *The big tree brought down several of its smaller neighbors as it fell.* **3** live or be near to. **4** a fellow human being. 1,2,4 *noun,* 3 *verb.*

neigh bor hood (nā′bər hùd), **1** region near some place or thing: *She lives in the neighborhood of the mill.* **2** place; district: *Is North Street in a good neighborhood?* **3** people living near one another; people of a place: *The whole neighborhood came to the big party.* **4** of a neighborhood: *a neighborhood newspaper.* 1-3 *noun,* 4 *adjective.*

in the neighborhood of, somewhere near; about: *The car cost in the neighborhood of $2500.*

neigh bor ing (nā′bər ing), living or being near; bordering; near: *We heard the bird calls from the neighboring woods. adjective.*

neigh bor ly (nā′bər lē), kindly; friendly. *adjective.*

nei ther (nē′ᴛʜər *or* nī′ᴛʜər), **1** not either: *Neither you nor I will go. Neither statement is true. Neither of the statements is true.* **2** nor yet; nor: *They didn't go; neither did we.* 1,2 *conjunction,* 1 *adjective,* 1 *pronoun.*

ne on (nē′on), a colorless, odorless gas, forming a very small part of the air. Tubes containing neon are used in electric signs or lamps. See picture. *noun.*

neph ew (nef′yü), son of one's brother or sister; son of one's brother-in-law or sister-in-law. *noun.*

Nep tune (nep′tün *or* nep′tyün), **1** the Roman god of the sea. **2** the fourth largest planet, so far from the earth that it cannot be seen without a telescope. *noun.*

nerve (nėrv), **1** fiber or bundle of fibers connecting the brain or spinal cord with the eyes, ears, muscles, and glands. **2** mental strength; courage. See picture. **3** rude boldness: *They had a lot of nerve to say that we were talking too loud. noun.*

get on one's nerves, bother one greatly.

nerv ous (nėr′vəs), **1** of the nerves: *a nervous disorder, nervous energy.* **2** easily excited or upset: *A person who has been overworking is likely to become nervous.* **3** restless or uneasy; timid: *Are you nervous about staying alone at night? adjective.*

nervous system, system of nerve fibers, nerve cells, and other nerve tissue in a person or animal. Your nervous system includes the brain and spinal cord, and controls all your body activities.

-ness, suffix meaning: being _____: Careful*ness* means *being* careful.

nest (nest), **1** structure shaped something like a bowl, built by birds out of twigs, leaves, or straw, as a place in which to lay their eggs and protect their young ones: *a robin's nest.* **2** structure or place used by insects, fishes, turtles, rabbits, or the like, for a similar purpose: *a squirrel's nest, a wasp's nest.* **3** the birds or animals living in a nest. **4** a warm, cozy place; place to sleep: *The little boy made a cozy nest among the sofa cushions and cuddled down in it.* **5** a group of different-sized things, all of which fit together: *a nest of measuring cups.* **6** place that swarms, usually with something bad: *a nest of thieves.* **7** make and use a nest: *The bluebirds are nesting here now.* 1-6 *noun,* 7 *verb.*

nes tle (nes′əl), **1** settle oneself comfortably or cozily: *She nestled down into the big chair.* **2** be sheltered: *The little house nestled among the trees.* **3** press close for comfort or in affection: *nestle up to one's mother or father, nestle a baby in one's arms.* See picture. *verb,* **nes tled, nes tling.**

net¹ (net), **1** an open fabric made of string, cord, or thread, knotted together in such a way as to leave large or small holes regularly arranged. A fish net is used for catching fish. A mosquito net keeps off mosquitoes. A hair net holds the hair in place. A tennis net is used in the game of tennis. **2** trap or snare: *The suspects were caught in the net of their own lies.* **3** catch in a net. See picture. 1,2 *noun,* 3 *verb,* **net ted, net ting.**

net² (net), **1** remaining after deductions; free from deductions. A net gain or profit is the actual gain after all working expenses have been paid. The net weight of a glass jar of candy is the weight of the candy itself. The net price of something is the actual price paid, after all deductions are made. **2** gain: *The sale netted me a good profit.* 1 *adjective,* 2 *verb,* **net ted, net ting.**

Neth er lands (neᴛʜ′ər ləndz), country in western Europe. *noun.*

net tle (net′l), **1** kind of plant having sharp leaf hairs that sting the skin when touched. **2** sting the mind; irritate; make angry; provoke; vex: *Their refusal to help nettled me.* 1 *noun,* 2 *verb,* **net tled, net tling.**

net work (net′wėrk′), **1** any system of lines that cross: *a network of vines, a network of railroads.* **2** group of radio or television stations that work together, so that what is broadcast by one may be broadcast by all. **3** net. *noun.*

neu tral (nü′trəl *or* nyü′trəl), **1** on neither side in a quarrel or war: *Switzerland was neutral during World War II.* **2** a neutral person or country; one not taking part in a war: *the rights of neutrals.* **3** having little or no color; grayish: *a neutral sky.* **4** position of gears when they do not transmit motion from the engine to the wheels or other working parts. 1,3 *adjective,* 2,4 *noun.*

neu tral ize (nü′trə līz *or* nyü′trə līz), **1** make neutral; keep war out of: *The city was neutralized so that peace talks could be held there.* **2** make of no effect; cancel the effect of; make up for the effect of: *I neutralized the bright colors in my room by using a tan rug.* *verb,* **neu tral ized, neu tral iz ing.**

neu tron (nü′tron *or* nyü′tron), a tiny particle that is neither positive nor negative electrically. Neutrons occur in the nucleus of all atoms except hydrogen. *noun.*

Ne vad a (nə vad′ə *or* nə vä′də), one of the western states of the United States. *noun.* [Nevada comes from a Spanish word meaning "snow-covered."]

nev er (nev′ər), **1** not ever; at no time: *She has never been to New York.* **2** not at all: *He will be never the wiser.* *adverb.*

nev er more (nev′ər môr′), never again. *adverb.*

nev er the less (nev′ər ᴛʜə les′), however; none the less; for all that; in spite of it: *She was very tired; nevertheless she kept on working.* *adverb.*

new (nü *or* nyü), **1** never having been before; now first made, thought out, known or heard of, felt or discovered: *a new invention, a new idea.* **2** lately grown, come, or made; not old: *a new bud.* **3** now first used; not worn or used up: *a new path.* **4** beginning again: *Sunrise marks a new day.* **5** as if new; fresh: *go on with new courage.* **6** different; changed: *have a new teacher, feel like a new person.* **7** not familiar; not yet used: *a new country to me, new to the work.* **8** later; modern; recent: *the new dances.* **9** just come: *a new arrival.* **10** more: *He sought new information on the subject.* **11** newly; recently or lately; freshly: *new-fallen snow.* 1-10 *adjective,* 11 *adverb.*

a hat	**i** it	**oi** oil	**ch** child	a in about
ā age	**ī** ice	**ou** out	**ng** long	e in taken
ä far	**o** hot	**u** cup	**sh** she	ə = i in pencil
e let	**ō** open	**ù** put	**th** thin	o in lemon
ē equal	**ô** order	**ü** rule	**ᴛʜ** then	u in circus
ėr term			**zh** measure	

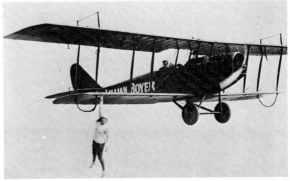

nerve (definition 2)—It takes great **nerve** to hang by one hand from an airplane.

American 19th Century Sculpture of Latona and her children, Apollo and Diane, William Henry Rinehart, Courtesy of The Metropolitan Museum of Art

nestle (definition 3)—The children **nestled** against their mother.

net¹ (definition 3)—The children **netted** a fish.

new born (nü′bôrn′ or nyü′bôrn′), **1** recently or only just born: *a newborn baby.* See picture. **2** ready to start a new life; born again. *adjective.*

new com er (nü′kum′ər or nyü′kum′ər), person who has just come or who came recently. *noun.*

New England, the northeastern part of the United States. Maine, New Hampshire, Vermont, Massachusetts, Rhode Island, and Connecticut are the New England states.

new fan gled (nü′fang′gəld or nyü′fang′gəld), lately come into fashion; of a new kind. *adjective.*

New Hamp shire (nü′ hamp′shər or nyü′ hamp′shər), one of the northeastern states of the United States. [*New Hampshire* was named in 1629 for Hampshire, a county in England.]

New Jer sey (nü′ jėr′zē or nyü′ jėr′zē), one of the northeastern states of the United States. [*New Jersey* was named in 1664 for the British island of Jersey.]

new ly (nü′lē or nyü′lē), lately; recently: *newly discovered, newly painted walls.* adverb.

New Mexico, one of the southwestern states of the United States. [*New Mexico* is a translation of the Spanish name *Nuevo México.* A Spanish explorer first gave this name to the area in 1562 to suggest that it would be as rich as the country of Mexico.]

new moon, moon when seen as a thin crescent.

news (nüz or nyüz), **1** something told as having just happened; information about something which has just happened or will soon happen: *The news that our teacher was leaving made us sad.* **2** report of a current happening or happenings in a newspaper or on television or radio. *noun.*

news boy (nüz′boi′ or nyüz′boi′), person who sells or delivers newspapers. *noun.*

news cast (nüz′kast′ or nyüz′kast′), a radio or television program devoted to current events and news bulletins. *noun.*

news pa per (nüz′pā′pər or nyüz′pā′pər), sheets of paper printed every day or week, telling the news, carrying advertisements, and having stories, pictures, articles, and useful information. *noun.*

news reel (nüz′rēl′ or nyüz′rēl′), motion picture showing current events. *noun.*

news stand (nüz′stand′ or nyüz′stand′), place where newspapers and magazines are sold. *noun.*

newt (nüt or nyüt), a small salamander that lives in water part of the time. See picture. *noun.*

New Testament, the part of the Bible which contains the life and teachings of Christ recorded by His followers, together with their own experiences and teachings.

New World, North America and South America.

New Year or **New Year's,** January 1; the first day or days of the year.

New Year's Day, January 1.

New York (nü′ yôrk′ or nyü′ yôrk′), one of the northeastern states of the United States. [*New York* was named in 1664 in honor of the Duke of York, who lived from 1633 to 1701, by his brother Charles II, king of England.]

newborn (definition 1)
The bear watched over her **newborn** cub.

nightingale—about 7 inches (18 centimeters) long

newt—about 4 inches (10 centimeters) long

next (nekst), **1** nearest: *Who is the girl next to you?* **2** following at once: *the next train. The next day after Sunday is Monday.* **3** the first time after this: *When you next come, bring it.* **4** in the place or time or position that is nearest: *I am going to do my arithmetic problems next. His name comes next.* **5** nearest to: *We live in the house next the church.* 1,2 *adjective,* 3,4 *adverb,* 5 *preposition.*

next door, in or at the next house or apartment: *He lives next door.*

next-door (nekst′dôr′), in or at the next house: *my next-door neighbor. adjective.*

nib ble (nib′əl), **1** eat away with quick small bites, as a rabbit or a mouse does. **2** bite gently or lightly: *A fish nibbles at the bait.* **3** a nibbling; small bite. 1,2 *verb,* **nib bled, nib bling;** 3 *noun.*

nice (nīs), **1** pleasing; agreeable; satisfactory: *a nice day, a nice ride, a nice child.* **2** thoughtful and kind: *They were nice to me.* **3** very fine; subtle: *a nice distinction, a nice shade of meaning.* **4** precise; exact; making very fine distinctions: *a nice ear for music.* **5** requiring care, skill, or tact: *a nice problem.* **6** particular; hard to please; fastidious; dainty: *nice in one's habits or dress. adjective,* **nic er, nic est.** [Earlier meanings of *nice* were "foolish" and "shy." It comes from a Latin word meaning "not knowing" or "knowing little."]

niche (nich), **1** recess or hollow in a wall for a statue or vase. **2** a suitable place or position; place for which a person is suited. *noun.*

nick (nik), **1** place where a small bit has been cut or broken out: *She cut nicks in a stick to keep score.* **2** make a nick or nicks in. 1 *noun,* 2 *verb.*

in the nick of time, just at the right moment: *We reached home in the nick of time; a minute later there was a downpour.*

nick el (nik′əl), **1** a hard, silvery-white metal that is used to plate other metals and is mixed with other metals to make alloys. **2** coin of the United States and Canada equal to 5 cents. Twenty nickels make one dollar. *noun.*

nick name (nik′nām′), **1** name added to a person's real name, or used instead of it: *"Ed" is a nickname for "Edward."* **2** give a nickname to: *They nicknamed the red-haired girl Rusty.* 1 *noun,* 2 *verb,* **nick named, nick nam ing.**

nic o tine (nik′ə tēn′), poison contained in the leaves of tobacco. *noun.* [*Nicotine* was formed from the name of Jacques Nicot, who lived from 1530 to 1600. He was the French ambassador to Portugal who introduced tobacco into France in 1560.]

niece (nēs), daughter of one's brother or sister; daughter of one's brother-in-law or sister-in-law. *noun.*

nigh (nī), **1** near. **2** nearly. 1,2 *adverb,* 1 *adjective,* 1 *preposition.*

night (nīt), **1** time between evening and morning; time from sunset to sunrise, especially when it is dark. **2** evening; nightfall. *noun.*

night fall (nīt′fôl′), the coming of night. *noun.*

night gown (nīt′goun′), a long, loose garment worn by a woman or child in bed. *noun.*

night in gale (nīt′n gāl), a small, reddish-brown bird of Europe. The nightingale sings sweetly at night as well as in the daytime. See picture. *noun.*

night ly (nīt′lē), **1** happening every night. **2** every night: *Performances are given nightly except on Sunday.* **3** happening at night: *nightly dew.* **4** at night: *Many animals come out only nightly.* 1,3 *adjective,* 2,4 *adverb.*

night mare (nīt′mer′ *or* nīt′mar′), **1** a very distressing dream. **2** a very distressing experience: *The hurricane was a nightmare. noun.*

night time (nīt′tīm′), the time between evening and morning. *noun.*

nimble (definition 1)
The **nimble** goat leaped from ledge to ledge.

nim ble (nim′bəl), **1** quick-moving; active and sure-footed; light and quick. See picture. **2** quick to understand and to reply; clever: *The student had a nimble mind and could think up an answer to almost any question. adjective,* **nim bler, nim blest.**

nim bly (nim′blē), quickly and lightly. *adverb.*

nine (nīn), **1** one more than eight; 9. Six and three make nine. **2** set of nine persons or things: *a baseball nine.* 1,2 *noun,* 1 *adjective.*

nine pins (nīn′pinz′), game in which nine large wooden pins are set up to be bowled over with a ball. *noun.*

nine teen (nīn′tēn′), nine more than ten; 19. *noun, adjective.*

nine teenth (nīn′tēnth′), **1** next after the 18th. **2** one of 19 equal parts. 1 *adjective,* 1,2 *noun.*

nine ti eth (nīn′tē ith), **1** next after the 89th. **2** one of 90 equal parts. 1 *adjective,* 1,2 *noun.*

nine ty (nīn′tē), nine times ten; 90. *noun, plural* **nine ties;** *adjective.*

ninth (nīnth), **1** next after the eighth. **2** one of nine equal parts. 1 *adjective,* 1,2 *noun.*

nip¹ (nip), **1** squeeze tight and quickly; pinch; bite: *The crab nipped my toe.* **2** a tight squeeze; pinch; sudden bite. **3** hurt at the tips; spoil; injure: *Some of our tomato plants were nipped by frost.* **4** have a sharp, biting effect on: *A cold wind nipped our ears.* **5** sharp cold; chill: *There is a nip in the air this frosty morning.* 1,3,4 *verb*, **nipped, nip ping;** 2,5 *noun.*

nip² (nip), a small drink. *noun.*

nip ple (nip′əl), **1** the part of a breast or udder through which an infant or a baby animal gets its mother's milk. **2** the rubber cap of a baby's bottle, through which the baby gets milk and other liquids. *noun.*

ni tro gen (nī′trə jən), a gas without color, taste, or odor which forms about four fifths of the air. All animals and plants need nitrogen. *noun.*

nit wit (nit′wit′), a very stupid person. *noun.*

no (nō), **1** word used to say that you can't or won't, or that something is wrong. *No means the same as shaking your head from side to side. Will you come? No. Can a cow fly? No.* **2** not any: *Dogs have no wings. Eat no more.* **3** vote against; person voting against: *The noes won.* 1 *adverb,* 2 *adjective,* 3 *noun, plural* **noes.**

no., number.

no bil i ty (nō bil′ə tē), **1** people of noble rank, title, or birth. Counts, countesses, marquises, and earls belong to the nobility. **2** noble birth; noble rank. **3** noble character. *noun, plural* **no bil i ties.**

no ble (nō′bəl), **1** high and great by birth, rank, or title: *a noble family.* **2** person high and great by birth, rank, or title. **3** high and great in character; showing greatness of mind; good: *a noble person, a noble deed.* **4** excellent; fine; splendid; magnificent: *Niagara Falls is a noble sight.* 1,3,4 *adjective,* **no bler, no blest;** 2 *noun.*

no ble man (nō′bəl mən), man of noble rank, title, or birth. *noun, plural* **no ble men.**

no ble wom an (nō′bəl wùm′ən), woman of noble rank, title, or birth. *noun, plural* **no ble wom en.**

no bly (nō′blē), in a noble manner; in a splendid way; as a noble person would do. *adverb.*

no bod y (nō′bod′ē), **1** no one; no person. **2** person of no importance. 1 *pronoun,* 2 *noun, plural* **no bod ies.**

noc tur nal (nok tèr′nl), **1** of the night: *Stars are a nocturnal sight.* **2** in the night: *a nocturnal visitor.* **3** active in the night: *The owl is a nocturnal bird. adjective.*

nod (nod), **1** bow (the head) slightly and raise it again quickly. **2** say yes by nodding: *Father quietly nodded his consent.* **3** a nodding of the head: *She gave us a nod as she passed.* **4** let the head fall forward and bob about when sleepy or falling asleep. **5** be sleepy; become careless and dull. **6** droop, bend, or sway back and forth: *Trees nod in the wind.* 1,2,4-6 *verb,* **nod ded, nod ding;** 3 *noun.*

No el (nō el′), **1** Christmas. **2** noel, a Christmas song. *noun, plural* **no els** for 2.

noise (noiz), **1** sound that is not musical or pleasant: *The noise kept me awake.* **2** sound: *the noise of rain on the roof.* **3** din of voices and movements; loud shouting: *They made so much noise that they were asked to leave the theater.* **4** tell; spread the news of: *It was noised through the school that the principal was quitting.* 1-3 *noun,* 4 *verb,* **noised, nois ing.**

noise less (noiz′lis), making no noise; making little noise: *a noiseless typewriter. adjective.*

nois i ly (noi′zə lē), in a noisy manner. *adverb.*

nois y (noi′zē), **1** making much noise: *a noisy child, a noisy crowd, a noisy machine.* **2** full of noise: *a noisy street, a noisy house, the noisy city.* **3** having much noise with it: *a noisy quarrel, a noisy game. adjective,* **nois i er, nois i est.**

no mad (nō′mad), member of a tribe which moves from place to place to have food or pasture for its cattle: *Many Arabs are nomads.* See picture. *noun.*

nom i nate (nom′ə nāt), **1** name as candidate for an office: *He was nominated for President, but he was never elected.* **2** appoint to an office: *In 1933 Roosevelt nominated the first woman cabinet member in United States history. verb,* **nom i nat ed, nom i nat ing.**

nom i na tion (nom′ə nā′shən), **1** naming as candidate for office: *The nominations for president of the club were written on the blackboard.* **2** selection for office; appointment to office. **3** being nominated: *Her friends were pleased by her nomination. noun.*

nom i nee (nom′ə nē′), person nominated to or for an office. *noun.*

non-, prefix meaning: **1** not; not a: *Non*breakable means *not* breakable. *Non*member means *not a* member. **2** opposite of; lack of: *Non*agreement means the *opposite of* or *lack of* agreement.

non cha lant (non′shə lənt), without enthusiasm; coolly unconcerned; indifferent: *She remained quite nonchalant during all the excitement. adjective.*

non con duc tor (non′kən duk′tər), substance which does not readily conduct heat, electricity, light, or sound. Rubber is a nonconductor of electricity. *noun.*

non de script (non′də skript), not easily described; not of any one particular kind: *We drove past a block of nondescript houses. adjective.*

none (nun), **1** not any: *We have none of that paper left.* **2** no one; not one: *None of these is a special case.* **3** no persons: *None have arrived.* **4** not at all: *Our supply is none too great.* 1-3 *pronoun,* 4 *adverb.*

non sense (non′sens), words, ideas, or acts without meaning; foolish talk or doings; plan or suggestion that is foolish: *That tale about the ghost that haunts the old mansion is nonsense. noun.*

non stop (non′stop′), without stopping: *We took a nonstop flight from New York to Paris. He flew nonstop from New York to Los Angeles. adjective, adverb.*

noo dle (nü′dl), a mixture of flour, water, and eggs, like macaroni, but dried into hard flat strips. *noun.*

nook (nùk), **1** a cozy little corner: *a nook facing the fire.* **2** a hidden spot; sheltered place: *There is a wonderful nook in the woods behind our house. noun.*

northern lights—The northern lights appear most often at night in the far north.

a hat	**i** it	**oi** oil	**ch** child	⎧ a in about
ā age	**ī** ice	**ou** out	**ng** long	⎪ e in taken
ä far	**o** hot	**u** cup	**sh** she	ə = ⎨ i in pencil
e let	**ō** open	**ù** put	**th** thin	⎪ o in lemon
ē equal	**ô** order	**ü** rule	**ŦH** then	⎩ u in circus
ėr term			**zh** measure	

north (nôrth), **1** direction to which a compass needle points; direction to the right as one faces the setting sun. **2** toward the north; farther toward the north: *Drive north for the next mile.* **3** coming from the north: *a north wind.* **4** in the north: *the north window of a house.* **5** part of any country toward the north. **6 the North,** the northern part of the United States; the states north of Maryland, the Ohio River, and Missouri. 1,5,6 *noun,* 2 *adverb,* 2-4 *adjective.*

north of, farther north than: *The United States is north of Mexico.*

North America, continent northwest of South America and west of the Atlantic Ocean. It is the third largest continent; only Asia and Africa are larger. The United States, Canada, and Mexico are countries in North America.

North American, 1 of North America; having something to do with North America or its people; from North America. **2** person born or living in North America.

North Car o li na (nôrth′ kar′ə lī′nə), one of the southeastern states of the United States. [*North Carolina* was named in honor of Charles I, king of England, who lived from 1600 to 1649. His name in Latin is Carolus.]

North Da ko ta (nôrth′ də kō′tə), one of the midwestern states of the United States. [*North Dakota* got its name from an American Indian tribe, the Dakota, meaning "allies" or "friends."]

north east (nôrth′ēst′), **1** halfway between north and east. **2** a northeast direction. **3** place that is in the northeast part or direction. **4** toward the northeast: *At this point the road turns northeast.* **5** coming from the northeast: *a northeast wind.* **6** in the northeast: *the northeast district.* 1,5,6 *adjective,* 2,3 *noun,* 4 *adverb.*

north east ern (nôrth′ē′stərn), **1** toward the northeast. **2** from the northeast. **3** of the northeast. *adjective.*

north er ly (nôr′ŦHər lē), **1** toward the north: *The windows face northerly.* **2** from the north: *a northerly wind. adjective, adverb.*

north ern (nôr′ŦHərn), **1** toward the north: *the northern side of a building.* **2** coming from the north: *a northern breeze.* **3** of or in the north: *They have traveled in northern countries.* **4 Northern,** of or in the northern part of the United States: *Boston is a Northern city. adjective.*

north ern er (nôr′ŦHər nər), **1** person born or living in the north. **2 Northerner,** person born or living in the northern part of the United States. *noun.*

northern lights, streamers and bands of light appearing in the sky in northern regions. See picture.

nomad—The nomads camped near the ruins for a few days.

noon (nün), 12 o'clock in the daytime; the middle of the day. *noun.*

noon day (nün′dā′), noon. *noun.*

no one, no person; nobody.

no-one (nō′wun), no one. *pronoun.*

noon time (nün′tīm′), noon. *noun.*

noose (nüs), **1** loop with a slip knot that tightens as the string or rope is pulled. Nooses are used especially in lassos and snares. **2** snare or bond. *noun.*

nor (nôr), and no: *We had neither food nor water left after three days of camping out. conjunction.*

nor mal (nôr′məl), **1** of the usual standard; regular; usual: *The normal temperature of the human body is 98.6 degrees.* **2** the usual state or level: *He is ten pounds above normal for his age.* **3** not diseased, defective, or insane. 1,3 *adjective,* 2 *noun.*

Norse (nôrs), **1** of ancient Scandinavia, its people, or their language. **2** people of ancient Scandinavia. **3** language of these people. 1 *adjective,* 2 *noun plural,* 3 *noun singular.*

notorious—Jesse James was a notorious outlaw.

noteworthy—The completion of the first transcontinental railroad was a noteworthy event.

novel (definition 1)—He used a novel form of transportation.

north ern most (nôr′ŦHərn mōst), farthest north. *adjective.*

North Pole, the northern end of the earth's axis.

North Star, a bright star almost directly above the North Pole.

north ward (nôrth′wərd), toward the north; north: *I walked northward. The orchard is on the northward slope of the hill. Rocks lay northward of the ship's course. adjective, adverb.*

north wards (nôrth′wərdz), northward. *adverb.*

north west (nôrth′west′), **1** halfway between north and west. **2** a northwest direction. **3** place that is in the northwest part or direction. **4** toward the northwest: *The road from Chicago to Minneapolis runs northwest.* **5** coming from the northwest: *a northwest wind.* **6** in the northwest. 1,5,6 *adjective,* 2,3 *noun,* 4 *adverb.*

north west ern (nôrth′wes′tərn), **1** toward the northwest. **2** from the northwest. **3** of the northwest. *adjective.*

nose (nōz), **1** the part of the face or head just above the mouth. The nose has openings for breathing and smelling. **2** sense of smell: *Most dogs have a good nose. A mouse has a good nose for cheese.* **3** smell; discover by smell; smell out: *The hounds nosed out the scent of the fox.* **4** smell; sniff (at): *The dog nosed about in the garden.* **5** rub with the nose: *The cat nosed its kittens.* **6** part that stands out, especially the bow of a ship, boat, or airplane: *We saw the little steamer's nose poking around the cliff.* **7** move forward carefully: *The boat nosed along between the rocks.* **8** search (for); pry (into): *Don't nose into my affairs.* 1,2,6 *noun,* 3-5,7,8 *verb,* **nosed, nos ing.**

under one's nose, in plain sight: *I lost my pencil, but found it again right under my nose.*

nose bleed (nōz′blēd′), flow of blood from the nose. *noun.*

nose cone, the cone-shaped front section of a missile or rocket, made to carry a bomb to a target or to carry instruments or passengers into space.

nose dive, **1** a swift plunge downward by an airplane. **2** a sudden, sharp drop: *The thermometer took a nose dive the first day of winter.*

nose-dive (nōz′dīv′), take a nose dive. *verb,* **nose-dived, nose-div ing.**

nos tril (nos′trəl), either of the two openings in the nose. Air is breathed into the lungs, and smells come into the sensitive parts of the nose, through the nostrils. *noun.*

not (not), word that says "no": *Cold is not hot. Six and two do not make ten. adverb.*

no ta ble (nō′tə bəl), **1** worth noticing; striking; remarkable; important: *a notable event, a notable person.* **2** person who is notable: *Many notables came to the reception at the White House.* 1 *adjective,* 2 *noun.*

no ta bly (nō′tə blē), **1** in a notable manner; to a notable degree: *Many countries are notably lacking in fertile soil and minerals.* **2** especially; particularly: *Some deserts, notably the Sahara and Death Valley, are extremely hot. adverb.*

no ta tion (nō tā′shən), a note to help the memory: *to make a notation in the margin of a book.* *noun.*

notch (noch), **1** nick or cut shaped like a V, made in an edge or on a curving surface: *People used to cut notches on a stick to keep count of numbers.* **2** make a notch or notches in. **3** a deep, narrow pass or gap between mountains. 1,3 *noun, plural* **notch es;** 2 *verb.*

note (nōt), **1** a short sentence, phrase, or single word, written down to remind one of what was in a book, a speech, or an agreement: *Sometimes our teacher has us take notes on what we read. I must make a note of that.* **2** write down as a thing to be remembered: *Our class notes the weather daily on a chart.* **3** comment, remark, or piece of information added concerning a word or a passage in a book, often to help pupils in studying the book: *A footnote is a note at the bottom of the page about something on the page.* **4** a very short letter: *a note of thanks.* **5** letter from one government to another: *England sent a note of protest to France.* **6** a written promise to pay a certain amount of money at a certain time: *The note showed that his loan is due on March 15.* **7** greatness; fame: *a person of note.* **8** observe; notice; give attention to: *Now note what I do next.* **9** (in music) the written sign to show the pitch and the length of a sound. **10** a single musical sound: *Sing this note for me.* **11** any one of the keys of a piano: *strike the wrong note.* **12** song or call of a bird. **13** a significant sound or way of expression: *There was a note of determination in her voice.* 1,3-7,9-13 *noun,* 2,8 *verb,* **not ed, not ing.**
take note of, give attention to; observe: *No one took any note of my leaving.*

note book (nōt′bùk′), book in which to write notes of things to be learned or remembered. *noun.*

not ed (nō′tid), well-known; specially noticed; famous: *Samson was noted for strength. adjective.*

note wor thy (nōt′wėr′ᴛʜē), worthy of notice; remarkable: *a noteworthy achievement.* See picture. *adjective.*

noth ing (nuth′ing), **1** not anything: *Nothing arrived by mail.* **2** thing that does not exist: *create a world out of nothing.* **3** thing or person of no value or importance: *Don't worry, it's nothing.* **4** zero. **5** not at all: *She is nothing like her sister in looks.* 1-4 *noun,* 5 *adverb.*

no tice (nō′tis), **1** heed; attention: *A sudden movement caught his notice.* **2** see; give attention to; observe: *I noticed a hole in my sock.* **3** information; warning: *The whistle blew to give notice that the boat was about to leave.* **4** a written or printed sign; paper posted in a public place; large sheet of paper giving information or directions: *We saw a notice of today's motion picture outside the theater.* **5** telling that one is leaving or must leave rented quarters or a job at a given time: *I gave two weeks' notice when I quit my job.* **6** a written or printed account in a newspaper: *There is a notice in the paper describing the wedding.*

a hat	i it	oi oil	ch child	a in about
ā age	ī ice	ou out	ng long	e in taken
ä far	o hot	u cup	sh she	ə = { i in pencil
e let	ō open	ù put	th thin	o in lemon
ē equal	ô order	ü rule	ᴛʜ then	u in circus
ėr term			zh measure	

1,3-6 *noun,* 2 *verb,* **no ticed, no tic ing.**
take notice of, give attention to; observe: *Take no notice of them.*

no tice a ble (nō′ti sə bəl), **1** easily seen or noticed: *Our kitten is very noticeable because its fur is yellow.* **2** worth noticing. *adjective.*

no ti fi ca tion (nō′tə fə kā′shən), **1** notifying. **2** notice: *She received a notification of the meeting. noun.*

no ti fy (nō′tə fī), let know; give notice to; announce to; inform: *Our teacher notified us that there would be a test on Monday. We have a letter notifying us that she will visit us soon. verb,* **no ti fied, no ti fy ing.**

no tion (nō′shən), **1** idea; understanding: *I have no notion of what you mean.* **2** opinion; view; belief: *One common notion is that red hair goes with a quick temper.* **3** intention: *He has no notion of risking his money.* **4** desire; fancy; whim: *We had a sudden notion to take a short vacation.* **5** a foolish idea or opinion: *Grow oranges in Alaska? What a notion!* **6 notions,** small useful articles, such as pins, needles, thread, or tape. *noun.*

no to ri ous (nō tôr′ē əs), well-known or commonly known, especially because of something bad: *Our neighbors are notorious for giving noisy parties.* See picture. *adjective.*

not with stand ing (not′wiᴛʜ stan′ding or not′wiᴛʜ stan′ding), **1** in spite of: *I bought it notwithstanding the price.* **2** nevertheless: *It is raining; but I shall go, notwithstanding.* 1 *preposition,* 2 *adverb.*

nought (nôt), naught. *noun.*

noun (noun), word used as the name of a person, place, thing, quality, or event. Words like *Lisa, table, kindness, skill,* and *party* are nouns. *noun.*

nour ish (nėr′ish), **1** make grow, or keep alive and well, with food; feed: *Milk is all we need to nourish our small baby.* **2** maintain; foster; support; encourage: *nourish a hope. verb.*

nour ish ment (nėr′ish mənt), food. *noun.*

Nov., November.

nov el (nov′əl), **1** of a new kind or nature; strange; new. See picture. **2** story with characters and a plot, long enough to fill one or more volumes. Novels are usually about people, scenes, and happenings such as might be met in real life. 1 *adjective,* 2 *noun.*

nov el ist (nov′ə list), person who writes novels. *noun.*

nov el ty (nov′əl tē), **1** newness: *After the novelty of washing dishes wore off, we did not want to do it any more.* **2** a new or unusual thing: *Staying up late was a novelty to the children, and they enjoyed it.* **3 novelties,** small, unusual articles, such as toys or cheap jewelry. *noun, plural* **nov el ties.**

nuzzle—His horse **nuzzled** him.

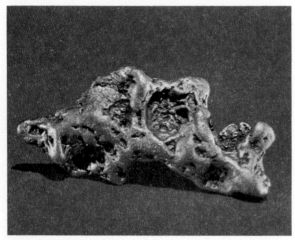

nugget (definition 1)—a nugget of gold

nucleus (definition 1)—nucleus of a plant cell

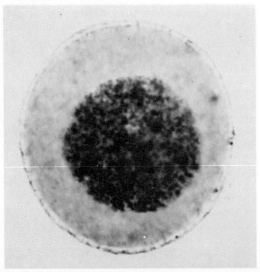

No vem ber (nō vem′bər), the 11th month of the year. It has 30 days. *noun.* [*November*, the Latin name for this month, came from a Latin word meaning "nine." The month was called this because it was the ninth month in the ancient Roman calendar.]

nov ice (nov′is), **1** beginner; one who is new to something: *Novices are likely to make some mistakes.* **2** person who is not yet a monk or nun, but is in a period of trial and preparation. *noun.*

now (nou), **1** at this time: *He is here now. Most people do not believe in ghosts now.* **2** by this time: *She must have reached the city now.* **3** this time: *by now, until now, from now on.* **4** at once: *Do it now!* **5** since; now that: *Now I am older, I have changed my mind. Now you mention it, I do remember.* **6** as things are; as it is: *Now I can never believe you again.* **7** then; next: *Now you see it; now you don't.* **8** a little while ago: *I just now saw him.* **9** *Now* is used in many sentences where it makes very little difference in the meaning: *Now what do you mean? Oh, come now! Now you knew that was wrong.* 1,2,4,6-9 *adverb,* 3 *noun,* 5 *conjunction.*

now and then or **now and again,** from time to time; once in a while: *I see him now and then, but not often.*

now a days (nou′ə dāz′), at the present day; in these times: *Nowadays people travel in automobiles rather than carriages. adverb.*

no where (nō′hwer or nō′hwar), in no place; at no place; to no place. *adverb.*

noz zle (noz′əl), tip put on a hose or pipe forming an outlet: *He adjusted the nozzle so that the water came out in a fine spray. noun.*

nu cle ar (nü′klē ər or nyü′klē ər), **1** having to do with nuclei or a nucleus, especially the nucleus of an atom: *nuclear particles.* **2** of or having to do with atoms or atomic energy; atomic: *a nuclear reactor, the nuclear age. adjective.*

nu cle us (nü′klē əs or nyü′klē əs), **1** a central part or thing around which other parts or things are collected. See picture. **2** a beginning, to which additions are to be made: *I hoped my dollar would become the nucleus of a growing bank account.* **3** proton, or group of protons and neutrons, forming the central part of an atom. A nucleus has a positive charge of electricity. *noun,* plural **nu cle i** (nü′klē ī or nyü′klē ī), **nu cle us es.**

nudge (nuj), **1** push slightly; jog with the elbow to attract attention. **2** a slight push or jog. 1 *verb,* **nudged, nudg ing;** 2 *noun.*

nug get (nug′it), **1** lump; valuable lump. See picture. **2** anything valuable: *nuggets of wisdom. noun.*

nui sance (nü′sns or nyü′sns), thing or person that annoys, troubles, offends, or is disagreeable: *Flies are a nuisance. noun.*

numb (num), **1** having lost the power of feeling or moving: *My fingers are numb with cold.* **2** make numb. **3** dull the feelings of: *The news of her death numbed them with grief.* 1 *adjective,* 2,3 *verb.*

num ber (num′bər), **1** the count or sum of a group of things or persons; amount: *The number* of students in our class is twenty. **2** word that tells exactly how many. Two, thirteen, twenty-one, and one hundred are such numbers. **3** word that tells rank or place in a series. Second and thirteenth are such numbers. **4** find out the number of; count. **5** figure or mark that stands for a number; numeral. 2, 7, and 9 are numbers. **6** give a number to: *The pages of this book are numbered.* **7** be or amount to a given number: *The states in the Union number 50. This city numbers a million people.* **8** quantity, especially a rather large quantity: *We saw a number of birds.* **9 numbers, a** arithmetic: *She is very clever at numbers.* **b** many: *There were numbers who stayed out of school that day.* **c** being more: *win a battle by force of numbers.* **10** reckon as one of a class or collection: *I number you among my best friends.* **11** issue of a magazine: *The May number has an unusually good story.* **12** one of a numbered series, often a particular numeral identifying a person or thing: *a telephone number, a house number.* **13** a single part of a program: *The program consisted of four musical numbers.* **14** limit; fix the number of: *Our old dog's days are numbered.* **15** (in grammar) a word form or ending which shows whether one or more is meant. *Boy, ox,* and *this* are in the singular number; *boys, oxen,* and *these* are in the plural number. 1-3,5,8,9, 11-13,15 *noun,* 4,6,7,10,14 *verb.*

without number, too many to be counted: *stars without number.*

num ber less (num/bər lis), very numerous; too many to count: *There are numberless fish in the sea. adjective.*

nu mer al (nü/mər əl *or* nyü/mər əl), figure or group of figures standing for a number. 7, 25, 463, III, and XIX are numerals. *noun.*

nu me ra tor (nü/mə rā/tər *or* nyü/mə rā/tər), number above the line in a fraction, which shows how many equal parts of the whole make up the fraction: *In ³/₈, 3 is the numerator and 8 is the denominator. noun.*

nu mer i cal (nü mer/ə kəl *or* nyü mer/ə kəl), having something to do with numbers; in numbers; by numbers: *numerical order. adjective.*

nu mer ous (nü/mər əs *or* nyü/mər əs), very many: *The child asked numerous questions. adjective.*

nun (nun), woman who gives up everything else for religion, and with other religious women lives a life of prayer and worship. Some nuns teach; others care for the sick. *noun.*

nup tial (nup/shəl), **1** of marriage or weddings. **2 nuptials,** a wedding or the wedding ceremony. 1 *adjective,* 2 *noun.*

nurse (nèrs), **1** person who takes care of the sick or the old, or is trained to do this: *Hospitals employ many nurses.* **2** be or act as a nurse for sick people; wait on or try to cure the sick. **3** cure or try to cure by care: *She nursed a bad cold by going to bed.* **4** woman who cares for and brings up the young children or babies of other persons. **5** act as a nurse; have charge of or bring up (another's baby or young child). **6** one who feeds and protects. **7** nourish; make grow; protect: *nurse a*

hatred in the heart, nurse a plant. **8** treat with special care: *He nursed his sore arm by using it very little.* **9** give milk to (a baby) at the breast. **10** suck milk from the breast of a mother. 1,4,6 *noun,* 2,3,5,7-10 *verb,* **nursed, nurs ing.**

nurse maid (nèrs/mād/), girl or woman employed to care for children. *noun.*

nurs er y (nèr/sər ē), **1** room set apart for the use and care of babies. **2** a place where babies and small children are cared for during the day: *a day nursery.* **3** piece of ground or place where young plants are raised for transplanting or sale. *noun. plural* **nurs er ies.**

nursery school, school for children not old enough to go to kindergarten.

nur ture (nèr/chər), **1** rear; bring up; care for; foster; train: *They nurtured the child as if she were their own.* **2** rearing; bringing up; training; education: *The two sisters had received very different nurture, one at home and the other at a convent.* **3** nourish; feed: *nurture resentment.* **4** nourishment; food. 1,3 *verb,* **nur tured, nur tur ing;** 2,4 *noun.*

nut (nut), **1** a dry fruit or seed with a hard woody or leathery shell and a kernel inside which is often good to eat. **2** kernel of a nut. **3** a small, usually metal block having a threaded hole, which screws on to a bolt to hold the bolt in place. **4** an odd or silly person. *noun.*

nut crack er (nut/krak/ər), instrument for cracking the shells of nuts. *noun.*

nut meg (nut/meg), a hard, spicy seed about as big as a marble, obtained from the fruit of a tree growing in the East Indies. The seed is grated and used for flavoring food. *noun.*

nu tri ent (nü/trē ənt *or* nyü/trē ənt), **1** nourishing: *the nutrient value of milk.* **2** a nourishing substance; food: *Children need more vitamins and nutrients than adults.* 1 *adjective,* 2 *noun.*

nu tri tion (nü trish/ən *or* nyü trish/ən), **1** food; nourishment: *A balanced diet provides nutrition for your body.* **2** series of processes by which food is used by animals and plants for growth and energy. *noun.*

nu tri tious (nü trish/əs *or* nyü trish/əs), nourishing; valuable as food: *Oranges and bread are nutritious. adjective.*

nuz zle (nuz/əl), rub with the nose; press the nose against. See picture. *verb,* **nuz zled, nuz zling.**

NW *or* **N.W.,** **1** northwest. **2** northwestern.

ny lon (nī/lon), an extremely strong, elastic, and durable substance, used to make clothing, stockings, or bristles. *noun.*

nymph (nimf), a Greek or Roman goddess of nature, who lived in seas, rivers, fountains, hills, woods, or trees. *noun.*

O o

O[1] or **o** (ō), the 15th letter of the English alphabet.
There are two *o*'s in *Ohio*. *noun, plural* **O's** or **o's.**

O[2] (ō), oh! *interjection.*

oaf (ōf), **1** a very stupid person. **2** a clumsy person.
noun.

oak (ōk), **1** a tree or shrub found in most parts of
the world, having nuts which are called acorns.
There are many kinds of oaks. **2** its hard, strong
wood, used in building and for flooring. **3** of an
oak: *oak leaves.* **4** made of oak wood: *an oak table.*
1,2 *noun,* 3,4 *adjective.*

oar (ôr), **1** a long pole with a broad, flat end, used
in rowing. Sometimes an oar is used to steer a
boat. **2** person who rows: *He is the best oar in the
crew. noun.*

oars man (ôrz′mən), **1** person who rows. **2** person
who rows well. *noun, plural* **oars men.**

o a sis (ō ā′sis), a fertile spot in the desert where
there is water. *noun, plural* **o a ses** (ō ā′sēz′).

oat (ōt), **1** a kind of cereal grass whose grain is
used in making oatmeal and as a food for horses
and other farm animals. **2 oats,** the grains of the
oat plant. *noun.*

oath (ōth), **1** a solemn promise or statement that
something is true, which God or some holy
person or thing is called on to witness: *I gave an
oath that I would tell the truth.* **2** name of God used
as an exclamation to add force or to express
anger. **3** a curse; word used in swearing: *The
pirate cursed us with fearful oaths. noun, plural*
oaths (ōᵺz *or* ōths).

oat meal (ōt′mēl′), **1** oats partially ground up and
flattened into small flakes. **2** a cooked cereal
made from this: *We often have oatmeal with cream
and sugar for breakfast. noun.*

o be di ence (ō bē′dē əns), doing what one is told
to do; submitting to authority or law: *They were
strict parents who demanded complete obedience
from their children. She acted in obedience to the
judge's order. noun.*

o be di ent (ō bē′dē ənt), doing what one is told to
do; willing to obey: *The obedient dog came at its
owner's whistle. adjective.*

ob e lisk (ob′ə lisk), a tapering, four-sided shaft of
stone with a top shaped like a pyramid. See
picture. *noun.*

o bey (ō bā′), **1** do what one is told to do: *The dog
obeyed and went home.* **2** follow the orders of: *You
must obey the court's decision.* **3** yield to the control
of: *A horse obeys the rein. verb.*

o bi (ō′bē), a long, broad sash worn by Japanese
around the waist of a kimono. See picture. *noun,
plural* **o bis.**

ob ject (ob′jikt *for 1-3;* əb jekt′ *for 4 and 5*),
1 something that can be seen or touched; thing:
What is that object by the fence? A dark object

obelisk

obi

oboe

moved between me and the door. **2** person or thing toward which feeling, thought, or action is directed: *She was the object of their affection. The rare disease became an object of study.* **3** thing aimed at; end; purpose; goal: *My object in coming here was to help you.* **4** make objections; be opposed; feel dislike: *Many people object to loud noise.* **5** give as a reason against something: *I objected that it was too cold for camping.* 1-3 *noun,* 4,5 *verb.*

ob jec tion (əb jek′shən), **1** something said in objecting; reason or argument against something: *One of the objections to the new plan was that it would cost too much.* **2** feeling of disapproval or dislike: *an energetic person with no objection to hard work. noun.*

ob jec tion a ble (əb jek′shə nə bəl), **1** likely to be objected to: *an objectionable movie.* **2** unpleasant: *an objectionable odor. adjective.*

ob jec tive (əb jek′tiv), **1** something aimed at: *My objective this summer will be learning to play tennis better.* **2** existing outside the mind as an actual object, and not merely in the mind as an idea; real. Buildings are objective; thoughts are subjective. **3** about outward things, not about the thoughts and feelings of the speaker, writer, or painter: *Scientists must be objective in their experiments. The witness gave an objective report of the accident.* 1 *noun,* 2,3 *adjective.*

ob li gate (ob′lə gāt), bind by law or a sense of duty: *A witness in court is obligated to tell the truth. verb,* **ob li gat ed, ob li gat ing.**

ob li ga tion (ob′lə gā′shən), **1** duty under the law; duty due to a promise or contract; duty on account of social relationship or kindness received: *Taxes are an obligation which may fall on everybody. The contractor is really under obligation to paint our house first. We have an obligation to our friends.* **2** binding power (of a law, promise, or sense of duty): *The one who did the damage is under obligation to pay for it. noun.*

o blige (ə blīj′), **1** bind by a promise, contract, or duty; compel; force: *The law obliges parents to send their children to school. I am obliged to leave early to catch my train.* **2** bind by a favor or service; do a favor to: *Kindly oblige me by closing the door. verb,* **o bliged, o blig ing.**

o blig ing (ə blī′jing), willing to do favors; helpful: *Her obliging nature wins friends. adjective.*

o blique (ə blēk′), slanting; not straight up and down; not straight across. *adjective.*

o blit e rate (ə blit′ə rāt′), blot out; remove all traces of; destroy: *The heavy rain obliterated all of the footprints. verb,* **o blit e rat ed, o blit e rat ing.**

o bliv i on (ə bliv′ē ən), condition of being entirely forgotten: *Many ancient cities have long since passed into oblivion. noun.*

o bliv i ous (ə bliv′ē əs), forgetful; not mindful: *The book was so interesting that I was oblivious of my surroundings. adjective.*

ob long (ob′lông), **1** longer than broad: *an oblong loaf of bread.* **2** rectangle that is not a square. See

a hat	i it	oi oil	ch child	a in about
ā age	ī ice	ou out	ng long	e in taken
ä far	o hot	u cup	sh she	ə = i in pencil
e let	ō open	u̇ put	th thin	o in lemon
ē equal	ô order	ü rule	ŦH then	u in circus
ėr term			zh measure	

picture. 1 *adjective,* 2 *noun.*

ob nox ious (əb nok′shəs), offensive; very disagreeable; hateful: *Their constant rudeness and bad manners made them obnoxious to me. adjective.*

o boe (ō′bō), a wooden wind instrument in which the tone is produced by a double reed. See picture. *noun.*

ob scene (əb sēn′), offending modesty or decency: *obscene language. adjective.*

ob scure (əb skyu̇r′), **1** not clearly expressed; hard to understand: *an obscure passage in a book.* **2** not well known; attracting no notice: *an obscure little village, an obscure poet, an obscure job in the government.* **3** hidden; not easily discovered: *an obscure path, an obscure meaning.* **4** not distinct; not clear: *an obscure shape, obscure sounds.* **5** dark; dim: *an obscure corner.* **6** make obscure; dim; darken; hide from view: *Clouds obscure the sun.* 1-5 *adjective,* **ob scur er, ob scur est;** 6 *verb,* **ob scured, ob scur ing.**

ob scur i ty (əb skyu̇r′ə tē), **1** lack of clearness; difficulty in being understood: *The obscurity of the book caused an argument over its meaning.* **2** condition of being unknown: *Abraham Lincoln rose from obscurity to fame. noun, plural* **ob scur i ties.**

ob serv ance (əb zėr′vəns), **1** act of observing or keeping laws or customs: *the observance of the Sabbath.* **2** act performed as a sign of worship or respect; religious ceremony. *noun.*

ob serv ant (əb zėr′vənt), **1** observing; quick to notice; watchful: *If you are observant in the fields and woods, you will find many flowers that others fail to notice.* **2** careful in observing (a law, rule, or custom): *A good driver is observant of the traffic rules. adjective.*

ob ser va tion (ob′zər vā′shən), **1** act, habit, or power of seeing and noting: *By trained observation a doctor can tell much about the condition of a patient.* **2** fact of being seen; notice; being seen: *The spy avoided observation.* **3** something seen and

oblongs (definition 2)

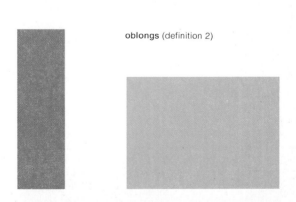

noted: *During science experiments she kept careful records of her observations.* **4** remark: *"Haste makes waste," was Father's observation when I spilled the milk.* noun.

ob serv a to ry (əb zėr′və tôr′ē), **1** place or building fitted up with a telescope for observing the stars and other heavenly bodies. **2** a high place or building giving a wide view. *noun, plural* **ob serv a to ries.**

ob serve (əb zėrv′), **1** see and note; notice: *Did you observe anything strange in her behavior?* **2** examine closely; study: *An astronomer observes the stars.* **3** remark; comment: *"Bad weather ahead," she observed.* **4** keep; follow in practice: *The monks observed silence for days at a time. The teacher asked us to observe the rule about not walking on the grass.* **5** show regard for; celebrate: *observe the Sabbath.* verb, **ob served, ob serv ing.**

ob serv er (əb zėr′vər), person who observes. noun.

ob so lete (ob′sə lēt), **1** no longer in use. See picture. **2** out of date: *We still use this machine though it is obsolete.* adjective.

ob sta cle (ob′stə kəl), something that stands in the way or stops progress; hindrance: *A tree fallen across the road was an obstacle to our car. He overcame the obstacle of blindness and became a musician.* noun.

ob sti nate (ob′stə nit), **1** stubborn; not giving in. See picture. **2** hard to control or treat: *an obstinate cough.* adjective.

ob struct (əb strukt′), **1** block up; make hard to pass through: *Fallen trees obstruct the road.* **2** be in the way of; hinder: *Trees obstruct our view of the ocean. A shortage of materials obstructed the work of the factory.* verb.

ob struc tion (əb struk′shən), **1** thing that obstructs; something in the way; obstacle: *The old path was blocked by such obstructions as boulders and fallen trees. Ignorance is an obstruction to progress.* **2** blocking; hindering: *the obstruction of progress by prejudices.* noun.

ob tain (əb tān′), get through effort; come to have: *obtain a job one applies for, obtain knowledge through study.* verb.

ob tain a ble (əb tā′nə bəl), able to be obtained. adjective.

ob tuse (əb tüs′ *or* əb tyüs′), **1** not sharp; blunt. **2** slow in understanding; stupid: *They were too obtuse to take the hint.* adjective.

obtuse angle, angle greater than a right angle. See picture.

ob vi ous (ob′vē əs), easily seen or understood; not to be doubted; plain: *It is obvious that two and two make four. The sickly child was in obvious need of good food and sunshine.* adjective.

oc ca sion (ə kā′zhən), **1** a particular time: *We have met them on several occasions.* **2** a special event: *The jewels were worn only on great occasions, such as a royal wedding or a coronation.* **3** a good chance; opportunity: *The trip we took together gave us an occasion to get better acquainted.* **4** a cause; reason: *The dog that was the occasion of the quarrel*

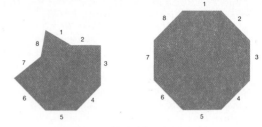

octagon—two kinds of octagons

obstinate (definition 1)—The **obstinate** horse tried to throw anyone who rode it.

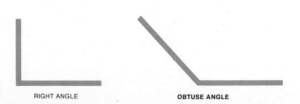

obsolete (definition 1)—Automobiles made horse-drawn buggies obsolete.

RIGHT ANGLE   OBTUSE ANGLE

had run away. **5** cause; bring about: *His strange behavior occasioned a good deal of talk.* 1-4 *noun*, 5 *verb.*

oc ca sion al (ə kā′zhə nəl), happening or coming now and then, or once in a while: *We had fine weather all through July except for an occasional thunderstorm. adjective.*

oc ca sion al ly (ə kā′zhə nə lē), now and then; once in a while; at times. *adverb.*

oc cu pan cy (ok′yə pən sē), occupying; holding (land, houses, a pew, or the like) by being in possession: *The occupancy of the land by farmers was opposed by the ranchers. noun.*

oc cu pant (ok′yə pənt), **1** person who occupies: *The occupant of the shack stepped out as I approached.* **2** person in actual possession of a house, estate, or office. *noun.*

oc cu pa tion (ok′yə pā′shən), **1** work a person does regularly or to earn a living; business; employment; trade: *Caring for the sick is a nurse's occupation.* **2** possession; occupying; being occupied: *the occupation of a town by the enemy, the occupation of a house by a family. noun.*

oc cu py (ok′yə pī), **1** take up; fill: *The building occupies an entire block. The lessons occupy the morning.* **2** keep busy; engage; employ: *Composing music occupied her attention.* **3** take possession of: *The enemy occupied our fort.* **4** hold; have in use: *A judge occupies an important position.* **5** live in: *Two families occupy the house next door.* verb, **oc cu pied, oc cu py ing.**

oc cur (ə kėr′), **1** happen; take place: *Storms often occur in winter.* **2** be found; exist: *"E" occurs in print more often than any other letter.* **3** come to mind; suggest itself: *Has it occurred to you to close the windows?* verb, **oc curred, oc cur ring.**

oc cur rence (ə kėr′əns), **1** occurring: *The occurrence of storms delayed our trip.* **2** happening; event: *an unexpected occurrence. noun.*

o cean (ō′shən), **1** the great body of salt water that covers almost three fourths of the earth's surface; the sea. **2** any of its four main divisions—the Atlantic, Pacific, Indian, and Arctic oceans. The waters around the Antarctic continent are considered by some to form a separate ocean. *noun.*

o cean og ra phy (ō′shə nog′rə fē), science that deals with the ocean and the plants and animals that live there. *noun.*

o ce lot (ō′sə lot *or* os′ə lot), a spotted animal somewhat like a leopard, but smaller. It is found from Texas south through Mexico and into parts of South America. See picture. *noun.*

o'clock (ə klok′), by the clock; according to the clock: *We have dinner at six o'clock. adverb.*

Oct., October.

oc ta gon (ok′tə gon), a figure having eight angles and eight sides. See picture. *noun.*

oc tag o nal (ok tag′ə nəl), having eight angles and eight sides. *adjective.*

oc tave (ok′tiv), **1** (in music) the interval between a tone and another tone having twice (or half) as many vibrations. From middle C to the C above it

a hat	**i** it	**oi** oil	**ch** child	a in about
ā age	**ī** ice	**ou** out	**ng** long	e in taken
ä far	**o** hot	**u** cup	**sh** she	ə = i in pencil
e let	**ō** open	**u̇** put	**th** thin	o in lemon
ē equal	**ô** order	**ü** rule	**ŦH** then	u in circus
ėr term			**zh** measure	

is an octave. **2** the eighth tone above (or below) a given tone, having twice (or half) as many vibrations per second. **3** series of tones or of keys of an instrument filling the interval between a tone and its octave. **4** the sounding together of a tone and its octave. *noun.*

Oc to ber (ok tō′bər), the tenth month of the year. It has 31 days. *noun.* [*October,* the Latin name for this month, came from a Latin word meaning "eight." The month was called this because it was the eighth month in the ancient Roman calendar.]

oc to pus (ok′tə pəs), **1** a sea animal having a soft body and eight arms with suckers on them. It is a mollusk. See picture. **2** anything like an octopus. *noun, plural* **oc to pus es, oc to pi** (ok′tə pī). [*Octopus* comes from a Greek word meaning "having eight feet."]

ocelot—about 3 feet (1 meter) long without the tail

octopus (definition 1)—from 6 inches (15 centimeters) to 20 feet (6 meters) across

odd (od), **1** strange; peculiar; unusual: *Her face is familiar; it's odd that I can't remember her name.* **2** leaving a remainder of 1 when divided by 2: *Three, five, and seven are odd numbers.* **3** being one of a pair or set of which the rest is missing: *Every time she does her laundry, she ends up with at least one odd sock.* **4** left over: *Pay the bill with this money and keep the odd change.* **5** extra; occasional: *He could not find regular work and had to take odd jobs. adjective.*

odd i ty (od′ə tē), **1** peculiarity; being strange or unusual: *the oddity of wearing a fur coat over a bathing suit.* **2** a strange, unusual, or peculiar person or thing. See picture. *noun, plural* **odd i ties.**

odd ly (od′lē), in a strange or unusual manner. *adverb.*

odds (odz), **1** difference in favor of one and against another; advantage. In betting, odds of 3 to 1 mean that the person giving odds will pay 3 if the bet is lost, or receive 1 if the bet is won. *The odds are in our favor and we should win.* **2** (in games) an extra allowance given to the weaker side. *noun plural or singular.*

at odds, quarreling; disagreeing: *The two brothers were often at odds.*

odds and ends, remnants; stray bits left over: *I went about the house picking up the odds and ends.*

o di ous (ō′dē əs), very displeasing; hateful; offensive: *an odious smell, odious lies. adjective.*

o dor (ō′dər), smell: *the odor of roses, the odor of garbage. noun.*

o dor less (ō′dər lis), without any odor: *Pure water is odorless. adjective.*

of (ov, uv, *or* əv), **1** belonging to: *the children of the family, a friend of my childhood, the news of the day, the driver of the car, the cause of the quarrel.* **2** made from: *a house of bricks, castles of sand.* **3** that has; with: *a house of six rooms.* **4** that is; named: *the city of Chicago.* **5** away from; from: *north of Boston, take leave of a friend.* **6** about; concerning; having to do with: *think well of someone, be fifteen years of age.* **7** out of; owing to: *expect much of a new medicine. She came of a noble family.* **8** among: *Many of my classmates were at the party. preposition.*

off (ôf), **1** from the usual position or condition: *I took off my hat.* **2** from; away from; far from: *He pushed me off my seat. We are miles off the main road.* **3** away; at a distance; to a distance: *go off on a journey. Christmas is only five weeks off.* **4** so as to stop or lessen: *Turn the water off. The game was called off.* **5** not on; not connected; loose: *The electricity is off. A button is off his coat.* **6** without work: *an afternoon off. She likes to read during off hours.* **7** wholly; in full: *She cleared off her desk.* **8** in a specified condition in regard to money or property: *How well off are the neighbors?* **9** on one's way: *It's late and we must be off.* **10** straight out from: *The boat anchored off the fort.* 1,3,4,6,7,9 *adverb,* 2,5,10 *preposition,* 5,6,8 *adjective.*

be off, go away; leave quickly: *I'm off now for the party.*

off and on, now and then: *He has lived in Europe off and on for ten years.*

of fend (ə fend′), pain; displease; hurt the feelings of; make angry: *My friend was offended by my laughter. verb.*

of fend er (ə fen′dər), **1** person who offends. **2** person who does wrong or breaks a law: *No smoking here; offenders will be fined $5. noun.*

of fense (ə fens′ *for 1-4;* ô′fens *for 5*), **1** breaking of the law; sin: *The punishment for that offense is two years in prison. Lying and cruelty are offenses.* **2** condition of being offended; hurt feelings; anger: *He tried not to cause offense.* **3** offending; hurting someone's feelings: *No offense was meant.* **4** something that offends or causes displeasure. **5** an attacking team or force: *Our football team has a good offense. noun.*

give offense, offend: *I did not mean to give offense to you.*

take offense, be offended: *I did not take offense at the coach's criticism of my playing.*

of fen sive (ə fen′siv), **1** giving offense; irritating; annoying: *"Shut up" is an offensive remark.* **2** unpleasant; disagreeable; disgusting: *The bad eggs had an offensive odor.* **3** used for attack; having something to do with attack: *offensive weapons, an offensive war for conquest.* **4** position or attitude of attack: *The army took the offensive.* **5** attack: *Our planes bombed the enemy lines on the night before the offensive.* 1-3 *adjective,* 4,5 *noun.*

of fer (ô′fər), **1** hold out to be taken or refused; present: *offer one's hand. She offered us her help.* **2** propose; suggest: *offer a price. She offered a few ideas to improve the plan.* **3** present in worship: *offer prayers.* **4** try; attempt: *The thieves offered no resistance to the policemen.* **5** present itself; occur: *She will come if the opportunity offers.* **6** act of offering: *an offer of money, an offer to sing, an offer of $20,000 for a house.* 1-5 *verb,* 6 *noun.*

of fer ing (ô′fər ing), **1** giving something as an act of worship. **2** contribution; gift. *noun.*

off hand (ôf′hand′ *for 1;* ôf′hand′ *for 2*), **1** at once; without previous thought or preparation: *The carpenter could not tell offhand the cost of his work.* **2** done or made without previous thought or preparation: *Her offhand opinion turned out to be quite accurate.* 1 *adverb,* 2 *adjective.*

of fice (ô′fis), **1** place in which the work of a business or profession is done; room or rooms in which to work: *The doctor's office is on the second floor.* **2** staff or persons carrying on work in such a place: *Half the office is on vacation.* **3** position, especially a public position: *accept or resign an office. The President holds the highest public office in the United States. noun.*

of fi cer (ô′fə sər), **1** person who commands others in the armed forces. Majors, generals, captains, and admirals are officers. **2** person who holds a public, church, or government office: *a health officer, a police officer.* **3** the president, vice-president, secretary, or treasurer of a club or society. *noun.*

of fi cial (ə fish′əl), **1** person who holds a public

ogre

oddity (definition 2)—A blue hot dog is quite an oddity.

a hat	i it	oi oil	ch child		a in about
ā age	ī ice	ou out	ng long		e in taken
ä far	o hot	u cup	sh she	ə =	i in pencil
e let	ō open	u̇ put	th thin		o in lemon
ē equal	ô order	ü rule	ŦH then		u in circus
ėr term			zh measure		

position or who is in charge of some public work or duty: *The mayor is a government official.* **2** person holding office; officer: *bank officials.* **3** of or having something to do with an office: *an official uniform, official business.* **4** having authority: *An official record is kept of the proceedings of Congress.* 1,2 *noun,* 3,4 *adjective.*

off set (ôf′set′), make up for: *Her speed offset the strength of her opponent and she won the tennis match.* See picture. *verb,* **off set, off set ting.**

off shoot (ôf′shüt′), shoot from a main stem; branch: *an offshoot of a plant. noun.*

off shore (ôf′shôr′), off or away from the shore: *The wind was blowing offshore. We saw offshore oil wells along the coast. adjective, adverb.*

off spring (ôf′spring′), the young of a person, animal, or plant; descendant: *All their offspring had red hair. noun, plural* **off spring** or **off springs.**

oft (ôft), often. *adverb.*

of ten (ô′fən), many times; frequently: *We often go to the seashore for a vacation. We see our neighbors often. adverb,* **of ten er, of ten est.**

of ten times (ô′fən tīmz′), often. *adverb.*

o gre (ō′gər), (in fairy tales) a giant or monster that was supposed to eat people. See picture. *noun.*

oh or **Oh** (ō), **1** word used before a person's name in beginning to speak: *Oh, Mary, look!* **2** word used to express surprise, joy, pain, and other feelings: *Oh, dear me! interjection.* Also spelled **O.**

O hi o (ō hī′ō), one of the north central states of the United States. *noun.* [*Ohio* got its name from the Ohio River. It may have come from an Iroquois Indian word meaning "fine" or "beautiful."]

oil (oil), **1** any of several kinds of thick, fatty or greasy liquids that are lighter than water, burn easily, and will not mix or dissolve in water but will dissolve in alcohol. Mineral oils, such as kerosene, are used for fuel; animal and vegetable oils, such as olive oil, are used in cooking and medicine. **2** petroleum. **3** put oil on or in: *oil the squeaky hinges of a door.* **4** paint made by grinding coloring matter in oil. 1,2,4 *noun,* 3 *verb.*

oil cloth (oil′klôth′), **1** cloth made waterproof by coating it with paint, used to cover shelves or tables. **2** cloth made waterproof by treating it with oil. *noun, plural* **oil cloths** (oil′klôŦHz′ or oil′klôths′).

oil painting, picture painted with colors made by mixing pigment with oil.

oil well, well drilled to get oil.

oil y (oi′lē), **1** of oil: *an oily smell.* **2** containing oil: *oily salad dressing.* **3** covered or soaked with oil: *oily rags.* **4** like oil; smooth; slippery. **5** too smooth; smooth in a disagreeable way: *an oily manner. adjective,* **oil i er, oil i est.**

old-fashioned (definition 1)—an old-fashioned valentine

onlooker—Onlookers surrounded me as I lay on the ground.

ominous—The sky looked very **ominous** just before the storm broke.

oint ment (oint′mənt), substance made from oil or fat, often containing medicine, used on the skin to heal it or to make it soft. *noun.*

OK or **O.K.** (ō′kā′), all right: *The new schedule was OK. "OK, OK!" he yelled. adjective, adverb, interjection.*

O kla ho ma (ō′klə hō′mə), one of the southwestern states of the United States. *noun.* [*Oklahoma* came from Choctaw Indian words meaning "red people."]

o kra (ō′krə), the sticky pods of a plant, used as a vegetable and in soups. *noun.* [*Okra* comes from a west African name for the okra plant.]

old (ōld), **1** not young; aged; having existed for a long time: *old people, an old oak tree.* **2** of age; in age: *The baby is ten months old.* **3** not new or recent; dating far back; ancient: *an old debt, an old castle.* **4** much worn by age or use: *an old coat.* **5** looking or seeming old; like an old person in some way: *That child is old for her years.* **6** skilled; having much experience: *He is an old hand at swimming.* **7** of long standing; over a long period of time: *We are old friends.* **8** former: *An old pupil came back to visit our teacher.* **9** the time of long ago; the past: *the knights of old.* 1-8 *adjective,* **old er, old est** or **eld er, eld est;** 9 *noun.*

old age, years of life from about 65 on.

old en (ōl′dən), old; of old; ancient: *In olden times very few people lived to old age. adjective.*

old-fash ioned (ōld′fash′ənd), **1** out-of-date; of an old style: *old-fashioned clothing.* See picture. **2** keeping to old ways or ideas: *My grandparents are quite old-fashioned. adjective.*

Old Testament, the earlier part of the Bible, which contains the religious and social laws of the Hebrews, a record of their history, their important literature, and writings of their prophets.

old-time (ōld′tīm′), of former times; like old times. *adjective.*

Old World, Europe, Asia, and Africa.

o le o mar gar ine (ō′lē ō mär′jər ən *or* ō′lē ō mär′jə rēn′), substitute for butter made from vegetable oils; margarine. *noun.*

ol ive (ol′iv), **1** kind of evergreen tree with gray-green leaves. The olive tree grows in the southern part of Europe and other warm regions. **2** fruit of this tree, with a hard stone and bitter pulp. Olives are eaten green or ripe, as a relish, and are used to make olive oil. **3** yellowish green; yellowish brown. 1,2 *noun,* 3 *adjective.*

olive oil, oil pressed from olives, used in cooking and medicine.

O lym pic games (ō lim′pik gāmz′), **1** contests in athletics, poetry, and music, held every four years by the ancient Greeks. **2** modern athletic contests imitating the athletic contests of these games, held every four years in a different country. Athletes from many nations compete in them.

om e let (om′lit), eggs beaten up with milk or water, fried or baked, and then folded over. *noun.*

o men (ō′mən), sign of what is to happen; object

or event that is believed to mean good or bad fortune: *Spilling salt is said to be an omen of bad luck.* noun.

om i nous (om′ə nəs), unfavorable; threatening. See picture. *adjective.*

o mis sion (ō mish′ən), **1** omitting or being omitted: *the omission of a paragraph in copying a story.* **2** thing omitted: *His song was the only omission from the program.* noun.

o mit (ō mit′), **1** leave out: *Many of my spelling mistakes are caused by omitting letters.* **2** fail to do; neglect: *They omitted making their beds.* verb,
o mit ted, o mit ting.

on (ôn), **1** above and supported by: *This book is on the table.* **2** touching so as to cover or be around: *I put the ring on my finger.* **3** close to: *a house on the shore.* **4** in the direction of; toward: *The protesters marched on the Capitol.* **5** against; upon: *The picture is on the wall.* **6** toward something: *Some played; the others looked on.* **7** farther: *March on.* **8** by means of; by the use of: *I just talked to her on the phone.* **9** in the condition of: *on duty.* **10** in or into a condition, process, manner, or action: *Turn the gas on.* **11** taking place: *The race is on.* **12** in use; operating: *The radio is on.* **13** at the time of; during: *They greeted us on our arrival.* **14** from a time; forward: *later on, from that day on.* **15** concerning: *a book on animals.* **16** for the purpose of: *He went on an errand.* **17** among: *I am not on the committee considering new members for our club.* 1-5,8,9,13,15-17 *preposition,* 6,7,10,14 *adverb,* 11,12 *adjective.*

on and on, without stopping: *We talked on and on through the whole afternoon.*

once (wuns), **1** one time: *Read it once more.* **2** at some one time in the past; formerly: *That small town was once the capital of the state.* **3** if ever; whenever: *Most people like to swim, once they have learned how.* 1,2 *adverb,* 3 *conjunction.*

at once, 1 immediately: *You must come at once.* **2** at the same time: *All three children spoke at once.*

once in a while, at one time or another; not too often: *We see our neighbors on the next farm once in a while.*

once upon a time, long ago: *Once upon a time there were dinosaurs.*

on com ing (ôn′kum′ing), approaching or advancing: *oncoming winter. adjective.*

one (wun), **1** the number 1. **2** a single: *one person, one apple.* **3** a single person or thing: *I like the ones in that box.* **4** some: *One day you will be sorry.* **5** some person or thing: *Two of you may go, but one must stay.* **6** any person, standing for people in general: *One does not like to be left out.* **7** the same: *All face one way.* **8** joined together; united: *The class was one in its approval.* **9** a certain: *A short speech was made by one Jane Smith.* 1,3 *noun,* 2,4,7-9 *adjective,* 5,6 *pronoun.*

at one, in agreement: *The two judges were at one about the winner.*

one by one, one after another: *They came out the door one by one.*

one self (wun self′), one's own self: *At the age of*

seven one ought to dress oneself. *pronoun.*

one-sid ed (wun′sī′did), **1** unfair; partial; seeing only one side of a question: *The umpire seemed one-sided in his decisions.* **2** uneven; unequal: *If one team is much better than the other, a game is one-sided. adjective.*

one-way (wun′wā′), moving or allowing movement in only one direction: *a one-way street, a one-way ticket. adjective.*

on ion (un′yən), vegetable with a bulb that is eaten raw and used in cooking. Onions have a sharp, strong smell and taste. *noun.*

on look er (ôn′lùk′ər), spectator; person who watches without taking part. See picture. *noun.*

on ly (ōn′lē), **1** by itself or themselves; one and no more: *Water is her only drink. This is the only road along the shore.* **2** just; merely: *She sold only two.* **3** and no one else; and nothing more; and that is all: *Only he remained. I did it only through friendship.* **4** except that; but: *He would have started, only it rained.* **5** best; finest: *He is the only writer for my taste.* **6** but then; it must be added that: *We had camped right beside a stream, only the water was not fit to drink.* 1,5 *adjective,* 2,3 *adverb,* 4,6 *conjunction.*

if only, I wish: *If only the sun would shine!*

only too, very: *She was only too glad to help us.*

on rush (ôn′rush′), a very strong or forceful forward rush: *He was knocked down by the onrush of water. noun.*

on set (ôn′set′), **1** beginning: *The onset of this disease is gradual.* **2** attack: *The onset of the enemy took us by surprise. noun.*

on slaught (ôn′slôt′), vigorous attack: *The pirates made an onslaught on the ship. noun.*

on to (ôn′tü), on to; to a position on: *throw a ball onto the roof, get onto a horse, a boat driven onto the rocks. preposition.*

on ward (ôn′wərd), on; further on; toward the front; forward: *The crowd around the store window began to move onward. An onward movement began. adverb, adjective.*

on wards (ôn′wərdz), onward. *adverb.*

ooze (üz), **1** pass out slowly through small openings; leak out little by little: *Blood still oozed from the cut. His courage oozed away as he waited.* **2** a slow flow. 1 *verb,* **oozed, ooz ing;** 2 *noun.*

o pal (ō′pəl), gem that shows beautiful changes of color. The common opal is milky white with colored lights. *noun.*

o paque (ō pāk′), **1** not letting light through; not transparent: *A brick wall is opaque.* **2** not shining; dark; dull: *an opaque star, an opaque light. adjective.*

o pen (ō′pən), **1** not shut; not closed; letting (anything or anyone) in or out: *The open windows*

a hat	**i** it	**oi** oil	**ch** child	a in about
ā age	**ī** ice	**ou** out	**ng** long	e in taken
ä far	**o** hot	**u** cup	**sh** she	ə = { i in pencil
e let	**ō** open	**ù** put	**ʹth** thin	o in lemon
ē equal	**ô** order	**ü** rule	**ŦH** then	u in circus
ėr term			**zh** measure	

let in the fresh air. **2** not having its door, gate, or lid closed; not shut up: *an open box, an open drawer, an open house.* **3** not closed in: *the open sea, an open field, an open car.* **4 the open, a** open or clear space; open country, open air. **b** public view or knowledge: *The secret is now out in the open.* **5** unfilled; not taken: *a position still open.* **6** able to be entered, used, or shared by all, or by a person or persons mentioned: *an open meeting, an open market. The race is open to girls under 15.* **7** not covered or protected; exposed: *an open fire, an open jar, open to temptation.* **8** not hidden or secret: *open war, open disregard of rules.* **9** ready to listen to new ideas and judge them fairly; not prejudiced: *She has an open mind.* **10** frank and sincere: *an open heart. Please be open with me.* **11** make or become open: *Open the window. The door opened.* **12** have an opening or passage: *This door opens into the dining room.* **13** spread out or unfold: *open a book, open a letter.* **14** come apart or burst open: *a crack where the earth had opened. The clouds opened and the sun shone through.* **15** start or set up; establish: *He opened a new store.* **16** begin: *open a debate. School opens in September.* 1-3,5-10 *adjective,* 4 *noun,* 11-16 *verb.*

open to, ready to take; willing to consider: *open to suggestions.*

open up, make or become open; open a way to: *The pioneers who opened up the American West included men, women, and children.*

open air, outdoors: *Children like to play in the open air.*

o pen heart ed (ō′pən här′tid), free in expressing one's real thoughts, opinions, and feelings; frank. *adjective.*

o pen ing (ō′pə ning), **1** hole; gap; an open or clear space: *an opening in a wall, an opening in the forest.* **2** the first part; the beginning: *The opening of the story took place in New York.* **3** first; beginning: *the opening words of her speech.* **4** a formal beginning: *The opening will be at three o'clock tomorrow afternoon.* **5** a job that is open or vacant: *an opening for a teller in a bank.* **6** a favorable chance or opportunity: *In talking with your mother, I made an opening to ask her about sending you to camp. As soon as I saw an opening, I got up quickly and left the room.* 1,2,4-6 *noun,* 3 *adjective.*

o pen ly (ō′pən lē), without secrecy; frankly. *adverb.*

op er a (op′ər ə), play that is mostly sung, with costumes, scenery, acting, and music to go with the singing. *noun.* [*Opera comes from a Latin word meaning "work" or "effort."*]

op e rate (op′ə rāt′), **1** be at work; run: *The machinery operates night and day.* **2** keep at work; manage: *operate an elevator. The company operates three factories.* **3** produce an effect; work; act: *Several causes operated to bring on the war.* **4** produce a desired effect: *The medicine operated quickly.* **5** do something to the body, usually with instruments, to improve health: *The doctor operated on the injured man, removing his damaged*

lung. verb, **op e rat ed, op e rat ing.**

op e ra tion (op′ə rā′shən), **1** working: *The operation of an airline needs many people.* **2** the way a thing works: *The operation of this machine is simple.* **3** doing; activity: *the operation of brushing one's teeth.* **4** something done to the body, usually with instruments, to improve health: *Taking out the tonsils is a common operation.* **5** movement of soldiers, ships, or supplies: *military and naval operations. noun.*

in operation, in action or in use: *The motor is now in operation.*

op e ra tor (op′ə rā′tər), person who operates: *a telegraph or telephone operator, the operators of a mine or railroad. noun.*

op e ret ta (op′ə ret′ə), a short, amusing opera with some spoken parts. *noun.*

o pin ion (ə pin′yən), **1** what one thinks; belief not so strong as knowledge; judgment: *I try to learn the facts and form my own opinions.* **2** judgment of worth; impression: *I have a good opinion of her.* **3** a formal judgment by an expert; professional advice: *He wanted the doctor's opinion about the cause of his headache. noun.*

o pi um (ō′pē əm), a powerful narcotic drug that causes sleep and eases pain. Opium is made from a kind of poppy. *noun.*

o pos sum (ə pos′əm), a small animal that lives in trees and carries its young in a pouch. When it is caught, it pretends to be dead. The opossum is common in the southern part of the United States. An opossum is often called a possum. See picture. *noun, plural* **o pos sums** or **o pos sum.**

op po nent (ə pō′nənt), person who is on the other side in a fight, game, or discussion; person fighting, struggling, or speaking against another: *She defeated her opponent in the election. noun.*

op por tu ni ty (op′ər tü′nə tē *or* op′ər tyü′nə tē), a good chance; favorable time; convenient occasion: *I had an opportunity to earn some money baby-sitting. I have had no opportunity to give him your message. noun, plural* **op por tu ni ties.**

op pose (ə pōz′), **1** be against; be in the way of; act, fight, or struggle against; try to hinder; resist: *Many people opposed building a new highway because of the cost.* **2** put in contrast: *Night is opposed to day. Love is opposed to hate. verb,* **op posed, op pos ing.**

op po site (op′ə zit), **1** placed against; as different in direction as can be; face to face; back to back: *The house straight across the street is opposite to ours.* **2** as different as can be; just contrary: *North and south are opposite directions. Sour is opposite to sweet.* **3** thing or person as different as can be: *Night is the opposite of day. A saint is the opposite of a sinner.* 1,2 *adjective,* 3 *noun.*

op po si tion (op′ə zish′ən), **1** action against; resistance: *There was some opposition to the workers' request for higher wages.* **2** contrast: *His views are in opposition to mine.* **3 Opposition,** a political party opposed to the party which is in power. *noun.*

op press (ə pres′), **1** govern harshly; keep down

unjustly or by cruelty: *The people were oppressed by the invaders.* **2** weigh down; lie heavily on; burden: *A sense of trouble ahead oppressed her spirits. verb.*

op pres sion (ə presh′ən), **1** oppressing; burdening: *The oppression of the people by the invaders caused much suffering.* **2** being oppressed or burdened: *They fought against oppression.* **3** cruel or unjust treatment. **4** a heavy, weary feeling. *noun.*

op pres sive (ə pres′iv), **1** hard to bear; burdensome: *The great heat was oppressive.* **2** harsh; severe; unjust: *Oppressive measures were taken to crush the rebellion. adjective.*

op ti cal (op′tə kəl), **1** of the eye or the sense of sight; visual: *an optical illusion. Being nearsighted is an optical defect.* **2** made to assist sight: *Telescopes and microscopes are optical instruments. adjective.*

op ti mis tic (op′tə mis′tik), **1** inclined to look on the bright side of things. **2** hoping for the best: *I am optimistic about the chance of good weather tomorrow. adjective.*

or (ôr), **1** The word *or* is used to suggest a choice. It connects words, and sometimes groups of words, of equal importance in a sentence. *You can go or stay. Is it sweet or sour?* **2** *Or* may state the only choice left: *Either eat this or go hungry.* **3** *Or* may state what will happen if the first does not happen: *Hurry, or you will be late.* **4** *Or* may explain what goes before or that two things are the same: *an igloo or Eskimo snow house. We had orchestra, or main floor, seats. conjunction.*

-or, suffix meaning person or thing that ___s: Act*or* means a *person that acts.* Generat*or* means a *thing that generates.*

o ral (ôr′əl), **1** spoken; using speech: *An oral agreement is not enough; we must have a written promise.* **2** of the mouth: *The oral opening in an earthworm is small. adjective.*

o ral ly (ôr′ə lē), **1** by spoken words. **2** by the mouth. *adverb.*

o range (ôr′inj), **1** the round, reddish-yellow, juicy fruit of a tree grown in warm climates. Oranges are good to eat. **2** reddish yellow. **1** *noun,* **2** *adjective.*

o range ade (ôr′inj ād′), drink made of orange juice, sugar, and water. *noun.*

o rang-ou tang (ô rang′ủ tang′), orangutan. *noun.*

o rang u tan (ô rang′ủ tan′), a large ape of the forests of islands off southeast Asia, having very long arms and long, reddish-brown hair. It lives mostly in trees and eats fruits and leaves. See picture. *noun.* [*Orangutan* comes from Malay words meaning "man of the woods."]

o ra tion (ô rā′shən), a formal public speech delivered on a special occasion. *noun.*

o ra tor (ôr′ə tər), **1** person who makes an oration. **2** person who can speak very well in public. *noun.*

o ra to ry (ôr′ə tôr′ē), **1** skill in public speaking; fine speaking. **2** art of public speaking. *noun.*

orb (ôrb), **1** sphere; globe. **2** sun, moon, planet, or star. *noun.*

or bit (ôr′bit), **1** path of the earth or any one of the planets about the sun. **2** path of any heavenly

body about another heavenly body. **3** path of an artificial satellite around the earth. **4** travel around the earth or some other heavenly body in an orbit: *Some artificial satellites can orbit the earth in less than an hour.* **1-3** *noun,* **4** *verb.*

or chard (ôr′chərd), **1** piece of ground on which fruit trees are grown. **2** the trees in an orchard: *The orchard should bear a good crop this year. noun.*

or ches tra (ôr′kə strə), **1** the musicians playing at a concert, an opera, or a play. **2** the violins, cellos, horns, and other instruments played together by the musicians in an orchestra. **3** the part of a theater just in front of the stage, where the musicians sit to play. **4** the main floor of a theater, especially the part near the front: *Buy two seats in the orchestra. noun.*

opossum
about 2½ feet
(75 centimeters)
long with the tail

orangutan
about 4½ feet
(1½ meters) tall

or ches tral (ôr kes′trəl), of an orchestra; composed for or performed by an orchestra. *adjective.*

or chid (ôr′kid), **1** plant with flowers that often have unusual shapes and colors. See picture. **2** light purple. **1** *noun,* **2** *adjective.*

or dain (ôr dān′), **1** order; decide; pass as a law: *The law ordains that all citizens shall have equal rights.* **2** officially appoint or consecrate as a minister in a Christian church. *verb.*

or deal (ôr dēl′), severe test or experience: *I dreaded the ordeal of going to the dentist. noun.*

or der (ôr′dər), **1** the way one thing follows another: *in order of size, in alphabetical order, copy them in order.* **2** condition in which every part or piece is in its right place: *put a room in order.* **3** put in proper condition; arrange: *order one's affairs.* **4** condition; state: *My affairs are in good order.* **5** way the world works; way things happen: *the order of nature.* **6** state or condition of things in which the law is obeyed and there is no trouble: *keep order. Order was established after the riot.* **7** command; telling what to do: *Our parents expect us to obey their orders.* **8** tell what to do; command; bid; give an order: *The teacher ordered the class to sit down.* **9** give orders or directions: *Please order dinner for me.* **10** paper saying that money is to be given or paid, or something handed over: *a postal money order.* **11** a spoken or written request for goods that one wants to buy or receive: *I gave the grocer an order for two dozen eggs, a loaf of bread, and two cans of tomatoes.* **12** goods so requested: *When will you be able to deliver our order?* **13** give (a store) an order for: *We need to order milk, eggs, and bread from the grocer.* **14** kind or sort: *have ability of a high order.* **15** society of monks, friars, or nuns: *the order of Saint Francis.* **1,2,4-7,10-12,14,15** *noun,* **3,8,9,13** *verb.*

by order, according to an order given by the proper person: *The bank was closed by order of the governor.*

in order, 1 in the right arrangement or condition: *Take the lowest first, then without stop the rest in order to the top.* **2** working right: *Everything is set in order for the voyage.*

in order to, as a means to; with a view to; for the purpose of: *She worked hard in order to win the prize.*

out of order, 1 in the wrong arrangement or condition: *He listed the states alphabetically, but California was out of order.* **2** not working right: *My watch is out of order.*

ordered pair, (in mathematics) any two numbers written in a special order with one first and the other second. (2,5) is an ordered pair.

or der ly (ôr′dər lē), **1** in order; with regular arrangement, method, or system: *an orderly arrangement of dishes on shelves; an orderly mind.* **2** keeping order; well-behaved or regulated: *an orderly class.* **3** soldier who attends a superior officer to carry orders. **4** a hospital attendant who keeps things clean and in order. **1,2** *adjective,* **3,4** *noun, plural* **or der lies.**

or di nance (ôrd′n əns), rule or law made by authority; decree: *Some cities have ordinances forbidding the use of soft coal. noun.*

or di nar i ly (ôrd′n er′ə lē), commonly; usually; normally: *We ordinarily go to the movies on Saturday. adverb.*

or di nar y (ôrd′n er′ē), **1** usual; common; normal: *My ordinary lunch is soup, a sandwich, and milk.* **2** somewhat below the average: *The speaker was ordinary and tiresome. adjective.*

out of the ordinary, unusual; not regular: *Such a long delay is out of the ordinary.*

ord nance (ôrd′nəns), **1** cannon; artillery. **2** military weapons of all kinds. *noun.*

ore (ôr), mineral or rock containing enough of a metal or metals to make mining it profitable: *Gold ore was discovered in California in 1848. noun.*

O re gon (ôr′ə gon *or* ôr′ə gən), one of the Pacific states of the United States. *noun.* [*Oregon* probably got its name from the Oregon River, a name once given to the Columbia River.]

or gan (ôr′gən), **1** a musical instrument that has pipes of different lengths and often several sets of keys. The tones are produced by air being blown through the pipes by a bellows. **2** a similar instrument with one or more sets of keys but without pipes. The tones are produced by electrical devices. **3** any part of an animal or plant fitted to do certain things in life. The eyes, ears, stomach, heart, and lungs are organs of the body. Stamens and pistils are organs of flowers. **4** means of action; instrument: *A court is an organ of government.* **5** newspaper or magazine that speaks for and gives the views of a political party or some other organization. *noun.*

or gan ic (ôr gan′ik), **1** of, having to do with, or gotten from plants or animals. Decaying grass and animal manure are organic fertilizers. **2** grown by using decaying plant and animal matter instead of artificial fertilizers: *organic foods. adjective.*

or gan ism (ôr′gə niz′əm), **1** a living body having organs; an individual animal or plant. **2** whole made up of related parts that work together. Human society may be spoken of as a social organism. *noun.*

or gan ist (ôr′gə nist), person who plays an organ. *noun.*

or gan i za tion (ôr′gə nə zā′shən), **1** group of persons united for some purpose. Churches, clubs, and political parties are organizations. **2** grouping and arranging parts to form a whole; organizing: *The organization of a big picnic takes time and thought.* **3** way in which a thing's parts are arranged to work together: *The organization of the human body is very complicated. noun.*

or gan ize (ôr′gə nīz), **1** put into working order; get together and arrange: *Let's organize a volleyball team.* **2** combine in a company, political party, or labor union: *organize the truckers. verb,* **or gan ized, or gan iz ing.**

o ri ent (ôr′ē ənt *for 1 and 2;* ôr′ē ent *for 3-5*), **1** the east. **2 the Orient,** the East; eastern countries. China and Japan are important nations of the

orchid (definition 1)

ornate—The dancers wore ornate headdresses.

a hat	i it	oi oil	ch child	
ā age	ī ice	ou out	ng long	a in about
ä far	o hot	u cup	sh she	e in taken
e let	ō open	u̇ put	th thin	ə = i in pencil
ē equal	ô order	ü rule	ŦH then	o in lemon
ėr term			zh measure	u in circus

Orient. **3** place so that it faces in any indicated direction: *The building is oriented north and south.* **4** adjust to a new situation; bring into the right relationship to surroundings: *I had to orient myself on coming to a new city. The college has a program to orient freshman students.* 1,2 *noun,* 3,4 *verb.* [*Orient* comes from a Latin word meaning "the place of the rising sun" or "the East."]

O ri en tal (ôr/ē en/tl), **1** Eastern; of the Orient: *Oriental customs.* **2** person born or living in the East, especially the Far East. The Chinese and Japanese are Orientals. **3** person whose ancestors came from the Far East. 1 *adjective,* 2,3 *noun.*

o ri gin (ôr/ə jin), **1** beginning; starting point; thing from which anything comes: *the origin of the quarrel, the origin of a disease.* **2** parentage; birth: *She is of Mexican origin. noun.*

o rig i nal (ə rij/ə nəl), **1** belonging to the beginning; first; earliest: *The Dutch were the original settlers of New York. The hat has been marked down from its original price.* **2** new; fresh; novel: *It is hard to plan original games for a party.* **3** inventive; able to do, make, or think something new: *Edison had an original mind.* **4** not copied, imitated, or translated from something else: *She wrote an original poem.* **5** thing from which another is copied, imitated, or translated: *The original of this picture is in Rome.* 1-4 *adjective,* 5 *noun.*

o rig i nal i ty (ə rij/ə nal/ə tē), **1** ability to do, make, or think up something new. **2** freshness; novelty. *noun.*

o rig i nal ly (ə rij/ə nə lē), **1** by origin: *a plant originally African.* **2** at first; in the first place: *a house originally small.* **3** in an original manner: *We want this room decorated originally. adverb.*

o rig i nate (ə rij/ə nāt), **1** cause to be; invent: *originate a new style of painting.* **2** come into being; begin; arise: *Where did that story originate? verb,* **o rig i nat ed, o rig i nat ing.**

o ri ole (ôr/ē ōl), **1** any of several American birds having yellow-and-black or orange-and-black feathers. **2** any of several European birds having yellow-and-black feathers. *noun.*

or na ment (ôr/nə mənt *for 1;* ôr/nə ment *for 2*), **1** something pretty; something to add beauty: *Lace, jewels, vases, and statues are ornaments.* **2** add beauty to; make more pleasing or attractive; decorate. 1 *noun,* 2 *verb.*

or na men tal (ôr/nə men/tl), **1** for ornament; used as an ornament: *ornamental plants.* **2** decorative: *ornamental designs in wallpaper. adjective.*

or nate (ôr nāt/), much adorned; much ornamented. See picture. *adjective.*

or ner y (ôr/nər ē), mean in disposition: *an ornery person. adjective,* **or ner i er, or ner i est.**

ostrich—up to 8 feet
(2½ meters) tall

otter (definition 1)—up to 4 feet (1 meter) long with the tail

WE MADE ALL OF THESE TODAY!

YOUR OUTPUT ISN'T VERY GOOD, BUT YOUR POTS OUTDO EVERYONE'S IN IMAGINATION!

IT TOOK ME A WEEK TO DO THE TEAPOT.

or phan (ôr′fən), **1** child whose parents are dead. **2** of or for such children: *an orphan asylum.* **3** without a father or mother or both. **4** make an orphan of: *The war orphaned the child.* **1** *noun,* **2,3** *adjective,* **4** *verb.*

or phan age (ôr′fə nij), home for orphans. *noun.*

or tho don tist (ôr′thə don′tist), dentist whose work is straightening teeth. *noun.*

or tho dox (ôr′thə doks), **1** generally accepted, especially in religion: *orthodox beliefs.* **2** having generally accepted views or opinions, especially in religion. **3** approved by convention; usual; customary. *adjective.*

os ten ta tious (os′ten tā′shəs), **1** done for display; intended to attract notice: *ostentatious jewels.* **2** showing off; liking to attract notice. *adjective.*

os trich (ôs′trich), a large bird of Africa that can run fast but cannot fly. Ostriches have two toes and are the largest of existing birds. They have large feathers or plumes which were used for decorating hats and fans. See picture. *noun, plural* **os trich es.**

oth er (uᴛн′ər), **1** remaining: *I am home, but the other members of the family are away.* **2** additional or further: *I have no other place to go.* **3** not the same as one or more already mentioned: *Come some other day.* **4** different: *Do you have a color other than red?* **5** the other one; not the same ones: *Each praises the other.* **6** other person or thing: *There are others to consider.* **7** in any different way; otherwise: *I could not do other than I did.* **1-4** *adjective,* **5,6** *pronoun,* **7** *adverb.*

every other, every second; alternate: *We have spelling every other day.*

the other day or **the other night,** recently.

oth er wise (uᴛн′ər wīz′), **1** in a different way; differently: *I could not act otherwise.* **2** different; in a different condition: *It might have been otherwise.* **3** in other ways: *It is windy, but otherwise a nice day.* **4** or else; if not: *Come at once; otherwise you will be too late.* **1,3** *adverb,* **2** *adjective,* **4** *conjunction.*

ot ter (ot′ər), **1** an animal somewhat like a weasel that has webbed toes with claws and is a good swimmer. Otters live near water and often swim or catch fish. See picture. **2** its short, thick, glossy fur. *noun, plural* **ot ters** or **ot ter.**

ouch (ouch), exclamation expressing sudden pain. *interjection.*

ought (ôt), **1** have a duty; be obliged: *You ought to obey your parents.* **2** be right or suitable: *Cruelty ought not to be allowed.* **3** be wise: *I ought to go before it rains.* **4** be expected: *At your age you ought to know better.* **5** be very likely: *It ought to be a fine day tomorrow. verb.*

ounce (ouns), **1** unit of weight, ¹/₁₆ of a pound in ordinary weight, and ¹/₁₂ of a pound in troy weight. **2** a unit for measuring liquids; fluid ounce. 16 ounces = 1 pint. **3** a little bit; very small amount: *An ounce of prevention is worth a pound of cure. noun.*

our (our), of us; belonging to us: *Our classes were*

interesting. We need our coats now. adjective.

ours (ourz), **1** of us; belonging to us: *This garden is ours.* **2** the one or ones belonging to us: *Ours is a large house. I like ours better than yours. pronoun.*

our selves (our selvz′), **1** *Ourselves* is used to make a statement stronger. *We ourselves will do the work.* **2** *Ourselves* is used instead of *we* or *us* in cases like: *We cook for ourselves. We help ourselves.* **3** us: *We cannot see ourselves as others see us. pronoun plural.*

-ous, suffix meaning full of _____: *Joyous* means *full of joy.*

oust (oust), force out; drive out: *The sparrows have ousted the bluebirds from their nest. verb.*

out (out), **1** away; forth: *The water will rush out. Spread the rug out.* **2** not in or at a usual place, as one's home or place of work: *My mother is out just now.* **3** (in baseball) no longer at bat or on base: *The outfielder caught the fly and the batter was out.* **4** not in use, action, control, or fashion: *The fire is out. The election results show that our present mayor is out. That style is out this year.* **5** through to the outside: *She went out the door.* **6** into the open; made public; made known; into being; so as to be seen: *The secret is out now. The new book will be out next month. Many flowers were coming out.* **7** to or at an end: *Let them fight it out.* **8** be made known; come out: *The facts will out.* **9** aloud; plainly: *Speak out so that all can hear.* **10** completely: *fit out a boat, clean out a closet.* **11** to others: *let out rooms. Give out the books.* **12** from a number; from among others: *Pick out an apple for me. She picked out a new coat.* 1,2,6,7,9-12 *adverb,* 3,4 *adjective,* 5 *preposition,* 8 *verb.*

out of, 1 from within: *He came out of the house.* **2** not within: *He is out of town.* **3** away from; beyond: *The airplane was soon out of sight. This style went out of fashion.* **4** without: *I am out of work. We are out of coffee.* **5** from: *My dress is made out of silk.* **6** from among: *three out of four people. We picked our puppy out of that litter.* **7** because of: *I went only out of curiosity.*

out-and-out (out′n out′), thorough; complete: *an out-and-out defeat. adjective.*

out board (out′bôrd′), outside the hull of a ship or boat. *adjective.*

outboard motor, a small motor attached to the stern of a boat or canoe.

out break (out′brāk′), **1** breaking out: *an outbreak of flu, outbreaks of anger.* **2** riot; public disturbance: *The outbreak ended when the police arrived. noun.*

out build ing (out′bil′ding), shed or building built against or near a main building: *Barns are outbuildings on a farm. noun.*

out burst (out′bėrst′), bursting forth: *an outburst of laughter, an outburst of anger. noun.*

out cast (out′kast′), person or animal cast out from home and friends: *Criminals are outcasts of society. That kitten was just a little outcast when we found it. noun.*

out come (out′kum′), result; consequence: *the outcome of a race. noun.*

a hat	i it	oi oil	ch child	a in about
ā age	ī ice	ou out	ng long	e in taken
ä far	o hot	u cup	sh she	ə = i in pencil
e let	ō open	u̇ put	th thin	o in lemon
ē equal	ô order	ü rule	ŦH then	u in circus
ėr term			zh measure	

out cry (out′krī′), **1** crying out; sudden cry or scream. **2** a strong expression of disapproval; protest: *The raising of taxes caused a public outcry. noun, plural* **out cries.**

out dat ed (out dā′tid), out-of-date; old-fashioned. *adjective.*

out did (out did′). See **outdo.** *She outdid all the other diving contestants. verb.*

out dis tance (out dis′təns), leave behind: *The winner outdistanced all the other runners in the race. verb,* **out dis tanced, out dis tanc ing.**

out do (out dü′), do more or better than; surpass: *She's such a good tennis player that I know I won't be able to outdo her.* See picture. *verb,* **out did, out done, out do ing.**

out done (out dun′). See **outdo.** *He has outdone his previous record for the race. verb.*

out door (out′dôr′), done, used, or living outdoors: *outdoor games. adjective.*

out doors (out′dôrz′), **1** out in the open air; not indoors or in the house: *Let's go outdoors to play.* **2** the world outside of houses; the open air: *We must protect the wildlife of the great outdoors.* 1 *adverb,* 2 *noun.*

out er (ou′tər), farther out; on the outside: *Shingles are used as an outer covering for many roofs. adjective.*

out er most (ou′tər mōst), farthest out. *adjective.*

outer space, 1 space beyond the earth's atmosphere: *The moon is in outer space.* **2** space beyond the solar system: *There are other suns in outer space.*

out field (out′fēld′), **1** the part of the baseball field beyond the diamond or infield. **2** the three players in the outfield. *noun.*

out field er (out′fēl′dər), a baseball player who plays in the outfield. *noun.*

out fit (out′fit), **1** all the articles necessary for any undertaking or purpose: *the outfit for a camping trip, a skiing outfit.* **2** furnish with everything necessary for any purpose; equip: *She outfitted herself for camp.* **3** group working together, such as a group of soldiers: *His father and mine were in the same outfit during the war.* 1,3 *noun,* 2 *verb,* **out fit ted, out fit ting.**

out go ing (out′gō′ing), **1** outward bound; departing: *outgoing steamships.* **2** friendly and helpful to others: *a very outgoing person. adjective.*

out grew (out grü′). See **outgrow.** *He used to stutter, but he outgrew it. verb.*

out grow (out grō′), **1** grow too large for: *outgrow one's clothes.* **2** grow beyond or away from; get rid of by growing older: *outgrow early friends, outgrow a babyish habit.* **3** grow faster or taller than: *By the time he was ten, he had outgrown his older brother. verb,* **out grew, out grown, out grow ing.**

out grown (out grōn´). See **outgrow**. *My last year's clothes are now outgrown.* verb.

out growth (out´grōth´), a natural development, product, or result: *This big store is an outgrowth of a little shop.* noun.

out ing (ou´ting), a short pleasure trip; walk or drive; holiday spent outdoors away from home: *On Sunday the family went on an outing to the beach.* noun.

out land ish (out lan´dish), not familiar; strange or ridiculous; odd: *an outlandish hat.* adjective.

out last (out last´), last longer than. verb.

out law (out´lô´), **1** a lawless person; criminal. **2** make or declare unlawful: *A group of nations agreed to outlaw war.* 1 noun, 2 verb.

out lay (out´lā´), **1** expense; laying out money; spending: *a large outlay for clothing.* **2** the amount spent: *an outlay of eleven dollars.* noun.

out let (out´let), **1** means or place of letting out or getting out; a way out; opening; exit: *the outlet of a lake, an outlet for one's energies.* **2** place in a wall for inserting an electric plug. noun.

out line (out´līn´), **1** line that shows the shape of an object: *The outline of Italy suggests a boot. We saw the outlines of the mountains against the evening sky.* **2** drawing or style of drawing that gives only outer lines: *Make an outline of the scene before you paint it.* **3** draw the outer line of anything: *Outline a map of America.* **4** a brief plan; rough draft: *Make an outline before trying to write a composition. The teacher gave a brief outline of the work planned for the term.* **5** give a plan of; sketch: *She outlined their trip abroad.* 1,2,4 noun, 3,5 verb, **out lined, out lin ing.**

out live (out liv´), live longer than; last longer than; survive; outlast: *She outlived her older sister. The idea was good once, but it has outlived its usefulness.* verb, **out lived, out liv ing.**

out look (out´lùk´), **1** what one sees on looking out; view: *The room has a pleasant outlook.* **2** what seems likely to happen; prospect: *The outlook for our picnic is bad, for it looks as if it's going to rain.* **3** way of thinking about things; attitude of mind; point of view: *a gloomy outlook on life.* noun.

out ly ing (out´lī´ing), lying outside the boundary; far from the center; remote: *We live in an outlying suburb of the city.* adjective.

out num ber (out num´bər), be more than; exceed in number: *They outnumbered us three to one.* verb.

out-of-date (out´əv dāt´), old-fashioned; not in present use: *A horse and buggy is an out-of-date means of traveling.* adjective.

out-of-door (out´əv dôr´), outdoor. adjective.

out-of-doors (out´əv dôrz´), **1** outdoor. **2** outdoors. 1 adjective, 2 noun, adverb.

out post (out´pōst´), **1** guard, or small number of soldiers, placed at some distance from an army or camp, to prevent surprise. **2** place where they are stationed. noun.

out put (out´pùt´), **1** amount produced; product or yield: *the daily output of automobiles.* **2** putting forth: *It will take a great output of energy for us to*

do such a difficult job well. noun.

out rage (out´rāj), **1** act showing no regard for the rights or feelings of others; very offensive act; shameful act of violence; offense; insult: *Setting the house on fire was an outrage.* **2** offend greatly; insult; do violence to: *The British government outraged the colonists by taxing them unfairly.* 1 noun, 2 verb, **out raged, out rag ing.**

out ra geous (out rā´jəs), shocking; very bad or insulting: *outrageous language.* adjective.

out ran (out ran´). See **outrun**. *He outran me easily.* verb.

out rig ger (out´rig´ər), framework ending in a float, extending outward from the side of a light boat or canoe to keep it from turning over. See picture. noun.

out right (out´rīt´), **1** altogether; entirely; not gradually: *We paid for our car outright.* **2** openly; without restraint: *We laughed outright.* **3** complete; thorough: *an outright criminal, an outright lie.* **4** downright; straightforward; direct: *an outright refusal.* 1,2 adverb, 3,4 adjective.

out run (out run´), **1** run faster than: *She can outrun her older sister.* **2** leave behind; run beyond; pass the limits of: *This month's expenses have outrun our budget.* verb, **out ran, out run, out run ning.**

out side (out´sīd´), **1** side or surface that is out; outer part: *polish the outside of a car, the outside of a house.* **2** on the outside; of or nearer the outside: *the outside leaves.* **3** on or to the outside; outdoors: *Run outside and play.* **4** space that is beyond or not inside: *Wait on the outside.* **5** out of; beyond the limits of: *Stay outside the house. That is outside my plans.* **6** highest; largest: *an outside estimate of the cost.* 1,4 noun, 2,6 adjective, 3 adverb, 5 preposition. **at the outside,** at the utmost limit: *I can do it in a week, at the outside.*

out sid er (out´sī´dər), person not belonging to a particular group, set, company, party, or district. noun.

out skirts (out´skèrts´), the outer parts or edges of a town or district; outlying parts: *They have a farm on the outskirts of town.* noun plural.

out spo ken (out´spō´kən), frank; not reserved: *an outspoken person, an outspoken criticism. Your own family is likely to be outspoken in its remarks about you.* adjective.

out spread (out´spred´ for 1; out spred´ for 2), **1** spread out; extended: *an eagle with outspread wings.* **2** spread out; extend. 1 adjective, 2 verb, **out spread, out spread ing.**

out stand ing (out stan´ding), **1** standing out from others; well-known; important: *an outstanding student.* **2** unpaid: *outstanding debts.* adjective.

out stretched (out´strecht´), stretched out; extended: *He welcomed his old friend with outstretched arms.* adjective.

out ward (out´wərd), **1** going toward the outside; turned toward the outside: *an outward motion. She gave one outward glance.* **2** toward the outside; away: *A porch extends outward from the house.* **3** outer: *To all outward appearances, it looks as if*

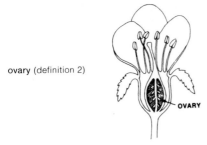

ovary (definition 2)

outrigger on a sailboat

oval (definitions 1, 2, and 3)

a hat	i it	oi oil	ch child	a in about
ā age	ī ice	ou out	ng long	e in taken
ä far	o hot	u cup	sh she	i in pencil
e let	ō open	ù put	th thin	ə = o in lemon
ē equal	ô order	ü rule	ŦH then	u in circus
ėr term			zh measure	

we'll have a good day. **4** on the outside: *She turned the coat with the lining outward.* **5** that can be seen; plain to see; on the surface: *outward behavior.* 1,3,5 *adjective,* 2,4 *adverb.*

out ward ly (out′wərd lē), **1** on the outside or outer surface. **2** in appearance: *Though frightened, the boy remained outwardly calm. adverb.*

out wards (out′wərdz), outward. *adverb.*

out weigh (out wā′), **1** weigh more than: *He outweighs me by ten pounds.* **2** exceed in value, importance, or influence: *The advantages of the plan outweigh its disadvantages. verb.*

out wit (out wit′), get the better of; be too clever for: *She usually outwits me and wins at checkers. verb,* **out wit ted, out wit ting.**

out worn (out′wôrn′), **1** worn out: *outworn clothes.* **2** out-of-date; outgrown: *outworn ideas. adjective.*

o val (ō′vəl). See picture. **1** shaped like an egg. **2** shaped like an ellipse. **3** something having an oval shape. 1,2 *adjective,* 3 *noun.*

o var y (ō′vər ē), **1** part of a female animal in which eggs are produced. **2** part of a plant enclosing the young seeds. See picture. *noun, plural* **o var ies.**

ov en (uv′ən), **1** an enclosed space usually in a stove, for baking, roasting, and sometimes broiling food. **2** a small furnace for heating or drying pottery. *noun.*

o ver (ō′vər), **1** above: *the sky over our heads. We have a captain over us.* **2** above and to the other side of; across: *leap over a wall. Can you climb over that hill?* **3** across a space or distance: *Come over to my house.* **4** down; out and down (from an edge or from an upright position): *If you go too near the edge, you may fall over.* **5** out and down from; down from the edge of: *The ball rolled over the side of the porch.* **6** about or upon, so as to cover: *Spread the canvas over the new cement.* **7** at all or various places on; on: *A smile came over her face. Farms were scattered over the valley.* **8** here and there on or in; round about; all through: *travel over the United States. I went over my notes before the test.* **9** from beginning to end; at some length: *read a newspaper over.* **10** again: *I had to write my paper over.* **11** during: *We were out of town over the weekend.* **12** at an end: *The play is over.* **13** about; concerning: *He is troubled over his health. I was upset over our argument.* **14** more than; beyond: *It cost over ten dollars.* **15** too; more; besides: *I ate two apples and had one left over.* **16** the other side up; upside down: *Turn over a page.* 1,2,5-8,11,13,14 *preposition,* 1,3,4,9,10,15,16 *adverb,* 12 *adjective.*

over again, once more: *Let's do that over again.*

over and above, besides; in addition to: *He had repairs to pay for over and above the cost of the car.*

over and over, again and again: *Practice the song over and over until you do it right.*

o ver alls (ō′vər ôlz′), loose trousers with a piece covering the chest. Overalls are usually worn over clothes to keep them clean. *noun plural.*

o ver arm (ō′vər ärm′), with the arm raised above the shoulder; overhand. *adjective.*

o ver ate (ō′vər āt′). See **overeat.** *I have a stomach ache because I overate. verb.*

o ver bear ing (ō′vər ber′ing or ō′vər bar′ing), inclined to dictate; forcing others to one's own will; masterful; domineering: *We found it hard to like our overbearing new neighbors. adjective.*

o ver board (ō′vər bôrd′), from a ship or boat into the water: *to fall overboard. adverb.*

o ver bur den (ō′vər bėrd′n), load with too great a burden. *verb.*

o ver came (ō′vər kām′). See **overcome.** *I finally overcame my fear. verb.*

o ver cast (ō′vər kast′), **1** cloudy; dark; gloomy: *The sky was overcast before the storm.* **2** cover (the sky or sun) with clouds or darkness. 1 *adjective,* 2 *verb,* **o ver cast, o ver cast ing.**

o ver charge (ō′vər chärj′), charge too high a price. *verb,* **o ver charged, o ver charg ing.**

o ver coat (ō′vər kōt′), a heavy coat worn over the regular clothing for warmth in cold weather. *noun.*

o ver come (ō′vər kum′), **1** get the better of; win the victory over; conquer; defeat: *overcome an enemy, overcome difficulties, overcome a fault.* **2** make weak or helpless: *The child was overcome by weariness and slept. verb,* **o ver came, o ver come, o ver com ing.**

o ver crowd (ō′vər kroud′), crowd too much; put in too much or too many. *verb.*

o ver did (ō′vər did′). See **overdo.** *verb.*

o ver do (ō′vər dü′), **1** do too much: *When getting over an illness you mustn't overdo.* **2** exaggerate: *The funny scenes in the play were overdone.* **3** cook too much: *The vegetables were overdone. verb,* **o ver did, o ver done, o ver do ing.**

o ver done (ō′vər dun′). See **overdo.** *verb.*

o ver dose (ō′vər dōs′), too big a dose. *noun.*

o ver dress (ō′vər dres′), wear clothes that are too fancy or formal. *verb.*

o ver due (ō′vər dü′ or ō′vər dyü′), more than due; due some time ago but not yet arrived or paid: *The train is overdue. This bill is overdue. adjective.*

o ver eat (ō′vər ēt′), eat too much. *verb,* **o ver ate, o ver eat en, o ver eat ing.**

o ver eat en (ō′vər ēt′n). See **overeat.** *Nearly everyone has overeaten at the picnic. verb.*

o ver flow (ō′vər flō′ for 1-6; ō′vər flō′ for 7), **1** flow over the bounds: *Rivers often overflow in the spring.* **2** cover; flood: *The river overflowed my garden.* **3** have the contents flowing over: *My cup is overflowing.* **4** flow over the top of: *Stop! The milk is overflowing the cup.* **5** extend out beyond; be too many for: *The crowd overflowed the little parlor and filled the hall.* **6** be very abundant: *an overflowing harvest, overflowing kindness.* **7** overflowing; excess: *The overflow from the glass ran onto the*

table. 1-6 *verb,* **o ver flowed, o ver flown** (ō′vər flōn′), **o ver flow ing;** 7 *noun.*

o ver grew (ō′vər grü′). See **overgrow.** *Vines overgrew the wall. verb.*

o ver grow (ō′vər grō′), **1** grow over: *The wall is overgrown with vines.* **2** grow too fast; become too big. *verb,* **o ver grew, o ver grown, o ver grow ing.**

o ver grown (ō′vər grōn′), **1** grown too big: *an overgrown child.* **2** See **overgrow.** *The vines have overgrown the wall.* 1 *adjective,* 2 *verb.*

o ver hand (ō′vər hand′), **1** with the hand raised above the shoulder: *an overhand throw, pitch overhand.* **2** with the knuckles upward. *adjective, adverb.*

o ver hang (ō′vər hang′ for 1; ō′vər hang′ for 2), **1** hang over; project over: *Trees overhang the street to form an arch of branches.* **2** something that projects: *The overhang of the roof shaded the flower bed beneath.* 1 *verb,* **o ver hung, o ver hang ing;** 2 *noun.*

o ver haul (ō′vər hôl′), **1** examine completely so as to make repairs or changes that are needed: *Once a year we overhaul our boat.* **2** gain upon; overtake: *An automobile can overhaul any horse. verb.*

o ver head (ō′vər hed′ for 1; ō′vər hed′ for 2 and 3), **1** over the head; on high; above: *the stars overhead.* **2** placed above; placed high up: *overhead wires.* **3** general expenses of running a business, such as rent, lighting, heating, taxes, and repairs. 1 *adverb,* 2 *adjective,* 3 *noun.*

o ver hear (ō′vər hir′), hear when one is not meant to hear: *They spoke so loud that I could not help overhearing what they said. verb,* **o ver heard, o ver hear ing.**

o ver heard (ō′vər hėrd′). See **overhear.** *I overheard what you told them. verb.*

o ver heat (ō′vər hēt′), heat too much: *My car got overheated when we drove through the mountains. verb.*

o ver hung (ō′vər hung′ for 1; ō′vər hung′ for 2), **1** hung from above: *an overhung door.* **2** See **overhang,** definition 1. *A big awning overhung the sidewalk.* 1 *adjective,* 2 *verb.*

o ver joy (ō′vər joi′), make very joyful. *verb.*

o ver joyed (ō′vər joid′), very joyful; filled with joy; delighted. *adjective.*

o ver laid (ō′vər lād′). See **overlay.** *The workmen overlaid the dome with gold. verb.*

o ver land (ō′vər land′), on land; by land: *travel overland from Maine to Texas, an overland route. adverb, adjective.*

o ver lap (ō′vər lap′), lap over; cover and extend beyond: *Shingles are laid to overlap each other. verb,* **o ver lapped, o ver lap ping.**

o ver lay (ō′vər lā′ for 1; ō′vər lā′ for 2), **1** put a coating over the surface of: *The dome is overlaid with gold.* **2** something laid over something else; covering; ornamental layer. 1 *verb,* **o ver laid, o ver lay ing;** 2 *noun.*

o ver load (ō′vər lōd′ for 1; ō′vər lōd′ for 2), **1** load too heavily: *overload a boat.* **2** too great a

load: *The overload of electric current blew the fuse.*
1 *verb,* 2 *noun.*

o ver look (ō′vər lùk′), 1 fail to see: *Here are some letters which you overlooked.* 2 pay no attention to; excuse: *I will overlook your bad behavior this time.* 3 have a view of from above; be higher than: *This high window overlooks half the city. verb.*

o ver lord (ō′vər lôrd′), person who is lord over another lord or other lords: *The duke was the overlord of the barons and knights. noun.*

o ver ly (ō′vər lē), excessively; too. *adverb.*

o ver night (ō′vər nīt′ *for 1;* ō′vər nīt′ *for 2 and 3*), 1 during the night: *stay overnight with friends.* 2 done or occurring during the night: *an overnight stop.* 3 for the night: *An overnight bag contains articles needed for one night's stay.* 1 *adverb,* 2,3 *adjective.*

o ver pass (ō′vər pas′), bridge over a road, railroad, or canal. *noun, plural* **o ver pass es.**

o ver pow er (ō′vər pou′ər), 1 overcome; master; overwhelm: *overpower an enemy. I was overpowered by the heat.* 2 be much greater or stronger than: *The wind brought a terrible smell which overpowered all others. Sudden anger overpowered every other feeling. verb.*

o ver ran (ō′vər ran′). See **overrun.** *verb.*

o ver rate (ō′vər rāt′), rate or estimate too highly: *I overrated my strength and had to ask for help. verb,* **o ver rat ed, o ver rat ing.**

o ver rule (ō′vər rül′), 1 rule or decide against (a plea, argument, or objection); set aside: *The president overruled my plan.* 2 prevail over: *I was overruled by the majority. verb,* **o ver ruled, o ver rul ing.**

o ver run (ō′vər run′), 1 spread over and spoil or harm in some way: *Weeds had overrun the old garden.* 2 spread over: *Vines overran the wall.* 3 run or go beyond; exceed: *The speaker overran the time set for her. verb,* **o ver ran, o ver run, o ver run ning.**

o ver saw (ō′vər sô′). See **oversee.** *verb.*

o ver seas (ō′vər sēz′ *for 1;* ō′vər sēz′ *for 2 and 3*), 1 across the sea; beyond the sea; abroad: *travel overseas.* 2 done, used, or serving overseas: *overseas military service.* 3 of countries across the sea; foreign: *overseas trade.* 1 *adverb,* 2,3 *adjective.*

o ver see (ō′vər sē′), look after and direct (work or workers); superintend; manage: *oversee a factory. verb,* **o ver saw, o ver seen, o ver see ing.**

o ver seen (ō′vər sēn′). See **oversee.** *verb.*

o ver se er (ō′vər sē′ər), person who oversees others or their work. *noun.*

o ver shad ow (ō′vər shad′ō), 1 be more important than: *Preparations for the school play soon overshadowed other student activities.* 2 cast a shadow over: *Storm clouds suddenly overshadowed the valley. verb.*

o ver shoe (ō′vər shü′), a waterproof shoe or boot, often made of rubber, worn over another shoe to keep the foot dry and warm. *noun.*

o ver shoot (ō′vər shüt′), 1 to shoot over: *overshoot a target.* 2 go beyond or past: *overshoot a runway. verb,* **o ver shot, o ver shoot ing.**

a hat	i it	oi oil	ch child	a in about
ā age	ī ice	ou out	ng long	e in taken
ä far	o hot	u cup	sh she	ə = i in pencil
e let	ō open	ù put	th thin	o in lemon
ē equal	ô order	ü rule	₮H then	u in circus
ėr term			zh measure	

o ver shot (ō′vər shot′ *for 1;* ō′vər shot′ *for 2*), 1 driven by water flowing over from above: *an overshot water wheel.* 2 See **overshoot.** 1 *adjective,* 2 *verb.*

o ver sight (ō′vər sīt′), 1 failure to notice or think of something: *Through an oversight, the kitten got no supper last night.* 2 watchful care: *While children are at school they are under their teacher's oversight and direction. noun.*

o ver sleep (ō′vər slēp′), sleep beyond (a certain hour); sleep too long. *verb,* **o ver slept, o ver sleep ing.**

o ver slept (ō′vər slept′). See **oversleep.** *I overslept and missed the bus. verb.*

o ver spread (ō′vər spred′), spread over: *Ivy overspread the cottage. verb,* **o ver spread, o ver spread ing.**

o ver stay (ō′vər stā′), stay beyond the time of: *Don't overstay your welcome. verb.*

o ver step (ō′vər step′), go beyond; exceed: *I'm afraid I've overstepped the rules. verb,* **o ver stepped, o ver step ping.**

o ver take (ō′vər tāk′), 1 come up with: *The blue car overtook ours.* 2 come upon suddenly: *A storm had overtaken the children. verb,* **o ver took, o ver tak en, o ver tak ing.**

o ver tak en (ō′vər tā′kən). See **overtake.** *verb.*

o ver threw (ō′vər thrü′). See **overthrow.** *verb.*

o ver throw (ō′vər thrō′ *for 1 and 2;* ō′vər thrō′ *for 3*), 1 take away the power of; defeat: *The people overthrew the tyrant.* 2 overturn; upset; knock down. 3 defeat; upset: *the overthrow of the government.* 1,2 *verb,* **o ver threw, o ver thrown, o ver throw ing;** 3 *noun.*

o ver thrown (ō′vər thrōn′). See **overthrow.** *verb.*

o ver time (ō′vər tīm′), 1 extra time; time beyond the regular hours: *I was paid for the overtime I worked.* 2 beyond the regular hours: *They worked overtime.* 1 *noun,* 2 *adverb.*

o ver tone (ō′vər tōn′), a fainter and higher tone heard along with the main tone. *noun.*

o ver took (ō′vər tùk′). See **overtake.** *verb.*

o ver ture (ō′vər chər), 1 proposal; offer: *The enemy is making overtures for peace.* 2 a musical composition played by the orchestra as an introduction to an opera or other long musical composition. *noun.*

o ver turn (ō′vər tėrn′ *for 1-3;* ō′vər tėrn′ *for 4*), 1 turn upside down. 2 upset; fall down; fall over: *The boat overturned.* 3 make fall down; overthrow; defeat; destroy the power of: *The rebels overturned the government.* 4 overturning. 1-3 *verb,* 4 *noun.*

o ver weight (ō′vər wāt′), having too much weight: *I am a little overweight for my height. adjective.*

owl—about 2 feet (60 centimeters) tall

SCOUNDREL! VILLAIN! LIAR! CROOK!

overwhelm (definition 1)
He was **overwhelmed** by the fury of her attack.

o ver whelm (ō′vər hwelm′), **1** crush; overcome completely. See picture. **2** cover completely as a flood would: *A great wave overwhelmed the boat.* *verb.*

o ver work (ō′vər wèrk′ for 1; ō′vər wèrk′ for 2), **1** too much or too hard work: *exhausted from overwork.* **2** work too hard or too long. 1 *noun*, 2 *verb.*

owe (ō), **1** have to pay; be in debt to: *I owe the grocer a dollar.* **2** be in debt: *I still owe for my share of the expenses.* **3** be obliged or indebted for: *We owe a great deal to our parents.* *verb,* **owed, ow ing.**

ow ing (ō′ing), due; owed: *pay what is owing.* *adjective.*

owing to, on account of; because of: *Owing to the bad weather, we cancelled our trip.*

owl (oul), bird with a big head, big eyes, and a short, hooked beak. Owls hunt mice and small birds at night. Some kinds have tufts of feathers on their heads called "horns" or "ears." You can tell an owl by the hoot it makes. See picture. *noun.*

owl et (ou′lit), **1** a young owl. **2** a small owl. *noun.*

own (ōn), **1** have; possess: *I own many books.* **2** of oneself; belonging to oneself or itself: *This is my own book.* **3** admit; confess: *I own you are right. I own to being afraid.* 1,3 *verb,* 2 *adjective.*

come into one's own, 1 get what belongs to one: *His inheritance was held in trust; not until he was twenty-one would he come into his own.* **2** get the success or credit that one deserves: *At the end of her twenties, she came into her own as a sculptor.*

of one's own, belonging to oneself: *You have a good mind of your own.*

on one's own, not ruled or directed by someone else: *When a young man, he traveled about the world on his own.*

own up, confess fully: *own up to a crime.*

own er (ō′nər), one who owns: *Who is the owner of this dog? noun.*

own er ship (ō′nər ship), being an owner; the possessing (of something); right of possession: *She claimed ownership of the abandoned wagon.* *noun.*

ox (oks), **1** the full-grown male of domestic cattle that cannot father young and is used to pull loads or for beef. **2** any of a group of animals that chew their cud and have horns and hoofs. Cattle, buffaloes, and bison belong to this group. *noun, plural* **ox en.**

ox bow (oks′bō′), piece of wood shaped like a U that is placed under and around the neck of an ox, with the upper ends inserted in the bar of the yoke. *noun.*

ox cart (oks′kärt′), cart drawn by oxen. *noun.*

ox en (ok′sən), more than one ox. *noun plural.*

ox ford (ok′sfərd), kind of low shoe. *noun.* [The *oxford* was named for Oxford, a city in England.]

ox i dize (ok′sə dīz), combine with oxygen. When a substance burns or rusts, it oxidizes. *verb,* **ox i dized, ox i diz ing.**

ox y gen (ok′sə jən), a gas without color, taste, or odor that forms about one fifth of the air. Animals and plants cannot live without oxygen. Fire will not burn without oxygen. *noun.*

oxygen tent, a small tent that can be filled with oxygen and placed over the head and shoulders of a sick person who has difficulty breathing.

oys ter (oi′stər), shellfish with a rough, irregular shell in two halves. Oysters are much used as food. They are found in shallow water along seacoasts. Some kinds produce pearls inside them. *noun.*

oz., ounce. *plural* **oz.** or **ozs.**

o zone (ō′zōn), form of oxygen with a sharp smell, produced by electricity and present in the air especially after a thunderstorm. *noun.*

Pp

a hat	i it	oi oil	ch child		a in about
ā age	ī ice	ou out	ng long		e in taken
ä far	o hot	u cup	sh she	ə =	i in pencil
e let	ō open	ů put	th thin		o in lemon
ē equal	ô order	ü rule	ŦH then		u in circus
ėr term			zh measure		

P or **p** (pē), the 16th letter of the English alphabet. There are two *p*'s in *papa. noun, plural* **P's** or **p's.** **mind one's P's and Q's,** be careful about what one says or does.

p., page.

pace (pās), **1** step: *He took three paces into the room.* **2** walk with regular steps: *The tiger paced back and forth in its cage.* **3** length of a step in walking; about 2¹/₂ feet: *There were perhaps ten paces between me and the bear.* **4** measure by paces: *We paced off the distance and found it to be 69 paces.* **5** way of stepping. The walk, trot, and gallop are some of the paces of the horse. **6** a particular pace of some horses in which the feet on the same side are lifted and put down together. **7** move at a pace: *Some horses are trained to pace.* **8** rate; speed: *to walk at a fast pace.* **1,3,5,6,8** *noun,* **2,4,7** *verb,* **paced, pac ing.**

keep pace with, keep up with; go as fast as: *They walked so fast I couldn't keep pace with them.*

set the pace, 1 set a rate of speed for others to keep up with. **2** be an example or model for others to follow.

pack animals

pa cif ic (pə sif′ik), peaceful: *American Indians made pacific advances toward the Pilgrims of Plymouth. The Quakers are a pacific people. adjective.*

Pa cif ic (pə sif′ik), **1** ocean west of North and South America. It extends to Asia and Australia. **2** of the Pacific Ocean. **3** on or near the Pacific Ocean: *The Pacific coast of the United States has beautiful scenery.* **4** of or on the Pacific coast of the United States: *Oregon is one of the Pacific states.* **1** *noun,* **2-4** *adjective.*

pac i fy (pas′ə fī), **1** make calm; quiet down; give peace to: *Can't you pacify that screaming baby? We tried to pacify our angry neighbor.* **2** bring peace to: *Soldiers were sent to pacify the country. verb,* **pac i fied, pac i fy ing.**

pack (pak), **1** bundle of things wrapped up or tied together for carrying: *The hikers carried packs on their backs.* **2** put together in a bundle, box, bale, or other container: *Pack your books in this box.* **3** fill with things; put one's things into: *Pack your trunk.* **4** press or crowd closely together: *A hundred people were packed into one small room.* **5** set; lot; a number together: *a pack of thieves, a pack of nonsense, a pack of lies.* **6** number of animals of the same kind hunting together: *Wolves hunt in packs; lions hunt alone.* **7** a complete set of playing cards, usually 52. **8** a large area of floating pieces of ice pushed together: *The ship forced its way through the pack.* **9** make tight with something that water, steam, or air cannot leak through: *The plumber packed the pipe joint with string.* **1,5-8** *noun,* **2-4,9** *verb.*

pack off, send away: *The child was packed off to bed.*

send packing, send away in a hurry: *She sent them packing.*

pack age (pak′ij), **1** bundle of things packed or wrapped together; box with things packed in it; parcel. **2** put in a package or wrapper: *packaged foods. Grocery stores package some fruits and vegetables.* **1** *noun,* **2** *verb,* **pack aged, pack ag ing.**

pack animal, animal used for carrying loads or packs. See picture.

pack et (pak′it), a small package; parcel: *a packet of letters. noun.*

pact (pakt), agreement: *The three nations signed a peace pact. noun.*

pad (pad), **1** a soft mass used for comfort, protection, or stuffing; cushion: *The baby's carriage has a pad.* **2** fill with something soft; stuff: *pad a chair.* **3** a cushionlike part on the bottom side of the feet of dogs, foxes, and some other animals. **4** foot of a dog, fox, or some similar animal. **5** the large floating leaf of the water lily. **6** number of sheets of paper fastened tightly together; tablet. **7** cloth soaked with ink to use with a rubber stamp. **8** use words just to fill space: *I padded my report so that it would fill the required 10 pages.* **9** a launching pad. **1,3-7,9** *noun,* **2,8** *verb,* **pad ded, pad ding.**

pad dle¹ (pad′l), **1** a short oar with a broad blade at one end or both ends, usually held with both hands in rowing a boat or canoe. **2** move (a boat or a canoe) with a paddle or paddles. **3** act of paddling; a turn at the paddle. **4** one of the broad boards fixed around a water wheel or a paddle wheel to push, or be pushed by, the water. **5** a broad piece of wood with a handle at one end, used for stirring, for mixing, for beating clothes, and in other ways. **6** beat with a paddle; spank. **1,3-5** *noun,* **2,6** *verb,* **pad dled, pad dling.**

pagoda

paddy

pad dle[2] (pad′l), move the hands or feet about in water: *Children love to paddle at the beach. verb,* **pad dled, pad dling.**

paddle wheel, wheel with paddles fixed around it for propelling a ship over the water.

pad dock (pad′ək), **1** a small, enclosed field near a stable or house, used for exercising animals or as a pasture. **2** pen for horses at a racetrack. *noun.*

pad dy (pad′ē), field of rice. See picture. *noun, plural* **pad dies.**

pad lock (pad′lok′), **1** lock that can be put on and removed. It hangs by a curved bar, hinged at one end and snapped shut at the other. **2** fasten with a padlock. **1** *noun,* **2** *verb.*

pa gan (pā′gən), **1** person who is not a Christian, Jew, or Moslem; one who worships many gods or no god; heathen. The ancient Greeks and Romans were pagans. **2** having something to do with pagans; heathen: *pagan customs.* **1** *noun,* **2** *adjective.*

page[1] (pāj), **1** one side of a sheet or piece of paper: *a page in this book.* **2** record: *the pages of history.* **3** happening or time considered as part of history: *The settling of the West is an exciting page in our history. noun.*

page[2] (pāj), **1** person who runs errands or delivers messages. Pages at hotels usually wear uniforms. **2** try to find (a person) at a hotel or club by having his or her name called out. **3** a youth who waits on a person of high position. **4** a youth who was preparing to be a knight. **1,3,4** *noun,* **2** *verb,* **paged, pag ing.**

pag eant (paj′ənt), **1** an elaborate spectacle; procession in costume; pomp; display: *The coronation of a new ruler is always a splendid pageant.* **2** a public entertainment that represents scenes from history, legend, or the like: *Our school gave a pageant of the coming of the Pilgrims to America. noun.*

pa go da (pə gō′də), temple having many stories forming a tower. There are pagodas in India, Japan, and China. See picture. *noun.*

paid (pād). See **pay.** *I have paid my bills. These bills are all paid. verb.*

pail (pāl), **1** a round container for carrying liquids, sand, or the like; bucket. **2** amount a pail holds. *noun.*

pail ful (pāl′fůl), amount that fills a pail. *noun, plural* **pail fuls.**

pain (pān), **1** a feeling of being hurt; suffering: *A cut gives pain. A toothache is a pain. The death of one we love causes us pain.* **2** cause to suffer; give pain: *Does your tooth pain you?* **1** *noun,* **2** *verb.*

take pains, be careful: *I took pains to write neatly.*

pain ful (pān′fəl), hurting; causing pain; unpleasant: *They both suffered painful injuries. It was my painful duty to tell them they had failed the test. adjective.*

pain less (pān′lis), without pain; causing no pain. *adjective.*

paint (pānt), **1** a solid coloring matter mixed with a liquid, that can be put on a surface to make a layer or film of white, black, or colored matter. **2** cover or decorate with paint: *paint a house.* **3** represent (an object) in colors: *The artist painted fairies and angels.* **4** make pictures. **5** picture vividly in words. **6** coloring matter put on the face or body. **7** put on like paint: *I painted iodine on my cut.* **1,6** *noun,* **2-5,7** *verb.*

paint brush (pānt′brush′), brush for putting on paint. *noun, plural* **paint brush es.**

paint er (pān′tər), **1** person who paints pictures; artist. **2** person who paints houses or woodwork. *noun.*

paint ing (pān′ting), **1** picture; something painted. **2** act of one who paints. *noun.*

pair (per *or* par), **1** set of two; two that go together: *a pair of shoes, a pair of horses.* **2** arrange or be arranged in pairs: *My socks are neatly paired in a drawer.* **3** a single thing consisting of two parts that cannot be used separately: *a pair of scissors, a pair of trousers.* **4** two animals that are mated. **5** join in a pair; mate: *Some animals pair for life.* **1,3,4** *noun, plural* **pairs** *or* **pair;** **2,5** *verb.*

pair off, arrange in pairs; form into pairs.

pa ja mas (pə jä′məz *or* pə jam′əz), clothes to sleep in, consisting of a shirt and loose trousers. *noun plural.* Also spelled **pyjamas.** [The word *pajamas* comes from a Hindu word meaning "leg garment."]

pal (pal), a close friend; playmate. *noun.*

pal ace (pal′is), **1** a grand house for a king, a queen, or a bishop to live in. **2** a very fine house or building. *noun.*

pal ate (pal′it), **1** roof of the mouth. The bony part in front is the hard palate, and the fleshy part in back is the soft palate. **2** sense of taste: *The new flavor pleased his palate. noun.*

pale (pāl), **1** without much color; whitish: *When you have been ill, your face is sometimes pale.* **2** not bright; dim: *pale blue. The bright stars are surrounded by hundreds of pale ones.* **3** turn pale: *Their faces paled at the bad news.* **1,2** *adjective,* **pal er, pal est;** 3 *verb,* **paled, pal ing.**

pale face (pāl′fās′), a white person. The American Indians are said to have called white people palefaces. *noun.*

Pal es tine (pal′ə stīn), region in southwestern Asia on the Mediterranean Sea. In olden times the Jews came there from Egypt. Jesus was born in Palestine. It is now divided chiefly between Israel and Jordan. *noun.*

pal ette (pal′it), **1** a thin board, usually oval or oblong, with a thumb hole at one end, used by artists to lay and mix colors on. **2** set of colors on this board. *noun.*

pal i sade (pal′ə sād′), **1** fence of long, strong, wooden stakes pointed at the top end and set firmly in the ground to enclose or defend. **2 palisades,** line of high, steep cliffs. *noun.*

pall[1] (pôl), **1** a heavy cloth of black, purple, or white velvet spread over a coffin, a hearse, or a tomb. **2** a dark, gloomy covering: *A thick pall of smoke shut out the sun from the city. noun.*

pall[2] (pôl), become distasteful or very tiresome because there has been too much of it: *Even the most tasty food palls if it is served every day. verb.*

pal let (pal′it), bed of straw; poor bed. *noun.*

pal lid (pal′id), lacking color; pale: *Illness may cause a pallid complexion. adjective.*

pal lor (pal′ər), lack of color from fear, illness, or death; paleness. *noun.*

palm[1] (päm), **1** the inside of the hand between the wrist and the fingers. **2** the width of a hand; 3 to 4 inches. **3** conceal in the hand: *The magician palmed the nickel.* **1,2** *noun,* 3 *verb.*

palm off, pass off or get accepted by tricks, fraud, or false representation.

palm[2] (päm), **1** any of many kinds of trees growing in warm climates. Most palms have tall trunks, no branches, and many large leaves at the top. See picture. **2** leaf or stalk of leaves of a palm tree as a symbol of victory or triumph. *noun.*

pal met to (pal met′ō), kind of palm with fan-shaped leaves, abundant on the southeastern coast of the United States. See picture. *noun, plural* **pal met tos** or **pal met toes.**

Palm Sunday, the Sunday before Easter.

pal o mi no (pal′ə mē′nō), a golden-tan horse whose mane and tail are usually lighter colored. See picture. *noun, plural* **pal o mi nos.**

palm[2] (definition 1)—palms on the island of Bali

palmetto

palomino

pal pi tate (pal′pə tāt), **1** beat very rapidly: *Your heart palpitates when you are excited.* See picture. **2** quiver; tremble: *His body palpitated with terror.* *verb,* **pal pi tat ed, pal pi tat ing.**

pal sy (pôl′zē), paralysis, most often a form of paralysis that comes late in life and causes trembling and muscular weakness. *noun, plural* **pal sies.**

pal try (pôl′trē), almost worthless; trifling; petty; mean: *I sold my old, rusted bicycle for a paltry sum of money. Pay no attention to paltry gossip. adjective,* **pal tri er, pal tri est.**

pam pas (ɒam′pəz), the vast grassy plains of South America, with no trees. *noun plural.*

pam per (pam′pər), indulge too much; allow too many privileges: *pamper a child, pamper a sick person, pamper one's appetite. verb.*

pam phlet (pam′flit), booklet in paper covers. *noun.*

pan (pan), **1** dish for cooking and other household uses, usually broad, shallow, and with no cover: *pots and pans.* **2** anything like this. Gold and other metals are sometimes obtained by washing ore in pans. The dishes on a pair of scales are called pans. **3** wash (gravel or sand) in a pan to separate the gold. 1,2 *noun,* 3 *verb,* **panned, pan ning.**

pan out, turn out or work out: *Their latest scheme panned out well.*

Pan a ma (pan′ə mä), isthmus or narrow neck of land that connects North and South America. *noun.*

Panama Canal, canal cut across the Isthmus of Panama to connect the Atlantic and Pacific oceans.

pan cake (pan′kāk′), a thin, flat cake made of batter and fried in a pan or on a griddle. *noun.*

pan cre as (pan′krē əs), gland near the stomach that helps digestion. *noun.*

pan da (pan′də), **1** a bearlike animal of Tibet and parts of China, mostly white with black legs, often called the **giant panda.** See picture. **2** a reddish-brown animal somewhat like a raccoon, that lives in the mountains of India. *noun.*

pane (pān), a single sheet of glass in a division of a window, a door, or a sash: *Big hailstones and sudden gusts of wind broke several panes of glass.* *noun.* [*Pane* comes from a Latin word meaning "cloth." Early panes were strips of cloth, oiled paper, and so forth.]

pan el (pan′l), **1** strip or surface that is different in some way from what is around it. A panel is often sunk below or raised above the rest, and used for a decoration. Panels may be in a door or other woodwork, on large pieces of furniture, or made as parts of a dress. **2** arrange in panels; furnish or decorate with panels: *The walls of the dining room were paneled with oak.* **3** list of persons called as jurors; members of a jury. **4** group formed for discussion: *A panel of experts gave its opinion on ways to solve the traffic problem.* **5** board containing the instruments, controls, or indicators used in operating an automobile, aircraft, computer, or other mechanism. 1,3-5 *noun,* 2 *verb.*

panda (definition 1)—about 5 feet (1½ meters) long

parachute (definition 1)

pang (pang), **1** a sudden, short, sharp pain: *the pangs of a toothache.* **2** a sudden feeling: *A pang of pity moved my heart. noun.*

pan ic (pan′ik), **1** a fear spreading through a multitude of people so that they lose control of themselves; unreasoning fear: *When the theater caught fire, there was a panic.* **2** be affected with panic: *The audience panicked when the fire broke out.* **1** *noun,* **2** *verb,* **pan icked, pan ick ing.** [*Panic* comes from a Greek word meaning "of Pan." Pan was a Greek god whose appearance was thought to cause terror among people who saw him.]

pan ic-strick en (pan′ik strik′ən), frightened out of one's wits. *adjective.*

pan o ram a (pan′ə ram′ə), a wide, unbroken view of a surrounding region: *a panorama of beach and sea. noun.*

pan sy (pan′zē), flower somewhat like a violet but much larger and having flat petals usually of several colors. See picture. *noun, plural* **pan sies.** [*Pansy* comes from an old French word meaning "thought." The flower was called this because it was considered the symbol of thought or remembrance.]

pant (pant), **1** breathe hard and quickly: *He is panting from playing tennis.* **2** a short, quick breath. **3** speak with short, quick breaths: *"Hurry, hurry,"* she panted. **4** be eager; long very much: *I am just panting for my turn.* **1,3,4** *verb,* **2** *noun.*

pan ther (pan′thər), **1** leopard, most often a black leopard. **2** puma. **3** jaguar. *noun, plural* **pan thers** or **pan ther.**

pan ties (pan′tēz), kind of underwear with short legs worn by women or children. *noun plural.*

pan to mime (pan′tə mīm), **1** play without words in which the actors express themselves by gestures. **2** gestures without words. *noun.*

pan try (pan′trē), a small room in which food, dishes, silver, or table linen is kept. *noun, plural* **pan tries.**

pants (pants), a two-legged outer garment reaching from the waist to the ankles or sometimes to the knees; trousers. *noun plural.*

pant suit (pant′süt′), a woman's or girl's suit consisting of a jacket and trousers. *noun.*

pa pa (pä′pə), father; daddy. *noun.*

pa pal (pā′pəl), of or having to do with the pope: *a papal letter. adjective.*

pa pa ya (pə pä′yə), the fruit of a palmlike tropical American tree. Papayas look somewhat like melons, have yellowish pulp, and are good to eat. *noun.*

pa per (pā′pər), **1** a material used for writing, printing, drawing, wrapping packages, and covering walls. Paper is made in thin sheets from wood pulp, rags, and straw. **2** piece or sheet of paper. **3** piece or sheet of paper with writing or printing on it; document: *Important papers were stolen.* **4** **papers,** documents telling who or what one is. **5** newspaper. **6** article; essay: *The professor read a paper on the teaching of English.* **7** made of paper: *paper dolls.* **8** like paper; thin: *almonds with paper shells.* **9** wallpaper. **10** cover with wallpaper:

a hat	i it	oi oil	ch child	a in about
ā age	ī ice	ou out	ng long	e in taken
ä far	o hot	u cup	sh she	ə = i in pencil
e let	ō open	u̇ put	th thin	o in lemon
ē equal	ô order	ü rule	ᴛ̶ʜ then	u in circus
ėr term			zh measure	

pansies

paper a room. **1-6,9** *noun,* **7,8** *adjective,* **10** *verb.*

on paper, in writing or print: *I like your idea, so let's get it down on paper.*

pa per back (pā′pər bak′), book with a paper binding or cover, usually sold at a low price. *noun.*

pa per boy (pā′pər boi′), person who delivers or sells newspapers; newsboy. *noun.*

paper clip, a flat, bent piece of wire forming a clip for holding papers together.

paper money, money made of paper, not metal. A dollar bill is paper money.

pa poose or **pap poose** (pa püs′), a North American Indian baby. The use of this word is often considered offensive. *noun.*

pa pri ka (pa prē′kə *or* pap′rə kə), kind of mild red pepper, used as a seasoning in food. *noun.*

pa py rus (pə pī′rəs), a tall water plant from which the ancient Egyptians, Greeks, and Romans made a kind of paper to write on. *noun, plural* **pa py ri** (pə pī′rī).

par (pär), **1** equality; equal level: *She is quite on a par with her brother in intelligence.* **2** an average or normal amount, degree, or condition: *A sick person feels below par. noun.*

par a ble (par′ə bəl), a brief story used to teach some truth or moral lesson. *noun.*

par a chute (par′ə shüt), **1** device shaped something like an umbrella, made of nylon or silk, used in descending safely through the air from a great height. See picture. **2** come down by a parachute: *The pilot of the burning plane parachuted safely to the ground.* **1** *noun,* **2** *verb,* **par a chut ed, par a chut ing.**

pa rade (pə rād′), **1** march for display; procession: *The circus had a parade.* **2** march in a procession; walk proudly as if in a parade. **3** group of people walking for display or pleasure. **4** a great show or display: *They were rich but modest and did not make a parade of their wealth.*

5 make a great show of: *parade one's wealth.* **6** a military display or review of troops. **7** come together in military order for review or inspection. 1,3,4,6 *noun,* 2,5,7 *verb,* **pa rad ed, pa rad ing.**

par a dise (par/ə dīs), **1** heaven. **2** place or condition of great happiness: *The summer camp was a paradise for her. noun.*

par a dox (par/ə doks), **1** statement that may be true but seems to say two opposite things: *"More haste, less speed" and "The child is father to the man" are paradoxes.* **2** statement that is false because it says two opposite things. *noun, plural* **par a dox es.**

par af fin (par/ə fin), a white, tasteless substance like wax, used for making candles and for sealing jars of jelly or jam. *noun.*

par a graph (par/ə graf), **1** group of sentences that are about the same idea; distinct part of a chapter, letter, or composition. Paragraphs usually begin on a new line and are indented. **2** divide into paragraphs. **3** a separate note or item of news in a newspaper. 1,3 *noun,* 2 *verb.*

par a keet (par/ə kēt), a small parrot with a slender body and a long tail. *noun.*

par al lel (par/ə lel), **1** at or being the same distance apart everywhere, like the two rails of a railroad track. See picture. **2** be at the same distance from throughout the length: *The street parallels the railroad.* **3** The imaginary parallel circles around the earth, marking degrees of latitude, are called parallels. **4** comparison to show likeness: *draw a parallel between this winter and last winter.* **5** be or find a case which is similar or parallel to: *Can you parallel that for friendliness?* **6** similar; corresponding: *parallel customs in different countries.* 1,6 *adjective,* 2,5 *verb,* 3,4 *noun.*

pa ral y sis (pə ral/ə sis), **1** lessening or loss of the power of motion or feeling in any part of the body: *Polio sometimes causes a paralysis of the legs.* **2** condition of helpless lack of activity; crippling: *The war caused a paralysis of trade. noun, plural* **pa ral y ses** (pə ral/ə sēz/).

par a lyze (par/ə līz), **1** cause a lessening or loss of the power of motion or feeling in any part of the body: *The patient's left arm was paralyzed.* **2** make powerless or helplessly inactive; cripple: *Fear paralyzed my mind. verb,* **par a lyzed, par a lyz ing.**

par a mount (par/ə mount), above others; chief in importance; supreme: *Truth is of paramount importance. adjective.*

par a pet (par/ə pet), **1** a low wall or mound of stone or earth to protect soldiers. **2** a low wall at the edge of a balcony, roof, or bridge. *noun.*

par a site (par/ə sīt), **1** animal or plant that lives on or in another from which it gets its food. Lice and tapeworms are parasites on animals. Mistletoe is a parasite on oak trees. **2** person who lives on others without making any useful and fitting return. *noun.*

par a sol (par/ə sôl), a light umbrella used as a protection from the sun. *noun.*

par a troop er (par/ə trü/pər), soldier trained to use a parachute for descent from an aircraft into a battle area. *noun.*

par cel (pär/səl), **1** bundle of things wrapped or packed together; package: *I had my arms filled with parcels and gifts.* **2** piece: *a parcel of land.* **3** lot; pack: *The peddler had a whole parcel of odds and ends in his sack. noun.*

parcel out, divide into portions or distribute in portions: *The two big nations parceled out the little country between them.*

parcel post, branch of the postal service which carries parcels.

parch (pärch), **1** dry by heating; roast slightly: *The Indians parched corn.* **2** make or become hot and dry or thirsty: *I am parched with the heat. verb.*

parch ment (pärch/mənt), **1** skin of sheep or goats, prepared for use as a writing material. **2** document written on parchment. **3** paper that looks like parchment. *noun.*

par don (pärd/n), **1** forgiveness. **2** forgive: *Our teacher pardoned our misbehavior.* **3** excuse: *I beg your pardon, but I didn't hear you.* **4** set free from punishment: *The governor pardoned the prisoner.* **5** setting free from punishment: *The pardon freed an innocent person.* 1,3,5 *noun,* 2,4 *verb.*

pare (per *or* par), **1** cut, trim, or shave off the outer part of; peel: *pare an apple.* **2** cut away little by little: *pare down expenses. verb,* **pared, par ing.**

par ent (per/ənt *or* par/ənt), **1** father or mother. **2** any animal or plant that produces offspring. **3** source; cause: *Too much leisure can be the parent of mischief. noun.*

par ent age (per/ən tij *or* par/ən tij), descent from parents; family line; ancestors. *noun.*

pa ren tal (pə ren/tl), of or having something to do with a parent or parents: *The teen-ager resented parental advice. adjective.*

pa ren the ses (pə ren/thə sēz/), more than one parenthesis. The pronunciations in this dictionary are enclosed in parentheses. *noun plural.*

pa ren the sis (pə ren/thə sis), either or both of two curved lines ( ) used to set off a word, phrase, or sentence inserted within a sentence to explain or qualify something. *noun, plural* **pa ren the ses.**

par ish (par/ish), **1** district that has its own church and clergyman. **2** people of a parish. **3** (in Louisiana) a county. *noun.*

park (pärk), **1** land set apart for the pleasure of the public: *Many cities have beautiful parks.* **2** land set apart for wild animals. **3** grounds around a fine house. **4** leave (an automobile or other vehicle) for a time in a certain place: *Park your car here.* 1-3 *noun,* 4 *verb.*

par ka (pär/kə), **1** a fur jacket with a hood, worn in Alaska and the northeastern part of Asia. **2** jacket with a hood. *noun.*

park way (pärk/wā/), a broad road with spaces planted with grass, trees, or flowers. *noun.*

par ley (pär/lē), **1** conference or informal talk to discuss terms or matters in dispute: *The general held a parley with the enemy.* **2** discuss matters, especially with an enemy. 1 *noun, plural* **par leys;** 2 *verb.*

a hat	i it	oi oil	ch child	⎧ a in about
ā age	ī ice	ou out	ng long	e in taken
ä far	o hot	u cup	sh she	ə = ⟨ i in pencil
e let	ō open	u̇ put	th thin	o in lemon
ē equal	ô order	ü rule	ŦH then	⎩ u in circus
ėr term			zh measure	

parallel (definition 1)—parallel stripes

parrot (definition 1)—about 1 foot (30 centimeters) tall

par lia ment (pär′lə mənt), council or congress that is the highest lawmaking body in some countries. The British Parliament consists of the House of Lords and the House of Commons. *noun.*

par lor (pär′lər), **1** room for receiving or entertaining guests; sitting room. **2** a decorated room used as a shop; shop: *a beauty parlor. noun.*

pa ro chi al (pə rō′kē əl), of or in a parish: *a parochial school. adjective.*

par rot (par′ət), **1** bird with a stout, hooked bill and often with bright-colored feathers. Some parrots can imitate sounds and repeat words and sentences. See picture. **2** person who repeats words or acts without understanding them. *noun.*

par ry (par′ē), **1** ward off; turn aside (a thrust, weapon, or question): *He parried the sword with his dagger. She parried our question by asking us one.* **2** act of parrying. 1 *verb,* **par ried, par ry ing;** 2 *noun, plural* **par ries.**

par sley (pär′slē), a garden plant with finely divided, fragrant leaves. Parsley is used to flavor food and to trim platters of meat or fish. *noun, plural* **par sleys.**

par snip (pär′snip), the long, tapering, whitish root of a garden plant. Parsnips are eaten as a vegetable. *noun.*

par son (pär′sən), **1** minister in charge of a parish. **2** any clergyman; minister. *noun.*

par son age (pär′sə nij), house provided for a minister by a church. *noun.*

part (pärt), **1** something less than the whole; not all: *He ate part of an apple.* **2** each of several equal quantities into which a whole may be divided; fraction: *A dime is a tenth part of a dollar.* **3** thing that helps to make up a whole: *A radio has many parts.* **4** share: *I had no part in the mischief.* **5** side in a dispute or contest: *She always takes her sister's part.* **6** character in a play or motion picture; role: *He played the part of Hamlet.* **7** the words spoken by a character: *She spoke the part of the heroine in our play.* **8** divide into two or more pieces. **9** force apart; divide: *Several mounted police parted the crowd.* **10** go apart; separate: *The friends parted in anger.* **11** a dividing line left in combing one's hair. **12** one of the voices or instruments in music. The four parts in singing are soprano, alto, tenor, and bass. **13** music for it. **14** less than the whole; partial: *a part payment on a car.* **15** partly; in some measure or degree: *part Irish.* 1-7,11-13 *noun,* 8-10 *verb,* 14 *adjective,* 15 *adverb.*

part with, give up; let go: *I hated to part with my savings.*

take part, take or have a share: *She took no part in the discussion.*

par take (pär tāk′), **1** eat or drink some: *Will you partake of our lunch?* **2** take or have a share: *They plan to partake in the celebration. verb,* **par took, par tak en, par tak ing.**

par tak en (pär tā′kən). See **partake.** *verb.*

par tial (pär′shəl), **1** not complete; not total: *My parents made a partial payment on our new car.* **2** inclined to favor one side more than another; favoring unfairly: *Parents should not be partial to any one of their children.* **3** having a liking for; favorably inclined: *I am partial to sports. adjective.*

par tial ly (pär′shə lē), in part; not generally or totally; partly. *adverb.*

par tic i pant (pär tis′ə pənt), person who shares or participates. *noun.*

par tic i pate (pär tis′ə pāt), have a share; take part: *The teacher participated in the children's games. verb,* **par tic i pat ed, par tic i pat ing.**

par ti ci ple (pär′tə sip′əl), a form of a verb which may also be used as an adjective. In the phrases *the girl writing at the blackboard* and *the stolen silver, writing* is a present participle and *stolen* is a past participle. *noun.*

par ti cle (pär′tə kəl), a very little bit: *I got a particle of dust in my eye. noun.*

par tic u lar (pər tik′yə lər), **1** apart from others; considered separately; single: *That particular chair is already sold.* **2** belonging to some one person, thing, group, or occasion: *His particular task is to care for the dog.* **3** different from others; unusual; special: *This vacation was of particular importance to her, for she was going to Brazil. He is a particular friend of mine.* **4** hard to please; wanting everything to be just right; very careful: *They are very particular; nothing but the best will do.* **5** an individual part; item; point: *All the particulars of the accident are now known.* 1-4 adjective, 5 noun.
in particular, especially: *We strolled around, not going anywhere in particular.*

par tic u lar ly (pər tik′yə lər lē), in a high degree; especially: *The teacher praised her particularly. I am particularly fond of him. She mentioned that point particularly. adverb.*

part ing (pär′ting), **1** departure; going away; taking leave: *The friends were sad at parting.* **2** given, taken, or done at parting: *a parting request, a parting shot.* 1 noun, 2 adjective.

par ti san (pär′tə zən), **1** a strong supporter of a person, party, or cause; one whose support is based on feeling rather than on reasoning. **2** of a partisan; like a partisan: *There are often partisan favors in politics.* 1 noun, 2 adjective.

par ti tion (pär tish′ən), **1** division into parts: *the partition of a person's wealth when he or she dies.* **2** divide into parts: *partition a territory into three states, partition a house into rooms.* **3** wall between rooms. 1,3 noun, 2 verb.

part ly (pärt′lē), in part; in some measure or degree: *They are partly to blame. adverb.*

part ner (pärt′nər), **1** one who shares: *My sister was the partner of my walks.* **2** member of a company or firm who shares the risks and profits of the business. **3** wife or husband. **4** companion in a dance. **5** player on the same team or side in a game. *noun.*

part ner ship (pärt′nər ship), being a partner; association; joint interest: *a business partnership, the partnership of marriage. noun.*

par took (pär tük′). See **partake.** *He partook of food and drink. verb.*

par tridge (pär′trij), **1** a wild bird somewhat like the quail and the pheasant. It is hunted and used for food. **2** (in the United States) the ruffed grouse or the quail. *noun, plural* **par tridg es** or **par tridge.**

part-time (pärt′tīm′), for part of the usual time: *A part-time job helped her finish college. adjective.*

par ty (pär′tē), **1** group of people having a good time together: *She invited her friends to a party.* **2** group of people doing something together: *a dinner party, a scouting party of three soldiers.* **3** group of people organized to gain political influence and control: *the Democratic Party.* **4** of or having something to do with a party of people: *They have strong party loyalties.* **5** one who takes part in, aids, or knows about: *He was a party to our secret.* **6** person: *The party you are telephoning is out.* 1-3,5,6 noun, plural **par ties;** 4 adjective.

pass (pas), **1** go by; move past: *The parade passed. We passed a truck. They pass our house every day.* **2** move on: *The days pass quickly. The salesman passed from house to house.* **3** go from person to person: *The property passed from father to daughter.* **4** hand around; hand from one to another: *Please pass the butter.* **5** throw (the ball) to another player in such games as basketball and football. **6** a throw of the ball to another player in such games as basketball and football. **7** get through or by: *The ship passed the channel. The bill passed Congress.* **8** move: *Pass your hand over the velvet and feel how soft it is.* **9** be successful in (an examination): *She passed Spanish.* **10** act of passing; success in an examination. **11** come to an end; die: *King Arthur passed in peace.* **12** go beyond; exceed; surpass: *Your story passes belief.* **13** use or spend: *We passed the days happily.* **14** change: *Water passes to a solid state when it freezes.* **15** take place; happen: *She can tell you all that has passed.* **16** be taken: *That cloth could pass for real silk.* **17** give a judgment or opinion: *Please pass upon this question.* **18** go without notice: *They were rude, but I let it pass.* **19** written permission: *No one can get in the fort without a pass.* **20** a free ticket: *a pass to the circus.* **21** state; condition: *Things have come to a strange pass when children give orders to their parents.* **22** a narrow road, path, or opening: *A pass crosses the mountains.* 1-5,7-9,11-18 verb, 6,10,19-22 noun.
pass away, come to an end; die.
pass off, use trickery or dishonesty to get something accepted as something else: *The criminal was caught passing off counterfeit money to stores.*
pass out, **1** give out; distribute: *Please pass out this test to the members of the class.* **2** faint; lose consciousness: *We carried him home after he passed out.*

pas sage (pas′ij), **1** hall or way through a building; passageway. **2** means of passing; a way through: *They opened a passage through the crowd.* **3** passing: *the passage of time.* **4** piece from a speech or writing: *a passage from the Bible.* **5** going across; voyage: *We had a stormy passage across the Atlantic.* **6** making into law by a favoring vote of a legislature: *the passage of a bill. noun.*

pas sage way (pas′ij wā′), way along which one can pass; passage. *noun.*

pas sen ger (pas′n jər), traveler in a train, bus, automobile, boat, or airplane, usually one that pays a fare. *noun.*

passenger pigeon, wild pigeon of North America, now extinct, that flew far in very large flocks. See picture.

pass er-by (pas′ər bī′), one that passes by. *noun, plural* **pass ers-by.**

pass ing (pas′ing), **1** going by; a departure. **2** done or given in passing: *a passing smile.* **3** allowing one to pass an examination or test: *Any mark above 75 will be a passing mark.* 1 noun, 2,3 adjective.
in passing, by the way; incidentally: *In passing, I'd like to compliment you on your excellent work.*

pas sion (pash′ən), **1** very strong feeling: *Hate and fear are passions.* **2** rage; violent anger: *He flew into a passion.* **3** love between a man and a woman. **4** very strong liking: *She has a passion for music.* **5** thing for which a strong liking is felt: *Music is her passion. noun.*

pas sion ate (pash′ə nit), **1** having or showing strong feelings: *a passionate believer in equal rights for all.* **2** easily moved by anger. **3** resulting from strong feeling: *He made a passionate speech against death sentences. adjective.*

pas sive (pas′iv), **1** not acting in return; being acted on without itself acting: *a passive mind, a passive disposition.* **2** not resisting; yielding or submitting to the will of another: *The children gave passive obedience to their strict parents. adjective.*

Pass o ver (pas′ō/vər), an annual Jewish holiday in memory of the escape of the Hebrews from Egypt, where they had been slaves. *noun.*

pass port (pas′pôrt), **1** paper or book giving one official permission to travel in a foreign country, under the protection of one's own government. **2** anything that gives one admission or acceptance: *A sense of curiosity can be a passport to knowledge. noun.*

passenger pigeons
about 16 inches (40 centimeters) long

pasture (definition 1)

a hat	i it	oi oil	ch child	⎧ a in about
ā age	ī ice	ou out	ng long	⎪ e in taken
ä far	o hot	u cup	sh she	ə = ⎨ i in pencil
e let	ō open	u̇ put	th thin	⎪ o in lemon
ē equal	ô order	ü rule	ᴛʜ then	⎩ u in circus
ėr term			zh measure	

pass word (pas′wėrd′), a secret word that allows a person speaking it to pass a guard. *noun.*

past (past), **1** gone by; ended: *Summer is past. Our troubles are past.* **2** just gone by: *The past year was full of trouble. For some time past I have been ill.* **3** time gone by; time before; what has happened: *Life began far back in the past. History is a study of the past.* **4** one's past life or history: *a nation with a glorious past. I cannot change my past.* **5** beyond: *half past two, a girl past twelve, to run past the house. The arrow went past the mark.* **6** passing by; by: *The bus goes past once an hour.* **7** expressing something that happened or existed in time gone by: *the past tense of a verb.* 1,2,7 *adjective,* 3,4 *noun,* 5 *preposition,* 6 *adverb.*

paste (pāst), **1** mixture, such as flour and water boiled together, that will stick paper together. **2** to stick with paste. **3** a soft mixture: *liver paste.* 1,3 *noun,* 2 *verb,* **past ed, past ing.**

paste board (pāst′bôrd′), a stiff material made of sheets of paper pasted together or of paper pulp pressed and dried. *noun.*

pas tel (pa stel′), **1** kind of chalklike crayon used in drawing. **2** drawing made with such crayons. **3** soft and pale: *pastel pink, pastel shades.* 1,2 *noun,* 3 *adjective.*

pas teur ize (pas′chə rīz′), heat (milk) hot enough and long enough to kill certain germs. *verb,* **pas teur ized, pas teur iz ing.** [*Pasteurize* was formed from the name of Louis Pasteur, who lived from 1822 to 1895. He was a French scientist who invented this way of keeping milk from spoiling.]

pas time (pas′tīm′), pleasant way of passing time; amusement; recreation. Games and sports are pastimes. *noun.*

pas tor (pas′tər), minister in charge of a church; spiritual guide. *noun.*

pas tor al (pas′tər əl), **1** of shepherds or country life: *The pastoral tribes of the mountains graze their sheep on the hillside.* **2** simple or naturally beautiful like the country: *a pastoral landscape.* **3** of a pastor: *a pastoral letter. adjective.*

pas try (pā′strē), **1** pies, tarts, or other baked food made with dough rich in butter or other shortening. **2** the dough for such food. *noun,* *plural* **pas tries.**

pas tur age (pas′chər ij), **1** growing grass and other plants for cattle, sheep, or horses to feed on. **2** pasture land. *noun.*

pas ture (pas′chər), **1** a grassy field or hillside; grassy land on which cattle, sheep, or horses can feed. See picture. **2** grass and other growing plants: *These lands afford good pasture.* **3** put (cattle, sheep, or horses) out to pasture. **4** feed on (growing grass). 1,2 *noun,* 3,4 *verb,* **pas tured, pas tur ing.**

pat (pat), **1** strike or tap lightly with something flat: *He patted the dough into a flat cake.* **2** tap with the hand as a sign of sympathy, approval, or affection: *pat a dog.* **3** a light stroke or tap with the hand or with something flat. **4** sound made by patting. **5** a small mass, especially of butter. **6** apt; suitable; to the point: *a pat reply.* 1,2 *verb,* **pat ted, pat ting;** 3-5 *noun,* 6 *adjective,* **pat ter, pat test.**

patch (pach), **1** piece put on to mend a hole or a tear, or as a decoration. **2** piece of cloth put over a wound or a sore. **3** pad over a hurt eye to protect it. **4** put patches on; mend; protect with a patch or patches. **5** piece together; make hastily. **6** a small, uneven spot: *a patch of brown on the skin.* **7** piece of ground: *a garden patch.* 1-3,6,7 *noun, plural* **patch es;** 4,5 *verb.*

patch up, 1 put an end to; settle: *patch up a quarrel.* **2** make right hastily or for a time: *patch up a leaking faucet.*

patch work (pach′werk′), **1** pieces of cloth of various colors or shapes sewed together. **2** made of such pieces of cloth. See picture. 1 *noun,* 2 *adjective.*

pat ent (pat′nt), **1** a government document which grants a person or company sole rights to make, use, or sell a new invention for a certain number of years. **2** given or protected by a patent. **3** get a patent for: *She patented her new invention.* 1 *noun,* 2 *adjective,* 3 *verb.*

pat ent leath er (pat′nt leⱦ′ər), leather with a very glossy, smooth surface, usually black. Some shoes are made of patent leather.

pa ter nal (pə tėr′nl), **1** of or like a father; fatherly: *paternal concern.* **2** related on the father's side of the family: *Everyone has two paternal grandparents and two maternal grandparents. adjective.*

path (path), **1** way made by people or animals walking. It is usually too narrow for automobiles or wagons. **2** line along which a person or thing moves; route; track: *The moon has a regular path through the sky.* **3** way of acting or behaving; way of life: *Some choose paths of glory; some choose paths of ease. noun, plural* **paths** (paⱦz *or* paths).

pa thet ic (pə thet′ik), pitiful; arousing pity: *The starving people were pathetic. adjective.*

path less (path′lis), having no path through or across it: *a pathless mountain. adjective.*

path way (path′wā′), path. *noun.*

pa tience (pā′shəns), **1** calm bearing of pain, of waiting, or of anything that annoys, troubles, or hurts: *The cat watched the mouse hole with patience.* **2** long, hard work; steady effort. *noun.*

pa tient (pā′shənt), **1** having patience; showing patience: *The teacher was patient with the class.* **2** person who is being treated by a doctor. 1 *adjective,* 2 *noun.*

pat i o (pat′ē ō), **1** an inner court or yard open to the sky. Houses in Spanish-speaking countries are often built around patios. See picture. **2** terrace for outdoor eating or lounging. *noun, plural* **pat i os.**

pa tri arch (pā′trē ärk), **1** father and ruler of a family or tribe. In the Bible, Abraham, Isaac, and Jacob were patriarchs. **2** a highly respected elderly man. *noun.*

pa tri ot (pā′trē ət), person who loves his or her country and gives it loyal support. *noun.* [*Patriot* comes from a Greek word meaning "a fellow countryman."]

pa tri ot ic (pā′trē ot′ik), **1** loving one's country. **2** showing love and loyal support of one's own country. *adjective.*

pa tri ot ism (pā′trē ə tiz′əm), love and loyal support of one's country. *noun.*

pa trol (pə trōl′), **1** go around in an area watching and guarding in order to protect life and property: *The police patrolled once every hour.* **2** a going of the rounds to watch or guard. **3** persons who patrol: *The patrol was changed at midnight.* **4** group of soldiers, ships, or airplanes, sent out to find out all they can about the enemy. 1 *verb,* **pa trolled, pa trol ling;** 2-4 *noun.*

pa tron (pā′trən), **1** person who buys regularly at a given store or goes regularly to a certain hotel or restaurant. **2** person who gives approval and support to some person, art, cause, or undertaking: *a patron of artists.* **3** guarding; protecting: *a patron saint.* 1,2 *noun,* 3 *adjective.*

pa tron age (pā′trə nij *or* pat′rə nij), **1** regular business given to a store, hotel, or restaurant by customers. **2** favor, encouragement, or support given by a patron. **3** power to give jobs or favors: *the patronage of a governor, mayor, or congressman. noun.*

pa tron ize (pā′trə nīz *or* pat′rə nīz), **1** be a regular customer of; give regular business to: *We patronize our neighborhood stores.* **2** act as a patron toward; support or protect: *patronize the ballet. verb,* **pa tron ized, pa tron iz ing.**

pat ter (pat′ər), **1** make rapid taps: *The rain pattered on the windowpane. Bare feet pattered along the hard floor.* **2** series of quick taps or the sound they make: *the patter of raindrops.* 1 *verb,* 2 *noun.*

pat tern (pat′ərn), **1** arrangement of forms and colors; design: *the patterns of wallpaper, rugs, cloth, and jewelry.* **2** model or guide for something to be made: *I used a paper pattern in cutting the cloth for my coat.* **3** a fine example; model to be followed: *He was a pattern of generosity.* **4** make according to a pattern: *Pattern yourself after her.* 1-3 *noun,* 4 *verb.*

pat ty (pat′ē), a small, round, flat piece of food: *a hamburger patty, a peppermint patty. noun, plural* **pat ties.**

pau per (pô′pər), a very poor person; person supported by charity. *noun.*

pause (pôz), **1** stop for a time; wait: *I paused for a moment to look in a store window.* **2** a brief stop or rest: *After a pause for lunch we returned to work.* 1 *verb,* **paused, paus ing;** 2 *noun.*

pave (pāv), **1** cover (a street, sidewalk, or driveway) with a pavement: *pave a road with concrete.* **2** prepare; make smooth or easy: *The invention paved the way for new discoveries. verb,* **paved, pav ing.**

pave ment (pāv′mənt), **1** covering or surface for

streets, sidewalks, or driveways, made of asphalt, concrete, gravel, or stones. **2** a paved road. *noun.*

pa vil ion (pə vil′yən), **1** a light building, usually one somewhat open, used for shelter or pleasure: *a bathing pavilion.* **2** a large tent with a floor raised on posts. **3** any building that houses an exhibition at a fair. *noun.*

pav ing (pā′ving), **1** material for pavement. **2** pavement. *noun.*

paw (pô), **1** foot of a four-footed animal having claws. Cats and dogs have paws. **2** strike or scrape with the paws or feet: *The cat pawed the mouse it had caught. The horse pawed the ground, eager to be going again.* **3** handle awkwardly or roughly: *Stop pawing the tomatoes, you'll bruise them.* **1** *noun,* **2,3** *verb.*

pawn[1] (pôn), **1** leave (something) with another person as security that borrowed money will be returned; pledge: *I pawned my watch to buy food until I could get work.* **2** something left as security. **1** *verb,* **2** *noun.*

pawn[2] (pôn), **1** the least important piece in the game of chess. Pawns are often given up to gain some advantage. **2** an unimportant person or thing used by somebody to gain some advantage. *noun.*

pay (pā), **1** give money to for things or work: *Pay the doctor.* **2** money given for things or work: *He gets his pay every Saturday.* **3** give money for: *Pay your fare. Pay your debts.* **4** give what is due: *She owes it and must pay.* **5** return for favors or hurts; reward or punish: *He paid them for their insults by causing them trouble.* **6** give; offer: *pay attention, pay a compliment.* **7** give a profit; be worthwhile: *It pays to be polite.* **1,3-7** *verb,* **paid, pay ing;** **2** *noun.*

pay back, 1 return borrowed money: *She paid back the money she borrowed.* **2** give the same treatment as received: *I hope to be able to pay back their help.*

pay ment (pā′mənt), **1** paying: *payment of debts.* **2** amount paid: *a monthly payment of $10.* **3** pay: *The pleasure of helping you is payment enough. noun.*

pay roll (pā′rōl′), **1** list of persons to be paid and the amount that each one is to receive. **2** the total amount to be paid to them. *noun.*

pea (pē), one of the round seeds, eaten as a vegetable, that are inside the long, green pod of a garden plant. *noun.*

peace (pēs), **1** freedom from strife of any kind; condition of quiet, order, and security: *peace in the family.* **2** freedom from war: *work for world peace.* **3** agreement between enemies to end war: *sign the peace.* **4** quiet; calm; stillness: *peace of mind. We enjoy the peace of the country. noun.*

hold one's peace, keep still: *Do not speak when you should hold your peace.*

peace a ble (pē′sə bəl), peaceful. *adjective.*

peace ful (pēs′fəl), **1** quiet; calm; full of peace: *It was peaceful in the mountains.* **2** liking peace; keeping peace: *peaceful neighbors. adjective.*

peace pipe, pipe smoked by North American Indians as a token or pledge of peace. See picture.

a hat	i it	oi oil	ch child	(a in about
ā age	ī ice	ou out	ng long	e in taken
ä far	o hot	u cup	sh she	ə = { i in pencil
e let	ō open	u̇ put	th thin	o in lemon
ē equal	ô order	ü rule	ᵺ then	(u in circus
ėr term			zh measure	

peace pipe

patio (definition 1)

patchwork (definition 2)—a patchwork quilt

peach (pēch), **1** a juicy, nearly round, yellowish-pink fruit having a downy skin and a rough stone inside. Peaches grow on trees and are good to eat. **2** yellowish pink. **1** *noun, plural* **peach es; 2** *adjective.*

pea cock (pē′kok′), a large bird with beautiful green, blue, and gold feathers. The tail feathers of the male have spots like eyes on them and can be spread out and held upright like a fan. *noun, plural* **pea cocks** or **pea cock.**

pea hen (pē′hen′), a female peacock. *noun.*

peak (pēk), **1** the pointed top of a mountain or hill: *snowy peaks.* **2** mountain that stands alone: *Pikes Peak.* **3** any pointed end or top: *the peak of a roof.* **4** the highest point: *reach the peak of one's profession.* **5** the front part or the brim of a cap, that stands out. *noun.*

peal (pēl), **1** a loud, long sound: *a peal of thunder, peals of laughter.* **2** the loud ringing of bells. **3** chime; set of bells. **4** sound out in a peal; ring: *The bells pealed forth their message of joy.* **1-3** *noun,* **4** *verb.*

pea nut (pē′nut′), the nutlike seed of a plant. Peanuts are contained in pods that ripen underground. They are roasted and used as food or pressed to get an oil for cooking. *noun.*

peanut butter, food made of peanuts ground until soft and smooth. It is spread on bread or crackers.

pear (per *or* par), a sweet, juicy, yellowish fruit rounded at one end and smaller toward the stem end. Pears grow on trees and are good to eat. *noun.*

pearl (pėrl), **1** a white or nearly white gem that has a soft shine like satin. Pearls are found inside the shell of a kind of oyster, or in other similar shellfish. **2** thing that looks like a pearl. See picture. **3** very pale, clear, bluish gray. **1,2** *noun,* **3** *adjective.*

pearl y (pėr′lē), like a pearl in color or luster: *pearly teeth. adjective,* **pearl i er, pearl i est.**

peas ant (pez′nt), **1** farmer of the working class in Europe. **2** of peasants: *peasant labor.* **1** *noun,* **2** *adjective.*

peas ant ry (pez′n trē), peasants. *noun.*

peat (pēt), kind of turf, used as fuel after being dried. Peat is made of partly rotted moss and plants. *noun.*

peb ble (peb′əl), a small stone, usually worn smooth and round by being rolled about by water. *noun.*

peb bly (peb′lē), having many pebbles; covered with pebbles: *The pebbly beach hurt our bare feet. adjective,* **peb bli er, peb bli est.**

pe can (pi kän′ *or* pi kan′), **1** nut that is shaped like an olive and has a smooth shell. Pecans are good to eat. **2** tree it grows on. Pecans grow in the southern United States. *noun.*

pec car y (pek′ər ē), a wild animal with hoofs that is somewhat like a pig. It is found in South America and as far north as Texas. See picture. *noun, plural* **pec car ies** or **pec car y.**

peck[1] (pek), **1** strike at and pick up with the beak: *The hen pecked corn.* **2** stroke made with the beak: *The hen gave me a peck.* **3** make by striking with the beak: *The woodpeckers pecked holes in the trees.* **4** hole or mark made by pecking. **5** make a pecking motion. **6** a stiff, unwilling kiss. **1,3,5** *verb,* **2,4,6** *noun.*

peck at, eat only a little, bit by bit: *Because he is not feeling well, he just pecks at his food.*

peck[2] (pek), **1** a unit of measure for grain, fruit, vegetables, and other dry things, equal to 8 quarts or one fourth of a bushel: *a peck of potatoes.* **2** container holding just a peck, to measure with. **3** a great deal: *a peck of trouble. noun.*

pe cul iar (pi kyü′lyər), **1** strange; odd; unusual: *A clock with no hands looks peculiar. It was peculiar that the fish market had no fish last Friday.* **2** special; belonging to one person or thing and not to another: *a type of pottery peculiar to the ancient Egyptians. adjective.*

pe cu li ar i ty (pi kyü′lē ar′ə tē), **1** being peculiar; strange or unusual quality: *We noticed the peculiarity of her manner at once.* **2** some little thing that is strange or odd: *One of his peculiarities is that his eyes are not the same color. noun, plural* **pe cu li ar i ties.**

pearl (definition 2)—The insect was covered with **pearls** of dew.

ped al (ped′l), **1** lever worked by the foot; the part on which the foot is placed to move any kind of machinery. Organs have pedals for changing the tone. The two pedals of a bicycle, pushed down one after the other, make it go. **2** work or use the pedals of; move by pedals: *I pedaled my bicycle slowly up the hill.* **1** *noun,* **2** *verb.*

ped dle (ped′l), **1** carry from place to place and sell: *The farmer peddled fruit from house to house.* **2** offer or deal out in small quantities: *peddle a new idea, peddle gossip.* **3** travel about with things to sell. *verb,* **ped dled, ped dling.**

ped dler (ped′lər), person who travels about selling things carried in a pack or in a cart. *noun.*

ped es tal (ped′i stəl), **1** base on which a column or a statue stands. **2** base of a tall vase or lamp. *noun.*

pe des tri an (pə des′trē ən), **1** person who goes on foot; walker: *Pedestrians have to watch for automobiles turning corners.* **2** going on foot; walking. **1** *noun,* **2** *adjective.*

pe di a tri cian (pē′dē ə trish′ən), doctor who specializes in children's diseases and the care of babies and children. *noun.*

ped i gree (ped′ə grē′), list of ancestors of a person or animal; family tree. *noun.*

peek (pēk), **1** look quickly and slyly; peep: *You must not peek while you are counting in hide-and-seek.* **2** a quick, sly look. **1** *verb,* **2** *noun.*

peel (pēl), **1** rind or outer covering of fruit or vegetables. **2** strip the skin, rind, or bark from: *peel an orange.* **3** strip: *I peeled the tape off my hand.* **4** come off: *The paint on the shed is peeling.* **1** *noun,* **2-4** *verb.*

peep[1] (pēp), **1** look through a small or narrow hole or crack. **2** look through a hole or crack; little look: *take a peep into the pantry.* **3** look when no one knows it. **4** a secret look: *take a peep at the presents.* **5** look out, as if peeping; come partly out: *Violets peeped among the leaves.* **6** the first looking or coming out: *at the peep of day.* **1,3,5** *verb,* **2,4,6** *noun.*

peep[2] (pēp), **1** cry of a young bird or chicken; sound like a chirp or a squeak. **2** make such a sound; chirp. **1** *noun,* **2** *verb.*

peer[1] (pir), **1** person of the same rank, ability, or qualities as another; equal: *She is so fine a writer that it would be hard to find her peer.* **2** person of British nobility such as a duke or baron. *noun.*

peer[2] (pir), **1** look closely to see clearly, as a near-sighted person does. See picture. **2** come out slightly; peep out: *The sun was peering from behind a cloud. verb.*

peer less (pir′lis), without an equal; matchless: *His peerless performance won him a prize. adjective.*

pee vish (pē′vish), cross; fretful; complaining: *A peevish child is unhappy and makes others unhappy. adjective.*

peg (peg), **1** pin or small bolt of wood or metal used to fasten parts together, to hang things on, to stop a hole, to make fast a rope or string on, or to mark the score in a game. **2** fasten or hold with pegs: *We must peg down our tent.* **3** work hard: *He pegged away at his studies so that he would get high marks.* **1** *noun,* **2,3** *verb,* **pegged, peg ging.**

take down a peg, humble; lower the pride of: *Three losses in a row took the team down a peg.*

Pe king ese (pē′kə nēz′), a small dog with long hair and a broad, flat face. *noun, plural* **Pe king ese.**

pel i can (pel′ə kən), a very large, fish-eating water bird with a huge bill and a pouch on the bottom side of the bill for scooping up fish. See picture. *noun.*

pel let (pel′it), a little ball of mud, paper, hail, snow, food, or medicine; pill. *noun.*

pell-mell (pel′mel′), in a rushing, tumbling mass or crowd: *The children dashed pell-mell down the beach and into the waves. adverb.*

pelt[1] (pelt), **1** throw things at; attack; assail: *We pelted each other with snowballs.* **2** beat heavily: *The rain came pelting down. verb.*

pelt[2] (pelt), skin of a sheep, goat, or small fur-bearing animal, before it is tanned. *noun.*

a hat	i it	oi oil	ch child	a in about
ā age	ī ice	ou out	ng long	e in taken
ä far	o hot	u cup	sh she	ə = i in pencil
e let	ō open	u̇ put	th thin	o in lemon
ē equal	ô order	ü rule	₮H then	u in circus
ėr term			zh measure	

peccary—about 3 feet (1 meter) long

peer[2] (definition 1)
She **peered** at the goldfish.

pelican—about 4 feet (1 meter) long. Pelicans bring food up from their stomachs to their pouches for their young to eat.

pen[1] (pen), **1** instrument used in writing with ink.
2 write: *I penned a brief note.* 1 *noun*, 2 *verb*,
penned, pen ning.

pen[2] (pen), **1** a small, closed yard for cows, sheep,
pigs, chickens, or other farm animals. **2** shut in a
pen. **3** shut in; confine closely: *The fox was penned
in a corner with no way of escape.* 1 *noun*, 2,3 *verb*,
penned, pen ning.

pe nal ize (pē′nl īz), **1** declare punishable by law
or by rule; set a penalty for: *Speeding on city streets
is penalized. Fouls are penalized in many games.*
2 inflict a penalty on; punish: *Our football team
was penalized five yards. verb,* **pe nal ized,
pe nal iz ing.**

pen al ty (pen′l tē), **1** punishment: *The penalty for
speeding is usually a fine.* **2** disadvantage placed on
a side or player for breaking the rules of some
game or contest. *noun, plural* **pen al ties.**

pen ance (pen′əns), **1** punishment borne to show
sorrow for sin, to make up for a wrong done, and
to obtain pardon for sin. **2** any act done to show
that one is sorry or repents: *They did penance for
cheating by staying after school. noun.*

pence (pens), more than one British penny. *noun
plural.*

pen cil (pen′səl), **1** a pointed tool to write or draw
with. **2** mark or write with a pencil. 1 *noun,* 2 *verb.*

pend ant (pen′dənt), a hanging ornament, such
as a locket. *noun.*

pend ing (pen′ding), **1** waiting to be decided or
settled: *while the agreement was pending.* **2** while
waiting for; until: *Pending your return, we'll get
everything ready.* **3** during: *pending the investigation.*
1 *adjective,* 2,3 *preposition.*

pen du lum (pen′jə ləm), weight hung from a
fixed point so that it is free to swing to and fro.
The movement of the works of a tall clock is often
timed by a pendulum. *noun.*

pen e trate (pen′ə trāt), **1** get into or through: *A
bullet can penetrate this wall, or two inches into that
wall.* **2** pierce through; make a way: *Our eyes could
not penetrate the darkness. Even where the trees were
thickest, the sunshine penetrated.* **3** soak through;
spread through: *The rain penetrated our clothes.
The aroma of fresh baked bread penetrated the whole
house.* **4** see into; understand: *I could not penetrate
the mystery. verb,* **pen e trat ed, pen e trat ing.**

pen e tra tion (pen′ə trā′shən), **1** act or power of
penetrating. **2** sharpness of intellect; insight. *noun.*

pen guin (pen′gwin), a sea bird with flippers for
diving and swimming in place of wings for flying.
Penguins live in Antarctica and other cold areas
of the Southern Hemisphere. See picture. *noun.*

pen i cil lin (pen′ə sil′ən), a very powerful drug
used to kill the bacteria that cause certain
diseases. It is made from a fungus mold. *noun.*
[*Penicillin* comes from a Latin word meaning "a
small brush" or "a painter's brush." Penicillin was
called this because the cells of the mold from
which it is made look like small brushes.]

pe nin su la (pə nin′sə lə), piece of land almost
surrounded by water, or extending far out into the
water. Florida is a peninsula. *noun.* [*Peninsula*

penguins—about 3 feet (1 meter) tall

pentagon

pentagon—The Pentagon in Washington, D.C., is a building with
five sides.

comes from Latin words meaning "almost"
and "island."]

pen i tence (pen′ə təns), sorrow for doing wrong;
repentance. *noun.*

pen i tent (pen′ə tənt), **1** sorry for doing wrong;
repenting: *The penitent student promised never to
cheat again.* **2** person who is sorry for sin,

especially one who is doing penance under the direction of a church. 1 *adjective*, 2 *noun*.

pen i ten tiar y (pen′ə ten′shər ē), prison for criminals. *noun*, *plural* **pen i ten tiar ies.**

pen knife (pen′nīf′), a small pocketknife. *noun*, *plural* **pen knives** (pen′nīvz′).

pen man (pen′mən), 1 writer. 2 person who has good handwriting. *noun*, *plural* **pen men.**

pen man ship (pen′mən ship), handwriting; writing with pen or pencil. *noun*.

pen nant (pen′ənt), flag, usually long and narrow, used on ships, in signaling, or as a school banner. In some sports, the best team wins a pennant. *noun*.

pen ni less (pen′ē lis), without a cent of money; very poor: *I've lost all my money and now I'm penniless. adjective.*

Penn syl van ia (pen′səl vā′nyə), one of the northeastern states of the United States. *noun*. [*Pennsylvania*, meaning "Penn's woods," was formed by combining the name Penn with a Latin word meaning "woods." It was named by King Charles II of England in 1681 in honor of the father of the colony's founder, William Penn.]

pen ny (pen′ē), 1 cent; coin of the United States and Canada. One hundred pennies make one dollar. 2 a British coin. One hundred pennies make one pound. 3 a former British coin equal to one twelfth of a shilling. Until 1971, 240 pennies made one pound. *noun*, *plural* **pen nies** or (for definitions 2 and 3) **pence.**

a pretty penny, a large sum of money.

pen sion (pen′shən), 1 a regular payment to a person which is not wages. Pensions are often paid because of long service, special merit, or injuries received. 2 give a pension to: *The company pensioned several employees who were sixty-five years old.* 1 *noun*, 2 *verb*.

pen sive (pen′siv), thoughtful in a serious or sad way: *She was in a pensive mood, and sat staring out the window. adjective.*

pen ta gon (pen′tə gon), a figure having five angles and five sides. See pictures. *noun*.

pent house (pent′hous′), apartment or other dwelling located on the top of a building. *noun*, *plural* **pent hous es** (pent′hou′ziz).

pe o ny (pē′ə nē), a garden plant with large, showy red, pink, or white flowers. *noun*, *plural* **pe o nies.**

peo ple (pē′pəl), 1 men, women, and children; persons: *There were ten people present.* 2 race; nation: *Asian peoples, the American people.* 3 persons in general; the public: *A democracy is a government of the people.* 4 persons of a place, class, or group: *city people, Southern people.* 5 the common people; the lower classes: *The French nobles oppressed the people.* 6 persons in relation to a superior: *a queen and her people.* 7 family; relatives: *He spends his holidays with his people.* 8 fill with people: *Many nations helped people America.* 1-7 *noun*, *plural* **peo ple** or (for definition 2) **peo ples;** 8 *verb*, **peo pled, peo pling.**

pep (pep), 1 spirit; energy; vim. 2 **pep up**, fill or inspire with energy; put new life into: *A brisk walk after dinner will pep you up.* 1 *noun*, 2 *verb*, **pepped, pep ping.**

pep per (pep′ər), 1 a seasoning with a hot taste, used for soups, meats, or vegetables. Pepper is made by grinding the berries of a vine grown in parts of Asia. 2 a hollow green or red vegetable that is eaten raw, cooked, or pickled. 3 season with pepper; sprinkle with pepper. 4 hit with small objects sent thick and fast: *We peppered them with snowballs.* 1,2 *noun*, 3,4 *verb*.

pep per mint (pep′ər mint), 1 a kind of mint grown for its oil which is used in medicine and candy. 2 candy flavored with peppermint oil. *noun*.

per (pər or pėr), 1 for each: *a pint of milk per child, ten cents per pound.* 2 through; by means of: *I send this per my son. preposition.*

per an num (pər an′əm), per year; yearly; for each year: *Her salary was $15,000 per annum.*

per cap i ta (pər kap′ə tə), for each person: *$100 divided by five people is $20 per capita.*

per ceive (pər sēv′), 1 be aware of through the senses; see, hear, taste, smell, or feel: *Did you perceive the colors of that bird?* 2 take in with the mind; observe: *I soon perceived that I could not make him change his mind. verb*, **per ceived, per ceiv ing.**

per cent (pər sent′), per cent. *noun*.

per cent, 1 hundredths; parts in each hundred: *Five per cent of 40 is 2.* 2 percentage: *A large per cent of the farm's apple crop was ruined.*

per cent age (pər sen′tij), 1 rate or proportion of each hundred; part of each hundred: *What percentage of children were absent?* 2 part; proportion: *A large percentage of schoolbooks now have pictures. noun.*

per cep ti ble (pər sep′tə bəl), that can be perceived: *The other ship was barely perceptible in the fog. adjective.*

per cep ti bly (pər sep′tə blē), in a perceptible way or amount. *adverb*.

per cep tion (pər sep′shən), 1 act of perceiving: *His perception of the change came in a flash.* 2 power of perceiving: *a keen perception.* 3 understanding that is the result of perceiving: *She had a clear perception of the problem, and soon solved it. noun.*

perch[1] (pėrch), 1 bar, branch, or anything else on which a bird can come to rest. 2 alight and rest; sit: *A robin perched on the branch.* 3 a rather high seat or position. 4 sit rather high: *He perched on a stool.* 5 place high up: *a village perched on a high hill.* 1,3 *noun*, *plural* **perch es;** 2,4,5 *verb*.

perch[2] (pėrch), a small freshwater fish, used for food. *noun*, *plural* **perch es** or **perch.**

per chance (pər chans′), perhaps. *adverb*.

a hat	i it	oi oil	ch child	⎧ a in about
ā age	ī ice	ou out	ng long	e in taken
ä far	o hot	u cup	sh she	ə = i in pencil
e let	ō open	u̇ put	th thin	o in lemon
ē equal	ô order	ü rule	ᴛʜ then	⎩ u in circus
ėr term			zh measure	

per co late (pėr′kə lāt), drip or drain through small holes or spaces: *Let the coffee percolate for seven minutes.* verb, **per co lat ed, per co lat ing.**

per cus sion (pər kush′ən), **1** striking of one thing against another with force; blow. **2** shock made by the striking of one thing against another with force. *noun.*

percussion instrument, a musical instrument played by striking it, such as a drum or cymbal. See picture.

pe ren ni al (pə ren′ē əl), **1** lasting through the whole year: *a perennial stream.* **2** lasting for a very long time: *the perennial beauty of the hills.* **3** living more than two years: *perennial garden plants.* **4** a perennial plant. Roses are perennials. 1-3 *adjective,* 4 *noun.*

per fect (pėr′fikt *for 1,3-5, and 7;* pər fekt′ *for 2 and 6*), **1** having no faults; not spoiled at any point: *a perfect spelling paper, a perfect apple, a perfect life.* **2** remove all faults from; make perfect; add the finishing touches to: *perfect an invention. The artist was perfecting his picture.* **3** completely skilled; expert: *a perfect golfer.* **4** having all its parts there; complete: *The set was perfect; nothing was missing or broken.* **5** exact: *a perfect copy, a perfect circle.* **6** carry through; complete: *perfect a plan.* **7** entire; utter: *She was a perfect stranger to us.* 1,3-5,7 *adjective,* 2,6 *verb.*

per fec tion (pər fek′shən), **1** perfect or faultless condition; highest excellence. **2** a perfect person or thing: *This restaurant serves desserts that are perfection.* **3** making complete or perfect: *Perfection of our plans will take another week.* noun.
to perfection, perfectly: *The orchestra played the difficult piece to perfection.*

per fo rate (pėr′fə rāt′), **1** make a hole or holes through: *The target was perforated by bullets.* **2** make a row or rows of holes through: *Sheets of postage stamps are perforated.* verb, **per fo rat ed, per fo rat ing.**

per form (pər fôrm′), **1** do: *Perform your duties well.* **2** put into effect; carry out: *The surgeon performed an operation.* **3** act, play, sing, or do tricks in public. See picture. *verb.*

per form ance (pər fôr′məns), **1** carrying out; doing: *in the performance of one's regular duties, the efficient performance of an automobile.* **2** thing performed; act; deed: *The child's kicks and screams made a disgraceful performance.* **3** the giving of a play, circus, or other show: *The evening performance is at 8 o'clock.* noun.

per form er (pər fôr′mər), person who performs, especially one who performs for the entertainment of others. *noun.*

per fume (pėr′fyüm *for 1 and 2;* pər fyüm′ *for 3*), **1** liquid having the sweet smell of flowers. **2** a sweet smell: *We enjoyed the perfume of the flowers.* **3** fill with sweet odor: *Flowers perfumed the air.* 1,2 *noun,* 3 *verb,* **per fumed, per fum ing.**

per haps (pər haps′), it may be; possibly: *Perhaps a letter will come to you today.* adverb.

per il (per′əl), chance of harm; danger: *This bridge is not safe; cross it at your peril.* noun.

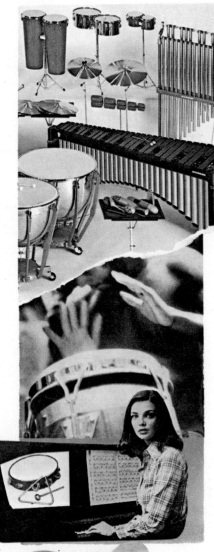

percussion instruments

perform (definition 3)—We went to the circus to see the animals **perform**.

a hat	**i** it	**oi** oil	**ch** child		a in about
ā age	**ī** ice	**ou** out	**ng** long		e in taken
ä far	**o** hot	**u** cup	**sh** she	**ə** =	i in pencil
e let	**ō** open	**u̇** put	**th** thin		o in lemon
ē equal	**ô** order	**ü** rule	**ŦH** then		u in circus
ėr term			**zh** measure		

per il ous (per′ə ləs), dangerous. *adjective.*

pe rim e ter (pə rim′ə tər), the distance around a figure such as a square, triangle, or oval. *noun.*

per i od (pir′ē əd), **1** portion of time: *She visited us for a short period.* **2** portion of time marked off by events that happen again and again; time after which the same things begin to happen again: *A month, from new moon to new moon, is a period.* **3** a certain series of years: *the period of World War II.* **4** portion of a game during which there is actual play. **5** one of the portions of time into which a school day is divided. **6** dot (.) marking the end of most sentences or showing an abbreviation, as in Mr. or Dec. *noun.*

per i od ic (pir′ē od′ik), occurring, appearing, or done again and again at regular intervals: *periodic attacks of malaria. The coming of the new moon is a periodic event. adjective.*

per i od i cal (pir′ē od′ə kəl), **1** magazine that appears regularly. **2** published at regular intervals, less often than daily. **3** periodic. **1** *noun,* **2,3** *adjective.*

per i od i cal ly (pir′ē od′ik lē), **1** at regular intervals. **2** every now and then. *adverb.*

per i scope (per′ə skōp), instrument that allows those in a submarine or trench to see a view of the surface. It is a tube with an arrangement of prisms or mirrors that reflect light rays down the tube. *noun.*

per ish (per′ish), be destroyed; die: *They perished in the fire. Flowers perish when frost comes. verb.*

per ish a ble (per′i shə bəl), liable to spoil or decay: *Fruit is perishable. adjective.*

perk (pėrk), raise smartly or briskly: *The dog perked its ears when it heard its owner. verb.*

perk up, brighten up; become lively and vigorous: *Perk up; things will get better.*

per ma nence (pėr′mə nəns), being permanent; lasting quality or condition: *the permanence of the sun. noun.*

per ma nent (pėr′mə nənt), lasting; intended to last; not for a short time only: *a permanent filling in a tooth. After doing odd jobs for a week, I got a permanent position as a clerk in a store. adjective.*

per me ate (pėr′mē āt), **1** spread through the whole of; pass through; soak through: *The smoke permeated the house.* **2** penetrate: *Water will easily permeate cotton. verb,* **per me at ed, per me at ing.**

per mis sion (pər mish′ən), consent; leave: *She asked the teacher's permission to leave early. noun.*

per mit (pər mit′ for 1; pėr′mit for 2), **1** let; allow: *My parents will not permit me to stay up late. The law does not permit smoking in this store.* **2** a formal written order giving permission to do something: *Have you a permit to fish in this lake?* **1** *verb,* **per mit ted, per mit ting;** **2** *noun.*

per pen dic u lar (pėr′pən dik′yə lər), **1** upright; standing straight up. See picture. **2** at right angles. One line is perpendicular to another when it makes a square corner with another. The floor of a room is perpendicular to the side walls and parallel to the ceiling. *adjective.*

per pe trate (pėr′pə trāt), do or commit (a crime, fraud, trick, or anything bad or foolish): *They were arrested for perpetrating a robbery. verb,* **per pe trat ed, per pe trat ing.**

per pet u al (pər pech′ü əl), **1** eternal; lasting forever: *the perpetual hills.* **2** lasting throughout life: *a perpetual income.* **3** continuous; never ceasing: *a perpetual stream of visitors. adjective.*

per pet u al ly (pər pech′ü ə lē), forever. *adverb.*

per pet u ate (pər pech′ü āt), make perpetual; keep from being forgotten: *A statue helps perpetuate the memory of a famous person. verb,* **per pet u at ed, per pet u at ing.**

perpendicular (definition 1) a perpendicular cliff

per plex (pər pleks′), trouble with doubt; puzzle; bewilder: *This problem even perplexed the teacher.* See picture. *verb.*

per plex i ty (pər plek′sə tē), **1** perplexed condition; confusion; being puzzled; not knowing what to do or how to act: *My perplexity was so great that I asked everyone for advice.* **2** something that perplexes: *There are many perplexities in such a complicated job. noun, plural* **per plex i ties.**

per se cute (pėr′sə kyüt), **1** treat badly; do harm to again and again; oppress: *That gang persecutes the children by attacking them on their way home.* **2** treat badly because of one's principles or beliefs: *Christians were persecuted in ancient Rome. verb,* **per se cut ed, per se cut ing.**

per se cu tion (pėr′sə kyü′shən), **1** persecuting: *The gang's persecution of the children was cruel.* **2** being persecuted: *The children's persecution by the gang made them afraid to walk home. noun.*

per se ver ance (pėr′sə vir′əns), sticking to a purpose or an aim; never giving up what one has set out to do: *By perseverance she finally learned to swim. noun.*

per se vere (pėr′sə vir′), continue steadily in doing something hard; persist. To try, try, try again is to persevere. *verb,* **per se vered, per se ver ing.**

per sim mon (pər sim′ən), the yellowish-orange, plumlike fruit of a North American tree. Persimmons are very bitter when green, but sweet and good to eat when very ripe. *noun.*

per sist (pər sist′), **1** stick to it; refuse to stop or be changed: *She persists in reading at the dinner table.* **2** last; stay; endure: *On some very high mountains snow persists throughout the year.* **3** say again and again; maintain: *He persisted that he was innocent of the crime. verb.*

per sist ence (pər sis′təns), **1** being persistent: *the persistence of a fly buzzing around one's head.* **2** continuing existence: *the stubborn persistence of a cough. noun.*

per sist ent (pər sis′tənt), **1** persisting; not giving up, especially in the face of dislike, disapproval, or difficulties: *a persistent worker.* **2** lasting; going on; continuing: *a persistent headache that lasted for three days. adjective.*

per son (pėr′sən), **1** man, woman, or child; human being: *Any person who wishes may come to the fair.* **2** the human body: *The person of the king was well guarded.* **3** bodily appearance: *He kept his person neat and trim. noun.*
in person, with or by one's own action or presence; personally: *Come in person; do not write or phone.*

per son age (pėr′sə nij), **1** person of importance. **2** person. **3** character in a book or a play. *noun.*

per son al (pėr′sə nəl), **1** belonging to a person; private: *a personal letter.* **2** done in person; directly by oneself, not through others or by letter: *a personal visit.* **3** of the body or bodily appearance: *personal charms.* **4** about or against a person or persons: *personal remarks, personal abuse. adjective.*

per son al i ty (pėr′sə nal′ə tē), **1** the personal or individual quality that makes one person be different or act differently from another: *A baby two weeks old does not have much personality.* **2** likable qualities of a person: *The boy is developing a personality.* **3** a well-known person: *personalities of the entertainment world. noun, plural* **per son al i ties.**

per son al ly (pėr′sə nə lē), **1** in person; not by the aid of others: *The owner of this store deals personally with customers.* **2** as far as oneself is concerned: *Personally, I like apples better than oranges.* **3** as a person: *I don't know her personally, but I've been told she is a talented writer. adverb.*

per spec tive (pər spek′tiv), **1** art of picturing objects on a flat surface so as to give the appearance of distance. See picture. **2** effect of the distance of events upon the mind: *Many happenings of last year seem less important when viewed in perspective. noun.*

per spi ra tion (pėr′spə rā′shən), **1** sweat: *The runner's forehead was damp with perspiration.* **2** sweating. *noun.*

per spire (pər spīr′), sweat: *The room was so hot I began to perspire. verb,* **per spired, per spir ing.**

per suade (pər swād′), win over to do or believe; make willing or sure by urging or arguing: *I knew I should study, but he persuaded me to go to the movies. verb,* **per suad ed, per suad ing.**

per sua sion (pər swā′zhən), **1** persuading: *All our attempts at persuasion were useless; she would not go.* **2** power of persuading: *He is a poor salesman because he lacks persuasion.* **3** a firm belief: *different political persuasions.* **4** a religious belief; religious denomination: *Even though we are not of the same persuasion, we believe many of the same things. noun.*

per sua sive (pər swā′siv), able to persuade; fitted to persuade: *Your persuasive argument convinced me. adjective.*

pert (pėrt), not serious or respectful; too free in speech or action: *Her pert reply annoyed us. adjective.*

per tain (pər tān′), **1** belong or be connected as a part or possession: *We own the house and the land pertaining to it.* **2** have to do with; be related; refer: *My question pertains to yesterday's homework.* **3** be appropriate: *We had turkey and everything else that pertains to Thanksgiving Day. verb.*

per ti nent (pėrt′n ənt), having something to do with what is being considered; relating to the matter in hand; to the point: *If your question is pertinent, I will answer it. adjective.*

per turb (pər tėrb′), disturb greatly; make uneasy or troubled: *My parents were perturbed by my grades. verb.*

pe ruse (pə rüz′), **1** read thoroughly and carefully. **2** read. *verb,* **pe rused, pe rus ing.**

per vade (pər vād′), go or spread throughout; be throughout: *The odor of pines pervades the air. verb,* **per vad ed, per vad ing.**

per verse (pər vėrs′), **1** contrary and willful; stubborn: *The perverse child did just what we told him not to do.* **2** wicked. *adjective.*

pe so (pā′sō), unit of money in various countries of Latin America and in the Philippines. *noun, plural* **pe sos.**

pes si mis tic (pes′ə mis′tik), **1** having a tendency to look on the dark side of things or to see all the difficulties and disadvantages. **2** expecting the worst: *I was pessimistic about passing the test because I hadn't studied. adjective.*

pest (pest), thing or person that causes trouble, injuries, or destruction; nuisance: *Flies are pests. Whining children are pests.* See picture. *noun.*

pes ter (pes′tər), annoy; trouble; vex: *Flies pester us. Don't pester me with foolish questions. verb.*

pes ti lence (pes′tl əns), disease that spreads rapidly, causing many deaths. Smallpox, yellow fever, and the plague are pestilences. *noun.*

pes tle (pes′əl), tool for pounding or crushing something to a powder in a mortar. *noun.*

pet (pet), **1** animal kept as a favorite and treated with affection. **2** treated as a pet: *a pet rabbit.* **3** stroke or pat; touch lovingly and gently: *She is petting the kitten.* **4** darling or favorite: *teacher's pet.* 1,4 *noun,* 2 *adjective,* 3 *verb,* **pet ted, pet ting.**

pet al (pet′l), one of the parts of a flower that are usually colored. A rose has many petals. *noun.*

pe tite (pə tēt′), little; of small size: *a petite young woman. adjective.*

pe ti tion (pə tish′ən), **1** a formal request to someone in authority for some privilege, right, or benefit: *The people on our street signed a petition asking the city council for a new sidewalk.* **2** ask earnestly; make a formal request to: *They petitioned the mayor to use his influence with the city council.* 1 *noun,* 2 *verb.*

pet rel (pet′rəl), a small black-and-white sea bird with long, pointed wings. *noun.*

pet ri fy (pet′rə fī), **1** turn into stone: *There is a petrified forest in Arizona.* **2** paralyze with fear, horror, or surprise: *The bird was petrified as the snake came near. verb,* **pet ri fied, pet ri fy ing.**

pe tro le um (pə trō′lē əm), an oily, dark-colored liquid that is found in the earth. Gasoline, kerosene, and many other products are made from petroleum. *noun.*

pet ti coat (pet′ē kōt), **1** skirt worn beneath a dress or outer skirt by women and girls. **2** skirt. *noun.*

pet ty (pet′ē), **1** small; having little importance or value: *Don't let petty disturbances upset you.* **2** mean: *A gossip has a petty mind.* **3** lower; subordinate: *a petty official. adjective,* **pet ti er, pet ti est.**

pet u lant (pech′ə lənt), likely to have little fits of bad temper; irritable over trifles; peevish. *adjective.*

pe tun ia (pə tü′nyə *or* pə tyü′nyə), a common garden plant that has white, pink, and purple flowers shaped like funnels. *noun.*

pew (pyü), bench in church for people to sit on, fastened to the floor and with a back. *noun.*

pe wee (pē′wē), a small American bird with an olive-colored or gray back. Its call sounds somewhat like its name. *noun.*

a hat	**i** it	**oi** oil	**ch** child	a in about
ā age	**ī** ice	**ou** out	**ng** long	e in taken
ä far	**o** hot	**u** cup	**sh** she	ə = i in pencil
e let	**ō** open	** u̇** put	**th** thin	o in lemon
ē equal	**ô** order	**ü** rule	**ŦH** then	u in circus
ėr term			**zh** measure	

perplex—The difficult jigsaw puzzle **perplexed** them.

perspective (definition 1) The yellow lines on the street seem to meet at the horizon because of perspective.

pew ter (pyü′tər), **1** alloy of tin with lead, copper, or other metals. **2** dishes or other utensils made of this. **3** made of pewter: *a pewter mug.* 1,2 *noun,* 3 *adjective.*

phan tom (fan′təm), **1** image in the mind which seems to be real: *phantoms of a dream.* **2** a vague, dim, or shadowy appearance; ghost. **3** like a ghost; unreal: *a phantom ship.* 1,2 *noun,* 3 *adjective.*

phar aoh (fer′ō), title given to the kings of ancient Egypt. *noun.*

phar ma cist (fär′mə sist), druggist. *noun.*

phar ma cy (fär′mə sē), **1** store where drugs and other medicines are sold; drugstore. **2** preparation of drugs and medicines; business of a druggist. *noun, plural* **phar ma cies.**

phase (fāz), **1** one of the changing states or stages of development of a person or thing: *At present his voice is changing; that is a phase all boys go through.* **2** one side, part, or view (of a subject): *What phase of arithmetic are you studying now?* **3** shape of the moon or of a planet as it is seen at a particular time. See picture. *noun.*

pheas ant (fez′nt), a bird with a long tail and brightly colored feathers that is hunted and used for food. Wild pheasants live in many parts of Europe and America. See picture. *noun, plural* **pheas ants** or **pheas ant.**

phe nom e na (fə nom′ə nə), more than one phenomenon. *noun plural.*

phe nom e nal (fə nom′ə nəl), extraordinary: *a phenomenal memory. adjective.*

phe nom e non (fə nom′ə non), **1** fact, event, or circumstance that can be observed: *Lightning is an electrical phenomenon. Fever and inflammation are phenomena of disease.* **2** something or someone extraordinary or remarkable: *An eclipse is an interesting phenomenon. The fond parents think their child is a phenomenon. noun, plural* **phe nom e na** or (for definition 2) **phe nom e nons.**

phi al (fī′əl), a small bottle; vial. *noun.*

phil an throp ic (fil′ən throp′ik), charitable; benevolent; kindly. *adjective.*

phi lan thro pist (fə lan′thrə pist), a person who helps humanity, often by giving large sums of money to worthy causes. *noun.*

Phil ip pine (fil′ə pēn′), of or having something to do with the Philippines or their people. *adjective.*

Phil ip pines (fil′ə pēnz′), country made up of 7000 islands in the Pacific Ocean southeast of Asia. The United States governed the Philippines before they gained independence in 1946. *noun plural.*

phi los o pher (fə los′ə fər), **1** person who studies philosophy a great deal. **2** author or founder of a system of philosophy. **3** person who is calm and reasonable under hard conditions, accepting life and making the best of it. *noun.*

phil o soph ic (fil′ə sof′ik), philosophical. *adjective.*

phil o soph i cal (fil′ə sof′ə kəl), **1** of philosophy. **2** wise, calm, and reasonable. *adjective.*

phi los o phy (fə los′ə fē), **1** study of the truth or principles of all real knowledge; study of the most general causes and principles of the universe. **2** explanation of the universe. **3** system for guiding life. **4** calm and reasonable attitude; accepting things as they are and making the best of them. *noun, plural* **phi los o phies.**

phlegm (flem), the thick mucus that appears in the nose and throat during a cold. *noun.*

phlox (floks), a common garden plant that has showy flower clusters of various colors. *noun, plural* **phlox es.**

phoe be (fē′bē), a small North American bird with a grayish-brown back, a yellowish-white breast, and a low crest on the head. It catches and eats insects as it flies. *noun.*

phone (fōn), telephone. *noun, verb,* **phoned, phon ing.**

pho net ic (fə net′ik), representing sounds made with the voice. Phonetic symbols are marks used to show pronunciation. We use ō as the phonetic symbol for the sound of *o* in *photo. adjective.*

pho no graph (fō′nə graf), instrument that reproduces sounds from records; record player. As a record turns, a special needle picks up its sounds, which are heard on a loudspeaker. *noun.*

phos phor us (fos′fər əs), a yellow or white waxy substance that burns slowly at ordinary temperatures and glows in the dark. *noun.*

pho to (fō′tō), photograph. *noun, plural* **pho tos.**

pho to graph (fō′tə graf), **1** picture made with a camera. A photograph is made by the action of the light rays from the thing pictured passing through the lens of the camera to the film. **2** take a photograph of. 1 *noun,* 2 *verb.*

pho tog ra pher (fə tog′rə fər), **1** person who takes photographs. **2** person whose business is taking photographs. *noun.*

pho tog ra phy (fə tog′rə fē), taking photographs. *noun.*

phrase (frāz), **1** combination of words: *He spoke in simple phrases, so that the children understood him.* **2** expression often used: *"Call up" is the common phrase for "make a telephone call to."* **3** express in a particular way: *I tried to phrase my excuse politely.* **4** group of words not containing a subject and verb and used as a single word. *In the house, coming by the church,* and *to eat too fast* are phrases. 1,2,4 *noun,* 3 *verb,* **phrased, phras ing.**

phys i cal (fiz′ə kəl), **1** of the body: *physical exercise, physical strength.* **2** of matter; material: *The tide is a physical force.* **3** according to the laws of nature: *It is a physical impossibility for the sun to rise in the west.* **4** dealing with the natural features of the earth. **Physical geography** teaches about the earth's formation, climate, clouds, and tides. *adjective.*

phys i cal ly (fiz′ik lē), in a physical manner; in physical respects; as regards the body: *She was in fine condition both physically and mentally. adverb.*

phy si cian (fə zish′ən), doctor of medicine. *noun.*

phys i cist (fiz′ə sist), person who is an expert in physics. *noun.*

phys ics (fiz′iks), the science that deals with matter and energy and their relationships to each other. Physics includes the study of mechanics, heat, light, sound, electricity, and magnetism. *noun.*

phys i ol o gy (fiz′ē ol′ə jē), science dealing with the normal working of living things or their parts: *animal physiology, human physiology. noun.*

phy sique (fə zēk′), body; bodily structure, organization, or development: *The swimmer had a strong physique. noun.*

pi an ist (pē an′ist *or* pē′ə nist), person who plays the piano. *noun.*

pi an o (pē an′ō), a musical instrument whose tones come from many wires. The wires are sounded by hammers that are worked by striking keys on a keyboard. *noun, plural* **pi an os.** [*Piano* was shortened from *pianoforte,* which came from an Italian word meaning "soft and loud." The piano was called this because of the many different tones that can be played on it.]

pi az za (pē az′ə *for 1;* pē ät′sə *or* pē az′ə *for 2*), **1** a large porch along one or more sides of a house. **2** an open public square in Italian towns. *noun.*

pic co lo (pik′ə lō), a small, shrill flute, sounding an octave higher than an ordinary flute. See picture. *noun, plural* **pic co los.**

pick[1] (pik), **1** choose; select: *I picked a winning horse at the races.* **2** choice or selection: *This red rose is my pick.* **3** the best part: *We got a high price for the pick of our peaches.* **4** pull away with the fingers; gather: *We pick fruit.* **5** pierce, dig into, or break up with some pointed tool: *pick ground, pick rocks.* **6** use something pointed to remove things from: *pick one's teeth, pick a bone.* **7** open with a pointed instrument or wire: *The burglar picked the lock on the garage.* **8** steal the contents of: *Someone picked my pocket.* **9** pluck at: *I picked the banjo.* **10** thing held in the fingers and used to pluck the strings of a musical instrument. **11** seek and find: *Don't pick a quarrel with them.* 1,4-9,11 *verb,* 2,3,10 *noun.*

pick at, 1 pull on with the fingers: *She picked at the scab on her finger.* **2** eat a bit at a time: *The bird picks at the bread. Don't pick at your food.*

pick on, 1 find fault with: *The teacher picked on him for always being late.* **2** annoy; tease: *My older brother and sister are always picking on me.*

pick out, 1 choose; select: *Pick out a coat you like.* **2** distinguish (a thing) from its surroundings: *Can you pick me out in this group picture?*

pick over, look over carefully: *to pick over vegetables before buying.*

pick up, 1 take up: *She picked up a hammer. The bus stopped at the corner to pick up passengers.* **2** get by chance: *I picked up a bargain at the sale.* **3** learn without being taught: *He picks up games easily.* **4** succeed in seeing or hearing: *She picked up a radio broadcast from Paris.* **5** tidy up; put in order: *pick up a room, pick up one's desk.*

pick[2] (pik), **1** pickax. **2** a sharp-pointed tool. Ice is broken into pieces with a pick. *noun.*

a hat	i it	oi oil	ch child	a in about
ā age	ī ice	ou out	ng long	e in taken
ä far	o hot	u cup	sh she	ə = i in pencil
e let	ō open	u̇ put	th thin	o in lemon
ē equal	ô order	ü rule	₮H then	u in circus
ėr term			zh measure	

pheasant—about 3½ feet (1 meter) long with the tail

phase (definition 3)—phases of the moon

piccolo

pick ax or **pick axe** (pik′aks′), tool with a heavy metal bar, pointed at one or both ends, attached through the center to a wooden handle. It is used for breaking up dirt or rocks. *noun, plural* **pick ax es.**

pick er el (pik′ər əl), a freshwater fish that is smaller than the pike and has a long, pointed head. It is used for food. *noun, plural* **pick er els** or **pick er el.**

pick et (pik′it), **1** a pointed stake or peg placed upright to make a fence or driven into the ground to tie a horse to. **2** enclose with pickets; fence. **3** tie to a picket: *Picket your horse here.* **4** a small group of soldiers, or a single soldier, posted at some place to watch for the enemy and guard against surprise. **5** person stationed by a labor union near a factory or store where there is a strike. Pickets try to prevent employees from working or customers from buying. **6** station as pickets: *The union picketed workers near the main entrance.* **7** station pickets at or near: *to picket a factory during a strike.* **1,4,5** *noun,* **2,3,6,7** *verb.*

pick le (pik′əl), **1** salt water, vinegar, or other liquid in which meat and vegetables can be preserved. **2** cucumber preserved in pickle. **3** any other vegetable preserved in pickle. **4** preserve in pickle: *pickle beets.* **5** trouble; difficulty: *I got in a bad pickle today.* **1-3,5** *noun,* **4** *verb,* **pick led, pick ling.**

pick pock et (pik′pok′it), person who steals from people's pockets. *noun.*

pick up (pik′up′), **1** picking up: *the daily pickup of mail.* **2** improvement: *a pickup in business, a pickup in one's health.* **3** going faster; increase in speed. **4** a small, light truck with an open back, used for light hauling. *noun.*

pic nic (pik′nik), **1** pleasure trip or party, with a meal in the open air: *We had a picnic at the beach.* **2** go on such a trip: *Our family often picnics at the beach.* **3** eat in picnic style: *We picnicked in the backyard.* **1** *noun,* **2,3** *verb,* **pic nicked, pic nick ing.**

pic nick er (pik′ni kər), person who picnics. *noun.*

pic to ri al (pik tôr′ē əl), **1** having something to do with pictures; expressed in pictures. **2** making a picture for the mind; vivid. **3** illustrated by pictures: *a pictorial history, a pictorial magazine. adjective.*

pic ture (pik′chər), **1** drawing, painting, portrait, or photograph; printed copy of any of these: *The book contains a good picture of a tiger.* **2** scene: *The trees and brook make a lovely picture.* **3** something beautiful: *The old castle was a picture in the bright sunlight.* **4** draw or paint; make into a picture: *The artist pictured life in the old West.* **5** likeness; image: *He is the picture of his father.* **6** form a picture of in the mind; imagine: *It is hard to picture life a hundred years ago.* **7** idea: *have a clear picture of the problem.* **8** a vivid description. **9** show by words; describe vividly: *The speaker pictured the suffering of the poor.* **10** motion picture. **11** image on a television set. **1-3,5,7,8,10,11** *noun,* **4,6,9** *verb,* **pic tured, pic tur ing.**

pillory (definition 1)

pier (definition 1)

pic tur esque (pik′chə resk′), **1** quaint or interesting enough to be used as the subject of a picture: *a picturesque old mill.* **2** making a picture for the mind; vivid: *picturesque language. adjective.*

pie (pī), fruit, meat, or the like, enclosed in pastry and baked: *apple pie, chicken pie. noun.*

piece (pēs), **1** one of the parts into which a thing is divided or broken; bit: *The cup broke in pieces.* **2** a limited part: *a piece of land containing two acres.* **3** a small quantity: *a piece of bread, a piece of wood.* **4** a single thing of a set or class: *This set of china has 144 pieces.* **5** a single composition in an art: *a piece of poetry, a piece of music.* **6** coin: *A nickel is a five=cent piece.* **7** example; instance: *That silly story is a piece of nonsense.* **8** make or repair by adding or joining pieces: *piece a quilt.* **9** join the pieces of. **1-7** *noun,* **8,9** *verb,* **pieced, piec ing.**

piece of one's mind, a scolding: *She gave them a piece of her mind for coming late again.*

piece meal (pēs′mēl′), **1** piece by piece; a little at a time: *work done piecemeal.* **2** piece from piece; to pieces; into fragments: *The lamb was torn piecemeal by the wolves. adverb.*

piece of eight, an old Spanish peso, used by the Spanish in Spain and America. It corresponded to the United States dollar.

pied (pīd), having patches of two or more colors; many-colored. *adjective.*

pier (pir), **1** structure built out over the water, and used as a walk or a landing place. See picture. **2** one of the solid supports on which the arches of a bridge rest; pillar. *noun.*

pierce (pirs), **1** go into; go through: *A tunnel pierces the mountain.* **2** make a hole in; bore into or through: *A nail pierced the tire of our car.* **3** force a way through or into: *The cold wind pierced our clothes. A sharp cry pierced the air.* **4** make a way through with the eye or mind: *pierce a disguise, pierce a mystery. verb,* **pierced, pierc ing.**

pi e ty (pī′ə tē), **1** being pious; reverence for God; religious character or conduct; holiness; goodness. **2** a pious act, remark, or belief. *noun, plural* **pi e ties.**

pig (pig), **1** a domestic animal with a stout, heavy body, hoofs, and a broad snout. It is raised for its meat. **2** a young pig. **3** person who seems or acts like a pig; one who is greedy, dirty, dull, sullen, or stubborn. *noun.*

pig eon (pij′ən), bird with a plump body and short legs; dove. *noun.*

pig eon-toed (pij′ən tōd′), having the toes or feet turned inward. *adjective.*

pig gy back (pig′ē bak′), on the back: *a piggyback ride. Flatcars often take trucks piggyback from one place to another. adjective, adverb.*

pig-head ed (pig′hed′id), stupidly obstinate or stubborn. *adjective.*

pig ment (pig′mənt), a coloring matter. Paint and dyes are made by mixing pigments with liquid. The color of a person's hair, skin, and eyes is due to pigment in the cells of the body. *noun.*

pig my (pig′mē), pygmy. *noun, plural* **pig mies;** *adjective.*

pig pen (pig′pen′), **1** pen where pigs are kept. **2** a filthy place. *noun.*

pig sty (pig′stī), pigpen. *noun, plural* **pig sties.**

pig tail (pig′tāl′), braid of hair hanging from the back of the head. *noun.*

pike[1] (pīk), spear with a long wooden handle which foot soldiers used to carry; spear. *noun.*

pike[2] (pīk), a large freshwater fish with a long, pointed head. *noun, plural* **pikes** or **pike.**

pile[1] (pīl), **1** many things lying one upon another in a more or less orderly way: *a pile of wood.* **2** mass like a hill or mound: *a pile of dirt.* **3** make into a pile; heap up; stack: *The campers piled the extra wood in a corner.* **4** gather or rise in piles: *Snow piled against the fences.* **5** a large amount: *I have a pile of work to do.* **6** cover with large amounts: *pile a plate with food.* **7** go in a confused, rushing crowd or group: *We piled out of the bus into the schoolyard. They all piled into the car.* 1,2,5 *noun,* 3,4,6,7 *verb,* **piled, pil ing.**

pile[2] (pīl), a heavy beam driven upright into the ground or the bed of a river to help support a bridge, wharf, or building. *noun.*

pile[3] (pīl), **1** a soft, thick nap on velvet, plush, and many carpets: *The pile of that rug is almost half an inch long.* **2** a soft, fine hair or down; wool. *noun.*

pil fer (pil′fər), steal in small quantities: *The children pilfered apples from the orchard. verb.*

a hat	i it	oi oil	ch child	(a in about
ā age	ī ice	ou out	ng long	e in taken
ä far	o hot	u cup	sh she	ə = { i in pencil
e let	ō open	u̇ put	th thin	o in lemon
ē equal	ô order	ü rule	ŦH then	u in circus
ėr term			zh measure	

pil grim (pil′grəm), **1** person who goes on a journey to a sacred or holy place as an act of religious devotion. In the Middle Ages, many people used to go as pilgrims to Jerusalem and to holy places in Europe. **2** traveler; wanderer. **3** **Pilgrim,** one of the English settlers who founded Plymouth, Massachusetts, in 1620. *noun.*

pil grim age (pil′grə mij), **1** a pilgrim's journey; journey to some sacred place. **2** a long journey. *noun.*

pill (pil), medicine made up into a tiny ball to be swallowed whole. *noun.*

pil lage (pil′ij), **1** plunder; rob with violence: *Pirates pillaged the towns along the coast.* **2** plunder; robbery. 1 *verb,* **pil laged, pil lag ing;** 2 *noun.*

pil lar (pil′ər), **1** a slender upright support; column. Pillars are usually made of stone, wood, or metal and used as supports or ornaments for a building. Sometimes a pillar stands alone as a monument. **2** anything slender and upright like a pillar. **3** an important support or supporter: *a person who is a pillar of the church. noun.*

pil lor y (pil′ər ē), **1** frame of wood with holes through which a person's head and hands were put. The pillory was formerly used as a punishment, being set up in a public place where the crowd could make fun of the offender. See picture. **2** put in the pillory. 1 *noun, plural* **pil lor ies;** 2 *verb,* **pil lor ied, pil lor y ing.**

pil low (pil′ō), **1** bag or case filled with feathers, down, or other soft material, usually to support the head when resting or sleeping. **2** rest on a pillow. 1 *noun,* 2 *verb.*

pil low case (pil′ō kās′), a cloth cover pulled over a pillow. *noun.*

pi lot (pī′lət), **1** person who steers a ship or boat. **2** person whose business is to steer ships in or out of a harbor or through dangerous waters. A ship takes on a pilot before coming into a strange harbor. **3** person who operates the controls of an aircraft in flight. **4** act as a pilot of; steer: *to pilot an airplane.* **5** guide; leader. **6** guide; lead: *The manager piloted us through the big factory.* 1-3,5 *noun,* 4,6 *verb.*

pim ple (pim′pəl), a small, sore, red swelling of the skin. *noun.*

pin (pin), **1** a short slender piece of wire with a point at one end and a head at the other, for fastening things together. **2** badge with a pin or clasp to fasten it to the clothing: *She wore her class pin.* **3** ornament which has a pin or clasp; brooch. **4** peg made of wood, metal, or plastic, used to fasten things together, hold something, or hang things on. **5** any of various fastenings, such as a clothespin or a safety pin. **6** fasten with a pin or pins; put a pin through. **7** hold fast in one position: *When the tree fell, its branches pinned the* *bear to the ground.* **8** a bottle-shaped piece of wood used in the game of bowling. 1-5,8 *noun*, 6,7 *verb*, **pinned, pin ning.**

on pins and needles, very anxious or uneasy: *I was on pins and needles until I found out I passed the test.*

pin a fore (pin′ə fôr′), **1** a child's apron that covers most of the dress. **2** a light dress without sleeves. *noun.*

pi ña ta (pē nyä′tə), pot filled with candy, fruit, and small toys, hung at Christmas time in Mexico and other Latin-American countries. Blindfolded children swing sticks in order to break the pot to get what is inside. *noun, plural* **pi ña tas.**

pin cers (pin′sərz), **1** tool for gripping and holding tight, made like scissors but with jaws instead of blades. **2** the large claw with which crabs, lobsters, and crayfish pinch or nip; pair of claws. See picture. *noun plural or singular.*

pinch (pinch), **1** squeeze with thumb and forefinger: *I pinched the baby's cheek playfully.* **2** act of pinching. **3** press so as to hurt; squeeze: *These new shoes pinch my feet.* **4** sharp pressure that hurts; a squeeze: *the pinch of tight shoes.* **5** sharp discomfort or distress: *the pinch of hunger.* **6** cause to shrink or become thin: *a face pinched by hunger.* **7** time of special need: *I will help you in a pinch.* **8** as much as can be taken up with the tips of finger and thumb: *a pinch of salt.* **9** be stingy; be stingy with: *The miser even pinched pennies.* 1,3,6,9 *verb*, 2,4,5,7,8 *noun, plural* **pinch es.**

pin cush ion (pin′kush′ən), a small cushion to stick pins in until they are needed. *noun.*

pine¹ (pīn), **1** tree that bears cones and has evergreen leaves shaped like needles. Many pines are of value for lumber, tar, and turpentine. **2** wood of the pine. *noun.*

pine² (pīn), long eagerly; yearn: *The homesick children pined to see their parents.* *verb*, **pined, pin ing.**

pine ap ple (pī′nap′əl), the large, juicy, tropical fruit of a plant with slender, stiff leaves. Pineapples look something like big pine cones and are good to eat. *noun.*

Ping-Pong (ping′pong′), a trademark for a game like tennis played on a large table, using small wooden rackets and a light, hollow ball. *noun.*

pin ion (pin′yən), **1** the last joint of a bird's wing. **2** bind; bind the arms of; bind (to something): *The bank robbers pinioned the guard's arms.* 1 *noun*, 2 *verb.*

pink (pingk), **1** a color that is a mixture of red and white; light or pale red. **2** having this color. **3** the highest degree or condition: *Exercise helps keep a person in the pink of health.* **4** a garden plant with spicy-smelling flowers of various colors, mostly white, pink, and red. A carnation is one kind of pink. 1,3,4 *noun*, 2 *adjective.*

pink eye (pingk′ī′), a disease that causes soreness of the thin lining that covers the inner eyelid and the front of the eyeball. You can catch pinkeye from someone who has it. *noun.*

pin na cle (pin′ə kəl), **1** a high peak or point of

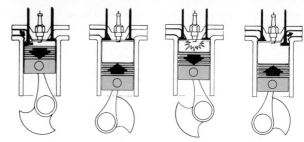

piston—The drawing shows how an automobile piston (shown in blue) moves inside a cylinder. A spark causes the gasoline vapor to explode and drive the piston.

rock. **2** the highest point: *at the pinnacle of her fame.* **3** a slender turret or spire. *noun.*

pint (pīnt), a unit for measuring liquids equal to half a quart or 16 fluid ounces. *noun.*

pin to (pin′tō), **1** spotted in two or more colors. **2** a spotted, white and black or white and brown horse. 1 *adjective*, 2 *noun, plural* **pin tos.**

pi o neer (pī′ə nir′), **1** person who settles in a part of a country, preparing it for others. See picture. **2** person who goes first, or does something first, and so prepares a way for others: *a pioneer in medical science.* **3** prepare or open up for others; take the lead: *Astronauts are pioneering in exploring outer space.* 1,2 *noun*, 3 *verb.*

pi ous (pī′əs), **1** religious; having or showing reverence for God. **2** done under pretense of religion: *a pious fraud.* *adjective.*

pipe (pīp), **1** tube through which a liquid or gas flows. **2** carry by means of a pipe or pipes. **3** supply with pipes: *Our street is being piped for gas.* **4** tube of clay, wood, or other material, with a bowl at one end, for smoking. **5** a musical instrument with a single tube into which the player blows. **6** play music on a pipe. **7** any one of the tubes in an organ. **8** make a shrill noise; sing in a shrill voice. **9** a shrill sound, voice, or song: *the pipe of the lark.* 1,4,5,7,9 *noun*, 2,3,6,8 *verb*, **piped, pip ing.**

pipe line (pīp′līn′), line of pipes for carrying oil or gas, usually over a considerable distance. *noun.*

pip er (pī′pər), person who plays on a pipe or bagpipe. *noun.*

pip ing (pī′ping), **1** a shrill sound: *the piping of frogs in the spring.* **2** shrill. **3** so as to hiss; boiling: *The tea is piping hot.* **4** pipes: *lead piping.* 1,4 *noun*, 2,3 *adjective.*

pique (pēk), **1** feeling of anger at being slighted; wounded pride: *In a pique, he left the party.* **2** wound the pride of: *It piqued her that we had a secret she did not share.* **3** arouse; stir up: *Our curiosity was piqued by the locked trunk.* 1 *noun*, 2,3 *verb*, **piqued, pi quing.**

pi ra cy (pī′rə sē), robbery on the sea. *noun, plural* **pi ra cies.**

pi rate (pī′rit), **1** person who attacks and robs ships; robber on the sea. **2** be a pirate; plunder; rob. 1 *noun*, 2 *verb*, **pi rat ed, pi rat ing.**

pis til (pis′tl), the part of a flower that produces seeds. See picture. *noun.*

pis tol (pis′tl), a small, short gun held and fired with one hand. *noun.*

pis ton (pis′tən), a short cylinder, or a flat, round piece of wood or metal, fitting closely inside a tube or hollow cylinder in which it is moved back and forth by some force (often the pressure of steam). A piston receives or transmits motion by means of a rod that is attached to it. See picture. *noun.*

pit[1] (pit), **1** a natural hole in the ground. **2** hole dug deep into the earth. A mine or the shaft of a mine is a pit. **3** a hollow place on the surface of anything: *the pit of the stomach.* **4** a little hollow place or scar, such as is left by smallpox. **5** mark with small pits or scars. **6** set to fight or compete; match: *She was pitted against her friend in the last round of the tennis match.* 1-4 *noun,* 5,6 *verb,* **pit ted, pit ting.**

pit[2] (pit), **1** the hard seed of a cherry, peach, plum, date, or similar fruit; stone. **2** remove the pits from (fruit). 1 *noun,* 2 *verb,* **pit ted, pit ting.**

pitch[1] (pich), **1** throw; fling; hurl; toss: *They were pitching horseshoes.* **2** (in baseball) to throw (a ball) to the player batting. **3** act of pitching; a throw or toss: *The first pitch was a strike.* **4** fix firmly in the ground; set up: *pitch a tent.* **5** fall or plunge forward: *I lost my balance and pitched down the stairs.* **6** plunge with the bow rising and then falling: *The ship pitched about in the storm.* **7** point; position; degree: *He has reached the highest pitch of success.* **8** degree of highness or lowness of a sound. **9** amount of slope: *Some roads in the Rocky Mountains have a very steep pitch.* 1,2,4-6 *verb,* 3,7-9 *noun, plural* **pitch es.**

pitch in, work hard: *All of us pitched in, and the job was soon finished.*

pitch into, attack.

pitch[2] (pich), a black, sticky substance made from tar or turpentine, used to cover the seams of wooden ships, to cover roofs, or to make pavements. *noun, plural* **pitch es.**

pitch er[1] (pich′ər), **1** container made of china, glass, or silver, with a lip at one side and a handle at the other. Pitchers are used for holding and pouring out water, milk, and other liquids. **2** amount that a pitcher holds. *noun.*

pitch er[2] (pich′ər), player on a baseball team who throws a ball to the batter to hit. *noun.*

pitch fork (pich′fôrk′), a large fork with a long handle for lifting and throwing hay. *noun.*

pit e ous (pit′ē əs), to be pitied; moving the heart; deserving pity: *A starving person is a piteous sight. adjective.*

pit fall (pit′fôl′), **1** a hidden pit to catch animals in. **2** any trap or hidden danger. *noun.*

pith (pith), **1** the central spongy tissue in the stems of certain plants. **2** anything like this tissue: *the pith of an orange.* **3** the important or essential part: *the pith of a speech. noun.*

pit i a ble (pit′ē ə bəl), **1** to be pitied; moving the heart; deserving pity. **2** deserving contempt; mean; to be scorned: *Their half-hearted attempts to help with the work were pitiable. adjective.*

a hat	**i** it	**oi** oil	**ch** child	a in about
ā age	**ī** ice	**ou** out	**ng** long	e in taken
ä far	**o** hot	**u** cup	**sh** she	ə = { i in pencil
e let	**ō** open	**u̇** put	**th** thin	o in lemon
ē equal	**ô** order	**ü** rule	**ᵀH** then	u in circus
ėr term			**zh** measure	

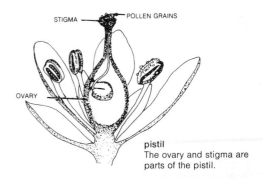

pistil
The ovary and stigma are parts of the pistil.

pincers (definition 2)—pincers of a crab

pioneer (definition 1)—The pioneers of the American West included explorers, trappers, and farming families.

pit i ful (pit′i fəl), **1** to be pitied; moving the heart; piteous; deserving pity: *The rabbit caught in the trap was a pitiful sight.* **2** deserving contempt; mean; to be scorned: *a pitiful excuse. adjective.*

pit i less (pit′ē lis), without pity or mercy. *adjective.*

pit y (pit′ē), **1** sympathy; sorrow for another's suffering or distress; feeling for the sorrows of others. **2** feel pity for: *I pitied the homeless puppy.* **3** cause for pity or regret; thing to be sorry for: *It is a pity to be kept in the house in fine weather.* **1,3** *noun, plural* **pit ies;** **2** *verb,* **pit ied, pit y ing.**
have pity on or **take pity on,** to show pity for: *Have pity on the poor beggar.*

piv ot (piv′ət), **1** shaft, pin, or point on which something turns. **2** mount on, attach by, or provide with a pivot. **3** turn on a pivot: *pivot on one's heel.* **4** a turn on a pivot or as if on a pivot: *With a quick pivot he threw the ball to his teammate.* **5** person or thing on which something turns, hinges, or depends; central point: *Being admitted to college was the pivot of her hopes.* **1,4,5** *noun,* **2,3** *verb.*

pix y or **pix ie** (pik′sē), fairy or elf. *noun, plural* **pix ies.**

piz za (pēt′sə), a spicy Italian dish made by baking a large flat layer of bread dough covered with cheese, tomato sauce, herbs, and other things. *noun.*

pk., peck. *plural* **pk.** or **pks.**

pl., plural.

plac ard (plak′ärd), notice to be posted in a public place; poster. *noun.*

place (plās), **1** the part of space occupied by a person or thing. **2** city, town, village, district, island, or the like: *What place do you come from?* **3** building or spot used for some particular purpose: *A store or office is a place of business.* **4** house; dwelling: *They have a beautiful place in the country.* **5** part or spot in a body or surface: *a sore place on one's foot. The dentist filled the decayed place in the tooth.* **6** the right position; usual position: *There is a time and place for everything. Each book is in its place on the shelf.* **7** rank; position; way of life: *She won first place in the contest. They have a high place in society.* **8** position in time; part of time occupied by an event: *The performance went too slowly in several places.* **9** space or seat for a person: *We took our places at the table.* **10** put in a particular spot, position, or condition: *Place the books on the table. The orphan was placed in a home. We placed an order for hats with this store. The people placed confidence in their leader.* **11** work; job; employment: *He tried to get a place in a store on Saturdays.* **12** duty; business: *It is not my place to find fault.* **1-9,11,12** *noun,* **10** *verb,* **placed, plac ing.**
in place of, instead of: *Use water in place of milk in that recipe.*
take place, happen; occur.

plac id (plas′id), pleasantly calm or peaceful; quiet: *a placid temper.* See picture. *adjective.*

plague (plāg), **1** a very dangerous disease that spreads rapidly from person to person and often

placid—We saw clouds reflected in the placid water.

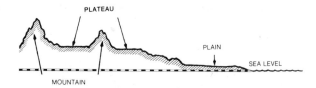

PLATEAU

PLAIN

SEA LEVEL

MOUNTAIN

plaid (definition 2)

causes death. **2** punishment thought to be sent by God. **3** thing or person that torments, vexes, annoys, troubles, offends, or is disagreeable. **4** vex; annoy; bother: *The people were plagued with high taxes.* **1-3** *noun,* **4** *verb,* **plagued, pla guing.**

plaid (plad), **1** a long piece of woolen cloth, usually having a pattern of checks or stripes in many colors, worn over one shoulder by the Scottish Highlanders. **2** any cloth with a pattern of checks or crisscross stripes. See picture. **3** pattern of this kind. **4** having a pattern of checks or stripes: *a plaid dress.* **1-3** *noun,* **4** *adjective.*

plain (plān), **1** clear; easy to understand; easily seen or heard: *The meaning is plain.* **2** clearly; in a plain manner. **3** without ornament or decoration; simple: *a plain coat.* **4** all of one color: *a plain blue shirt.* **5** not rich or highly seasoned: *plain food.* **6** common; ordinary; simple in manner: *They were plain, hard-working people.* **7** not pretty or handsome; homely: *a plain face.* **8** frank; honest; sincere: *plain speech.* **9** a flat stretch of land: *Cattle wandered over the western plains.* 1,3-8 *adjective,* 2 *adverb,* 9 *noun.*

plain-spo ken (plān′spō′kən), plain or frank in speech. *adjective.*

plain tive (plān′tiv), mournful; sad: *a plaintive song. adjective.*

plan (plan), **1** way of making or doing something that has been worked out beforehand: *Our summer plans were upset by mother's illness.* **2** think out beforehand how something is to be made or done; decide on methods and materials: *I plan to reach New York by train on Tuesday, and stay two days.* **3** make a plan of: *Have you planned your trip?* **4** drawing or diagram to show how a garden, a floor of a house, a park, or the like, is arranged. 1,4 *noun,* 2,3 *verb,* **planned, plan ning.**

plane[1] (plān), **1** any flat or level surface. **2** flat; level. **3** level; grade: *Try to keep your work on a high plane.* **4** airplane. 1,3,4 *noun,* 2 *adjective.*

plane[2] (plān), **1** a carpenter's tool with a blade for smoothing wood. **2** smooth (wood) with a plane. 1 *noun,* 2 *verb,* **planed, plan ing.**

plan et (plan′it), one of the heavenly bodies that move around the sun. Mercury, Venus, the earth, Mars, Jupiter, Saturn, Uranus, Neptune, and Pluto are planets. *noun.* [*Planet* comes from Greek words meaning "wandering stars." People of ancient times thought of the planets as stars that moved about while the other stars stayed in one place.]

plan e tar i um (plan′ə ter′ē əm *or* plan′ə tar′ē əm), a building with special equipment for showing the movements of the sun, moon, planets, and stars. These movements are shown by projecting lights on the inside of a dome. *noun.*

plan e tar y (plan′ə ter′ē), of a planet; having something to do with planets. *adjective.*

plank (plangk), a long, flat piece of sawed timber thicker than a board. *noun.*

walk the plank, be put to death by being forced to walk along and off a plank extending from a ship's side over the water. Pirates used to make their prisoners do this.

plank ton (plangk′tən), the small animals and plants that float or drift in water, especially at or near the surface. Plankton provides food for many fish. *noun.*

plant (plant), **1** any living thing that is not an animal. Trees, bushes, vines, grass, vegetables, and seaweed are all plants. **2** a living thing that has leaves, roots, and a soft stem, and is small in contrast with a tree or shrub: *a tomato plant, a house plant.* **3** a young growth ready to be set out in another place: *The farmer set out 100 cabbage plants.* **4** put in the ground to grow: *She planted sunflower seeds in the backyard.* **5** set firmly; put; place: *The climbers planted a flag on the top of the mountain. I planted my feet far apart.* **6** establish (a colony or city); settle. **7** put in (ideas or feelings): *Parents try to plant ideals in their children.*

8 building, machinery, and tools used in manufacturing some article or in producing something. 1-3,8 *noun,* 4-7 *verb.*

plan ta tion (plan tā′shən), a large farm or estate on which cotton, tobacco, sugar cane, or rubber trees are grown. The work on a plantation is done by laborers who live there. *noun.*

plant er (plan′tər), **1** person who owns or runs a plantation: *a cotton planter.* **2** machine for planting: *a corn planter.* **3** a box, stand, or other container, usually decorative, for plants. *noun.*

plas ma (plaz′mə), the clear, almost colorless, liquid part of blood, in which the corpuscles or blood cells float. *noun.*

plas ter (plas′tər), **1** a soft mixture of lime, sand, and water that hardens as it dries. **2** cover (a wall or ceiling) with plaster. **3** spread with anything thickly: *His shoes were plastered with mud.* **4** a medical preparation consisting of some substance spread on cloth, that will stick to the body and protect cuts or relieve pain. 1,4 *noun,* 2,3 *verb.*

plas tic (plas′tik), **1** any of various substances that can be shaped or molded when hot and become hard when cooled. Some plastics are very strong and tough. Vinyl and nylon are plastics. **2** made of a plastic: *a plastic bottle, a plastic dish.* **3** easily molded or shaped: *Clay, wax, and plaster are plastic substances.* 1 *noun,* 2,3 *adjective.*

plate (plāt), **1** dish, usually round, that is almost flat. Our food is served on plates. **2** something having a similar shape: *A plate is passed in our church to receive the collection.* **3** food served to one person at a meal: *The fund-raising dinner cost $50 a plate.* **4** dishes or utensils of silver or gold: *The family plate included a silver pitcher and the usual knives, forks, and spoons.* **5** dishes or utensils covered with a thin layer of silver or gold. **6** cover with a thin layer of silver, gold, or some other metal. **7** a thin, flat sheet or piece of metal: *a license plate.* **8** a thin, flat piece of metal or plastic on which something is engraved. Plates are used for printing pictures. **9** a thin sheet of glass or metal coated with chemicals that are sensitive to light. Plates are sometimes used in taking photographs. **10** (in baseball) the home base. 1-5,7-10 *noun,* 6 *verb,* **plat ed, plat ing.**

pla teau (pla tō′), plain in the mountains, or very high above sea level; large, high plain. See picture. *noun, plural* **pla teaus, pla teaux** (pla tōz′).

plat form (plat′fôrm), **1** a raised level surface: *There is a platform beside the track at the railroad station. The hall has a platform for speakers.* **2** plan of action or statement of beliefs of a group: *The platform of the new political party demands lower taxes. noun.*

plat i num (plat′n əm), a heavy, precious metal that looks like silver. Platinum does not tarnish or melt easily. It is used for making chemical and industrial equipment and in jewelry. *noun.*

pla toon (plə tün′), **1** the part of an army commanded by a lieutenant. Two or more squads make a platoon. **2** a small group. *noun.*

plat ter (plat′ər), a large, shallow dish for holding or serving food, especially meat and fish. *noun.*

plau si ble (plô′zə bəl), **1** appearing true, reasonable, or fair: *She gave a plausible excuse for being late.* **2** apparently worthy of confidence but often not really so: *a plausible liar. adjective.*

play (plā), **1** fun; sport; something done to amuse oneself: *The children are happy at play.* **2** have fun; do something in sport; perform: *The kitten plays with its tail. He played a joke on his sister.* **3** take part in (a game): *Children play tag and ball.* **4** take part in a game against: *Our team played the sixth-grade team.* **5** a turn, move, or act in a game: *It is your play next. She made a good play at checkers.* **6** put into action in a game: *Play your card.* **7** story written for or acted on the stage: *"Romeo and Juliet" is a famous play.* **8** act a part; act the part of: *The famous actress played Juliet.* **9** act: *play sick, play the fool, play fair.* **10** action: *fair play, foul play. He brought all his strength into play to move the rock.* **11** make believe; pretend in fun: *Let's play the hammock is a boat.* **12** make music; produce (music) on an instrument. **13** perform on (a musical instrument): *play a piano.* **14** cause to produce recorded or broadcast sound: *play a record, play the radio.* **15** move lightly or quickly: *A breeze played on the water.* **16** a light, quick movement: *the play of sunlight on leaves.* **17** freedom for action or motion: *We gave our fancies full play in telling what we could do with a million dollars.* **18** cause to act or to move: *play a hose on a burning building. The ship played its light along the coast.* **19** act carelessly; do foolish things: *Don't play with matches.* **20** gamble: *They like to play the horses.* 1,5,7,10,16,17 *noun,* 2-4,6,8,9,11-15,18-20 *verb.*

play on or **play upon,** take advantage of; make use of: *She played on her mother's good nature to get what she wanted.*

play er (plā′ər), **1** person who plays: *a baseball player, a card player.* **2** actor in a theater. **3** thing or device that plays: *A phonograph is a record player. noun.*

play ful (plā′fəl), **1** full of fun; fond of playing: *a playful puppy.* **2** joking; not serious: *a playful remark. adjective.*

play ground (plā′ground′), place for outdoor play. *noun.*

play house (plā′hous′), **1** a small house for a child to play in. **2** a toy house for a child; doll house. **3** theater. *noun, plural* **play hous es** (plā′hou′ziz).

playing card, one of a set of cards to play games with.

play mate (plā′māt′), person who plays with another. *noun.*

WHAT A RIDICULOUS PLIGHT!

plow (definition 2)

play pen (plā′pen′), a small folding enclosure for a baby or young child to play in. *noun.*

play room (plā′rüm′), room for children to play in. *noun.*

play thing (plā′thing′), thing to play with; toy. *noun.*

play wright (plā′rīt′), writer of plays; dramatist. *noun.*

plaz a (plaz′ə), a public square in a city or town. *noun.*

plea (plē), **1** request; asking: *The homeless people made a plea for help.* **2** excuse; defense: *The plea of the man who drove past the red light was that he did not see it. noun.*

plead (plēd), **1** offer reasons for or against something; argue: *The students pleaded their need for more time to finish the test.* **2** ask earnestly; make an earnest appeal: *When the rent was due, the poor family pleaded for more time.* **3** offer as an excuse: *The woman who stole pleaded poverty.* **4** speak for or against in a court of law: *He had a good lawyer to plead his case.* **5** answer to a charge in a court of law: *An accused person has the choice of pleading guilty or not guilty.* verb, **plead ed** or **pled, plead ing.**

pleas ant (plez′nt), **1** that pleases; giving pleasure: *a pleasant swim on a hot day.* **2** friendly; easy to get along with: *She is a pleasant person.* **3** fair; not stormy: *a pleasant day.* adjective.

please (plēz), **1** be agreeable to: *Toys please children. Sunshine and flowers please most people.* **2** be agreeable: *Such a fine meal cannot fail to please.* **3** wish; think fit: *Do what you please.* **4** be so kind as to; be good or nice enough to. *Please* is used with requests and commands as a means of being polite. *Would you please go to the store for some milk? Please come here.* verb, **pleased, pleas ing.**
be pleased, 1 be moved to pleasure. **2** like; choose.
if you please, if you like; with your permission.

pleas ing (plē′zing), giving pleasure; pleasant: *a very pleasing young man, a pleasing smile.* adjective.

pleas ur a ble (plezh′ər ə bəl), pleasant; agreeable. adjective.

pleas ure (plezh′ər), **1** feeling of being pleased; delight; joy: *His pleasure in the gift was obvious.* **2** something that pleases; cause of joy or delight: *It would be a pleasure to see you again.* **3** sport; play; anything that amuses: *She takes her pleasure in riding and hunting.* **4** desire; choice: *What is your pleasure in this matter?* noun.

pleat (plēt), **1** a flat, usually narrow, fold made in cloth by doubling it on itself. **2** fold or arrange in pleats: *pleat a skirt.* **1** noun, **2** verb.

pled (pled). See **plead.** *The lawyer pled her case.* verb.

pledge (plej), **1** an earnest promise: *They signed a pledge to give money to charity.* **2** promise earnestly: *We pledge allegiance to the flag.* **3** something that secures or makes safe; security: *She left the jewelry as a pledge for the loan.* **4** give as security. **5** something given to show favor or love. **1,3,5** noun, **2,4** verb, **pledged, pledg ing.**

plen te ous (plen′tē əs), plentiful. adjective.

plen ti ful (plen′ti fəl), more than enough; ample; abundant: *a plentiful supply of food.* adjective.

plen ty (plen′tē), full supply; all that one needs; a large enough number or amount: *You have plenty of time to catch the train.* noun.

pli a ble (plī′ə bəl), **1** easily bent; flexible; supple: *Willow twigs are pliable.* **2** easily influenced; yielding: *He is too pliable to be a good leader.* adjective.

pli ant (plī′ənt), **1** bending easily; pliable: *pliant leather.* **2** easily influenced; yielding: *a pliant nature.* adjective.

pli ers (plī′ərz), small pincers with long jaws for bending or cutting wire or holding small objects. noun plural or singular.

plight[1] (plīt), bad state; serious condition: *He was in a sad plight when he became ill and had no money.* See picture. noun.

plight[2] (plīt), pledge; promise earnestly: *plight one's loyalty.* verb.

a hat	**i** it	**oi** oil	**ch** child		**a** in about
ā age	**ī** ice	**ou** out	**ng** long		**e** in taken
ä far	**o** hot	**u** cup	**sh** she	**ə** =	**i** in pencil
e let	**ō** open	**u̇** put	**th** thin		**o** in lemon
ē equal	**ô** order	**ü** rule	**ŦH** then		**u** in circus
ėr term			**zh** measure		

plod (plod), **1** walk heavily; trudge: *The old man plods wearily along the road.* **2** proceed in a slow or dull way; work patiently with effort: *He plods away at his lessons until he learns them.* verb, **plod ded, plod ding.**

plop (plop), **1** sound like that of a flat object striking water without a splash. **2** make such a sound. **1** noun, **2** verb, **plopped, plop ping.**

plot (plot), **1** a secret plan, especially to do something wrong: *They formed a plot to rob the bank.* **2** plan; plan secretly with others to do something wrong: *The rebels plotted against the government.* **3** plan or main story of a play, novel, or poem: *Some people like plots filled with action and adventure.* **4** a small piece of ground: *a garden plot.* **5** map or diagram. **6** make a map or diagram of: *The nurse plotted a chart to show the patient's temperature over several days.* **7** mark the position of (something) on a map or diagram: *The nurse plotted the patient's temperature over several days.* **1,3-5** noun, **2,6,7** verb, **plot ted, plot ting.**

plough (plou), plow. noun, verb.

plov er (pluv′ər), bird with a short tail, a short bill, and long, pointed wings. noun.

plow (plou), **1** a big, heavy farm instrument for cutting the soil and turning it over. **2** turn up (the soil) with a plow: *plow a field.* See picture. **3** snowplow. **4** use a plow. **5** move through anything as a plow does; advance slowly and with effort: *The ship plowed through the waves.* **1,3** noun, **2,4,5** verb. Also spelled **plough.**

plow share (plou′sher′ or plou′shar′), blade of a plow; part of a plow that cuts the soil. noun.

pluck (pluk), **1** pick; pull off: *He plucked flowers in the garden.* **2** pull; pull at; tug; jerk: *She plucked at the loose threads of her coat.* **3** act of picking or pulling. **4** pull the feathers out of: *pluck a chicken.* **5** courage: *The cat showed pluck in fighting the dog.* **1,2,4** verb, **3,5** noun.

pluck y (pluk′ē), having or showing courage: *a plucky dog.* adjective, **pluck i er, pluck i est.**

plug (plug), **1** piece of wood or other substance used to stop up a hole. **2** stop up or fill with a plug. **3** device to make an electrical connection. Some plugs screw into sockets; others have prongs. **4** work steadily; plod: *We plugged away at our typewriters.* **1,3** noun, **2,4** verb, **plugged, plug ging.**
plug in, make an electrical connection by inserting a plug: *Plug in the television set.*

plum (plum), **1** a round, juicy fruit with smooth skin and a stone or pit. Plums are red, green, purple, or yellow. They grow on trees and are good to eat. **2** raisin in a pudding or cake. **3** something good: *This new job is a fine plum for her.* noun.

plumb line

plumage—The rooster had bright **plumage**.

plum age (plü′mij), feathers of a bird. See picture. *noun.*

plumb (plum), **1** a small weight. A plumb is hung on the end of a line used to measure the depth of water or to see if a wall is vertical. **2** test by a plumb line: *Our line was not long enough to plumb the depths of the lake.* **1** *noun,* **2** *verb.*

plumb er (plum′ər), person whose work is putting in and repairing water pipes and fixtures in buildings: *When the water pipe froze, we sent for a plumber. noun.*

plumb ing (plum′ing), **1** work or trade of a plumber. **2** the water pipes and fixtures in a building: *bathroom plumbing. noun.*

plumb line, line with a plumb at the end, used to find the depth of water or to see if a wall is vertical. See picture.

plume (plüm), **1** a large, long feather; feather. **2** a feather, bunch of feathers, or tuft of hair worn as an ornament on a hat or helmet. **3** smooth or arrange the feathers of: *The eagle plumed its wing.* **1,2** *noun,* **3** *verb,* **plumed, plum ing.**

plump[1] (plump), pleasantly round and full: *plump cheeks, a plump figure. adjective.*

plump[2] (plump), **1** fall or drop heavily or suddenly: *All out of breath, she plumped down on a chair.* **2** a sudden plunge; a heavy fall. **3** sound made by a plunge or fall. **4** heavily or suddenly: *He ran plump into me.* **1** *verb,* **2,3** *noun,* **4** *adverb.*

plun der (plun′dər), **1** rob by force; rob: *The pirates entered the harbor and began to plunder the town.* **2** things stolen; booty; loot: *They carried off the plunder in their ships.* **3** act of robbing by force: *In olden times soldiers often gained great wealth by plunder of a conquered city.* **1** *verb,* **2,3** *noun.*

plunge (plunj), **1** throw or thrust with force into a liquid or into a place: *Plunge your hand into the water.* **2** throw oneself into water, danger, or a fight: *She plunged into the lake to save the drowning swimmer.* **3** rush; dash: *The runner plunged ahead five yards.* **4** jump or thrust; dive: *a sudden plunge into the sea.* **5** pitch suddenly and violently: *The ship plunged about in the storm.* **1-3,5** *verb,* **plunged, plung ing;** **4** *noun.*

plur al (plùr′əl), **1** more than one in number: *"Cat" is singular; "cats" is plural.* **2** showing more than one in number: *the plural ending -s, the plural noun "fishes."* **3** form of a word to show that it means more than one. *Books is the plural of book; men is the plural of man; we is the plural of I; these is the plural of this.* **1,2** *adjective,* **3** *noun.*

plus (plus), **1** added to: *3 plus 2 equals 5.* **2** and also: *The work of an engineer requires intelligence plus experience.* **3** and more: *Her mark was B plus.* **4** the sign (+) meaning that the quantity following it is to be added. **1,2** *preposition,* **3** *adjective,* **4** *noun.*

plush (plush), fabric like velvet but thicker and softer. *noun.*

Plu to (plü′tō), **1** Greek and Roman god of the region of the dead. **2** planet that is farthest from the sun. *noun.*

plu to ni um (plü tō′nē əm), a radioactive metal

produced artificially from uranium. Plutonium is used as a source of atomic energy. *noun.*

ply[1] (plī), **1** work with; use: *The dressmaker plies her needle.* **2** keep up work on; work at or on: *ply one's trade. We plied the water with our oars.* **3** urge again and again: *She plied me with questions to make me tell her what was in the package.* **4** go back and forth regularly between certain places: *The bus plies from the station to the hotel.* verb, **plied, ply ing.**

ply[2] (plī), thickness, fold, or twist: *Three-ply rope is made up of three twists. noun, plural* **plies.**

ply wood (plī′wùd′), board or boards made of several thin layers of wood glued together. *noun.*

p.m. or **P.M.,** time from noon to midnight: *School ends at 3 p.m.* [The abbreviations *p.m.* and *P.M.* stand for the Latin words *post meridiem,* meaning "after noon."]

pneu mat ic (nü mat′ik *or* nyü mat′ik), **1** filled with air; containing air: *a pneumatic tire.* **2** worked by air: *a pneumatic drill. adjective.*

pneu mo nia (nü mō′nyə *or* nyü mō′nyə), an infectious disease that causes soreness and swelling of the lungs and often a high fever and a hard, dry cough. Pneumonia often follows a bad cold or other disease. *noun.*

p.o. or **P.O.,** post office.

poach[1] (pōch), **1** trespass on (another's land), especially to hunt or fish. **2** take (game or fish) without any right. *verb.*

poach[2] (pōch), cook (an egg) by breaking it into boiling water. *verb.*

pock (pok), pimple, mark, or pit left on the skin by smallpox and certain other diseases. *noun.*

pock et (pok′it), **1** a small bag sewed into clothing for carrying money or other small articles. **2** put in one's pocket. **3** meant to be carried in a pocket: *a pocket handkerchief.* **4** small enough to go in a pocket: *a pocket camera.* **5** hole in the earth containing gold or other ore: *The miner struck a pocket of silver.* **6** take secretly or dishonestly: *One partner pocketed all the profits.* **7** any current or condition in the air which causes an airplane to drop suddenly. 1,5,7 *noun,* 2,6 *verb,* 3,4 *adjective.*

pock et book (pok′it bùk′), **1** a woman's purse. **2** wallet; billfold. *noun.*

pock et ful (pok′it fùl′), as much as a pocket will hold. *noun, plural* **pock et fuls.**

pock et knife (pok′it nīf′), a small knife with one or more blades that fold into the handle. *noun, plural* **pock et knives** (pok′it nīvz′).

pod (pod), shell or case in which plants like beans and peas grow their seeds. *noun.*

po em (pō′əm), form of writing in verse; an arrangement of words in lines with a regularly repeated accent and often with rhyme. *noun.*

po et (pō′it), person who writes poems. Emily Dickinson and Walt Whitman were poets. *noun.*

po et ic (pō et′ik), **1** having something to do with poems or poets. **2** suitable for poems or poets. *Nevermore* is a poetic word. **3** showing imagination: *She told the story in poetic language. adjective.*

a hat	i it	oi oil	ch child	a in about
ā age	ī ice	ou out	ng long	e in taken
ä far	o hot	u cup	sh she	ə = { i in pencil
e let	ō open	ù put	th thin	o in lemon
ē equal	ô order	ü rule	ŦH then	u in circus
ėr term			zh measure	

po et i cal (pō et′ə kəl), poetic. *adjective.*

po et ry (pō′i trē), **1** poems: *Have you read much poetry?* **2** art of writing poems: *Shakespeare and Milton were masters of English poetry. noun.*

poin set ti a (poin set′ē ə), plant with large scarlet leaves that look like flower petals. Poinsettias are much used as Christmas decorations. *noun.* [*Poinsettia* was named for Joel Poinsett, who lived from 1779 to 1851. He was an American official in Mexico who introduced the plant in the United States.]

point (point), **1** a sharp end: *the point of a needle.* **2** sharpen: *Please point my pencil.* **3** dot; punctuation mark: *A period is a point.* **4** (in mathematics) something that has position without length or width. Two lines meet or cross at a point. **5** place; spot: *Stop at this point.* **6** degree; stage: *freezing point, boiling point.* **7** item; small part: *The speaker replied to the argument point by point.* **8** a special quality or feature: *Courage and endurance were her good points.* **9** the main idea or purpose: *I did not get the point of his argument.* **10** give force to (speech or action): *The teacher pointed the lesson by writing three key words on the blackboard.* **11** aim: *The archer pointed the arrow at the target.* **12** show position or direction with the finger: *He pointed the way to the village over the hills.* **13** direction. North, northeast, south, and southwest are some of the 32 points of the compass. **14** piece of land with a sharp end sticking out into the water; cape. **15** unit of scoring or measuring: *We won the game by three points.* 1,3,4-9,13-15 *noun,* 2,10-12 *verb.*

beside the point, having nothing to do with the subject; not appropriate.

make a point of, insist on: *I made a point of arriving on time.*

on the point of, just about (to do): *She was on the point of going out when a neighbor came in.*

point out, show or call attention to; indicate: *Please point out my mistakes.*

to the point, appropriate to the subject at hand; apt: *His speech was brief and to the point.*

point ed (poin′tid), **1** having a point or points: *a pointed roof.* **2** sharp; piercing: *a pointed wit.* **3** directed; aimed: *a pointed remark. adjective.*

point er (poin′tər), **1** person or thing that points. **2** a long, tapering stick used in pointing things out on a map or blackboard. **3** hand of a clock or meter. **4** a short-haired hunting dog. A pointer is trained to show where game is by standing still with its head and body pointing toward it. See picture. **5 Pointers,** the two stars in the Big Dipper which point to the North Star. *noun.*

point less (point′lis), without meaning or purpose: *a pointless question. adjective.*

point of view, 1 position from which one looks at something. **2** attitude of mind: *Farmers and campers have different points of view toward rain.*

poise (poiz), balance: *She has perfect poise both of mind and of body and never seems embarrassed. The athlete poised the weight in the air before throwing it. Poise yourself on your toes. noun, verb,* **poised, pois ing.**

poi son (poi′zn), **1** a substance that is very dangerous to life and health when it is breathed or swallowed. Arsenic and lead are poisons. **2** kill or harm by poison. **3** put poison in or on: *poison food, poison arrows.* **4** anything deadly or harmful: *The poison of jealousy ended their friendship.* **5** have a very harmful effect on: *Lies poison the mind.* 1,4 *noun,* 2,3,5 *verb.*

poison ivy, a climbing plant that looks like ivy, and causes a painful rash on most people if they touch it. See picture.

poi son ous (poi′zn əs), **1** containing poison; very harmful to life and health: *The rattlesnake's bite is poisonous.* **2** having a harmful effect: *a poisonous lie. adjective.*

poke (pōk), **1** push against with something pointed; thrust into: *poke the ashes of a fire. He poked me in the ribs with his elbow.* **2** thrust; push: *The dog poked its head out of the car window.* **3** poking; thrust; push. **4** go in a lazy way; loiter: *She felt tired and just poked around the house all day.* 1,2,4 *verb,* **poked, pok ing;** 3 *noun.*

pok er[1] (pō′kər), a metal rod for stirring a fire. *noun.*

pok er[2] (pō′kər), a card game in which the players bet on the value of the cards that they hold in their hands. *noun.*

pok y or **pok ey** (pō′kē), slow; dull. *adjective,* **pok i er, pok i est.**

po lar (pō′lər), of or near the North or South Pole: *It is very cold in the polar regions. adjective.*

polar bear, a large white bear of the arctic regions. See picture.

pole[1] (pōl), **1** a long, slender piece of wood or the like: *a telephone pole, a totem pole.* **2** make (a boat) go with a pole. 1 *noun,* 2 *verb,* **poled, pol ing.**

pole[2] (pōl), **1** either end of the earth's axis. The North Pole and the South Pole are opposite each other. **2** either of two parts where opposite forces are strongest. A magnet or a battery has both a positive pole and a negative pole. *noun.*

pole cat (pōl′kat′), **1** a small, dark-brown European animal somewhat like a weasel. It has a very strong, unpleasant smell. **2** skunk. *noun.*

pole star (pōl′stär′), the North Star, a star that is almost directly above the North Pole, and was formerly much used as a guide by sailors. *noun.*

po lice (pə lēs′), **1** persons whose duty is keeping order and arresting people who break the law. **2** department of government that keeps order and arrests persons who break the law. **3** keep in order: *police the streets.* 1,2 *noun,* 3 *verb,* **po liced, po lic ing.**

po lice man (pə lēs′mən), member of the police. *noun, plural* **po lice men.**

po lice wom an (pə lēs′wùm′ən), woman who is a member of the police. *noun, plural* **po lice wom en.**

pol i cy[1] (pol′ə sē), plan of action; way of management: *government policies. It is a poor policy to promise more than you can do. noun, plural* **pol i cies.**

pol i cy[2] (pol′ə sē), a written agreement about insurance: *My fire insurance policy states that I shall receive $15,000 if my house burns down. noun, plural* **pol i cies.**

po li o (pō′lē ō), a disease most often of children that causes fever, paralysis of various muscles, and sometimes death; infantile paralysis; poliomyelitis. Unless you are vaccinated against polio, you can catch the disease if you are around someone who has it. *noun.*

po li o my e li tis (pō′lē ō mī′ə lī′tis), polio. *noun.*

pol ish (pol′ish), **1** make smooth and shiny: *polish shoes.* **2** become smooth and shiny; take on a polish: *The silverware polished beautifully.* **3** substance used to give smoothness or shine: *silver polish.* **4** smoothness; polished condition: *The polish of the furniture reflected our faces like a mirror.* 1,2 *verb,* 3,4 *noun, plural* **pol ish es.**

po lite (pə līt′), **1** behaving properly; having or showing good manners: *The polite girl gave the old man her seat on the bus.* **2** refined; elegant: *to learn the customs of polite society. adjective,* **po lit er, po lit est.**

po lit i cal (pə lit′ə kəl), **1** having something to do with citizens or the government: *Treason is a political offense. Who shall have the right to vote is a political question.* **2** of politicians or their methods: *a political party, political meetings. adjective.*

polar bear—about 4 feet (1 meter) high at the shoulder and about 8 feet (2½ meters) long

pol i ti cian (pol′ə tish′ən), person who gives much time to political affairs; person who is experienced in politics: *Politicians are busy near election time. noun.*

pol i tics (pol′ə tiks), **1** management of political affairs; science and art of government: *The senator was engaged in politics for many years.* **2** political principles or opinions: *Her politics are very liberal. noun singular or plural.*

pol ka (pōl′kə *or* pō′kə), **1** kind of lively dance. **2** music for it. *noun.*

pol ka dot (pō′kə dot′), dot or round spot repeated to form a pattern on cloth.

poll (pōl), **1** voting; collection of votes: *The class had a poll to decide where it would have its picnic.* **2** number of votes cast: *If it rains on election day, there is usually a light poll.* **3 polls,** place where votes are cast and counted: *The polls will be open all day.* **4** list of persons, especially a list of voters. **5** receive (as votes) at an election: *The mayor polled a record vote.* **6** vote; cast (a vote): *A large vote was polled for president.* **7** take the votes of: *poll a village.* **8** a survey of public opinion about a particular subject. 1-4,8 *noun,* 5-7 *verb.*

pol len (pol′ən), a fine, yellowish powder produced by the anthers of flowers. Grains of pollen carried to the pistils of flowers fertilize them. *noun.*

pol li wog (pol′ē wog), tadpole. *noun.*

pol lute (pə lüt′), make dirty; defile: *The water at the bathing beach was polluted by refuse from the factory.* verb, **pol lut ed, pol lut ing.**

pol lu tion (pə lü′shən), a making dirty or impure: *Exhaust from automobiles causes air pollution. noun.*

po lo (pō′lō), game like hockey, played on horseback with long-handled mallets and a wooden ball. *noun.*

pol y gon (pol′ē gon), figure having three or more angles and straight sides. See picture. *noun.*

pol yp (pol′ip), a rather simple form of water animal consisting largely of a stomach with fingerlike tentacles around the edge to gather in food. Polyps often grow in colonies, with their bases connected. Corals are polyps. See picture. *noun.*

pome gran ate (pom′gran′it), the reddish-yellow fruit of a small tree. Pomegranates have thick skin, red pulp, and many seeds. The pulp and seeds have a pleasant, slightly sour taste. *noun.*

pom mel (pum′əl *or* pom′əl), **1** part of a saddle that sticks up at the front. **2** a rounded knob on the handle of a sword. **3** strike or beat; beat with the fists. 1,2 *noun,* 3 *verb.*

pomp (pomp), stately or showy display; magnificence: *The new ruler was crowned with great pomp. noun.*

pom pon (pom′pon), an ornamental ball of feathers, silk, wool, or the like, worn on a hat or on shoes. *noun.*

pom pous (pom′pəs), fond of display; acting too proudly; trying to seem magnificent: *The leader of the band bowed in a pompous manner. adjective.*

pon cho (pon′chō), a large piece of cloth, often waterproof, with a slit in the middle for the head to go through. Ponchos are worn in South America as cloaks. Waterproof ponchos are used in the army and navy and by hikers and campers. *noun, plural* **pon chos.**

pond (pond), body of still water, smaller than a lake: *a duck pond. noun.*

pon der (pon′dər), think over; consider carefully: *ponder a problem. verb.*

a hat	i it	oi oil	ch child	a in about
ā age	ī ice	ou out	ng long	e in taken
ä far	o hot	u cup	sh she	ə = i in pencil
e let	ō open	u̇ put	th thin	o in lemon
ē equal	ô order	ü rule	ŦH then	u in circus
ėr term			zh measure	

polygons

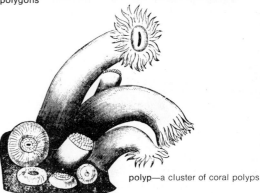
polyp—a cluster of coral polyps

poison ivy

pon der ous (pon′dər əs), **1** very heavy. **2** heavy and clumsy: *A hippopotamus is ponderous.* **3** dull; tiresome: *The speaker talked in a ponderous way.* *adjective.*

pon iard (pon′yərd), dagger. *noun.*

pon toon (pon tün′), **1** a low, flat-bottomed boat. **2** such a boat, or some other floating structure, used as one of the supports of a temporary bridge. **3** either of two boat-shaped parts of an airplane, used for landing on or taking off from water. *noun.*

po ny (pō′nē), kind of small horse. Ponies are usually less than 5 feet (1½ meters) tall at the shoulder. *noun, plural* **po nies.**

pony express, system of carrying letters and small packages in the western United States in 1860 and 1861 by riders on fast ponies or horses.

poo dle (pü′dl), an intelligent pet dog with thick, curly hair. *noun.* [*Poodle* comes from a German word meaning "puddle dog." The breed was called this because it is fond of water.]

pool[1] (pül), **1** tank of water to swim or bathe in: *a swimming pool.* **2** a small pond; small body of still water: *a wading pool.* **3** puddle: *a pool of grease under a car. noun.*

pool[2] (pül), **1** game played with 16 hard balls on a special table with six pockets. A long stick called a cue is used to hit certain balls into the pockets. **2** put (things or money) together for common advantage: *We plan to pool our savings to buy a boat.* **3** things or money put together by different persons for common advantage: *a car pool.* 1,3 *noun,* 2 *verb.*

poor (pùr), **1** having few things or nothing: *The children were so poor that they had no shoes.* **2** the poor, those who have little or nothing. **3** not good in quality; lacking something needed: *poor soil, a poor crop, poor milk, a poor cook, a poor story.* **4** needing pity; unfortunate: *This poor child is hurt.* 1,3,4 *adjective,* 2 *noun.*

poor ly (pùr′lē), **1** not sufficiently: *A desert is poorly supplied with water.* **2** badly; not well: *The student did poorly on the test. adverb.*

pop (pop), **1** make a short, quick, explosive sound: *The firecrackers popped in bunches.* **2** a short, quick, explosive sound: *We heard the pop of a cork.* **3** burst open; cause to burst open: *The balloon popped. We popped some popcorn.* **4** move, go, or come suddenly or unexpectedly: *Our neighbor popped in for a short call.* **5** thrust or put suddenly: *She popped her head out through the window.* **6** a bubbling soft drink: *strawberry pop.* 1,3-5 *verb,* **popped, pop ping;** 2,6 *noun.*

pop corn (pop′kôrn′), **1** kind of corn, the kernels of which burst open and puff out when heated. **2** the white, puffed-out kernels. *noun.*

pope or **Pope** (pōp), head of the Roman Catholic Church: *the last three popes, the Pope. noun.* [*Pope* comes from a Greek word meaning "father" or "papa."]

pop lar (pop′lər), **1** tree that grows rapidly and produces light, soft wood. The cottonwood is one kind of poplar. **2** its wood. *noun.*

pop py (pop′ē), kind of plant with delicate, showy red, yellow, or white flowers. Opium is made from one kind of poppy. *noun, plural* **pop pies.**

Pop si cle (pop′sə kəl), a trademark for flavored, sweetened ice that is molded onto a stick. *noun.*

pop u lace (pop′yə lis), the common people. *noun.*

pop u lar (pop′yə lər), **1** liked by most people: *a popular song.* **2** liked by acquaintances or associates: *His good nature makes him the most popular boy in the school.* **3** of the people; by the people; representing the people: *a popular election. The United States has a popular government.* **4** widespread among many people; common: *It is a popular belief that black cats bring bad luck.* **5** suited to the people: *popular prices, books on popular science. adjective.*

pop u lar i ty (pop′yə lar′ə tē), fact or condition of being liked by most people. *noun.*

pop u late (pop′yə lāt), **1** live in; inhabit: *a densely populated city.* **2** furnish with inhabitants: *Europe helped populate America. verb,* **pop u lat ed, pop u lat ing.**

pop u la tion (pop′yə lā′shən), **1** people of a city, country, or district. **2** the number of people. *noun.*

pop u lous (pop′yə ləs), full of people; having many people per square mile: *the most populous state of the United States. adjective.*

por ce lain (pôr′sə lin), very fine earthenware; china: *Teacups are often made of porcelain.* See picture. *noun.*

porcelain—figures made of porcelain

porch (pôrch), a covered entrance or addition to a building: *Our house has a big sleeping porch at the back. noun, plural* **porch es.**

por cu pine (pôr′kyə pīn), animal covered with spines or quills. See picture. *noun.* [*Porcupine* comes from Latin words meaning "pig" and "thorn."]

pore[1] (pôr), look at or study long and steadily: *I pored over the book trying to find the answer. verb,* **pored, por ing.**

pore[2] (pôr), a very small opening. Sweat comes through the pores in the skin. *noun.*

pork (pôrk), meat of a pig or hog used for food. *noun.*

po rous (pôr′əs), full of pores or tiny holes: *Cloth is porous. Aluminum is not porous. adjective.*

por poise (pôr′pəs), a sea animal with a blunt, rounded snout. It looks like a small whale. *noun, plural* **por pois es** or **por poise.**

por ridge (pôr′ij), food made of oatmeal or other cereal boiled in water or milk until it thickens. *noun.*

port[1] (pôrt), **1** harbor; place where ships and boats can be sheltered from storms. **2** place where ships and boats can load and unload; city or town by a harbor: *New York City is an important port. noun.*

port[2] (pôrt), **1** porthole. **2** opening in a cylinder or pipe for steam, air, or water to pass through. *noun.*

port[3] (pôrt), **1** side of a ship or aircraft to the left of a person facing the bow or front. **2** on the left side of a ship, boat, or aircraft. **1** *noun,* **2** *adjective.*

port[4] (pôrt), a strong, sweet, dark-red wine. *noun.*

port a ble (pôr′tə bəl), capable of being carried or moved; easily carried: *a portable typewriter. adjective.*

por tage (pôr′tij), **1** carrying of boats or provisions overland from one river or lake to another. **2** place over which this is done. *noun.*

por tal (pôr′tl), door, gate, or entrance, usually an impressive one. *noun.*

port cul lis (pôrt kul′is), a strong gate or grating of iron that can be raised or lowered, used to close the gateway of an ancient castle or fortress. *noun, plural* **port cul lis es.**

por tend (pôr tend′), indicate beforehand; give warning of: *Black clouds portend a storm. verb.*

por tent (pôr′tent), a warning, usually of coming evil; sign; omen: *The black clouds were a portent of bad weather. noun.*

por ter[1] (pôr′tər), **1** person employed to carry burdens or baggage: *Give your bags to the porter.* **2** attendant in a sleeping car of a railway train. *noun.*

por ter[2] (pôr′tər), person who guards a door or entrance: *The porter let them in. noun.*

port hole (pôrt′hōl′), **1** opening in a ship's side to let in light and air. **2** opening in a ship or wall through which to shoot. *noun.*

por ti co (pôr′tə kō), roof supported by columns, forming a porch or a covered walk. See picture. *noun, plural* **por ti coes** or **por ti cos.**

por tion (pôr′shən), **1** part or share: *A portion of each school day is devoted to arithmetic.* **2** divide into parts or shares: *The money was portioned out among the children.* **1** *noun,* **2** *verb.*

port ly (pôrt′lē), fat or large in a dignified or stately way: *a portly English gentleman. adjective,* **port li er, port li est.**

por trait (pôr′trit *or* pôr′trāt), picture of a person, especially of the face. See picture. *noun.*

por tray (pôr trā′), **1** make a likeness of in a drawing or painting; make a picture of: *portray a historical scene.* **2** picture in words; describe: *The book "Black Beauty" portrays the life of a horse.* **3** act the part of in a play or motion picture: *The actor portrayed a newspaper reporter. verb.*

a hat	i it	oi oil	ch child	a in about
ā age	ī ice	ou out	ng long	e in taken
ä far	o hot	u cup	sh she	ə = i in pencil
e let	ō open	ů put	th thin	o in lemon
ē equal	ô order	ü rule	₮H then	u in circus
ėr term			zh measure	

portrait of Pocahontas

porcupine—about 2½ feet (75 centimeters) long with the tail

portico

National Portrait Gallery, Smithsonian Institution, Washington, D.C.

pose (pōz), **1** position of the body; way of holding the body: *a natural pose, a pose taken in exercising.* **2** hold a position: *She posed an hour for her portrait.* See picture. **3** put in a certain position; put: *The photographer posed him before taking his picture.* **4** attitude assumed for effect; pretense; affectation: *Her interest in people is real; it isn't just a pose.* **5** take a false position for effect: *They posed as a rich couple although they had little money.* **1,4** *noun,* **2,3,5** *verb,* **posed, pos ing.**

po si tion (pə zish′ən), **1** place where a thing or person is: *The flowers grew in a sheltered position behind the house.* **2** way of being placed: *Put the baby in a comfortable position.* **3** proper place: *The band got into position to march in the parade.* **4** job: *He has a position in a bank.* **5** rank; standing, especially high standing: *She was raised to the position of manager.* **6** way of thinking; set of opinions: *What is your position on this question?* *noun.*

pos i tive (poz′ə tiv), **1** permitting no question; without doubt; sure: *We have positive knowledge that the earth moves around the sun.* **2** too sure: *A positive manner annoys some people.* **3** definite; emphatic: *"No. I will not," was his positive refusal.* **4** that can be thought of as real and present: *Light is a positive thing; darkness is only the absence of light.* **5** that surely does something or adds something; practical: *Don't just make a negative criticism; give us some positive help.* **6** showing agreement or approval: *a positive answer to a question.* **7** of the kind of electricity produced on glass when it is rubbed with silk. *adjective.*

pos i tive ly (poz′ə tiv lē), **1** in a positive way: *The audience reacted positively to our play.* **2** to a great extreme; absolutely: *I was positively furious at them for being so rude.* *adverb.*

pos se (pos′ē), group of citizens called together by a sheriff to help maintain law and order: *The posse chased the bandits across the prairie.* *noun.* [*Posse* comes from Latin words of the Middle Ages meaning "power of the county."]

pos sess (pə zes′), **1** own; have: *My aunt possessed great intelligence and determination.* **2** hold as property; hold; occupy. **3** control; influence strongly: *She was possessed by the desire to be rich.* **4** control by an evil spirit: *He fought like one possessed.* *verb.*

pos ses sion (pə zesh′ən), **1** possessing; holding: *I have in my possession the books you lost.* **2** ownership: *On her 21st birthday she came into possession of $50,000.* **3** thing possessed; property: *Please move your possessions from my room.* **4** territory under the rule of a country: *Guam is a possession of the United States.* **5** self-control. *noun.*

pos ses sive (pə zes′iv), **1** showing possession. *My, your, his,* and *our* are possessive adjectives because they indicate who possesses or owns. **2** the possessive form of a word. **3** word showing possession. In "your book," *your* is a possessive. **1** *adjective,* **2,3** *noun.*

pos ses sor (pə zes′ər), person who possesses; owner; holder. *noun.*

pos si bil i ty (pos′ə bil′ə tē), **1** being possible: *There is a possibility that the train may be late.* **2** a possible thing, person, or event: *A whole week of rain is a possibility.* *noun, plural* **pos si bil i ties.**

pos si ble (pos′ə bəl), **1** able to be; able to be done; able to happen: *Come if possible. It is possible to cure tuberculosis.* **2** capable of being true or a fact: *It is possible that they are lost.* **3** able to be done or chosen properly: *the only possible action, the only possible candidate.* *adjective.*

pos si bly (pos′ə blē), **1** no matter what happens: *I cannot possibly go.* **2** perhaps: *Possibly you are right.* *adverb.*

pos sum (pos′əm), opossum. *noun, plural* **pos sums** or **pos sum.**

post¹ (pōst), **1** piece of timber, metal, or other solid substance firmly set up, usually to support something else: *the posts of a door, a hitching post.* **2** fasten (a notice) up in a place where it can easily be seen: *The list of winners will be posted soon.* **3** make known by means of a posted notice; make public: *post a reward.* **1** *noun,* **2,3** *verb.*

post² (pōst), **1** place where a soldier or police officer is stationed; place where one is supposed to be when one is on duty: *At the sound of the guns, the soldiers rushed to their posts.* **2** place where soldiers are stationed; fort. **3** station at a post: *They posted guards at the door.* **4** job or position: *the post of secretary, a diplomatic post.* **5** a trading station, especially in unsettled country; trading post. **1,2,4,5** *noun,* **3** *verb.*

post³ (pōst), **1** system for carrying letters, papers, or packages; the mail: *I shall send the package by post.* **2** a single delivery of mail: *This morning's post has come.* **3** send by mail; put into the mailbox; mail: *post a letter.* **4** travel with haste; hurry: *The messenger posted through the forest with a letter for the king.* **5** supply with up-to-date information; inform: *be well posted on current events.* **1,2** *noun,* **3-5** *verb.*

post age (pō′stij), amount paid on anything sent by mail. *noun.*

postage stamp, an official stamp placed on mail to show that postage has been paid.

post al (pō′stəl), having to do with mail and post offices: *postal regulations, a postal clerk. adjective.*

postal card, post card.

Postal Service, the service that takes charge of mail for the government.

post card, card about 3¹/₂ by 5¹/₂ inches, for sending a message by mail. Some post cards have pictures on one side.

post er (pō′stər), a large printed sheet or notice put up on a wall. *noun.*

pos ter i ty (po ster′ə tē), **1** generations of the future: *Posterity may travel to distant planets.* **2** anyone's children, and their children, and their children, and so on and on. *noun.*

pos tern (pō′stərn *or* pos′tərn), a back door or gate: *the postern of a castle. noun.*

post man (pōst′mən), person who carries and delivers mail for the government. *noun, plural* **post men.**

pose (definition 2)—The children **posed** for their picture.

potter[1]

a hat	i it	oi oil	ch child		a in about
ā age	ī ice	ou out	ng long		e in taken
ä far	o hot	u cup	sh she	ə =	i in pencil
e let	ō open	ù put	th thin		o in lemon
ē equal	ô order	ü rule	ŦH then		u in circus
ėr term			zh measure		

po sy (pō′zē), **1** flower. **2** bunch of flowers; bouquet. *noun, plural* **po sies.**

pot (pot), **1** kind of round container. There are many different kinds and shapes of pots. They are made of iron, tin, earthenware, and other substances. A pot may hold food or drink or contain earth for flowers to grow in. **2** amount a pot will hold: *a small pot of beans.* **3** put into a pot: *I potted the young tomato plants.* **1,2** *noun,* **3** *verb,* **pot ted, pot ting.**

pot ash (pot′ash′), any of several substances made from certain minerals or wood ashes and used in making soap and fertilizers. *noun.*

po tas si um (pə tas′ē əm), a soft, silver-white element. Potassium is necessary for the growth of plants, and is used in making soap and fertilizers. *noun.*

po ta to (pə tā′tō), **1** a round or oval, hard, starchy vegetable with a thin skin. It is one of the most widely used vegetables in Europe and America. Potatoes grow underground. **2** sweet potato. *noun, plural* **po ta toes.**

po tent (pōt′nt), powerful; having great power; strong: *a potent remedy for a disease. adjective.*

po ten tate (pōt′n tāt), **1** person having great power. **2** ruler. Kings, queens, and emperors are potentates. *noun.*

po ten tial (pə ten′shəl), possible as opposed to actual; capable of coming into being or action: *There is a potential danger of being bitten when playing with a strange dog. adjective.*

po tion (pō′shən), a drink, especially one used as a medicine or poison, or in magic. *noun.*

pot shot (pot′shot′), **1** a shot fired without careful aim at a close target. **2** criticism, usually made in a careless way. *noun.*

pot ter[1] (pot′ər), person who makes pots, dishes, or vases out of clay. See picture. *noun.*

pot ter[2] (pot′ər), keep busy in a rather useless way; putter: *I like to potter in the garden on weekends. verb.*

pot ter y (pot′ər ē), **1** pots, dishes, or vases made from clay and hardened by heat. **2** art or business of making them. **3** place where such pots, dishes, or vases are made. *noun, plural* **pot ter ies.**

pouch (pouch), **1** bag or sack: *a tobacco pouch.* **2** a natural part of some animals that is like a bag or pocket. A kangaroo has a pouch for carrying its young. A chipmunk has cheek pouches for carrying food. *noun, plural* **pouch es.**

poul try (pōl′trē), birds raised for their meat or eggs, such as chickens, turkeys, geese, or ducks. *noun.*

pounce (pouns), **1** jump suddenly and seize: *The cat pounced upon the mouse.* **2** a sudden swoop. **1** *verb,* **pounced, pounc ing; 2** *noun.*

post mark (pōst′märk′), **1** an official mark stamped on mail to cancel the postage stamp and record the place and date of mailing. **2** stamp with a postmark. **1** *noun,* **2** *verb.*

post mas ter (pōst′mas′tər), person in charge of a post office. *noun.*

post office, place where mail is handled and postage stamps are sold.

post paid (pōst′pād′), with the postage paid for. *adjective.*

post pone (pōst pōn′), put off till later; put off to a later time; delay: *The ball game was postponed because of rain. verb,* **post poned, post pon ing.**

post script (pōst′skript), addition to a letter, written below the writer's name. *noun.*

pos ture (pos′chər), **1** position of the body; way of holding the body: *Good posture is important to health.* **2** take a position: *The dancer postured before the mirror, bending and twisting her body.* **1** *noun* **2** *verb,* **pos tured, pos tur ing.**

post war (pōst′wôr′), after the war. *adjective.*

prairie schooner

prairie dog—about 15 inches (38 centimeters) long with the tail

pound¹ (pound), **1** a unit of weight equal to 16 ounces in ordinary weight and 12 ounces in troy weight. **2** unit of money in Great Britain equal to 100 pence. £1.00 means one pound. The pound is worth more than two dollars. *noun, plural* **pounds** or **pound.**

pound² (pound), **1** hit hard again and again; hit heavily: *She pounded the door with her fist.* **2** beat hard; throb: *After running fast you can feel your heart pound.* **3** make into a powder or pulp by pounding: *They pounded the grains of corn into meal. verb.*

pound³ (pound), an enclosed place in which to keep stray animals: *a dog pound. noun.*

pour (pôr), **1** cause to flow in a steady stream: *I poured the milk from the bottle into the cups.* **2** flow in a steady stream: *The crowd poured out of the theater. The rain poured down.* **3** rain heavily. **4** a heavy rain; downpour. 1-3 *verb,* 4 *noun.*

pout (pout), **1** thrust or push out the lips, as a displeased or sulky child does. **2** a pushing out of the lips when displeased or sulky. 1 *verb,* 2 *noun.*

pov er ty (pov′ər tē), **1** condition of being poor: *Their tattered clothing and broken furniture indicated their poverty.* **2** poor quality: *The poverty of the soil makes the crops small.* **3** a small amount: *A boring person's talk shows poverty of ideas. noun.*

pow der (pou′dər), **1** solid reduced to dust by pounding, crushing, or grinding. **2** make into powder; become powder: *The soil powdered in the heat.* **3** some special kind of powder: *face powder, bath powder.* **4** sprinkle or cover with powder. **5** put powder on the face: *powder one's nose.* **6** sprinkle: *The ground was lightly powdered with snow.* **7** gunpowder: *Soldiers used to carry their powder in a powder horn.* 1,3,7 *noun,* 2,4-6 *verb.*

powder horn, flask made of the horn of an animal, used to carry gunpowder.

pow der y (pou′dər ē), **1** of powder. **2** like powder; in the form of powder. **3** sprinkled or covered with powder. *adjective.*

pow er (pou′ər), **1** strength; might; force: *Penicillin is a medicine of great power.* **2** ability to do or act: *I will give you all the help in my power.* **3** authority; right; control; influence: *Congress has power to declare war.* **4** person or thing that has authority or influence; important nation: *Five powers held a peace conference.* **5** energy or force that can do work: *Running water can be used to operate a turbine and produce electric power.* **6** provide with power or energy: *a boat powered by an outboard motor.* **7** operated by a motor; equipped with its own motor: *a power drill.* 1-5 *noun,* 6 *verb,* 7 *adjective.*

in power, having control or authority.

pow er ful (pou′ər fəl), having great power or force; mighty; strong: *a powerful person, a powerful medicine, a powerful argument, a powerful nation. adjective.*

pow er house (pou′ər hous′), building containing boilers, engines, or generators for producing electric power. *noun, plural* **pow er hous es** (pou′ər hou′ziz).

pow er less (pou′ər lis), without power; helpless: *The mouse was powerless in the cat's claws. adjective.*

power saw, saw worked by a motor, not by hand.

pow wow (pou′wou′), **1** ceremony of the North American Indians, usually accompanied by magic, feasting, and dancing, performed for the cure of disease, success in hunting, or for other purposes. **2** council or conference of or with North American Indians. **3** any conference or meeting. **4** hold a powwow; confer. 1-3 *noun,* 4 *verb.*

pp., pages.

pr., pair.

prac ti ca ble (prak′tə kə bəl), **1** able to be done; capable of being put into practice: *a practicable idea.* **2** able to be used: *a practicable road. adjective.*

prac ti cal (prak′tə kəl), **1** having something to do with action or practice rather than thought or theory: *Earning a living is a practical matter.* **2** fit for actual practice: *a practical plan.* **3** useful: *An outdoor swimming pool is more practical in Florida than in Minnesota.* **4** having good sense: *A practical person does not spend time and money foolishly. adjective.*

practical joke, trick played on someone.

prac ti cal ly (prak′tik lē) **1** really; so far as what the results will be; in effect: *She is only a clerk, but she is in the store so much that she practically runs the business.* **2** almost; nearly: *Our house is around the corner, so we are practically home.* **3** in a practical way; in a useful way: *You must stop wishing and start thinking practically. adverb.*

prac tice (prak′tis), **1** action done many times over for skill: *Practice makes perfect.* **2** skill gained by experience or exercise: *He was out of practice at batting.* **3** do (some act) again and again to learn to do it well: *She practiced pitching the ball. I practice on the piano every day.* **4** do usually; make a custom of: *Practice what you preach.* **5** follow, observe, or use day after day: *We should practice kindness to others.* **6** the usual way; custom: *It is the practice at the factory to blow a whistle at noon.* **7** work at or follow as a profession, art, or occupation: *practice medicine.* **8** working at or following a profession: *She is engaged in the practice of law.* **9** business of a doctor or a lawyer: *The old doctor sold his practice to a younger doctor.* 1,2,6,8,9 *noun,* 3-5,7 *verb,* **prac ticed, prac tic ing.**

prac ticed (prak′tist), skilled; expert; experienced: *Years of study have made him a practiced musician. adjective.*

prair ie (prer′ē), a large area of level or rolling land with grass but few or no trees. *noun.*

prairie dog, animal like a woodchuck but smaller. Prairie dogs bark. See picture.

prairie schooner, a large covered wagon used in crossing the plains of North America before the railroads were built. See picture.

praise (prāz), **1** saying that a thing or person is good; words that tell the worth or value of a thing or person: *Everyone heaped praise upon the winning team.* **2** speak well of: *The coach praised the team for its fine playing.* **3** worship in words or song: *praise God.* 1 *noun,* 2,3 *verb,* **praised, prais ing.**

praise wor thy (prāz′wėr′ᴛнē), worthy of praise; deserving approval. *adjective.*

prance (prans), **1** spring about on the hind legs: *Horses prance when they feel lively.* **2** move gaily or proudly: *The children pranced about in their new Halloween costumes. verb,* **pranced, pranc ing.**

prank (prangk), a playful trick; piece of mischief: *On April Fools' Day people play pranks on each other. noun.*

prat tle (prat′l), **1** tell freely and carelessly, as some children do. **2** talk in a foolish way; babble. *verb,* **prat tled, prat tling.**

pray (prā), **1** ask from God; speak to God in worship: *They prayed for God's help.* **2** ask earnestly: *pray a person's forgiveness.* **3** please: *Pray come with me. verb.*

prayer (prer *or* prar), **1** act of praying. **2** thing prayed for: *Our prayers were granted.* **3** form of words to be used in praying: *the Lord's Prayer.* **4** form of worship. **5** an earnest request. *noun.*

pre-, prefix meaning: **1** before: *Prewar preparations* mean preparations made *before* a war. **2** beforehand; in advance: To *preview* means to view *beforehand.* Prepay means to pay *in advance.*

preach (prēch), **1** speak on a religious subject; deliver (a sermon): *Our minister preaches on Sunday morning.* **2** make known by preaching; proclaim: *preach the gospel.* **3** urge; recommend strongly: *The coach was always preaching exercise and fresh air.* **4** give earnest advice: *Some people are always preaching about good manners. verb.*

preach er (prē′chər), person who preaches; clergyman; minister. *noun.*

pre car i ous (pri ker′ē əs *or* pri kar′ē əs), uncertain; not safe; not secure; dangerous: *A racing-car driver leads a precarious life. Her hold on the branch was precarious. adjective.*

pre cau tion (pri kô′shən), **1** care taken beforehand: *Locking doors is a precaution against thieves.* **2** taking care beforehand: *Proper precaution is wise. noun.*

pre cede (prē sēd′), **1** go before; come before: *A precedes B in the alphabet. The band preceded the floats in the parade.* **2** be higher than in rank or importance: *A major precedes a captain. verb,* **pre ced ed, pre ced ing.**

prec e dent (pres′ə dənt), action that may serve as an example or reason for later action: *Last year's school picnic set a precedent for having one this year. A decision of a court often serves as a precedent in other courts. noun.*

pre ced ing (prē sē′ding), going before; coming before; previous: *Turn back and look on the preceding page for the answer. adjective.*

pre cept (prē′sept), rule or direction: *"If at first you don't succeed, try, try again" is a familiar precept. noun.*

pre cinct (prē′singkt), **1** part or district of a city: *a police precinct. There are over 300 election precincts in that city.* **2** space within a boundary: *Do not leave the school precincts during school hours. noun.*

pre cious (presh′əs), **1** having great value. Gold and silver are often called the precious metals. Diamonds and rubies are precious stones. **2** much loved; dear: *a precious child. adjective.*

prec i pice (pres′ə pis), a very steep cliff or slope. *noun.* [*Precipice* comes from a Latin word meaning "a headlong fall."]

pre cip i tate (pri sip′ə tāt *for 1,3, and 4;* pri sip′ə tit *for 2*), **1** hasten the beginning of; bring about suddenly: *precipitate a war.* **2** with great haste and force; plunging or rushing; hasty; rash: *a precipitate action.* **3** throw down, fling, hurl, send, or plunge in a violent, sudden, or headlong way: *precipitate a rock down a cliff, precipitate oneself into a struggle.* **4** condense (water vapor) from the air in the form of rain, dew, or snow. 1,3,4 *verb,* **pre cip i tat ed, pre cip i tat ing;** 2 *adjective.*

predatory
Snakes are predatory;
some snakes prey on
birds' eggs.

pre cip i ta tion (pri sip′ə tā′shən), **1** throwing down or falling headlong. **2** a sudden bringing on: *the precipitation of a quarrel.* **3** sudden haste; unwise or rash rapidity. **4** the depositing of moisture in the form of rain, dew, or snow. **5** something that is precipitated, such as rain, dew, or snow. *noun.*

pre cise (pri sīs′), **1** exact; accurate; definite: *The directions they gave us were so precise that we found our way easily. The precise sum was 34 cents.* **2** careful. See picture. **3** strict: *We had precise orders to come home by nine o'clock. adjective.*

pre ci sion (pri sizh′ən), accuracy; being exact: *the precision of a machine. noun.*

pre clude (pri klüd′), shut out; make impossible; prevent: *The heavy thunderstorm precluded our going to the beach. verb,* **pre clud ed, pre clud ing.**

pre co cious (pri kō′shəs), developed earlier than usual. See picture. *adjective.* [*Precocious* comes from a Latin word meaning "to ripen early."]

pred a to ry (pred′ə tôr′ē), preying upon other animals. Lions are predatory animals; hawks are predatory birds. See picture. *adjective.*

pred e ces sor (pred′ə ses′ər), person holding a position or office before another. *noun.*

pre dic a ment (pri dik′ə mənt), an unpleasant, difficult, or bad situation: *She was in a predicament when she missed the last train home. noun.*

pred i cate (pred′ə kit), word or words in a sentence that tell what is said about the subject. In "Dogs bark," "The dogs dug holes," and "The dogs are beagles," *bark, dug holes,* and *are beagles* are all predicates. *noun.*

pre dict (pri dikt′), tell beforehand; prophesy: *The Weather Service predicts rain for tomorrow. verb.*

pre dic tion (pri dik′shən), thing predicted; prophecy: *The official predictions about the weather often come true. noun.*

pre dom i nant (pri dom′ə nənt), **1** having more power, authority, or influence than others; superior: *The United States is probably the predominant nation in the Western Hemisphere today.* **2** most extensive; most noticeable: *Green was the predominant color in the forest. adjective.*

pre dom i nate (pri dom′ə nāt), be greater in power, strength, influence, or numbers: *Sunny days predominate over rainy days in desert regions. verb,* **pre dom i nat ed, pre dom i nat ing.**

preen (prēn), **1** smooth or arrange (the feathers) with the beak. See picture. **2** dress or groom (oneself) carefully. *verb.*

pref ace (pref′is), introduction to a book, writing, or speech: *Does your history book have a preface written by the author? noun.*

pre fer (pri fėr′), **1** like better; choose rather: *I will come later, if you prefer. She prefers swimming to fishing.* **2** put forward; present: *The policeman preferred charges of speeding against the driver. verb,* **pre ferred, pre fer ring.**

pref er a ble (pref′ər ə bəl), to be preferred; more desirable. *adjective.*

pref er a bly (pref′ər ə blē), by choice: *She needs an assistant, preferably a college graduate. adverb.*

precise (definition 2)—Watchmakers must be very **precise** in their work.

precocious
The precocious little girl could use many difficult words.

YOUR PRECARIOUS PREDICAMENT REFLECTS A LACK OF PRECAUTION.

preen (definition 1)
The swan preened itself.

prehistoric—the skeleton of a prehistoric animal

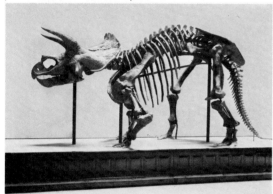

a hat	**i** it	**oi** oil	**ch** child	⎧ a in about
ā age	**ī** ice	**ou** out	**ng** long	e in taken
ä far	**o** hot	**u** cup	**sh** she	ə = ⎨ i in pencil
e let	**ō** open	**u̇** put	**th** thin	o in lemon
ē equal	**ô** order	**ü** rule	**ŦH** then	⎩ u in circus
ėr term			**zh** measure	

pref er ence (pref′ər əns), **1** act or attitude of liking better: *My preference is for beef rather than lamb.* **2** thing preferred; first choice: *My preference in reading is a mystery story.* **3** favoring one above another: *A teacher should not show preference for any student. noun.*

pre fix (prē′fiks *for 1;* prē fiks′ *for 2*), **1** syllable, syllables, or word put at the beginning of a word to change its meaning or make another word, as *pre-* in *prepaid, under-* in *underline, dis-* in *disappear, un-* in *unlike,* and *re-* in *reopen.* **2** put before: *We prefix Mr. to a man's name and Ms. to a woman's name.* **1** *noun, plural* **pre fix es; 2** *verb.*

preg nant (preg′nənt), soon to have a baby; with one or more babies growing inside the female's body. *adjective.*

pre his to ric (prē′hi stôr′ik), of or belonging to times before histories were written: *Prehistoric peoples used stone tools.* See picture. *adjective.*

prej u dice (prej′ə dis), **1** opinion formed without taking time and care to judge fairly: *Many people have a prejudice against foreigners.* **2** cause a prejudice in; fill with prejudice: *One unfortunate experience prejudiced them against all lawyers.* **3** harm or injury: *I will do nothing to the prejudice of my cousin in this matter.* **4** harm or injure. **1,3** *noun,* **2,4** *verb,* **prej u diced, prej u dic ing.**

prel ate (prel′it), clergyman of high rank, such as a bishop. *noun.*

pre lim i nar y (pri lim′ə ner′ē), **1** coming before the main business; leading to something more important: *After the preliminary exercises of prayer and song, the speaker of the day gave an address.* **2** a preliminary step; something preparatory: *An examination is a preliminary to entering that school.* **1** *adjective,* **2** *noun, plural* **pre lim i nar ies.**

prel ude (prel′yüd), anything serving as an introduction; preliminary performance: *We heard the organist play a prelude to the church service. noun.*

pre ma ture (prē′mə chu̇r′, prē′mə tu̇r′, *or* prē′mə tyu̇r′), before the proper time; too soon: *Their arrival an hour before the party began was premature. adjective.*

pre med i tate (prē med′ə tāt), plan beforehand: *a premeditated murder. verb,* **pre med i tat ed, pre med i tat ing.**

pre mier (pri mir′), prime minister; chief officer. *noun.*

pre mi um (prē′mē əm), **1** reward; prize: *Some magazines give premiums for obtaining new subscriptions.* **2** money paid for insurance: *I pay premiums on my life insurance four times a year.* **3** unusual or unfair value: *It's possible to put too high a premium on neatness. noun.*

pre paid (prē pād′). See **prepay.** *Send this shipment prepaid. verb.*

prep a ra tion (prep′ə rā′shən), **1** preparing; making ready: *I sharpened the knife in preparation for carving the meat.* **2** being ready. **3** thing done to get ready: *He made thorough preparations for his trip by carefully planning which way to go.* **4** a specially made medicine or food or mixture of any kind: *The preparation included camphor. noun.*

pre par a to ry (pri par′ə tôr′ē), preparing; making ready. *Preparatory schools fit pupils for college. adjective.*

pre pare (pri per′ *or* pri par′), **1** make ready; get ready: *prepare lessons, prepare dinner.* **2** make by a special process: *prepare steel from iron. verb,* **pre pared, pre par ing.**

pre pay (prē pā′), pay for in advance: *to prepay a bill. verb,* **pre paid, pre pay ing.**

prep o si tion (prep′ə zish′ən), word that shows certain relations between other words. *With, for, by,* and *in* are prepositions in the sentence "Someone *with* rugs *for* sale walked *by* our house *in* the morning." *noun.*

pre pos ter ous (pri pos′tər əs), against nature, reason, or common sense; absurd; senseless; foolish: *It would be preposterous to shovel coal with a teaspoon. That the moon is made of green cheese is a preposterous notion. adjective.*

pre scribe (pri skrīb′), **1** lay down as a rule to be followed; order; direct: *Good citizens do what the laws prescribe.* **2** order as medicine or treatment: *The doctor prescribed penicillin. verb,* **pre scribed, pre scrib ing.**

pre scrip tion (pri skrip′shən), **1** order; direction. **2** a written direction or order for preparing and using a medicine: *a prescription for a cough. noun.*

pres ence (prez′ns), **1** being present in a place: *I just learned of their presence in the city.* **2** place where a person is: *The messenger was admitted to the king's presence.* **3** appearance; bearing: *The queen is a person of noble presence.* **4** something present, especially a ghost or spirit. *noun.*

in the presence of, in the sight or company of: *I signed my name in the presence of two witnesses.*

presence of mind, ability to think calmly and quickly when taken by surprise.

pres ent¹ (prez′nt), **1** being in the place or thing in question; at hand; not absent: *Every member of the class was present. Oxygen is present in the air.* **2** at this time; being or occurring now: *the present ruler, present prices.* **3** now; this time; the time being: *That is enough for the present. At present people need courage.* **4** expressing something happening or existing at the time being: *the present tense of a verb.* 1,2,4 *adjective,* 3 *noun.*

pre sent² (pri zent′ for 1 and 3-7; prez′nt for 2), **1** give: *They presented flowers to their teacher.* **2** gift; something given: *a birthday present.* **3** introduce; make acquainted; bring (a person) before somebody: *He was presented at court. Ms. Smith, may I present Mr. Brown?* **4** offer to view or notice: *The new library presents a fine appearance.* **5** bring before the public: *Our class presented a play.* **6** offer; set forth in words: *The speaker presented arguments for her side.* **7** hand in; send in: *The grocer presented his bill.* 1,3-7 *verb,* 2 *noun.*

present with, give to: *Our class presented the school with a picture.*

pre sent a ble (pri zen′tə bəl), **1** fit to be seen: *make a house presentable for company.* **2** suitable in appearance, dress, or manners for being introduced into society or company. *adjective.*

pres en ta tion (prez′n tā′shən), **1** act of giving; delivering: *the presentation of a gift.* **2** the gift that is presented. **3** offering to be considered: *the presentation of a plan.* **4** an offering to be seen; exhibition; showing: *the presentation of a play or motion picture.* **5** a formal introduction: *the presentation of a lady to the queen. noun.*

pres ent ly (prez′nt lē), **1** before long; soon: *The clock will strike presently.* **2** at the present time; now: *She is presently in fourth grade. adverb.*

pres er va tion (prez′ər vā′shən), **1** preserving; keeping safe: *Doctors work for the preservation of our health.* **2** being preserved; being kept safe: *Egyptian mummies have been in a state of preservation for thousands of years. noun.*

pre serv a tive (pri zėr′və tiv), any substance that will prevent decay or injury: *Paint is a preservative for wood surfaces. Salt is a preservative for meat. noun.*

pre serve (pri zėrv′), **1** keep from harm or change; keep safe; protect. **2** keep up; maintain. **3** keep from spoiling: *Ice helps to preserve food.* **4** prepare (food) to keep it from spoiling. Boiling with sugar, salting, smoking, and pickling are different ways of preserving food. **5** **preserves,** fruit cooked with sugar and sealed from the air: *Try our homemade plum preserves.* **6** place where wild animals, fish, or trees and plants are protected: *People are not allowed to hunt in that preserve.* 1-4 *verb,* **pre served, pre serv ing;** 5,6 *noun.*

pre serv er (pri zėr′vər), person or thing that saves and protects from danger. Life preservers help to save people from drowning. *noun.*

pre side (pri zīd′), **1** hold the place of authority; have charge of a meeting: *Our principal will preside at our election of school officers.* **2** have authority; have control: *The manager presides over the business of this store. verb,* **pre sid ed, pre sid ing.**

pres i den cy (prez′ə dən sē), **1** office of president: *She was elected to the presidency of the Junior Club.* **2** time during which a president is in office: *The United States entered World War II in the presidency of Franklin D. Roosevelt. noun, plural* **pres i den cies.**

pres i dent (prez′ə dənt), **1** the chief officer of a company, college, society, or club. **2** **President,** the highest officer of a modern republic. *noun.*

pres i dent-e lect (prez′ə dənt i lekt′), president who has been elected but not yet inaugurated. *noun.*

pres i den tial (prez′ə den′shəl), having something to do with a president or presidency: *a presidential election, a presidential candidate. adjective.*

press¹ (pres), **1** use force or weight against; push with steady force: *Press the button to ring the bell.* **2** squeeze; squeeze out: *Press all the juice from the oranges.* **3** make smooth; flatten: *press clothes with an iron.* **4** clasp; hug: *I pressed the puppy to me.* **5** push; force; pressure: *The press of many duties keeps the principal very busy.* **6** machine for pressing: *an ironing press.* **7** a printing press. **8** company that prints books, magazines, or newspapers: *Many editors, writers, and printers work for the press.* **9** newspapers, magazines, radio, and television, and the people who report for them: *Our school picnic was reported by the press.* **10** keep on pushing one's way; push ahead with eagerness or haste: *We pressed on in spite of the strong wind.* **11** a crowd: *The little boy was lost in the press.* **12** to crowd; throng: *The people pressed about the famous actor.* **13** urge; keep asking (somebody) earnestly: *Because it was so stormy, we pressed our guest to stay all night.* 1-4,10,12,13 *verb,* 5-9,11 *noun, plural* **press es.**

press² (pres), force into service, usually naval or military. Naval officers used to visit towns and ships to press men for the fleet. *verb.*

press ing (pres′ing), requiring immediate action or attention; urgent: *A person with a broken leg is in pressing need of a doctor's help. She left town quickly on some pressing business. adjective.*

pres sure (presh′ər), **1** the continued action of a weight or force: *The small box was flattened by the pressure of the heavy book on it. The pressure of the wind filled the sails of the boat.* **2** force per unit of area: *There is a pressure of 20 pounds to the square inch on this tire.* **3** state of trouble or strain: *the pressure of poverty, working under pressure.* **4** a forceful influence: *I was under pressure from the others to change my mind.* **5** force or urge by exerting pressure: *The car dealer tried to pressure my parents into buying a car.* **1-4** *noun,* **5** *verb,* **pres sured, pres sur ing.**

pres tige (pre stēzh′), reputation, influence, or distinction, based on what is known about one's abilities, achievements, or associations: *Her prestige rose when her classmates learned that she knew how to ski. noun.*

pres to (pres′tō), **1** very quickly. **2** very quick. **1** *adverb,* **2** *adjective.*

pre sum a ble (pri zü′mə bəl), able to be presumed or taken for granted; probable; likely: *Unless they lose their way, noon is the presumable time of their arrival. adjective.*

pre sum a bly (pri zü′mə blē), probably. *adverb.*

pre sume (pri züm′), **1** suppose; take for granted without proving: *You'll play out of doors, I presume, if there is sunshine.* **2** take upon oneself; venture; dare: *May I presume to tell you you are wrong?* **3** take an unfair advantage: *Don't presume on his good nature by borrowing from him every week. verb,* **pre sumed, pre sum ing.**

pre sump tion (pri zump′shən), **1** unpleasant boldness: *It is presumption to go to a party when one has not been invited.* **2** thing taken for granted: *Since she left the house last, the presumption was that she locked the door.* **3** act of presuming. *noun.*

pre sump tu ous (pri zump′chü əs), forward; too bold; daring too much. *adjective.*

pre tence (prē′tens), pretense. *noun.*

pre tend (pri tend′), **1** make believe: *Let's pretend that we are grown-ups.* **2** claim falsely: *I pretended to like the meal so that my host would be pleased.* **3** claim: *I don't pretend to be a musician. verb.*

pre tense (prē′tens), **1** make-believe; pretending: *My anger was all pretense.* **2** a false appearance: *Under pretense of dropping a pencil, the student looked at a classmate's test.* **3** a false claim: *They made a pretense of knowing our secret.* **4** display; showing off: *a person who is quiet and free from pretense. noun.* Also spelled **pretence.**

pre ten sion (pri ten′shən), **1** claim: *The young prince has pretensions to the throne.* **2** putting forward of a claim; laying claim to. **3** doing things for show or to make a fine appearance; showy display: *We were annoyed by the pretensions of our wealthy neighbor. noun.*

pre ten tious (pri ten′shəs), **1** making claims to excellence or importance: *a pretentious person.* **2** doing things for show or to make a fine appearance: *a pretentious style of entertaining guests. adjective.*

pre text (prē′tekst), a false reason concealing the real reason; misleading excuse; pretense: *She did*

---

a hat	i it	oi oil	ch child		a in about
ā age	ī ice	ou out	ng long		e in taken
ä far	o hot	u cup	sh she	ə =	i in pencil
e let	ō open	u̇ put	th thin		o in lemon
ē equal	ô order	ü rule	ᴛʜ then		u in circus
ėr term			zh measure		

not go, on the pretext of being too busy. noun.

pret ti ly (prit′ə lē), in a pretty manner. *adverb.*

pret ti ness (prit′ē nis), pleasing appearance. *noun.*

pret ty (prit′ē), **1** pleasing; attractive: *a pretty face, a pretty dress, a pretty tune.* **2** not at all pleasing: *This is a pretty mess, indeed.* **3** fairly; rather: *It is pretty late.* **1,2** *adjective,* **pret ti er, pret ti est;** **3** *adverb.*

pret zel (pret′səl), a crisp cracker, usually in the form of a knot or stick, salted on the outside. *noun.*

pre vail (pri vāl′), **1** exist in many places; be in general use: *Making resolutions on New Year's Day is a custom that still prevails.* **2** be the most usual or strongest: *Sadness prevailed in our minds.* **3** be the stronger; win the victory; succeed: *prevail against an enemy. Reason prevailed over emotion. verb.*

prevail on or **prevail upon,** persuade: *Can't I prevail upon you to stay for dinner?*

pre vail ing (pri vā′ling), in general use; common: *The prevailing summer winds here are from the west. adjective.*

prev a lence (prev′ə ləns), widespread occurrence; general use: *the prevalence of complaints about the weather, the prevalence of automobiles. noun.*

prev a lent (prev′ə lənt), widespread; in general use; common: *Colds are prevalent in the winter. adjective.*

pre vent (pri vent′), **1** keep (from): *Illness prevented him from doing his work.* **2** keep from happening: *Rain prevented the game.* **3** hinder: *I'll meet you at six if nothing prevents. verb.*

pre vent a ble (pri ven′tə bəl), able to be prevented. *adjective.*

pre ven tion (pri ven′shən), **1** preventing; hindering: *the prevention of fire.* **2** something that prevents. *noun.*

pre ven tive (pri ven′tiv), **1** able to prevent or hinder: *preventive measures against disease.* **2** something that prevents: *Vaccination is a preventive against polio.* **1** *adjective,* **2** *noun.*

pre view (prē′vyü′), **1** a previous view, inspection, or survey: *a preview of things to come.* **2** view beforehand. **3** an advance showing of scenes from a motion picture, play, or television program. **1,3** *noun,* **2** *verb.*

pre vi ous (prē′vē əs), coming or being before; earlier: *He did better in the previous lesson. adjective.*

previous to, before: *Previous to her departure she gave a party.*

pre vi ous ly (prē′vē əs lē), at a previous time; before. *adverb.*

prey (prā), **1** animal hunted or seized for food: *Mice and birds are the prey of cats.* **2** habit of hunting and killing other animals for food: *Hawks are birds of prey.* **3** person or thing injured; victim: *be a prey to fear, be a prey to disease. noun.*

prey on or **prey upon, 1** hunt or kill for food: *Cats prey upon mice.* **2** do harm; be a strain upon: *Worry about debts preyed on her mind.*

price (prīs), **1** amount for which a thing is sold or can be bought; cost to the buyer: *The price of this hat is $10.* **2** put a price on; set the price of: *The hat was priced at $10.* **3** ask the price of; find out the price of: *Mother is pricing cars.* **4** reward offered for the capture of a person alive or dead: *Every member of the gang has a price on his head.* **5** what must be given or done to obtain a thing; amount paid for any result: *The Pilgrims paid a heavy price for staying in America; half of them died during the first winter.* 1,4,5 *noun,* 2,3 *verb,* **priced, pric ing.**

beyond price or **without price,** so valuable that it cannot be bought: *a painting beyond price.*

price less (prīs/lis), very, very valuable: *Many museums have collections of priceless paintings by famous artists. adjective.*

prick (prik), **1** a sharp point. **2** a little hole or mark made by a sharp point. **3** make a little hole or mark on with a sharp point: *I pricked the map with a pin to show our route.* **4** pain like that made by a sharp point. **5** cause sharp pain to: *Thorns prick. The cat pricked me with its claws.* **6** act of pricking. 1,2,4,6 *noun,* 3,5 *verb.*

prick le (prik/əl), **1** a small, sharp point; thorn. **2** feel a prickly or smarting sensation: *My skin prickled as I listened to the scary story.* 1 *noun,* 2 *verb,* **prick led, prick ling.**

prick ly (prik/lē), **1** having many sharp points or thorns: *a prickly rosebush, a prickly porcupine.* **2** sharp and stinging; smarting: *Heat sometimes causes a prickly redness of the skin. adjective,* **prick li er, prick li est.**

prickly pear, the pear-shaped fruit of a kind of cactus. Prickly pears are good to eat. See picture.

pride (prīd), **1** a high opinion of one's own worth or possessions: *Pride in our city should make us help to keep it clean.* **2** pleasure or satisfaction in something concerned with oneself: *take pride in a hard job well done.* **3** something that one is proud of: *Their oldest child is their great pride.* **4** too high an opinion of oneself: *Pride goes before a fall.* **5 pride oneself on,** be proud of: *We pride ourselves on our clean streets. I pride myself on my memory.* 1-4 *noun,* 5 *verb,* **prid ed, prid ing.**

pried (prīd). See **pry.** *verb.*

priest (prēst), **1** clergyman or minister of a Christian church. **2** a special servant of a god: *priests of Apollo. noun.*

priest ess (prē/stis), woman who serves at an altar or in sacred rites. *noun, plural* **priest ess es.**

priest ly (prēst/lē), **1** of or having something to do with a priest: *priestly robes.* **2** like a priest; suitable for a priest: *a priestly desire to help those in need. adjective,* **priest li er, priest li est.**

prim (prim), precise, formal, and proper: *a prim manner. adjective,* **prim mer, prim mest.**

pri mar i ly (prī/mer/ə lē *or* prī mer/ə lē), **1** above all; chiefly; principally: *That student is primarily interested in science.* **2** at first; originally. *adverb.*

pri mar y (prī/mer/ē), **1** first in time; first in order; original: *The primary causes of the war go back many years.* **2** chief; first in importance: *The primary reason for eating a balanced diet is good health.* **3** election in which members of a political party choose candidates for office. Primaries are held before the regular election. 1,2 *adjective,* 3 *noun, plural* **pri mar ies.**

primary accent, 1 the strongest accent in the pronunciation of a word. **2** mark (/) used to show this.

primary color, red, yellow, or blue.

primary school, the first three or four grades of the elementary school.

pri mate (prī/māt), one of a group of mammals that have very advanced brains, and hands with thumbs that can be used to hold on to things. Primates are the most highly developed mammals. Apes, monkeys, and human beings are primates. *noun.*

prime[1] (prīm), **1** first in rank; chief: *His prime object was to get enough to eat.* **2** first in time or order; primary: *the prime causes of war.* **3** first in quality; first-rate; excellent: *prime ribs of beef. adjective.*

prime[2] (prīm), the best part; best time; best condition: *A person of forty is in the prime of life. noun.*

prime[3] (prīm), **1** prepare by putting something in or on. New wood is primed with a special first coat of paint so that the final coat will not soak in. **2** pour water into (a pump) to start action. *verb,* **primed, prim ing.**

prime minister, the chief minister in certain governments. The prime minister is the head of the cabinet.

prim er (prim/ər), **1** a first book in reading. **2** a first book; beginner's book: *a primer in arithmetic. noun.*

pri me val (prī mē/vəl), **1** of or having something to do with the earliest age of the earth: *In its primeval state the earth was without any forms of life.* **2** ancient: *primeval forests untouched by the ax. adjective.*

prim ing (prī/ming), powder or other material used to set fire to an explosive. *noun.*

prim i tive (prim/ə tiv), **1** of early times; of long ago: *Primitive people often lived in caves.* **2** very simple; such as people had early in human history: *A primitive way of making fire is by rubbing two sticks together. adjective.*

prim rose (prim/rōz/), **1** a plant having showy, bell-shaped or funnel-shaped flowers of various colors. There are many kinds of primroses. The common one of Europe has pale-yellow flowers. **2** pale yellow. 1 *noun,* 2 *adjective.*

prince (prins), **1** son of a king or queen; son of a king's or queen's son. **2** ruler of a small state or country. **3** the greatest or best of a group; chief: *a prince of artists, a merchant prince. noun.*

prince ly (prins′lē), **1** of a prince or his rank; royal. **2** like a prince; noble. **3** fit for a prince; magnificent: *Some presidents of businesses earn princely salaries. adjective,* **prince li er, prince li est.**

prin cess (prin′ses), **1** daughter of a king or queen; daughter of a king's or queen's son. **2** wife or widow of a prince. *noun, plural* **prin cess es.**

prin ci pal (prin′sə pəl), **1** main; chief; most important: *Chicago is the principal city of Illinois.* **2** the chief person; one who gives orders. **3** head of a school. **4** sum of money on which interest is paid. **1** *adjective,* **2-4** *noun.*

prin ci pal ly (prin′sə pə lē), for the most part; above all; chiefly. *adverb.*

prin ci ple (prin′sə pəl), **1** basic truth or law; truth that is a foundation for other truths: *the principle of free speech.* **2** a basic belief: *religious principles.* **3** rule of action or conduct: *I make it a principle to save some money each week.* **4** goodness; honesty; high standard of behavior: *a person of principle.* **5** rule of science explaining how things act: *the principle by which a machine works. noun.*

print (print), **1** use type to stamp words on (paper): *Who prints this newspaper?* **2** cause to be printed; publish: *print books. Most newspapers are printed daily.* **3** words in ink stamped by type: *This book has clear print.* **4** make letters the way they look in print instead of writing them: *Print your name clearly. Most children learn to print before learning to write.* **5** mark (cloth or paper) with patterns or designs: *This machine prints wallpaper.* **6** cloth with a pattern pressed on it: *She has two dresses made of print.* **7** picture made in a special way; printed picture or design. **8** stamp; produce (marks or figures) by pressure; impress. **9** mark made by pressing or stamping, such as a footprint. **10** photograph produced from a negative. **1,2,4,5,8** *verb,* **3,6,7,9,10** *noun.*

print er (prin′tər), person whose business or work is printing or setting type. *noun.*

print ing (prin′ting), **1** the producing of books, newspapers, magazines, or pamphlets by stamping in ink or dye from movable types or plates. **2** printed words. **3** all the copies printed at one time. **4** letters made like those in print. *noun.*

printing press, machine for printing.

pri or[1] (prī′ər), coming before; earlier: *I can't go with you because I have a prior engagement. adjective.*

prior to, earlier than; before.

pri or[2] (prī′ər), head of a priory or monastery for men. Priors usually rank below abbots. *noun.*

pri or ess (prī′ər is), woman at the head of a convent or priory for women. *noun, plural* **pri or ess es.**

pri or i ty (prī ôr′ə tē), greater importance; coming before in order or importance: *Fire engines have priority over other traffic. noun, plural* **pri or i ties.**

pri or y (prī′ər ē), a religious house governed by a prior or prioress. *noun, plural* **pri or ies.**

a hat	i it	oi oil	ch child	a in about
ā age	ī ice	ou out	ng long	e in taken
ä far	o hot	u cup	sh she	ə = i in pencil
e let	ō open	ù put	th thin	o in lemon
ē equal	ô order	ü rule	ᴛʜ then	u in circus
ėr term			zh measure	

prickly pears

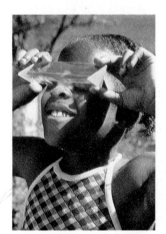

prism
The girl looked through the prism.

prism (priz′əm), a transparent solid object with two ends that are triangles and three sides that are rectangles. A prism separates white light passing through it into the colors of the rainbow. See picture. *noun.*

pris on (priz'n), **1** a public building in which criminals are confined: *The convicted killer was sentenced to prison for life.* **2** any place where a person or animal is shut up unwillingly: *The small apartment was a prison to the big dog.* noun.

pris on er (priz'n ər), **1** person who is under arrest or held in a jail or prison. **2** person who is kept shut up unwillingly, or who is not free to move. **3** person taken by the enemy in war. noun.

pri va cy (prī'və sē), **1** condition of being private; being away from others: *in the privacy of one's home.* **2** secrecy: *He told me his reasons in strict privacy.* noun, plural **pri va cies.**

pri vate (prī'vit), **1** not for the public; for one person or a few special people: *a private road, a private house, a private letter.* **2** personal; not public: *the private life of a king, a private opinion. A diary is private.* **3** secret; confidential: *News reached her through private channels.* **4** having no public office: *a private citizen.* **5** soldier or marine of the lowest rank: *His brother was promoted from private to corporal last week.* 1-4 adjective, 5 noun.
in private, secretly: *The rebels met in private to plot against the government.*

pri va tion (prī vā'shən), lack of the comforts or necessities of life; hardship: *Because of privation during the war, many people were homeless.* noun.

priv i lege (priv'ə lij), a special right, advantage, or favor: *My sister has the privilege of driving the family car.* noun.

priv i leged (priv'ə lijd), having some privilege or privileges: *Royalty are privileged people.* adjective.

priv y (priv'ē), **1** private. **2** secret. adjective.
privy to, having secret or private knowledge of: *The Vice-President was privy to the plans of the President.*

prize[1] (prīz), **1** reward won after trying against other people: *Prizes will be given for the three best stories.* **2** given as a prize. **3** worthy of a prize: *prize vegetables.* **4** reward worth working for. 1,4 noun, 2,3 adjective.

prize[2] (prīz), thing or person captured in war, especially an enemy's ship and its cargo taken at sea. noun.

prize[3] (prīz), value highly: *She prizes her new bicycle.* verb, **prized, priz ing.**

prize fight (prīz'fīt'), a boxing match between prizefighters. noun.

prize fight er (prīz'fī'tər), person who fights or boxes for money. noun.

pro[1] (prō), **1** in favor of; for: *We talked about the problem pro and con.* **2** reason in favor of. *The pros and cons of a question are the arguments for and against it.* 1 adverb, 2 noun, plural **pros.**

pro[2] (prō), professional. noun, plural **pros;** adjective.

prob a bil i ty (prob'ə bil'ə tē), **1** quality or fact of being likely or probable; good chance: *There is a probability of rain.* **2** something likely to happen: *A storm is a probability for tomorrow.* noun, plural **prob a bil i ties.**
in all probability, probably: *In all probability I will go with you.*

procession (definition 1)

prob a ble (prob'ə bəl), **1** likely to happen: *Cooler weather is probable after this shower.* **2** likely to be true: *Something he ate is the probable cause of his upset stomach.* adjective.

prob a bly (prob'ə blē), more likely than not. adverb.

pro ba tion (prō bā'shən), trial or testing of conduct, character, or qualifications: *He was admitted to the sixth grade on probation.* noun.

probe (prōb), **1** search into; examine thoroughly; investigate: *probe the causes of crime. She probed her thoughts and feelings in an effort to find out why she acted as she did.* **2** a thorough examination· investigation: *a probe of illegal gambling.* **3** a slender instrument for exploring something. A doctor or dentist uses a probe to explore the depth or direction of a wound or cavity. A Geiger counter uses a probe to detect the amount of radiation in radioactive matter, such as rock. **4** spacecraft carrying scientific instruments to record or report back information about planets or other objects in outer space: *a lunar probe.* **5** examine with a probe. 1,5 verb, **probed, prob ing;** 2-4 noun.

prob lem (prob'ləm), **1** question; difficult question: *How to do away with poverty is a problem that concerns the government.* **2** matter of doubt or difficulty: *The president of a large company has to deal with many problems.* **3** something to be worked out: *a problem in arithmetic.* **4** that causes difficulty: *a problem child.* 1-3 noun, 4 adjective.

pro ce dure (prə sē'jər), way of doing things: *What is your procedure in making bread?* noun.

pro ceed (prə sēd'), **1** go on after having stopped; move forward: *Please proceed with your story. The train proceeded at the same speed as before.* **2** carry on any activity: *I proceeded to light the fire.* **3** come forth; issue; go out: *Heat proceeds from fire.* verb.

pro ceed ing (prə sē'ding), **1** what is done; action; conduct. **2 proceedings, a** action in a case in a court of law. **b** record of what was done at the meetings of a society or club. noun.

pro ceeds (prō'sēdz'), money obtained from a sale or some other activity or transaction: *The proceeds from the school play will be used to buy a new curtain for the stage.* noun plural.

proc ess (pros'es), **1** set of actions or changes in a special order: *By what process is cloth made from wool?* **2** treat or prepare by some special method:

This cloth has been processed to make it waterproof.
1 *noun, plural* **proc ess es;** 2 *verb.*

in process, 1 in the course or condition: *In process of time the house will be finished.* **2** in the course or condition of being done: *The author has just finished one book and has another in process.*

pro ces sion (prə sesh′ən), **1** something that moves forward; persons marching or riding: *a funeral procession.* See picture. **2** an orderly moving forward: *We formed lines to march in procession onto the platform. noun.*

pro claim (prə klām′), make known publicly and officially; declare publicly: *War was proclaimed. The President proclaimed this week as National Dog Week. verb.*

proc la ma tion (prok′lə mā′shən), an official announcement; public declaration: *The queen issued a proclamation ending the war. noun.*

pro cure (prə kyùr′), **1** get by care or effort; obtain; secure: *procure a position in a bank. It is hard to procure water in a desert.* **2** bring about; cause: *The lawyer procured the prisoner's release. verb,* **pro cured, pro cur ing.**

prod (prod), **1** poke or jab with something pointed: *prod an animal with a stick.* **2** stir up; urge on; goad: *My parents keep prodding me to clean my room.* **3** poke; thrust: *That prod in the ribs hurt.* **4** stick with a sharp point; goad. 1,2 *verb,* **prod ded, prod ding;** 3,4 *noun.*

prod i gal (prod′ə gəl), **1** spending too much; wasting money or other things; wasteful: *America has been prodigal of its forests.* **2** abundant; lavish. **3** person who is wasteful or extravagant: *The father welcomed the prodigal back home.* 1,2 *adjective,* 3 *noun.*

pro di gious (prə dij′əs), **1** very great; huge; vast: *The ocean contains a prodigious amount of water.* **2** wonderful; marvelous. *adjective.*

prod i gy (prod′ə jē), marvel; wonder. An infant prodigy is a child remarkably brilliant in some way. *noun, plural* **prod i gies.**

pro duce (prə düs′ *or* prə dyüs′ *for 1-4;* prod′üs *or* prod′yüs *for 5*), **1** make; bring into existence: *This factory produces stoves.* **2** bring about; cause: *Hard work produces success.* **3** bring forth; supply; yield: *Hens produce eggs.* **4** bring forward; show: *Produce your proof. Our class produced a play.* **5** what is produced; yield: *Vegetables are a garden's produce.* 1-4 *verb,* **pro duced, pro duc ing;** 5 *noun.*

pro duc er (prə dü′sər *or* prə dyü′sər), **1** one that produces, especially a person who grows or manufactures things that are used by others. **2** person in charge of presenting a play, a motion picture, or a television or radio show. *noun.*

prod uct (prod′əkt), **1** that which is produced; result of work or of growth: *factory products, farm products.* **2** number resulting from multiplying two or more numbers together: *40 is the product of 5 and 8. noun.*

pro duc tion (prə duk′shən), **1** act of producing; manufacture: *the production of automobiles.* **2** something that is produced: *the yearly production of a farm. noun.*

a hat	**i** it	**oi** oil	**ch** child		a in about
ā age	**ī** ice	**ou** out	**ng** long		e in taken
ä far	**o** hot	**u** cup	**sh** she	ə =	i in pencil
e let	**ō** open	**u̇** put	**th** thin		o in lemon
ē equal	**ô** order	**ü** rule	**ᵺ** then		u in circus
ėr term			**zh** measure		

pro duc tive (prə duk′tiv), **1** producing much; fertile: *a productive farm, a productive writer.* **2** producing food or other useful articles: *Farming is productive labor. adjective.*

pro fane (prə fān′), **1** without respect for God or holy things: *profane language.* **2** treat (holy things) with disrespect or abuse: *profane a church by stabling horses in it.* 1 *adjective,* 2 *verb,* **pro faned, pro fan ing.**

pro fan i ty (prə fan′ə tē), **1** swearing; use of profane language. **2** being profane; lack of reverence. *noun, plural* **pro fan i ties.**

pro fess (prə fes′), **1** claim to have; claim: *She professed the greatest respect for the law. I don't profess to be an expert in chemistry.* **2** declare one's belief in: *Christians profess the Christian religion.* **3** declare openly: *He professed his loyalty to the United States. verb.*

pro fes sion (prə fesh′ən), **1** occupation requiring special education, such as law, medicine, teaching, or the ministry. **2** the people engaged in such an occupation: *The medical profession favors this law.* **3** an open declaration; act of professing: *a profession of friendship, a profession of faith. noun.*

pro fes sion al (prə fesh′ə nəl), **1** of or having something to do with a profession: *Our doctor has a professional gravity very unlike his ordinary joking manner.* **2** engaged in a profession: *A lawyer or a doctor is a professional person.* **3** making a business or trade of something which others do for pleasure: *professional musicians.* **4** person who does this. 1-3 *adjective,* 4 *noun.*

pro fes sor (prə fes′ər), teacher of the highest rank in a college or university. *noun.*

pro fi cient (prə fish′ənt), skilled; expert; advanced in any art, science, or subject: *She was very proficient in music. adjective.*

pro file (prō′fīl), **1** a side view, especially of the human face. See picture. **2** outline. *noun.*

profile (definition 1)

prof it (prof′it), **1** the gain from a business; what is left when the cost of goods and of carrying on the business is subtracted from the amount of money taken in: *The profits in this business are not large.* **2** make a gain from business; make a profit. **3** advantage; benefit: *What profit is there in worrying?* **4** get advantage; gain; benefit: *A wise person profits from mistakes.* 1,3 *noun,* 2,4 *verb.*

prof it a ble (prof′ə tə bəl), **1** yielding profit: *The sale held by the Girl Scouts was very profitable.* **2** useful; giving a gain or benefit: *We spent a profitable afternoon in the library. adjective.*

prof it a bly (prof′ə tə blē), with profit. *adverb.*

pro found (prə found′), **1** very deep: *a profound sigh, a profound sleep.* **2** felt strongly; very great: *profound despair, profound sympathy.* **3** going far deeper than what is easily understood; having or showing great knowledge or understanding: *a profound book, a profound thinker. adjective.*

pro fuse (prə fyüs′), **1** very abundant: *profuse thanks.* **2** very generous; extravagant: *profuse spending. He was profuse in his praise of the book. adjective.*

pro fu sion (prə fyü′zhən), a very large quantity; abundance: *a profusion of books, a profusion of roses. noun.*

pro gram (prō′gram), **1** list of items or events set down in order with a list of the performers. There are concert programs, theater programs, and programs of a meeting. **2** items making up an entertainment: *The entire program was delightful.* **3** plan of what is to be done: *a school program, a business program, a government program. noun.*

prog ress (prog′res for 1 and 3; prə gres′ for 2 and 4), **1** advance; growth; development; improvement: *the progress of science. The class showed rapid progress in its studies.* **2** get better; advance; develop: *We progress in learning step by step.* **3** moving forward; going ahead: *make rapid progress on a journey.* **4** move forward; go ahead: *The building of the new school progressed quickly during the summer.* 1,3 *noun,* 2,4 *verb.*

pro gres sion (prə gresh′ən), moving forward; going ahead: *Creeping is a slow method of progression. noun.*

pro gres sive (prə gres′iv), **1** making progress; advancing to something better; improving: *a progressive nation.* **2** favoring progress; wanting improvement or reform in government, religion, or business. **3** person who favors improvement and reform in government, religion, or business: *Our doctor is a progressive in her beliefs.* 1,2 *adjective,* 3 *noun.*

pro hib it (prō hib′it), **1** forbid by law or authority: *Picking flowers in the park is prohibited.* See picture. **2** prevent: *Rainy weather and fog prohibited flying. verb.*

pro hi bi tion (prō′ə bish′ən), **1** act of prohibiting or forbidding: *The prohibition of swimming in the city's reservoirs is sensible.* **2** law or laws against making or selling alcoholic liquors. *noun.*

proj ect (proj′ekt for 1,2 and 6; prə jekt′ for 3-5), **1** a plan; scheme: *a project for slum clearance.* **2** undertaking; special assignment. See picture. **3** throw or cast forward: *A cannon projects shells.* **4** cause to fall on a surface: *Motion pictures are projected on the screen. The tree projects a shadow on the grass.* **5** stick out: *The rocky point projects far into the water.* **6** group of apartment buildings built and run as a unit: *They live in a big housing project.* 1,2,6 *noun,* 3-5 *verb.*

pro jec tile (prə jek′təl), any object that can be thrown, hurled, or shot, such as a stone or bullet. *noun.*

pro jec tion (prə jek′shən), **1** part that projects or sticks out: *rocky projections on the face of a cliff.* **2** sticking out. **3** throwing or casting forward: *the projection of a shell from a cannon, the projection of a photographic image on a screen. noun.*

pro jec tor (prə jek′tər), apparatus for projecting a picture on a screen. *noun.*

pro lif ic (prə lif′ik), **1** producing many offspring: *Rabbits are prolific.* **2** producing much: *a prolific tree, a prolific garden, a prolific writer. adjective.*

pro long (prə lông′), make longer; extend; stretch: *Good care may prolong a sick person's life. I enjoyed myself so much at my grandparents' that they asked me to prolong my visit. verb.*

prom (prom), a formal dance given by a college or high-school class. *noun.*

prom e nade (prom′ə nād′ *or* prom′ə näd′), **1** a walk for pleasure or for show: *The Easter promenade is well known as a fashion show.* **2** to walk about for pleasure or for show: *We promenaded back and forth on the ship's deck.* **3** a public place for such a walk: *The resort had a promenade along the beach.* 1,3 *noun,* 2 *verb,* **prom e nad ed, prom e nad ing.**

prom i nence (prom′ə nəns), **1** being prominent, distinguished, or conspicuous: *the prominence of Washington as a leader, the prominence of football as a sport.* **2** something that juts out or projects, especially upward. A hill is a prominence. *noun.*

prom i nent (prom′ə nənt), **1** well-known; important: *a prominent citizen.* **2** easy to see: *A single tree in a field is prominent.* **3** standing out; projecting: *Some insects have prominent eyes. adjective.*

prom ise (prom′is), **1** words said or written, binding a person to do or not to do something: *You can count on her to keep her promise.* **2** give one's word; make a promise: *They promised to stay till we came.* **3** make a promise of: *promise help.* **4** indication of what may be expected: *The clouds give promise of rain.* **5** indication of giving hope of success in the future: *She shows promise as a musician.* **6** give hope; give hope of: *The rainbow promises fair weather.* 1,4,5 *noun,* 2,3,6 *verb,* **prom ised, prom is ing.**

prom is ing (prom′is sing), giving hope of success in the future; likely to turn out well: *The promising young pianist has a great deal of talent. adjective.*

prom on to ry (prom′ən tôr′ē), a high point of land or rock extending into a body of water; headland. See picture. *noun, plural* **prom on to ries.**

pro mote (prə mōt′), **1** raise in rank or importance: *Pupils who pass this test will be promoted to the next higher grade.* **2** help to grow or develop; help to success: *A kindly feeling toward other countries will promote peace.* **3** recommend the use of; try to sell by advertising: *A series of TV commercials promotes the new soap. verb,* **pro mot ed, pro mot ing.**

pro mo tion (prə mō′shən), **1** advance in rank or importance: *The clerk was given a promotion and an increase in salary.* **2** helping to grow or develop; helping along to success: *The doctors were busy in the promotion of a health campaign. noun.*

prompt (prompt), **1** quick; on time; ready and willing: *to be prompt to obey.* **2** done at once; made without delay: *a prompt answer.* **3** cause (someone) to do something: *His curiosity prompted him to ask questions.* **4** remind (a speaker or actor) of the words or actions needed: *Please prompt me if I forget my lines.* **1,2** *adjective,* **3,4** *verb.*

prone (prōn), **1** inclined; liable: *He is prone to forget to do his chores.* **2** lying face down: *be prone on the bed.* **3** lying flat: *fall prone on the ground. adjective.*

prong (prông), one of the pointed ends of a fork or antler. *noun.*

prong horn (prông′hôrn′), antelope (definition 2). *noun, plural* **prong horns** *or* **prong horn.**

pro noun (prō′noun), word used to indicate without naming, such as *you, it, they, him, we, whose, this,* or *whoever;* word used instead of a noun. In "John and Mary did not go because they were sick," *they* is a pronoun used in the second part of the sentence to avoid repeating *John and Mary. noun.*

pro nounce (prə nouns′), **1** make the sounds of; speak: *Pronounce your words clearly.* **2** declare (a person or thing) to be: *The doctor pronounced her cured.* **3** declare solemnly or positively: *The judge pronounced sentence on the prisoner. verb,* **pro nounced, pro nounc ing.**

pro nounced (prə nounst′), strongly marked; decided: *She has pronounced opinions on politics. adjective.*

pro nun ci a tion (prə nun′sē ā′shən), **1** way of pronouncing. This book gives the pronunciation of each main word. **2** making the sounds of words; speaking. *noun.*

proof (prüf), **1** way or means of showing beyond doubt the truth of something: *Is what you say a guess or have you proof?* **2** act of testing; trial: *That box looks big enough; but let us put it to the proof.* **3** of tested value against something: *This fabric is wrinkle-proof.* **1,2** *noun,* **3** *adjective.*

proof read (prüf′rēd′), read and mark errors to be corrected. *verb,* **proof read** (prüf′red′), **proof read ing.**

prop (prop), **1** hold up by placing a support under or against: *Prop the clothes line with a stick. He was propped up in bed with pillows.* **2** thing or person used to support another: *I used the book as a prop behind my painting.* **1** *verb,* **propped, prop ping;** **2** *noun.*

a hat	i it	oi oil	ch child	⎧ a in about
ā age	ī ice	ou out	ng long	⎪ e in taken
ä far	o hot	u cup	sh she	ə = ⎨ i in pencil
e let	ō open	u̇ put	th thin	⎪ o in lemon
ē equal	ô order	ü rule	₮H then	⎩ u in circus
ėr term			zh measure	

promontory— A **promontory** rose high above the river.

project (definition 2)—He watered the plants in the class science **project.**

prohibit (definition 1)—Docking boats at the pier was **prohibited.**

prop a gan da (prop/ə gan/də), **1** systematic efforts to spread opinions or beliefs: *Propaganda is most effective where there is no freedom of the press.* **2** opinions or beliefs spread by such efforts: *During the war, the enemy spread false propaganda about us. noun.*

prop a gate (prop/ə gāt), **1** produce offspring; reproduce: *Trees propagate themselves by seeds.* **2** cause to increase in number by the production of young: *Cows and sheep are propagated on farms.* **3** spread (news or knowledge): *The scientist propagated his new theory about life in outer space. verb,* **prop a gat ed, prop a gat ing.**

pro pel (prə pel/), drive forward; force ahead: *propel a boat by oars, a person propelled by ambition. verb,* **pro pelled, pro pel ling.**

pro pel lant (prə pel/ənt), something that propels, especially the fuel of a rocket. *noun.*

pro pel ler (prə pel/ər), a revolving part with blades, for propelling boats and aircraft. See picture. *noun.*

prop er (prop/ər), **1** right for the occasion; fitting: *Night is the proper time to sleep.* **2** in the strict sense of the word: *Puerto Rico is not part of the United States proper.* **3** decent; respectable: *proper conduct.* **4** belonging to one or a few; not common to all. *Mary Jones* and *John Jones* are proper names. A **proper noun,** such as *Kansas* or *Moses,* starts with a capital letter and refers to a particular person, place, or thing. *adjective.*

prop er ly (prop/ər lē), **1** in a proper, correct, or suitable manner: *Eat properly.* **2** rightly; justly: *An honest person is properly angry at the offer of a bribe.* **3** strictly: *Properly speaking, a whale is not a fish. adverb.*

prop er ty (prop/ər tē), **1** thing or things owned; possession or possessions: *This house is her property. That book is my property; please return it to me.* **2** piece of land or real estate: *He owns some property out West.* **3** quality or power belonging specially to something: *Soap has the property of removing dirt. Copper has several important properties. noun, plural* **prop er ties.**

proph e cy (prof/ə sē), **1** telling what will happen; foretelling future events. **2** thing told about the future. *noun, plural* **proph e cies.**

proph e sy (prof/ə sī), **1** tell what will happen; foretell; predict: *The fortuneteller prophesied that I would have good luck in the future.* **2** speak when or as if inspired by God. *verb,* **proph e sied, proph e sy ing.**

proph et (prof/it), **1** person who tells what will happen: *Don't be a bad-luck prophet.* **2** a religious leader who speaks as the voice of God: *Jeremiah was a prophet of the Old Testament. noun.*

pro por tion (prə pôr/shən), **1** relation of two things; a size, number, or amount compared to another: *Each girl's pay will be in proportion to the work she does. Mix water and orange juice in the proportions of three to one by taking three measures of water to every measure of orange juice.* See picture. **2** proper relation between parts. **3** fit (one thing to another) so that they go together: *The designs in that rug are well proportioned.* **4** part; share: *A large proportion of Nevada is desert.* **5 proportions, a** size; extent: *He left an art collection of considerable proportions.* **b** dimensions: *The dining room of the castle had the proportions of our entire apartment.* 1,2,4,5 *noun,* 3 *verb.*

pro pos al (prə pō/zəl), **1** plan; scheme; suggestion: *The club will now hear this member's proposal.* **2** offer of marriage. **3** act of proposing: *Proposal is easier than performance. noun.*

pro pose (prə pōz/), **1** put forward; suggest: *She proposed that we take turns at the swing.* **2** present (the name of someone) for an office: *I am proposing Jack for president.* **3** intend; plan: *She proposes to save half of all she earns.* **4** make an offer of marriage. *verb,* **pro posed, pro pos ing.**

prop o si tion (prop/ə zish/ən), **1** what is offered to be considered; proposal: *She made a proposition to buy out her partner's interest in the store.* **2** statement. EXAMPLE: "All men are created equal." **3** statement that is to be proved true. EXAMPLE: Resolved: that our school should have a bank. **4** problem to be solved: *a proposition in arithmetic. noun.*

pro pri e tor (prə prī/ə tər), owner. *noun.*

pro pri e ty (prə prī/ə tē), **1** quality of being proper; fitness. **2** proper behavior: *They acted with propriety. Propriety demands good table manners. noun, plural* **pro pri e ties.**

pro pul sion (prə pul/shən), **1** driving forward or onward. **2** a propelling force or impulse: *Most large aircraft are powered by propulsion of jet engines. noun.*

prose (prōz), the ordinary form of spoken or written language; plain language not arranged in verses. *noun.*

pros e cute (pros/ə kyüt), **1** bring before a court of law: *Reckless drivers will be prosecuted.* **2** carry out; follow up: *They started an inquiry into the cause of the fire, and prosecuted it for several weeks. verb,* **pros e cut ed, pros e cut ing.**

pros e cu tion (pros/ə kyü/shən), **1** the carrying on of a lawsuit: *The prosecution will be stopped if the stolen money is returned.* **2** side that starts action against another in a court of law. The prosecution makes certain charges against the defense. **3** carrying out; following up: *They were dedicated to the prosecution of their plan. noun.*

pros pect (pros/pekt), **1** the act of looking forward; expectation: *The prospect of a vacation is pleasant.* **2** outlook for the future: *Without a high school education the prospect of getting a good job is poor.* **3** view; scene: *The prospect from the mountain was grand.* **4** search or look: *prospect for gold.* **5** person who may become a customer, buyer, or candidate: *The salesman called on several prospects.* 1-3,5 *noun,* 4 *verb.*

pro spec tive (prə spek/tiv), expected; likely to be: *a prospective client, a prospective raise in pay. adjective.*

pros pec tor (pros/pek tər), person who explores or examines a region, searching for gold, silver, oil, uranium, or other valuable resources. *noun.*

propeller of a ship

proportion
(definition 1)
She was tiny
in proportion
to the dog.

a hat	**i** it	**oi** oil	**ch** child		⎧ a in about
ā age	**ī** ice	**ou** out	**ng** long		⎪ e in taken
ä far	**o** hot	**u** cup	**sh** she	**ə** =	⎨ i in pencil
e let	**ō** open	**u̇** put	**th** thin		⎪ o in lemon
ē equal	**ô** order	**ü** rule	**ᵵH** then		⎩ u in circus
ėr term			**zh** measure		

have a large dog for our protection. **2** thing or person that prevents damage: *A hat is a protection from the sun.* noun.

pro tec tive (prə tek′tiv), **1** protecting; being a defense: *the hard protective covering of a turtle.* **2** preventing injury to those around: *a protective device on a machine.* adjective.

pro tec tor (prə tek′tər), person or thing that protects; defender. noun.

pro tein (prō′tēn), one of the substances containing nitrogen which are a necessary part of the cells of animals and plants. Foods such as meat, milk, cheese, eggs, and beans contain protein. noun.

pro test (prō′test *for 1;* prə test′ *for 2-4*), **1** statement that denies or objects strongly: *They yielded only after protest.* **2** make objections; object: *We protested against staying after school.* **3** object to: *She protested the referee's decision.* **4** declare solemnly; assert: *to protest one's innocence.* **1** noun, **2-4** verb.

under protest, unwillingly; though objecting.

Prot es tant (prot′ə stənt), **1** member of any of certain Christian churches which split off from the Roman Catholic Church. **2** of Protestants or their religion. **1** noun, **2** adjective.

pro ton (prō′ton), a tiny particle having one unit of positive electricity. All atoms are made up of electrons and protons. noun.

pro to plasm (prō′tə plaz′əm), living matter; the living substance of all plant and animal cells. Protoplasm is a colorless substance somewhat like white of egg. noun.

pro to zo an (prō′tə zō′ən), a very simple animal that is made up of only one cell. Most protozoans live in water and are so small that they can be seen only through a microscope. noun.

pro trude (prō trüd′), stick out; project: *Her teeth protrude too far.* verb, **pro trud ed, pro trud ing.**

proud (proud), **1** thinking well of oneself. **2** thinking too well of oneself; haughty. **3** very pleasing to one's feelings or one's pride: *It was a proud moment for her when she was given the award.* **4** grand; magnificent: *The big ship was a proud sight.* adjective.

proud of, thinking well of; being well satisfied with: *be proud of oneself, be proud of one's family.*

prove (prüv), **1** show that (a thing) is true and right: *Prove your statement.* **2** turn out; be found to be: *The book proved interesting.* **3** try out; test: *prove a new product.* verb, **proved, proved** or **prov en, prov ing.**

prov en (prü′vən), proved. See **prove.** verb.

prov erb (prov′ėrb′), a short, wise saying used for a long time by many people. "Haste makes waste" is a proverb. noun.

pros per (pros′pər), **1** be successful; have good fortune; flourish: *Their business prospered.* **2** make successful. verb.

pros per i ty (pros per′ə tē), success; good fortune; prosperous condition: *a time of peace and prosperity.* noun, plural **pros per i ties.**

pros per ous (pros′pər əs), **1** successful; thriving; doing well; fortunate: *a prosperous merchant.* **2** favorable; helpful: *prosperous weather for growing wheat.* adjective.

pros trate (pros′trāt), **1** lay down flat; cast down: *The captives prostrated themselves before the conqueror.* **2** lying flat with face downward: *They were humbly prostrate in prayer.* **3** lying flat: *I stumbled and fell prostrate on the floor.* **4** make very weak or helpless; exhaust: *Sickness often prostrates people.* **5** overcome; helpless: *They were prostrate with grief.* **1,4** verb, **pros trat ed, pros trat ing; 2,3,5** adjective.

pro tect (prə tekt′), shield from harm or danger; shelter; defend; guard: *Protect yourself from danger. Protect the baby's eyes from the sun.* verb.

pro tec tion (prə tek′shən), **1** act of protecting; condition of being kept from harm; defense: *We*

pro vide (prə vīd/), **1** give what is needed or wanted; supply; furnish: *Sheep provide us with wool.* **2** take care for the future: *provide for old age.* **3** arrange in advance; state as a condition beforehand: *Our club's rules provide that dues must be paid monthly.* **4** get ready; prepare: *They provided a good dinner. verb,* **pro vid ed, pro vid ing.**

pro vid ed (prə vī/did), on the condition that; if: *She will go provided her friends can go also. conjunction.*

prov i dence (prov/ə dəns), God's care and help: *Trusting in providence, the Pilgrims sailed for the unknown world. noun.*

prov i dent (prov/ə dənt), careful in providing for the future; having or showing foresight: *Provident people save some money for the future. adjective.*

prov ince (prov/əns), **1** one of the main divisions of a country. Canada is divided into provinces instead of into states. **2** proper work or activity: *Astronomy is not within the province of Grade 4. noun.*

pro vin cial (prə vin/shəl), **1** of a province: *provincial government.* **2** person born or living in a province. **3** having the manners, speech, dress, or point of view of people living in a province. **1,3** *adjective,* **2** *noun.*

pro vi sion (prə vizh/ən), **1** statement making a condition: *Our library has a provision that hands must be clean before books are taken out.* **2** act of providing; preparation: *They made provision for their children's education.* **3 provisions,** a supply of food and drinks: *They took plenty of provisions on their trip.* **4** supply with provisions: *The cabin was well provisioned with canned goods.* **1-3** *noun,* **4** *verb.*

pro vi sion al (prə vizh/ə nəl), for the time being; temporary: *a provisional agreement. adjective.*

prov o ca tion (prov/ə kā/shən), **1** act of provoking. **2** something that stirs one up; cause of anger: *Their insults were a provocation.* See picture. *noun.*

pro voke (prə vōk/), **1** make angry; vex: *She provoked him by her teasing.* **2** stir up; excite: *An insult provokes a person to anger.* **3** call forth; bring about; cause; start into action: *The senator's*

speech provoked much discussion. *verb,* **pro voked, pro vok ing.**

prow (prou), **1** the pointed front part of a ship or boat; bow. **2** something like it: *the prow of an aircraft. noun.*

prowl (proul), **1** go about slowly and secretly hunting for something to eat or steal: *Many wild animals prowl at night.* **2** wander: *He got up and prowled about his room.* **3** prowling: *It was only a wild animal on its nightly prowl.* **1,2** *verb,* **3** *noun.*

prox y (prok/sē), agent; deputy; substitute. *noun, plural* **prox ies.**

pru dence (prüd/ns), wise thought before acting; good judgment. *noun.*

pru dent (prüd/nt), planning carefully ahead of time; sensible; discreet: *Prudent people save part of their wages. adjective.*

prune¹ (prün), kind of sweet plum that is dried: *We had stewed prunes for breakfast. noun.*

prune² (prün), **1** cut out useless parts from: *Prune that tree. The editor pruned the writer's manuscript.* **2** cut off; cut out: *Prune all the dead branches. verb,* **pruned, prun ing.**

pry¹ (prī), look with curiosity; peep: *to pry into another's private affairs. verb,* **pried, pry ing.**

pry² (prī), **1** raise or move by force: *Pry up that stone with your pickax.* **2** lever for prying. **3** get with much effort: *We finally pried the secret out of him.* **1,3** *verb,* **pried, pry ing; 2** *noun, plural* **pries.**

P.S., postscript.

psalm (säm), a sacred song or poem, especially one of the Psalms of the Old Testament. *noun.*

pshaw (shô), exclamation expressing impatience, contempt, or dislike. *interjection, noun.*

psy chi a trist (sī kī/ə trist), doctor who treats mental and emotional disorders. *noun.*

psy chol o gist (sī kol/ə jist), person who is an expert in psychology. *noun.*

psy chol o gy (sī kol/ə jē), science of the mind. Psychology tries to explain why people act, think, and feel as they do. *noun, plural* **psy chol o gies.**

pt., pint. *plural* **pt.** or **pts.**

ptar mi gan (tär/mə gən), any of several kinds of grouse found in mountainous and cold regions. See picture. *noun, plural* **ptar mi gans** or **ptar mi gan.**

pub lic (pub/lik), **1** of the people: *public affairs.* **2** all the people: *inform the public.* **3** for the people; serving the people: *public meetings, public libraries.* **4** of the affairs or service of the people: *a public official.* **5** known to many or all; not private: *a matter of public knowledge.* **1,3-5** *adjective,* **2** *noun.* **in public,** publicly; openly; not in private or secret: *stand up in public for what you believe.*

pub li ca tion (pub/lə kā/shən), **1** book, newspaper, or magazine; anything that is published: *This newspaper is a weekly publication.* **2** the printing and selling of books, newspapers, or magazines. *noun.*

pub lic i ty (pub lis/ə tē), **1** public notice: *the publicity that actors desire.* **2** measures used for getting, or the process of getting, public notice: *I worked on the publicity for the concert. noun.*

provocation (definition 2)—He kicked his brother without provocation.

Courtesy of The Museum of Modern Art/ Film Stills Archive

puff (definition 6)—Some toads puff out their throats to make loud calls.

ptarmigan—about 13 inches (33 centimeters) long

pucker (definition 1) She puckered her lips.

a hat	i it	oi oil	ch child	a in about
ā age	ī ice	ou out	ng long	e in taken
ä far	o hot	u cup	sh she	ə = i in pencil
e let	ō open	ů put	th thin	o in lemon
ē equal	ô order	ü rule	ŦH then	u in circus
ėr term			zh measure	

pub lic ly (pub′lik lē), **1** in a public manner; openly. **2** by the public. *adverb.*

public opinion, opinion of the people in a country or community: *make a survey of public opinion.*

public school, 1 (in the United States) a free school maintained by taxes. **2** (in Great Britain) a private boarding school.

pub lish (pub′lish), **1** prepare and offer (a book, paper, map, or piece of music) for sale or distribution. **2** make publicly or generally known: *Don't publish the faults of your friends. verb.*

pub lish er (pub′li shər), person or company whose business is to produce and sell books, newspapers, or magazines: *Look at the bottom of the title page of this book for the publisher's name. noun.*

puck (puk), a rubber disk used in the game of ice hockey. *noun.*

puck er (puk′ər), **1** draw into wrinkles or irregular folds: *pucker one's brow, pucker cloth in sewing.* See picture. **2** wrinkle; irregular fold: *This coat does not fit; there are puckers at the shoulders.* 1 *verb,* 2 *noun.*

pud ding (půd′ing), a soft, cooked food, usually sweet, such as rice pudding. *noun.*

pud dle (pud′l), **1** a small pool of water, especially dirty water: *a puddle of rain water.* **2** a small pool of any liquid: *a puddle of ink. noun.*

pudg y (puj′ē), short and fat or thick: *a child's pudgy hand. adjective,* **pudg i er, pudg i est.**

pueb lo (pweb′lō), an Indian village built of adobe and stone. There were once many pueblos in the southwestern part of the United States. *noun, plural* **pueb los.** [*Pueblo* comes from a Spanish word meaning both "village" and "people."]

Puer to Ri co (pwer′tō rē′kō), island in the eastern part of the West Indies, associated with the United States in foreign affairs, but ruling itself in local affairs.

puff (puf), **1** blow with short, quick blasts: *The bellows puffed on the fire.* **2** a short, quick blast: *A puff of wind blew my hat off.* **3** breathe quick and hard: *She puffed as she climbed the stairs.* **4** give out puffs; move with puffs: *The engine puffed out of the station.* **5** smoke: *puff a cigar.* **6** swell with air or pride: *puff out one's cheeks. He puffed out his chest when the teacher praised his work.* See picture. **7** act or process of swelling. **8** a soft, round mass: *a puff of cotton, a puff of hair.* **9** a small pad for putting powder on the skin. **10** light pastry filled with whipped cream, jam, or the like: *a cream puff.* 1,3-6 *verb,* 2,7-10 *noun.*

puff y (puf′ē), **1** puffed out; swollen: *My eyes were puffy from crying.* **2** coming in puffs. *adjective,* **puff i er, puff i est.**

pug nose (pug′ nōz′), a short, turned-up nose.

pull (pùl), **1** move (something) by grasping it and drawing toward oneself: *Pull the door open.* **2** move, usually with effort or force: *pull a sled uphill.* **3** take hold of and tug: *pull a person's hair, pull at someone's sleeve.* **4** take hold of and draw out with the fingers or a clutching tool held in the fingers: *pull weeds. She pulled out the nails with the claw of a hammer. The dentist decided to pull my bad tooth.* **5** move; go: *We had to pull over to the side of the road to change the flat tire.* **6** pick; pluck: *pull flowers.* **7** tear; rip: *The baby pulled the toy to pieces.* **8** stretch too far; strain: *I pulled a muscle in my leg while skiing.* **9** row: *Pull for the shore as fast as you can!* **10** act of pulling; tug: *The boy gave a pull at the rope.* **11** effort of pulling; effort: *It was a hard pull to get up the hill.* 1-9 *verb,* 10,11 *noun.*

pull oneself together, get control of one's mind or energies: *I stopped crying and started to pull myself together.*

pull through, get through a difficult or dangerous situation: *The doctor thinks that the patient will pull through.*

pul let (pùl′it), a young hen, usually less than a year old. *noun.*

pul ley (pùl′ē), wheel with a grooved rim in which a rope can run, and so lift weights, or change the direction of the pull: *Our flag is raised to the top of a pole by a rope and two pulleys.* See picture. *noun,* plural **pul leys.**

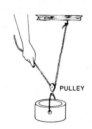

pulp (pulp), **1** the soft, fleshy part of any fruit or vegetable. **2** the soft inner part of a tooth, containing blood vessels and nerves. **3** any soft, wet mass. Paper is made from wood ground to a pulp. *noun.*

pul pit (pùl′pit), **1** platform in a church from which the minister preaches. **2** preachers or preaching: *the influence of the pulpit. noun.*

pul sate (pul′sāt), **1** beat; throb. **2** vibrate; quiver. *verb,* **pul sat ed, pul sat ing.**

pulse (puls), **1** the beating of the arteries caused by the rush of blood that the heart pumps into them. By feeling your pulse in the artery of your wrist, you can count the number of times your heart beats each minute. **2** any regular, measured beat: *the pulse of an engine.* **3** beat; throb; vibrate: *My heart pulsed with joy.* 1,2 *noun,* 3 *verb,* **pulsed, puls ing.**

pul ve rize (pul′və rīz′), **1** grind to powder. **2** become dust. *verb,* **pul ve rized, pul ve riz ing.**

pu ma (pyü′mə), a wild, brownish-yellow animal somewhat like a cat but larger that is found in many parts of North and South America; cougar; panther; mountain lion. *noun.*

pum ice (pum′is), a light, glassy rock having many tiny holes in it. Pumice comes from volcanoes and is used for cleaning and polishing. *noun.*

pum mel (pum′əl), strike or beat; beat with the fists; pommel. *verb.*

pump (pump), **1** machine for forcing liquids, air, or gases into or out of things: *a water pump, an oil pump.* See picture. **2** move (liquids, air, or gases) by a pump: *Pump water from the well into the pail.* **3** blow air into: *Pump up the car's tires.* **4** get information out of: *Don't let them pump you.* 1 *noun,* 2-4 *verb.*

pump kin (pump′kin *or* pung′kin), the large, roundish, orange fruit of a trailing vine, used for making pies and for jack-o'-lanterns. *noun.*

pun (pun), **1** the humorous use of a word where it can have different meanings: *"We must all hang together or we shall all hang separately" is a famous pun by Benjamin Franklin.* **2** make puns. 1 *noun,* 2 *verb,* **punned, pun ning.**

punch¹ (punch), **1** hit with the fists: *to punch someone on the arm.* **2** a quick thrust or blow. **3** tool for making holes. **4** pierce a hole in: *The conductor punched the ticket.* **5** herd or drive cattle: *Cowboys punch cows for a living.* 1,4,5 *verb,* 2,3 *noun,* plural **punch es.**

punch² (punch), drink made of different liquids, often fruit juices, mixed together. *noun,* plural **punch es.**

punc tu al (pungk′chü əl), prompt; on time: *He is punctual to the minute. adjective.*

punc tu ate (pungk′chü āt), **1** use periods, commas, and other marks in writing or printing to help make the meaning clear. **2** give emphasis or force to: *She punctuated her remarks with gestures. verb,* **punc tu at ed, punc tu at ing.**

punc tu a tion (pungk′chü ā′shən), use of periods, commas, and other marks to help make the meaning of a sentence clear. Punctuation does for writing or printing what pauses and change of voice do for speech. *noun.*

punctuation mark, mark used in writing or printing to help make the meaning clear. Periods, commas, question marks, semicolons, and colons are punctuation marks.

punc ture (pungk′chər), **1** hole made by something pointed. **2** make such a hole in. **3** spoil or destroy as if by a puncture: *His plans to buy a car were punctured when he lost his job.* 1 *noun,* 2,3 *verb,* **punc tured, punc tur ing.**

pun gent (pun′jənt), sharp; biting: *a pungent pickle, pungent criticism, a pungent wit. adjective.*

pun ish (pun′ish), **1** cause pain, loss, or discomfort to for some fault or offense: *The parents punished the naughty children.* **2** cause pain, loss, or discomfort for: *The law punishes crime. verb.*

pun ish a ble (pun′i shə bəl), **1** liable to punishment. **2** deserving punishment. *adjective.*

pun ish ment (pun′ish mənt), **1** punishing; being punished. **2** pain, suffering, or loss: *Her punishment for stealing was a year in prison. noun.*

pupa of a butterfly

a hat	i it	oi oil	ch child	(a in about
ā age	ī ice	ou out	ng long	{ e in taken
ä far	o hot	u cup	sh she	ə = { i in pencil
e let	ō open	u̇ put	th thin	{ o in lemon
ē equal	ô order	ü rule	ᵺ then	(u in circus
ėr term			zh measure	

punt (punt), **1** kick (a football) before it touches the ground after dropping it from the hands. **2** such a kick. 1 *verb*, 2 *noun.*

pu ny (pyü′nē), **1** weak; of less than usual size and strength. **2** not important; petty. *adjective,* **pu ni er, pu ni est.**

pup (pup), **1** a young dog; puppy. **2** a young fox, wolf, coyote, or seal. *noun.*

pu pa (pyü′pə), an insect while it is changing from a wormlike larva into an adult. Many pupae are enclosed in a tough case or cocoon and can't move about. A caterpillar becomes a pupa and then a butterfly. See picture. *noun, plural* **pu pae** (pyü′pē), **pu pas.**

pu pil[1] (pyü′pəl), person who is learning in school or is being taught by someone. *noun.* [*Pupil*[1] comes from Latin words meaning "an orphan." Originally these words meant "a little boy" and "a little girl."]

pu pil[2] (pyü′pəl), the opening in the center of the eye which looks like a black spot. The pupil is the only place where light can enter the eye. *noun.* [*Pupil*[2] comes from a Latin word meaning "a little doll." The center of the eye was called this because when you look into the eye of another person you can see a tiny image of yourself.]

pup pet (pup′it), **1** a small doll. In a puppet show the puppets are often moved by wires. See picture. **2** anybody who is not independent, waits to be told how to act, and does what somebody else says. *noun.*

pup py (pup′ē), a young dog. *noun, plural* **pup pies.**

pur chase (pėr′chəs), **1** get by paying a price; buy: *We purchased a new car.* **2** thing bought: *That hat was a good purchase.* **3** a firm hold to help move something, or to keep from slipping: *Wind the rope twice around the tree to get a better purchase.* 1 *verb,* **pur chased, pur chas ing;** 2,3 *noun.*

pur chas er (pėr′chə sər), buyer. *noun.*

pure (pyu̇r), **1** not mixed with anything else; genuine: *pure gold.* **2** perfectly clean; not dirty: *pure water.* **3** nothing else than; mere: *They won by pure luck.* **4** with no evil; without sin: *a pure mind. adjective,* **pur er, pur est.**

pure bred (pyu̇r′bred′), of pure breed; having ancestors known to have all belonged to one breed: *purebred cows. adjective.*

purge (pėrj), wash away all that is not clean; remove what is harmful: *We must purge the city of dishonest officials. verb,* **purged, purg ing.**

pur i fi ca tion (pyu̇r′ə fə kā′shən), purifying; being purified. *noun.*

pur i fy (pyu̇r′ə fī), make pure: *Filters are used to purify water. verb,* **pu ri fied, pu ri fy ing.**

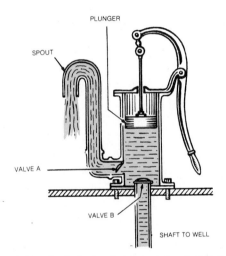

PLUNGER

SPOUT

VALVE A

VALVE B

SHAFT TO WELL

pump (definition 1)—As the handle is raised, the plunger moves downward forcing water through valve A and out the spout. As the handle is pushed down, the plunger moves upward pulling water up through valve B from the shaft.

puppet (definition 1)—hand puppets

Pur i tan (pyür′ə tən), **1** person who wanted simpler forms of worship and stricter morals than others did in the Protestant Church during the 1500's and 1600's. Many Puritans settled in New England. **2 puritan**, person who is very strict in morals and religion. *noun.*

pur i ty (pyür′ə tē), **1** freedom from dirt or mixture; clearness; cleanness: *the purity of drinking water.* **2** freedom from evil; innocence: *a person of purity and goodness. noun, plural* **pur i ties.**

pur ple (pėr′pəl), **1** a dark color that is a mixture of red and blue. **2** having this color: *purple grapes.* **1** *noun,* **2** *adjective.*

pur plish (pėr′plish), somewhat purple. *adjective.*

pur port (pər pôrt′ for 1 and 2; pėr′pôrt for 3), **1** claim: *The letter purported to be from the governor.* **2** mean; have as its main idea: *a statement purporting certain facts.* **3** meaning; main idea: *The purport of her letter was that she could not come.* **1,2** *verb,* **3** *noun.*

pur pose (pėr′pəs), a plan; aim; intention; something one has in mind to get or do: *Her purpose in coming to see us was to ask for a donation to the hospital fund. noun.*

on purpose, with a purpose; not by accident: *He tripped me on purpose.*

pushup

pussy willows

pur pose ful (pėr′pəs fəl), having a purpose. *adjective.*

pur pose ly (pėr′pəs lē), on purpose: *Did you leave the door open purposely? adverb.*

purr (pėr), **1** a low, murmuring sound such as a cat makes when pleased. **2** make this sound. **1** *noun,* **2** *verb.*

purse (pėrs), **1** a small bag or container to hold coins, usually carried in a handbag or pocket. **2** a woman's handbag. **3** sum of money: *A purse was made up for the victims of the fire.* **4** draw together; press into folds or wrinkles: *She pursed her lips and whistled.* **1-3** *noun,* **4** *verb,* **pursed, purs ing.**

pur sue (pər sü′), **1** follow to catch or kill; chase: *The dogs pursued the rabbit.* **2** follow; proceed along: *He pursued a wise course by taking no chances.* **3** strive for; try to get; seek: *pursue pleasure.* **4** carry on; keep on with: *She pursued the study of music for four years.* **5** follow closely and annoy: *The student continued to pursue the teacher with questions. verb,* **pur sued, pur su ing.**

pur su er (pər sü′ər), person who pursues. *noun.*

pur suit (pər süt′), **1** act of pursuing; chase: *The dog is in pursuit of the cat.* **2** occupation: *Fishing is his favorite pursuit; reading is mine. noun.*

pus (pus), a thick, yellowish-white liquid found in infected sores. *noun.*

push (push), **1** move (something) away by pressing against it: *Push the door; don't pull it.* **2** press hard: *We pushed with all our strength.* **3** thrust: *Trees push their roots down into the ground.* **4** go forward by force: *push on at a rapid pace.* **5** urge; make go forward: *He pushed his plans strongly. Please push this job and get it done this week.* **6** urge the use or sale of. **7** force; power to succeed: *She has plenty of push.* **8** act of pushing: *Give the door a push.* **1-6** *verb,* **7,8** *noun, plural* **push es.**

push cart (push′kärt′), a light cart pushed by hand: *The peddler's pushcart was filled with fruit. noun.*

push up (push′up′), an exercise done by lying face down and raising the body with the arms while keeping the back straight and the toes on the ground. See picture. *noun.*

puss (pus), cat. *noun, plural* **puss es.**

puss y (pus′ē), cat. *noun, plural* **puss ies.**

pussy willow, a small North American willow with silky, gray catkins. See picture.

put (put), **1** place; lay; set; cause to be in some place or position: *I put sugar in my tea. Put away your toys. Put on your coat.* **2** cause to be in some state, condition, position, or relation: *Put your room in order. Put the question in writing. The murderer was put to death.* **3** express: *The teacher puts things clearly.* **4** apply: *I put my writing skill to good use.* **5** impose: *put a tax on gasoline. verb,* **put, put ting.**

put about, (of a ship) change direction.

put across, 1 carry out successfully: *The salesman put the deal across.* **2** get accepted or understood: *He could not put across his point of view to the audience.*

put down, 1 put an end to: *The rebellion was quickly put down.* **2** write down.

put in, 1 spend (time): *Put in a full day of work.* **2** enter a place for safety or supplies: *The ship put in at Hong Kong.*

put off, 1 lay aside; make wait: *Don't put off going to the dentist or your teeth will suffer from neglect.* **2** go away; start out: *The Mayflower put off for America in 1620.*

put on, 1 present on a stage; produce: *The class put on a play.* **2** take on or add to oneself: *put on weight.* **3** pretend: *Her surprise was all put on; she*

a hat	**i** it	**oi** oil	**ch** child	⎧ a in about
ā age	**ī** ice	**ou** out	**ng** long	⎪ e in taken
ä far	**o** hot	**u** cup	**sh** she	ə = ⎨ i in pencil
e let	**ō** open	**u̇** put	**th** thin	⎪ o in lemon
ē equal	**ô** order	**ü** rule	**ᴛʜ** then	⎩ u in circus
ėr term			**zh** measure	

puzzle (definition 3)—The shape of the statue **puzzled** him.

pyramid (definition 2)
At the left is a
skyscraper shaped
like a pyramid.
Below are stone
pyramids in Egypt.

knew we were coming beforehand. **4** apply or exert: *put on pressure.*

put out, 1 extinguish; make an end to; destroy: *put out a fire, put out one's eye.* **2** provoke; offend: *You must not be put out by the train delay.* **3** go; turn; proceed: *The ship put out to sea.*

put through, carry out with success: *The Congresswoman put her bill through Congress.*

put up, 1 offer: *put up a house for sale.* **2** give or show: *put up a brave front.* **3** build: *put up a monument.* **4** lay aside (work). **5** propose for election or adoption: *His name was put up for president of the club.* **6** pack up or preserve (fruit): *put up six jars of blackberries.* **7** provide lodging or food for: *They put us up for the night.* **8** get (a person) to do: *put someone up to mischief.*

put up with, bear with patience; endure.

pu trid (pyü′trid), rotten; foul: *The meat became putrid in the hot sun. adjective.*

putt (put), **1** strike (a golf ball) gently and carefully in an effort to make it roll into the hole. **2** the stroke itself: *A good putt requires control.* 1 *verb,* 2 *noun.*

put ter[1] (put′ər), keep busy in an aimless or useless way: *I like to putter around the garden. verb.*

putt er[2] (put′ər), a golf club used in putting. *noun.*

put ty (put′ē), **1** a soft mixture of powdered chalk and linseed oil, used for fastening panes of glass in window frames. **2** stop up, fill up, or cover with putty: *We puttied the holes in the woodwork.* 1 *noun,* plural **put ties;** 2 *verb,* **put tied, put ty ing.**

puz zle (puz′əl), **1** a hard problem: *How to get all my things into one trunk is a puzzle.* **2** problem or task to be done for fun: *A famous Chinese puzzle has seven pieces of wood to fit together.* **3** make unable to understand something; confuse: *How the cat got out puzzled us.* See picture. **4** be confused. **5** use one's mind on something hard: *They puzzled over their arithmetic for an hour.* 1,2 *noun,* 3-5 *verb,* **puz zled, puz zling.**

pyg my (pig′mē), **1** a very small person; dwarf. The Pygmies living in Africa and Asia are less than five feet high. **2** very small: *a pygmy mind.* 1 *noun,* plural **pyg mies;** 2 *adjective.* Also spelled **pigmy.**

py ja mas (pə jä′məz *or* pə jam′əz), pajamas. *noun plural.*

pyr a mid (pir′ə mid), **1** a solid object with a base and with triangular sides that meet in a point. **2** anything having the form of a pyramid. See pictures. *noun.*

pyre (pīr), pile of wood for burning a dead body. *noun.*

py thon (pī′thon), a large snake of Asia, Africa, and Australia that kills its prey by squeezing. *noun.*

Q q

Q or **q** (kyü), the 17th letter of the English alphabet. *Q* is followed by *u* in most English words. *noun, plural* **Q's** *or* **q's.**

qt., quart. *plural* **qt.** *or* **qts.**

quack[1] (kwak), **1** sound a duck makes. **2** make such a sound. 1 *noun*, 2 *verb*.

quack[2] (kwak), **1** a dishonest person who pretends to be a doctor. **2** an ignorant pretender to knowledge or skill of any sort: *Don't pay a quack to tell your fortune.* **3** used by quacks: *quack medicine.* **4** not genuine: *a quack doctor.* 1,2 *noun*, 3,4 *adjective*.

quad ru ped (kwod′rə ped), animal that has four feet. *noun*.

quad ru plet (kwod′rə plit *or* kwo drü′plit), **1** one of four children born at the same time of the same mother. **2** group of four. *noun*.

quail[1] (kwāl), a plump, wild bird that is hunted and used for food. A bobwhite is one kind of quail. See picture. *noun, plural* **quails** *or* **quail.**

quail[2] (kwāl), be afraid; lose courage; shrink back with fear. See picture. *verb*.

quaint (kwānt), strange or odd in an interesting, pleasing, or amusing way: *Old photographs seem quaint to us today.* *adjective*.

quake (kwāk), **1** shake; tremble: *They quaked with fear.* **2** earthquake. 1 *verb*, **quaked, quak ing;** 2 *noun*.

qual i fi ca tion (kwol′ə fə kā′shən), **1** that which makes a person fit for a job, task, office, or function: *To know the way is one qualification for a guide.* **2** that which limits or changes, and makes less free and full: *They accepted the plan with only one qualification.* *noun*.

qual i fy (kwol′ə fī), **1** make fit or competent: *Can you qualify yourself for the job?* **2** become fit; show oneself fit: *He qualified for a driver's license.* **3** limit; make less strong; change somewhat: *Qualify your statement that dogs are loyal by adding "usually."* *verb*, **qual i fied, qual i fy ing.**

qual i ty (kwol′ə tē), **1** something special about a person or object that makes it what it is: *One quality of iron is hardness; one quality of sugar is sweetness. She has many fine qualities.* **2** nature, kind, or character of something: *the quality of a sound, the refreshing quality of a drink.* **3** grade of excellence: *food of poor quality.* **4** merit; excellence: *Look for quality rather than quantity.* *noun, plural* **qual i ties.**

qualm (kwäm), **1** a sudden disturbing feeling in the mind; uneasiness; misgiving or doubt: *I tried the test with some qualms.* **2** disturbance or scruple of conscience: *I had no qualms about playing instead of working on such a sunny day.* *noun*.

quan ti ty (kwon′tə tē), **1** amount: *Use equal quantities of nuts and raisins in the cake.* **2** a large

quartz—common quartz

quail[1]—about 10 inches
(25 centimeters) long

amount; large number: *The baker buys flour in quantity. She owns quantities of books.* noun, plural **quan ti ties.**

quar an tine (kwôr′ən tēn′), **1** keep (a person, animal, plant, or ship) away from others for a time to prevent the spread of an infectious disease: *People with smallpox are quarantined.* **2** condition of being quarantined: *The ship was in quarantine because several of the crew had smallpox.* **1** *verb,* **quar an tined, quar an tin ing; 2** *noun.* [*Quarantine* comes from an Italian word meaning "forty." It was called this because people thought to have a disease that could easily spread used to be kept away from others for forty days.]

quar rel (kwôr′əl), **1** an angry dispute; fight with words: *The children had a quarrel over the division of the candy.* **2** fight with words; dispute or disagree angrily: *The two friends quarreled and now they don't speak to each other.* **3** cause for a dispute: *A bully likes to pick quarrels.* **4** find fault: *It is useless to quarrel with fate, because one does not have control over it.* **1,3** *noun,* **2,4** *verb.*

quar rel some (kwôr′əl səm), too ready to quarrel; fond of fighting and disputing: *A quarrelsome person has few friends.* *adjective.*

quar ry (kwôr′ē), place where stone is dug, cut, or blasted out for use in building. *noun, plural* **quar ries.**

quart (kwôrt), **1** a unit for measuring liquids equal to one fourth of a gallon: *a quart of milk.* **2** a unit for measuring dry things equal to one eighth of a peck: *a quart of berries.* *noun.*

quar ter (kwôr′tər), **1** one of four equal parts; half of a half; one fourth: *a quarter of an apple, a quarter of lamb. A quarter of an hour is 15 minutes.* **2** divide into fourths: *She quartered the apple.* **3** coin of the United States and Canada equal to 25 cents. Four quarters make one dollar. **4** one of four equal periods of play in certain games, such as football, basketball, or soccer. **5** one fourth of a year; 3 months: *Many savings banks pay interest every quarter.* **6** one of the four periods of the moon, lasting about 7 days each. **7** direction: *We learned that each of the four points of the compass is called a quarter. From what quarter did the wind blow?* **8** region; section; place: *The quarter where they live is near the railroad.* **9 quarters,** a place to live or stay in: *The circus has its winter quarters in the South. The servants have quarters in a cottage.* **10** give a place to live: *Soldiers were quartered in all the houses of the town.* **11** mercy shown in sparing the life of a defeated enemy: *The pirates gave no quarter to their victims.* **1,3-9,11** *noun,* **2,10** *verb.*
at close quarters, very close together; almost touching: *The cars had to pass at close quarters on the narrow mountain road.*

quar ter back (kwôr′tər bak′), player who stands behind the center in football. The quarterback begins each play by handing the ball to a running back, passing it to a teammate, or running with it himself. *noun.*

quar ter ly (kwôr′tər lē), **1** four times a year: *make quarterly payments on one's insurance.* **2** once each

quench (definition 1)—The cold, clear water **quenched** his thirst.

quarter of a year: *Some magazines are published quarterly.* **1** *adjective,* **2** *adverb.*

quar ter mas ter (kwôr′tər mas′tər), (in the army) an officer who has charge of providing quarters, clothing, food, and ammunition for troops. *noun.*

quar tet or **quar tette** (kwôr tet′), **1** group of four singers or players performing together. **2** piece of music for four voices or instruments. **3** any group of four. *noun.*

quartz (kwôrts), a very hard kind of rock. Common quartz is colorless and transparent, but amethyst, jasper, and many other colored stones are also quartz. See picture. *noun.*

qua ver (kwā′vər), **1** shake; tremble: *The animal quavered with fear.* **2** sing or say in trembling tones. **3** trembling of the voice. **1,2** *verb,* **3** *noun.*

quay (kē), a solid landing place for ships, often built of stone. *noun.*

queen (kwēn), **1** wife of a king. **2** woman who rules a country and its people. **3** woman who is very beautiful or important: *the queen of society.* **4** a female bee or ant that lays eggs. There is usually only one queen in a hive of bees. **5** a playing card with the picture of a queen on it. It is above a jack and below a king. **6** the most powerful piece in the game of chess. *noun.*

queer (kwir), **1** strange; odd; peculiar: *That was a queer remark for her to make.* **2** not well; faint; giddy: *The motion of the ship made him feel queer.* *adjective.*

quell (kwel), put down; overcome: *The police quelled the riot.* *verb.*

quench (kwench), **1** put an end to; stop. See picture. **2** drown out; put out: *quench a fire.* *verb.*

quer y (kwir/ē), **1** question. **2** ask; ask about; inquire into. **3** express doubt about. **1** *noun, plural* **quer ies; 2,3** *verb,* **quer ied, quer y ing.**

quest (kwest), search; hunt: *She went to the library in quest of something to read. noun.*

ques tion (kwes/chən), **1** thing asked in order to find out: *The teacher answered the children's questions about the story.* **2** ask in order to find out: *Then the teacher questioned the children about what happened in the story.* **3** doubt; dispute: *I question the truth of their story.* **4** matter to be talked over: *What is the question you have raised?* **5** matter to be voted upon: *The president asked if the club members were ready for the question.* **1,4,5** *noun,* **2,3** *verb.*

beside the question, off the subject.

beyond question, without a doubt: *The statements in that book are true beyond question.*

out of the question, not to be considered.

without question, without a doubt: *That is without question the best book I've ever read.*

ques tion a ble (kwes/chə nə bəl), open to question; doubtful; uncertain: *Whether your statement is true is questionable. adjective.*

question mark, mark (?) put after a question in writing or printing.

queue (kyü), **1** braid of hair hanging down the back. **2** number of persons, automobiles, or trucks arranged in a line waiting their turn: *There was a long queue at the theater. noun.*

quick (kwik), **1** fast and sudden; swift: *The cat made a quick jump. Many weeds have a quick growth.* **2** lively; ready; active: *a quick wit.* **3** quickly. **4** the tender, sensitive flesh under a fingernail or toenail: *Some people bite their nails down to the quick.* **5** the tender, sensitive part of one's feelings: *Their insults cut me to the quick.* **1,2** *adjective,* **3** *adverb,* **4,5** *noun.*

quick en (kwik/ən), **1** move more quickly; hasten: *Quicken your pace.* **2** stir up; make alive: *She quickened the hot ashes into flames. Reading adventure stories quickens my imagination.* **3** become more active or alive: *His pulse quickened. verb.*

quick sand (kwik/sand/), soft wet sand, very deep, that will not hold up one's weight. Quicksand may swallow up people and animals. *noun.*

quick-wit ted (kwik/wit/id), having a quick mind; clever. *adjective.*

qui et (kwī/ət), **1** making no sound; with little or no noise: *quiet footsteps, a quiet room.* **2** still; moving very little: *a quiet river.* **3** at rest; not busy: *a quiet evening at home.* **4** peaceful; with nothing to fear: *a quiet mind.* **5** gentle; not offending others: *quiet manners, a quiet person.* **6** state of rest; stillness; peace: *read in quiet.* **7** make or become quiet: *Soft words quieted the frightened child. The*

wind quieted down. **8** not showy or bright: *Gray is a quiet color.* **1-5,8** *adjective,* **6** *noun,* **7** *verb.*

quill (kwil), **1** a large stiff feather. **2** pen made from a feather. **3** a stiff sharp hair or spine like the end of a feather. A porcupine has quills on its back. *noun.*

quilt (kwilt), **1** cover for a bed, usually made of two pieces of cloth with a soft pad between, held in place by stitching. **2** make quilts. **3** stitch together with a soft lining: *a quilted jacket.* **1** *noun,* **2,3** *verb.*

qui nine (kwī/nīn), a bitter medicine used for malaria and fevers. *noun.*

quin tet or **quin tette** (kwin tet/), **1** group of five singers or players. **2** piece of music for five voices or instruments. **3** any group of five. *noun.*

quin tu plet (kwin/tə plit, kwin tü/plit, *or* kwin tyü/plit), **1** one of five children born at the same time of the same mother. **2** group of five. *noun.*

quit (kwit), **1** stop: *They quit work at five.* **2** leave: *Her big sister is quitting school this June. verb,* **quit** or **quit ted, quit ting.**

quite (kwīt), **1** completely; entirely: *a hat quite out of fashion. I am quite alone.* **2** really; truly: *quite a change in the weather.* **3** very; rather; somewhat: *It is quite hot. adverb.*

quit ter (kwit/ər), person who shirks or gives up easily. *noun.*

quiv er[1] (kwiv/ər), **1** shake; shiver; tremble: *quiver with excitement.* **2** shaking or trembling: *A quiver of his mouth showed that he was about to cry.* **1** *verb,* **2** *noun.*

quiv er[2] (kwiv/ər), case to hold arrows. *noun.*

quiz (kwiz), **1** a short or informal test: *Each week the teacher gives us a quiz in spelling.* **2** examine by questions; test the knowledge of. **1** *noun, plural* **quiz zes; 2** *verb,* **quizzed, quiz zing.**

quo ta (kwō/tə), the share of a total due from or to a particular district, state, or person: *Each class had its quota of tickets to sell for the school fair. noun.*

quo ta tion (kwō tā/shən), somebody's words repeated exactly by another person; passage quoted from a book or speech: *From what author does this quotation come? See picture. noun.*

quotation mark, one of a pair of marks (" ") put at the beginning and end of a quotation.

quote (kwōt), **1** repeat exactly the words of another or a passage from a book: *The students often quote their teacher. The newspaper quoted from the congresswoman's speech.* **2** quotation. **1** *verb,* **quot ed, quot ing; 2** *noun.*

quo tient (kwō/shənt), number arrived at by dividing one number by another: *If you divide 26 by 2, the quotient is 13. noun.*

"The only way to have a friend is to be one."—Emerson

---

quotation from Ralph Waldo Emerson's *Essays*

Rr

a hat	i it	oi oil	ch child	⎧ a in about
ā age	ī ice	ou out	ng long	⎪ e in taken
ä far	o hot	u cup	sh she	ə = ⎨ i in pencil
e let	ō open	u̇ put	th thin	⎪ o in lemon
ē equal	ô order	ü rule	₮H then	⎩ u in circus
ėr term			zh measure	

R or r (är), the 18th letter of the English alphabet. There are two r's in carry. noun, plural **R's** or **r's**. **the three R's,** reading, writing, and arithmetic. The three R's were called this because reading, writing, and arithmetic were humorously spelled reading, 'riting, and 'rithmetic.

rab bi (rab′ī), teacher of the Jewish religion; leader of a Jewish congregation. noun, plural **rab bis.**

rab bit (rab′it), **1** animal about as big as a cat, with soft fur and long ears. A rabbit can make long jumps. Rabbits are sometimes raised for food or fur. **2** its fur. noun.

rab ble (rab′əl), **1** a disorderly crowd; mob. **2 the rabble,** the lower class of persons: The proud nobles scorned the rabble. noun.

ra bies (rā′bēz), a disease that causes damage to brain cells, and paralyzes the body of warm-blooded animals. Rabies is most often caught from the bite of a dog that has the disease. It is a fatal disease unless it is treated with a serum. noun.

rac coon (ra kün′), **1** a small, grayish animal with a bushy ringed tail, that lives in wooded areas near water, and is active at night. See picture. **2** its fur. noun. Also spelled **racoon.** [Raccoon comes from a Powhatan Indian word meaning "he scratches with the hands." The animal was probably called this because it scratches trees and digs to find food.]

race¹ (rās), **1** any contest of speed: a horse race, a boat race. **2** run to see who will win. **3** run a race with; try to beat in a contest of speed: I'll race you home. **4** run, move, or go swiftly: I raced home from school. **5** make go faster than necessary: Don't race the motor. **6** a strong or rapid current of water. 1,6 noun, 2-5 verb, **raced, rac ing.**

race² (rās), **1** a great division of all human beings that passes on certain physical characteristics from one generation to another. **2** group of persons, animals, or plants having the same ancestors, far back in the past: the human race, the canine race. **3** group of people of the same kind: the brave race of pioneers. noun.

rac er (rā′sər), **1** person, animal, boat, or car that takes part in races. **2** a large, harmless North American snake that can move very rapidly. noun.

race track (rās′trak′), ground laid out for racing, usually round or oval. noun.

ra cial (rā′shəl), **1** having something to do with a race of persons, animals, or plants; characteristic of a race: racial traits. **2** of or involving races: racial discrimination. adjective.

rack (rak), **1** frame with bars, shelves, or pegs to hold, arrange, or keep things on: a tool rack, a baggage rack. **2** instrument once used for torturing people by stretching them. **3** hurt very much: racked with grief. A toothache racked her jaw. 1,2 noun, 3 verb.

rack et¹ (rak′it), **1** loud noise; din; loud talk: Don't make a racket when others are reading. **2** a dishonest scheme for getting money from people, often by threatening to hurt them or what belongs to them. noun.

rack et² (rak′it), an oval wooden or metal frame with a network of strings and having a long handle. It is used to hit the ball in games like tennis. noun.

ra coon (ra kün′), raccoon. noun.

ra dar (rā′där), instrument for determining the distance, direction, and speed of unseen objects by the reflection of radio waves. noun. [Radar comes from the words radio detecting and ranging which describe what this instrument does. It was formed by combining the first two letters of radio and the first letter of each of the other words.]

raccoon (definition 1)
32 inches (80 centimeters) long with the tail

ra di ance (rā′dē əns), brightness: the radiance of the sun. noun.

ra di ant (rā′dē ənt), **1** shining; bright; beaming: a radiant smile. **2** sent off in rays from some source; radiated: We get radiant heat from the sun. adjective.

radiant energy, energy in the form of rays or waves. Heat, light, X rays, and radio waves are forms of radiant energy.

ra di ate (rā′dē āt), **1** give out rays of: The sun radiates light and heat. **2** come out in rays: Heat radiates from hot steam pipes. **3** give out; send forth: His face radiates joy. **4** spread out from a center: Roads radiate from the city in every direction. verb, **ra di at ed, ra di at ing.**

ra di a tion (rā′dē ā′shən), **1** giving out rays, as of light or heat. **2** rays sent or given out. noun.

ra di a tor (rā′dē ā′tər), **1** device for heating a

room, consisting of pipes through which hot water or steam passes. **2** device for cooling water. The radiator of an automobile gives off heat very fast and so cools the water inside it. *noun.*

rad i cal (rad/ə kəl), **1** going to the root; fundamental: *To lose weight I had to make radical changes in my eating habits.* **2** extreme; favoring extreme changes or reforms. **3** person who favors extreme changes or reforms; person with extreme opinions. 1,2 *adjective,* 3 *noun.*

ra di i (rā/dē ī), more than one radius. *noun plural.*

ra di o (rā/dē ō), **1** a way of sending and receiving sounds through the air without using wires to connect the sender and the receiver: *Music is broadcast by radio.* **2** the device on which these sounds may be heard or from which they may be sent. **3** of radio; used in radio; sent by radio: *a radio set, radio program.* **4** transmit or send out by radio: *The ship radioed a call for help.* 1,2 *noun, plural* **ra di os** for 2; 3 *adjective,* 4 *verb.*

ra di o ac tive (rā/dē ō ak/tiv), of, having, or caused by radioactivity. Radium and uranium are radioactive metals. *adjective.*

ra di o ac tiv i ty (rā/dē ō ak tiv/ə tē), **1** the property that certain metals have of giving off rays or tiny particles from their atomic nuclei. **2** the rays or particles given off. *noun.*

rad ish (rad/ish), a small, crisp root with a red or white skin, used as a relish and in salads. *noun.*

ra di um (rā/dē əm), a radioactive metal, used in treating cancer. *noun.*

ra di us (rā/dē əs), **1** any line going straight from the center to the outside of a circle or a sphere. Any spoke of a wheel is a radius. See picture. **2** a circular area measured by the length of its radius: *The explosion could be heard within a radius of ten miles. noun, plural* **ra di i** or **ra di us es.**

raft (raft), a floating platform made of wood or other material. A rubber **life raft** is held up by a tube filled with air. *noun.*

raft er (raf/tər), a slanting beam of a roof. See picture. *noun.*

rag (rag), **1** a torn or waste piece of cloth: *Use a clean rag to rub this mirror bright.* **2 rags,** tattered or worn-out clothes: *The beggar was dressed in rags.* **3** a small piece of cloth: *a polishing rag.* **4** made from rags: *a rag doll, a rag rug.* 1-3 *noun,* 4 *adjective.*

rage (rāj), **1** violent anger: *a voice quivering with rage.* See picture. **2** talk or act violently; storm: *Keep your temper; don't rage.* See picture. **3** what everybody wants for a short time; the fashion: *Red ties were all the rage last year.* 1,3 *noun,* 2 *verb,* **raged, rag ing.**

rag ged (rag/id), **1** worn or torn into rags: *ragged clothing.* **2** wearing torn or badly worn-out clothing: *a ragged beggar.* **3** not smooth and tidy; rough: *an old dog's ragged coat, a ragged garden.* **4** having loose shreds or bits: *a ragged wound. adjective.*

rag weed (rag/wēd/), a coarse weed whose pollen is one of the most common causes of hay fever. *noun.*

rage (definition 2)—The fire **raged** through the forest.

rage (definition 1)—He seethed with **rage.**

radius (definition 1)
Each line from C (center)
is a radius.

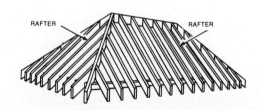

RAFTER   RAFTER

raid (rād), **1** attack; a sudden attack: *The pirates planned a raid on the harbor.* **2** attack suddenly: *The enemy raided our camp.* **3** entering and seizing what is inside: *The hungry girls made a raid on the refrigerator.* **4** force a way into; enter and seize what is in: *The police raided the house looking for stolen jewels.* 1,3 *noun,* 2,4 *verb.*

rail[1] (rāl), **1** bar of wood or of metal. There are stair rails, fence rails, or rails protecting monuments. Bars laid along the ground for a railroad track are called rails. **2** railroad: *We travel by rail and by boat. noun.*

rail[2] (rāl), complain bitterly: *They railed at their hard luck. verb.*

rail ing (rā′ling), **1** fence made of rails. **2** rail used as a guard or support on a stairway or platform; handrail. *noun.*

rail road (rāl′rōd′), **1** road or track with parallel steel rails on which the wheels of the cars go. Engines pull trains on railroads. **2** tracks, stations, trains, and the people who manage them. **3** work on a railroad. 1,2 *noun,* 3 *verb.*

rail way (rāl′wā′), **1** railroad. **2** track made of rails. *noun.*

rai ment (rā′mənt), clothing; garments. *noun.*

rain (rān), **1** water falling in drops from the clouds: *The rain spattered the windows.* **2** the fall of such drops: *a hard rain.* **3** fall in drops of water: *It rained all day.* **4** a thick, fast fall of anything: *a rain of bullets.* **5** fall like rain: *Sparks rained down from the burning building.* **6** send like rain: *The guests rained rice on the bride and groom.* 1,2,4 *noun,* 3,5,6 *verb.*

rain bow (rān′bō′), bow or arch of colored light seen in the sky opposite the sun, or in mist or spray. The seven colors of the rainbow are violet, indigo, blue, green, yellow, orange, and red. Rainbows occur when the sun's rays are bent and reflected by drops of water. *noun.*

rain coat (rān′kōt′), a waterproof coat worn for protection from rain. *noun.*

rain drop (rān′drop′), drop of rain. *noun.*

rain fall (rān′fôl′), **1** shower of rain. **2** amount of water in the form of rain, sleet, or snow that falls within a given time: *The yearly rainfall in New York is much greater than that in Arizona. noun.*

rain y (rā′nē), **1** having rain; having much rain: *April is a rainy month.* **2** bringing rain: *The sky is filled with dark, rainy clouds.* **3** wet with rain: *rainy streets. adjective,* **rain i er, rain i est.**

raise (rāz), **1** lift up; put up: *raise the flag. Children in school raise their hands to answer a question.* **2** cause to rise: *The automobiles raised a cloud of dust. Dough for bread is raised by yeast.* **3** put or take into a higher position; make higher or nobler: *to raise a clerk to a manager.* **4** make higher or larger; increase in degree, amount, price, or pay: *raise prices, raise the rent, raise one's courage.* **5** an increase in amount, price, or pay: *I got a raise in my allowance.* **6** bring together; get together; gather: *to raise funds for a hospital.* **7** bring up; make grow; help to grow: *The farmer raises chickens and corn. Parents raise their children.*

8 cause; bring about: *A funny remark raises a laugh.* **9** build; build up; set up: *to raise a monument to a famous person.* **10** rouse; stir up: *The dogs had raised a rabbit and were chasing it.* **11** bring back to life: *raise the dead.* **12** put an end to: *Our soldiers raised the siege of the fort by driving away the enemy.* 1-4,6-12 *verb,* **raised , rais ing;** 5 *noun.*

rai sin (rā′zn), a sweet, dried grape. *noun.*

ra jah or **ra ja** (rä′jə), ruler or chief in India, and in some other Eastern countries. *noun.*

rake (rāk), **1** a long-handled tool having a bar at one end with teeth in it. A rake is used for smoothing the soil or gathering together loose leaves, hay, or straw. **2** move with a rake: *Rake the leaves off the grass.* **3** make clear, clean, or smooth with a rake: *Rake the yard.* **4** search carefully: *She raked the newspaper ads, hoping to find a bicycle for sale.* **5** fire guns along the length of (a ship or a line of soldiers). 1 *noun,* 2-5 *verb,* **raked, rak ing.**

ral ly (ral′ē), **1** bring together; bring together again; get in order again: *The commander was able to rally the fleeing troops.* **2** come together for a common purpose or action: *The people rallied to rebuild the dike before the river flooded their homes.* **3** come to help: *She rallied to the side of her injured friend.* **4** recover health and strength: *My sick friend has begun to rally.* **5** coming together; meeting of many people: *a political rally.* 1-4 *verb,* **ral lied, ral ly ing;** 5 *noun, plural* **ral lies.**

ram (ram), **1** a male sheep. See picture. **2** butt against; strike head-on; strike violently: *One ship rammed the other ship.* **3** push hard; drive down or in by heavy blows. **4** machine or part of a machine that strikes heavy blows. A **battering ram** knocks walls down. 1,4 *noun,* 2,3 *verb,* **rammed, ram ming.**

ram (definition 1)—about 2 feet (60 centimeters) high at the shoulder

ram ble (ram′bəl), **1** wander about: *We rambled here and there through the woods.* **2** a walk for pleasure, not to go to any special place. **3** talk or write about first one thing and then another with no clear connections. 1,3 *verb,* **ram bled, ram bling;** *noun.*

ram bling (ram′bling), **1** wandering about. **2** going from one thing to another without clear connections: *a rambling speech.* **3** extending in irregular ways in various directions; not planned in an orderly way: *a rambling old farmhouse. adjective.*

ramp (ramp), a sloping way connecting two different levels, especially of a building or road; slope: *The passengers walked up the ramp to board their plane. noun.*

ram part (ram′pärt), a wide bank of earth, often with a wall on top, built around a fort to help defend it. *noun.*

ram rod (ram′rod′), **1** rod for ramming down the ammunition in a gun that is loaded from the muzzle. **2** rod for cleaning the barrel of a gun. *noun.*

ran (ran). See **run.** *The dog ran after the cat. verb.*

ranch (ranch), **1** a very large farm and its buildings. Many ranches are used for raising cattle. **2** any farm, especially one used to raise one kind of animal or crop: *a chicken ranch, a fruit ranch.* **3** work on a ranch; manage a ranch. 1,2 *noun,* 3 *verb.*

ranch er (ran′chər), person who owns, manages, or works on a ranch. *noun.*

ran dom (ran′dəm), by chance; with no plan: *I don't know the answer, but I'll take a random guess. adjective.*

at random, by chance: *She took a book at random from the shelf.*

rang (rang). See **ring².** *The telephone rang. verb.*

range (rānj), **1** distance between certain limits; extent: *a range of colors to choose from, a range of prices from $5 to $25, the range of hearing.* **2** extend between certain limits: *prices ranging from $5 to $10.* **3** distance a gun can shoot. **4** place to practice shooting: *a rifle range.* **5** land for grazing. **6** wander over; rove; roam: *Dinosaurs once ranged the earth. Our talk ranged over all that had happened on our vacation.* **7** row or line of mountains: *Mount Rainier is in the Cascade Range.* **8** row or line: *ranges of books in perfect order.* **9** put in a row or rows: *Range the books by size.* **10** put in groups or classes. **11** district in which certain plants or animals live. **12** run in a line; extend: *a boundary ranging east and west.* **13** be found; occur: *a plant ranging from Canada to Mexico.* **14** stove for cooking: *Gas and electric ranges have replaced the coal and wood range.* 1,3-5,7,8,11,14 *noun,* 2,6,9,10,12,13 *verb,* **ranged, rang ing.**

rang er (rān′jər), **1** person employed to guard a forest. **2** one of a body of armed men employed in ranging over a region to police it. **3** person or thing that ranges; rover. *noun.*

rank¹ (rangk), **1** row or line, usually of soldiers, placed side by side. **2 ranks** or **the rank and file, a** common soldiers. **b** common people. **3** arrange in a row or line. **4** position; grade; class: *The rank of major is higher than the rank of captain.* **5** high position: *A duke is a man of rank.* **6** have a certain place or position in relation to other persons or things: *I ranked high on the spelling test.* **7** put in some special order in a list: *Rank the states in order of size.* 1,2,4,5 *noun,* 3,6,7 *verb.*

rank² (rangk), **1** growing in a thick, coarse way: *rank grass, a rank growth of weeds.* **2** having an unpleasant, strong smell or taste: *rank meat, rank tobacco.* **3** strongly marked; extreme: *rank ingratitude, rank nonsense. adjective.*

ran kle (rang′kəl), be sore; cause soreness; continue to give pain: *The memory of the insult still rankles in my mind. verb,* **ran kled, ran kling.**

ran sack (ran′sak), **1** search thoroughly through: *We ransacked the house for my lost ring.* **2** rob; plunder: *The invading army ransacked the city and carried off its treasures. verb.*

ran som (ran′səm), **1** price paid or demanded before a captive is set free: *The robber held the travelers prisoners for ransom.* **2** obtain the release of (a captive) by paying a price: *They ransomed the kidnaped child with a great sum of money.* **3** the freeing of a captive by paying the price that is demanded: *the ransom of a prisoner.* 1,3 *noun,* 2 *verb.*

rap (rap), **1** a quick, light blow; light, sharp knock: *a rap on the door.* **2** knock sharply; tap: *The chairman rapped on the table for order.* **3** say sharply: *rap out an answer.* 1 *noun,* 2,3 *verb,* **rapped, rap ping.**

rap id (rap′id), **1** very quick; swift: *a rapid walk, a rapid worker.* **2 rapids,** part of a river where the water rushes quickly, often over rocks lying near the surface. See picture. 1 *adjective,* 2 *noun.*

ra pid i ty (rə pid′ə tē), quickness; swiftness; speed. *noun.*

ra pi er (rā′pē ər), a long and light sword used for thrusting. *noun.*

rapt (rapt), **1** lost in delight. **2** so busy thinking of or enjoying one thing that one does not know what else is happening. **3** showing that a person is rapt: *a rapt smile. He listened to the story with rapt attention.* See picture. *adjective.*

rap ture (rap′chər), very great joy; extreme happiness: *The children watched in rapture as the magician pulled a rabbit out of a hat. noun.*

rap tur ous (rap′chər əs), full of rapture; feeling rapture; expressing rapture. *adjective.*

rare¹ (rer *or* rar), **1** seldom seen or found. See picture. **2** not happening often: *Snow is rare in Florida.* **3** unusually good: *Edison had rare powers as an inventor.* **4** thin; not dense: *The higher we go above the earth, the rarer the air is. adjective,* **rar er, rar est.**

rare² (rer *or* rar), not cooked much: *a rare steak. adjective,* **rar er, rar est.**

rare ly (rer′lē *or* rar′lē), seldom; not often: *A person who is usually on time is rarely late. adverb.*

rar i ty (rer′ə tē *or* rar′ə tē), **1** something rare: *A person over a hundred years old is a rarity.*

rapt

a hat	**i** it	**oi** oil	**ch** child		a in about
ā age	**ī** ice	**ou** out	**ng** long		e in taken
ä far	**o** hot	**u** cup	**sh** she	**ə** =	i in pencil
e let	**ō** open	**ů** put	**th** thin		o in lemon
ē equal	**ô** order	**ü** rule	**ŦH** then		u in circus
ėr term			**zh** measure		

2 fewness; scarcity: *The rarity of diamonds makes them valuable.* **3** thinness; lack of density: *The rarity of the air on high mountains is bad for some people. noun, plural* **rar i ties.**

ras cal (ras′kəl), **1** a bad, dishonest person. **2** a mischievous person: *That little rascal ate all the cookies. noun.*

rash¹ (rash), too hasty; careless; reckless; taking too much risk: *It is rash to cross the street without looking both ways. adjective.*

rash² (rash), breaking out with many small red spots on the skin. *Scarlet fever causes a rash. noun, plural* **rash es.**

rasp (rasp), **1** make a harsh, grating sound: *The file rasped as she worked.* **2** a harsh, grating sound: *the rasp of crickets, a rasp in a person's voice.* **3** grate on; irritate: *Their constant quarreling began to rasp my nerves.* **1,3** *verb,* **2** *noun.*

rasp ber ry (raz′ber′ē), a small fruit that grows on bushes. Raspberries are usually red or black, but some kinds are white or yellow. They are good to eat. *noun, plural* **rasp ber ries.**

rat (rat), **1** a long-tailed gnawing animal like a mouse, but larger. Rats are gray, black, brown, or white. **2** a mean, hateful person. *noun.*
smell a rat, suspect a trick or scheme.

rate (rāt), **1** quantity, amount, or degree, measured in proportion to something else: *The car was going at the rate of 40 miles an hour. The rate of interest is 6 cents on the dollar.* **2** price: *We pay the regular rate.* **3** put a value on: *We rated the house as worth $30,000.* **4** consider; regard: *He was rated as one of the richest men in town.* **5** class; grade: *first rate, second rate.* **6** be ranked; be considered: *She rdtes high as a musician.* **1,2,5** *noun,* **3,4,6** *verb,* **rat ed, rat ing.**
at any rate, anyway; in any case.

rath er (raŦH′ər), **1** more willingly: *I would rather go today than tomorrow.* **2** more properly; with better reason: *This is rather for your parents to decide than for you.* **3** more truly: *We sat up till one o'clock Monday night, or, rather, Tuesday morning.* **4** to some extent; somewhat; more than a little: *After working so long he was rather tired. adverb.*

rat i fi ca tion (rat′ə fə kā′shən), confirmation; approval: *the ratification of a treaty by the Senate. noun.*

rat i fy (rat′ə fī), confirm; approve: *The two countries will ratify the agreement made by their representatives. verb,* **rat i fied, rat i fy ing.**

ra ti o (rā′shē ō), **1** relation between two numbers or quantities meant when we say *times as many* or *times as much.* "They have sheep and cows in the ratio of 10 to 3" means that they have ten sheep for every three cows, or $3\frac{1}{3}$ times as many sheep as cows. **2** quotient. The ratio between two

rapid (definition 2)—The boat was swept along by the **rapids**.

rare¹ (definition 1)—This picture shows both sides of a rare Jewish coin that is almost 1900 years old.

rattlesnake—3 to 6 feet (1 to 1½ meters) long

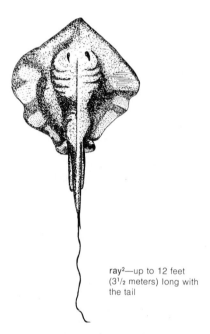

ray²—up to 12 feet (3½ meters) long with the tail

ravage (definition 1)—The town was ravaged by fire and flood.

quantities is the number of times one contains the other. The ratio of 3 to 6 is ³/₆ or ¹/₂; the ratio of 6 to 3 is ⁶/₃ or 2. The ratios of 3 to 5 and 6 to 10 are the same. *noun, plural* **ra ti os.**

ra tion (rash′ən *or* rā′shən), **1** a fixed allowance of food; daily allowance of food for a person or animal. **2** portion of anything dealt out: *rations of sugar, rations of coal.* **3** allow only certain amounts to: *ration citizens when supplies are scarce.* **4** distribute in limited amounts: *Food was rationed to the public during the war.* **5** supply with rations: *ration an army.* 1,2 *noun,* 3-5 *verb.*

ra tion al (rash′ə nəl), **1** sensible; reasonable; reasoned out: *When very angry, people seldom act in a rational way.* **2** able to think and reason clearly: *Human beings are rational animals.* **3** of reason; based on reasoning: *There is a rational explanation for thunder and lightning. adjective.*

rat tle (rat′l), **1** make or cause to make a number of short, sharp sounds: *The window rattled in the wind. They rattled the dishes.* **2** number of short, sharp sounds: *the rattle of empty bottles.* **3** move with short, sharp sounds: *The old car rattled down the street.* **4** toy or instrument that makes a noise when it is shaken: *The baby shook the rattle.* **5** series of horny pieces at the end of a rattlesnake's tail. **6** talk or say quickly; talk on and on: *She rattled off the names of all the planets.* **7** disturb; confuse; upset: *I was so rattled that I forgot my speech.* 1,3,6,7 *verb,* **rat tled, rat tling;** 2,4,5 *noun.*

rat tler (rat′lər), rattlesnake. *noun.*

rat tle snake (rat′l snāk′), a poisonous snake with a thick body and a broad head, that makes a buzzing noise with rattles at the end of its tail. See picture. *noun.*

rau cous (rô′kəs), hoarse; harsh-sounding: *We heard the raucous caw of a crow in the field of corn. adjective.*

rav age (rav′ij), **1** lay waste; damage greatly; destroy. See picture. **2** violence; destruction; great damage: *the ravages of war.* 1 *verb,* **rav aged, rav ag ing;** 2 *noun.*

rave (rāv), **1** talk wildly. An excited, angry person may rave. **2** talk with too much enthusiasm: *They raved about the food. verb,* **raved, rav ing.**

rav el (rav′əl), to fray; separate into threads: *The sweater has raveled at the elbow. verb.*

ra ven (rā′vən), **1** a large black bird like a crow but larger. **2** deep glossy black: *raven hair.* 1 *noun,* 2 *adjective.*

rav en ous (rav′ə nəs), **1** very hungry: *I hadn't eaten all day and was ravenous.* **2** greedy. *adjective.*

ra vine (rə vēn′), a long, deep, narrow valley: *The river had worn a ravine between the two hills. noun.*

rav ish (rav′ish), **1** fill with delight: *I was ravished by the beauty of the countryside.* **2** carry off by force: *The wolf ravished the lamb from the flock. verb.*

rav ish ing (rav′i shing), very delightful; enchanting: *jewels of ravishing beauty. adjective.*

raw (rô), **1** not cooked: *raw meat.* **2** in the natural state; not manufactured, treated, or prepared:

Raw milk has not been pasteurized. **3** not experienced; not trained: *a raw recruit.* **4** damp and cold: *a raw wind.* **5** with the skin off; sore: *a raw spot on a horse where the harness rubbed.* *adjective.*

raw hide (rô′hīd′), **1** skin of cattle that has not been tanned. **2** rope or whip made of this. *noun.*

raw material, substance in its natural state; any product that comes from mines, farms, forests, or the like before it is prepared for use in factories, mills, and similar places. Coal, coffee beans, iron ore, cotton, and hides are raw materials.

ray[1] (rā), **1** line or beam of light: *rays of the sun.* **2** line or stream of heat, light, or other radiant energy. **3** a thin line like a ray, coming out from a center. **4** part like a ray. The petals of a daisy and the arms of a starfish are rays. **5** a slight trace; faint gleam: *A ray of hope pierced our gloom. noun.*

ray[2] (rā), a fish with a wide, flat body and very wide fins. See picture. *noun.*

ray on (rā′on), fiber or fabric made from cellulose, and used instead of silk, cotton, and other similar fabrics. *noun.*

raze (rāz), tear down; destroy completely: *The old school was razed to the ground, and a new one was built. verb,* **razed, raz ing.**

ra zor (rā′zər), tool with a sharp blade to shave with. *noun.*

rd., road.

R.D., Rural Delivery.

re-, prefix meaning: **1** again: *Re*open means to open *again.* **2** back: *Re*pay means to pay *back.*

reach (rēch), **1** get to; arrive at; come to: *Your letter reached me yesterday. We reached an agreement.* **2** stretch out or hold out an arm or a hand: *He reached in the dark and turned on the lights.* **3** stretch; extend: *The United States reaches from ocean to ocean.* **4** touch: *I cannot reach the top of the wall. The anchor reached bottom.* **5** move to touch or seize something; try to get: *I reached for the rope.* **6** get at; influence: *Some people can be reached by flattery.* **7** take or pass with the hand: *Please reach me the newspaper.* **8** get in touch with (someone): *I could not reach you by telephone.* **9** reaching; stretching out: *By a long reach, the drowning man grasped the rope.* **10** extent or distance of reaching: *Food and water were left within reach of the sick dog.* **11** range; power; capacity: *I'm afraid this difficult lesson is beyond my reach.* **12** a long stretch or extent: *vast reaches of snow in the Antarctic.* 1-8 *verb,* 9-12 *noun, plural* **reach es.**

re act (rē akt′), **1** act back; have an effect on the one that is acting: *Unkindness often reacts on the unkind person.* **2** act in response: *Dogs react to kindness by showing affection. verb.*

react against, act unfavorably toward or take an unfavorable attitude toward: *Some individuals react against fads.*

re ac tion (rē ak′shən), action in response to some influence: *Our reaction to a joke is to laugh. The doctor observed carefully the patient's reactions to the tests. noun.*

a hat	i it	oi oil	ch child	(a in about
ā age	ī ice	ou out	ng long	e in taken
ä far	o hot	u cup	sh she	ə = { i in pencil
e let	ō open	u̇ put	th thin	o in lemon
ē equal	ô order	ü rule	₮ң then	(u in circus
ėr term			zh measure	

re ac tor (rē ak′tər), device for splitting atoms to produce atomic energy without causing an explosion. *noun.*

read[1] (rēd), **1** get the meaning of (writing or print): *read a book. The blind read by touching special raised print with their fingertips.* **2** learn from writing or print: *I read of the event in the paper.* **3** speak out loud the words of writing or print: *Please read this story to me.* **4** show by letters, figures, or signs: *The thermometer reads 70 degrees. The ticket reads "From New York to Boston."* **5** study: *to read law.* **6** get the real meaning of; understand: *Although she was smiling, I could read unhappiness in her eyes.* **7** give the meaning of; interpret: *The fortuneteller told my future by reading tea leaves.* *verb,* **read** (red), **read ing.**

read[2] (red), **1** having knowledge gained by reading; informed: *He is widely read in history.* **2** See **read**[1]. *I read that book last year.* 1 *adjective,* 2 *verb.*

read a ble (rē′də bəl), easy to read; interesting. *adjective.*

read er (rē′dər), **1** person who reads. **2** book for learning and practicing reading. *noun.*

read i ly (red′l ē), **1** quickly: *The bright student answered readily.* **2** easily: *readily available.* **3** willingly. *adverb.*

read i ness (red′ē nis), **1** being ready: *Everything is in readiness for the party.* **2** quickness; promptness. **3** ease. **4** willingness. *noun.*

read ing (rē′ding), **1** getting the meaning of written or printed words. **2** a speaking out loud of written or printed words. **3** the written or printed matter read or to be read. **4** amount shown by letters, figures, or signs on the scale of an instrument: *The reading of the thermometer was 96 degrees. noun.*

read y (red′ē), **1** prepared for action or use at once; prepared: *Dinner is ready. We were ready to start at nine.* **2** willing: *I am ready to forget our argument.* **3** quick; prompt: *a ready welcome, a ready wit.* **4** likely; liable: *Don't be too ready to find fault.* **5** easy to get at; easy to reach: *ready money.* **6** make ready; prepare: *The expedition readied itself during the summer.* 1-5 *adjective,* **read i er, read i est;** 6 *verb,* **read ied, read y ing.**

read y-made (red′ē mād′), ready for immediate use; made for anybody who will buy: *This store sells ready-made clothes. adjective.*

re al (rē′əl), **1** existing as a fact; not imagined; not made up; actual; true: *real pleasure, the real reason.* **2** genuine: *real diamonds.* **3** very; extremely: *Come again real soon.* 1,2 *adjective,* 3 *adverb.*

real estate, land together with the buildings, fences, trees, water, and minerals that belong with it.

re al is tic (rē′ə lis′tik), like the real thing; lifelike: *a realistic picture, a realistic story. adjective.*

re al i ty (rē al′ə tē), **1** actual existence; true state of affairs: *I doubt the reality of what I saw; I must have dreamed it.* **2** a real thing; actual fact: *Slaughter and destruction are the terrible realities of war. noun, plural* **re al i ties.**

in reality, really; in fact: *We thought she was serious, but in reality she was joking.*

re al i za tion (rē′ə lə zā′shən), **1** realizing or being realized: *the realization of all your hopes.* **2** understanding: *The explorers had a full realization of the dangers they would face. noun.*

re al ize (rē′ə līz), **1** understand clearly: *I realize how hard you worked.* **2** make real: *Her uncle's present made it possible for her to realize the dream of going to college. verb,* **re al ized, re al iz ing.**

re al ly (rē′ə lē), **1** actually; truly; in fact: *We all should learn to accept things as they really are.* **2** indeed: *Oh, really? adverb.*

realm (relm), **1** kingdom: *the British realm.* **2** region; range; extent: *This is beyond the realm of my understanding.* **3** a particular field of something: *the realm of biology, the realm of poetry. noun.*

ream (rēm), 480, 500, or 516 sheets of paper of the same size and quality. *noun.*

reap (rēp), **1** cut (grain). **2** gather (a crop). **3** cut grain or gather a crop from: *They reaped the field.* **4** get as a return or reward: *Kind acts often reap happy smiles. verb.*

reap er (rē′pər), person or machine that cuts grain or gathers a crop. *noun.*

re ap pear (rē′ə pir′), come into sight again. *verb.*

rear[1] (rir), **1** the back part; back: *The kitchen is in the rear of the house.* **2** at the back; in the back: *Leave by the rear door of the bus.* **3** the last part of an army or a fleet. *1,3 noun, 2 adjective.*

rear[2] (rir), **1** make grow; help to grow; bring up: *They reared their children to respect others.* **2** set up; build: *The Romans reared temples to their gods.* **3** raise; lift up: *The snake reared its head.* **4** (of an animal) to rise on the hind legs: *The spirited horse reared. See picture. verb.*

rear admiral, a naval officer next in rank above a captain.

re ar range (rē′ə rānj′), **1** arrange in a new or different way: *They rearranged the furniture for the party.* **2** arrange again: *I had to rearrange my papers after the wind blew them on the floor. verb,* **re ar ranged, re ar rang ing.**

rea son (rē′zn), **1** cause; motive: *I have my reasons for doing it this way.* **2** explanation: *What is your reason for being so late?* **3** think things out; solve new problems: *Most animals can't reason.* **4** power to think: *That poor old man has lost his reason.* **5** right thinking; common sense: *The stubborn child was at last brought to reason.* **6** consider; discuss; argue: *Reason with her and try to make her change her mind. 1,2,4,5 noun, 3,6 verb.*

stand to reason, be reasonable and sensible: *It stands to reason that you can't do your best if you're tired.*

rea son a ble (rē′zn ə bəl), **1** according to reason;

sensible; not foolish: *When we are angry, we do not always act in a reasonable way.* **2** not asking too much; fair; just: *a reasonable person.* **3** not high in price; inexpensive: *a reasonable price.* **4** able to reason: *Human beings are reasonable animals. adjective.*

rea son a bly (rē′zn ə blē), in a reasonable manner; with reason. *adverb.*

rea son ing (rē′zn ing), **1** process of drawing conclusions from facts. **2** reasons; arguments. *noun.*

re as sure (rē′ə shùr′), **1** restore to confidence: *The calmness of the crew during the storm reassured the ship's passengers.* **2** assure again or anew. *verb,* **re as sured, re as sur ing.**

reb el (reb′əl *for 1 and 2;* ri bel′ *for 3 and 4*), **1** person who resists or fights against authority instead of obeying: *The rebels armed themselves against the government.* **2** defying law or authority: *a rebel army.* **3** resist or fight against law or authority: *Unfair taxes made the colonists rebel.* **4** feel a great dislike or opposition: *We rebelled at having to stay in on so fine a day. 1 noun, 2 adjective, 3,4 verb,* **re belled, re bel ling.** [*Rebel* is from a Latin word meaning "one who makes war again." This usually referred to a person who had already been conquered in war, but kept on fighting anyway, hoping to regain freedom.]

re bel lion (ri bel′yən), **1** a fight against one's government; revolt: *The American colonists were in rebellion against the British king.* **2** resistance: *The prisoners rose in rebellion against their guards. noun.*

re bel lious (ri bel′yəs), **1** defying authority; acting like a rebel: *a rebellious army.* **2** hard to manage; hard to treat; disobedient: *The rebellious child would not obey the rules. adjective.*

re birth (rē′bėrth′), a new birth; being born again: *a rebirth of national pride. noun.*

re born (rē bôrn′), born again. *adjective.*

re bound (ri bound′ *for 1;* rē′bound′ *for 2*), **1** spring back. **2** springing back: *You hit the ball on the rebound in handball. 1 verb, 2 noun.*

re buff (ri buf′), **1** a blunt or sudden check to a person who makes advances, offers help, or makes a request. See picture. **2** give a rebuff to: *The friendly dog was rebuffed by a kick. 1 noun, 2 verb.*

re build (rē bild′), build again or anew. *verb,* **re built, re build ing.**

re built (rē bilt′). See rebuild. *verb.*

re buke (ri byük′), **1** express disapproval of; reprove: *The teacher rebuked the child for throwing paper on the floor.* **2** expression of disapproval; scolding: *The child feared the teacher's rebuke. 1 verb,* **re buked, re buk ing;** *2 noun.*

re call (ri kôl′), **1** call back to mind; remember: *I can recall stories read to me when I was very young.* **2** call back; order back: *The doctor was recalled to the hospital.* **3** take back; withdraw: *I shall recall my order for a new coat because I have had one given to me.* **4** act of calling back; fact of being called back. *1-3 verb, 4 noun.*

re cap ture (rē kap′chər), capture again; have

again. *verb*, **re cap tured, re cap tur ing.**

re cede (ri sēd⁄), **1** go backward; move backward: *Houses and trees seem to recede as you ride past in a train.* **2** slope backward: *a chin that recedes. verb,* **re ced ed, re ced ing.**

re ceipt (ri sēt⁄), **1** a written statement that money, a package, or a letter has been received: *Sign the receipt for this parcel.* **2** write on (a bill or invoice) that something has been received or paid for: *Pay the bill and ask the grocer to receipt it.* **3 receipts,** money received: *Our expenses were less than our receipts.* **4** receiving; being received: *On receipt of the news he went home.* **1,3,4** *noun,* **2** *verb.*

re ceive (ri sēv⁄), **1** take (something offered or sent): *receive gifts.* **2** be given; get: *I received a letter from my friend.* **3** take in; support; bear; hold: *The boat received a heavy load.* **4** take or let into the mind; accept: *receive new ideas, receive news, receive an education.* **5** experience; suffer; endure: *receive blows, receive punishment.* **6** let into one's house or society; accept: *The people of the neighborhood were glad to receive the new couple.* **7** (in radio or television) to change radio waves broadcast through the air into sounds, or sounds and pictures: *Our television receives well since we had a new antenna put on. verb,* **re ceived, re ceiv ing.**

re ceiv er (ri sē⁄vər), **1** person who receives: *The receiver of a gift should thank the giver.* **2** thing that receives: *Public telephones have coin receivers for nickels, dimes, and quarters.* **3** part of the telephone held to the ear. **4** device that receives sounds, or sounds and pictures, sent by radio waves: *a radio receiver, a television receiver. noun.*

re cent (rē⁄snt), **1** done or made not long ago: *recent events.* **2** not long past; modern: *a recent period of history. adjective.*

re cep ta cle (ri sep⁄tə kəl), any container or place used to put things in. Bags, baskets, and vaults are all receptacles. *noun.*

re cep tion (ri sep⁄shən), **1** act of receiving: *Her calm reception of the bad news surprised us.* **2** being received: *Her reception as a club member pleased her.* **3** manner of receiving: *We were given a warm reception on returning home.* **4** party or entertainment to welcome people: *Our school gave a reception for our new principal.* **5** quality of the sound in a radio or sound and picture in a television set: *Reception was poor because we were so far from the transmitter. noun.*

re cep tive (ri sep⁄tiv), able, quick, or ready to receive ideas, suggestions, or impressions: *a receptive mind. adjective.*

re cess (rē⁄ses *or* ri ses⁄ *for 1,3, and 4;* ri ses⁄ *for 2*), **1** time during which work stops: *Our school has an hour's recess at noon.* **2** take a recess: *The committee recessed for lunch.* **3** part of a wall or other flat surface set back from the rest: *The bench was in the recess of the wall.* **4** an inner place or part: *the recesses of a cave, the recesses of one's secret thoughts.* **1,3,4** *noun,* **2** *verb.*

rec i pe (res⁄ə pē), **1** set of directions for preparing something to eat: *Please give me your recipe for*

a hat	i it	oi oil	ch child	⎰a in about
ā age	ī ice	ou out	ng long	e in taken
ä far	o hot	u cup	sh she	ə = ⎨ i in pencil
e let	ō open	ù put	th thin	o in lemon
ē equal	ô order	ü rule	ᴛʜ then	⎱u in circus
ėr term			zh measure	

rear² (definition 4)

cookies. **2** set of directions for preparing anything or reaching some result: *a recipe for happiness.* noun.

re cip i ent (ri sip′ē ənt), person who receives something: *The recipients of the prizes had their names printed in the paper.* noun.

re cit al (ri sī′tl), **1** telling facts in detail: *I hope that my lengthy recital of my problems hasn't bored you.* **2** story; account. **3** a musical entertainment, usually given by a single performer: *My music teacher will give a recital Tuesday afternoon.* noun.

rec i ta tion (res′ə tā′shən), **1** reciting a prepared lesson by pupils before a teacher. **2** repeating something from memory before an audience. noun.

rectangles

re cite (ri sīt′), **1** say over; repeat: *He can recite that poem from memory.* **2** say part of a lesson; answer a teacher's questions: *The teacher called on me to recite.* **3** give an account of in detail: *She recited the day's adventures. verb,* **re cit ed, re cit ing.**

reck less (rek′lis), rash; heedless; careless: *Reckless driving causes many automobile accidents.* adjective.

reck on (rek′ən), **1** find the number or value of; count: *Reckon the cost before you decide.* **2** consider; judge: *He is reckoned the best speller in the class.* **3** think; suppose. **4** depend; rely: *Can we reckon on your help? verb.*

reck on ing (rek′ə ning), **1** count; calculation: *By my reckoning we are miles from home.* **2** settling an account: *a day of reckoning.* **3** calculation of the position of a ship or aircraft. noun.

re claim (ri klām′), **1** bring back to a useful, good condition: *The farmer reclaimed the swamp by draining it. Society reclaims criminals by teaching them skills.* **2** get from discarded things: *reclaim rubber from old tires.* **3** demand or ask for the return of: *She reclaimed her luggage at the end of the trip. verb.*

recreation—Sports and games are forms of recreation.

rec la ma tion (rek′lə mā′shən), bringing back to a useful, good condition: *the reclamation of deserts by irrigation.* noun.

re cline (ri klīn′), lean back; lie down: *I reclined on the couch. verb,* **re clined, re clin ing.**

rec luse (rek′lüs *or* ri klüs′), person who lives shut up or withdrawn from the world. noun.

rec og ni tion (rek′əg nish′ən), **1** knowing again; recognizing. **2** being recognized: *By a good disguise he escaped recognition.* **3** acknowledgment: *We insisted on complete recognition of our rights.* **4** favorable notice; attention: *The actor soon won recognition from the public.* noun.

rec og nize (rek′əg nīz), **1** know again: *You have grown so much that I scarcely recognized you.* **2** acknowledge; accept; admit: *They recognized and did their duty. verb,* **rec og nized, rec og niz ing.**

re coil (ri koil′), **1** draw back; shrink back: *Most people would recoil at seeing a snake in the path.* **2** spring back: *The gun recoiled after I fired it.* **3** springing back. **1,2** *verb,* **3** *noun.*

rec ol lect (rek′ə lekt′), remember. *verb.*

rec ol lec tion (rek′ə lek′shən) **1** act or power of calling back to mind. **2** memory; remembrance:

recorder (definition 4)

This has been the hottest summer within my recollection. **3** thing remembered. *noun.*

rec om mend (rek/ə mend/), **1** speak in favor of; suggest favorably: *The teacher recommended her for the job. Can you recommend a good adventure story?* **2** advise: *The doctor recommended that the patient stay in bed.* **3** make pleasing or attractive: *The location of the camp recommends it as a summer home. verb.*

rec om men da tion (rek/ə men dā/shən), **1** act of recommending. **2** anything that recommends a person or thing. **3** words of advice or praise. *noun.*

rec om pense (rek/əm pens), **1** reward; pay back; pay (a person): *The travelers recompensed the man who so carefully directed them.* **2** make a fair return for (an action, anything lost, damage done, or hurt received): *The insurance company recompensed her for the loss of her car.* **3** payment; reward; return: *She received $2000 in recompense for the loss of her car.* **1,2** *verb,* **rec om pensed, rec om pens ing; 3** *noun.*

rec on cile (rek/ən sīl), **1** make friends again: *The children had quarreled but were soon reconciled.* **2** settle (a quarrel or difference): *The teacher reconciled the dispute between the two pupils.* **3** make agree; bring into harmony: *It is impossible to reconcile their story with the facts.* **4** make satisfied; make no longer opposed: *It is hard to reconcile oneself to being sick a long time. verb,* **rec on ciled, rec on cil ing.**

rec on cil i a tion (rek/ən sil/ē ā/shən), **1** bringing together again in friendship. **2** settlement or adjustment of disagreements or differences: *a reconciliation of opposite points of view. noun.*

rec on noi ter (rek/ə noi/tər *or* rē/kə noi/tər), **1** approach and examine or observe in order to learn something: *Our scouts will reconnoiter the enemy's position before we attack.* **2** approach a place and make a first survey of it: *It seemed wise to reconnoiter before entering the town. verb.*

re con struct (rē/kən strukt/), construct again; rebuild; make over. *verb.*

re cord (ri kôrd/ *for 1,2, and 6;* rek/ərd *for 3-5,7-9*), **1** set down in writing so as to keep for future use: *Listen to the speaker and record what he says.* **2** put in some permanent form; keep for remembrance: *We record history in books.* **3** the thing written or kept. **4** an official written account: *The secretary kept a record of what was done at the meeting.* **5** disk used on a phonograph. A record plays the sounds copied on its very small grooves. **6** put (music, words, or sounds) on such a disk or on specially treated wire or tape. **7** the known facts about what a person, animal, or ship has done: *She has a fine record at school.* **8** the best yet done; best amount, rate, or speed yet reached: *Who holds the record for the high jump?* **9** making or affording a record: *a record wheat crop.* **1,2,6** *verb,* **3-5,7,8** *noun,* **9** *adjective.*

break a record, make a better record.

re cord er (ri kôr/dər), **1** person whose business is to make and keep records. **2** machine or part of a machine that records. A cashier's recorder adds

up and prints the amount of sales made. **3** tape recorder. **4** a wooden musical instrument somewhat like a flute. See picture. *noun.*

re cord ing (ri kôr/ding), record used on a phonograph, or a plastic tape used on a tape recorder. *noun.*

record player, instrument that reproduces sounds from records; phonograph.

re count[1] (ri kount/), tell in detail; give an account of: *He recounted all the happenings of the day. verb.*

re count[2] *or* **re-count** (rē kount/ *for 1;* rē/kount/ *for 2*), **1** count again: *She recounted the money to check the sum.* **2** a second count: *make a recount of the votes.* **1** *verb,* **2** *noun.*

re course (rē/kôrs), **1** turning for help or protection; appealing: *Our recourse in illness is to a doctor.* **2** person or thing appealed to or turned to for help or protection: *His only recourse in trouble was his family. noun.*

re cov er (ri kuv/ər), **1** get back (something lost, taken away, or stolen): *recover one's temper or health, recover a lost purse.* **2** make up for (something lost or damaged): *recover lost time.* **3** get well; get back to a normal condition: *She is recovering from a cold. verb.*

re-cov er (rē kuv/ər), put a new cover on: *We had our couch re-covered. verb.*

re cov er y (ri kuv/ər ē), **1** coming back to health or normal condition: *We heard of your recovery from fever.* **2** getting back something that was lost, taken away, stolen, or sent out: *the recovery of a space capsule.* **3** getting back to a proper position or condition: *He started to fall, but made a quick recovery. noun, plural* **re cov er ies.**

rec re a tion (rek/rē ā/shən), play; amusement. Walking, gardening, and reading are quiet forms of recreation. See picture. *noun.*

re cross (rē krôs/), cross again. *verb.*

re cruit (ri krüt/), **1** a newly enlisted soldier or sailor. **2** get (people) to join an army, navy, or air force. **3** new member of any group or class: *The Nature Club needs recruits.* **4** get (new members); get (people) to join: *recruit new members.* **1,3** *noun,* **2,4** *verb.*

rec tan gle (rek/tang/gəl), a four-sided figure with four right angles. See picture. *noun.*

rec tan gu lar (rek tang/gyə lər), shaped like a rectangle. *adjective.*

rec ti fy (rek/tə fī), make right; put right; adjust; remedy: *The storekeeper admitted her mistake and was willing to rectify it. verb,* **rec ti fied, rec ti fy ing.**

rec tor (rek/tər), clergyman who is in charge of a parish or congregation. *noun.*

re cur (ri ker/), **1** come up again; occur again; be repeated: *Leap year recurs every four years.* **2** return in thought or speech: *Old memories often recurred to him. She recurred to the matter of cost. verb,* **re curred, re cur ring.**

re cy cle (rē sī′kəl), to treat or process (something) in order that it may be used again. Paper, aluminum, and glass products are commonly recycled. See picture. *verb,* **re cy cled, re cy cling.**

red (red), **1** the color of blood or of a ruby. **2** having this color: *a red rose.* **3 Red,** a Communist or, sometimes, any extreme radical. **1,3** *noun,* **2** *adjective.*

see red, become very angry: *I saw red and before I knew it I had hit him hard.*

red blood cell, a cell in the blood that carries oxygen from the lungs to various parts of the body.

red cap (red′kap′), porter at a railroad or bus station whose uniform usually includes a red cap. *noun.*

red coat (red′kōt′), (in former times) a British soldier. *noun.*

Red Cross, an international organization to care for the sick and wounded in war, and to relieve suffering caused by floods, fire, diseases, and other calamities. Its badge is a red cross on a white background.

red deer, deer with reddish-brown fur. There used to be a great many red deer in England.

red den (red′n), **1** make or become red. **2** blush. *verb.*

red dish (red′ish), somewhat red. *adjective.*

re deem (ri dēm′), **1** buy back: *The property on which money was lent was redeemed when the loan was paid back.* **2** pay off: *We redeemed the mortgage.* **3** make up for: *A very good feature will sometimes redeem several bad ones.* **4** fulfill; carry out; make good: *We redeem a promise by doing what we said we would.* **5** set free; rescue; save; deliver: *redeemed from sin. verb.*

re demp tion (ri demp′shən), **1** buying back; paying off. **2** ransom. **3** deliverance; rescue. **4** deliverance from sin; salvation. *noun.*

red head ed (red′hed′id), having red hair. *adjective.*

red-hot (red′hot′), very hot. *adjective.*

re dis cov er (rē′dis kuv′ər), discover again or anew. *verb.*

re dou ble (rē dub′əl), **1** double again. **2** double; increase greatly: *The swimmer redoubled her speed as she neared the finish line.* **3** double back: *The fox redoubled on its trail to escape the hunters. verb,* **re dou bled, re dou bling.**

re dress (ri dres′ for 1; rē′dres for 2), **1** set right; repair; remedy: *King Arthur tried to redress wrongs in his kingdom.* **2** setting right; relief: *Anyone who has been injured deserves redress.* **1** *verb,* **2** *noun.*

re duce (ri düs′ or ri dyüs′), **1** make less; make smaller; decrease: *We have reduced expenses this year. She is trying to reduce her weight.* **2** become less in weight: *His doctor advised him to reduce.* **3** bring down; lower: *Their misfortunes reduced them to poverty.* **4** change to another form: *The*

chalk was reduced to powder. If you reduce 3 ft., 6 in. to inches you have 42 inches. **5** bring to a different condition; change: *The teacher soon reduced the noisy class to order.* **6** conquer: *The army reduced the fort by a sudden attack. verb,* **re duced, re duc ing.**

re duc tion (ri duk′shən), **1** reducing or being reduced: *a reduction of ten pounds in weight.* **2** amount by which a thing is reduced: *The reduction in cost was $5. noun.*

red wood (red′wu̇d′), **1** an evergreen tree of California and Oregon that bears cones and grows to a height of over 300 feet. **2** its brownish-red wood. *noun.*

reed (rēd), **1** a kind of tall grass that grows in wet places. Reeds have hollow, jointed stalks. **2** anything made from the stalk of a reed, such as a pipe to blow on or an arrow. **3** a thin piece of wood, metal, or plastic in a musical instrument that produces sound when a current of air moves it. *noun.*

reed instrument, a musical instrument that makes sound by means of a vibrating reed or reeds. Oboes, clarinets, English horns, and saxophones are reed instruments.

reef[1] (rēf), a narrow ridge of rocks, sand, or coral at or near the surface of water. See picture. *noun.*

reef[2] (rēf), **1** the part of a sail that can be rolled or folded up to reduce its size. **2** reduce the size of (a sail) by rolling or folding up a part of it. **1** *noun,* **2** *verb.*

reek (rēk), **1** a strong, unpleasant smell: *We noticed the reek of cooking cabbage as we entered the hall.* **2** send out a strong, unpleasant smell: *The beach reeks of dead fish.* **1** *noun,* **2** *verb.*

reel[1] (rēl), **1** roller or spool for winding thread, yarn, a fish line, rope, wire, string, or anything that can be wound. **2** something wound on a reel: *two reels of motion-picture film.* **3** wind on a reel. **4** draw with a reel or by winding: *She reeled in a fish.* **1,2** *noun,* **3,4** *verb.*

reel off, say, write, or make in a quick, easy way: *He can reel off stories by the hour.*

reel[2] (rēl), **1** sway, swing, or rock under a blow or shock: *She reeled when the ball struck her.* **2** sway in standing or walking: *The dazed boy reeled down the street.* **3** be in a whirl; be dizzy: *My head was reeling after the fast dance. verb.*

reel[3] (rēl), **1** a lively dance. **2** music for it. *noun.*

re e lect or **re-e lect** (rē′i lekt′), elect again. *verb.*

re e lec tion or **re-e lec tion** (rē′i lek′shən), election again; election for the second time. *noun.*

re en ter or **re-en ter** (rē en′tər), enter again; go in again: *reenter a room, reenter public life. verb.*

re en try (rē en′trē), entering again or returning, especially of a rocket or spacecraft into the earth's atmosphere. *noun, plural* **re en tries.**

re-en try (rē en′trē), reentry. *noun, plural* **re-en tries.**

re es tab lish or **re-es tab lish** (rē′ə stab′lish), establish again; restore. *verb.*

re fer (ri fėr′), **1** send or direct for information, help, or action: *Our teacher refers us to many good*

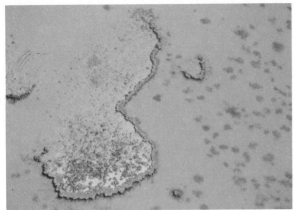

reef¹—a photograph of the Great Barrier Reef along the coast of Australia, as viewed from an airplane

recycle—She brought in old cans so that they could be recycled.

refinery

a hat	i it	oi oil	ch child	⎰a in about
ā age	ī ice	ou out	ng long	e in taken
ä far	o hot	u cup	sh she	ə = ⎨ i in pencil
e let	ō open	u̇ put	th thin	o in lemon
ē equal	ô order	ü rule	ŦH then	⎱u in circus
ėr term			zh measure	

books. **2** hand over; submit: *Let's refer the dispute to the umpire.* **3** turn for information or help: *A person refers to a dictionary to find the meaning of words.* **4** direct attention to or speak about: *The speaker referred to the Bible.* **5** assign to or think of as caused by: *They referred their failure to bad luck.* *verb,* **re ferred, re fer ring.**

ref e ree (ref′ə rē′), **1** judge of play in games and sports: *the referee in a football game.* **2** person to whom something is referred for decision or settlement. **3** act as a referee. 1,2 *noun,* 3 *verb,* **ref e reed, ref e ree ing.**

ref er ence (ref′ər əns), **1** direction of the attention: *The report contained many references to newspaper articles.* **2** statement referred to: *You will find that reference on page 16.* **3** something used for information or help: *A dictionary is a book of reference.* **4** used for information or help: *a reference library.* **5** person who can give information about another person's character or ability: *He gave his principal as a reference.* **6** statement about someone's character or ability: *When she left the company, she received an excellent reference from her boss.* **7** relation; respect; regard: *The test is to be taken by all pupils without reference to age or grade.* 1-3,5-7 *noun,* 4 *adjective.*
make reference to, mention: *Don't make any reference to the bad news.*

re fill (rē fil′ *for 1;* rē′fil′ *for 2*), **1** fill again. **2** something to refill with: *Refills can be bought for some kinds of pens and pencils.* 1 *verb,* 2 *noun.*

re fine (ri fīn′), **1** make pure; become pure: *Sugar, oil, and metals are refined before they are used.* **2** make or become fine, polished, or cultivated: *Visiting with polite people helped refine their manners.* *verb,* **re fined, re fin ing.**

re fined (ri fīnd′), **1** freed from impurities: *refined sugar.* **2** free from coarseness or vulgarity; well-bred: *refined tastes, refined manners, a refined voice.* *adjective.*

re fine ment (ri fīn′mənt), **1** fine quality of feeling, taste, manners, or language: *Good manners and correct speech are marks of refinement.* **2** act or result of refining: *Gasoline is produced by the refinement of petroleum.* *noun.*

re fin er y (ri fī′nər ē), building and machinery for purifying metal, sugar, petroleum, or other things. See picture. *noun, plural* **re fin er ies.**

re fit (rē fit′), fit, prepare, or equip for use again: *The old ship was refitted for the voyage.* *verb,* **re fit ted, re fit ting.**

re flect (ri flekt′), **1** turn back or throw back (light, heat, sound, or the like): *The sidewalks reflect heat on a hot day.* **2** give back an image of: *The mirror reflects my face.* **3** reproduce or show like a mirror: *The newspaper reflected the owner's opinions.*

reflection (definition 3)

4 think; think carefully: *Take time to reflect before doing important things.* **5** cast blame, reproach, or discredit: *The children's spoiled behavior reflected on their parents.* **6** serve to cast or bring: *A brave act reflects credit on the person who does it. verb.*

re flec tion (ri flek/shən), **1** act of reflecting. **2** something reflected. **3** likeness; image. See picture. **4** thinking; careful thinking: *On reflection, the plan seemed too dangerous.* **5** idea or remark resulting from careful thinking. **6** remark or action that casts blame or discredit. *noun.*

re flec tor (ri flek/tər), any thing, surface, or device that reflects light, heat, sound, or the like, especially a piece of glass or metal for reflecting light in a particular direction. *noun.*

re flex (rē/fleks), an automatic action that takes place when some nerve cells are stimulated. Sneezing and shivering are reflexes. *noun.*

re fo rest (rē fôr/ist), plant again with trees. *verb.*

re form (ri fôrm/), **1** make better; improve by removing faults: *Some prisons try to reform criminals instead of just punishing them.* **2** become better: *They promised to reform if given another chance.* **3** improvement; change intended to be an improvement: *The new government made many reforms.* **1,2** *verb*, **3** *noun.*

re-form (rē fôrm/), **1** form again. **2** take a new shape. *verb.*

ref or ma tion (ref/ər mā/shən), change for the better; improvement. *noun.*

re form a to ry (ri fôr/mə tôr/ē), **1** institution for reforming young offenders against the laws; prison for young criminals. **2** serving to reform; intended to reform. **1** *noun, plural* **re form a to ries; 2** *adjective.*

re form er (ri fôr/mər), person who reforms, or tries to reform, some state of affairs, custom, or practice. *noun.*

re fract (ri frakt/), bend (a ray of light, sound waves, or a stream of electrons) from a straight course. Water refracts light. See picture. *verb.*

re frain¹ (ri frān/), hold oneself back: *Refrain from wrongdoing. verb.*

re frain² (ri frān/), phrase or verse repeated regularly in a song or poem. In "The Star-Spangled Banner" the refrain is "O'er the land of the free and the home of the brave." *noun.*

re fresh (ri fresh/), make fresh again; renew: *His bath refreshed him. She refreshed her memory by a glance at the book. verb.*

re fresh ing (ri fresh/ing), **1** able to refresh: *a cool, refreshing drink.* **2** welcome as a pleasing change. *adjective.*

re fresh ment (ri fresh/mənt), **1** refreshing; being refreshed. **2** thing that refreshes. **3 refreshments,** food or drink: *Cake and lemonade were the refreshments at our party. noun.*

re frig e rate (ri frij/ə rāt/), make or keep (food or drinks) cool or cold: *Milk, meat, and ice cream must be refrigerated to prevent spoiling. verb,* **re frig e rat ed, re frig e rat ing.**

re frig e ra tor (ri frij/ə rā/tər), something that keeps things cool. An electric refrigerator keeps

refract—Because water refracts light, the ruler appears bent.

refuge—The bobcat took **refuge** in the rocks.

food cool without ice. *noun.*

ref uge (ref′yüj), shelter or protection from danger or trouble. See picture. *noun.*

ref u gee (ref′yə jē′), person who flees for refuge or safety, especially to a foreign country, in time of war, persecution, or disaster: *Many refugees came from Europe to America. The homeless refugees from the flooded town were helped by the Red Cross.* *noun.*

re fund (ri fund′ *for 1;* rē′fund *for 2 and 3*), **1** pay back: *If these shoes do not wear well, the shop will refund your money.* **2** return of money paid. **3** money paid back. 1 *verb,* 2,3 *noun.*

re fus al (ri fyü′zəl), act of refusing: *a refusal to lend money. noun.*

re fuse[1] (ri fyüz′), **1** say no to: *He refuses the offer. The teacher refused me permission to leave class early.* **2** say no: *She is free to refuse.* **3** say one will not do, give, or allow something: *They refuse to obey. verb,* **re fused, re fus ing.**

ref use[2] (ref′yüs), useless stuff; waste; rubbish: *The street-cleaning department took away all refuse from the streets. noun.*

re fute (ri fyüt′), show (a claim, opinion, or argument) to be false or incorrect: *How would you refute the statement that the cow jumped over the moon? verb,* **re fut ed, re fut ing.**

re gain (ri gān′), **1** get again; recover: *regain health.* **2** get back to; reach again: *You can regain the main road by turning left two miles ahead. verb.*

re gal (rē′gəl), **1** belonging to a king or queen; royal: *regal power.* **2** fit for a king or queen; stately; splendid; magnificent: *It was a regal banquet. adjective.*

re gale (ri gāl′), entertain very well; delight with something pleasing: *Grandmother regaled us with stories about her childhood. verb,* **re galed, re gal ing.**

re gard (ri gärd′), **1** think of; consider: *Our school band is regarded as the best in the state.* **2** care for; respect: *Please regard the rights of others.* **3** thoughtfulness for others and their feelings; care: *Have regard for the feelings of others.* **4** look at; look closely at; watch: *The cat regarded me anxiously when I picked up her kittens.* **5** look; steady look: *The man's regard seemed fixed upon some distant object.* **6** good opinion; esteem: *The teacher has high regard for your ability.* **7 regards,** good wishes; an expression of esteem: *She sends her regards.* 1,2,4 *verb,* 3,5-7 *noun.*

as regards, with respect to; concerning: *As regards money, I have enough.*

in regard to or **with regard to,** concerning; regarding: *The teacher spoke to me in regard to being late.*

re gard ing (ri gär′ding), concerning; about: *A letter regarding the field trip to the museum was sent to my parents. preposition.*

re gard less (ri gärd′lis), with no heed; careless: *The bridge will be built, regardless of the cost. adjective.*

re gat ta (ri gat′ə), a boat race or a series of boat races. See picture. *noun.*

a hat	**i** it	**oi** oil	**ch** child	a in about
ā age	**ī** ice	**ou** out	**ng** long	e in taken
ä far	**o** hot	**u** cup	**sh** she	ə = i in pencil
e let	**ō** open	**ù** put	**th** thin	o in lemon
ē equal	**ô** order	**ü** rule	**ᴛʜ** then	u in circus
ėr term			**zh** measure	

re gent (rē′jənt), person who rules when the regular ruler is absent, unfit, or too young: *The Queen will be the regent till her son grows up. noun.*

re gime (ri zhēm′ *or* rä zhēm′), system of government or rule: *the Communist regime in China. noun.*

reg i ment (rej′ə mənt), the part of an army commanded by a colonel. Two or more battalions make a regiment. *noun.*

re gion (rē′jən), **1** any large part of the earth's surface: *the region of the equator.* **2** place; space; area: *an unhealthful region, a mountainous region.* **3** part of the body: *the region of the heart. noun.*

reg is ter (rej′ə stər), **1** write in a list or record: *Register the names of the new pupils.* **2** have one's name written in a list or record: *You must register before you can vote.* **3** list; record: *A register of attendance is kept in our school.* **4** book in which a list or record is kept: *Look up his record in the register.* **5** have (a letter, package, or other mail) recorded in the post office, paying extra postage for special care in delivering: *She registered the letter containing the check.* **6** thing that records. A cash register shows the amount of money taken in. **7** indicate; record: *The thermometer registers 90 degrees.* **8** show (surprise, joy, anger, or other feeling) by the expression on one's face or by actions. **9** range of a voice or an instrument. **10** opening in a wall or floor in a device to control the amount of heated or cooled air that passes through. 1,2,5,7,8 *verb,* 3,4,6,9,10 *noun.*

reg is tra tion (rej′ə strā′shən), **1** act of registering. **2** entry in a register. **3** number of people registered: *Registration for camp is higher than last year. noun.*

regatta

re gret (ri gret′), **1** feel sorry for or about: *We regretted his absence.* **2** feel sorry; mourn: *He wrote regretting that he could not visit us.* **3** feeling of being sorry; sorrow; sense of loss: *It is a matter of regret that I could not see my mother before leaving.* **4** regrets, a polite reply declining an invitation: *She could not come to the party, but she sent regrets.* 1,2 *verb,* **re gret ted, re gret ting;** 3,4 *noun.*

re gret ful (ri gret′fəl), sorry; sorrowful; feeling or expressing regret. *adjective.*

re gret ta ble (ri gret′ə bəl), to be regretted; giving cause for regret. *adjective.*

reg u lar (reg′yə lər), **1** fixed by custom or rule; usual: *Six o'clock was her regular hour of rising.* **2** following some rule or principle; according to rule: *A period is the regular ending for a sentence.* **3** coming again and again at the same time: *I make regular visits to the dentist.* **4** steady; habitual: *A regular customer trades often at the same store.* **5** well-balanced; even in size, spacing, or speed: *regular teeth, regular breathing.* **6** orderly; methodical: *He leads a regular life.* **7** properly fitted or trained: *The regular cook in our cafeteria is sick.* **8** member of a regularly paid group of any kind: *The fire department was made up of regulars and volunteers.* 1-7 *adjective,* 8 *noun.*

reg u lar i ty (reg′yə lar′ə tē), order; system; steadiness; being regular. *noun.*

reg u late (reg′yə lāt), **1** control by rule, principle, or system: *The government regulates the coining of money.* **2** put in condition to work properly: *My watch is losing time; I will have to have it regulated.* **3** keep at some standard: *This instrument regulates the temperature of the room. verb,* **reg u lat ed, reg u lat ing.**

reg u la tion (reg′yə lā′shən), **1** control by rule, principle, or system. **2** rule; law: *traffic regulations.* **3** required by some rule: *Soldiers wear a regulation uniform.* 1,2 *noun,* 3 *adjective.*

re hears al (ri hér′səl), rehearsing; performance beforehand for practice or drill. *noun.*

re hearse (ri hèrs′), practice for a public performance: *We rehearsed our parts for the school play. verb,* **re hearsed, re hears ing.**

reign (rān), **1** period of power of a ruler: *The queen's reign lasted fifty years.* **2** rule: *A king reigns over his kingdom.* **3** act of ruling; royal power: *The reign of a wise ruler benefits the country.* **4** exist everywhere; prevail: *On a still night silence reigns.* 1,3 *noun,* 2,4 *verb.*

rein (rān), **1** a long, narrow strap or line fastened to a bridle or bit, and used to guide and control an animal. The reins are held in the hands of the driver or rider. **2** means of control and direction: *When the President was ill, the Vice-President took the reins of government.* **3** guide and control: *She reined her horse well. Rein your tongue.* 1,2 *noun,* 3 *verb.*

give rein to, let move or act freely, without control: *give rein to one's feelings.*

rein deer (rān′dir′), a large deer with branching antlers that lives in northern regions. It is used to pull sleighs and also for meat, milk, and hides.

See picture. *noun, plural* **rein deer.**

re in force (rē′in fôrs′), **1** strengthen with new force or materials: *reinforce a garment with an extra thickness of cloth, reinforce a wall or a bridge.* **2** strengthen: *reinforce an argument, reinforce a plea, reinforce a supply. verb,* **re in forced, re in forc ing.**

re in force ment (rē′in fôrs′mənt), **1** strengthening; being strengthened. **2** something that strengthens. **3** reinforcements, extra soldiers, warships, or planes: *Reinforcements were sent to the battlefield. noun.*

re it e rate (rē it′ə rāt′), repeat again; say or do several times: *The teacher reiterated her request for order in the classroom. verb,* **re it e rat ed, re it e rat ing.**

re ject (ri jekt′), **1** refuse to take: *She rejected our help. He tried to join the army but was rejected because of poor health.* **2** throw away: *Reject all apples with soft spots. verb.*

re jec tion (ri jek′shən), **1** rejecting or being rejected: *The inspector ordered the rejection of the faulty parts.* **2** thing rejected: *All rejections by the inspector were destroyed at once. noun.*

re joice (ri jois′), be glad; be filled with joy: *I rejoiced to hear of her success. verb,* **re joiced, re joic ing.**

re join[1] (rē join′), join again; unite again: *After my telephone conversation, I rejoined my friends in the kitchen. verb.*

re join[2] (ri join′), answer; reply: *"Come with me!" "Not on your life," he rejoined. verb.*

re lapse (ri laps′), **1** fall or slip back into a former state or way of acting: *After one cry of surprise, he relapsed into silence.* **2** falling or slipping back into a former state or way of acting: *She seemed to be getting over her illness but had a relapse.* 1 *verb,* **re lapsed, re laps ing;** 2 *noun.*

re late (ri lāt′), **1** give an account of; tell: *The traveler related her adventures.* **2** connect in thought or meaning: *"Better" and "best" are related to "good." verb,* **re lat ed, re lat ing.**

re lat ed (ri lā′tid), belonging to the same family: *Cousins are related. adjective.*

re la tion (ri lā′shən), **1** act of telling; account: *We enjoyed the relation of the traveler's adventures.* **2** connection in thought or meaning: *Your answer has no relation to the question.* **3** connection or dealings between persons, groups, or countries: *The relation of twins is a close one. Our firm has business relations with their firm.* **4** person who belongs to the same family as another; relative. *noun.*

in relation to or **with relation to,** in reference to; in regard to; about; concerning: *We must plan in relation to the future.*

re la tion ship (ri lā′shən ship), **1** connection: *What is the relationship of clouds to rain?* **2** condition of belonging to the same family. *noun.*

rel a tive (rel′ə tiv), **1** person who belongs to the same family as another, such as a father, brother, aunt, nephew, or cousin. **2** compared to each other: *We discussed the relative characteristics of*

relic (definition 1)—These relics found in Israel are more than 3000 years old. At the top is a jar; the three pieces below are oil lamps.

a hat	**i** it	**oi** oil	**ch** child	a in about
ā age	**ī** ice	**ou** out	**ng** long	e in taken
ä far	**o** hot	**u** cup	**sh** she ə =	i in pencil
e let	**ō** open	**u̇** put	**th** thin	o in lemon
ē equal	**ô** order	**ü** rule	**ᴛʜ** then	u in circus
ėr term			**zh** measure	

snakes and lizards. **3** depending for meaning on a relation to something else: *East is a relative term; for example, Chicago is east of California but west of New York.* 1 *noun,* 2,3 *adjective.*

relative to, 1 about; concerning: *The teacher asked me some questions relative to my plans for the summer.* **2** in proportion to; in comparison with; for: *He is strong relative to his size.*

rel a tive ly (rel′ə tiv lē), in relation to something else; comparatively: *I am relatively tall for my age.* *adverb.*

re lax (ri laks′), **1** loosen up; make or become less stiff or firm: *Relax your muscles to rest them. Relax when you dance.* **2** make or become less strict or severe; lessen in force: *Discipline is relaxed on the last day of school.* **3** weaken: *Don't relax your efforts now; keep trying. verb.*

re lax a tion (rē′lak sā′shən), **1** loosening: *the relaxation of the muscles.* **2** lessening of strictness, severity, or force: *the relaxation of discipline over the holidays.* **3** recreation; amusement: *Walking and reading are relaxations. noun.*

re lay (rē′lā *or* ri lā′), **1** a fresh supply: *New relays of men were sent to fight the fire.* **2** take and carry farther: *Messengers will relay your message.* 1 *noun,* 2 *verb,* **re layed, re lay ing.**

re lay race (rē′lā rās′), race in which each member of a team runs or swims only a certain part of the distance. See picture.

re lease (ri lēs′), **1** let go: *Release the catch and the box will open.* **2** let loose; set free: *She released him from his promise.* **3** relieve: *The nurse will be released from duty at seven o'clock.* **4** letting go; setting free: *The end of the war brought the release of the prisoners.* **5** freedom; relief: *This medicine will give you a release from pain.* 1-3 *verb,* **re leased, re leas ing;** 4,5 *noun.*

re lent (ri lent′), become less harsh; be more tender and merciful: *After I pleaded for hours, my parents finally relented and let me go on the trip.* *verb.*

re lent less (ri lent′lis), without pity; not relenting; harsh: *The storm raged all night with relentless fury.* *adjective.*

rel e vant (rel′ə vənt), bearing upon or connected with the matter in hand; to the point: *relevant questions. adjective.*

re li a ble (ri lī′ə bəl), worthy of trust; able to be depended on: *Send her to the bank for the money; she is reliable. adjective.*

re li ance (ri lī′əns), trust; confidence; dependence: *I have complete reliance in my friend.* *noun.*

rel ic (rel′ik), **1** thing left from the past. See picture. **2** something belonging to a holy person, kept as a sacred memorial. *noun.*

reindeer—about 4 feet (1 meter) high at the shoulder

relay race—The runner on the left is finishing his part of the race. While still running, he hands a thin, metal rod to his teammate on the right.

relief (definition 6)

renovate—They are renovating the building.

re lief (ri lēf′), **1** the lessening of, or freeing from, a pain, burden, or difficulty: *It was a relief to hear I had passed the exam.* **2** something that lessens or frees from pain, burden, or difficulty; aid; help: *Relief was quickly sent to the sufferers from the great fire.* **3** freedom from a post of duty: *This nurse is on duty from seven in the morning until seven at night, with only two hours' relief.* **4** change of persons on duty. **5** persons who relieve others from duty; person who does this: *The nurse's relief arrives at seven.* **6** projection of figures and designs from a surface in sculpture, drawing, or painting. See picture. *noun.*

on relief, receiving money to live on from public funds: *Many of those who lost their jobs had to go on relief.*

relief map, map that shows the different heights of a surface by using shading, colors, or solid materials such as clay.

re lieve (ri lēv′), **1** make less; make easier; reduce the pain or trouble of: *What will relieve a headache? We telephoned to relieve our parents' uneasiness.* **2** set free: *Your coming relieves me of writing a long letter.* **3** free (a person on duty) by taking his or her place. **4** bring aid to; help: *Food and medicine were sent to relieve the flood victims.* **5** give variety to: *The colorful new couch relieves this dull room. verb,* **re lieved, re liev ing.**

re li gion (ri lij′ən), **1** belief in and worship of God or gods. **2** a particular system of faith and worship: *the Christian religion, the Moslem religion. noun.*

re li gious (ri lij′əs), **1** of religion; connected with religion: *religious meetings, religious books, religious differences.* **2** much interested in religion; devoted to religion: *They are a religious family; they pray before each meal.* **3** very careful; strict: *I gave religious attention to the doctor's orders. adjective.*

re lin quish (ri ling′kwish), give up; let go: *The small dog relinquished its bone to the big dog. She has relinquished all hope of going to Europe this year. verb.*

rel ish (rel′ish), **1** a pleasant taste; good flavor: *Hunger gives relish to simple food.* **2** something to add flavor to food. Olives and pickles are relishes. **3** liking; enjoyment: *The hungry children ate with great relish. The teacher has no relish for old jokes.* **4** like the taste of; like; enjoy: *That cat relishes cream.* 1-3 *noun,* 4 *verb.*

re load (rē lōd′), load again. *verb.*

re luc tance (ri luk′təns), unwillingness; slowness in action because of unwillingness: *She took part in the game with reluctance. noun.*

re luc tant (ri luk′tənt), unwilling; slow to act because unwilling: *The teacher led the reluctant boy to the principal. I am reluctant to go out in very cold weather. adjective.*

re ly (ri lī′), depend; trust: *Rely on your own efforts. I relied upon your promise. verb,* **re lied, re ly ing.**

re main (ri mān′), **1** continue in a place; stay: *We shall remain at the lake till September.* **2** continue; last; keep on: *The town remains the same year after year.* **3** be left: *A few apples remain on the tree. If* *you take 2 from 5, 3 remains.* **4 remains, a** what is left: *The remains of the meal were fed to the dog.* **b** a dead body: *Washington's remains are buried at Mount Vernon.* 1-3 *verb,* 4 *noun.*

re main der (ri mān′dər), part left over; rest: *If you take 2 from 9 the remainder is 7. After studying an hour, she spent the remainder of the afternoon playing. noun.*

re mark (ri märk′), **1** say in a few words; state; comment: *She remarked that it was a beautiful day.* **2** something said in a few words; short statement: *The president made a few remarks.* **3** notice; observe: *Did you remark that queer cloud?* 1,3 *verb,* 2 *noun.*

re mark a ble (ri mär′kə bəl), worthy of notice; unusual: *He has a remarkable memory. adjective.*

re mark a bly (ri mär′kə blē), notably; unusually: *The day of the blizzard was remarkably cold. adverb.*

rem e dy (rem′ə dē), **1** means of removing or relieving diseases or any bad condition; cure: *Aspirin is used as a remedy for headaches.* **2** cure; put right; make right: *A nap remedied my weariness.* 1 *noun, plural* **rem e dies;** 2 *verb,* **rem e died, rem e dy ing.**

re mem ber (ri mem′bər), **1** call back to mind: *I can't remember that man's name.* **2** have (something) return to the mind: *Then I remembered where I was.* **3** keep in mind; take care not to forget: *Remember me when I am gone.* **4** keep in mind as deserving a reward or gift; make a gift to: *Uncle remembered us in his will.* **5** mention (a person) as sending friendly greetings: *She asked to be remembered to you. verb.*

re mem brance (ri mem′brəns), **1** act of remembering; memory: *I hold my old friend in fond remembrance.* **2** keepsake; any thing or action that makes one remember a person; souvenir. *noun.*

re mind (ri mīnd′), make (one) think of something; cause to remember: *This picture reminds me of a story I heard. verb.*

re mind er (ri mīn′dər), something to help one remember. *noun.*

re mit (ri mit′), **1** send money to a person or place: *Enclosed is our bill; please remit.* **2** refrain from carrying out; cancel: *The governor is remitting the prisoner's punishment.* **3** make less; decrease: *After we had rowed the boat into calm water, we remitted our efforts. verb,* **re mit ted, re mit ting.**

rem nant (rem′nənt), a small part left: *a remnant of silk. This town has only a remnant of its former population. noun.*

re mod el (rē mod′l), make over; change or alter: *The old barn was remodeled into a house. verb.*

re morse (ri môrs′), a deep, painful regret for having done wrong: *I felt remorse for hurting my friend's feelings, so I apologized. noun.*

re mote (ri mōt′), **1** far away; far off: *The North Pole is a remote part of the world.* **2** out of the way; secluded: *Mail comes to this remote village only once a week.* **3** distant: *She is a remote relative; a third cousin, to be exact.* **4** slight; faint: *I haven't the remotest idea what you mean. adjective,* **re mot er, re mot est.**

a hat	i it	oi oil	ch child	a in about
ā age	ī ice	ou out	ng long	e in taken
ä far	o hot	u cup	sh she	ə = i in pencil
e let	ō open	ù put	th thin	o in lemon
ē equal	ô order	ü rule	ᵮH then	u in circus
ėr term			zh measure	

re mov al (ri mü′vəl), **1** taking away: *After the removal of the soup, fish was served.* **2** change of place: *The store announced its removal to larger quarters.* **3** dismissal from an office or position. *noun.*

re move (ri müv′), **1** move from a place or position; take off; take away: *Remove your hat.* **2** get rid of; put an end to: *The demonstration removed any doubts we had about the invention's usefulness.* **3** dismiss from an office or position: *The mayor removed the chief of police for failing to do his duty. verb,* **re moved, re mov ing.**

re name (rē nām′), give a new name to; name again. *verb,* **re named, re nam ing.**

rend (rend), pull apart violently; tear; split: *Wolves will rend a lamb in pieces. Lightning rent the tree. verb,* **rent, rend ing.**

ren der (ren′dər), **1** cause to become; make: *Fright rendered me speechless.* **2** give; do: *render a suggestion. She rendered us a great service by her help.* **3** hand in; report: *The treasurer rendered an account of all the money spent.* **4** give in return: *Render thanks for your blessings.* **5** bring out the meaning of; represent: *The actor rendered the part of the villain well.* **6** play or sing (music). *verb.*

ren dez vous (rän′də vü), **1** appointment to meet at a fixed place or time; meeting by agreement. **2** a meeting place; gathering place: *The family's favorite rendezvous was the garden. noun, plural* **ren dez vous** (rän′də vüz). [*Rendezvous* comes from French words meaning "present yourselves!"]

ren e gade (ren′ə gād), deserter from a religious faith, political party, or other group; traitor. *noun.*

re new (ri nü′ *or* ri nyü′), **1** make new again; make like new; restore: *Rain renews the greenness of the field.* **2** begin again; say, do, or give again: *She renewed her efforts to fix the broken bicycle.* **3** replace by new material or a new thing of the same sort; fill again: *to renew a prescription. The well renews itself no matter how much water is taken away.* **4** give or get for a new period: *We renewed the lease for another year. verb.*

re new al (ri nü′əl *or* ri nyü′əl), renewing or being renewed: *When hot weather comes there will be a renewal of interest in swimming. noun.*

re nounce (ri nouns′), **1** give up; give up entirely; declare that one gives up: *He renounces his claim to the money.* **2** cast off; refuse to recognize as one's own: *The people renounced the dictator. verb,* **re nounced, re nounc ing.**

ren o vate (ren′ə vāt), make like new; restore to good condition. See picture. *verb,* **ren o vat ed, ren o vat ing.**

re nown (ri noun′), fame: *A doctor who finds a cure for a disease wins renown. noun.*

re nowned (ri nound′), famous. *adjective.*

rent[1] (rent), **1** a regular payment for the use of property. **2** pay for the use of (property): *We rent a house from them.* **3** receive regular pay for the use of (property): *They rent several other houses.* **4** be rented: *This farm rents for $1500 a year.* 1 *noun*, 2-4 *verb.*

for rent, that can be had in return for rent paid: *That vacant apartment is for rent.*

rent[2] (rent), **1** a torn place; tear; split: *There is a rent in your pants.* **2** torn; split. **3** See **rend.** *The tree was rent by the wind.* 1 *noun*, 2 *adjective*, 3 *verb.*

rent al (ren′tl), amount received or paid as rent: *The yearly rental of her house is $2400. noun.*

re o pen (rē ō′pən), **1** open again: *School will reopen in September.* **2** discuss again or further: *The matter is settled and cannot be reopened. verb.*

re or gan ize (rē ôr′gə nīz), organize anew; form again; arrange in a new way: *Classes will be reorganized after the first four weeks. verb,* **re or gan ized, re or gan iz ing.**

re paid (ri pād′). See **repay.** *I repaid the money I had borrowed. All debts should be repaid. verb.*

re pair (ri per′ or ri par′), **1** put in good condition again; mend: *He repairs shoes.* **2** act or work of repairing: *Repairs on the school building are made during the summer.* **3** condition fit to be used: *The state keeps the roads in repair.* **4** condition for use: *The house was in very bad repair.* **5** make up for: *How can I repair the harm done?* 1,5 *verb*, 2-4 *noun*

re pair man (ri per′man′ or ri par′man′), person whose work is repairing machines. *noun, plural* **re pair men.**

rep a ra tion (rep′ə rā′shən), compensation for wrong or injury done: *France demanded reparations from Germany after World War I. noun.*

re past (ri past′), meal; food: *Breakfast at our house is a light repast. noun.*

re pay (ri pā′), **1** pay back; give back: *She repaid the money she had borrowed.* **2** make return for: *No thanks can repay such kindness.* **3** make return to: *The boy's success repaid the teacher for her efforts. verb,* **re paid, re pay ing.**

re peal (ri pēl′), **1** take back; withdraw; do away with: *The law was finally repealed.* **2** act of repealing; withdrawal; abolition: *He voted for the repeal of that law.* 1 *verb*, 2 *noun.*

re peat (ri pēt′), **1** do or make again: *repeat an error.* **2** say again: *repeat a word for emphasis.* **3** say over; recite: *She can repeat many poems from memory.* **4** say after another says: *Repeat the pledge to the flag after me.* **5** tell to another or others: *I promised not to repeat the secret.* **6** repeating: *a repeat of a previous performance.* **7** thing repeated: *a television repeat.* 1-5 *verb*, 6,7 *noun.*

re peat ed (ri pē′tid), said, done, or made more than once: *Her repeated efforts at last won success. adjective.*

re pel (ri pel′), **1** force back; drive back; drive away: *They repelled the enemy. We can repel bad thoughts.* **2** force apart or away by some inherent force: *The positive poles of two magnets repel each other.* **3** be displeasing to; cause dislike in: *Spiders and worms repel me. verb,* **re pelled, re pel ling.**

re pent (ri pent′), **1** feel sorry for doing wrong and seek forgiveness: *The thief repented.* **2** feel sorry for; regret: *They bought a white rug and repented their choice. verb.*

re pent ance (ri pen′təns), sorrow for doing wrong; regret. *noun.*

re pent ant (ri pen′tənt), repenting; feeling regret; sorry for doing wrong. *adjective.*

rep e ti tion (rep′ə tish′ən), **1** repeating; doing again; saying again: *Repetition helps learning. Any repetition of the offense will be punished.* **2** a repeated occurrence; thing repeated. *noun.*

re place (ri plās′), **1** fill or take the place of: *A substitute replaced our teacher.* **2** get another in place of: *I will replace the cup I broke.* **3** put back; put in place again: *Replace the books on the shelves. verb,* **re placed, re plac ing.**

re place ment (ri plās′mənt), **1** replacing or being replaced: *The law required the replacement of all wooden freight cars by steel cars.* **2** something or someone that replaces. *noun.*

represent (definition 1)—The 50 stars in our flag represent the 50 states.

repose (definition 1)—Do not disturb his repose.

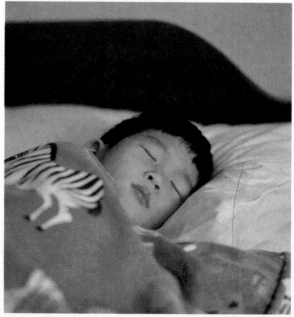

re plen ish (ri plen′ish), fill again; provide a new supply for: *replenish a food supply. You had better replenish the fire. verb.*

rep li ca (rep′lə kə), copy; reproduction: *The young artist made a replica of the famous painting. noun.*

re ply (ri plī′), **1** answer by words or action: *He replied with a shout. The enemy replied to the attack with heavy gun fire.* **2** act of replying: *I didn't hear your reply to the question.* **1** *verb,* **re plied, re ply ing; 2** *noun, plural* **re plies.**

re port (ri pôrt′), **1** account of something seen, heard, or read about. **2** anything formally expressed, generally in writing: *a school report.* **3** give or bring an account of; make a report of; state formally: *Our treasurer reports that all dues are paid up.* **4** repeat (what one has heard or seen); bring back an account of; describe; tell: *The radio reports the news and weather. The divers reported the treasures they had found in the sunken ship.* **5** present oneself: *Report for work at eight o'clock.* **6** sound of a shot or an explosion: *the report of a gun.* **1,2,6** *noun,* **3-5** *verb.*

report card, a report sent regularly by a school to parents or guardians, giving information on a student's work and behavior.

re port er (ri pôr′tər), **1** person who reports. **2** person who gathers news for a newspaper, magazine, or radio or television station. *noun.*

re pose (ri pōz′), **1** rest; sleep. See picture. **2** lie at rest: *The cat reposed upon the cushion.* **3** lay to rest: *Repose yourself in the hammock.* **4** quietness; ease: *She has repose of manner.* **1,4** *noun,* **2,3** *verb,* **re posed, re pos ing.**

rep re sent (rep′ri zent′), **1** stand for; be a sign or symbol of. See picture. **2** act in place of; speak and act for: *We chose a committee to represent us.* **3** act the part of: *Each child will represent an animal at the party.* **4** describe; set forth: *He represented the plan as safe, but it was not.* **5** show in a picture; give a likeness of; portray: *This painting represents the signing of the Declaration of Independence. verb.*

rep re sen ta tion (rep′ri zen tā′shən), **1** act of representing. **2** condition or fact of being represented: *"Taxation without representation is tyranny."* **3** likeness; picture; model. *noun.*

rep re sent a tive (rep′ri zen′tə tiv), **1** person appointed or elected to act or speak for others: *He is the club's representative at the convention.* **2** having its citizens represented by chosen persons: *a representative government.* **3** representing: *Images representative of animals were made by the children out of clay.* **4** example; type: *The tiger is a common representative of the cat family.* **5** serving as an example of; typical: *Oak and maple are representative American hardwoods.* **1,4** *noun,* **2,3,5** *adjective.*

re press (ri pres′), **1** prevent from acting; check: *She repressed an impulse to cough.* **2** keep down; put down; suppress: *The government repressed a revolt. verb.*

re pres sion (ri presh′ən), **1** repressing: *The repression of a laugh made him choke.* **2** being

a hat	i it	oi oil	ch child		a in about
ā age	ī ice	ou out	ng long		e in taken
ä far	o hot	u cup	sh she	ə =	i in pencil
e let	ō open	u̇ put	th thin		o in lemon
ē equal	ô order	ü rule	ᵀᴴ then		u in circus
ėr term			zh measure		

repressed: *Repression made the people revolt against the government. noun.*

re proach (ri prōch′), **1** blame: *Their conduct was above reproach.* **2** to blame; censure: *They reproached me for being late.* **3** a cause of blame or disgrace: *That run-down building is a reproach to the owners.* **4** words of blame. **1,3,4** *noun, plural* **re proach es; 2** *verb.*

re proach ful (ri prōch′fəl), full of reproach; expressing reproach. *adjective.*

re pro duce (rē′prə düs′ *or* rē′prə dyüs′), **1** produce again: *The painting was destroyed and could never be reproduced.* **2** make a copy of: *Can you reproduce my handwriting?* **3** produce offspring: *Most plants reproduce by seeds. verb,* **re pro duced, re pro duc ing.**

re pro duc tion (rē′prə duk′shən), **1** reproducing; being reproduced: *the reproduction of sounds.* **2** a copy: *the reproduction of a famous painting.* **3** process by which animals and plants produce individuals like themselves. *noun.*

re proof (ri prüf′), words of blame or disapproval; blame. *noun.*

re prove (ri prüv′), find fault with; blame: *I reproved the children for teasing the cat. verb,* **re proved, re prov ing.**

rep tile (rep′təl), one of a group of cold-blooded animals that have a backbone and are usually covered with scales. Reptiles creep or crawl. Snakes, lizards, turtles, alligators, and crocodiles are reptiles. *noun.*

re pub lic (ri pub′lik), nation or state in which the citizens elect representatives to manage the government, which is usually headed by a president. The United States and Mexico are republics. *noun.* [*Republic* comes from Latin words meaning "public thing," that is, something that belongs to the public or the people.]

re pub li can (ri pub′lə kən), **1** of a republic; like that of a republic: *Many countries have a republican form of government.* **2** person who favors a republic: *The republicans fought to overthrow the king.* **3 Republican, a** of the Republican Party. **b** member of the Republican Party. **1,3a** *adjective,* **2,3b** *noun.*

Republican Party, one of the two main political parties in the United States.

re pu di ate (ri pyü′dē āt), **1** refuse to accept; reject: *repudiate a rumor.* **2** refuse to acknowledge or pay: *repudiate a debt.* **3** cast off; disown: *repudiate a son. verb,* **re pu di at ed, re pu di at ing.**

re pulse (ri puls′), **1** drive back; repel: *Our soldiers repulsed the enemy.* **2** driving back; being driven back: *After the second repulse, the enemy surrendered.* **3** refuse to accept; reject: *She coldly* *repulsed him.* **4** refusal; rejection: *Her repulse was quite unexpected.* 1,3 *verb,* **re pulsed, re puls ing;** 2,4 *noun.*

re pul sive (ri pul′siv), causing disgust or strong dislike: *Snakes are repulsive to some people.* *adjective.*

rep u ta ble (rep′yə tə bəl), having a good reputation; well thought of: *a reputable citizen.* *adjective.*

rep u ta tion (rep′yə tā′shən), **1** what people think and say the character of a person or thing is; character in the opinion of others; name; repute: *This store has an excellent reputation for fair dealing.* **2** good name; good reputation: *Cheating at the game ruined that player's reputation. noun.*

re pute (ri pyüt′), **1** reputation: *This is a district of bad repute because there are so many robberies here.* **2** consider; suppose; suppose to be: *He is reputed the richest man in the city.* 1 *noun,* 2 *verb,* **re put ed, re put ing.**

re quest (ri kwest′), **1** ask for; ask as a favor: *She requested a loan from the bank.* **2** ask: *He requested her to go with him.* **3** act of asking: *Your request for a ticket was made too late.* **4** what is asked for: *She granted my request.* 1,2 *verb,* 3,4 *noun.*

re quire (ri kwīr′), **1** need: *We require more spoons for our party.* **2** demand; order; command: *The rules required us all to be present. verb,* **re quired, re quir ing.**

re quire ment (ri kwīr′mənt), **1** need; thing needed: *Patience is a requirement in teaching.* **2** demand; thing demanded: *to fulfill the requirements for graduation. noun.*

req ui si tion (rek′wə zish′ən), **1** act of requiring. **2** demand made, especially a formal written demand: *The principal signed a requisition for new books.* **3** demand or take by authority: *requisition supplies.* 1,2 *noun,* 3 *verb.*

re read (rē rēd′), read again: *reread a good book. verb,* **re read** (rē red′), **re read ing.**

res cue (res′kyü), **1** save from danger, capture, or harm; free; deliver: *to rescue someone from drowning.* **2** saving or freeing from harm or danger: *The fireman was praised for his brave rescue of the children in the burning house. A dog was chasing our cat when your sister came to the rescue.* 1 *verb,* **res cued, res cu ing;** 2 *noun.*

res cu er (res′kyü ər), one that rescues. *noun.*

re search (ri sėrch′ *or* rē′sėrch′), a careful hunting for facts or truth; inquiry; investigation: *Medical research has done much to lessen disease. noun, plural* **re search es.**

re sem blance (ri zem′bləns), likeness; similar appearance: *Twins often show great resemblance. noun.*

re sem ble (ri zem′bəl), be like; have likeness to in form, figure, or qualities. See picture. *verb,* **re sem bled, re sem bling.**

re sent (ri zent′), feel injured and angry at; feel indignation at: *Our cat seems to resent having anyone sit in its chair. verb.*

re sent ful (ri zent′fəl), feeling resentment; injured and angry; showing resentment. *adjective.*

re sent ment (ri zent′mənt), the feeling that one has at being injured or insulted; indignation: *Everyone feels resentment at being treated unfairly. noun.*

res er va tion (rez′ər vā′shən), **1** keeping back; hiding in part; something not expressed: *I did not mention it, but I had reservations about staying out so late.* **2** a limiting condition: *The United States accepted the plan with reservations plainly stated.* **3** land set aside for a special purpose. The government has set apart Indian reservations. **4** arrangement to keep a thing for a person; securing of lodging or seating in advance: *Please make reservations for rooms at a hotel in Portland and seats at the theater that night. noun.*

re serve (ri zėrv′), **1** keep back; hold back: *Mother reserved judgment until she had heard both sides of the argument.* **2** set apart: *He reserves his evenings to spend them with his family.* **3** save for use later: *Reserve enough money for your fare home.* **4** something kept back for future use; store: *a reserve of food or energy. Banks must keep a reserve of money.* **5 reserves,** soldiers kept ready to help in battle: *Reserves will be sent to help the soldiers fighting at the front.* **6** public land set apart for a special purpose: *a forest reserve.* **7** keeping back; holding back; reservation: *You may speak before her without reserve.* **8** self-restraint in action or speech. **9** a silent manner that keeps people from making friends easily. 1-3 *verb,* **re served, re serv ing;** 4-9 *noun.*

re served (ri zėrvd′), **1** kept in reserve; kept by special arrangement. **2** set apart. **3** having or showing self-restraint. **4** inclined to keep to oneself: *A reserved person does not make friends easily. adjective.*

res er voir (rez′ər vwär), **1** place where water is collected and stored for use. See picture. **2** anything to hold a liquid: *A fountain pen has an ink reservoir.* **3** place where anything is collected and stored: *His mind was a reservoir of facts.* **4** a great supply: *a reservoir of weapons. noun.*

re side (ri zīd′), **1** live (in or at a place) for a long time; dwell: *This family has resided in our town for 100 years.* **2** be; exist: *The power to declare war resides in Congress. verb,* **re sid ed, re sid ing.**

res i dence (rez′ə dəns), **1** house or home; the place where a person lives: *The President's residence is the White House in Washington, D.C.* **2** residing; living; dwelling: *Long residence in France made them very fond of the French.* **3** period of residing in a place: *They spent a residence of ten years in France. noun.*

res i dent (rez′ə dənt), **1** person living in a place, not a visitor: *The residents of the town are proud of its new library.* **2** staying; dwelling in a place: *Resident owners live on their property.* **3** living in a place while on duty: *That doctor is a resident physician at the hospital.* 1 *noun,* 2,3 *adjective.*

res i den tial (rez′ə den′shəl), of or having something to do with homes; suitable for homes or residences: *They live in a large residential district outside the city. adjective.*

res i due (rez′ə dü *or* rez′ə dyü), what remains after a part is taken; remainder: *The syrup had dried up, leaving a sticky residue. Her will directed that after payment of all debts, the residue of her property should go to her children.* noun.

re sign (ri zīn′), give up a job, office, or position: *The editor resigned her position on the school paper.* verb.

resign oneself, submit quietly; yield: *He had to resign himself to a week in bed when he hurt his back.*

res ig na tion (rez′ig nā′shən), **1** act of resigning: *There have been so many resignations from the committee that a new one must be formed.* **2** a written statement giving notice that one resigns. **3** patient acceptance; quiet submission: *He bore the pain with resignation.* noun.

re signed (ri zīnd′), accepting what comes without complaint. adjective.

res in (rez′n), a sticky substance that flows from some trees. Resin is used in medicine and in varnishes. When pine resin is heated it yields turpentine; the hard, yellow substance that remains is called rosin. noun.

re sist (ri zist′), **1** act against; strive against; oppose: *The window resisted his efforts to open it.* **2** strive successfully against; keep from; withstand: *I could not resist laughing.* **3** withstand the action or effect of: *A healthy body resists disease.* verb.

re sist ance (ri zis′təns), **1** act of resisting: *The bank clerk made no resistance to the robbers.* **2** power to resist: *Some people have very little resistance to colds.* **3** opposition; opposing force; thing or act that resists: *An airplane can overcome the resistance of the air and go in the desired direction, but an ordinary balloon just drifts.* noun.

re sist ant (ri zis′tənt), resisting. adjective.

res o lute (rez′ə lüt), determined; firm: *She was resolute in her attempt to climb to the top of the mountain. The captain's resolute words cheered the team.* adjective.

res o lu tion (rez′ə lü′shən), **1** thing decided on; thing determined: *He made a resolution to get up early.* **2** power of holding firmly to a purpose; determination: *The pioneers' resolution overcame their hardships.* **3** a formal expression of opinion: *The club passed a resolution thanking the teacher for her help.* noun.

re solve (ri zolv′), **1** make up one's mind; determine; decide: *I resolved to do better work in the future.* **2** thing determined on; thing decided: *He kept his resolve to do better.* **3** firmness in carrying out a purpose; determination: *Helen Keller was a woman of great resolve.* **4** decide by vote: *It was resolved that our class should have a picnic.* **5** answer and explain; solve: *Their letter resolved all our doubts.* 1,4,5 *verb,* **re solved, re solv ing;** 2,3 *noun.*

re solved (ri zolvd′), determined; firm; resolute. adjective.

res o nant (rez′n ənt), **1** resounding; continuing to sound. **2** tending to increase sounds or to make them last longer. adjective.

resemble—The domes on this building **resemble** onions.

reservoir (definition 1)

re sort (ri zôrt′), **1** go; go often: *Many people resort to the beaches in hot weather.* **2** place people go to, usually for recreation: *There are many summer resorts in the mountains.* **3** turn for help: *The parents resorted to punishment to make the child obey.* **4** act of turning for help: *The resort to force is forbidden in this school.* **5** person or thing turned to for help: *Friends are the best resort in trouble.* 1,3 *verb,* 2,4,5 *noun.*

re sound (ri zound′), **1** give back sound; echo: *The hills resounded when we shouted.* **2** sound loudly: *Radios resound from every house.* **3** be filled with sound: *The room resounded with the children's shouts.* **4** be much talked about: *The fame of the first flight across the Atlantic resounded all over the world. verb.*

re source (ri sôrs′ *or* rē′sôrs), **1** any supply that will meet a need. We have resources of money, of knowledge, and of strength. **2 resources,** the actual and possible wealth of a country: *natural resources, human resources.* **3** any means of getting success or getting out of trouble: *Climbing a tree is a cat's resource when chased by a dog.* **4** skill in meeting difficulties or getting out of trouble. *noun.*

re source ful (ri sôrs′fəl), good at thinking of ways to do things. See picture. *adjective.*

re spect (ri spekt′), **1** honor; esteem: *The children always showed great respect for their grandparents.* **2** feel or show honor or esteem for: *We respect an honest person.* **3** care; consideration: *We should show respect for school buildings, parks, and other public property.* **4** care for; show consideration for: *Respect the ideas and feelings of others.* **5 respects,** expressions of respect; regards: *Give them my respects. We must pay our respects to the governor.* **6** feature; point; matter; detail: *The plan is unwise in many respects.* **7** relation; reference: *We must plan with respect to the future.* 1,3,5-7 *noun,* 2,4 *verb.*

re spect a ble (ri spek′tə bəl), **1** worthy of respect; having a good reputation: *They are very respectable people.* **2** fairly good; moderate in size or quality: *His record in school was always respectable, but never brilliant.* **3** good enough to use; fit to be seen: *respectable clothes. adjective.*

re spect ful (ri spekt′fəl), showing respect; polite: *I always try to be respectful to older people. adjective.*

re spect ing (ri spek′ting), regarding; about; concerning: *A discussion arose respecting the merits of different automobiles. preposition.*

re spec tive (ri spek′tiv), belonging to each; particular; individual: *The classes went to their respective rooms. adjective.*

re spec tive ly (ri spek′tiv lē), as regards each of several persons or things in turn or in the order mentioned: *Pat, José, and Kathy are 6, 8, and 10 years old, respectively. adverb.*

res pi ra tion (res′pə rā′shən), breathing: *A bad cold can make respiration difficult. noun.*

res pir a to ry (res′pər ə tôr′ē), having something to do with breathing. The lungs are respiratory organs. *adjective.*

resourceful—The **resourceful** children raked leaves to earn money.

resplendent
He was **resplendent** in his costume.

res pite (res′pit), time of relief and rest; lull: *A thick cloud brought a respite from the glare of the sun. noun.*

re splend ent (ri splen′dənt), very bright; shining; splendid: *a face resplendent with joy.* See picture. *adjective.*

re spond (ri spond′), 1 answer; reply: *He responded briefly to the question.* 2 act in answer; react: *A dog responds to kind treatment by loving its owner. She responded quickly to the medicine and was well in a few days. verb.*

re sponse (ri spons′), answer by word or act: *Her response to my letter was prompt. She laughed in response to his joke. noun.*

re spon si bil i ty (ri spon′sə bil′ə tē), 1 being responsible; sense of duty: *A little child does not feel much responsibility.* 2 thing for which one is responsible: *Keeping my room clean and feeding the cat are my responsibilities. noun, plural* **re spon si bil i ties.**

re spon si ble (ri spon′sə bəl), 1 obliged or expected to account for; accountable; answerable: *You are responsible for the care of your schoolbooks.* 2 deserving credit or blame: *Rain was responsible for the small attendance.* 3 trustworthy; reliable: *The class chose a responsible pupil to take care of its money.* 4 involving obligation or duties: *The President holds a very responsible position. adjective.*

re spon sive (ri spon′siv), 1 making answer; responding: *a responsive glance.* 2 easily moved; responding readily: *a very friendly person with a responsive nature. adjective.*

rest[1] (rest), 1 sleep: *The children had a good night's rest.* 2 be still or quiet; sleep: *Lie down and rest.* 3 ease after work or effort: *I left the swimming pool for a short rest.* 4 quiet; freedom from anything that tires, troubles, disturbs, or pains: *The medicine gave the patient some rest from pain.* 5 be free from work, effort, care, or trouble: *Teachers can rest during summer vacation.* 6 absence of motion; stillness: *The driver brought the car to a rest. The lake was at rest.* 7 give rest to; refresh by rest: *Stop and rest your horse.* 8 be supported; lean; lie: *The ladder rested against the wall. The roof of the porch rests on columns.* 9 place for support; lay: *rest one's head in one's hands. I rested the rake against the fence.* 10 support; something to lean on. 11 look; be fixed: *Our eyes rested on the open book.* 12 be at ease: *Don't let her rest until she promises to visit us.* 13 depend; rely; trust; be based: *Our hope rests on you.* 14 be found; be present; lie: *In a democracy, government rests with the people. The blame rested on all of them.* 15 (in music) a pause. 16 mark to show such a pause. 17 be dead; lie in the grave: *The old man rests with his ancestors in the old village cemetery.* 1,3,4,6,10,15,16 *noun,* 2,5,7-9,11-14,17 *verb.*

rest[2] (rest), 1 what is left; those that are left: *The sun was out in the morning but it rained for the rest of the day. One horse was running ahead of the rest.* 2 continue to be; remain: *We can offer suggestions, but the final decision rests with you.* 1 *noun,* 2 *verb.*

a hat	i it	oi oil	ch child	a in about
ā age	ī ice	ou out	ng long	e in taken
ä far	o hot	u cup	sh she	ə = { i in pencil
e let	ō open	u̇ put	th thin	o in lemon
ē equal	ô order	ü rule	ŦH then	u in circus
ėr term			zh measure	

res taur ant (res′tər ənt), place to buy and eat a meal. *noun.*

rest ful (rest′fəl), 1 full of rest; giving rest: *She had a restful nap.* 2 quiet; peaceful. *adjective.*

rest less (rest′lis), 1 unable to rest; uneasy: *The dog seemed restless, as if it sensed some danger.* 2 without rest or sleep; not restful: *The sick child passed a restless night.* 3 rarely or never still or quiet; always moving: *Some nervous people are very restless. adjective.*

res to ra tion (res′tə rā′shən), 1 restoring or being restored; bringing back to a former condition: *the restoration of health, the restoration of a king.* 2 something restored: *The house we slept in was a restoration of a colonial mansion. noun.*

re store (ri stôr′), 1 bring back; establish again: *The police restored order.* 2 bring back to a former condition or to a normal condition: *The old house has been restored. He is restored to health.* 3 give back; put back: *She restored the money she had found to its owner. verb,* **re stored, re stor ing.**

re strain (ri strān′), hold back; keep down; keep in check; keep within limits: *I could not restrain my curiosity to see what was in the box. We restrained the excited dog when guests came. verb.*

re straint (ri strānt′), 1 restraining or being restrained: *Noisy people sometimes need restraint.* 2 means of restraining. 3 tendency to restrain natural feeling; reserve: *He was very angry, but he spoke with restraint. noun.*

re strict (ri strikt′), keep within limits; confine: *Our club membership is restricted to twelve. verb.*

re stric tion (ri strik′shən), 1 something that restricts; limiting condition or rule: *The restrictions on the use of the playground are: No fighting; no damaging property.* 2 restricting or being restricted: *This park is open to the public without restriction. noun.*

rest room, washroom or bathroom in a public building.

re sult (ri zult′), 1 that which happens because of something; what is caused: *The result of the fall was a broken leg.* 2 a good or useful effect: *The new medicine got results.* 3 be a result; follow as a consequence: *Sickness often results from eating too much.* 4 have as a result; end: *Eating too much often results in sickness.* 1,2 *noun,* 3,4 *verb.*

re sume (ri züm′), 1 begin again; go on: *Resume reading where we left off.* 2 take again: *Those standing may resume their seats. verb,* **re sumed, re sum ing.**

re sump tion (ri zump′shən), resuming: *the resumption of duties after absence. noun.*

res ur rect (rez′ə rekt′), 1 raise from the dead; bring back to life. 2 bring back to sight or into use: *resurrect an old custom. verb.*

res ur rec tion (rez/ə rek/shən), **1** coming to life again; rising from the dead. **2 Resurrection,** the rising again of Christ after His death and burial. **3** coming back to sight or into use: *the resurrection of an old custom. noun.*

re tail (rē/tāl), **1** sale of goods in small quantities directly to the user: *Our grocer buys at wholesale and sells at retail.* **2** in small lots or quantities: *The wholesale price of this coat is $30; the retail price is $40.* **3** selling in small quantities: *a retail merchant, the retail trade.* **4** sell in small quantities. **1** *noun,* **2,3** *adjective,* **4** *verb.*

re tail er (rē/tā lər), a retail merchant or dealer. *noun.*

re tain (ri tān/), **1** continue to have or hold; keep: *A china teapot retains heat for quite a long time. Our baseball team retained a lead throughout the game.* **2** keep in mind; remember: *She retained the tune but not the words of the song.* **3** employ by payment of a fee: *I retained the best lawyer in the state. verb.*

re tal i ate (ri tal/ē āt), pay back a wrong or injury; return like for like, usually to return evil for evil: *If we insult them, they will retaliate. verb,* **re tal i at ed, re tal i at ing.**

re tal i a tion (ri tal/ē ā/shən), a paying back of a wrong or injury; return of evil for evil. *noun.*

re tard (ri tärd/), make slow; delay the progress of; keep back; hinder: *Lack of education retards progress. Bad roads retarded the car. verb.*

ret i na (ret/n ə), layer of cells at the back of the eyeball that is sensitive to light and receives the images of things looked at. *noun.*

re tire (ri tīr/), **1** give up an office or occupation: *Our teachers retire at 65.* **2** remove from an office or occupation. **3** go away, especially to a place which is more quiet or private: *They retired to the country.* **4** withdraw; draw back; send back: *The government retires worn or torn dollar bills from use.* **5** go back; retreat: *The enemy retired before the advance of our troops.* **6** go to bed: *We retire early. verb,* **re tired, re tir ing.**

re tired (ri tīrd/), **1** withdrawn from one's occupation: *a retired teacher.* **2** secluded; shut off; hidden: *a retired spot. adjective.*

re tire ment (ri tīr/mənt), **1** retiring or being retired; withdrawal: *The teacher's retirement from teaching was regretted by the school.* **2** a quiet way or place of living: *The artist lived in retirement, away from city life. noun.*

re tir ing (ri tī/ring), shrinking from society or publicity; shy: *Our neighbor is a quiet, retiring person. adjective.*

re tort (ri tôrt/), **1** reply quickly or sharply: *"It's none of your business," he retorted.* **2** a sharp or witty reply: *"Why are your teeth so sharp?" asked Red Ridinghood. "The better to eat you with," was the wolf's retort.* **1** *verb,* **2** *noun.*

re trace (ri trās/), go back over: *We retraced our steps to where we started. verb,* **re traced, re trac ing.**

re tract (ri trakt/), **1** draw back or in: *The dog snarled and retracted its lips.* **2** withdraw; take back: *retract an offer, retract an opinion. verb.*

re treat (ri trēt/), **1** go back; move back; withdraw: *The enemy retreated before the advance of our soldiers.* **2** act of going back or withdrawing: *The army's retreat was orderly.* **3** signal for retreat: *The drums beat a retreat.* **4** a safe, quiet place; place of rest or refuge: *She went to her mountain retreat for the weekend.* **1** *verb,* **2-4** *noun.*

re trieve (ri trēv/), **1** get again; recover: *retrieve a lost pocketbook.* **2** bring back to a former or better condition; restore: *retrieve one's fortunes.* **3** make good; make amends for; repair: *retrieve a mistake, retrieve a loss.* **4** find and bring to a person: *Some dogs can be trained to retrieve game. verb,* **re trieved, re triev ing.**

re triev er (ri trē/vər), dog trained to find killed or wounded game and bring it to a hunter. See picture. *noun.*

re turn (ri tėrn/), **1** go back; come back: *Return home for your report card. My sister will return this summer.* **2** going back; coming back; happening again: *We look forward all winter to our return to the country. We wish you many happy returns of your birthday.* **3** bring back; give back; send back; put back; pay back: *Return that book to the library. I left a message for her to return my telephone call.* **4** bringing back; giving back; sending back; putting back; paying back: *Such bad behavior was a poor return for kindness.* **5** profit; amount received: *The returns from the sale were more than a hundred dollars.* **6** yield: *The concert returned about $50 over expenses.* **7** report; account: *The election returns are all in. I must make out my income-tax return.* **8** report or announce officially: *The jury returned a verdict of guilty.* **9** reply; answer: *"Not I," he returned crossly.* **10** having something to do with a return: *a return ticket to the point of starting.* **11** sent, given, or done in return: *a return game.* **1,3,6,8,9** *verb,* **2,4,5,7** *noun,* **10,11** *adjective.*

in return, as a return: *If you will loan me your skates now, I'll loan you my tennis racket next summer in return.*

re un ion (rē yü/nyən), coming together again: *We have a family reunion at Thanksgiving. noun.*

re u nite (rē/yü nīt/), bring together again; come together again. See picture. *verb,* **re u nit ed, re u nit ing.**

Rev., Reverend.

re veal (ri vēl/), **1** make known: *Promise never to reveal my secret.* **2** display; show: *His smile revealed his even white teeth. verb.*

rev eil le (rev/ə lē), signal on a bugle or drum to waken soldiers or sailors in the morning: *The bugler blew reveille. noun.* [Reveille is from a French word meaning "wake up!"]

rev el (rev/əl), **1** take great pleasure: *The children revel in country life.* **2** a noisy good time; merrymaking: *A parade and fireworks were planned for the Fourth of July revels.* **3** make merry. **1,3** *verb,* **rev eled, rev el ing; 2** *noun.*

rev e la tion (rev/ə lā/shən), **1** act of making known: *We all waited for the revelation of the winner's name.* **2** thing made known: *Her true nature was a revelation to me. noun.*

retriever—2 feet (60 centimeters) high at the shoulder

a hat	i it	oi oil	ch child	a in about
ā age	ī ice	ou out	ng long	e in taken
ä far	o hot	u cup	sh she	ə = i in pencil
e let	ō open	u̇ put	th thin	o in lemon
ē equal	ô order	ü rule	ᴛH then	u in circus
ėr term			zh measure	

reunite—The soldier was **reunited** with his family.

2 Reverend, title for clergymen: *The Reverend Thomas A. Johnson. adjective.*

rev er ent (rev′ər ənt), feeling reverence; showing reverence: *He gave reverent attention to the sermon. adjective.*

rev er ie (rev′ər ē), dreamy thoughts; dreamy thinking of pleasant things: *She was so lost in reverie that she did not hear the bell ring. He loved to indulge in reveries about his future. noun.*

re verse (ri vėrs′), **1** the opposite or contrary: *She did the reverse of what I suggested.* **2** turned backward; opposite or contrary in position or direction: *Play the reverse side of that phonograph record.* **3** the back: *His name is on the reverse of the medal.* **4** turn the other way; turn inside out; turn upside down: *Reverse your order in line.* **5** arrangement of gears that reverses the movement of machinery: *Drive the automobile in reverse until you get out of the garage.* **6** change to the opposite; repeal: *The higher court reversed the lower court's decision.* **7** a change to bad fortune; setback: *They used to be rich, but they met with reverses in their business.* 1,3,5,7 *noun,* 2 *adjective,* 4,6 *verb,* **re versed, re vers ing.**

re vert (ri vėrt′), go back; return: *My thoughts reverted to the last time that I had seen her. verb.*

re view (ri vyü′), **1** study again; look at again: *Review today's lesson for tomorrow.* **2** studying again: *Before the examinations we have a review of the term's work.* **3** look back on: *Before falling asleep, she reviewed the day's happenings.* **4** looking back on; survey: *A review of the trip was pleasant.* **5** look at with care; examine: *A superior court may review decisions of a lower court.* **6** examination; inspection: *A review of the troops will be held during the general's visit to the camp.* **7** inspect formally: *The admiral reviewed the fleet.* **8** account of a book, play, concert, or any public performance, giving its merits and faults: *Reviews of new books, motion pictures, and plays appear in the newspapers.* 1,3,5,7 *verb,* 2,4,6,8 *noun.*

re vile (ri vīl′), call bad names; abuse with words: *The pedestrian reviled the reckless driver. verb,* **re viled, re vil ing.**

re vise (ri vīz′), **1** read carefully in order to correct; look over and change; examine and improve: *She has revised the long story she wrote to make it shorter.* **2** change; alter: *I revised my opinion of the plan. verb,* **re vised, re vis ing.**

re viv al (ri vī′vəl), **1** bringing or coming back to life or consciousness. **2** being restored to vigor or health. **3** bringing or coming back to style or use: *Most Western movies on television are a revival of the motion pictures of years ago.* **4** special services or efforts made to awaken or increase interest in religion. *noun.*

re venge (ri venj′), **1** harm done in return for a wrong; vengeance; returning evil for evil. **2** desire for vengeance. **3** do harm in return for: *I will revenge that insult.* 1,2 *noun,* 3 *verb,* **re venged, re veng ing.**
be revenged or **revenge oneself,** get revenge.

rev e nue (rev′ə nü or rev′ə nyü), money coming in; income: *The government got much revenue from taxes last year. noun.*

re ver be rate (ri vėr′bə rāt′), echo back: *The deep, rumbling sound of the organ reverberated in the huge church. verb,* **re ver be rat ed, re ver be rat ing.**

re vere (ri vir′), love and respect deeply; honor greatly; show reverence for: *We revere sacred things. People revered the great saint. verb,* **re vered, re ver ing.**

rev er ence (rev′ər əns), feeling of deep respect, mixed with wonder, fear, and love. *noun.*

rev er end (rev′ər ənd), **1** worthy of great respect.

rhea—about 5 ft. (1½ meters) tall

rib (definition 2)—The curved pieces of wood on the canoe are ribs.

rhinoceros—5½ feet (1½ meters) high at the shoulder

re vive (ri vīv′), **1** bring back or come back to life or consciousness: *The lifeguard revived the half-drowned swimmer.* **2** come back to a fresh, lively condition: *Flowers revive in water.* **3** restore; make or become fresh: *Hot cocoa revived us after a long, cold walk.* **4** bring back or come back to notice, use, fashion, memory, or activity: *An old play is sometimes revived on the stage. verb,* **re vived, re viv ing.**

re voke (ri vōk′), take back; repeal; cancel; withdraw: *revoke a driver's license. verb,* **re voked, re vok ing.**

re volt (ri vōlt′), **1** act or state of rebelling: *The town is in revolt.* **2** turn away from and fight against a leader; rise against the government's authority: *The people revolted against the dictator.* **3** turn away with disgust: *revolt at a bad smell.* **4** cause to feel disgust: *Senseless cruelty revolts me.* **1** *noun,* **2-4** *verb.*

rev o lu tion (rev′ə lü′shən), **1** a complete change in government: *The era of the American Revolution, from 1763 to 1783, ended with the war which gave independence to the colonies.* **2** a complete change: *The automobile caused a revolution in ways of traveling.* **3** movement around some point in a circle or curve: *One revolution of the earth around the sun takes a year.* **4** act or fact of turning around a center: *The wheel of the motor turns at a rate of more than one thousand revolutions a minute. noun.*

rev o lu tion ar y (rev′ə lü′shə ner′ē), **1** of a revolution; connected with a revolution. **2** bringing or causing great changes: *Radio and television were two revolutionary inventions of this century. adjective.*

Revolutionary War, the war fought by the American colonies from 1775 to 1783 to gain their independence from England.

rev o lu tion ize (rev′ə lü′shə nīz), change completely; produce a very great change in: *The automobile, radio, and television have revolutionized country life. verb,* **rev o lu tion ized, rev o lu tion iz ing.**

re volve (ri volv′), **1** move in a circle; move in a curve round a point: *The moon revolves around the earth.* **2** turn round a center: *The wheels of a moving car revolve. verb,* **re volved, re volv ing.**

re volv er (ri vol′vər), pistol that can be fired several times without being loaded again. *noun.*

re ward (ri wôrd′), **1** return made for something done. **2** money payment given or offered. Rewards are given for the capture of criminals and the return of lost property. **3** give a reward to. **4** give a reward for. **1,2** *noun,* **3,4** *verb.*

re word (rē wėrd′), put in other words. *verb.*

re write (rē rīt′), write again; write in a different form. *verb,* **re wrote** (rē rōt′), **re writ ten** (rē rit′n), **re writ ing.**

R.F.D., Rural Free Delivery.

rhe a (rē′ə), a large bird of South America that is much like the ostrich but smaller and has three toes instead of two. See picture. *noun.*

rheu mat ic fe ver (rü mat′ik fē′vər), a disease most often of children that causes fever, pain in the joints, and often damage to the heart.

rheu ma tism (rü′mə tiz′əm), disease that causes soreness, swelling, and stiffness of the joints or muscles. *noun.*

rhi noc er os (rī nos′ər əs), a large, thick-skinned animal of Africa and Asia with hoofs and with one or two upright horns on the snout. Rhinoceroses eat grass and other plants. See picture. *noun, plural* **rhi noc er os es** or **rhi noc er os.** [*Rhinoceros* is from Greek words meaning "nose" and "horn."]

Rhode Is land (rōd′ ī′lənd), one of the northeastern states of the United States. [*Rhode Island* probably got its name from Rhodes, an island in the eastern Mediterranean Sea. The name was originally given to Aquidneck Island in Narragansett Bay because it was thought to be about the size of the island of Rhodes.]

rho do den dron (rō′də den′drən), an evergreen shrub with beautiful pink, purple, or white flowers. *noun.* [*Rhododendron* comes from Greek words meaning "rose tree."]

rhu barb (rü′bärb), the sour stalks of a garden plant having very large leaves. The stalks are used for making sauce or pies. *noun.*

rhyme (rīm), **1** sound alike in the last part: *"Long" and "song" rhyme. "Go to bed" rhymes with "sleepy head."* **2** a word or line having the same last sound as another: *"Cat" is a rhyme for "mat." "Hey! diddle, diddle" and "The cat and the fiddle" are rhymes.* **3** verses or poetry with a regular return of similar sounds. **4** agreement in the final sounds of words or lines. **5** make rhymes. **6** use a word with another that rhymes with it: *rhyme "love" and "dove."* 1,5,6 *verb,* **rhymed, rhym ing;** 2-4 *noun.* Also spelled **rime.**

rhythm (riⷮH′əm), movement with a regular repetition of a beat, accent, rise and fall, or the like: *the rhythm of dancing, the rhythm of music, the rhythm of the tides. noun.*

rhyth mic (riⷮH′mik), rhythmical: *the rhythmic beat of the heart. adjective.*

rhyth mi cal (riⷮH′mə kəl), having rhythm; of rhythm: *the rhythmical sound of the music. adjective.*

rib (rib), **1** one of the curved bones that go from the backbone around the heart and lungs to the front of the body. **2** something like a rib. The curved timbers in a ship's frame are called ribs. The thick vein of a leaf is also called a rib. An umbrella has ribs. See picture. *noun.*

rib bon (rib′ən), **1** strip or band of silk, satin, velvet, or other fine material. Bows for the hair, belts, and badges are often made of ribbon. **2** anything like such a strip: *a typewriter ribbon. Her dress was torn to ribbons by the thorns and briers she had come through. noun.*

rice (rīs), the grain of a kind of cereal grass, or the plant that it grows on. Rice is grown in warm climates and is an important food in India, China, and Japan. See picture. *noun.*

rich (rich), **1** having much money, land, goods, or other property: *Henry Ford and John D. Rockefeller were rich men.* **2 the rich,** rich people.

a hat	**i** it	**oi** oil	**ch** child	⎧ a in about
ā age	**ī** ice	**ou** out	**ng** long	e in taken
ä far	**o** hot	**u** cup	**sh** she	ə = ⎨ i in pencil
e let	**ō** open	**u̇** put	**th** thin	o in lemon
ē equal	**ô** order	**ü** rule	**ⷮH** then	⎩ u in circus
ėr term			**zh** measure	

3 abounding; well supplied: *a country rich in oil.* **4** fertile; producing much: *a rich soil, a rich mine.* **5** valuable; worthy: *a rich harvest, a rich suggestion.* **6** costly; elegant: *rich dresses, rich jewels, rich carpets.* **7** containing plenty of butter, eggs, and flavoring: *a rich fruit cake.* **8** deep; full: *a rich red, a rich tone.* 1,3-8 *adjective,* 2 *noun.*

rich es (rich′iz), wealth; abundance of property; much money, land, or goods. *noun plural.*

rick ets (rik′its), disease of childhood, caused by improper feeding and lack of sunshine. It results in softening, and sometimes bending, of the bones. *noun.*

rick et y (rik′ə tē), **1** weak; liable to fall or break down; shaky: *a rickety old chair.* **2** feeble in the joints. *adjective.*

ric o chet (rik′ə shā′), **1** the skipping or jumping motion of an object after it bounces or glances off a flat surface: *the ricochet of a stone thrown along the surface of water.* **2** move in this way: *The bullets struck the ground and ricocheted through the grass.* 1 *noun,* 2 *verb,* **ric o cheted** (rik′ə shād′), **ric o chet ing** (rik′ə shā′ing).

rid (rid), make free: *What will rid a house of mice? verb,* **rid** or **rid ded, rid ding.**

get rid of, 1 get free from: *I can't get rid of this cold.* **2** do away with: *Poison will get rid of the rats in the barn.*

rid den (rid′n). See **ride.** *I had ridden my horse all day. verb.*

rid dle[1] (rid′l), a puzzling question, statement, or problem. EXAMPLE: *When is a door not a door?* ANSWER: *When it is ajar. noun.*

rid dle[2] (rid′l), pierce with holes: *Insects had riddled the old tree stump. verb,* **rid dled, rid dling.**

rice—The woman is planting rice.

ride (rīd), **1** sit on a horse and make it go. **2** sit on something and make it go: *ride a camel, ride a bicycle.* **3** be carried along: *ride on a train, ride in a car.* **4** be carried on: *The eagle rides the wind.* **5** trip on horseback, in an automobile, on a train, or on any other thing that carries: *On Sundays we take a ride into the country.* See picture. **6** move or float on the water: *The ship rides at anchor in the harbor.* **7** carry; cause to ride: *She rode her little brother piggyback.* 1-4,6,7 *verb,* **rode, rid den, rid ing;** 5 *noun.*

rid er (rī′dər), person who rides: *The West is famous for its riders. noun.*

ridge (rij), **1** the long and narrow upper part of something: *the ridge of an animal's back.* **2** line where two sloping surfaces meet: *the ridge of a roof.* **3** a long, narrow chain of hills or mountains: *the Blue Ridge of the Appalachian Mountains.* **4** any raised narrow strip: *the ridges in plowed ground, the ridges on corduroy cloth. noun.*

ridge pole (rij′pōl′), the horizontal timber along the top of a roof or tent. *noun.*

rid i cule (rid′ə kyül), **1** laugh at; make fun of: *Many people ridiculed the Wright brothers' airplane.* **2** laughter in mockery; words or actions that make fun of somebody or something: *I was hurt by the ridicule of my classmates.* 1 *verb,* **rid i culed, rid i cul ing;** 2 *noun.*

ri dic u lous (ri dik′yə ləs), deserving ridicule; absurd; laughable: *It would be ridiculous to walk backward all the time. adjective.*

ri fle (rī′fəl), **1** gun with spiral grooves in its long barrel which spin or twist the bullet as it is shot. A rifle is usually fired from the shoulder. **2** search thoroughly and rob; steal. 1 *noun,* 2 *verb,* **ri fled, ri fling.**

ri fle man (rī′fəl mən), **1** soldier armed with a rifle. **2** person skilled in the use of the rifle. *noun, plural* **ri fle men.**

rift (rift), split; cleft; break; crack: *There's a rift in the clouds; perhaps the sun will come out soon. noun.*

rig (rig), **1** fit (a ship) with masts, sails, and ropes; fit out: *My sister and brother rigged a toy boat for me.* **2** arrangement of masts and sails on a ship. A schooner has a fore-and-aft rig; that is, the sails are set lengthwise on the ship. **3** outfit; equipment: *a camper's rig, an oil-drilling rig.* **4** fit out; equip: *rig out a football team with uniforms.* **5** to dress: *On Halloween the children rig themselves up in funny clothes.* **6** set of clothes; costume: *His rig consisted of a silk hat and overalls.* **7** put together in a hurry or by using odds and ends: *The girls rigged up a tent in the yard with a rope and a blanket.* **8** arrange in an unfair way: *The race was rigged.* 1,4,5,7,8 *verb,* **rigged, rig ging;** 2,3,6 *noun.*

rig ging (rig′ing), **1** ropes, chains, and cables used to support and work the masts and sails on a ship. **2** tackle; equipment: *Do you need all that rigging for a trip of only two days? noun.*

right (rīt), **1** good; just; lawful: *She did the right thing when she told the truth.* **2** in a way that is good, just, or lawful: *He acted right when he told the truth.* **3** that which is right, just, good, true: *Do right, not wrong.* **4** a just claim; something that is due to a person: *Each member of the club has a right to vote. I demanded my rights.* **5** correct; true: *the right answer.* **6** correctly; truly: *She guessed right.* **7** fitting; suitable; proper: *Learn to say the right thing at the right time.* **8** properly; well: *It's faster to do a job right the first time.* **9** well; healthy; in good condition: *I don't feel right; I think I'm getting the flu.* **10** meant to be seen; most important: *the right side of cloth.* **11** make correct; set right: *right a wrong.* **12** put right; get into the proper position: *The boys righted the boat. The ship righted after the big wave passed.* **13** opposite of left; belonging or having something to do with the side of anything that is turned east when the main side is turned north. You have a right hand and a left hand. Your right side is toward the east when you face north. Most people eat, write, and work with their right hands. **14** to the right hand: *turn right.* **15** the right-hand side: *Turn to your right.* **16** exactly: *Your cap is right where you left it.* **17** at once; immediately: *Stop playing right now.* **18** very: *the Right Honorable Lord Mayor.* **19** in a straight line; directly: *Look me right in the eye.* **20** completely: *My hat was knocked right off.* 1,5,7,9,10,13 *adjective,* 2,6,8,14,16-20 *adverb,* 3,4,15 *noun,* 11,12 *verb.*

by right or **by rights,** rightly; properly; correctly: *This book ought to be mine by right.*

right away, at once; immediately.

right angle, angle of 90 degrees. The angles in a square or in the capital letters F, L, and T are right angles. See picture.

right eous (rī′chəs), **1** doing right; virtuous; behaving justly: *a righteous person.* **2** proper; just; right: *righteous anger. adjective.*

right ful (rīt′fəl), **1** according to law; by right: *the rightful owner of this dog.* **2** just and right; proper: *I took my rightful place alongside the others. adjective.*

right-hand (rīt′hand′), **1** on the right. **2** of, for, or with the right hand. **3** most helpful or useful: *He is the scoutmaster's right-hand man. adjective.*

right-hand ed (rīt′han′did), using the right hand more easily and more readily than the left. *adjective.*

right ly (rīt′lē), **1** justly; fairly. **2** correctly: *She guessed rightly that it would rain.* **3** properly; in a suitable manner. *adverb.*

rig id (rij′id), **1** stiff; firm; not bending: *Hold your arm rigid.* **2** strict; not changing: *In our home, it is a rigid rule to wash one's hands before eating. adjective.*

rig or (rig′ər), strictness; severity: *the rigor of a long, cold winter. noun.*

rig or ous (rig′ər əs), **1** very severe; harsh; strict: *the rigorous discipline in the army.* **2** exact; thoroughly logical and scientific: *the rigorous methods of science. adjective.*

rill (ril), a tiny stream; little brook. *noun.*

rim (rim), **1** edge, border, or margin on or around anything: *the rim of a wheel, the rim of a cup.* **2** form a rim around: *Wild flowers and grasses rimmed the little pool.* 1 *noun,* 2 *verb,* **rimmed, rim ming.**

a hat	i it	oi oil	ch child	(a in about
ā age	ī ice	ou out	ng long	e in taken
ä far	o hot	u cup	sh she	ə = { i in pencil
e let	ō open	ù put	th thin	o in lemon
ē equal	ô order	ü rule	ŦH then	(u in circus
èr term			zh measure	

right angles

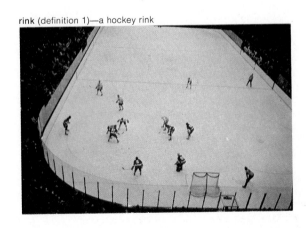

ride (definition 5)—We took a **ride** on the roller coaster.

rink (definition 1)—a hockey rink

rime (rīm), rhyme. *verb,* **rimed, rim ing;** *noun.*

rind (rīnd), a firm outer covering. We do not eat the rind of oranges, melons, and cheese. *noun.*

ring[1] (ring), **1** circle: *You can tell the age of a tree by counting the number of rings in its wood; one ring grows every year. The elves danced in a ring.* **2** a thin circle of metal or other material: *a wedding ring, a key ring, a napkin ring.* **3** put a ring around; enclose; form a circle around. **4** an enclosed space (for races or games): *a circus ring, a ring for a fight.* 1,2,4 *noun,* 3 *verb,* **ringed, ring ing.**

ring[2] (ring), **1** give forth a clear sound, as a bell does: *Did the telephone ring?* **2** cause to give forth a clear, ringing sound: *Ring the bell.* **3** cause a bell to sound: *Did you ring?* **4** sound of a bell: *Did you hear a ring?* **5** sound like that of a bell: *On a cold night we can hear the ring of skates on ice.* **6** hear a sound like that of a bell ringing: *My ears ring.* **7** sound loudly: *The room rang with laughter.* **8** seem; appear to be: *Her words rang true.* **9** call up on a telephone: *I'll ring you tomorrow.* 1-3,6-9 *verb,* **rang, rung, ring ing;** 4,5 *noun.*

ring lead er (ring′lē′dər), person who leads others in opposition to authority or law: *the ringleaders of the mutiny. noun.*

ring let (ring′lit), **1** curl: *The baby's hair was in ringlets.* **2** a little ring: *Drops of rain made ringlets in the pond. noun.*

ring side (ring′sīd′), **1** place just outside a ring or arena, especially at a circus or fight. **2** place affording a close view. *noun.*

rink (ringk), **1** sheet of ice for skating. See picture. **2** a smooth floor for roller-skating. *noun.*

rinse (rins), **1** wash with clean water: *Rinse all the soap out of your hair after you wash it.* **2** wash lightly: *Rinse your mouth with warm water.* **3** rinsing: *Give the plate a final rinse in cold water.* 1,2 *verb,* **rinsed, rins ing;** 3 *noun.*

ri ot (rī′ət), **1** disturbance; confusion; disorder; a wild, violent public disturbance: *a riot in a prison.* **2** behave in a wild, disorderly way. **3** a bright display: *The garden was a riot of color.* 1,3 *noun,* 2 *verb.*

run riot, 1 act without restraint: *The crowd ran riot and could not be controlled.* **2** grow wildly: *The daisies run riot in this field.*

ri ot ous (rī′ə təs), **1** taking part in a riot: *The leaders of the riotous mob were arrested.* **2** noisily cheerful; disorderly: *Sounds of riotous glee came from the playhouse. adjective.*

rip (rip), **1** cut roughly; tear apart; tear off: *Rip the cover off this box.* **2** cut or pull out (the threads in the seams of a garment). **3** a torn place; seam burst in a garment: *Please sew up this rip in my sleeve.* 1,2 *verb,* **ripped, rip ping;** 3 *noun.*

ripe (rīp), **1** full-grown and ready to be gathered

and eaten: *ripe fruit, ripe grain, ripe vegetables.* **2** fully developed; mature: *a person ripe in knowledge.* **3** ready: *a country ripe for revolution. adjective,* **rip er, rip est.**

rip en (rī/pən), become ripe; make ripe. *verb.*

rip ple (rip/əl), **1** a very little wave: *Throw a stone into still water and watch the ripples spread in rings.* **2** anything that seems like a tiny wave. See picture. **3** sound that reminds one of little waves: *a ripple of laughter in the crowd.* **4** make little ripples on: *A breeze rippled the water.* 1-3 *noun,* 4 *verb,* **rip pled, rip pling.**

rise (rīz), **1** get up from a lying, sitting, or kneeling position; stand up; get up: *Please rise from your seat when you recite.* **2** get up from sleep or rest: *I rise at 7 every morning.* **3** go up; come up: *The kite rises in the air. Bread rises. Mercury rises in a thermometer on a hot day. Fish rise to the surface.* **4** go higher; increase: *Butter rose five cents in price. The wind rose rapidly. My anger rose at that remark.* **5** going up; increase: *a rise in prices, the rise of a balloon.* **6** advance in importance or rank: *He rose from office clerk to president of the company.* **7** slope upward: *Hills rise in the distance.* **8** an upward slope: *The rise of the hill is gradual. The house is situated on a rise.* **9** come above the horizon: *The sun rises in the morning.* **10** start; begin: *The river rises from a spring. Quarrels often rise from trifles.* **11** origin; beginning: *the rise of a river, the rise of a storm, the rise of a new problem.* **12** become more cheerful; improve: *Our spirits rose at the good news.* **13** revolt; rebel: *The peasants rose against the nobles.* 1-4,6,7,9,10,12,13 *verb,* **rose, ris en, ris ing;** 5,8,11 *noun.*

give rise to, bring about; start; begin; cause: *Their sudden wealth gave rise to rumors about where the money came from.*

ris en (riz/n). See **rise.** *The sun had risen long before I woke up. verb.*

risk (risk), **1** chance of harm or loss; danger: *There is less risk of getting sick if you eat properly.* **2** expose to the chance of harm or loss: *You risk your neck trying to climb that tree.* **3** take the risk of: *They risked defeat in fighting the larger army.* 1 *noun,* 2,3 *verb.*

run a risk or **take a risk,** expose oneself to the chance of harm or loss: *In order to win the war we had to take the risk of offending neutral nations.*

risk y (ris/kē), full of risk; dangerous. *adjective,* **risk i er, risk i est.**

rite (rīt), a solemn ceremony. Most religions have rites for marriage and burial. Secret societies have their special rites. *noun.*

rit u al (rich/ü əl), form or system of rites. The rites of marriage and burial are part of the ritual of most religions. *noun.*

ri val (rī/vəl), **1** person who wants and tries to get the same thing as another; one who tries to equal or do better than another: *The two girls were rivals for the same class office.* **2** wanting the same thing as another; being a rival: *A rival store tried to get our grocer's trade.* **3** try to equal or outdo: *The stores rival each other in beautiful window displays.*

4 equal; match: *The sunset rivaled the sunrise in beauty.* 1 *noun,* 2 *adjective,* 3,4 *verb.*

ri val ry (rī/vəl rē), effort to obtain something another person wants; competition: *There is rivalry among business firms for trade. noun, plural* **ri val ries.**

riv er (riv/ər), **1** a large natural stream of water that flows into a lake, ocean, or the like. **2** any abundant stream or flow: *rivers of blood. noun.*

riv er side (riv/ər sīd/), **1** bank of a river: *We walked along the riverside.* **2** beside a river: *The riverside path is much used.* 1 *noun,* 2 *adjective.*

riv et (riv/it), **1** a metal bolt with a head at one end. The end opposite the head is hammered to form another head after it is passed through the things to be joined. Rivets are often used to fasten heavy steel beams together. See picture. **2** fasten with a rivet or rivets. **3** fasten firmly; fix firmly: *Their eyes were riveted on the speaker.* 1 *noun,* 2,3 *verb.*

riv u let (riv/yə lit), a very small stream. *noun.*

roach (rōch), insect often found in kitchens or around water pipes; cockroach. *noun, plural* **roach es.**

road (rōd), **1** way between places; way made for automobiles, trucks, or other vehicles to travel on: *the road from New York to Boston.* **2** way: *the road to ruin, a road to peace. noun.*

road map, a flat drawing of a part of the earth's surface showing roads for automobile travel.

road side (rōd/sīd/), **1** side of a road: *Flowers grew along the roadside.* **2** beside a road: *a roadside inn.* 1 *noun,* 2 *adjective.*

road way (rōd/wā/), **1** road. **2** part of a road used by wheeled vehicles: *Do not walk in the roadway. noun.*

roam (rōm), go about with no special plan or aim; wander: *roam through the fields. verb.*

roan (rōn), **1** yellowish or reddish brown sprinkled with gray or white. **2** a horse with a red, brown, or black coat with white hairs mixed in. 1 *adjective,* 2 *noun.*

roar (rôr), **1** make a loud deep sound; make a loud noise: *The lion roared. The wind roared at the windows.* **2** a loud deep sound; loud noise: *the roar of the cannon, a roar of laughter.* **3** laugh loudly: *The audience roared at the clown.* 1,3 *verb,* 2 *noun.*

roast (rōst), **1** cook by the dry heat of an oven, an open fire, or hot charcoal: *I will roast the meat for an hour. We roasted marshmallows at camp.* **2** piece of baked meat; piece of meat to be roasted. **3** roasted: *roast beef, roast pork.* **4** prepare by heating: *roast coffee, roast a metal ore.* **5** make or become very hot. 1,4,5 *verb,* 2 *noun,* 3 *adjective.*

rob (rob), take away from by force; steal: *Thieves robbed the bank of thousands of dollars. Some children robbed the orchard. They said they would not rob again. verb,* **robbed, rob bing.**

rob ber (rob/ər), person who robs; thief. *noun.*

rob ber y (rob/ər ē), act of robbing; theft; stealing: *a bank robbery. noun, plural* **rob ber ies.**

robe (rōb), **1** a long, loose, outer garment: *The priests wore robes.* **2** garment that shows rank or

office: *a judge's robe, the queen's robes of state.*
3 covering or wrap: *a beach robe.* **4** put a robe on; dress. 1-3 *noun,* 4 *verb,* **robed, rob ing.**

rob in (rob′ən), **1** a large North American bird with a reddish breast. **2** a smaller European bird with an orange breast. *noun.*

ro bot (rō′bət), machine made in imitation of a human being; a mechanical device that does routine work in response to commands. See picture. *noun.* [*Robot* comes from a Czech word meaning "work."]

ro bust (rō bust′ *or* rō′bust), strong and healthy; sturdy: *a robust person, a robust mind. adjective.*

rock[1] (rok), **1** a large mass of stone: *The ship was wrecked on the rocks.* **2** piece of stone: *She threw a rock in the lake.* **3** hard mineral matter that is not metal; stone. The earth's crust is made up of rock under a layer of soil. **4** something firm like a rock; support; defense: *Christ is called the Rock of Ages. noun.*

rock[2] (rok), **1** move backward and forward, or from side to side; sway: *My chair rocks. The waves rocked the ship.* **2** a rocking movement. **3** rock'n'roll. 1 *verb,* 2,3 *noun.*

rock er (rok′ər), **1** one of the curved pieces on which a cradle or rocking chair rocks. **2** rocking chair. *noun.*

rock et (rok′it), **1** device consisting of a tube open at one end in which an explosive or fuel is rapidly burned. The burning explosive or fuel creates gases that escape from the open end and force the tube and whatever is attached to it upward or forward. Some rockets, such as those used in fireworks displays, shoot into the air and burst into showers of sparks. Larger rockets are used in weapons of war and to send spacecraft beyond the earth's atmosphere. **2** go like a rocket; move very, very fast: *The singing group rocketed to fame with its first hit record. The racing car rocketed across the finish line to victory.* 1 *noun,* 2 *verb.*

rocking chair, chair mounted on rockers, or on springs, so that it can rock back and forth.

rocking horse, a toy horse on rockers for children to ride.

rock 'n' roll (rok′ən rōl′), **1** a kind of popular music with a strong beat and simple melody. **2** a lively dance done to this music. *noun.*

rock salt, the common salt got from mines; salt in large crystals. Rock salt is often used to melt ice on roads and sidewalks.

rock y[1] (rok′ē), **1** full of rocks: *a rocky shore.* **2** made of rock. **3** like rock; hard; firm: *rocky determination. adjective,* **rock i er, rock i est.**

rock y[2] (rok′ē), shaky; likely to rock: *That table seems a bit rocky to me; put a piece of wood under the short leg. adjective,* **rock i er, rock i est.**

rod (rod), **1** a thin straight pole or bar of wood, metal, or plastic: *a fishing rod, a curtain rod.* **2** stick used to beat or punish. **3** a unit of length equal to $5\frac{1}{2}$ yards or $16\frac{1}{2}$ feet. A square rod is $30\frac{1}{4}$ square yards or $272\frac{1}{4}$ square feet. *noun.*

rode (rōd). See **ride.** *We rode ten miles yesterday. verb.*

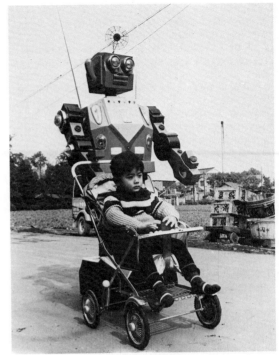

robot pushing a child in a baby carriage

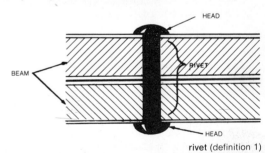

rivet (definition 1)

ripple (definition 2)—ripples in sand

ro dent (rōd′nt), any of a group of animals with four large front teeth that they often use to gnaw wood. Rats, mice, and squirrels are rodents. See picture. *noun.*

ro de o (rō′dē ō *or* rō dā′ō), a contest or exhibition of skill in roping cattle or riding horses and steers. See picture. *noun, plural* **ro de os.**

roe[1] (rō), a small deer of Europe and Asia. *noun, plural* **roes** *or* **roe.**

roe[2] (rō), fish eggs. *noun.*

roe buck (rō′buk′), a male roe deer. *noun.*

rogue (rōg), **1** a tricky or dishonest person; rascal. **2** a mischievous person: *The little rogue has his grandpa's glasses on.* **3** animal with a savage nature that lives apart from the herd: *An elephant that is a rogue is very dangerous. noun.*

rogues' gallery, collection of photographs of known criminals.

ro guish (rō′gish), **1** dishonest; having to do with rogues. **2** playfully mischievous: *with a roguish twinkle in his eyes. adjective.*

role (rōl), **1** an actor's part in a play: *She played the leading role in the school play.* **2** part played in real life: *The parental role is one of love and guidance. noun.* [*Role* comes from a French word meaning "roll." The actor's part was called this because it used to be written on a roll of paper.]

roll (rōl), **1** move along by turning over and over: *The ball rolled away.* **2** turn round and round on itself or on something else; wrap; be wrapped round: *She rolled the string into a ball. The boy rolled himself up in a blanket.* **3** something rolled up: *a roll of film, a roll of paper.* **4** a rounded or rolled-up mass: *a roll of cookie dough.* **5** move on wheels: *roll a baby carriage. The automobile rolls along.* **6** move smoothly; sweep along: *Waves roll in on the beach. The years roll on.* **7** move with a side-to-side motion: *to roll one's eyes. The ship rolled in the waves.* **8** act of rolling; motion from side to side: *The ship's roll made many people sick.* **9** rise and fall again and again: *rolling country, rolling waves.* **10** make flat or smooth with a roller; spread out with a rolling pin: *Roll the dough thin for these cookies.* **11** make deep, loud sounds: *Thunder rolls.* **12** a deep, loud sound: *the roll of thunder.* **13** beat (a drum) with rapid, continuous strokes. **14** a rapid, continuous beating on a drum. **15** trill: *roll your r's.* **16** list of names; list: *I will call the roll to find out who is absent.* **17** kind of bread or cake: *a sweet roll.* 1,2,5-7,9-11,13,15 *verb,* 3,4,8,12,14,16,17 *noun.*

roll up, pile up; increase: *Bills roll up fast.*

roll call, calling a list of names to find out who is present.

roll er (rō′lər), **1** thing that rolls; cylinder on which something is rolled along or rolled up. The shades for many windows are raised and lowered on rollers. **2** cylinder of metal, stone, or wood used for smoothing, pressing, or crushing. A heavy roller is used in making and repairing roads. **3** a long, swelling wave: *Rollers broke on the beach. noun.*

roll er coast er (rō′lər kō′stər), railway for

rodeo

rodent
Hamsters are rodents.

rooster

amusement, consisting of inclined tracks along which small cars roll and make sudden drops and turns.

roller skate, a shoe or metal base with four small wheels, used for skating on a floor, sidewalk, or other smooth surface.

roll er-skate (rō′lər skāt′), move on roller skates: *The children roller-skated to the park. verb,* **roll er-skat ed, roll er-skat ing.**

rolling pin, cylinder of wood, plastic, or glass with a handle at each end, for rolling out dough.

Ro man (rō′mən), **1** of or having something to do with Rome. **2** person born or living in Rome. **3** citizen of ancient Rome. **4** of or having something to do with the Roman Catholic Church. **5** roman, style of type most used in printing and typewriting. This sentence is in roman. 1,4 *adjective,* 2,3,5 *noun.*

Roman Catholic, 1 of, having something to do with, or belonging to the Christian church that recognizes the pope as the supreme head. **2** member of this church.

ro mance (rō mans′), **1** a love story. **2** story of adventure: *"The Arabian Nights" and "Treasure Island" are romances.* **3** a story or poem telling of heroes: *Have you read the romances about King Arthur and his knights?* **4** real happenings that are like stories of heroes and are full of love, excitement, or noble deeds: *The children dreamed of traveling in search of romance. The explorer's life was filled with romance.* **5** a love affair: *"Cinderella" is the story of the romance between a beautiful girl and a prince.* **6** think or talk in a romantic way: *Stop romancing and get down to work.* 1-5 *noun,* 6 *verb,* **ro manced, ro manc ing.**

Roman numerals, numerals like XXIII, LVI, and MDCCLX, in which I = 1, V = 5, X = 10, L = 50, C = 100, D = 500, and M = 1000.

ro man tic (rō man′tik), **1** characteristic of romances or romance; appealing to fancy and the imagination: *He likes to read romantic tales of love and war. She thinks it would be romantic to be an explorer.* **2** having ideas or feelings suited to romance: *The old couple remembered the days when they were young and romantic.* **3** suited to a romance: *The band played soft, romantic music. adjective.*

Rome (rōm), **1** city in southern Europe, the capital of Italy. **2** an ancient city in the same place, the capital of an ancient empire. *noun.*

romp (romp), **1** play in a rough, boisterous way; rush, tumble, and punch in play: *On rainy days the children liked to romp in the basement.* **2** a rough, lively play or frolic: *A pillow fight is a romp.* 1 *verb,* 2 *noun.*

romp ers (rom′pərz), a loose outer garment, worn by young children at play. *noun plural.*

roof (rüf), **1** the top covering of a building. **2** something like it: *the roof of a cave, the roof of a car, the roof of the mouth.* **3** cover with or as if with a roof: *Tall trees roofed the road through the woods.* 1,2 *noun, plural* **roofs;** 3 *verb.*

roof ing (rü′fing), material used for roofs.

a hat	i it	oi oil	ch child	a in about
ā age	ī ice	ou out	ng long	e in taken
ä far	o hot	u cup	sh she	ə = { i in pencil
e let	ō open	u̇ put	th thin	o in lemon
ē equal	ô order	ü rule	₮H then	u in circus
ėr term			zh measure	

Shingles are a common roofing for houses. *noun.*

rook[1] (ru̇k), a European bird much like a crow that often nests in trees near buildings. *noun.*

rook[2] (ru̇k), one of the pieces in the game of chess. *noun.*

rook ie (ru̇k′ē), **1** an inexperienced recruit. **2** beginner. *noun.*

room (rüm), **1** part of a house, or other building, with walls of its own: *a dining room.* **2** people in a room: *The whole room laughed.* **3** space: *The street was so crowded that the cars did not have room to move. There is room for one more in the automobile.* **4** opportunity: *There is room for improvement in her work.* **5** occupy a room; live in a room: *Three girls from our town roomed together at college.* 1-4 *noun,* 5 *verb.*

room er (rü′mər), person who lives in a rented room or rooms in another's house; lodger. *noun.*

room i ness (rü′mē nis), ample space; abundance of room. *noun.*

room mate (rüm′māt′), person who shares a room with another or others. *noun.*

room y (rü′mē), large; spacious; having plenty of room: *Her new apartment is quite roomy. adjective,* **room i er, room i est.**

roost (rüst), **1** bar, pole, or perch on which birds rest or sleep. **2** sit as birds do on a roost; settle for the night. **3** place for birds to roost in. 1,3 *noun,* 2 *verb.*

roost er (rü′stər), a full-grown male chicken. See picture. *noun.*

root[1] (rüt), **1** part of a plant that grows down into the soil, holds the plant in place, and absorbs food and water from the soil. **2** any underground part of a plant. **3** something like a root in shape, position, or use: *the root of a tooth, the roots of the hair.* **4** part from which other things grow and develop; cause; source: *"The love of money is the root of all evil."* **5** become fixed in the ground; send out roots and begin to grow: *Some plants root more quickly than others.* **6** fix firmly: *He was rooted to the spot by surprise.* **7** pull, tear, or dig (up or out) by the roots; get rid of completely. **8** word from which other words are made. *Room is the root of roominess, roomer, roommate, and roomy.* 1-4,8 *noun,* 5-7 *verb.*

root[2] (rüt), **1** dig with the snout: *The pigs rooted up the garden.* **2** rummage: *She rooted through the closet looking for her old shoes. verb.*

root[3] (rüt), cheer or support a team or a member of a team enthusiastically. *verb.*

root beer, a soft drink flavored with the juice of the roots of certain plants.

rope (rōp), **1** a strong thick line or cord made by twisting smaller cords together. **2** tie, bind, or fasten with a rope. **3** enclose or mark off with a rope. **4** catch (a horse, calf, or other animal) with a lasso. **5** a number of things twisted or strung together: *a rope of onions, a rope of pearls.* 1,5 *noun,* 2-4 *verb,* **roped, rop ing.**

ro sar y (rō′zər ē), **1** string of beads for keeping count in saying a series of prayers. **2** series of prayers. *noun, plural* **ro sar ies.**

rose[1] (rōz), **1** flower that grows on a bush with thorny stems. Roses are red, pink, white, or yellow and usually smell very sweet. **2** the bush itself. **3** pinkish red: *Her dress was rose.* **4** something shaped like a rose, or suggesting a rose. See picture. 1,2,4 *noun,* 3 *adjective.*

rose[2] (rōz). See **rise.** *The cat rose and stretched. verb.*

rose bud (rōz′bud′), bud of a rose. *noun.*

rose bush (rōz′bůsh′), shrub or vine that bears roses. *noun, plural* **rose bush es.**

ro sette (rō zet′), ornament shaped like a rose. Rosettes are often made of ribbon. See picture. *noun.*

Rosh Ha sha nah or **Rosh Ha sha na** (rosh′ hə shä′nə), the Jewish New Year. It usually occurs in September.

ros in (roz′n), a hard, yellow substance that remains when turpentine is evaporated from pine resin. Rosin is rubbed on violin bows, and on the shoes of acrobats and ballet dancers to keep them from slipping. *noun.*

ros y (rō′zē), **1** like a rose; pinkish-red: *rosy cheeks.* **2** bright; cheerful: *a rosy future. adjective,* **ros i er, ros i est.**

rot (rot), **1** become rotten; decay; spoil: *So much rain will make the fruit rot.* **2** cause to decay. **3** process of rotting; decay. **4** any of several diseases of plants and animals, especially sheep. 1,2 *verb,* **rot ted, rot ting;** 3,4 *noun.*

ro tate (rō′tāt), **1** move around a center or axis; turn in a circle; revolve. Wheels, tops, and the earth rotate. **2** change in a regular order; cause to take turns: *rotate crops in a field. verb,* **ro tat ed, ro tat ing.** [*Rotate* comes from a Latin word meaning "wheel."]

ro ta tion (rō tā′shən), a turning round a center; turning in a circle: *the rotation of a top. The earth's rotation causes night and day. noun.*

in rotation, in turn; in regular succession: *We all had a chance to recite in rotation.*

rotation of crops, the varying from year to year of crops grown in the same field to keep the soil from losing its fertility.

rote (rōt). **by rote,** by memory without thought of the meaning: *learn a lesson by rote. noun.*

ro tor (rō′tər), **1** the rotating part of a machine or apparatus. **2** system of rotating blades by which a helicopter is able to fly. See picture. *noun.*

rot ten (rot′n), **1** decayed; spoiled: *a rotten egg.* **2** foul; bad-smelling; disgusting: *a rotten smell.* **3** weak; unsound; not in good condition: *rotten beams in a floor.* **4** corrupt; dishonest: *rotten government. adjective.*

rouge (rüzh), **1** a red powder, paste, or liquid for coloring the cheeks or lips. **2** color with rouge.

1 *noun,* **2** *verb,* **rouged, roug ing.**

rough (ruf), **1** not smooth; not level; not even: *rough boards, the rough bark of oak trees, a rough, rocky hill.* **2** stormy: *rough weather, a rough sea.* **3** likely to hurt others; harsh; not gentle: *rough manners.* **4** without luxury and ease: *He led a rough life at his summer camp.* **5** without polish or fine finish: *rough diamonds.* **6** not completed; done as a first try; without details: *a rough drawing, a rough idea.* **7** coarse and tangled: *rough fur, a dog with a rough coat of hair.* **8** unpleasant; hard; severe: *She had a rough time in the hospital.* **9** make rough; roughen: *A strong wind roughed up the waves.* **10** shape or sketch roughly: *rough out a plan, rough in the outlines of a face.* **11** roughly: *Those older boys play too rough for me.* 1-8 *adjective,* 9,10 *verb,* 11 *adverb.*

rough it, live without comforts and conveniences: *They have been roughing it in the woods this summer.*

rough age (ruf′ij), the coarser parts or kinds of food. Bran, fruit skins, and straw are roughage. *noun.*

rough en (ruf′ən), make rough; become rough. *verb.*

rough ly (ruf′lē), **1** in a rough manner. **2** approximately: *From New York to Los Angeles is roughly three thousand miles. adverb.*

round (round), **1** shaped like a ball or circle or tree trunk: *Oranges are round. A ring is round. Most candles are round.* **2** anything shaped like a ball or circle or tree trunk. The rungs of a ladder are sometimes called rounds. **3** plump: *a short, round figure.* **4** make or become round: *The carpenter rounded the corners of the table.* **5** around: *Wheels go round. They built a fence round the yard.* **6** go around; make a turn to the other side of: *The car rounded the corner at high speed.* **7 rounds,** a fixed course ending where it begins: *The watchman makes his rounds of the building.* **8** movement in a circle or about an axis: *the earth's yearly round.* **9** series (of duties or events); routine: *a round of pleasures, a round of duties.* **10** section of a game or sport: *a round in a boxing match, a round of cards.* **11** discharge of guns by a group of soldiers at the same time. **12** powder or bullets for one such discharge, or for a single shot: *Three rounds of ammunition were left in the rifle.* **13** an act that a number of people do together: *a round of cheers. She was greeted by a round of applause.* **14** a short song sung by several persons or groups beginning one after the other. "Row, Row, Row Your Boat" is a round. **15** full; complete; large: *a round dozen, a good round sum of money.* **16** change a number to the nearest hundredth, tenth, ten, hundred, and so on. 7578 rounded off to the nearest hundred would be 7600. **17** frank; blunt: *She told us what she thought of us in round terms.* 1,3,15,17 *adjective,* 2,7-14 *noun,* 4,6,16 *verb,* 5 *adverb,* 5 *preposition.*

round out, finish; complete: *round out an unfinished paragraph, round out a career and retire.*

round up, 1 drive or bring (cattle or horses) together: *The cowboys rounded up the cattle.*

2 gather together; collect: *to round up some kids to play baseball.*

round a bout (round′ə bout′), indirect: *a roundabout route, in a roundabout way. adjective.*

round house (round′hous′), building for storing or repairing locomotives. It is built about a platform that turns around. *noun, plural* **round hous es** (round′hou′ziz).

round ish (roun′dish), somewhat round. *adjective.*

round number, number in even tens, hundreds, thousands, and so on. 3874 in round numbers would be 3900 or 4000.

round-shoul dered (round′shōl′dərd), having the shoulders bent forward. *adjective.*

round trip, trip to a place and back again.

round up (round′up′), **1** act of driving or bringing cattle together from long distances. **2** the people and horses that do this. **3** any similar gathering: *a roundup of old friends. noun.*

rouse (rouz), wake up; stir up; excite; arouse: *I was roused by the ring of the telephone. The dogs roused a deer from the bushes. She was roused to anger by the insult. verb,* **roused, rous ing.**

rose[1] (definition 4)

rosettes

rotor (definition 2)

rout[1] (rout), **1** flight of a defeated army in disorder: *The enemy's retreat soon became a rout.* **2** put to flight: *Our soldiers routed the enemy.* **3** a complete defeat. **4** defeat completely: *The baseball team routed its opponents by a score of ten to one.* **1,3** *noun,* **2,4** *verb.*

rout[2] (rout), **1** dig (out); get by searching. **2** put (out); force (out): *Mother routed us out of bed early the day of the picnic.* **3** dig with the snout: *The pigs were routing for nuts under the trees. verb.*

route (rüt *or* rout), **1** way to go; road: *Will you go to the coast by the northern route?* **2** arrange the way to go for: *The automobile club routed us on our vacation to Canada.* **3** send by a certain way or road: *The signs routed us around the construction work and over a side road.* **4** a fixed, regular course or area of a person making deliveries or sales: *a newspaper route, a milk route.* **1,4** *noun,* **2,3** *verb,* **rout ed, rout ing.**

rou tine (rü tēn′), **1** a fixed, regular method of doing things; habitual doing of the same things in the same way: *Getting up and going to bed are parts of your daily routine.* **2** using routine: *routine methods.* **1** *noun,* **2** *adjective.*

rove (rōv), wander; wander about; roam: *She loved to rove through the woods near her house. verb,* **roved, rov ing.**

rov er (rō′vər), wanderer. *noun.*

row[1] (rō), line of people or things: *The children stood in a row in front of the row of chairs. Corn is planted in rows. noun.*

row[2] (rō), **1** use oars to move a boat: *Row to the island.* **2** carry in a rowboat: *Row us to the island.* **3** trip in a rowboat: *It's only a short row to the island.* **1,2** *verb,* **3** *noun.*

row[3] (rou), a noisy quarrel; noise: *The children had a row over the bicycle. What's all this row about? noun.*

row boat (rō′bōt′), boat moved by oars. *noun.*

row dy (rou′dē), **1** a rough, disorderly, quarrelsome person. **2** rough; disorderly; quarrelsome. **1** *noun, plural* **row dies; 2** *adjective,* **row di er, row di est.**

roy al (roi′əl), **1** of kings and queens: *the royal family.* **2** belonging to a king or queen: *royal power, a royal palace.* **3** from or by a king or queen: *a royal command.* **4** of a kingdom: *a royal army or navy.* **5** suitable for a king or queen; splendid: *a royal welcome, a royal feast.* **6** like a king or queen; noble; majestic: *The lion is a royal beast. adjective.*

roy al ty (roi′əl tē), **1** a royal person; royal persons. Kings, queens, princes, and princesses are royalty. **2** rank or dignity of a king or queen; royal power: *The crown is the symbol of royalty. noun, plural* **roy al ties.**

rubble—They found a doll in the mud and **rubble** of the vacant lot.

ruff (definition 1)

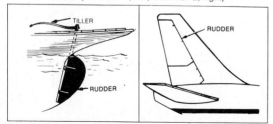

rudder (definition 1, left; definition 2, right)

rub (rub), **1** move one thing back and forth against another: *Rub your hands to warm them. He rubbed soap on his hands.* **2** push and press along the surface of: *The nurse rubbed my lame back. That door rubs on the floor.* **3** make or bring by rubbing: *rub silver bright. Don't rub my skin off.* **4** clean, smooth, or polish by moving one thing firmly against another: *Rub the silver with a soft cloth.* **5** act of rubbing: *Give the silver a rub with the polish.* 1-4 *verb*, **rubbed, rub bing;** 5 *noun.*

rub ber (rub′ər), **1** an elastic substance made from the juice of certain tropical plants or by a chemical process. Rubber will not let air or water through. **2** something made from this substance. We wear rubbers on our feet when it rains. Pencils often have rubbers for erasing pencil marks. **3** made of rubber: *a rubber tire.* 1,2 *noun,* 3 *adjective.*

rubber band, a circular strip of rubber, used to hold things together.

rubber stamp, stamp made of rubber, used with ink for printing dates, signatures, or other special imprints.

rub bish (rub′ish), **1** trash; waste; worthless or useless stuff: *Pick up the rubbish and burn it.* **2** silly words and thoughts; nonsense: *Gossip is often a lot of rubbish. noun.*

rub ble (rub′əl), rough broken stone or bricks. See picture. *noun.*

ru by (rü′bē), **1** a clear, hard, red precious stone. Real rubies are very rare. **2** deep, glowing red: *ruby lips, ruby wine.* 1 *noun, plural* **ru bies;** 2 *adjective.*

rud der (rud′ər), **1** a movable flat piece of wood or metal at the rear end of a boat or ship by which it is steered. See picture. **2** a similar piece on an aircraft. See picture. *noun.*

rud di ness (rud′ē nis), healthy redness of skin; redness. *noun.*

rud dy (rud′ē), **1** red: *the ruddy glow of a fire.* **2** having a fresh, healthy, red look: *ruddy cheeks. adjective,* **rud di er, rud di est.**

rude (rüd), **1** impolite; not courteous: *It is rude to stare at people or to point.* **2** rough; coarse; roughly made or done: *Prehistoric people made rude tools from stone.* **3** very forceful; violent; rough in manner or behavior: *Rude hands seized the barking dog.* **4** not having learned much; primitive: *Rude tribes lived in the jungle surrounding the river. adjective,* **rud er, rud est.**

rude ness (rüd′nis), roughness; coarseness; bad manners; violence: *His rudeness is inexcusable. noun.*

ru di ment (rü′də mənt), **1** part to be learned first; beginning: *the rudiments of arithmetic.* **2** something in an early stage: *the rudiments of wings on a baby chick. noun.*

ru di men tar y (rü′də men′tər ē), **1** to be learned or studied first; elementary: *It is almost impossible to learn multiplication without knowing the rudimentary steps of addition.* **2** in an early stage of development: *rudimentary wings. adjective.*

rue (rü), be sorry for; repent; regret: *She will rue*

the day she left school. verb, **rued, ru ing.**

rue ful (rü′fəl), **1** sorrowful; unhappy; mournful: *a rueful expression.* **2** causing sorrow or pity: *a rueful sight. adjective.*

ruff (ruf), **1** a deep frill stiff enough to stand out, worn around the neck by men and women in the 1500's and 1600's. See picture. **2** collar of specially marked feathers or hairs on the neck of a bird or other animal. *noun.*

ruf fi an (ruf′ē ən), a rough, brutal, or cruel person. *noun.*

ruf fle (ruf′əl), **1** make rough or uneven; wrinkle: *A breeze ruffled the lake. The hen ruffled its feathers when the dog barked.* **2** strip of cloth, ribbon, or lace gathered along one edge and used for trimming. **3** gather into a ruffle. **4** disturb; annoy: *Nothing can ruffle her calm temper.* **1,3,4** *verb,* **ruf fled, ruf fling; 2** *noun.*

rug (rug), a heavy floor covering: *a rag rug, a fur rug.* Rugs usually cover only part of a room's floor. *noun.*

rug ged (rug′id), **1** covered with rough edges; rough and uneven: *rugged rocks, rugged ground.* **2** sturdy and vigorous; able to do and endure much: *Pioneers were rugged people.* **3** strong and irregular: *rugged features.* **4** harsh; stern: *rugged times.* **5** stormy: *rugged weather. adjective.*

ru in (rü′ən), **1** building or wall that has fallen to pieces: *That ruin was once a famous castle.* **2** very great damage; destruction; overthrow: *The ruin of property caused by the earthquake was enormous. His enemies planned the duke's ruin.* **3** a fallen or decayed condition: *The house had gone to ruin from neglect.* **4** cause of destruction, decay, or downfall: *Reckless spending will be your ruin.* **5** destroy; spoil: *The rain ruined our picnic.* **1-4** *noun,* **5** *verb.*

ru in ous (rü′ə nəs), **1** bringing ruin; causing destruction: *The heavy frost in late spring was ruinous to the crops.* **2** fallen into ruins; ruined: *a building in a ruinous condition. adjective.*

rule (rül), **1** statement of what to do and what not to do; principle governing conduct or action: *Obey the rules of the game.* **2** set of rules: *Different kinds of monks live under different rules.* **3** decide: *My parents ruled in my favor in the dispute between my sister and me. The judge ruled against them.* **4** control; govern: *The majority rules in a democracy.* **5** control; government: *the rule of the majority.* **6** period of power of a ruler; reign: *The Revolutionary War took place during the rule of George III.* **7** a regular method; thing that usually happens or is done; what is usually true: *Fair weather is the rule in June.* **8** a straight strip of wood or metal used to measure or as a guide in drawing; ruler. **9** mark with lines: *She used a ruler to rule the paper.* **1,2,5-8** *noun,* **3,4,9** *verb,* **ruled, rul ing.**

as a rule, usually: *As a rule, hail falls in summer.*

rule out, decide against: *He did not rule out a possible camping trip this summer.*

rul er (rü′lər), **1** person who rules. **2** a straight strip of wood or metal used in drawing lines or in measuring. *noun.*

rum (rum), a strong alcoholic drink made from sugar cane or molasses. *noun.*

rum ble (rum′bəl), **1** make a deep, heavy, continuous sound. **2** a deep, heavy, continuous sound: *We hear the far-off rumble of thunder.* **3** move with such a sound: *The train rumbled along over the tracks.* **1,3** *verb,* **rum bled, rum bling; 2** *noun.*

ru mi nant (rü′mə nənt), animal that chews the cud. Cows, sheep, and camels are ruminants. *noun.*

rum mage (rum′ij), **1** search thoroughly by moving things about: *I rummaged three drawers before I found my gloves.* **2** search in a disorderly way: *I rummaged in my drawer for a pair of gloves.* **3** a thorough search in which things are moved about. **1,2** *verb,* **rum maged, rum mag ing; 3** *noun.*

rummage sale, sale of odds and ends or old clothing, usually held to raise money for charity.

rum my (rum′ē), a card game in which points are scored by forming sets of three or more cards. *noun.*

ru mor (rü′mər), **1** story or statement talked of as news without any proof that it is true: *The rumor spread that a new school would be built here.* **2** vague, general talk: *Rumor has it that the new girl went to school in France.* **3** tell or spread by rumor: *It was rumored that the government was going to increase taxes.* **1,2** *noun,* **3** *verb.*

rump (rump), the hind part of the body of an animal, where the legs join the back. A rump steak is a cut of beef from this part. *noun.*

rum ple (rum′pəl), crumple; crush; wrinkle: *rumple sheets of paper, rumple a suit. verb,* **rum pled, rum pling.**

rum pus (rum′pəs), a noisy disturbance or uproar; row. *noun, plural* **rum pus es.**

run (run), **1** go by moving the legs quickly; go faster than walking: *A horse can run faster than a person.* **2** go in a hurry; hasten: *Run for help.* **3** make a quick trip: *Let's run over to the lake for the weekend.* **4** escape; flee: *Run for your life.* **5** cause to run; cause to move: *run a horse up and down the track.* **6** do by running: *run errands.* **7** go; move; keep going: *This train runs from Chicago to St. Louis. Does your watch run well?* **8** go on: *Prices of hats run as high as $50.* **9** creep; grow; climb: *Vines run along the sides of the brick wall.* **10** pass or cause to pass quickly: *The thought that I might forget my speech ran through my mind.* **11** stretch; extend: *Shelves run along the walls.* **12** drive; force; thrust: *He ran a splinter into his hand.* **13** flow; flow with: *The street ran oil after an oil truck overturned.* **14** discharge fluid, mucus, or pus: *My nose runs whenever I have a cold.* **15** get; become: *Never run* into debt. *The well ran dry.* **16** spread: *The color ran when the shirt was washed.* **17** continue; last: *a lease to run two years.* **18** take part in a race or contest. **19** be a candidate for election: *He will run for President.* **20** expose oneself to: *run a risk of taking cold.* **21** move or cause to move easily or smoothly; operate or cause to operate: *The engine ran all day without overheating. Can you run this machine?* **22** act of running: *set out at a run. The dog came on the run.* **23** trip: *The train makes a run of one hundred miles in two hours.* **24** to conduct; manage: *run a business.* **25** unit of score in baseball or cricket. **26** time; period; spell: *a run of good luck, a run of wet weather.* **27** series of regular performances: *This play has had a run of two years.* **28** onward movement; progress; course; trend: *the run of events.* **29** a sudden demand or series of demands: *a run on a bank to draw out money.* **30** usual kind or sort: *the general run of children's books.* **31** freedom to go over or through, or to use: *The guests were given the run of the house.* **32** go about without restraint: *The children were allowed to run about the streets.* **33** number of fish moving together: *a run of salmon.* **34** stretch of ground or an enclosed place for animals: *a chicken run.* **35** drop stitches; ravel: *Nylon stockings often run.* **36** place where stitches have slipped out or become undone: *a run in a stocking.* **37** get past or through: *Enemy ships tried to run the blockade.* 1-21,24,32,35,37 *verb,* **ran, run, run ning;** 22,23,25-31,33,34,36 *noun.*

in the long run, on the whole; in the end: *In the long run we will have to investigate the mystery.*

run across, meet by chance: *I ran across an old friend in town today.*

run down, 1 stop going or working: *The clock has run down.* **2** chase till caught: *The fox ran down the hare.* **3** knock down by running against: *We stand a good chance of being run down by a car in this traffic.* **4** say bad things about: *run down a person, run down the food at a restaurant.* **5** make tired or ill: *She is run down from working too hard.*

run for it, run for safety: *As soon as they heard the siren, they ran for it.*

run in, pay a short visit: *My neighbor runs in to see me when she pleases.*

run into, 1 meet by chance: *I ran into an old friend at the library.* **2** crash into: *A large steamship ran into the tugboat.*

run out, come to an end: *After three minutes his time ran out on the telephone call.*

run out of, use up; have no more: *Mother ran out of eggs and had to borrow some from her neighbor.*

run over, 1 ride or drive over: *The car ran over some glass.* **2** overflow: *The waiter filled his cup too full and the coffee ran over onto the table.*

run through, 1 spend fast and foolishly: *My cousin ran through a whole week's allowance in one day.* **2** pierce. **3** review or rehearse: *The teacher ran through the homework assignment a second time.*

run a way (run′ə wā′), **1** person or animal that runs away. **2** running with nobody to guide or stop it; out of control: *a runaway horse.* **3** having

run away: *a runaway child.* **1** *noun,* 2,3 *adjective.*

run-down (run′doun′), **1** tired; sick. **2** falling to pieces; partly ruined: *a run-down old building.* **3** no longer going or working: *a run-down watch.* *adjective.*

rung[1] (rung). See **ring**[2]. *The bell has rung. verb.*

rung[2] (rung), **1** a round rod or bar used as a step of a ladder. **2** crosspiece set between the legs of a chair or as part of the back or arm of a chair. *noun.*

run ner (run′ər). See picture. **1** person, animal, or thing that runs; racer: *A runner arrived out of breath.* **2** in baseball, a player on the team at bat who either is on base or is running to the next base. **3** one of the narrow pieces upon which a sleigh, sled, or ice skate slides. **4** a long narrow strip: *We have a runner of carpet in our hall, and runners of linen and lace on bureaus.* **5** person or ship that tries to evade somebody; smuggler: *a blockade runner.* **6** a slender stem that takes root along the ground, thus producing new plants. *Strawberry plants spread by runners. noun.*

run ner-up (run′ər up′), player or team that takes second place in a contest. *noun.*

run ning (run′ing), **1** act of a person or thing that runs. **2** flowing; moving; not stopping: *I heard the running water of the falls. A running jump is one made with a run first.* **1** *noun,* **2** *adjective.*

running mate, candidate in an election who is paired with another candidate from the same political party who is running for a more important office.

runt (runt), animal, person, or plant which is smaller than the usual size. *noun.*

run way (run′wā′), **1** a smooth, level strip of land on which aircraft land and take off. **2** way, track, groove, trough, or the like, along which something moves or slides. **3** the beaten track of deer or other animals. *noun.*

rup ture (rup′chər), **1** breaking or being broken: *The rupture of a blood vessel usually causes the mark of a bruise.* **2** breaking off of friendly relations. **3** break; burst; break off. **4** the sticking out of some organ of the body through the muscular wall that surrounds it and should hold it in. 1,2,4 *noun,* 3 *verb,* **rup tured, rup tur ing.**

rur al (rür′əl), in the country; belonging to the country; like that of the country: *Rural life is quiet. adjective.*

rural delivery or **rural free delivery,** free delivery of mail in country districts by regular mail carriers.

ruse (rüz), trick or scheme to mislead others. *noun.*

rush[1] (rush), **1** move or go with speed and force: *The river rushed past.* **2** send, push, or force with speed or haste: *Rush this order, please.* **3** go or act with great haste: *They rush into things without knowing anything about them.* **4** attack with much speed and force: *The soldiers rushed the enemy.* **5** act of rushing; dash: *The rush of the flood swept everything before it.* **6** busy haste; hurry: *the rush of city life. What is your rush? Wait a minute.* **7** great or sudden effort of many people to go somewhere or get something: *The Christmas rush is hard on clerks.* **8** eager demand; pressure: *A sudden rush of business kept everyone working hard.* **9** requiring speed: *A rush order must be filled at once.* 1-4 *verb,* 5-8 *noun, plural* **rush es;** 9 *adjective.*

rush² (rush), a grasslike plant with a hollow stem that grows in wet soil or marshy places. The seats of chairs are sometimes made of rushes. *noun, plural* **rush es.**

rush hour, the time of day when traffic is heaviest or when trains and buses are most crowded.

rus set (rus′it), yellowish brown; reddish brown. See picture. *adjective.*

Rus sia (rush′ə), **1** the Soviet Union, a country reaching from eastern Europe across Asia to the Pacific Ocean. It is made up of 15 republics. **2** a former country in eastern Europe and northwestern Asia. It is now a large part of the Soviet Union. *noun.*

Rus sian (rush′ən), **1** of or having something to do with Russia, its people, or their language. **2** person born or living in Russia. **3** language of Russia. 1 *adjective,* 2,3 *noun.*

rust (rust), **1** the reddish-brown or orange coating that forms on iron or steel when exposed to air or moisture. **2** become covered with this: *Don't let the tools rust by leaving them out in the rain.* **3** become spoiled by not being used: *Don't let your mind rust during vacation.* **4** a plant disease that spots leaves and stems. 1,4 *noun,* 2,3 *verb.*

rus tic (rus′tik), **1** belonging to the country; rural; suitable for the country. **2** simple; plain; like those of country people: *Their rustic speech and ways made them uncomfortable in the royal palace.* **3** rough; awkward. **4** country person. 1-3 *adjective,* 4 *noun.*

rus tle (rus′əl), **1** a light, soft sound of things gently rubbing together. **2** make or cause to make this sound: *Leaves rustled in the breeze. The wind rustled the papers.* **3** steal (cattle or horses). 1 *noun,* 2,3 *verb,* **rus tled, rus tling.**

rustle up, 1 gather; find: *If I am to go on the trip, I must rustle up some money.* **2** get ready; prepare: *The cook rustled up some food.*

rus tler (rus′lər), a cattle thief. *noun.*

rust y (rus′tē), **1** covered with rust; rusted: *a rusty knife.* **2** made by rust: *a rusty spot.* **3** colored like rust. **4** damaged by lack of use: *My skating is rusty because I haven't skated all winter. adjective,* **rust i er, rust i est.**

rut (rut), **1** track made in the ground by wheels. **2** make ruts in. **3** a fixed or established way of acting: *Some people become so set in their ways that they get in a rut.* 1,3 *noun,* 2 *verb,* **rut ted, rut ting.**

ruth less (rüth′lis), having no pity; showing no mercy; cruel: *a ruthless dictator. adjective.*

rye (rī), **1** the grain of a kind of cereal grass, or the plant that it grows on. Rye grows in cool climates and is used for making flour and as food for farm animals. **2** made from rye grain or flour: *rye bread.* 1 *noun,* 2 *adjective.*

russet—The leaves in the fall are scarlet, yellow, and **russet.**

runner (definitions 1, 2, 3, and 6)

S s

S or **s** (es), the 19th letter of the English alphabet. There are two s's in *sister. noun, plural* **S's** or **s's.**

S or **S., 1** south. **2** southern.

Sab bath (sab′əth), day of the week used for rest and worship. Sunday is the Christian Sabbath. Saturday is the Jewish Sabbath. *noun.*

sa ber (sā′bər), a heavy, curved sword with a sharp edge, used by cavalry. *noun.*

sa ble (sā′bəl), **1** a flesh-eating animal somewhat like a weasel but larger. It has dark-brown, glossy fur. See picture. **2** its fur. Sable is one of the most costly furs. *noun.*

sac (sak), part like a bag in an animal or plant, often one that holds liquids. The human bladder is a sac. *noun.*

sa chem (sā′chəm), chief of a North American Indian tribe. *noun.*

sack[1] (sak), **1** a large bag made of coarse cloth. Sacks are used for holding grain, flour, potatoes, and charcoal. **2** such a bag with what is in it: *two sacks of corn.* **3** any bag with what is in it: *a sack of candy.* **4** put into a sack or sacks: *sack grain.* 1-3 *noun,* 4 *verb.*

sack[2] (sak), **1** plunder (a captured city): *The soldiers sacked the town.* **2** act of plundering (a captured city). 1 *verb,* 2 *noun.*

sac ra ment (sak′rə mənt), a solemn religious ceremony of the Christian church. Baptism is a sacrament. *noun.*

sa cred (sā′krid), **1** belonging to or dedicated to God; holy: *A church is a sacred building.* **2** connected with religion; religious: *sacred music.* **3** worthy of reverence: *the sacred memory of a dead hero.* **4** that must not be violated or disregarded: *She made a sacred promise. adjective.*

sac ri fice (sak′rə fīs), **1** act of offering to a god. **2** thing offered: *The ancient Hebrews killed animals on the altars as sacrifices to God.* **3** give or offer to a god. See picture. **4** giving up one thing for another: *Our teacher does not approve of any sacrifice of studies to sports.* **5** give up: *to sacrifice one's life for another.* **6** loss: *They sold their house at a sacrifice because they needed the money.* **7** sell at a loss. 1,2,4,6 *noun,* 3,5,7 *verb,* **sac ri ficed, sac ri fic ing.**

sad (sad), **1** not happy; full of sorrow: *You feel sad if your best friend goes away.* **2** causing sorrow: *The death of a pet is a sad loss. adjective,* **sad der, sad dest.**

sad den (sad′n), make or become sad: *The bad news saddened her. verb.*

sad dle (sad′l), **1** seat for a rider on a horse's back, on a bicycle, or on other like things. See pictures. **2** thing shaped like a saddle. A ridge between two mountain peaks is called a saddle. **3** put a saddle on: *Saddle the horse.* **4** burden: *to be*

sacrifice (definition 3)—The ancient Greeks **sacrificed** animals to their gods.

saddles (definition 1)

Western saddle

English saddle

saddled with too much work. 1,2 *noun,* 3,4 *verb,*
sad dled, sad dling.
in the saddle, in a position of control.

sa fa ri (sə fär′ē), journey or hunting expedition in
eastern Africa. *noun, plural* **sa fa ris.** [*Safari* comes
from an Arabic word meaning "a journey."]

safe (sāf), **1** free from harm or danger: *Keep money
in a safe place.* **2** not harmed: *She returned from the
mountain climbing expedition safe and sound.* **3** out
of danger; secure: *We feel safe with the dog in the
house.* **4** not causing harm or danger: *Is it safe to
leave the house unlocked? A soft rubber ball is a safe
plaything.* **5** careful: *a safe guess, a safe move.* **6** that
can be depended on: *a safe guide.* **7** (in baseball)
reaching a base without being put out. **8** place or
container for keeping things safe. 1-7 *adjective,*
saf er, saf est; 8 *noun.*

safe guard (sāf′gärd′), **1** keep safe; guard against
hurt or danger; protect: *Pure food laws safeguard
our health.* **2** protection; defense: *Keeping clean is a
safeguard against disease.* 1 *verb,* 2 *noun.*

safe keep ing (sāf′kē′ping), protection; keeping
safe; care. *noun.*

safe ty (sāf′tē), **1** freedom from harm or danger:
*There is a lifeguard at the swimming pool to assure
your safety.* **2** bringing no harm or danger; making
harm unlikely: *a safety pin, a safety match.* 1 *noun,*
2 *adjective.*

sag (sag), **1** sink under weight or pressure; bend
down in the middle. **2** hang down unevenly: *Your
coat sags in the back.* **3** become less firm or elastic;
yield through weakness, weariness, or lack of
effort; droop; sink: *Our courage sagged.* **4** a
sagging. 1-3 *verb,* **sagged, sag ging;** 4 *noun.*

sa ga (sä′gə), any story of heroic deeds. *noun.*

sage[1] (sāj), a wise man. *noun.*

sage[2] (sāj), the dried leaves of a plant, used as a
seasoning in food. *noun.*

sage brush (sāj′brush′), a grayish-green, bushy
plant, common on the dry plains of western North
America. *noun.*

said (sed), **1** See **say.** *He said he would come. She
had said "No" every time.* **2** named or mentioned
before: *the said witness, the said sum of money.*
1 *verb,* 2 *adjective.*

sail (sāl), **1** piece of cloth that catches the wind to
make a ship move on the water. **2** something like
a sail, such as the part of a windmill that catches
the wind. **3** trip on a boat with sails: *Let's go for a
sail.* **4** travel on water by the action of wind on
sails. **5** travel on a steamship. **6** move smoothly
like a ship with sails: *The swans sail along the lake.
The eagle sailed by. The dancers sailed across the
room.* **7** sail upon, over, or through: *sail the seas.*
8 manage a ship or boat: *The boys are learning to
sail.* **9** begin a trip by water: *She sailed from New
York.* 1-3 *noun,* 4-9 *verb.*

make sail or **set sail,** begin a trip by water: *We
will set sail for Europe next week.*

sail boat (sāl′bōt′), boat that is moved by sails.
Schooners and sloops are kinds of sailboats.
noun.

sail or (sā′lər), **1** person whose work is handling a

sailboat or other vessel. In these days most sailors
are on steamships. **2** member of a ship's crew.
Members of the United States Navy who are not
officers are called sailors. **3** like a sailor's: *Her
blouse has a sailor collar.* 1,2 *noun,* 3 *adjective.*

saint (sānt), **1** a very holy person. **2** person
declared to be a saint by a church. **3** person who
is very humble, patient, or like a saint in other
ways. *noun.*

Saint Ber nard (sānt′ bər närd′), a big,
powerful, brown-and-white dog with a large head.
Saint Bernards were once trained to rescue
travelers lost in the snow of the Swiss mountains.

saint ly (sānt′lē), like a saint; very holy; very
good. *adjective,* **saint li er, saint li est.**

sake (sāk), **1** cause; account; interest: *Do not go to
any trouble for our sakes.* **2** purpose; end: *We
moved to the country for the sake of peace and quiet.*
noun.

sal ad (sal′əd), raw green vegetables, such as
lettuce and celery, served with a dressing. Often
cold meat, fish, eggs, cooked vegetables, or fruits
are used along with, or instead of, the raw green
vegetables. *noun.* [*Salad* may have come from
Latin words of the Middle Ages, meaning "salted
herb."]

sal a man der (sal′ə man′dər), animal shaped like
a lizard, but belonging to the same group as frogs
and toads. Salamanders live in damp places. See
picture. *noun.*

sal ar y (sal′ər ē), fixed pay for regular work.
Teachers, government officials, and business
executives receive salaries. *noun, plural* **sal ar ies.**
[*Salary* comes from a Latin word meaning "money
given to soldiers for buying salt." In ancient times
salt was scarce, and therefore very expensive.]

salamander—about 5 inches (13 centimeters) long

sale (sāl), **1** act of selling; exchange of goods for money: *the sale of a house.* **2 sales,** the amount sold: *Today's sales were larger than yesterday's.* **3** selling at lower prices than usual: *This store is having a sale on suits.* noun.

for sale, to be sold: *That car is for sale.*

on sale, for sale at lower prices than usual: *The grocer has coffee on sale today.*

sales man (sālz/mən), man whose work is selling. *noun, plural* **sales men.**

sales wom an (sālz/wùm/ən), woman whose work is selling. *noun, plural* **sales wom en.**

sa li va (sə lī/və), liquid produced by glands in the mouth to keep it moist, help in chewing, and start digestion. *noun.*

sal i var y (sal/ə ver/ē), of or producing saliva: *the salivary glands.* adjective.

sal low (sal/ō), having a sickly, yellowish color. *adjective.*

sal ly (sal/ē), **1** rush forth suddenly; go out; set out briskly: *We sallied forth at dawn.* **2** a sudden rushing forth: *The men in the fort made a brave sally.* **1** *verb,* **sal lied, sal ly ing;** **2** *noun, plural* **sal lies.**

salm on (sam/ən), **1** a large food fish with silvery scales and yellowish-pink flesh. See picture. **2** yellowish pink. **1** *noun, plural* **salm ons** or **salm on; 2** *adjective.*

sa loon (sə lün/), place where alcoholic drinks are sold and drunk. *noun.*

salt (sôlt), **1** a white substance found in the earth and in sea water. Salt is used to season and preserve food. **2** containing salt: *The ocean is a great body of salt water.* **3** mix or sprinkle with salt. **4** preserve or season with salt: *salt the soup.* **5** a chemical compound of a metal and an acid. Baking soda is a salt. **1,5** *noun,* **2** *adjective,* **3,4** *verb.*

salt away or **salt down, 1** pack with salt to preserve: *The fish were salted down in a barrel.* **2** store away: *She is salting away money for her retirement.*

salt wa ter (sôlt/wô/tər), **1** consisting of or containing salt water: *a saltwater solution.* **2** living in the sea or in water like sea water: *saltwater fish.* adjective.

salt y (sôl/tē), containing salt; tasting of salt. Sweat and tears are salty. *adjective,* **salt i er, salt i est.**

sal u ta tion (sal/yə tā/shən), **1** greeting; saluting: *The man raised his hat in salutation.* **2** something uttered, written, or done to salute. You begin a letter with a salutation, such as "Dear Mr. Jones" or "Dear Sue." *noun.*

sa lute (sə lüt/), **1** honor in a formal manner by raising the hand to the head, by firing guns, or by dipping flags: *We salute the flag every day at school. The soldier saluted the officer.* **2** meet with kind words, a bow, a kiss, or other greeting; greet: *The old gentleman walked along the avenue saluting his friends.* **3** act of saluting; sign of welcome or honor: *The queen gracefully acknowledged the salutes of the crowd.* **4** position of the hand or a gun in saluting. **1,2** *verb,* **sa lut ed,**

sa lut ing; 3,4 *noun.* [*Salute* comes from a Latin word meaning "to wish good health to" or "to greet."]

sal vage (sal/vij), **1** act of saving a ship or its cargo from wreck or capture. **2** payment for saving it. **3** rescue of property from fire, flood, or shipwreck. **4** save from fire, flood, or shipwreck. **1-3** *noun,* **4** *verb,* **sal vaged, sal vag ing.**

sal va tion (sal vā/shən), **1** saving; being saved. **2** person or thing that saves. Christians believe that Christ is the salvation of the world. **3** saving the soul; deliverance from sin and from punishment for sin. *noun.*

salve (sav), **1** a soft, greasy substance put on wounds and sores; healing ointment: *Is this salve good for burns?* **2** put salve on. **3** something soothing: *The kind words were salve to his hurt feelings.* **4** soothe; smooth over: *She salved her conscience by the thought that her lie harmed no one.* **1,3** *noun,* **2,4** *verb,* **salved, salv ing.**

same (sām), **1** not another: *We came back the same way we went.* **2** just alike; not different: *Her name and mine are the same.* **3** not changed: *It is the same beautiful place.* **4** just spoken of: *We were talking about my aunt. This same aunt will be visiting us next week.* **5** the same person or thing. **6 the same,** in the same manner: *"Sea" and "see" are pronounced the same.* **1-4** *adjective,* **5** *pronoun,* **6** *adverb.*

all the same, regardless; nevertheless: *All the same, I'm glad to be at home again.*

just the same, 1 in the same manner: *The stairs creaked just the same as ever.* **2** nevertheless: *Just the same, I am planning to go.*

sam pan (sam/pan), any of various small boats of China and nearby regions. A sampan is sculled by one or more oars at the stern; it usually has a single sail. *noun.*

sam ple (sam/pəl), **1** part to show what the rest is like; one thing to show what the others are like: *Here are some samples of drapery material for you to choose from.* **2** take a part of; test a part of: *We sampled the cake and found it very good.* **1** *noun,* **2** *verb,* **sam pled, sam pling.**

san a to ri um (san/ə tôr/ē əm), place for treating people who are sick or recovering from an illness. People who have a long, slow disease like tuberculosis often go to sanatoriums. *noun.*

sanc tion (sangk/shən), **1** permission with authority; support; approval: *You need the owner's sanction to cross this property.* **2** approve; authorize; allow: *Her conscience does not sanction stealing.* **1** *noun,* **2** *verb.*

sanc tu ar y (sangk/chü er/ē), **1** a sacred place. A church is a sanctuary. **2** refuge or protection: *We found sanctuary from the storm in an abandoned cabin. noun, plural* **sanc tu ar ies.**

sand (sand), **1** tiny grains of worn-down rock: *the sands of the seashore, the sands of the desert.* **2** spread sand over: *The highway department sanded the icy road.* **3** scrape, smooth, polish, or clean with sand or sandpaper: *sand the edges of a piece of wood.* **1** *noun,* **2,3** *verb.*

san dal (san′dl), **1** kind of shoe made of a sole fastened to the foot by straps. **2** kind of slipper. *noun.*

sand box (sand′boks′), box for holding sand, especially for children to play in. *noun, plural* **sand box es.**

sand pa per (sand′pā′pər), **1** strong paper with sand glued on it, used for smoothing, cleaning, or polishing. **2** smooth, clean, or polish with sandpaper. 1 *noun,* 2 *verb.*

sand pip er (sand′pī′pər), a small bird with a long bill, living on sandy shores. See picture. *noun.*

sand stone (sand′stōn′), kind of rock formed mostly of sand. *noun.*

sand storm (sand′stôrm′), storm of wind that bears along clouds of sand. *noun.*

sand wich (sand′wich), **1** two or more slices of bread with meat, jelly, cheese, or some other filling between them. **2** put in (between): *I was sandwiched between two large boxes in the back seat of the car.* 1 *noun, plural* **sand wich es;** 2 *verb.* [*Sandwich* was named for the fourth Earl of Sandwich, a British official who lived from 1718 to 1792. He is said to have invented this kind of food so that he would not have to stop in the middle of a card game to eat a regular meal.]

sand y (san′dē), **1** containing sand; consisting of sand: *sandy soil.* **2** covered with sand: *Most of the shore is rocky, but there is a sandy beach.* **3** yellowish red: *She has sandy hair. adjective,* **sand i er, sand i est.**

sane (sān), **1** having a healthy mind; not crazy. **2** having or showing good sense; sensible: *A person with a sane attitude toward driving doesn't take chances. adjective,* **san er, san est.**

sang (sang). See **sing.** *The bird sang for us yesterday. verb.*

san i tar i um (san′ə ter′ē əm), sanatorium. *noun.*

san i tar y (san′ə ter′ē), **1** of or having to do with health; favorable to health; preventing disease: *sanitary regulations in a hospital.* **2** free from dirt and filth: *Food should be kept in a sanitary place. adjective.*

san i ta tion (san′ə tā′shən), working out ways to improve health conditions; practical application of sanitary measures. *noun.*

san i ty (san′ə tē), **1** soundness of mind; mental health. **2** soundness of judgment; sensibleness. *noun.*

sank (sangk). See **sink.** *The ship sank before help reached us. verb.*

sap¹ (sap), liquid that circulates through a plant, carrying water and food as blood does in animals. Rising sap carries water and dissolved minerals; sap going downward carries water and dissolved food. Maple syrup is made from the sap of some maple trees. *noun.*

sap² (sap), weaken; use up: *The extreme heat and humidity sapped her strength. verb,* **sapped, sap ping.**

sap ling (sap′ling), a young tree. *noun.*

sap phire (saf′īr), **1** a hard, clear, bright-blue

a hat	i it	oi oil	ch child	a in about
ā age	ī ice	ou out	ng long	e in taken
ä far	o hot	u cup	sh she	ə = { i in pencil
e let	ō open	ů put	th thin	o in lemon
ē equal	ô order	ü rule	‡H then	u in circus
ėr term			zh measure	

sandpiper—about 9 inches (23 centimeters) long

salmon (definition 1)—up to 19 inches (48 centimeters) long

precious stone. **2** bright blue: *a sapphire sky.* 1 *noun,* 2 *adjective.*

sar casm (sär′kaz′əm), **1** a sneering or cutting remark. **2** act of making fun of a person to hurt his feelings; harsh or bitter irony: *"How unselfish you are!" said the girl in sarcasm as her sister took the biggest piece of cake. noun.* [*Sarcasm* comes from a Greek word meaning "speak bitterly" or "tear the flesh."]

sar cas tic (sär kas′tik), using sarcasm; sneering; bitterly cutting: *"Don't hurry!" was my brother's sarcastic comment as I slowly dressed. adjective.*

sar dine (sär dēn′), one of several kinds of small fish preserved in oil for food. *noun, plural* **sar dines** or **sar dine.**

sa ri (sär′ē), a long piece of cotton or silk worn wound round the body with one end thrown over the head or shoulder. It is the outer garment of Hindu women. See picture. *noun, plural* **sa ris.**

sash[1] (sash), a long, broad strip of cloth or ribbon, worn as an ornament around the waist or over one shoulder. *noun, plural* **sash es.**

sash[2] (sash), frame for the glass of a window or door. *noun, plural* **sash es.**

sat (sat). See **sit.** *Yesterday I sat in a train all day. The cat has sat at that mouse hole for hours. verb.*

Sa tan (sāt′n), the evil spirit; the enemy of goodness; the Devil. *noun.*

satch el (sach′əl), a small bag, especially one for carrying clothes or books. *noun.*

sat el lite (sat′l īt), **1** a heavenly body that revolves around a planet or other larger heavenly body. The moon is a satellite of the earth. **2** an artificial object shot by a rocket into an orbit around the earth or other heavenly body. Such satellites are used to send weather and other scientific information back to earth; they also transmit television programs across the earth. See picture. **3** country that claims to be independent but is actually under the control of another. East Germany is a satellite of the Soviet Union. *noun.*

sat in (sat′n), **1** silk or rayon cloth with one very smooth, glossy side. **2** of satin; like satin; smooth and glossy. **1** *noun,* **2** *adjective.*

sat is fac tion (sat′i sfak′shən), **1** fulfillment; satisfying: *The satisfaction of hunger requires food.* **2** condition of being satisfied, or pleased and contented: *She felt satisfaction at having done well.* **3** anything that makes us feel pleased or contented: *It is a great satisfaction to have things turn out just the way you want. noun.*

sat is fac tor i ly (sat′i sfak′tər ə lē), in a satisfactory manner. *adverb.*

sat is fac tor y (sat′i sfak′tər ē), satisfying; good enough to satisfy; adequate: *If you do satisfactory work in the fourth grade, you will pass to the fifth grade. adjective.*

sat is fy (sat′i sfī), **1** give enough to; fulfill (desires, hopes, or demands); put an end to (needs or wants): *He satisfied his hunger with a sandwich and milk.* **2** make contented; please: *Are you satisfied now?* **3** pay; make right: *After the accident he satisfied all claims for the damage he had caused.* **4** set free from doubt; convince: *She is satisfied that it was an accident. verb,* **sat is fied, sat is fy ing.**

sat u rate (sach′ə rāt′), soak thoroughly; fill full: *During the fog, the air was saturated with moisture. verb,* **sat u rat ed, sat u rat ing.**

Sat ur day (sat′ər dē), the seventh day of the week; the day after Friday. *noun.* [*Saturday* comes from an earlier English word meaning "Saturn's day." It referred to the planet Saturn.]

Sat urn (sat′ərn), **1** the Roman god of agriculture. **2** the second largest planet. Saturn has a system of many rings around it. *noun.*

sa tyr (sā′tər), (in Greek myths) a creature of the woods, part man and part beast. *noun.*

sari

satellite (definition 2)—a communications satellite

saxophone

sauce (sôs), **1** something, usually a liquid, served with a food to make it taste better. We eat cranberry sauce with turkey and many different sauces with ice cream. **2** stewed fruit. *noun.*

sauce pan (sôs′pan′), a small pan with a handle, used for stewing, boiling, or other like things. *noun.*

sau cer (sô′sər), a shallow dish to set a cup on. *noun.*

sau cy (sô′sē), showing lack of respect; rude: *saucy language, saucy conduct. adjective,* **sau ci er, sau ci est.**

sauer kraut (sour′krout′), cabbage cut fine, salted, and allowed to sour. *noun.*

saun ter (sôn′tər), **1** walk along slowly and happily; stroll: *People sauntered through the park on summer evenings.* **2** a stroll. **1** *verb,* **2** *noun.*

sau sage (sô′sij), chopped pork, beef, or other meats, seasoned and usually stuffed into a thin tube. *noun.*

sav age (sav′ij), **1** member of a primitive, uncivilized people. **2** not civilized: *savage customs.* **3** fierce; cruel; ready to fight: *a savage dog.* **4** a fierce, brutal, or cruel person. **5** wild or rugged: *savage mountain scenery.* **1,4** *noun,* **2,3,5** *adjective.*

sav age ry (sav′ij rē), **1** fierceness; cruelty; brutality. **2** wildness. **3** an uncivilized condition. *noun, plural* **sav age ries.**

save[1] (sāv), **1** make safe from harm, danger, hurt, or loss; rescue: *The dog saved the boy's life. She saved her garden from the frost.* **2** keep safe from harm, danger, hurt, or loss; protect: *save one's honor.* **3** lay aside; store up: *save money, save rubber bands.* **4** keep from spending or wasting: *Save your strength.* **5** avoid expense or waste: *Save in every way you can.* **6** prevent; make less: *save work, save trouble.* **7** treat carefully to lessen wear or weariness: *Large print saves one's eyes.* **8** set free from sin and its results. *verb,* **saved, sav ing.**

save[2] (sāv), except; but: *I work every day save Sunday. preposition.*

sav ing (sā′ving), **1** tending to save up money; avoiding waste; economical. **2** savings, money saved. **3** way of saving money or time: *It will be a saving to take this shortcut.* **4** save; except; with the exception of: *Saving a few crusts, we had eaten nothing all day.* **1** *adjective,* **2,3** *noun,* **4** *preposition.*

sav ior (sā′vyər), one who saves or rescues. *noun.*

sa vor (sā′vər), **1** taste or smell; flavor: *The soup has a savor of onion.* **2** enjoy the taste or smell of: *We savored the soup.* **1** *noun,* **2** *verb.*

sa vor y (sā′vər ē), pleasing in taste or smell: *The savory smell of roasting turkey greeted us as we entered the house. adjective,* **sa vor i er, sa vor i est.**

saw[1] (sô), **1** tool for cutting, made of a thin blade with sharp teeth on the edge. **2** cut with a saw: *to saw wood.* **3** make with a saw: *Boards are sawed from logs.* **4** use a saw: *Can you saw straight?* **5** be sawed: *Pine saws more easily than oak.* **1** *noun,* **2-5** *verb,* **sawed, sawed** or **sawn, saw ing.**

saw[2] (sô). See **see**[1]. *I saw a robin yesterday. verb.*

saw dust (sô′dust′), particles of wood made by sawing. *noun.*

saw horse (sô′hôrs′), frame for holding wood that is being sawed. *noun.*

saw mill (sô′mil′), building where machines saw timber into planks or boards. *noun.*

sawn (sôn), sawed. See **saw**[1]. *verb.*

sax o phone (sak′sə fōn), a brass musical wind instrument with keys for the fingers and a reed mouthpiece. See picture. *noun.* [*Saxophone* was formed from the name of its Belgian inventor, Adolphe Sax, who lived from 1814 to 1894, and a Greek word meaning "sound."]

say (sā), **1** speak: *What did you say? "Thank you," she said.* **2** put into words; declare: *Say what you think.* **3** recite; repeat: *Say your prayers.* **4** about; approximately: *You can learn to dance in, say, ten lessons.* **5** express an opinion: *It is hard to say which shirt is nicer.* **6** chance to say something: *If you have all had your say, we will vote on the matter.* **7** power; authority: *Who has the final say in this matter?* **1-3,5** *verb,* **said, say ing;** **4** *adverb,* **6,7** *noun.*

say ing (sā′ing), **1** something said; statement. **2** proverb: *"Haste makes waste" is a saying. noun.*

says (sez). See **say**. *He says he'll be late. verb.*

scab (skab), crust that forms over a sore as it heals: *A scab started to form on my scraped knee. noun.*

scab bard (skab′ərd), sheath or case for the blade of a sword, dagger, or knife. *noun.*

scaf fold (skaf′əld), **1** a temporary structure for holding workmen and materials. See picture. **2** a raised platform on which criminals are put to death. *noun.*

scaffold (definition 1)—used to bring materials to the various floors of a building under construction

scald (skôld), **1** burn with hot liquid or steam: *I scalded myself with hot grease.* **2** burn caused by hot liquid or steam: *The scald on his hand came from lifting a pot cover carelessly.* **3** pour boiling liquid over: *Scald the dishes before drying them.* **4** heat almost to boiling, but not quite: *Scald the milk.* 1,3,4 *verb,* 2 *noun.*

scale[1] (skāl), **1** the dish or pan of a balance. **2 scales,** balance; instrument for weighing: *She weighed some meat on the scales. noun.*

scale[2] (skāl), **1** one of the thin, flat, hard plates forming the outer covering of some fishes, snakes, and lizards. **2** a thin layer like a scale: *My sunburn caused my skin to peel off in scales.* **3** remove scales from: *She scaled the fish with a knife.* **4** come off in scales: *The paint is scaling off the house.* 1,2 *noun,* 3,4 *verb,* **scaled, scal ing.**

scale[3] (skāl), **1** series of steps or degrees; scheme of graded amounts: *The salary scale for this job ranges from $8000 to $10,000 a year.* **2** series of marks made along a line at regular distances to use in measuring. A thermometer has a scale. **3** instrument marked in this way, used for measuring. **4** size of a plan, map, drawing, or model compared with what it represents: *This map is drawn to the scale of one inch for each 100 miles.* **5** relative size or extent: *An ambassador must entertain on a large scale.* **6** reduce by a certain amount in relation to other amounts: *To draw this map, mileage was scaled down to one inch for each 100 miles.* **7** (in music) a series of tones ascending or descending in pitch: *She practices scales on the piano.* **8** climb: *They scaled the wall by ladders.* 1-5,7 *noun,* 6,8 *verb,* **scaled, scal ing.**

scal lop (skol'əp), **1** a shellfish somewhat like a clam. In some kinds the large muscle that opens and closes the shell is good to eat. See picture. **2** bake with sauce and bread crumbs in a dish: *scalloped oysters, scalloped tomatoes.* **3** one of a series of curves on the edge of anything: *This cuff has scallops.* **4** make with such curves: *She scalloped the edge of the quilt.* 1,3 *noun,* 2,4 *verb.*

scalp (skalp), **1** skin on the top and back of the head, usually covered with hair. **2** cut or tear the scalp from. 1 *noun,* 2 *verb.*

scal y (skā'lē), covered with scales; having scales like a fish: *This iron pipe is scaly with rust. adjective,* **scal i er, scal i est.**

scamp (skamp), rascal; rogue. *noun.*

scam per (skam'pər), run quickly: *The mice scampered away when the cat came. verb.*

scan (skan), look at closely; examine with care: *You should scan every word of the contract before you sign it. verb,* **scanned, scan ning.**

scan dal (skan'dl), **1** a shameful action that brings disgrace or shocks public opinion: *It was a scandal for the city treasurer to take tax money for personal use.* **2** damage to reputation; disgrace. **3** public talk about a person which will hurt that person's reputation; evil gossip; slander. *noun.*

scan dal ize (skan'dl īz), offend by something thought to be wrong or improper; shock: *Our great-grandparents would be scandalized by many of the things we do today. verb,* **scan dal ized, scan dal iz ing.**

scan dal ous (skan'dl əs), **1** disgraceful; shameful; shocking. **2** spreading scandal or slander: *a scandalous piece of gossip. adjective.*

scant (skant), **1** not enough in size or quantity: *Her coat was short and scant.* **2** barely enough; barely full; bare: *Use a scant cup of butter in the cake. You have a scant hour to pack. adjective.*

scant y (skan'tē), **1** not enough: *His scanty clothing did not keep out the cold.* **2** barely enough; meager: *Drought caused a scanty harvest. adjective,* **scant i er, scant i est.**

scar (skär), **1** mark left by a healed cut, wound, burn, or sore: *My vaccination scar is small.* **2** any mark like this: *See the scars your shoes have made on the chair.* **3** mark with a scar: *He scarred the wood with the hammer when he missed the nail.* 1,2 *noun,* 3 *verb,* **scarred, scar ring.**

scarce (skers or skars), hard to get; rare: *Very old stamps are scarce. adjective,* **scarc er, scarc est.**

scarce ly (skers'lē or skars'lē), **1** not quite; barely: *We could scarcely see the ship through the thick fog.* **2** decidedly not: *He can scarcely have said that. adverb.*

scar ci ty (sker'sə tē or skar'sə tē), too small a supply; lack; rarity: *There is a scarcity of nurses. noun, plural* **scar ci ties.**

scare (sker or skar), **1** frighten: *We were scared and ran away.* **2** fright: *I had a sudden scare when I saw a dog running toward me.* **3** a widespread state of fright or panic: *a bomb scare at the airport.* Such scares are often exaggerated and without foundation or reason. **4** frighten (away); drive off: *The watchdog scared away the robber by barking.* 1,4 *verb,* **scared, scar ing;** 2,3 *noun.*

scare crow (sker'krō' or skar'krō'), figure of a person dressed in old clothes, set in a field to frighten birds away from growing crops. *noun.*

scarf (skärf), a long, broad strip of silk, lace, or other material, worn about the neck, shoulders, or head. *noun, plural* **scarfs, scarves** (skärvz).

scar let (skär'lit), very bright red. *adjective.*

scarlet fever, a disease most often of children that causes a scarlet rash, sore throat, and fever. You can catch scarlet fever if you are around someone who has it.

scar y (sker'ē or skar'ē), causing fright or alarm: *scary sounds, a scary movie. adjective,* **scar i er, scar i est.**

scat ter (skat'ər), **1** throw here and there; sprinkle: *I scattered salt on the sidewalk to melt the ice.* **2** separate and drive off in different directions: *The police scattered the disorderly crowd.* **3** separate and go in different directions: *The chickens scattered in fright when the truck honked at them. verb.*

scav en ger (skav'ən jər), animal that feeds on dead and decaying animals or plants. Vultures are scavengers. *noun.*

scene (sēn), **1** time, place, and circumstances of a play or story: *The scene of the book is laid in Boston in the year 1775.* **2** the painted screens or hangings used in a theater to represent places: *The scene*

a hat	i it	oi oil	ch child	⎧ a in about
ā age	ī ice	ou out	ng long	⎪ e in taken
ä far	o hot	u cup	sh she	ə = ⎨ i in pencil
e let	ō open	ù put	th thin	⎪ o in lemon
ē equal	ô order	ü rule	ŦH then	⎩ u in circus
ėr term			zh measure	

scepter—At her coronation, Queen Elizabeth II held a **scepter** in her right hand.

scallop (definition 1) shell up to 3 inches (8 centimeters) long

scene (definition 4)—five scenes of family life, painted by a fourteen-year-old

represents a city street. **3** part of an act of a play: *The king comes to the castle in Act I, Scene 2.* **4** view; picture: *The white sailboats in the blue water made a pretty scene.* See picture. **5** show of strong feeling in front of others: *The child kicked and screamed and made a dreadful scene.* noun. [*Scene* comes from a Greek word, originally meaning "tent" or "booth." Later, the word was used to mean "background for plays" and "stage of a theater."]

scen er y (sē′nər ē), **1** the general appearance of a place: *She enjoys mountain scenery very much.* **2** the painted hangings or screens used in a theater to represent places: *The scenery pictures a garden in the moonlight.* noun, plural **scen er ies.**

scen ic (sē′nik), **1** of or having something to do with natural scenery: *The scenic splendors of Yellowstone National Park are famous.* **2** having much fine scenery: *a scenic highway.* adjective.

scent (sent), **1** smell: *The scent of roses filled the air. The dog scented a rabbit and ran off after it.* **2** sense of smell: *Many dogs have a keen scent.* **3** smell left in passing: *The dogs followed the fox by the scent.* **4** means by which a thing or a person can be traced: *The police are on the scent of the thieves.* **5** have a suspicion of; be aware of: *I scent a trick in their offer.* **6** perfume: *She used too much scent.* **7** fill with odor; perfume: *scented writing paper.* 1-4,6 *noun,* 1,5,7 *verb.*

scep ter (sep′tər), rod or staff carried by a ruler as a symbol of royal power or authority. See picture. noun.

sched ule (skej′ùl), **1** a written or printed statement of details; list: *A timetable is a schedule of the coming and going of trains.* **2** make a schedule of; enter in a schedule. 1 *noun,* 2 *verb,* **sched uled, sched ul ing.**

scheme (skēm), **1** program of action; plan: *He has a scheme for extracting salt from sea water.* **2** plot: *a scheme to cheat the government.* **3** plan; plot: *They were scheming to smuggle the stolen jewels into the country.* **4** system of connected things, parts, or thoughts: *The color scheme of the room is blue and gold.* 1,2,4 *noun,* 3 *verb,* **schemed, schem ing.**

schol ar (skol′ər), **1** person having much knowledge: *The professor was a famous scholar.* **2** pupil at school; learner. noun.

schol ar ly (skol′ər lē), **1** of a scholar; like that of a scholar: *scholarly habits.* **2** having much knowledge. adjective.

schol ar ship (skol′ər ship), **1** possession of knowledge gained by study; quality of learning and knowledge. **2** money given to help a student continue his or her studies: *The college offered her a scholarship of one thousand dollars.* noun.

school[1] (skül), **1** place for teaching and learning:

schooner

scooter

score (definition 4)—She tried to score a basket.

Children go to school to learn. **2** learning in school; instruction: *Most children start school when they are about five years old.* **3** regular meetings of teachers and pupils for teaching and learning. **4** time or period of such meetings: *stay after school.* **5** pupils who are taught and their teachers: *Our school will be in a new building next fall.* **6** group of people holding the same beliefs or opinions: *the French school of painting.* **7** a particular department or group in a university: *a medical school, a law school.* **8** teach; train; discipline: *School yourself to control your temper.* **9** of or having something to do with a school or schools. 1-7 *noun,* 8 *verb,* 9 *adjective.*

school² (skül), a large number of the same kind of fish or water animals swimming together: *a school of mackerel. noun.*

school book (skül′bůk′), book for study in schools. *noun.*

school boy (skül′boi′), boy attending school. *noun.*

school girl (skül′gėrl′), girl attending school. *noun.*

school house (skül′hous′), building used as a school. *noun, plural* **school hous es** (skül′hou′ziz).

school ing (skü′ling), instruction in school; education received at school. *noun.*

school mas ter (skül′mas′tər), man who teaches in a school, or is its principal. *noun.*

school mate (skül′māt′), companion at school. *noun.*

school mis tress (skül′mis′tris), woman who teaches in a school, or is its principal. *noun, plural* **school mis tress es.**

school room (skül′rüm′), room in which pupils are taught. *noun.*

school teach er (skül′tē′chər), person who teaches in a school. *noun.*

school work (skül′wėrk′), a student's work in school. *noun.*

school yard (skül′yärd′), piece of ground around or near a school, used for play or games. *noun.*

schoon er (skü′nər), ship with two or more masts and sails set lengthwise. See picture. *noun.*

schwa (shwä), **1** an unstressed vowel sound such as *a* in *about* or *o* in *lemon.* **2** the symbol ə, used to represent this sound. *noun.*

sci ence (sī′əns), **1** knowledge based on observed facts and tested truths arranged in an orderly system. **2** branch of such knowledge. Biology, chemistry, physics, and astronomy are **natural sciences.** Economics is a **social science.** Agriculture and engineering are **applied sciences.** *noun.*

sci en tif ic (sī′ən tif′ik), **1** using the facts and laws of science: *a scientific method, a scientific farmer.* **2** of or having something to do with science; used in science: *scientific books, scientific instruments. adjective.*

sci en tist (sī′ən tist), person who has expert knowledge of some branch of science. Persons specially trained in and familiar with the facts and laws of such fields of study as biology, chemistry, mathematics, physics, geology, and astronomy are scientists. *noun.*

scis sors (siz′ərz), tool or instrument for cutting that has two sharp blades so fastened that they will work toward each other. *noun plural or singular.*

scoff (skôf), make fun to show one does not believe something; mock: *We scoffed at the idea of swimming in three inches of water. verb.*

scold (skōld), **1** find fault with; blame with angry words: *I scolded them for misbehaving.* **2** find fault; talk angrily: *Don't scold so much.* **3** person who scolds. 1,2 *verb,* 3 *noun.*

scoop (sküp), **1** tool like a small shovel for dipping out or shoveling up things. A kitchen utensil to take out flour or sugar is a scoop. A large ladle is a scoop. **2** part of a dredge or steam shovel that holds coal, sand, or other like things. **3** amount taken up at one time by a scoop: *Use two scoops of flour and one of sugar.* **4** take up or out with a scoop, or as a scoop does: *You scoop up snow with your hands to make snowballs.* **5** hollow out; dig out; make by scooping: *The children scooped holes in the sand.* 1-3 *noun,* 4,5 *verb.*

scoot er (skü′tər), a child's vehicle consisting of a board for the feet between two wheels, one in front of the other, steered by a handlebar and pushed by one foot against the ground. See picture. *noun.*

scope (skōp), **1** distance the mind can reach; extent of view: *Very hard words are not within the scope of a child's understanding.* **2** space; opportunity: *A class discussion gives scope for new ideas. noun.*

scorch (skôrch), **1** burn slightly; burn on the outside: *The cake tastes scorched.* **2** a slight burn. **3** dry up; wither: *The grass is scorched by so much hot sunshine.* 1,3 *verb,* 2 *noun, plural* **scorch es.**

score (skôr), **1** record of points made in a game, contest, or test: *The score was 9 to 2 in favor of our school.* **2** make as points in a game, contest, or test: *score two runs in the second inning.* **3** keep a record of the number of points made in a game or contest: *The teacher will appoint some pupil to score for both sides.* **4** make as an addition to the score; gain; win: *She scored five runs for our team.* See picture. **5** group or set of twenty: *A score or more were present at the party.* **6** a written or printed piece of music arranged for different instruments or voices: *She was studying the score of the piece she was learning to play.* 1,5,6 *noun,* 2-4 *verb,* **scored, scor ing.**

settle a score, get even for an injury or wrong: *He had an old score to settle.*

scorn (skôrn), **1** look down upon; think of as mean or low; despise: *Most people scorn tattletales.* **2** reject or refuse as low or wrong: *The judge scorned to take a bribe.* **3** a feeling that a person or act is mean or low; contempt: *Most pupils feel scorn for those who cheat.* 1,2 *verb,* 3 *noun.*

scorn ful (skôrn′fəl), showing contempt; mocking; full of scorn: *They spoke of our old car in a scornful way. adjective.*

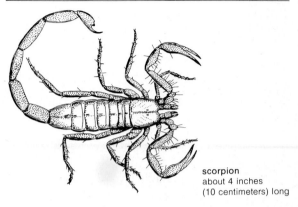

scorpion
about 4 inches
(10 centimeters) long

scor pi on (skôr′pē ən), a small animal belonging to the same group as the spider and having a poisonous sting in its tail. See picture. *noun.*

Scotch (skoch), Scottish. *adjective, noun.*

Scotch tape, trademark for a very thin, transparent or opaque adhesive tape used for mending or sealing.

Scot land (skot′lənd), division of Great Britain north of England. *noun.*

Scot tish (skot′ish), **1** of or having something to do with Scotland or its people. **2** people of Scotland. 1 *adjective,* 2 *noun plural.*

scoun drel (skoun′drəl), a very bad person without honor or good principles; villain; rascal: *The scoundrels set fire to the barn. noun.*

scour[1] (skour), clean or polish by hard rubbing: *I scoured the sink with cleanser. verb.*

scour[2] (skour), move quickly over or through in search or pursuit: *We scoured the house for my pet snake. verb.*

scourge (skėrj), **1** whip. **2** any means of punishment. **3** punish. **4** some thing or person that causes great trouble or misfortune. Formerly, an outbreak of disease was called a scourge. 1,2,4 *noun,* 3 *verb,* **scourged, scourg ing.**

scout (skout), **1** person sent to find out what the enemy is doing. A scout usually wears a uniform; a spy does not. **2** thing that acts as a scout. Some ships and airplanes are scouts. **3** act as a scout; hunt around to find something: *Go and scout for firewood for the picnic.* **4** person belonging to the Boy Scouts or Girl Scouts. 1,2,4 *noun,* 3 *verb.*

scout mas ter (skout′mas′tər), adult in charge of a troop of Boy Scouts. *noun.*

scow (skou), a large boat with a flat bottom used to carry freight, sand, or other like things. *noun.*

scowl (skoul), **1** look angry or sullen by lowering the eyebrows; frown: *Something must be troubling you, for you're scowling.* **2** an angry, sullen look; frown. 1 *verb,* 2 *noun.*

scram ble (skram′bəl), **1** make one's way by climbing or crawling: *We scrambled up the steep, rocky hill.* **2** climb or walk over rough ground: *It was a long scramble through bushes and over rocks to the top of the hill.* **3** struggle with others for something: *The players scrambled to get the ball.* **4** struggle to possess: *the scramble for wealth and power.* **5** scrambling; any disorderly struggle or activity: *The pile of boys on the football seemed a wild scramble of arms and legs.* **6** cook (eggs) with the whites and yolks mixed together. 1,3,6 *verb*, **scram bled, scram bling;** 2,4,5 *noun*.

scrap¹ (skrap), **1** a small piece; little bit; small part left over: *The cook gave some scraps of meat to the dog.* See picture. **2** make into scraps; break up. **3** throw aside as useless or worn out. 1 *noun*, 2,3 *verb*, **scrapped, scrap ping.**

scrap² (skrap), a fight, quarrel, or struggle: *Those two dogs are always scrapping. verb,* **scrapped, scrap ping.**

scrap book (skrap′bùk′), book in which pictures or clippings are pasted and kept. *noun.*

scrape (skrāp), **1** rub with something sharp or rough; make smooth or clean by doing this: *Scrape your muddy shoes with this old knife.* **2** remove by rubbing with something sharp or rough: *We need to scrape the peeling paint off the house before we repaint it.* **3** scratch or graze by rubbing against something rough: *She fell and scraped her knee on the sidewalk.* **4** act of scraping. **5** a scraped place. **6** rub with a harsh sound: *The branch scraped against the window.* **7** give a harsh sound; grate. **8** a harsh, grating sound: *the scrape of the bow of a violin.* **9** collect by scraping or with difficulty: *I was so hungry I scraped every crumb from my plate. I've finally scraped together enough money for a bicycle.* **10** difficulty; position hard to get out of: *Children often get into scrapes.* 1-3,6,7,9 *verb*, **scraped, scrap ing;** 4,5,8,10 *noun*.

scrap er (skrā′pər), tool for scraping: *We removed the loose paint with a scraper. noun.*

scratch (skrach), **1** break, mark, or cut slightly with something sharp or rough: *Your feet have scratched the chair.* **2** mark made by scratching: *There are deep scratches on this desk.* **3** tear or dig with the nails or claws: *The cat scratched me.* **4** a very slight cut: *That scratch on your hand will soon be well.* **5** rub or scrape to relieve itching: *Don't scratch your mosquito bites.* **6** rub with a harsh noise; rub: *I scratched the match on a rock.* **7** sound of scratching: *the scratch of a pen.* **8** write in a hurry or carelessly. **9** scrape out; strike out; draw a line through. 1,3,5,6,8,9 *verb*, 2,4,7 *noun*, *plural* **scratch es.**

from scratch, with no advantages; from the beginning: *They had to borrow money and start their business from scratch.*

scrawl (skrôl), **1** write or draw poorly or carelessly. **2** poor, careless handwriting. 1 *verb*, 2 *noun*.

scraw ny (skrô′nē), lean; thin; skinny: *Turkeys have scrawny necks. adjective,* **scraw ni er, scraw ni est.**

scrap¹ (definition 1)—Her dress was made of **scraps** of cloth.

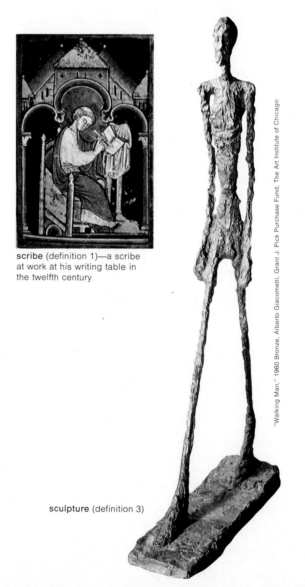

scribe (definition 1)—a scribe at work at his writing table in the twelfth century

"Walking Man," 1960 Bronze. Alberto Giacometti, Grant J. Pick Purchase Fund, The Art Institute of Chicago

sculpture (definition 3)

scream (skrēm), **1** make a loud, sharp, piercing cry. People scream in fright, in anger, and in excitement. **2** a loud, sharp, piercing cry. 1 *verb*, 2 *noun*.

screech (skrēch), **1** cry out sharply in a high voice; shriek: *Someone screeched, "Help! Help!"* **2** a shrill, harsh scream or sound: *The screeches brought the police.* 1 *verb*, 2 *noun*, *plural* **screech es.**

screen (skrēn), **1** a covered frame that hides, protects, or separates: *We keep the trunk behind a screen.* **2** wire woven together with small openings in between: *We have screens at the windows to keep out flies.* **3** anything like a screen: *A screen of trees hides our house from the road.* **4** shelter, protect, or hide with, or as with, a screen: *We have screened our porch to keep out flies.* **5** surface on which motion pictures, television images, or slides appear or are shown. **6** sieve for sifting sand, gravel, coal, seed, or other like things. **7** sift with a screen or as with a screen: *screen sand. Many government agencies screen their employees for loyalty.* 1-3,5,6 *noun*, 4,7 *verb*.

screw (skrü), **1** kind of nail, with a ridge twisted evenly round its length: *Turn the screw to the right to tighten it.* **2** cylinder with a ridge winding around it. **3** anything that turns like a screw or looks like one. **4** turn as one turns a screw; twist: *screw a lid on a jar.* **5** fasten or tighten with a screw or screws: *The carpenter screwed the hinges to the door.* **6** propeller that moves a boat or ship. 1-3,6 *noun*, 4,5 *verb*.

screw driv er (skrü′drī′vər), tool for putting in or taking out screws by turning them. *noun*.

scrib ble (skrib′əl), **1** write or draw carelessly or hastily. **2** make marks that do not mean anything. **3** something scribbled. 1,2 *verb*, **scrib bled, scrib bling;** 3 *noun*.

scribe (skrīb), **1** person whose occupation is writing. Before printing was invented, there were many scribes. See picture. **2** (in ancient times) a teacher of the Jewish law. *noun*.

scrim mage (skrim′ij), **1** a rough fight or struggle. **2** play in football that takes place when the two teams are lined up and the ball is snapped back. *noun*.

script (skript), **1** handwriting; written letters, figures, signs, or characters. **2** style of printing that looks like handwriting. **3** manuscript of a play, actor's part, or radio or television broadcast. *noun*.

Scrip ture (skrip′chər), **1** the Bible. **2** the Scriptures or the Holy Scriptures, the Bible. **3** scripture, any sacred writing. *noun*.

scroll (skrōl), **1** roll of parchment or paper, especially one with writing on it. See picture. **2** ornament resembling a partly unrolled sheet of paper, or having a spiral or coiled form. *noun*.

scrub[1] (skrub), **1** rub hard; wash or clean by rubbing: *The floor needs to be scrubbed with a brush and soap.* **2** scrubbing: *Give your face and hands a good scrub.* 1 *verb*, **scrubbed, scrub bing;** 2 *noun*.

scrub[2] (skrub), **1** low, stunted trees or shrubs. **2** anything small or below the usual size: *The stray we found is a little scrub of a dog.* **3** small; poor; inferior. A scrub ball team is made up of inferior, substitute, or untrained players. 1,2 *noun*, 3 *adjective*.

a hat	i it	oi oil	ch child	(a in about
ā age	ī ice	ou out	ng long	e in taken
ä far	o hot	u cup	sh she	ə = { i in pencil
e let	ō open	u̇ put	th thin	o in lemon
ē equal	ô order	ü rule	ŦH then	(u in circus
ėr term			zh measure	

scruff (skruf), skin at the back of the neck; the back of the neck. *noun*.

scru ple (skrü′pəl), feeling of uneasiness that keeps a person from doing something: *She has scruples about ever telling a lie. noun*.

scru pu lous (skrü′pyə ləs), **1** very careful to do what is right. **2** attending thoroughly to details; very careful: *A restaurant has to be scrupulous about cleanliness. adjective*.

scu ba (skü′bə), portable breathing equipment, including one or more tanks of compressed air, used by underwater swimmers or divers. *noun*. [*Scuba* comes from the words *self contained underwater breathing apparatus*. It was formed by using the first letter of each of those words.]

scuff (skuf), **1** walk without lifting the feet; shuffle. **2** wear or injure the surface of by hard use: *scuff one's shoes. verb*.

scuf fle (skuf′əl), **1** struggle or fight in a rough, confused manner: *The children were scuffling over the ball.* **2** a confused, rough struggle or fight: *I lost my hat in the scuffle.* 1 *verb*, **scuf fled, scuf fling;** 2 *noun*.

scull (skul), **1** oar worked with a side twist over the end of a boat to make it go. **2** one of a pair of oars used, one on each side, by a single rower. **3** make (a boat) go by a scull or by sculls. 1,2 *noun*, 3 *verb*.

sculp tor (skulp′tər), person who carves or models figures. Sculptors make statues of marble and bronze. *noun*.

sculp ture (skulp′chər), **1** art of carving or modeling figures. Sculpture includes the cutting of statues from blocks of marble, stone, or wood, casting in bronze, and modeling in clay or wax. **2** make figures this way; carve or model. **3** sculptured work; piece of such work: *There are many famous sculptures in the museums.* See picture. **4** cover or ornament with sculpture. 1,3 *noun*, 2,4 *verb*, **sculp tured, sculp tur ing.**

scroll (definition 1)

scum (skum), **1** a thin layer that rises to the top of a liquid: *When the jelly boils, you skim off the scum. Green scum floated on the pond.* **2** undesirable people: *the scum of the town. noun.*

scur ry (skėr′ē), **1** run quickly; scamper; hurry: *We could hear the mice scurry about in the walls.* **2** a hasty running; hurrying: *With much fuss and scurry, we at last got started.* **1** *verb,* **scur ried, scur ry ing; 2** *noun, plural* **scur ries.**

scur vy (skėr′vē), **1** disease caused by a lack of vegetables and fruits. It causes swollen and bleeding gums, extreme weakness, and spots that look like bruises on the skin. Scurvy used to be common among sailors when they had little to eat except bread and salt meat. **2** mean; contemptible; base: *a scurvy fellow, a scurvy trick.* **1** *noun,* **2** *adjective,* **scur vi er, scur vi est.**

scut tle[1] (skut′l), kind of bucket for holding or carrying coal. *noun.*

scut tle[2] (skut′l), scamper; scurry: *The dogs scuttled off into the woods. verb,* **scut tled, scut tling.**

scut tle[3] (skut′l), cut holes through the bottom or sides of (a ship) to sink it: *After the pirates captured the ship, they scuttled it. verb,* **scut tled, scut tling.**

scythe (sīᴛн), a long, slightly curved blade on a long handle, used for mowing or reaping. *noun.*

SE or **S.E., 1** southeast. **2** southeastern.

sea (sē), **1** the great body of salt water that covers almost three fourths of the earth's surface; the ocean. **2** any large body of salt water, smaller than an ocean: *the North Sea, the Mediterranean Sea.* **3** a large, heavy wave: *A high sea swept over the ship's deck.* **4** swell of the ocean. **5** an overwhelming amount or number: *a sea of trouble. noun.*

at sea, 1 out on the sea: *We were at sea out of sight of land for ten days.* **2** puzzled; confused: *I can't understand this problem; I'm all at sea.*

follow the sea, be a sailor: *When I saw the ocean for the first time, I dreamed of following the sea.*

go to sea, 1 become a sailor: *The captain had gone to sea when he was barely seventeen.* **2** begin a voyage: *The family went to sea last month.*

put to sea, begin a voyage: *Our fleet put to sea from Boston.*

sea board (sē′bôrd′), land near the sea; seacoast; seashore: *New York City is on the Atlantic seaboard. noun.*

sea coast (sē′kōst′), land along the sea: *the seacoast of North America. noun.*

sea far ing (sē′fer′ing *or* sē′far′ing), going, traveling, or working on the sea: *a hardy seafaring people. adjective.*

sea food (sē′füd′), saltwater fish and shellfish that are good to eat. *noun.*

sea go ing (sē′gō′ing), **1** going by sea; seafaring. **2** fit for going to sea: *a seagoing tugboat. adjective.*

sea gull, any gull, especially one living on or near the sea.

sea horse, a small fish with a head that looks somewhat like a horse's head. See picture.

seal[1] (sēl), **1** design stamped on a piece of wax or other soft material, used to show ownership or authority. The seal of the United States is attached to important government papers. See picture. **2** stamp for marking things with such a design: *a seal with one's initials on it.* **3** piece of wax, paper, or metal on which the design is stamped. **4** mark with a seal: *The treaty was signed and sealed by both governments.* **5** close very tightly; fasten: *Seal the letter before mailing it. I sealed the jars of fruit. Her promise sealed her lips.* **6** settle; determine: *The judge's words sealed the prisoner's fate.* **7** give a sign that (a thing) is true: *They sealed their bargain by shaking hands.* **8** a special kind of stamp: *Christmas seals.* **1-3,8** *noun,* **4-7** *verb.*

seal[2] (sēl), **1** a sea animal with large flippers, usually living in cold regions. Some kinds have very valuable fur. **2** its fur. **3** leather made from the skin of a seal. *noun, plural* **seals** or **seal.**

sea level, surface of the sea. Mountains, plains, and ocean beds are measured as so many feet or meters above or below sea level.

sealing wax, kind of wax, soft when heated, used for sealing letters or packages. It is made of resin and shellac.

sea lion, a large seal of the Pacific coast.

seal skin (sēl′skin′), skin or fur of the seal, prepared for use. *noun.*

seam (sēm), **1** line formed by sewing together two pieces of cloth, canvas, leather, and the like: *the seams of a coat, the seams of a sail.* **2** any line where edges join: *The seams of the boat must be filled in or they will leak.* **3** any mark or line like a seam: *The old sword cut had left a seam in his face.* **4** mark with seams, furrows, wrinkles, and the like; scar. **5** layer: *a seam of coal.* **1-3,5** *noun,* **4** *verb.*

sea man (sē′mən), **1** sailor. **2** sailor who is not an officer. *noun, plural* **sea men.**

seam stress (sēm′stris), woman whose work is sewing. *noun, plural* **seam stress es.**

sea plane (sē′plān′), airplane that can rise from and land on water. See picture. *noun.*

sea port (sē′pôrt′), port or harbor on the seacoast; city or town with a harbor that ships can reach from the sea: *San Francisco is a seaport. noun.*

sear (sir), **1** burn the surface of: *The hot iron seared my hand.* **2** dry up; wither. *verb.*

search (sėrch), **1** try to find by looking; seek; look for (something): *We searched all day for the lost kitten.* **2** look through; go over carefully; examine, especially for something concealed: *The police searched the prisoners to see if they had weapons.* **3** act of searching; examination: *She found her book after a long search.* **1,2** *verb,* **3** *noun, plural* **search es.**

in search of, trying to find; looking for: *The children went in search of their lost dog.*

search ing (sėr′ching), examining carefully; thorough: *a searching look, a searching examination. adjective.*

search light (sėrch′līt′), **1** a powerful light that can throw a bright beam in any direction. **2** beam of light so thrown. *noun.*

sea shell (sē′shel′), shell of any shellfish, such as an oyster or conch. *noun.*

sea shore (sē′shôr′), land at the edge of a sea; shore. *noun.*

sea sick (sē′sik′), sick because of a ship's motion. *adjective.*

sea side (sē′sīd′), **1** seashore. **2** of or at the seaside: *a seaside hotel.* **1** *noun,* **2** *adjective.*

sea son (sē′zn), **1** one of the four periods of the year; spring, summer, autumn, or winter. **2** any period of time marked by something special: *the holiday season, the harvest season.* **3** improve the flavor of: *Season your egg with salt.* **4** give interest or character to: *She seasoned her speech with humor.* **5** make or become fit for use by a period of keeping or treatment: *Wood is seasoned for building by drying and hardening it.* **1,2** *noun,* **3-5** *verb.*

in season, at the right time.

sea son al (sē′zn əl), having to do with the seasons; depending on a season; happening at regular intervals: *Monsoon rains are seasonal in Asia and Africa. adjective.*

sea son ing (sē′zn ing), something that gives a better flavor: *Salt, pepper, and spices are seasonings. noun.*

seat (sēt), **1** thing to sit on. Chairs, benches, and stools are seats. *Take a seat, please.* **2** place to sit. **3** place in which one has the right to sit. When we say that someone has a seat in Congress, we mean that that person is a member of Congress. **4** that part of a chair, bench, stool, and the like, on which one sits: *This bench has a broken seat.* **5** that part of the body on which one sits, or the clothing covering it: *The seat of her jeans is patched.* **6** set or place on a seat: *Please seat yourself in a comfortable chair.* **7** have seats for: *Our school auditorium seats one thousand pupils.* **8** an established place or center: *A university is a seat of learning. The seat of our government is in Washington, D.C.* **1-5,8** *noun,* **6,7** *verb.*

be seated, sit down.

seat belt, belt attached to the seat of an automobile or airplane, used to hold its occupant in the seat in the event of a crash, jolt, or bump.

sea ward (sē′wərd), toward the sea: *Our house faces seaward. adjective, adverb.*

sea way (sē′wā′), an inland waterway that is deep enough to permit ocean shipping: *Ocean-going freighters reach Detroit by passing through the St. Lawrence Seaway. noun.*

sea weed (sē′wēd′), any plant or plants growing in the sea. *noun.*

sec., second; seconds.

se clud ed (si klü′did), shut off from others; undisturbed: *a secluded cottage in the woods. adjective.*

se clu sion (si klü′zhən), keeping apart or being shut off from others; retirement: *She lives in seclusion apart from her friends. noun.*

sec ond[1] (sek′ənd), **1** next after the first: *the second seat from the front, the second prize.* **2** below the first; inferior: *the second officer on a ship, cloth*

a hat	i it	oi oil	ch child	⎧ a in about
ā age	ī ice	ou out	ng long	e in taken
ä far	o hot	u cup	sh she	ə = ⎨ i in pencil
e let	ō open	u̇ put	th thin	o in lemon
ē equal	ô order	ü rule	ᴛʜ then	⎩ u in circus
ėr term			zh measure	

seal[1] (definition 1)—the seal of the President of the United States

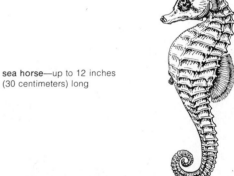

sea horse—up to 12 inches (30 centimeters) long

seaplane

of second quality. **3** another; other: *Napoleon has been called a second Caesar.* **4** person or thing that is second. **5 seconds,** goods below first quality: *These stockings are seconds and have some slight defects.* **6** person who supports or aids another: *The prizefighter had a second.* **7** support; back up; assist: *One member made a motion to adjourn the meeting, and another seconded it.* 1-3 *adjective,* 4-6 *noun,* 7 *verb.*

**sec ond² ** (sek′ənd), one of the 60 very short equal periods of time that make up a minute. The time between the ticks of some clocks is a second. *noun.*

sec ond ar y (sek′ən der′ē), **1** next after the first in order, place, time, or importance: *A secondary industry uses products produced by other industries as its raw materials.* **2** having less importance: *Reading fast is secondary to reading well. adjective.*

secondary accent, 1 accent in a word that is stronger than no accent but weaker than the strongest accent. The second syllable of *ab bre′ vi a′tion* has a secondary accent. **2** mark (′) used to show this.

secondary school, school attended after elementary school; high school.

sec ond-class (sek′ənd klas′), **1** of or belonging to the class next after the first: *second-class mail.* **2** by the second grade of passenger seating and service offered by a ship, airplane, or train: *We could afford only to travel second-class.* **3** of inferior grade or quality. 1,3 *adjective,* 2 *adverb.*

sec ond-hand (sek′ənd hand′), **1** not original; obtained from another: *second-hand information.* **2** not new; used already by another: *a second-hand car.* **3** dealing in used goods: *a second-hand bookstore. adjective.*

sec ond ly (sek′ənd lē), in the second place. *adverb.*

se cre cy (sē′krə sē), **1** condition of being secret or being kept secret. **2** ability to keep things secret. *noun.*

se cret (sē′krit), **1** kept from the knowledge of others: *a secret errand, a secret weapon.* **2** keeping to oneself what one knows: *Be as secret as the grave.* **3** known only to a few: *a secret sign.* **4** kept from sight; hidden: *a secret drawer.* **5** something secret or hidden: *Can you keep a secret?* **6** a hidden cause or reason: *I wish I knew the secret of her success.* 1-4 *adjective,* 5,6 *noun.*

in secret, secretly; privately; not openly: *I have said nothing in secret that I would not say openly.*

sec re tar y (sek′rə ter′ē), **1** person who writes letters and keeps records for a person, company, club, committee, and the like: *Our club has a secretary who keeps the minutes of the meeting.* **2** person who has charge of a department of the government. The Secretary of the Treasury is the head of the Treasury Department. **3** a writing desk with a set of drawers, and often with shelves for books. See picture. *noun, plural* **sec re tar ies.**

se crete (si krēt′), **1** keep secret; hide. **2** make; prepare; produce: *Glands in the mouth secrete saliva. verb,* **se cret ed,** **se cret ing.**

se cre tion (si krē′shən), **1** substance that is secreted by some part of an animal or plant: *Bile is the secretion of the liver.* **2** producing and discharging of such a substance. *noun.*

sect (sekt), group of people having the same principles, beliefs, or opinions: *Each religious sect in the town had its own church. noun.*

sec tion (sek′shən), **1** part cut off; part; division; slice: *Cut the pie into eight equal sections.* **2** division of a book: *Our arithmetic book has several sections on fractions.* **3** region; part of a country, city, community, or group: *the business section of a town.* **4** cut into sections; divide into sections: *section an orange.* **5** representation of a thing as it would appear if cut straight through. **6** district one mile square. A township usually contains 36 sections. 1-3,5,6 *noun,* 4 *verb.*

se cure (si kyur′), **1** safe against loss, attack, escape, or danger: *This is a secure hiding place.* **2** make safe; protect: *You cannot secure yourself against all risks and dangers.* **3** sure; certain; that can be counted on: *We know in advance that our victory is secure.* **4** free from care or fear: *He hoped for a secure old age.* **5** firmly fastened; not liable to break or fall: *The boards of this bridge do not look secure.* **6** make firm or fast: *Secure the locks on the doors and windows.* **7** get; obtain: *We have secured our tickets for the school play.* 1,3-5 *adjective,* 2,6,7 *verb,* **se cured,** **se cur ing.**

se cur i ty (si kyur′ə tē), **1** freedom from danger, care, or fear; feeling or condition of being safe: *It gave us a sense of security to have the lifeguard nearby while we swam.* **2** something that secures or makes safe: *My watchdog is a security against burglars. noun, plural* **se cur i ties.**

se dan (si dan′), **1** a closed automobile seating four or more persons. **2** sedan chair. *noun.*

sedan chair, a covered chair carried on poles by two men. Sedan chairs were much used during the 1600's and 1700's. See picture.

sedge (sej), a grasslike plant that grows in wet places. Sedges have solid, three-sided stems. *noun.*

sed i ment (sed′ə mənt), **1** matter that settles to the bottom of a liquid. **2** earth and stones deposited by water, wind, or ice: *When the Nile River overflows, it leaves sediment on the land it covers. noun.*

sed i men tar y (sed′ə men′tər ē), **1** of sediment; having something to do with sediment. **2** formed by the depositing of sediment. Shale is a sedimentary rock. *adjective.*

se duce (si düs′ *or* si dyüs′), tempt to wrongdoing; persuade to do wrong: *Benedict Arnold was seduced by the offer of great wealth, and betrayed his own country to the enemy. verb,* **se duced,** **se duc ing.**

see¹ (sē), **1** look at; be aware of by using the eyes: *See that black cloud.* **2** have the power of sight: *The blind do not see.* **3** understand; be aware of with the mind: *I see what you mean.* **4** find out: *I will see what needs to be done.* **5** take care; make sure: *See that the work is done properly.* **6** have knowledge or experience of: *That coat has seen hard wear.* **7** go with; attend; escort: *She saw her friend home safely.* **8** call on: *I went to see a friend.* **9** receive a visit from: *She is too ill to see anyone.* **10** visit; attend: *We saw the new book fair. verb,* **saw, seen, see ing.**

see through, 1 understand the real character or hidden purpose of: *I saw through their excuses.* **2** go through with; finish: *I mean to see this job through.* **3** watch over or help through difficulty: *His friends saw him through his time of illness.*

see to, look after; take care of: *They saw to it that their children had good educations.*

see[2] (sē), district under a bishop's authority. *noun.*

seed (sēd), **1** part of a plant from which a flower, vegetable, or other plant grows: *We planted seeds in the garden. Part of every crop is saved for seed.* **2** sow with seed; scatter seed over: *The farmer seeded the field with corn. Dandelions seed themselves.* **3** produce seeds; shed seeds. **4** remove the seeds from: *I seeded the grapes.* **5** source or beginning of anything: *the seeds of trouble.* 1,5 *noun, plural* **seeds** or **seed**; 2-4 *verb.*

seed case (sēd′kās′), any pod or other dry, hollow fruit that contains seeds. *noun.*

seed ling (sēd′ling), a very young plant. *noun.*

seek (sēk), **1** try to find; look for; hunt; search: *seek for something lost. We are seeking a new home.* **2** try to get: *Some people seek wealth. Friends sought her advice.* **3** try; attempt: *Nations are seeking to make peace with one another. verb,* **sought, seek ing.**

seem (sēm), **1** look like; appear to be: *This apple seemed good but was rotten inside. The dog seems to like that bone. Does this room seem hot to you?* **2** appear to oneself: *I still seem to hear the music.* **3** appear to exist: *There seems no need to wait longer. verb.*

seem ing ly (sē′ming lē), apparently; as far as appearances go: *This hill is, seemingly, the highest around here. adverb.*

seen (sēn). See **see**[1]. *Have you seen Father? verb.*

seep (sēp), ooze; trickle: *Water seeps through sand. verb.*

see saw (sē′sô′), **1** plank resting on a support near its middle so that the ends can move up and down. **2** a children's game in which the children sit at opposite ends of such a plank and move up and down. **3** move up and down on such a plank: *The two children seesawed in the playground.* 1,2 *noun,* 3 *verb.*

seethe (sēᵺ), **1** be excited; be disturbed: *She seethed with anger at being unjustly fired from her job.* **2** bubble and foam: *Water seethed under the falls. verb,* **seethed, seeth ing.**

seg ment (seg′mənt), piece or part cut off, marked off, or broken off; division; section: *An orange is easily pulled apart into its segments. noun*

seg re gate (seg′rə gāt), to separate one racial group from others by having separate schools, restaurants, theaters, and the like. *verb,* **seg re gat ed, seg re gat ing.**

seg re ga tion (seg′rə gā′shən), separation of one racial group from others, especially in

secretary (definition 3)

sedan chair

schools, restaurants, and other public places. The United States Supreme Court ruled in 1954 that segregation in public schools is unconstitutional. *noun.*

seine (sān), a fishing net that hangs straight down in the water. A seine has floats at the upper edge and weights at the lower. See picture. *noun.*

seis mo graph (sīz′mə graf), instrument for recording earthquakes. *noun.*

seize (sēz), **1** take hold of suddenly; clutch; grasp: *In fright I seized her arm.* **2** take possession of by force: *The soldiers seized the city.* *verb,* **seized, seiz ing.**

sei zure (sē′zhər), **1** act of seizing. **2** condition of being seized. **3** a sudden attack of disease. *noun.*

sel dom (sel′dəm), rarely; not often: *I am seldom ill.* *adverb.*

se lect (si lekt′), **1** choose; pick out: *Select the book you want.* **2** picked as best; chosen specially: *She is one of a select group of skiers chosen to compete.* **3** careful in choosing; particular as to friends, company, or associates: *He was asked to join a very select club.* **1** *verb,* **2,3** *adjective.*

se lec tion (si lek′shən), **1** choice: *This library has a good selection of mystery stories.* **2** person, thing, or group chosen: *This book of stories is my selection.* *noun.*

self (self), **1** one's own person: *Your self is you. My self is I.* **2** one's own welfare or interests: *It is good to think more of others and less of self.* **3** character of a person; nature of a person or thing: *She does not seem like her former self.* *noun, plural* **selves.**

self-ad dressed (self′ə drest′), addressed to oneself: *Send a self-addressed envelope along with your order.* *adjective.*

self-con fi dence (self′kon′fə dəns), belief in one's own ability, power, or judgment; confidence in oneself. *noun.*

self-con scious (self′kon′shəs), embarrassed, especially by the presence or the thought of other people and their attitude toward one; shy. *adjective.*

self-con trol (self′kən trōl′), control of one's actions or feelings. *noun.*

self-de fense (self′di fens′), defense of one's own person, property, or reputation. *noun.*

self-gov ern ment (self′guv′ərn mənt), government of a group by its own members: *We have self-government through our elected representatives.* *noun.*

self ish (sel′fish), caring too much for oneself; caring too little for others. Selfish people put their own interests first. *adjective.*

self-re spect (self′ri spekt′), respect for oneself; proper pride. *noun.*

self same (self′sām′), very same: *We study the selfsame books that you do.* *adjective.*

sell (sel), **1** exchange for money or other payment: *We plan to sell our house.* **2** deal in; keep for sale: *The butcher sells meat.* **3** be on sale; be sold: *Strawberries sell at a high price in January.* **4** give up; betray: *The traitor sold his country for money.* *verb,* **sold, sell ing.**

seine—African fishermen using a seine. It is lowered into the water and pulled to shore.

sell er (sel′ər), person who sells: *A druggist is a seller of drugs.* *noun.*

selves (selvz), more than one self: *She has two selves—one that likes to save money and one that likes to spend it.* noun plural.

sem a phore (sem′ə fôr), device for signaling. Railroad semaphores are posts or other structures with movable arms. Hand-held flags in different positions are another kind of semaphore, used chiefly on ships. *noun.*

sem i cir cle (sem′i sėr′kəl), half a circle: *We sat in a semicircle around the fire.* *noun.*

sem i co lon (sem′i kō′lən), mark of punctuation (;) that shows a separation not so complete as that shown by a period. EXAMPLE: *We arrived much later than we had intended; consequently there was almost no time left for swimming.* *noun.*

sem i fi nal (sem′i fī′nl), **1** one of the two rounds or matches that settles who will play in the final one, which follows: *The team that will face the state champions defeated our team in the semifinal.* **2** having something to do with such a round or match: *Our team lost in the semifinal game.* **1** *noun,* **2** *adjective.*

sem i nar y (sem′ə ner′ē), school or college for training students to be priests, ministers, or rabbis. *noun, plural* **sem i nar ies.**

sen ate (sen′it), **1** a governing or lawmaking assembly. The highest council of state in ancient Rome was called the senate. **2** the upper and smaller branch of an assembly that makes laws. The Congress of the United States is the Senate and the House of Representatives. *noun.* [*Senate* comes from a Latin word meaning "an old man." The original Roman senate was called this because it was made up of a group of old men.]

sen a tor (sen′ə tər), member of a senate. *noun.*

send (send), **1** cause to go from one place to another: *to send someone for a doctor, to send someone on an errand.* **2** cause to be carried: *We sent the letter by air mail.* **3** cause to come, occur, or be: *Send help at once.* **4** drive; throw: *send a ball. The volcano sent clouds of smoke into the air.* *verb,* **sent, send ing.**

sen ior (sē′nyər), 1 the older (used of a father whose son has the same name): *John Parker, Senior, is the father of John Parker, Junior.* 2 older: *a senior citizen.* 3 an older person: *I am my sister's senior by seven years.* 4 higher in rank or longer in service: *Mr. Jones is the senior member of the firm of Jones and Brown.* 5 person of higher rank or longer service. 6 student who is a member of the graduating class of a high school or college. 7 of or having something to do with these students: *the senior class, the senior year.* 1,2,4,7 *adjective,* 3,5,6 *noun.*

se ñor (sā nyôr′), a Spanish word meaning: 1 Mr. or sir. 2 a gentleman. *noun, plural* **se ño res** (sā nyōr′ās).

se ño ra (sā nyōr′ä), a Spanish word meaning: 1 Mrs. or madam. 2 a lady. *noun, plural* **se ño ras.**

se ño ri ta (sā′nyō rē′tä), a Spanish word meaning: 1 Miss. 2 a young lady. *noun, plural* **se ño ri tas.**

sen sa tion (sen sā′shən), 1 action of the senses; power to see, hear, feel, taste, or smell: *Blindness is the loss of the sensation of sight.* 2 feeling: *Ice gives a sensation of coldness. I have a sensation of dizziness when I walk along cliffs.* 3 strong or excited feeling: *The announcement of peace caused a sensation throughout the nation.* *noun.*

sen sa tion al (sen sā′shə nəl), 1 arousing strong or excited feeling: *The player's sensational catch made the crowd cheer.* 2 trying to arouse strong or excited feeling: *a sensational newspaper story.* *adjective.*

sense (sens), 1 power of the mind to know what happens outside itself. Sight, smell, taste, hearing, and touch are the five senses. *A dog has a keen sense of smell.* 2 feeling: *The extra lock on the door gives us a sense of security.* 3 feel; understand: *I sense that you would rather not go.* 4 understanding; appreciation: *Everyone thinks he has a good sense of humor.* 5 senses, a clear or sound state of mind: *They must be out of their senses to climb that steep cliff.* 6 judgment; intelligence: *She had the good sense to stay out of the argument.* 7 meaning: *What sense does the word have in each sentence?* 1,2,4-7 *noun,* 3 *verb,* **sensed, sens ing.**

make sense, have a meaning; be reasonable: *"Cow cat bless Monday" doesn't make sense.*

sense less (sens′lis), 1 unconscious: *A hard blow on the head knocked him senseless.* 2 foolish; stupid: *a senseless idea.* *adjective.*

sen si bil i ty (sen′sə bil′ə tē), 1 ability to feel or perceive: *Some drugs lessen a person's sensibilities.* 2 fineness of feeling: *She has an unusual sensibility for colors.* *noun, plural* **sen si bil i ties.**

sen si ble (sen′sə bəl), having good sense; showing good judgment; wise: *She is too sensible to do anything foolish.* *adjective.*

sen si tive (sen′sə tiv), 1 receiving impressions readily: *The eye is sensitive to light.* 2 easily affected or influenced: *The mercury in the thermometer is sensitive to changes in temperature.* 3 easily hurt or offended: *to be sensitive about one's weight.* *adjective.*

a hat	i it	oi oil	ch child	a in about
ā age	ī ice	ou out	ng long	e in taken
ä far	o hot	u cup	sh she	ə = i in pencil
e let	ō open	u̇ put	th thin	o in lemon
ē equal	ô order	ü rule	ᵀH then	u in circus
ėr term			zh measure	

sen sor y (sen′sər ē), of or having to do with sensation or the senses. The eyes and ears are sensory organs. *adjective.*

sent (sent). See send. *They sent the trunks last week. She was sent on an errand.* *verb.*

sen tence (sen′təns), 1 group of words that expresses a complete thought. "Boys and girls" is not a sentence. "The boys and girls are here" is a sentence. 2 decision by a judge on the punishment of a criminal. 3 the punishment itself. 4 pronounce punishment on: *The judge sentenced the thief to five years in prison.* 1-3 *noun,* 4 *verb,* **sen tenced, sen tenc ing.**

sen ti ment (sen′tə mənt), 1 mixture of thought and feeling. Admiration, patriotism, and loyalty are sentiments. 2 feeling, especially tender feeling: *My sister is full of sentiment.* 3 thought or saying that expresses feeling. 4 a personal opinion. *noun.*

sen ti men tal (sen′tə men′tl), 1 having or showing much tender feeling: *sentimental poetry.* 2 likely to act from feelings rather than from logical thinking; having too much sentiment. 3 of sentiment; dependent on sentiment: *These old family photographs have sentimental value. adjective.*

sen ti nel (sen′tə nəl), person stationed to keep watch and guard against surprises. *noun.*

sen try (sen′trē), soldier stationed at a place to keep watch and guard against surprises. *noun, plural* **sen tries.**

se pal (sē′pəl), one of the leaflike parts which make up the calyx, or outer covering, of a flower. In a carnation, the sepals make a green cup at the base of the flower. In a tulip, the sepals are bright, just like the petals. *noun.*

sep a rate (sep′ə rāt′ *for 1-3;* sep′ər it *for 4 and 5*), 1 be between; keep apart; divide: *The Atlantic Ocean separates America from Europe.* 2 go, draw, or come apart: *The children separated in all directions. The rope separated under the strain.* 3 put apart; take away: *Separate your books from mine.* 4 apart from others: *in a separate room.* 5 divided; not joined: *separate seats.* 1-3 *verb,* **sep a rat ed, sep a rat ing;** 4,5 *adjective.*

sep a ra tion (sep′ə rā′shən), 1 act of separating; dividing; taking apart. 2 condition of being apart; being separated: *The friends were glad to meet after so long a separation.* *noun.*

Sept., September.

Sep tem ber (sep tem′bər), the ninth month of the year. It has 30 days. *noun.* [*September,* the Latin name for this month, came from a Latin word meaning "seven." The month was called this because it was the seventh month in the ancient Roman calendar.]

sep ul cher (sep′əl kər), place for putting the bodies of persons who have died; tomb. *noun.*

se quel (sē′kwəl), **1** something that follows as a result of some earlier happening; a result of something; outcome: *Among the sequels of the party were many stomach aches.* **2** a complete story continuing an earlier one about the same characters: *"Son of Lassie" is a sequel to the movie "Lassie Come Home."* *noun.*

se quence (sē′kwəns), **1** the coming of one thing after another; succession; order of succession: *Arrange the names in alphabetical sequence.* **2** connected series: *a sequence of lessons on one subject.* *noun.*

se quoi a (si kwoi′ə), an evergreen tree of California that bears cones and grows to a height of over 300 feet. *noun.* [The *sequoia* was named in honor of Sequoya, a Cherokee Indian who invented a way of writing his own language. He lived from 1770 to 1843.]

se ra pe (sə rä′pē), shawl or blanket, often having bright colors, worn by Spanish Americans. *noun.*

ser e nade (ser′ə nād′), **1** music played or sung outdoors at night, especially by a lover under his sweetheart's window. **2** sing or play to in this way. **1** *noun,* **2** *verb,* **ser e nad ed, ser e nad ing.**

se rene (sə rēn′), **1** peaceful; calm: *serene happiness, a serene smile.* **2** clear; bright; not cloudy: *a serene sky.* *adjective.*

se ren i ty (sə ren′ə tē), **1** quiet peace; calmness. **2** clearness; brightness. *noun, plural* **se ren i ties.**

serf (sėrf), **1** slave who could not be sold off the land but passed from one owner to another with the land. **2** person treated almost like a slave; person who is mistreated or underpaid. *noun.*

ser geant (sär′jənt), **1** an army or marine officer ranking next above a corporal. **2** officer in the air force next above the lowest rank. **3** a police officer ranking next above an ordinary policeman. *noun.*

ser i al (sir′ē əl), **1** story published, broadcast, or televised one part at a time in a magazine or newspaper or on the radio or television. **2** of a series; arranged in a series; making a series: *in serial order, a serial number.* **1** *noun,* **2** *adjective.*

ser ies (sir′ēz), **1** number of things alike in a row: *A series of rooms opened off the long hall.* **2** number of things placed one after another: *names in an alphabetical series.* **3** number of things or events happening one after the other: *A series of rainy days spoiled their vacation.* *noun, plural* **ser ies.**

ser i ous (sir′ē əs), **1** thoughtful; grave: *a serious face.* **2** in earnest; not fooling: *Are you joking or serious?* **3** important; needing thought: *Choice of one's life work is a serious matter.* **4** important because it may do much harm; dangerous: *The patient was in serious condition.* *adjective.*

ser mon (sėr′mən), **1** a public talk on religion or something connected with religion, usually given by a clergyman. **2** a serious talk about conduct or duty: *After the guests left, the children got a sermon on their table manners.* *noun.*

ser pent (sėr′pənt), snake, especially a big snake. *noun.*

ser um (sir′əm), **1** the clear, pale-yellow, watery part of the blood, which separates from the clot when blood thickens. **2** liquid used to prevent or cure a disease, obtained from the blood of an animal that has been made immune to the disease. Polio vaccine is a serum. *noun.*

serv ant (sėr′vənt), **1** person employed in a household. Cooks and nursemaids are servants. **2** person employed by another. Police and firefighters are public servants. **3** person devoted to any service: *a servant of God.* *noun.*

serve (sėrv), **1** work for; be a servant; work: *to serve a worthwhile cause, to serve customers in a store, to serve in the army.* **2** wait on at table; bring food to: *The waiter served us.* **3** put (food or drink) on the table: *The waitress served the soup. Dinner is served.* **4** supply; furnish; supply with something needed: *The dairy serves us with milk.* **5** supply enough for: *One pie will serve six persons.* **6** be useful; be what is needed; be used: *A flat stone served as a table.* **7** be favorable or suitable; satisfy: *The ship will sail when the wind and tide serve.* **8** pass; spend: *The thief served a term in prison.* **9** deliver; present: *She was served with a notice to appear in court.* **10** put (the ball) in play by hitting it in tennis and similar games. *verb,* **served, serv ing.**

serve one right, be just what one deserves: *The punishment served him right.*

serv ice (sėr′vis), **1** helpful act or acts; aid; being useful to others: *They performed many services for their community.* **2** supply; arrangements for supplying: *Bus service was good.* **3** occupation or employment as a servant: *She is in service with a wealthy family.* **4 services, a** performance of duties: *He no longer needs the services of a doctor.* **b** work in the service of others: *We pay for services such as repairs, maintenance, and utilities.* **5** advantage; benefit; use: *This coat has given me great service.* **6** department of government or public employment, or the persons working in it: *the diplomatic service.* **7** army, navy, or air force: *We were in the service together.* **8** a religious meeting; religious ceremony: *They attend services on Friday evening. The marriage service was performed at the home of the bride.* **9** manner of serving food or the food served: *The service in this restaurant is excellent.* **10** number of things to be used together at the table: *a silver tea service.* **11** make fit for service; keep fit for service: *The mechanic serviced our automobile.* **12** act or manner of putting the ball in play in tennis and similar games. **1-10,12** *noun,* **11** *verb,* **serv iced, serv ic ing.**

serv ice a ble (sėr′vi sə bəl), **1** useful for a long time; able to stand much use: *We want to buy a serviceable used car.* **2** capable of giving good service; useful. *adjective.*

serv ice man (sėr′vis man′), member of the armed forces. *noun, plural* **serv ice men.**

ser vile (sėr′vəl), **1** like that of slaves; fit for a slave; mean: *servile flattery.* **2** of slaves: *a servile revolt, servile work.* *adjective.*

ser vi tude (sėr′və tüd *or* sėr′və tyüd), **1** slavery;

a hat	i it	oi oil	ch child	⎧ a in about
ā age	ī ice	ou out	ng long	e in taken
ä far	o hot	u cup	sh she	ə = ⎨ i in pencil
e let	ō open	ů put	th thin	o in lemon
ē equal	ô order	ü rule	ŦH then	⎩ u in circus
ėr term			zh measure	

set (definitions 2, 3, and 12)

bondage. **2** forced labor as a punishment: *The criminal was sentenced to five years' servitude. noun.*

ses sion (sesh′ən), **1** sitting or meeting of a court, council, or legislature. **2** series of such sittings. **3** term or period of such sittings: *This year's session of Congress was unusually long.* **4** meeting: *an important session with the manager.* **5** a single, continuous course or period of lessons and study: *Our school has two sessions, one in the morning and one in the afternoon. noun.*

in session, meeting: *Congress is now in session.*

set (set). See picture. **1** put in some place; put; place: *Set the box on its end.* **2** put in the right place, position, or condition for use; arrange; put in proper order: *The hunter sets his traps. Set the table for dinner. Set the clock. The doctor set my broken leg.* **3** put in some condition or relation: *A spark set the woods on fire. The slaves were set free.* **4** fix; arrange; appoint: *The teacher set a time limit for the examination.* **5** fixed or appointed beforehand; established: *a set time, set rules.* **6** ready: *I am all set to try again.* **7** provide for others to follow: *set a good example.* **8** put in a fixed, rigid, or settled state: *set one's teeth.* **9** fixed; rigid: *a set smile.* **10** become fixed; make or become firm or hard: *Jelly sets as it cools.* **11** put in a frame or other thing that holds: *set a diamond in gold.* **12** go down; sink: *The sun sets in the west.* **13** group; things or people belonging together: *a set of dishes.* **14** the scenery of a play or for a motion picture. **15** device for receiving or sending by radio, television, telephone, or telegraph. **16** form; shape; the way a thing is put or placed: *There was a stubborn set to her jaw.* **17** begin to move; start: *We set out to hike ten miles.* **18** begin to apply; begin to apply oneself: *set to work.* **19** (in music) adapt; fit: *set words to music.* **20** put (a hen) to sit on eggs to hatch them; place (eggs) under a hen to be hatched. 1-4,7,8,10-12,17-20 *verb,* **set, set ting;** 5,6,9 *adjective,* 13-16 *noun.*

set about, start work upon; begin: *set about washing.*

set down, put into writing.

set forth, 1 make known; express; declare: *set forth one's opinions on a subject.* **2** start to go: *set forth on a trip around the world.*

set in, begin: *Winter set in early.*

set off, 1 explode: *to set off a string of firecrackers.* **2** start to go: *set off for home.* **3** increase by contrast: *The green dress set off her red hair.*

set on or **set upon, 1** attack. **2** urge to attack.

set up, 1 build: *set up a monument.* **2** begin; start: *He sold his old business and set up a new one.*

set back (set′bak′), check to progress; reverse: *The team suffered a setback when its best player became sick. noun.*

severe—The **severe** weather made even walking difficult.

setter (definition 2)—about 2 feet (60 centimeters) high at the shoulder

settee

set tee (se tē′), sofa or long bench with a back and, usually, arms. See picture. *noun.*

set ter (set′ər), **1** person or thing that sets: *a setter of type, a setter of jewels.* **2** a long-haired hunting dog, trained to stand motionless and point its nose toward the game that it scents. See picture. *noun.*

set ting (set′ing), **1** frame or other thing in which something is set. The mounting of a jewel is a setting. **2** scenery of a play. **3** place and time of a play or story. **4** surroundings; background. **5** music composed to go with certain words. **6** See **set.** *You may help me by setting the table.* 1-5 *noun,* 6 *verb.*

set tle[1] (set′l), **1** determine; decide; agree (upon): *Let's settle this argument. Have you settled on a day for the picnic?* **2** put or be put in order; arrange: *I must settle all my affairs before going away for the winter.* **3** pay: *We have settled all our bills.* **4** take up residence (in a new country or place): *Our cousin intends to settle in California.* **5** establish colonies in: *The English settled New England.* **6** set or be set in a fairly permanent position, place, or way of life: *At last we are settled in our new home.* **7** come to rest in a particular place; become set or fixed: *My cold has settled in my lungs.* **8** place in or come to a desired or comfortable position: *The cat settled itself in the chair for a nap.* **9** make quiet; become quiet: *This medicine will settle your stomach. I had just settled down for a nap when the phone rang.* **10** go down; sink: *Our house has settled several inches since it was built. verb,* **set tled, set tling.**

set tle[2] (set′l), a long bench. *noun.*

set tle ment (set′l mənt), **1** act of settling or condition of being settled. **2** putting in order; arrangement: *No settlement of the dispute is possible unless each side yields some point.* **3** payment: *Settlement of all claims against the company will be made shortly.* **4** the settling of persons in a new country: *The settlement of the English along the Atlantic coast gave England claim to that section.* **5** colony: *England had many settlements along the Atlantic coast.* **6** group of buildings and the people living in them: *Ships brought supplies to the colonists' settlements.* **7** place in a poor, neglected neighborhood where work for its improvement is carried on: *Hull House is a famous settlement on the west side of Chicago. noun.*

set tler (set′lər), **1** person who settles. **2** person who settles in a new country. *noun.*

sev en (sev′ən), one more than six; 7. *noun, adjective.*

sev en teen (sev′ən tēn′), seven more than ten; 17. *noun, adjective.*

sev en teenth (sev′ən tēnth′), **1** next after the 16th. **2** one of 17 equal parts. *adjective, noun.*

sev enth (sev′ənth), **1** next after the sixth: *Saturday is the seventh day of the week.* **2** one of seven equal parts: *A day is one seventh of a week. adjective, noun.*

sev en ti eth (sev′ən tē ith), **1** next after the 69th. **2** one of 70 equal parts. *adjective, noun.*

sev en ty (sev′ən tē), seven times ten; 70. *noun, plural* **sev en ties;** *adjective.*

sev er (sev′ər), **1** cut apart; cut off: *The sailor severed the rope with a knife.* **2** part; divide; separate: *The rope severed and the swing fell down.* **3** break off: *The two nations severed friendly relations. verb.*

sev er al (sev′ər əl), **1** more than two or three but not many; some; a few: *gain several pounds. Several have given their consent.* **2** different; individual: *The children went their several ways after school.* **1,2** *adjective,* **1** *noun.*

se vere (sə vir′), **1** very strict; stern; harsh: *The judge imposed a severe sentence on the criminal.* **2** sharp; violent: *I have a severe headache.* See picture. **3** serious; dangerous: *a severe illness.* **4** very plain or simple; without ornament: *She wore a severe black dress.* **5** difficult: *The new car had to pass severe safety tests. adjective,* **se ver er, se ver est.**

se ver i ty (sə ver′ə tē), **1** strictness; sternness; harshness: *the severity of a punishment.* **2** simplicity of style or taste; plainness: *I like the severity of modern architecture better than the ornamentation of earlier buildings.* **3** violence; sharpness: *the severity of storms, the severity of pain, the severity of grief.* **4** seriousness. *noun, plural* **se ver i ties.**

sew (sō), **1** work with a needle and thread. You can sew by hand or with a machine. **2** fasten with stitches: *sew on a button, sew a hem on a sewing machine.* **3** close with stitches: *The doctor sewed up the wound. verb,* **sewed, sewed** or **sewn, sew ing.**

sew age (sü′ij), the waste matter which passes through sewers. *noun.*

sew er (sü′ər), an underground drain to carry off waste water and refuse. *noun.*

sew ing (sō′ing), **1** work done with a needle and thread. **2** something to be sewed. *noun.*

sewing machine, machine for sewing or stitching cloth.

sewn (sōn), sewed. See **sew.** *She has sewn patches on her jeans. verb.*

sex (seks), **1** one of the two divisions of human beings or animals. Men, bulls, and roosters are of the male sex; women, cows, and hens are of the female sex. **2** character of being male or female: *People were admitted without regard to age or sex. noun, plural* **sex es.**

sex ton (sek′stən), man who takes care of a church. The sexton keeps the church clean and warm. *noun.*

shab by (shab′ē), **1** much worn: *His old suit looks shabby.* **2** wearing old or much worn clothes: *She is always shabby.* **3** mean; not generous; unfair: *That's a shabby way to treat a friend. adjective,* **shab bi er, shab bi est.**

shack (shak), **1** a roughly built hut or cabin: *We built a shack of old boards in the backyard.* **2** house in bad condition: *Those run-down shacks are being torn down to make way for new housing. noun.*

shack le (shak′əl), **1** a metal band fastened around the ankle or wrist of a prisoner or slave. Shackles are usually fastened to each other, the

a hat	i it	oi oil	ch child	⎡a in about
ā age	ī ice	ou out	ng long	⎢e in taken
ä far	o hot	u cup	sh she	ə = ⎨i in pencil
e let	ō open	u̇ put	th thin	⎢o in lemon
ē equal	ô order	ü rule	ŦH then	⎣u in circus
ėr term			zh measure	

wall, or the floor by chains. **2** put shackles on. **3** anything that prevents freedom of action or thought: *Fear and prejudice are shackles.* **4** restrain; hamper. **1,3** *noun,* **2,4** *verb,* **shack led, shack ling.**

shad (shad), a food fish of the North Atlantic coast of America. Shad have many small, loose bones. *noun, plural* **shad** or **shads.**

shade (shād), **1** a partly dark place, not in the sunshine: *Let's sit in the shade of that tree.* **2** a slight darkness or coolness given by something that cuts off light: *Big trees cast shade.* **3** something that shuts out light: *Pull down the shades of the windows.* **4** keep light from: *A big hat shades the eyes.* **5** lightness or darkness of color: *I want to see silks in all shades of blue.* **6** a very small difference; little bit: *Your coat is a shade longer than your dress.* **7** ghost; spirit: *the shades of departed heroes.* **1-3,5-7** *noun,* **4** *verb,* **shad ed, shad ing.**

shad ing (shā′ding), **1** use of black or color to give the effect of shade in a picture. **2** a slight variation or difference of color, character, or quality. *noun.*

shad ow (shad′ō), **1** shade made by some person, animal, or thing. Sometimes a person's shadow is much longer than he is, and sometimes much shorter. **2** darkness; partial shade: *Don't turn on the light; we like to sit in the shadow.* **3** a little bit; small degree; slight suggestion: *He is innocent beyond a shadow of a doubt.* **4** ghost. **5** follow closely, usually secretly: *The detective shadowed the suspected burglar.* **1-4** *noun,* **5** *verb.*

shad ow y (shad′ō ē), like a shadow; dim; faint: *shadowy outlines in the pale moonlight. adjective.*

shad y (shā′dē), **1** in the shade. **2** giving shade. **3** of doubtful honesty or character: *They were arrested for being involved in a shady business deal. adjective,* **shad i er, shad i est.**

shaft (shaft), **1** bar to support parts of a machine that turn, or to help move parts. **2** a deep passage sunk in the earth. The entrance to a mine is called a shaft. **3** passage that is like a well; long, narrow space: *an elevator shaft.* **4** arrow, spear, or lance. **5** the long, slender stem of an arrow, spear, or lance. **6** one of the two wooden poles between which a horse is harnessed to a carriage or other vehicle. **7** the main part of a column. *noun.*

shag gy (shag′ē), **1** covered with a thick, rough mass of hair or wool, or something resembling them: *a shaggy dog.* **2** long, thick, and rough: *My cousin has shaggy eyebrows. adjective,* **shag gi er, shag gi est.**

shake (shāk), **1** move quickly backwards and forwards, up and down, or from side to side: *shake a rug. The baby shook the rattle. The branches of the old tree shook in the wind.* **2** bring, throw, or scatter by or as if by movement: *She shook the snow off her clothes.* **3** clasp (hands) in greeting another: *shake hands.* **4** tremble: *The kitten was shaking with cold.* **5** make tremble: *The explosion shook the whole town.* **6** disturb; make less firm: *His lie shook my faith in his honesty.* **7** act of shaking: *A shake of her head was the answer.* 1-6 *verb,* **shook, shak en, shak ing;** 7 *noun.*

shake up, 1 shake hard: *Shake up a mixture of oil and vinegar for the salad.* **2** jar in body or nerves: *I was much shaken up by the experience.*

shak y (shā′kē), **1** shaking: *a shaky voice.* **2** liable to break down; weak: *a shaky porch.* **3** not reliable; not to be depended on: *a shaky bank, a shaky supporter.* *adjective,* **shak i er, shak i est.**

shale (shāl), rock formed from hardened clay or mud in thin layers that split easily. *noun.*

shall (shal). *Shall* is used to express future time, command, obligation, and necessity. *We shall come soon. You shall go to the party, I promise you. Shall I drink the milk? verb, past tense* **should.**

shal low (shal′ō), **1** not deep: *shallow water, a*

shamrock
(definition 1)

shark[1]—The diver is photographing a great white shark. This is a very dangerous kind of shark, which may reach a length of 25 feet (7½ meters) or more.

shallow dish, a shallow mind.* **2 shallows,** a shallow place: *The children splashed in the shallows of the pond.* **1** *adjective,* **2** *noun.*

sham (sham), **1** fraud; pretense: *Their claim to be descended from royalty is a sham.* **2** false; pretended; imitation: *a sham battle fought for practice, sham antiques.* **3** pretend: *He shammed sickness so he wouldn't have to work.* **1** *noun,* 2 *adjective,* 3 *verb,* **shammed, sham ming.**

sham ble (sham′bəl), walk awkwardly or unsteadily: *The exhausted hikers shambled into camp. verb,* **sham bled, sham bling.**

sham bles (sham′bəlz), confusion; mess; general disorder: *to make a shambles of a clean room. noun plural or singular.*

shame (shām), **1** a painful feeling of having done something wrong, improper, or silly: *to blush with shame.* **2** cause to feel shame: *My silly mistake shamed me.* **3** drive or force by shame: *I was shamed into cleaning my room after guests saw it.* **4** disgrace; dishonor: *to bring shame to one's family.* **5** bring disgrace upon: *to shame one's family.* **6** fact to be sorry about; pity: *It is a shame to be so wasteful. What a shame you can't come to the party!* 1,4,6 *noun,* 2,3,5 *verb,* **shamed, sham ing.**

put to shame, 1 make ashamed; disgrace: *Her bad behavior put her family to shame.* **2** surpass: *His careful work put all the rest to shame.*

shame ful (shām′fəl), causing shame; bringing disgrace. *adjective.*

shame less (shām′lis), **1** without shame. **2** not modest. *adjective.*

sham poo (sham pü′), **1** wash (the hair). **2** washing the hair. **3** preparation used for shampooing. **1** *verb,* **sham pooed, sham poo ing;** 2,3 *noun, plural* **sham poos.**

sham rock (sham′rok), **1** a bright-green leaf that is divided into three parts. The shamrock is the national emblem of Ireland. See picture. **2** a plant such as white clover, that has leaves like this. *noun.*

shank (shangk), **1** the part of the leg between the knee and the ankle. **2** the similar part in animals. **3** cut of meat from the upper part of the leg of an animal. **4** any part like a leg, stem, or shaft. The shank of a fishhook is the straight part between hook and loop. *noun.*

shan't (shant), shall not.

shan ty (shan′tē), a roughly built hut or cabin. *noun, plural* **shan ties.**

shape (shāp), **1** form; figure; appearance: *An apple is different in shape from a banana. A witch was supposed to take the shape of a cat or a bat. A white shape stood beside his bed.* **2** form: *The child shapes clay into balls.* **3** develop; take shape: *Her plan is shaping well.* **4** adapt in form: *Hats are shaped to fit our heads.* **5** condition: *Athletes exercise to keep themselves in good shape.* **6** order; definite form; proper arrangement: *Take time to get your thoughts into shape.* 1,5,6 *noun,* 2-4 *verb,* **shaped, shap ing.**

take shape, have or take on a definite form: *The general outline of the novel began to take shape.*

shape less (shāp′lis), 1 without definite shape: *a shapeless old hat.* 2 having a shape that is not attractive: *a shapeless figure. adjective.*

shape ly (shāp′lē), having a pleasing shape. *adjective,* **shape li er, shape li est.**

share (sher *or* shar), 1 part belonging to one person; part; portion: *Each child received an equal share of the property. You've done more than your share of the work.* 2 each of the parts into which the ownership of a company or corporation is divided: *The ownership of this railroad is divided into several million shares.* 3 use together; enjoy together; have in common: *The sisters share the same room.* 4 divide into parts, each taking a part: *The child shared his candy with his sister.* 5 have a share; take part: *Everyone shared in making the picnic a success.* 1,2 *noun,* 3-5 *verb,* **shared, shar ing.**

shark[1] (shärk), a large and ferocious fish that eats other fish. Certain kinds are sometimes dangerous to human beings. See picture. *noun.*

shark[2] (shärk), a dishonest person who preys on others. *noun.*

sharp (shärp), 1 having a thin cutting edge or a fine point: *a sharp knife.* 2 having a point; not rounded: *a sharp corner on a box.* 3 with a sudden change of direction: *a sharp turn.* 4 very cold: *sharp weather.* 5 severe; biting: *sharp words.* 6 feeling somewhat like a cut or prick; acting keenly on the senses: *a sharp taste, a sharp pain.* 7 clear; distinct: *the sharp contrast between black and white.* 8 quick; brisk: *a sharp walk.* 9 fierce; violent: *a sharp struggle.* 10 being aware of things quickly: *sharp ears.* 11 watchful; wide-awake: *The sentry kept a sharp watch for the enemy.* 12 quick in mind; shrewd; clever: *a sharp lawyer.* 13 promptly; exactly: *Come at one o'clock sharp.* 14 in a sharp manner; in an alert manner; keenly: *Look sharp!* 15 high in pitch; shrill: *a sharp voice.* 16 above the true pitch in music: *sing sharp.* 17 tone one half step above natural pitch: *music written in C sharp.* 18 sign in music (#) that shows this. 1-12,15 *adjective,* 13,14,16 *adverb,* 17,18 *noun.*

sharp en (shär′pən), 1 make sharp: *Sharpen the pencil. Sharpen your wits.* 2 become sharp. *verb.*

sharp shoot er (shärp′shü′tər), person who shoots very well, especially with a rifle. *noun.*

shat ter (shat′ər), 1 break into pieces: *A stone shattered the window.* 2 destroy; disturb greatly: *Our hopes for a picnic were shattered by the rain. verb.*

shave (shāv), 1 remove hair with a razor; cut hair from (the face, chin, or some other part of a person's body) with a razor: *Father shaves every day. The actor shaved his head in order to portray a bald man.* 2 cutting off of hair with a razor. 3 cut off (hair) with a razor. 4 cut off in thin slices: *She shaved the chocolate.* 5 come very close to; graze: *The car shaved the corner.* 6 a narrow miss or escape: *The car missed her, but it was a close shave.* 1,3-5 *verb,* **shaved, shaved** or **shav en, shav ing;** 2,6 *noun.*

shav en (shā′vən), 1 shaved. 2 closely cut.

a hat	**i** it	**oi** oil	**ch** child	(a in about
ā age	**ī** ice	**ou** out	**ng** long	e in taken
ä far	**o** hot	**u** cup	**sh** she	**ə** = i in pencil
e let	**ō** open	**u̇** put	**th** thin	o in lemon
ē equal	**ô** order	**ü** rule	**ŦH** then	u in circus
ėr term			**zh** measure	

3 shaved. See **shave.** 1,2 *adjective,* 3 *verb.*

shav ing (shā′ving), 1 a very thin piece or slice: *Shavings of wood are cut off by a plane.* 2 act or process of cutting hair from the face, chin, or some other part of a person's body with a razor: *He washed his face after shaving. noun.*

shawl (shôl), a square or oblong piece of cloth to be worn about the shoulders or head. *noun.*

she (shē), 1 girl, woman, or female animal spoken about or mentioned before: *My sister says she likes to read and her reading helps her in school.* 2 anything thought of as female and spoken about or mentioned before: *She was a fine old ship.* 3 a female: *Is the baby a he or a she?* 1,2 *pronoun,* plural **they;** 3 *noun.*

sheaf (shēf), bundle of things of the same sort: *a sheaf of arrows. They were bringing sheaves of wheat. noun,* plural **sheaves.**

shear (shir), 1 cut with shears or scissors. 2 cut the wool or fleece from: *to shear sheep.* 3 cut close; cut off; cut. *verb,* **sheared, sheared** or **shorn, shear ing.**

shears (shirz), 1 large scissors: *barber's shears.* 2 any cutting instrument resembling scissors: *grass shears, tin shears. noun plural.*

sheath (shēth), 1 case or covering for the blade of a sword, dagger, or knife. 2 any similar covering, especially on an animal or plant. *noun,* plural **sheaths** (shēŦHz *or* shēths).

sheathe (shēŦH), 1 put (a sword, dagger, or knife) into a sheath. 2 enclose in a case or covering: *a mummy sheathed in linen, doors sheathed in metal. verb,* **sheathed, sheath ing.**

sheaves (shēvz), more than one sheaf. *noun plural.*

shed[1] (shed), building used for the shelter or storage of goods or vehicles, usually having only one story: *a train shed, a wagon shed. noun.*

shed[2] (shed), 1 pour out; let flow: *shed tears, shed blood.* 2 throw off: *The snake shed its skin. The umbrella sheds water.* 3 scatter abroad; give forth: *The sun sheds light. Flowers shed perfume. verb,* **shed, shed ding.**

she'd (shēd), 1 she had. 2 she would.

sheen (shēn), brightness; luster: *Satin and polished silver have a sheen. noun.*

sheep (shēp), 1 animal with a thick coat and hoofs that chews its cud. Sheep are somewhat like goats and cattle, and they are raised for wool, meat, and skin. 2 person who is weak, timid, or stupid: *"Are you men or are you sheep?" cried the captain. noun,* plural **sheep.**

sheep ish (shē′pish), 1 awkwardly bashful or embarrassed: *a sheepish smile.* 2 like a sheep; timid; weak; stupid. *adjective.*

sheep skin (shēp′skin′), skin of a sheep, especially with the wool on it. *noun.*

sheer[1] (shir), **1** very thin; almost transparent: *Those sheer curtains will let the light through.* **2** unmixed with anything else; complete: *sheer nonsense, sheer weariness.* **3** straight up and down; steep. See picture. *adjective.*

sheer[2] (shir), turn from a course; turn aside; swerve. *verb.*

sheet (shēt), **1** a large piece of cloth, usually of linen or cotton, used to sleep on or under. **2** a broad, thin piece of anything: *a sheet of glass.* **3** a single piece of paper. **4** a broad, flat surface: *a sheet of water. noun.*

sheik (shēk), an Arab chief or head of a family, village, or tribe. *noun.*

shelf (shelf), **1** a thin, flat piece of wood, stone, metal, or other material, fastened to a wall or frame to hold things, such as books or dishes. **2** anything like a shelf: *The ship hit a shelf of coral. noun, plural* **shelves.**

shell (shel), **1** the hard outside covering of certain animals. Oysters, turtles, and beetles all have shells. **2** the hard outside covering of a nut, seed, or fruit. **3** the hard outside covering of an egg. **4** take out of a shell: *The cook is shelling peas.* **5** separate (grains of corn) from the cob. **6** something like a shell. The framework of a house and a very light racing boat are called shells. **7** case filled with gunpowder to be fired from a rifle, pistol, or cannon. **8** fire cannon at; bombard with shells: *The enemy shelled the town.* 1-3,6,7 *noun,* 4,5,8 *verb.*

shell out, hand over (money); pay out: *We had to shell out five dollars for the movie.*

she'll (shēl), **1** she shall. **2** she will.

shel lac (shə lak/), **1** varnish made with alcohol that gives a smooth, shiny appearance to wood, metal, or the like. **2** put shellac on. 1 *noun,* 2 *verb,* **shel lacked, shel lack ing.**

shell fish (shel/fish/), a water animal with a shell. Oysters, clams, crabs, and lobsters are shellfish. Shellfish are very different from regular fish. *noun, plural* **shell fish es** or **shell fish.**

shel ter (shel/tər), **1** something that covers or protects from weather, danger, or attack: *Trees are a shelter from the sun.* **2** protect; shield; hide: *shelter runaway slaves.* **3** protection; refuge: *We took shelter from the storm in a barn.* 1,3 *noun,* 2 *verb.*

shelve (shelv), **1** put on a shelf. **2** lay aside: *Let us shelve that argument.* **3** furnish with shelves. *verb,* **shelved, shelv ing.**

shelves (shelvz), more than one shelf. *noun plural.*

shep herd (shep/ərd), **1** person who takes care of sheep. **2** take care of: *to shepherd a flock.* **3** guide; direct: *The teacher shepherded the children safely out of the burning building.* **4** person who cares for and protects. 1,4 *noun,* 2,3 *verb.*

shep herd ess (shep/ər dis), woman who takes care of sheep. *noun, plural* **shep herd ess es.**

sher bet (shėr/bət), a frozen dessert made of fruit juice, sugar, and water or milk. *noun.*

sher iff (sher/if), the most important law-enforcing officer of a county. A sheriff appoints deputies who help to keep order. *noun.*

sher ry (sher/ē), a strong wine. Its color varies from pale yellow to brown. *noun, plural* **sher ries.**

she's (shēz), **1** she is. **2** she has.

shied (shīd). See **shy.** *The horse shied and threw the rider. It had never shied like that before. verb.*

shield (shēld), **1** piece of armor carried on the arm to protect the body in battle. **2** anything used to protect: *I turned up my collar as a shield against the cold wind.* **3** something shaped like a shield. **4** protect; defend: *They shielded me from unjust punishment.* 1-3 *noun,* 4 *verb.*

shift (shift), **1** move or change from one place, position, or person, to another; change: *I shifted the heavy bag from one hand to the other. Don't try to shift the blame to someone else. The wind has shifted to the southeast.* **2** change of direction, position, or attitude: *a shift of the mind, a shift in policy.* **3** group of workers who work during the same period of time: *She is on the night shift this week.* **4** time during which such a group works. **5** manage to get along: *He left home at an early age and had to shift for himself.* **6** change the position of (the gears of an automobile). 1,5,6 *verb,* 2-4 *noun.*

shift less (shift/lis), lazy; inefficient. *adjective.*

shift y (shif/tē), tricky; not straightforward. *adjective,* **shift i er, shift i est.**

shil ling (shil/ing), a former British coin equal to 12 pence. Twenty shillings made one pound. *noun.*

shim mer (shim/ər), **1** gleam faintly: *Both the sea and the sand shimmered in the moonlight.* **2** a faint gleam or shine. See picture. 1 *verb,* 2 *noun.*

shin (shin), **1** the front part of the leg from the knee to the ankle. **2** climb by holding fast with the arms and legs and drawing oneself up: *I shinned up the tree.* 1 *noun,* 2 *verb,* **shinned, shin ning.**

shine (shīn), **1** send out light; be bright with light; glow: *The sun shines. His face is shining with soap and water.* **2** light; brightness: *the shine of a lamp.* **3** luster; polish: *the shine of a new penny.* **4** fair weather; sunshine: *We'll be there rain or shine.* **5** do very well; be bright: *She shines at sports. He is a shining athlete.* **6** make bright; polish: *I have to shine my shoes.* 1,5,6 *verb,* **shone** or **shined, shin ing;** 2-4 *noun.*

shin gle (shing/gəl), **1** a thin piece of wood, used to cover roofs and walls. Shingles are laid in overlapping rows with the thicker ends showing. **2** cover with such pieces: *shingle a roof.* 1 *noun,* 2 *verb,* **shin gled, shin gling.**

shin y (shī/nē), **1** reflecting light; bright: *A new penny is shiny.* **2** worn to a glossy smoothness: *a coat shiny from hard wear. adjective,* **shin i er, shin i est.**

ship (ship), **1** any large vessel for travel on water, such as a steamship, frigate, or galley. **2** a large sailing vessel, especially one with three or more masts. **3** airship, airplane, or spacecraft. **4** put or take on board a ship. **5** travel on a ship; sail. **6** send or carry from one place to another by a ship, train, truck, or airplane: *Did he ship it by express or by freight?* **7** take a job on a ship: *He*

a hat	i it	oi oil	ch child	a in about
ā age	ī ice	ou out	ng long	e in taken
ä far	o hot	u cup	sh she	ə = { i in pencil
e let	ō open	u̇ put	th thin	o in lemon
ē equal	ô order	ü rule	₮ʜ then	u in circus
ėr term			zh measure	

shimmer (definition 2)
The shimmer of the moonlight on the water made a golden pathway.

sheer¹ (definition 3)
From the top of the canyon it was a sheer drop of hundreds of feet to the river below.

shipped as cook. 1-3 noun, 4-7 verb, **shipped, ship ping.**

-ship, suffix meaning: **1** office, position, or occupation of _____: Governorship means the office of governor. **2** quality or condition of being _____: Partnership means the condition of being a partner. **3** act, power, or skill of _____: Workmanship means the skill of a workman.

ship board (ship′bôrd′). **on shipboard,** on or inside a ship. noun.

ship load (ship′lōd′), a full load for a ship. noun.

ship ment (ship′mənt), **1** act of shipping goods: The oranges were crated for shipment. **2** goods sent at one time to a person or company: We received two shipments of boxes from the factory. noun.

ship per (ship′ər), person who ships goods. noun.

ship ping (ship′ing), **1** the sending of goods by water, rail, or air. **2** ships: Much of the world's shipping passes through the Panama Canal each year. **3** ships of a nation, city, or business: British merchant shipping. noun.

ship shape (ship′shāp′), **1** trim; in good order. **2** in a trim, neat manner. 1 adjective, 2 adverb.

ship wreck (ship′rek′), **1** destruction or loss of a ship: Only two people were saved from the shipwreck. **2** a wrecked ship. **3** destruction; ruin: the shipwreck of one's hopes. **4** suffer shipwreck. 1-3 noun, 4 verb.

ship yard (ship′yärd′), place near the water where ships are built or repaired. noun.

shirk (shėrk), avoid or get out of doing (work or a duty): You will lose your job if you continue to shirk responsibility. See picture. verb.

shirt (shėrt), **1** garment for the upper part of a man's body. **2** undergarment for the upper part of the body. noun.

shiv er (shiv′ər), **1** shake with cold or fear: She crept shivering into bed. **2** shaking from cold or fear. 1 verb, 2 noun.

shoal (shōl), **1** place in a sea, lake, or stream where the water is shallow. **2** sandbank or sand bar that makes the water shallow: The ship was wrecked on the shoals. noun.

shock¹ (shok), **1** a sudden, violent shake, blow, or crash: Earthquake shocks are often felt in Japan. The two trains collided with a terrible shock. **2** a sudden, violent, or upsetting disturbance: Her death was a great shock to her family. **3** cause to feel surprise, horror, or disgust: That child's bad language shocks everyone. **4** a great weakening of the body that sometimes causes a person to become unconscious. Shock may set in after a severe injury, great loss of blood, or after a person suddenly becomes very upset. **5** disturbance produced by an electric current passing through the body. **6** give an electric shock to. 1,2,4,5 noun, 3,6 verb.

shock[2] (shok), **1** group of stalks of corn or bundles of grain set up on end together. **2** make into shocks. **1** *noun,* **2** *verb.*

shock[3] (shok), a thick, bushy mass: *a shock of red hair. noun.*

shock ing (shok/ing), **1** causing intense, painful surprise: *shocking news.* **2** offensive; disgusting: *a shocking sight.* **3** very bad: *shocking manners. adjective.*

shod (shod). See **shoe.** *The blacksmith shod the horses. verb.*

shoe (shü), **1** an outer covering for a person's foot. Shoes are often made of leather. **2** thing like a shoe in shape or use. **3** horseshoe. **4** furnish with a shoe or shoes: *A blacksmith shoes horses. Her feet were shod with silver slippers.* **1-3** *noun,* **4** *verb,* **shod, shoe ing.**

shoe lace (shü/lās/), cord, braid, or leather strip for fastening a shoe. *noun.*

shoe mak er (shü/mā/kər), person who makes or mends shoes. *noun.*

shoe string (shü/string/), **1** shoelace. **2** a very small amount of money: *They started in business on a shoestring. noun.*

shone (shōn). See **shine.** *The sun shone all last week. It has not shone since. verb.*

shoo (shü), **1** an exclamation used to scare away hens, birds, and other animals. **2** scare or drive away by calling "Shoo!": *Shoo those flies away.* **1** *interjection,* **2** *verb,* **shooed, shoo ing.**

shook (shuk). See **shake.** *They shook hands. verb.*

shoot (shüt), **1** hit with a bullet, shot, or arrow: *He shot a rabbit.* **2** send swiftly: *A bow shoots an arrow. She shot question after question at us.* **3** fire or use (a gun or other shooting weapon): *shoot a rifle. We shot at the target.* **4** send a bullet: *This gun shoots straight.* **5** move suddenly and rapidly: *A car shot by us. Flames shoot up from a burning house. Pain shot up his arm from his hurt finger.* **6** pass quickly along, through, over, or under: *Only a shallow boat can shoot this stretch of rapids.* **7** come forth from the ground; grow; grow rapidly: *Buds shoot forth in the spring. The corn is shooting up in the warm weather.* **8** a new part growing out; young branch: *See the new shoots on that bush.* **9** take (a picture) with a camera; photograph. **1-7,9** *verb,* **shot, shoot ing; 8** *noun.*

shooting star, meteor.

shop (shop), **1** place where things are sold; store: *a small dress shop.* **2** visit stores to look at or to buy things: *We shopped all morning for a coat.* **3** place where things are made or repaired: *He works in a carpenter's shop.* **4** place where a certain kind of work is done: *We get our hair cut at a barber shop.* **1,3,4** *noun,* **2** *verb,* **shopped, shop ping.**

shop keep er (shop/kē/pər), person who owns or manages a shop or store. *noun.*

shop lift (shop/lift/), steal goods from a store while pretending to be a customer. *verb.*

shop ping (shop/ing), act of visiting stores to look at or to buy things: *I do the shopping on Saturdays. noun.*

shopping center, a group of stores built as a unit on or near a main road. Most shopping centers have large areas for parking automobiles.

shore (shôr), **1** land at the edge of a sea, lake, or large river. **2** land near a sea. **3** land: *Our marines serve on both the sea and shore. noun.*

off shore, in or on the water; not far from the shore: *The yacht was anchored off shore.*

shorn (shôrn). See **shear.** *The sheep was shorn of its wool. verb.*

short (shôrt), **1** not long; of small extent from end to end: *a short time, a short life, a short street.* **2** not tall: *a short man, short grass.* **3** not coming up to the right amount, measure, or standard: *I am short by a dime.* **4** so brief as to be rude: *She was so short with me that I felt hurt.* **5** in a short manner; suddenly: *The horse stopped short.* **6** A **short vowel** is a vowel like *a* in *hat,* *e* in *leg,* *i* in *it,* *o* in *hot,* or *u* in *hut.* **7 shorts, a** short, loose trousers reaching to above the knees. Shorts are worn by men, women, or children in hot weather or when playing tennis, running races, or taking part in other sports. **b** a similar men's or boys' undergarment. **1-4,6** *adjective,* **5** *adverb,* **7** *noun.*

cut short, end suddenly: *We cut short our vacation because of the bad weather.*

fall short, 1 fail to reach: *The ball fell short of her.* **2** be insufficient: *The corn crop falls short this year.*

for short, in order to make shorter: *Robert was called Rob for short.*

in short, briefly: *I will give you the details later; in short, the party has been canceled.*

run short, 1 not have enough: *Let me know if you run short of money before then.* **2** not be enough: *Our food supply ran short.*

short of, 1 not up to; less than: *Nothing short of your best work will satisfy me.* **2** not having enough of: *He is short of funds right now.*

short age (shôr/tij), lack; too small an amount: *There is a shortage of grain because of poor crops. noun.*

short circuit, a side circuit of electricity like that formed when insulation wears off wires which touch each other. A short circuit may blow a fuse or cause a fire.

short-cir cuit (shôrt/sėr/kit), make a short circuit in. *verb.*

short com ing (shôrt/kum/ing), fault; defect: *Rudeness is a serious shortcoming. noun.*

short cut (shôrt/kut/), a quicker way. *noun.*

short en (shôrt/n), **1** make shorter; cut off: *The new highway shortens the trip. She has had all her dresses shortened.* **2** become shorter: *The days shorten in November in this country. verb.*

short en ing (shôrt/n ing), butter, lard, or other fat, used to make pastry or cake crisp or easily crumbling. *noun.*

short hand (shôrt/hand/), **1** method of rapid writing which uses symbols in place of letters, sounds, and words. **2** writing in such symbols. See picture. *noun.*

short horn (shôrt/hôrn/), breed of cattle with short horns, raised for beef. *noun.*

short ly (shôrt/lē), **1** in a short time; before long; soon: *I will be with you shortly.* **2** in a few words; briefly. *adverb.*

short sight ed (shôrt/sī/tid), **1** nearsighted; not able to see far. **2** lacking in foresight; not prudent. *adjective.*

short stop (shôrt/stop/), a baseball player stationed between second and third base. *noun.*

short-tem pered (shôrt/tem/pərd), easily made angry; quick-tempered. *adjective.*

shot[1] (shot), **1** discharge of a gun or cannon: *We heard two shots.* **2** act of shooting. **3** tiny balls of lead or steel; bullets. **4** a single ball of lead or steel for a gun or cannon. **5** attempt to hit by shooting: *That was a good shot, and it hit the mark.* **6** distance a weapon can shoot; range: *We were within rifle shot of the fort.* **7** person who shoots: *He is a good shot.* **8** something like a shot. An aimed stroke or throw in a game is sometimes called a shot. **9** dose of a drug in the form of an injection: *A polio shot is an injection of vaccine to protect against getting polio.* **10** an attempt; try: *I think I'll take a shot at that job. noun, plural* **shots** or (for definition 3) **shot.**

shot[2] (shot), **1** See **shoot.** *Many years ago he shot a rival and was himself shot in revenge.* **2** woven so as to show a play of colors: *blue silk shot with gold.* **1** *verb,* **2** *adjective.*

shot gun (shot/gun/), gun with no grooves in its barrel, for firing cartridges filled with small shot. *noun.*

should (shùd), **1** See **shall.** "I said that I should come next week" means that I said, "I shall come next week." **2** ought to: *You should try to make fewer mistakes.* **3** *Should* is used to express uncertainty. *If it should rain, I should not go.* **4** *Should* is used in speaking of something which might have happened but did not. *I should have gone if you had asked me. verb.*

shoul der (shōl/dər), **1** part of the body to which an arm, foreleg, or wing is attached. **2** part of a garment that covers a shoulder. **3 shoulders,** the two shoulders and the upper part of the back: *The man carried a trunk on his shoulders.* **4** bear (a burden or blame): *She shouldered the responsibility of sending her niece through college.* **5** something that sticks out like a shoulder: *Don't drive on the shoulder of the road.* **6** push with the shoulders: *She shouldered her way through the crowd.* **1-3,5** *noun,* **4,6** *verb.*

shoulder blade, the flat bone of the shoulder.

should n't (shùd/nt), should not.

shorthand (definition 2) for "Your letter was received today." (Gregg system)

shout (shout), **1** call or cry loudly and vigorously: *I shouted for help when the boat sank. Somebody shouted, "Fire!" The crowd shouted with laughter.* **2** a loud, vigorous call or cry: *Shouts of joy rang through the halls.* **3** talk or laugh very loudly. **1,3** *verb,* **2** *noun.*

shove (shuv), **1** push; move forward or along by force from behind: *Help me shove this bookcase into place.* **2** push roughly or rudely against; jostle: *The people shoved to get on the crowded car.* **3** push: *We gave the boat a shove which sent it far out into the water.* **1,2** *verb,* **shoved, shov ing; 3** *noun.*

shov el (shuv/əl), **1** tool with a broad scoop, used to lift and throw loose matter: *a snow shovel, a coal shovel. A steam shovel is worked by steam.* **2** lift and throw with a shovel: *She shoveled the snow from the walk.* **3** make with a shovel: *They shoveled a path through the snow.* **4** throw or lift as if with a shovel: *The hungry girl shoveled the food into her mouth.* **1** *noun,* **2-4** *verb.*

show (shō), **1** let be seen; put in sight: *She showed me her rock collection. The dog showed its teeth.* **2** be in sight; appear; be seen: *The hole in his stocking shows above his shoe. Amusement showed in his face.* **3** point out: *She showed us the way to town.* **4** direct; guide: *Show them out.* **5** make clear to; explain to: *The teacher showed the children how to do the problem.* **6** grant; give: *show mercy, show favor.* **7** display: *The jewels made a fine show.* **8** display for effect: *He put on a show of learning to impress us.* **9** any kind of public exhibition or display: *We are going to the flower show and to the automobile show.* **10** play, motion picture, or television program: *We saw a good show on television last night.* **1-6** *verb,* **showed, shown** or **showed, show ing; 7-10** *noun.*

show off, make a show (of); display: *show off fine clothes.*

show up, put in an appearance: *We were going to play ball, but the other team didn't show up.*

show er (shou/ər), **1** a short fall of rain. **2** wet with a shower; sprinkle; spray. **3** anything like a fall of rain: *a shower of hail, a shower of tears, a shower of sparks from an engine.* **4** come in a shower. **5** send in a shower; pour down: *to shower gifts upon someone.* **6** bath in which water pours down on the body from an overhead nozzle. **7** take a bath in this manner. **1,3,6** *noun,* **2,4,5,7** *verb.*

shown (shōn), showed. See **show.** *She has shown us how to play the game. We were shown many tricks. verb.*

show-off (shō/ôf/), person who shows off by always trying to attract attention: *The child is a show-off whenever company comes. noun.*

show y (shō/ē), **1** making a display; likely to attract attention; conspicuous: *A peony is a showy* *flower.* **2** too bright and gay to be in good taste. *adjective,* **show i er, show i est.**

shrank (shrangk). See **shrink.** *That shirt shrank in the wash.* verb.

shrap nel (shrap/nəl), **1** shell filled with fragments of metal and powder, set to explode in the air and scatter the fragments over a wide area. **2** fragments scattered by such a shell. *noun.* [*Shrapnel* was named for Henry Shrapnel, a British army officer who invented it in 1784. He lived from 1761 to 1842.]

shred (shred), **1** a very small piece torn off or cut off; very narrow strip; scrap: *The wind tore the sail to shreds.* **2** fragment; particle; bit: *There's not a shred of evidence that he took the money.* **3** tear or cut into small pieces: *Shredded paper is used in packing dishes.* **1,2** *noun,* **3** *verb,* **shred ded or shred, shred ding.**

shrew (shrü), **1** a bad-tempered, quarrelsome woman. **2** a small animal like a mouse, that has a long snout and brownish fur. Shrews eat insects and worms. See picture. *noun.*

shrewd (shrüd), having a sharp mind; showing a keen wit; clever: *He is a shrewd businessman.* *adjective.*

shriek (shrēk), **1** a loud, sharp, shrill sound: *We heard the shriek of the engine's whistle.* **2** make a loud, sharp, shrill sound. People sometimes shriek because of terror, anger, pain, or amusement. **1** *noun,* **2** *verb.*

shrill (shril), **1** having a high pitch; high and sharp in sound; piercing: *Crickets and katydids make shrill noises.* **2** make a shrill sound. **1** *adjective,* **2** *verb.*

shril ly (shril/ē), in shrill tones. *adverb.*

shrimp (shrimp), **1** a small shellfish with a long tail. Some shrimps are used for food. See picture. **2** a small or insignificant person. *noun, plural* **shrimps** or (for definition 1) **shrimp.**

shrine (shrīn), **1** a sacred place; place where sacred things are kept. A shrine may be the tomb of a saint, an altar in a church, or a box holding a holy object. **2** any place or object sacred because of its history; something sacred because of memories connected with it: *Independence Hall is visited as a shrine.* *noun.*

shrink (shringk), **1** draw back: *The dog shrank from the whip. That shy girl shrinks from meeting strangers.* **2** become smaller: *Wool shrinks in hot water.* **3** make smaller: *Hot water shrinks wool.* *verb,* **shrank** or **shrunk, shrunk** or **shrunk en, shrink ing.**

shriv el (shriv/əl), dry up; wither; shrink and wrinkle: *The hot sunshine shriveled the grass.* *verb.*

shroud (shroud), **1** cloth or garment in which a dead person is wrapped for burial. **2** wrap for burial. **3** something that covers, conceals, or veils: *The fog was a shroud over the city.* **4** cover; conceal; veil: *The earth is shrouded in darkness.* **5** rope from a mast to the side of a ship. Shrouds help support the mast. **1,3,5** *noun,* **2,4** *verb.*

shrub (shrub), a woody plant smaller than a tree, usually with many separate stems starting from or near the ground. The lilac bush and the coffee plant are shrubs. *noun.*

shrub ber y (shrub/ər ē), **1** shrubs. **2** place planted with shrubs. *noun, plural* **shrub ber ies.**

shrug (shrug), **1** raise (the shoulders) as an expression of dislike, doubt, indifference, or impatience: *He merely shrugged his shoulders when we asked for directions.* **2** raising the shoulders in this way: *She replied with a shrug.* **1** *verb,* **shrugged, shrug ging; 2** *noun.*

shrunk (shrungk). See **shrink.** *These woolen socks have shrunk and I can't get them on.* verb.

shrunk en (shrung/kən), **1** grown smaller; shriveled. **2** See **shrink. 1** *adjective,* **2** *verb.*

shuck (shuk), **1** husk; pod. **2** remove the shucks from: *shuck corn.* **1** *noun,* **2** *verb.*

shud der (shud/ər), **1** tremble with horror, fear, or cold: *I shudder at the sight of snakes.* **2** trembling; quivering. **1** *verb,* **2** *noun.*

shuf fle (shuf/əl), **1** walk without lifting the feet: *We shuffled along the slippery sidewalk.* **2** scrape or drag (the feet). **3** a scraping or dragging movement of the feet. **4** mix (cards) so as to change the order. **5** push about; thrust or throw with clumsy haste: *Instead of cleaning her room, she shuffled everything into a drawer.* **6** move this way and that: *shuffle a stack of papers.* **7** movement this way and that: *After a hasty shuffle of his papers, the speaker began to talk.* **1,2,4-6** *verb,* **shuf fled, shuf fling; 3,7** *noun.*

shun (shun), keep away from; avoid: *She shuns housework.* *verb,* **shunned, shun ning.**

shut (shut), **1** close (a container or opening) by pushing or pulling a lid, door, or some part into place: *shut a box, shut a window.* **2** bring together the parts of: *Shut your eyes. Shut the book.* **3** close tight; close securely; close doors or other openings of: *We shut the house for the winter by boarding up the windows.* **4** become closed; be closed. **5** enclose; confine; keep (from going out): *Shut the kitten in the basket.* *verb,* **shut, shut ting.**

shut down, close (a factory or the like) for a time; stop work: *We've got to shut down until there is a demand for our product.*

shut off, close; obstruct; check; turn off: *Shut off the radio.*

shut out, 1 keep from coming in: *The curtains shut out the light.* **2** defeat (a team) without allowing it to score: *The pitcher shut out the other team, limiting them to three hits.*

shut up, 1 shut the doors and windows of. **2** stop talking: *It was rude of you to tell me to shut up.*

shut out (shut/out/), defeat of a team without allowing it to score. *noun.*

shut ter (shut/ər), **1** a movable cover for a window: *We closed the shutters as the storm approached.* **2** a movable cover or slide for closing an opening. The device that opens and closes in front of the film in a camera is the shutter. *noun.*

shut tle (shut/l), **1** device used in weaving that carries the thread back and forth across the piece being woven. **2** the sliding holder for the lower thread in a sewing machine, which moves back and forth once for each stitch. **3** move quickly to and fro. **4** bus, train, or airplane that runs regularly back and forth over a short distance. 1,2,4 *noun,* 3 *verb,* **shut tled, shut tling.**

shy (shī), **1** uncomfortable in company; bashful: *He is shy and dislikes parties.* **2** easily frightened away; timid: *A deer is a shy animal.* **3** start back or aside suddenly: *The horse shied at the newspaper blowing along the ground.* 1,2 *adjective,* **shy er, shy est,** or **shi er, shi est;** 3 *verb,* **shied, shy ing.**

sick (sik), **1** in poor health; having some disease; ill. **2** vomiting; inclined to vomit; feeling nausea. **3** for a sick person: *sick pay.* **4** the **sick,** sick people: *The sick need special care.* **5** weary; tired: *I'm sick of school.* **6** affected with sorrow or longing: *to be sick at heart.* 1-3,5,6 *adjective,* 4 *noun.*

sick bed (sik′bed′), bed of a sick person. *noun.*

sick en (sik′ən), make or become sick: *The sight of blood sickens some people. The bird sickened from being kept in a cage. verb.*

sick le (sik′əl), tool consisting of a short, curved blade on a short handle, for cutting grass. *noun.*

sick ly (sik′lē), **1** often sick; not strong; not healthy. **2** of or having something to do with sickness: *Her skin is a sickly yellow.* **3** causing sickness: *That place has a sickly climate.* **4** faint; weak; pale: *a sickly glow. adjective,* **sick li er, sick li est.**

sick ness (sik′nis), **1** illness; poor health; disease. **2** nausea; vomiting. *noun, plural* **sick ness es.**

side (sīd), **1** surface or line bounding a thing: *the sides of a square, a side of a box.* **2** one of the two surfaces of an object that is not the front, back, top, or bottom: *There is a door at the side of the house.* **3** either of the two surfaces of paper or cloth: *Write only on one side of the paper.* **4** a particular surface: *the outer and inner sides of a hollow ball, the side of the moon toward the earth.* **5** slope of a hill or bank. **6** either the right or the left part of a thing; either part or region beyond a central line: *the east side of a city, our side of the street, turn to one side.* **7** either the right or the left part of the body: *I felt a sharp pain in my side.* **8** group of persons who stand up for their beliefs, opinions, or ways of doing things against another group: *Both sides are ready for the contest. We'll choose sides for a game of softball.* **9** position, course, or part of one person or party against another: *It is pleasant to be on the winning side.* **10** part of a family; line of descent: *The man is English on his mother's side.* **11** at one side; on one side: *a side door, the side aisles of a theater.* **12** from one side: *a side view.* **13** toward one side: *a side glance.* **14** less important: *a side issue.* **15** side with, take sides: *The sisters always side with each other.* 1-10 *noun,* 11-14 *adjective,* 15 *verb,* **sid ed, sid ing.**

by one's side, near one: *My family was by my side during my illness.*

side by side, beside one another: *They walked side by side.*

side effect, an additional effect, usually one that

sidelong—They gave each other **sidelong** glances.

shrimp (definition 1) about 2 inches (5 centimeters) long

shrew (definition 2)—about 6 inches (15 centimeters) long with the tail

is unpleasant: *Many drugs produce side effects such as headache or upset stomach in some people.*

side long (sīd′lông′), to one side; toward the side. See picture. *adjective.*

side show (sīd/shō/), a small show in connection with a main one: *the sideshow of a circus. noun.*

side step (sīd/step/), 1 step aside. 2 avoid by stepping aside: *sidestep a responsibility. verb,* **side stepped, side step ping.**

side track (sīd/trak/), 1 a short railroad track to which a train may be switched from a main track. 2 switch (a train) to a sidetrack. 3 put aside; turn aside: *The teacher refused to be sidetracked by questions on other subjects.* 1 *noun,* 2,3 *verb.*

side walk (sīd/wôk/), place to walk at the side of a street, usually paved. *noun.*

side ways (sīd/wāz/), 1 to one side; toward one side: *walk sideways.* 2 from one side: *a sideways glimpse.* 3 with one side toward the front: *stand sideways, place a book sideways on a shelf. adverb, adjective.*

side wise (sīd/wīz/), sideways. *adverb, adjective.*

siege (sēj), 1 the surrounding of a fortified place by an army trying to capture it: *Troy was under a siege for ten years.* 2 any long or persistent effort to overcome resistance: *a siege of illness. noun.*
lay siege to, besiege: *The Greeks laid siege to Troy for ten years.*

si er ra (sē er/ə), chain of hills or mountains whose peaks suggest the teeth of a saw. *noun.* [*Sierra* is from a Spanish word meaning "a saw."]

si es ta (sē es/tə), nap or rest taken at noon or in the afternoon. *noun.*

sieve (siv), utensil having holes that let liquids and smaller pieces pass through, but not the larger pieces: *Shaking flour through a sieve removes lumps. noun.*

sift (sift), 1 to separate large pieces from small by shaking in a sieve: *Sift the gravel and put the larger stones in another pile.* 2 put through a sieve: *Sift sugar on the top of the cake.* 3 fall through, or as if through, a sieve: *The snow sifted softly down.* 4 examine very carefully: *The jury sifted the evidence before making its decision. verb.*

sigh (sī), 1 let out a very long, deep breath because one is sad, tired, or relieved: *We heard her sigh with relief.* 2 act or sound of sighing: *a sigh of relief.* 3 make a sound like a sigh: *The wind sighed in the treetops.* 4 wish very much; long: *He sighed for home.* 1,3,4 *verb,* 2 *noun.*

sight (sīt), 1 power of seeing: *Birds have better sight than dogs.* 2 act of seeing; look: *love at first sight.* 3 range of seeing: *We live in sight of the school.* 4 thing seen; view; glimpse: *I can't stand the sight of blood.* 5 something worth seeing: *Niagara Falls is one of the sights of the world.* 6 something that looks bad or odd: *Your room is a sight.* 7 see: *At last Columbus sighted land.* 8 device to guide the eye in taking aim or observing: *the sights on a rifle.* 9 aim or observation taken by such devices. 10 look at through sights; point to; aim at; aim: *I sighted carefully and fired at the target.* 1-6,8,9 *noun,* 7,10 *verb.*
at sight or **on sight,** as soon as seen: *She reads music at sight.*
catch sight of, see: *I caught sight of her.*
out of sight of, 1 where one cannot see: *Columbus was out of sight of land for several weeks.* 2 where one cannot be seen by: *out of sight of the neighbors.*

sight less (sīt/lis), blind. *adjective.*

sight see ing (sīt/sē/ing), going around to see objects or places of interest: *a weekend of sightseeing. noun.*

sign (sīn), 1 any mark or thing used to mean, represent, or point out something: *The sign reads, "Keep off the grass." The signs for add, subtract, multiply, and divide are* +, −, ×, *and* ÷. 2 put one's name on; write one's name. A person signs a letter, a note promising to pay a debt, or a check. We sign for telegrams or parcels. 3 motion or gesture used to mean, represent, or point out something: *She made the sign of the cross. A nod is a sign of agreement. We talked to the deaf man by signs.* 4 indication: *There are no signs of life about the house.* 5 indication of a coming event: *Dawn is the first sign of a new day. The coming of robins is a sign of spring.* 6 trace: *The hunters found signs of deer.* 1,3-6 *noun,* 2 *verb.*
sign off, stop broadcasting: *The show signs off at midnight.*
sign up, enlist or join by written agreement: *I signed up as a member of the scouts.*

sig nal (sig/nəl), 1 sign giving notice of something: *A red light is a signal of danger.* 2 make a signal or signals (to): *She signaled the car to stop by raising her hand.* 3 make known by a signal or signals: *A bell signals the end of a school period.* 4 used as a signal or in signaling: *a signal flag.* 5 remarkable; striking: *The airplane was a signal invention.* 1 *noun,* 2,3 *verb,* 4,5 *adjective.*

sig na ture (sig/nə chər), 1 a person's name written by that person. 2 signs printed at the beginning of a staff to show the pitch, key, and time of a piece of music. *noun.*

sign board (sīn/bôrd/), board having a sign, notice, or advertisement on it. *noun.*

sig net (sig/nit), a small seal: *The order was sealed with the king's signet. noun.*

sig nif i cance (sig nif/ə kəns), 1 importance; consequence: *The President wants to see you on a matter of significance.* 2 meaning: *I understood the significance of her look. noun.*

sig nif i cant (sig nif/ə kənt), 1 full of meaning; important; of consequence: *July 4, 1776, is a significant date for Americans.* 2 having a meaning; expressive: *Smiles are significant of pleasure.* 3 having or expressing a hidden meaning: *A significant nod from his friend warned him to stop talking. adjective.*

sig ni fy (sig/nə fī), 1 be a sign of; mean: *"Oh!" signifies surprise.* 2 make known by signs, words, or actions: *They waved to signify that they saw us. verb,* **sig ni fied, sig ni fy ing.**

sign language, language in which motions, especially of the hands, stand for words and ideas.

sign post (sīn/pōst/), post having signs, notices, or directions on it. *noun.*

si lence (sī/ləns), 1 absence of sound or noise;

silhouette (definition 1)

silhouette (definition 3)—The roosting gulls were **silhouetted** against the sky.

silo—A tall **silo** stood close to the barn.

stillness: *The teacher asked for silence.* **2** keeping still; not talking: *Silence gives consent.* **3** not mentioning: *Mother passed over his foolish remarks in silence.* **4** stop the noise of; make silent; quiet: *Please silence that barking dog.* 1-3 *noun,* 4 *verb,* **si lenced, si lenc ing.**

si lent (sī′lənt), **1** quiet; still; noiseless: *a silent house.* **2** not speaking; saying little or nothing: *The stranger was silent about his early life. Pupils must be silent during the study hour.* **3** not spoken; not said out loud: *a silent prayer. The "e" in "time" is a silent letter.* See picture. **4** taking no open or active part. *A silent partner in a business has no share in managing the business. adjective.*

sil hou ette (sil′ü et′), **1** an outline portrait cut out of black paper or filled in with some single color. See picture. **2** a dark image outlined against a lighter background. **3** show in outline. See picture. 1,2 *noun,* 3 *verb,* **sil hou et ted, sil hou et ting.** [*Silhouette* was named for Étienne de Silhouette, who lived from 1709 to 1767. He was a French official in charge of finance in 1759. Because he greatly pared down the large state expenses, the sharply cut outline pictures were called *Silhouettes* in fun.]

silk (silk), **1** a fine, soft thread spun by silkworms. **2** cloth made from this thread. **3** anything like silk: *corn silk.* **4** of silk; like silk: *She sewed the silk dress with silk thread.* 1-3 *noun,* 4 *adjective.*

silk en (sil′kən), **1** made of silk: *The king wore silken robes.* **2** like silk; smooth, soft, and glossy: *silken hair. adjective.*

silk worm (silk′wėrm′), a moth caterpillar that spins silk to make a cocoon. *noun.*

silk y (sil′kē), like silk; smooth, soft, and glossy: *A kitten has silky fur. adjective,* **silk i er, silk i est.**

sill (sil), piece of wood or stone across the bottom of a door, window, or house frame. *noun.*

sil ly (sil′ē), without sense or reason; foolish; ridiculous: *Baby talk is silly. adjective,* **sil li er, sil li est.**

si lo (sī′lō), an airtight building or pit in which green food for farm animals is preserved. See picture. *noun, plural* **si los.**

silt (silt), very fine particles of earth, sand, or similar things, carried by moving water and deposited as sediment: *The harbor is being choked up with silt. noun.*

sil ver (sil′vər), **1** a shining white precious metal. Silver is used to make coins, jewelry, spoons, knives, and forks. **2** coins made of this or a similar metal: *a pocketful of silver.* **3** utensils or dishes made of or covered with silver; silverware. **4** made of or covered with silver: *a silver spoon.* **5** cover or coat with silver or a similar metal: *silver a mirror.* **6** shining whitish gray: *a silver slipper.* **7** make or become a shining whitish gray: *The old man's hair had silvered.* 1-3 *noun,* 4,6 *adjective,* 5,7 *verb.*

sil ver smith (sil′vər smith′), person who makes articles of silver. *noun.*

sil ver ware (sil′vər wer′ *or* sil′vər war′), **1** silver things; utensils or dishes made from silver. **2** metal knives, forks, and spoons for eating. *noun.*

sil ver y (sil′vər ē), like silver; like that of silver: *Moonbeams are silvery. The bell has a silvery sound. adjective.*

sim i lar (sim′ə lər), **1** much the same; alike; like: *A creek and a brook are similar.* **2** having the same shape but often a different size: *similar triangles. adjective.*

sim i lar i ty (sim′ə lar′ə tē), likeness; resemblance. *noun, plural* **sim i lar i ties.**

sim mer (sim′ər), **1** keep at or just below the boiling point; boil gently: *Simmer the milk, do not boil it. The soup should simmer for a few hours to improve its taste.* **2** be on the point of just breaking out: *simmering rebellion. I simmered with anger, but said nothing. verb.*

sim ple (sim′pəl), **1** easy to do or understand: *a simple problem. This book is in simple language.* **2** without ornament; not rich or showy; plain: *simple food, simple clothing.* **3** having few parts; not complex. **4** natural; not affected; not showing off: *She has a pleasant, simple manner.* **5** stupid; dull; having little mental ability: *"Simple Simon met a pieman." adjective,* **sim pler, sim plest.**

sim ple ton (sim′pəl tən), a silly person; fool. *noun.*

sim plic i ty (sim plis′ə tē), **1** being simple: *simplicity of structure.* **2** freedom from difficulty; clearness: *The simplicity of that book makes it suitable for children.* **3** plainness: *Hospital rooms are furnished with simplicity. noun, plural* **sim plic i ties.**

sim pli fy (sim′plə fī), make plainer or easier; make simple or more simple: *"Tho" is a simplified spelling of "though." verb,* **sim pli fied, sim pli fy ing.**

sim ply (sim′plē), **1** in a simple manner: *to explain a problem simply.* **2** without much ornament; without pretense or affectation; plainly: *The nurse was simply dressed.* **3** merely; only: *We simply need a little information.* **4** absolutely: *simply perfect. adverb.*

si mul ta ne ous (sī′məl tā′nē əs), done, existing, or happening at the same time: *The two simultaneous shots sounded like one. adjective.*

sin (sin), **1** breaking the law of God on purpose. **2** break the law of God. **3** wrongdoing of any kind; immoral act. Lying, stealing, dishonesty, and cruelty are sins. **4** do wrong. 1,3 *noun,* 2,4 *verb,* **sinned, sin ning.**

since (sins), **1** from a past time till now: *The sun has been up since five.* **2** after the time that; from the time when: *He has been home only once since he went to New York.* **3** after: *She has worked hard since she left school.* **4** from then till now: *I caught cold Saturday and have been in bed ever since.* **5** at some time between then and now: *He at first refused the position, but has since accepted it.*

6 before now; ago: *The ancient city had long since been deserted.* **7** because: *Go, since you are bored.* **1** *preposition,* 2,3,7 *conjunction,* 4-6 *adverb.*

sin cere (sin sir′), free from pretense or deceit; genuine; real; honest: *sincere thanks. I made a sincere effort to pass my exams. adjective,* **sin cer er, sin cer est.**

sin cer i ty (sin ser′ə tē), freedom from pretense or deceit; honesty: *We do business with him because of his sincerity. noun, plural* **sin cer i ties.**

sin ew (sin′yü), **1** a tough, strong band or cord that joins muscle to bone; tendon: *You can see the sinews between muscle and bone in this cooked chicken leg.* **2** strength; energy. **3** means of strength; source of power: *Freedom of speech is one of the sinews of democracy. noun.*

sin ful (sin′fəl), full of sin; wicked; wrong: *a sinful person, a sinful act. adjective.*

sing (sing), **1** make music with the voice: *You sing very well.* **2** make pleasant, musical sounds: *Birds sing.* **3** bring, send, or put with or by singing: *Sing the baby to sleep.* **4** tell in song or poetry: *The poet sang of love.* **5** make a ringing, whistling, humming, or buzzing sound: *The teakettle sang on the stove. verb,* **sang** *or* **sung, sung, sing ing.**

singe (sinj), **1** burn a little: *The chicken was singed to remove the fine hairs.* **2** a slight burn. **1** *verb,* **singed, singe ing;** **2** *noun.*

sing er (sing′ər), person or bird that sings: *Our canary is a fine singer. noun.*

sin gle (sing′gəl), **1** one and no more; only one: *The spider hung by a single thread.* **2** for only one; individual: *The sisters share one room with two single beds in it.* **3** not married: *a single man.* **4** having only one on each side: *The knights engaged in single combat.* **5** pick from others: *She was singled out for praise.* **6** having only one set of petals. Most cultivated roses have double flowers with many petals; wild roses have single flowers with five petals. **7** in baseball, a hit that allows the batter to reach first base. 1-4,6 *adjective,* 5 *verb,* **sin gled, sin gling;** 7 *noun.*

single file, line of persons or things arranged one behind another: *march in single file.*

sin gle-hand ed (sing′gəl han′did), without help from others. See picture. *adjective, adverb.*

sin gly (sing′glē), **1** by itself; separately: *Let us consider each point singly.* **2** one by one; one at a time: *Misfortunes never come singly.* **3** by one's own efforts; without help. *adverb.*

sin gu lar (sing′gyə lər), **1** extraordinary; unusual: *"Treasure Island" is a story of singular interest.* **2** strange; queer; peculiar: *The detectives were puzzled by the singular nature of the crime.* **3** one in number. *Dog is singular; dogs is plural.* **4** the singular number in grammar. *Ox is the singular of oxen.* 1-3 *adjective,* 4 *noun.*

sin is ter (sin′ə stər), **1** showing ill will; threatening: *a sinister rumor, a sinister look.* **2** bad; evil; dishonest: *a sinister plan. adjective.* [Sinister is from a Latin word, originally meaning "left" or "on the left side." Later, it came to mean "unlucky" because of the belief that omens seen on the left side were unlucky.]

sink (singk), **1** go down; fall slowly; go lower and lower: *The sun is sinking in the west.* **2** go or make go under: *The ship sank. The submarine sank two ships.* **3** make or become lower or weaker: *Her voice sank to a whisper.* **4** go deeply: *Let the lessons sink into your mind.* **5** make go deep; dig: *They are sinking a well.* **6** a shallow basin or tub with a pipe to drain it: *The dishes are in the kitchen sink.* 1-5 *verb,* **sank** or **sunk, sunk, sink ing;** 6 *noun.*

sin ner (sin′ər), person who sins or does wrong: *The sinner who repented was forgiven. noun.*

sip (sip), **1** drink little by little: *She sipped her tea.* **2** a very small drink: *She took a sip.* 1 *verb,* **sipped, sip ping;** 2 *noun.*

si phon (sī′fən), **1** a bent tube through which liquid can be drawn over the edge of one container into another at a lower level by air pressure. **2** draw off or pass through a siphon: *They siphoned some gasoline from their car to ours.* 1 *noun,* 2 *verb.*

sir (sėr), **1** title of respect or honor used to a man instead of his name. We begin business letters to men with "Dear Sir." **2 Sir,** the title of a knight: *Sir Walter Scott.* **3** Mr. or Master: *You, sir, have no business here; get out. noun.*

sire (sīr), **1** a male ancestor; forefather. **2** a male parent; father: *Lightning was the sire of the race horse Danger.* **3** be the father of: *Lightning sired Danger.* **4** title of respect formerly used to a great noble and now used to a king. 1,2,4 *noun,* 3 *verb,* **sired, sir ing.**

si ren (sī′rən), kind of whistle that makes a loud, piercing sound. *noun.*

sir up (sir′əp *or* sėr′əp), syrup. *noun.*

sis ter (sis′tər), **1** daughter of the same parents. A girl is a sister to the other children of her parents. **2** a close friend or companion. **3** a female member of the same union, club, or religious organization. **4** nun: *Sisters of Charity. noun.*

single-handed
She tamed lions and tigers **single-handed.**

sis ter hood (sis′tər hůd), **1** bond between sisters; feeling of sister for sister: *There was a strong feeling of sisterhood among the women who worked together for the right to vote.* **2** persons joined as sisters; association of women with some common aim, characteristic, belief, or profession. *noun.*

sis ter-in-law (sis′tər in lô′), **1** sister of one's husband or wife. **2** wife of one's brother. *noun, plural* **sis ters-in-law.**

sis ter ly (sis′tər lē), of or like a sister; friendly; kindly: *sisterly teasing. My friend took a sisterly interest in helping me solve my problem. adjective.*

sit (sit), **1** rest on the lower part of the body, with the weight off the feet: *She sat in a chair.* **2** seat; cause to sit: *I sat the child in the chair.* **3** be placed; be: *The clock has sat on that shelf for years.* **4** have a seat in an assembly; be a member of a council: *sit in Congress.* **5** hold a session: *The court sits next month.* **6** place oneself in a position for having one's picture made; pose: *sit for a portrait.* **7** press or weigh: *His responsibilities sit heavy on his mind.* **8** perch: *The birds were sitting on the fence rail.* **9** cover eggs so that they will hatch; brood. **10** take care of children while their parents are away for a short time: *I sit for the woman next door while she's at work.* **11** fit: *Her coat sits well. verb,* **sat, sit ting.**

sit down, take a seat: *We sat down by the roadside to have our picnic.*

sit on *or* **sit upon,** have a seat on (a jury, committee, commission, or council): *He sat upon the State Hospital Commission.*

sit up, 1 raise the body to a sitting position: *Stop slumping and sit up on your chair.* **2** keep such a position: *The sick man sat up at last.* **3** stay up instead of going to bed: *They sat up talking all night.*

site (sīt), position or place (of anything): *The house on the hill has one of the best sites in town. The site for the new school has not yet been chosen. noun.*

sit ting (sit′ing), **1** meeting or session of a court of law, legislature, commission, or anything like it: *The hearing lasted through six sittings.* **2** time of remaining seated: *He read five chapters at one sitting.* **3** that sits or has to do with sitting: *be in bed in a sitting position.* 1,2 *noun,* 3 *adjective.*

sitting room, room to sit in; parlor; living room.

sit u ate (sich′ü āt), place or locate: *The school is situated so that it can be reached easily from all parts of town. verb,* **sit u at ed, sit u at ing.**

sit u a tion (sich′ü ā′shən), **1** circumstances; case; condition: *It is a very disagreeable situation to be alone and without money in a strange city.* **2** place to work; job or position: *She is trying to find a situation.* **3** position; location: *Our house has a beautiful situation on a hill. noun.*

skunk (definition 1)—about 2 feet (60 centimeters) long with the tail

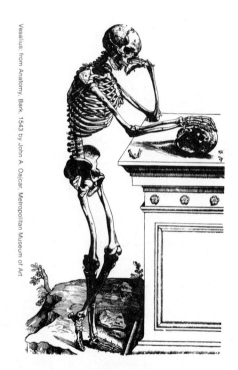

Vesalius: from Anatomy, Bark, 1543 by John A. Oajcar, Metropolitan Museum of Art

skeleton (definition 1)

skeins of yarn

six (siks), one more than five; 6: *Six apples are half a dozen apples.* noun, plural **six es;** *adjective.*

six pence (siks′pəns), **1** six British pennies; 6 pence. **2** a former British coin having this value. *noun.*

six-shoot er (siks′shü′tər), revolver that can fire six shots without being loaded again. *noun.*

six teen (sik′stēn′), six more than ten; 16: *There are sixteen ounces in a pound.* noun, adjective.

six teenth (sik′stēnth′), **1** next after the 15th. **2** one of 16 equal parts: *An ounce is one sixteenth of a pound.* adjective, noun.

sixth (siksth), **1** next after the fifth. **2** one of six equal parts. *adjective, noun.*

six ti eth (sik′stē ith), **1** next after the 59th. **2** one of 60 equal parts. *adjective, noun.*

six ty (sik′stē), six times ten; 60. *noun,* plural **six ties;** *adjective.*

size (sīz), **1** amount of surface or space a thing takes up: *The two boys are of the same size. We need a house of larger size.* **2** one of a series of measures: *His collar size is fourteen.* **3 size up,** form an opinion of: *We sized up the candidates before we voted.* 1,2 *noun,* 3 *verb,* **sized, siz ing.**

siz zle (siz′əl), **1** make a hissing sound, as fat does when it is frying or burning. **2** a hissing sound. 1 *verb,* **siz zled, siz zling;** 2 *noun.*

skate¹ (skāt), **1** frame with a blade fixed to a shoe so that a person can glide over ice. **2** roller skate. **3** glide or move along on skates. 1,2 *noun,* 3 *verb,* **skat ed, skat ing.**

skate² (skāt), a broad, flat fish that often has a pointed nose. *noun,* plural **skates** or **skate.**

skate board (skāt′bôrd′), a narrow board with roller-skate wheels attached to each end, used for gliding or moving on any hard surface. *noun.*

skat er (skā′tər), person who skates. *noun.*

skein (skān), a small bundle of yarn or thread. See picture. *noun.*

skel e ton (skel′ə tən), **1** bones of a body, fitted together in their natural places. The skeleton is a frame that supports the muscles and organs of the body. See picture. **2** frame: *the steel skeleton of a building. noun.* [*Skeleton* comes from Greek words meaning "a dried-up body."]

skeleton key, key made to open many locks.

skep tic (skep′tik), person who is skeptical; doubter. *noun.*

skep ti cal (skep′tə kəl), inclined to doubt; questioning the truth of theories and apparent facts; not believing easily. *adjective.*

sketch (skech), **1** a rough, quickly done drawing, painting, or design. **2** make a sketch of; draw roughly. **3** a short description, story, or play. 1,3 *noun,* plural **sketch es;** 2 *verb.*

sketch y (skech′ē), **1** having or giving only outlines or main features. **2** incomplete; done very roughly: *I didn't like the book because of its sketchy plot. adjective,* **sketch i er, sketch i est.**

ski (skē), **1** one of a pair of long, slender pieces of hard wood, plastic, or metal fastened by straps or special harness to the shoes to enable a person to glide over snow. **2** glide over the snow on skis.

1 *noun, plural* **skis** or **ski;** 2 *verb,* **skied, ski ing.**

skid (skid), **1** slip or slide sideways while moving: *The car skidded on the slippery road.* **2** a sideways slip or slide: *The car went into a skid on the icy road.* **3** piece of wood or metal to prevent a wheel from turning. **4** slide along without turning. 1,4 *verb,* **skid ded, skid ding;** 2,3 *noun.*

skies (skīz). See **sky.** *The skies are cloudy. noun plural.*

skiff (skif), **1** a light rowboat. **2** a small, light boat. *noun.*

skill (skil), **1** ability gained by practice or knowledge: *The trained teacher managed the children with skill.* **2** ability to do things well with one's body or with tools: *It takes great skill to tune a piano. noun.*

skilled (skild), **1** having skill; trained; experienced: *A carpenter is a skilled worker.* **2** showing skill; requiring skill: *Plastering is skilled labor. adjective.*

skil let (skil′it), a shallow pan with a handle, used for frying. *noun.*

skill ful or **skil ful** (skil′fəl), **1** having skill; expert: *a skillful surgeon.* **2** showing skill: *That is a skillful piece of work. adjective.*

skim (skim), **1** remove from the top: *The cook skims the fat from the soup.* **2** take something from the top of: *The dairy skims milk to remove the cream for making butter.* **3** move lightly over; glide: *The pebble I threw skimmed the surface of the water. Skaters were skimming over the ice. A hawk skimmed by.* **4** read hastily; read with omissions: *It took me an hour to skim the book. verb,* **skimmed, skim ming.**

skim milk or **skimmed milk,** milk from which the cream has been removed.

skimp y (skim′pē), scanty; not enough: *I was hungry all afternoon after my skimpy lunch. adjective,* **skimp i er, skimp i est.**

skin (skin), **1** the outer covering of human and animal bodies, plants, fruits, and seeds: *Their skin was tanned from playing in the sun. Peach skins are fuzzy.* **2** hide; pelt: *The skin of a calf makes soft leather.* **3** take the skin off: *She fell and skinned her knee. The hunter skinned the deer.* **4** container made of skin for holding liquids. 1,2,4 *noun,* 3 *verb,* **skinned, skin ning.**

by the skin of one's teeth, very narrowly; barely: *She got home by the skin of her teeth before it rained.*

skin diver, person skilled in skin diving.

skin diving, swimming about under water for long periods of time with rubber flippers and other gear.

skin ny (skin′ē), very thin; very lean: *You will get skinny if you don't eat more. adjective,* **skin ni er, skin ni est.**

skip (skip), **1** leap lightly; spring; jump: *The children skipped merrily down the street.* **2** leap lightly over: *The girls skipped rope.* **3** a light spring, jump, or leap: *The child gave a skip of joy.* **4** send bounding along a surface: *I like to skip stones on the lake.* **5** pass over; fail to notice; omit: *Skip any questions you can't answer.* 1,2,4,5 *verb,* **skipped, skip ping;** 3 *noun.*

skip per (skip′ər), **1** captain of a ship, especially of a small trading or fishing boat. **2** any captain or leader. *noun.*

skir mish (skėr′mish), **1** a slight fight between small groups: *The scouts of our army had a skirmish with a small group of the enemy.* **2** any slight conflict, argument, or contest. **3** take part in a skirmish. 1,2 *noun, plural* **skir mish es;** 3 *verb.*

skirt (skėrt), **1** part of a dress that hangs from the waist. **2** a woman's or girl's garment that hangs from the waist. **3** **skirts,** the outer part of a place, group of people, or anything like it; outskirts. **4** pass along the border or edge of: *The new highway skirts the city instead of going through it.* 1-3 *noun,* 4 *verb.*

skit (skit), a short play or story that often contains humor: *a television skit. Five members of our class were elected to write a skit. noun.*

skulk (skulk), **1** keep out of sight to avoid danger, work, or duty; hide for a bad purpose; sneak; lurk. **2** move in a stealthy, sneaking way: *The wolf was skulking in the woods near the sheep. verb.*

skull (skul), the bony framework of the head and face in human beings and other animals with backbones. The skull encloses and protects the brain. *noun.*

skunk (skungk), **1** a black, bushy-tailed animal of North America about the size of a cat, usually with white stripes along the back. Skunks spray out a strong, unpleasant-smelling liquid when they are frightened or attacked. See picture. **2** fur of this animal. **3** a mean, contemptible person. *noun.*

sky (skī), **1** the space overhead that seems to cover the earth like a bowl; the area of clouds; the heavens: *a blue sky, a cloudy sky.* **2** heaven. *noun, plural* **skies.** [*Sky* comes from an old Norse word meaning "cloud."]

sky div ing (skī′dī′ving), act or sport of diving from an airplane and dropping for a great distance before releasing the parachute. *noun.*

sky lark (skī′lärk′), **1** a small bird of Europe that sings very sweetly as it flies toward the sky. **2** play; frolic: *The children were skylarking in the orchard.* 1 *noun,* 2 *verb.*

sky light (skī′līt′), window in a roof or ceiling. *noun.*

sky line (skī′līn′), **1** line at which earth and sky seem to meet; horizon. **2** outline of mountains, trees, or buildings, as seen against the sky: *The tall buildings of New York make a remarkable skyline. noun.*

sky rock et (skī′rok′it), **1** firework that goes up high in the air and bursts into a shower of stars and sparks. **2** rise suddenly; rise much and quickly: *The movie star skyrocketed to fame. The price of sugar has skyrocketed.* 1 *noun,* 2 *verb.*

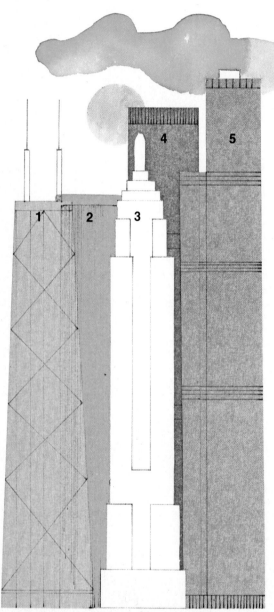

skyscrapers—five of the world's tallest skyscrapers
1 John Hancock Center, Chicago—1107 feet (337 meters) tall
2 Standard Oil Building, Chicago—1136 feet (346) meters) tall
3 Empire State Building, New York—1250 feet (381 meters) tall
4 World Trade Center, New York—1350 feet (411 meters) tall
5 Sears Tower, Chicago—1454 feet (443 meters) tall

sky scrap er (skī′skrā′pər), a very tall building. See picture. *noun.*

slab (slab), a broad, flat, thick piece (of stone, wood, meat, or anything solid): *This sidewalk is made of slabs of stone. The butcher cut slices from the slab of bacon. noun.*

slack (slak), **1** not tight or firm; loose: *a slack rope.* **2** part that hangs loose: *Pull in the slack of the rope.* **3** careless: *a slack worker.* **4** slow: *The horse was moving at a slack pace.* **5** not active; not brisk; dull: *Business is slack at this season.* 1,3-5 *adjective,* 2 *noun.*

slack en (slak′ən), **1** make or become slower: *Business slackens in the winter.* **2** make or become looser: *Slacken your hold on the rope. verb.*

slacks (slaks), trousers for casual wear. *noun plural.*

slag (slag), **1** the rough, hard waste left after metal is separated from ore by melting it. **2** a light, spongy lava. *noun.*

slain (slān). See **slay.** *The sheep were slain by wolves. verb.*

slam (slam), **1** shut with force and noise; close with a bang: *She slammed the window down. The door slammed.* **2** throw, push, hit, or move hard with force: *He slammed himself down on his bed. That car slammed into a truck.* **3** a violent and noisy closing or striking; bang: *The door blew shut with a slam.* 1,2 *verb,* **slammed, slam ming;** 3 *noun.*

slan der (slan′dər), **1** a false spoken statement meant to harm a person's reputation: *The candidate for mayor accused his opponent of slander.* **2** talk falsely about. 1 *noun,* 2 *verb.*

slang (slang), words, phrases, or meanings not accepted as good English when speaking or writing formal English. Slang is often very vivid and expressive and is used in familiar talk between friends but is not usually appropriate in school themes. Slang is mostly made up of new words or meanings that are popular for only a short time. See picture. *noun.*

slant (slant), **1** slope: *Most handwriting slants to the right.* **2** a slanting direction or position; slope: *Has your roof a sharp slant?* **3** sloping: *a slant roof.* 1 *verb,* 2 *noun,* 3 *adjective.*

slap (slap), **1** blow with the open hand or with something flat. **2** strike with the open hand or with something flat: *He slapped at the fly with a folded newspaper. I slapped the table with my hand.* **3** put or throw with force: *She slapped the book down on the table.* 1 *noun,* 2,3 *verb,* **slapped, slap ping.**

slash (slash), **1** cut with a sweeping stroke of a sword, knife, or whip; gash: *He slashed the bark off the tree with his knife.* **2** make a slashing stroke: *She slashed at the vines growing across the path.* **3** a sweeping, slashing stroke: *the slash of a sword.* **4** cut or wound made by such a stroke. **5** cut down severely; reduce a great deal: *Salaries were slashed when business became bad.* **6** a sharp cutting down; great reduction: *a slash in prices.* 1,2,5 *verb,* 3,4,6 *noun, plural* **slash es.**

slat (slat), a long, thin, narrow piece of wood or metal. *noun.*

slate (slāt), **1** a bluish-gray rock that splits easily into thin, smooth layers. Slate is used to cover roofs and for blackboards. **2** a thin piece of this rock. People used to write on slates, but now they use paper. **3** dark bluish gray. 1,2 *noun*, 3 *adjective*.

slaugh ter (slô′tər), **1** the killing of an animal or animals for food; butchering: *the slaughter of a steer, fatten hogs for slaughter.* **2** brutal killing; much or needless killing: *The battle resulted in a frightful slaughter.* **3** kill an animal or animals for food; butcher: *Millions of cattle are slaughtered every year in the stockyards.* 1,2 *noun*, 3 *verb*.

slave (slāv), **1** person who is owned by another. **2** person who is controlled or ruled by some desire, habit, or influence: *a slave of drink, a slave to one's emotions.* **3** person who works like a slave. **4** work like a slave: *We slaved all day cleaning the house.* **5** of slaves; done by slaves: *slave labor.* 1-3 *noun*, 4 *verb*, **slaved, slav ing;** 5 *adjective*.

slav er y (slā′vər ē), **1** condition of being a slave. Many African Negroes were captured and sold into slavery. **2** custom of owning slaves. Where slavery is permitted, certain people own other people. **3** condition like that of a slave. **4** hard work like that of a slave. *noun*.

slav ish (slā′vish), **1** of or having something to do with a slave or slaves. **2** weakly submitting; like slaves; fit for slaves: *slavish obedience.* **3** lacking originality and independence: *a slavish reproduction. adjective.*

slay (slā), kill with violence: *A hunter slays wild animals. verb,* **slew, slain, slay ing.**

sled (sled), **1** framework of boards mounted on runners for use on snow or ice. Sleds pulled by dogs are in common use in the Arctic. **2** ride or coast on a sled. 1 *noun*, 2 *verb*, **sled ded, sled ding.**

sledge ham mer (slej′ham′ər), a large, heavy hammer, usually swung with both hands. *noun*.

sleek (slēk), **1** soft and glossy; smooth: *sleek hair.* **2** having smooth, soft skin, hair, or fur: *a sleek cat.* **3** smooth in speech and manners: *a sleek salesman.* **4** smooth: *He sleeked down his hair.* 1-3 *adjective*, 4 *verb*.

sleep (slēp), **1** rest body and mind; be without ordinary thought or movement: *We sleep at night. Most animals sleep.* **2** rest of body and mind occurring naturally and regularly: *Most people need eight hours of sleep a day.* **3** be in a condition like sleep: *The seeds slept in the ground all winter.* **4** condition like sleep. The last sleep means death. 1,3 *verb*, **slept, sleep ing;** 2,4 *noun*.

sleep away, pass or spend in sleeping: *She slept away the whole morning.*

sleep i ly (slē′pə lē), in a sleepy manner: *The baby opened its eyes sleepily. adverb.*

sleeping bag, a warmly lined, canvas or nylon bag to sleep in out of doors.

sleeping car, a railroad car with berths for passengers to sleep in.

sleep less (slēp′lis), without sleep; not sleeping; restless: *The hot weather caused me to have a sleepless night. adjective.*

a hat	**i** it	**oi** oil	**ch** child	a in about
ā age	**ī** ice	**ou** out	**ng** long	e in taken
ä far	**o** hot	**u** cup	**sh** she	**ə =** i in pencil
e let	**ō** open	** u̇** put	**th** thin	o in lemon
ē equal	**ô** order	**ü** rule	**ŦH** then	u in circus
ėr term			**zh** measure	

sleep y (slē′pē), **1** ready to go to sleep; inclined to sleep: *He never gets enough rest and is always sleepy.* **2** quiet; not active: *a sleepy little mountain town. adjective,* **sleep i er, sleep i est.**

sleet (slēt), **1** half-frozen rain; snow or hail mixed with rain. Sleet forms when rain falls through a layer of cold air. **2** come down in sleet: *It sleeted; then it snowed; then it rained.* 1 *noun*, 2 *verb*.

sleeve (slēv), part of a garment that covers the arm. *noun*.

sleigh (slā), **1** carriage or cart mounted on runners for use on snow or ice. See picture. **2** travel or ride in a sleigh. 1 *noun*, 2 *verb*.

slang

sleigh (definition 1)—The **sleighs** raced over the icy road.

slen der (slen′dər), **1** long and thin; not big around; slim: *a slender child. A pencil is a slender piece of wood.* **2** slight; small: *a slender meal, a slender income, a slender hope. adjective.*

slept (slept). See **sleep.** *The child slept soundly. I haven't slept well for weeks. verb.*

slew (slü). See **slay.** *Jack slew the giant. verb.*

slice (slīs), **1** a thin, flat, broad piece cut from something: *a slice of bread, a slice of meat, a slice of cake.* **2** cut into slices: *Slice the bread. We ate sliced peaches.* **3** cut (off) as a slice. **1** *noun,* **2,3** *verb,* **sliced, slic ing.**

slick (slik), **1** sleek; smooth: *slick hair.* **2** sly; tricky. **3** make sleek or smooth. **4** slippery; greasy: *a road slick with mud.* **5** a smooth place or spot. *Oil makes a slick on the surface of water.* **1,2,4** *adjective,* **3** *verb,* **5** *noun.*

slid (slid). See **slide.** *The minutes slid rapidly by. She has slid past us. verb.*

slide (slīd), **1** move smoothly, as a sled moves on snow or ice: *The bureau drawers slide in and out.* **2** move easily, quietly, or secretly: *The thief quickly slid behind the curtains.* **3** pass by degrees; slip: *He has slid into bad habits.* **4** pass or put quietly or secretly: *I slid the note into my pocket.* **5** act of sliding: *The children each take a slide in turn.* **6** a smooth surface for sliding on: *The frozen brook makes a good slide.* **7** track, rail, or smooth channel on which something slides. **8** mass of snow and ice or dirt and rocks sliding down: *The slide cut off the valley from the rest of the world.* **9** a small, thin sheet of glass or plastic. *Objects are put on slides in order to look at them under a microscope. Slides of photographic film with pictures on them are put in a projector and shown on a screen.* **1-4** *verb,* **slid, slid ing;** **5-9** *noun.*

slight (slīt), **1** not much; not important; small: *I have a slight headache.* **2** not big around; slender: *She is a slight girl.* **3** pay too little attention to; neglect: *I felt slighted because I was not asked to the party.* **4** slighting treatment; act showing neglect or lack of respect: *Cinderella suffered many slights from her sisters.* **1,2** *adjective,* **3** *verb,* **4** *noun.*

slight ly (slīt′lē), **1** in a slight manner. **2** to a slight degree; somewhat; a little: *I knew him slightly. adverb.*

slim (slim), **1** slender; thin: *He was very slim, being 6 feet tall and weighing only 130 pounds.* **2** small; slight; weak: *We had a slim attendance at the football game because of the rain. adjective,* **slim mer, slim mest.**

slime (slīm), **1** soft, sticky mud or something like it: *The stagnant pond is covered with slime.* **2** a sticky substance given off by certain animals, such as snails, slugs, and fish. *noun.*

slim y (slī′mē), **1** covered with slime: *The pond is too slimy to swim in.* **2** of slime; like slime: *a slimy secretion. adjective,* **slim i er, slim i est.**

sling (sling), **1** strip of leather with a string fastened to each end, for throwing stones. **2** throw with a sling. **3** throw; cast; hurl: *We slung stones over the edge of the cliff.* **4** a hanging loop of cloth fastened around the neck to support a hurt arm.

5 rope, band, or chain by which heavy objects are lifted, carried, or held: *We lowered the heavy boxes over the railing by a sling.* **6** hang in a sling; hang so as to swing loosely: *The bag was slung over her shoulder.* **1,4,5** *noun,* **2,3,6** *verb,* **slung, sling ing.**

sling shot (sling′shot′), a Y-shaped stick with a rubber band fastened to its prongs, used to shoot pebbles. *noun.*

slink (slingk), move in a secret, guilty manner; sneak: *After stealing the meat, the dog slunk away. verb,* **slunk, slink ing.**

slip[1] (slip), **1** go or move smoothly, quietly, easily, or quickly: *She slipped out of the room. Time slips by.* **2** slide; move out of place: *The knife slipped and cut him.* **3** slide suddenly without wanting to: *He slipped on the icy sidewalk.* **4** slipping: *My broken leg was caused by a slip on a banana peel.* **5** cause to slip; put, pass, or draw smoothly, quietly, or secretly: *I slipped the bolt into place and locked the door. Slip the note into her hand.* **6** put or take (something) easily or quickly: *Slip on your coat and come with us. Slip off your shoes.* **7** a sleeveless garment worn under a dress. **8** pass without notice; pass through neglect; escape: *Don't let this opportunity slip.* **9** get loose from; get away from; escape from: *The dog has slipped its collar. Your name has slipped my mind.* **10** make a mistake or error: *I slipped and mailed the wrong letter.* **11** mistake; error: *He makes slips in pronouncing words. That remark was a slip of the tongue.* **1-3,5,6,8-10** *verb,* **slipped, slip ping;** **4,7,11** *noun.* **let slip,** tell without meaning to: *Don't let the secret slip about the surprise party.*

slip[2] (slip), **1** a narrow strip of paper, wood, or other material. **2** a small branch or twig cut from a plant to grow a new plant: *She has promised us slips from that bush. noun.*

slip per (slip′ər), a light, low shoe that is slipped on easily: *a pair of bedroom slippers. noun.*

slip per y (slip′ər ē), **1** causing or likely to cause slipping: *A wet street is slippery. The steps are slippery with ice.* **2** slipping away easily: *Wet soap is slippery.* **3** not to be depended on; tricky. *adjective,* **slip per i er, slip per i est.**

slit (slit), **1** cut or tear along a line; make a long, straight cut or tear in: *slit cloth into strips, slit a skirt to make a pocket.* **2** a straight, narrow cut, tear, or opening: *a slit in a bag, the slit in the letter box.* **1** *verb,* **slit, slit ting;** **2** *noun.*

sliv er (sliv′ər), **1** a long, thin piece that has been split off, broken off, or cut off; splinter. **2** split or break into slivers. **1** *noun,* **2** *verb.*

slo gan (slō′gən), word or phrase used by a business, political party, or any group to advertise its purpose; motto: *"Service with a smile" was the store's slogan. noun.*

sloop (slüp), sailboat having one mast, a mainsail, a jib, and sometimes other sails. *noun.*

slop (slop), **1** spill liquid upon; spill; splash: *I slopped water on the floor.* **2** liquid carelessly spilled or splashed about. **3** dirty water; liquid garbage: *kitchen slops.* **4** weak liquid food, such as gruel. **1** *verb,* **slopped, slop ping;** **2-4** *noun.*

slope (slōp), **1** go up or down at an angle; slant: *The land slopes toward the sea. That house has a sloping roof.* **2** any line, surface, or land that goes up or down from a level: *If you roll a ball up a slope, it will roll down again.* **3** amount of slope: *The floor of the theater has a slope of four feet from the back seats to the front seats.* **1** *verb,* **sloped, slop ing; 2,3** *noun.*

slop py (slop′ē), **1** very wet; slushy: *sloppy ground, sloppy weather.* **2** careless; slovenly: *use sloppy language, do sloppy work. adjective,* **slop pi er, slop pi est.**

slosh (slosh), splash in slush, mud, or water: *The children sloshed through the puddles and got all wet. verb.*

slot (slot), **1** a small, narrow opening: *Put your money in the slot to get a stick of gum from this machine.* **2** make a slot or slots in. **1** *noun,* **2** *verb,* **slot ted, slot ting.**

sloth (slôth), **1** unwillingness to work or exert oneself; laziness; idleness: *Sloth keeps many people from taking any exercise.* **2** a very slow-moving animal of South America that lives in trees. Sloths hang upside down from tree branches. See picture. *noun.*

sloth ful (slôth′fəl), lazy; sluggish. *adjective.*

slouch (slouch), **1** stand, sit, walk, or move in an awkward, drooping manner: *She slouched in her chair.* **2** bending forward of head and shoulders; awkward, drooping way of standing, sitting, or walking. **3** an awkward, slovenly, or inefficient person. **1** *verb,* **2,3** *noun, plural* **slouch es.**

slov en ly (sluv′ən lē), untidy, dirty, or careless in dress, appearance, habits, or work. *adjective,* **slov en li er, slov en li est.**

slow (slō), **1** taking a long time; taking longer than usual; not fast or quick: *a slow journey. He is slow to anger.* **2** behind time; running at less than proper speed: *The slow runners couldn't keep up.* **3** showing time earlier than the correct time: *The clock was slow and I was late for school.* **4** make slow or slower; reduce the speed of: *slow down a car.* **5** become slow; go slower: *Slow up when you drive through a town.* **6** in a slow manner or way; slowly: *Drive slow past a school.* **7** sluggish; inactive: *Business is slow.* **8** dull; not interesting: *a slow party.* **9** not quick to understand: *a slow pupil.* **1-3,7-9** *adjective,* **4,5** *verb,* **6** *adverb.*

slug[1] (slug), **1** a slow-moving animal like a snail, without a shell or with only a very small shell. Slugs live mostly in forests, gardens, and damp places feeding on plants. See picture. **2** piece of lead or other metal for firing from a gun. **3** a round metal piece or counterfeit coin inserted in a machine instead of a genuine coin. *noun.*

slug[2] (slug), **1** hit hard. **2** a hard blow with the fist. **1** *verb,* **slugged, slug ging; 2** *noun.*

slug gish (slug′ish), slow-moving; not active: *When I stay up late, I am often sluggish the next day. The stream was so sluggish that I could hardly tell which way it flowed. adjective.*

sluice (slüs), **1** structure with a gate for holding back or controlling the water of a canal, river, or

slug[1] (definition 1)—about 1 inch (2¹/₂ centimeters) long

sloth (definition 2)—about 2 feet (60 centimeters) long

lake. **2** gate that controls the flow of water. When the water behind a dam gets too high, the sluices are opened. **3** let out or draw off (water) by opening a sluice. **4** flush or cleanse with a rush of water; pour or throw water over. **5** a long, sloping trough through which water flows, used to wash gold from sand, dirt, or gravel. **6** channel for carrying off overflow or surplus water. **1,2,5,6** *noun,* **3,4** *verb,* **sluiced, sluic ing.**

slum (slum), a run-down, overcrowded part of a city or town. Poverty, dirt, and unhealthy living conditions are common in the slums. *noun.*

slum ber (slum′bər), **1** sleep lightly; doze. **2** a light sleep: *I awoke from my slumber.* **3** pass in sleep: *The baby slumbers away the hours.* **4** be like a person asleep; be inactive: *The volcano had slumbered for years.* 1,3,4 *verb,* 2 *noun.*

slump (slump), **1** drop heavily; fall suddenly: *slump into a chair.* **2** a heavy or sudden fall: *a slump in prices.* 1 *verb,* 2 *noun.*

slung (slung). See **sling.** *They slung some stones and ran away. She has slung the bag over her shoulder. verb.*

slunk (slungk). See **slink.** *The dog slunk away ashamed. verb.*

slur (slėr), **1** pass lightly over; go through hurriedly or in a careless way. **2** pronounce in an incomplete or indistinct way: *Many persons slur "How do you do."* **3** a slurred pronunciation or sound. **4** blot or stain (upon reputation); insulting or slighting remark: *a slur on a person's good name.* 1,2 *verb,* **slurred, slur ring;** 3,4 *noun.*

slush (slush), partly melted snow; snow and water mixed. *noun.*

sly (slī), **1** able to fool, trick, or deceive; cunning; crafty; tricky; wily: *The sly cat stole the meat while the cook's back was turned. They asked many sly questions.* **2** playfully mischievous or knowing: *Waiting for the surprise party to begin, the children exchanged many sly looks and smiles.* **3** acting secretly or stealthily. *adjective,* **sly er, sly est,** or **sli er, sli est.**

on the sly, in a sly way; secretly: *The teacher caught me reading a comic book on the sly.*

sly ly (slī′lē), in a sly manner; secretly. *adverb.*

smack¹ (smak), **1** a slight taste or flavor: *This sauce has a smack of lemon.* **2** trace; touch: *The old sailor still had a smack of the sea about him.* **3** have a taste, trace, or touch (of): *That plan smacks of dishonesty.* 1,2 *noun,* 3 *verb.*

smack² (smak), **1** open (the lips) quickly so as to make a sharp sound: *He smacked his lips at the thought of cake.* **2** such a movement of the lips. **3** the sharp sound made in this way. **4** kiss loudly. **5** a loud kiss. **6** slap: *She smacked the horse on its rump.* **7** directly; squarely: *I fell smack on my face.* 1,4,6 *verb,* 2,3,5 *noun,* 7 *adverb.*

smack³ (smak), a small sailboat with one mast. *noun.*

small (smôl), **1** not large; little; not large as compared with other things of the same kind: *A cottage is a small house.* **2** not great in amount, degree, extent, duration, value, or strength: *a small dose, small hope of success. The cent is our smallest coin.* **3** not important: *This is only a small matter now.* **4** having little land or capital: *a small farmer. They own a small business.* **5** mean; petty: *A person with a small nature is not generous.* **6** that part which is small; a small, slender, or narrow part: *the small of the back.* 1-5 *adjective,* 6 *noun.*

small hours, the early hours in the morning.

small intestine, the long, winding tube that receives partly digested food from the stomach. The small intestine completes the digestion of the food and sends it into the blood.

small letter, an ordinary letter, not a capital.

small pox (smôl′poks′), a disease that causes fever and a rash of sores like blisters on the skin. The rash often leaves permanent scars shaped like little pits. Unless you are vaccinated against smallpox, you can catch the disease if you are around someone who has it. *noun.*

small talk, talk about matters having little importance; chat.

smart (smärt), **1** feel sharp pain: *Her eyes smarted from the wind.* **2** cause sharp pain: *The cut smarts.* **3** feel distress or irritation: *She smarted from the scolding.* **4** sharp; severe: *He gave the horse a smart blow.* **5** keen; active; lively: *They walked at a smart pace.* **6** clever; bright: *a smart student.* **7** fresh and neat; in good order: *a smart uniform.* **8** stylish; fashionable: *smart new clothes.* **9** in a smart manner. 1-3 *verb,* 4-8 *adjective,* 9 *adverb.*

smash (smash), **1** break or be broken into pieces with violence and noise: *to smash a window with a stone. The dish smashed.* **2** ruin or become ruined; shatter; destroy: *smash a person's hopes.* **3** rush violently; crash: *The car smashed into the tree.* **4** a violent breaking; shattering; crash: *Two cars were involved in the smash.* **5** sound of a smash or crash: *the smash of broken glass.* **6** a crushing defeat; disaster. 1-3 *verb,* 4-6 *noun, plural* **smash es.**

smear (smir), **1** cover or stain with anything sticky, greasy, or dirty: *My clothes are smeared with mud.* **2** rub or spread (oil, grease, or paint). **3** a mark or stain left by smearing: *There are smears of paint on the wallpaper.* **4** receive a mark or stain; be smeared: *Wet paint smears easily.* **5** harm; soil; spoil: *smear a person's good reputation.* 1,2,4,5 *verb,* 3 *noun.*

smell (smel), **1** detect or recognize by breathing in through the nose: *Can you smell the smoke?* **2** sense of smelling: *Smell is keener in dogs than in people.* **3** use this sense: *We smell with our noses.* **4** sniff at: *Smell this flower. The dog smelled the stranger's legs.* **5** odor: *The smell of burning rubber is not pleasant.* **6** give out a smell: *The garden smelled of roses.* **7** give out a bad smell: *That dirty, wet dog smells.* **8** act of smelling: *Have a smell of this rose.* 1,3,4,6,7 *verb,* **smelled** or **smelt, smell ing;** 2,5,8 *noun.*

smelt¹ (smelt), melt (ore) in order to get the metal out of it. *verb.*

smelt² (smelt), a small food fish with silvery scales. *noun, plural* **smelts** or **smelt.**

smelt³ (smelt), smelled. See **smell.** *verb.*

smile (smīl), **1** look pleased or amused; show pleasure, favor, kindness, or amusement by an upward curve of the mouth. **2** show scorn or disdain by a curve of the mouth: *to smile bitterly.* **3** bring, put, or drive by smiling: *Smile your tears away.* **4** act of smiling: *a friendly smile, a smile of pity.* **5** a favoring look or regard; pleasant look. 1-3 *verb,* **smiled, smil ing;** 4,5 *noun.*

smite (smīt), strike; strike hard; hit hard: *The hero smote the giant with his sword. verb,* **smote, smit ten, smit ing.**

smith (smith), **1** person who makes or shapes

things out of metal. **2** blacksmith. *noun.*

smith y (smith′ē), workshop of a smith, especially a blacksmith. *noun, plural* **smith ies.**

smit ten (smit′n). See **smite.** *I was smitten with curiosity. verb.*

smock (smok), a loose outer garment worn to protect clothing. *noun.*

smog (smog), a combination of smoke and fog in the air: *Automobile exhaust fumes are a major cause of smog. noun.* [*Smog* was formed by blending the words *smoke* and *fog.*]

smoke (smōk), **1** mixture of gases and carbon that can be seen rising in a cloud from anything burning. **2** something like this. **3** give off smoke or steam, or something like it: *The fireplace smokes.* **4** draw the smoke from (a pipe, cigar, or cigarette) into the mouth and puff it out again. **5** act or period of smoking tobacco. **6** cure (meat or fish) by treating with smoke in order to preserve it. **1,2,5** *noun,* **3,4,6** *verb,* **smoked, smok ing.**

smoke out, drive out by smoke: *We tried to smoke the woodchuck out of its hole.*

smoke house (smōk′hous′), building or place in which meat or fish is treated with smoke to keep it from spoiling. *noun, plural* **smoke hous es** (smōk′hou′ziz).

smok er (smō′kər), person who smokes tobacco. *noun.*

smoke stack (smōk′stak′), a tall chimney. *noun.*

smok y (smō′kē), **1** giving off much smoke: *a smoky fire.* **2** full of smoke. **3** darkened or stained with smoke. **4** like smoke or suggesting smoke: *a smoky gray, a smoky taste. adjective,* **smok i er, smok i est.**

smol der (smōl′dər), **1** burn and smoke without flame: *The campfire smoldered for hours after the blaze died down.* **2** a slow, smoky burning without flame. **3** exist or continue in a suppressed condition: *The people's discontent smoldered for years before it broke out into open rebellion.* **1,3** *verb,* **2** *noun.* Also spelled **smoulder.**

smooth (smüŦH), **1** having an even surface, like glass, silk, or still water; flat; level: *smooth stones.* **2** free from unevenness or roughness: *smooth sailing.* **3** without lumps: *smooth gravy.* **4** make

snail (definition 1)—about 2 inches (5 centimeters) long

a hat	i it	oi oil	ch child	a in about
ā age	ī ice	ou out	ng long	e in taken
ä far	o hot	u cup	sh she	ə = { i in pencil
e let	ō open	u̇ put	th thin	o in lemon
ē equal	ô order	ü rule	ŦH then	u in circus
ėr term			zh measure	

smooth or smoother; make flat, even, or level: *I smoothed out the ball of paper and read it.* **5** make easy: *Your tact smoothed the way to an agreement.* **6** polished; pleasant; polite: *That sales clerk has a smooth manner.* **7** in a smooth manner. **1-3,6** *adjective,* **4,5** *verb,* **7** *adverb.*

smooth down, calm; soothe: *I tried to smooth down my parents' anger.*

smote (smōt). See **smite.** *The blacksmith smote the horseshoe with a hammer. verb.*

smoth er (smuŦH′ər), **1** make unable to get air; kill by depriving of air: *The gas almost smothered the coal miners but they got out in time.* **2** be unable to breathe freely; suffocate: *We are smothering in this stuffy room.* **3** cover thickly: *In the fall the grass is smothered with leaves.* **4** put out by covering thickly: *Smother the fire with sand before you leave.* **5** keep back; check: *I smothered a cough. Her smothered laughter finally broke out.* **6** cloud of dust, smoke, or spray. **1-5** *verb,* **6** *noun.*

smoul der (smōl′dər), smolder. *verb, noun.*

smudge (smuj), **1** a dirty mark; smear. **2** mark with dirty streaks; smear: *The child's drawing was smudged.* **1** *noun,* **2** *verb,* **smudged, smudg ing.**

smug (smug), self-satisfied; too pleased with one's own goodness, cleverness, or accomplishments: *Nothing disturbs the smug beliefs of some prim, narrow-minded people. adjective,* **smug ger, smug gest.**

smug gle (smug′əl), **1** bring in or take out of a country secretly and against the law: *It is a crime to smuggle goods into the United States.* **2** bring, take, or put secretly: *I tried to smuggle my puppy into the house. verb,* **smug gled, smug gling.**

smug gler (smug′lər), **1** person who smuggles. **2** ship used in smuggling. *noun.*

snack (snak), a light meal: *He eats a snack before going to bed. noun.*

snag (snag), **1** tree or branch held fast in a river or lake. Snags are dangerous to boats. **2** any sharp or rough projecting point, such as the broken end of a branch. **3** catch on a snag: *I snagged my sweater on a nail.* **4** a hidden or unexpected obstacle: *Our plans hit a snag.* **1,2,4** *noun,* **3** *verb,* **snagged, snag ging.**

snail (snāl), **1** a small animal with a soft body that crawls very slowly. Most snails have shells on their backs into which they can pull back for protection. See picture. **2** a lazy, slow-moving person. *noun.*

snake (snāk), **1** a long, slender, crawling reptile with a dry, scaly skin and no legs. Some snakes are poisonous. **2** a sly, treacherous person. **3** move, wind, or curve like a snake: *The narrow road snaked through the mountains.* **1,2** *noun,* **3** *verb,* **snaked, snak ing.**

snowshoes—hunters on snowshoes stalking deer in deep snow

snowflakes (magnified many times)

snare drum

snap (snap), **1** make or cause to make a sudden, sharp sound: *This wood snaps as it burns.* **2** a quick, sharp sound: *The box shut with a snap.* **3** break suddenly or sharply: *The violin string snapped because it was fastened too tight.* **4** a sudden breaking or the sound of breaking: *One snap made the knife useless.* **5** make a sudden, quick bite or snatch: *The turtle snapped at the child's hand. The dog snapped up the meat.* **6** seize suddenly: *snap up a bargain. I snapped at the chance to earn some money.* **7** a quick, sudden bite or snatch: *The dog made a snap at a fly.* **8** speak quickly and sharply: *"Silence!" snapped the captain.* **9** move quickly and sharply: *The soldiers snapped to attention. You better snap it up or you'll never get the job done.* **10** a quick, sharp way: *She moves with snap and energy.* **11** A **cold snap** is a few days of cold weather. **12** made or done suddenly: *A snap judgment is likely to be wrong.* **13** fastener; clasp: *One of the snaps of your dress is unfastened.* **14** a thin, crisp cooky: *a ginger snap.* **15** take a snapshot of. 1,3,5,6,8,9,15 *verb*, **snapped, snap ping;** 2,4,7,10,11,13,14 *noun*, 12 *adjective.*

snap drag on (snap′drag′ən), a garden plant with spikes of showy flowers of various colors. *noun.*

snap shot (snap′shot′), photograph taken in an instant with a small camera. *noun.*

snare (sner *or* snar), **1** noose for catching small animals and birds: *The boys made snares to catch rabbits.* **2** catch with a snare: *One day they snared a skunk.* **3** a trap: *Flattery is a snare in which we are sometimes caught.* **4** to trap. 1,3 *noun*, 2,4 *verb*, **snared, snar ing.**

snare drum, a small drum with strings stretched across the bottom to make a rattling sound. See picture.

snarl¹ (snärl), **1** growl sharply and show one's teeth: *The dog snarled at the stranger.* **2** a sharp, angry growl. **3** say or express with a snarl: *The bully snarled out threats.* **4** sharp, angry words: *to reply with a nasty snarl.* 1,3 *verb*, 2,4 *noun.*

snarl² (snärl), tangle: *snarls in your hair. noun.*

snatch (snach), **1** seize suddenly: *The hawk snatched the chicken and flew away.* **2** act of snatching: *The boy made a snatch at the ball.* **3** a small amount; bit; scrap: *We heard snatches of their conversation as they raised their voices from time to time.* 1 *verb*, 2,3 *noun*, plural **snatch es.**

snatch at, 1 try to seize or grasp; seize; grasp: *I snatched at the rail as I fell.* **2** take advantage of eagerly: *She snatched at the chance to travel.*

sneak (snēk), **1** move in a sly or stealthy way: *The man sneaked about the barn watching for a chance to steal the cow.* **2** get, put, or pass in a sly or stealthy way: *The children sneaked the puppy into the house.* **3** act like a thief or a person who is ashamed to be seen: *She sneaked in by the back way.* **4** person who sneaks; sneaking, cowardly person. **5** stealthy; underhand: *a sneak attack.* 1-3 *verb*, 4 *noun*, 5 *adjective.*

sneak ers (snē′kərz), light canvas shoes with rubber soles, used for games and sports. *noun plural.*

sneer (snir), **1** show scorn or contempt by looks or words: *People sneered at claims that a machine could be made to fly.* **2** look or words expressing scorn or contempt: *The Wright brothers ignored people's sneers and built an airplane.* **3** say with scorn or contempt: *"Bah!" he sneered with a curl of his lip.* 1,3 *verb,* 2 *noun.*

sneeze (snēz), **1** expel air suddenly and violently through the nose and mouth. A person sneezes when he has a cold. *The pepper made her sneeze.* **2** a sudden, violent expelling of air through the nose and mouth. 1 *verb,* **sneezed, sneez ing;** 2 *noun.*

snick er (snik′ər), **1** a sly or silly laugh; giggle. **2** laugh in this way: *The children were snickering to each other.* 1 *noun,* 2 *verb.*

sniff (snif), **1** draw air through the nose in short, quick breaths that can be heard: *The man who had a cold was sniffing.* **2** smell with sniffs: *The dog sniffed at the stranger.* **3** try the smell of: *I sniffed the soup before I tasted it.* **4** draw in through the nose with the breath: *She sniffed steam to clear her head.* **5** act or sound of sniffing: *He cleared his nose with a loud sniff.* **6** a single breathing in of something; breath. 1-4 *verb,* 5,6 *noun.*

snif fle (snif′əl), **1** sniff again and again as one does from a cold in the head or in trying to stop crying. **2** a sniffling; a loud sniff. **3** the sniffles, a slight cold in the head. 1 *verb,* **snif fled, snif fling;** 2,3 *noun.*

snip (snip), **1** cut with a small, quick stroke or series of strokes with scissors: *She snipped the thread.* **2** act of snipping: *With a few snips, she had cut her hair.* **3** a small piece cut off: *Pick up the snips of thread from the floor.* 1 *verb,* **snipped, snip ping;** 2,3 *noun.*

snipe (snīp), **1** a marsh bird with a long bill. **2** shoot from a hidden place at an enemy one at a time, as a sportsman shoots at game. 1 *noun,* plural **snipes** or **snipe;** 2 *verb,* **sniped, snip ing.**

snip er (snī′pər), a hidden sharpshooter. *noun.*

snob (snob), person who cares too much for rank, wealth, or position, and too little for real merit. *noun.*

snoop (snüp), **1** go about in a sneaking, prying way; pry. See picture. **2** person who snoops. 1 *verb,* 2 *noun.*

snooze (snüz), **1** sleep; doze; take a nap: *The dog snoozed on the porch in the sun.* **2** doze; nap. 1 *verb,* **snoozed, snooz ing;** 2 *noun.*

snore (snôr), **1** breathe during sleep with a harsh, rough sound: *The child had a stuffy nose and snored all night.* **2** the sound made. 1 *verb,* **snored, snor ing;** 2 *noun.*

snor kel (snôr′kəl), **1** shaft for taking in air and discharging gases, which allows submarines to remain under water for a very long time. It is like a periscope in shape. **2** a curved tube which enables swimmers to breathe under water while swimming near the surface. *noun.*

snort (snôrt), **1** force the breath violently through the nose with a loud, harsh sound: *The horse snorted.* **2** make a sound like this: *The engine snorted.* **3** act or sound of snorting. **4** say with a snort: *"Indeed!" snorted my aunt.* 1,2,4 *verb,* 3 *noun.*

snout (snout), **1** the part of an animal's head that extends forward and contains the nose, mouth, and jaws. Pigs, dogs, and crocodiles have snouts. **2** anything like an animal's snout. *noun.*

snow (snō), **1** frozen water vapor in soft, white flakes that fall to earth and spread upon it as a white layer. **2** a fall of snow. **3** fall as snow: *snow all day.* 1,2 *noun,* 3 *verb.*

snow in, shut in by snow: *The mountain village was snowed in for almost a week after the blizzard.*

snow ball (snō′bôl′), **1** ball made of snow pressed together. **2** throw balls of snow at: *The children snowballed each other.* **3** shrub with white flowers in large clusters like balls. 1,3 *noun,* 2 *verb.*

snow bank (snō′bangk′), a large mass or drift of snow, especially at the side of a road. *noun.*

snow capped (snō′kapt′), having its top covered with snow: *a snowcapped mountain. adjective.*

snow drift (snō′drift′), bank of snow piled up by the wind. *noun.*

snow fall (snō′fôl′), **1** a fall of snow. **2** amount of snow falling within a certain time and area: *The snowfall in that one storm was 16 inches. noun.*

snow flake (snō′flāk′), a small, feathery piece of snow. See picture. *noun.*

snow man (snō′man′), mass of snow made into a figure somewhat like that of a person. *noun,* plural **snow men.**

snow mo bile (snō′mō bēl), tractor or other vehicle for use in snow. Some snowmobiles have skis or runners in front. *noun.*

snow plow (snō′plou′), machine for clearing away snow from streets, railroad tracks, and roads. *noun.*

snow shoe (snō′shü′), a light wooden frame with strips of leather stretched across it. Trappers in the far North wear snowshoes on their feet to keep from sinking in deep, soft snow. See picture. *noun.*

snoop (definition 1)—He had a bad habit of **snooping** into other people's business.

snow storm (snō'stôrm'), storm with much snow. *noun.*

snow y (snō'ē), **1** having snow: *a snowy day.* **2** covered with snow: *a snowy roof.* **3** like snow; white as snow: *The old woman has snowy hair.* *adjective,* **snow i er, snow i est.**

snub (snub), **1** treat coldly, scornfully, or with contempt: *Ever since we argued, my neighbor snubs me when we meet.* **2** cold, scornful, or disdainful treatment. **3** short and turned up at the tip: *a snub nose.* **1** *verb,* **snubbed, snub bing; 2** *noun,* **3** *adjective.*

snuff¹ (snuf), **1** draw in through the nose; draw up into the nose: *He snuffs up steam to relieve a cold.* **2** sniff; smell: *The dog snuffed at the tracks of the fox.* **3** powdered tobacco to be taken into the nose. **1,2** *verb,* **3** *noun.*

snuff² (snuf), put out (a candle). *verb.*
snuff out, put an end to suddenly and completely: *The dictator snuffed out the people's hopes for freedom.*

snug (snug), **1** comfortable; warm; sheltered: *The cat has found a snug corner behind the stove.* **2** neat; trim; compact: *The cabins on the boat are snug.* **3** fitting closely: *That coat is a little too snug.* *adjective,* **snug ger, snug gest.**

snug gle (snug'əl), nestle; cuddle. *verb,* **snug gled, snug gling.**

so (sō), **1** in that way; in the same way or degree: *Hold your pen so. The chair is broken and has been so for a long time. Do not walk so fast. Is that really so?* **2** in such a way; to such a degree: *He is not so tall as his brother.* **3** very: *You are so kind.* **4** very much: *My head aches so.* **5** therefore: *The dog seemed hungry, so we fed it.* **6** So is sometimes used alone to ask a question or to exclaim: *So! late again! The train is late. So?* **7** more or less: *a pound or so.* **1-5** *adverb,* **6** *interjection,* **7** *pronoun.*
and so, 1 likewise; also: *He is here, and so is she.* **2** accordingly: *I said I would go, and so I shall.*
so as or **so that,** with the result or purpose: *I go to bed early so as to get enough sleep. The boy studies so that he will do well.*

soak (sōk), **1** make very wet; wet through: *The rain soaked my clothes.* **2** become very wet. **3** let remain in water or other liquid until wet clear through: *Soak the clothes all night before you wash them.* **4** go; enter; make its way: *Water will soak through the earth.* **5** act or process of soaking: *Give the clothes a long soak.* **1-4** *verb,* **5** *noun.*
soak up, take up; suck: *Sponges soak up water.*

soap (sōp), **1** substance used for washing, usually made of a fat and lye. **2** rub with soap: *Soap your hands well.* **1** *noun,* **2** *verb.*

soap suds (sōp'sudz'), bubbles and foam made with soap and water. *noun plural.*

soap y (sō'pē), **1** covered with soap or soapsuds. **2** containing soap: *soapy water.* **3** of or like soap: *The water has a soapy taste.* *adjective,* **soap i er, soap i est.**

soar (sôr), **1** fly at a great height; fly upward: *The eagle soared without flapping its wings.* **2** rise beyond what is common and ordinary: *Prices are* soaring. *Her hopes soared when she was called in for a job interview. verb.*

sob (sob), **1** cry or sigh with short, quick breaths: *"I have lost my penny," the child sobbed. She sobbed herself to sleep.* **2** catching of short, quick breaths because of grief or some other emotion. **3** make a sound like a sob: *The wind sobbed.* **4** utter with sobs: *He sobbed out his sad story.* **1,3,4** *verb,* **sobbed, sob bing; 2** *noun.*

so ber (sō'bər), **1** not drunk. **2** temperate; moderate: *The Puritans led sober, hard-working lives.* **3** quiet; serious; solemn: *He looked sober at the thought of missing the picnic.* **4** calm; sensible; free from exaggeration: *The judge's sober opinion was not influenced by prejudice or strong feeling.* **5** make or become sober: *The class sobered when the teacher entered the room.* **1-4** *adjective,* **5** *verb.*

so-called (sō'kôld'), called so, but really not so: *Her so-called friend hasn't phoned her. adjective.*

soc cer (sok'ər), game played between two teams of eleven players each, using a round ball. The ball may be struck with any part of the body except the hands and arms. See picture. *noun.*

so cia ble (sō'shə bəl), **1** liking company; friendly: *They are a sociable family and entertain a great deal.* **2** with conversation and companionship: *We had a sociable afternoon together. adjective.*

so cial (sō'shəl), **1** concerned with human beings as a group: *History and geography are social studies.* **2** living or liking to live with others: *People are social beings.* **3** for companionship or friendliness: *a social club.* **4** liking company: *She has a social nature.* **5** connected with fashionable society: *The mayor and his wife are the social leaders of our town.* **6** a social gathering or party. **1-5** *adjective,* **6** *noun.*

so cial ism (sō'shə liz'əm), system in which the means of production and distribution of goods are owned and controlled by the government or by the community as a whole. *noun.*

so cial ist (sō'shə list), person who favors or supports socialism. *noun.*

so ci e ty (sə sī'ə tē), **1** group of persons joined together for a common purpose or by common interests. A club, a lodge, or an association may be called a society. **2** all the people; human beings living together as a group: *Society must work hard for world peace.* **3** the people of any particular time or place: *American society, 20th-century society.* **4** company; companionship: *I enjoy your society.* **5** fashionable people or their doings: *His parents are leaders of society. noun, plural* **so ci e ties.**

sock¹ (sok), a short, close-fitting knitted covering of wool, cotton, or other fabric for the foot and leg, especially one that reaches about halfway to the knee. *noun.*

sock² (sok), **1** strike or hit hard. **2** a hard blow. **1** *verb,* **2** *noun.*

sock et (sok'it), a hollow part or piece for receiving and holding something. A candlestick has a socket for a candle. A light bulb is screwed into a socket. Your eyes are set in sockets. *noun.*

sod (sod), **1** ground covered with grass. **2** piece or layer of this containing the grass and its roots. See picture. **3** cover with sods: *We must have the bare spots of our lawn sodded.* 1,2 *noun,* 3 *verb,* **sod ded, sod ding.**

so da (sō′də), **1** baking soda. **2** soda water flavored with fruit juice or syrup, and often containing ice cream. *noun.*

soda fountain, counter with places for holding soda water, flavored syrups, ice cream, and soft drinks.

soda water, water charged with carbon dioxide to make it bubble and fizz.

so di um (sō′dē əm), a soft, silver-white metal that occurs only in combination with other substances. Salt and soda contain sodium. *noun.*

so fa (sō′fə), a long, upholstered seat or couch having a back and arms. *noun.*

soft (sôft), **1** not hard; not stiff; yielding easily to touch: *Feathers, cotton, and wool are soft.* **2** not hard compared with other things of the same sort: *Pine is softer than oak. Lead is softer than steel.* **3** smooth; pleasant to the touch; not rough or coarse: *the soft hair of a kitten, soft silk.* **4** quietly pleasant; mild: *a soft spring morning, soft words, the soft light of candles.* **5** gentle; kind; tender: *soft voice, soft eyes, soft heart.* **6** weak: *He became soft from idleness and luxury. adjective.*

soft ball (sôft′bôl′), **1** kind of baseball game. A larger ball and lighter bats are used in softball than in baseball. **2** ball used in this game. *noun.*

soft coal, coal that burns with a yellow, smoky flame; bituminous coal.

soft drink, drink that does not contain alcohol.

soft en (sôf′ən), **1** make softer: *Lotion softens the skin.* **2** become softer: *Soap softens in water. verb.*

soft wood (sôft′wùd′), any wood that is easily cut. Pine is a softwood; oak is a hardwood. *noun.*

sog gy (sog′ē), **1** soaked; thoroughly wet: *The wash on the line was soggy from the rain.* **2** damp and heavy: *soggy bread. adjective,* **sog gi er, sog gi est.**

soil[1] (soil), **1** ground; earth; dirt: *Roses grow best in rich soil.* **2** land; country: *This is my native soil. noun.*

soil[2] (soil), **1** make or become dirty: *to soil one's clothes.* **2** disgrace; dishonor: *to soil one's good name. verb.*

so journ (sō′jėrn′), **1** dwell for a time: *The Jews sojourned in the land of Egypt.* **2** a brief stay; stay that is not permanent: *During his sojourn in Paris his French improved.* 1 *verb,* 2 *noun.*

so lar (sō′lər), **1** of the sun: *a solar eclipse.* **2** measured by the earth's motion in relation to the sun: *solar time.* **3** working by means of the sun's light or heat. A solar battery traps sunlight and changes it into electrical energy. *adjective.*

solar system, the sun and all the planets, satellites, and comets that revolve around it. See picture.

sold (sōld). See **sell.** *She sold her car a week ago. She has sold it to a friend. verb.*

sol der (sod′ər), **1** metal that can be melted and

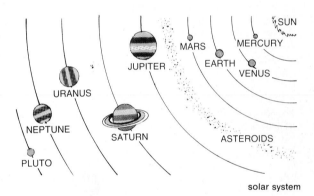

sod (definition 2)—The pioneer family lived in a house made of sod.

SUN
MARS
MERCURY
JUPITER
EARTH
VENUS
URANUS
NEPTUNE
SATURN
ASTEROIDS
PLUTO

solar system

soccer

used for joining or mending metal surfaces or parts. **2** fasten, mend, or join with solder: *She soldered the broken wires together.* 1 *noun,* 2 *verb.*

sol dier (sōl′jər), **1** person who serves in an army. **2** person in the army who is not a commissioned officer. **3** person who serves in any cause: *Christian soldiers. noun.* [*Soldier* comes from a Latin word meaning "a Roman gold coin." Soldiers were called this because they served in an army for pay.]

sole[1] (sōl), **1** one and only; single: *He was the sole heir to the fortune when his aunt died.* **2** only: *We three were the sole survivors from the wreck. adjective.*

sole[2] (sōl), **1** the bottom or under surface of the foot. **2** bottom of a shoe, slipper, or boot. **3** piece of leather or rubber cut in the same shape. **4** put a sole on: *I must have my shoes soled.* 1-3 *noun,* 4 *verb,* **soled, sol ing.**

sole[3] (sōl), flatfish much used for food. *noun,* *plural* **soles** or **sole.**

sole ly (sōl′lē), **1** alone: *I am solely responsible for providing the lunch.* **2** only: *Bananas grow outdoors solely in warm climates. adverb.*

sol emn (sol′əm), **1** serious; grave; earnest: *a solemn voice. He gave his solemn promise to do better.* See picture. **2** causing serious thoughts: *The organ played solemn music. adjective.*

so lem ni ty (sə lem′nə tē), **1** solemn feeling; seriousness; impressiveness: *The solemnity of the occasion was felt even by the children.* **2** a solemn, formal ceremony: *Passover is observed with solemnities. noun, plural* **so lem ni ties.**

so lic it (sə lis′it), **1** ask earnestly; try to get: *The new business is soliciting trade through newspaper advertising.* **2** make appeals or requests: *solicit for contributions to a charity. verb.*

sol id (sol′id), **1** not liquid or gaseous: *Water becomes solid when it freezes.* **2** substance that is not a liquid or a gas. Iron, wood, and ice are solids. **3** not hollow: *A bar of iron is solid; a pipe is hollow.* **4** strongly put together; hard; firm: *They were glad to leave the boat and put their feet on solid ground.* **5** alike throughout: *The cloth is a solid blue.* **6** firmly united: *The country was solid for peace.* **7** that can be depended on: *a solid citizen.* **8** whole; entire: *I spent a solid hour on my arithmetic.* **9** undivided; continuous: *a solid row of houses.* 1,3-9 *adjective,* 2 *noun.*

so lid i fy (sə lid′ə fī), make or become solid; harden: *Extreme cold solidifies water into ice. verb,* **so lid i fied, so lid i fy ing.**

sol i tar y (sol′ə ter′ē), **1** alone; single; only: *A solitary rider was seen in the distance.* **2** without companions; away from people; lonely: *She leads a solitary life in her cabin in the mountains. adjective.*

sol i tude (sol′ə tüd *or* sol′ə tyüd), being alone: *I like solitude in the evening so that I can read. noun.*

so lo (sō′lō), **1** piece of music for one voice or instrument: *to sing a solo.* **2** arranged for one voice or instrument: *a solo part.* **3** without a partner, teacher, or associate; alone: *a solo flight across the ocean.* 1 *noun, plural* **so los;** 2,3 *adjective.*

sop, sopping wet—The baby mountain lions were **sopping wet** after the rain storm.

solemn

sombrero

so lo ist (sō′lō ist), person who performs a solo. *noun.*

sol u ble (sol′yə bəl), **1** capable of being dissolved or made into liquid: *Salt is soluble in water.* **2** capable of being solved: *soluble puzzles. This problem is soluble. adjective.*

so lu tion (sə lü′shən), **1** the solving of a problem: *That problem was hard; its solution required many hours.* **2** explanation: *The police are seeking a solution of the crime.* **3** liquid or mixture formed by dissolving: *Every time you put sugar in lemonade you are making a solution.* **4** being dissolved: *Sugar and salt can be held in solution in water. noun.*

solve (solv), find the answer to; clear up; explain: *The detective solved the mystery. He has solved all the problems in the lesson. verb,* **solved, solv ing.**

som ber (som′bər), **1** dark; gloomy: *A cloudy winter day is somber.* **2** melancholy; dismal: *His losses made him very somber. adjective.*

som brer o (som brer′ō), a broad-brimmed hat worn in the southwestern United States, Mexico, and Spain. See picture. *noun, plural* **som brer os.**

some (sum), **1** certain or particular, but not known or named: *Some dogs are larger than others.* **2** a number of: *Ask some people to help you.* **3** a quantity of: *Drink some milk.* **4** a certain number or quantity: *She kept some and gave the rest away.* **5** a; any: *Can't you find some person who will help you?* **6** about: *Some twenty people asked for work.* 1-3,5 *adjective,* 4 *pronoun,* 6 *adverb.*

some bod y (sum′bod′ē), **1** person not known or named; some person; someone: *Somebody has taken my pen.* **2** person of importance: *This restaurant treats you as if you are really somebody.* 1 *pronoun,* 2 *noun, plural* **some bod ies.**

some day (sum′dā), at some future time. *adverb.*

some how (sum′hou), in a way not known or not stated; in one way or another: *I'll finish this work somehow. adverb.*

some one (sum′wun), some person; somebody: *Someone has to lock up the house. pronoun.*

som er sault (sum′ər sôlt), roll or jump, turning the heels over the head. *noun, verb.*

some thing (sum′thing), **1** some thing; a particular thing not named or known: *I'm sure I've forgotten something.* **2** a part; a certain amount; a little: *There is something of his father in his smile.* **3** somewhat; to some extent or degree: *She and her sister look something alike.* 1,2 *noun,* 3 *adverb.*

some time (sum′tīm), **1** at one time or another: *Come to see us sometime.* **2** at an indefinite point of time: *It happened sometime last March. adverb.*

some times (sum′tīmz), now and then; at times: *They come to visit sometimes. adverb.*

some what (sum′hwot), **1** to some degree; slightly: *My hat is somewhat like yours.* **2** some part; some amount: *A joke loses somewhat of its fun when you hear it the second time.* 1 *adverb,* 2 *noun.*

some where (sum′hwer *or* sum′hwar), **1** in or to some place; in or to one place or another: *It is somewhere about the house.* **2** at some time: *It happened somewhere in the past. adverb.*

a hat	i it	oi oil	ch child	⌠a in about
ā age	ī ice	ou out	ng long	⎪e in taken
ä far	o hot	u cup	sh she	ə = ⎨i in pencil
e let	ō open	u̇ put	th thin	⎪o in lemon
ē equal	ô order	ü rule	₮H then	⌡u in circus
ėr term			zh measure	

son (sun), a male child. A boy is the son of his father and mother. *noun.*

so nar (sō′när), a device for discovering and locating objects under water by the reflection of sound waves. *noun.* [*Sonar* comes from the words *sound navigation ranging,* which describe what this device does. It was formed from the first two letters of *sound* and *navigation* and the first letter of *ranging.*]

so na ta (sə nä′tə), piece of music for one or two instruments, having three or four movements in contrasted rhythms but related keys. *noun.*

song (sông), **1** something to sing; short poem set to music. **2** sound like music made by a bird: *the song of the canary.* **3** poetry that has a musical sound. *noun.*

for a song, very cheap: *buy things for a song.*

song bird (sông′bėrd′), bird that sings. *noun.*

son-in-law (sun′in lô′), husband of one's daughter. *noun, plural* **sons-in-law.**

son net (son′it), a short poem, especially one of 14 lines with rhyme. *noun.*

so no rous (sə nôr′əs), **1** giving out or having a deep, loud sound: *a big, sonorous church bell.* **2** full and rich in sound. *adjective.*

soon (sün), **1** in a short time; before long: *I will see you again soon.* **2** before the usual or expected time; early: *Why have you come so soon?* **3** promptly; quickly: *As soon as I hear, I will let you know.* **4** readily; willingly: *I would as soon get it over with. adverb.*

soot (sut), a black substance in the smoke from burning coal, wood, oil, or other fuel. Soot makes smoke dark and collects on the inside of chimneys. *noun.*

soothe (sü₮H), **1** quiet; calm; comfort: *The father soothed the crying child.* **2** make less painful; ease: *Heat soothes some aches; cold soothes others. verb,* **soothed, sooth ing.**

sooth say er (süth′sā′ər), person who claims to tell what will happen. *noun.*

sop (sop), **1** dip or soak: *sop bread in milk.* **2** take up (water or other liquid): *Please sop up that water with a cloth. verb,* **sopped, sop ping.**

sopping wet, thoroughly wet, or drenched. See picture.

soph o more (sof′ə môr), student in the second year of high school or college. *noun.*

so pran o (sə pran′ō), **1** the highest female or boys' singing voice. **2** singer with such a voice. **3** part sung by such a voice. *noun, plural* **so pran os.**

sor cer er (sôr′sər ər), person who supposedly practices magic with the aid of evil spirits; magician. *noun.*

sor cer ess (sôr′sər is), woman who supposedly

practices magic with the aid of evil spirits; witch. *noun, plural* **sor cer ess es.**

sor cer y (sôr′sər ē), magic thought to be performed by the aid of evil spirits; witchcraft: *The prince had been changed into a lion by sorcery. noun.*

sor did (sôr′did), dirty; filthy. See picture. *adjective.*

sore (sôr), 1 painful; aching; smarting: *a sore finger.* 2 a painful place on the body where the skin or flesh is broken or bruised. 3 offended; angered: *She is sore at having to stay home.* 4 causing misery, anger, or offense: *Their defeat is a sore subject with the members of the team.* 1,3,4 *adjective,* **sor er, sor est;** 2 *noun.*

so ro ri ty (sə rôr′ə tē), club or society of women or girls, especially at a college. *noun, plural* **so ro ri ties.**

sor rel (sôr′əl), plant with sour leaves. *noun.*

sor row (sor′ō), 1 grief; sadness; regret: *We felt sorrow at the loss of our kitten.* 2 cause of grief or sadness; trouble; suffering; misfortune: *His sorrows have aged him.* 3 feel or show grief, sadness, or regret; be sad; feel sorrow: *She sorrowed over the lost money.* 1,2 *noun,* 3 *verb.*

sor row ful (sor′ə fəl), 1 full of sorrow; feeling sorrow; sad: *A funeral is a sorrowful occasion.* 2 causing sorrow. *adjective.*

sor ry (sor′ē), 1 feeling pity, regret, or sympathy; sad: *I am sorry that you are sick.* 2 wretched; poor; pitiful: *The hungry, shivering dog was a sorry sight. adjective,* **sor ri er, sor ri est.**

sort (sôrt), 1 kind; class: *What sort of work do you do? I like this sort of candy best.* 2 arrange by kinds or classes; arrange in order: *Sort these cards according to their colors.* 3 separate from others; put: *The farmer sorted out the best apples for eating.* 1 *noun,* 2,3 *verb.*

out of sorts, ill, cross, or uncomfortable.

S O S (es′ō′es′), an urgent call for help.

sought (sôt). See seek. *For days she sought a safe hiding place. He was sought and found. verb.*

soul (sōl), 1 the part of the human being that thinks, feels, and makes the body act; spiritual part of a person. Many religions believe that the soul and the body are separated in death and that the soul lives forever. 2 energy of mind or feelings; spirit: *She puts her whole soul into her work.* 3 cause of inspiration and energy: *Florence Nightingale was the soul of the movement to reform nursing.* 4 a special feeling or spirit among Black Americans, expressed especially through music. 5 person: *Don't tell a soul. noun.*

sound[1] (sound), 1 what can be heard: *the sound of music, the sound of thunder.* 2 one of the simple elements that make up speech: *a vowel sound.* 3 make a sound or noise: *The trumpet sounds for battle. The wind sounds like an animal howling.* 4 pronounce: *Sound each syllable.* 5 be pronounced: *"Rough" and "ruff" sound just alike.* 6 cause to sound: *Sound the trumpets; beat the drums.* 7 order or direct by a sound: *Sound the retreat.* 8 make known; announce; utter: *The trumpets sounded the call to battle. Everyone*

sounded his praises. 9 seem: *That excuse sounds queer.* 1,2 *noun,* 3-9 *verb.*

within sound, near enough to hear.

sound[2] (sound), 1 free from disease; healthy: *a sound body, a sound mind.* 2 free from injury, decay, or defect: *sound walls, a sound ship, sound fruit.* 3 strong; safe; secure: *a sound business firm.* 4 correct; right; reasonable; reliable: *sound advice.* 5 thorough; hearty: *a sound whipping, a sound sleep.* 6 deeply; thoroughly: *The child was sound asleep.* 1-5 *adjective,* 6 *adverb.*

sound[3] (sound), 1 measure the depth of (water) by letting down a weight fastened on the end of a line. 2 examine or test by a line arranged to bring up a sample. 3 try to find out the views of; test; examine: *We sounded our landlady on the subject of having pets in the apartment.* 4 go toward the bottom; dive: *The whale sounded. verb.*

sound[4] (sound), 1 a long, narrow channel of water joining two larger bodies of water, or between the mainland and an island: *Long Island Sound.* 2 inlet or arm of the sea: *Puget Sound. noun.*

sound ly (sound′lē), 1 deeply; heavily: *The tired child slept soundly.* 2 vigorously; heartily; thoroughly: *We were scolded soundly.* 3 with good judgment: *to make a decision soundly. adverb.*

sound proof (sound′prüf′), 1 not letting sound pass through. 2 make soundproof: *The halls at school are soundproofed.* 1 *adjective,* 2 *verb.*

soup (süp), a liquid food made by boiling meat, vegetables, or fish in water, milk, or the like. *noun.*

sour (sour), 1 having a taste like vinegar or lemon juice; sharp and biting: *This green fruit is sour.* 2 fermented; spoiled. Sour milk is healthful, but most foods are not good to eat when they have become sour. 3 disagreeable; bad-tempered; peevish: *a sour face, a sour remark.* 4 make sour; become sour; turn sour: *The milk soured while it stood in the hot sun.* 5 make or become peevish, bad-tempered, or disagreeable. 1-3 *adjective,* 4,5 *verb.*

source (sôrs), 1 person or place from which anything comes or is obtained: *A newspaper gets news from many sources. Mines are the chief source of diamonds.* 2 beginning of a brook or river; fountain; spring. *noun.*

south (south), 1 direction to one's right as one faces the rising sun; direction just opposite north. 2 toward the south; farther toward the south: *Drive south forty miles.* 3 from the south: *a south wind.* 4 in the south: *the south window of the house.* 5 part of any country toward the south. 6 the South, the southern part of the United States; the states south of Pennsylvania, the Ohio River, and Missouri. 1,5,6 *noun,* 2-4 *adjective,* 2 *adverb.*

south of, further south than: *New York is south of Boston.*

South America, continent southeast of North America and west of the Atlantic Ocean. It is the fourth largest continent; only Asia, Africa, and North America are larger. Brazil, Argentina, and Peru are countries in South America.

South American, 1 of South America; having

something to do with South America or its people; from South America. **2** person born or living in South America.

South Car o li na (south′ kar′ə lī′nə), one of the southeastern states of the United States. [*South Carolina* was named in honor of Charles I, king of England, who lived from 1600 to 1649. His name in Latin is Carolus.]

South Da ko ta (south′ də kō′tə), one of the midwestern states of the United States. [*South Dakota* got its name from an American Indian tribe, the Dakota, meaning "allies" or "friends."]

south east (south′ēst′), **1** halfway between south and east. **2** a southeast direction. **3** place that is in the southeast part or direction. **4** toward the southeast. **5** from the southeast: *a southeast wind.* **6** in the southeast: *the southeast district.* 1,5,6 *adjective,* 2,3 *noun,* 4 *adverb.*

south east ern (south′ē′stərn), **1** toward the southeast. **2** from the southeast. **3** of the southeast. *adjective.*

south er ly (suᴛʜ′ər lē), **1** toward the south: *The windows face southerly.* **2** from the south: *a southerly wind. adjective, adverb.*

south ern (suᴛʜ′ərn), **1** toward the south: *the southern side of a building.* **2** from the south: *a southern breeze.* **3** of or in the south: *They have traveled in southern countries.* **4** **Southern,** of or in the southern part of the United States: *a Southern city. adjective.*

south ern er (suᴛʜ′ər nər), **1** person born or living in the south. **2** **Southerner,** person born or living in the southern part of the United States. *noun.*

south ern most (suᴛʜ′ərn mōst), farthest south. *adjective.*

South Pole, the southern end of the earth's axis.

south ward (south′wərd), toward the south; south: *I walked southward. The orchard is on the southward slope of the hill. adverb, adjective.*

south wards (south′wərdz), southward. *adverb.*

south west (south′west′), **1** halfway between south and west. **2** a southwest direction. **3** place that is in the southwest part or direction. **4** toward the southwest. **5** from the southwest: *a southwest wind.* **6** in the southwest. 1,5,6 *adjective,* 2,3 *noun,* 4 *adverb.*

south west er (south′wes′tər *for 1;* sou′wes′tər *for 2*), **1** wind or storm from the southwest. **2** waterproof hat with a broad brim behind to protect the neck. *noun.* Also spelled **sou'wester.**

south west ern (south′wes′tərn), **1** toward the southwest. **2** from the southwest. **3** of or in the southwest. *adjective.*

sou ve nir (sü′və nir′), something given or kept for remembrance; remembrance; keepsake: *She bought a pair of moccasins as a souvenir of her trip out West. noun.*

sou' west er (sou′wes′tər), southwester. *noun.*

sov er eign (sov′rən), **1** supreme ruler; king or queen; monarch. Queen Victoria was the sovereign of Great Britain from 1837 to 1901. **2** greatest in rank or power: *a sovereign court.* **3** independent of the control of other

governments: *When the thirteen colonies won the Revolutionary War, America became a sovereign nation.* **4** above all others; supreme; greatest: *Character is of sovereign importance.* 1 *noun,* 2-4 *adjective.*

sov er eign ty (sov′rən tē), supreme power or authority: *The revolutionaries rejected the sovereignty of the king. noun, plural* **sov er eign ties.**

So vi et Un ion (sō′vē et yü′nyən), Russia; a country reaching from eastern Europe across Asia to the Pacific Ocean. It is made up of 15 republics.

sow[1] (sō), **1** scatter (seed) on the ground; plant (seed); plant seed in: *She sowed grass seed in the yard.* See picture. **2** scatter (anything); spread abroad: *The rebels sowed discontent among the people. verb,* **sowed, sown** or **sowed, sow ing.**

sow[1] (definition 1)—They **sowed** the freshly plowed field.

sordid—He lived in a **sordid** shack near the city dump.

sow[2] (sou), a fully grown female pig. *noun.*

sown (sōn). See **sow**[1]. *The field had been sown with oats. verb.*

soy bean (soi′bēn′), bean widely grown in Asia and North America. Soybeans are used in making flour and oil, and as a food. *noun.*

space (spās), **1** the unlimited room or place extending in all directions: *The earth moves through space.* **2** limited place or room: *Is there space in the car for another person?* **3** outer space: *the conquest and exploration of space, a rocket launched into space.* **4** of or having to do with outer space: *a space satellite, space flight, space vehicles.* **5** distance: *The road is bad for a space of two miles.* **6** length of time: *Many changes occur within the space of a lifetime.* **7** fix the space or spaces of; divide into spaces. **8** separate by spaces: *Space your words evenly when you write.* 1-3,5,6 *noun,* 4 *adjective,* 7,8 *verb,* **spaced, spac ing.**

space craft (spās′kraft′), vehicle or vehicles used for flight in outer space. *noun, plural* **space craft.**

space ship (spās′ship′), spacecraft. *noun.*

space suit (spās′süt′), an airtight suit that protects travelers in outer space from radiation, heat, and lack of oxygen. *noun.*

space walk (spās′wôk′), act of moving or floating in space while outside a spacecraft. *noun.*

spa cious (spā′shəs), containing much space; with plenty of room: *a spacious house. adjective.*

spade (spād), **1** tool for digging; kind of shovel. **2** dig with a spade: *Spade up the garden.* 1 *noun,* 2 *verb,* **spad ed, spad ing.**

spa ghet ti (spə get′ē), the same mixture of flour and water as macaroni, but made up in slender sticks. Spaghetti is thinner than macaroni and not hollow. *noun.* [*Spaghetti* comes from an Italian word, originally meaning "thin strings."]

Spain (spān), country in southwestern Europe. *noun.*

span (span), **1** part between two supports: *The bridge crossed the river in a single span.* **2** distance between two supports: *The arch had a fifty-foot span.* **3** short space of time: *His span of life is nearly over.* **4** extend over: *A bridge spanned the river.* See picture. **5** measure by the hand spread out: *This post can be spanned by one's two hands.* **6** distance between the tip of a person's thumb and the tip of the little finger when the hand is spread out; about 9 inches. 1-3,6 *noun,* 4,5 *verb,* **spanned, span ning.**

span gle (spang′gəl), **1** a small piece of glittering metal used for decoration: *The costume was covered with spangles.* **2** any small, bright bit: *This rock shows spangles of gold.* **3** decorate with spangles: *The dress was spangled with gold.* **4** sprinkle with small, bright bits: *The sky is spangled with stars.* 1,2 *noun,* 3,4 *verb,* **span gled, span gling.**

span iel (span′yəl), dog, usually of small or medium size, with long, silky hair and drooping ears. *noun.* [*Spaniel* was shortened from an old French word meaning "a Spanish dog." The spaniel first came from Spain.]

span
(definition 4)

Span ish (span′ish), **1** of or having something to do with Spain, its people, or their language. **2** people of Spain. **3** language of Spain. Spanish is spoken also in Mexico, most parts of Central America and South America, and many other places. 1 *adjective,* 2 *noun plural,* 3 *noun singular.*

spank (spangk), **1** strike with the open hand, a slipper, or with something flat: *She was spanked for being naughty.* **2** blow with the open hand, a slipper, or with something flat; slap. 1 *verb,* 2 *noun.*

spar[1] (spär), a stout pole used to support or extend the sails of a ship; mast, yard, or boom of a ship. *noun.*

spar[2] (spär), **1** make motions of attack and defense with the arms and fists; box. **2** dispute: *Two people were sparring about who would win the election. verb,* **sparred, spar ring.**

spare (sper *or* spar), **1** show mercy to; refrain from harming or destroying: *He spared his enemy. Her jokes spared no one, not even herself.* **2** make (a person) free from labor or pain: *They did the work to spare you the trouble.* **3** get along without; omit; do without: *I can't spare the car today, so you'll have to take the bus.* **4** use in small quantities or not at all; be saving of: *spare no expense.* **5** free for other use: *spare time.* **6** extra; in reserve: *a spare tire.* **7** thin; lean: *Lincoln was a tall, spare man.* **8** small in quantity; scanty: *I'm still hungry after that spare meal.* 1-4 *verb,* **spared, spar ing;** 5-8 *adjective,* **spar er, spar est.**

spar ing (sper′ing *or* spar′ing), economical; frugal: *a sparing use of sugar. adjective.*

spark (spärk), **1** a small bit of fire: *The burning wood threw off sparks.* **2** flash given off when electricity jumps across an open space. An electric spark ignites the gasoline vapor in the engine of an automobile. **3** a bright flash; gleam: *We saw a spark of light through the trees.* **4** flash; gleam; sparkle. **5** a small amount: *I haven't a spark of interest in the plan.* **6** a glittering bit: *The moving sparks we saw were fireflies.* **7** send out small bits of fire; produce sparks. 1-3,5,6 *noun,* 4,7 *verb.*

spar kle (spär'kəl), **1** send out little sparks: *The fireworks sparkled.* **2** a little spark. **3** shine; glitter; flash: *The jewels in the crown sparkled. I like the sparkle of her eyes.* **4** be brilliant; be lively: *This author's wit sparkles.* 1,3,4 *verb,* **spar kled, spar kling;** 2,3 *noun.*

spar row (spar'ō), a small, brownish-gray bird. English sparrows and some other kinds live near houses; others live in woods and fields. *noun.*

sparse (spärs), thinly scattered; occurring here and there: *the sparse population of the country, sparse hair.* *adjective,* **spars er, spars est.**

spasm (spaz'əm), **1** a sudden, abnormal, uncontrollable contraction of a muscle or muscles: *The sick dog kept twitching its legs in a spasm.* **2** any sudden, brief fit or spell of unusual energy or activity: *a spasm of temper, a spasm of enthusiasm.* *noun.*

spat[1] (spat), a slight quarrel. *noun.*

spat[2] (spat). See **spit**[1]. *The cat spat at the dog.* *verb.*

spat ter (spat'ər), **1** scatter or dash in drops: *spatter mud.* **2** fall in drops: *Rain spatters on the sidewalk.* **3** act or sound of spattering: *We listened to the spatter of the rain on the roof.* **4** spot caused by something splashed. **5** sprinkle or spot with something that soils or stains: *spatter a white dress with mud.* 1,2,5 *verb,* 3,4 *noun.*

spat u la (spach'ə lə), tool with a broad, flat, flexible blade, used for mixing, spreading, scraping, or stirring soft substances, such as plaster or frosting, and for mixing powders. *noun.*

spawn (spôn), **1** the eggs of fish, frogs, shellfish, and other animals growing or living in water. **2** the young newly hatched from these eggs. **3** produce eggs. 1,2 *noun,* 3 *verb.*

speak (spēk), **1** say words; talk: *A person with a cold often has trouble speaking distinctly.* **2** make a speech: *Who is going to speak at the meeting?* **3** say; tell; express; make known: *Speak the truth. Their eyes speak of suffering.* **4** use (a language): *Do you speak French?* *verb,* **spoke, spo ken, speak ing.**

speak for, speak in the interest of; represent: *My lawyer will speak for me.*

speak of, mention; refer to: *She spoke of this matter to me. Speaking of school, how do you like the new gym? I have no complaints to speak of.*

speak out or **speak up,** speak loudly, clearly, or freely: *No one dared to speak out against the big bully. The children all spoke up in favor of having a party.*

speak er (spē'kər), **1** person who speaks. **2** person who presides over an assembly: *the Speaker of the House of Representatives.* **3** loudspeaker. *noun.*

spear[1] (spir), **1** weapon with a long shaft and a sharp-pointed head. **2** pierce with a spear: *The Indian speared a fish.* **3** pierce or stab with anything sharp: *spear string beans with a fork.* 1 *noun,* 2,3 *verb.*

spear[2] (spir), sprout or shoot of a plant: *a spear of grass.* *noun.*

spear head (spir'hed'), **1** the sharp-pointed striking end of a spear. **2** the driving force in an attack or any undertaking. **3** lead or clear the way

a hat	i it	oi oil	ch child	a in about
ā age	ī ice	ou out	ng long	e in taken
ä far	o hot	u cup	sh she	ə = i in pencil
e let	ō open	u̇ put	th thin	o in lemon
ē equal	ô order	ü rule	ŦH then	u in circus
ėr term			zh measure	

for; head: *Our group spearheaded the efforts to clean up the lake.* 1,2 *noun,* 3 *verb.*

spear mint (spir'mint'), a kind of mint grown for its oil which is used for flavoring. *noun.*

spe cial (spesh'əl), **1** of a particular kind; distinct from others; not general: *A safe has a special lock. Have you any special color in mind for your new coat?* **2** more than ordinary; unusual; exceptional: *Lions and tigers are a topic of special interest.* **3** having a particular purpose, function, or use: *The railroad ran special trains on holidays. Send the letter by a special messenger.* **4** a special person or thing, such as a special train or bus. 1-3 *adjective,* 4 *noun.*

spe cial ist (spesh'ə list), person who pursues one particular branch of study, business, or occupation. A heart specialist is a doctor who treats diseases of the heart. *noun.*

spe cial ize (spesh'ə līz), pursue some special branch of study or work: *Some doctors specialize in taking care of children.* *verb,* **spe cial ized, spe cial iz ing.**

spe cial ly (spesh'ə lē), in a special manner or degree; particularly; unusually. *adverb.*

spe cial ty (spesh'əl tē), **1** special study; special line of work, profession, or trade: *Straightening teeth is that dentist's specialty.* **2** product or article to which special attention is given: *This store makes a specialty of children's clothes.* *noun, plural* **spe cial ties.**

spe cies (spē'shēz), group of animals or plants that have certain permanent characteristics in common. All species of apples belong to the same family. Wheat is a species of grass. The lion is one species of cat. *noun, plural* **spe cies.**

spe cif ic (spi sif'ik), definite; precise; particular: *There was no specific reason for the quarrel.* *adjective.*

spec i fi ca tion (spes'ə fə kā'shən), **1** a detailed statement of particulars: *She made careful specification as to the kinds of cake and candy for her party.* **2** a detailed description of the dimensions or materials for a building, road, dam, boat, or like thing to be made or constructed. *noun.*

spec i fy (spes'ə fī), mention or name definitely: *Did you specify any particular time for us to call? He delivered the paper as specified.* *verb,* **spec i fied, spec i fy ing.**

spec i men (spes'ə mən), one of a group or class taken to show what the others are like; sample: *He collects specimens of all kinds of rocks.* *noun.*

speck (spek), **1** a small spot; stain: *Can you clean the specks off this wallpaper?* **2** a tiny bit; particle: *a speck in the eye.* **3** mark with specks: *This fruit is badly specked.* 1,2 *noun,* 3 *verb.*

spec ta cle (spek′tə kəl), **1** thing to look at; sight: *The children at play among the flowers made a charming spectacle. A quarrel is an unpleasant spectacle.* **2** a public show or display: *The parade was a fine spectacle.* **3 spectacles**, glasses. *noun.*

spec tac u lar (spek tak′yə lər), making a great display: *Motion pictures present spectacular scenes like battles, processions, storms, or races.* See picture. *adjective.*

spec ta tor (spek′tā tər), person who looks on without taking part: *There were many spectators at the game. noun.*

spec ter (spek′tər), ghost. *noun.*

spec trum (spek′trəm), the band of colors formed when a beam of light is broken up by being passed through a prism or by some other means. A rainbow has all the colors of the spectrum: red, orange, yellow, green, blue, indigo, and violet. See picture. *noun, plural* **spec tra** (spek′trə), **spec trums.**

spec u late (spek′yə lāt), **1** think carefully; reflect; meditate; consider: *The philosopher speculated about time and space.* **2** guess; conjecture: *She refused to speculate about the possible winner.* **3** buy or sell when there is a large risk: *He became poor after speculating in what turned out to be worthless oil wells. verb,* **spec u lat ed, spec u lat ing.**

spec u la tion (spek′yə lā′shən), **1** careful thought; reflection: *Former speculations about electricity were often mere guesses.* **2** guessing; conjecture: *His estimates of the cost were based on speculation.* **3** buying or selling when there is a large risk: *Her speculations in the stock market made her a thousand dollars. noun.*

sped (sped). See **speed.** *The police car sped down the road. verb.*

speech (spēch), **1** act of speaking; talk. **2** power of speaking: *Animals lack speech.* **3** manner of speaking: *I could tell by their speech that they were from the South.* **4** what is said; the words spoken: *We made the usual farewell speeches.* **5** a public talk: *The President gave an excellent speech.* **6** language: *The native speech of most Americans is English. noun, plural* **speech es.**

speech less (spēch′lis), **1** not able to speak: *Animals are speechless. I was speechless with anger.* **2** silent: *Her frown gave a speechless message. adjective.*

speed (spēd), **1** swift or rapid movement: *The cat pounced on the mouse with amazing speed.* **2** go fast: *The boat sped over the water.* **3** make go fast: *Let's all help speed the work.* **4** rate of movement: *The children ran at full speed.* **5** go faster than is safe or lawful: *The car was stopped for speeding.* **6** give success to: *God speed you.* 1,4 *noun,* 2,3,5,6 *verb,* **sped** or **speed ed, speed ing.**

speed i ly (spē′dl ē), quickly; with speed; soon. *adverb.*

speed om e ter (spē dom′ə tər), instrument to indicate speed. Automobiles have speedometers. *noun.*

speed way (spēd′wā′), road or track for fast driving. *noun.*

spectacular—The sunset was **spectacular.**

spectrum

sphinx (definition 1)

speed y (spē′dē), fast; rapid; quick; swift: *speedy workers, a speedy change, a speedy decision.* *adjective,* **speed i er, speed i est.**

spell[1] (spel), **1** write or say the letters of (a word) in order: *Some words are easy to spell. We learn to spell in school.* **2** mean: *Those clouds spell a storm.* *verb,* **spelled** or **spelt, spell ing.**

spell[2] (spel), **1** word or set of words supposed to have magic power. **2** fascination; charm: *We were under the spell of the beautiful music. noun.*

spell[3] (spel), **1** period of work or duty: *The sailor's spell at the wheel was four hours.* **2** period or time of anything: *The child has spells of coughing. There was a long spell of rainy weather in August.* **3** work in place of (another person) for a while: *I'll spell you at cutting the grass.* **1,2** *noun,* **3** *verb,* **spelled, spell ing.**

spell bound (spel′bound′), too interested to move; fascinated; enchanted: *The children were spellbound by the circus performance. adjective.*

spell er (spel′ər), **1** person who spells words. **2** book for teaching spelling. *noun.*

spell ing (spel′ing), **1** writing or saying the letters of a word in order: *She is poor at spelling.* **2** the way a word is spelled: *"Ax" has two spellings, "ax" and "axe." noun.*

spelt (spelt), spelled. See **spell**[1]. *verb.*

spend (spend), **1** pay out: *I spent ten dollars shopping for food today.* **2** pay out money: *Earn before you spend.* **3** use; use up: *Spend more time on that lesson.* **4** pass: *We spent last summer at the seashore.* **5** wear out: *The storm has spent its force.* *verb,* **spent, spend ing.**

spend thrift (spend′thrift′), **1** person who wastes money. **2** wasteful. **1** *noun,* **2** *adjective.*

spent (spent), **1** See **spend.** *Saturday was spent at the beach.* **2** used up. **3** worn out; tired: *a spent swimmer, a spent horse.* **1** *verb,* **2,3** *adjective.*

sperm cell (spėrm′ sel′), cell in a male for producing young when combined with an egg cell.

sperm whale (spėrm′ hwāl′), a large whale with a square head that is valuable for its oil. See picture.

sphere (sfir), **1** a round solid object. Every point on the surface of a sphere is the same distance from the center. See picture. **2** ball; globe. The sun, moon, earth, and stars are spheres. A baseball is a sphere. **3** place or surroundings in which a person or thing exists, acts, or works: *A teacher's sphere is the classroom.* **4** range; extent; region: *England's sphere of influence. noun.*

sphinx (sfingks), **1** statue of a lion's body with the head of a man, ram, or hawk. The **Great Sphinx** is a huge statue with a man's head and a lion's body, near Cairo, Egypt. See picture. **2** **Sphinx,** (in Greek mythology) a monster with the head of a woman, the body of a lion, and wings. The Sphinx proposed a riddle to everyone who passed by and killed those unable to guess it. **3** a puzzling, mysterious person. *noun, plural* **sphinx es.**

spice (spīs), **1** seasoning. Pepper, cinnamon, cloves, ginger, and nutmeg are common spices.

sperm whale—capturing a sperm whale

sphere (definition 1)

2 put spice in; season: *spiced peaches.* **3** something that adds flavor or interest: *"Variety is the spice of life."* **4** add flavor or interest to: *The principal spiced her speech with stories and jokes.* **1,3** *noun,* **2,4** *verb,* **spiced, spic ing.**

spick-and-span (spik′ən span′), new; fresh; spruce; smart; neat and clean: *a spick-and-span room. adjective.*

spic y (spī′sē), **1** flavored with spice: *The cookies were rich and spicy.* **2** like spice: *Those apples have a spicy smell and taste.* **3** lively; keen: *spicy conversation full of gossip. adjective,* **spic i er, spic i est.**

spi der (spī/dər), **1** a small animal with eight legs, no wings, and a body divided into two parts. Many spiders spin webs to catch insects for food. See picture. **2** something like or suggesting a spider. *noun.*

spied (spīd). See **spy.** *She spied her friend in the crowd. Who spied on us? verb.*

spig ot (spig/ət), faucet. *noun.*

spike[1] (spīk), **1** a large, strong nail. **2** fasten with spikes: *The work crew laid the track by spiking the rails to the ties.* **3** a sharp-pointed piece or part: *The baseball players wore shoes with spikes.* **4** provide with spikes: *The runners wore spiked shoes to keep from slipping.* **5** pierce or injure with a spike. **6** put an end or stop to; make useless; block: *The government spiked the rumors of an increase in taxes.* 1,3 *noun,* 2,4-6 *verb,* **spiked, spik ing.**

spike[2] (spīk), **1** ear of grain. **2** a long, pointed flower cluster. *noun.*

spill (spil), **1** let (liquid or any matter in loose pieces) run or fall: *spill milk, spill salt.* **2** fall or flow out: *Water spilled from the pail.* **3** cause to fall from a horse, car, boat, or the like: *The boat upset and spilled us into the water.* **4** such a fall: *He got a bad spill trying to ride that horse.* 1-3 *verb,* **spilled** or **spilt, spill ing;** 4 *noun.*

spilt (spilt), spilled. See **spill.** *verb.*

spin (spin), **1** turn or cause to turn around rapidly: *The wheels are spinning. The child spun the top.* **2** feel as if one were whirling around; feel dizzy: *My head is spinning.* **3** draw out and twist (cotton, flax, or wool) into thread. See picture. **4** make (a thread, web, or cocoon) by giving out from the body sticky material that hardens into thread. A spider spins a web. **5** produce; draw out; tell: *They sat around the campfire spinning stories.* **6** act of spinning. **7** a rapid run, ride, or drive: *Get your bicycle and come for a spin with me.* **8** run, ride, or drive rapidly. **9** a rapid turning around of an airplane as it falls. 1-5,8 *verb,* **spun, spin ning;** 6,7,9 *noun.*

spin ach (spin/ich), the green leaves of a garden plant, cooked and eaten as a vegetable or used uncooked in a salad. *noun.*

spi nal (spī/nl), of the spine or backbone; having to do with the backbone. *adjective.*

spinal column, backbone.

spinal cord, the thick, whitish cord of nerve tissue in the backbone or spine. Nerves to various parts of the body branch off from the spinal cord.

spin dle (spin/dl), **1** rod or pin used in spinning to twist, wind, and hold thread. **2** any rod or pin that turns around or on which something turns. Axles and shafts are spindles. *noun.*

spine (spīn), **1** series of small bones down the middle of the back; backbone. **2** a stiff, sharp-pointed growth on plants or animals. The thorns of a cactus and the quills of a porcupine are spines. See picture. *noun.*

spine less (spīn/lis), **1** having no spine: *A turtle is spineless.* **2** without courage: *a spineless coward.* **3** having no spines: *a spineless cactus. adjective.*

spider—about 1 inch (2½ centimeters) long

spin (definition 3)—She **spun** the wool into yarn.

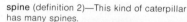

spine (definition 2)—This kind of caterpillar has many spines.

a hat	i it	oi oil	ch child	⎧ a in about
ā age	ī ice	ou out	ng long	e in taken
ä far	o hot	u cup	sh she	ə = ⎨ i in pencil
e let	ō open	u̇ put	th thin	o in lemon
ē equal	ô order	ü rule	ᴛʜ then	⎩ u in circus
ėr term			zh measure	

spire (definition 1)—The cathedral had two tall spires.

spinning wheel

spiral (definition 2)

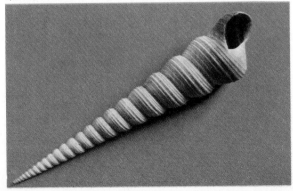

spinning wheel, a large wheel with a spindle, arranged for spinning cotton, flax, or wool into thread or yarn. See picture.

spin ster (spin′stər), woman who has not married. *noun.* [An earlier meaning of *spinster* was "a woman who spins." Later, the word was added after an unmarried woman's name to show what her occupation was.]

spi ral (spī′rəl), **1** a winding and gradually widening coil. A watch spring is a spiral. The thread of a screw is a spiral. **2** coiled: *a spiral staircase. Some sea shells have a spiral shape.* See picture. **3** move in a spiral: *The flaming airplane spiraled to earth.* **1** *noun,* **2** *adjective,* **3** *verb.*

spire (spīr), **1** the top part of a tower or steeple that narrows to a point. See picture. **2** anything tapering and pointed. A blade of grass is sometimes called a spire of grass. *The sun shone on the mountain's rocky spires. noun.*

spir it (spir′it), **1** soul: *Some religions teach that at death the spirit leaves the body.* **2** a human being's moral, religious, or emotional nature. **3** a supernatural being. God is a spirit. Ghosts and fairies are spirits. **4 spirits, a** state of mind; disposition; temper: *I am in good spirits.* **b** strong alcoholic liquor. Whiskey or brandy is called spirits. **5** person; personality: *You have been a brave spirit. She is a moving spirit in the community.* **6** influence that stirs up and rouses: *A spirit of progress is good for people.* **7** courage; vigor; liveliness: *A race horse must have spirit.* **8** what is really meant as opposed to what is said or written: *The spirit of a law is more important than its words.* **9** carry (away or off) secretly: *The gold has been spirited away.* **1-8** *noun,* **9** *verb.*

out of spirits, sad; gloomy.

spir it ed (spir′ə tid), lively; dashing; brave: *a spirited race horse. adjective.*

spir i tu al (spir′ə chü əl), **1** of or having something to do with the spirit or spirits. **2** caring much for the things of the spirit or soul. **3** sacred; religious: *a spiritual leader.* **4** a religious song which originated among the Negroes of the southern United States. **1-3** *adjective,* **4** *noun.*

spit¹ (spit), **1** throw out saliva from the mouth. **2** throw out: *The gun spits fire. He spat curses.* **3** the liquid produced in the mouth; saliva. **4** make a hissing sound. **1,2,4** *verb,* **spat** or **spit, spit ting; 3** *noun.*

spit² (spit), a sharp-pointed, slender rod or bar on which meat is roasted. *noun.*

spite (spīt), **1** ill will; grudge: *He broke my new radio out of spite.* **2** show ill will toward; annoy: *They let the weeds grow in their yard to spite their neighbors.* **1** *noun,* **2** *verb,* **spit ed, spit ing.**

in spite of, not prevented by; notwithstanding:

The schools were open in spite of the snowstorm.

spite ful (spīt′fəl), full of spite; eager to annoy; behaving with ill will and malice. *adjective.*

splash (splash), **1** cause (water, mud, or the like) to fly about so as to wet or soil: *The swimmers splashed each other with water.* **2** dash liquid about: *The baby likes to splash in the tub.* **3** dash in scattered masses or drops. See picture. **4** wet, spatter, or soil: *Our car is all splashed with mud.* **5** act or sound of splashing; splashing: *The boat upset with a loud splash.* **6** spot of liquid splashed upon a thing: *She has splashes of grease on her clothes.* **1-4** *verb,* **5,6** *noun, plural* **splash es.**

splash down (splash′doun′), the landing of a capsule or other spacecraft in the ocean after reentry. *noun.*

splat ter (splat′ər), splash; spatter. *verb, noun.*

splen did (splen′did), **1** brilliant; glorious; magnificent; grand: *a splendid sunset, a splendid palace, splendid jewels, a splendid victory.* **2** very good; fine; excellent: *a splendid chance. adjective.*

splen dor (splen′dər), **1** great brightness; brilliant light: *The sun set in a golden splendor.* **2** magnificent show; pomp; glory. *noun.*

splice (splīs), **1** join together (ropes) by weaving together ends which have been pulled out into separate strands. **2** join together (two pieces of timber) by overlapping. **3** join together (film, tape, or wire) by gluing or cementing the ends. **4** joining of ropes, timbers, film, or the like, by splicing: *How neat a splice can you make?* **1-3** *verb,* **spliced, splic ing;** **4** *noun.*

splint (splint), **1** arrangement of wood, metal, or plaster to hold a broken bone in place. **2** a thin strip of wood, such as is used in making baskets. *noun.*

splin ter (splin′tər), **1** a thin, sharp piece of wood, bone, glass, or the like: *I have a splinter in my hand. The mirror broke into splinters.* **2** split or break into splinters: *He splintered the locked door with an ax. The mirror splintered.* **1** *noun,* **2** *verb.*

split (split), **1** break or cut from end to end, or in layers: *We split the logs into firewood. The baker split the cake and filled it with jelly.* **2** separate into parts; divide: *The huge tree split when it was struck by lightning. Let's split the cost of the dinner between us.* **3** divide into different groups, parties, or factions. **4** division in a group, party, or faction: *There was a split in the club for a time, but harmony was soon restored.* **5** splitting; break; crack: *Frost caused the split in the rock.* **6** an acrobatic trick of sinking to the floor with the legs spread far apart in opposite directions. **7** divide (a molecule, atom, or atomic nucleus) into two or more smaller parts. **1-3,7** *verb,* **split, split ting;** **4-6** *noun.*

spoil (spoil), **1** damage or injure (something) so as to make it unfit or useless; ruin; destroy: *The rain spoiled the picnic.* **2** be damaged; become bad or unfit for use: *The fruit spoiled because I kept it too long.* **3** injure the character or disposition of: *That child is being spoiled by too much attention.* **4** **spoils,** things taken by force; things won: *The soldiers carried the spoils back to their own land.* **1-3** *verb,*

splash

spoiled or spoilt, spoil ing; **4** *noun.*

spoilt (spoilt), spoiled. See **spoil.** *verb.*

spoke¹ (spōk). See **speak.** *She spoke about that yesterday. verb.*

spoke² (spōk), one of the bars from the center of a wheel to the rim. *noun.*

spo ken (spō′kən), **1** See **speak.** *She has spoken about coming to visit.* **2** expressed with the mouth; uttered; told: *There were no written directions for the test, only spoken ones.* **1** *verb,* **2** *adjective.*

spokes man (spōks′mən), person who speaks for another or others: *I am the spokesman for my class in the student council. noun, plural* **spokes men.**

sponge (spunj), **1** a water animal with a light, elastic skeleton. **2** the skeleton of this animal which has many holes. It is used for soaking up water in bathing or cleaning. **3** a similar article made artificially of rubber or plastic. **4** wipe or rub with a wet sponge; make clean or damp in this way: *Sponge up the spilled water. Sponge the mud spots off the car.* **5** something like a sponge, such as a pad of gauze used by doctors, bread dough, a kind of cake, or a kind of pudding. **6** live or profit at the expense of another in a selfish way: *They are sponging on their relatives instead of working.* **1-3,5** *noun,* **4,6** *verb,* **sponged, spong ing.**

spon gy (spun′jē), **1** like a sponge; soft, light, and full of holes: *spongy moss, spongy dough.* **2** hard and full of holes: *a spongy rock. adjective,* **spon gi er, spon gi est.**

spon sor (spon′sər), **1** person who is responsible for a person or thing: *the sponsor of a law, the sponsor of a student applying for a scholarship.* **2** person who stands with the parents at an infant's baptism, agreeing to assist in the child's religious upbringing if necessary; godfather or godmother. **3** company, store, or other business firm that pays the costs of a radio or television program advertising its products. **4** act as sponsor for: *The parents' organization at our school sponsors our scout troop.* **1-3** *noun,* **4** *verb.*

spon ta ne ous (spon tā/nē əs), of one's own choice; natural; of itself: *Both sides burst into spontaneous cheers at the skillful play. A pile of oily rags will sometimes break into a spontaneous flame.* **Spontaneous combustion** occurs when something sets itself on fire. *adjective.*

spook (spük), ghost; specter. *noun.*

spool (spül), cylinder of wood or metal on which thread or wire is wound. *noun.*

spoon (spün), **1** a small, shallow bowl at the end of a handle. Spoons are used to take up or stir food or drink. **2** take up in a spoon. **1** *noun,* **2** *verb.*

spoon ful (spün/fül), as much as a spoon can hold. *noun, plural* **spoon fuls.**

spore (spôr), **1** a single cell capable of growing into a new plant or animal. Ferns produce spores; mold grows from spores. **2** germ; seed. *noun.*

sport (spôrt), **1** game or contest requiring some skill and usually a certain amount of physical exercise. Baseball, golf, football, tennis, swimming, racing, hunting, and fishing are outdoor sports; bowling and basketball are indoor sports. **2** any pastime or amusement: *They spend Saturdays in sport and play.* **3** amuse oneself; play: *Lambs sport in the fields. The kitten sports with its tail.* **4** playful joking; fun: *That was great sport.* **5** object of jokes and ridicule: *The awkward beginner was the sport of the experienced golfers.* **6** person who behaves in a fair and honorable manner and is a good loser: *to be a sport.* **1,2,4-6** *noun,* **3** *verb.*

make sport of, ridicule: *Don't make sport of her.*

sport ing (spôr/ting), **1** of, interested in, or engaging in sports. **2** playing fair: *It was a sporting gesture for the loser to shake the winner's hand.* **3** willing to take a chance. **4** involving risk; uncertain: *She took a sporting chance in climbing up the cliff. adjective.*

sports man (spôrts/mən), **1** person who takes part in sports, especially hunting, fishing, or racing. **2** person who likes sports. **3** person who plays fair. *noun, plural* **sports men.**

sports man ship (spôrts/mən ship), **1** qualities or conduct of a sportsman; fair play. **2** ability in sports. *noun.*

spot (spot), **1** a small mark or stain that discolors or disfigures: *You have grease spots on your suit. That spot on her arm is a bruise.* **2** a blemish or flaw in character or reputation: *His record is without spot.* **3** small part unlike the rest: *The shirt is blue with white spots.* **4** make or become spotted: *I have spotted the tablecloth. This silk spots from water.* **5** place: *From this spot you can see the ocean.* **6** ready; on hand: *He paid spot cash for the horse.* **7** pick out; find out; recognize: *I spotted my sister in the crowd. The teacher spotted every mistake in my paper.* **8** figure or dot on a playing card, domino, or die to show its kind and value. **1-3,5,8** *noun,* **4,7** *verb,* **spot ted, spot ting;** **6** *adjective.*

on the spot, 1 at that very place. **2** at once: *Your orders will be carried out on the spot.* **3** in trouble or difficulty: *He put me on the spot by asking a question I could not answer.*

a hat	i it	oi oil	ch child	a in about
ā age	ī ice	ou out	ng long	e in taken
ä far	o hot	u cup	sh she	ə = i in pencil
e let	ō open	ů put	th thin	o in lemon
ē equal	ô order	ü rule	ŦH then	u in circus
ėr term			zh measure	

spot less (spot/lis), without a spot: *a spotless white shirt. adjective.*

spot light (spot/līt/), **1** a strong light thrown upon a particular place or person. **2** lamp that gives the light: *a spotlight in a theater.* **3** light up with a spotlight or spotlights: *At night the baseball field is spotlighted.* **4** public notice; anything that directs attention on a person or thing: *Movie stars are often in the spotlight.* **1,2,4** *noun,* **3** *verb.*

spot ty (spot/ē), **1** having spots; spotted. **2** not of uniform quality: *Your work is spotty. adjective,* **spot ti er, spot ti est.**

spouse (spous), husband or wife: *Mr. Smith is Mrs. Smith's spouse, and she is his spouse. noun.*

spout (spout), **1** throw out (a liquid) in a stream or spray: *The fountain spouted up high. A whale spouts water when it breathes.* **2** flow out with force: *Water spouted from a break in the pipe.* **3** stream; jet: *A spout of water shot up from the hole in the pipe.* **4** pipe for carrying off water: *Rain runs down a spout from our roof to the ground.* **5** tube or lip by which liquid is poured. **6** speak in loud and very emotional tones: *The inexperienced actor spouted his lines.* **1,2,6** *verb,* **3-5** *noun.*

sprain (sprān), **1** injure (a joint or muscle) by a sudden twist or wrench: *I sprained my ankle.* **2** injury caused by a sudden twist or wrench: *The sprain took a long time to heal.* **1** *verb,* **2** *noun.*

sprang (sprang). See **spring.** *She sprang from her chair. verb.*

sprawl (sprôl), **1** lie or sit with the arms and legs spread out, especially ungracefully: *The people sprawled on the beach in their bathing suits.* **2** spread out in an irregular or awkward manner: *His large handwriting sprawled across the page.* **3** act or position of sprawling. **1,2** *verb,* **3** *noun.*

spray[1] (sprā), **1** liquid going through the air in small drops: *We were wet with the sea spray.* **2** something like this: *A spray of bullets hit the target.* **3** instrument that sends a liquid out as spray. **4** sprinkle; scatter spray on: *Spray this liquid on your throat. Spray the apple tree to kill the worms.* **1-3** *noun,* **4** *verb.*

spray[2] (sprā), a small branch or piece of some plant with its leaves, flowers, or fruit: *a spray of lilacs, a spray of berries. noun.*

spread (spred), **1** cover or cause to cover a large or larger area; stretch out; unfold; open out: *spread rugs on the floor, spread one's arms. The bird spread its wings.* **2** move farther apart: *Spread out your fingers.* **3** extend; lie: *Fields of corn spread out before us.* **4** scatter; distribute: *We spread the news. She spread grain for the chickens.* **5** cover with a thin layer: *I spread each slice with butter.* **6** put as a thin layer: *Spread the paint evenly.* **7** act of spreading: *fight the spread of infection, encourage* *the spread of knowledge.* **8** width; extent; amount of spreading: *The spread of the airplane's wings was sixty feet.* **9** covering for a bed or table. **10** put food on (a table). **11** food put on the table; feast. **12** article of food to spread on bread, crackers, rolls, or the like. *Butter and jam are spreads.* 1-6,10 *verb,* **spread, spread ing;** 7-9,11,12 *noun.*

spree (sprē), **1** a lively frolic; gay time. **2** spell of drinking intoxicating liquor. *noun.*

sprig (sprig), shoot, twig, or small branch: *a sprig of lilac. noun.*

spright ly (sprīt′lē), lively; gay: *a sprightly kitten. adjective,* **spright li er, spright li est.**

spring (spring). See picture. **1** leap or jump; rise or move suddenly and lightly: *The dog sprang at the thief. I sprang to my feet.* **2** leap or jump: *She made a spring over the fence.* **3** fly back or away: *The door sprang open.* **4** cause to spring; cause to act by a spring: *spring a trap.* **5** an elastic device that returns to its original shape after being pulled or held out of shape. *Beds have wire springs. The spring in a clock makes it go.* **6** elastic quality: *There is no spring left in these old rubber bands.* **7** season when plants begin to grow; season of the year between winter and summer: *Robins return in the spring.* **8** of or for spring; coming in spring: *Tulips are spring flowers. Spring wheat is wheat sown in the spring.* **9** a small stream of water coming from the earth. **10** come from some source; arise; grow: *A wind has sprung up. Plants spring from seeds.* **11** begin to move, act, or grow suddenly; burst forth: *Towns spring up where oil is discovered.* **12** bring out, produce, or make suddenly: *spring a surprise on someone.* **13** crack, split, bend, strain, or break: *Cracks all along the wall showed where it had sprung.* 1,3,4,10-13 *verb,* **sprang** or **sprung, sprung, spring ing;** 2,5-7,9 *noun,* 8 *adjective.*

spring board (spring′bôrd′), board used to give added spring in diving, jumping, and vaulting. *noun.*

spring time (spring′tīm′), the season of spring: *Flowers bloom in the springtime. noun.*

spring y (spring′ē), elastic: *His step was springy. adjective,* **spring i er, spring i est.**

sprin kle (spring′kəl), **1** scatter in drops or tiny bits: *I sprinkled sand on the icy sidewalk.* **2** spray or cover with small drops: *She sprinkled the flowers with water.* **3** sprinkling; small quantity: *The cook put a sprinkle of nuts on the cake.* **4** rain a little. **5** a light rain. 1,2,4 *verb,* **sprin kled, sprin kling;** 3,5 *noun.*

sprint (sprint), **1** run at top speed for a short distance. **2** a short race at top speed. 1 *verb,* 2 *noun.*

sprock et (sprok′it), **1** one of a set of parts sticking out from the rim of a wheel and arranged to fit into the links of a chain. The sprockets keep the chain from slipping. See picture. **2** wheel made with sprockets, sometimes called a **sprocket wheel.** See picture. *noun.*

sprout (sprout), **1** begin to grow; shoot forth: *Seeds sprout. Buds sprout in the spring. Weeds have*

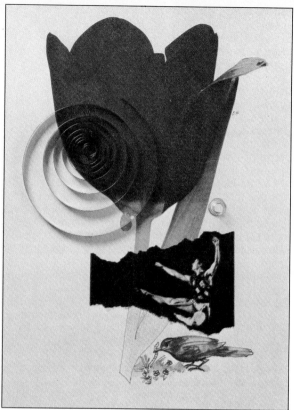

spring (definitions 1, 2, 5, 7, and 8)

sprouted in the garden. **2** cause to grow: *The rain has sprouted the corn.* **3** shoot of a plant: *The gardener was setting out sprouts.* 1,2 *verb,* 3 *noun.*

spruce[1] (sprüs), **1** kind of evergreen tree with leaves shaped like needles. **2** its wood. *noun.*

spruce[2] (sprüs), **1** neat; trim: *You look very spruce in your new suit.* **2** make spruce; become spruce: *He spruced himself up for dinner.* 1 *adjective,* **spruc er, spruc est;** 2 *verb,* **spruced, spruc ing.**

sprung (sprung). See **spring.** *The mouse sprung the trap. The trap was sprung. verb.*

spry (sprī), lively; nimble: *The spry old woman traveled all over the country. adjective,* **spry er, spry est,** or **spri er, spri est.**

spud (spud), **1** tool with a narrow blade for digging up or cutting the roots of weeds. **2** potato. *noun.*

spun (spun). See **spin.** *The car skidded and spun on the ice. The thread was spun from silk. verb.*

spunk (spungk), courage; pluck; spirit: *a little puppy full of spunk. noun.*

spur (spėr), **1** a pricking instrument worn on a rider's heel for urging a horse on. See picture. **2** prick with spurs: *The riders spurred their horses on.* **3** ride quickly. **4** something like a spur; point sticking out. *A cock has spurs on his legs. A spur of rock stuck out from the mountain.* **5** anything that urges on; goad: *Ambition was the spur that made him work.* **6** urge on: *Anger spurred her to* *speak unkindly.* **7** any short branch: *a spur of a railroad.* 1,4,5,7 *noun,* 2,3,6 *verb,* **spurred, spur ring.**

spurn (spėrn), refuse with scorn; scorn: *The judge spurned the bribe. verb.*

spurt (spėrt), **1** flow suddenly in a stream or jet; gush out; squirt: *Water spurted from the fountain.* **2** a sudden rushing forth; jet: *a spurt of blood from a cut.* **3** a great increase of effort or activity for a short time: *To win the race he put on a spurt of speed.* **4** put forth great energy for a short time; show great activity for a short time: *The runners spurted near the end of the race.* 1,4 *verb,* 2,3 *noun.*

sput ter (sput′ər), **1** make spitting or popping noises: *fat sputtering in the frying pan. The firecrackers sputtered.* **2** throw out (drops of spit, bits of food, etc.) in excitement or in talking too fast. **3** say (words or sounds) in haste and confusion. **4** confused talk. **5** sputtering; sputtering noise. 1-3 *verb,* 4,5 *noun.*

spy (spī), **1** person who keeps secret watch on the actions of others. **2** person who tries to get information about the enemy, usually in time of war by visiting the enemy's territory in disguise. **3** keep secret watch: *He saw two men spying on him from behind a tree.* **4** act as a spy; be a spy. **5** catch sight of; see: *She was the first to spy the mountains on the horizon.* 1,2 *noun,* plural **spies;** 3-5 *verb,* **spied, spy ing.**

spy glass (spī′glas′), a small telescope. *noun,* plural **spy glass es.**

squab (skwob), a young pigeon. *noun.*

squab ble (skwob′əl), **1** a petty, noisy quarrel: *Children's squabbles annoy their parents.* **2** take part in a petty, noisy quarrel: *I won't squabble over a nickel.* 1 *noun,* 2 *verb,* **squab bled, squab bling.**

squad (skwod), **1** a small number of soldiers grouped for drill, inspection, or work. A squad is the smallest part of an army. **2** any small group of persons working together: *A squad of boys cleaned up the yard. noun.*

squad ron (skwod′rən), **1** part of a naval fleet used for special service: *a destroyer squadron.* **2** formation of eight or more airplanes that fly or fight together. **3** unit of cavalry. **4** any group. *noun.*

squal id (skwol′id), very dirty; degraded; wretched: *a squalid tenement. adjective.*

squall[1] (skwôl), a sudden, violent gust of wind, often with rain, snow, or sleet. *noun.*

squall[2] (skwôl), **1** cry out loudly; scream violently: *The baby squalled.* **2** a loud, harsh cry: *The parrot's squall was heard all over the house.* 1 *verb,* 2 *noun.*

squal or (skwol′ər), misery and dirt; filth. *noun.*

squan der (skwon′dər), spend foolishly; waste: *to squander time and money. verb.*

square (skwer *or* skwar), **1** figure with four equal sides and four right angles (▢). **2** having this shape: *a square box. This table is square.* **3** anything having this shape or nearly this shape: *I gave the child a square of chocolate.* **4** make square in shape: *square the corners of a board.* **5** mark out in squares: *The children squared off the sidewalk for their game.* **6** space in a city or town bounded by

a hat	**i** it	**oi** oil	**ch** child	⎧ a in about
ā age	**ī** ice	**ou** out	**ng** long	e in taken
ä far	**o** hot	**u** cup	**sh** she	**ə** = ⎨ i in pencil
e let	**ō** open	** u̇** put	**th** thin	o in lemon
ē equal	**ô** order	**ü** rule	**ᴙ** then	⎩ u in circus
ėr term			**zh** measure	

streets on all sides: *This square is full of stores.* **7** distance along one side of such a space; block: *We lived three squares from the school.* **8** open space in a city or town bounded by streets on four sides, often planted with grass or trees: *There is a fountain in the square opposite the city hall.* **9** any similar open space, such as at the meeting of streets. **10** having length and width. A square meter is the area of a square whose edges are each one meter long. **11** forming a right angle: *This table has four square corners.* **12** instrument shaped like a T or an L, used for drawing right angles and testing the squareness of anything. See picture. **13** make straight, level, or even:

square (definition 12)

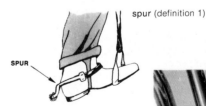

spur (definition 1)

sprocket (definitions 1 and 2)

square a picture on a wall. **14** adjust; settle: *Let us square our accounts.* **15** agree; conform: *My thoughts on the subject square with yours.* **16** just; fair; honest: *You will get a square deal at this shop.* **17** satisfying: *At our house we have three square meals each day.* 1,3,6-9,12 *noun,* 2,10,11,16,17 *adjective,* **squar er, squar est;** 4,5,13-15 *verb,* **squared, squar ing.**

square dance, dance performed by a set of couples arranged about a square space or in some set form.

square foot, a unit of area one foot long and one foot wide. A rug 9 ft. long and 6 ft. wide covers 54 square feet.

square inch, a unit of area one inch long and one inch wide.

squash[1] (skwosh), **1** press until soft or flat; crush: *She squashed the bug. This package was squashed in the mail.* **2** game somewhat like handball and tennis, played in a walled court with rackets and a hollow rubber ball. 1 *verb,* 2 *noun.*

squash[2] (skwosh), the fruit of a trailing vine, used as a vegetable or for making pies. Squash have several different shapes and are usually yellow, green, or white. *noun, plural* **squash** or **squash es.** [*Squash*[2] comes from a Narragansett Indian word meaning "the green things that may be eaten raw."]

squat (skwot), **1** crouch on the heels. **2** sit on the ground or floor with the legs drawn up closely beneath or in front of the body: *We squatted around the fire.* **3** crouching: *A squat figure sat in front of the fire.* **4** act of squatting. **5** settle on another's land without title or right. **6** settle on public land to acquire ownership of it. **7** short and thick; low and broad: *That is a squat teapot.* 1,2,5,6 *verb,* **squat ted** or **squat, squat ting;** 3,7 *adjective,* **squat ter, squat test;** 4 *noun.*

squaw (skwô), a North American Indian woman or wife. The use of this word is often considered offensive. *noun.*

squawk (skwôk), **1** make a loud, harsh sound: *Hens and ducks squawk when frightened.* **2** a loud, harsh sound. **3** complain loudly. **4** a loud complaint. 1,3 *verb,* 2,4 *noun.*

squeak (skwēk), **1** make a short, sharp, shrill sound: *A mouse squeaks.* **2** such a sound: *We heard the squeak of the stairs.* 1 *verb,* 2 *noun.*

squeak y (skwē′kē), squeaking: *a squeaky door.* *adjective,* **squeak i er, squeak i est.**

squeal (skwēl), **1** make a long, sharp, shrill cry: *A pig squeals when it is hurt.* **2** such a cry. **3** inform on another. 1,3 *verb,* 2 *noun.*

squeeze (skwēz), **1** press hard: *Don't squeeze the kitten, or you will hurt it.* **2** a tight pressure: *She gave her sister's arm a squeeze.* **3** hug: *He squeezed his child.* **4** force by pressing: *I can't squeeze another thing into my trunk.* **5** yield to pressure: *Sponges squeeze easily.* **6** force a way: *He squeezed through the crowd.* **7** crush; crowd: *It's a tight squeeze to get five people in that little car.* 1,3-6 *verb,* **squeezed, squeez ing;** 2,7 *noun.*

squid (skwid), a sea animal like an octopus but

having ten arms instead of eight. *noun, plural* **squids** or **squid.**

squint (skwint), **1** look with the eyes partly closed. **2** sidelong look; hasty look; look. **3** look sideways. **4** tendency to look sideways. **5** looking sideways. **6** be cross-eyed. **7** cross-eyed. 1,3,6 *verb,* 2,4 *noun,* 5,7 *adjective.*

squire (skwīr), **1** (in Great Britain) a country gentleman, especially the chief landowner in a district. **2** a young man of noble family who attended a knight till he himself was made a knight. See picture. *noun.*

squirm (skwėrm), wriggle; writhe; twist: *The restless girl squirmed in her seat.* *verb.*

squir rel (skwėr′əl), **1** a small, bushy-tailed animal that usually lives in trees and eats nuts. **2** its gray, reddish, or dark-brown fur. *noun.*

squirt (skwėrt), **1** force out (liquid) through a narrow opening: *to squirt water through a tube.* **2** come out in a jet or stream: *Water squirted from the hose.* **3** squirting: *The children soaked one another with squirts of water from the hose.* 1,2 *verb,* 3 *noun.*

Sr., Senior.

St., 1 Saint. **2** Street.

stab (stab), **1** pierce or wound with a pointed weapon. **2** thrust or blow made with a pointed weapon. **3** wound made by stabbing. **4** wound sharply or deeply in the feelings: *He was stabbed to the heart when his friend betrayed him.* 1,4 *verb,* **stabbed, stab bing;** 2,3 *noun.*

sta bil i ty (stə bil′ə tē), **1** being fixed in position; firmness: *A concrete wall has more stability than a light wooden fence.* **2** permanence: *the stability of a lifelong friendship.* **3** steadfastness of character or purpose: *She has the stability to see the job through to its completion.* *noun, plural* **sta bil i ties.**

sta ble[1] (stā′bəl), **1** building where horses or cattle are kept and fed: *She took riding lessons at the stable.* **2** group of animals housed in such a building: *a stable of race horses.* **3** put or keep in a stable. 1,2 *noun,* 3 *verb,* **sta bled, sta bling.**

sta ble[2] (stā′bəl), not likely to move or change; steadfast; firm; steady: *Concrete reinforced with steel is stable. The world needs a stable peace.* *adjective.*

stack (stak), **1** a large pile of hay or straw. Haystacks are often round and arranged so as to shed water. **2** pile of anything: *a stack of wood.* **3** number of rifles arranged to form a cone or pyramid. **4** pile or arrange in a stack: *stack hay, stack guns.* **5** chimney. 1-3,5 *noun,* 4 *verb.*

sta di um (stā′dē əm), place shaped like an oval or a U, consisting of tiers of seats around an open field: *The stadium was filled for the final baseball game.* *noun.*

staff (staf), **1** stick; pole; rod: *The old man leaned on his staff. The flag hangs on a staff.* **2** something that supports or sustains. Bread is called the staff of life because it will support life. **3** group assisting a chief; group of employees: *Our school has a staff of twenty teachers.* **4** group of officers that makes plans for an army but does no

stags

fighting. **5** provide with officers or employees. **6** the five lines and the four spaces between them on which music is written. 1-4,6 *noun, plural* **staves** or **staffs** for 1 and 2, **staffs** for 3, 4, and 6; 5 *verb.*

stag (stag), a full-grown male deer. See picture. *noun.*

stage (stāj), **1** one step or degree in a process; period of development. Frogs pass through a tadpole stage. **2** the raised platform in a theater on which the actors perform. **3 the stage,** the theater; the drama; actor's profession: *write for the stage.* **4** scene of action: *Bunker Hill was the stage of a famous battle.* **5** arrange: *The play was very well staged. The class staged a surprise party for the teacher's birthday.* **6** section of a rocket or missile having its own engine and fuel. A three-stage rocket has three engines, one in each stage, which separate one after another from the rocket after use. **7** stagecoach. **8** distance between two places on a journey. 1-4,6-8 *noun,* 5 *verb,* **staged, stag ing.**

by easy stages, slowly; often stopping: *We climbed the mountain by easy stages.*

stage coach (stāj′kōch′), coach carrying passengers and parcels over a regular route. *noun.*

stagger (definition 2)—The news that he had lost his entire fortune **staggered** him.

stag ger (stag′ər), **1** sway or reel (from weakness, a heavy load, or being drunk): *I staggered and fell under the heavy load of books.* **2** make sway or reel. See picture. **3** swaying or reeling. **4** become unsteady; waver: *The troops staggered under the severe attack.* **5** arrange to be at different times: *Vacations were staggered so that only one person was away at a time.* 1,2,4,5 *verb,* 3 *noun.*

stag nant (stag′nənt), **1** not running or flowing; foul from standing still: *stagnant air, stagnant water.* **2** not active; sluggish: *During the summer business is often stagnant. adjective.*

stain (stān), **1** soil; spot: *The tablecloth is stained where food has been spilled.* **2** spot: *I have an ink stain on my shirt.* **3** spot by wrongdoing or disgrace; dishonor: *His crimes stained the family honor.* **4** mark of disgrace; dishonor: *His character is without stain.* **5** color; dye: *She stained the chair green.* **6** coloring or dye: *Paint the table with a brown stain.* 1,3,5 *verb,* 2,4,6 *noun.*

stair (ster *or* star), **1** one of a series of steps for going from one level or floor to another. **2 stairs,** a set of such steps: *the top of the stairs. noun.*

stair case (ster′kās′ *or* star′kās′), stairs. *noun.*

stair way (ster′wā′ *or* star′wā′), way up and down by stairs; stairs: *the back stairway. noun.*

stake¹ (stāk), **1** stick or post pointed at one end for driving into the ground. **2** fasten to a stake or with a stake: *stake down a tent.* **3** mark with stakes;

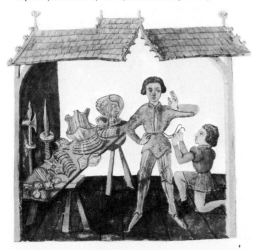

squire (definition 2)—a squire attending a knight

stalactites and stalagmites

stall¹ (definition 1)

stamen—The flower had yellow stamens.

mark the boundaries of: *The miners staked out their claims.* 1 *noun,* 2,3 *verb,* **staked, stak ing.**

stake² (stāk), **1** risk (money or something valuable) on the result of a game or on any chance: *She staked five dollars on the black horse.* **2** money risked; what is staked: *The gamblers played for high stakes.* **3** the prize in a race or contest: *The stakes were divided up among the winners.* **4** something to gain or lose; an interest; a share in a property: *Each of us has a stake in the future of our country.* 1 *verb,* **staked, stak ing;** 2-4 *noun.*

at stake, to be won or lost: *His honor is at stake.*

sta lac tite (stə lak′tīt), formation of lime, shaped like an icicle, hanging from the roof of a cave. It is formed by dripping water that contains lime. See picture. *noun.*

sta lag mite (stə lag′mīt), formation of lime, shaped like a cone, built up on the floor of a cave. It is formed by water dripping from a stalactite. See picture. *noun.*

stale (stāl), **1** not fresh: *stale bread.* **2** no longer new or interesting: *a stale joke.* **3** out of condition: *The horse has gone stale from too much running. adjective,* **stal er, stal est.**

stalk¹ (stôk), **1** the main stem of a plant. **2** any slender, supporting part of a plant or animal. A flower may have a stalk. The eyes of a lobster are on stalks. *noun.*

stalk² (stôk), **1** approach or pursue without being seen or heard: *The hungry lion stalked a zebra.* **2** spread silently and steadily: *Disease stalked through the land.* **3** walk in a slow, stiff, or proud manner: *She stalked into the room and threw herself into a chair.* **4** stalking. 1-3 *verb,* 4 *noun.*

stall¹ (stôl), **1** place in a stable for one animal. See picture. **2** a small place for selling things: *At the public market different things were sold in different stalls under one big roof.* **3** seat in the choir of a church. **4** put or keep in a stall: *The horses were safely stalled.* **5** stop or bring to a standstill, usually against one's wish: *The engine stalled. We were stalled in the mud.* 1-3 *noun,* 4,5 *verb.*

stall² (stôl), **1** delay: *You have been stalling long enough.* **2** pretense to avoid doing something: *Her excuse was just a stall.* 1 *verb,* 2 *noun.*

stal lion (stal′yən), a male horse that can father young. *noun.*

stal wart (stôl′wərt), **1** strongly built. **2** strong and brave: *a stalwart knight.* **3** firm; steadfast: *a stalwart refusal. adjective.*

sta men (stā′mən), the part of a flower that contains the pollen. A stamen consists of an anther supported by a slender stem called a filament. The stamens are surrounded by the petals. See picture. *noun.*

stam mer (stam′ər), **1** repeat the same sound in an effort to speak; hesitate in speaking. EXAMPLE: I s-s-see a d-d-dog. **2** stammering; stuttering: *He has a nervous stammer.* 1 *verb,* 2 *noun.*

stamp (stamp), **1** a small piece of paper with a sticky back that is put on letters, papers, or parcels to show that a charge has been paid; postage stamp. **2** put a stamp on: *stamp a letter.*

3 bring down one's foot with force: *He stamped his foot in anger. I stamped on the spider.* **4** act of stamping: *The horse gave a stamp of its hoof.* **5** pound; crush; trample; tread: *Stamp out the fire.* **6** instrument that cuts, shapes, or impresses a design on (paper, wax, or metal); thing that puts a mark on: *The stamp had her name on it.* **7** mark made by such an instrument. **8** make a mark on: *She stamped the papers with the date.* **9** show to be of a certain quality or character: *His speech stamps him as an educated man.* **10** impression; marks: *Their faces bore the stamp of suffering.* 1,4,6,7,10 *noun,* 2,3,5,8,9 *verb.*

stam pede (stam pēd′), **1** a sudden scattering or headlong flight of a frightened herd of cattle or horses. **2** any headlong flight of a large group: *a stampede of a frightened crowd from a burning building.* **3** scatter or flee in a stampede. **4** general rush: *a stampede to newly discovered gold fields.* **5** make a general rush. **6** cause to stampede: *Thunder stampeded the cattle.* 1,2,4 *noun,* 3,5,6 *verb,* **stam ped ed, stam ped ing.**

stand (stand), **1** be upright on one's feet: *Don't stand if you are tired, but sit down.* **2** rise to one's feet: *The children stood to salute the flag.* **3** be set upright; be placed; be located: *The box stands over there.* **4** set upright: *Stand the box here.* **5** be in a certain place, rank, or scale: *Pillars stand on each side of the door. He stood first in his class for service to the school.* **6** take or keep a certain position: *"Stand back!" called the policeman to the crowd.* **7** be in a special condition: *She stands innocent of the crime. The poor child stood in need of food and clothing.* **8** be unchanged; hold good; remain the same: *The rule against being late will stand.* **9** stay in place; last: *The old house has stood for a hundred years.* **10** bear; endure: *Those plants cannot stand cold and die in the winter.* **11** stop moving; halt; stop: *The cars stood and waited for the light to change.* **12** a halt; stop. **13** stop for defense: *We made a last stand against the enemy.* **14** place where a person stands; position: *The monitor took her stand in the hall.* **15** a raised place where people can sit or stand: *The mayor sat on the reviewing stand at the parade.* **16** something to put things on or in: *Leave your wet umbrella in the stand in the hall.* **17** place or fixtures for a small business: *a newspaper stand, a fruit stand.* **18** group of growing trees or plants: *a stand of timber.* 1-11 *verb,* **stood, stand ing;** 12-18 *noun.*

stand by, 1 be near. **2** side with; help; support: *stand by a friend.* **3** be or get ready for use or action: *The radio operator was ordered to stand by.*
stand for, 1 represent; mean: *What does the abbreviation "St." stand for?* **2** be on the side of; take the part of; uphold: *Our school stands for fair play.* **3** put up with: *The teacher said she would not stand for talking during class.*
stand out, 1 project: *His ears stood out.* **2** be noticeable or prominent: *Certain facts stand out.* **3** refuse to yield: *stand out against popular opinion.*
stand up for, take the part of; defend; support: *stand up for a friend.*

stand up to, meet or face boldly: *stand up to an enemy.*
stan dard (stan′dərd), **1** anything taken as a basis of comparison; model: *Your work is not up to the class standard.* **2** used as a standard; according to rule: *standard spelling, standard pronunciation.* **3** having recognized excellence or authority: *Use a standard encyclopedia to look up the facts for your report.* **4** flag, emblem, or symbol: *The dragon was the standard of China.* 1,4 *noun,* 2,3 *adjective.*
stan dard ize (stan′dər dīz), make standard in size, shape, weight, quality, or strength: *Bicycle tires are standardized. verb,* **stan dard ized, stan dard iz ing.**
stand ing (stan′ding), **1** position; reputation: *a person of good standing.* **2** duration: *a friendship o, long standing.* **3** straight up; erect: *standing timber.* **4** done from an erect position: *a standing jump.* **5** established; permanent: *a standing invitation, a standing army.* **6** not flowing; stagnant: *standing water.* 1,2 *noun,* 3-6 *adjective.*
stand point (stand′point′), point of view; mental attitude: *From my standpoint, you are wrong. noun.*
stand still (stand′stil′), a complete stop; halt. *noun.*
stank (stangk). See **stink.** *The dead fish stank. verb.*
stan za (stan′zə), group of lines of poetry, usually four or more, arranged according to a fixed plan; verse of a poem: *They sang the first and last stanzas of "America." noun.*
sta ple[1] (stā′pəl), **1** piece of metal with pointed ends bent into a U shape. Staples are driven into wood to hold a hook, pin, or bolt. **2** a bent piece of wire used to hold together papers or parts of a book. **3** fasten with staples: *staple pages together.* 1,2 *noun,* 3 *verb,* **sta pled, sta pling.**
sta ple[2] (stā′pəl), **1** the most important or principal article grown or manufactured in a place: *Cotton is the staple in many Southern states.* **2** most important; principal: *Bread is a staple food. Weather was their staple subject of conversation.* **3** raw material. 1,3 *noun,* 2 *adjective.*
star (stär), **1** any of the heavenly bodies appearing as bright points seen in the sky at night. **2** any heavenly body that is not the moon, a planet, comet, or meteor. **3** figure having usually five points, sometimes six, like these: ☆ ✩. **4** person having brilliant qualities: *an athletic star.* **5** a famous person in some art or profession, especially one who plays the lead in a performance: *a movie star.* **6** chief; best; leading; excellent: *the star player on a football team.* **7** be prominent; be a leading performer; excel: *She has starred in many motion pictures.* 1-5 *noun,* 6 *adjective,* 7 *verb,* **starred, star ring.**

star board (stär′bərd), **1** the right side of a ship, boat, or aircraft when you are facing forward. **2** on the right side of a ship, boat, or aircraft. 1 *noun*, 2 *adjective*.

starch (stärch), **1** a white, tasteless food substance. Potatoes, wheat, rice, and corn contain much starch. **2** preparation of it used to stiffen clothes or curtains. **3** stiffen (clothes or curtains) with starch. 1,2 *noun*, 3 *verb*.

starch y (stär′chē), **1** like starch; containing starch. **2** stiffened with starch. *adjective*, **starch i er, starch i est.**

stare (ster *or* star), **1** look long and directly with the eyes wide open. A person stares in wonder, surprise, stupidity, curiosity, or from rudeness. *The little girl stared at the toys in the window.* **2** a long and direct look with the eyes wide open. See picture. **3** be very striking or glaring: *His eyes stared with anger.* 1,3 *verb*, **stared, star ing;** 2 *noun*.

star fish (stär′fish′), a star-shaped sea animal with a flattened body. Starfish are not fish. See picture. *noun, plural* **star fish es** *or* **star fish.**

stark (stärk), **1** downright; complete: *That fool is talking stark nonsense.* **2** entirely; completely: *The boys went swimming stark naked.* **3** stiff: *The rat lay stark in death.* 1,3 *adjective*, 2 *adverb*.

star light (stär′līt′), **1** light from the stars. **2** lighted by the stars. 1 *noun*, 2 *adjective*.

star ling (stär′ling), a common European and American bird which nests about buildings and flies in large flocks. *noun*.

star lit (stär′lit′), lighted by the stars: *a starlit night. adjective.*

star ry (stär′ē), **1** lighted by stars; containing many stars: *a starry sky.* **2** shining like stars: *starry eyes. adjective,* **star ri er, star ri est.**

Stars and Stripes, the flag of the United States.

start (stärt), **1** begin to move, go, or act: *The train started on time.* **2** begin: *start reading a book.* **3** set going; put into action: *start a car, start a fire.* **4** setting in motion: *We pushed the car to give the motor a start.* **5** beginning to move, go, or act: *see a race from start to finish.* **6** move suddenly: *I started in surprise.* **7** a sudden movement; jerk: *I awoke with a start.* **8** come or rise suddenly; spring suddenly: *Tears started from her eyes.* 1-3,6,8 *verb*, 4,5,7 *noun*.

star tle (stär′tl), **1** frighten suddenly; surprise: *The dog jumped at the girl and startled her.* **2** move suddenly in fear or surprise. *verb,* **star tled, star tling.**

star va tion (stär vā′shən), suffering from extreme hunger; being starved: *Starvation caused his death. noun.*

starve (stärv), **1** die because of hunger. **2** suffer severely because of hunger. **3** weaken or kill with hunger: *The enemy starved the men in the fort into surrendering.* **4** feel very hungry. *verb,* **starved, starv ing.**

starve for, suffer from lack of: *That lonely child is starving for affection.*

stare

statue

starfish—about 4 inches (10 centimeters) across

state (stāt), **1** condition of a person or thing. Ice is water in a solid state. *The crowd was in a state of excitement. The house is in a bad state of repair.* **2** group of people occupying a given area and organized under a government; nation. **3** one of several organized political groups of people which together form a nation: *The state of Alaska is one of the United States.* **4** of or having to do with a state: *a state road, state police.* **5** position in life; rank: *a person of humble state.* **6** tell in speech or writing; express; say: *State your opinion of the new school rules.* **7** high style of living; dignity; pomp: *The royal family lived in great state.* **8** with ceremony; of ceremony: *state occasions, state robes.* 1-3,5,7 *noun,* 4,8 *adjective,* 6 *verb,* **stat ed, stat ing.**

stat ed (stā′tid), fixed; settled: *School begins daily at a stated time.* *adjective.*

state ly (stāt′lē), having dignity; grand; majestic: *The Capitol at Washington is a stately building.* *adjective,* **state li er, state li est.**

state ment (stāt′mənt), **1** something stated; account; report: *Her statement was correct.* **2** act of stating; manner of stating something: *The statement of an idea helps me to remember it.* *noun.*

states man (stāts′mən), person skilled in the management of public or national affairs. *noun, plural* **states men.**

stat ic (stat′ik), **1** at rest; standing still: *Life does not remain static, but changes constantly.* **2** electrical disturbances in the air. Static interferes with radio and television broadcasting by causing crackling sounds in the receiver. 1 *adjective,* 2 *noun.*

sta tion (stā′shən), **1** place to stand in; place which a person is appointed to occupy in the performance of some duty: *The policeman took his station at the corner.* **2** building or place used for a definite purpose. A place where soldiers live, a harbor for ships, and the police headquarters of a district are all called stations. **3** a regular stopping place: *the bus station.* **4** place or equipment for sending out or receiving programs or messages by radio or television. **5** place: *She stationed herself at the door to collect tickets. The soldier was stationed at Fort Hays.* **6** social position; rank: *A serf was a person of humble station in life.* 1-4,6 *noun,* 5 *verb.*

sta tion ar y (stā′shə ner′ē), **1** having a fixed station or place; not movable: *A factory engine is stationary.* **2** standing still; not moving: *A parked car is stationary.* **3** without change: *The population of this town has been stationary for ten years at about 5000 people.* *adjective.*

sta tion er y (stā′shə ner′ē), writing materials such as paper, cards, and envelopes. *noun.*

station wagon, a closed automobile with a rear door for loading and unloading and seats in the rear that can be folded down, for use as a light truck.

stat ue (stach′ü), image of a person or animal carved in stone or wood, cast in bronze, or modeled in clay or wax: *Nearly every city has a*

a hat	**i** it	**oi** oil	**ch** child	a in about
ā age	**ī** ice	**ou** out	**ng** long	e in taken
ä far	**o** hot	**u** cup	**sh** she	ə = i in pencil
e let	**ō** open	**u̇** put	**th** thin	o in lemon
ē equal	**ô** order	**ü** rule	**ŦH** then	u in circus
ėr term			**zh** measure	

statue of some famous person. See picture. *noun.*

stat ure (stach′ər), **1** height: *a young woman of average stature.* **2** development; physical, mental, or moral growth; accomplishment: *Thomas Jefferson was a man of great stature among his countrymen. noun.*

sta tus (stā′təs), **1** social or professional standing; position: *the status of a doctor.* **2** condition; state: *Diplomats are interested in the status of world affairs. noun.*

stat ute (stach′üt), a law: *The statutes for the United States are made by Congress. noun.*

staunch (stônch), **1** strong; firm: *staunch walls, a staunch defense.* **2** loyal; steadfast: *staunch friends, a staunch supporter of the law. adjective.*

stave (stāv), **1** one of the curved pieces of wood which form the sides of a barrel, tub, or the like. **2 stave off,** put off; keep back; delay or prevent: *The lost campers ate birds' eggs to stave off starvation.* 1 *noun,* 2 *verb,* **staved** or **stove, stav ing.**

staves (stāvz), **1** more than one staff. See **staff** (definitions 1 and 2). **2** more than one stave. *noun plural.*

stay[1] (stā), **1** remain; continue to be: *Stay still. Stay here till I tell you to move. The cat stayed out all night. Shall I go or stay?* **2** live for a while; dwell: *She is staying with her aunt for a few weeks.* **3** staying; stop; time spent: *a stay at the seashore.* **4** stop; halt: *We have no time to stay.* **5** put an end to for a while; satisfy: *He ate some bread and butter to stay his hunger till time for dinner.* **6** put off; hold back; delay: *The teacher stayed judgment till she could hear both sides.* **7** last; endure: *The runner was unable to stay to the final lap of the race.* 1,2,4-7 *verb,* 3 *noun.*

stay[2] (stā), support; prop; brace: *The oldest child was the family's stay. noun, verb.*

stay[3] (stā), **1** a strong rope, often made of wire, which supports the mast of a ship. **2** any rope or chain attached to something to steady it. *noun.*

stead (sted), place: *Our regular baby-sitter could not come, but sent her brother in her stead. noun.*

stand in good stead, be of advantage or service to: *My ability to swim stood me in good stead when the boat upset.*

stead fast (sted′fast′), firmly fixed; constant; not moving or changing: *a steadfast companion, a steadfast defender of liberty. adjective.*

stead i ly (sted′l ē), in a steady manner; firmly; uniformly. *adverb.*

stead i ness (sted′ē nis), being steady; firmness. *noun.*

stead y (sted′ē), **1** changing little; uniform; regular: *He is making steady progress at school.* **2** firmly fixed; firm; not swaying or shaking: *This*

post is steady as a rock. Hold the ladder steady.
3 not easily excited; calm: *steady nerves.* **4** having good habits; reliable: *He is a steady young man.* **5** make steady; keep steady: *Steady the ladder while I climb to the roof.* **6** become steady: *Our sails filled as the wind steadied from the east.* 1-4 *adjective,* **stead i er, stead i est;** 5,6 *verb,* **stead ied, stead y ing.**

steak (stāk), slice of meat or fish for broiling or frying. *Steak often means beefsteak. noun.*

steal (stēl), **1** take something that does not belong to one; take dishonestly: *Robbers stole the money.* **2** take, get, or do secretly: *She stole time from her lessons to read a story.* **3** take, get, or win by artful or charming ways: *The baby stole our hearts.* **4** move secretly or quietly: *She had stolen softly out of the house.* **5** in baseball, run to second, third, or home base, as the pitcher throws the ball to the catcher. **6** act of stealing. 1-5 *verb,* **stole, sto len, steal ing;** 6 *noun.*

stealth (stelth), secret or sly action: *He obtained the letter by stealth, taking it while nobody was in the room. noun.*

stealth y (stel'thē), done in a secret manner; secret; sly: *The cat crept in a stealthy way toward the bird. adjective,* **stealth i er, stealth i est.**

steam (stēm), **1** water in the form of vapor or gas. Boiling water gives off steam. Steam is used to produce electricity, and for heating and cooking. **2** give off steam: *The cup of coffee was steaming.* **3** move by steam: *The ship steamed off.* **4** cook, soften, or freshen by steam: *to steam vegetables.* **5** power; energy; force: *I have worked all day and am running out of steam.* 1,5 *noun,* 2-4 *verb.*

steam boat (stēm'bōt'), boat moved by steam. See picture. *noun.*

steam engine, engine worked by steam. Ships and generators which produce electricity may be driven by steam engines.

steam er (stē'mər), steamboat; steamship. *noun.*

steam roll er (stēm'rō'lər), a heavy roller, formerly run by steam but now usually by an engine burning gasoline or oil, used to crush and level materials in making roads. *noun.*

steam ship (stēm'ship'), ship moved by steam. *noun.*

steam shovel, machine for digging, formerly run by steam but now usually by an engine burning gasoline or oil.

steed (stēd), horse, especially a spirited riding horse or a war horse. *noun.*

steel (stēl), **1** iron mixed with carbon so that it is very hard, strong, and tough. Most tools are made from steel. **2** something made from steel. A sword or a rod of steel for sharpening knives can be called a steel. **3** made of steel. **4** make hard or strong like steel: *I tried to steel myself against possible failure.* 1,2 *noun,* 3 *adjective,* 4 *verb.*

steel wool, a mass or pad of long, fine steel threads. Steel wool is used in cleaning or polishing surfaces.

steep[1] (stēp), **1** having a sharp slope; almost straight up and down: *The hill is steep.*

2 unreasonable: *a steep price. adjective.*

steep[2] (stēp), soak: *Let the tea steep in boiling water for five minutes. verb.*

stee ple (stē'pəl), a high tower on a church. Steeples usually have spires. *noun.*

steer[1] (stir), **1** guide the course of: *steer a car.* **2** be guided: *This car steers easily.* **3** direct one's way or course: *Steer for the harbor. Steer away from trouble. verb.*

steer[2] (stir), a young male of beef cattle, usually two to four years old, that cannot father young. *noun.*

stem[1] (stem), **1** the main part of a plant above the ground. The stem supports the branches. The trunk of a tree and the stalks of corn are stems. **2** part of a flower, a fruit, or a leaf that joins it to the plant or tree. **3** remove the stem from (a leaf, fruit, or vegetable). **4** anything like the stem of a plant: *the stem of a goblet, the stem of a pipe.* 1,2,4 *noun,* 3 *verb,* **stemmed, stem ming.**

stem from, come from; to have as a source or cause: *Our difficulties stem from poor planning.*

stem[2] (stem), **1** stop; check; dam up. **2** make progress against: *When you swim upstream you have to stem the current. verb,* **stemmed, stem ming.**

sten cil (sten'səl), **1** a thin sheet of metal, paper, or cardboard, having letters or designs cut through it. When it is laid on a surface and ink or color is spread on, these letters or designs are made on the surface. **2** mark, paint, or make with a stencil: *to stencil one's name on a box.* 1 *noun,* 2 *verb.*

step (step), **1** a movement made by lifting the foot and putting it down again in a new position; one motion of the leg in walking, running, or dancing. **2** distance covered by one such movement: *I was three steps from the phone when it stopped ringing.* **3** move the legs as in walking, running, or dancing: *Step lively!* **4** a short distance; little way: *The school is only a step from our house.* **5** walk a short distance: *Step this way.* **6** way of walking or dancing: *a quick step.* **7** measure (off) by taking steps: *Step off the distance from the door to the window.* **8** put the foot down: *Don't step on that bug.* **9** sound made by putting the foot down: *I hear steps upstairs.* **10** place for the foot in going up or coming down. A stair or a rung of a ladder is a step. **11** footprint: *I see steps in the mud.* **12** degree in a scale; grade in rank: *A colonel is two steps above a captain.* 1,2,4,6,9-12 *noun,* 3,5,7,8 *verb,* **stepped, step ping.**

in step, 1 making one's steps fit those of another person or persons. **2** making one's actions or ideas agree with those of another person or persons.

keep step, move the same leg at the same time that another person does.

out of step, not in step.

step up, make go faster or higher; increase: *step up the production of automobiles, step up the pressure in a boiler.*

take steps, put into effect or carry out measures

considered to be necessary or desirable: *The principal took steps to stop needless absence from school.*

step fa ther (step′fä′ᵺər), man who has married one's mother after the death or divorce of one's real father. *noun.*

step lad der (step′lad′ər), ladder with flat steps instead of rungs. *noun.*

step moth er (step′muᵺ′ər), woman who has married one's father after the death or divorce of one's real mother. *noun.*

ster e o (ster′ē ō *or* stir′ē ō), a record player giving the effect of lifelike sound by using two or more sets of equipment. *noun, plural* **ster e os.**

ster ile (ster′əl), **1** free from living germs: *Bandages should be kept sterile.* **2** barren; not fertile: *Sterile land does not produce good crops. adjective.*

ster i lize (ster′ə līz), make free from living germs: *The water had to be sterilized by boiling to make it fit to drink. verb,* **ster i lized, ster i liz ing.**

ster ling (stèr′ling), **1** containing 92.5 per cent pure silver. *Sterling* is stamped on solid silver knives, forks, spoons, and jewelry. **2** genuine; reliable: *A job with so many responsibilities requires a person of sterling character.* **3** British money: *pay in sterling.* **4** of British money; payable in British money. 1,2,4 *adjective,* 3 *noun.*

stern¹ (stèrn), **1** severe; strict; harsh: *Our teacher's stern frown silenced us.* **2** hard; not yielding; firm: *stern necessity. adjective.*

stern² (stèrn), the rear part of a ship, boat, or aircraft. *noun.*

steth o scope (steth′ə skōp), instrument used by doctors when listening to sounds in the lungs, heart, or other part of the body. See picture. *noun.*

stew (stü *or* styü), **1** cook by slow boiling: *The cook stewed the chicken for a long time.* **2** food cooked by slow boiling: *beef stew.* 1 *verb,* 2 *noun.*

stew ard (stü′ərd *or* styü′ərd), **1** person who has charge of the food and table service for a club, ship, railroad train, airplane, or bus. **2** man employed on a ship or airplane to wait upon passengers. **3** person who manages another's property: *He is the steward of that great estate. noun.*

stew ard ess (stü′ər dis *or* styü′ər dis), woman employed on a ship or airplane to wait upon passengers. *noun, plural* **stew ard ess es.**

stick¹ (stik), **1** a long, thin piece of wood: *Put some sticks on the fire.* **2** such a piece of wood shaped for a special use: *a walking stick.* **3** something like a stick in shape: *a stick of candy. noun.*

stick² (stik), **1** pierce with a pointed instrument; stab: *She stuck her fork into the potato.* **2** fasten by thrusting the point or end into or through something: *He stuck a flower in his buttonhole.* **3** put into a position: *Don't stick your head out of the window.* **4** be thrust; extend from, out of, through, or up: *The sweater shrunk so that my arms stick out of the sleeves.* **5** fasten; attach: *Stick a stamp on the letter.* **6** keep close: *The puppy stuck to my heels.* **7** be or become fastened; become fixed; be at a standstill: *Our car stuck in the mud. Two*

a hat	**i** it	**oi** oil	**ch** child	a in about
ā age	**ī** ice	**ou** out	**ng** long	e in taken
ä far	**o** hot	**u** cup	**sh** she	ə = i in pencil
e let	**ō** open	**ù** put	**th** thin	o in lemon
ē equal	**ô** order	**ü** rule	**ᵺ** then	u in circus
ėr term			**zh** measure	

pages of the book stuck together. **8** bring to a stop: *Our work was stuck by the breakdown of the machinery.* **9** keep on; hold fast: *Let's stick to the task until we've finished it.* **10** puzzle: *That problem in arithmetic stuck me.* **11** take advantage of; burden: *I got stuck washing dishes when everyone else went out. verb,* **stuck, stick ing.**

stick up for, stand up for; support; defend.

stick er (stik′ər), a label that has gum or glue on the back of it so that it can be fastened to something. *noun.*

stethoscope—veterinarian using a stethoscope

steamboats

stick y (stik′ē), **1** that sticks: *sticky glue.* **2** that makes things stick: *sticky paper to catch flies.* adjective, **stick i er, stick i est.**

stiff (stif), **1** not easily bent: *He wore a stiff collar.* **2** hard to move: *The old hinges on the barn door are stiff.* **3** not able to move easily: *My neck is stiff.* **4** firm: *Beat the egg whites until they are stiff.* **5** not easy or natural in manner; formal: *The magician made a stiff bow to the audience. This author writes in a stiff style.* **6** strong: *a stiff breeze.* **7** hard to deal with; hard: *a stiff test.* **8** more than seems suitable: *They are asking a stiff price for their house. adjective.*

stiff en (stif′ən), make or become stiff: *I stiffened the shirt with starch. She stiffened with anger. The wind is stiffening. verb.*

sti fle (stī′fəl), **1** stop the breath of; smother: *The smoke stifled the firefighters.* **2** be unable to breathe freely: *I am stifling in this close room.* **3** keep back; stop; suppress: *stifle a cry, stifle a yawn, stifle business activity. verb,* **sti fled, sti fling.**

stig ma (stig′mə), **1** mark of disgrace or shame. **2** part of the pistil of a plant which receives the pollen. *noun.*

stile (stīl), **1** step or steps for getting over a fence or wall. **2** turnstile. *noun.*

still (stil), **1** without motion: *Sit still. The lake is still today.* **2** without noise; quiet: *a still night. The room was so still that you could have heard a pin drop.* **3** make or become quiet: *I stilled the crying baby. The storm stilled.* **4** even; yet: *You can read still better if you will try.* **5** and yet; but yet; nevertheless: *He was hungry; still he would not eat.* **6** even to this time; even to that time: *Was the store still open?* 1,2 *adjective,* 3 *verb,* 4-6 *adverb,* 5 *conjunction.*

stilt (stilt), one of a pair of poles, each with a support for the foot at some distance above the ground. Stilts are used in walking through shallow water, or by children for amusement. *noun.*

stilt ed (stil′tid), stiffly dignified: *a stilted manner of speaking. adjective.*

stim u lant (stim′yə lənt), **1** food, drug, or medicine that speeds up the activity of the body or some part of the body for a short time. Tea and coffee are stimulants. **2** something that excites, stirs, or stimulates: *Advertising is a stimulant to sales. noun.*

stim u late (stim′yə lāt), spur on; stir up; rouse to action: *The new factory helped to stimulate growth in the town. verb,* **stim u lat ed, stim u lat ing.**

stim u lus (stim′yə ləs), something that stirs to action or effort: *Ambition is a great stimulus. noun, plural* **stim u li** (stim′yə lī).

sting (sting), **1** prick with a small point; wound: *Bees, wasps, and hornets sting. A bee stung her.* **2** prick; wound: *She put mud on the sting to take away the pain.* **3** the sharp-pointed part of an insect, animal, or plant that pricks or wounds and often poisons. **4** pain sharply: *I was stung by the insult.* **5** sharp pain: *The ball team felt the sting of defeat.* **6** cause a feeling like that of a sting: *Mustard stings the tongue.* 1,4,6 *verb,* **stung, sting ing;** 2,3,5 *noun.*

sting er (sting′ər), **1** part of an insect or animal that stings. **2** anything that stings. *noun.*

stin gi ness (stin′jē nis), meanness about spending or giving money. *noun.*

stin gy (stin′jē), mean about spending or giving money: *He tried to save money without being stingy. adjective,* **stin gi er, stin gi est.**

stink (stingk), **1** a very bad smell. **2** have a bad smell: *Decaying fish stink.* 1 *noun,* 2 *verb,* **stank** or **stunk, stunk, stink ing.**

stint (stint), **1** keep on short allowance; be saving or careful in using or spending; limit: *The parents stinted themselves on food to give it to the children.* **2** limit: *That generous man gives without stint.* **3** task assigned: *She did a stint as a reporter for the local newspaper.* 1 *verb,* 2,3 *noun.*

stir (stėr), **1** move: *The wind stirs the leaves.* **2** move about: *No one was stirring in the house.* **3** mix by moving around with a spoon, fork, stick, or some other implement or device: *Stir the sugar in the lemonade.* **4** affect strongly; set going; excite: *The ghost story stirred our imaginations.* **5** movement: *There was a stir in the bushes where the children were hiding.* **6** excitement: *The queen's coming caused a great stir.* **7** act of stirring: *Give the mixture a hard stir.* 1-4 *verb,* **stirred, stir ring;** 5-7 *noun.*

stir ring (stėr′ing), **1** moving; active; lively: *stirring times.* **2** rousing; exciting: *a stirring speech. adjective.*

stir rup (stėr′əp), support for the rider's foot, that hangs from a saddle. See picture. *noun.*

stitch (stich), **1** one complete movement of a threaded needle through cloth in sewing: *Take short stitches.* **2** one complete movement in knitting, crocheting, or embroidering. **3** loop of thread or yarn made by a stitch: *Rip out these long stitches. The doctor took the stitches out of my cut.* **4** make stitches in; fasten with stitches: *I stitched a patch on my jeans. The doctor stitched the cut.* **5** sew. 1-3 *noun, plural* **stitch es;** 4,5 *verb.*

stock (stok), **1** things for use or for sale; supply used as it is needed: *This store keeps a large stock of toys.* **2** cattle or other farm animals; livestock: *The farm was sold with all its stock.* **3** lay in a supply of; supply: *Our camp is well stocked with food for a short stay.* **4** keep regularly for use or for sale: *A toy store stocks toys.* **5** kept on hand regularly for use or for sale: *Nails and screws are stock items in a hardware store.* **6** in common use; commonplace; everyday: *The weather is a stock subject of conversation.* **7** shares in a company. The profits of a company are divided among the owners of stock. **8** people who have come from the same ancestor; family: *The senator is from old New England stock.* **9** part used as a support or handle: *the stock of a rifle.* **10** trunk or stump of a tree; main stem of a plant. **11 the stocks,** a framework with holes for the feet, and sometimes for the hands, used as a punishment. See picture. 1,2,7-11 *noun,* 3,4 *verb,* 5,6 *adjective.*

in stock, on hand; ready for use or sale.

out of stock, no longer on hand; lacking.

stock ade (sto kād′), defense or pen made of

large, strong posts fixed upright in the ground: *A heavy stockade around the cabins protected the pioneers from attack.* noun.

stock ing (stok′ing), a close-fitting knitted covering of wool, cotton, silk, nylon, or other fabric for the foot and leg. noun.

stock y (stok′ē), having a solid or sturdy form or build; thick for its height: *a stocky little child, a stocky building.* adjective, **stock i er, stock i est.**

stock yard (stok′yärd′), place with pens and sheds for cattle, sheep, hogs, and horses, often connected with a railroad or market. noun.

stole (stōl). See **steal.** *Who stole my money?* verb.

sto len (stō′lən). See **steal.** *The money was stolen by a thief.* verb.

stom ach (stum′ək), **1** the large muscular bag in the body which first receives the food, and digests some of it before passing it on to the intestines. **2** part of the body containing the stomach: *The ball hit me in the stomach.* **3** appetite. **4** put up with; bear; endure: *I cannot stomach violent movies.* **5** liking: *I have no stomach for killing harmless creatures.* 1-3,5 noun, 4 verb.

stirrup on a Western saddle

stock (definition 11)—the stocks

stomp (stomp), **1** to stamp with the foot: *The crowd cheered and stomped.* **2** such a stamping: *the stomp of heavy boots.* 1 verb, 2 noun.

stone (stōn), **1** the hard mineral matter of which rocks are made up; hard matter that is not metal. Stone, such as granite and marble, is much used in building. **2** piece of rock: *The children threw stones into the pond.* **3** made of stone: *a stone wall, a stone house.* **4** having something to do with stone. **5** gem; jewel: *The royal diamonds are fine stones.* **6** throw stones at; drive by throwing stones: *The cruel children stoned the dog.* **7** a hard seed: *peach stones.* **8** take stones or seeds out of: *stone cherries.* 1,2,5,7 noun, 3,4 adjective, 6,8 verb, **stoned, ston ing.**

Stone Age, the earliest known period of human culture, in which people used tools and weapons made from stone.

ston y (stō′nē), **1** having many stones: *The beach is stony.* **2** without expression or feeling: *a stony stare.* adjective, **ston i er, ston i est.**

stood (stu̇d). See **stand.** *I stood on the corner for five minutes. I had stood in line all morning to buy tickets to the game.* verb.

stool (stül), **1** seat without back or arms. **2** a similar article used to rest the feet on. noun.

stoop[1] (stüp), **1** bend forward: *I stooped to pick up the money.* **2** a forward bend: *She walks with a stoop.* **3** carry head and shoulders bent forward: *The old man stoops.* **4** lower oneself; descend: *He stooped to cheating.* 1,3,4 verb, 2 noun.

stoop[2] (stüp), porch or platform at the entrance of a house. noun.

stop (stop), **1** keep (from moving, acting, doing, being, or working): *I stopped the child from breaking the toy. I stopped the clock.* **2** put an end to; check: *stop a noise.* **3** stay; halt: *She stopped at the bank for a few minutes.* **4** come to an end; cease; leave off (moving, acting, doing, being, or working): *The baby stopped crying. The rain is stopping.* **5** close (a hole or opening) by filling (it): *I stopped up the hole in the boat.* **6** block (a way); obstruct: *A big box stops up the doorway.* **7** act of stopping; closing; filling up; blocking; hindering; checking: *Her sudden stop startled us. The singing came to a stop.* **8** place where a stop is made: *a bus stop.* **9** thing that stops, such as a cork, block, or plug. **10** device that controls the pitch of a musical instrument. 1-6 verb, **stopped, stop ping;** 7-10 noun.

stop light (stop′līt′), **1** a red light at the rear end of a vehicle, that turns on when the brakes are put on. **2** traffic light. noun.

stop page (stop′ij), act of stopping: *The foreman called for a stoppage of operations to oil the machinery.* noun.

stop per (stop/ər), plug or cork for closing the opening of a bottle, tube, or container. *noun.*

stop watch (stop/woch/), watch which has a hand that can be stopped or started at any instant. A stopwatch indicates fractions of a second and is used for timing races. *noun, plural* **stop watch es.**

stor age (stôr/ij), **1** act or fact of storing goods: *the storage of furs in summertime.* **2** condition of being stored. Cold storage is used to keep eggs and meat from spoiling. **3** place for storing: *She has put her furniture in storage. noun.*

storage battery, a battery that can be charged again, after it has discharged its electricity, by passing an electric current through it. Automobiles have storage batteries.

store (stôr), **1** place where goods are kept for sale: *a clothing store.* **2** something put away for use later; supply; stock: *We put up stores of preserves and jellies every year.* **3** put away for use later; lay up: *The squirrel stores away nuts.* 1,2 *noun,* 3 *verb,* **stored, stor ing.**
in store, on hand; saved for the future.

store house (stôr/hous/), place where things are stored: *The factory has many storehouses for its products. A library is a storehouse of information. noun, plural* **store hous es** (stôr/hou/ziz).

store keep er (stôr/kē/pər), person who has charge of a store. *noun.*

store room (stôr/rüm/), room where things are stored. *noun.*

stork (stôrk), a large bird with long legs, a long neck, and a long bill. Storks are found in most warm parts of the world. See picture. *noun.*

storm (stôrm), **1** a strong wind with rain, snow, hail, or thunder and lightning. In deserts there are storms of sand. **2** a heavy fall of rain, snow, or hail; violent outbreak of thunder and lightning. **3** blow hard; rain; snow; hail. **4** violent outburst or disturbance: *a storm of tears, a storm of angry words.* **5** be violent; rage. **6** rush violently: *I stormed from the room in anger.* **7** attack violently: *The enemy stormed the castle.* **8** violent attack: *The castle was taken by storm.* 1,2,4,8 *noun,* 3,5-7 *verb.*

storm y (stôr/mē), **1** having storms; likely to have storms; troubled by storms: *a stormy sea, stormy weather, a stormy night.* **2** rough and disturbed; violent: *They had stormy quarrels. adjective,* **storm i er, storm i est.**

sto ry¹ (stôr/ē), **1** account of some happening or group of happenings: *Tell us the story of your life.* **2** such an account, either true or made-up, intended to interest the reader or hearer; tale: *fairy stories, stories of adventure.* **3** falsehood: *That's not true; you're telling stories. noun, plural* **sto ries.**

sto ry² (stôr/ē), set of rooms on the same level or floor of a building: *That house has two stories. noun, plural* **sto ries.**

stout (stout), **1** fat and large: *That boy could run faster if he weren't so stout.* **2** strongly built; firm; strong: *The fort has stout walls.* **3** brave; bold: *Robin Hood was a stout fellow. adjective.*

stove¹ (stōv), apparatus for cooking and heating. There are wood, coal, gas, oil, and electric stoves. *noun.*

stove² (stōv). See **stave.** *They barely stove off starvation when they were lost in the forest. verb.*

stove pipe (stōv/pīp/), a metal pipe that carries smoke and gases from a stove to a chimney. *noun.*

stow (stō), **1** pack: *The cargo was stowed in the ship's hold.* **2** pack things closely in; fill by packing: *The girls stowed their packs with supplies for the hike. verb.*
stow away, hide on a ship, airplane, train, or bus to get a free ride or to make an escape.

stow a way (stō/ə wā/), person who hides on a ship, airplane, train, or bus to get a free passage or to make an escape. *noun.*

strad dle (strad/l), **1** walk, stand, or sit with the legs wide apart: *straddle over a fence watching cars go by.* **2** have a leg on each side of (a horse, bicycle, chair, ditch, or the like). *verb,* **strad dled, strad dling.**

strag gle (strag/əl), **1** wander in a scattered fashion: *Cows straggled along the lane.* **2** spread in an irregular, rambling manner: *Vines straggled over the yard. It was a straggling little town. verb,* **strag gled, strag gling.**

straight (strāt), **1** without a bend or curve: *a straight line, a straight path, straight hair.* **2** in a line; directly: *Walk straight. Go straight home.* **3** going in a line; direct: *a straight course, a straight aim or throw.* **4** frank; honest; upright: *a straight answer.* **5** frankly; honestly; uprightly: *Live straight.* **6** right; correct: *straight thinking, a straight thinker.* **7** in proper order or condition: *Set the room straight. Our accounts are straight.* **8** showing no emotion or humor: *I kept a straight face, though I wanted to laugh.* 1,3,4,6-8 *adjective,* 2,5 *adverb.*
straight away or **straight off,** at once.

straight en (strāt/n), **1** make straight: *He straightened the bent pin. Straighten your shoulders.* **2** become straight. **3** put in the proper order or condition: *straighten out accounts. Straighten up your room. verb.*

straight for ward (strāt/fôr/wərd), **1** honest; frank: *a straightforward answer.* **2** going straight ahead; direct. *adjective.*

straight way (strāt/wā/), at once; immediately: *I will leave straightway. adverb.*

strain¹ (strān), **1** draw tight; stretch: *The weight strained the rope.* **2** pull hard: *The dog strained at its leash.* **3** force or weight that stretches: *The strain on the rope made it break.* **4** stretch as much as possible: *She strained the truth in telling that story.* **5** use to the utmost. See picture. **6** injure by too much effort or by stretching: *The runner strained her leg.* **7** injury caused by too much effort or by stretching: *The injury to his back was only a slight strain.* **8** any severe or wearing pressure: *The strain of overwork can make you ill.* **9** effect of such pressure on the body or mind. **10** press or pour through a strainer: *Babies eat food that has been strained.* **11** part of a piece of music; melody; song. 1,2,4-6,10 *verb,* 3,7-9,11 *noun.*

strain[2] (strān), **1** family line; stock: *I am proud of my Irish strain.* **2** an inherited quality: *There is a strain of musical talent in that family.* **3** trace or streak: *That horse has a mean strain.* *noun.*

strain er (strā′nər), thing that strains. A filter and a sieve are strainers. *noun.*

strait (strāt), **1** a narrow channel connecting two larger bodies of water: *The Strait of Gibraltar connects the Mediterranean Sea and the Atlantic Ocean.* **2 straits,** difficulty; need; distress: *The family is in desperate straits for money. noun.*

strand[1] (strand), **1** bring or come into a helpless position: *She was stranded a thousand miles from home with no money.* **2** run aground; drive on the shore: *The ship was stranded on the rocks. verb.*

strand[2] (strand), **1** one of the threads, strings, or wires that are twisted together to make a rope or cable: *This is a rope of three strands.* **2** thread or string: *a strand of hair, a strand of pearls. noun.*

strange (strānj), **1** unusual; queer; peculiar: *a strange experience, strange clothing, a strange quiet.* **2** not known, seen, or heard of before; not familiar: *She is moving to a strange place. A strange cat is on our steps.* **3** not used to: *He is strange to the work but will soon learn.* **4** out of place; not at home: *The poor child felt strange in the palace. adjective,* **strang er, strang est.**

stran ger (strān′jər), **1** person not known, seen, or heard of before: *She is a stranger to us.* **2** person or thing new to a place: *I am a stranger in New York.* **3** person from another country: *The king received the strangers with kindness. noun.*

stran gle (strang′gəl), **1** kill by squeezing the throat to stop the breath. **2** choke; suffocate: *This tight collar is nearly strangling me. verb,* **stran gled, stran gling.**

strap (strap), **1** a narrow strip of leather, cloth, or other material used for fastening things or holding things together: *Put a strap around the trunk. The strap on my sandal broke.* **2** fasten with a strap: *We strapped the trunk.* **3** beat with a strap. **1** *noun,* **2,3** *verb,* **strapped, strap ping.**

strap ping (strap′ing), tall, strong, and healthy: *a fine, strapping youngster. adjective.*

stra ta (strā′tə). See **stratum.** *noun plural.*

strat a gem (strat′ə jəm), scheme or trick for deceiving the enemy; trick; trickery: *The spy got into the castle by the stratagem of dressing as a beggar. noun.*

stra te gic (strə tē′jik), **1** of strategy; based on strategy; useful in strategy: *a strategic retreat.* **2** important in strategy: *The Panama Canal is a strategic link in our national defense. adjective.*

strat e gy (strat′ə jē), **1** planning and directing of military movements and operations. **2** the skillful planning and management of anything: *Strategy helped our team win the game. noun, plural* **strat e gies.**

stra tum (strā′təm), layer of material, especially one of several parallel layers placed one upon another: *In digging the well, the men struck first a stratum of sand, then several strata of rock.* See picture. *noun, plural* **stra ta** *or* **stra tums.**

stork—about 3 feet (1 meter) high

strain[1] (definition 5)—The runners strained every muscle to reach the finish line.

stratum—Many different strata of rock were visible in the canyon walls.

straw (strô), **1** the stalks or stems of grain after drying and threshing. Straw is used for bedding for horses and cows, for making hats, and for many other purposes. **2** hollow stem or stalk; something like it. Straws made of plastic or waxed paper are used for sucking up drinks. **3** made of straw: *a straw hat.* **1,2** *noun,* **3** *adjective.*

straw ber ry (strô′ber′ē), the small, juicy, red fruit of a plant that grows close to the ground. Strawberries are good to eat. *noun, plural* **straw ber ries.**

stray (strā), **1** lose one's way; wander; roam: *Our dog has strayed off somewhere.* **2** wandering; lost: *A stray cat is crying at the door.* **3** wanderer; lost animal: *That cat is a stray that we took in.* **4** scattered; here and there: *The beach was empty except for a few stray swimmers.* **1** *verb,* **2,4** *adjective,* **3** *noun.*

streak (strēk), **1** a long, thin mark or line: *You have a streak of dirt on your face. We saw the streaks of lightning.* **2** layer: *Bacon has streaks of fat and streaks of lean.* **3** vein; strain; element: *Watch out for her mean streak.* **4** put long, thin marks or lines on: *The children streaked their faces with watercolors.* **5** a short period: *a streak of bad luck.* **6** move very fast; go at full speed: *She streaked past us to win the race.* **1-3,5** *noun,* **4,6** *verb.*
like a streak, very fast: *When her dog saw her, it ran like a streak to greet her.*

stream (strēm), **1** flow of water in a channel or bed. Small rivers and large brooks are both called streams. *Because of the lack of rain many streams dried up.* **2** any steady flow: *a stream of lava, a stream of light, a stream of words.* **3** flow: *Rain water streamed down the gutters.* **4** move steadily; move swiftly: *The crowd streamed out of the theater.* **5** float or wave: *The flags streamed in the wind.* **1,2** *noun,* **3-5** *verb.*

stream er (strē′mər), **1** any long, narrow flowing thing: *Streamers of colored paper decorated the gym for the dance.* **2** a long, narrow flag. *noun.*

stream line (strēm′līn′), **1** streamlined: *a streamline racing car.* **2** give a streamlined shape to. **3** bring up to date; make more efficient: *to streamline train service between Chicago and New York.* **1** *adjective,* **2,3** *verb,* **stream lined, stream lin ing.**

stream lined (strēm′līnd′), having a shape that offers the least possible resistance to air or water. The fastest automobiles, airplanes, and trains have streamlined bodies. See picture. *adjective.*

street (strēt), **1** road in a city or town, usually with buildings on both sides. **2** people who live in the buildings on a street: *The whole street came to the party.* **3** place or way for automobile and other traffic to go: *Be careful crossing the street. noun.*

street car (strēt′kär′), car that runs on rails in the streets and carries passengers. *noun.*

strength (strengkth), **1** quality of being strong; power; force; vigor: *I do not have the strength to lift that heavy box. Steel is valued for its strength.* **2** degree of strength; intensity: *Some flavorings lose their strength in cooking. noun.*

on the strength of, relying on: *My parents bought me the dog on the strength of my promise to take care of it.*

strength en (strengk′thən), make or grow stronger: *Daily exercise strengthens my muscles. verb.*

stren u ous (stren′yü əs), **1** very active: *We had a strenuous day moving into our new house.* **2** full of energy: *Beavers are strenuous workers.* **3** needing much energy or effort: *Running is strenuous exercise. adjective.*

strep throat (strep′ thrōt′), a serious throat inflammation caused by bacteria and producing fever, aching muscles, and headache.

stress (stres), **1** pressure; force; strain: *The stress on the rope caused it to break. Under the stress of being in front of an audience I forgot my lines.* **2** put pressure upon. **3** emphasis; importance: *That school lays stress upon arithmetic and reading.* **4** lay stress on; emphasize: *Stress the important words of a sentence.* **5** the greater force or stronger tone of voice given to certain syllables or words; accent. In *hero,* the stress is on the first syllable. **6** pronounce with stress: *"Accept" is stressed on the second syllable.* **1,3,5** *noun, plural* **stress es;** **2,4,6** *verb.*

stretch (strech), **1** draw out; extend to full length: *The bird stretched its wings. She stretched herself out on the grass to rest.* **2** extend one's body or arms and legs: *I stretched out on the couch.* **3** continue over a distance; extend from one place to another; fill space; spread: *The forest stretches for miles.* **4** reach out; hold out: *The child stretched out a hand for the candy.* **5** draw out to greater size: *Stretch this shoe a little.* **6** become longer or wider without breaking: *Rubber stretches.* **7** draw tight; strain: *to stretch a rubber band until it breaks.* **8** exaggerate: *stretch the truth.* **9** an unbroken length; extent: *A stretch of sand hills lay between the road and the ocean.* **10** act of stretching; condition of being stretched: *With a stretch I was able to reach the high shelf.* **1-8** *verb,* **9,10** *noun.*

stretch er (strech′ər), canvas stretched on a frame for carrying the sick, wounded, or dead. *noun.*

strew (strü), **1** scatter; sprinkle: *She strewed seeds in her garden.* **2** cover with something scattered or sprinkled: *In fall the ground was strewn with colorful leaves. verb,* **strewed, strewed** or **strewn, strew ing.**

strewn (strün), strewed. See **strew.** *verb.*

streamlined

strick en (strik/ən), **1** hit, wounded, or affected by (a weapon, disease, trouble, sorrow, or the like): *a stricken deer. They fled from the stricken city. The stricken man was taken immediately to a hospital.* **2** struck. See **strike.** 1 *adjective,* 2 *verb.*

stricken in years, old.

strict (strikt), **1** very careful in following a rule or in making others follow it: *Our teacher is strict but fair.* **2** harsh; severe: *a strict parent, strict discipline.* **3** exact; precise: *He told the strict truth.* **4** perfect; complete; absolute: *The secret was told in strict confidence. adjective.*

strid den (strid/n). See **stride.** *He had stridden away angrily. verb.*

stride (strīd), **1** walk with long steps: *She strode rapidly down the street.* **2** pass with one long step: *I strode over the brook.* **3** long step: *The child could not keep up with his father's stride.* **4** sit or stand with one leg on each side of: *stride a fence.* 1,2,4 *verb,* **strode, strid den, strid ing;** 3 *noun.*

strife (strīf), quarreling; fighting: *bitter strife between rivals. noun.*

strike (strīk), **1** hit: *to strike a person in anger. The ship struck a rock.* **2** give; deal forth or out: *to strike a blow in self-defense.* **3** set or be set on fire by hitting or rubbing: *Strike a match.* **4** have a strong effect on the mind or feelings of; impress: *The plan strikes me as silly.* **5** sound: *The clock strikes twelve times at noon.* **6** find or come upon suddenly: *After years of prospecting the old man finally struck gold.* **7** sudden success in finding rich ore in mining or oil in boring: *They made a rich strike in the Yukon.* **8** stop work to get better pay, shorter hours, or to force an employer to meet some other demand: *The coal miners struck when the company refused to improve safety conditions in the mines.* **9** stopping work in this way: *The workers were home for six weeks during the strike last year.* **10** baseball pitched over the plate and between the batter's shoulders and knees. A strike is called by the umpire when the batter does not swing at such a pitch, or if he swings at any pitch and misses, or if he hits a foul ball. 1-6,8 *verb,* **struck, struck** or **strick en, strik ing;** 7,9,10 *noun.*

on strike, stopping work to get more pay, shorter hours, or to force an employer to meet some other demand: *Most of the workers voted to go on strike.*

strike out, 1 cross out; rub out. **2** in baseball, put out or be put out on three strikes: *Two batters struck out. The pitcher struck out six batters.*

strike up, begin: *The two girls struck up a friendship.*

strik ing (strī/king), **1** attracting attention; very noticeable: *a striking color, a striking performance.* **2** on strike: *The striking miners will soon return to work. adjective.*

string (string), **1** a small cord or very thin rope: *The package is tied with red string.* **2** cord or thread with things on it: *She wore a string of beads around her neck.* **3** put on a string: *The child is stringing beads.* **4** a special cord for musical instruments or bows: *the strings of a violin.* **5 strings,** violins,

a hat	i it	oi oil	ch child	a in about
ā age	ī ice	ou out	ng long	e in taken
ä far	o hot	u cup	sh she	ə = { i in pencil
e let	ō open	u̇ put	th thin	o in lemon
ē equal	ô order	ü rule	ŦH then	u in circus
ėr term			zh measure	

cellos, and other stringed instruments. **6** furnish with strings: *She had her tennis racket strung.* **7** anything used for tying: *apron strings.* **8** tie with string or rope; hang with a string or rope: *We dry herbs by stringing them from rafters in the barn.* **9** number of things in a line or row: *A string of cars came down the street.* 1,2,4,5,7,9 *noun,* 3,6,8 *verb,* **strung, strung** or **stringed, string ing.**

string out, stretch; extend: *The program was strung out too long.*

string bean, a long, green or yellow pod containing smooth, somewhat flat seeds. String beans grow on bushes·or vines and are eaten as a vegetable.

stringed in stru ment (stringd/ in/strə mənt), a musical instrument having strings. A harp, a violin, and a guitar are stringed instruments.

string y (string/ē), like a string or strings. *adjective,* **string i er, string i est.**

strip¹ (strip), **1** make bare or naked; undress. **2** take off the covering of: *The boy stripped the banana by taking off the skin.* **3** take away: *The birds stripped the fruit from the trees.* **4** rob: *Thieves stripped the house of everything valuable.* **5** tear off the teeth of (a gear). *verb,* **stripped, strip ping.**

strip² (strip), a long, narrow, flat piece (of cloth, paper, bark, or the like). *noun.*

stripe (strīp), **1** a long, narrow band. The stripes on a uniform show a person's rank. *A tiger has stripes. The American flag has thirteen stripes.* **2** mark with stripes: *The stick of candy was striped with red.* 1 *noun,* 2 *verb,* **striped, strip ing.**

striped (strīpt), having stripes; marked with stripes: *Zebras are striped. adjective.*

strive (strīv), **1** try hard; work hard: *Strive to succeed.* **2** struggle; fight: *The swimmer strove against the tide. verb,* **strove** or **strived, striv en, striv ing.**

striv en (striv/ən). See **strive.** *She has striven hard to make the business a success. verb.*

strode (strōd). See **stride.** *He strode into the room. verb.*

stroke¹ (strōk), **1** act of striking; blow: *I drove in the nail with several strokes of the hammer. The house was hit by a stroke of lightning.* **2** sound made by striking: *We arrived at the stroke of three o'clock.* **3** a single complete movement to be made again and again: *He rowed with a strong stroke of the oars.* **4** movement or mark made by a pen, pencil, or brush: *She writes with a heavy down stroke.* **5** a very successful effort; feat: *a stroke of genius.* **6** a single effort; act: *I felt lazy and didn't do a stroke of work all day.* **7** a sudden attack of illness, especially a paralysis caused by injury to the brain when a blood vessel breaks or becomes blocked. *noun.*

stroke² (strōk), **1** move the hand gently along: *She* *likes to stroke her kitten.* **2** such a movement: *I brushed the crumbs away with one stroke.* 1 *verb,* **stroked, strok ing;** 2 *noun.*

stroll (strōl), **1** take a quiet walk for pleasure; walk. **2** a leisurely walk: *We went for a stroll in the park.* **3** go from place to place: *strolling gypsies.* 1,3 *verb,* 2 *noun.*

strong (strông), having much strength, power, force, or vigor: *We need someone strong to move the piano. A strong wind blew down the trees. A strong nation has many able citizens and great resources. Strong tea has more flavor than weak tea.* adjective, **strong er** (strông′gər), **strong est** (strông′gəst).

strong hold (strông′hōld′), a strong place; safe place; fort: *The robbers have a stronghold in the mountains.* noun.

strove (strōv). See **strive.** *They strove hard, but did not win the game.* verb.

struck (struk). See **strike.** *The clock struck four. The barn was struck by lightning.* verb.

struc tur al (struk′chər əl), **1** used in building. Structural steel is steel made into beams and girders. **2** of or having to do with structure or structures: *Ferns and daisies have structural differences.* adjective.

struc ture (struk′chər). See picture. **1** a building; something built: *The city hall is a large stone structure.* **2** anything composed of parts arranged together: *The human body is a wonderful structure.* **3** way parts are put together; manner of building; construction: *The structure of the schoolhouse was excellent.* **4** arrangement of parts: *the structure of an atom, the structure of a flower.* noun.

strug gle (strug′əl), **1** make great efforts with the body; try hard; work hard against difficulties: *The poor have to struggle for a living. The swimmer struggled against the tide. I struggled to keep back my tears.* **2** great effort; hard work: *It was a struggle for the widow to send her six children to college. Making the baby eat his spinach is a struggle.* **3** fight: *The dog struggled fiercely with the wildcat.* **4** fighting; conflict: *The struggle between the two enemy countries went on for years.* 1,3 *verb,* **strug gled, strug gling;** 2,4 *noun.*

strum (strum), play by running the fingers lightly or carelessly across the strings or keys: *strum a guitar.* verb, **strummed, strum ming.**

strung (strung). See **string.** *The children strung along after the teacher. The vines had been strung on poles.* verb.

strut[1] (strut), **1** walk in a vain, important manner: *The rooster struts about the barnyard.* **2** a strutting walk. 1 *verb,* **strut ted, strut ting;** 2 *noun.*

strut[2] (strut), a supporting piece; brace. noun.

stub (stub), **1** a short piece that is left: *the stub of a pencil.* **2** strike (one's toe) against something: *I stubbed my toe on a rock.* 1 *noun,* 2 *verb,* **stubbed, stub bing.**

stub ble (stub′əl), **1** the lower ends of stalks of grain left in the ground after the grain is cut: *The stubble hurt her bare feet.* **2** any short, rough growth: *He had three days' stubble on his unshaven face.* noun.

structure (definitions 1, 2, and 4)

stub born (stub′ərn), **1** fixed in purpose or opinion; not giving in to argument or requests: *The stubborn boy refused to listen to reasons for not going out in the rain.* **2** hard to deal with: *a stubborn cough.* adjective.

stub by (stub′ē), short and thick: *stubby fingers.* adjective, **stub bi er, stub bi est.**

stuc co (stuk′ō), **1** plaster for covering the outer walls of buildings. **2** cover with stucco: *We had our house stuccoed last year.* 1 *noun, plural* **stuc coes** or **stuc cos;** 2 *verb.*

stuck (stuk). See **stick²**. *She stuck out her tongue. We were stuck in the mud.* verb.

stud (stud), **1** head of a nail, knob, or the like, sticking out from a surface: *The belt was ornamented with silver studs.* **2** set with studs or something like studs: *The crown was studded with jewels.* **3** be set or scattered over: *Little islands studded the harbor.* 1 *noun,* 2,3 *verb,* **stud ded, stud ding.**

stu dent (stüd′nt *or* styüd′nt), **1** person who studies: *She is a student of birds.* **2** person who is studying in a school, college, or university: *That high school has 3000 students.* noun.

stu di o (stü′dē ō *or* styü′dē ō), **1** workroom of a painter, sculptor, photographer, or other artist. **2** place where motion pictures are made. **3** place from which a radio or television program is broadcast. *noun, plural* **stu di os.**

stu di ous (stü′dē əs *or* styü′dē əs), **1** fond of study: *That studious boy likes school.* **2** careful; thoughtful; showing careful consideration: *The clerk made a studious effort to please customers.* adjective.

stud y (stud′ē), **1** effort to learn by reading or thinking: *After an hour's hard study, I knew my lesson.* **2** try to learn: *She studied her spelling lesson for half an hour. He is studying to be a doctor.* **3** careful examination; investigation: *A careful study of the map showed us the shortest way home.* **4** examine carefully: *We studied the map to find the shortest road home.* **5** subject that is studied; branch of learning. *History, music, and law are studies.* **6** room for study, reading, or writing: *The author was at work in her study.* **7** consider with care; think out; plan: *The mayor is studying ways to cut expenses.* **8** deep thought: *The judge was absorbed in study about the case.* 1,3,5,6,8 *noun, plural* **stud ies;** 2,4,7 *verb,* **stud ied, stud y ing.**

stuff (stuf), **1** what a thing is made of; material: *She bought some white stuff for curtains. That boy has good stuff in him.* **2** worthless material; useless things: *Their attic is full of old stuff.* **3** pack full; fill: *I stuffed the pillow with feathers.* **4** stop up; block; choke up: *My head is stuffed up by a cold.* **5** fill the skin of (a dead animal) to make it look as it did when alive: *We saw many stuffed birds at the museum.* **6** fill (a chicken, turkey, fish, or other animal) with stuffing. **7** force; push; thrust: *I stuffed my things into a closet.* **8** fill too much with food: *I stuffed myself at dinner last night.* 1,2 *noun,* 3-8 *verb.*

stuff ing (stuf′ing), **1** material used to fill or pack something. **2** a seasoned mixture of bread crumbs with sausage or oysters, chestnuts, or some other food, used to stuff a chicken, turkey, fish, or other animal. noun.

stuff y (stuf′ē), **1** lacking fresh air: *a stuffy room.* **2** lacking freshness or interest; dull: *a stuffy speech.* **3** stopped up: *A cold makes my head feel stuffy.* adjective, **stuff i er, stuff i est.**

stum ble (stum′bəl), **1** slip or trip by striking the foot against something: *stumble over a stool in the dark.* **2** walk in an unsteady way: *The tired hikers*

a hat	i it	oi oil	ch child	a in about
ā age	ī ice	ou out	ng long	e in taken
ä far	o hot	u cup	sh she	ə = { i in pencil
e let	ō open	u̇ put	th thin	o in lemon
ē equal	ô order	ü rule	ŦH then	u in circus
ėr term			zh measure	

stumbled along. **3** speak or act in a clumsy or hesitating way: *The actors made many blunders as they stumbled through the play.* **4** come by accident or chance: *While in the country, she stumbled upon some fine old pieces of furniture.* verb, **stum bled, stum bling.**

stump (stump), **1** the lower end of a tree or plant left after the main part is cut off: *We sat on top of a stump.* **2** anything left after the main or important part is removed: *the stump of a pencil, the stump of a candle. The dog wagged its stump of a tail.* **3** walk in a stiff, clumsy way: *The lame man stumped along.* **4** make unable to answer or do; cause to be at a loss: *The riddle stumped me.* 1,2 *noun,* 3,4 *verb.*

stun (stun), **1** make senseless; knock unconscious: *He was stunned by the fall.* **2** daze; bewilder; shock; overwhelm: *She was stunned by the news of her friend's death.* verb, **stunned, stun ning.**

stung (stung). See **sting**. *A wasp stung him. He was stung on the neck.* verb.

stunk (stungk). See **stink**. *The garbage dump stunk. The rotten eggs had stunk up the kitchen.* verb.

stun ning (stun′ing), **1** excellent; very attractive; good-looking: *a stunning outfit.* **2** that stuns or dazes; bewildering: *a stunning blow.* adjective.

stunt¹ (stunt), check in growth or development: *Lack of proper food stunts a child.* verb.

stunt² (stunt), feat to attract attention; performance. See picture. noun.

stunt

stu pen dous (stü pen′dəs *or* styü pen′dəs), amazing; marvelous; immense: *Niagara Falls is a stupendous sight. adjective.*

stu pid (stü′pid *or* styü′pid), **1** not intelligent; dull: *a stupid person, a stupid remark.* **2** not interesting; boring: *a stupid book. adjective.*

stu pid i ty (stü pid′ə tē *or* styü pid′ə tē), **1** lack of intelligence. **2** a stupid act or idea. *noun, plural* **stu pid i ties.**

stu por (stü′pər *or* styü′pər), a dazed condition; loss or lessening of the power to feel: *I lay in a stupor for some time after I was hit on the head. noun.*

stur dy (stėr′dē), **1** strong; stout: *a sturdy child, a sturdy chair.* **2** firm; not yielding: *sturdy resistance, sturdy defenders. adjective,* **stur di er, stur di est.**

stur geon (stėr′jən), a large food fish whose body has a tough skin with rows of bony plates. *noun, plural* **stur geons** *or* **stur geon.**

stut ter (stut′ər), **1** repeat the same sound in an effort to speak. EXAMPLE: C-c-c-c-can't th-th-th-they c-c-c-come? **2** act or habit of stuttering. **1** *verb,* **2** *noun.*

style (stīl), **1** fashion: *My clothes are out of style.* **2** manner; method; way: *the Gothic style of architecture. She learned several styles of swimming.* **3** way of writing or speaking: *Books for children should have a clear, easy style.* **4** good style: *She dresses in style.* **5** name; call: *She styles herself a poet.* **6** the stemlike part of the pistil of a flower. At the top of the style is the stigma. **1-4,6** *noun,* **5** *verb,* **styled, styl ing.**

styl ish (stī′lish), having style; in the current fashion; fashionable: *stylish clothes. adjective.*

sub di vide (sub′də vīd′), divide into smaller parts: *A builder bought the farm, subdivided it into lots, and built homes on them. verb,* **sub di vid ed, sub di vid ing.**

sub di vi sion (sub′də vizh′ən), **1** division into smaller parts. **2** part of a part. **3** tract of land divided into building lots. *noun.*

sub due (səb dü′ *or* səb dyü′), **1** overcome by superior force; conquer: *The Spanish subdued the Indian tribes in Mexico.* **2** keep down; hold back: *We subdued a desire to laugh.* **3** tone down; soften: *Pulling down the shades subdued the light in the room. verb,* **sub dued, sub du ing.**

sub ject (sub′jikt *for 1-5,8-10;* səb jekt′ *for 6 and 7),* **1** something thought about, discussed, or studied: *The subject for our composition was "An Exciting Moment."* **2** something learned or taught; course of study in some branch of knowledge: *English, science, and arithmetic are some of the subjects we take up in school.* **3** person who is under the power, control, or influence of another: *The people are the subjects of the king.* **4** under the power or influence of: *We are subject to our country's laws.* **5** under some power or influence: *the subject nations of an empire.* **6** bring under some power or influence: *Rome subjected all Italy to its rule.* **7** cause to undergo or experience something: *The school subjected new students to many tests.* **8** likely to have: *I am subject to colds.*

9 depending on; on the condition of: *I bought the car subject to your approval.* **10** word or group of words about which something is said in a sentence. *I is the subject of the following sentences: I see the cat. I am seen by the cat. I can see.* **1-3,10** *noun,* **4,5,8,9** *adjective,* **6,7** *verb.*

sub lime (sə blīm′), noble; majestic; grand. See picture. *adjective.*

sub ma rine (sub′mə rēn′ *for 1;* sub′mə rēn′ *for 2),* **1** boat that can go under water. Submarines are used in warfare for attacking enemy ships and launching guided missiles. **2** under the surface of the sea; underwater: *submarine plants, submarine warfare.* **1** *noun,* **2** *adjective.*

sub merge (səb mėrj′), **1** put under water; cover with water: *A big wave submerged us. At high tide this path is submerged.* **2** cover; bury: *His talent was submerged by his shyness.* **3** go below the surface of the water: *The submarine submerged to escape enemy attack. verb,* **sub merged, sub merg ing.**

sub mis sion (səb mish′ən), **1** yielding to the power, control, or authority of another: *The defeated general showed his submission by giving up his sword.* **2** humble obedience: *He bowed in submission to the king's order. noun.*

sub mis sive (səb mis′iv), yielding to the power, control, or authority of another; obedient; humble. *adjective.*

sub mit (səb mit′), **1** yield to the power, control, or authority of some person or group; surrender; yield: *They submitted to the will of the majority.* **2** refer to the consideration or judgment of another or others: *The secretary submitted a report of the last meeting. verb,* **sub mit ted, sub mit ting.**

sub or di nate (sə bôrd′n it *for 1-3;* sə bôrd′n āt *for 4),* **1** lower in rank: *In the army, lieutenants are subordinate to captains.* **2** having less importance; secondary; dependent: *An errand boy has a subordinate position.* **3** a subordinate person or thing. **4** place in a lower order or rank; make subject to or dependent on: *We subordinated our wishes to those of our guests.* **1,2** *adjective,* **3** *noun,* **4** *verb,* **sub or di nat ed, sub or di nat ing.**

sub scribe (səb skrīb′), **1** promise to give or pay (a sum of money): *I subscribed $5 to the hospital fund.* **2** promise to take and pay for: *We subscribe to several magazines.* **3** write (one's name) at the end of a document, or the like; sign (one's name): *The men who subscribed to the Declaration of Independence are now famous.* **4** give one's consent or approval; agree: *She does not subscribe to my opinion. verb,* **sub scribed, sub scrib ing.**

sub scrib er (səb skrī′bər), person who subscribes: *The magazines make a special offer to new subscribers. noun.*

sub scrip tion (səb skrip′shən), **1** subscribing. **2** money subscribed; contribution: *Their subscription to the Fresh Air Fund was $5.* **3** right to receive something, obtained by paying a certain sum: *My subscription to the newspaper expired. noun.*

sub se quent (sub′sə kwənt), coming after; following after; later: *Subsequent events proved that*

sublime—The scenery in the mountains was sublime.

subway (definition 1)

a hat	i it	oi oil	ch child	a in about
ā age	ī ice	ou out	ng long	e in taken
ä far	o hot	u cup	sh she	ə = i in pencil
e let	ō open	u̇ put	th thin	o in lemon
ē equal	ô order	ü rule	ŦH then	u in circus
ėr term			zh measure	

substance in different forms. **2** the real, main, or important part of anything: *The substance of an education is its effect on your life, not just learning lessons.* **3** real meaning: *Give the substance of the speech in your own words.* **4** wealth; property: *a man of substance. noun.*

sub stan tial (səb stan′shəl), **1** real; actual: *People and things are substantial; dreams and ghosts are not.* **2** strong; firm; solid: *That house is substantial enough to last a hundred years.* **3** large; important; ample: *Your work shows substantial improvement.* **4** in the main; in substance: *The stories told by the children were in substantial agreement.* **5** well-to-do; wealthy. *adjective.*

sub stan tial ly (səb stan′shə lē), **1** essentially; mainly: *This report is substantially correct.* **2** really; actually. **3** solidly; strongly: *a substantially built house. adverb.*

sub sti tute (sub′stə tüt *or* sub′stə tyüt), **1** thing used instead of another; person taking the place of another: *Margarine is a common substitute for butter.* **2** put in the place of another: *We substituted brown sugar for molasses in these cookies.* **3** take the place of another: *The principal substituted for our teacher, who is ill.* **1** *noun,* **2,3** *verb,* **sub sti tut ed, sub sti tut ing.**

sub sti tu tion (sub′stə tü′shən *or* sub′stə tyü′shən), use of one thing for another; putting (one person or thing) in place of another; taking the place of another. *noun.*

sub tle (sut′l), **1** not obvious; delicate; fine: *There is a subtle odor of burning leaves in the fall air. Subtle jokes are often hard to understand.* **2** having a keen, quick mind; discerning; acute: *She is a subtle observer of slight differences in things.* **3** sly; crafty; tricky: *a subtle scheme to get some money. adjective,* **sub tler, sub tlest.**

sub tract (səb trakt′), take away: *Subtract 2 from 10 and you have 8. verb.*

sub trac tion (səb trak′shən), process of subtracting one number from another: *$10 - 2 = 8$ is a simple subtraction. noun.*

sub tra hend (sub′trə hend), number to be subtracted from another: *In $10 - 2 = 8$, the subtrahend is 2. noun.*

sub urb (sub′ėrb′), district, town, or village just outside or near a city: *Many people who work in the city live in the suburbs. noun.*

sub ur ban (sə bėr′bən), **1** having to do with a suburb; in a suburb: *We have excellent suburban train service.* **2** characteristic of a suburb or its inhabitants. *adjective.*

sub way (sub′wā′), **1** an underground electric railroad running beneath the surface of the streets in a city. See picture. **2** an underground passage. *noun.*

she was right. *The story will be continued in subsequent chapters. adjective.*

sub se quent ly (sub′sə kwənt lē), afterward; later. *adverb.*

sub side (səb sīd′), **1** grow less; die down; become less active: *The waves subsided when the wind stopped. Her fever subsided after she took the medicine.* **2** sink to a lower level: *Several days after the rain stopped, the flood waters subsided. verb,* **sub sid ed, sub sid ing.**

sub stance (sub′stəns), **1** what a thing consists of; matter; material: *Ice and water are the same*

suc ceed (sək sēd′), **1** turn out well; do well; have success: *The plan succeeded.* **2** come next after; follow; take the place of: *John Adams succeeded Washington as President. Week succeeds week. verb.*

suc cess (sək ses′), **1** a favorable result; wished-for ending; good fortune: *Success in school comes from intelligence and work.* **2** gaining wealth or position: *She has had success in business.* **3** person or thing that succeeds: *The circus was a great success. noun.*

suc cess ful (sək ses′fəl), having success; ending in success; prosperous; fortunate: *The books of a successful writer are liked by the public. adjective.*

suc ces sion (sək sesh′ən), **1** group of things happening one after another; series: *A succession of accidents spoiled our automobile trip.* **2** the coming of one person or thing after another. **3** right of succeeding to an office, property, or rank: *There was a dispute about the rightful succession to the throne.* **4** order or arrangement of persons having such a right of succeeding: *The queen's oldest son is next in succession to the throne. noun.*

in succession, one after another: *We visited our sick friend several days in succession.*

suc ces sive (sək ses′iv), coming one after another; following in order: *It has rained for three successive days. adjective.*

suc ces sor (sək ses′ər), one who follows or succeeds another in office, position, or ownership of property; thing that comes after another in a series: *John Adams was Washington's successor as President. noun.*

such (such), **1** of that kind; of the same kind or degree: *Such perfect diamonds as those are quite rare. The child had such a fever that he nearly died.* **2** of the kind already spoken of or suggested: *She does not like tea and coffee and such drinks.* **3** to the extent described; so great, so bad, or so good: *They are such liars! Such weather!* **4** such a person or thing: *Take from the blankets such as you need.* **1-3** *adjective,* **4** *pronoun.*

such as, 1 similar to; like: *A good friend such as you is rare.* **2** for example: *members of the dog family, such as the wolf and the fox.*

suck (suk), **1** draw into the mouth: *Lemonade can be sucked through a straw.* **2** draw something from with the mouth: *suck oranges.* **3** drink; take; absorb: *Plants suck up moisture from the earth. A sponge sucks in water.* **4** hold in the mouth and lick: *The child sucked a lollipop.* **5** act of sucking: *The baby took one suck at the bottle and pushed it away.* **1-4** *verb,* **5** *noun.*

suck er (suk′ər), **1** animal or thing that sucks. **2** a freshwater fish with large, fleshy lips that suck in food. **3** a part of the body of some animals for sucking and holding fast. **4** a shoot growing from an underground stem or root. **5** piece of hard candy, usually on the end of a small stick. *noun.*

suc tion (suk′shən), process of drawing liquids or gases into a space by sucking out or removing part of the air. We draw liquid through a straw by suction. Some pumps work by suction. *noun.*

sud den (sud′n), **1** not expected: *a sudden stop, a sudden storm, a sudden idea.* **2** quick; rapid: *The cat made a sudden jump at the mouse. adjective.*

all of a sudden, unexpectedly or quickly.

suds (sudz), **1** soapy water. **2** bubbles and foam on soapy water; soapsuds. *noun plural.*

sue (sü), **1** start a lawsuit against: *He sued the railroad because his cow was killed by the engine.* **2** beg or ask (for); plead: *Messengers came suing for peace. verb,* **sued, su ing.**

suede (swād), a soft leather that has a velvety nap on one or both sides. *noun.*

su et (sü′it), the hard fat of cattle or sheep. Suet is used in cooking and for making tallow. *noun.*

suf fer (suf′ər), **1** have pain, grief, or injury: *He suffers from headaches.* **2** have or feel (pain, grief, or injury): *She suffered a broken leg while skiing.* **3** experience harm or loss: *Crops suffered during the dry spell.* **4** bear with patiently; endure: *I will not suffer such insults. verb.*

suf fer ing (suf′ər ing), pain: *Hunger causes suffering. noun.*

suf fi cient (sə fish′ənt), as much as is needed; enough: *The poor child did not have sufficient clothing for the winter. adjective.*

suf fi cient ly (sə fish′ənt lē), as much as is needed; enough. *adverb.*

suf fix (suf′iks), syllable or syllables put at the end of a word to change its meaning or to make another word, as *-ly* in *badly, -ness* in *goodness,* and *-ful* in *spoonful. noun, plural* **suf fix es.**

suf fo cate (suf′ə kāt), **1** kill by stopping the breath. **2** keep from breathing; hinder in breathing. **3** gasp for breath; choke. **4** die for lack of air. *verb,* **suf fo cat ed, suf fo cat ing.**

suf fo ca tion (suf′ə kā′shən), choking or smothering. *noun.*

suf frage (suf′rij), right to vote: *The United States granted suffrage to women in 1920.* See picture. *noun.*

sug ar (shug′ər), **1** a sweet substance obtained chiefly from sugar cane or sugar beets and widely used in food products. Most plants manufacture sugar. **2** put sugar in; sweeten with sugar: *Sugar your tea.* **3** cover with sugar; sprinkle with sugar: *to sugar doughnuts.* **4** form crystals of sugar: *Maple syrup will sugar if cooked.* **1** *noun,* **2-4** *verb.*

sugar beet, a large beet with a white root from which sugar is made.

sugar cane, a very tall grass with a strong, jointed stem and flat leaves, growing in warm regions. Sugar cane is one of the chief sources of sugar.

sugar maple, a maple tree. Maple sugar and maple syrup are made from the sweet sap of this tree. See picture.

sug gest (səg jest′), **1** bring to mind; call up the thought of: *The thought of summer suggests swimming, tennis, and hot weather.* **2** put forward; propose: *She suggested a swim, and we all agreed.* **3** show in an indirect way; hint: *His yawns suggested that he would like to go to bed. verb.*

sug ges tion (səg jes′chən), **1** act of suggesting:

The suggestion of a swim made the children jump with joy. **2** thing suggested: *The picnic was an excellent suggestion.* **3** a very small amount; slight trace: *She spoke with just a suggestion of a French accent. noun.*

su i cide (sü′ə sīd), **1** killing oneself on purpose. **2** person who kills himself on purpose. *noun.*
commit suicide, kill oneself on purpose.

suit (süt), **1** set of clothes to be worn together. A man's suit consists of a coat, trousers, and sometimes a vest. *The knight wore a suit of armor.* **2** case in a court of law: *She started a suit to collect the money she was owed.* **3** make suitable; make fit: *to suit a punishment to the crime.* **4** be good for; agree with: *A cold climate suits apples and wheat, but not oranges and tea.* **5** be suitable; be convenient; fit; please; satisfy: *Which time suits you best? It is hard to suit everybody.* **6** be becoming to: *That blue sweater suits you.* **7** request; asking; wooing: *The prince's suit was successful, and Cinderella married him.* 1,2,7 *noun,* 3-6 *verb.*

suit a ble (sü′tə bəl), right for the occasion; fitting; proper: *Simple clothes are suitable for school wear. The park gives the children a suitable playground. adjective.*

suit case (süt′kās′), a flat traveling bag. *noun.*

suite (swēt), **1** set of connected rooms to be used by one person or family: *She has a suite of rooms at the hotel—a living room, bedroom, and bath.* **2** set of furniture that matches. **3** any set or series of like things. *noun.*

sui tor (sü′tər), man who is courting a woman: *The princess had many suitors. noun.*

sul fur (sul′fər), a light-yellow substance that burns with a blue flame and a stifling odor. Sulfur is used in making matches and gunpowder. *noun.* Also spelled **sulphur.**

sulk (sulk), **1** be sulky. **2** fit of sulking. 1 *verb,* 2 *noun.*

sulk y (sul′kē), **1** silent because of bad humor; sullen: *Some children become sulky when they cannot have their own way.* **2** a light carriage with two wheels, for one person. See picture. 1 *adjective,* **sulk i er, sulk i est;** 2 *noun, plural* **sulk ies.**

sul len (sul′ən), **1** silent because of bad humor or anger: *The sullen child wouldn't even speak to me.* **2** gloomy; dismal: *The sullen skies threatened rain. adjective.*

sul phur (sul′fər), sulfur. *noun.*

sul tan (sult′n), the ruler of certain Moslem countries. Turkey was ruled by a sultan until 1922. *noun.*

sul try (sul′trē), hot, close, and moist: *We expect some sultry weather during July. adjective,* **sul tri er, sul tri est.**

sum (sum), **1** amount of money: *We paid a large sum for our new house.* **2** number arrived at by adding two or more numbers together: *The sum of 2 and 3 and 4 is 9.* **3** problem in arithmetic: *He can do easy sums in his head, but he has to use pencil and paper for hard ones.* **4** the whole amount; total

a hat	i it	oi oil	ch child	a in about
ā age	ī ice	ou out	ng long	e in taken
ä far	o hot	u cup	sh she	ə = i in pencil
e let	ō open	u̇ put	th thin	o in lemon
ē equal	ô order	ü rule	ᵀʜ then	u in circus
ėr term			zh measure	

suffrage—a demonstration for woman suffrage

sulky (definition 2)

sugar maple—collecting sap from sugar maples

amount: *The sum of scientific knowledge has increased greatly in this century.* **5 sum up,** express or tell briefly: *Sum up the main points of the lesson in three sentences. The judge summed up the evidence.* 1-4 *noun,* 5 *verb,* **summed, sum ming.**

su mac (sü′mak *or* shü′mak), shrub or small tree with leaves that turn scarlet in the autumn and long clusters of red fruit. *noun.*

sum ma rize (sum′ə rīz′), make a summary of; give only the main points of; express briefly: *summarize the story of a book.* verb, **sum ma rized, sum ma riz ing.**

sum mar y (sum′ər ē), **1** a brief statement giving the main points: *This history book has a summary at the end of each chapter.* **2** brief; short. **3** direct and prompt; without delay: *The teacher took summary action by sending us straight to the principal.* 1 *noun, plural* **sum mar ies;** 2,3 *adjective.*

sum mer (sum′ər), **1** the warmest season of the year; season of the year between spring and autumn. **2** of or for summer; coming in summer: *summer heat, summer clothes, summer holidays.* **3** spend the summer: *to summer at the seashore.* 1 *noun,* 2 *adjective,* 3 *verb.*

sum mer time (sum′ər tīm′), summer season; summer. *noun.*

sum mit (sum′it), the highest point; top: *the summit of a mountain, to reach the summit of success.* See picture. *noun.*

sum mon (sum′ən), **1** call with authority; order to come; send for: *I was summoned to the principal's office.* **2** stir to action; rouse: *We summoned our courage and entered the deserted house.* verb.

sum mons (sum′ənz), **1** a formal order or notice to appear before a court of law or judge, especially to answer a charge: *I received a summons for speeding.* **2** an urgent call; a summoning command, message, or signal: *I hurried in response to my friend's summons for help.* noun, plural **sum mons es.**

sump tu ous (sump′chü əs), costly; magnificent; rich: *sumptuous jewels, a sumptuous banquet.* adjective.

sun (sun), **1** the heavenly body around which the earth and the other planets revolve. The sun is the brightest heavenly body in the sky. It lights and warms the earth. **2** the light and warmth of the sun: *The cat likes to sit in the sun.* **3** put in the light and warmth of the sun: *The swimmers sunned themselves on the beach.* **4** any heavenly body like the sun. Many stars are suns and have planets traveling around them. **5** something bright like the sun. 1,2,4,5 *noun,* 3 *verb,* **sunned, sun ning.**

sun beam (sun′bēm′), ray of sunlight: *A sunbeam brightened the child's hair to gold.* noun.

sun bon net (sun′bon′it), a large bonnet that shades the face and neck. *noun.*

sun burn (sun′bėrn′), **1** burning the skin by the sun's rays. A sunburn is often red and painful. **2** burn the skin by the sun's rays: *He is sunburned from a day on the beach.* **3** become burned by the sun: *Her skin sunburns quickly.* 1 *noun,* 2,3 *verb,* **sun burned** or **sun burnt, sun burn ing.**

summit—the snow-covered summit of Mt. Everest, the world's highest mountain

sundial

French Horology, XVIII century. The Metropolitan Museum of Art, Gift of Mrs. Stephen D. Tucker, 1903

sunflowers

sun burnt (sun′bėrnt′), sunburned. See **sunburn**. *verb.*

sun dae (sun′dē), dish of ice cream with syrup, crushed fruits, or nuts over it. *noun.*

Sun day (sun′dē), the first day of the week. *noun.* [*Sunday* comes from an earlier English word meaning "day of the sun."]

Sunday school, 1 school held on Sunday for teaching religion. **2** its members.

sun di al (sun′dī′əl), instrument for telling the time of day by the position of a shadow cast by the sun. See picture. *noun.*

sun down (sun′doun′), sunset: *We'll be home by sundown. noun.*

sun fish (sun′fish′), **1** a small, freshwater fish of North America, used for food. **2** a large sea fish with tough flesh. *noun, plural* **sun fish es** or **sun fish.**

sun flow er (sun′flou′ər), a tall plant having large yellow flowers with brown centers. See picture. *noun.*

sung (sung). See **sing**. *Many songs were sung at the concert. verb.*

sun glass es (sun′glas′iz), spectacles to protect the eyes from the glare of the sun. They are usually made of colored glass. *noun plural.*

sunk (sungk). See **sink**. *The ship had sunk to the bottom. verb.*

sunk en (sung′kən), **1** that has sunk in water: *a sunken ship.* **2** submerged; underwater: *a sunken rock.* **3** situated below the general level: *a sunken living room.* **4** fallen in; hollow: *sunken eyes. adjective.*

sun light (sun′līt′), light of the sun: *Outdoor sunlight is very good for the health. noun.*

sun lit (sun′lit′), lighted by the sun. *adjective.*

sun ny (sun′ē), **1** having much sunshine: *a sunny day.* **2** lighted or warmed by the sun: *a sunny room.* **3** like the sun. **4** bright; cheerful; happy: *The baby gave a sunny smile. adjective,* **sun ni er, sun ni est.**

sun rise (sun′rīz′), the coming up of the sun; first appearance of the sun in the morning. *noun.*

sun set (sun′set′), the going down of the sun; last appearance of the sun in the evening. *noun.*

sun shine (sun′shīn′), **1** the shining of the sun; light of the sun. **2** brightness; cheerfulness; happiness. *noun.*

sun stroke (sun′strōk′), a sudden illness with fever and dry skin that is caused by too much heat from the sun. *noun.*

sun up (sun′up′), sunrise. *noun.*

su perb (sù pėrb′), **1** grand; stately; majestic; magnificent; splendid: *Mountain scenery is superb. The queen's jewels are superb.* **2** very fine; first-rate; excellent: *The singer gave a superb performance. adjective.*

su per fi cial (sü′pər fish′əl), **1** on the surface; at the surface: *His burns were superficial and soon healed.* **2** not thorough; shallow: *Girls used to receive only a superficial education. adjective.*

su per high way (sü′pər hī′wā), highway for fast traveling. *noun.*

su per in tend (sü′pər in tend′), oversee and direct (work or workers); manage (a place or institution). *verb.*

su per in tend ent (sü′pər in ten′dənt), person who oversees, directs, or manages; supervisor: *a superintendent of schools, a superintendent of a factory. noun.*

su per i or (sə pir′ē ər), **1** above the average; very good; excellent: *superior work in school.* **2** higher in quality; better; greater: *a superior blend of coffee. We lost the game to a superior team.* **3** higher in position, rank, or importance: *a superior officer.* **4** person who is superior: *As a violin player, he has no superior. A captain is a lieutenant's superior.* **5** showing a feeling of being above others; proud: *Her superior attitude caused her to be disliked.* **6** head of a monastery or convent. **1-3,5** *adjective,* **4,6** *noun.*

superior to, 1 higher than; above: *Apes are considered superior to most other animals in intelligence.* **2** better than; greater than: *This restaurant's food is superior to any other.*

su per i or i ty (sə pir′ē ôr′ə tē), superior state or quality: *No one doubts the superiority of modern ways of traveling over those of olden times. noun.*

su per la tive (sə pėr′lə tiv), **1** of the highest kind; above all others; supreme: *Solomon is said to have been a man of superlative wisdom.* **2** *Fairest, fastest,* and *best* are the superlatives of *fair, fast,* and *good.* **1** *adjective,* **2** *noun.*

su per man (sü′pər man′), person having more than human powers. *noun, plural* **su per men.**

su per mar ket (sü′pər mär′kit), a large store for groceries in which customers select items from open shelves and pay for them just before leaving. *noun.*

su per nat ur al (sü′pər nach′ər əl), above or beyond what is natural: *Angels and devils are supernatural beings. adjective.*

su per sede (sü′pər sēd′), **1** take the place of; cause to be set aside; displace: *Electric lights have superseded gas lights in American homes.* **2** fill the place of; replace: *A new governor superseded the old one. verb,* **su per sed ed, su per sed ing.**

su per son ic (sü′pər son′ik), **1** greater than the speed of sound in the air. **2** able to move at a speed greater than the speed of sound: *a supersonic jet. adjective.*

su per sti tion (sü′pər stish′ən), **1** an unreasoning fear of what is unknown or mysterious. **2** belief or practice founded on ignorant fear or mistaken reverence: *A common superstition considered 13 an unlucky number. noun.*

su per sti tious (sü′pər stish′əs), full of superstition; likely to believe superstitions; caused by superstition: *a superstitious habit, a superstitious belief. adjective.*

a hat	i it	oi oil	ch child	
ā age	ī ice	ou out	ng long	a in about
ä far	o hot	u cup	sh she	e in taken
e let	ō open	ů put	th thin	ə = { i in pencil
ē equal	ô order	ü rule	₮ʜ then	o in lemon
ėr term			zh measure	u in circus

su per vise (sü′pər vīz), look after and direct (work, workers, or a process); oversee; manage: *Morning recess is supervised by teachers. verb,* **su per vised, su per vis ing.**

su per vi sion (sü′pər vizh′ən), management; direction; oversight: *The house was built under the careful supervision of an architect. noun.*

su per vi sor (sü′pər vī′zər), person who supervises: *The music supervisor has charge of the school band, chorus, and orchestra. noun.*

sup per (sup′ər), the evening meal; meal eaten early in the evening if dinner is near noon, or late in the evening if dinner is at six or later. *noun.*

sup per time (sup′ər tīm′), time at which supper is served. *noun.*

sup plant (sə plant′), 1 take the place of: *Machinery has supplanted hand labor in making shoes.* 2 take the place of by unfair methods: *The queen's cousin plotted to supplant her. verb.*

sup ple (sup′əl), 1 bending easily: *a supple birch tree, supple leather, a supple dancer.* See picture. 2 readily adapting to different ideas, circumstances, or people; yielding: *The children's supple natures will enable them to make friends quickly in their new neighborhood. adjective,* **sup pler, sup plest.**

sup ple ment (sup′lə mənt *for 1;* sup′lə ment *for 2*), 1 something added to complete a thing, or to make it larger or better: *We get a supplement to our encyclopedia every year.* 2 add to; complete: *I supplement my diet with vitamin pills.* 1 *noun,* 2 *verb.*

sup pli ca tion (sup′lə kā′shən), a humble, earnest request or prayer: *supplications to God. noun.*

sup ply (sə plī′), 1 furnish; provide: *The school supplies books for the children. A well supplies us with water.* 2 quantity ready for use; stock; store: *Our school gets its supplies of books, paper, pencils, and chalk from the city. We have a large supply of vegetables in the freezer.* 3 **supplies,** the food and equipment necessary for an army, expedition, or the like. 4 make up for; fill: *Rocks and stumps supplied the place of chairs at the picnic.* 1,4 *verb,* **sup plied, sup ply ing;** 2,3 *noun, plural* **sup plies.**

sup port (sə pôrt′), 1 keep from falling; hold up: *Walls support the roof.* 2 give strength or courage to; keep up; help: *Hope supports us in trouble.* 3 provide for: *Parents usually support their children.* 4 be in favor of; back: *She supports the proposed law.* 5 help prove; bear out: *The facts support his claim.* 6 help; aid: *He needs the support of a scholarship.* 7 person or thing that supports; prop: *The neck is the support of the head.* 1-5 *verb,* 6,7 *noun.*

sup pose (sə pōz′), 1 consider as possible: *Suppose we are late, what will the teacher say?* 2 believe; think; imagine: *I suppose she will come as usual. verb,* **sup posed, sup pos ing.**

sup posed (sə pōzd′), considered as possible or probable; assumed: *The supposed beggar was really a prince. adjective.*

sup pos ing (sə pō′zing), if: *Supposing it rains, shall we go? conjunction.*

sup press (sə pres′), 1 put an end to; put down; stop by force: *to suppress a riot.* 2 keep in; hold back; keep from appearing: *She suppressed a yawn. verb.*

sup pres sion (sə presh′ən), 1 putting down by force or authority; putting an end to: *Troops were used in the suppression of the revolt.* 2 keeping in; holding back: *The suppression of facts may be as dishonest as the telling of lies. noun.*

su prem a cy (sə prem′ə sē), supreme authority or power. *noun, plural* **su prem a cies.**

su preme (sə prēm′), 1 highest in rank or authority: *a supreme ruler.* 2 highest in degree; greatest; utmost; extreme: *With supreme effort, we moved the piano. adjective.*

Supreme Being, God.

Supreme Court, the highest court in the United States, which meets at Washington, D.C. It consists of a chief justice and eight associate justices.

sure (shür), 1 free from doubt; certain: *Are you sure you locked the door? Make sure you have the key.* 2 to be trusted; safe; reliable: *You can trust him; he is a sure messenger.* 3 never missing, slipping, or failing: *sure aim.* 4 firm: *stand on sure ground.* 5 surely. 1-4 *adjective,* **sur er, sur est;** 5 *adverb.*

sure-foot ed (shür′füt′id), not liable to stumble, slip, or fall. *adjective.*

sure ly (shür′lē), 1 certainly: *Surely you must come again.* 2 firmly; without mistake; without missing, slipping, or failing: *The goat leaped surely from rock to rock. adverb.*

surf (sėrf), waves or swell of the sea breaking on the shore. The surf is high just after a storm. *noun.*

sur face (sėr′fis), 1 the outside of anything: *the surface of a mountain. An egg has a smooth surface.* 2 any face or side of a thing: *A cube has six surfaces. The upper surface of the plate has pictures on it.* 3 the outward appearance: *She seems rough, but you will find her very kind below the surface.* 4 of the surface; on the surface; having something to do with the surface: *a surface view.* 5 put a surface on; make smooth: *The town must surface this road.* 6 arise to the surface of the water: *The submarine surfaced.* 1-3 *noun,* 4 *adjective,* 5,6 *verb,* **sur faced, sur fac ing.**

surf board (sėrf′bôrd′), a long, narrow board for riding the surf. See picture. *noun.*

surge (sėrj), 1 rise and fall; move like waves: *A wave surged over us. The crowd surged through the streets.* 2 a swelling wave; a sweep or rush of waves: *Our boat was upset by a surge.* 3 something like a wave: *A surge of anger.* 1 *verb,* **surged, surg ing;** 2,3 *noun.*

sur geon (sėr′jən), doctor who performs operations: *A surgeon removed my tonsils. noun.*

sur ger y (sėr′jər ē), art and science of treating diseases or injuries by operations and instruments: *Malaria can be cured by medicine, but a ruptured appendix requires surgery. noun, plural* **sur ger ies.**

surfboard
He rode the **surfboard** just ahead of the crest of the wave.

surrey

supple (definition 1)

a hat	i it	oi oil	ch child	a in about
ā age	ī ice	ou out	ng long	e in taken
ä far	o hot	u cup	sh she	ə = { i in pencil
e let	ō open	ù put	th thin	o in lemon
ē equal	ô order	ü rule	ŦH then	u in circus
ėr term			zh measure	

sur gi cal (sėr′jə kəl), **1** of surgery; having something to do with surgery: *a surgical patient.* **2** used in surgery: *surgical instruments. adjective.*

sur ly (sėr′lē), bad-tempered and unfriendly; rude; gruff: *They got a surly answer from their grouchy neighbor. adjective,* **sur li er, sur li est.**

sur mise (sər mīz′), **1** guess: *We surmised that the delay was caused by some accident.* **2** guessing: *His guilt was a matter of surmise; there was no proof.* **1** *verb,* **sur mised, sur mis ing; 2** *noun.*

sur mount (sər mount′), **1** rise above: *That mountain surmounts all the peaks near it.* **2** be above or on top of: *A statue surmounts the monument.* **3** overcome: *We surmounted all objections to the plan. verb.*

sur name (sėr′nām′), a last name; family name: *Smith is the surname of John Smith. noun.*

sur pass (sər pas′), **1** do better than; be greater than; excel: *She surpasses her sister in arithmetic.* **2** be too much or too great for; go beyond; exceed: *The beauty of the sunset surpassed description. verb.*

sur plus (sėr′pləs), **1** amount over and above what is needed; extra quantity left over; excess: *The bank keeps a large surplus of money in reserve.* **2** more than is needed; extra; excess: *Surplus wheat is put in storage or shipped abroad.* **1** *noun,* **2** *adjective.*

sur prise (sər prīz′), **1** feeling caused by something happening suddenly or unexpectedly: *His face showed surprise at the news.* **2** cause to feel surprise; astonish: *The victory surprised us.* **3** something unexpected: *Our grandparents always have a surprise for us when we visit them.* **4** surprising; that is not expected; coming as a surprise: *a surprise party, a surprise visit.* **5** catch unprepared; come upon suddenly: *The enemy surprised the fort during the night.* **6** catching unprepared; coming upon suddenly: *The fort was captured by surprise.* **1,3,6** *noun,* **2,5** *verb,* **sur prised, sur pris ing; 4** *adjective.*

sur pris ing (sər prī′zing), causing surprise or wonder: *a surprising recovery. adjective.*

sur ren der (sə ren′dər), **1** give up; give (oneself or itself) up; yield: *The captain had to surrender to the enemy. As the storm got worse, we surrendered all hope of going camping. We surrendered ourselves to sleep.* **2** act of surrendering: *The surrender of the fort came at dawn.* **1** *verb,* **2** *noun.*

sur rey (sėr′ē), a light carriage with four wheels and two seats. See picture. *noun, plural* **sur reys.** [The *surrey* was named for Surrey, a county in southeastern England, where it was first made.]

sur round (sə round′), shut in on all sides; be around; extend around: *A high fence surrounds the field. They surrounded their children with love. verb.*

swan—about 4 feet (1 meter) long

swamp (definition 1)

swallow²—about 7 inches (18 centimeters) long

sur round ings (sə roun′dingz), surrounding things or conditions: *the peaceful surroundings of the mountains.* noun plural.

sur veil lance (sər vā′ləns), watch kept over a person: *The police kept the criminal under surveillance.* noun.

sur vey (sər vā′ for 1 and 3; sėr′vā for 2, 4, and 5), **1** look over; view; examine: *The buyers surveyed the goods offered for sale.* **2** a general look; view; examination; inspection: *We were pleased with our first survey of the house.* **3** measure for size, shape, position, or boundaries: *The land is being surveyed before it is divided into house lots.* **4** a careful measurement: *A survey showed that the northern boundary was not correct.* **5** plan or description of such a measurement: *She pointed out the route of the railroad on the government survey.* 1,3 *verb,* 2,4,5 *noun, plural* **sur veys.**

sur vey or (sər vā′ər), person who surveys, especially land. noun.

sur viv al (sər vī′vəl), **1** act or fact of surviving; continuance of life; living or lasting longer than others. **2** person, thing, custom, or belief that has lasted from an earlier time: *Many superstitions are survivals of ancient times.* noun.

sur vive (sər vīv′), **1** live longer than; remain alive after: *He survived his wife by three years. Only ten of the crew survived the shipwreck.* **2** continue to exist; remain: *These cave paintings have survived for over 15,000 years. verb,* **sur vived, sur viv ing.**

sur vi vor (sər vī′vər), person, animal, or plant that remains alive; thing that continues to exist: *She is the only survivor of a family of nine. There were two survivors from the plane crash.* noun.

sus cep ti ble (sə sep′tə bəl), easily influenced by feelings or emotions; very sensitive: *Poetry appealed to his susceptible nature.* adjective.

susceptible of, capable of receiving, undergoing, or being affected by: *Her ideas are susceptible of consideration.*

susceptible to, easily affected by; liable to; open to: *Young children are susceptible to many diseases. Vain people are susceptible to flattery.*

sus pect (sə spekt′ for 1-3; sus′pekt for 4), **1** imagine to be so; think likely: *The old fox suspected danger and did not touch the trap. I suspect that they have been delayed.* **2** believe guilty, false, or bad without proof: *The police suspected them of being thieves.* **3** feel no confidence in; doubt: *Her guilty look made me suspect the truth of her excuse.* **4** person suspected: *The police have arrested two suspects in connection with the bank robbery.* 1-3 *verb,* 4 *noun.*

sus pend (sə spend′), **1** hang down by attaching to something above: *The lamp was suspended from the ceiling.* **2** hold in place as if by hanging: *We saw the smoke suspended in the still air.* **3** stop for a while: *We suspended building operations during the winter.* **4** remove or exclude for a while from some privilege or job: *They were suspended from school for a week for bad conduct.* **5** keep undecided; put off: *Suspend judgment until all the facts are known.* verb.

sus pend ers (sə spen′dərz), straps worn over the shoulders to hold up the trousers. *noun plural.*

sus pense (sə spens′), **1** condition of being uncertain: *The detective story kept me in suspense until the last chapter.* **2** anxious uncertainty; anxiety: *The class waited in suspense while the teacher graded the tests. noun.*

sus pen sion (sə spen′shən), suspending or being suspended: *the suspension of a driver's license for speeding. noun.*

suspension bridge, bridge hung on cables or chains between towers. See picture.

sus pi cion (sə spish′ən), **1** state of mind of a person who suspects; suspecting: *The real thief tried to turn suspicion toward others.* **2** condition of being suspected. *noun.*

above suspicion, not to be suspected: *My friend is honest and, therefore, above suspicion.*

on suspicion, because of being suspected: *They were arrested on suspicion of robbery.*

under suspicion, suspected.

sus pi cious (sə spish′əs), **1** causing one to suspect: *Someone suspicious was hanging around the house.* **2** feeling suspicion; suspecting: *Our dog is suspicious of strangers.* **3** showing suspicion: *The dog gave suspicious sniffs at my leg. adjective.*

sus tain (sə stān′), **1** keep up; keep going: *His cheerfulness sustained us through our troubles. She cannot sustain this pace for long.* **2** hold up; support; bear: *Arches sustain the weight of the roof.* **3** suffer; experience: *She sustained a great loss in the death of her husband.* **4** allow; admit; favor: *The court sustained our claim.* **5** agree with; confirm: *The results of the experiment sustain the scientist's theory. verb.*

SW or S.W., 1 southwest. **2** southwestern.

swag ger (swag′ər), **1** walk with a bold, rude, or superior air; strut about or show off in a vain or insolent way: *The villain in the play swaggered onto the stage.* **2** boast or brag noisily. **3** a swaggering way of walking or acting: *The villain moved around the stage with a swagger.* **1,2** *verb,* **3** *noun.*

swal low[1] (swol′ō), **1** take into the stomach through the throat: *We swallow all our food and drink.* **2** take in; absorb: *The waves swallowed up the swimmer.* **3** believe too easily; accept without question or suspicion: *No one will swallow that ridiculous story.* **4** put up with; take meekly; accept without opposing or resisting: *You don't have to swallow their insults.* **5** take back: *swallow words said in anger.* **6** keep back; keep from expressing: *She swallowed her displeasure and smiled.* **7** swallowing: *I took the bitter medicine at one swallow.* **8** amount swallowed at one time: *There are only about four swallows of water left in the bottle.* **1-6** *verb,* **7,8** *noun.*

swal low[2] (swol′ō), a small bird that has long, pointed wings and can fly very fast. Some kinds have deeply forked tails. See picture. *noun.*

swam (swam). See **swim.** *When the boat sank, we swam to shore. verb.*

swamp (swomp), **1** wet, soft land: *We will drain the swamp on our farm so that we can plant crops there.*

suspension bridge

See picture. **2** plunge or sink in a swamp or in water: *The horses were swamped in the stream.* **3** fill with water and sink: *The waves swamped the boat.* **4** overwhelm or be overwhelmed as by a flood; make or become helpless: *to be swamped with homework.* **1** *noun,* **2-4** *verb.*

swamp y (swom′pē), **1** like a swamp; soft and wet: *The front yard is swampy from the heavy rain.* **2** containing swamps: *a swampy region. adjective,* **swamp i er, swamp i est.**

swan (swon), a large, graceful water bird with a long, slender, curving neck. The adult is usually pure white. See picture. *noun.*

swap (swop), trade: *The children swapped toys. verb,* **swapped, swap ping.**

swarm (swôrm), **1** group of bees that leave a hive and fly off together to start a new colony. **2** fly off together to start a new colony of bees. **3** group of bees settled together in a hive. **4** a large group of insects, animals, or people moving about together: *Swarms of children played in the park.* **5** fly or move about in great numbers; be in very great numbers: *The mosquitoes swarmed about us.* **6** be crowded: *The lobby of the theater swarmed with people during intermission.* **1,3,4** *noun,* **2,5,6** *verb.*

swarth y (swôr′ŦHē), having a dark skin: *The sailor was swarthy from the sun of the tropics. adjective,* **swarth i er, swarth i est.**

swat (swot), hit sharply or violently: *swat a fly. verb,* **swat ted, swat ting.**

sway (swā), **1** swing back and forth; swing from side to side, or to one side: *The dancers swayed to the music. The pail swayed in her hands as she ran.* **2** make move; cause to sway: *The wind swayed the branches.* **3** swinging back and forth or from side to side: *The sway of the pail caused some milk to spill out.* **4** move to one side; turn aside: *The horse swayed left at the crossroads.* **5** change in opinion or feeling: *Nothing could sway him after he had made up his mind.* **6** influence; control; rule: *The speaker's words swayed the audience.* **7** an influence, control, or rule: *a country under the sway of a dictator.* 1,2,4-6 *verb,* 3,7 *noun.*

swear (swer *or* swar), **1** make a solemn statement, appealing to God or some other sacred being or object: *A witness at a trial is asked, "Do you swear to tell the truth, the whole truth, and nothing but the truth, so help you God?"* **2** promise; vow: *The governor swore to uphold the constitution. I swear I will tell no one.* **3** bind by an oath; require to promise: *Members of the club were sworn to secrecy.* **4** use profane language; curse: *The pirates raged and swore when they were captured. verb,* **swore, sworn, swear ing.**

sweat (swet), **1** moisture coming through the skin: *After mowing the lawn she wiped the sweat from her face.* **2** give out moisture through the pores of the skin: *We sweated because it was very hot.* **3** fit or condition of sweating: *I was in a cold sweat from fear.* **4** moisture given out by something or gathered on its surface. **5** give out moisture; collect moisture from the air: *A pitcher of ice water sweats on a hot day.* 1,3,4 *noun,* 2,5 *verb,* **sweat ed** or **sweat, sweat ing.**

sweat er (swet′ər), a knitted jacket, usually of wool or nylon, worn for warmth. *noun.*

sweep (swēp). See picture. **1** clean or clear (a floor, deck, or the like) with a broom or brush; use a broom or something like one to remove dirt: *The campers swept the floor of their cabin every morning.* **2** move, drive, or take away with a broom or as with a broom or brush: *They swept the dust into a pan. The wind sweeps the snow into drifts.* **3** remove with a sweeping motion; carry along: *A flood swept away the bridge.* **4** act of sweeping; clearing away; removing: *I made a clean sweep of all my debts.* **5** pass over with a steady movement: *Her fingers swept the strings of the harp. His eyes swept the crowd, looking for his friend.* **6** move swiftly; pass swiftly: *The hawk swept down on the mouse. The wind sweeps over the valley.* **7** a steady, driving motion or swift onward course of something: *the sweep of the wind across the prairie.* **8** move with dignity: *The queen swept into the room.* **9** move or extend in a long course or curve: *The shore sweeps to the south for miles.* **10** a swinging or curving motion: *He cut the grass with strong sweeps of his scythe.* **11** a continuous extent; stretch: *The house looks upon a wide sweep of farming country.* **12** reach; range; extent: *The mountain is beyond the sweep of your eye.* **13** person who sweeps chimneys or streets. 1-3,5,6,8,9 *verb,* **swept, sweep ing;** 4,7,10-13 *noun.*

sweep (definitions 1, 2, and 3)

sweep er (swē′pər), person or thing that sweeps: *a carpet sweeper.* noun.

sweep ing (swē′ping), **1** passing over a wide space: *Her sweeping glance took in the whole room.* **2** having wide range: *a sweeping victory, a sweeping statement.* adjective.

sweep ings (swē′pingz), dust or scraps swept out or up. noun plural.

sweep stakes (swēp′stāks′), **1** system of gambling on horse races or other contests. People buy tickets, and the money they pay goes to the holder or holders of winning tickets. **2** the race or contest. noun.

sweet (swēt), **1** having a taste like sugar or honey: *Pears are much sweeter than lemons.* **2** having a pleasant taste or smell: *Perfume is sweet.* **3** pleasant; agreeable: *a sweet child, a sweet smile, sweet music.* **4** fresh; not sour, salty, bitter, or spoiled: *sweet cream.* **5** something sweet. **6 sweets,** candy or other sweet things. **7** in a sweet manner. 1-4 adjective, 5,6 noun, 7 adverb.

sweet corn, kind of corn eaten by people when it is young and tender.

sweet en (swēt′n), **1** make sweet: *He sweetened his coffee with sugar.* **2** become sweet: *Those pears will sweeten as they ripen.* verb.

sweet en ing (swēt′n ing), something that sweetens. Sugar is a sweetening. noun.

sweet heart (swēt′härt′), a loved one; lover. noun.

sweet ish (swē′tish), somewhat sweet. adjective.

sweet pea, a climbing plant with delicate, fragrant flowers of various colors.

sweet potato, the thick, sweet, orange root of a vine, eaten as a vegetable.

swell (swel), **1** grow bigger; make bigger: *Rain swelled the river. Bread dough swells as it rises.* **2** be larger or thicker in a particular place; stick out: *A barrel swells in the middle.* **3** increase in amount, degree, or force: *Savings may swell into a fortune.* **4** act of swelling; increase in amount, degree, or force. **5** rise above the level: *Rounded hills swell gradually from the village plain.* **6** part that rises or swells out. **7** long, unbroken wave or waves: *The boat rocked in the swell.* **8** grow louder; make louder: *The sound swelled to a roar. All joined in to swell the chorus.* **9** a swelling tone or sound. **10** stylish; grand. **11** excellent; very satisfactory. 1-3,5,8 verb, **swelled, swelled** or **swol len, swell ing;** 4,6,7,9 noun, 10,11 adjective.

swell ing (swel′ing), an increase in size; swollen part: *There is a swelling on her head where she bumped it.* noun.

swel ter (swel′tər), suffer from heat. verb.

swept (swept). See **sweep.** *He swept the room. It was swept clean.* verb.

swept-back (swept′bak′), extending outward and sharply backward. Most fast airplanes have swept-back wings. See picture. adjective.

swerve (swėrv), **1** turn aside: *The car swerved and hit a tree.* **2** turning aside: *The swerve of the ball made it hard to hit.* 1 verb, **swerved, swerv ing;** 2 noun.

a hat	i it	oi oil	ch child	(a in about
ā age	ī ice	ou out	ng long	e in taken
ä far	o hot	u cup	sh she	ə = { i in pencil
e let	ō open	ù put	th thin	o in lemon
ē equal	ô order	ü rule	₮H then	(u in circus
ėr term			zh measure	

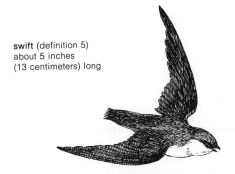

swift (definition 5)
about 5 inches
(13 centimeters) long

swept-back—an airplane with swept-back wings

swift (swift), **1** moving very fast; able to move very fast: *a swift automobile.* **2** coming or happening quickly: *a swift answer.* **3** quick, rapid, or prompt to act: *He is swift to repay a kindness.* **4** in a swift manner. **5** a small bird with long wings. A swift looks somewhat like a swallow. See picture. 1-3 adjective, 4 adverb, 5 noun.

swim (swim), **1** move along on or in the water by using arms, legs, or fins: *Fish swim. Most girls and boys like to swim.* **2** swim across: *He swam the river.* **3** make swim: *She swam her horse across the stream.* **4** float: *The roast lamb was swimming in gravy.* **5** be overflowed or flooded with: *His eyes were swimming with tears.* **6** act, time, motion, or distance of swimming: *Her swim had tired her. She had had an hour's swim.* **7** the swim, activities; what is going on: *An active and sociable person likes to be in the swim.* **8** go smoothly; glide: *Clouds swam across the sky.* **9** be dizzy: *Whirling around makes my head swim.* 1-5,8,9 verb, **swam, swum, swim ming;** 6,7 noun.

swim mer (swim/ər), person or animal that swims. *noun.*

swin dle (swin/dl), **1** cheat; defraud: *Honest merchants do not swindle their customers.* **2** act of swindling; fraud. 1 *verb,* **swin dled, swin dling;** 2 *noun.*

swin dler (swin/dlər), person who cheats or defrauds. *noun.*

swine (swīn), a hog or pig. *noun, plural* **swine.**

swing (swing), **1** move back and forth, especially with a regular motion: *The hammock swings. We swing our arms as we walk.* **2** move in a curve: *She swung the automobile around the corner.* **3** act or manner of swinging: *He brought the hammer down with a long swing.* **4** seat hung from ropes in which one may sit and swing. **5** hang: *We swung the hammock between two trees.* **6** move with a free, swaying motion: *The children came swinging down the street.* **7** movement; activity: *It's hard to get into the swing of school after vacation.* **8** a marked, swinging rhythm: *The song "Dixie" has a swing.* 1,2,5,6 *verb,* **swung, swing ing;** 3,4,7,8 *noun.*
in full swing, going on actively and completely: *By five o'clock the party was in full swing.*

swirl (swėrl), **1** move or drive along with a twisting motion; whirl: *dust swirling in the air, a stream swirling over rocks.* **2** a swirling movement; whirl; eddy. **3** twist; curl: *a lock of hair swirled against the neck.* **4** a twist or curl. 1,3 *verb,* 2,4 *noun.*

swish (swish), **1** move with a thin, light, hissing or brushing sound: *The whip swished through the air.* **2** make such a sound: *The long gown swished as she danced across the floor.* **3** cause to swish: *The cow swished its tail.* **4** a swishing movement or sound: *the swish of little waves on the shore.* 1-3 *verb,* 4 *noun, plural* **swish es.**

switch (swich), **1** a slender stick used in whipping. **2** whip; strike: *I switched the horse to make it gallop.* **3** stroke; lash: *The big dog knocked a vase off the table with a switch of its tail.* **4** move or swing like a switch: *The horse switched its tail to drive off the flies.* **5** device for making or breaking a connection in an electric circuit. **6** pair of movable rails by which a train can shift from one track to another. **7** change, turn, or shift by using a switch: *Switch off the light.* **8** change or shift: *switch places. They switched hats.* **9** change; turn; shift: *a last-minute switch in plans.* 1,3,5,6,9 *noun, plural* **switch es;** 2,4,7,8 *verb.*

switch board (swich/bôrd/), panel with electric switches and plugs for connecting telephone lines. *noun.*

swol len (swō/lən), **1** swelled: *a swollen ankle.* **2** See **swell.** *Her ankle has swollen considerably since she fell.* 1 *adjective,* 2 *verb.*

swoon (swün), faint: *He swoons at the sight of blood. Cold water will bring her out of the swoon.* *verb, noun.*

swoop (swüp), **1** come down with a rush, as a hawk does; sweep rapidly down upon in a sudden attack: *Bats swooped down from the roof of the cave.* **2** a rapid downward sweep; sudden, swift descent or attack: *With one swoop the hawk seized*

the chicken and flew away. **3** snatch: *The nurse swooped up the running child.* 1,3 *verb,* 2 *noun.*

sword (sôrd), **1** weapon, usually metal, with a long, sharp blade fixed in a handle or hilt. **2 the sword,** fighting or military power: *"Those that live by the sword shall perish by the sword." "The pen is mightier than the sword."* *noun.*

sword fish (sôrd/fish/), a very large sea fish that has a swordlike bone sticking out from its upper jaw. *noun, plural* **sword fish es** or **sword fish.**

swords man (sôrdz/mən), **1** person skilled in using a sword. **2** person using a sword. *noun, plural* **swords men.**

swore (swôr). See **swear.** *He swore that he was telling the truth.* *verb.*

sworn (swôrn), **1** See **swear.** *A solemn oath of loyalty was sworn by all the knights.* **2** having taken an oath; bound by an oath: *There were ten sworn witnesses.* **3** declared or promised with an oath: *We have her sworn statement before us.* 1 *verb,* 2,3 *adjective.*

swum (swum). See **swim.** *I have never swum before.* *verb.*

swung (swung). See **swing.** *He swung his arms as he walked. The door had swung open.* *verb.*

syc a more (sik/ə môr), kind of shade tree with large leaves and light-colored bark that peels off in tiny scales. *noun.*

syl lab ic (sə lab/ik), **1** of, having to do with, or made up of syllables. **2** forming a separate syllable by itself. The second *l* sound in *little* (lit/l) is syllabic. *adjective.*

syl lab i cate (sə lab/ə kāt), divide into syllables. *verb,* **syl lab i cat ed, syl lab i cat ing.**

syl lab i ca tion (sə lab/ə kā/shən), division into syllables. *noun.*

syl la ble (sil/ə bəl), **1** word or part of a word pronounced as a unit that usually consists of a vowel alone or a vowel with one or more consonants. There are three syllables (sil, ə, and bəl) in the pronunciation of the word *syllable.* Certain consonant sounds may be used as a vowel sound in syllables, such as the (l) in *bottle* (bot/l) or the (n) in *hidden* (hid/n). **2** letter or group of letters representing a syllable in writing and printing. A word of two or more syllables can be divided with a hyphen at the end of a line. *noun.*

sym bol (sim/bəl), something that stands for or represents something else: *The lion is the symbol of courage; the lamb, of meekness; the olive branch, of peace; the cross, of Christianity. The marks +, −, ×, and ÷ are symbols for add, subtract, multiply, and divide.* See picture. *noun.*

sym bol ize (sim/bə līz), **1** be a symbol of; stand for; represent: *A dove symbolizes peace.* **2** represent by a symbol or symbols: *The Indians and the settlers symbolized their friendship by smoking the peace pipe.* **3** use symbols. *verb,* **sym bol ized, sym bol iz ing.**

sym me try (sim/ə trē), **1** a regular, balanced form or arrangement on opposite sides of a line or around a center. See pictures. **2** a well-balanced arrangement of parts; harmony: *A swollen cheek* spoiled the symmetry of his face. *noun, plural* **sym me tries.**

sym pa thet ic (sim′pə thet′ik), **1** having or showing kind feelings toward others; sympathizing: *She is an unselfish and sympathetic friend.* **2** approving; agreeing: *The teacher was sympathetic to the class's plan for a trip to the museum.* **3** enjoying the same things and getting along well together. *adjective.*

sym pa thet i cal ly (sim′pə thet′ik lē), in a sympathetic way; with kindness: *The doctor spoke sympathetically while he bandaged my leg. adverb.*

sym pa thize (sim′pə thīz), **1** feel or show sympathy: *The boy sympathized with his little sister who had hurt herself.* **2** share in or agree with a feeling or opinion: *Her parents sympathize with her plans to be a painter. verb,* **sym pa thized, sym pa thiz ing.**

sym pa thy (sim′pə thē), **1** sharing another's sorrow or trouble: *We feel sympathy for a person who is ill.* **2** having the same feeling: *The sympathy between the twins was so great that they always smiled or cried at the same things.* **3** agreement; favor: *I am in sympathy with your plan. noun, plural* **sym pa thies.**

sym pho ny (sim′fə nē), **1** an elaborate musical composition for an orchestra. **2** harmony of sounds. **3** harmony of colors: *In autumn the woods are a symphony in red, brown, and yellow. noun, plural* **sym pho nies.**

symp tom (simp′təm), sign; indication: *Fever is a symptom of illness. noun.*

syn a gogue (sin′ə gôg), building used by Jews for religious instruction and worship. *noun.*

syn o nym (sin′ə nim), word that means the same or nearly the same as another word. *Keen* is a synonym of *sharp. noun.*

syn on y mous (si non′ə məs), having the same or nearly the same meaning. "Little" and "small" are synonymous. *adjective.*

syn thet ic (sin thet′ik), made by human skill; not natural: *synthetic rubber. Nylon is a synthetic fiber. adjective.*

syr up (sir′əp *or* sėr′əp), a sweet, thick liquid. Sugar boiled with water or fruit juices makes a syrup. A cough syrup contains medicine to relieve coughing. Maple syrup is made from the sap of maple trees. *noun.* Also spelled **sirup.**

sys tem (sis′təm), **1** set of things or parts forming a whole: *a mountain system, a railroad system, the digestive system, the nervous system.* **2** ordered group of facts, principles, or beliefs: *a system of government, a system of education.* **3** plan; scheme; method: *She has a system for getting the work done in half the time.* **4** an orderly way of getting things done: *He works by a system, not by chance. noun.*

sys tem at ic (sis′tə mat′ik), **1** according to a system; having a system, method, or plan: *systematic work.* **2** orderly in arranging things or in getting things done: *a very systematic person. adjective.*

sys tem at i cal ly (sis′tə mat′ik lē), with system; according to some plan or method. *adverb.*

symbol—The eagle is the symbol of the United States.

symmetry (definition 1)—two kinds of symmetry

T t

T or **t** (tē), the 20th letter of the English alphabet. There are two *t*'s in *tablet*. *noun, plural* **T's** or **t's.**

tab (tab), a small flap. Tabs stick out from caps to cover the ears, from cards used in filing, and from envelopes or cans for opening them. *noun.*

tab er nac le (tab′ər nak′əl), **1** place of worship for a large audience. **2** a Jewish temple. **3 Tabernacle,** the covered, wooden framework used by the Jews as a place of worship during their journey from Egypt to Palestine. *noun.*

ta ble (tā′bəl), **1** piece of furniture having a smooth, flat top on legs. **2** food put on a table to be eaten: *Our hosts set a good table.* **3** persons seated at a table: *The whole table joined in the conversation.* **4** information in a very brief form; list: *a table of contents in the front of a book, the multiplication table.* **5** a thin, flat piece of wood, stone, metal, or the like; tablet: *The Ten Commandments were written on tables of stone.* See picture. *noun.*

turn the tables, reverse conditions or circumstances completely: *They won the first game but we turned the tables on them and won the second.*

ta ble cloth (tā′bəl klôth′), cloth for covering a table: *Spread the tablecloth and set the table for dinner. noun, plural* **ta ble cloths** (tā′bəl klô̄ŦHz′ or tā′bəl klôths′).

ta ble land (tā′bəl land′), a high plain; plateau. *noun.*

ta ble spoon (tā′bəl spün′), **1** a large spoon used to serve food. **2** a unit of measure in cooking equal to 3 teaspoons or one half fluid ounce. *noun.*

ta ble spoon ful (tā′bəl spün′fùl), as much as a tablespoon holds. *noun, plural* **ta ble spoon fuls.**

tab let (tab′lit), **1** a thin, flat sheet of stone, wood, ivory, or other material, used to write or draw on. The ancient Romans used tablets as we use pads of paper. See picture. **2** number of sheets of writing paper fastened together at the edge. **3** a small, flat surface with an inscription. **4** a small, flat piece of medicine or candy: *That box contains twelve aspirin tablets. noun.*

tack (tak), **1** a short, sharp-pointed nail or pin having a broad, flat head: *We bought some carpet tacks.* **2** fasten with tacks: *She tacked mosquito netting over the windows.* **3** attach; add: *He tacked a postscript to the end of the letter.* **4** sail in a zigzag course against the wind: *The ship was tacking, trying to make the harbor.* **5** direction in which a ship moves in regard to the position of its sails. **6** course of action or conduct: *Ordering rather than asking her to help was the wrong tack to take.* 1,5,6 *noun,* 2-4 *verb.*

tack le (tak′əl), **1** equipment; apparatus; gear. **Fishing tackle** means the rod, line, hooks, or

table (definition 5)
and **tablet** (definition 1)

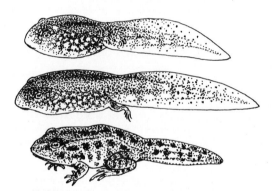

tadpole at different stages of growth

other equipment used in catching fish. **2** ropes and pulleys for lifting, lowering, and moving heavy things. The sails of a ship are raised and moved by tackle. **3** try to deal with: *We have a difficult problem to tackle.* **4** lay hold of; seize: *John tackled the boy with the football and pulled him to the ground.* **5** act of tackling. **6** a football player between the guard and the end on either side of the line. 1,2,5,6 *noun,* 3,4 *verb,* **tack led, tack ling.**

ta co (tä′kō), tortilla filled with chopped meat, chicken, or cheese, and served hot. *noun, plural* **ta cos.**

tact (takt), ability to say and do the right things; skill in dealing with people or handling difficult situations: *Father's tact kept him from talking about things likely to be unpleasant to his guests. noun.*

tact ful (takt′fəl), **1** having tact. See picture. **2** showing tact: *A tactful reply does not hurt a person's feelings. adjective.*

tac tics (tak′tiks), **1** art or science of arranging military or naval forces, or of putting them in a certain position. **2** the operations themselves: *The tactics of pretending to cross the river and of making a retreat fooled the enemy.* **3** procedures to gain advantage or success; methods: *When coaxing failed, they changed their tactics and began to threaten. noun.*

tad pole (tad′pōl′), a very young frog or toad, at the stage when it has a tail and lives in water. See picture. *noun.*

taf fy (taf′ē), kind of chewy candy. *noun, plural* **taf fies.**

tag[1] (tag), **1** piece of card, paper, leather, or the like, to be tied or fastened to something: *Each coat in the store has a tag with the price mark on it.* **2** supply with a tag or tags: *All her trunks and suitcases are tagged with her name and address.* **3** follow closely: *The baby tagged after his brother.* 1 *noun,* 2,3 *verb,* **tagged, tag ging.**

tag[2] (tag), **1** a children's game in which one player who is "it" chases the others and tries to touch them. The first one touched is then "it" and must chase the others. **2** touch or tap with the hand. 1 *noun,* 2 *verb,* **tagged, tag ging.**

tail (tāl), **1** the part that sticks out from the back of an animal's body. Rabbits have short tails. Mice have long tails. **2** something like an animal's tail: *Rags tied together made the tail of my kite.* **3** part of an airplane at the rear of the body. **4** the hind part of anything; back; rear: *Boys fastened their sleds to the tail of a cart. A crowd of children formed the tail of the procession.* **5** follow close behind: *Children tailed after the parade.* **6** coming from behind: *a tail wind.* 1-4 *noun,* 5 *verb,* 6 *adjective.*

tai lor (tā′lər), **1** person whose business is making, altering, or repairing clothes. **2** make by tailor's work: *The suit was well tailored.* 1 *noun,* 2 *verb.*

tail spin (tāl′spin′), a downward movement of an airplane with the nose first and the tail spinning in a circle above. *noun.*

taint (tānt), **1** stain or spot; trace of decay, corruption, or disgrace: *No taint of scandal ever touched the mayor.* **2** give a taint to; spoil: *Flies*

sometimes taint what they touch. *Rumors about taking bribes tainted the judge's reputation.* 1 *noun,* 2 *verb.*

take (tāk), **1** lay hold of: *I took her hand when we crossed the street.* **2** seize; capture: *Wild animals are taken in traps.* **3** catch hold; lay hold: *The fire has taken. The medicine seems to be taking; the fever is better.* **4** accept: *Take my advice. The dealer won't take a cent less for the car.* **5** receive: *I took the gift with a smile of thanks.* **6** win: *Our team took six games. He took first prize.* **7** get; have: *take a seat.* **8** absorb: *Marble takes a high polish.* **9** use; make use of: *I hate to take medicine. We took a train to go to Boston.* **10** need; require: *It takes time and patience to learn how to drive an automobile.* **11** choose; select: *Take the shortest way home.* **12** remove: *Please take the wastebasket away and empty it.* **13** subtract: *If you take 2 from 7, you have 5.* **14** go with; escort: *He likes to take his dog out for a walk.* **15** carry: *Take your lunch along.* **16** do; make; obtain by a special method: *Take a walk. Please take my photograph.* **17** feel: *She takes pride in her schoolwork.* **18** act; have effect: *The inoculation did not take.* **19** suppose: *I take it you won't go to school since you feel sick.* **20** regard; consider: *Let us take an example.* **21** engage; hire; lease: *take a cottage for the summer.* **22** receive and pay for; receive regularly: *take a newspaper.* **23** become affected by: *take cold.* **24** please; attract; charm: *The song took our fancy. verb,* **took, tak en, tak ing.**

take after, be like; resemble: *She takes after her mother.*

take back, withdraw; retract: *I apologized and took back my rude remark.*

take in, 1 make smaller: *Please take in the waist of my pants.* **2** understand: *She took in the situation at a glance.*

take off, 1 rise from the ground or water into the air: *The airplane took off so smoothly I didn't realize exactly when we rose from the runway.* **2** rush off: *I took off at the first sign of trouble.*

take on, agree to do; take upon oneself: *I plan to take on more jobs when school lets out this June.*

take to, 1 form a liking for: *Good students take to books.* **2** go to: *The cat took to the woods and became wild.*

take up, 1 soak up; absorb: *A sponge takes up liquid.* **2** make smaller: *The tailor took up the hem of the dress.* **3** begin; undertake: *He took up piano lessons in the summer.*

tak en (tā′kən). See take. *I have taken this toy from the shelf. verb.*

take off (tāk′ôf′), the leaving of the ground in leaping or in beginning a flight in an aircraft; taking off. *noun.*

a hat	i it	oi oil	ch child	ə = { a in about
ā age	ī ice	ou out	ng long	e in taken
ä far	o hot	u cup	sh she	i in pencil
e let	ō open	u̇ put	th thin	o in lemon
ē equal	ô order	ü rule	₮H then	u in circus
ėr term			zh measure	

tale (tāl), **1** story: *a tale about ghosts. Grandfather told the children tales of his boyhood.* **2** falsehood; lie. *noun.*

tell tales, tell something that will get a person into trouble.

tal ent (tal′ənt), a special natural ability; ability: *She has a talent for music. noun.*

tal ent ed (tal′ən tid), having natural ability; gifted: *a talented musician. adjective.*

talk (tôk), **1** use words; speak: *Baby is learning to talk.* **2** use in speaking: *Can you talk French?* **3** the use of words; spoken words; speech; conversation: *The old friends met for a good talk.* **4** an informal speech: *The coach gave the team a talk about the need for more team spirit.* **5** bring, put, drive, or influence by talk: *We talked her into joining the club.* **6** discuss: *talk politics, talk business.* **7** spread ideas by other means than speech: *talk by signs.* **8** spread rumors; gossip: *I try never to talk about anyone, because the facts could prove me wrong.* 1,2,5-8 *verb,* 3,4 *noun.*

talk a tive (tô′kə tiv), having the habit of talking a great deal; fond of talking: *He is a merry, talkative old man who knows everyone on our street. adjective.*

tall (tôl), **1** higher than the average; high: *New York has many tall buildings.* **2** having the height of; in height: *The tree is a hundred feet tall.* **3** hard to believe; exaggerated: *That is a pretty tall story. adjective.*

tal low (tal′ō), the fat of sheep and cattle after it has been melted. Tallow is used for making candles and soap. *noun.*

tal ly (tal′ē), **1** something, such as a sheet or pad of paper, on which a score or account is kept. **2** mark made for a certain number of objects in keeping account. **3** mark on a tally; count up: *tally a score.* **4** account; reckoning; score: *a tally of a game.* **5** agree; correspond: *Your account tallied with mine.* 1,2,4 *noun, plural* **tal lies;** 3,5 *verb,* **tal lied, tal ly ing.**

tal on (tal′ən), claw of a bird of prey; claw. See picture. *noun.*

tam bou rine (tam′bə rēn′), a small drum with jingling metal disks around the side, played by striking it with the knuckles or by shaking it. See picture. *noun.*

tame (tām), **1** taken from the wild state and made obedient: *a tame bear.* **2** gentle; without fear: *The birds are so tame that they will eat from our hands.* **3** make tame; break in: *The lion was tamed for the circus.* **4** become tame: *White rats tame easily.* **5** deprive of courage; tone down; subdue: *The bad news tamed our spirits.* **6** dull: *The party was tame because we were sleepy.* 1,2,6 *adjective,* **tam er, tam est;** 3-5 *verb,* **tamed, tam ing.**

tam per (tam′pər), meddle; meddle in an improper way: *Do not tamper with the lock. verb.*

tan (tan), **1** yellowish brown: *tan shoes.* **2** the brown color of a person's skin caused by being in the sun and air: *His arms and legs had a dark tan.* **3** make or become brown by exposure to sun and air: *Sun and wind had tanned her face. If you lie on the beach in the sun you will tan.* **4** make (a hide)

tapestry

tambourine

into leather by soaking in a special liquid.
1 *adjective*, **tan ner, tan nest;** 2 *noun*, 3,4 *verb*,
tanned, tan ning.

tang (tang), a strong taste or flavor: *the tang of
mustard. noun.*

tan ge rine (tan/jə rēn/), the reddish-orange, juicy
fruit of a tree grown in warm climates. Tangerines
look somewhat like small oranges. They have
loose peel, and their segments separate easily.
noun. [*Tangerine* comes from the name of Tangier,
a seaport in Morocco, northern Africa. The fruit
was originally called "Tangerine orange" because
it looked like an orange and was first exported
from Tangier.]

tan gle (tang/gəl), 1 twist and twine together in a
confused mass: *The kitten had tangled the ball of
twine.* 2 a confused or tangled mass: *The climbing
vines are all one tangle and need to be pruned and
tied up.* 3 a bewildering confusion; mess: *We tried
to sort out the truth from a tangle of lies.* 1 *verb*,
tan gled, tan gling; 2,3 *noun.*

tank (tangk), 1 a large container for liquid or gas.
An automobile has a fuel tank. 2 put or store in a
tank: *The plane tanked up on gas.* 3 a heavily
armored combat vehicle carrying machine guns
and usually a cannon, moving on an endless track
on each side. Tanks can travel over rough ground,
fallen trees, and other obstacles. 1,3 *noun*, 2 *verb.*

tank er (tang/kər), ship, airplane, or truck with
tanks for carrying oil or other liquid. *noun.*

tan ner (tan/ər), person whose work is making
hides into leather by tanning them. *noun.*

tan ta lize (tan/tl īz), torment by keeping
something desired in sight but out of reach; tease
by holding out hopes that are repeatedly
disappointed: *They tantalized the hungry dog by
pretending to feed it.* verb, **tan ta lized,
tan ta liz ing.** [*Tantalize* was formed from the
name of Tantalus, a king in Greek myths. His
punishment in the world of the dead was having
to stand up to his chin in water under branches
filled with fruit. Yet, whenever he tried to drink or
eat, the water or fruit drew back from his reach.]

tan trum (tan/trəm), fit of bad temper: *Little
children sometimes have tantrums when they do not
get what they want. noun.*

tap¹ (tap), 1 strike lightly: *I tapped on the window.*
2 a light blow: *There was a tap at the door.* 3 make,
put, or move by light blows: *tap a message, tap a
rhythm, tap the ashes out of a pipe.* 1,3 *verb*,
tapped, tap ping; 2 *noun.*

tap² (tap), 1 stopper or plug to close a hole in a
barrel containing liquid. 2 means of turning on or
off a flow of liquid; faucet. 3 make a hole in to let
out liquid: *tap sugar maples.* 1,2 *noun*, 3 *verb*,
tapped, tap ping.
on tap, ready for use: *I keep an extra box of
stationery on tap so that I won't run out of it
unexpectedly.*

tape (tāp), 1 a long, narrow strip of cloth, paper,
plastic, or some other material: *fancy tape to tie
packages. Put the bandage on with adhesive tape.*
2 something like such a strip. The strip

stretched across the finish line in a race is called
the tape. 3 fasten with tape; wrap with tape: *The
doctor taped up the wound.* 4 a plastic or paper
tape on which sounds or images can be recorded.
5 to record on such a tape: *The parade was taped
to show on a television news program in the evening.*
1,2,4 *noun*, 3,5 *verb*, **taped, tap ing.**

tape measure, a long strip of cloth or steel
marked in inches and feet, or in metric units, for
measuring.

ta per (tā/pər), 1 make or become gradually
smaller toward one end: *The church spire tapers off
to a point.* 2 grow less gradually; diminish: *Their
business tapered to nothing as people moved away.*
3 a very slender candle. 1,2 *verb*, 3 *noun.*

tape recorder, machine that records sound on
plastic tape and plays the sound back after it is
recorded.

tap es try (tap/ə strē), fabric with pictures or
designs woven in it, used to hang on walls or to
cover furniture. See picture. *noun, plural*
tap es tries.

tape worm (tāp/wėrm/), a long, flat worm that
lives in the intestines of people and animals. *noun.*

tap i o ca (tap/ē ō/kə), a starchy food obtained
from the root of a tropical plant. It is used for
puddings. *noun.*

ta pir (tā/pər), a large piglike animal of tropical
America and southern Asia with hooves and a
flexible snout. See picture. *noun.*

tap root (tap/rüt/), a main root growing
downward. *noun.*

taps (taps), signal on a bugle or drum to put out
lights at night. Taps are also sounded at military
funerals. *noun plural.*

tapir—about 3 feet (1 meter) high at the shoulder

talons

tar[1] (tär), **1** a black, sticky substance obtained from wood or coal. Tar is used to cover and patch roads and to keep telephone poles and other timber from rotting. **2** cover or smear with tar; soak in tar. Tarred paper is used on sheds to keep out water. *The street in front of our house is tarred.* **3** the brownish-black residue from the smoke of cigarettes, cigars, or pipes. 1,3 *noun*, 2 *verb*, **tarred, tar ring.**

tar and feather, pour heated tar on and cover with feathers as a punishment.

tar[2] (tär), sailor. *noun.*

ta ran tu la (tə ran′chə lə), a large, hairy, poisonous spider whose bite is painful but not dangerous. See picture. *noun.* [*Tarantula* comes from the name of Taranto, a seaport in southeastern Italy where the spider is commonly found.]

tar dy (tär′dē), behind time; late: *I was tardy for school yesterday. adjective,* **tar di er, tar di est.**

tar get (tär′git), **1** mark for shooting at; thing aimed at. A target is often a circle, but anything may be used as a target. **2** object of abuse, scorn, or criticism: *Their crazy plan was the target of many jokes. noun.*

tar iff (tar′if), **1** a list of duties or taxes on imports or exports. **2** any duty or tax in such a list: *There is a very high tariff on imported jewelry. noun.*

tar nish (tär′nish), **1** dull the luster or brightness of: *Salt will tarnish silver.* **2** lose luster or brightness: *The brass doorknobs tarnished.* **3** loss of luster or brightness. 1,2 *verb,* 3 *noun.*

tar pau lin (tär pô′lən), sheet of canvas, or other coarse cloth, made waterproof. *noun.*

tar pon (tär′pon), a large, silver-colored fish found in the warmer parts of the Atlantic Ocean. *noun, plural* **tar pons** or **tar pon.**

tar ry (tar′ē), **1** remain; stay: *We tarried another day to see all the sights.* **2** wait; delay: *Why do you tarry so long? verb,* **tar ried, tar ry ing.**

tart[1] (tärt), **1** having a sharp taste; sour: *Some apples are tart.* **2** sharp: *A tart reply is sometimes impolite. adjective.*

tart[2] (tärt), pastry filled with cooked fruit, jam, or the like. In Canada and the United States, a tart is small and open on the top so that the fruit shows; in England, any fruit pie is a tart. *noun.*

tar tan (tärt′n), **1** a plaid woolen cloth. Each Scottish clan has its own pattern of tartan. **2** the pattern or design itself. **3** made of tartan. 1,2 *noun,* 3 *adjective.*

tar tar (tär′tər), substance that collects on the teeth. If not removed by brushing the teeth, tartar will harden into a crust. *noun.*

task (task), **1** work to be done; piece of work; duty: *His task is to set the table.* **2** put work on; force to work: *The coach tasked the team members beyond their strength.* 1 *noun,* 2 *verb.*

take to task, blame, scold, or reprove: *The teacher took the student to task for not studying.*

tas sel (tas′əl), **1** a hanging bunch of threads, small cords, beads, or the like, fastened together at one end. **2** something like this: *Corn has tassels.*

3 grow tassels: *Corn tassels just before the ears form.* 1,2 *noun,* 3 *verb.*

taste (tāst), **1** flavor; what is special about (something) to the sense organs of the mouth. Sweet, sour, salt, and bitter are the four most important tastes. *I think this milk is sour; it has a funny taste.* **2** try the flavor of (something) by taking a little into the mouth: *The cook tastes everything to see if it is right.* **3** sense by which one is aware of the flavor of things: *Her taste is unusually keen.* **4** get the flavor of by the sense of taste: *I taste almond in this cake. When I have a cold, I can taste nothing.* **5** have a particular flavor: *The soup tastes of onion.* **6** eat or drink a little bit of: *The children barely tasted their breakfast the day they went to the circus.* **7** a little bit; sample: *Give me just a taste of the pudding. The snowstorm will give you a taste of northern winter.* **8** experience; have: *Having tasted freedom, the bird would not return to its cage.* **9** liking: *Suit your own taste.* **10** ability to know and enjoy what is beautiful and excellent: *Some people have taste in art.* **11** manner or style that shows such ability: *Their house is furnished in excellent taste.* 1,3,7,9-11 *noun,* 2,4-6,8 *verb,* **tast ed, tast ing.**

taste less (tāst′lis), **1** without taste: *Some hot foods are tasteless and unpleasant when they become cold.* **2** without good taste; in poor taste. *adjective.*

tast y (tā′stē), tasting good; pleasing to the taste. *adjective,* **tast i er, tast i est.**

tat ter (tat′ər), a torn piece; rag: *After the storm the flag hung in tatters upon the mast. noun.*

tat tered (tat′ərd), **1** torn; ragged. **2** wearing torn or ragged clothes. *adjective.*

tat tle (tat′l), **1** tell tales or secrets. **2** talk foolishly; gossip. *verb,* **tat tled, tat tling.**

tat tle tale (tat′l tāl′), person who tells tales on others; person who reveals private or secret matters from ill will. *noun.*

tat too (ta tü′), **1** mark (the skin) with designs or patterns by pricking it and putting in colors: *The sailor had a ship tattooed on his arm.* **2** mark or design tattooed on the skin. 1 *verb,* 2 *noun, plural* **tat toos.**

taught (tôt). See **teach.** *That teacher taught my mother. She has taught arithmetic for years. verb.*

taunt (tônt), **1** make fun of in a bitter or insulting way; mock; jeer at: *My classmates taunted me for being teacher's pet.* **2** a bitter or insulting remark; mocking; jeering. 1 *verb,* 2 *noun.*

taut (tôt), **1** drawn tight; tense: *a taut rope.* **2** in neat condition; tidy: *The captain insists on a taut ship. adjective.*

tav ern (tav′ərn), **1** place where alcoholic drinks are sold and drunk. **2** inn. *noun.*

taw ny (tô′nē), brownish yellow. *adjective,* **taw ni er, taw ni est.**

tax (taks), **1** money paid by people for the support of the government and the cost of public works and services. **2** put a tax on. People who own property are taxed in order to provide clean streets, good roads, protection against crime, and free education. **3** burden, duty, or demand that

a hat	i it	oi oil	ch child		a in about
ā age	ī ice	ou out	ng long		e in taken
ä far	o hot	u cup	sh she	ə =	i in pencil
e let	ō open	u̇ put	th thin		o in lemon
ē equal	ô order	ü rule	ᵀʜ then		u in circus
ėr term			zh measure		

tarantula
body 1 to 2 inches (2½ to 5 centimeters) long

teal—about 14 inches (36 centimeters) long.

team (definition 2)—a team of 33 mules

oppresses; strain: *Climbing stairs is a tax on a weak heart.* **4** lay a heavy burden on; be hard for: *The work taxed my strength. Reading in a poor light taxes the eyes.* **5** find fault with; accuse: *My parents taxed me with not doing my share of the housework.* 1,3 *noun, plural* **tax es** for 1; 2,4,5 *verb.*

tax a tion (tak sā′shən), **1** act or system of taxing: *Taxation is necessary to provide roads, schools, and police.* **2** amount people pay for the support of the government; taxes. *noun.*

tax i (tak′sē), **1** taxicab. **2** ride in a taxi. **3** move slowly on the ground or water: *The airplane taxied off the field after landing.* 1 *noun, plural* **tax is**; 2,3 *verb*, **tax ied, tax i ing** or **tax y ing.**

tax i cab (tak′sē kab′), automobile for hire, usually with a meter for recording the fare. *noun.*

tax pay er (taks′pā′ər), person who pays a tax or is required by law to do so. *noun.*

tea (tē), **1** a common drink made by pouring boiling water over the dried and prepared leaves of a shrub grown chiefly in China, Japan, and India. **2** the leaves themselves. **3** shrub these leaves grow on. **4** drink made from some other plant or from meat: *sage tea.* **Beef tea** is a strong broth made from beef. **5** a light meal in the late afternoon or early evening, at which tea is served. **6** an afternoon reception at which tea is served. *noun.*

teach (tēch), **1** help to learn; show how to do; make understand: *He is teaching his dog to shake hands.* **2** give lessons in: *He teaches music.* **3** give lessons; act as teacher: *She teaches for a living.* *verb*, **taught, teach ing.**

teach er (tē′chər), person who teaches, especially one who teaches in a school. *noun.*

teach ing (tē′ching), **1** work or profession of a teacher. **2** what is taught: *religious teachings. noun.*

tea cup (tē′kup′), cup for drinking tea. *noun.*

tea ket tle (tē′ket′l), kettle with a handle and a spout for heating water. *noun.*

teal (tēl), a small wild duck that is related to the mallard. See picture. *noun, plural* **teals** or **teal.**

team (tēm), **1** number of people working or acting together, especially one of the sides in a game or a match: *a football team, a debating team.* **2** two or more horses or other animals harnessed together to work. See picture. **3** join together in a team: *Everybody teamed up to clean the room after the party.* 1,2 *noun*, 3 *verb.*

team mate (tēm′māt′), a fellow member of a team. *noun.*

team ster (tēm′stər), person whose work is hauling things with a truck or driving a team of horses. *noun.*

team work (tēm′wėrk′), the acting together of a number of people to make the work of a group

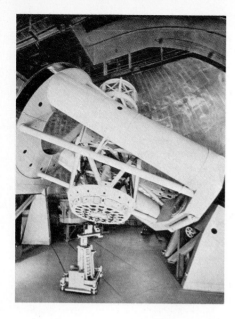

telescope (definition 1)
two different telescopes

tempest (definition 1)—The **tempest** drove the
ship southward.

successful and effective: *Football requires
teamwork even more than individual skill. noun.*

tea pot (tē′pot′), container with a handle and a
spout for making and serving tea. *noun.*

tear[1] (tir), drop of salty water coming from the
eye. *noun.*

in tears, shedding tears or crying: *The baby is in
tears because he is hungry.*

tear[2] (ter *or* tar), **1** pull apart by force: *tear a box
open. I tore the paper in half.* **2** make by pulling
apart: *She tore a hole in her jeans.* **3** pull hard; pull
violently: *Tear out the page.* **4** cut badly; wound:
The jagged stone tore my skin. **5** make miserable;
distress: *She was torn by sorrow.* **6** become torn:
Lace tears easily. **7** a torn place: *She has a tear in
her jacket.* **8** move with great force or haste: *An
automobile came tearing down the road.* 1-6,8 *verb*,
tore, torn, tear ing; 7 *noun.*

tear down, destroy: *to tear down an old building.*

tear ful (tir′fəl), **1** full of tears; weeping. **2** causing
tears; sad: *Getting lost was a tearful experience.
adjective.*

tease (tēz), **1** vex or worry by jokes, questions,
requests, or the like; annoy: *The children teased the
dog until it snapped at them.* **2** beg: *That child teases
for everything he sees.* **3** person who teases. 1,2
verb, **teased, teas ing;** 3 *noun.*

tea spoon (tē′spün′), **1** a small spoon often used
to stir tea or coffee. **2** a unit of measure in
cooking equal to one-third tablespoon. *noun.*

tea spoon ful (tē′spün′fül), as much as a
teaspoon holds. *noun, plural* **tea spoon fuls.**

tech ni cal (tek′nə kəl), **1** of or having something
to do with a mechanical or industrial art or with
applied science: *This technical school trains
engineers, chemists, and architects.* **2** of or having
something to do with the special facts of a
science or art: *"Transistor" and "protein" are
technical words.* **3** of or having to do with the
method or ability of an artist's performance: *Her
singing showed technical skill, but her voice was
weak. adjective.*

tech ni cian (tek nish′ən), person who knows the
technical details and methods of a subject or a
job. *noun.*

tech nique (tek nēk′), **1** method or ability of an
artist's performance; technical skill: *The pianist's
technique was excellent.* **2** a special method or
system used to do something. *noun.*

ted dy bear (ted′ē ber′ *or* ted′ē bar′), a child's
furry toy bear. [The word *teddy* comes from *Teddy*,
a nickname for Theodore Roosevelt. He was
president of the United States from 1901 to 1909.
A cartoon showed him refusing to shoot a bear
cub when he was hunting. Soon, stuffed toy
animals were being sold that came to be known
as "teddy bears."]

te di ous (tē′dē əs *or* tē′jəs), long and tiring: *A
boring talk that you cannot understand is tedious.
adjective.*

tee (tē), **1** a mark or place where a player starts
to play each hole in golf. **2** a short wooden or
plastic peg on which a golf ball can be placed

and then hit. *noun.*

tee off, hit (a golf ball) from a tee.

teem (tēm), be full; abound; swarm: *The swamp teemed with mosquitoes. verb.*

teen ag er (tēn′ā′jər), person in his or her teens. *noun.*

teens (tēnz), the years of life from 13 to 19. *noun plural.*

tee pee (tē′pē), tepee. *noun.*

tee shirt, T-shirt.

tee ter (tē′tər), rock unsteadily; sway. *verb.*

tee ter-tot ter (tē′tər tot′ər), seesaw. *noun.*

teeth (tēth), more than one tooth: *You often show your teeth when you smile. noun plural.*

in the teeth of, straight against; in the face of: *He advanced in the teeth of the wind.*

teethe (tēᴛʜ), grow teeth; cut teeth: *Babies teethe. verb,* **teethed, teeth ing.**

tel e cast (tel′ə kast′), **1** to broadcast by television. **2** a television program. **1** *verb,* **tel e cast** or **tel e cast ed, tel e cast ing; 2** *noun.*

tel e gram (tel′ə gram), message sent by telegraph: *Father sent a telegram telling us what train to take. noun.*

tel e graph (tel′ə graf), **1** way of sending coded messages over wires by means of electricity. **2** device used for sending these messages. **3** send (a message) by telegraph: *Mother telegraphed that she would arrive home by the afternoon plane.* **1,2** *noun,* **3** *verb.*

tel e phone (tel′ə fōn), **1** instrument for talking between distant points over wires by means of electricity. **2** talk through a telephone; send (a message) by telephone. **3** make a telephone call to. **1** *noun,* **2,3** *verb,* **tel e phoned, tel e phon ing.** [*Telephone* was formed from Greek words meaning "far off," and "sound" or "voice."]

telephone book or **telephone directory,** list of names, addresses, and telephone numbers.

tel e scope (tel′ə skōp), **1** an instrument for making distant objects appear nearer and larger. The stars are studied by means of telescopes. See pictures. **2** force together, one inside another, like the sliding tubes of some telescopes: *When the two railroad trains crashed into each other, the cars were telescoped.* **3** be forced together in this way. **1** *noun,* **2,3** *verb,* **tel e scoped, tel e scop ing.**

tel e vise (tel′ə vīz), send by television: *televise a baseball game. verb,* **tel e vised, tel e vis ing.**

tel e vi sion (tel′ə vizh′ən), **1** a way of sending and receiving over wires or through the air pictures of things and events and the sounds that go with them. **2** device on which these pictures and sounds may be seen and heard. *noun.*

tell (tel), **1** put in words; say: *Tell us a story. Tell the truth.* **2** tell to; inform: *Tell us about it.* **3** make known: *Don't tell where the candy is.* **4** recognize; know: *I can't tell which house is yours.* **5** say to; order; command: *Do as you are told. verb,* **told, tell ing.**

tell on, inform on; tell tales about.

tell er (tel′ər), **1** person who tells: *Our teacher is a good teller of stories.* **2** person who counts. A teller

in a bank takes in, gives out, and counts money. *noun.*

a hat	i it	oi oil	ch child	a in about
ā age	ī ice	ou out	ng long	e in taken
ä far	o hot	u cup	sh she	ə = i in pencil
e let	ō open	u̇ put	th thin	o in lemon
ē equal	ô order	ü rule	ᴛʜ then	u in circus
ėr term			zh measure	

tem per (tem′pər), **1** state of mind; disposition; condition: *a sweet temper. She was in no temper to be kept waiting.* **2** angry state of mind: *fly into a temper. In my temper I slammed the door.* **3** calm state of mind: *He became angry and lost his temper.* **4** moderate; soften: *Temper justice with mercy.* **5** bring or be brought to a proper or desired condition by mixing or preparing. Painters temper their colors by mixing them with oil. Steel is tempered by heating it and working it until it has the proper degree of hardness and toughness. **6** the hardness or toughness of the mixture: *The temper of the clay was right for shaping.* **1-3,6** *noun,* **4,5** *verb.*

tem per a ment (tem′pər ə mənt), a person's nature; make-up; disposition: *a nervous temperament. noun.*

tem per a men tal (tem′pər ə men′tl), subject to moods and whims; easily irritated; sensitive. *adjective.*

tem per ance (tem′pər əns), **1** being moderate in action, speech, or habits; self-control: *Temperance should be applied not only to food and drink but also to work and play.* **2** using little or no alcoholic drinks. *noun.*

tem per ate (tem′pər it), **1** not very hot, and not very cold: *Seattle has a temperate climate.* **2** moderate; using self-control: *She spoke in a temperate manner, not favoring either side.* **3** moderate in using alcoholic drinks: *A temperate person doesn't drink too much. adjective.*

temperate zone or **Temperate Zone,** either of two regions between the tropics and polar circles: *The United States is in the north temperate zone.*

tem per a ture (tem′pər ə chər), **1** degree of heat or cold. The temperature of freezing water is 32 degrees Fahrenheit, or 0 degrees Celsius. **2** a body temperature higher than normal (98.6 degrees Fahrenheit, or 37 degrees Celsius): *A sick person may have a temperature. noun.*

tem pest (tem′pist), **1** a violent storm with much wind. See picture. **2** a violent disturbance: *a tempest of anger. noun.*

tem pes tu ous (tem pes′chü əs), **1** stormy: *It was a tempestuous night.* **2** violent: *a tempestuous fit of anger. adjective.*

tem ple[1] (tem′pəl), **1** building used for the service or worship of a god or gods: *Greek temples were beautifully built.* **2** **Temple,** any of three temples in ancient Jerusalem built at different times by the Jews. Solomon built the first Temple. **3** any building set apart for worship, especially a Jewish synagogue. *noun.*

tem ple[2] (tem′pəl), the flattened part on either side of the forehead. *noun.*

tem po (tem′pō), in music, the time or rate of movement; proper speed of movement: *the correct tempo for a dance tune. noun, plural* **tem pos.**

tem po rar i ly (tem′pə rer′ə lē), for a short time; for the present: *They are living in a hotel temporarily. adverb.*

tem po rar y (tem′pə rer′ē), lasting for a short time only: *This is just a temporary job. adjective.*

tempt (tempt), **1** make or try to make (a person) do something: *Extreme hunger can tempt a person to steal food.* **2** appeal strongly to; attract. See picture. **3** provoke: *It is tempting fate to go in that old boat. verb.*

temp ta tion (temp tā′shən), **1** tempting: *No temptation could make her break her promise.* **2** being tempted: *The Lord's Prayer says, "Lead us not into temptation."* **3** thing that tempts: *Money left carelessly about is a temptation. noun.*

ten (ten), one more than nine; 10. *noun, adjective.*

te na cious (ti nā′shəs), **1** holding fast. See picture. **2** stubborn; persistent: *a tenacious salesman. adjective.*

te nac i ty (ti nas′ə tē), **1** firmness in holding fast. See picture. **2** stubbornness; persistence. **3** firmness in holding together. **4** sticky quality; sticky condition. *noun.*

ten ant (ten′ənt), **1** person paying rent for the temporary use of land or buildings of another person: *That building has apartments for one hundred tenants.* **2** person or thing that occupies: *Birds are tenants of the trees.* **3** hold or occupy as a tenant; inhabit: *That old house is not tenanted.* 1,2 *noun,* 3 *verb.*

tend[1] (tend), **1** be apt; be likely; incline (to): *Fruit tends to decay. I tend to sleep late on weekends.* **2** move (toward); be directed: *The road tends to the south here. verb.*

tend[2] (tend), take care of; look after; attend to: *He tends shop for his parents. The shepherd tends the flock of sheep. verb.*

ten den cy (ten′dən sē), inclination; leaning: *a tendency to fight. Wood has a tendency to swell if it gets wet. noun, plural* **ten den cies.**

ten der[1] (ten′dər), **1** not hard or tough; soft: *The meat is tender. Stones hurt the little child's tender feet.* **2** delicate; not strong and hardy: *The leaves in spring are green and tender.* **3** kind; affectionate; loving: *She spoke tender words to the baby.* **4** gentle; not rough or crude: *He patted the dog with tender hands.* **5** young: *Two years old is a tender age.* **6** sensitive; painful; sore: *a tender wound. Automobiles are a tender subject with Dad since he wrecked his.* **7** feeling pain or grief easily: *a person with a tender heart. adjective.*

ten der[2] (ten′dər), **1** offer formally: *She tendered her thanks.* **2** a formal offer: *She refused his tender of marriage.* **3** thing offered. **Legal tender** means money that must be accepted as payment for a debt. 1 *verb,* 2,3 *noun.*

tend er[3] (ten′dər), **1** person or thing that tends another. **2** a small boat carried or towed by a ship

tempt (definition 2)—He was **tempted** to spend his entire allowance on ice cream.

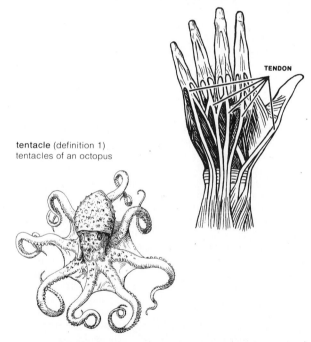

tentacle (definition 1)
tentacles of an octopus

TENDON

THIS DOG CERTAINLY IS TENACIOUS

YES, ITS TENACITY IS REMARKABLE

and used to land passengers. **3** the car that carries coal and water, attached to a locomotive. *noun.*

ten der foot (ten′dər fut′), **1** newcomer to the pioneer life of the western United States. **2** person not used to rough living and hardships. **3** an inexperienced person; beginner. *noun, plural* **ten der foots, ten der feet** (ten′dər fēt′).

ten don (ten′dən), a tough, strong band or cord of tissue that joins a muscle to a bone; sinew. See picture. *noun.*

ten dril (ten′drəl), a threadlike part of a climbing plant, that attaches itself to something and helps support the plant. *noun.*

ten e ment (ten′ə mənt), an old building, especially in a poor section of a city. A tenement is divided into sets of rooms occupied by separate families. *noun.*

Ten nes see (ten′ə sē′), one of the south central states of the United States. *noun.* [*Tennessee* got its name from a Cherokee Indian village called Tanasie.]

ten nis (ten′is), game played by two or four players on a special court, in which a ball is hit back and forth over a net with a racket. *noun.*

ten or (ten′ər), **1** the highest singing voice of a man. **2** singer with such a voice. **3** part sung by such a voice. *noun.*

tense[1] (tens), **1** stretched tight; strained to stiffness: *a tense rope, a face tense with pain.* **2** stretch tight; stiffen: *She tensed her muscles for the leap.* **3** strained: *tense nerves, a tense moment.* **1,3** *adjective,* **tens er, tens est;** **2** *verb,* **tensed, tens ing.**

tense[2] (tens), form of a verb that shows the time of the action or state expressed by the verb. *I dance* is in the present tense. *I danced* is in the past tense. *I will dance* is in the future tense. *noun.*

ten sion (ten′shən), **1** a stretching. **2** a stretched condition: *The tension of the bow gives speed to the arrow.* **3** strain: *Tension is sometimes brought on by overwork. noun.*

tent (tent), **1** a movable shelter made of cloth or skins supported by a pole or poles. **2** live in a tent: *We sang "We are tenting tonight on the old camp ground."* **1** *noun,* **2** *verb.*

ten ta cle (ten′tə kəl), **1** a long, slender, flexible growth on the head or around the mouth of an animal, used to touch, hold, or move: *An octopus has eight tentacles.* See picture. **2** a sensitive, hairlike growth on a plant. *noun.*

tenth (tenth), **1** next after the ninth. **2** one of ten equal parts. *adjective, noun.*

te pee (tē′pē), tent used by North American Indians, made of hides sewn together and stretched over poles arranged in the shape of a cone. See picture. *noun.* Also spelled **teepee.**

tep id (tep′id), slightly warm; lukewarm. *adjective.*

term (tėrm), **1** word or group of words used in connection with some special subject, science, art, or business: *medical terms. "Acid," "base," and "salt" are terms commonly used in chemistry.* **2** name; call: *He might be termed handsome.* **3** a set

period of time; length of time that a thing lasts: *The President's term of office is four years.* **4** one of the periods into which the school year is divided: *Most schools have a fall term and a spring term.* **5 terms, a** conditions: *The terms of the peace were very hard for the defeated nation.* **b** personal relations: *We are on very good terms with all our neighbors.* **1,3-5** *noun,* **2** *verb.*

ter mi nal (tėr′mə nəl), **1** at the end; forming the end part. Terminal buds grow at the end of stems. **2** end; end part. A terminal is either end of a railroad line, bus line, airline, or shipping route where sheds, hangars, garages, and offices to handle freight and passengers are located. **3** device for making an electrical connection: *the terminals of a battery.* **4** device by which a person and a computer may communicate. A terminal usually has a keyboard like a typewriter and a screen like a television. **1** *adjective,* **2-4** *noun.*

ter mi nate (tėr′mə nāt), **1** bring to an end; put an end to; end: *The lawyers terminated their partnership and each opened a separate office.* **2** come to an end: *The contract terminates tomorrow. verb,* **ter mi nat ed, ter mi nat ing.**

ter mi na tion (tėr′mə nā′shən), ending; end: *Termination of the contract left both parties free to do business elsewhere. noun.*

ter mi nus (tėr′mə nəs), an end of a railroad line, bus line, airline, or shipping route. *noun, plural* **ter mi ni** (tėr′mə nī), **ter mi nus es.**

ter mite (tėr′mīt), insect that has a soft, pale body. Termites eat the wood of buildings, furniture, and other material containing cellulose. *noun.*

tepee

ter race (ter′is), **1** a paved outdoor space near a house for lounging or dining. **2** a flat, raised piece of land with vertical or sloping sides, especially one of a series of such levels placed one above the other. **3** form into a terrace or terraces; furnish with terraces: *a terraced garden.* 1,2 *noun,* 3 *verb,* **ter raced, ter rac ing.**

ter rar i um (tə rer′ē əm), a glass enclosure in which plants or small land animals are kept. See picture. *noun.*

ter res tri al (tə res′trē əl), of the earth; not of the heavens: *this terrestrial globe. adjective.*

ter ri ble (ter′ə bəl), causing great fear; dreadful; awful: *The terrible storm destroyed many lives. adjective.*

ter ri bly (ter′ə blē), **1** in a terrible manner; dreadfully: *The child was terribly afraid of the thunder.* **2** extremely; very: *I am terribly sorry I stepped on your toes. adverb.*

ter ri er (ter′ē ər), a small, active, intelligent dog that was once used to chase prey into its burrow. Well-known kinds include fox terriers, Irish terriers, and Scotch terriers. *noun.*

ter rif ic (tə rif′ik), **1** causing great fear; terrifying: *A terrific earthquake shook Japan.* **2** very great or severe: *A terrific hot spell ruined many of the crops.* **3** very good; wonderful: *She is a terrific tennis player. adjective.*

ter ri fy (ter′ə fī), fill with great fear; frighten very much: *Terrified by the sight of the bear, we ran into the cabin. verb,* **ter ri fied, ter ri fy ing.**

ter ri to ry (ter′ə tôr′ē), **1** land; region: *Much territory in the northern part of Africa is desert.* **2** land belonging to a government; land under the rule of a distant government: *Alaska was a territory of the United States until 1958. noun, plural* **ter ri to ries.**

ter ror (ter′ər), **1** great fear: *The child has a terror of thunder.* **2** cause of great fear: *Pirates were once the terror of the sea. noun.*

ter ror ize (ter′ə rīz′), **1** fill with terror: *The sight of the growling dog terrorized the little child.* **2** rule by causing terror. *verb,* **ter ror ized, ter ror iz ing.**

test (test), **1** examination; trial: *The teacher gave us a test in arithmetic. People who want a license to drive an automobile must pass a test.* **2** means of trial: *Trouble is a test of character.* **3** examination of a substance to see what it is or what it contains: *A test showed that the water was pure.* **4** put to a test of any kind; try out: *That water was tested for purity. The doctor tested the girl's eyes.* 1-3 *noun,* 4 *verb.* [*Test* is from an old French word meaning "a small pot in which to treat ore to find out how much metal it has." From this the meaning "any means of finding out" developed.]

tes ta ment (tes′tə mənt), **1** written instructions telling what to do with a person's property after his or her death; will. **2 Testament, a** a main division of the Bible; the Old Testament or the New Testament. **b** the New Testament. *noun.*

tes ti fy (tes′tə fī), give evidence; say as a witness; declare: *The witness testified that the speeding car had crashed into the truck. Other witnesses were*

unwilling to testify. *verb,* **tes ti fied, tes ti fy ing.**

tes ti mo ny (tes′tə mō′nē), **1** statement used for evidence or proof: *A witness gave testimony that the accused man was at home all day.* **2** evidence: *The pupils presented their teacher with a watch in testimony of their respect and affection. noun, plural* **tes ti mo nies.**

test tube, a thin glass tube closed at one end, used in making chemical tests.

tet a nus (tet′n əs), disease that causes violent spasms, stiffness of many muscles, and even death. You can be protected against it by inoculation. *noun.*

teth er (teᴛʜ′ər), **1** rope or chain for fastening an animal so that it can graze or move only within a certain limit: *The cow had broken its tether and was in the garden.* **2** fasten with a tether: *The horse is tethered to a stake.* 1 *noun,* 2 *verb.*

Tex as (tek′səs), one of the southwestern states of the United States. *noun.* [*Texas* got its name from a group of American Indians living in the area who were called *Tejas* by the Spanish. This name came from an American Indian word meaning "friends" or "allies."]

text (tekst), **1** the main body of reading matter in a book: *This history book contains 300 pages of text, and about 50 pages of maps and pictures.* **2** the original words of a writer. A text is often changed here and there when it is copied. **3** a short passage in the Bible: *The minister preached on the text "Blessed are the merciful."* **4** topic; subject: *Town improvement was the speaker's text.* **5** textbook. *noun.*

text book (tekst′bùk′), book for regular study by pupils. Most books used in schools are textbooks. *noun.*

tex tile (tek′stəl *or* tek′stīl), **1** a woven fabric; cloth: *Beautiful textiles are sold in Paris.* **2** suitable for weaving: *Linen, cotton, silk, nylon, and wool are common textile materials.* **3** of or having something to do with weaving: *the textile arts, the textile industry.* 1 *noun,* 2,3 *adjective.*

tex ture (teks′chər), **1** arrangement of threads woven together: *Homespun is cloth that has a loose texture. A piece of burlap has a much coarser texture than a linen handkerchief.* **2** arrangement of the parts of anything; structure; feel: *Velvet has a soft, smooth texture. The texture of marble makes it take a polish. noun.*

-th¹, suffix meaning: number _____ in order or position in a series. Six*th* means *number* six *in order or position in a series.* The suffix *-eth* is used to form numbers like *fiftieth* and *sixtieth.*

-th², suffix meaning: **1** act or process of _____ing: Grow*th* means *act or process of* growing. **2** quality, state, or condition of being _____: Tru*th* means *quality, state, or condition of being* true.

than (ᴛʜan), **1** in comparison with: *She is taller than her sister.* **2** compared to that which: *You know better than I do.* **3** except; besides: *How else can we come than by train? conjunction.*

thank (thangk), say that one is pleased and grateful for something given or done: *She thanked* *her teacher for helping her. verb.*

have oneself to thank, be to blame: *You have yourself to thank if you eat too much.*

thank ful (thangk′fəl), feeling thanks; grateful: *I am thankful for your help. adjective.*

thank less (thangk′lis), **1** ungrateful: *The thankless child expressed no appreciation for our gift.* **2** not likely to get thanks: *Giving advice is usually a thankless act. adjective.*

thanks (thangks), **1** I thank you: *Thanks for your good wishes.* **2** act of thanking; expression of pleasure and gratitude: *I return the book to you with my sincere thanks.* **3** feeling of kindness received; gratitude: *You have our thanks for everything you have done. noun plural.*

thanks to, owing to or because of: *Thanks to his efforts, the garden is a great success.*

thanks giv ing (thangks giv′ing), **1** giving thanks. **2** expression of thanks: *They offered a thanksgiving to God for their escape. noun.*

Thanksgiving Day, day set apart as a holiday on which to give thanks for past blessings. In the United States, Thanksgiving Day is the fourth Thursday in November.

that (ŦHat), **1** *That* is used to point out some one person or thing or idea. We use *this* for the thing nearer us, and *that* for the thing farther away from us. *Do you know that woman? Shall we buy this book or that one? I like that better.* **2** *That* is also used to connect a group of words. *I know that 6 and 4 are 10.* **3** *That* is used to show purpose. *Study that you may learn.* **4** *That* is used to show result. *I ran so fast that I was five minutes early.* **5** who; whom: *Is he the man that sells dogs? She is the girl that you saw in school.* **6** which: *Bring the box that will hold most.* **7** on which; at or in which: *It was the day that school began. The year that we went to England was 1970.* **8** to that extent; to such a degree; so: *The baby cannot stay up that long.* **1** *adjective, plural* **those;** **1,5-7** *pronoun, plural* **those;** **2-4** *conjunction;* **8** *adverb.*

thatch (thach), **1** straw, rushes, or the like, used as a roof or covering. **2** make or cover with thatch. See picture. **1** *noun,* **2** *verb.*

that's (ŦHats), that is.

thaw (thô), **1** melt (ice, snow, or anything frozen); free from frost: *The sun at noon thaws the ice on the streets. It thawed early last spring.* **2** weather above the freezing point (32 degrees Fahrenheit, or 0 degrees Celsius); time of melting: *In January we usually have a thaw.* **3** become less cold, less formal, or less reserved: *His shyness thawed under the teacher's kindness.* **1,3** *verb,* **2** *noun.*

the[1] (ŦHə, ŦHi, *or* ŦHē), a certain; a particular: *The dog I saw had no tail. The girl driving the car is my sister. definite article.*

the[2] (ŦHə *or* ŦHi), by how much; by that much: *The longer you work, the more you get. The later I sit up, the sleepier I become. adverb.*

the a ter *or* **the a tre** (thē′ə tər), **1** place where plays are acted or motion pictures are shown. **2** place that looks like a theater in its arrangement of seats: *The surgeon performed an operation before*

a hat	**i** it	**oi** oil	**ch** child	⎧ a in about
ā age	**ī** ice	**ou** out	**ng** long	⎪ e in taken
ä far	**o** hot	**u** cup	**sh** she	ə = ⎨ i in pencil
e let	**ō** open	** u̇** put	**th** thin	⎪ o in lemon
ē equal	**ô** order	**ü** rule	**ŦH** then	⎩ u in circus
ėr term			**zh** measure	

the medical students in the operating theater. **3** place of action: *France has been the theater for many wars.* **4** plays; writing, acting in, or producing plays; drama: *He was interested in the theater and tried to write plays himself. noun.*

the at ri cal (thē at′rə kəl), of or having something to do with the theater or actors: *theatrical performances, a theatrical company. adjective.*

thee (ŦHē), an old word meaning **you.** "Bless thee" means "bless you." *pronoun.*

theft (theft), stealing: *The prisoner was jailed for theft. noun.*

their (ŦHer *or* ŦHar), of them; belonging to them: *They like their fine, new school. adjective.*

theirs (ŦHerz *or* ŦHarz), the one or ones belonging to them: *Our house is white; theirs is brown. pronoun.*

terrarium

thatch (definition 2)—These people are thatching a roof.

them (ᴛнem), the persons, animals, or things spoken about: *The books are new; take care of them.* pronoun.

theme (ᴛнēm), **1** subject; topic: *The theme of her speech was equal rights for all Americans.* **2** a short written composition: *Our school themes must be written in ink and on white paper.* **3** the principal melody in a piece of music. **4** melody used to identify a particular radio or television program. *noun.*

them selves (ᴛнem selvz′), **1** *Themselves* is used to make a statement stronger. *The teachers themselves said the test was too hard.* **2** *Themselves* is used instead of *them* in cases like: *They hurt themselves sliding downhill.* **3** their normal or usual selves: *The children are sick and are not themselves this morning.* pronoun.

then (ᴛнen), **1** at that time: *Father talked of his childhood, and recalled that prices were lower then.* **2** that time: *By then we shall know the result of the election.* **3** soon afterward: *The noise stopped and then began again.* **4** next in time or place: *First comes spring, then summer.* **5** at another time: *Now one team was ahead and then the other.* **6** also; besides: *The circus is too good to miss, and then it costs very little.* **7** in that case; therefore: *If she painted the best picture, then she should receive the first prize.* **1,3-7** adverb, **2** noun.

thence (ᴛнens), from that place; from there: *We went to Italy; thence we went to France.* adverb.

thence forth (ᴛнens′fôrth′), from then on; from that time forward: *Women won the same rights as men; thenceforth they could vote.* adverb.

the ol o gy (thē ol′ə jē), **1** teachings concerning God and His relations to human beings and to the universe. **2** study of religion and religious beliefs. *noun, plural* **the ol o gies.**

the or y (thē′ər ē), **1** explanation; explanation based on thought; explanation based on observation and reasoning: *According to one scientific theory of life, the more complicated animals developed from the simpler ones.* **2** principles or methods of a science or art rather than its practice: *the theory of music.* **3** idea or opinion about something: *I think the fire was started by a careless smoker. What is your theory?* *noun, plural* **the or ies.**

there (ᴛнer *or* ᴛнar), **1** in that place; at that place; at that point: *Sit there. Finish reading the page and stop there.* **2** to or into that place: *We are going there tomorrow.* **3** that place: *We go to New York first and from there to Boston.* **4** in that matter: *You are mistaken there.* **5** *There* is also used in sentences in which the verb comes before its subject. *There are three new houses on our street. Is there a drugstore near here?* **6** *There* is used to call attention to some person or thing. *There goes the bell.* **7** *There* is also used to express some feeling. *There, there! Don't cry.* **1,2,4-6** adverb, **3** noun, **7** interjection.

there a bout (ᴛнer′ə bout′ *or* ᴛнar′ə bout′), thereabouts. *adverb.*

there a bouts (ᴛнer′ə bouts′ *or* ᴛнar′ə bouts′),

1 near that place: *She lives in the main part of town, on Front Street or thereabouts.* **2** near that time: *He went home in the late afternoon, at 5 o'clock or thereabouts.* **3** near that number or amount: *It was very cold and the temperature fell to zero or thereabouts.* adverb.

there af ter (ᴛнer af′tər *or* ᴛнar af′tər), after that; afterward: *He was very ill as a child and was considered delicate thereafter.* adverb.

there by (ᴛнer bī′ *or* ᴛнar bī′), **1** by means of that; in that way: *He wished to travel and thereby study the customs of other countries.* **2** in connection with that: *She won the game, and thereby is quite a story.* **3** near there: *A farm lay thereby.* adverb.

there fore (ᴛнer′fôr *or* ᴛнar′fôr), for that reason; as a result of that: *She had to work last night and therefore had little time to study.* adverb.

there's (ᴛнerz *or* ᴛнarz), there is.

thermometer—The thermometer is registering a temperature of 75 degrees Fahrenheit, or 24 degrees Celsius.

thimble

ther mom e ter (thər mom′ə tər), instrument for measuring temperature. Most thermometers contain mercury or alcohol in a narrow tube. When the temperature outside goes up, the liquid rises by expanding; when the temperature goes down, the liquid drops by contracting. See picture. *noun.* [*Thermometer* was formed from Greek words meaning "heat" and "measure."]

ther mo stat (thėr′mə stat), an automatic device for regulating temperature: *Most furnaces and ovens are controlled by thermostats.* noun.

these (ᴛнēz). *These* is used to point out persons, things, or ideas. *These days are cold. These two problems are hard. These are my books.* adjective, pronoun plural of **this.**

they (ᴛнā), **1** the persons, animals, things, or ideas spoken about: *I had three books yesterday. Do you know where they are? They are on the table.* **2** some people; any people; persons: *They say we should have a new school.* pronoun plural.

they'd (ᴛнād), **1** they had. **2** they would.

they'll (ᴛнāl), **1** they will. **2** they shall.

they're (ᴛнer), they are.

they've (ᴛнāv), they have.

thick (thik), **1** with much space from one side to

the opposite side; not thin: *The castle has thick stone walls.* **2** measuring between two opposite sides: *This brick is 8 inches long, 4 inches wide, and 2 1/2 inches thick.* **3** set close together; dense: *She has thick hair. It is a thick forest.* **4** many and close together; abundant: *The troops were greeted by bullets thick as hail.* **5** like glue or syrup; not like water: *Thick liquids pour much more slowly than thin liquids.* **6** not clear; foggy: *The weather was thick and the airports were shut down.* **7** not clear in sound; hoarse: *She had a thick voice because of a cold.* **8** stupid; dull: *He has a thick head.* **9** thickly: *The cars came thick and fast.* **10** the hardest part; place where there is the most danger or activity: *They were in the thick of the fight.* **11** very friendly; intimate. 1-8,11 *adjective,* 9 *adverb,* 10 *noun.*
through thick and thin, in good times and bad: *They were friends through thick and thin.*

thick en (thik′ən), make thick or thicker; become thick or thicker: *The cook thickens the gravy with flour. The pudding will thicken as it cools. verb.*

thick et (thik′it), shrubs, bushes, or small trees growing close together: *We crawled into the thicket and hid. noun.*

thick ly (thik′lē), **1** in a thick manner; closely; densely: *Most of New York City is thickly settled.* **2** in great numbers; in abundance: *Weeds grow thickly in the rich soil.* **3** frequently: *The houses came more thickly as we got closer to the city.* **4** in tones that are hoarse or hard to understand. *adverb.*

thick ness (thik′nis), **1** being thick: *The thickness of the walls shuts out all sound.* **2** distance between two opposite sides; the third measurement of a solid, not length nor width: *The length of the board is 10 feet, the width 6 inches, the thickness 2 inches.* **3** layer: *The pad was made up of three thicknesses of cloth. noun, plural* **thick ness es.**

thief (thēf), person who steals, especially one who steals secretly and usually without using force: *A thief stole the bicycle from the yard. noun, plural* **thieves.**

thieve (thēv), steal: *She saw a student thieving at school today. verb,* **thieved, thiev ing.**

thieves (thēvz), more than one thief. *noun plural.*

thigh (thī), part of the leg between the hip and the knee. *noun.*

thim ble (thim′bəl), a small metal cap worn on the finger to protect it when pushing the needle in sewing. See picture. *noun.*

thin (thin), **1** with little space from one side to the opposite side; not thick: *thin paper, thin wire. The ice on the pond is too thin for skating.* **2** having little flesh; slender; lean: *a thin person.* **3** not set close together; scanty: *He has thin hair.* **4** not dense: *The air on the tops of high mountains is thin.* **5** few and far apart; not abundant: *The actors played to a thin audience.* **6** like water; not like glue or syrup; not as thick as usual: *This gravy is too thin.* **7** not deep or strong; having little depth, fullness, or intensity: *a thin color, a thin voice.* **8** easily seen through; flimsy: *It was a thin excuse that satisfied no one.* **9** make thin; become thin: *Hunger had*

a hat	**i** it	**oi** oil	**ch** child	a in about
ā age	**ī** ice	**ou** out	**ng** long	e in taken
ä far	**o** hot	**u** cup	**sh** she	ə = { i in pencil
e let	**ō** open	**ů** put	**th** thin	o in lemon
ē equal	**ô** order	**ü** rule	**ŦH** then	u in circus
ėr term			**zh** measure	

thinned their cheeks. 1-8 *adjective,* **thin ner, thin nest;** 9 *verb,* **thinned, thin ning.**

thine (ŦHīn), an old word meaning: **1** yours. "It is thine" means "it is yours." **2** your (used only before a vowel or *h*). "Thine eyes" means "your eyes." 1 *pronoun,* 2 *adjective.*

thing (thing), **1** any object or substance; what you can see or hear or touch or taste or smell: *All the things in the house were burned. Put these things away.* **2 things, a** personal belongings: *We packed up all our things and moved.* **b** clothes: *I packed my things and took the train.* **3** whatever is spoken or thought of; act; deed; fact; event; idea: *It was a good thing to do. A strange thing happened. That is a strange thing to think of.* **4** matter; affair: *Let's settle this thing between us. How are things going?* **5** person or animal: *I felt sorry for the poor thing. noun.*

think (thingk), **1** have ideas; use the mind: *I want to think about that question before I answer it.* **2** have in the mind: *He thought that he would go.* **3** have an opinion; believe: *Do you think it will rain? We thought it might snow.* **4** consider: *They think their child a genius. verb,* **thought, think ing.**
think of, 1 imagine: *She doesn't like apple pie. Think of that!* **2** remember: *I can't think of his name.*

third (thėrd), **1** next after the second: *C is the third letter of the alphabet.* **2** one of three equal parts: *We divided the cake into thirds. adjective, noun.*

thirst (thėrst), **1** a dry, uncomfortable feeling in the mouth or throat caused by having had nothing to drink: *The traveler in the desert suffered from thirst.* **2** desire for something to drink: *She satisfied her thirst with a glass of water.* **3** feel thirst; be thirsty. **4** a strong desire: *have a thirst for adventure.* **5** have a strong desire: *Some people thirst for power.* 1,2,4 *noun,* 3,5 *verb.*

thirst y (thėr′stē), **1** feeling thirst; having thirst: *The dog is thirsty; please give it some water.* **2** without water or moisture; dry: *The land seemed thirstier than a desert. adjective,* **thirst i er, thirst i est.**

thir teen (thėr′tēn′), three more than ten; 13. *noun, adjective.*

thir teenth (thėr′tēnth′), **1** next after the 12th. **2** one of 13 equal parts. *adjective, noun.*

thir ti eth (thėr′tē ith), **1** next after the 29th. **2** one of 30 equal parts: *A day is about one thirtieth of a month. adjective, noun.*

thir ty (thėr′tē), three times ten; 30. *noun, plural* **thir ties;** *adjective.*

this (ŦHis), **1** *This* is used to point out some one person, thing, or idea as present, or near, or spoken of before. We use *that* for the thing farther away from us and *this* for the thing nearer us.

School begins at eight this year. This is my brother. Shall we buy this or that? **2** present; near; spoken of: *this minute, this child, this idea.* **3** to this degree or extent; so: *You can have this much.* **1,2** *adjective, plural* **these;** **1** *pronoun, plural* **these;** **3** *adverb.*

this tle (this′əl), plant with a prickly stalk and leaves and usually with purple flowers. The purple thistle is the national flower of Scotland. See picture. *noun.*

tho or **tho'** (ᴛʜō), though. *conjunction, adverb.*

thong (thông), **1** a narrow strip of leather, especially one used as a fastening: *The ancient Greeks laced their sandals on with thongs.* **2** lash of a whip. *noun.*

tho rax (thôr′aks), **1** the part of the body between the neck and the abdomen; chest. It contains the heart and the lungs. **2** the second of the three parts of the body of an insect. It is between the head and the abdomen. *noun, plural* **tho rax es, tho ra ces** (thôr′ə sēz′).

thorn (thôrn), **1** a sharp point on a stem or branch of a tree or other plant: *Roses have thorns.* **2** tree or other plant with thorns: *Thorns sprang up and choked the wheat. noun.*

thorn y (thôr′nē), **1** full of thorns: *I scratched my hands on the thorny bush.* **2** troublesome; annoying: *It took her a long time to solve the thorny problem. adjective,* **thorn i er, thorn i est.**

thor ough (thėr′ō), **1** complete: *Please make a thorough search for the lost money.* **2** doing all that should be done: *The doctor was very thorough in examining the patient. adjective.*

thor ough bred (thėr′ō bred′), **1** of pure breed. **2** a thoroughbred animal, most often a horse. See picture. **3** a well-bred or thoroughly trained person. **1** *adjective,* **2,3** *noun.*

thor ough fare (thėr′ō fer′ or thėr′ō far′), **1** passage, road, or street open at both ends: *A city street is a public thoroughfare.* **2** main road; highway: *The interstate highway that goes from Chicago to San Francisco is one of the main thoroughfares in the United States. noun.*
no thoroughfare, people are forbidden to go through.

those (ᴛʜōz). *Those is used to point out several persons or things. She owns that dog; the boys own those dogs. That is his book; those are my books. adjective, pronoun plural of* **that.**

thou (ᴛʜou), an old word meaning **you.** God is sometimes addressed as Thou. *pronoun singular.*

though (ᴛʜō), **1** in spite of the fact that: *We take our medicine, though we do not like it. Though it was pouring, the girls went to school.* **2** even supposing that: *Though I fail, I shall try again.* **3** however: *I am sorry for our quarrel; you began it, though.* **1,2** *conjunction,* **3** *adverb.* Also spelled **tho** or **tho'.**
as though, as if: *You look as though you were tired.*

thought (thôt), **1** what a person thinks; idea; notion: *Her thought was to have a picnic.*
2 thinking: *Thought helps us solve problems.* **3** care; attention; regard: *Show some thought for others than yourself.* **4** See **think.** *We thought it would snow yesterday.* **1-3** *noun,* **4** *verb.*

thought ful (thôt′fəl), **1** full of thought; thinking. See picture. **2** careful of others; considerate: *She is always thoughtful of her parents. adjective.*

thought less (thôt′lis), **1** without thought; doing things without thinking; careless: *Thoughtless drivers cause many automobile accidents.* **2** showing little or no care or regard for others: *It is thoughtless of them to keep us waiting so long. adjective.*

thou sand (thou′znd), ten hundred; 1000. *noun, adjective.*

thou sandth (thou′zndth), **1** next after the 999th. **2** one of 1000 equal parts. *adjective, noun.*

thrash (thrash), **1** beat: *They were thrashed for stealing apples.* **2** move violently; toss: *Unable to sleep, the patient thrashed about in the bed.* **3** thresh (wheat, rye, or other grain). *verb.*

thrash er (thrash′ər), a North American songbird that has a long tail and is somewhat like a thrush. *noun.*

thread (thred), **1** cotton, silk, flax, or some similar material spun out into a fine cord. You sew with thread. **2** pass a thread through: *Can you thread a needle? I threaded beads onto a string.* **3** something long and slender like a thread: *The spider hung by a thread.* **4** the main thought that connects the parts of a story or speech: *Something distracted her and she lost the thread of their conversation.* **5** make one's way through; make (one's way) carefully: *He threaded his way through the crowd.* **6** the sloping ridge that winds around a bolt, screw, or pipe joint. The thread of a nut interlocks with the thread of a bolt. **1,3,4,6** *noun,* **2,5** *verb.*

thread bare (thred′ber′ or thred′bar′), **1** having the nap worn off; worn so much that the threads show: *a threadbare coat.* **2** wearing clothes worn to the threads; shabby: *a threadbare beggar.* **3** old and worn: *Saying "I forgot" is a threadbare excuse. adjective.*

threat (thret), **1** statement of what will be done to hurt or punish someone: *The teacher's threat to keep the class after school stopped the noise.* **2** sign or cause of possible evil or harm: *Those black clouds are a threat of rain. noun.*

threat en (thret′n), **1** make a threat against; say what will be done to hurt or punish: *The teacher threatened to fail all the students that did no homework.* **2** say threats: *They threaten and scold too much.* **3** give warning of (coming trouble): *Black clouds threaten rain.* **4** be a cause of possible evil or harm to: *A flood threatened the city. verb.*

three (thrē), one more than two; 3. Three feet make one yard. *noun, adjective.*

three fold (thrē′fōld′), **1** three times as much or as many. **2** having three parts. **1,2** *adjective,* **1** *adverb.*

three score (thrē′skôr′), three times twenty; 60. *adjective.*

thresh (thresh), **1** separate the grain or seeds from (wheat, rye, or other grain). Nowadays most farmers use a machine to thresh their wheat. **2** toss about; thrash. *verb.*

thresh er (thresh′ər), person or thing that

threshes, especially a person or machine that threshes wheat, rye, or other grain. *noun.*

thresh old (thresh′ōld), **1** piece of wood or stone under a door. **2** doorway. **3** point of entering; beginning point: *The scientist was on the threshold of an important discovery. noun.*

threw (thrü). See **throw.** *He threw the ball at me. verb.*

thrice (thrīs), three times: *He knocked thrice. adverb.*

thrift (thrift), absence of waste; saving; economical management; habit of saving: *By thrift they managed to get along on their small income. A bank account encourages thrift. noun.*

thrift y (thrif′tē), careful in spending; economical; saving: *a thrifty shopper. adjective,* **thrift i er, thrift i est.**

thrill (thril), **1** a shivering, exciting feeling: *She gets a thrill whenever she sees a parade.* **2** give a shivering, exciting feeling to: *Stories of adventure thrilled him.* **3** have a shivering, exciting feeling: *The children thrilled at the sight of the parade.* **4** tremble: *Her voice thrilled with excitement.* 1 *noun,* 2-4 *verb.*

thrive (thrīv), be successful; grow rich; grow strong; prosper: *Flowers will not thrive without sunshine. verb,* **throve** or **thrived, thrived** or **thriv en** (thriv′ən), **thriv ing.**

throat (thrōt), **1** the front of the neck: *I wrapped a scarf around my throat.* **2** passage from the mouth to the stomach or the lungs: *A chicken bone got stuck in the dog's throat.* **3** any narrow passage: *The throat of the valley was blocked by fallen rocks. noun.*

throb (throb), **1** beat rapidly or strongly: *The long climb up the hill made her heart throb. The wounded arm throbbed with pain.* **2** a rapid or strong beat: *A throb of pain shot through his head.* 1 *verb,* **throbbed, throb bing;** 2 *noun.*

throne (thrōn), **1** chair on which a king, queen, bishop, or other person of high rank sits during ceremonies. **2** the power or authority of a king, queen, or other ruler: *The throne of England commands respect but does not command armies. noun.*

throng (thrông), **1** a crowd; multitude. **2** crowd; fill with a crowd: *People thronged the theater to see the new movie.* **3** come together in a crowd; go or press in large numbers: *The people thronged to see the parade.* 1 *noun,* 2,3 *verb.*

throt tle (throt′l), **1** valve for regulating the supply of steam or gasoline to an engine. **2** lever or pedal working such a valve. The throttle of a car is called an accelerator. **3** stop or lessen by closing such a valve: *throttle a steam engine.* **4** choke; strangle: *The thief throttled the dog to keep it from barking.* 1,2 *noun,* 3,4 *verb,* **throt tled, throt tling.**

through (thrü), **1** from end to end of; from side to side of; between the parts of: *They drove through a snowstorm. I bored holes through a board.* **2** from beginning to end; from one side to the other: *She read the book all the way through.* **3** here and there in; over: *We traveled through New England and saw*

a hat	i it	oi oil	ch child	a in about
ā age	ī ice	ou out	ng long	e in taken
ä far	o hot	u cup	sh she	ə = { i in pencil
e let	ō open	u̇ put	th thin	o in lemon
ē equal	ô order	ü rule	ŦH then	u in circus
ėr term			zh measure	

thoughtful

thistle

thoroughbred (definition 2)

many old towns. **4** because of; by reason of: *The family refused help through pride.* **5** by means of: *I learned of the new book through my teacher.* **6** completely: *I walked home in the rain and my clothes are wet through.* **7** going all the way without change: *a through train from New York to Chicago.* **8** having reached the end of; finished with: *We are through school at three o'clock.* **9** having reached the end; finished: *I will soon be through.* 1,3-5,8 *preposition,* 2,6 *adverb,* 7,9 *adjective.* Also spelled **thru.**

through out (thrü out′), **1** all the way through; through all; in every part of: *The Fourth of July is celebrated throughout the United States.* **2** in every part: *The house is well built throughout.* 1 *preposition,* 2 *adverb.*

throve (thrōv). See **thrive.** *The plants throve in the rich soil. verb.*

throw (thrō), **1** cast; toss; hurl: *throw a ball. I threw water on the fire.* **2** act of throwing; a cast, toss, or hurl: *That was a good throw from left field to the catcher.* **3** bring to the ground: *He was thrown when his horse bucked.* **4** put carelessly or in haste: *I threw a coat over my shoulders.* 1,3,4 *verb,* **threw, thrown, throw ing;** 2 *noun.*

throw away, 1 get rid of; discard: *Throw away those old shoes.* **2** waste: *Don't throw away your opportunities.*

throw in, add as a gift: *Our grocer often throws in an extra apple or two.*

throw off, 1 get rid of: *throw off a cold.* **2** cause to lose: *The fox threw the hounds off its trail by doubling back several times.*

throw over, give up; discard; abandon: *throw over an old friend.*

thrown (thrōn). See **throw.** *She has thrown her old toys away. verb.*

thru (thrü), through. *preposition, adverb, adjective.*

thrush (thrush), any of a large group of songbirds that includes the robin and the bluebird. *noun, plural* **thrush es.**

thrust (thrust), **1** push with force: *He thrust his hands into his pockets.* **2** a push with force: *She hid the book behind the pillow with a quick thrust.* **3** stab; pierce: *I thrust the knife into the apple.* **4** a stab: *A thrust with the pin broke the balloon.* 1,3 *verb,* **thrust, thrust ing;** 2,4 *noun.*

thud (thud), **1** a dull sound. A heavy blow or fall may cause a thud. *The book hit the floor with a thud.* **2** hit, move, or strike with a thud: *The heavy box fell and thudded on the floor.* 1 *noun,* 2 *verb,* **thud ded, thud ding.**

thumb (thum), **1** the short, thick finger of the hand. **2** part that covers the thumb: *There was a hole in the thumb of the mitten.* **3** soil or wear by handling with the thumbs: *Some of the books were badly thumbed.* **4** turn the pages of rapidly, with a thumb or as if with a thumb: *I didn't read the book; I just thumbed through it.* 1,2 *noun,* 3,4 *verb.*

under one's thumb, under one's power or influence: *Several members of the club are under the president's thumb.*

thumb tack (thum′tak′), tack with a broad, flat head, that can be pressed into a wall or board with the thumb. *noun.*

thump (thump), **1** strike with something thick and heavy; pound: *She thumped the table with her fist.* **2** a blow with something thick and heavy; heavy knock: *a thump on the head.* **3** the dull sound made by a blow, knock, or fall: *We heard a thump when the book fell.* **4** make a dull sound: *The hammer thumped against the wood.* **5** beat violently: *His heart thumped as he walked past the cemetery at night.* 1,4,5 *verb,* 2,3 *noun.*

thun der (thun′dər), **1** the loud noise that often follows a flash of lightning. It is caused by a disturbance of the air resulting from the discharge of electricity. **2** give forth thunder: *It thundered a few times, but no rain fell.* **3** any noise like thunder: *the thunder of Niagara Falls, a thunder of applause.* **4** make a noise like thunder: *The cannon thundered throughout the night.* 1,3 *noun,* 2,4 *verb.*

thun der bolt (thun′dər bōlt′), **1** a flash of lightning and the thunder that follows it. **2** something sudden, startling, and terrible: *The news of the accident came as a thunderbolt. noun.*

thun der cloud (thun′dər kloud′), a dark cloud that brings thunder and lightning. *noun.*

thun der ous (thun′dər əs), **1** producing thunder. **2** making a noise like thunder: *The famous actor received a thunderous burst of applause at the end of the play. adjective.*

thun der show er (thun′dər shou′ər), shower with thunder and lightning. *noun.*

thun der storm (thun′dər stôrm′), storm with thunder and lightning. *noun.*

thun der struck (thun′dər struk′), overcome as if hit by a thunderbolt; astonished; amazed: *We were thunderstruck by the news of war. adjective.*

Thurs day (thėrz′dē), the fifth day of the week; the day after Wednesday. *noun.* [*Thursday* is from an earlier English word meaning "Thur's day." Thur or Thunor is a name of the god of thunder.]

thus (ᴛHus), **1** in this way; in the following manner: *The speaker spoke thus: "Ladies and Gentlemen, parents, fellow students."* **2** therefore: *We hurried and thus arrived on time.* **3** to this extent; to this degree; so: *Thus far may you go and no farther. adverb.*

thwart (thwôrt), **1** oppose and defeat; keep from doing something: *Lack of money thwarted her plans for college.* **2** seat across a boat, on which a rower sits. 1 *verb,* 2 *noun.*

thy (ᴛHī), an old word meaning **your.** "Thy name" means "your name." *adjective.*

thyme (tīm), a small plant with sweet-smelling leaves. The leaves are used for seasoning. *noun.*

thy roid (thī′roid), gland in the neck that affects growth. *noun.*

thy self (ᴛHī self′), an old word meaning **yourself.** *pronoun.*

tick[1] (tik), **1** sound made by a clock or watch. **2** make such a sound: *The clock ticked.* **3** a sound like it: *the tick of a moth against a windowpane.* **4** mark off: *The clock ticked away the minutes.* **5** a small mark. We use ✓ or / as a tick. *I put a tick*

a hat	i it	oi oil	ch child	(a in about
ā age	ī ice	ou out	ng long	e in taken
ä far	o hot	u cup	sh she	ə = { i in pencil
e let	ō open	u̇ put	th thin	o in lemon
ē equal	ô order	ü rule	ᵮH then	u in circus
ėr term			zh measure	

tide (definition 1)
top, a ship at high tide;
bottom, the same ship at low tide

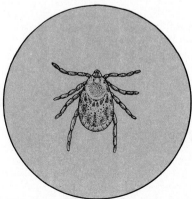

tick²—about ¹⁄₄ inch (5 millimeters) long

next to each chore I had completed on the list.
6 mark with a tick; check: *She ticked off the items one by one.* 1,3,5 *noun,* 2,4,6 *verb.*

tick² (tik), a tiny eight-legged animal, related to the spider, that lives on animals and sucks their blood. See picture. *noun.*

tick et (tik′it), **1** card or piece of paper that gives its holder a right or privilege: *a ticket to the theater.* **2** a written order to appear in court, given to a person accused of breaking a traffic law or a parking regulation: *a ticket for speeding, a parking ticket.* **3** card or piece of paper attached to something to show its price, what it is or consists of, or some similar information. **4** put a ticket on: *All items are ticketed with the price.* 1-3 *noun,* 4 *verb.*

tick le (tik′əl), **1** touch lightly, causing little thrills, shivers, or wriggles: *He tickled the baby's feet and made her laugh.* **2** have a feeling like this: *My nose tickles from the dust.* **3** a tingling or itching feeling. **4** amuse; excite pleasantly: *The funny story tickled me.* 1,2,4 *verb,* **tick led, tick ling;** 3 *noun.*

tick lish (tik′lish), **1** sensitive to tickling: *The bottoms of the feet are ticklish.* **2** requiring careful handling; delicate; risky: *Telling your friends their faults is a ticklish business.* **3** easily upset; unstable: *A canoe is a ticklish craft. adjective.*

tid al (tī′dl), of tides; having tides; caused by tides. A tidal river is affected by the ocean's tide. *adjective.*

tidal wave, a large, destructive ocean wave produced by an earthquake or strong wind.

tid bit (tid′bit′), a very pleasing bit of food, news, or information. *noun.*

tide (tīd), **1** the rise and fall of the ocean about every twelve hours, caused by the pull of the moon and the sun. See picture. **2** anything that rises and falls like the tide: *the tide of public opinion.* **3 tide over,** help along for a time: *His savings will tide him over his illness.* 1,2 *noun,* 3 *verb,* **tid ed, tid ing.**

ti di ness (tī′dē nis), neatness. *noun.*

ti dings (tī′dingz), news; information: *joyful tidings. noun plural.*

ti dy (tī′dē), **1** neat and in order: *a tidy room.* **2** make neat; put in order: *We tidied the room.* **3** considerable; fairly large: *$500 is a tidy sum of money.* 1,3 *adjective,* **ti di er, ti di est;** 2 *verb,* **ti died, ti dy ing.**

tie (tī), **1** fasten with string or the like; bind: *Please tie this package.* **2** arrange to form a bow or knot: *Tie your shoelace.* **3** fasten; form a bow: *That ribbon doesn't tie well.* **4** tighten and fasten the string or strings of: *tie one's shoes.* **5** necktie: *He always wears a shirt and tie.* **6** thing that ties; fastening; bond; connection: *family ties, ties of friendship.* **7** a heavy piece of timber or iron. The

tiger—about 9 feet (2½ meters) long with the tail

tightrope

timberline

rails of a railroad track rest on ties. **8** equality in points: *The game ended in a tie, 3 to 3.* **9** make the same score; be equal in points: *The two teams tied.* **10** (in music) a curved line joining two notes of the same pitch. 1-4,9 *verb,* **tied, ty ing;** 5-8,10 *noun.*

tier (tir), one of several rows one above another: *tiers of seats in a football stadium. noun.*

ti ger (tī′gər), a large, fierce animal of Asia that has dull-yellow fur striped with black. See picture. *noun.*

tight (tīt), **1** firm; held firmly; packed or put together firmly: *a tight knot.* **2** firmly: *The rope was tied too tight.* **3** fitting closely; close: *tight clothing.* **4** not letting water, air, or gas in or out: *The tight roof kept rain from leaking in.* **5** hard to deal with or manage; difficult: *A lie got her in a tight spot.* **6** almost even; close: *It was a tight race.* **7** hard to get; scarce: *Money is tight just now.* **8** stingy: *He is tight with his money.* 1,3-8 *adjective,* 2 *adverb.*

tight en (tīt′n), make or become tight: *He tightened his belt. The rope tightened as I pulled it. verb.*

tight rope (tīt′rōp′), rope stretched tight on which acrobats perform. See picture. *noun.*

tights (tīts), a tight-fitting garment, usually covering the lower part of the body and the legs, worn by acrobats, dancers, or gymnasts. *noun, plural.*

ti gress (tī′gris), a female tiger. *noun, plural* **ti gress es.**

tile (tīl), **1** a thin piece of baked clay, stone, or plastic. Tiles are used for covering roofs, paving floors, and ornamenting. **2** put tiles on or in: *tile a bathroom floor.* 1 *noun,* 2 *verb,* **tiled, til ing.**

till[1] (til), until; up to the time of; up to the time when: *The child played till eight. Walk till you come to a white house. preposition, conjunction.*

till[2] (til), cultivate (land); plow: *Farmers till before planting. verb.*

till[3] (til), a small drawer for money under or behind a counter. *noun.*

till er (til′ər), bar or handle used to turn the rudder in steering a boat. *noun.*

tilt (tilt), **1** tip or cause to tip; slope; slant: *You tilt your head forward when you bow.* **2** a slope; slant: *the tilt of a wobbly table.* **3** fight with lances. Knights used to tilt on horseback. 1,3 *verb,* 2 *noun.* **full tilt,** at full speed; with full force: *The wagon ran full tilt down the hill.*

tim ber (tim′bər), **1** wood for building and making things. Houses, ships, and furniture are made from timber. **2** a large piece of wood used in building. Beams and rafters are timbers. **3** trees or forests that could provide wood for building: *Half their land is covered with timber. noun.*

tim ber line (tim′bər līn′), line beyond which trees will not grow on mountains and in the polar regions because of the cold. See picture. *noun.*

time (tīm), **1** all the days there have been or ever will be; the past, present, and future. Time is measured in years, months, days, hours, minutes, and seconds. **2** a part of the past, present, or future: *A minute is a short time. A long time ago* *people lived in caves.* **3** period of history; age: *We are living in the time of space exploration.* **4** some point in time: *The time the game begins is two o'clock, November 8. What time is it right now?* **5** the right part or point of time: *It is time to eat dinner.* **6** occasion: *This time we will succeed.* **7** a way of counting the hours that pass: *standard time, daylight-saving time.* **8** condition of life: *War brings hard times.* **9** an experience during a certain period: *Everyone had a good time at the party.* **10** rate of movement in music; rhythm: *march time, waltz time.* **11** to measure the speed of: *I timed the horse at half a mile per minute.* **12** do at regular times; do in rhythm with; set the time of: *The dancers time their steps to the music.* **13** choose the moment or occasion for: *I timed my request for a raise so as to catch my boss in a good mood.* **14** times, multiplied by. The sign for this in arithmetic is ×. *Four times three is twelve. Twenty is five times four.* 1-10 *noun,* 11-13 *verb,* **timed, tim ing;** 14 *preposition.*

at times, now and then; once in a while: *Most people at times have wished to have power to do what they want to do.*

bide one's time, wait for a good chance: *If you bide your time you will probably get a better buy.*

for the time being, for the present; for now: *The baby is asleep for the time being.*

from time to time, now and then; once in a while: *From time to time we visit my grandparents.*

in no time, shortly; before long: *We hurried and arrived home in no time.*

in time, 1 after a while: *I think that in time we may win.* **2** soon enough: *Will she arrive in time to have dinner with us?* **3** in the right rate of movement in music, dancing, or marching.

keep time, 1 (of a watch or clock) go correctly: *My watch keeps good time.* **2** sound or move at the right rate: *The marchers kept time to the music.*

on time, 1 at the right time; not late: *We get to school on time each day.* **2** with time in which to pay; on credit: *He bought a car on time.*

tell time, know what time it is by the clock.

time after time or **time and again,** again and again: *I made the same mistake time after time.*

time ly (tīm′lē), at the right time: *The timely arrival of the firemen prevented the fire from destroying the building. adjective,* **time li er, time li est.**

time piece (tīm′pēs′), clock or watch. *noun.*

time ta ble (tīm′tā′bəl), schedule showing the times when trains, boats, buses, or airplanes come and go. *noun.*

tim id (tim′id), easily frightened; shy: *The timid child was afraid of the dark. adjective.*

ti mid i ty (tə mid′ə tē), timid behavior; shyness. *noun.*

tin (tin), **1** a soft, silver-white metal. Tin is used to plate other metals and is mixed with other metals to form alloys. **2** thin sheets of iron or steel coated with tin. **3** made of or lined with tin: *tin cans.* **4** any can, box, or pan made of or lined with tin: *a pie tin.* 1,2,4 *noun,* 3 *adjective.*

tin der (tin′dər), **1** anything that catches fire

a hat	**i** it	**oi** oil	**ch** child	⎧ a in about
ā age	**ī** ice	**ou** out	**ng** long	⎪ e in taken
ä far	**o** hot	**u** cup	**sh** she	**ə** = ⎨ i in pencil
e let	**ō** open	**ù** put	**th** thin	⎪ o in lemon
ē equal	**ô** order	**ü** rule	**ŦH** then	⎩ u in circus
ėr term			**zh** measure	

easily. **2** material used to catch fire from a spark: *Before matches were invented people struck flint and steel together to light tinder. noun.*

tin foil (tin′foil′), a very thin sheet of aluminum, tin, or tin and lead, used as a wrapping for candy, tobacco, or similar articles. *noun.*

tinge (tinj), **1** color slightly: *A drop of ink will tinge a glass of water.* **2** a slight coloring or tint: *There was a tinge of red in the leaves.* **3** add a trace of some quality to; change a very little: *Sad memories tinged her present joy.* **4** trace; very small amount: *She likes just a tinge of lemon in her tea. There was a tinge of blame in his voice.* 1,3 *verb,* **tinged, tinge ing** or **ting ing;** 2,4 *noun.*

tin gle (ting′gəl), **1** have a feeling of thrills or a pricking, stinging feeling: *He tingled with excitement on his first airplane trip.* **2** a pricking, stinging feeling: *The cold caused a tingle in my fingers.* 1 *verb,* **tin gled, tin gling;** 2 *noun.*

tink er (ting′kər), **1** person who mends pots, pans, kettles, and other metal household articles. **2** work or repair in an unskilled or clumsy way: *The children were tinkering with the clock and broke it.* **3** work or keep busy in a rather useless way: *I was tinkering in my workshop.* 1 *noun,* 2,3 *verb.*

tin kle (ting′kəl), **1** make or cause to make short, light, ringing sounds: *Little bells tinkle. She tinkled the side of the glass with her spoon.* **2** series of short, light, ringing sounds: *the tinkle of sleigh bells.* 1 *verb,* **tin kled, tin kling;** 2 *noun.*

tin sel (tin′səl), **1** very thin sheets, strips, or threads of glittering metal or plastic, used to trim Christmas trees. **2** anything showy but having little value. *noun.*

tint (tint), **1** a shade of a color: *The picture was painted in several tints of blue.* **2** a delicate or pale color. **3** put a tint on; color slightly: *The walls were tinted gray.* 1,2 *noun,* 3 *verb.*

ti ny (tī′nē), very small: *a tiny baby chicken. adjective,* **ti ni er, ti ni est.**

tip[1] (tip), **1** the end part; end: *the tips of the fingers.* **2** a small piece put on the end of something: *Buy rubber tips to put on the legs of a stool.* **3** put a tip on; furnish with a tip: *spears tipped with steel.* 1,2 *noun,* 3 *verb,* **tipped, tip ping.**

tip[2] (tip), **1** slope; slant: *She tipped the table toward her.* **2** a slope; slant: *There is such a tip to that table that everything slips off it.* **3** upset; overturn: *I tipped over my glass of water.* **4** take off (a hat) in greeting: *The old gentleman tipped his hat to his neighbor, when they passed on the sidewalk.* **5** empty out; dump: *She tipped the money in her purse onto the table.* 1,3-5 *verb,* **tipped, tip ping;** 2 *noun.*

tip[3] (tip), **1** a small present of money in return for service: *She gave the waiter a tip.* **2** give a small present of money to: *Did you tip the porter?* **3** piece of secret information: *He had a tip that the black horse would win the race.* **4** a useful hint or suggestion: *Someone gave me a tip about pitching the tent where trees would shade it.* 1,3,4 *noun*, 2 *verb*, **tipped, tip ping.**

tip off, 1 give secret information to: *They tipped me off about a good bargain.* **2** warn: *Someone tipped off the criminals and they escaped before the police arrived.*

tip toe (tip′tō′), **1** the tips of the toes. **2** walk on the tips of the toes: *She tiptoed quietly up the stairs.* 1 *noun*, 2 *verb*, **tip toed, tip toe ing.**

on tiptoe, 1 on the tips of one's toes: *walk on tiptoe.* **2** eager: *The children were on tiptoe for vacation to begin.*

tip top (tip′top′), **1** the very top; highest point. **2** first-rate; excellent. 1 *noun*, 2 *adjective.*

tire[1] (tīr), **1** make weary: *The work tired me.* **2** become weary: *An elderly person may tire easily.* *verb*, **tired, tir ing.**

tire[2] (tīr), band of rubber or metal around a wheel. Some rubber tires have inner tubes for holding air; others hold the air in the tire itself or are made of solid rubber. *Put more air in the tires.* *noun.*

tired (tīrd), weary; wearied; exhausted: *I'm tired, but I must get back to work.* *adjective.*

tire less (tīr′lis), **1** never becoming tired; requiring little rest: *a tireless worker.* **2** never stopping: *tireless efforts.* *adjective.*

tire some (tīr′səm), tiring; not interesting: *a tiresome speech.* *adjective.*

tis sue (tish′ü), **1** mass of cells forming some part of an animal or plant: *The teacher showed pictures of muscle tissues, brain tissues, and skin tissues.* **2** a thin, soft paper that absorbs moisture easily. *noun.*

tissue paper, a very thin, soft paper, used for wrapping or covering things.

ti tle (tī′tl), **1** the name of a book, poem, picture, song, and the like: *"Goldilocks and the Three Bears" is the title of a famous story for little children.* **2** name showing rank, occupation, or condition in life. King, duke, lord, countess, captain, doctor, professor, Madame, and Miss are titles. **3** first-place position; championship: *He won the school tennis title.* **4** a written deed showing a legal right to the possession of property. When a house is sold, the seller gives title to the buyer. *noun.*

title page, page at the front of a book that gives the title and the name of the author and the publisher.

to (tü, tù, *or* tə), **1** in the direction of: *Go to the right.* **2** as far as; until: *This apple is rotten to the core. I will be your friend to the end.* **3** for the purpose of; for: *She soon came to the rescue.* **4** into: *She tore the letter to pieces.* **5** along with; with: *We danced to the music.* **6** compared with: *The score was 9 to 5.* **7** in agreement with: *Going without food is not to my liking.* **8** on: *Fasten it to the wall.* **9** about; concerning: *What did he say to that?* **10** *To* is used to show action toward. *Give the book to me. Speak to her.* **11** *To* is used with verbs. *He likes to read. The birds began to sing.* *preposition.*

toad (tōd), a small animal somewhat like a frog, that lives most of the time on land rather than in water. Toads have a rough, brown skin that suggests a lump of earth. See picture. *noun.*

toad stool (tōd′stül′), a poisonous mushroom. *noun.*

toast[1] (tōst), **1** slices of bread browned by heat. **2** brown by heat: *We toasted the bread.* **3** heat thoroughly: *He toasted his feet before the open fire.* 1 *noun*, 2,3 *verb.*

toast[2] (tōst), **1** take a drink and wish good fortune to: *We toasted our hosts.* **2** person or thing whose health is proposed and drunk. **3** act of drinking to the health of a person or thing. 1 *verb*, 2,3 *noun.*

toast er (tō′stər), thing that toasts: *Turn on the electric toaster.* *noun.*

to bac co (tə bak′ō), **1** the prepared leaves of certain plants, used for smoking or chewing or as snuff. **2** one of these plants. *noun, plural* **to bac cos** or **to bac coes.**

to bog gan (tə bog′ən), **1** a long, narrow, flat sled without runners. The front of a toboggan curves upwards. **2** slide downhill on such a sled. 1 *noun*, 2 *verb.*

to day or **to-day** (tə dā′), **1** this day; the present time: *Today is Wednesday.* **2** on or during this day: *What are you doing today?* **3** at the present time; now: *Pollution is a major problem today.* 1 *noun*, 2,3 *adverb.*

tod dle (tod′l), walk with short, unsteady steps, as a baby does. *verb*, **tod dled, tod dling.**

toe (tō), **1** one of the five end parts of the foot. **2** the part of a stocking, shoe, or slipper that covers the toes: *have a hole in the toe of a sock.* **3** touch or reach with the toes: *Toe this line.* 1,2 *noun*, 3 *verb*, **toed, toe ing.**

toe nail (tō′nāl′), the nail growing on a toe. *noun.*

to geth er (tə geŦH′ər), **1** with each other; in company: *They were standing together.* **2** into one gathering, company, mass, or body: *The principal called the school together. The tailor will sew these pieces together and make a suit.* **3** at the same time: *You cannot have day and night together.* **4** without a stop or break; continuously: *He reads for hours together.* *adverb.*

toil (toil), **1** hard work; labor. See picture. **2** work hard: *toil with one's hands for a living.* **3** move with difficulty, pain, or weariness: *Carrying heavy loads, they toiled up the mountain.* 1 *noun*, 2,3 *verb.*

toi let (toi′lit), **1** bathroom. **2** a porcelain bowl with a seat attached and with a drain at the bottom to flush the bowl clean. Waste matter from the body is disposed of in a toilet. **3** process of dressing. Bathing, combing the hair, and putting on one's clothes are all parts of one's toilet. *I made a hurried toilet.* **4** of or for the toilet: *Combs and brushes are toilet articles.* 1-3 *noun*, 4 *adjective.*

to ken (tō′kən), **1** a mark or sign (of something): *Black is a token of mourning.* **2** sign of friendship; keepsake: *She received many birthday tokens.* **3** piece of metal stamped for a higher value than the metal is worth. Tokens are used on some buses and trains instead of money. **4** piece of metal or plastic indicating a right or privilege: *This token will admit you to the swimming pool.* *noun.*

told (tōld). See **tell.** *You told me that last week. We were told to wait.* *verb.*

tol er a ble (tol′ər ə bəl), **1** able to be endured; bearable: *The pain has become tolerable.* **2** fairly good: *My grandparents are in tolerable health.* *adjective.*

tol er ance (tol′ər əns), willingness to be patient toward people whose opinions or ways differ from one's own: *The principal's tolerance of their bad behavior surprised us.* *noun.*

tol er ant (tol′ər ənt), willing to let other people do as they think best; willing to endure beliefs and actions of which one does not approve: *to be tolerant toward all religious beliefs.* *adjective.*

tol e rate (tol′ə rāt′), **1** allow; permit: *The teacher won't tolerate any disorder.* **2** bear; endure; put up with: *I cannot tolerate swimming in icy water.* *verb,* **tol e rat ed, tol e rat ing.**

toll[1] (tōl), **1** to sound with single strokes slowly and regularly repeated: *On Sunday all the church bells toll.* **2** stroke or sound of a bell being tolled. **1** *verb,* **2** *noun.*

toll[2] (tōl), **1** tax or fee paid for some right or privilege: *We pay a toll when we use that bridge.* **2** charge for a certain service. *There is a toll on long-distance telephone calls.* *noun.*

toll booth (tōl′büth′), place where tolls are collected before or after going over a bridge, road, or turnpike or through a tunnel. *noun, plural* **toll booths** (tōl′büᴛHz′ *or* tōl′büths′).

toll gate (tōl′gāt′), tollbooth. *noun.*

toll road, road on which tolls are charged; turnpike.

tom a hawk (tom′ə hôk), a light ax used by North American Indians as a weapon and a tool. See picture. *noun.*

to ma to (tə mā′tō *or* tə mä′tō), a juicy, red or yellow fruit eaten as a vegetable, either raw or cooked. Tomatoes grow on a spreading garden plant that has hairy leaves and stems and yellow flowers. *noun, plural* **to ma toes.**

tomb (tüm), grave or vault for a dead body, often above ground. *noun.*

tom boy (tom′boi′), a girl who likes to take part in so-called boys' games and activities. *noun.*

tomb stone (tüm′stōn′), stone that marks a tomb or grave. *noun.*

tom cat (tom′kat′), a male cat. *noun.*

to mor row (tə môr′ō), **1** the day after today. **2** the near future: *Houses of tomorrow may be heated by the sun.* **3** on the day after today. **1,2** *noun,* **3** *adverb.*

tom-tom (tom′tom′), a kind of drum, usually beaten with the hands. *noun.*

ton (tun), a unit of weight equal to 2000 pounds in the United States and Canada, and 2240 pounds in Great Britain. A **long ton** is 2240 pounds; a **short ton** is 2000 pounds. A **metric ton** is 1000 kilograms. *noun.*

a hat	i it	oi oil	ch child	ə = { a in about
ā age	ī ice	ou out	ng long	e in taken
ä far	o hot	u cup	sh she	i in pencil
e let	ō open	ů put	th thin	o in lemon
ē equal	ô order	ü rule	ᴛH then	u in circus
ėr term			zh measure	

toad—up to 5½ inches (14 centimeters) long

tomahawks

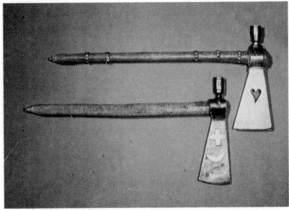

toil (definition 1)

tone (tōn), **1** any sound considered with reference to its quality, pitch, strength, or source: *angry tones, gentle tones, the deep tone of an organ.* **2** quality of sound: *a voice that is soft in tone.* **3** a musical sound, especially one of definite pitch and character. **4** difference in pitch between two notes. C and D are one tone apart. **5** manner of speaking or writing: *I disliked their disrespectful tone.* **6** spirit; character; style: *A tone of quiet elegance prevails in their home.* **7** normal, healthy condition; vigor: *Regular exercise will keep your body in tone.* **8** effect of color and of light and shade in a picture: *I like the soft green tone of that painting.* **9** shade of color: *The room is furnished in tones of brown.* **10 tone down,** soften: *Tone down your voice.* 1-9 *noun,* 10 *verb,* **toned, ton ing.**

tongs (tôngz), tool for seizing, holding, or lifting. Different kinds of tongs are used for picking up ice, logs, sugar, and other things. *noun plural.*

tongue (tung), **1** the movable piece of flesh in the mouth. The tongue is used in tasting and, by people, for talking. **2** an animal's tongue used as food: *We ate cold tongue and salad.* **3** power of speech: *Have you lost your tongue?* **4** way of speaking; speech; talk: *My friend has a quick tongue.* **5** the language of a people: *the English tongue.* **6** something shaped or used like a tongue: *Tongues of flame leaped from the fire.* **7** the strip of leather under the laces of a shoe. *noun.*

hold one's tongue, keep quiet; be silent: *Try to hold your tongue while someone else is talking.*

tongue-tied (tung′tīd′), unable to speak, especially because of shyness, embarrassment, surprise, or shock. *adjective.*

ton ic (ton′ik), **1** anything that gives strength; medicine to give strength: *Cod-liver oil is a tonic.* **2** giving strength; bracing: *The mountain air is tonic.* 1 *noun,* 2 *adjective.*

to night (tə nīt′), **1** the night of this day; this night: *I must finish this work by tonight.* **2** on or during this night: *Do you think it will snow tonight?* 1 *noun,* 2 *adverb.*

ton nage (tun′ij), **1** the carrying capacity of a ship. **2** total amount of shipping in tons. **3** weight in tons. *noun.*

ton sil (ton′səl), either of the two small, oval masses of tissue on the sides of the throat, just back of the mouth. See picture. *noun.*

ton sil li tis (ton′sə lī′tis), soreness and swelling of the tonsils. *noun.*

too (tü), **1** also; besides: *The dog is hungry, and thirsty too. We, too, are going away.* **2** more than what is proper or enough: *I ate too much.* **3** very; exceedingly: *I am only too glad to help. adverb.*

took (tùk). See **take.** *She took the car an hour ago. verb.*

tool (tül), **1** a knife, hammer, saw, shovel, or any instrument used in doing work: *Plumbers, mechanics, carpenters, and shoemakers need tools.* **2** person or thing used by another like a tool: *Books are a scholar's tools. He is a tool of the party boss.* **3** work or shape with a tool: *to tool beautiful designs in leather with a knife.* 1,2 *noun,* 3 *verb*

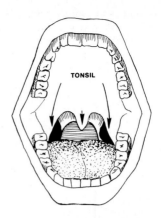

tornado in Nebraska

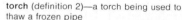
torch (definition 2)—a torch being used to thaw a frozen pipe

toot (tüt), **1** sound of a horn, whistle, or other wind instrument. **2** give forth a short blast of sound: *He heard the train whistle toot three times.* **3** sound (a horn, whistle, or other wind instrument) in short blasts. **1** *noun,* **2,3** *verb.*

tooth (tüth), **1** one of the hard, bonelike parts in the mouth, used for biting and chewing. **2** something like a tooth. Each one of the projecting parts of a comb, rake, or saw is a tooth. *noun, plural* **teeth.**

tooth ache (tüth′āk′), pain in a tooth. *noun.*

tooth brush (tüth′brush′), a small brush for cleaning the teeth. *noun, plural* **tooth brush es.**

toothed (tütht *or* tüŦHd), **1** having teeth. **2** notched: *the toothed surface of a gear. adjective.*

tooth paste (tüth′pāst′), paste used in cleaning the teeth. *noun.*

tooth pick (tüth′pik′), a small, pointed piece of wood or plastic for removing bits of food from between the teeth. *noun.*

top[1] (top), **1** the highest point or part: *the top of a mountain.* **2** the upper part, end, or surface: *the top of a table, a shoe top.* **3** the highest or leading place or rank: *She is at the top of her class.* **4** the highest point, pitch, or degree: *They were yelling at the top of their voices.* **5** part of a plant that grows above ground: *Beet tops are somewhat like spinach.* **6** head: *The baby was all bundled up from top to toe.* **7** highest; greatest: *the top shelf. The runners set off at top speed.* **8** put a top on: *I will top the box.* **9** be on top of; be the top of: *A church tops the hill.* **10** reach the top of: *Call me when you see a gray car topping the hill.* **11** rise high; rise above: *The sun topped the horizon.* **12** be higher or greater than; do better than; outdo; excel: *His story topped all the rest.* **13** remove the top part of: *top a tree.* **1-6** *noun,* **7** *adjective,* **8-13** *verb,* **topped, top ping.**

top[2] (top), toy that spins on a point. *noun.*

to paz (tō′paz), a hard precious stone that occurs in crystals of various forms and colors. Clear yellow topaz is used in jewelry. *noun, plural* **to paz es.**

top coat (top′kōt′), a lightweight overcoat. *noun.*

top ic (top′ik), subject that people think, write, or talk about: *I chose women's rights as the topic for my report. noun.*

top most (top′mōst), highest: *I need a ladder to reach the apples on the topmost branches. adjective.*

to pog ra phy (tə pog′rə fē), **1** the accurate and detailed description of places. **2** the surface features of a place or region. The topography of a region includes hills, valleys, streams, lakes, bridges, tunnels, and roads. *noun, plural* **to pog ra phies.**

top ple (top′əl), **1** fall forward; tumble down: *The chimney toppled over on the roof.* **2** throw over or down; overturn: *The wind toppled the tree. verb,* **top pled, top pling.**

top soil (top′soil′), the upper part of the soil; surface soil: *Farmers need rich topsoil for their crops. noun.*

top sy-tur vy (top′sē tėr′vē), **1** upside down.

a hat	i it	oi oil	ch child		a in about
ā age	ī ice	ou out	ng long		e in taken
ä far	o hot	u cup	sh she	ə =	i in pencil
e let	ō open	u̇ put	th thin		o in lemon
ē equal	ô order	ü rule	ŦH then		u in circus
ėr term			zh measure		

2 in confusion or disorder: *On moving day everything in the house was topsy-turvy. adverb, adjective.*

torch (tôrch), **1** light to be carried around or stuck in a holder on a wall. A piece of pine wood or anything that burns easily makes a good torch. The Statue of Liberty holds a torch. **2** device that shoots out a very hot flame. A torch is used to melt metal and burn off paint. See picture. *noun, plural* **torch es.**

tore (tôr). See **tear**[2]. *Yesterday I tore my jeans on a nail. verb.*

tor ment (tôr ment′ *for 1 and 4;* tôr′ment *for 2 and 3),* **1** cause very great pain to: *Severe headaches tormented him.* **2** cause of very great pain: *A bad burn can be a torment.* **3** very great pain: *She suffered torments from her toothache.* **4** worry or annoy very much: *Don't torment me with silly questions.* **1,4** *verb,* **2,3** *noun.*

torn (tôrn). See **tear**[2]. *I had torn up the plant by the roots. The coat was torn at the elbow. verb.*

tor na do (tôr nā′dō), a very violent and destructive whirlwind. A tornado extends down from a mass of dark clouds as a twisting funnel and moves over the land in a narrow path. See picture. *noun, plural* **tor na does** *or* **tor na dos.**

tor pe do (tôr pē′dō), **1** a large, cigar-shaped shell that contains explosives and travels through water by its own power. **2** attack or destroy with a torpedo or torpedoes. **3** an explosive device put on a railroad track, which makes a very loud noise for a signal when a wheel of the engine runs over it. **1,3** *noun, plural* **tor pe does;** **2** *verb,* **tor pe doed, tor pe do ing.**

tor rent (tôr′ənt), **1** a violent, rushing stream of water: *The mountain torrent dashed over the rocks.* **2** a heavy downpour. See picture. **3** any violent,

torrent (definition 2)—The rain came down in a **torrent** during the thunderstorm.

rushing stream; flood: *a torrent of lava from a volcano, a torrent of questions. noun.*

tor rid (tôr′id), very hot: *July is usually a torrid month. adjective.*

Torrid Zone, the very warm region between the two temperate zones. The equator divides the Torrid Zone.

tor til la (tôr tē′yə), a thin, flat, round cake made of corn meal, commonly eaten in Spanish America. Tortillas are baked on a flat surface and served hot. *noun.*

tor toise (tôr′təs), 1 turtle with a high, arched shell that lives only on land. See picture. 2 any turtle. *noun, plural* **tor tois es** or **tor toise.**

tor ture (tôr′chər), 1 act of inflicting very severe pain. Torture has been used to make people give evidence about crimes, or to make them confess. 2 very severe pain: *You can suffer tortures from a toothache.* 3 cause very severe pain to: *It is cruel to torture animals.* 1,2 *noun,* 3 *verb,* **tor tured, tor tur ing.**

toss (tôs), 1 throw lightly with the palm of the hand upward; cast; fling: *She tossed the ball to the baby.* 2 throw about; pitch about: *The ship is tossed by the waves. He tossed on his bed all night.* 3 lift quickly; throw upward· *She tossed her head.* 4 throw a coin to decide something by the side that falls upward. 5 throw; tossing: *A toss of a coin decided who should play first.* 1-4 *verb,* 5 *noun, plural* **toss es.**

tot (tot), a little child. *noun.*

to tal (tō′tl), 1 whole; entire: *The total cost of the house and land will be $30,000.* 2 the whole amount: *Our expenses reached a total of $100. Add the different sums to get the total.* 3 find the sum of; add: *Total that column of figures.* 4 reach an amount of; amount to: *The money spent yearly on chewing gum totals millions of dollars.* 5 complete: *The lights went out and we were in total darkness.* 1,5 *adjective,* 2 *noun,* 3,4 *verb.*

to tal ly (tō′tl ē), wholly; entirely; completely: *We were totally unprepared for a surprise attack. adverb.*

to tem (tō′təm), 1 a natural object, often an animal, taken as the emblem of a tribe, clan, or family. 2 image of such an object. Totems are often carved and painted on poles. *noun.*

tot ter (tot′ər), 1 walk with shaky, unsteady steps: *The old man tottered across the room.* 2 be unsteady; shake as if about to fall: *The old wall tottered in the gale and fell. verb.*

touch (tuch), 1 put the hand or some other part of the body on or against and feel: *I touched the pan to see whether it was still hot.* 2 put (one thing) against another: *He touched the post with his umbrella.* 3 be against; come against: *Your sleeve is touching the butter.* 4 touching or being touched: *A bubble bursts at a touch.* 5 sense by which a person perceives things by feeling, handling, or coming against them: *The blind develop a keen touch.* 6 communication; connection: *She kept in touch with her family while she was overseas.* 7 a slight amount; little bit: *We had a touch of frost.* 8 a light, delicate stroke with a brush, pencil, or pen; detail:

The artist finished the picture with a few touches. 9 strike lightly or gently: *She touched the strings of the harp to see if it was in tune.* 10 injure slightly: *The flowers were touched by the frost.* 11 affect with some feeling: *The sad story touched our hearts.* 12 have to do with; concern: *The matter touches your interests.* 13 reach; come up to: *His head almost touches the ceiling. Nobody in our class can touch her in science.* 14 act or manner of playing a musical instrument: *The piano player has an excellent touch.* 1-3,9-13 *verb,* 4-8,14 *noun, plural* **touch es.**

touch down, land an aircraft: *The pilot touched down at a small country airfield.*

touch on or **touch upon,** mention; treat lightly: *Our conversation touched on many subjects.*

touch up, change a little; improve: *The photographer touched up a photograph.*

touch down (tuch′doun′), 1 score made in football by putting the ball on the ground behind the opponents′ goal line. 2 act of landing an airplane: *The pilot made an unexpected touchdown because of engine trouble. noun.*

touch football, game having rules similar to those of football except that the person carrying the ball is touched rather than tackled.

touch ing (tuch′ing), 1 arousing tender feeling: *"A Christmas Carol" is a touching story.* 2 concerning; about: *They asked many questions touching my home and school life.* 1 *adjective,* 2 *preposition.*

touch y (tuch′ē), apt to take offense at trifles: *He is tired and very touchy this afternoon. adjective,* **touch i er, touch i est.**

tough (tuf), 1 bending without breaking: *Leather is tough; cardboard is not.* 2 hard to cut, tear, or chew: *The steak was so tough I couldn′t eat it.* 3 strong; hardy: *a tough plant. Donkeys are tough little animals and can carry big loads.* 4 hard; difficult: *Dragging the load uphill was tough work for the horses.* 5 hard to influence; stubborn: *a tough person to deal with.* 6 rough; disorderly: *That is a tough neighborhood.* 7 a rough person: *A gang of toughs attacked them.* 1-6 *adjective,* 7 *noun.*

tough en (tuf′ən), make or become tough: *I toughened my muscles by doing exercises. My muscles finally toughened. verb.*

tour (tür), 1 travel from place to place: *Our scout troop toured by bus for a week.* 2 travel through: *Last year they toured Mexico.* 3 a long journey: *The family made a tour through Europe.* 4 a short journey: *Our class made a tour of the historic old battlefield.* 5 walk around in: *The class will tour the museum.* 1,2,5 *verb,* 3,4 *noun.*

tour ist (tür′ist), person traveling for pleasure: *Each year many tourists go to Canada. noun.*

tour na ment (tėr′nə mənt), 1 contest of many persons in some sport: *a golf tournament.* 2 contest between two groups of knights on horseback who fought for a prize. *noun.*

tour ni quet (tür′nə kit), something used to stop bleeding by pressing a blood vessel, such as a bandage tightened by twisting with a stick. *noun.*

toxic—This mushroom is toxic.

towboat

a hat	i it	oi oil	ch child	(a in about
ā age	ī ice	ou out	ng long	e in taken
ä far	o hot	u cup	sh she	ə = { i in pencil
e let	ō open	u̇ put	th thin	o in lemon
ē equal	ô order	ü rule	ŦH then	(u in circus
ėr term			zh measure	

tow (tō), **1** pull by a rope or chain: *The tug is towing three barges.* **2** act of towing. **3** condition of being pulled along by a rope or chain: *The launch had the sailboat in tow.* **4** what is towed: *Each tug had a tow of three barges.* **5** the rope or chain used. **1** *verb,* **2-5** *noun.*

to ward (tôrd *or* tə wôrd/), **1** in the direction of; to: *He walked toward the north.* **2** with respect to; about; concerning: *What is her attitude toward the proposed new library?* **3** near: *Toward morning the storm ended.* **4** for: *Will you give something toward our new hospital?* preposition.

to wards (tôrdz *or* tə wôrdz/), toward. *preposition.*

tow boat (tō/bōt/), a powerful boat with a flat bottom used to tow or push barges on rivers. See picture. *noun.*

tow el (tou/əl), piece of cloth or paper for wiping and drying something wet. We have hand towels, bath towels, and dish towels. *noun.*

tow er (tou/ər), **1** a high structure. A tower may stand alone or form part of a church, castle, or other building. Some towers are forts or prisons. **2** rise high up: *The new skyscraper towers over the older buildings.* **1** *noun,* **2** *verb.*

tow er ing (tou/ər ing), **1** very high: *a towering peak.* **2** very great: *Making electricity from atomic power is a towering achievement.* **3** very violent: *a towering rage. adjective.*

town (toun), **1** a large group of houses and buildings, smaller than a city: *Do you live in a town or in the country?* **2** any large place with many people living in it: *I hear that Boston is a fine town.* **3** people of a town: *The whole town was having a holiday. noun.*

town cri er (toun/ krī/ər), (in former times) person who called out the news on the streets of a city or town.

town hall, building used for a town's business.

town ship (toun/ship), part of a county in the United States and Canada having certain powers of government. *noun.*

tox ic (tok/sik), poisonous: *Fumes from an automobile are toxic.* See picture. *adjective.* [*Toxic* comes from a Latin word meaning "poison."]

toy (toi), **1** something for a child to play with; plaything. Dolls are toys; so are electric trains. **2** thing that has little value or importance. **3** of, made as, or like a toy. **4** amuse oneself; play; trifle: *I toyed with my pencil. Don't toy with matches.* **1,2** *noun,* **3** *adjective,* **4** *verb.*

trace (trās), **1** mark or sign of the former existence of something: *The explorer found traces of an ancient city.* **2** footprint or other mark left; track; trail: *We saw traces of rabbits and squirrels on the snow.* **3** follow by means of marks, tracks, or signs: *The dog traced the fox to its den.* **4** follow the

tortoise (definition 1)—shell up to 10 inches (25 centimeters) long

train (definition 3)—He carried the **train** of her gown.

track (definition 7)

track (definition 9)—tracks on a tractor

course of: *We traced the river to its source. The Aldens trace their family back three hundred years to John Alden, one of the Pilgrims.* **5** a very small amount; little bit: *There was not a trace of gray in her hair.* **6** mark out: *The spy traced a plan of the fort.* **7** copy by following the lines of with a pencil or pen: *He put thin paper over the map and traced it.* **1,2,5** noun, **3,4,6,7** verb, **traced, trac ing.**

tra che a (trā′kē ə), windpipe. noun, plural **tra che ae** (trā′kē ē′), **tra che as.**

trac ing (trā′sing), copy of something made by putting thin paper over it and following the lines of it with a pencil or pen. noun.

track (trak), **1** a line of parallel steel rails for cars to run on: *railroad tracks.* **2** mark left: *The dirt road showed many automobile tracks.* **3** footprint: *We saw bear tracks near the camp.* **4** follow by means of footprints, smell, or any mark left by anything that has passed by: *We tracked the deer and photographed it.* **5** make footprints or other marks on: *Don't track the floor with your muddy feet.* **6** path; trail; rough road: *A track runs through the woods to the farmhouse.* **7** course for running or racing. See picture. **8** contests in running, jumping, throwing, and similar sports performed around or inside a track: *I'm going out for track this year.* **9** one of the endless belts of linked steel plates on which a tank, bulldozer, or tractor moves. See picture. **1-3,6-9** noun, **4,5** verb.

keep track of, keep within one's sight or attention: *There was so much noise it was difficult for me to keep track of what you said.*

track less (trak′lis), without paths or trails: *The region near the South Pole is a trackless wilderness.* adjective.

track meet, series of contests in running, jumping, throwing, and similar sports.

tract (trakt), **1** stretch of land or water; area: *A tract of desert land has little value.* **2** system of related parts or organs in the body. The stomach and intestines are parts of the digestive tract. noun.

trac tion (trak′shən), friction: *Wheels slip on ice because there is too little traction.* noun.

trac tor (trak′tər), engine which moves on wheels or on two endless tracks, used for pulling wagons, trucks, plows, or other vehicles. noun.

trade (trād), **1** buying and selling; exchange of goods; commerce: *The United States has much trade with foreign countries.* **2** buy and sell; exchange goods; be in commerce: *Some American companies trade all over the world.* **3** an exchange: *an even trade.* **4** exchange; make an exchange: *He traded a stick of gum for a ride on her bicycle. If you don't like your book, I'll trade with you.* **5** bargain; deal: *I made a good trade.* **6** kind of work; business, especially one requiring skilled work: *the carpenter's trade.* **7** people in the same kind of work or business: *Carpenters, plumbers, and electricians are all members of the building trade.* **1,3,5-7** noun, **2,4** verb, **trad ed, trad ing.**

trade in, give (an automobile, refrigerator, or other article) as payment or part payment for

a hat	i it	oi oil	ch child	a in about
ā age	ī ice	ou out	ng long	e in taken
ä far	o hot	u cup	sh she	ə = { i in pencil
e let	ō open	ù put	th thin	o in lemon
ē equal	ô order	ü rule	ŦH then	u in circus
ėr term			zh measure	

something, especially for a newer model.

trade on, take advantage of: *People sometimes trade on their wealth to gain influence in government.*

trade-in (trād/in/), thing given or accepted as payment or part payment for something. *noun.*

trade mark (trād/märk/), mark, picture, name, word, symbol, or letters owned and used by a manufacturer or merchant. A trademark identifies the product for the buyer. *noun.*

trad er (trā/dər), **1** person who trades: *The trappers sold furs to traders.* **2** ship used in trading. *noun.*

trades man (trādz/mən), storekeeper; shopkeeper. *noun, plural* **trades men.**

trade wind, wind blowing steadily toward the equator.

trading post, store or station of a trader, especially on the frontier or in unsettled country. Trading posts used to sell food, weapons, clothes, and other articles to Indians and trappers in exchange for hides and furs.

tra di tion (trə dish/ən), **1** the handing down of beliefs, opinions, customs, and stories from parents to children, especially by word of mouth or by practice. **2** what is handed down in this way: *According to the old tradition, the first American flag was made by Betsy Ross. noun.*

tra di tion al (trə dish/ə nəl), **1** of tradition. **2** handed down by tradition: *Shaking hands upon meeting is a traditional custom.* **3** according to tradition: *traditional furniture.* **4** customary: *A Memorial Day parade is traditional in almost every town. adjective.*

traf fic (traf/ik), **1** people, automobiles, wagons, ships, or the like coming and going along a way of travel: *Police control the traffic in large cities.* **2** buying and selling; trade: *Governments are trying to stop the illegal drug traffic.* **3** carry on trade; buy; sell; exchange: *The traders trafficked with the natives for ivory.* **4** business done by a railroad line, steamship line, or airline; number of passengers or amount of freight carried. 1,2,4 *noun,* 3 *verb,* **traf ficked, traf fick ing.**

traffic light, set of electric lights used to control traffic at a corner or intersection. The lights are usually colored red for stop, green for go, and yellow for caution. They are flashed automatically every few seconds or minutes.

trag e dy (traj/ə dē), **1** a serious play having an unhappy ending. **2** a very sad or terrible happening: *Her sudden death was a tragedy to her friends. noun, plural* **trag e dies.**

trag ic (traj/ik), **1** of tragedy; having something to do with tragedy: *a tragic actor, a tragic poet.* **2** very sad; dreadful: *a tragic death, a tragic accident. adjective.*

trail (trāl), **1** path across a wild or unsettled region: *The scouts followed mountain trails for days.* **2** track or smell: *The dogs found the trail of the rabbit.* **3** hunt by track or smell: *The dogs trailed the rabbit.* **4** anything that follows along behind: *As the car sped down the road, it left a trail of dust behind it.* **5** follow along behind; follow: *The dog*

trailed its master constantly. **6** pull or drag along behind: *The child trailed a toy horse after him.* **7** grow along: *Poison ivy trailed by the road.* 1,2,4 *noun,* 3,5-7 *verb.*

trail er (trā/lər), **1** vehicle used for carrying freight. It is usually pulled by a truck. **2** vehicle like a house on wheels usually pulled by an automobile. When parked, it is used as a house or office. *noun.*

train (trān), **1** a connected line of railroad cars moving along together: *A very long freight train of 100 cars rolled by.* **2** line of people, animals, wagons, trucks, or the like, moving along together: *The early settlers crossed the continent by wagon train.* **3** part that hangs down and drags along. See picture. **4** group of followers: *the king and his train.* **5** series; succession: *A long train of misfortunes overcame the hero.* **6** order of succession; sequence: *I lost my train of thought when I was interrupted.* **7** bring up; rear; teach: *They trained their child to be thoughtful of others.* **8** make skillful by teaching and practice: *train people as nurses. Saint Bernard dogs were trained to hunt for travelers lost in the snow.* **9** make fit by exercise and diet: *The runners trained for races.* **10** point; aim: *train guns upon a fort.* **11** bring into a particular position; make grow in a particular way: *We trained the vines around the post.* 1-6 *noun,* 7-11 *verb.*

train ing (trā/ning), **1** practical education in some art, profession, or trade: *training for teachers.* **2** development of strength and endurance: *physical training.* **3** good condition maintained by exercise and care: *The athlete kept in training by not overeating and not smoking. noun.*

train man (trān/mən), **1** brakeman or railroad worker in a train crew, of lower rank than a conductor. *noun, plural* **train men.**

trait (trāt), quality of mind or character; feature; characteristic: *Courage, love of fair play, and common sense are desirable traits. noun.*

trai tor (trā/tər), **1** person who betrays his or her country: *Benedict Arnold became a traitor by helping the British during the Revolutionary War.* **2** person who betrays a trust, a duty, or a friend. *noun.*

tramp (tramp), **1** walk heavily: *They tramped across the floor in their heavy boots.* **2** step heavily (on): *He tramped on the flowers.* **3** sound of a heavy step: *the tramp of marching feet.* **4** walk; go on foot: *The hikers tramped through the mountains.* **5** a long, steady walk; hike: *The friends took a tramp together over the hills.* **6** person who wanders about and lives by begging or doing odd jobs. **7** a freight ship that takes a cargo when and where it can. 1,2,4 *verb,* 3,5-7 *noun.*

tram ple (tram/pəl), **1** tread heavily on; crush: *The* herd of wild cattle trampled the farm crops. **2** tread heavily; tramp. **3** act or sound of trampling: *We heard the trample of many feet.* 1,2 *verb,* **tram pled, tram pling;** 3 *noun.*

trample on or **trample upon,** treat with scorn, harshness, or cruelty: *The dictator trampled on the rights of the people.*

tram po line (tram′pə lēn′), piece of canvas or other sturdy fabric stretched on a metal frame, used for tumbling. *noun.*

trance (trans), **1** condition somewhat like sleep in which a person no longer responds to the surroundings. A person may be in a trance from some illnesses or from hypnotism. Some people can even put themselves into trances. **2** a dreamy or absorbed condition which is like a trance: *She sat in a trance, thinking of her past life. noun.*

tran quil (trang′kwəl), calm; peaceful; quiet: *the tranquil morning air. adjective.*

tran quil iz er (trang′kwə lī′zər), a drug that relaxes muscles, reduces tension, and lowers blood pressure. *noun.*

tran quil li ty (trang kwil′ə tē), tranquil condition; calmness; peacefulness; quiet. *noun.*

trans act (tran zakt′), attend to; manage; do; carry on (business): *He transacts business daily. verb.*

trans ac tion (tran zak′shən), **1** carrying on (of business): *She attends to the transaction of important matters herself.* **2** a business deal: *A record is kept of all the firm's transactions. noun.*

trans con ti nen tal (tran′skon tə nen′tl), crossing a continent: *a transcontinental railroad. adjective.*

trans fer (tran sfėr′ *for 1, 2, and 5;* tran′sfėr *for 3, 4, and 6*), **1** change or move from one place to another: *The clerk was transferred to another department. Please have my trunks transferred to the Union Station.* **2** change (a drawing, design, or pattern) from one surface to another: *You transfer the embroidery design from the paper to cloth by pressing it with a warm iron.* **3** transferring or being transferred: *a transfer to a different school.* **4** thing transferred; drawing, pattern, or design printed from one surface onto another. **5** change from one bus, train, or airline to another. **6** ticket allowing a passenger to change from one bus, train, or airline to another. 1,2,5 *verb,* **trans ferred, trans fer ring;** 3,4,6 *noun.*

trans form (tran sfôrm′), **1** change in form or appearance: *The blizzard transformed the bushes into mounds of white.* **2** change in condition, nature, or character: *A tadpole becomes transformed into a frog.* See picture. *verb.*

trans for ma tion (tran′sfər mā′shən), transforming: *the transformation of a caterpillar into a butterfly. noun.*

trans fu sion (tran sfyü′zhən), **1** causing to pass from one container or holder to another. **2** transferring blood from one person or animal to another: *The injured driver was bleeding badly and needed a transfusion at once. noun.*

tran sis tor (tran zis′tər), a small electronic device

used to amplify or control the flow of electrons in an electric circuit. Transistors have replaced tubes in many radios and televisions. *noun.*

tran sit (tran′sit), **1** passing across or through. **2** carrying across or through: *The goods were damaged in transit.* **3** instrument used in surveying to measure angles. *noun.*

transform (definition 2)
The movie was about a man who was **transformed** into a wolf.

tran si tion (tran zish′ən), change or passing from one condition, place, or thing to another: *Lincoln's life was a transition from poverty to power. noun.*

trans late (tran slāt′), **1** change from one language into another: *translate a book from French into English.* **2** express (one thing) in terms of another: *translate words into action. verb,* **trans lat ed, trans lat ing.**

trans la tion (tran slā′shən), **1** change into another language: *the translation of the Bible from Hebrew to English.* **2** change from one position or condition to another: *the translation of a promise into a deed.* **3** result of translating; version. *noun.*

trans lu cent (tran slü′snt), letting light through, but not able to be seen through: *Frosted glass is translucent.* See picture. *adjective.*

trans mis sion (tran smish′ən), **1** sending over; passing on; passing along; letting through: *Mosquitoes are the only means of transmission of malaria.* **2** part of an automobile which transmits power from the engine to the rear axle. **3** passing through space of radio or television waves from the transmitting station to the receiving station: *When transmission is good, even foreign stations can be heard. noun.*

trans mit (tran smit′), **1** send over; pass on; pass along; let through: *I will transmit the money by special messenger. Rats transmit disease.* **2** send out (signals, voice, music, or pictures) by radio or television: *Some station is transmitting every hour of the day. verb,* **trans mit ted, trans mit ting.**

trans mit ter (tran smit′ər), device that sends out sounds, or sounds and pictures, by radio waves: *Radio stations and television stations have transmitters. noun.*

tran som (tran′səm), window over a door or other window, usually hinged for opening. *noun.*

trans par ent (tran sper′ənt *or* tran spar′ənt), easily seen through: *A transparent excuse doesn't fool anyone.* See picture. *adjective.*

trans plant (tran splant′ *for 1-3;* tran′splant *for 4*), **1** plant again in a different place: *We start the flowers indoors and then transplant them to the garden.* **2** remove from one place to another: *Ten farmers were transplanted to the island by the government.* **3** transfer (skin, an organ, or the like) from one person, animal, or part of the body to another: *transplant a kidney.* **4** transfer of skin, an organ, or the like from one person, animal, or part of the body to another: *a heart transplant.* 1-3 *verb,* 4 *noun.*

trans port (tran spôrt′ *for 1, 5, and 7;* tran′spôrt *for 2-4 and 6*), **1** carry from one place to another: *Wheat is transported from the farms to the mills.* **2** carrying from one place to another: *Trucks are much used for transport.* **3** a ship used to carry troops and supplies. **4** airplane that transports passengers, mail, or freight. **5** carry away by strong feeling: *She was transported with joy by the good news.* **6** strong feeling: *a transport of rage.* **7** send away to another country as a punishment: *Years ago, England transported many of its criminals to Australia.* 1,5,7 *verb,* 2-4,6 *noun.*

trans por ta tion (tran′spər tā′shən), **1** transporting: *The railroad allows free transportation for a certain amount of a passenger's baggage.* **2** being transported. **3** means of transport. **4** cost of transport; ticket for transport: *Her transportation was provided by her company. noun.*

trap (trap), **1** thing or means for catching animals. **2** trick or other means for catching someone off guard: *The police set traps to catch the robbers.* **3** catch in a trap: *The bear was trapped.* **4** set traps for animals: *to trap a mouse.* **5** trap door. **6** bend in a pipe to catch small objects and to keep gas from backing up. 1,2,5,6 *noun,* 3,4 *verb,* **trapped, trap ping.**

trap door, door in a floor or roof.

tra peze (trə pēz′), a short, horizontal bar hung by ropes like a swing, used in gymnasiums and circuses. *noun.*

trap per (trap′ər), person who traps, especially one who traps wild animals for their furs. See picture. *noun.*

trash (trash), **1** broken or torn bits, such as leaves, twigs, or husks: *Rake up the trash in the yard.* **2** worthless stuff; rubbish: *That magazine is simply trash. noun.*

trav el (trav′əl), **1** go from one place to another; journey: *She is traveling in Europe this summer.* **2** going in trains, airplanes, ships, cars, and the like, from one place to another: *She loves travel.* **3** go from place to place selling things: *He travels for a large firm.* **4** move; proceed; pass: *Sound travels in waves.* 1,3,4 *verb,* 2 *noun.*

trav el er (trav′ə lər), a person who travels. *noun.*

a hat	i it	oi oil	ch child	⎧ a in about
ā age	ī ice	ou out	ng long	⎪ e in taken
ä far	o hot	u cup	sh she	ə = ⎨ i in pencil
e let	ō open	ů put	th thin	⎪ o in lemon
ē equal	ô order	ü rule	ᴛʜ then	⎩ u in circus
ėr term			zh measure	

transparent—A plant seen through transparent glass.

translucent—The same plant seen through translucent glass.

trapper

trawl (trôl), **1** net dragged along the bottom of the sea. **2** fish or catch fish with a net by dragging it along the bottom of the sea. 1 *noun,* 2 *verb.*

tray (trā), **1** a flat, shallow holder or container with a rim around it: *The waiter carries the dishes on a tray.* **2** a shallow box that fits into a trunk or cabinet: *Dentists keep many of their instruments in trays. noun.*

treach er ous (trech/ər əs), **1** not to be trusted; not faithful; not loyal: *The treacherous soldier carried reports to the enemy.* **2** having a false appearance of strength or security; not reliable; deceiving: *That thin ice is treacherous. adjective.*

treach er y (trech/ər ē), **1** breaking of faith; treacherous behavior; deceit: *King Arthur's kingdom was destroyed by treachery.* **2** treason. *noun, plural* **treach er ies.**

tread (tred), **1** walk; step; set the foot down: *Don't tread on the flower beds.* **2** press under the feet; trample; crush: *In Italy, we watched people tread grapes to make wine.* **3** make, form, or do by walking: *Cattle had trodden a path to the pond.* **4** way of walking; step: *to walk with a heavy tread.* **5** part of stairs or a ladder that a person steps on: *The stair treads were covered with rubber to prevent slipping.* **6** part of a wheel or tire that touches the ground: *The treads of rubber tires are grooved to improve traction.* 1-3 *verb,* **trod, trod den** or **trod, tread ing;** 4-6 *noun.*

trea dle (tred/l), lever or pedal worked by the foot to operate a machine. *noun.*

tread mill (tred/mil/), **1** device for producing a turning motion by having a person or animal walk on the moving steps of a wheel or of a sloping, endless belt. See picture. **2** any wearisome or monotonous round of work or of life. *noun.*

trea son (trē/zn), being false to one's country or ruler. Helping the enemies of one's country is treason. *noun.* [*Treason* comes from a Latin word meaning "a delivering" or "a handing down." The same Latin word is also the source of the word *tradition.*]

treas ure (trezh/ər), **1** wealth or riches stored up; valuable things: *The pirates buried treasure along the coast.* **2** any thing or person that is much loved or valued: *The silver teapot was the old couple's chief treasure.* **3** value highly: *She treasures her train more than all her other toys.* 1,2 *noun,* 3 *verb,* **treas ured, treas ur ing.**

treas ur er (trezh/ər ər), person in charge of money. The treasurer of a club pays its bills. *noun.*

treas ur y (trezh/ər ē), **1** place where money is kept. **2** money owned; funds: *We voted to pay for the party out of the club treasury.* **3 Treasury,** department of the government that has charge of the income and expenses of a country. The Treasury of the United States collects federal taxes, mints money, supervises national banks, and prevents counterfeiting. **4** place where treasure is kept. *noun, plural* **treas ur ies.**

treat (trēt), **1** act toward: *The children treated the puppy with care.* **2** think of; consider; regard: *She treated her mistake as a joke.* **3** deal with to relieve or cure: *The dentist is treating my toothache.* **4** deal with; discuss: *This magazine treats the progress of medicine.* **5** express in literature or art: *The author treats the characters of his story so that you feel you know them.* **6** give food, drink, or amusement: *She treated her friends to ice cream.* **7** gift of food, drink, or amusement: *"This is my treat,"* she said. **8** anything that gives pleasure: *Being in the country was a treat to the city children.* 1-6 *verb,* 7,8 *noun.*

treat of, deal with the subject of: *"The Medical Journal" treats of the progress of medicine.*

treadmill (definition 1)—The horses are on a treadmill.

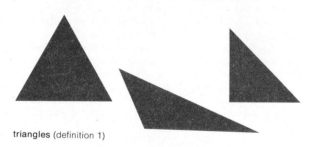

triangles (definition 1)

triangle (definition 3)

treat ment (trēt'mənt), **1** act or process of treating: *My cold won't respond to treatment.* **2** way of treating: *This cat has suffered from bad treatment.* **3** thing done or used to treat something else, such as a disease. *noun.*

trea ty (trē'tē), a formal agreement, especially one between nations, signed and approved by each nation. *noun, plural* **trea ties.**

tre ble (treb'əl), **1** three times: *His salary is treble mine.* **2** make or become three times as much: *She trebled her money by buying a dog for $25 and selling it for $75.* **3** the highest part in music; soprano. **1** *adjective,* **2** *verb,* **tre bled, tre bling;** **3** *noun.*

tree (trē), **1** a large plant with a woody trunk and usually having branches and leaves at some distance from the ground. **2** a wooden object used for some special purpose: *a clothes tree, a shoe tree.* **3** anything like a tree. A **family tree** is a diagram with branches showing how the members of a family are related. **4** chase up a tree: *The cat was treed by a dog.* **1-3** *noun,* **4** *verb,* **treed, tree ing.**

tree less (trē'lis), without trees: *a treeless plain.* *adjective.*

tree top (trē'top'), top or uppermost part of a tree. *noun.*

trek (trek), **1** travel slowly by any means; travel: *The pioneers trekked across the great western plains by covered wagon.* **2** journey: *It was a long trek over the mountains.* **1** *verb,* **trekked, trek king;** **2** *noun.*

trel lis (trel'is), frame of light strips of wood or metal crossing one another with open spaces in between; lattice, especially one supporting growing vines. *noun, plural* **trel lis es.**

trem ble (trem'bəl), **1** shake because of fear, excitement, weakness, cold, or the like: *The child's voice trembled with fear. My hands trembled from the cold.* **2** move gently: *The leaves trembled in the breeze.* **3** trembling: *There was a tremble in her voice as she began to recite.* **1,2** *verb,* **trem bled, trem bling;** **3** *noun.*

tre men dous (tri men'dəs), **1** dreadful; very severe: *The army suffered a tremendous defeat.* **2** enormous; very great: *That is a tremendous house for a family of three. adjective.*

trem or (trem'ər), **1** a shaking or trembling: *a nervous tremor in the voice.* **2** thrill of emotion or excitement. *noun.*

trench (trench), **1** a long, narrow ditch with earth thrown up in front to protect soldiers. **2** a deep furrow; ditch: *dig a trench for a sewer pipe. noun, plural* **trench es.**

trend (trend), **1** the general direction; course; tendency: *The trend of modern living is away from many old customs.* **2** have a general direction; tend; run: *Modern life trends toward less formal customs.* **1** *noun,* **2** *verb.*

tres pass (tres'pəs), **1** go on somebody's property without any right: *The farmer put up "No Trespassing" signs to keep hunters off his farm.* **2** go beyond the limits of what is right, proper, or polite: *I won't trespass on your kind hospitality any longer.* **3** act of trespassing. **4** do wrong; sin.

a hat	**i** it	**oi** oil	**ch** child	**a** in about
ā age	**ī** ice	**ou** out	**ng** long	**e** in taken
ä far	**o** hot	**u** cup	**sh** she	**ə** = **i** in pencil
e let	**ō** open	**u̇** put	**th** thin	**o** in lemon
ē equal	**ô** order	**ü** rule	**ᵺ** then	**u** in circus
ėr term			**zh** measure	

5 wrong; sin: *"Forgive us our trespasses as we forgive those who trespass against us."* **1,2,4** *verb,* **3,5** *noun, plural* **tres pass es.**

tress (tres), lock, curl, or braid of hair: *golden tresses. noun, plural* **tress es.**

tres tle (tres'əl), **1** a frame used as a support for a flat surface. **2** a framework of steel or wood used to support a highway or railroad bridge. *noun.*

tri al (trī'əl), **1** the examining and deciding a case in court: *The suspect was brought to trial.* **2** process of trying or testing: *The mechanic gave the motor another trial to see if it would start.* **3** for a try or test: *a trial model, a trial run.* **4** being tried or tested: *He is employed for two weeks on trial.* **5** trouble; hardship: *The pioneers suffered many trials.* **1,2,4,5** *noun,* **3** *adjective.*

tri an gle (trī'ang'gəl), **1** figure having three sides and three angles. See picture. **2** something shaped like a triangle. **3** a musical instrument made of a triangle of steel that is struck with a steel rod. See picture. *noun.*

tri an gu lar (trī ang'gyə lər), shaped like a triangle; three-cornered. *adjective.*

trib al (trī'bəl), of a tribe: *tribal customs. adjective.*

tribe (trīb), **1** group of people united by race and customs under the same leaders: *an American Indian tribe.* **2** class or set of people: *A tribe of hungry children rushed into the house. noun.*

tribes man (trībz'mən), member of a tribe. *noun, plural* **tribes men.**

trib u tar y (trib'yə ter'ē), stream that flows into a larger stream or body of water: *The Ohio River is one of the tributaries of the Mississippi River. noun, plural* **trib u tar ies.**

trib ute (trib'yüt), **1** money paid by one nation to another for peace or protection or because of some agreement. **2** any forced payment: *The pirates demanded tribute from passing ships.* **3** acknowledgment of thanks or respect; compliment: *Labor Day is a tribute to workers. noun.*

trick (trik), **1** something done to deceive or cheat: *The false message was a trick to get her to leave the house.* **2** deceive; cheat: *We were tricked into buying a stolen car.* **3** a clever act; feat of skill: *We enjoyed the tricks of the trained animals.* **4** the best way of doing or dealing with something: *She is teaching me the trick of restoring old furniture.* **5** piece of mischief; prank: *Hiding my lunch was a mean trick.* **6** play tricks. **7** of, like, or done as a trick or stunt: *trick riding, trick shooting.* **8** a peculiar habit or way of acting: *He has a trick of pulling at his collar.* **9** cards played in one round of a card game. **1,3-5,8,9** *noun,* **2,6** *verb,* **7** *adjective.*

trick er y (trik'ər ē), use of tricks; deception; cheating. *noun, plural* **trick er ies.**

trick le (trik′əl), **1** flow or fall in drops or in a small stream: *Tears trickled down her cheeks. The brook trickled through the valley.* **2** a small flow or stream. **3** come, go, pass, or move forward slowly and unevenly: *An hour before the show started, people began to trickle into the theater.* **1,3** *verb,* **trick led, trick ling; 2** *noun.*

trick y (trik′ē), **1** full of tricks; deceiving: *A fox is trickier than a sheep.* **2** not doing what is expected; dangerous or difficult to deal with: *The back door has a tricky lock.* *adjective,* **trick i er, trick i est.**

tri cy cle (trī′sə kəl *or* trī′sik′əl), a three-wheeled vehicle usually worked by pedals. Children often ride tricycles before they are old enough for bicycles. *noun.*

tried (trīd), **1** tested; proved: *a person of tried abilities.* **2** See **try.** *I tried to call you.* **1** *adjective,* **2** *verb.*

tri fle (trī′fəl), **1** thing that is of very little value or small importance. **2** a small amount; little bit: *She was a trifle late.* **3** a small amount of money: *The picture cost only a trifle.* **4** talk or act lightly, not seriously: *Don't trifle with serious matters.* **5** play or toy (with); handle: *He trifled with his pencil.* **6** spend (time, effort, or money) on things having little value: *They trifled away the whole morning.* **1-3** *noun,* **4-6** *verb,* **tri fled, tri fling.**

tri fling (trī′fling), **1** having little value; not important; small: *The friends treated their quarrel as only a trifling matter.* **2** silly; shallow: *Their conversation was nothing but trifling gossip.* *adjective.*

trig ger (trig′ər), **1** the small lever pulled back by the finger in firing a gun. **2** lever that releases a spring when pulled or pressed. **3** set off (an explosion): *A spark triggered the explosion.* **4** begin; start: *I broke the glass that triggered the fire alarm.* **1,2** *noun,* **3,4** *verb.*

trill (tril), **1** sing, play, sound, or speak with a trembling sound: *Some birds trill their songs.* **2** act or sound of trilling. **1** *verb,* **2** *noun.*

trim (trim), **1** put in good order; make neat by cutting away parts: *The gardener trims the hedge. The barber trimmed my hair.* **2** neat; in good condition or order: *The entire family works together to keep a trim house.* **3** good condition or order: *Is our team in trim for the game?* **4** condition; order: *That ship is in poor trim for a voyage.* **5** decorate: *The children were trimming the Christmas tree.* **6** arrange (the sails) to fit wind and direction. **7** defeat; beat. **1,5-7** *verb,* **trimmed, trim ming; 2** *adjective,* **trim mer, trim mest; 3,4** *noun.*

trim ming (trim′ing), **1** anything used to trim or decorate; ornament: *trimming for a dress.* **2** defeat; beating. **3 trimmings, a** parts cut away in trimming, clipping, paring, or pruning. **b** everything needed to make something complete and festive: *We ate turkey with all the trimmings.* *noun.*

trin ket (tring′kit), any small fancy article, bit of jewelry, or the like: *The baby played with the trinkets on the bracelet.* *noun.*

tri o (trē′ō), **1** piece of music for three voices or instruments. **2** group of three singers or players performing together. **3** any group of three. *noun, plural* **tri os.**

trip (trip), **1** journey; voyage: *a trip to Europe.* **2** stumble: *He tripped on the stairs.* **3** cause to stumble and fall: *The loose board on the stairs tripped her.* **4** make a mistake; do something wrong: *He tripped on that difficult question.* **5** cause to make a mistake: *The difficult question tripped me.* **6** take light, quick steps: *The children came tripping down the path to meet us.* **1** *noun,* **2-6** *verb,* **tripped, trip ping.**

tripe (trīp), walls of the first and second stomachs of an ox, steer, or cow, used as food. *noun.*

tri ple (trip′əl), **1** three times as much or as many: *a triple portion of cake, get triple pay.* **2** having three parts: *a triple crown.* **3** make or become three times as much or as many: *The number of club members has tripled this year.* **4** in baseball, a hit that allows the batter to reach third base. **1,2** *adjective,* **3** *verb,* **tri pled, tri pling; 4** *noun.*

tri plet (trip′lit), **1** one of three children born at the same time from the same mother. **2** group of three. *noun.*

tri pod (trī′pod), a three-legged support or stand for a camera, telescope, or the like. *noun.*

tri umph (trī′umf), **1** victory; success: *final triumph over the enemy. The conquest of outer space is one of the great triumphs of modern science.* **2** gain victory; win success: *Our team triumphed over theirs.* **3** joy because of victory or success: *We welcomed the team home with cheers of triumph.* **1,3** *noun,* **2** *verb.*

tri um phal (trī um′fəl), celebrating a victory: *a triumphal march.* *adjective.*

tri um phant (trī um′fənt), **1** victorious; successful: *a triumphant army.* **2** joyful because of victory or success: *The winners spoke in triumphant tones about their skillful play.* *adjective.*

triv i al (triv′ē əl), not important: *Your composition has only a few trivial mistakes.* *adjective.*

trod (trod). See **tread.** *The path was trod by many feet.* *verb.*

trod den (trod′n). See **tread.** *The cattle had trodden down the corn.* *verb.*

troll[1] (trōl), **1** sing in a rich, loud voice. **2** sing in succession. When three people troll a round, the soprano sings one line, the alto comes in next with the same line, and then the bass sings it, and so on, while the others keep on singing. **3** song whose parts are sung in succession; round: *"Three Blind Mice" is a well-known troll.* **4** fish with a moving line, usually by trailing the line behind the boat near the surface: *I trolled for bass.* See picture. **1,2,4** *verb,* **3** *noun.*

troll[2] (trōl), (in stories) an ugly giant or dwarf living in caves or underground. See picture. *noun.*

trol ley (trol′ē), **1** pulley at the end of a pole which moves against a wire to carry electricity to a streetcar or an electric engine. A **trolley car** or **trolley bus** is a streetcar or bus having such a pulley. **2** a basket or carriage hung from a pulley which runs on an overhead track. *noun, plural* **trol leys.**

trom bone (trom′bōn), a brass wind instrument with a loud tone, usually with a long sliding piece for varying the length of the tube. See picture. *noun.*

troop (trüp), **1** group or band of persons: *a troop of children.* **2** herd, flock, or swarm: *a troop of deer.* **3** unit of cavalry, usually commanded by a captain. **4 troops,** soldiers: *The government sent troops to put down the revolt.* **5** gather in troops or bands; move together: *The children trooped around the teacher.* **6** walk; go; go away: *The younger children trooped off after the older ones.* 1-4 *noun,* 5,6 *verb.*

troop er (trü′pər), **1** soldier in a troop of cavalry. **2** a mounted policeman. The state police of some states are called troopers, because they were originally organized as mounted troops. *noun.*

tro phy (trō′fē), an award, often in the form of a statue or cup, given as a sign of victory. A trophy is often awarded as a prize in a race or contest. See picture. *noun, plural* **tro phies.**

trop i cal (trop′ə kəl), of the tropics: *Bananas are tropical fruit. adjective.*

trop ics (trop′iks), regions near the equator. The hottest parts of the earth are in the tropics. *noun plural.*

trot (trot), **1** the gait of a horse between a walk and a gentle gallop. In a trot, the right forefoot and the left hind foot are lifted at the same time. **2** ride at a trot: *The riders trotted home.* **3** go or cause to go at a trot: *The pony trotted through the field. We trotted our horses through the woods.* **4** run, but not fast: *The child trotted after me.* **5** a slow running. 1,5 *noun,* 2-4 *verb,* **trot ted, trot ting.**

trou ble (trub′əl), **1** distress; worry; difficulty: *The noisy students made trouble for their teacher.* **2** cause distress or worry to; disturb: *Lack of business troubled the grocer. I am troubled by headaches.* **3** disturbance; disorder: *political troubles.* **4** extra work; bother; effort: *Take the trouble to do careful work.* **5** require extra work or effort of: *May I trouble you to pass the sugar?* **6** cause oneself inconvenience: *Don't trouble to come to the door; I can let myself in.* **7** illness; disease: *She has stomach trouble.* 1,3,4,7 *noun,* 2,5,6 *verb,* **trou bled, trou bling.**

trou ble some (trub′əl səm), causing trouble; annoying; full of trouble: *Last year we had noisy, troublesome neighbors. adjective.*

trough (trôf), **1** a long, narrow container for holding food or water: *He led the horses to the watering trough.* **2** something shaped like this: *The baker used a trough for kneading dough.* **3** a long hollow between two ridges: *the trough between two waves. noun.*

trounce (trouns), beat; thrash: *The victors trounced the losing team. verb,* **trounced, trounc ing.**

troupe (trüp), band or company, especially a group of actors, singers, or acrobats. *noun.*

trou sers (trou′zərz), a two-legged outer garment reaching from the waist to the ankles or knees. *noun plural.*

trout (trout), a freshwater food fish that is related to the salmon. *noun, plural* **trouts** or **trout.**

a hat	**i** it	**oi** oil	**ch** child	a in about
ā age	**ī** ice	**ou** out	**ng** long	e in taken
ä far	**o** hot	**u** cup	**sh** she	ə = { i in pencil
e let	**ō** open	**u̇** put	**th** thin	o in lemon
ē equal	**ô** order	**ü** rule	**ŦH** then	u in circus
ėr term			**zh** measure	

trombone

trophy—She proudly displayed her trophy.

trow el (trou′əl), **1** tool with a broad, flat blade for spreading or smoothing plaster or mortar. **2** tool with a curved blade for taking up plants or loosening dirt. See picture. *noun.*

troy weight (troi′ wāt′), a standard system of weights used for gems and precious metals. One pound troy equals a little over four fifths of an ordinary pound. 12 troy ounces = 1 troy pound. [The word *troy* comes from Troyes, a city in northern France. Formerly, a fair was held there at which this system of weights was supposed to have been used.]

tru ant (trü′ənt), **1** student who stays away from school without permission. **2** person who neglects duty. **3** neglecting duty: *The truant factory worker left the machine running without watching it.* 1,2 *noun,* 3 *adjective.*

truce (trüs), stop in fighting; peace for a short time: *A truce was declared between the two armies. noun.*

truck (truk), **1** a strongly built motor vehicle for carrying heavy loads. **2** carry on a truck: *truck freight to the warehouse.* **3** frame with two or more pairs of wheels for supporting the end of a railroad car or a locomotive. 1,3 *noun,* 2 *verb.*

trudge (truj), **1** go on foot; walk. **2** walk wearily or with effort. **3** a hard or weary walk: *It was a long trudge up the hill.* 1,2 *verb,* **trudged, trudg ing;** 3 *noun.*

true (trü), **1** agreeing with fact; not false: *It is true that 4 and 6 are 10. The story I told is true; I did not make it up.* **2** real; genuine: *true gold, true kindness.* **3** faithful; loyal: *my truest friend, true to your promises.* **4** agreeing with a standard; right; proper; correct; exact; accurate: *This is a true copy of my letter.* **5** rightful; lawful: *the true heir to the property.* **6** in a true manner; truly; exactly: *Your words ring true.* 1-5 *adjective,* **tru er, tru est;** 6 *adverb.*

tru ly (trü′lē), **1** in a true manner; exactly; rightly; faithfully: *Tell me truly what you think.* **2** really; in fact: *It was truly a beautiful sight. adverb.*

trum pet (trum′pit), **1** a brass wind instrument that has a powerful tone, commonly a curved tube with a flaring bell at one end. See picture. **2** thing shaped like a trumpet. Ear trumpets were once used to help persons who were not able to hear well. **3** blow a trumpet. **4** a sound like that of a trumpet. **5** make a sound like a trumpet: *An elephant trumpeted.* **6** announce loudly or widely: *They trumpeted the news all over town.* 1,2,4 *noun,* 3,5,6 *verb.*

trun dle (trun′dl), **1** roll along; push along: *The worker trundled a wheelbarrow full of cement.* **2** a small wheel. 1 *verb,* **trun dled, trun dling;** 2 *noun.*

trundle bed, a low bed moving on small wheels.

trunk (trungk), **1** the main stem of a tree, as distinct from the branches and the roots. **2** the main part of anything: *the trunk of a column.* **3** main; chief: *a trunk highway.* **4** a big box for holding clothes and other articles when traveling. **5** an enclosed compartment in an automobile for storing baggage, a spare tire, and similar things.

6 a human or animal body but not including the head, arms, and legs. **7** the long, flexible snout of an elephant, used by the animal to grasp objects, and to feed itself. **8 trunks,** very short pants worn by swimmers, boxers, acrobats, and athletes. 1,2,4-8 *noun,* 3 *adjective.*

trust (trust), **1** firm belief in the honesty, truthfulness, justice, or power of a person or thing; faith: *Children put trust in their parents.* **2** believe firmly in the honesty, truth, justice, or power of; have faith in: *They are people you can trust.* **3** rely on; depend on: *If you can't trust your memory, write things down.* **4** person or thing trusted: *God is our trust.* **5** hope; believe: *I trust you will soon feel better.* **6** duty or responsibility that a person takes on when given confidence or authority: *Congress has a public trust.* **7** commit to the care of; leave without fear: *Can I trust the keys to them?* 1,4,6 *noun,* 2,3,5,7 *verb.*

trus tee (tru stē′), person responsible for the property or affairs of another person or of an institution: *A trustee will manage the children's property until they grow up. noun.*

trust ful (trust′fəl), ready to confide; ready to have faith; trusting; believing: *That trustful boy would lend money to any of his friends. adjective.*

trust ing (trus′ting), trustful. *adjective.*

trust wor thy (trust′wer′ᴛнē), able to be depended on; reliable: *The class chose a trustworthy student for treasurer. adjective.*

trust y (trus′tē), **1** able to be depended on; reliable: *She left her new car with a trusty friend.* **2** prisoner who is given special privileges because of good behavior. 1 *adjective,* **trust i er, trust i est;** 2 *noun, plural* **trust ies.**

truth (trüth), **1** that which is true: *Tell the truth.* **2** quality or nature of being true, exact, honest, sincere, or loyal. *noun, plural* **truths** (trüᴛнz *or* trüths).

truth ful (trüth′fəl), **1** telling the truth: *He is a truthful boy and will tell what really happened.* **2** true; agreeing with the facts: *You can count on her for a truthful report. adjective.*

try (trī), **1** attempt; make an effort: *He tried to do the work. Try harder if you wish to succeed.* **2** experiment on or with; test: *Try this candy and see if you like it.* **3** find out about; test: *We try each car before we sell it.* **4** attempt: *Each girl had three tries at the high jump.* **5** investigate in a court of law: *They were tried and found guilty of robbery.* **6** put to severe test; strain: *Don't try your eyes by reading in a poor light. Her carelessness tries my patience.* 1-3,5,6 *verb,* **tried, try ing;** 4 *noun, plural* **tries.**

try on, put on to test the fit or looks: *I tried on several coats.*

try out, 1 test or sample: *Try out this new recipe for apple pie.* **2** show someone how well you can do: *I tried out for the swimming team.*

try ing (trī′ing), hard to endure; annoying; distressing: *a trying day. adjective.*

try out (trī′out′), test made to determine fitness for a specific purpose: *Tryouts for our football*

trumpet (definition 1)

trowel
(definition 2)

tuba

a hat	i it	oi oil	ch child	⎧a in about
ā age	ī ice	ou out	ng long	e in taken
ä far	o hot	u cup	sh she	ə = ⎨i in pencil
e let	ō open	u̇ put	th thin	o in lemon
ē equal	ô order	ü rule	ᵀH then	⎩u in circus
ėr term			zh measure	

team will start a week after school opens. noun.

T-shirt (tē′shėrt′), **1** a light, close-fitting knitted shirt with short sleeves and no collar, worn for sports. **2** undershirt resembling this. *noun.*

tub (tub), **1** a large, open container for washing or bathing. **2** bathtub. **3** bath: *He takes a cold tub every morning.* **4** a round, wooden container for holding butter, lard, or something similar. **5** as much as a tub can hold. *noun.*

tu ba (tü′bə *or* tyü′bə), a large brass wind instrument that has a very deep tone. See picture. *noun.*

tube (tüb *or* tyüb), **1** a long pipe of metal, glass, rubber, plastic, or other material. Tubes are used to hold or carry liquids or gases. **2** a small cylinder of thin, easily bent metal with a cap that screws on the open end, used for holding toothpaste, ointment, paint, or some similar material. **3** pipe or tunnel through which something travels: *The railroad runs under the river in a tube.* **4** anything like a tube: *the bronchial tubes.* *noun.*

tu ber (tü′bər *or* tyü′bər), the thick part of an underground stem. A potato is a tuber. *noun.*

tu ber cu lo sis (tü bėr′kyə lō′sis *or* tyü bėr′kyə lō′sis), a disease that destroys various tissues of the body, but most often the lungs. You can catch tuberculosis if you are around someone who has it. *noun.*

tuck (tuk), **1** thrust into some narrow space or into some out-of-the-way place: *She tucked the book under her arm. He tucked the letter in his pocket.* **2** thrust the edge or end of (a garment or covering) closely into place: *Tuck your shirt in. He tucked a napkin under his chin.* **3** cover snugly: *Tuck the children in bed.* **4** pull or gather in a fold or folds: *She tucked up her sleeves before washing her hands.* **5** fold sewed in a garment: *The pants were too big, so I put a tuck in them.* **6** sew a fold in a garment for trimming or to make it shorter or tighter: *The baby's dress was beautifully tucked with tiny stitches.* 1-4,6 *verb,* 5 *noun.*

Tues day (tüz′dē *or* tyüz′dē), the third day of the week; the day after Monday. *noun.* [*Tuesday* is from an earlier English word meaning "Tiw's day." Tiw is a name of the god of war.]

tuft (tuft), bunch of feathers, hair, grass, or other soft and flexible things, held together at one end: *The goat had a tuft of hair on its chin.* *noun.*

tug (tug), **1** pull with force or effort; pull hard: *We tugged the boat in to shore. The dog tugged at the rope.* **2** a hard pull: *The baby gave a tug at my hair.* **3** tugboat. **4** tow by a tugboat. 1,4 *verb,* **tugged, tug ging;** 2,3 *noun.*

tug boat (tug′bōt′), a small, powerful boat used to tow or push other boats. *noun.*

turban (definition 1)

tuning fork

tug-of-war (tug′əv wôr′ *or* tug′ə wôr′), **1** contest between two teams pulling at the ends of a rope, each trying to drag the other over a line marked between them. See picture. **2** any hard struggle. *noun, plural* **tugs-of-war.**

tu i tion (tü ish′ən *or* tyü ish′ən), money paid for instruction: *The college raised its tuition $300. noun.*

tu lip (tü′lip *or* tyü′lip), a plant having long, narrow leaves and cup-shaped flowers of various colors. Tulips grow from bulbs and bloom in the spring. *noun.* [*Tulip* comes from a Persian word meaning "turban." It was called this because the flower resembles a turban.]

tum ble (tum′bəl), **1** fall headlong or in a helpless way: *The child tumbled down the stairs.* **2** a fall by tumbling: *The tumble only bruised the child.* **3** throw over or down; cause to fall: *The strong winds tumbled a tree in our yard.* **4** roll or toss about: *The sick child tumbled restlessly in the bed.* **5** move in a hurried or awkward way: *He tumbled out of bed.* **6** perform leaps, somersaults, or other feats o1 agility. 1,3-6 *verb,* **tum bled, tum bling;** 2 *noun.*

tum ble-down (tum′bəl doun′), ready to fall down; not in good condition: *a tumble-down shack in the mountains. adjective.*

tum bler (tum′blər), **1** person who performs leaps or springs; acrobat. **2** a drinking glass. **3** contents of a glass: *drink a tumbler of water. noun.*

tum ble weed (tum′bəl wēd′), plant growing in the western United States, that breaks off from its roots and is blown about by the wind. *noun.*

tu mult (tü′mult *or* tyü′mult), **1** noise; uproar: *The sailors' voices could not be heard above the tumult of the storm.* **2** a violent disturbance or disorder: *The shout of "Fire!" caused a tumult in the theater. noun.*

tu mul tu ous (tü mul′chü əs *or* tyü mul′chü əs), **1** very noisy or disorderly; violent: *a tumultuous celebration.* **2** greatly disturbed: *tumultuous emotion.* **3** rough; stormy: *Tumultuous waves beat upon the rocks. adjective.*

tu na (tü′nə), a large sea fish used for food. It sometimes grows to a length of ten feet or more. *noun, plural* **tu nas** *or* **tu na.**

tun dra (tun′drə), a vast, level, treeless plain in the arctic regions. The ground beneath its surface is frozen even in summer. Much of Alaska and northern Canada is tundra. *noun.*

tune (tün *or* tyün), **1** piece of music; air or melody: *hymn tunes.* **2** the proper pitch: *The piano is out of tune. Please sing in tune.* **3** outlook or manner: *They'll change their tune when they see this.* **4** agreement; harmony: *I hope my ideas are in tune with the times.* **5** put in tune: *We should have the piano tuned.* 1-4 *noun,* 5 *verb,* **tuned, tun ing.**

tune in, adjust a radio or television set to hear or see (what is wanted).

tune up, put (an engine or other mechanism) into the best working order.

tune ful (tün′fəl *or* tyün′fəl), musical; melodious: *A robin has a tuneful song. adjective.*

tung sten (tung′stən), a rare metal used in making steel and for electric light bulb filaments. *noun.*

tug-of-war (definition 1)—The children had a **tug-of-war.**

tu nic (tü′nik *or* tyü′nik), **1** garment like a shirt or gown, worn by the ancient Greeks and Romans. **2** any garment like this. **3** a short, close-fitting coat, especially one worn by soldiers or police officers. *noun.*

tuning fork, a small steel instrument that makes a musical tone of a certain pitch when it is struck. See picture.

tun nel (tun′l), **1** an underground passage: *The railroad passes under the mountain through a tunnel.* **2** make a tunnel: *The mole tunneled in the ground. The railroad crew are going to tunnel through the mountain.* **1** *noun,* **2** *verb.*

tur ban (tėr′bən), **1** scarf wound around the head or around a cap, worn by men in parts of India and in some other countries. See picture. **2** any hat or headdress like this, such as a big handkerchief tied around the head. *noun.*

tur bine (tėr′bən), engine or motor in which a wheel with vanes is made to revolve by the force of water, steam, or air. Turbines are often used to turn generators that produce electric power. *noun.*

tur bu lence (tėr′byə ləns), disorder; tumult; commotion. *noun.*

tur bu lent (tėr′byə lənt), **1** disorderly; unruly; violent: *A turbulent mob rushed into the store.* **2** greatly disturbed: *muddy, turbulent water.* *adjective.*

tu reen (tə rēn′), a deep, covered dish for serving soup. *noun.*

turf (tėrf), **1** the upper surface of the soil covered with grass and other small plants, including their roots and the soil clinging to them; sod. **2** piece of this. **3** place where horses race. **4** horse racing. *noun.*

Turk (tėrk), person born or living in Turkey. *noun.*

tur key (tėr′kē), **1** a large North American bird with brown or white feathers and a bare head and neck. **2** its flesh, used for food. *noun, plural* **tur keys.**

talk turkey, speak in a frank, blunt way.

Tur key (tėr′kē), country in western Asia and southeastern Europe. *noun.*

Turk ish (tėr′kish), **1** of or having something to do with Turkey, its people, or their language. **2** language of Turkey. **1** *adjective,* **2** *noun.*

tur moil (tėr′moil), commotion; disturbance; tumult: *Unexpected guests put us in a turmoil.* *noun.*

turn (tėrn), **1** move round as a wheel does; rotate: *The merry-go-round turned.* **2** cause to move round as a wheel does: *I turned the crank three times.* **3** motion like that of a wheel: *At each turn the screw goes in further.* **4** move part way around; change from one side to the other: *Turn over on your back.* **5** take a new direction: *The road turns to the north here.* **6** give a new direction to: *She turned her steps to the north.* **7** change of direction: *A turn to the left brought him in front of us.* **8** place where there is a change in direction: *a turn in the road.* **9** change; change and become: *They turned pale with fright.* **10** spoil; sour: *Hot weather turns milk.* **11** a change: *Matters have taken a turn for the worse. The patient has taken a turn for the better.*

a hat	i it	oi oil	ch child	a in about
ā age	ī ice	ou out	ng long	e in taken
ä far	o hot	u cup	sh she	ə = i in pencil
e let	ō open	ů put	th thin	o in lemon
ē equal	ô order	ü rule	ŦH then	u in circus
ėr term			zh measure	

12 give form to; make: *He can turn pretty compliments.* **13** form; style: *A scholar often has a serious turn of mind.* **14** change the attitudes of; unsettle: *Too much praise may turn a person's head.* **15** twist; one round in a coil of rope: *Give that rope a few more turns around the tree.* **16** time or chance to do something; opportunity: *It is her turn to bat.* **17** deed; act: *One good turn deserves another.* **18** a walk, drive, or ride: *We all enjoyed a turn in the park before dinner.* **19** make sick: *The sight of blood turns my stomach.* **20** become dizzy. **1,2,4-6,9,10, 12,14,19,20** *verb,* **3,7,8,11,13,15-18** *noun.*

by turns, one after another: *The campers slept by turns, to guard against wild animals.*

in turn, in proper order: *Each should go in turn.*

take turns, act one after another in proper order: *They took turns watching the baby.*

turn down, 1 fold down: *turn down the covers on the bed.* **2** bend downward. **3** refuse: *turn down a plan.*

turn in, 1 turn and go in: *I turned in at your house to see you.* **2** go to bed: *It's late and I'm going to turn in now.* **3** give or give back: *turn in homework, turn in a library book.* **4** exchange: *turn in an old appliance for a new model.*

turn off, 1 shut off: *Is the tap turned off or do I hear the water dripping?* **2** put out (a light): *Turn off the lights.*

turn on, 1 start the flow of; put on. **2** put on (a light). **3** attack; resist; oppose: *The cat turned on the dog that was chasing it.* **4** depend on: *The success of the picnic turns on the weather.*

turn out, 1 put out; shut off: *Turn out that big spotlight.* **2** drive out: *We turned the stray dog out of our yard.* **3** come out; go out: *Everyone turned out for the circus.* **4** make; produce: *This author turns out two novels a year.* **5** result: *How did the game turn out?* **6** be found or known: *The rumor turned out to be true.*

turn over, 1 give; hand over; transfer: *turn over a job to someone.* **2** think carefully about; consider in different ways: *turn over an idea in the mind.*

tur nip (tėr′nəp), the large, fleshy, roundish root of a garden plant, eaten as a vegetable. *noun.*

turn out (tėrn′out′), gathering of people: *There was a good turnout at the picnic.* *noun.*

turn pike (tėrn′pīk′), **1** highway on which tolls are charged; toll road. **2** any main highway. *noun.*

turn stile (tėrn′stīl′), post with bars that turn, set in an entrance or exit. The bars are turned to let one person through at a time. *noun.*

turn ta ble (tėrn′tā′bəl), **1** a revolving platform with a track for turning locomotives around. **2** the round, revolving platform of a phonograph upon which records are placed. *noun.*

tur pen tine (tėr′pən tīn), **1** mixture of oil and

resin obtained from various cone-bearing trees. **2** an oil distilled from this mixture. Turpentine is used in mixing paints and varnishes, and in medicine. *noun.*

tur quoise (tėr′koiz *or* tėr′kwoiz), **1** a clear blue or greenish-blue precious stone, used in jewelry. **2** greenish blue. 1 *noun,* 2 *adjective.* [*Turquoise* comes from old French words meaning "Turkish stone." The stone was called this because it was first brought into Europe through a Turkish territory.]

tur ret (tėr′it), **1** a small tower, often on the corner of a building. See picture. **2** a low armored structure that revolves and has guns mounted inside it. The heavy gun of an armored tank is mounted in a turret which makes up the entire upper portion of the tank. *noun.*

tur tle (tėr′tl), reptile with a soft, rounded body enclosed in a hard shell into which many kinds can draw their head and legs. Turtles live in fresh water, salt water, or on land. Those living on land are often called tortoises. *noun.*

tur tle neck (tėr′tl nek′), **1** a round, high, closely fitting collar, usually worn turned down over itself. **2** garment with such a collar. **3** having such a collar. 1,2 *noun,* 3 *adjective.*

tusk (tusk), a very long, pointed tooth that sticks out of the mouth. Elephants, walruses, and wild boars have tusks. *noun.*

tus sle (tus′əl), **1** struggle; wrestle; scuffle: *They tussled over the ball.* **2** a severe struggle or hard contest. 1 *verb,* **tus sled, tus sling;** 2 *noun.*

tu tor (tü′tər *or* tyü′tər), **1** a private teacher. See picture. **2** teach; instruct: *Students are sometimes tutored at home when they are sick.* 1 *noun,* 2 *verb.*

TV, television.

twang (twang), **1** a sharp ringing sound: *The bow made a twang when I shot the arrow.* **2** make a sharp ringing sound: *The banjos twanged.* **3** a sharp nasal tone: *The visitor spoke with a twang.* **4** speak with a sharp nasal tone. 1,3 *noun,* 2,4 *verb.*

tweed (twēd), **1** a woolen cloth with a rough surface. Tweed usually has two or more colors. See picture. **2 tweeds,** clothes made of tweed. *noun.*

tweed (definition 1)

tweet (twēt), the note of a young bird: *We heard the "tweet, tweet" from a nest in the tree. noun, interjection.*

twelfth (twelfth), **1** next after the 11th. **2** one of 12 equal parts. *adjective, noun.*

twelve (twelv), one more than 11; 12. A year has twelve months. *noun, adjective.*

twen ti eth (twen′tē ith), **1** next after the 19th. **2** one of 20 equal parts. *adjective, noun.*

twen ty (twen′tē), two times ten; 20. *noun, plural* **twen ties;** *adjective.*

twice (twīs), **1** two times: *Twice two is four.* **2** doubly: *twice as much. adverb.*

twid dle (twid′l), twirl: *twiddle one's pencil. verb,* **twid dled, twid dling.**

twig (twig), a slender shoot of a tree or other plant; very small branch: *Dry twigs are good to start a fire with. noun.*

twi light (twī′līt′), **1** the faint light reflected from the sky before the sun rises and after it sets. **2** of twilight; like that of twilight: *the twilight hour.* 1 *noun,* 2 *adjective.*

twin (twin), **1** one of two persons or animals born at the same time from the same mother. Twins sometimes look just alike. **2** being a twin: *Have you met my twin sister?* **3** one of two persons or things exactly alike. **4** being one of two things very much or exactly alike: *Twin candlesticks stood on the shelf.* **5** having two like parts. 1,3 *noun,* 2,4,5 *adjective.*

twine (twīn), **1** a strong thread or string made of two or more strands twisted together. **2** twist together: *We twined holly into wreaths.* **3** wind: *The vine twines around the tree.* 1 *noun,* 2,3 *verb,* **twined, twin ing.**

twinge (twinj), **1** a sudden, sharp pain: *a twinge of rheumatism, a twinge of remorse.* **2** feel such pain. 1 *noun,* 2 *verb,* **twinged, twing ing.**

twin kle (twing′kəl), **1** shine with quick little gleams: *The stars twinkled. His eyes twinkled when he laughed.* **2** twinkling; sparkle; gleam: *She has a merry twinkle in her eye.* **3** move quickly: *The dancer's feet twinkled.* 1,3 *verb,* **twin kled, twin kling;** 2 *noun.*

twirl (twėrl), **1** revolve rapidly; spin; whirl. See picture. **2** twirling; spin; whirl; turn: *a twirl in a dance.* 1 *verb,* 2 *noun.*

twist (twist), **1** turn with a winding motion; wind: *I twisted the cap off the jar.* **2** to wind together; wind: *This rope is twisted from many threads.* **3** curve; crook; bend: *twist a piece of wire into a loop. The path twists in and out among the rocks.* **4** a curve; crook; bend: *It is full of twists.* **5** force out of shape or place: *I fell and twisted my ankle.* **6** change the meaning of: *Don't twist what I say into something different.* **7** twisting; being twisted. **8** anything made by twisting: *a twist of bread.* 1-3,5,6 *verb,* 4,7,8 *noun.*

twist er (twis′tər), whirlwind; tornado. *noun.*

twitch (twich), **1** move with a quick jerk: *The cat's paw twitched when I touched it.* **2** a quick, jerky movement of some part of the body. 1 *verb,* 2 *noun, plural* **twitch es.**

twit ter (twit′ər), **1** sound made by birds; chirping. **2** make such a sound: *Birds begin to twitter just before sunrise.* **3** an excited condition: *My nerves are in a twitter when I have to speak in public.* **4** tremble with excitement. 1,3 *noun,* 2,4 *verb.*

two (tü), one more than one; 2. We count one, two, three, four. *noun, plural* **twos;** *adjective.*

two fold (tü′fōld′), **1** two times as much or as many; double. **2** having two parts: *This is a twofold shipment; part is coming now and the rest later.* 1,2 *adjective,* 1 *adverb.*

-ty[1], suffix meaning: _____ tens: Seven*ty* means seven *tens.*

-ty[2], suffix meaning quality, condition, or fact of being _____: Safe*ty* means *condition or quality of being* safe. The form *-ity* is often used instead of *-ty,* as in *timidity.*

ty ing (tī′ing). See **tie.** *He is tying his shoes. verb.*

type (tīp), **1** kind, class, or group alike in some important way: *three types of local government. She is the type of person I like, kind and friendly.* **2** person or thing having the characteristics of a kind, class, or group; representative; symbol: *He is a fine type of schoolboy.* **3** the general form, style, or character of some kind, class, or group: *She is above the ordinary type of student.* **4** piece of metal or wood having on its upper surface a raised letter for use in printing. **5** collection of such pieces: *set the manuscript for a book in type.* **6** write with a typewriter: *type a letter asking for a job.* **7** find out the type of; classify: *type a person's blood.* 1-5 *noun,* 6,7 *verb,* **typed, typ ing.**

type writ er (tīp′rī′tər), machine for writing which reproduces letters similar to printed ones. *noun.*

type writ ing (tīp′rī′ting), work done on a typewriter: *Your typewriting is very fast. noun.*

type writ ten (tīp′rit′n), written with a typewriter: *a typewritten letter. adjective.*

ty phoid fe ver (tī′foid fē′vər), an infectious and often fatal disease that causes a high fever and soreness and swelling of the intestines. The germ that causes typhoid fever enters the body with impure food or water. People can be inoculated against the disease.

ty phoon (tī fün′), a violent storm; hurricane. *noun.* [*Typhoon* comes from Chinese words meaning "big wind."]

typ i cal (tip′ə kəl), being a type; representative: *The typical Thanksgiving dinner consists of turkey, cranberry sauce, several vegetables, and mince or pumpkin pie. adjective.*

typ ist (tī′pist), person operating a typewriter; person trained in typewriting. *noun.*

ty ran ni cal (tə ran′ə kəl), cruel; unjust; of or like a tyrant: *a tyrannical ruler. adjective.*

tyr an ny (tir′ə nē), **1** cruel or unjust use of power: *Cinderella escaped from the tyranny of her stepmother.* **2** a tyrannical act: *The colonists rebelled against the king's tyrannies.* **3** government by an absolute ruler. *noun, plural* **tyr an nies.**

ty rant (tī′rənt), **1** person who uses his power cruelly or unjustly: *A good teacher is never a tyrant.* **2** a cruel or unjust ruler. *noun.*

a hat	i it	oi oil	ch child	ə = { a in about
ā age	ī ice	ou out	ng long	e in taken
ä far	o hot	u cup	sh she	i in pencil
e let	ō open	u̇ put	th thin	o in lemon
ē equal	ô order	ü rule	ᴛʜ then	u in circus
ėr term			zh measure	

twirl (definition 1) The skater **twirled** like a top.

turrets (definition 1)

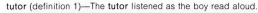
tutor (definition 1)—The **tutor** listened as the boy read aloud.

U u

U or **u** (yü), the 21st letter of the English alphabet. There are two *u*'s in *usual*. *noun, plural* **U's** or **u's.**

ud der (ud′ər), the baglike part that hangs down from the belly of a cow, female goat, or other female animal. Milk comes from the udder. *noun.*

ugh (ug *or* u), word used to express strong dislike, disgust, or horror: *Ugh! A snake! interjection.*

ug li ness (ug′lē nis), ugly appearance; being ugly. *noun.*

ug ly (ug′lē), **1** very unpleasant to look at: *an ugly house.* **2** disagreeable; unpleasant; bad; offensive: *an ugly smell, ugly language.* **3** threatening; dangerous: *The wound looked sore and ugly.* See picture. **4** cross; bad-tempered; quarrelsome: *The boss is in an ugly mood today. adjective,* **ug li er, ug li est.**

u ku le le (yü′kə lā′lē), a small guitar having four strings. *noun.*

ul ti mate (ul′tə mit), **1** last; final: *People who drive too fast seldom realize that the ultimate result of their speeding could be an accident.* **2** basic; fundamental: *The brain is the ultimate source of ideas. adjective.*

um brel la (um brel′ə), a light, folding frame covered with cloth or plastic, used as a protection against rain or sun. *noun.* [*Umbrella* comes from a Latin word meaning "shade."]

um pire (um′pīr), **1** person who rules on the plays in a game: *The umpire called the player safe.* See picture. **2** person chosen to settle a dispute. **3** act as umpire in (a game or dispute). 1,2 *noun,* 3 *verb,* **um pired, um pir ing.**

UN or **U.N.,** United Nations.

un-, prefix meaning: **1** not: *Unchanged means not changed.* **2** do the opposite of: *Unfasten means to do the opposite of fasten. Undress means to do the opposite of dress.*

un a ble (un ā′bəl), not able: *A newborn baby is unable to walk or talk. adjective.*

un ac cent ed (un ak′sen tid), not pronounced with force; not accented. In *unattended* the second and fourth syllables are unaccented. *adjective.*

un ac count a ble (un′ə koun′tə bəl), **1** not able to be accounted for or explained. **2** not responsible: *A wild animal is unaccountable for its actions. adjective.*

un ac cus tomed (un′ə kus′təmd), **1** not accustomed: *Polar bears are unaccustomed to hot weather.* **2** not familiar; unusual or strange: *He was unaccustomed to the routine of his new job. adjective.*

un aid ed (un ā′did), not aided; without help. *adjective.*

u nan i mous (yü nan′ə məs), **1** in complete agreement; agreed: *The children were unanimous in their wish to go to the beach.* **2** showing complete

agreement: *a unanimous vote,* ... n a Latin word

... ut weapons: *an unarmed robber. adjective.*

un as sum ing (un′ə sü′ming), modest; not putting on airs: *The people of the village were delighted by the unassuming manners of the king and queen. adjective.*

un at tend ed (un′ə ten′did), **1** alone; not accompanied or attended. **2** not taken care of; not attended to. *adjective.*

un a void a ble (un′ə voi′də bəl), not able to be avoided: *an unavoidable delay, an unavoidable accident. adjective.*

un a ware (un′ə wer′ *or* un′ə war′), **1** not aware; unconscious: *We were unaware of the approaching storm.* See picture. **2** unawares. 1 *adjective,* 2 *adverb.*

un a wares (un′ə werz′ *or* un′ə warz′), **1** without being expected; by surprise: *She came in and caught us unawares.* **2** without knowing: *to approach danger unawares. adverb.*

un bear a ble (un ber′ə bəl *or* un bar′ə bəl), not able to be suffered or endured: *The pain from a severe toothache is almost unbearable. adjective.*

un beat en (un bēt′n), **1** not defeated. **2** not traveled: *unbeaten paths. adjective.*

un be com ing (un′bi kum′ing), **1** not becoming; not flattering: *unbecoming clothes.* **2** not fitting; not proper: *unbecoming behavior. adjective.*

un be liev a ble (un′bi lē′və bəl), not able to be believed: *He told an unbelievable story. adjective.*

un born (un bôrn′), not yet born; still to come; of the future: *unborn generations. adjective.*

un break a ble (un brā′kə bəl), not breakable; not easily broken: *Some plastic phonograph records are unbreakable. adjective.*

un bro ken (un brō′kən), **1** not broken; whole: *an unbroken dish.* **2** continuous; not interrupted: *He had eight hours of unbroken sleep.* **3** not tamed: *an unbroken colt. adjective.*

un buck le (un buk′əl), **1** unfasten the buckle or buckles of. **2** unfasten. *verb,* **un buck led, un buck ling.**

un but ton (un but′n), unfasten the button or buttons of. *verb.*

un called-for (un kôld′fôr′), **1** unnecessary and improper: *an uncalled-for remark.* **2** not called for. *adjective.*

un can ny (un kan′ē), strange and mysterious; weird: *The trees took uncanny shapes in the half darkness. adjective.*

un cer tain (un sėrt′n), **1** not certain; doubtful: *She came so late that she was uncertain of her welcome.* **2** likely to change; not to be depended on: *This dog has an uncertain temper. adjective.*

un cer tain ty (un sėrt′n tē), **1** uncertain state or condition; doubt. **2** something uncertain. *noun, plural* **un cer tain ties.**

un chain (un chān′), let loose; set free. *verb.*

un changed (un chānjd′), not changed; the same: *unchanged tradition. adjective.*

un civ i lized (un siv′ə līzd), not civilized; barbarous; savage: *uncivilized manners. The cave dwellers of Europe were uncivilized people of the Stone Age. adjective.*

un cle (ung′kəl), **1** brother of one's father or mother. **2** husband of one's aunt. *noun.*

un clean (un klēn′), **1** dirty; not clean. **2** not pure morally; evil. *adjective.*

un coil (un koil′), unwind. *verb.*

un com fort a ble (un kum′fər tə bəl), **1** not comfortable: *an uncomfortable chair.* **2** troubled; not at ease: *I felt uncomfortable when they stared at me.* **3** disagreeable; causing discomfort: *an uncomfortable situation. adjective.*

un com mon (un kom′ən), **1** rare; unusual. **2** remarkable. *adjective.*

un con cerned (un′kən sėrnd′), not concerned; not interested; free from care or anxiety; indifferent. *adjective.*

un con di tion al (un′kən dish′ə nəl), without conditions; absolute: *The enemy refused our demand for unconditional surrender. adjective.*

un con scious (un kon′shəs), **1** not conscious: *He was knocked unconscious by the blow.* **2** not aware: *Unconscious of the time, she kept on reading and missed her piano lesson.* **3** not meant; not intended: *unconscious neglect. adjective.*

un con sti tu tion al (un′kon stə tü′shə nəl *or* un′kon stə tyü′shə nəl), not allowed by a constitution; not in agreement with a constitution: *The judges declared the law unconstitutional. adjective.*

un cooked (un kukt′), not cooked; raw. *adjective.*

un couth (un küth′), awkward; clumsy; crude: *uncouth manners. adjective.*

un cov er (un kuv′ər), **1** remove the cover from. **2** reveal; expose; make known. **3** remove one's hat or cap in respect: *The men uncovered as the flag passed by. verb.*

un cul ti vat ed (un kul′tə vā′tid), wild; not developed or cultivated: *uncultivated land. adjective.*

un curl (un kėrl′), straighten out. *verb.*

un daunt ed (un dôn′tid), not afraid; not discouraged; fearless: *She was undaunted even though her house was ruined by the flood. The general was undaunted as he faced the enemy. adjective.*

un de cid ed (un′di sī′did), **1** not decided; not settled. **2** not having one's mind made up. *adjective.*

un de ni a ble (un′di nī′ə bəl), plain; certain; not able to be denied: *undeniable facts. adjective.*

un der (un′dər), **1** below; beneath: *The book fell under the table. The swimmer went under.* **2** lower: *the under lip.* **3** lower than; lower down than; not so high as: *There was a tiny bruise just under his eye.* **4** less than: *The coat will cost under twenty dollars.* **5** according to; because of: *under the law. We acted under orders. The class learned a great deal under her teaching.* **6** during the rule or time of: *England under Queen Victoria.* **1,3-6** *preposition,* **1** *adverb,* **2** *adjective.*

a hat	i it	oi oil	ch child	a in about
ā age	ī ice	ou out	ng long	e in taken
ä far	o hot	u cup	sh she	ə = i in pencil
e let	ō open	u̇ put	th thin	o in lemon
ē equal	ô order	ü rule	ᵀH then	u in circus
ėr term			zh measure	

ugly (definition 3)—The **ugly** sky signaled us that a storm was coming.

unaware (definition 1)—The painter was **unaware** of the cow licking his picture.

umpire (definition 1)

under-, prefix meaning: **1** below; beneath: *Under*line the title of a book means to draw a line *below* the title. An *under*ground passage means a passage that is *beneath* the ground. **2** not enough; not sufficiently: *Under*nourished people means people who are *not sufficiently* nourished.

un der brush (un/dər brush/), bushes, shrubs, and small trees growing under large trees in woods or forests. *noun.*

un der clothes (un/dər klōz/), underwear. *noun plural.*

un der de vel oped (un/dər di vel/əpt), **1** not normally developed: *underdeveloped muscles.* **2** poorly developed in industry and way of living: *The underdeveloped countries need trained workers.* See picture. *adjective.*

un der fed (un/dər fed/), fed too little; not well nourished. *adjective.*

un der foot (un/dər fút/), **1** under one's feet; on the ground; underneath. **2** in the way: *She complained because the cat was always underfoot. adverb.*

un der go (un/dər gō/), **1** go through; pass through; be subjected to: *The town is undergoing many changes as more and more people are moving in.* **2** endure; suffer: *The pioneers underwent many hardships. verb,* **un der went, un der gone, un der go ing.**

un der gone (un/dər gôn/). See **undergo.** *The town has undergone many changes. verb.*

un der ground (un/dər ground/ for 1 and 4; un/dər ground/ for 2, 3, 5, and 6), **1** beneath the surface of the ground: *Miners work underground.* **2** being, working, or used beneath the surface of the ground: *an underground passage.* **3** place or space beneath the surface of the ground: *In London the subway system is called the underground.* **4** in secrecy: into concealment: *The thief went underground after the robbery.* **5** secret: *The revolt against the government was an underground plot.* **6** a secret organization working against an unpopular government, especially during military occupation: *The French underground protected many American fliers shot down over France during World War II.* **1,4** *adverb,* **2,5** *adjective,* **3,6** *noun.*

un der growth (un/dər grōth/), bushes, shrubs, and small trees growing under large trees in woods or forests. *noun.*

un der hand (un/dər hand/), **1** secret; sly; not open or honest. **2** secretly; slyly. **3** with the hand below the shoulder: *to pitch underhand, an underhand pitch.* **1,3** *adjective,* **2,3** *adverb.*

un der hand ed (un/dər han/did), underhand; secret; sly: *an underhanded trick. adjective.*

un der line (un/dər līn/), draw a line under: *In writing, we underline titles of books. verb,* **un der lined, un der lin ing.**

un der mine (un/dər mīn/), **1** dig under; make a passage or hole under: *The soldiers undermined the wall.* **2** wear away the foundations of: *The waves had undermined the cliff.* **3** weaken by secret or unfair means: *Some people tried to undermine the congresswoman's influence by spreading lies about*

underdeveloped (definition 2)—In some underdeveloped countries people harvest grain by hand.

her. **4** weaken or destroy gradually: *Many severe colds had undermined her health. verb,* **un der mined, un der min ing.**

un der neath (un/dər nēth/), beneath; below; under: *We can sit underneath this tree. Someone was pushing up from underneath. preposition, adverb.*

un der nour ished (un/dər nėr/isht), not sufficiently nourished. *adjective.*

un der pants (un/dər pants/), panties worn next to the skin under other clothing. *noun plural.*

un der pass (un/dər pas/), path underneath; road under railroad tracks or under another road. *noun, plural* **un der pass es.**

un der rate (un/dər rāt/), rate or estimate too low; put too low a value on. *verb,* **un der rat ed, un der rat ing.**

un der sea (un/dər sē/), being, working, or used beneath the surface of the sea: *an undersea cable, undersea exploration. adjective.*

un der shirt (un/dər shėrt/), shirt worn next to the skin under other clothing. *noun.*

un der side (un/dər sīd/), surface lying underneath; bottom side: *The underside of the stone was covered with ants. noun.*

un der stand (un/dər stand/), **1** get the meaning of: *Now I understand the teacher's question.* **2** get the meaning: *I have told him three times, but he still doesn't understand.* **3** know well; know how to deal with: *A good teacher understands children.* **4** be informed; learn: *I understand that she is moving to another town.* **5** take as a fact; believe: *It is understood that you will come. verb,* **un der stood, un der stand ing.**

un der stand ing (un/dər stan/ding), **1** comprehension; knowledge: *a clear understanding of the problem.* **2** intelligence; ability to learn and know: *That scholar is a man of understanding.* **3** that understands; intelligent and sympathetic: *an understanding reply.* **4** knowledge of each other's meaning and wishes: *You and I must come to an understanding.* **1,2,4** *noun,* **3** *adjective.*

un der stood (un/dər stúd/). See **understand.** *Have you understood the lesson? I understood what she said. verb.*

un der take (un′dər tāk′), **1** try; attempt: *undertake to reach home before dark.* **2** agree to do; take upon oneself: *I will undertake the feeding of your dogs while you are away.* **3** promise. *verb,* **un der took, un der tak en, un der tak ing.**

un der tak er (un′dər tā′kər), person who prepares the dead for burial and takes charge of funerals. *noun.*

un der tak ing (un′dər tā′king), **1** something undertaken; task; enterprise. **2** promise; pledge. *noun.*

un der tone (un′dər tōn′), **1** a low or very quiet tone: *talk in undertones.* **2** a subdued color; color seen through other colors: *There was an undertone of brown beneath all the gold and crimson of autumn.* **3** something beneath the surface: *an undertone of sadness in her gaiety. noun.*

un der took (un′dər tùk′). See **undertake.** *He failed because he undertook more than he could do. verb.*

un der wa ter (un′dər wô′tər), **1** below the surface of the water: *an underwater current, to swim underwater.* **2** made for use under the water: *A submarine is an underwater boat.* **1,2** *adjective,* **1** *adverb.*

un der wear (un′dər wer′ *or* un′dər war′), clothing worn under one's outer clothes, especially next to the skin. *noun.*

un der weight (un′dər wāt′), having too little weight; below the normal or required weight. *adjective.*

un der went (un′dər went′). See **undergo.** *Transportation underwent a great change with the development of the automobile. verb.*

un de sir a ble (un′di zī′rə bəl), objectionable; disagreeable: *The drug was taken off the market because it had undesirable effects on persons who used it. adjective.*

un did (un did′). See **undo.** *I undid my shoes. The fire in the artist's studio undid many years of work. verb.*

un dis put ed (un′dis pyü′tid), not disputed; not doubted. *adjective.*

un dis turbed (un′dis tėrbd′), not disturbed; not troubled; calm. *adjective.*

un do (un dü′), **1** unfasten; untie: *Please undo the package. I undid the string.* **2** do away with: *What's done cannot be undone.* **3** wipe out; cancel; destroy: *Workers repair the road each year, but heavy winter storms undo their work. verb,* **un did, un done, un do ing.**

un do ing (un dü′ing), **1** wiping out; canceling; destroying. **2** cause of destruction or ruin: *Gambling was this man's undoing.* **3** reversing the effect of something. *noun.*

un done (un dun′), **1** not done; not finished. **2** ruined: *"Alas! We are undone," cried the villain.* **3** untied; unfastened. **4** See **undo. 1-3** *adjective,* **4** *verb.*

un doubt ed (un dou′tid), not doubted; accepted as true. *adjective.*

un dress (un dres′), take the clothes off; strip. *verb.*

a hat	**i** it	**oi** oil	**ch** child	
ā age	**ī** ice	**ou** out	**ng** long	a in about
ä far	**o** hot	**u** cup	**sh** she	e in taken
e let	**ō** open	**ù** put	**th** thin	ə = i in pencil
ē equal	**ô** order	**ü** rule	**ᴛʜ** then	o in lemon
ėr term			**zh** measure	u in circus

un due (un dü′ *or* un dyü′), **1** not fitting; improper; not right: *They made rude, undue remarks about people in the restaurant.* **2** too great; too much: *A miser gives undue importance to money. adjective.*

un du ly (un dü′lē *or* un dyü′lē), **1** improperly. **2** excessively; too much: *unduly harsh. adverb.*

un dy ing (un dī′ing), deathless; immortal; eternal: *undying fame, undying beauty. adjective.*

un earth (un ėrth′), **1** dig up: *unearth a buried city.* **2** discover; find out: *unearth a plot. verb.*

un eas i ly (un ē′zə lē), in an uneasy manner; restlessly. *adverb.*

un eas i ness (un ē′zē nis), lack of ease or comfort; restlessness; anxiety. *noun.*

un eas y (un ē′zē), **1** restless; disturbed; anxious. **2** not comfortable. **3** not easy in manner; awkward. *adjective,* **un eas i er, un eas i est.**

un ed u cat ed (un ej′ə kā′tid), not educated; not taught or trained. *adjective.*

un em ployed (un′em ploid′), **1** not employed; not in use: *an unemployed skill.* **2** not having a job; having no work: *an unemployed person.* **3 the unemployed,** people out of work: *Some of the unemployed sought aid from the government.* **1,2** *adjective,* **3** *noun.*

un em ploy ment (un′em ploi′mənt), lack of employment; being out of work. *noun.*

un e qual (un ē′kwəl), **1** not the same in amount, size, number, or value: *unequal sums of money.* **2** not fair; one-sided: *an unequal contest.* **3** not enough; not adequate: *Their strength was unequal to the task.* **4** not regular; not even: *unequal vibrations. adjective.*

un e ven (un ē′vən), **1** not level: *uneven ground.* **2** not equal: *an uneven contest.* **3** leaving a remainder of 1 when divided by 2; odd: *1, 3, 5, 7, and 9 are uneven numbers. adjective.*

un ex pect ed (un′ek spek′tid), not expected: *We had an unexpected, but welcome, visit from our grandmother last week. adjective.*

un fail ing (un fā′ling), **1** never failing; always ready when needed; loyal: *an unfailing friend.* **2** never running short: *an unfailing supply of water. adjective.*

un fair (un fer′ *or* un far′), unjust: *an unfair decision. You were unfair to trick your little sister into giving you all the candy. adjective.*

un faith ful (un fāth′fəl), **1** not faithful; not true to duty or one's promises; faithless. **2** not exact; not accurate. *adjective.*

un fa mil iar (un′fə mil′yər), **1** not well known; unusual; strange: *That face is unfamiliar to me.* **2** not acquainted: *He is unfamiliar with the Greek language. adjective.*

un fas ten (un fas′n), undo; untie; loosen; open. *verb.*

un fa vor a ble (un fā′vər ə bəl), not favorable; adverse; harmful. *adjective.*

un feel ing (un fē′ling), **1** cruel; hardhearted: *a cold, unfeeling person.* **2** not able to feel; numb. *adjective.*

un fin ished (un fin′isht), **1** not finished; not complete: *unfinished homework, an unfinished symphony.* **2** without some special finish; rough; not polished or painted: *unfinished furniture. adjective.*

un fit (un fit′), **1** not fit; not suitable. **2** not good enough. *adjective.*

un fold (un fōld′), **1** open the folds of; spread out: *unfold a napkin, unfold your arms.* **2** reveal; show; explain: *unfold the plot of a story.* **3** open; develop: *Buds unfold into flowers. verb.*

un fore seen (un′fôr sēn′), not known beforehand; unexpected. *adjective.*

un for get ta ble (un′fər get′ə bəl), not able to be forgotten; worth remembering. *adjective.*

un for tu nate (un fôr′chə nit), **1** not lucky; having bad luck. **2** not suitable; not fitting: *The child's outburst of temper was an unfortunate thing for the guest to see.* **3** an unfortunate person. **1,2** *adjective,* **3** *noun.*

un friend ly (un frend′lē), **1** not friendly. **2** not favorable. *adjective.*

un furl (un fėrl′), spread out; shake out; unfold: *Unfurl the sail. The flag unfurled. verb.*

un fur nished (un fėr′nisht), not furnished; without furniture. *adjective.*

un gain ly (un gān′lē), awkward; clumsy: *Long arms and large hands can give a person an ungainly appearance.* See picture. *adjective.*

un god ly (un god′lē), **1** not devout; not religious. **2** wicked; sinful. **3** very annoying. *adjective.*

un grate ful (un grāt′fəl), not grateful; not thankful. *adjective.*

un guard ed (un gär′did), **1** not protected: *an unguarded camp.* **2** careless: *In an unguarded moment, she gave away the secret. adjective.*

un hand (un hand′), let go; take the hands from; release. *verb.*

un hap pi ly (un hap′ə lē), **1** not happily: *live unhappily.* **2** unfortunately: *Unhappily I missed seeing him.* **3** in an unsuitable way. *adverb.*

un hap pi ness (un hap′ē nis), **1** sadness; sorrow. **2** bad luck. *noun.*

un hap py (un hap′ē), **1** without gladness; sad; sorrowful: *an unhappy face.* **2** unlucky: *an unhappy accident.* **3** not suitable: *an unhappy selection of colors. adjective,* **un hap pi er, un hap pi est.**

un health y (un hel′thē), **1** not possessing good health; not well: *an unhealthy child.* **2** coming from or showing poor health: *an unhealthy paleness.* **3** hurtful to health; unwholesome: *an unhealthy climate. adjective,* **un health i er, un health i est.**

un heard (un hėrd′), not listened to; not heard: *unheard melodies. adjective.*

un heard-of (un hėrd′uv′), **1** never heard of; unknown: *The electric light was unheard-of 200 years ago.* **2** not known before: *unheard-of prices, unheard-of bad manners. adjective.*

unison (definition 1)—The runners moved their legs in **unison.**

unicorn

un hitch (un hich′), free from being hitched; unfasten: *She unhitched the wagon from her bicycle so she could ride faster.* verb.

un hook (un hùk′), **1** loosen from a hook. **2** undo by loosening a hook or hooks. **3** become unhooked; become undone. *verb.*

U NI CEF (yü′nə sef), United Nations Children's Fund. *noun.*

u ni corn (yü′nə kôrn), an imaginary animal like a horse, but having a single, long horn in its forehead. See picture. *noun.*

un i den ti fied (un′ī den′tə fīd), not identified; not recognized. *adjective.*

u ni form (yü′nə fôrm), **1** always the same; not changing: *The earth turns at a uniform rate.* **2** all alike; not varying: *All the bricks have a uniform size.* **3** clothes worn by the members of a group when on duty. Soldiers, policemen, and nurses wear uniforms so that they may be easily recognized. **4** clothe or furnish with a uniform. 1,2 *adjective,* 3 *noun,* 4 *verb.*

u ni form i ty (yü′nə fôr′mə tē), uniform condition or character; sameness throughout. *noun, plural* **u ni form i ties.**

u ni fy (yü′nə fī), unite; make or form into one: *Several small states were unified into one nation.* *verb,* **u ni fied, u ni fy ing.**

un im por tant (un′im pôrt′nt), not important; insignificant; trifling. *adjective.*

un in hab it ed (un′in hab′ə tid), not lived in; without inhabitants: *an uninhabited wilderness.* *adjective.*

un in tel li gi ble (un′in tel′ə jə bəl), not able to be understood: *There was so much static on the radio that the whole program was unintelligible.* *adjective.*

un ion (yü′nyən), **1** joining of two or more persons or things into one: *The United States was formed by the union of thirteen former British colonies.* **2** group of persons, states, or nations joined for some common purpose; combination: *the Soviet Union.* **3 the Union,** the United States. **4** group of workers joined together to protect and promote their interests; labor union. *noun.*

u nique (yü nēk′), **1** having no like or equal; being the only one of its kind: *a unique specimen of rock, a unique experience. The astronaut described his experience as unique.* See picture. **2** very uncommon or unusual; rare; remarkable: *His style of singing is rather unique. adjective.*

u ni son (yü′nə sən), **1** agreement. See picture. **2** agreement in pitch of two or more tones or voices; sounding together at the same pitch. *noun.*

u nit (yü′nit), **1** a single thing or person. **2** any group of things or persons considered as one: *The family is a social unit.* **3** one of the individuals or groups of which a whole is composed: *The body consists of units called cells.* **4** a standard quantity or amount: *A foot is a unit of length; a pound is a unit of weight.* **5** a special part, division, or section: *the beginning unit of a book. Tomorrow the teacher is going to ask us questions about the stories we have read in this unit. noun.*

a hat	**i** it	**oi** oil	**ch** child	a in about
ā age	**ī** ice	**ou** out	**ng** long	e in taken
ä far	**o** hot	**u** cup	**sh** she	ə = i in pencil
e let	**ō** open	**ù** put	**th** thin	o in lemon
ē equal	**ô** order	**ü** rule	**ŦH** then	u in circus
ėr term			**zh** measure	

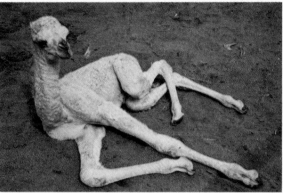

ungainly—The newborn camel was very **ungainly.**

u nite (yü nīt′), join together; make one; become one: *Several firms were united to form one company. The class united in singing "America." verb,* **u nit ed, u nit ing.**

United Nations, 1 a world-wide organization devoted to establishing world peace and promoting economic and social welfare. The United Nations charter was put into effect October 24, 1945. **2** the nations that belong to this organization.

United States, country in North America, extending from the Atlantic to the Pacific and from the Gulf of Mexico to Canada. Alaska, the 49th state, lies northwest of Canada. Hawaii, the 50th state, is an island group in the Pacific.

United States of America, United States.

u ni ty (yü′nə tē), **1** oneness: *The group's unity of purpose helped them get results.* **2** harmony: *Brothers and sisters should live together in unity. noun, plural* **u ni ties.**

u ni ver sal (yü′nə vėr′səl), **1** of all; belonging to all; concerning all; done by all: *Food is a universal need.* **2** existing everywhere: *The law of gravity is universal. adjective.*

u ni ver sal ly (yü′nə vėr′sə lē), **1** in every instance; without exception. **2** everywhere. *adverb.*

u ni verse (yü′nə vėrs′), all things; everything there is. Our world is but a small part of the universe. *noun.*

u ni ver si ty (yü′nə vėr′sə tē), institution of higher education. Universities usually have schools of law, medicine, teaching, and business, as well as colleges for general instruction. *noun, plural* **u ni ver si ties.**

un just (un just′), not just; not fair. *adjective.*

un kempt (un kempt′), **1** not combed. **2** neglected; untidy: *unkempt clothes, an unkempt appearance. adjective.*

un kind (un kīnd′), harsh; cruel. *adjective.*

un kind ly (un kīnd′lē), **1** harsh; unkind. **2** in an unkind way; harshly. **1** *adjective,* **2** *adverb.*

un known (un nōn′), **1** not known; not familiar; strange; unexplored: *the dark, unknown depths of the sea.* **2** person or thing that is unknown: *The diver descended into the unknown.* **1** *adjective,* **2** *noun.*

un lace (un lās′), undo the laces of. *verb,* **un laced, un lac ing.**

un law ful (un lô′fəl), contrary to the law; against the law; forbidden; illegal. *adjective.*

un learn ed (un lėr′nid *for 1;* un lėrnd′ *for 2*), **1** not educated; ignorant: *They were unlearned and could not read or write.* **2** not learned; known without being learned: *Swallowing is unlearned behavior. adjective.*

un less (un les′), if not; except if: *I won't go unless you do. conjunction.*

un like (un līk′), **1** not like; different: *The two problems are quite unlike.* **2** different from: *One kitten was acting unlike the others.* **1** *adjective,* **2** *preposition.*

un like ly (un līk′lē), **1** not likely; not probable: *She is unlikely to win the race.* **2** not likely to succeed: *an unlikely undertaking. adjective.*

un lim it ed (un lim′ə tid), without limits. *adjective.*

un load (un lōd′), **1** remove (a load). **2** take the load from. **3** get rid of: *I don't want to unload my troubles on you.* **4** remove powder, shot, bullets, or shells from a gun. **5** discharge a cargo: *The ship is unloading. verb.*

un lock (un lok′), **1** open the lock of; open (anything firmly closed). **2** disclose; reveal: *Science has unlocked the mystery of the atom.* **3** become unlocked. *verb.*

un loose (un lüs′), let loose; set free; release. *verb,* **un loosed, un loos ing.**

un luck y (un luk′ē), not lucky; unfortunate; bringing bad luck. *adjective,* **un luck i er, un luck i est.**

un manned (un mand′), without a crew: *an unmanned space flight. adjective.*

un mar ried (un mar′ēd), not married; single. *adjective.*

un mis tak a ble (un′mə stā′kə bəl), not able to be mistaken or misunderstood; clear; plain; evident. *adjective.*

un moved (un müvd′), **1** not moved; firm. **2** not disturbed; indifferent. *adjective.*

un nat ur al (un nach′ər əl), **1** not natural; not normal. **2** horrible; shocking. *adjective.*

un nec es sar y (un nes′ə ser′ē), not necessary; needless. *adjective.*

un nerve (un nėrv′), deprive of firmness or self-control: *The sight of blood unnerves some people. verb,* **un nerved, un nerv ing.**

un no ticed (un nō′tist), not noticed; not observed; not receiving any attention. *adjective.*

un num bered (un num′bərd), **1** not numbered; not counted. **2** too many to count: *There are unnumbered fish in the ocean. adjective.*

un ob served (un′əb zėrvd′), not observed; not noticed; disregarded. *adjective.*

un oc cu pied (un ok′yə pīd), **1** not occupied; vacant: *The driver pulled her car into the unoccupied parking space.* **2** not in action or use; idle: *an unoccupied mind. adjective.*

un of fi cial (un′ə fish′əl), not official. *adjective.*

un pack (un pak′), **1** take out (things packed in a box, trunk, or other container): *I unpacked my clothes.* **2** take things out of: *unpack a trunk. verb.*

un paid (un pād′), not paid: *Their unpaid bills amounted to $200. adjective.*

un par al leled (un par′ə leld), having no parallel; unequaled; matchless: *an unparalleled achievement. adjective.*

un pleas ant (un plez′nt), not pleasant; disagreeable. *adjective.*

un pop u lar (un pop′yə lər), not popular; not generally liked; disliked. *adjective.*

un pre pared (un′pri perd′ *or* un′pri pard′), **1** not made ready; not worked out ahead: *an unprepared speech.* **2** not ready: *a person unprepared to answer. adjective.*

un prin ci pled (un prin′sə pəld), lacking good moral principles; bad. *adjective.*

un ques tion a ble (un kwes′chə nə bəl), beyond dispute or doubt; certain: *Having a high school diploma is an unquestionable advantage when looking for a good job. adjective.*

un ques tion a bly (un kwes′chə nə blē), beyond dispute or doubt; certainly. *adverb.*

un rav el (un rav′əl), **1** separate the threads of; pull apart: *The kitten unraveled the ball of yarn.* **2** come apart: *This sweater is unraveling at the elbow.* **3** bring out of a tangled state: *The detective unraveled the mystery. verb.*

un re al (un rē′əl), not real; imaginary; fanciful. *adjective.*

un rea son a ble (un rē′zn ə bəl), **1** not reasonable: *an unreasonable dislike of animals.* **2** not moderate; excessive: *$50 is an unreasonable price for a pair of shoes. adjective.*

un rea son a bly (un rē′zn ə blē), **1** in a way that is not reasonable; foolishly. **2** extremely. *adverb.*

un re li a ble (un′ri lī′ə bəl), not reliable; not to be depended on; irresponsible. *adjective.*

un rest (un rest′), **1** restlessness; lack of ease and quiet. **2** agitation or disturbance amounting almost to rebellion. *noun.*

un ri valed (un rī′vəld), having no rival; without an equal. *adjective.*

un roll (un rōl′), **1** open or spread out (something rolled). **2** become opened or spread out. **3** reveal; display; make known: *The movie unrolls a tale of mystery and adventure. verb.*

un rul y (un rü′lē), hard to rule or control; lawless: *an unruly horse, a disobedient and unruly child, an unruly section of a country. adjective.*

un safe (un sāf′), dangerous. *adjective.*

un said (un sed′), not said: *Everything he had meant to say remained unsaid. adjective.*

un sat is fac tor y (un′sat i sfak′tər ē), not good enough to satisfy. *adjective.*

un sat is fied (un sat′i sfīd), not satisfied; not contented. *adjective.*

un scram ble (un skram′bəl), reduce from confusion to order: *After the wind died down, I unscrambled the papers that had blown on the floor.* verb, **un scram bled, un scram bling.**

un screw (un skrü′), **1** take out the screw or screws from. **2** loosen or take off by turning: *unscrew an electric light bulb.* verb.

un scru pu lous (un skrü′pyə ləs), not careful about right or wrong; without principles: *The unscrupulous student cheated on the test.* adjective.

un seat (un sēt′), **1** displace from a seat. **2** throw (a rider) from a saddle. **3** remove from office: *unseat a senator, unseat a government.* verb.

un seem ly (un sēm′lē), not proper; not suitable: *Laughter is often unseemly in a courtroom.* adjective, **un seem li er, un seem li est.**

un seen (un sēn′), **1** not seen: unnoticed: *an unseen error.* **2** not able to be seen; invisible: *an unseen spirit.* adjective.

un self ish (un sel′fish), caring for others; generous. adjective.

un set tle (un set′l), disturb; make or become unstable; shake; weaken: *The shock unsettled my nerves.* verb, **un set tled, un set tling.**

un set tled (un set′ld), **1** disordered; not in proper condition or order: *an unsettled mind. Our house is still unsettled.* **2** liable to change; uncertain: *The weather is unsettled.* **3** not adjusted or disposed of: *an unsettled estate, an unsettled bill.* **4** not determined or decided: *an unsettled question.* **5** not inhabited: *Some parts of the world are still unsettled.* adjective.

un shak en (un shā′kən), not shaken; firm: *unshaken courage, an unshaken belief in liberty.* adjective.

un sheathe (un shēŦH′), draw (a sword, knife, or the like) from a sheath. verb, **un sheathed, un sheath ing.**

un sight ly (un sīt′lē), ugly or unpleasant to look at: *The room was an unsightly mess.* adjective.

un skilled (un skild′), **1** not skilled; not trained; not expert: *unskilled workers, an unskilled athlete.* **2** not requiring special skills or training: *unskilled labor.* adjective.

un skill ful (un skil′fəl), awkward; clumsy. adjective.

un sound (un sound′), **1** not sound; not in good condition: *unsound walls, an unsound business, an unsound mind.* **2** not based on truth or fact: *an unsound doctrine, an unsound theory.* **3** not restful; disturbed: *an unsound sleep.* adjective.

un speak a ble (un spē′kə bəl), **1** not able to be expressed in words: *unspeakable joy.* **2** extremely bad; so bad that it is not spoken of. adjective.

un speak a bly (un spē′kə blē), beyond words; extremely: *unspeakably rude.* adverb.

un sta ble (un stā′bəl), not firmly fixed; easily moved, shaken, or overthrown. adjective.

un stead y (un sted′ē), **1** not steady; shaky: *an unsteady voice, an unsteady flame.* **2** likely to change; not reliable: *an unsteady mind, unsteady winds.* adjective, **un stead i er, un stead i est.**

un stressed (un strest′), unaccented. In *upward,*

a hat	i it	oi oil	ch child	a in about
ā age	ī ice	ou out	ng long	e in taken
ä far	o hot	u cup	sh she	ə = i in pencil
e let	ō open	u̇ put	th thin	o in lemon
ē equal	ô order	ü rule	ŦH then	u in circus
ėr term			zh measure	

the second syllable is unstressed. adjective.

un suc cess ful (un′sək ses′fəl), not successful; having no success. adjective.

un suit a ble (un sü′tə bəl), not suitable; unfit. adjective.

un sus pect ed (un′sə spek′tid), **1** not suspected. **2** not thought of: *an unsuspected danger.* adjective.

un think a ble (un thing′kə bəl), not able to be imagined. adjective.

un think ing (un thing′king), **1** not thinking; thoughtless; careless. **2** showing little or no thought: *blind, unthinking anger.* adjective.

un ti dy (un tī′dē), not neat; not in order: *an untidy house.* adjective, **un ti di er, un ti di est.**

un tie (un tī′), loosen; unfasten; undo: *untie a knot. She was untying bundles.* verb, **un tied, un ty ing.**

un til (un til′), **1** up to the time of: *It was cold from November until April.* **2** up to the time when: *We waited until the sun had set.* **3** before: *She did not leave until morning.* **4** to the degree or place that: *I worked until I was too tired to do more.* 1,3 preposition, 2,4 conjunction.

un time ly (un tīm′lē), **1** at a wrong time or season: *Snow in May is untimely.* **2** too early; too soon: *We were saddened by the young man's untimely death.* 1,2 adjective, 2 adverb.

un tir ing (un tī′ring), tireless: *an untiring runner, untiring efforts to succeed.* adjective.

un told (un tōld′), **1** not told; not revealed: *an untold secret.* **2** too many or too much to be counted: *There are untold stars in the sky.* **3** very great: *untold wealth. Wars do untold damage.* adjective.

un touched (un tucht′), not touched: *The cat left the milk untouched. The miser was untouched by the poor man's story.* adjective.

un to ward (un tôrd′ or un′tə wôrd′), **1** unfavorable; unfortunate: *an untoward wind, an untoward accident.* **2** perverse; stubborn; willful: *The untoward child was very hard to manage.* adjective.

un trained (un trānd′), not trained; without discipline or education: *Babies have untrained minds.* adjective.

un true (un trü′), **1** not true to the facts; false. **2** not faithful: disloyal. **3** not true to a standard or rule; not exact; inaccurate. adjective.

un truth (un trüth′), **1** lack of truth; falsity. **2** lie; falsehood. noun, plural **un truths** (un trüŦHz′ or un trüths′).

un used (un yüzd′), **1** not in use; not being used: *an unused room.* **2** never having been used: *unused drinking cups.* **3** not accustomed: *The actor's hands were unused to labor.* adjective.

un u su al (un yü′zhü əl), not in common use; not common; rare; beyond the ordinary. adjective.

un veil (un vāl/), remove a veil from; uncover; disclose; reveal: *The sun broke through the mist and unveiled the mountains. verb.*

un wel come (un wel/kəm), not welcome; not wanted: *The bees were unwelcome guests at our picnic. adjective.*

un wield y (un wēl/dē), hard to handle or manage; bulky and clumsy: *a large, unwieldy package.* See picture. *adjective,* **un wield i er, un wield i est.**

un will ing (un wil/ing), not willing; not consenting. *adjective.*

un wind (un wīnd/), **1** wind off; take from a spool, ball, or the like. **2** to become unrolled or uncoiled. *verb,* **un wound, un wind ing.**

un wise (un wīz/), not wise; not showing good judgment; foolish: *It is unwise to delay going to the doctor if you are sick. adjective.*

un wit ting ly (un wit/ing lē), not knowingly; unconsciously; not intentionally. *adverb.*

un wor thy (un wėr/ᴛнē), not worthy; not deserving: *Such a silly story is unworthy of belief. adjective,* **un wor thi er, un wor thi est.**

un wound (un wound/). See **unwind.** *I unwound the ball of string. verb.*

un wrap (un rap/), remove a wrapping from; open. *verb,* **un wrapped, un wrap ping.**

un yield ing (un yēl/ding), firm; not giving in: *My parents were unyielding in their refusal. adjective.*

up (up). See picture. **1** to a higher place or condition: *The butterfly flew up. Prices have gone up.* **2** in a higher place or condition: *We live up in a skyscraper. The sun is up.* **3** to a higher place on; at a higher place in: *The cat ran up the tree.* **4** along: *They walked up the street.* **5** to, near, or at the upper part of: *We sailed up the river.* **6** out of bed: *The children were up at dawn. Please get up before you are late.* **7** completely; entirely: *The house burned up.* **8** at an end; over: *His time is up now.* **9** to or in an even position; not back of: *catch up in a race. Keep up with the times.* **10** into storage or a safe place; aside; by: *Squirrels lay up nuts for the winter.* **1,2,6-10** *adverb,* **2,6** *adjective,* **3-5** *preposition.*

up to, 1 doing; about to do: *She is up to some mischief.* **2** equal to; capable of doing: *Do you feel up to going out so soon after being sick?*

up braid (up brād/), find fault with; blame; reprove: *The teacher upbraided the students for not doing their homework. verb.*

up held (up held/). See **uphold.** *The higher court upheld the lower court's decision. verb.*

up hill (up/hil/ *for 1 and 3;* up/hil/ *for 2*), **1** up the slope of a hill; upward: *It is an uphill road all the way.* **2** upward: *We walked a mile uphill.* **3** difficult: *an uphill fight.* **1,3** *adjective,* **2** *adverb.*

up hold (up hōld/), **1** give support to; confirm: *The principal upheld the teacher's decision.* **2** hold up; not let down; support: *We uphold the good name of our school. verb,* **up held, up hold ing.**

up hol ster (up hōl/stər), provide (seats or other furniture) with coverings, springs, or stuffing: *upholster a sofa. verb.*

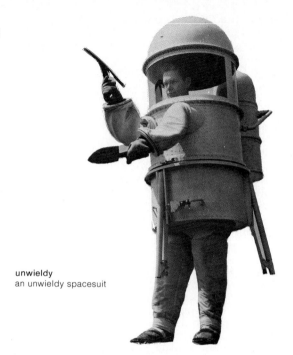

unwieldy
an unwieldy spacesuit

up hol ster y (up hōl/stər ē), **1** materials used for covering seats or other furniture: *That chair comes with cloth, plastic, or leather upholstery.* **2** the business of upholstering. *noun, plural* **up hol ster ies.**

up keep (up/kēp/), **1** maintenance: *the upkeep of a house.* **2** cost of operating and repair: *The upkeep of a yacht is expensive. noun.*

up land (up/lənd), **1** high land. **2** of high land; living or growing on high land: *upland flowers.* **1** *noun,* **2** *adjective.*

up lift (up lift/ *for 1;* up/lift/ *for 2*), **1** lift up; raise; elevate. **2** movement toward improvement. **1** *verb,* **2** *noun.*

up on (ə pôn/), on. *preposition.*

up per (up/ər), higher: *the upper lip, the upper floor, the upper notes of a singer's voice. adjective.*

upper hand, control; advantage: *Do what the doctor says or that cold may get the upper hand.*

up per most (up/ər mōst), **1** highest; topmost. **2** most prominent; having the most force or influence. **3** in, at, or near the top. **4** first: *The safety of the passengers was uppermost in the pilot's mind.* **1,2** *adjective,* **3,4** *adverb.*

up right (up/rīt/), **1** standing up straight; erect: *an upright post.* **2** straight up: *Hold yourself upright.* **3** something standing erect; vertical part or piece. **4** good; honest: *an upright citizen.* **1,4** *adjective,* **2** *adverb,* **3** *noun.*

up ris ing (up/rī/zing), **1** revolt: *a prison uprising.* **2** act of rising up. *noun.*

up roar (up/rôr/), **1** a noisy disturbance: *The town was in an uproar when a lion escaped from the circus.* **2** a loud or confused noise. *noun.*

up root (up rüt/), **1** tear up by the roots: *The storm uprooted many trees.* **2** remove completely: *Many* *families were uprooted from their homes because of the flood. verb.*

up set (up set′ *for 1, 4, and 7;* up′set′ *for 2, 3, 5, 6, and 8*), **1** tip over; overturn: *I upset my glass of milk. Moving about in a boat may upset it.* **2** tipping over; overturn. **3** tipped over; overturned. **4** disturb greatly; disorder: *Rain upset our plans for a picnic. The bad news upset me.* **5** a great disturbance; disorder. **6** greatly disturbed; disordered: *an upset stomach.* **7** defeat unexpectedly in a contest: *The independent candidate upset the mayor in the election.* **8** an unexpected defeat: *The hockey team suffered an upset.* 1,4,7 *verb,* **up set, up set ting;** 2,5,8 *noun,* 3,6 *adjective.*

up shot (up′shot′), conclusion; result: *The upshot of our discussion was a better understanding of one another. noun.*

up side down (up′sīd′ doun′), **1** having what should be on top at the bottom: *The slice of bread and butter fell upside down on the floor.* **2** in or into complete disorder: *The children turned the house upside down.*

up stairs (up′sterz′ *or* up′starz′), **1** up the stairs: *The boy ran upstairs.* **2** on or to an upper floor: *She lives upstairs. He is waiting in an upstairs hall.* **3** the upper floor or floors: *That small cottage has no upstairs.* 1,2 *adverb,* 2 *adjective,* 3 *noun.*

up start (up′stärt′), **1** person who has suddenly risen from a humble position to wealth, power, or importance. **2** a person who is very bold, conceited, and unpleasant. *noun.*

up stream (up′strēm′), against the current of a stream; up a stream: *It is hard to swim upstream. We had an upstream campsite. adverb, adjective.*

up-to-date (up′tə dāt′), **1** extending to the present time: *an up-to-date bank balance.* **2** keeping up with the times in style or ideas; modern: *an up-to-date store. adjective.*

up turn (up tėrn′ *for 1;* up′tėrn′ *for 2 and 3*), **1** turn up. **2** an upward turn: *The airplane made a sudden upturn to avoid the mountain.* **3** improvement: *As business improved, his income took an upturn.* 1 *verb,* 2,3 *noun.*

up ward (up′wərd), **1** toward a higher place: *She climbed upward until she reached the apple.* **2** toward a higher or greater rank, amount, age, or the like: *From ten years of age upward, she had studied French.* **3** above; more: *Children of twelve years and upward must pay full fare.* 1-3 *adverb,* 2 *adjective.*
upward of, more than: *Repairs to the car will cost upward of $100.*

up wards (up′wərdz), upward. *adverb.*

u ra ni um (yu̇ rā′nē əm), a heavy, white, radioactive metal that is used as a source of atomic energy. *noun.*

Ur a nus (yu̇r′ə nəs), the third largest planet in the solar system and the seventh in distance from the sun. *noun.*

ur ban (ėr′bən), **1** of or having something to do with cities or towns: *an urban district, urban planning.* **2** living in a city or cities: *Most urban people are familiar with pollution.* **3** characteristic of cities: *urban life. adjective.*

a hat	**i** it	**oi** oil	**ch** child		a in about
ā age	**ī** ice	**ou** out	**ng** long		e in taken
ä far	**o** hot	**u** cup	**sh** she	**ə** =	i in pencil
e let	**ō** open	**u̇** put	**th** thin		o in lemon
ē equal	**ô** order	**ü** rule	**ᴛʜ** then		u in circus
ėr term			**zh** measure		

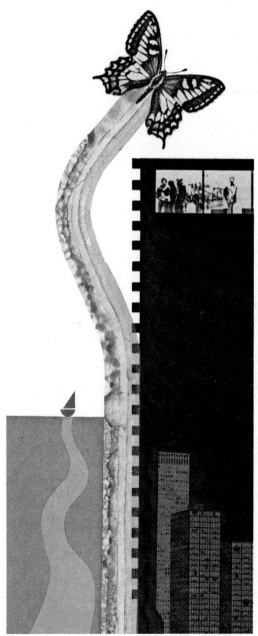

up (definitions 1, 2, and 5)

ur chin (ėr′chən), **1** a small child. **2** a mischievous child. **3** a poor, ragged child: *Urchins played in the street. noun.*

urge (ėrj), **1** push; force; drive: *The rider urged on his horse with whip and spurs. Hunger urged me to find some food.* **2** a driving force or impulse: *I had an urge to see my old friend again.* **3** ask earnestly; plead with: *She urged us to stay longer.* **4** plead or argue earnestly for; recommend strongly: *I urged the acceptance of the new plan.* 1,3,4 *verb*, **urged, urg ing;** 2 *noun.*

ur gent (ėr′jənt), demanding immediate·action or attention; pressing: *an urgent duty, an urgent message. adjective.*

ur ine (yùr′ən), a liquid waste product that is separated from the blood by the kidneys, goes to the bladder, and is discharged from the body. *noun.*

urn (ėrn), **1** vase with a foot. Urns were used in Greece and Rome to hold the ashes of the dead. See picture. **2** coffeepot or teapot with a faucet, used for making or serving coffee or tea at the table. *noun.*

us (us). *We* and *us* mean the person speaking plus the person or persons addressed or spoken about. *We learn because our teacher helps us. Mother went with us to the theater. pronoun.*

U.S., United States.

U.S.A., United States of America.

us a ble (yü′zə bəl), that can be used; fit for use. *adjective.*

us age (yü′sij *or* yü′zij), **1** manner or way of using; treatment: *This car has had rough usage.* **2** the customary way of using words: *The usage of the best writers and speakers determines what is good English. noun.*

use (yüz *for 1-3;* yüs *for 4-11*), **1** put into action or service: *We use our legs in walking. We use spoons to eat soup.* **2** act toward; treat: *Use others as you would have them use you.* **3** consume or expend by using: *We used most of the money. He uses tobacco.* **4** using: *the use of tools.* **5** being used: *methods long out of use.* **6** usefulness: *a thing of no practical use.* **7** purpose that a thing is used for: *find a new use for something.* **8** way of using: *poor use of material.* **9** need; occasion: *A camper has use for a hatchet. I had no further use for it.* **10** power of using; ability to use: *to lose the use of an arm.* **11** right or privilege of using: *I have the use of a friend's boat this summer.* 1-3 *verb*, **used, us ing;** 4-11 *noun.*

used to (yüst tü), **1** accustomed to: *Eskimos are used to cold weather.* **2** formerly did: *You used to come at ten o'clock, but now you come at noon.*

used (yüzd), not new; that has belonged to someone else: *a used car. adjective.*

use ful (yüs′fəl), of use; giving service; helpful: *a useful suggestion. They made themselves useful about the house. adjective.*

use less (yüs′lis), of no use; worthless: *A television set would be useless without electricity. adjective.*

us er (yü′zər), one that uses. *noun.*

ush er (ush′ər), **1** person who shows people to their seats in a church, theater, or public hall.

urn (definition 1)

2 conduct; escort; show: *We ushered our guests to the door.* 1 *noun,* 2 *verb.*

u su al (yü′zhü əl), commonly seen, found, or happening; ordinary; customary: *Snow is usual in the Rocky Mountains during winter. His usual bedtime is 8 p.m. adjective.*

as usual, in the usual manner; at the usual time; in the usual way: *We met, as usual, on the way to school.*

u su al ly (yü′zhü ə lē), commonly; ordinarily; customarily: *We usually eat dinner at six. adverb.*

U tah (yü′tô *or* yü′tä), one of the western states of the United States. *noun.* [*Utah* got its name from the Ute, an American Indian tribe that lived in the area. The name of the tribe may have come from a Ute word meaning "person" or "people."]

u ten sil (yü ten′səl), **1** container or implement used for practical purposes. Pots and pans are kitchen utensils. **2** implement or tool used for some special purpose. Pens and pencils are writing utensils. *noun.* [*Utensil* comes from a Latin word meaning "able to be used."]

u til i ty (yü til′ə tē), **1** usefulness: *A fur coat has more utility in winter than in summer.* **2** a useful thing. **3** company that performs a public service. Railroads, bus lines, and gas and electric companies are utilities. *noun, plural* **u til i ties.**

u ti lize (yü′tl īz), make use of; put to some practical use: *The cook will utilize the bones to make soup. verb,* **u ti lized, u ti liz ing.**

ut most (ut′mōst), **1** greatest possible; greatest; highest: *Sunshine is of the utmost importance to health.* **2** farthest; extreme: *She walked to the utmost edge of the cliff.* **3** the extreme limit; the most that is possible: *He enjoyed himself to the utmost at the circus.* 1,2 *adjective,* 3 *noun.*

ut ter[1] (ut′ər), complete; total; absolute: *utter surprise, utter darkness, utter defeat. adjective.*

ut ter[2] (ut′ər), **1** speak; make known; express: *the last words she uttered, utter one's thoughts.* **2** give out or forth: *to utter a sigh of relief. verb.*

ut ter ly (ut′ər lē), completely; totally; absolutely. *adverb.*

V v

V or **v** (vē), the 22nd letter of the English alphabet. There are two *v*'s in *vivid. noun, plural* **V's** or **v's.**

va can cy (vā′kən sē), **1** being vacant; emptiness. **2** an unoccupied position:' *The retirement of two clerks made two vacancies in the store.* **3** room, space, or apartment for rent: *There was a vacancy in the motel. There was a vacancy in the parking lot. noun, plural* **va can cies.**

va cant (vā′kənt), **1** not occupied: *a vacant chair, a vacant house.* **2** empty; not filled: *a vacant space.* **3** empty of thought or intelligence: *a vacant smile. adjective.*

va cate (vā′kāt), go away from and leave empty; make vacant: *They will vacate the house at the end of the month. verb,* **va cat ed, va cat ing.**

va ca tion (vā kā′shən), time of rest from school, business, or other duties: *Our school has a spring vacation each year. noun.*

vac ci nate (vak′sə nāt), give a person a shot of vaccine as a protection against a disease. Children who are vaccinated against measles, smallpox, whooping cough, diphtheria, and tetanus will not catch these diseases. *verb,* **vac ci nat ed, vac ci nat ing.**

vac ci na tion (vak′sə nā′shən), act or process of vaccinating: *Vaccination has made smallpox a very rare disease. noun.*

vac cine (vak′sēn′), preparation of dead or weakened germs or viruses of a particular disease, used to inoculate a person in order to prevent or lessen the effects of that disease. Salk vaccine is used against polio. *noun.* [*Vaccine* is from a Latin word meaning "of a cow." It was called this because the vaccine used against smallpox was obtained from cows.]

valentine (definition 1)

vac u um (vak′yü əm *or* vak′yùm), **1** an empty space without even air in it. **2** an enclosed space from which almost all air or gas has been removed. **3** an empty space; void: *Their child's death left a vacuum in the parents' lives.* **4** clean with a vacuum cleaner: *I vacuumed the rugs.* 1-3 *noun,* 4 *verb.*

vacuum cleaner, machine for cleaning carpets, curtains, floors, or the like, by suction.

vag a bond (vag′ə bond), **1** wanderer; idle wanderer; tramp. **2** wandering: *The gypsies lead a vagabond life.* 1 *noun,* 2 *adjective.*

vague (vāg), not definite; not clear; not distinct: *In a fog everything looks vague. His vague statement confused them. adjective,* **va guer, va guest.**

vain (vān), **1** having too much pride in one's looks, ability, or achievements: *Some good-looking people are vain.* **2** of no use; unsuccessful: *I made vain attempts to reach her by telephone.* **3** of no value or importance; worthless; empty: *a vain boast. adjective.*

in vain, without effect or without success: *Their shouts for help were in vain, for no one could hear them.*

val en tine (val′ən tīn), **1** a greeting card or small gift sent on Saint Valentine's Day, February 14. See picture. **2** sweetheart chosen on this day. *noun.*

val et (val′it *or* val′ā), **1** servant who takes care of a man's clothes and gives him personal service. **2** worker in a hotel who cleans or presses clothes. *noun.*

val iant (val′yənt), brave; courageous: *a valiant leader, a valiant deed. adjective.*

val id (val′id), **1** supported by facts or authority; sound; true: *a valid argument.* **2** having force in law: *A contract made by an insane person is not valid.* **3** having force; holding good; effective: *Illness is a valid excuse for being absent from school. adjective.*

val ley (val′ē), **1** low land between hills or mountains: *Most large valleys have rivers running through them.* **2** a wide region drained by a great river system: *the Mississippi valley. noun, plural* **val leys.**

val or (val′ər), bravery; courage. *noun.*

val u a ble (val′yü ə bəl), **1** having value; being worth something: *valuable information, a valuable friend.* **2** worth much money: *a valuable ring. He has a valuable stamp collection.* **3** articles of value: *She keeps her jewelry and other valuables in a safe.* 1,2 *adjective,* 3 *noun.*

val u a tion (val′yü ā′shən), **1** value estimated or determined: *The jeweler's valuation of the necklace was $10,000.* **2** estimating or determining of the value of something. *noun.*

val ue (val′yü), **1** the real worth; proper price: *We bought the house for less than its value.* **2** high worth; excellence, usefulness, or importance: *the value of education, the value of milk as a food.* **3** rate at a certain value or price; estimate the value of: *The land is valued at $5000.* **4** estimated worth: *The dealer placed a value of $500 on the old car.* **5** think highly of; regard highly: *We all value our teacher's opinion of our work.* **6 values,** *pl.* things or ideas believed to be important and desirable in one's life. 1,2,4,6 *noun,* 3,5 *verb,* **val ued, val u ing.**

valve (valv), **1** a movable part that controls the flow of a liquid or gas through a pipe by opening and closing the passage. A faucet contains a valve. **2** part of the body that works like a valve. The valves of the heart are membranes that control the flow of blood into and out of the heart. **3** one of the parts of shells like those of oysters and clams. *noun.*

van (van), **1** a covered truck or wagon for moving furniture and household articles. **2** a small, enclosed truck designed for light hauling or for recreation. *noun.*

van dal (van′dl), person who destroys or damages beautiful or valuable things on purpose. *noun.* [Our word *vandal* comes from the name of the Vandals, an uncivilized people who invaded parts of Europe and Africa long ago. In A.D. 455 they captured and looted the city of Rome.]

van dal ism (van′dl iz′əm), destroying or damaging beautiful or valuable things on purpose. *noun.*

vane (definition 1)

vane (vān), **1** a flat piece of metal or wood that turns around a rod; weather vane. Vanes are often placed on the tops of buildings; they turn with the wind and show its direction. See picture. **2** blade of a windmill, of a propeller, or the like. *noun.*

van guard (van′gärd′), **1** the front part of an army; soldiers marching in front to clear the way and guard against surprise. **2** the foremost position. *noun.*

va nil la (və nil′ə), flavoring used in ice cream, candy, and perfume. It is made from the bean of a tropical plant. *noun.*

van ish (van′ish), **1** disappear; disappear suddenly: *The sun vanished behind a cloud.* **2** pass away; cease to be: *Dinosaurs have vanished from the earth.* *verb.*

van i ty (van′ə tē), **1** too much pride in one's looks or ability: *Good looks or talent sometimes cause vanity.* **2** lack of real value: *the vanity of wealth.* *noun, plural* **van i ties.**

van quish (vang′kwish), conquer; defeat; overcome. *verb.*

va por (vā′pər), **1** steam from boiling water; moisture in the air that can be seen; fog; mist: *the vapor of the morning mist.* **2** gas formed from a substance that is usually a liquid or a solid: *We could smell the gasoline vapor as the gas tank of the car was being filled.* *noun.*

va por iz er (vā′pə rī′zər), device that changes a liquid into a vapor. One kind of vaporizer releases steam into a room, in order to ease the breathing of someone with a cold. *noun.*

var i a ble (ver′ē ə bəl *or* var′ē ə bəl), **1** apt to change; changeable; uncertain: *variable opinions, variable winds. The weather is more variable in New York than it is in California.* **2** able to be varied: *These adjustable curtain rods are of variable length.* **3** something that is likely to vary or change: *A number of variables influence the weather.* 1,2 *adjective,* 3 *noun.*

var i a tion (ver′ē ā′shən *or* var′ē ā′shən), **1** varying; change: *variations in colors.* **2** amount of change: *There was a variation of 30 degrees in the temperature yesterday.* **3** a varied or changed form. *noun.*

var ied (ver′ēd *or* var′ēd), **1** of different kinds; having variety: *a varied assortment of candies.* **2** changed; altered. *adjective.*

va ri e ty (və rī′ə tē), **1** lack of sameness; difference or change: *Variety is the spice of life.* **2** number of different kinds: *This shop has a variety of toys.* **3** kind or sort: *Which varieties of cake did you buy? noun, plural* **va ri e ties.**

var i ous (ver′ē əs *or* var′ē əs), **1** different; differing from one another: *various opinions as to how to raise children.* **2** several; many: *We looked at various houses, but have decided to buy this one. adjective.*

var nish (vär′nish), **1** a liquid that gives a smooth, glossy appearance to wood, metal, or the like. Varnish is often made from resin dissolved in oil or alcohol. **2** the smooth hard surface made by this liquid when it dries: *The varnish on the table was scratched.* **3** put varnish on. **4** give a false or deceiving appearance to: *varnish over the truth with a lie.* 1,2 *noun, plural* **var nish es;** 3,4 *verb.*

var y (ver′ē *or* var′ē), **1** change; make or become different: *The driver can vary the speed of an automobile.* **2** be different; differ: *Stars vary in brightness. verb,* **var ied, var y ing.**

vase (vās), holder or container used for ornament or for holding flowers. See picture. *noun.*

vault¹ (definition 1)
vault of a cathedral

vault² (definition 2)—athlete doing a pole vault

vase made in China 500 years ago

a hat	i it	oi oil	ch child	a in about
ā age	ī ice	ou out	ng long	e in taken
ä far	o hot	u cup	sh she	ə = { i in pencil
e let	ō open	ú put	th thin	o in lemon
ē equal	ô order	ü rule	₮H then	u in circus
ėr term			zh measure	

vas sal (vas′əl), **1** person who held land from a lord or superior, to whom in return he gave help in war or some other service. A great noble could be a vassal of the king and have many other vassals of his own. **2** like a vassal; subordinate: *a vassal nation.* **3** servant. 1,3 *noun,* 2 *adjective.*

vast (vast), very, very large; immense: *Texas and Alaska cover vast territories. A billion dollars is a vast amount of money. adjective.*

vat (vat), tank; large container for liquids: *a vat of dye. noun.*

Vat i can (vat′ə kən), **1** the buildings grouped about the palace of the pope in Rome. **2** the government, office, or authority of the pope. *noun.*

vault¹ (vôlt), **1** an arched roof or ceiling; series of arches. See picture. **2** an arched space or passage. **3** something like an arched roof. The vault of heaven means the sky. **4** make in the form of a vault: *The roof was vaulted.* **5** an underground cellar or storehouse. **6** place for storing valuable things and keeping them safe. Vaults are often made of steel. **7** place for burial. 1-3,5-7 *noun,* 4 *verb.*

vault² (vôlt), **1** jump or leap over by using the hands or a pole: *She vaulted the fence.* **2** such a jump or leap. See picture. **3** jump; leap: *He vaulted over the wall.* 1,3 *verb,* 2 *noun.*

veal (vēl), meat from a calf. *noun.*

veer (vir), **1** change in direction; shift; turn: *The wind veered to the south. The talk veered to ghosts.* **2** shift; turn. 1 *verb,* 2 *noun.*

veg e ta ble (vej′ə tə bəl), **1** plant whose fruit, seeds, leaves, roots, or other parts are used for food. Peas, corn, lettuce, tomatoes, and beets are vegetables. **2** the part of such a plant which is used for food. **3** any plant. **4** of plants; like plants; having something to do with plants: *the vegetable kingdom, vegetable life.* **5** of or made from vegetables: *vegetable soup.* 1-3 *noun,* 4,5 *adjective.*

veg e tar i an (vej′ə ter′ē ən), **1** person who eats vegetables but no meat. **2** eating vegetables but no meat. **3** containing no meat. 1 *noun,* 2,3 *adjective.*

veg e ta tion (vej′ə tā′shən), plant life; growing plants: *There is not much vegetation in deserts. noun.*

ve he ment (vē′ə mənt), **1** having or showing strong feeling: *loud and vehement quarrels.* **2** forceful; violent: *a vehement burst of energy. adjective.*

ve hi cle (vē′ə kəl), **1** any means of carrying, conveying, or transporting, such as a car, carriage, cart, wagon, or sled. Automobiles and trucks are motor vehicles. Rockets and satellites are space vehicles. **2** means by which something is communicated, shown, or done: *Language is the vehicle of thought. noun.*

vendor

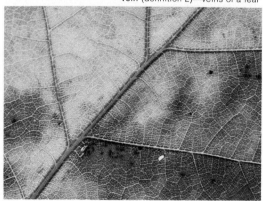

vein (definition 2)—veins of a leaf

veil (vāl), **1** piece of very thin material worn to protect or hide the face, or as an ornament. **2** piece of material worn so as to fall over the head and shoulders. **3** cover with a veil: *Some Moslem women veil their faces before going into public.* **4** anything that screens or hides: *A veil of clouds hid the sun.* **5** cover; hide: *Fog veiled the shore. The spy veiled his plans in secrecy.* 1,2,4 *noun,* 3,5 *verb.*

take the veil, become a nun.

vein (vān), **1** one of the blood vessels or tubes that carry blood to the heart from all parts of the body. **2** rib of a leaf or of an insect's wing. See picture. **3** crack or seam in rock filled with a different material: *a vein of copper.* **4** any streak or marking of a different shade or color in wood or marble. **5** special character or disposition; state of mind; mood: *a vein of cruelty, a joking vein. noun.*

ve loc i ty (və los/ə tē), **1** swiftness; quickness: *He threw the ball with the velocity of a bullet.* **2** rate of motion; speed: *The velocity of light is about 186,000 miles per second.* See picture. *noun, plural* **ve loc i ties.**

vel vet (vel/vit), **1** a thick, soft cloth. Velvet may be made of silk, rayon, cotton, or some combination of these. **2** made of velvet: *a velvet jacket.* **3** like velvet: *Our kitten has soft, velvet paws.* 1 *noun,* 2,3 *adjective.*

vel vet y (vel/və tē), smooth and soft like velvet. *adjective.*

vend (vend), sell; peddle: *They were vending fruit from a cart. verb.*

vend ing ma chine (ven/ding mə shēn/), machine from which one obtains candy, stamps, or other small articles, when a coin is dropped in.

ven dor (ven/dər), seller; peddler. See picture. *noun.*

ven er a ble (ven/ər ə bəl), worthy of reverence; deserving respect because of age, character, or importance: *a venerable teacher, venerable customs. adjective.*

ven e rate (ven/ə rāt/) regard with reverence; revere: *He venerates his father's memory. verb,* **ven e rat ed, ven e rat ing.** [*Venerate* comes from a Latin word meaning "respected or loved deeply." The Latin word came from the name of Venus, the Roman goddess of love.]

ven e ra tion (ven/ə rā/shən), deep respect; reverence. *noun.*

Ve ne tian blind (və nē/shən blīnd/), a window blind made of many horizontal slats. The blind can be raised and lowered, or the slats can be tilted so that they overlap, to regulate the light that is let in.

venge ance (ven/jəns), revenge; punishment in return for a wrong: *She swore vengeance against her hateful enemies. noun.*

with a vengeance, with great force or violence: *By six o'clock it was raining with a vengeance.*

ven i son (ven/ə sən), deer meat; flesh of a deer, used for food. *noun.*

ven om (ven/əm), **1** the poison of some snakes, spiders, scorpions, lizards, and similar animals. **2** spite; malice: *They spoke of their enemies with venom. noun.*

vent (vent), **1** hole; opening, especially one serving as an outlet: *He used a pencil to make air vents in the box top so his frog could breathe.* **2** outlet; way out: *Her great energy found vent in hard work. They gave vent to their grief in tears.* **3** let out; express freely: *Don't vent your anger on the dog.* 1,2 *noun,* 3 *verb.*

ven ti late (ven/tl āt), **1** change the air in: *We ventilate a room by opening windows.* **2** make known publicly; discuss openly. *verb,* **ven ti lat ed, ven ti lat ing.**

ven ti la tion (ven/tl ā/shən), **1** change of air; act or process of supplying with fresh air. **2** means of supplying fresh air: *Air conditioning provides ventilation in the summer. noun.*

ven ti la tor (ven/tl ā/tər), any apparatus or means, such as an opening, an air conditioner, or a fan, for changing or improving the air in a room, airplane, or any enclosed space. *noun.*

ven ture (ven/chər), **1** a risky or daring undertaking: *Our courage was equal to any venture. A lucky venture in oil stock made them rich.* **2** expose to risk or danger: *She ventured her life to rescue me.* **3** dare: *No one ventured to interrupt the speaker.* **4** dare to come or go: *They ventured out on the thin ice and fell through.* **5** dare to say or make: *He ventured an objection.* 1 *noun,* 2-5 *verb,* **ven tured, ven tur ing.**

veranda

a hat	i it	oi oil	ch child	(a in about
ā age	ī ice	ou out	ng long	e in taken
ä far	o hot	u cup	sh she	ə = { i in pencil
e let	ō open	ú put	th thin	o in lemon
ē equal	ô order	ü rule	ᵀʜ then	u in circus
ėr term			zh measure	

Ve nus (vē′nəs), **1** the Roman goddess of love and beauty. **2** the most brilliant planet, second in distance from the sun. *noun.*

ve ran da (və ran′də), a large porch along one or more sides of a house. See picture. *noun.*

verb (vėrb), word that tells what is or what is done; part of speech that expresses action or being. *Do, go, come, be, sit, think, know,* and *eat* are verbs. *noun.*

ver bal (vėr′bəl), **1** in words; of words: *A description is a verbal picture.* **2** expressed in spoken words; oral: *a verbal promise. adjective.*

ver dict (vėr′dikt), **1** decision of a jury: *The jury returned a verdict of "Not guilty."* **2** decision; judgment: *the verdict of history. noun.*

ver i fy (ver′ə fī), **1** prove to be true; confirm: *The driver's report of the accident was verified by two women who had seen it happen.* **2** find out the truth of; test the correctness of: *You can verify the spelling of a word by looking in a dictionary. verb,* **ver i fied, ver i fy ing.**

ver mil ion (vər mil′yən), bright red. *adjective.*

ver min (vėr′mən), small troublesome or destructive animals. Fleas, lice, rats, and mice are vermin. *noun plural or singular.*

Ver mont (vər mont′), one of the northeastern states of the United States. *noun.* [*Vermont* was formed from French words meaning "green mountain."]

ver sa tile (vėr′sə təl), able to do many things well: *She is a versatile student; she is skilled in science, art, mathematics, English, German, and history. adjective.*

verse (vėrs), **1** poetry; lines of words with a regularly repeated accent and often with rhyme. **2** a single line of poetry. **3** group of lines of poetry: *Sing the first verse of "America."* **4** a short division of a chapter in the Bible. *noun.*

versed (vėrst), experienced; practiced; skilled: *Our doctor is well versed in medicine. adjective.*

ver sion (vėr′zhən), **1** one particular statement, account, or description: *Each of the three girls gave her own version of what happened.* **2** a translation from one language to another: *a version of the Bible. noun.*

ver te bra (vėr′tə brə), one of the bones of the backbone. See picture. *noun, plural* **ver te brae** (vėr′tə brē), **ver te bras.**

ver te brate (vėr′tə brit), **1** animal that has a backbone. Fishes, amphibians, reptiles, birds, and mammals are vertebrates. **2** having a backbone. **1** *noun,* **2** *adjective.*

ver ti cal (vėr′tə kəl), straight up and down; perpendicular to a level surface; upright. A person standing up straight is in a vertical position. *adjective.*

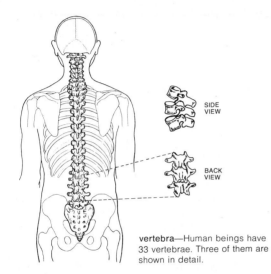

SIDE VIEW

BACK VIEW

vertebra—Human beings have 33 vertebrae. Three of them are shown in detail.

velocity

ver y (ver′ē), **1** much; greatly; extremely: *The sunshine is very hot in July.* **2** absolutely; exactly: *He stood in the very same place for an hour.* **3** same: *The very people who supported the plan are against it now.* **4** even; mere; sheer: *The very thought of summer vacation makes her happy.* **5** absolute; complete: *The storm meant the very end of our hopes for a picnic.* **6** actual: *They were caught in the very act of stealing.* **1,2** adverb, **3-6** adjective, **ver i er, ver i est.**

ves pers or **Ves pers** (ves′pərz), a church service held in the late afternoon or early evening. *noun plural.*

ves sel (ves′əl), **1** ship; large boat: *Ocean liners and other vessels are usually docked by tugboats.* **2** a hollow holder or container. Cups, bowls, pitchers, bottles, barrels, and tubs are vessels. **3** tube carrying blood or other fluid. Veins and arteries are blood vessels. *noun.*

vest (vest), **1** a short, sleeveless garment worn over a shirt or blouse. **2** clothe or robe: *The vested priest stood before the altar.* **3** furnish with powers, authority, rights, or functions: *Congress is vested with the power to make laws.* **4** put in the possession or control of a person or persons: *The management of the hospital is vested in a board of trustees.* **1** noun, **2-4** verb.

ves tige (ves′tij), all that remains; trace: *Ghost stories are vestiges of a former widespread belief in ghosts.* *noun.*

vest ment (vest′mənt), garment worn by a clergyman in performing sacred duties. *noun.*

vet er an (vet′ər ən), **1** person who has served in the armed forces. **2** having had much experience in war: *Veteran troops fought side by side with the young soldiers.* **3** person who has had much experience in some position or occupation: *a veteran of Congress.* **4** grown old in service; experienced: *a veteran teacher.* **1,3** noun, **2,4** adjective.

vet er i nar i an (vet′ər ə ner′ē ən), doctor or surgeon who treats animals. See picture. *noun.*

vet er i nar y (vet′ər ə ner′ē), **1** having something to do with the medical or surgical treatment of animals. **2** veterinarian. **1** adjective, **2** noun, plural **vet er i nar ies.**

veterinarian

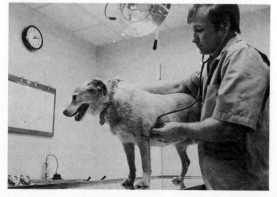

ve to (vē′tō), **1** right or power to forbid or prevent: *The President has the power of veto over most bills passed in Congress.* **2** the use of this right or power: *The governor's veto kept the bill from becoming a law.* **3** prohibition; refusal of consent: *Our plan met with a veto from the boss.* **4** refuse to consent to: *Her parents vetoed her plan to buy a car.* **1-3** noun, plural **ve toes**; **4** verb. [*Veto* comes from a Latin word meaning "I forbid." Originally, it was used by officials who represented the people in ancient Rome to oppose proposed laws.]

vex (veks), **1** annoy; anger by trifles; provoke: *It is vexing to have to wait for anyone.* **2** disturb; trouble: *Cape Hatteras is much vexed by storms.* verb.

vex a tion (vek sā′shən), **1** vexing; being vexed: *Their faces showed their vexation at the delay.* **2** thing that vexes: *Rain on Saturday was a vexation to the children.* noun.

vi a (vī′ə), by way of; by a route that passes through: *We are going from New York to Paris via London.* preposition.

vi a duct (vī′ə dukt), bridge for carrying a road or railroad over a valley, a part of a city, a river, or the like. noun.

vi al (vī′əl), a small glass or plastic bottle for holding medicines or the like; phial. noun.

vi brate (vī′brāt), **1** move rapidly back and forth: *A snake's tongue vibrates. A piano string vibrates and makes a sound when a key is struck.* **2** quiver; be moved: *The dog vibrated with fear during the storm.* verb, **vi brat ed, vi brat ing.**

vi bra tion (vī brā′shən), a rapid movement back and forth; quivering motion; vibrating: *The buses shake the house so much that we feel the vibration.* noun.

vic ar (vik′ər), **1** clergyman who has charge of one chapel in a parish. **2** person acting in place of another. Roman Catholics sometimes refer to the pope as the vicar of Christ. noun.

vice (vīs), **1** an evil habit or tendency: *Lying and cruelty are vices.* **2** evil; wickedness. **3** fault; bad habit: *They believed that gambling was a vice.* noun.

vice-pres i dent (vīs′prez′ə dənt), officer next in rank to the president, who takes the president's place when necessary. If the President of the United States dies or resigns, the Vice-President becomes President. noun.

vice roy (vīs′roi), person ruling a country or province as the deputy of the sovereign. noun.

vi ce ver sa (vī′sə vėr′sə), the other way round: *John blamed Mary, and vice versa (Mary blamed John).*

vi cin i ty (və sin′ə tē), **1** region near or about a place; neighborhood: *There are no houses for sale in this vicinity.* **2** nearness in place; closeness: *The vicinity of the school to the house was an advantage on rainy days.* noun, plural **vi cin i ties.**

vi cious (vish′əs), **1** evil; wicked: *The criminal led a vicious life.* **2** having bad habits or a bad disposition; savage: *a vicious animal.* **3** spiteful; malicious: *I won't listen to such vicious gossip.* **4** unpleasantly severe: *a vicious headache.* adjective.

vic tim (vik′təm), **1** person or animal sacrificed, injured, or destroyed: *victims of war, victims of an accident.* **2** person badly treated or taken advantage of; dupe: *the victim of a swindler. noun.*

vic tor (vik′tər), winner; conqueror. *noun.*

vic to ri ous (vik tôr′ē əs), **1** conquering; having won a victory: *a victorious team.* **2** having something to do with victory; ending in victory: *a victorious shout. adjective.*

vic to ry (vik′tər ē), defeat of an enemy or opponent: *The game ended in a victory for our school. noun, plural* **vic to ries.**

vid e o (vid′ē ō), **1** of or used in sending or receiving images in television. **2** television. **1** *adjective,* **2** *noun.* [*Video* comes from a Latin word meaning "I see."]

vid e o tape (vid′ē ō tāp′), **1** a magnetic tape that records and reproduces both sound and picture for television. **2** to record on videotape. **1** *noun,* **2** *verb,* **vid e o taped, vid e o tap ing.**

vie (vī), strive for superiority; contend in rivalry; compete: *The children vied with each other to be first in line. verb,* **vied, vy ing.**

view (vyü), **1** act of seeing; sight: *It was our first view of the ocean.* **2** power of seeing; range of the eye: *A ship came into view.* **3** see; look at: *They viewed the scene with pleasure.* **4** thing seen; scene. See picture. **5** picture of some scene: *Various views of the coast hung on the walls.* **6** a mental picture; idea: *This book will give you a general view of the way the pioneers lived.* **7** way of looking at or considering a matter; opinion: *Children take a different view of school from that of their teachers.* **8** consider; regard: *The plan for having classes on Saturday was not viewed with favor by the students.* **1,2,4-7** *noun,* **3,8** *verb.*

in view, 1 in sight: *As the noise grew louder, the airplane came in view.* **2** under consideration: *Keep the teacher's advice in view as you try to improve your work.*

in view of, considering; because of: *In view of the fact that she is the best player on the team, she should be the captain.*

on view, to be seen; open for people to see: *The exhibit is on view from 9 a.m. to 5 p.m.*

with a view to, with the purpose or intention of: *He worked hard after school with a view to earning money for a new bicycle.*

view point (vyü′point′), attitude of mind: *A heavy rain that is good from the viewpoint of farmers may be bad from the viewpoint of tourists. noun.*

vig il (vij′əl), keeping awake during the usual hours of sleep for some purpose; act of watching; watch: *All night the parents kept vigil over the sick child. noun.*

vig i lance (vij′ə ləns), watchfulness; alertness; caution: *The cat watched the mouse hole with vigilance. noun.*

vig i lant (vij′ə lənt), watchful; alert; wide-awake: *The dog kept vigilant guard. adjective.*

vig or (vig′ər), **1** active strength or force: *The principal argued with vigor that the new school*

view (definition 4)—The view from the shore was beautiful.

should have a library. **2** healthy energy or power: *A person's vigor lessens with old age. noun.*

vig or ous (vig′ər əs), full of vigor; strong and active; energetic; forcible: *The old man is still vigorous and lively. Doctors wage a vigorous war against disease. adjective.*

vi king or **Vi king** (vī′king), one of the daring seamen from northwest Europe who raided the coasts of Europe during the A.D. 700's, 800's, and 900's. The vikings were great warriors and explorers. They even came to North America. *noun.*

vile (vīl), **1** very bad: *The weather today was vile—rainy, windy, and cold.* **2** foul; disgusting: *A vile smell hung in the air around the garbage dump.* **3** evil; immoral: *a vile crime.* **4** poor; mean; lowly: *I worked at a vile job for low wages. adjective,* **vil er, vil est.**

vil la (vil′ə), house in the country or suburbs, sometimes at the seashore. A villa is usually a large or elegant residence. *noun.*

vil lage (vil′ij), **1** group of houses, usually smaller than a town. **2** people of a village: *The whole village was out to see the fire. noun.*

vil lag er (vil′i jər), person who lives in a village. *noun.*

vil lain (vil′ən), a very wicked person: *The villain stole the money and cast the blame on a friend. noun.*

vim (vim), force; energy; vigor: *The campers were full of vim after a good night's sleep. noun.*

vin di cate (vin′də kāt), **1** clear from suspicion, dishonor, or any charge of wrongdoing: *The verdict of "Not guilty" vindicated them.* **2** defend successfully against opposition; uphold; justify: *The heir vindicated her claim to the fortune. verb,* **vin di cat ed, vin di cat ing.**

vine (vīn), **1** plant with a long, slender stem that grows along the ground or that climbs by attaching itself to a wall, tree, or other support. Melons and pumpkins grow on vines. Ivy is a vine. See picture. **2** grapevine. *noun.*

vin e gar (vin′ə gər), a sour liquid produced by the fermenting of cider, wine, beer, ale, or the like. Vinegar is used in salad dressing, in flavoring food, and in preserving food. *noun.*

vine yard (vin′yərd), place planted with grapevines. *noun.*

vi nyl (vī′nl), any of various tough plastics, used in flooring, toys, and phonograph records. *noun.*

vi o la (vē ō′lə), a musical instrument shaped like a violin, but slightly larger, and lower in pitch. See picture. *noun.*

vi o late (vī′ə lāt), **1** break (a law, rule, agreement, promise, or instructions); act contrary to; fail to perform: *Speeding violates the traffic regulations.* **2** break in upon; disturb: *The sound of automobile horns violated the usual calm of Sunday morning.* **3** treat with disrespect or contempt: *They violated the graves by overturning the tombstones. verb,* **vi o lat ed, vi o lat ing.**

vi o la tion (vī′ə lā′shən), **1** breaking (of a law, rule, agreement, promise, or instructions): *He was fined $10 for his violation of the traffic law.* **2** treatment (of a holy thing) with contempt. *noun.*

vi o la tor (vī′ə lā′tər), person who violates. *noun.*

vi o lence (vī′ə ləns), **1** rough force in action: *She slammed the door with violence.* **2** rough or harmful action or treatment: *the violence of war. The dictator ruled with violence.* **3** harm; injury: *The storm did violence to the rosebushes. noun.*

vi o lent (vī′ə lənt), **1** acting or done with strong, rough force: *a violent blow.* **2** caused by strong, rough force: *a violent death.* **3** showing or caused by very strong feeling or action: *violent language, a violent rage.* **4** severe; extreme; very great: *a violent pain, violent heat. adjective.*

vi o let (vī′ə lit), **1** a small plant with purple, blue, yellow, or white flowers. Many common violets grow wild and bloom in the spring. **2** bluish purple. **1** *noun,* **2** *adjective.*

vi o lin (vī′ə lin′), a musical instrument with four strings played with a bow. See picture. *noun.*

vi o lin ist (vī′ə lin′ist), person who plays the violin. *noun.*

vi o lon cel lo (vī′ə lən chel′ō), cello. *noun, plural* **vi o lon cel los.**

vi per (vī′pər), **1** a poisonous snake, especially one with a thick body. Rattlesnakes are vipers. **2** a spiteful, treacherous person. *noun.*

vir gin (vėr′jən), **1** maiden. **2** of a virgin. **3** pure; spotless. Virgin snow is newly fallen snow. **4** not yet used: *virgin soil, a virgin forest.* **1** *noun,* **2-4** *adjective.*

Vir gin ia (vər jin′yə), one of the southeastern states of the United States. *noun.* [*Virginia* was formed in 1584 from a Latin word meaning "virgin." The area was named in honor of Elizabeth I of England, who lived from 1533 to 1603. She was called the Virgin Queen.]

viola and violin—The girl is playing a violin; the boy is playing a viola.

vine (definition 1)

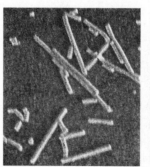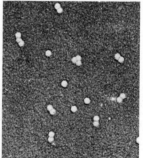

virus—two types of viruses, 50,000 times actual size. The pictures were taken with a special, very powerful microscope.

Virgin Islands, group of islands in the West Indies, several of which belong to the United States.

vir tu al (vėr′chü əl), real; actual; being something in effect, though not so in name; for all practical purposes: *The battle was won with so great a loss of soldiers that it was a virtual defeat. She is the virtual president, though her title is vice-president. adjective.*

vir tu al ly (vėr′chü ə lē), really; actually; in effect, though not in name: *If you travel by jet plane, Los Angeles and New York are virtually neighbors. adverb.*

vir tue (vėr′chü), **1** goodness; moral excellence: *a person of the highest virtue.* **2** a particular moral excellence: *Justice is a virtue.* **3** a good quality: *They praised the virtues of their small car.* **4** power to produce good results: *There is little virtue in that medicine. noun.*

vir tu ous (vėr′chü əs), good; moral; righteous: *virtuous conduct, a virtuous life. adjective.*

vi rus (vī′rəs), a living substance that can cause certain infectious diseases. Viruses are so small that they cannot be seen through most microscopes. Viruses cause such diseases in human beings as rabies, polio, chicken pox, and the common cold. See picture. *noun, plural* **vi rus es.**

vis count (vī′kount), nobleman ranking below an earl or count and above a baron. *noun.*

vise (vīs), tool having two jaws moved by a screw, used to hold an object firmly while work is being done on it. See picture. *noun.*

vis i bil i ty (viz′ə bil′ə tē), **1** condition or quality of being visible: *In a fog the visibility is very poor.* **2** distance at which things are visible: *Fog and rain decreased visibility to about 50 feet. noun.*

vis i ble (viz′ə bəl), **1** able to be seen: *The shore was barely visible through the fog.* **2** apparent; obvious: *A pauper has no visible means of support. adjective.*

vis i bly (viz′ə blē), so as to be visible; plainly: *After the long hike the children were visibly weary. adverb.*

vi sion (vizh′ən), **1** power of seeing; sense of sight: *I have to wear glasses because my vision is poor.* **2** act or fact of seeing; sight: *The vision of the table loaded with food made our mouths water.* **3** power of perceiving by the imagination or by clear thinking: *the vision of a prophet, a person of great vision.* **4** something seen in the imagination, in a dream, or in one's thoughts: *The gambler had visions of great wealth. noun.*

vis it (viz′it), **1** go to see; come to see: *Would you like to visit New Orleans?* **2** make a call; stay with; make a stay; be a guest: *I visited my friend last week.* **3** act of visiting; short stay: *My aunt paid us a visit last week.* **4** come upon; distress; afflict: *They were visited by many troubles.* **1,2,4** *verb,* **3** *noun.*

vis i tor (viz′ə tər), person who visits; person who is visiting; guest: *Visitors from the East arrived last night. noun.*

vi sor (vī′zər), **1** the movable front part of a

vise

visor (definition 2)

helmet, covering the face. **2** brim of a cap, that sticks out in front. See picture. **3** shade that can be lowered from above to the inside of a car windshield to shield the eyes from the sun. *noun.*

vis ta (vis′tə), **1** view seen through a narrow opening or passage: *Between the two rows of trees I saw a vista of the lake.* **2** such an opening or passage itself: *a shady vista of elms.* **3** a mental view: *Education should open up new vistas. noun.*

vis u al (vizh′ü əl), **1** of sight; having something to do with sight: *Being near-sighted is a visual defect. Telescopes and microscopes are visual aids.* **2** visible; that can be seen. *adjective.*

vi tal (vī′tl), **1** of life; having something to do with life: *Growth and decay are vital processes.* **2** necessary to life: *Eating is a vital function. The heart is a vital organ.* **3** very necessary; essential; very important: *Pure water is vital to the welfare of a community.* **4** causing death, failure, or ruin: *a vital wound, a vital blow to an industry.* **5** full of life and spirit; lively: *Vital children are seldom idle or dull. adjective.*

vi tal i ty (vī tal′ə tē), **1** ability to continue living; power to live: *One's vitality can be lessened by a long illness.* **2** strength or vigor of mind or body: *Exercise helps maintain vitality. noun, plural* **vi tal i ties.**

vi ta min (vī′tə mən), **1** any of certain special substances necessary for the normal growth and proper nourishment of the body. Vitamins are found especially in milk, butter, raw fruits and vegetables, cod-liver oil, and the outside part of wheat and other grains. Lack of vitamins causes certain diseases as well as generally poor health. **2** of or containing vitamins: *a vitamin tablet, a vitamin deficiency.* **1** *noun,* **2** *adjective.*

vi va cious (vī vā′shəs *or* vi vā′shəs), lively, sprightly; animated; gay: *a vivacious manner, a vivacious person. adjective.*

viv id (viv′id), **1** strikingly bright; brilliant; strong and clear. See picture. **2** lively; full of life: *Her description of the party was so vivid that I almost felt I had been there.* **3** strong and distinct: *I have a vivid memory of the fire. adjective.*

vix en (vik′sən), a female fox. *noun.*

vo cab u lar y (vō kab′yə ler′ē), **1** stock of words used by a person or group of people: *Reading will increase your vocabulary. The vocabulary of science has grown tremendously in the past 20 years.* **2** list of words, usually in alphabetical order, with their meanings: *There is a vocabulary in the back of our French book. noun, plural* **vo cab u lar ies.**

vo cal (vō′kəl), **1** of the voice; having to do with the voice or speaking: *The tongue is a vocal organ.* **2** made with the voice: *I like vocal music better than instrumental.* **3** having a voice; giving forth sound: *The zoo was vocal with the roar of the lions.* **4** aroused to speech; inclined to talk freely: *He became vocal with anger. adjective.*

vocal cords, two bands of elastic tissue in the throat. They can be pulled tight or let loose while breathing to help make the sounds of the voice.

vo ca tion (vō kā′shən), a particular occupation, business, profession, or trade: *Architecture is her vocation. noun.*

vod ka (vod′kə), a strong alcoholic drink made from potatoes, rye, barley, or corn. *noun.* [*Vodka* is from a Russian word meaning "water."]

vogue (vōg), **1** fashion: *Hoop skirts were in vogue many years ago.* **2** popularity: *That song had a great vogue at one time. noun.*

voice (vois), **1** sound made through the mouth, especially by people in speaking, singing, or shouting: *The voices of the children could be heard coming from the playground.* **2** power to make sounds through the mouth: *His voice was gone because of a sore throat.* **3** anything like speech or song: *the voice of the wind.* **4** ability as a singer: *That child has a very good voice.* **5** singer: *a choir of fifty voices.* **6** express; utter: *They voiced their approval.* **7** expression: *They gave voice to their joy.* **8** expressed opinion or choice: *Her voice was for compromise.* **9** right to express an opinion or choice: *Have we any voice in this matter at all?* **1-5,7-9** *noun,* **6** *verb,* **voiced, voic ing.**

void (void), **1** an empty space: *The death of his dog left an aching void in the boy's heart.* **2** empty; vacant: *a void space.* **3** without force; not binding in law: *Any contract made by a child is void.* **1** *noun,* **2,3** *adjective.*

vol can ic (vol kan′ik), **1** of or caused by a volcano; having to do with volcanoes: *a volcanic eruption.* **2** like a volcano; liable to break out violently: *a volcanic temper. adjective.*

vol ca no (vol kā′nō), mountain having an opening through which steam, ashes, and lava are forced out. *noun, plural* **vol ca noes** *or* **vol ca nos.** [*Volcano* comes from the Latin name of Vulcan, the Roman god of fire.]

vol ley (vol′ē), **1** shower of stones, bullets, or other missiles: *A volley of arrows rained down upon the attacking knights.* **2** a noisy burst of many things at once: *a volley of angry words.* **3** discharge of a number of guns at once. **4** discharge or be discharged in a volley: *Cannon volleyed on all sides.* **1-3** *noun, plural* **vol leys; 4** *verb.*

vol ley ball (vol′ē bôl′), **1** game played by two teams of players with a large ball and a high net. The ball is hit with the hands back and forth over the net without letting it touch the ground. See picture. **2** ball used in this game. *noun.*

volt (vōlt), unit for measuring the force of electric energy. *noun.* [*Volt* was named for Alessandro Volta, who lived from 1745 to 1827. He was an Italian scientist who invented one of the first electric batteries.]

volt age (vōl′tij), strength of electric force, measured in volts. A current of high voltage is used in transmitting electric power over long distances. *noun.*

vol u ble (vol′yə bəl), ready to talk much; having the habit of talking much: *She is a voluble speaker. adjective.*

vol ume (vol′yəm), **1** book: *We own a library of five hundred volumes.* **2** book forming part of a set or series: *You can find what you want to know in the ninth volume of this encyclopedia.* **3** space occupied: *The storeroom has a volume of 400 cubic feet.* **4** amount; quantity: *Volumes of smoke poured from the chimneys of the factory.* **5** amount of sound; fullness of tone: *An organ has much more volume than a violin or flute. noun.*

vol un tar i ly (vol′ən ter′ə lē), of one's own choice; without force or compulsion: *We returned the lost dog voluntarily to its owner. adverb.*

vol un tar y (vol′ən ter′ē), **1** acting, done, made, or given of one's own choice; not forced; not compelled: *a voluntary worker. My decision to quit my job was voluntary.* **2** intended; done on purpose: *Voluntary disobedience will be punished.* **3** controlled by the will: *Talking is voluntary; hiccupping is not voluntary. adjective.*

vol un teer (vol′ən tir′), **1** person who enters any service by choice; one who is not drafted. Some soldiers are volunteers. **2** person who serves without pay. In some towns, the firefighters are volunteers. **3** offer one's services: *She volunteered for the committee.* **4** offer freely: *He volunteered to*

help. **5** of volunteers: *a volunteer fire department.*
6 serving as a volunteer: *a volunteer fireman, a volunteer leader.* 1,2 *noun,* 3,4 *verb,* 5,6 *adjective.*

vom it (vom′it), **1** throw up what has been eaten.
2 substance thrown up from the stomach. **3** throw out with force: *The chimneys vomited smoke.* 1,3 *verb,* 2 *noun.*

vote (vōt), **1** a formal expression of a wish or choice on a proposal, motion, or candidate for office. In an election the person receiving the most votes is elected. **2** right to give such an expression. Children don't have the vote, and adult citizens can lose it by being convicted of certain crimes. **3** ballot: *More than a million votes were counted.* **4** votes considered together: *the labor vote, the vote of the people.* **5** give a vote: *I voted for that senator.* **6** pass, determine, or grant by a vote: *Money for a new school was voted by the board.* **7** declare: *The children all voted the trip a great success.* 1-4 *noun,* 5-7 *verb,* **vot ed, vot ing.**

vot er (vō′tər), **1** person who votes. **2** person who has the right to vote: *Women have been voters in the United States only since 1920.* noun.

vouch (vouch), be responsible; give a guarantee (for): *I can vouch for the truth of the story. The principal vouched for the boy's honesty.* verb.

vow (vou), **1** a solemn promise: *a vow of secrecy, marriage vows.* **2** promise made to God: *a nun's vows.* **3** make a vow: *I vowed never to leave home again.* **4** make a vow to do, give, get, or the like: *vow revenge. The knight vowed loyalty to the king.* 1,2 *noun,* 3,4 *verb.*

vow el (vou′əl), **1** a speech sound that is spelled by the letters *a, e, i, o, u,* and sometimes *y.* **2** letter or combination of letters that stands for a vowel sound. *noun.*

voy age (voi′ij), **1** a journey or travel by water; cruise: *We had a pleasant voyage to England.* **2** a journey or travel through the air or through space: *an airplane voyage, the earth's voyage around the sun.* **3** make or take a voyage; go by sea or air: *We voyaged across the Atlantic Ocean.* 1,2 *noun,* 3 *verb,* **voy aged, voy ag ing.**

voy ag er (voi′i jər), person who makes a voyage; traveler. *noun.*

vul gar (vul′gər), showing a lack of good breeding, manners, or taste; not refined; coarse: *to use vulgar language. adjective.*

vul gar i ty (vul gar′ə tē), **1** lack of good breeding, manners, or taste; lack of refinement; coarseness.
2 vulgar act or word: *Their vulgarities annoyed me terribly. noun, plural* **vul gar i ties.**

vul ner a ble (vul′nər ə bəl), **1** capable of being wounded or injured; open to attack: *The army's retreat left the city vulnerable to attack by the enemy.* **2** sensitive to criticism, temptations, or influences: *Most people are vulnerable to ridicule. adjective.*

vul ture (vul′chər), **1** a large bird of prey related to eagles and hawks that eats the flesh of dead animals. See picture. **2** person who steals from another; greedy, ruthless person. *noun.*

vy ing (vī′ing). See **vie.** *Members of the class were vying with each other for a part in the play.* verb.

a hat	i it	oi oil	ch child	(a in about
ā age	ī ice	ou out	ng long	e in taken
ä far	o hot	u cup	sh she	ə = { i in pencil
e let	ō open	u̇ put	th thin	o in lemon
ē equal	ô order	ü rule	₮н then	u in circus
ėr term			zh measure	

vivid (definition 1)—vivid colors

volleyball (definition 1)

vulture (definition 1)—about 2½ feet (75 centimeters) long

W w

W or **w** (dub′əl yü), the 23rd letter of the English alphabet. There are two *w*'s in *window*. *noun, plural* **W's** or **w's.**

W or **W.,** **1** west. **2** western.

wad (wod), **1** a small, soft mass: *I plugged my ears with wads of cotton.* **2** a tight roll; compact mass or bundle: *a wad of bills, a wad of chewing gum.* **3** make into a wad: *I wadded up the paper and threw it away.* **4** a round plug of cloth, cardboard, paper, or the like, used to hold the powder and shot in place in a gun or cartridge. **5** to stuff with a wad. 1,2,4 *noun,* 3,5 *verb,* **wad ded, wad ding.**

wad dle (wod′l), **1** walk with short steps and an awkward, swaying motion, as a duck does: *The small child waddled from the house carrying a large toy.* **2** act of waddling: *He made us laugh by imitating the waddle of a duck.* 1 *verb,* **wad dled, wad dling;** 2 *noun.*

wade (wād), **1** walk through water, snow, sand, mud, or anything that hinders free motion: *wade across a brook.* **2** make one's way with difficulty: *Must I wade through that dull book?* **3** get across or pass through by wading: *We waded the stream.* *verb,* **wad ed, wad ing.**

wa fer (wā′fər), a very thin cake or biscuit. *noun.*

waf fle (wof′əl), cake made of batter and cooked in a special griddle that makes the cakes very thin in places, usually eaten while hot with butter and syrup. *noun.*

waft (waft), **1** carry over water or through air: *The waves wafted the boat to shore.* **2** a breath or puff of air, wind, or scent: *A waft of fresh air came through the open window.* **3** a waving movement: *a waft of the hand.* 1 *verb,* 2,3 *noun.*

wag (wag), **1** move from side to side or up and down: *A dog wags its tail.* **2** wagging motion: *She refused with a wag of her head.* 1 *verb,* **wagged, wag ging;** 2 *noun.*

wage (wāj), **1 wages, a** amount paid for work: *His wages are $100 a week.* **b** something given in return: *The wages of poor eating is poor health.* **2** carry on: *Doctors wage war against disease.* 1 *noun,* 2 *verb,* **waged, wag ing.**

wa ger (wā′jər), **1** make a bet; bet; gamble: *I'll wager the black horse will win the race.* **2** act of betting; bet: *The wager of $10 was promptly paid.* 1 *verb,* 2 *noun.*

wag on (wag′ən), a four-wheeled vehicle for carrying loads: *a milk wagon. noun.*

waif (wāf), **1** a homeless or neglected child. **2** anything without an owner; stray thing or animal. *noun.*

wail (wāl), **1** cry loud and long because of grief or pain: *The baby wailed.* **2** a long cry of grief or pain. **3** a sound like such a cry: *the wail of a hungry coyote.* **4** make a mournful sound: *The wind wailed*

around the old house. **5** lament; mourn. 1,4,5 *verb,* 2,3 *noun.*

waist (wāst), **1** the part of the body between the ribs and the hips. **2** garment or part of a garment covering the body from the neck or shoulders to the hips. *noun.*

wait (wāt), **1** stay or stop doing something till someone comes or something happens: *Let's wait in the shade.* **2** act or time of waiting: *I had a long wait at the doctor's office.* **3** be ready; look forward: *The children wait impatiently for vacation.* **4** be left undone; be put off: *That matter can wait.* **5** delay or put off: *Please wait dinner for me.* **6** act as a servant; change plates, pass food, or attend to the wants of persons at table. 1,3-6 *verb,* 2 *noun.*

lie in wait, stay hidden ready to attack: *Robbers lay in wait for the travelers.*

wait on or **wait upon, 1** be a servant to: *wait on hotel guests.* **2** call upon (a superior): *The victorious general waited upon the queen.*

wait er (wā′tər), man who waits on table in a hotel or restaurant. *noun.*

wai tress (wā′tris), woman who waits on table in a hotel or restaurant. *noun, plural* **wai tress es.**

wake[1] (wāk), **1** stop sleeping: *I usually wake at dawn. She wakes at seven every morning.* **2** cause to stop sleeping: *The noise of the traffic always wakes the baby. Wake him up early.* **3** be awake; stay awake: *all her waking hours.* **4** become alive or active: *Flowers wake in the spring.* **5** make alive or active: *He needs some interest to wake him up.* **6** watching. **7** an all-night watch kept beside the body of a dead person. 1-5 *verb,* **waked** or **woke, wak ing;** 6,7 *noun.*

wake[2] (wāk), track left behind a moving ship. *noun.*

in the wake of, following; behind; after: *floods coming in the wake of a hurricane, a dog following in the wake of its master.*

wake ful (wāk′fəl), **1** not able to sleep. **2** without sleep. **3** watchful. *adjective.*

wak en (wā′kən), wake. *verb.*

walk (wôk), **1** go on foot. In walking, a person always has one foot on the ground. *Walk down to the post office with me.* **2** go over, on, or through: *We walked the length of the trail.* **3** cause to walk; make go slowly: *The rider walked the horse up the hill.* **4** act of walking, especially for pleasure or exercise: *We went for a walk in the country.* **5** accompany or escort in walking; to conduct while walking: *to walk a guest to the door. I walk the dog every morning.* **6** distance to walk: *It is a short walk to the school.* **7** way of walking; gait: *We could tell she was happy from her lively walk.* **8** place for walking: *There are many pretty walks in the park.* **9** way of living: *A doctor and a street cleaner are in different walks of life.* **10** in baseball, a going to first base after the pitcher throws four balls. 1-3,5 *verb,* 4,6-10 *noun.*

walk ie-talk ie (wô′kē tô′kē), a small, portable radio set that can be used to receive and send messages. It is operated by a battery and has an antenna. *noun, plural* **walk ie-talk ies.**

walruses—up to 11 feet (3½ meters) long

wampum

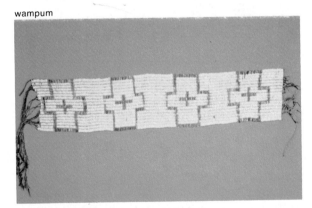

a hat	**i** it	**oi** oil	**ch** child	a in about
ā age	**ī** ice	**ou** out	**ng** long	e in taken
ä far	**o** hot	**u** cup	**sh** she	ə = i in pencil
e let	**ō** open	**u̇** put	**th** thin	o in lemon
ē equal	**ô** order	**ü** rule	**ᵺ** then	u in circus
ėr term			**zh** measure	

with a pattern in color, for pasting on and covering walls. **2** put wallpaper on. **1** *noun,* **2** *verb.*

wal nut (wôl′nut), **1** a rather large, almost round nut with a division between its two halves. The meat of the walnut is eaten by itself or used in cakes and cookies. **2** tree it grows on. **3** wood of this tree. Some kinds of walnut are used in making furniture. *noun.*

wal rus (wôl′rəs), a large sea animal of the arctic regions, resembling a seal but having long tusks. Walruses are hunted for their hides, ivory tusks, and blubber oil. See picture. *noun, plural* **wal rus es** or **wal rus.** [*Walrus* comes from Dutch words meaning "whale" and "horse."]

waltz (wôlts), **1** a smooth, even, gliding dance with three beats to a measure. **2** music for it. **3** dance a waltz. **1,2** *noun, plural* **waltz es;** **3** *verb.*

wam pum (wom′pəm), beads made from shells, formerly used by North American Indians as money and for ornament. See picture. *noun.*

wan (won), **1** pale: *Her face looked wan after her long illness.* **2** faint; weak; looking worn or tired: *The sick boy gave the doctor a wan smile. adjective,* **wan ner, wan nest.**

wand (wond), a slender stick or rod: *The magician waved her wand and a rabbit popped out of the hat. noun.*

wan der (won′dər), **1** move here and there without any special purpose: *We wandered around the fair, looking at exhibits.* **2** go from the right way; stray: *The dog wandered off and got lost. The speaker wandered away from the subject.* **3** not be able to think sensibly: *A high fever can sometimes make a person's mind wander. verb.*

wan der er (won′dər ər), person or animal that wanders. *noun.*

wane (wān), **1** lose size; become smaller gradually: *The moon wanes after it has become full.* **2** lose power, influence, or importance: *Many great empires have waned.* **3** lose strength or intensity: *The light of day wanes in the evening. verb,* **waned, wan ing.**

on the wane, growing less; waning: *Their chances of winning the game were on the wane.*

want (wont), **1** wish for; wish: *We want a new car. I want to become an engineer.* **2** thing desired or needed: *They live simply and have few wants.* **3** lack; be without: *The fund for a new hospital wants only a few thousand dollars of the sum needed.* **4** lack; need; condition of being without something desired or needed: *The plant died from want of water.* **5** need: *That plant wants water.* **6** a lack of food, clothing, or shelter; great poverty: *The old couple are now in want.* **7** need food, clothing, and shelter; be very poor: *Waste not, want not.* **1,3,5,7** *verb,* **2,4,6** *noun.*

wall (wôl), **1** side of a house, room, or other hollow thing. **2** structure of stone, brick, or other material built up to enclose, divide, support, or protect. Cities used to be surrounded by high walls to keep out enemies. **3** anything like a wall in looks or use: *The flood came in a wall of water twelve feet high. A wall of people waited to watch the parade.* **4** enclose, divide, protect, or fill with a wall: *The garden is walled. They walled up the old doorway.* **1-3** *noun,* **4** *verb.*

drive to the wall, make desperate or helpless: *Poverty drove the family to the wall.*

wal let (wol′it), a small, flat leather case for carrying paper money or cards in one's pocket or handbag; billfold. *noun.*

wal lop (wol′əp), **1** beat soundly; thrash. **2** hit very hard. **3** a very hard blow: *The wallop knocked me down.* **4** power to hit very hard blows. **1,2** *verb,* **3,4** *noun.*

wal low (wol′ō), **1** roll about; flounder: *The pigs wallowed in the mud. The boat wallowed helplessly in the stormy sea.* **2** to live contentedly in filth or wickedness. **3** to live or delight in some form of pleasure or manner of life: *wallow in wealth, wallow in sentimentality. verb.*

wall pa per (wôl′pā′pər), **1** paper, usually printed

warbler (definition 1)—5 inches (13 centimeters) long

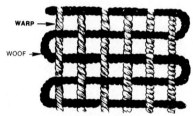

warp (definition 3)

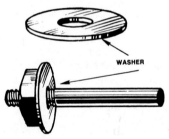

washer (definition 3)

wasps on their nest (about life-size).

want ing (won′ting), **1** lacking; missing: *The machine had some of its parts wanting.* **2** without; less; minus: *a year wanting three days.* **3** not satisfactory; not coming up to a standard or need: *Some people are wanting in courtesy. The vegetables were weighed and found wanting.* 1,3 *adjective,* 2 *preposition.*

wan ton (won′tən), **1** done in a reckless, heartless, or malicious way; done without reason or excuse: *a wanton attack, wanton mischief, wanton cruelty.* **2** not moral: *a sinful and wanton life.* *adjective.*

war (wôr), **1** fighting carried on by armed force between nations or parts of a nation. **2** any fighting or struggle; strife; conflict: *Doctors carry on war against disease.* **3** occupation or art of fighting with weapons: *Soldiers are trained for war.* **4** fight; make war: *Germany warred against France.* **5** used in war; having to do with war; caused by war: *war crimes, war casualties.* 1-3 *noun,* 4 *verb,* **warred, war ring;** 5 *adjective.*

war ble (wôr′bəl), **1** sing in a quick, vibrating, tuneful way: *Birds warbled in the trees.* **2** make a sound something like a bird warbling: *The brook warbled over its rocky bed.* **3** a bird's song or a sound like it. 1,2 *verb,* **war bled, war bling;** 3 *noun.*

war bler (wôr′blər), **1** any of several kinds of small songbirds, often brightly colored. See picture. **2** one that warbles; singer. *noun.*

ward (wôrd), **1** division of a hospital or prison. **2** district of a city or town. **3** person under the care of a guardian or of a court. *noun.*

ward off, keep away or turn aside: *He warded off the blow with his arm.*

-ward, suffix meaning: toward _____: Back*ward* means *toward* the back. Home*ward* means *toward* home.

ward en (wôrd′n), keeper; guard. The person in charge of a prison is called the warden. *noun.*

ward robe (wôrd′rōb′), **1** stock of clothes: *a summer wardrobe.* **2** room, closet, or piece of furniture for holding clothes. *noun.*

ware (wer *or* war), **1 wares,** articles for sale; manufactured goods: *The peddler sold his wares from door to door.* **2** kind of manufactured thing or article for sale: *Household wares are on the third floor at this store.* *noun.*

ware house (wer′hous′ *or* war′hous′), place where goods are kept; storehouse. *noun, plural* **ware hous es** (wer′hou′ziz *or* war′hou′ziz).

war fare (wôr′fer′ *or* wôr′far′), war; fighting. *noun.*

war i ly (wer′ə lē *or* war′ə lē), cautiously; with care: *We climbed warily up the dangerous path.* *adverb.*

war like (wôr′līk′), **1** fit for war; ready for war; fond of war: *warlike tribes.* **2** threatening war: *a warlike speech.* **3** of war; having to do with war: *warlike music. adjective.*

warm (wôrm), **1** more hot than cold; giving forth gentle heat: *a warm fire. She sat in the warm sunshine.* **2** having a feeling of heat: *be warm from* *running.* **3** able to make or keep something warm: *We wear warm clothes in winter.* **4** having or showing lively feelings; enthusiastic: *a warm welcome, a warm friend, a warm heart.* **5** easily excited: *a warm temper.* **6** exciting; lively: *a warm dispute.* **7** suggesting heat. Red, orange, and yellow are called warm colors. **8** make or become warm: *warm a room.* **9** make or become cheered, interested, or friendly: *The speaker warmed to his subject.* 1-7 *adjective,* 8,9 *verb.*

warm-blood ed (wôrm′blud′id), **1** having blood that stays at about the same temperature no matter what the temperature is of the air or water around the animal. Mammals and birds are warm-blooded. The temperature of mammals is about 99 degrees Fahrenheit (37 degrees Celsius), and the temperature of birds is about 104 degrees Fahrenheit (40 degrees Celsius). Cats are warm-blooded; snakes are cold-blooded. **2** with much feeling; eager; ardent. *adjective.*

warmth (wôrmth), **1** being warm: *We enjoyed the warmth of the open fire.* **2** warm feeling: *the warmth of our host's welcome.* **3** liveliness of feelings or emotions: *She spoke with warmth of the natural beauty of the mountains. noun.*

warn (wôrn), **1** give notice to in advance; put on guard against danger, evil, or harm: *The clouds warned us that a storm was coming.* **2** give notice to; inform: *The whistle warned visitors that the ship was ready to sail. verb.*

warn ing (wôr′ning), something that warns; notice given in advance. *noun.*

warp (wôrp), **1** bend or twist out of shape: *This old floor has warped so that it is not level.* **2** make not as it should be; cause not to work as it should: *Prejudice warps our judgment.* **3** the threads running lengthwise in a fabric. The warp is crossed by the woof. See picture. 1,2 *verb,* 3 *noun.*

war path (wôr′path′), way taken by a fighting expedition of North American Indians. *noun, plural* **war paths** (wôr′paτHz′ or wôr′paths′).

on the warpath, 1 ready for war: *The two enemy tribes are on the warpath again.* **2** looking for a fight; angry.

war rant (wôr′ənt), **1** reason which gives a right; authority: *They had no warrant for their action.* **2** a written order giving authority for something: *The police obtained a warrant to search the house.* **3** guarantee; promise; good and sufficient reason: *He had no warrant for his hopes.* **4** justify: *Nothing can warrant such rudeness.* **5** give one's word for; guarantee; promise: *The company warranted the quality of their cameras.* 1-3 *noun,* 4,5 *verb.*

war ri or (wôr′ē ər), a person experienced in fighting battles. *noun.*

war ship (wôr′ship′), ship armed and manned for war. *noun.*

wart (wôrt), **1** a small, hard lump on the skin. **2** a similar lump on a plant. *noun.*

war y (wer′ē or wãr′ē), **1** on one's guard against danger or deception: *a wary fox.* **2** cautious; careful: *We gave wary answers to all of the stranger's questions. adjective,* **war i er, war i est.**

a hat	i it	oi oil	ch child	a in about
ā age	ī ice	ou out	ng long	e in taken
ä far	o hot	u cup	sh she	ə = i in pencil
e let	ō open	u̇ put	th thin	o in lemon
ē equal	ô order	ü rule	₮H then	u in circus
ėr term			zh measure	

wary of, cautious about; careful about: *Be wary of gossip.*

was (woz or wuz). See **be.** *Once there was a queen. I was late to school yesterday. The candy was eaten. verb.*

wash (wosh), **1** clean with water: *wash one's face, wash dishes, wash clothes.* **2** remove (dirt, stains, paint, or the like) by or as by scrubbing with soap and water: *Can you wash that spot out?* **3** wash oneself; wash one's face and hands: *You should always wash before eating.* **4** wash clothes: *I have to wash today.* **5** washing or being washed: *This floor needs a good wash.* **6** quantity of clothes washed or to be washed: *Take the wash from the dryer.* **7** undergo washing without damage: *Some silks wash perfectly.* **8** carry or be carried along or away by water or other liquid: *Wood is often washed ashore by waves. The road washed out during the storm.* **9** wear by water: *The cliffs are being slowly washed away by the waves.* **10** motion, rush, or sound of water: *We listened to the wash of the waves against the boat.* **11** liquid for special use: *a mouth wash, a hair wash.* **12** a thin coating of color or metal. **13** the rough or broken water left just behind by a moving ship. **14** disturbance in air made by an airplane or any of its parts. 1-4,7-9 *verb,* 5,6,10-14 *noun, plural* **wash es.**

wash bowl (wosh′bōl′), bowl for holding water to wash one's face and hands. *noun.*

wash er (wosh′ər), **1** person who washes. **2** machine that washes. **3** a flat ring of metal, rubber, leather, or the like. Washers are used with bolts or nuts, or to make joints tight. See picture. *noun.*

wash ing (wosh′ing), clothes washed or to be washed: *send washing to the laundry. noun.*

washing machine, machine that washes clothes.

Wash ing ton (wosh′ing tən), **1** the capital of the United States. Washington is situated along the Potomac River between Maryland and Virginia. **2** one of the Pacific states of the United States. *noun.* [*Washington* was named in honor of George Washington, the first president of the United States. He lived from 1732 to 1799.]

wash room (wosh′rüm′), room where people can wash themselves, usually a public bathroom. *noun.*

wash stand (wosh′stand′), **1** bowl with pipes and faucets for running water to wash one's face and hands. **2** stand for holding a basin or pitcher for washing. *noun.*

was n't (woz′nt or wuz′nt), was not.

wasp (wosp), insect that has a slender body and a powerful sting. Hornets and yellow jackets are kinds of wasps. See picture. *noun.*

waste (wāst), **1** make poor use of; spend uselessly; fail to get full value or benefit from: *Though they had much work to do, they wasted their time doing nothing.* **2** poor use; useless spending; failure to get the most out of something: *Buying that suit was a waste of money; it is already starting to wear out.* **3** thrown away as useless or worthless: *a pile of waste lumber.* **4** useless or worthless material; stuff to be thrown away. Garbage or sewage is waste. **5** left over; not used: *waste food.* **6** stuff that is left over. Bunches of cotton waste are used to clean machinery. **7** bare; wild. **8** desert; wilderness: *We traveled through treeless wastes. Before us stretched a waste of snow and ice.* **9** wear down little by little; destroy gradually: *The patient was wasted by disease.* **10** wearing down little by little; gradual destruction or decay: *Both waste and repair are constantly going on in our bodies.* **11** spoil; ruin; destroy: *The soldiers wasted the fields and towns of the enemy.* 1,9,11 *verb,* **wast ed, wast ing;** 2,4,6,8,10 *noun,* 3,5,7 *adjective.*
lay waste, destroy; damage greatly: *War laid waste the land.*
waste bas ket (wāst′bas′kit), basket or other container for paper thrown away. *noun.*
waste ful (wāst′fəl), using or spending too much: *to be wasteful of water. adjective.*
waste land (wāst′land′), land that is not cultivated and does not produce anything. *noun.*
watch (woch), **1** look carefully: *The medical students watched while the surgeon performed the operation.* **2** look at: *Are you watching that show on television? We watched the kittens play.* **3** look or wait with care and attention; be very careful: *She watched for a chance to cross the street.* **4** a careful looking; attitude of attention: *Be on the watch for automobiles when you cross the street.* **5** keep guard: *The sentry watched throughout the night.* **6** protecting; guarding: *She kept watch over the house while we were gone.* **7** person or persons kept to guard: *A call for help aroused the night watch.* **8** period of time for guarding: *a watch in the night.* **9** stay awake for some purpose: *The nurse watches with the sick.* **10** staying awake for some purpose. **11** device for telling time, small enough to be carried in a pocket or worn on the wrist. 1-3,5,9 *verb,* 4,6-8,10,11 *noun, plural* **watch es.**
watch dog (woch′dôg′), dog kept to guard property. *noun.*
watch ful (woch′fəl), on the lookout; wide-awake; watching carefully: *You should always be watchful for cars when you cross the street. adjective.*
watch man (woch′mən), person who keeps watch; guard: *A watchman guards the bank at night. noun, plural* **watch men.**
watch tow er (woch′tou′ər), tower from which a person watches for enemies, fires, ships, or any approaching danger. *noun.*
watch word (woch′wėrd′), **1** a secret word that allows a person to pass a guard; password: *We gave the watchword, and the guard let us pass.* **2** motto; slogan: *"Smile!" is our watchword. noun.*

water lily

water buffaloes—5 feet (1½ meters) high at the shoulder

watercolor (definition 3)

wa ter (wô′tər), **1** the liquid that fills the ocean, rivers, lakes, and ponds, and falls from the sky as rain. We use water for drinking and washing. **2** a liquid like water. When you cry, water runs from your eyes. **3** sprinkle or wet with water: *I watered the grass.* **4** supply with water: *Our valley is well watered by rivers and brooks.* **5** weaken by adding water: *It is against the law to sell watered milk.* **6** fill with water; discharge water: *Strong sunlight will make your eyes water. The cake made my mouth water.* **7** done or used in or on water: *water sports.* **8** growing or living in or near water: *water plants, water insects.* 1,2 noun, 3-6 verb, 7,8 adjective.

throw cold water on, discourage: *My parents threw cold water on my plan to camp in the mountains by myself.*

tread water, keep oneself from sinking by moving the feet up and down in a treading motion.

water buffalo, buffalo of Asia, often used to pull loads. See picture.

wa ter col or (wô′tər kul′ər), **1** paint mixed with water instead of oil. **2** art of painting with watercolors. **3** picture made with watercolors. See picture. *noun.*

wa ter course (wô′tər kôrs′), **1** stream of water; river; brook. **2** channel for water: *In the summer many watercourses dry up. noun.*

wa ter fall (wô′tər fôl′), fall of water from a high place. *noun.*

wa ter front (wô′tər frunt′), land at the water's edge, especially the part of a city beside a river, lake, or harbor. *noun.*

water hole, hole in the ground where water collects; small pond; pool.

water lily, a water plant having flat, floating leaves and showy, fragrant flowers. The flowers of the common American water lily are white, or sometimes pink. See picture.

water main, a large pipe for carrying water.

wa ter mel on (wô′tər mel′ən), a large, juicy melon with red or pink pulp and hard green rind. *noun.*

water power, the power from flowing or falling water. Water power can be used to drive machinery and to generate electricity.

wa ter proof (wô′tər prüf′), **1** able to keep water from coming through: *An umbrella should be waterproof.* **2** make waterproof: *These hiking shoes have been waterproofed.* 1 adjective, 2 verb.

wa ter shed (wô′tər shed′), ridge between the regions drained by two different river systems. On one side of a watershed, rivers and streams flow in one direction; on the other side, they flow in the opposite direction. *noun.*

water ski, one of a pair of skis for gliding over water while being towed at the end of a rope by a motorboat.

wa ter-ski (wô′tər skē′), glide over the water on water skis. *verb,* **wa ter-skied, wa ter-ski ing.**

wa ter tight (wô′tər tīt′), **1** so tight that no water can get in or out. Large ships are often divided into watertight compartments by watertight partitions. **2** leaving no opening for misunderstanding or criticism; perfect: *a watertight argument. adjective.*

wa ter way (wô′tər wā′), **1** river, canal, or other body of water that ships can go on. **2** channel for water. *noun.*

water wheel, wheel turned by water and used to do work. The grindstones of grain mills used to be run by water wheels.

wa ter works (wô′tər wèrks′), **1** system of pipes, reservoirs, and pumps for supplying a city with water. **2** building with machinery for pumping water. *noun plural or singular.*

wa ter y (wô′tər ē), **1** full of water; wet: *watery soil.* **2** full of tears; tearful: *watery eyes.* **3** containing too much water: *watery soup.* **4** of water; like water. *adjective,* **wa ter i er, wa ter i est.**

watt (wot), unit of electric power: *My lamp uses 60 watts; my toaster uses 1000 watts. noun.* [The *watt* was named for James Watt, who lived from 1736 to 1819. He was a Scottish engineer and inventor who perfected the steam engine.]

wave (wāv), **1** a moving ridge or swell of water: *The raft rose and fell on the waves.* **2** any movement like this. Light, heat, and sound travel in waves. **3** a swell or sudden increase of some condition or emotion; flood or rush of anything: *A wave of cold weather is sweeping over the country. The announcement brought a wave of enthusiasm.* **4** move as waves do; move up and down; sway: *The tall grass waved in the breeze.* **5** move back and forth: *wave a flag. Wave your hand.* **6** signal or direct by moving the hand or an object back and forth: *The children waved good-by to their parents. The policeman waved the speeding driver to the side of the road.* **7** act of waving: *a wave of the hand.* **8** curve or series of curves: *waves in a person's hair.* **9** give a wavelike form to: *wave one's hair.* 1-3,7,8 noun, 4-6,9 verb, **waved, wav ing.**

wa ver (wā′vər), **1** move back and forth; flutter: *a wavering voice.* **2** flicker: *a wavering light.* **3** be undecided; hesitate: *We are still wavering between a picnic and a trip to the zoo.* **4** become unsteady; begin to give way: *Their determination began to waver.* **5** act of wavering. 1-4 verb, 5 noun.

wav y (wā′vē), having waves or curves: *a wavy line, wavy hair. adjective,* **wav i er, wav i est.**

wax¹ (waks), **1** a yellowish substance made by bees for constructing their honeycomb. Wax is hard when cold, but can be easily shaped when warm. **2** any substance like this. Most of the wax used for candles is really paraffin. **3** substance containing wax for polishing floors, furniture, cars, or the like. **4** rub, stiffen, or polish with wax or something like wax: *We wax that floor once a month.* 1-3 noun, plural **wax es** for 2 and 3; 4 verb.

a hat	**i** it	**oi** oil	**ch** child	⎧ a in about
ā age	**ī** ice	**ou** out	**ng** long	⎪ e in taken
ä far	**o** hot	**u** cup	**sh** she	ə = ⎨ i in pencil
e let	**ō** open	**u̇** put	**th** thin	⎪ o in lemon
ē equal	**ô** order	**ü** rule	**ᴛʜ** then	⎩ u in circus
ėr term			**zh** measure	

wax[2] (waks), **1** grow bigger or greater; increase: *The moon waxes till it becomes full, and then wanes.* **2** become: *The party waxed merry. verb.*

way (wā), **1** manner; style: *I decided to wear my hair in a new way.* **2** means; method: *Scientists are finding new ways to prevent disease.* **3** point; feature; detail; respect: *The plan is bad in several ways.* **4** direction: *Look this way.* **5** coming or going; moving along a course: *Our guide led the way through the museum.* **6** distance: *The sun is a long way off.* **7** means of moving along a course; path: *The scouts found a way through the forest.* **8** space for passing or going ahead: *Automobiles must make way for a fire engine.* **9** habit; custom: *She's always on time; it's her way.* **10** one's wish; will: *Just once I'd like to have my own way.* **11** condition; state: *The patient was in a bad way.* **12** at or to a distance; far: *The cloud of smoke stretched way out to the pier.* 1-11 *noun,* 12 *adverb.*

by way of, 1 by the route of; through: *She went to India by way of Japan.* **2** as; for: *By way of an answer he just nodded.*

give way, 1 retreat; make way; yield. See picture. **2** break down or fail: *The old bridge finally gave way and collapsed.* **3** abandon oneself to emotion: *give way to despair.*

under way, going on; in motion; in progress: *The committee finally got its plan under way.*

way far er (wā′fer′ər *or* wā′far′ər), traveler. *noun.*

way laid (wā′lād′). See **waylay.** *I waylaid him when he entered the meeting. verb.*

way lay (wā′lā′), **1** lie in wait for; attack on the way: *Robin Hood waylaid travelers and robbed them.* **2** stop (a person) on his or her way: *Newspaper reporters waylaid the mayor and asked her many questions. verb,* **way laid, way lay ing.**

way side (wā′sīd′), **1** edge of a road or path: *We ate lunch on the wayside.* **2** along the edge of a road or path: *We slept in a wayside inn.* 1 *noun,* 2 *adjective.*

way ward (wā′wərd), turning from the right way; disobedient; willful: *The wayward student never did any homework. adjective.*

we (wē), **1** the persons speaking: *We are glad to see you.* **2** the person speaking. An author, a ruler, or a judge sometimes uses *we* to mean *I.* pronoun plural.

weak (wēk), lacking strength; not strong: *A weak fort can be easily captured. Long sickness had made the patient weak. A weak law lacks authority. A person with a weak character is easily influenced by others. A weak mind is a feeble one. Weak tea has less flavor than strong tea. adjective.*

weak en (wē′kən), make or become weak or weaker: *You can weaken tea by adding water. We are almost to the top of the mountain; let's not weaken now. verb.*

weak ling (wēk′ling), a weak person or animal. *noun.*

weak ly (wēk′lē), **1** in a weak manner: *He called weakly for help.* **2** weak; feeble; sickly: *a weakly animal.* 1 *adverb,* 2 *adjective,* **weak li er, weak li est.**

weather vane

way, give way (definition 1)—Neither goat would **give way** and let the other pass.

weasel—about 16 inches (40 centimeters) long with the tail

weak ness (wēk'nis), **1** being weak; lack of power, force, or vigor: *Weakness kept him in bed.* **2** a weak point; slight fault: *Putting things off is her weakness.* **3** fondness; a liking that one is a little ashamed of: *a weakness for sweets. noun, plural* **weak ness es.**

wealth (welth), **1** riches; many valuable possessions; property: *people of wealth, the wealth of a city.* **2** all things that have money value; resources: *The wealth of our country includes its mines and forests as well as its factories.* **3** abundance; large quantity: *a wealth of hair, a wealth of words. noun.*

wealth y (wel'thē), having wealth; rich. *adjective,* **wealth i er, wealth i est.**

wean (wēn), **1** accustom (a child or young animal) to food other than its mother's milk. **2** accustom (a person) to do without something; cause to turn away: *to wean someone from a bad habit. verb.*

weap on (wep'ən), **1** any object or instrument used in fighting. Swords, spears, arrows, clubs, guns, cannons, and shields are man-made weapons. Animals use claws, horns, teeth, and stings as weapons. **2** any means of attack or defense: *Drugs are effective weapons against many diseases. noun.*

wear (wer *or* war), **1** have on the body: *wear a coat, wear a beard, wear black, wear a ring.* **2** have; show: *The gloomy old house wore an air of sadness.* **3** wearing; being worn: *Clothing for summer wear is being shown in the shops. This suit has been in constant wear for two years.* **4** things worn or to be worn; clothing: *The store sells children's wear.* **5** last long; give good service: *These jeans wear well. Their friendship wore well.* **6** lasting quality; service: *There is still much wear in these shoes.* **7** use up; be used up: *The pencil is worn to a stub.* **8** damage from use: *The rug shows wear.* **9** make by rubbing, scraping, or washing away: *Walking wore a hole in my shoe.* **10** tire: *They were worn with toil and care.* 1,2,5,7,9,10 *verb,* **wore, worn, wear ing;** 3,4,6,8 *noun.*

wear out, 1 wear or use until no longer fit for use: *These shoes are worn out.* **2** tire out; weary: *She is worn out by too much work.*

wear i ly (wir'ə lē), in a weary manner: *The tired hikers walked slowly and wearily along the road. adverb.*

wear i ness (wir'ē nis), weary condition; tired feeling: *After tramping all day the hikers were overcome with weariness. noun.*

wear i some (wir'ē səm), wearying; tiring; tiresome: *a long, boring, and wearisome tale. adjective.*

wear y (wir'ē), **1** tired: *weary feet, a weary brain.* **2** tiring: *a weary wait.* **3** make or become weary; tire: *Walking all day wearied the tourists.* 1,2 *adjective,* **wear i er, wear i est;** 3 *verb,* **wear ied, wear y ing.**

wea sel (wē'zəl), a small, quick, sly animal with a slender body and short legs. Weasels eat many small animals such as mice, rats, and birds. See picture. *noun.*

a hat	i it	oi oil	ch child	⌈ a in about
ā age	ī ice	ou out	ng long	e in taken
ä far	o hot	u cup	sh she	ə = ⌊ i in pencil
e let	ō open	ů put	th thin	o in lemon
ē equal	ô order	ü rule	ŦH then	u in circus
ėr term			zh measure	

weath er (weŦH'ər), **1** condition of the air at a certain place and time. Weather includes temperature, wind, and moisture information. **2** expose to the weather: *Wood turns gray if weathered for a long time.* **3** go or come through safely: *The ship weathered the storm.* 1 *noun,* 2,3 *verb.*

weath er-beat en (weŦH'ər bēt'n), worn by the wind, rain, and other forces of the weather: *an old farmer's weather-beaten face, a weather-beaten old barn. adjective.*

weath er cock (weŦH'ər kok'), a weather vane, especially one in the shape of a rooster. *noun.*

weath er man (weŦH'ər man'), person who forecasts the weather. *noun, plural* **weath er men.**

weather vane, a flat piece of metal or wood that turns around a rod. Weather vanes are often placed on the tops of buildings; they turn with the wind and show its direction. See picture.

weave (wēv), **1** form (threads or strips) into a thing or fabric. People weave thread into cloth, straw into hats, and reeds into baskets. See picture. **2** make out of thread, strips, or strands of the same material. A spider weaves a web. *She is weaving a rug.* **3** method or pattern of weaving: *Homespun is a cloth of coarse weave.* **4** combine into a whole: *The author wove three plots together into one story.* **5** make by combining parts: *The story he wove was exciting.* **6** go by twisting and turning: *a car weaving in and out of traffic.* 1,2,4-6 *verb,* **wove, wo ven** or **wove, weav ing;** 3 *noun.*

weav er (wē'vər), **1** person who weaves. **2** person whose work is weaving. *noun.*

weave (definition 1)—She **wove** thread into beautiful cloth.

web (definition 1)—a spider web

web (web), **1** something woven. A spider spins a web. See picture. **2** a whole piece of cloth made at one time. **3** anything like a web: *a web of lies.* **4** skin joining the toes of ducks and other swimming birds and some water animals such as frogs and beavers. *noun.*

webbed (webd), **1** formed like a web or with a web. **2** having the toes joined by a web. Ducks have webbed feet. *adjective.*

web-foot ed (web′fut′id), having the toes joined by a web. *adjective.*

wed (wed), **1** marry. **2** unite. *verb*, **wed ded, wed ded** or **wed, wed ding.**

we'd (wēd), **1** we had. **2** we should. **3** we would.

wed ded (wed′id), **1** married. **2** united. **3** devoted. *adjective.*

wed ding (wed′ing), **1** marriage ceremony. **2** an anniversary of it. A golden wedding is the fiftieth anniversary of a marriage. *noun.*

wedge (wej), **1** piece of wood or metal thick at one end and tapering to a thin edge at the other. A wedge is driven in between objects to be separated or into anything to be split. See picture. **2** something shaped like a wedge or used like a wedge: *Wild geese fly in a wedge. Their grand party was an entering wedge into society.* **3** split or separate with a wedge. **4** thrust or pack in tightly; squeeze: *She wedged herself through the narrow opening. The hiker's foot was wedged between the rocks.* **1,2** *noun,* **3,4** *verb,* **wedged, wedg ing.**

wed lock (wed′lok), married life; marriage. *noun.*

Wednes day (wenz′dē), the fourth day of the week; the day after Tuesday. *noun.* [*Wednesday* is from an earlier English word meaning "Woden's day." Woden was one of the most important of the old English gods.]

wee (wē), very small; tiny. *adjective,* **we er, we est.**

weed (wēd), **1** a useless or troublesome plant: *Weeds choked out the vegetables and flowers in the garden.* **2** take weeds out of: *Please weed the garden now.* **1** *noun,* **2** *verb.*

weed out, remove as useless or worthless: *I weeded out the old magazines that I no longer wanted.*

weed y (wē′dē), full of weeds: *a weedy garden. adjective,* **weed i er, weed i est.**

week (wēk), **1** seven days, one after another. **2** time from Sunday through Saturday: *He is away most of the week but comes home on Sundays.* **3** the working days of a seven-day period: *A school week is usually five days. noun.*

week day (wēk′dā′), any day of the week except Sunday or (now often) Saturday. *noun.*

week end (wēk′end′), Saturday and Sunday as a time for recreation or visiting: *a weekend in the country. noun.*

week ly (wēk′lē), **1** of a week; for a week; lasting a week: *Her weekly wage is $100.* **2** done or happening once a week: *She writes a weekly letter to her grandmother.* **3** once each week; every week: *I play tennis weekly.* **4** newspaper or magazine published once a week. **1,2** *adjective,* **3** *adverb,* **4** *noun, plural* **week lies.**

weep (wēp), cry; shed tears: *I wept for joy when I won the award. verb,* **wept, weep ing.**

wee vil (wē′vəl), a small beetle whose larvae eat grain, nuts, fruits, or the stems of leaves. Weevils do much damage to the grain and cotton crops. *noun.*

weigh (wā), **1** find out how heavy a thing is. We weigh persons, cattle, coal, and many other things. **2** measure by weight: *The grocer weighed out five pounds of potatoes.* **3** have as a measure by weight: *I weigh 110 pounds.* **4** bend by weight; burden: *The boughs of the apple tree are weighed down with fruit. They were weighed down with many troubles.* **5** bear down; be a burden: *Don't let this mistake weigh on your mind.* **6** balance in the mind; consider carefully: *He weighs his words before speaking.* **7** lift up (an anchor): *The ship weighed anchor and sailed away. verb.*

weight (wāt), **1** how heavy a thing is; amount a thing weighs: *The dog's weight is 50 pounds.* **2** quality that makes all things tend toward the center of the earth; heaviness: *Gas has hardly any weight.* **3** system of units for expressing weight: *troy weight.* **4** piece of metal used in weighing things: *a pound weight.* **5** a heavy thing or mass: *A weight keeps the papers in place.* **6** load; burden: *The pillars support the weight of the roof. The good news took a weight off my mind.* **7** load down; burden: *to be weighted with troubles.* **8** add weight to; put weight on: *They weighted the elevator too heavily.* **9** influence; importance; value: *the weight of public opinion.* **1-6,9** *noun,* **7,8** *verb.*

weight less (wāt′lis), **1** having little or no weight: *weightless snow.* **2** being free from the pull of gravity. See picture. *adjective.*

weight y (wā′tē), **1** heavy: *a weighty suitcase.* **2** too heavy; burdensome: *It is difficult to prepare for the weighty responsibilities of the presidency.* **3** important; influential: *a weighty speaker. adjective,* **weight i er, weight i est.**

weird (wird), **1** unearthly; mysterious; wild; strange: *We were awakened by a weird shriek.* **2** odd; fantastic; queer: *The shadows made weird figures on the wall. adjective.*

weld (definition 1)—The worker is welding the bow of a ship.

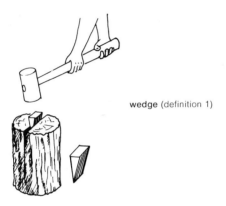

wedge (definition 1)

weightless (definition 2)—Astronauts know what it is like to float in space while in a **weightless** condition.

a hat	i it	oi oil	ch child	a in about
ā age	ī ice	ou out	ng long	e in taken
ä far	o hot	u cup	sh she	ə = i in pencil
e let	ō open	u̇ put	th thin	o in lemon
ē equal	ô order	ü rule	ŦH then	u in circus
ėr term			zh measure	

wel come (wel′kəm), **1** greet kindly: *We always welcome guests at our house.* **2** kind reception: *You will always have a welcome here.* **3** receive gladly: *We welcome new ideas.* **4** gladly received: *a welcome visitor, a welcome letter, a welcome rest from work.* **5** gladly or freely permitted: *You are welcome to pick the flowers.* **6** You say "You are welcome" when someone thanks you. **7** exclamation of friendly greeting: *Welcome, everyone!* 1,3 *verb,* **wel comed, wel com ing;** 2 *noun,* 4-6 *adjective,* 7 *interjection.*

weld (weld), **1** join (pieces of metal) together by bringing the parts that touch to the melting point, so that they flow together and become one piece in cooling. See picture. **2** a welded joint. **3** unite closely: *Working together for a month welded them into a strong team.* 1,3 *verb,* 2 *noun.*

wel fare (wel′fer′ *or* wel′far′), **1** health, happiness, and prosperity; being well; doing well: *My uncle asked about the welfare of everyone in our family.* **2** aid provided by the government to poor or needy people. *noun.*
on welfare, receiving aid from the government because of hardship or need.

well[1] (wel), **1** all right; in a satisfactory, favorable, or good manner: *Is everything going well at school? The job was well done.* **2** good; right: *It is well you came along.* **3** thoroughly: *He knew the lesson well. Shake the medicine well before taking it.* **4** much; to a considerable degree: *The fair brought in well over a hundred dollars.* **5** fairly; reasonably: *I couldn't very well refuse their request.* **6** in good health: *I am very well.* **7** *Well* is sometimes used to show mild surprise or merely to fill in. *Well! Well! Here she is. Well, I'm not sure.* 1,3-5 *adverb,* **bet ter, best;** 2,6 *adjective,* 7 *interjection.*

well[2] (wel), **1** hole dug or bored in the ground to get water, oil, or gas: *I pumped a bucket of water from the well.* **2** spring; fountain; source: *A scholar is a well of ideas.* **3** something like a well in shape or use. The reservoir of a fountain pen is a well. **4** shaft for stairs or elevator, extending through the floors of a building. **5** spring; rise; gush: *Water wells from a spring beneath the rock. Tears welled up in the child's eyes.* 1-4 *noun,* 5 *verb.*

we'll (wel), **1** we shall. **2** we will.

well-bal anced (wel′bal′ənst), **1** rightly balanced, adjusted, or regulated: *A well-balanced diet includes plenty of fruit and vegetables.* **2** sensible; sane: *She has a well-balanced outlook on life.* *adjective.*

well-be haved (wel′bi hāvd′), showing good manners or conduct: *The children were well-behaved. adjective.*

well-be ing (wel′bē′ing), welfare; health and happiness. *noun.*

well-bred (wel′bred′), well brought up; having or showing good manners. *adjective.*

well-known (wel′nōn′), **1** clearly known; familiar: *My feelings are well-known to you.* **2** generally or widely known; famous: *a well-known actor. adjective.*

well-man nered (wel′man′ərd), polite; courteous: *The well-mannered boy always remembered to say "please" and "thank you." adjective.*

well-nigh (wel′nī′), very nearly; almost. *adverb.*

well-to-do (wel′tə dü′), having enough money to live well; prosperous. *adjective.*

welt (welt), streak or ridge made on the skin, often by a blow. *noun.*

wel ter (wel′tər), **1** roll or tumble about; wallow. **2** rolling or tumbling about: *All we saw was a welter of arms, legs, and bodies.* **3** commotion; confusion. 1 *verb,* 2,3 *noun.*

wend (wend), direct (one's way): *We wended our way home. verb.*

went (went). See **go.** *I went home promptly after school. verb.*

wept (wept). See **weep.** *The children wept over the loss of their dog. verb.*

were (wėr). See **be.** *Our plans for a picnic were upset by the rain. If I were rich, I would help the poor. verb.*

we're (wir), we are.

weren't (wėrnt), were not.

wharf

west (west), **1** direction of the sunset. **2** toward the west; farther toward the west: *Walk west three blocks.* **3** from the west: *a warm west wind.* **4** in the west: *The kitchen is in the west wing of the house.* **5** the part of any country toward the west. **6 the West, a** the western part of the United States. **b** the countries in Europe and America as distinguished from those in Asia. 1,5,6 *noun,* 2-4 *adjective,* 2 *adverb.*

west of, farther west than: *Kansas is west of Pennsylvania.*

west er ly (wes′tər lē), **1** toward the west. **2** from the west: *a westerly wind. adjective; adverb.*

west ern (wes′tərn), **1** toward the west. **2** from the west. **3** of or in the west. **4 Western, a** of or in the western part of the United States. **b** of or in the countries in Europe or America. **5** story, motion picture, or television show about life in the western part of the United States, especially cowboy life. 1-4 *adjective,* 5 *noun.*

West Indies, islands in the Atlantic Ocean between Florida and South America.

West Virginia, one of the southeastern states of the United States. [*West Virginia* got its name from the state of Virginia. After the beginning of the Civil War, the western part of the state of Virginia formed its own government. It became a separate state in 1863.]

west ward (west′wərd), toward the west; west: *I walked westward. The orchard is on the westward slope of the hill. adverb, adjective.*

west wards (west′wərdz), westward. *adverb.*

wet (wet), **1** covered or soaked with water or other liquid: *wet hands, a wet sponge.* **2** watery: *eyes wet with tears.* **3** not yet dry: *Don't touch wet paint.* **4** make wet: *Wet the cloth and wipe off the window.* **5** rainy: *wet weather.* **6** wetness; rain: *Come in out of the wet.* 1-3,5 *adjective,* **wet ter, wet test;** 4 *verb,* **wet** or **wet ted, wet ting;** 6 *noun.*

we've (wēv), we have.

whack (hwak), **1** a sharp, resounding blow. **2** strike with such a blow: *The batter whacked at the ball and hit it out of the park.* 1 *noun,* 2 *verb.*

whale (hwāl), **1** animal shaped like a huge fish and living in the sea. Oil from whales used to be burned in lamps. See picture. **2** hunt and catch whales. 1 *noun, plural* **whales** or **whale;** 2 *verb,* **whaled, whal ing.**

whale bone (hwāl′bōn′), an elastic, horny substance growing in place of teeth in the upper jaw of certain whales. Thin strips of whalebone were used for stiffening in clothing. *noun.*

whal er (hwā′lər), **1** hunter of whales. **2** ship used for hunting and catching whales. *noun.*

wharf (hwôrf), platform built on the shore or out from the shore, beside which ships can load and unload. See picture. *noun, plural* **wharves** (hwôrvz) or **wharfs.**

what (hwot), **1** *What* is used in asking questions about persons or things. *What is your name? What time is it?* **2** that which: *I know what you mean. Put back what money is left.* **3** whatever; anything that; any that: *Do what you please. Take what supplies you will need.* **4** how much; how: *What does it matter?* **5** partly: *What with the wind and what with the rain, our walk was spoiled.* **6** *What* is often used to show surprise, liking, dislike, or other feeling. *What a pity! What happy times! What! Are you late again?* 1-3 *pronoun,* 1-3,6 *adjective,* 4-6 *adverb,* 6 *interjection.*

what ev er (hwot ev′ər), **1** anything that: *Do whatever you like.* **2** any (person or thing) that; any: *Take whatever books you need.* **3** no matter who; at all: *Any person whatever can tell you the way.* **4** no matter what: *Do it, whatever happens. Whatever excuse you make will not be accepted.* **5** *Whatever* is used for emphasis instead of *what. Whatever do you mean?* 1,4,5 *pronoun,* 2-4 *adjective.*

what's (hwots), **1** what is: *What's the latest news?* **2** what has: *What's been going on here lately?*

wheat (hwēt), the grain of a kind of cereal grass, or the plant that it grows on. The grain is used to make flour. See picture. *noun.*

whee dle (hwē′dl), **1** persuade by flattery, smooth words, or caresses; coax: *The children wheedled their parents into letting them go to the picnic.* **2** get by wheedling: *They finally wheedled the secret out of me. verb,* **whee dled, whee dling.**

wheel (hwēl), **1** a round frame that turns on its center. **2** anything round like a wheel or moving like one. A ship's wheel is used in steering. Clay is shaped into dishes on a potter's wheel. **3** turn: *The rider wheeled her horse about.* **4** move on wheels: *I wheeled the load of bricks on the wheelbarrow.* **1,2** *noun,* **3,4** *verb.*

at the wheel, at the steering wheel of an automobile.

wheel bar row (hwēl′bar′ō), a small vehicle which has one wheel and two handles. A wheelbarrow holds a small load which one person can push. *noun.*

wheel ie (hwē′lē), a stunt in which a moving bicycle, motorcycle, or car is balanced only on its back wheel or wheels. *noun.*

wheeze (hwēz), **1** breathe with difficulty and a whistling sound. **2** a whistling sound caused by difficult breathing. **3** make a sound like this: *The old engine wheezed.* **1,3** *verb,* **wheezed, wheez ing; 2** *noun.*

whelk (hwelk), a small animal with a spiral shell. One kind is used for food in Europe. See picture. *noun.*

whelp (hwelp), puppy or cub; young dog, wolf, bear, lion, tiger, or seal. *noun.*

when (hwen), **1** at what time: *When does school close?* **2** at the time that: *Stand up when your name is called.* **3** at any time that: *The dog comes when it is called.* **4** at which time; and then: *We had just started on our walk when it began to rain.* **5** although: *We have only three books when we need five.* **6** what time; which time: *Since when have they had a car?* **1** *adverb,* **2-5** *conjunction,* **6** *pronoun.*

when ev er (hwen ev′ər), when; at whatever time; at any time that: *Please come whenever you wish. You may come whenever possible. conjunction, adverb.*

where (hwer *or* hwar), **1** in what place; at what place: *Where do you live? Where is she?* **2** to what place: *Where are you going?* **3** from what place: *Where did you get that story?* **4** what place: *Where did it come from?* **5** in which; at which: *That is the house where I was born.* **6** to which: *I know the place where he is going.* **7** in what way; in what respect: *Where is the harm in trying?* **8** in the place in which; at the place at which: *Your coat is where you left it.* **1-3,7** *adverb,* **4** *noun,* **5,6,8** *conjunction.*

where a bouts (hwer′ə bouts′ *or* hwar′ə bouts′), **1** where; near what place: *Whereabouts are my books?* **2** place where a person or thing is: *Do you know the whereabouts of the cottage?* **1** *adverb, conjunction,* **2** *noun.*

a hat	i it	oi oil	ch child	a in about
ā age	ī ice	ou out	ng long	e in taken
ä far	o hot	u cup	sh she	ə = { i in pencil
e let	ō open	u̇ put	th thin	o in lemon
ē equal	ô order	ü rule	₮н then	u in circus
ėr term			zh measure	

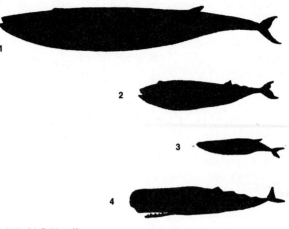

whale (definition 1)
1. blue whale—about 90 feet (27 meters) long
2. humpback whale—about 45 feet (14 meters) long
3. Minke whale—about 28 feet (8 meters) long
4. sperm whale—about 50 feet (15 meters) long

wheat—two kinds of wheat

whelks—The shells are 2 to 3 inches (5 to 8 centimeters) long.

where as (hwer az′ or hwar az′), **1** but; while; on the contrary: *Some children like school, whereas others do not.* **2** considering that; since: *"Whereas the people of the colonies have been grieved and burdened with taxes . . . ."* *conjunction.*

where by (hwer bī′ or hwar bī′), by what; by which: *There is no other way whereby she can do it.* *adverb, conjunction.*

where on (hwer ôn′ or hwar ôn′), on which; on what: *Summer cottages occupy the land whereon the old farmhouse stood.* *adverb, conjunction.*

where up on (hwer′ə pôn′ or hwar′e pôn′), **1** upon what; upon which. **2** at which; after which. *adverb, conjunction.*

wher ev er (hwer ev′ər or hwar ev′ər), where; to whatever place; in whatever place: *Sit wherever you like. Wherever did he go?* *conjunction, adverb.*

whet (hwet), **1** sharpen by rubbing: *whet a knife.* **2** make keen or eager: *The smell of food whetted my appetite. An exciting story whets your interest.* *verb,* **whet ted, whet ting.**

wheth er (hweŦH′ər), **1** *Whether* is used in expressing choices. *It matters little whether we go or stay. He does not know whether to work or rest.* **2** if: *He asked whether he might be excused.* **3** either: *Whether sick or well, she is always cheerful.* *conjunction.*

whet stone (hwet′stōn′), stone for sharpening knives or tools. *noun.*

whew (hwyü), word expressing surprise or dismay: *Whew! it's cold! interjection.*

whey (hwā), the watery part of milk that separates from the curd when milk sours or when cheese is made. *noun.*

which (hwich), **1** *Which* is used in asking questions about persons or things. *Which is the best plan? Which book do you want to read?* **2** *Which* is also used in connecting a group of words with some other word in the sentence. *Read the book which you have. Be careful which way you turn.* **3** the one that; any that: *Here are three boxes. Choose which you like best.* **1-3** *pronoun,* **1,2** *adjective.*

which ev er (hwich ev′ər), **1** any one; any that: *Take whichever you want. Buy whichever hat you like.* **2** no matter which: *Whichever you choose will be fine. Whichever side wins, I shall be satisfied.* *pronoun, adjective.*

whiff (hwif), **1** a slight puff of air, smoke, or odor: *a whiff of smoke.* **2** blow; puff. **1** *noun,* **2** *verb.*

while (hwīl), **1** time; space of time: *They kept us waiting a long while. The postman came a while ago.* **2** during the time that; in the time that; as: *While I was speaking, he said nothing. Summer is pleasant while it lasts.* **3** although: *While I like the color of the hat, I do not like its shape.* **4** pass or spend in some easy or pleasant manner: *The children while away many afternoons on the beach.* **1** *noun,* **2,3** *conjunction,* **4** *verb,* **whiled, whil ing.**

worth one's while, worth one's time, attention, or effort: *If you help me with the painting, I'll make it worth your while—I'll pay you ten dollars.*

whim (hwim), a sudden fancy or notion: *I had a whim to take a plane somewhere. noun.*

whim per (hwim′pər), **1** cry with low, broken sounds, in the way that a sick child or dog does. **2** a whimpering cry. **3** complain in a cross, childish way; whine. **1,3** *verb,* **2** *noun.*

whim si cal (hwim′zə kəl), having many odd notions or fancies; fanciful; odd: *a whimsical drawing.* See picture. *adjective.*

whine (hwīn), **1** make a low, complaining cry or sound: *The dog whined to go out with us.* **2** a low, complaining cry or sound. **3** complain in a cross, childish way: *Some people are always whining about trifles.* **4** say with a whine. **1,3,4** *verb,* **whined, whin ing; 2** *noun.*

whin ny (hwin′ē), **1** sound that a horse makes. **2** make such a sound. **1** *noun, plural* **whin nies; 2** *verb,* **whin nied, whin ny ing.**

whip (hwip), **1** thing to strike or beat with, usually a stick or handle with a lash at the end. **2** strike; beat: *The jockey whipped the horse to make it go faster.* **3** move, put, or pull quickly and suddenly: *She whipped off her coat.* **4** defeat in a fight or contest: *She whipped her opponent in the election.* **5** beat (cream, eggs, or the like) to a froth. **1** *noun,* **2-5** *verb,* **whipped, whip ping.**

whip poor will (hwip′ər wil′), a North American bird whose call sounds somewhat like its name. It is active at night or twilight. See picture. *noun.*

whir (hwėr), **1** noise that sounds like whir-r-r: *the whir of machinery.* **2** move quickly with such a noise: *The motor whirs.* **1** *noun,* **2** *verb,* **whirred, whir ring.**

whirl (hwėrl), **1** turn or swing round and round; spin: *The leaves whirled in the wind.* **2** move round and round: *whirl a lasso. We whirled about the room.* **3** move or carry quickly: *We were whirled away in an airplane.* **4** a whirling movement: *The dancer suddenly made a whirl.* **5** a dizzy or confused condition: *My thoughts are in a whirl.* **1-3** *verb,* **4,5** *noun.*

whirl pool (hwėrl′pül′), current of water whirling round and round rapidly and violently. *noun.*

whirl wind (hwėrl′wind′), current of air whirling violently round and round; whirling storm of wind. *noun.*

whisk (hwisk), **1** sweep or brush from a surface: *She whisked the crumbs from the table.* **2** a quick sweep: *He brushed away the dirt with a few whisks of the broom.* **3** move quickly: *The mouse whisked into its hole. I whisked the letter out of sight.* **4** a light, quick movement. **5** beat (cream, eggs, or the like) to a froth. **1,3,5** *verb,* **2,4** *noun.*

whisk broom, a small broom for brushing clothes.

whisk er (hwis′kər), **1** one of the hairs growing on a man's face. **2 whiskers,** the hair or part of a beard that grows on a man's cheeks. **3** a long, stiff hair growing near the mouth of a cat, rat, or other animal. *noun.*

whis key (hwis′kē), a strong alcoholic drink made from grain. Some kinds of whiskey are half alcohol. *noun, plural* **whis keys.**

whis ky (hwis′kē), whiskey. *noun, plural* **whis kies.**

whippoorwill—about 10 inches (25 centimeters) long

a hat	**i** it	**oi** oil	**ch** child	⎧ a in about
ā age	**ī** ice	**ou** out	**ng** long	⎪ e in taken
ä far	**o** hot	**u** cup	**sh** she	**ə** = ⎨ i in pencil
e let	**ō** open	**u̇** put	**th** thin	⎪ o in lemon
ē equal	**ô** order	**ü** rule	**ŦH** then	⎩ u in circus
ėr term			**zh** measure	

whis per (hwis′pər), **1** speak very softly and low. **2** a very soft, low spoken sound. **3** speak to in a whisper: *I whispered to my friend in class.* **4** tell secretly or privately: *It is whispered that their business is failing.* **5** something told secretly or privately: *No whisper about having a new teacher has come to our ears.* **6** make a soft, rustling sound: *The wind whispered in the pines.* **7** a soft, rustling sound: *The wind was so gentle that we could hear the whisper of the leaves.* 1,3,4,6 *verb,* 2,5,7 *noun.*

whis tle (hwis′əl), **1** make a clear, shrill sound: *The girl whistled and her dog ran to her quickly.* **2** sound made by whistling. **3** instrument for making whistling sounds. The whistles used by factories, ships, and trains to signal or to warn are tubes through which air or steam is blown. **4** blow a whistle: *The policeman whistled for the automobile to stop. The engineer whistled to warn the people at the train crossing.* **5** produce by whistling: *whistle a tune.* **6** move with a shrill sound: *The wind whistled around the house.* 1,4-6 *verb,* **whis tled, whis tling;** 2,3 *noun.*

white (hwīt), **1** the color of snow, salt, or the paper on which this book is printed. **2** having this color: *My grandparents have white hair.* **3** part that is white or whitish: *Take the whites of four eggs.* **4** pale: *They turned white with fear.* **5** light-colored:

whimsical

a white wine, white meat. **6** having a light-colored skin. **7** person who has light-colored skin. **8** spotless; pure; innocent. 1,3,7 *noun,* 2,4-6,8 *adjective,* **whit er, whit est.**

white blood cell, a colorless cell in the blood that destroys disease germs.

white cap (hwīt′kap′), wave with a foaming white crest. *noun.*

white flag, a plain white flag that means "We have quit fighting," or "We give up."

White House, 1 the official residence of the President of the United States, in Washington, D.C. **2** office, authority, or opinion of the President of the United States.

whit en (hwīt′n), make white; become white: *Sunshine helps to whiten clothes. They whitened when they heard the bad news. verb.*

white wash (hwīt′wosh′), **1** liquid for whitening walls, woodwork, or other surfaces. Whitewash is usually made of lime and water. **2** whiten with whitewash. **3** cover up the faults or mistakes of. 1 *noun,* 2,3 *verb.*

whith er (hwiŦH′ər), where; to what place; to which place. *adverb, conjunction.*

whit ish (hwī′tish), somewhat white. *adjective.*

whit tle (hwit′l), **1** cut shavings or chips from (wood) with a knife, usually for fun. **2** cut or shape with a knife: *The class learned how to whittle animals from wood. verb,* **whit tled, whit tling.**

whiz (hwiz), **1** a humming or hissing sound. **2** move or rush with such a sound: *An arrow whizzed past his head.* 1 *noun, plural* **whiz zes;** 2 *verb,* **whizzed, whiz zing.**

who (hü), **1** *Who* is used in asking questions about persons. *Who goes there? Who is your friend? Who told you?* **2** *Who* is also used in connecting a group of words with some word that refers to a person in the sentence. *The girl who spoke is my best friend. We saw people who were working in the fields.* **3** the person that; any person that; one that: *Who is not for us is against us. pronoun.*

whoa (hwō *or* wō), stop: *"Whoa there!" said the cowgirl to her horse. interjection.*

who'd (hüd), **1** who had. **2** who would.

who ev er (hü ev′ər), **1** who; any person that: *Whoever wants the book may have it.* **2** no matter who: *Whoever else leaves you, I won't. pronoun.*

whole (hōl), **1** having all its parts; complete: *They gave us a whole set of dishes.* **2** full; entire: *He worked the whole day. We ate the whole melon.* **3** all of a thing; the total: *Three thirds make a whole.* **4** thing complete in itself; a system: *the complex whole of civilization.* **5** not injured or broken: *I came out of the bicycle accident with a whole skin.* **6** in one piece: *The dog swallowed the meat whole.* **7** well; healthy. 1,2,5-7 *adjective,* 3,4 *noun.*

whole heart ed (hōl′här′tid), earnest; sincere; hearty; cordial: *The school gave the team its wholehearted support. adjective.*

whole number, a number such as 1, 2, 3, 4, 5, and so on, which is not a fraction or a mixed number. 15 and 106 are whole numbers; $^1/_2$ and $^7/_8$ are fractions; $1^3/_8$ and $23^2/_3$ are mixed numbers.

whole sale (hōl′sāl′), **1** sale of goods in large quantities, usually to storekeepers or others who will in turn sell them to users: *Our grocer buys at wholesale and sells at retail.* **2** in large lots or quantities: *The wholesale price of this coat is $30; the retail price is $50.* **3** selling in large quantities: *a wholesale fruit business.* **4** sell in large quantities: *They wholesale these jackets at $10 each.* 1 *noun,* 2,3 *adjective,* 2 *adverb,* 4 *verb,* **whole saled, whole sal ing.**

whole some (hōl′səm), **1** healthful; good for the health: *Milk is a wholesome food.* **2** healthy-looking; suggesting health: *a clean, wholesome face.* **3** good for the mind or morals: *The students had a wholesome interest in learning. adjective.*

whole-wheat (hōl′hwēt′), **1** made of the entire wheat kernel: *whole-wheat flour.* **2** made from whole-wheat flour: *whole-wheat bread. adjective.*

who'll (hül), **1** who will. **2** who shall.

whol ly (hō′lē), completely; entirely; totally: *The patient was wholly cured. adverb.*

whom (hüm), what person; which person. *Whom is a form of who, just as him is a form of he. Whom do you like best? He does not know whom to believe. The girl to whom I spoke is my cousin. pronoun.*

whoop (hüp), **1** a loud cry or shout: *The winner gave a whoop of joy.* **2** shout loudly. **3** the loud, gasping sound a person with whooping cough makes after a fit of coughing. **4** make this noise. 1,3 *noun,* 2,4 *verb.*

whoop ing cough (hüp′ing kôf′), a disease most often of children that causes fits of coughing that end with a loud, gasping sound. Unless you are vaccinated against whooping cough, you can catch the disease if you are around someone who has it.

whooping crane, a large white crane having a loud, hoarse cry. It is now almost extinct.

who's (hüz), **1** who is. **2** who has.

whose (hüz), of whom; of which: *The girl whose work got the prize is the youngest in her class. Whose book is this? pronoun.*

why (hwī), **1** for what reason: *Why did the baby cry? I do not know why they are late.* **2** because of which: *That is the reason why we left.* **3** *Why* is sometimes used to show surprise, doubt, or just to fill in, without adding any important meaning to what is said. *Why it's all gone! Why, yes, I will if you wish.* 1 *adverb,* 1,2 *conjunction,* 3 *interjection.*

wick (wik), cord of twisted thread on an oil lamp or candle. When the wick is lit, it draws the oil or melted wax up to be burned. *noun.*

wick ed (wik′id), **1** bad; evil; sinful: *a wicked person, wicked deeds.* **2** mischievous; playfully sly: *a wicked smile.* **3** unpleasant; severe: *A wicked*

snowstorm swept through the northern part of the state. *adjective.*

wick ed ness (wik′id nis), **1** sin; being wicked. **2** a wicked thing or act. *noun, plural* **wick ed ness es.**

wick er (wik′ər), **1** a slender, easily bent branch or twig. **2** twigs, branches, or any slender, easily bent material that is woven together. Wicker is used in making baskets and furniture. **3** made of wicker. 1,2 *noun,* 3 *adjective.*

wick et (wik′it), **1** a small door or gate: *The big door has a wicket in it.* **2** a small window: *Buy your tickets at this wicket.* **3** (in croquet) a wire arch stuck in the ground to knock the ball through. **4** (in cricket) either of the two sets of sticks that one side tries to hit with the ball. *noun.*

wide (wīd), **1** filling much space from side to side; not narrow; broad: *a wide street. The ship sailed across the wide ocean. They went forth into the wide world.* **2** extending a certain distance from side to side: *The door is three feet wide.* **3** having great range; including many different things: *A trip around the world gives wide experience. Wide reading gives wide understanding of other times and places.* **4** far open: *The child stared with wide eyes.* **5** to the full extent: *Open your mouth wide. The gates stand wide open.* **6** far from a named point or object: *The club raised little money; it was wide of its goal. The shot was wide of the mark.* 1-4,6 *adjective,* **wid er, wid est;** 5 *adverb.*

wide-a wake (wīd′ə wāk′), **1** fully awake; with the eyes wide open. **2** alert; keen; knowing: *A watchdog must be a wide-awake guard against danger. adjective.*

wide-eyed (wīd′īd′), with the eyes wide open: *The children watched the baby rabbits with wide-eyed interest. adjective.*

wid en (wīd′n), make or become wide or wider: *We widened the path through the forest. The river widens as it flows. verb.*

wide spread (wīd′spred′), **1** spread widely: *widespread wings.* **2** spread over a wide space: *a widespread flood.* **3** occurring in many places or among many persons far apart: *a widespread belief. adjective.*

wid ow (wid′ō), **1** woman whose husband is dead and who has not married again. **2** make a widow of: *She was widowed when she was only thirty years old.* 1 *noun,* 2 *verb.*

wid ow er (wid′ō ər), man whose wife is dead and who has not married again. *noun.*

width (width), **1** how wide a thing is; distance across; breadth: *The room is 12 feet in width.* **2** piece of a certain width: *Two widths of cloth will make the curtains. noun.*

wield (wēld), hold and use; manage; control: *The worker wielded a hammer. A writer wields the pen. The people wield the power in a democracy. verb.*

wie ner (wē′nər), frankfurter. *noun.* [*Wiener* comes from German words meaning "Viennese sausage." Vienna is an Austrian city.]

wife (wīf), a married woman. *noun, plural* **wives.** [*Wife* is from an earlier English word, which originally meant "woman."]

willful (definition 1)—The willful donkey would not obey its owner.

a hat	i it	oi oil	ch child	(a in about
ā age	ī ice	ou out	ng long	e in taken
ä far	o hot	u cup	sh she	ə = { i in pencil
e let	ō open	u̇ put	th thin	o in lemon
ē equal	ô order	ü rule	₮H then	(u in circus
ėr term			zh measure	

5 not checked; not held back: *a wild rush for the ball.* **6** violent: *Wild waves came roaring onto the shore.* **7** rash; crazy: *a wild scheme.* **8** in a wild manner; to a wild degree. 1,2,4-7 *adjective,* 3 *noun,* 8 *adverb.*

wild cat (wīld′kat′), a wild animal like a common cat, but larger. A lynx is one kind of wildcat. *noun.*

wil der ness (wil′dər nis), a wild place; region with no people living in it. *noun, plural* **wil der ness es.**

wild fire (wīld′fīr′), a fire that is hard to put out. *noun.*
like wildfire, very rapidly: *The news spread like wildfire.*

wild fowl, birds ordinarily hunted, such as wild ducks or geese, partridges, quails, and pheasants.

wild life (wīld′līf′), wild animals and plants: *The campers saw many kinds of wildlife. noun.*

wile (wīl), **1** trick to deceive; cunning way: *The witch by her wiles persuaded the prince to go with her.* **2** coax; lure; entice: *The sunshine wiled me from my work.* 1 *noun,* 2 *verb,* **wiled, wil ing.**

wil ful (wil′fəl), willful. *adjective.*

will[1] (wil), **1** am going to; is going to; are going to: *He will come tomorrow.* **2** am willing to; is willing to; are willing to: *I will go if you do.* **3** wish; desire: *We cannot always do as we will.* **4** be able to; can: *The pail will hold four gallons.* **5** must: *Don't argue with me; you will do it at once!* **6** do often or usually: *I will read for hours at a time. verb, past tense* **would.**

will[2] (wil), **1** power of the mind to decide and do: *A good leader must have a strong will.* **2** decide by using this power; use the will: *She willed to keep awake.* **3** determine; decide: *Fate has willed it otherwise.* **4** purpose; determination: *the will to live.* **5** wish; desire: *"Thy will be done."* **6** a legal statement of a person's wishes about what shall be done with property left after the person's death. **7** give by such a statement: *They willed all their property to their children.* **8** feeling toward another: *Most of us feel good will toward people we like and ill will toward people we dislike.* 1,4-6,8 *noun,* 2,3,7 *verb.*

will ful (wil′fəl), **1** wanting or taking one's own way; stubborn. See picture. **2** intended; done on purpose: *willful murder, willful waste. adjective.* Also spelled **wilful.**

will ing (wil′ing), **1** ready; consenting: *He is willing to wait.* **2** cheerfully ready: *willing obedience. adjective.*

wil low (wil′ō), **1** kind of tree or shrub with tough, slender branches and narrow leaves. The branches of most willows bend easily and are used to make furniture and baskets. **2** its wood. *noun.*

wigwam—Part of the wigwam is cut away to show the framework.

wig (wig), an artificial covering of natural or false hair for the head. English judges and lawyers wear wigs in court. *noun.*

wig gle (wig′əl), **1** wriggle; move with short, quick movements from side to side: *The puppy wiggled out of my arms.* **2** such a movement. 1 *verb,* **wig gled, wig gling;** 2 *noun.*

wig wag (wig′wag′), **1** move back and forth. **2** signal by movements of arms, flags, or lights, according to a code. **3** such signaling. 1,2 *verb,* **wig wagged, wig wag ging;** 3 *noun.*

wig wam (wig′wom), hut of poles covered with bark, mats, or skins, made by certain North American Indians. See picture. *noun.*

wild (wīld), **1** living or growing in the forests or fields; not tamed; not cultivated: *The tiger is a wild animal. The daisy is a wild flower.* **2** with no people living in it: *Airplanes now fly from California to Europe over the wild region of the far north.* **3** wilds, wild country. **4** not civilized; savage: *He is reading about the wild tribes of ancient times in Europe.*

windmill in Nantucket, Massachusetts, around 1875

wintry

wilt (wilt), **1** become limp and drooping; wither: *Flowers wilt when they do not get enough water.* **2** lose strength and vigor. *verb.*

wil y (wī′lē), tricky; cunning; crafty; sly: *a wily thief. The wily fox got away. adjective,* **wil i er, wil i est.**

win (win), **1** be successful over others; get victory or success: *The tortoise won over the hare in the end. We all hope our team will win.* **2** get victory or success in: *He won the race.* **3** success; victory: *We had five wins and no defeats.* **4** get by effort, ability, or skill; gain: *win fame, win a prize.* **5** gain the favor of; persuade: *The speaker soon won his audience. She has completely won the other scientists over to her opinion.* **6** get to; reach, often by effort: *win the summit of a mountain.* 1,2,4-6 *verb,* **won, win ning;** 3 *noun.*

wince (wins), **1** draw back suddenly; flinch slightly: *I winced when the dentist's drill touched my tooth.* **2** act of wincing: *The dentist saw my wince and stopped drilling for a moment.* 1 *verb,* **winced, winc ing;** 2 *noun.*

winch (winch), machine for lifting or pulling, turned by hand with a crank or by an engine. See picture. *noun, plural* **winch es.**

wind¹ (wind), **1** air in motion. The wind varies in force from a slight breeze to a strong gale. **2** a strong wind; gale: *Winds blowing at ninety miles an hour toppled a tree on our roof.* **3** breath; power of breathing: *A runner needs good wind.* **4** put out of breath; cause difficulty in breathing: *Walking up the steep hill winded the hiker.* 1-3 *noun,* 4 *verb.*

get wind of, find out about; get a hint of: *Don't let Mother get wind of our plans for a surprise party on her birthday.*

wind² (wīnd), **1** move this way and that; go in a crooked way; change direction; turn: *A brook winds through the woods. We wound our way through the narrow streets.* **2** fold, wrap, or place about something: *She wound her arms around her new puppy.* **3** cover with something put, wrapped, or folded around: *The patient's arm was wound with bandages.* **4** roll into a ball or on a spool: *We took turns winding yarn. Thread comes wound on spools.* **5** bend; turn; twist: *The road takes a wind to the south.* **6** twist or turn around something: *The vine winds around a pole.* **7** make (some machine) go by turning some part of it: *wind a clock.* 1-4,6,7 *verb,* **wound, wind ing;** 5 *noun.*

wind up, 1 end; settle; conclude: *The committee wound up its meeting in time for dinner.* **2** in baseball, make a rocking movement of the arms and body just before pitching the ball.

wind break (wind′brāk′), shelter from the wind. *We pitched our tent next to the stone wall, so that it would serve as a windbreak. noun.*

wind fall (wind′fôl′), **1** fruit blown down by the wind. **2** an unexpected piece of good luck. *noun.*

wind ing (wīn′ding), bending; turning: *narrow, winding streets. adjective.*

wind instrument, a musical instrument sounded by blowing air into it. Horns, flutes, and trombones are wind instruments.

wing (definition 7)—The bird **winged** its way to the south.

a hat	**i** it	**oi** oil	**ch** child	(a in about
ā age	**ī** ice	**ou** out	**ng** long	e in taken
ä far	**o** hot	**u** cup	**sh** she	ə = { i in pencil
e let	**ō** open	**ů** put	**th** thin	o in lemon
ē equal	**ô** order	**ü** rule	**₮H** then	(u in circus
ėr term			**zh** measure	

winch

wind lass (wind′ləs), machine for pulling or lifting things. The windlass is a kind of winch used to hoist water from a well or an anchor out of the water. *noun, plural* **wind lass es.**

wind mill (wind′mil′), mill or machine worked by the action of the wind upon a wheel of vanes or sails mounted on a tower. Windmills are mostly used to pump water. See picture. *noun.*

win dow (win′dō), **1** opening in a wall or roof to let in light or air. **2** such an opening with its frame and glass. *noun.* [*Window* comes from old Norse words meaning "wind" and "eye."]

win dow pane (win′dō pān′), piece of glass in a window. *noun.*

win dow sill (win′dō sil′), piece of wood or stone across the bottom of a window. *noun.*

wind pipe (wind′pīp′), passage by which air is carried from the throat to the lungs; trachea. *noun.*

wind shield (wind′shēld′), sheet of glass to keep off the wind. Automobiles have windshields. *noun.*

wind storm (wind′stôrm′), storm with much wind but little or no rain. *noun.*

wind y (win′dē), **1** having much wind: *a windy* street, windy weather. **2** made of wind; empty: *windy talk. adjective,* **wind i er, wind i est.**

wine (wīn), **1** an alcoholic drink made from the fermented juice of grapes. **2** the fermented juice of other fruits or plants: *currant wine, dandelion wine. noun.*

wing (wing), **1** one of the movable parts of a bird, insect, or bat used in flying, or a similar part in a bird or insect that does not fly. Birds have one pair of wings; insects have usually two pairs. **2** anything like a wing in shape or use: *the wings of an airplane.* **3** part that sticks out from the main part or body, especially the part of a building that sticks out sideways from the main part: *The house has a wing at each side.* **4** either of the side portions of an army or fleet ready for battle. **5** either of the spaces to the right or left of the stage in a theater. **6** player on either the right or left side of the center in hockey. **7** fly. See picture. **8** wound in the wing or arm: *The bullet winged the bird but did not kill it.* 1-6 *noun,* 7,8 *verb.*
on the wing, in flight.

winged (wingd *or* wing′id), **1** having wings. **2** swift; rapid: *a winged messenger. adjective.*

wing spread (wing′spred′), distance between the tips of the wings when they are spread. *noun.*

wink (wingk), **1** close the eyes and open them again quickly: *The bright light made me wink.* **2** close and open one eye on purpose as a hint or signal: *I winked at my sister to keep still.* **3** winking. **4** twinkle: *The stars winked.* **5** a very short time: *quick as a wink.* 1,2,4 *verb,* 3,5 *noun.*
wink at, pretend not to see: *My parents knew I came home past my bedtime, but they winked at it.*

win ner (win′ər), person or thing that wins: *The winner of the contest got a prize. noun.*

win ning (win′ing), **1** victorious; successful: *a winning team.* **2** charming; attractive: *a winning smile.* **3 winnings,** what is won: *The gamblers pocketed their winnings.* 1,2 *adjective,* 3 *noun.*

win ter (win′tər), **1** the coldest season of the year; season of the year between fall and spring. **2** of or for the winter; coming in winter: *winter clothes, winter weather.* **3** pass the winter: *Robins winter in the South.* **4** keep or feed during winter: *We wintered our cattle in the warm valley.* 1 *noun,* 2 *adjective,* 3,4 *verb.*

win ter green (win′tər grēn′), a small evergreen plant with bright-red berries. An oil made from its leaves is used in medicine and candy. *noun.*

win ter time (win′tər tīm′), season of winter. *noun.*

win·try (win′trē), **1** of winter; like winter: *wintry weather, a wintry sky.* See picture. **2** not warm or friendly; chilly: *a wintry manner, a wintry smile, a wintry greeting. adjective,* **win tri er, win tri est.**

withdraw (definition 1)—The turtle withdrew its head into its shell.

wistful

wipe (wīp), **1** rub in order to clean or dry: *We wipe our shoes on the mat. We wipe the dishes with a towel.* **2** take (away, off, or out) by rubbing: *Wipe away your tears. I wiped off the dust.* **3** act of wiping: *He gave his face a hasty wipe.* 1,2 *verb,* **wiped, wip ing;** 3 *noun.*

wipe out, destroy completely: *Whole cities were wiped out by the barbarians that swept over Europe.*

wire (wīr), **1** metal drawn out into a thin rod or thread: *a telephone wire.* **2** made of wire: *a wire fence.* **3** supply with wire: *wire a house for electricity.* **4** fasten with wire: *She wired the two*

pieces together. **5** telegraph: *He sent a message by wire.* **6** to telegraph: *She wired a birthday greeting.* **7** telegram: *The news of his arrival came in a wire.* 1,5,7 *noun,* 2 *adjective,* 3,4,6 *verb,* **wired, wir ing.**

wire less (wīr′lis), **1** using no wires; transmitting by radio waves instead of by electric wires. **2** radio. 1 *adjective,* 2 *noun, plural* **wire less es.**

wire tap ping (wīr′tap′ing), the making of a secret connection with telephone or telegraph wires to listen to or to record the messages sent over them. *noun.*

wir ing (wī′ring), system of wires to carry an electric current. *noun.*

wir y (wī′rē), **1** like wire. **2** lean, strong, and tough. *adjective,* **wir i er, wir i est.**

Wis con sin (wi skon′sən), one of the north central states of the United States. *noun.* [*Wisconsin* may have come from *Ouisconsing,* a French form of the American Indian name of the Wisconsin River.]

wis dom (wiz′dəm), being wise; knowledge and good judgment based on experience: *The leader's wisdom guided the group through difficulties. noun.*

wise (wīz), **1** having or showing knowledge and good judgment: *a wise judge, wise advice, wise plans.* **2** having knowledge or information: *We are none the wiser for his explanations. adjective,* **wis er, wis est.**

wish (wish), **1** have a desire for; be glad to have or do; want: *They wish to come with us. Do you wish to go home?* **2** have a desire; express a hope: *He wished for a new house.* **3** wishing; desire: *I have no wish to be rich. What is your wish?* **4** saying of a wish: *Please give her my best wishes for a Happy New Year.* **5** wish (something) for someone; have a hope for: *We wish peace for all people. I wish you a Happy New Year.* **6** thing wished for: *She got her wish.* 1,2,5 *verb,* 3,4,6 *noun, plural* **wish es.**

wish bone (wish′bōn′), the forked bone in the front of the breastbone in poultry and other birds. *noun.*

wish ful (wish′fəl), having or expressing a wish; desiring: *His boast about winning the race was only wishful thinking. adjective.*

wisp (wisp), **1** a small bundle; small bunch: *a wisp of hair.* **2** a small portion of anything; slight bit: *a wisp of smoke. noun.*

wis ter i a (wi stir′ē ə), a climbing shrub with large, drooping clusters of purple, blue, or white flowers. *noun.* [*Wisteria* was named for Caspar Wistar, an American doctor who lived from 1761 to 1818.]

wist ful (wist′fəl), longing; yearning: *Her wistful expression showed her sadness at moving away from her friends.* See picture. *adjective.*

wit (wit), **1** the power to perceive quickly and express cleverly ideas that are unusual, striking, and amusing: *Her wit made even troubles seem amusing.* **2** person with such power: *Benjamin Franklin was a wit.* **3** understanding; mind; sense: *People with quick wits learn easily. You can answer the riddle if you keep your wits about you. The beggar did not have wit enough to earn a living. noun.*

witch (wich), **1** person supposed to have magic power. Witches generally used their power to do evil. **2** an ugly old woman. *noun, plural* **witch es.**

witch craft (wich′kraft′), what a witch does or is supposed to be able to do; magic power. *noun.*

with (wiᴛʜ *or* with). *With* shows that persons or things are taken together in some way. **1** in the company of: *Come with me.* **2** among: *They will mix with the crowd.* **3** having: *He is a man with brains. She received a telegram with good news.* **4** by means of: *I cut the meat with a knife.* **5** using; showing: *Work with care.* **6** added to: *Do you want sugar with your tea?* **7** in regard to: *We are pleased with the house.* **8** in proportion to: *Her pay increased with her skill.* **9** because of: *We almost died with laughter.* **10** in the keeping or service of: *Leave the dog with me.* **11** from: *I hate to part with my favorite things.* **12** against: *The English fought with the Germans. preposition.*

with draw (wiᴛʜ drô′ *or* with drô′), **1** draw back; draw away. See picture. **2** take back; remove: *The owner of the store agreed to withdraw the charge of theft if the robbers returned the money.* **3** go away: *She withdrew from the room. verb,* **with drew, with drawn, with draw ing.**

with draw al (wiᴛʜ drô′əl *or* with drô′əl), withdrawing or being withdrawn: *a withdrawal of money from a bank account. noun.*

with drawn (wiᴛʜ drôn′ *or* with drôn′). See **withdraw.** *He was withdrawn from the game because of illness. verb.*

with drew (wiᴛʜ drü′ *or* with drü′). See **withdraw.** *The coach withdrew the player from the game when he was hurt. verb.*

with er (wiᴛʜ′ər), **1** make or become dry and lifeless; dry up; fade; shrivel: *The hot sun withers the grass. Flowers wither after they are cut. Age had withered the old woman's face.* **2** cause to feel ashamed or confused: *I was withered by their scornful looks. verb.*

with held (with held′ *or* wiᴛʜ held′). See **withhold.** *The witness withheld information from the police. verb.*

with hold (with hōld′ *or* wiᴛʜ hōld′), **1** refuse to give: *There will be no school play if the principal withholds consent.* **2** hold back; keep back: *Tell the whole story; don't withhold anything. verb,* **with held, with hold ing.**

with in (wiᴛʜ in′ *or* with in′), **1** not beyond; inside the limits of; not more than: *The task was within their power.* **2** in or into the inner part of; inside of: *By the use of X rays, doctors can see within the body.* **3** in or into the inner part; inside: *The house has been painted within and without.* 1,2 *preposition,* 3 *adverb.*

with out (wiᴛʜ out′ *or* with out′), **1** with no; not having; free from; lacking: *A cat walks without noise. I drink tea without sugar.* **2** so as to leave out, avoid, or neglect: *She walked past without noticing us.* **3** outside of; beyond: *Children were playing within and without the house.* **4** outside; on the outside: *The house is painted without and within.* 1-3 *preposition,* 4 *adverb.*

with stand (with stand′ *or* wiᴛʜ stand′), stand against; hold out against; resist; oppose, especially successfully; endure: *The pioneers had to withstand hardships in their move West. These shoes will withstand hard wear. verb,* **with stood, with stand ing.**

with stood (with stu̇d′ *or* wiᴛʜ stu̇d′). See **withstand.** *The family withstood many hardships. verb.*

wit less (wit′lis), lacking sense; stupid; foolish: *Crossing the street without looking in both directions is a witless thing to do. adjective.*

wit ness (wit′nis), **1** person who saw something happen; spectator: *There were several witnesses to the accident.* **2** see: *He witnessed the accident.* **3** person who takes an oath to tell the truth in a court of law. **4** evidence; testimony: *A person who gives false witness in court may be fined or jailed.* **5** testify to; give evidence of: *Her whole manner witnessed her surprise.* **6** person who signs a document to show that he or she saw the writer of the document sign it. **7** sign (a document) as witness: *witness a will.* 1,3,4,6 *noun, plural* **wit ness es;** 2,5,7 *verb.*

bear witness, give evidence; testify: *Her fingerprints bore witness to her guilt. His blushes bear witness to his embarrassment.*

wit ty (wit′ē), full of wit; clever and amusing: *A witty person makes witty remarks. adjective,* **wit ti er, wit ti est.**

wives (wīvz), more than one wife. *noun plural.*

wiz ard (wiz′ərd), **1** man supposed to have magic power. **2** a very clever person; expert: *She is a wizard at mathematics. noun.*

wk., week.

wob ble (wob′əl), **1** move unsteadily from side to side; shake; tremble: *A baby wobbles when it begins to walk alone.* **2** a wobbling motion. 1 *verb,* **wob bled, wob bling;** 2 *noun.*

wob bly (wob′lē), unsteady; shaky; wavering. *adjective,* **wob bli er, wob bli est.**

woe (wō), **1** great grief, trouble, or distress: *Disease and poverty are terrible woes.* **2** an exclamation of grief, trouble, or distress: *"Woe is me! What shall I do?"* 1 *noun,* 2 *interjection.*

woe ful (wō′fəl), **1** full of woe; sad; sorrowful; wretched: *The lost child had a woeful expression.* **2** pitiful: *You have made a woeful mistake. adjective.*

woke (wōk). See **wake**[1]. *I woke before they did. verb.*

wolf (wu̇lf), **1** a wild animal somewhat like a dog. Wolves sometimes kill sheep and other livestock, but they almost never attack human beings. **2** a cruel, greedy person. **3** eat greedily: *The starving man wolfed down the food.* 1,2 *noun, plural* **wolves;** 3 *verb.*

woodpeckers
about 9 inches
(23 centimeters) long

woodchuck—about 2 feet (60 centimeters) long with
the tail

wolverine—about
3½ feet (1 meter)
long with the tail

wolf hound (wùlf′hound′), a large dog of any of various kinds once used in hunting wolves. *noun.*

wol ve rine or **wol ve rene** (wùl′və rēn′), a heavily built, meat-eating animal living in the northern parts of the world. See picture. *noun.*

wolves (wùlvz), more than one wolf. *noun plural.*

wom an (wùm′ən), **1** an adult female person. When a girl grows up, she becomes a woman. **2** a female servant: *The princess told her woman to wait outside. noun, plural* **wom en.** [*Woman* comes from an earlier English word *wifman.* This was formed from words meaning "woman or wife" and "a human being."]

wom an hood (wùm′ən hùd), **1** condition or time of being a woman: *The girl was about to enter womanhood.* **2** character or qualities of a woman. **3** women as a group: *the womanhood of the United States. noun.*

wom an kind (wùm′ən kīnd′), women as a group. *noun.*

wom an li ness (wùm′ən lē nis), womanly quality; womanly behavior. *noun.*

wom an ly (wùm′ən lē), **1** having qualities that are by tradition admired in a woman: *a womanly sympathy and understanding.* **2** suitable for a woman: *Tennis is as much a womanly as it is a manly sport. adjective.*

wom en (wim′ən), more than one woman. *noun plural.*

Wom en's Lib e ra tion (wim′ənz lib′ə rā′shən), the efforts of women to achieve equality for women in all areas of life.

won (wun). See **win.** *Which side won yesterday? We have won four games. verb.*

won der (wun′dər), **1** a strange and surprising thing or event: *The Grand Canyon is one of the wonders of the world. It is a wonder that he refused such a good offer.* **2** the feeling caused by what is strange and surprising: *The baby looked with wonder at the snow.* **3** feel wonder: *We wonder at the splendor of the stars.* **4** be surprised or astonished: *I shouldn't wonder if she wins the prize.* **5** be curious about; wish to know: *I wonder what time it is.* 1,2 *noun,* 3-5 *verb.*

won der ful (wun′dər fəl), **1** causing wonder; marvelous; remarkable: *a wonderful adventure, the wonderful creations of nature.* **2** excellent; splendid; fine: *We had a wonderful time at the party. adjective.*

won der ment (wun′dər mənt), wonder; surprise: *He stared at the huge bear in wonderment. noun.*

won drous (wun′drəs), wonderful. *adjective.*

won't (wōnt), will not.

woo (wü), **1** make love to; seek to marry. **2** seek to win; try to get: *Some people woo fame; some woo wealth.* **3** try to persuade. *verb.*

wood (wùd), **1** the hard substance beneath the bark of trees and shrubs. Wood is used for making houses, boats, boxes, and furniture. **2** trees cut up for use: *The carpenter brought wood to build a playhouse. Put some wood on the fire.* **3** made of wood; wooden: *a wood house.* **4** woods, **a** a large number of growing trees; small forest: *The children go to the woods behind the farm for wild* flowers and for nuts. **b** area covered by a forest or forests: *Many campers go to the Maine woods.* 1,2,4 *noun,* 3 *adjective.*

wood chuck (wùd′chuk′), an animal with a thick body, short legs, and a bushy tail; ground hog. Woodchucks grow fat in summer and sleep in their holes in the ground all winter. See picture. *noun.*

wood cut ter (wùd′kut′ər), person who cuts down trees or chops wood. *noun.*

wood ed (wùd′id), covered with trees: *The house stood on a wooded hill.* *adjective.*

wood en (wùd′n), **1** made of wood. **2** stiff as wood; awkward. **3** dull; lifeless: *a face with a wooden expression.* *adjective.*

wood land (wùd′lənd), **1** land covered with trees. **2** of or in the woods; having something to do with the woods: *woodland sounds, woodland animals.* **1** *noun,* **2** *adjective.*

wood peck er (wùd′pek′ər), bird with a hard, pointed bill for pecking holes in trees to get insects. The flicker is one kind of woodpecker. See picture. *noun.*

wood pile (wùd′pīl′), pile of wood, especially wood for fuel. *noun.*

wood shed (wùd′shed′), shed for storing wood. *noun.*

woods man (wùdz′mən), **1** person used to life in the woods and skilled in hunting, fishing, trapping, and the like. **2** person whose work is cutting down trees; lumberjack. *noun, plural* **woods men.**

wood wind (wùd′wind′), any of a group of wind instruments which were originally made of wood, some of which are now made of metal. Clarinets, flutes, oboes, and bassoons are woodwinds. *noun.*

wood work (wùd′werk′), things made of wood; wooden parts inside a house, especially doors, stairs, and moldings. *noun.*

wood work ing (wùd′wer′king), making or shaping things of wood: *He is skilled in woodworking.* *noun.*

wood y (wùd′ē), **1** having many trees; covered with trees: *a woody hillside.* **2** consisting of wood: *the woody parts of a shrub.* **3** like wood: *Turnips become woody when they are old.* *adjective,* **wood i er, wood i est.**

woof (wüf), the threads running from side to side across a woven fabric. The woof crosses the warp. *noun.*

wool (wùl), **1** the soft curly hair or fur of sheep and some other animals. **2** short, thick, curly hair. **3** something like wool. **4** yarn, cloth, or garments made of wool: *People in cold climates often wear wool in the winter. noun.*

wool en or **wool len** (wùl′ən), **1** made of wool: *a woolen suit.* **2** cloth made of wool. **3** woolens, cloth or clothing made of wool: *We put our woolens in plastic bags to protect them against moths.* **4** of wool; having something to do with wool; that makes things from wool: *a woolen mill.* 1,4 *adjective,* 2,3 *noun.*

wool ly (wùl′ē), **1** consisting of wool: *the woolly*

a hat	i it	oi oil	ch child	⎧ a in about
ā age	ī ice	ou out	ng long	⎪ e in taken
ä far	o hot	u cup	sh she	ə = ⎨ i in pencil
e let	ō open	ù put	th thin	⎪ o in lemon
ē equal	ô order	ü rule	ŦH then	⎩ u in circus
ėr term			zh measure	

coat of a sheep. **2** like wool. **3** covered with wool or something like it. *adjective,* **wool li er, wool li est.**

wool y (wùl′ē), woolly. *adjective,* **wool i er, wool i est.**

word (werd), **1** a sound or a group of sounds that has meaning and is a unit of speech. We speak words when we talk. **2** the writing or printing that stands for a word: *This page is filled with words.* **3** words, angry talk; quarrel; dispute: *I had sharp words with them.* **4** a short talk: *May I have a word with you?* **5** speech: *She is honest in word and deed.* **6** a brief expression: *The teacher gave us a word of advice.* **7** command; order: *On a ship, the captain's word is law.* **8** promise: *She kept her word. He is a man of his word.* **9** news: *I have had no word from them in months.* **10** put into words: *She worded the message clearly.* 1-9 *noun,* 10 *verb.*

word ing (wer′ding), way of saying a thing; choice of words; use of words: *Careful wording helps you make clear to others what you really mean.* *noun.*

word y (wer′dē), using too many words. *adjective,* **word i er, word i est.**

wore (wôr). See **wear.** *I wore out my shoes in two months. verb.*

work (werk), **1** effort in doing or making something: *Gardening can be hard work.* **2** something to do; occupation; employment: *My friend is out of work.* **3** something made or done; result of effort: *The artist considers that picture to be his greatest work.* **4** that on which effort is put: *We carried our work out onto the porch.* **5** works, the moving parts of a machine: *the works of a watch.* **6** do work; labor: *Most people must work to earn money.* **7** work for pay; be employed: *She works at an airplane factory.* **8** put effort on: *They worked their farm with success.* **9** act; operate: *This pump will not work. The plan worked well.* **10** cause to do work: *That company works its employees hard.* **11** make or get by effort: *The injured man worked his way across the room on his hands and knees. He worked his way through college.* **12** bring about; cause; do: *The plan worked harm.* **13** go slowly or with effort: *The ship worked to windward.* **14** become (up, round, loose, or the like): *The handle has worked loose.* **15** make: *She worked a piece of copper into a tray.* 1-5 *noun,* 6-15 *verb.*

work out, 1 plan; develop: *Each group must work out its own program.* **2** solve: *I have to work out a few math problems.* **3** turn out; succeed: *Everything worked out fine. My part-time job after school didn't work out.*

work bench (werk′bench′), a strong, heavy table used by a carpenter, or by any person who works with tools and materials. *noun, plural* **work bench es.**

work book (wèrk′bùk′), book containing outlines for the study of some subject or questions to be answered; book in which a pupil answers questions and does some written work. *noun.*

work er (wèr′kər), 1 person that works. 2 bee, ant, wasp, or other insect that works for its community and usually does not produce young. *noun.*

work ing (wèr′king), 1 operation; action; method of work: *Do you understand the working of this machine?* 2 that works: *The class constructed a working model of a helicopter.* 3 of, for, or used in working: *working hours, working clothes.* 1 *noun,* 2,3 *adjective.*

work man (wèrk′mən), 1 worker. 2 person who works with his or her hands or with machines. *noun, plural* **work men.**

work man ship (wèrk′mən ship), 1 art or skill in a worker or in the work done: *Good workmanship requires long practice.* 2 quality or manner of work. *noun.*

work out (wèrk′out′), 1 exercise; practice: *They had a good workout running around the track before breakfast.* 2 trial; test: *The mechanic gave the car a thorough workout after repairing it. noun.*

work room (wèrk′rüm′), room where work is done. *noun.*

work shop (wèrk′shop′), 1 shop or building where work is done. 2 group of people working or studying on a special project: *a teachers' workshop. noun.*

world (wèrld), 1 the earth: *Ships can sail around the world.* 2 all of certain parts, people, or things of the earth: *the insect world, the world of books, the world of fashion.* 3 all people; the public: *The whole world knows it.* 4 the things of this life and the people devoted to them: *Monks live apart from the world.* 5 any planet, especially when considered as inhabited: *Has the earth ever been visited by creatures from another world?* 6 all things; everything; the universe. 7 great deal; very much; large amount: *Sunshine does children a world of good. noun.*

world ly (wèrld′lē), 1 of this world; not of heaven: *worldly wealth.* 2 caring much for the interests and pleasures of this world. *adjective,* **world li er, world li est.**

World War I, war fought from 1914 to 1918. The United States, Great Britain, France, Russia, and their allies were on one side; Germany, Austria-Hungary, and their allies were on the other side.

World War II, war fought from 1939 to 1945. The United States, Great Britain, the Soviet Union, and their allies were on one side; Germany, Italy, Japan, and their allies were on the other side.

world wide (wèrld′wīd′), spread throughout the world: *Gasoline now has worldwide use. adjective.*

worm (wèrm), 1 a small, slender, crawling or creeping animal. Most worms have soft bodies and no legs. 2 something like a worm in shape or movement, such as the thread of a screw. 3 move like a worm; crawl or creep like a worm: *The children wormed their way under the fence.* 4 get by persistent and secret means: *He wormed himself into our confidence.* 5 a weak, disgusting, or pitiful person. 6 **worms,** disease caused by worms in the body: *Our dog was cured of a bad case of worms.* 1,2,5,6 *noun,* 3,4 *verb.*

worm y (wèr′mē), 1 having worms; containing many worms: *wormy apples.* 2 damaged by worms: *wormy wood. adjective,* **worm i er, worm i est.**

worn (wôrn), 1 See **wear.** *I have worn these jeans all week.* 2 damaged by use: *worn rugs.* 3 tired; wearied: *The sick man's face was worn.* 1 *verb,* 2,3 *adjective.*

worn-out (wôrn′out′), 1 used until no longer fit for use: *a worn-out sweater.* 2 very tired; exhausted: *a worn-out horse. adjective.*

wor ry (wèr′ē), 1 feel anxious; be uneasy: *Don't worry about little things. They will worry if we are late.* 2 make anxious; trouble: *The problem worried him.* 3 care; anxiety; trouble; uneasiness: *Worry kept her awake.* 4 annoy; bother; vex: *Don't worry me right now with so many questions.* 5 seize and shake with the teeth; bite at; snap at: *The cat worried the mouse.* 1,2,4,5 *verb,* **wor ried, wor ry ing;** 3 *noun, plural* **wor ries.**

worse (wèrs), 1 less well; more ill: *The patient seems even worse today.* 2 less good; more evil: *Disobeying your parents was bad enough, but lying to them about it was worse. See picture.* 3 in a more severe or evil manner or degree: *It is raining worse than ever today.* 4 that which is worse: *Loss of her property was a terrible thing, but worse followed.* 1,2 *adjective, comparative of* **bad;** 3 *adverb,* 4 *noun.*

wor ship (wėr′ship), **1** great honor and respect: *the worship of God, hero worship.* **2** pay great honor and respect to: *People go to church to worship God.* **3** ceremonies or services in honor of God. Prayers and hymns are part of worship. **4** take part in a religious service. **5** consider extremely precious; hold very dear; adore: *A miser worships money. She worships her mother.* 1,3 *noun,* 2,4,5 *verb.*

wor ship er (wėr′ship ər), person who worships: *The church was filled with worshipers. noun.*

worst (wėrst), **1** least well; most ill: *This is the worst I've been since I got sick.* **2** least good; most evil: *That was the worst movie I've ever seen.* See picture. **3** in the worst manner or degree: *The children behave worst when they are tired.* **4** that which is worst: *Today was bad, but the worst is yet to come.* **5** beat; defeat: *to worst an enemy.* 1,2 *adjective, superlative of* **bad;** 3 *adverb,* 4 *noun,* 5 *verb.*

worth (wėrth), **1** good or important enough for; deserving of: *That book is worth reading. New York is a city worth visiting.* **2** merit; usefulness; importance: *We should read books of real worth.* **3** value: *She got her money's worth out of that coat.* **4** quantity that a certain amount will buy: *He bought a dollar's worth of stamps.* **5** equal in value to: *This book is worth five dollars. That toy is worth little.* **6** having property that amounts to: *That man is worth a million dollars.* 1,5,6 *adjective,* 2-4 *noun.*

worth less (wėrth′lis), without worth; good-for-nothing; useless: *Throw those worthless, broken toys away. adjective.*

worth while (wėrth′hwīl′), worth time, attention, or trouble; having real merit: *This is a worthwhile book; you should read it. adjective.*

wor thy (wėr′ᴛнē), **1** having worth or merit: *Helping the poor is a worthy cause.* **2** deserving; meriting: *Her courage was worthy of high praise. Bad acts are worthy of punishment. adjective,* **wor thi er, wor thi est.**

would (wůd), **1** See **will**[1]. *She said that she would come. They would go in spite of our warning.* **2** *Would* is also used: **a** to express future time: *Would he never go?* **b** to express action done again and again: *The children would play for hours on the beach.* **c** to express a wish: *I would I were rich.* **d** to sound more polite than *will* sounds: *Would you help us, please? verb.*

would n't (wůd′nt), would not.

wound[1] (wünd), **1** hurt or injury caused by cutting, stabbing, or shooting: *a knife wound, a bullet wound.* **2** injure by cutting, stabbing, or shooting; hurt: *The hunter wounded the deer.* **3** any hurt or injury to feelings or reputation: *Being fired from a job can be a wound to a person's pride.* **4** injure in feelings or reputation: *Their unkind words wounded me.* 1,3 *noun,* 2,4 *verb.*

wound[2] (wound). See **wind**[2]. *I wound the string into a tight ball. It is wound too loosely. verb.*

wove (wōv). See **weave.** *The spider wove a new web after the first was destroyed. verb.*

wo ven (wō′vən). See **weave.** *This cloth is closely woven. verb.*

wow (wou), exclamation of surprise, joy, or wonder: *Wow! I can sure use a gift like that. interjection.*

wran gle (rang′gəl), **1** argue or dispute in a noisy or angry way; quarrel: *The children wrangled about who should sit on the front seat.* **2** (in the western United States and Canada) to herd or tend (horses or cattle) on the range. *verb,* **wran gled, wran gling.**

wrap (rap), **1** cover by winding or folding something around: *She wrapped herself in a shawl.* **2** wind or fold as a covering: *Wrap a shawl around yourself.* **3** cover with paper and tie up or fasten: *Have you wrapped her birthday presents yet?* **4** cover; hide: *The mountain peak is wrapped in clouds.* **5** an outer covering. Shawls, scarfs, coats, and furs are wraps. 1-4 *verb,* **wrapped** or **wrapt, wrap ping;** 5 *noun.*

wrapped up in, devoted to; thinking chiefly of: *She is so wrapped up in her work that she never sees her old friends any more.*

wrap per (rap′ər), **1** person or thing that wraps. **2** a covering or cover: *Some magazines are mailed in paper wrappers. noun.*

wrap ping (rap′ing), paper, cloth, or the like in which something is wrapped. *noun.*

wrapt (rapt), wrapped. See **wrap.** *verb.*

wrath (rath), very great anger; rage. *noun.*

wrath ful (rath′fəl), very angry; showing wrath: *The wrathful lion turned on the hunters. His wrathful eyes flashed. adjective.*

wreak (rēk), **1** give expression to; work off (feelings or desires): *I wreaked my anger on my brother by yelling at him.* **2** inflict (vengeance or punishment). *verb.*

wreath (rēth), **1** ring of flowers or leaves twisted together: *We hang wreaths in the windows at Christmas.* **2** something suggesting a wreath: *a wreath of smoke. noun, plural* **wreaths** (rēᴛнz).

wreathe (rēᴛн), **1** make into a wreath: *The children wreathed a chain of daisies.* **2** decorate or adorn with wreaths: *The inside of the schoolhouse was wreathed with flowers for the graduation ceremony.* **3** make a ring around; encircle: *Mist wreathes the hills. verb,* **wreathed, wreath ing.**

wreck (rek), **1** destruction of a ship, building, train, automobile, truck, or airplane: *The hurricane caused many wrecks. Reckless driving causes many wrecks on the highway.* **2** any destruction or serious injury: *Heavy rains caused the wreck of many crops.* **3** what is left of anything that has been destroyed or much injured: *The waves cast the wreck of a ship upon the shore.* **4** cause the wreck of; destroy; ruin: *A broken rail wrecked the freight train just outside of town.* **5** person who has lost his health or money: *He was a wreck from overwork.* 1-3,5 *noun,* 4 *verb.*

wreck age (rek′ij), **1** what is left by a wreck or wrecks: *The shore was covered with the wreckage of the ship.* **2** wrecking: *They felt defeated by the wreckage of their plans. noun.*

wreck er (rek′ər), **1** person whose work is tearing down buildings. **2** person, car, train, or machine that removes wrecks. **3** person or ship that recovers wrecked or disabled ships or their cargoes. *noun.*

wren (ren), a small songbird with a slender bill and a short tail. Wrens often build their nests near houses. See picture. *noun.*

wrench (rench), **1** a violent twist or twisting pull: *She broke the branch off the tree with a sudden wrench.* **2** twist or pull violently: *She wrenched the knob off when she was trying to open the door. The policeman wrenched the gun out of the man's hand.* **3** injure by twisting: *She wrenched her back doing gymnastics.* **4** injury caused by twisting: *He gave his ankle a wrench when he jumped off the car.* **5** source of grief or sorrow: *It was a wrench to leave our old home.* **6** tool to hold and turn nuts, bolts, pieces of pipe, or the like. See picture. 1,4-6 *noun, plural* **wrench es;** 2,3 *verb.*

wrest (rest), **1** twist, pull, or tear away with force; wrench away: *She bravely wrested the knife from the attacker.* **2** take by force: *An enemy wrested the power from the duke. verb.*

wres tle (res′əl), **1** try to throw or force (an opponent) to the ground. **2** a wrestling match. **3** struggle: *We often wrestle with temptation. I have been wrestling with this problem for an hour.* 1,3 *verb,* **wres tled, wres tling;** 2 *noun.*

wres tler (res′lər), person who wrestles, especially as a sport. *noun.*

wres tling (res′ling), sport or contest in which each of two opponents tries to throw or force the other to the ground. The rules for wrestling do not allow using the fists or certain holds on the body. *noun.*

wretch (rech), **1** a very unfortunate or unhappy person. **2** a very bad person. *noun, plural* **wretch es.**

wretch ed (rech′id), **1** very unfortunate or unhappy. **2** very unsatisfactory; miserable: *a wretched hut.* **3** very bad: *a wretched traitor. adjective.*

wrig gle (rig′əl), **1** twist and turn: *Children wriggle when they are restless.* **2** move by twisting and turning: *The worm wriggled out of my hand when I tried to put it on the hook.* **3** make one's way by slyness and tricks: *That child can wriggle out of any difficulty.* **4** wriggling. 1-3 *verb,* **wrig gled, wrig gling;** 4 *noun.*

wring (ring), **1** twist with force; squeeze hard: *Wring out your wet bathing suit.* **2** get by twisting or squeezing; force out: *The boy wrung water from his wet bathing suit.* **3** get by force, effort, or persuasion: *to wring a secret out of someone.* **4** clasp and hold firmly: *She wrung her old friend's hand.* **5** cause pain or pity in: *Their poverty wrung his heart.* **6** a twist or squeeze. 1-5 *verb,* **wrung, wring ing;** 6 *noun.*

wren—about 5 inches (13 centimeters) long with the tail

wrinkle (definition 1)—The elephant's face had many **wrinkles.**

wrench (definition 6)—The jaws have ridged surfaces for gripping. They can be moved together or apart by means of a screw.

wring er (ring′ər), machine for squeezing water from wet clothes. *noun.*

wrin kle (ring′kəl), **1** ridge; fold: *the wrinkles in an old person's face, to press out the wrinkles in a shirt.* See picture. **2** make a wrinkle or wrinkles in: *She wrinkled her forehead.* **3** have wrinkles; acquire wrinkles: *This shirt will not wrinkle.* **1** *noun,* **2,3** *verb,* **wrin kled, wrin kling.**

wrist (rist), the joint connecting hand and arm. *noun.*

wrist band (rist′band′), band of a sleeve fitting around the wrist. *noun.*

wrist watch (rist′woch′), a small watch worn on a strap around the wrist. *noun, plural* **wrist watch es.**

writ (rit), **1** something written; piece of writing. The Bible is Holy Writ. **2** a formal order directing a person to do or not to do something: *A writ from the judge ordered the prisoner's release from jail.* *noun.*

write (rīt), **1** make letters or words with pen, pencil, or chalk: *You can read and write.* **2** mark with letters or words: *Please write on both sides of the paper.* **3** put down the letters or words of: *Write your name and address.* **4** make up stories, books, poems, articles, or the like; compose: *He writes for the magazines.* **5** be a writer: *Her ambition was to write.* **6** write a letter: *I write to my friend every week.* **7** write a letter to: *She wrote her parents that she would be home for New Year's.* **8** show plainly: *Fear was written on his face.* *verb,* **wrote, writ ten, writ ing.**

write down, put into writing: *I will write down your directions.*

write out, 1 put in writing: *He wrote out a check.* **2** write in full: *He wrote out his speech and memorized it.*

write up, write a description or account of, especially a full or detailed account: *The reporter wrote up his interview with the mayor for the newspaper.*

writ er (rī′tər), **1** person who writes. **2** person whose occupation is writing; author. *noun.*

writhe (rīŦH), **1** twist and turn; twist about: *writhe in pain. The snake writhed along the branch.* See picture. **2** suffer mentally; be very uncomfortable. *verb,* **writhed, writh ing.**

writ ing (rī′ting), **1** act of making letters or words with pen, pencil, chalk, or the like. **2** written form: *Put your ideas in writing.* **3** handwriting: *Your writing is hard to read.* **4** something written; a letter, paper, document, or the like. **5** literary work; book or other literary production: *the writings of Benjamin Franklin. noun.*

writ ten (rit′n). See **write.** *I have written a letter. verb.*

wrong (rông), **1** not right; bad: *Stealing is wrong.* **2** not true; not correct; not what it should be: *She gave the wrong answer.* **3** not proper; not suitable: *Heavy boots would be the wrong thing to wear for tennis.* **4** out of order: *Something is wrong with the car.* **5** badly; in an incorrect way: *I did my homework wrong and had to do it over.* **6** anything not right; wrong thing or action: *Two wrongs do not make a right.* **7** injury; harm: *You can do an innocent person a wrong by spreading false rumors.* **8** do wrong to; treat unfairly; injure: *It is often hard to forgive someone who has wronged you.* **9** not meant to be seen; least important: *the wrong side of cloth.* **1-4,9** *adjective,* **5** *adverb,* **6,7** *noun,* **8** *verb.*

go wrong, 1 turn out badly: *Everything went wrong today.* **2** stop being good and become bad: *The cashier went wrong and stole money from the cash register.*

in the wrong, at fault; guilty: *I was in the wrong.*

wrong do er (rông′dü′ər), person who does wrong. *noun.*

wrong ful (rông′fəl), **1** wrong. **2** unlawful. *adjective.*

wrote (rōt). See **write.** *He wrote his mother a long letter last week. verb.*

wrought (rôt), **1** made: *The gate was wrought with great skill.* **2** an old form of **worked.** **1** *adjective,* **2** *verb.*

wrung (rung). See **wring.** *She wrung out the wet cloth and hung it up. Her heart is wrung with pity for the poor. verb.*

wry (rī), twisted; turned to one side: *She made a wry face to show her disgust. adjective,* **wri er, wri est.**

Wy o ming (wī ō′ming), one of the western states of the United States. *noun.* [*Wyoming* got its name from Wyoming Valley, Pennsylvania. The name *Wyoming* comes from a Delaware Indian word meaning "upon the great plain." It became popular after a poem called "Gertrude of Wyoming" was published. A member of Congress proposed it as the name of the western land that became the state of Wyoming.]

writhe (definition 1)—The wrestlers **writhed** on the mat.

"The Wrestlers," George Loks. Museum of Fine Arts, Boston. Charles Henry Hayden Fund

X x

X or **x** (eks), **1** the 24th letter of the English alphabet. There are very few words that begin with *x*. **2** an unknown quantity. **3** anything shaped like an X. *noun, plural* **X's** or **x's.**

Xer ox (zir′oks), **1** trademark for a process of copying letters or other documents by making photographic prints of them. **2** make a copy or copies of by using a Xerox copying machine. **1** *noun,* **2** *verb.*

Xmas (kris′məs *or* eks′məs), Christmas. *noun.*

xylophone

X ray (definition 2)—X ray of a flower

X ray, 1 ray which can go through substances that ordinary rays of light cannot penetrate. X rays are used to locate breaks in bones or bullets lodged in the body, and to treat certain diseases. **2** picture made by means of X rays. See picture.

X-ray (eks′rā), **1** examine, photograph, or treat with X rays: *The doctor X-rayed my knee for broken bones.* **2** of, by, or having something to do with X rays: *an X-ray examination of one's teeth.* **1** *verb,* **2** *adjective.*

xy lo phone (zī′lə fōn), a musical instrument consisting of two rows of wooden bars of varying lengths, which are sounded by striking with wooden hammers. See picture. *noun.* [*Xylophone* was formed from Greek words meaning "wood" and "sound."]

Y y

Y or **y** (wī), **1** the 25th letter of the English alphabet. There are two *y*'s in *yearly* and *yesterday.* **2** anything shaped like a Y. *noun, plural* **Y's** or **y's.**

-y[1], suffix meaning: **1** full of _____: Bump*y* means *full of* bumps. **2** containing _____: Salt*y* means *containing* salt. **3** having _____: Cloud*y* means *having* clouds. **4** characterized by _____: Funn*y* means *characterized by* fun. **5** inclined to _____: Sleep*y* means *inclined to* sleep.

-y[2], suffix meaning: **1** small _____: Doll*y* means a *small doll.* **2** dear _____: Dadd*y* means *dear dad.*

yacht (yot), **1** boat for pleasure trips or for racing. **2** sail or race on a yacht. **1** *noun,* **2** *verb.* [*Yacht* comes from an old Dutch word meaning "a chasing ship." The boat was called this because it originally was a kind of light, fast ship suitable for chasing other ships.]

yak (yak), a long-haired ox of central Asia, raised for its meat, milk, and hair. See picture. *noun.* [*Yak* comes from the Tibetan name of the animal.]

yam (yam), **1** the thick, sweet, orange root of a vine of warm regions, eaten as a vegetable. **2** the sweet potato: *We like candied yams. noun.* [*Yam* comes from a Senegalese word meaning "to eat." Senegalese is a west African language.]

yank (yangk), **1** pull with a sudden motion; jerk; tug: *The dentist yanked the tooth.* **2** a sudden pull; jerk; tug: *I gave the door a yank.* **1** *verb,* **2** *noun.*

Yan kee (yang′kē), **1** person born or living in New England. **2** person born or living in the North, especially during the Civil War. **3** person born or living in the United States; American. *noun.*

yap (yap), **1** a quick, sharp bark; yelp. **2** bark in a quick, sharp way; yelp: *The little dog yapped at every strange person who came to the door.* **1** *noun,* **2** *verb,* **yapped, yap ping.**

yard[1] (yärd), **1** piece of ground near or around a house, barn, school, or other building: *You can play outside, but you must not leave the yard.* **2** piece of enclosed ground for some special purpose or business: *a chicken yard.* **3** space with many tracks where railroad cars are stored, shifted around, serviced, or made up into new trains: *My cousin works in the railroad yards. noun.*

yard[2] (yärd), **1** a unit of length equal to 36 inches; 3 feet: *I bought three yards of blue cloth for curtains.* **2** beam or pole fastened across a mast and used to support a sail. *noun.*

yard stick (yärd′stik′), **1** stick one yard long, used for measuring. **2** standard of judgment or comparison: *What yardstick do you use to decide whether your conduct is right or wrong? noun.*

yarn (yärn), **1** any spun thread, especially that prepared for weaving or knitting: *I'm knitting a scarf from this yarn.* **2** tale; story: *The old sailor made up his yarns as he told them. noun.*

yawn (yôn), **1** open the mouth wide because one is sleepy, tired, or bored. **2** act of opening the mouth in this way. **3** open wide: *The canyon yawned beneath our feet.* **1,3** *verb,* **2** *noun.*

yd., yard. *plural* **yd.** or **yds.**

ye (yē), an old word meaning **you.** *If ye are thirsty, drink. pronoun plural.*

yea (yā), **1** yes. **2** indeed. **3** vote or voter in favor of something. **1,2** *adverb,* **3** *noun.*

year (yir), **1** 12 months or 365 days; January 1 to December 31. Leap year has 366 days. **2** 12 months reckoned from any point: *I will see you again a year from today.* **3** the part of a year spent in a certain activity: *Our school year is 9 months.* **4 years,** age: *young in years but old in experience. I hope to live to your years. noun.*

year book (yir′buk′), book or report published every year. Yearbooks often report facts of the year. The graduating class in a school or college usually publishes a yearbook, with pictures of its members. *noun.*

year ling (yir′ling), **1** animal one year old. **2** one year old: *a yearling colt.* **1** *noun,* **2** *adjective.*

year ly (yir′lē), **1** once a year; in every year: *I take a yearly trip to New York.* **2** lasting a year: *The earth makes a yearly revolution around the sun.* **3** for a year: *a yearly salary of $10,000.* **1-3** *adjective,* **1** *adverb.*

yearn (yėrn), feel a longing or desire; desire earnestly: *He yearns for home. verb.*

yearn ing (yėr′ning), an earnest or strong desire; longing. *noun.*

yak—about 5½ feet (1½ meters) high at the shoulder

a hat	**i** it	**oi** oil	**ch** child	⎧ a in about
ā age	**ī** ice	**ou** out	**ng** long	e in taken
ä far	**o** hot	**u** cup	**sh** she	ə = ⎨ i in pencil
e let	**ō** open	**u̇** put	**th** thin	o in lemon
ē equal	**ô** order	**ü** rule	**ₜₕ** then	⎩ u in circus
ėr term			**zh** measure	

yeast (yēst), the substance that causes dough for bread to rise and beer to ferment. Yeast consists of many tiny, one-celled plants that grow quickly in a liquid containing sugar. *noun.*

yeast cake, a small block or cake of compressed yeast.

yell (yel), **1** cry out with a strong, loud sound: *I yelled with pain when the door slammed on my finger.* **2** a strong, loud cry. **3** say with a yell: *We yelled our good-bys to our friends as the bus moved away.* **4** a special shout or cheer used by a school or college at sports events. **1,3** *verb,* **2,4** *noun.*

yel low (yel′ō), **1** the color of gold, butter, or ripe lemons. **2** having this color. **3** make or become yellow: *Paper yellows with age.* **4** having a yellowish skin. **5** yolk of an egg. **6** cowardly. **1,5** *noun,* **2,4,6** *adjective,* **3** *verb.*

yellow fever, a dangerous, infectious disease of warm climates that causes high fever and turns the skin yellow. It is transmitted by the bite of a certain kind of mosquito. Yellow fever was once common in some southern parts of the United States.

yel low ish (yel′ō ish), somewhat yellow. *adjective.*

yellow jacket, wasp marked with bright yellow.

yelp (yelp), **1** the quick, sharp bark or cry of a dog or fox. **2** make such a bark or cry. **1** *noun,* **2** *verb.*

yen (yen), unit of money in Japan. *noun, plural* **yen.**

yeo man (yō′mən), **1** (in the United States Navy) a petty officer who has charge of supplies and accounts and acts as a secretary or clerk. **2** (in Great Britain) a person who owned a small amount of land and usually farmed it himself. *noun, plural* **yeo men.**

yes (yes), **1** word used to show agreement or consent: *"Yes, five and two are seven," he said. Will you go? Yes.* **2** a vote for; person voting for: *The yeses won.* **3** and what is more: *"Your work is good, yes, very good," said the teacher.* **1,3** *adverb,* **2** *noun, plural* **yes es** or **yes ses.**

yes ter day (yes′tər dē), **1** the day before today: *Yesterday was cold and rainy.* **2** on the day before today: *It rained yesterday.* **3** the recent past: *We are often amused by the fashions of yesterday.* **1,3** *noun,* **2** *adverb.*

yet (yet), **1** up to the present time; thus far: *The work is not yet finished.* **2** now; at this time: *Don't go yet.* **3** then; at that time: *It was not yet dark.* **4** still; even now: *She is doing her homework yet.* **5** sometime: *I may yet get rich.* **6** also; again: *Yet once more I forbid you to go.* **7** moreover: *He won't do it for you nor yet for me.* **8** but; nevertheless; however: *The work is good, yet it could be better.* **1-8** *adverb,* **8** *conjunction.*

yew (yü), **1** an evergreen tree of Europe and Asia.

Some kinds of yew are now widely grown in the United States as shrubs. **2** the wood of this tree. *noun.*

yield (yēld), **1** produce: *This land yields good crops. Mines yield ore.* **2** amount yielded; product: *This year's yield from the silver mine was very large.* **3** give; grant: *Her parents yielded their consent to her plans.* **4** give up; surrender: *The enemy yielded to our soldiers.* **5** give way: *The door yielded to his touch.* **6** give place: *We yield to nobody in love of freedom.* **1,3-6** *verb,* **2** *noun.*

yo del (yō′dl), **1** sing with frequent changes from the ordinary voice to a forced shrill voice and back again. **2** act or sound of yodeling. **1** *verb,* **2** *noun.*

yo gurt (yō′gərt), kind of slightly fermented liquid food made from milk, thickened by the action of bacteria. Yogurt is often sweetened and flavored. *noun.*

yoke (definitions 1 and 2)

yoke (yōk), **1** a wooden frame to fasten two work animals together. See picture. **2** pair fastened together with a yoke: *The plow was drawn by a yoke of oxen.* **3** any frame connecting two other parts: *I tried to carry two buckets on a yoke, one at each end.* **4** put a yoke on; fasten with a yoke: *The farmer yoked the oxen before hitching them to the wagon.* **5** part of a garment fitting the neck and shoulders closely. **1-3,5** *noun,* **4** *verb,* **yoked, yok ing.**

yolk (yōk), the yellow part of an egg. *noun.*

Yom Kip pur (yom kip′ər), a Jewish fast day of atoning for sins. It occurs ten days after Rosh Hashanah, the Jewish New Year.

yon (yon), yonder. *adjective, adverb.*

yon der (yon′dər), **1** over there; within sight, but not near: *Look at that wild duck yonder!* **2** situated over there; being within sight, but not near: *On yonder hill stands a ruined castle.* **1** *adverb,* **2** *adjective.*

yore (yôr). **of yore,** long past; now long since gone: *Outbreaks of the plague were common in days of yore. noun.*

you (yü *or* yə), **1** the person or persons spoken to: *Are you ready? Then you may go.* **2** one; anybody:

You never can tell. You push this button to get a light. pronoun singular or plural.

you'd (yüd *or* yəd), **1** you had. **2** you would.

you'll (yül *or* yəl), **1** you will. **2** you shall.

young (yung), **1** in the early part of life or growth; not old: *A puppy is a young dog.* **2** young ones: *An animal will fight to protect its young.* **3** having the looks or qualities of youth or of a young person: *She looks and acts young for her age.* **4** not so old as another or the other: *Young Mr. Jones worked for his father.* **1,3,4** *adjective,* **young er** (yung′gər), **young est** (yung′gist); **2** *noun.*

young ster (yung′stər), **1** child: *She is a lively youngster.* **2** a young person: *The old woman was as spry as a youngster. noun.*

your (yùr *or* yər), **1** belonging to you: *Wash your hands.* **2** having to do with you: *We enjoyed your visit.* **3** *Your* is used as part of some titles. *Your Highness, Your Lordship, Your Honor. adjective.*

you're (yùr *or* yər), you are.

yours (yùrz), **1** the one or ones belonging to you: *This pencil is yours. My hands are clean; yours are dirty.* **2** at your service: *I am yours to command.* **3** *Yours* is used at the end of a letter with some other word. *Yours truly, Sincerely yours.* pronoun singular or plural.

your self (yùr self′ *or* yər self′), **1** *Yourself* is used to make a statement stronger. *You yourself know the story is not true.* **2** *Yourself* is used instead of *you* in cases like: *Did you hurt yourself? Ask yourself what you really want. Try to do it by yourself.* **3** your real self: *Now that your cold is better, you'll feel like yourself again.* pronoun, plural **your selves.**

your selves (yùr selvz′ *or* yər selvz′). See **yourself.** *You can all see for yourselves that the room is empty.* pronoun plural.

youth (yüth), **1** fact or quality of being young: *She has all the vigor of youth.* **2** the time between being a child and being an adult. **3** a young man. **4** young people. **5** the first or early stage of anything: *Many of our beliefs go back to the youth of this country.* noun, plural **youths** (yüths *or* yü⁴Hz), **youth.**

youth ful (yüth′fəl), **1** young. **2** of youth: *youthful energy, youthful pleasures.* **3** lively; fresh; having the looks or qualities of youth: *My grandmother has a very gay and youthful spirit. adjective.*

you've (yüv *or* yəv), you have.

yowl (youl), **1** a long, distressful, or dismal cry; howl. **2** howl: *That dog is always yowling.* **1** *noun,* **2** *verb.*

yo yo (yō′yō), a small toy consisting of a deeply grooved disk which is spun out and reeled in by means of an attached string. *noun, plural* **yo yos.**

yr., year. *plural* **yr.** *or* **yrs.**

yuc ca (yuk′ə), plant found in dry, warm regions of North and Central America. The yucca has stiff, narrow leaves and white, bell-shaped flowers. *noun.*

yule *or* **Yule** (yül), **1** Christmas. **2** yuletide. *noun.*

yule tide *or* **Yule tide** (yül′tīd′), Christmas time; the Christmas season. *noun.*

Zz

a hat	**i** it	**oi** oil	**ch** child	a in about
ā age	**ī** ice	**ou** out	**ng** long	e in taken
ä far	**o** hot	**u** cup	**sh** she	ə = { i in pencil
e let	**ō** open	**u̇** put	**th** thin	o in lemon
ē equal	**ô** order	**ü** rule	**ᴛʜ** then	u in circus
ėr term			**zh** measure	

Z or z (zē), the 26th and last letter of the English alphabet. There are two *z*'s in *zigzag*. *noun, plural* **Z's or z's.**

zeal (zēl), eager desire or effort; earnest enthusiasm: *We worked with zeal to finish the project. noun.*

zeal ous (zel′əs), full of zeal; eager; earnest: *The children made zealous efforts to clean up the house for the party. adjective.*

ze bra (zē′brə), a wild animal of Africa with hoofs that is somewhat like a horse or a donkey but striped with dark bands on white. See picture. *noun, plural* **ze bras** or **ze bra.**

ze bu (zē′bü *or* zē′byü), an animal like an ox but with a large hump. The zebu is a domestic animal in Asia and eastern Africa. See picture. *noun.*

ze nith (zē′nith), **1** the point in the heavens directly overhead; the point where a vertical line would pierce the sky. To an observer at the North Pole, the North Star would be about at the zenith. **2** the highest point: *At the zenith of its power Rome dominated all the known world. noun.*

Zep pe lin (zep′ə lən), a large airship shaped like a cigar with pointed ends. It has compartments filled with gas. *noun.* [*Zeppelin* was named for Count Ferdinand von Zeppelin, the German army officer who invented it. He lived from 1838 to 1917.]

zer o (zir′ō), **1** the figure 0: *There are three zeros in 40,006.* **2** point marked as 0 on the scale of a thermometer. **3** temperature that corresponds to 0 on the scale of a thermometer. **4** of or at zero: *The other team's score was zero.* **5** nothing. **6** not any; none at all: *The weather station at the airport announced zero visibility.* **7** a very low point: *The team's spirit sank to zero after its fifth defeat in a row.* 1-3,5,7 *noun, plural* **zer os** or **zer oes;** 4,6 *adjective.*

zest (zest), **1** keen enjoyment; relish: *The hungry children ate with zest.* **2** a pleasant or exciting quality or flavor: *Wit gives zest to conversation. noun.*

Zeus (züs), the chief god of the ancient Greeks. The Romans called him Jupiter. *noun.*

zig zag (zig′zag′), **1** with short, sharp turns from one side to the other: *We traveled in a zigzag direction. The path ran zigzag up the hill.* **2** move in a zigzag way: *Lightning zigzagged across the sky.* **3** a zigzag line or course. See picture. **4** one of the short, sharp turns of a zigzag. 1 *adjective, adverb,* 2 *verb,* **zig zagged, zig zag ging;** 3,4 *noun.*

zinc (zingk), a bluish-white metal very little affected by air and moisture. Zinc is used as a coating for iron, in electric batteries, and in paint. *noun.*

zebra—up to 5 feet (1½ meters) high at the shoulder

zigzags (definition 3)

zebu—up to 5 feet (1½ meters) high at the shoulder

zin ni a (zin′ē ə), a garden plant grown for its showy flowers of many colors. See picture. *noun.* [*Zinnia* was named for Johann Zinn, a German botanist. He lived from 1727 to 1759.]

zip (zip), fasten or close with a zipper: *I zipped up my jacket. verb,* **zipped, zip ping.**

Zip   Code, 1 system of numbers which identify the postal delivery areas into which the United States and its larger cities have been divided. **2** a number in this system. [*Zip* was formed from the first letters of the words *zone improvement plan.*]

zip per (zip′ər), **1** a sliding fastener for clothing, shoes, or the like: *a zipper on a jacket.* **2** fasten or close with a zipper: *Zipper up your jacket before you go out in the cold.* 1 *noun,* 2 *verb.*

zith er (zith′ər), a musical instrument having 30 to 40 strings, played with the fingers. See picture. *noun.*

zo di ac (zō′dē ak), an imaginary belt of the heavens extending on both sides of the path of the sun and including the path of the planets and the moon. The zodiac is divided into 12 equal parts, called signs, named after 12 groups of stars. See picture. *noun.* [*Zodiac* comes from the Greek words meaning "circle of the animal figures." The zodiac was called this because each of the twelve parts was originally represented by an animal figure.]

zom bie (zom′bē), corpse supposedly brought to a condition resembling life by a supernatural power. People who practice voodoo believe in zombies. *noun, plural* **zom bies.**

zone (zōn), **1** any of the five great divisions of the earth's surface, bounded by imaginary lines going around the earth parallel to the equator. **2** any region or area especially considered or set off. A combat zone is a district where fighting is going on. **3** area or district in a city or town under special restrictions as to building. **4** divide into zones: *The city was zoned for factories and residences.* 1-3 *noun,* 4 *verb,* **zoned, zon ing.**

zoo (zü), place where animals are kept and shown: *There are often many tame animals in a children's zoo. noun, plural* **zoos.**

zo o log i cal (zō′ə loj′ə kəl), **1** of animals and animal life. **2** having to do with zoology. *adjective.*

zo ol o gist (zō ol′ə jist), person who is an expert in zoology. *noun.*

zo ol o gy (zō ol′ə jē), the science of animals; the study of animals and animal life. Zoology is a branch of biology. *noun.* [*Zoology* comes from Greek words meaning "animal" and "account or discussion."]

zoom (züm), **1** move suddenly upward: *The airplane zoomed.* **2** a sudden upward flight: *The airplane made a zoom and left the mountain far below.* **3** move suddenly and rapidly: *The car zoomed past us, going 80 miles an hour.* 1,3 *verb,* 2 *noun.*

zuc chi ni (zü kē′nē), kind of dark-green squash shaped like a cucumber. It is eaten as a vegetable. *noun, plural* **zuc chi ni** or **zuc chi nis.**

zinnias

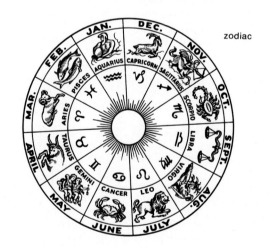
zither

zodiac

Picture Credits

Using This Dictionary

p. 9 (top)	UNICEF Collection
p. 9 (middle)	© Jeffrey C. Stoll / Jacana / Liaison
p. 9 (bottom)	Photograph taken at the Milwaukee County Zoo by William B. Parker
p. 10 (left)	© Grossa / Jacana / Liaison
p. 10 (right)	Jerry Hennen
p. 12	Photograph taken at the Milwaukee County Zoo by William B. Parker
p. 14	French or Flemish, Late 15th or early 16th century, "The Hunt of the Unicorn," Silk and Wool, Silver and Silver gilt threads, From the Chateau of Verteiu; The Metropolitan Museum of Art, The Cloister Collection, Gift of John D. Rockefeller, Jr.; 1937
p. 18	Norman Owen Tomalin / Bruce Coleman, Inc.
p. 19	New York Zoological Society Photo
p. 22	Photographs taken at the Milwaukee County Zoo by William B. Parker
p. 23	The Smithsonian Institution
p. 32	Courtesy of The Trustees of the British Museum
p. 34 (right)	From the collection of Cynthia Zilliac
p. 36	John Padour
p. 45 (top)	Information Canada Photothèque
p. 45 (middle)	Lynn M. Stone
p. 49 (bottom)	From the collection of G. Russell-Dempsey

Dictionary

absurdity	Oppenheim, Meret, *Object* (Le Déjeuner en fourrure) (1936) The Museum of Modern Art, New York
accordion	J. Lochridge
achievement	NASA
adept	Lynn Millar / Rapho / Photo Researchers
adorn	John Padour
agile	The Museum of Modern Art Film Stills Archive
alligator	Lynn M. Stone
aloft	United Press International
alphabet	ALPHABET SAMPLER Index of American Design National Gallery of Art, Washington, D.C.
amuse	Folger Shakespeare Library
anaconda	Allan Roberts
angel	"Angel," Jehan Barbet de Lyon Copyright The Frick Collection, New York
anteater	New York Zoological Society Photo
antelope	Lynn M. Stone
antenna	Turtox / Cambosco MacMillan Science Company Chicago, Illinois 60620 U.S.A.
antique	Courtesy of the Ford Motor Company Dearborn, Michigan
aqueduct	Spanish National Tourist Office
arch	Arch of Titus, Rome Alinari / Art Reference Bureau
armadillo	L. R. Ditto / Bruce Coleman, Inc.
armor	Courtesy of The Metropolitan Museum of Art
arrowhead	Danish National Museum
art	UNICEF Collection
aster	Gretchen Garner
attempt	P. C. and Connie Peri
attire	Carlton C. McAvey
austere	"American Gothic," Grant Wood Courtesy of The Art Institute of Chicago
autograph	Bob Adelman
bacteria	Courtesy of Dr. R. Wyckoff National Institute of Health
badger	John H. Gerard

bald eagle	From the collection of Cynthia Zilliac
bamboo	Lynn M. Stone
battlement	Spanish National Tourist Office
beetle	S. Kuribayashi / Katherine Young
bill	"The Circus is Coming" 1871 Charles C. Ward The Metropolitan Museum of Art Bequest of Susan Vanderpoel Clark, 1967
bison	"Buffs., Feb. 1820," T. R. Peale Courtesy of The American Philosophical Society
blackbird	From the collection of Cynthia Zilliac
blacken	Ruth A. Cordner / Root Resources
blimp	Courtesy of Goodyear Tire and Rubber Company
bloodhound	H. Armstrong Roberts
bluebird	From the collection of Cynthia Zilliac
blue jay	From the collection of Cynthia Zilliac
bobcat	John H. Gerard
bobsled	A. F. P. from Pictorial
box	"Interior of the Park Theatre, New York City," Painting by John Searle Watercolor on paper, November, 1822 Courtesy of The New York Historical Society, New York City
boxers	"Both Members of This Club" George Bellows National Gallery of Art, Washington, D.C. Gift of Chester Dale
brand	Courtesy of The State Highway Commission of Montana, Helena, Montana
breaker	David Muench / Van Cleve Photography
breathtaking	David Muench / Van Cleve Photography
breeches	The Franklin D. Roosevelt Library
bristle	Emmy Haas
bulldozer	Courtesy of the Caterpillar Tractor Company
bullfight	Walter S. Clark, Jr.
bust	"Sioux Indian Man" Sculpture by Malvina Hoffman, Courtesy of The Field Museum of Natural History
cable	Courtesy of Bell Laboratories
cactus	Carlton C. McAvey
canoe	Walter Chandoha
capsule	NASA
cardinal	From the collection of Cynthia Zilliac
cart	UNICEF Collection
cascade	William B. Parker
castle	R. Everts / ZEFA
caterpillar	Lynn M. Stone
cattail	Gretchen Garner
ceramics	Sgraffito-Ware Plate Index of American Design National Gallery of Art, Washington, D.C.
chalice	Tassilo Cup Courtesy of Kremsmunster Abbey, Austria
chandelier	The Family Dining Room of The Governor's Palace in Williamsburg, Virginia Colonial Williamsburg Photograph
chaps	Library of Congress
cheetah	M. P. Kahl / Bruce Coleman, Inc.
chemist	Courtesy of the Chemistry Department Northwestern University
chipmunk	Carlton C. McAvey
clinch	Photo by Paris Match
clipper	Library of Congress
coat of arms	Folger Shakespeare Library
collar	From the collection of G. Russell-Dempsey
colonnade	Raymond V. Schoder, S.J.
comet	Courtesy of Hale Observatories
condor	F. Erize / Bruce Coleman, Inc.
consume	General Dynamics Corporation

contemplation	Portrait of Christina Rossetti by D. G. Rossetti, The Mansell Collection
contradictory	Culver Pictures
conventional	Library of Congress
cooperate	P. C. and Connie Peri
coral	Anne L. Daubilet / Animals, Animals © 1975
court	Folger Shakespeare Library
coyote	Information Canada Photothèque Ottawa, Canada
crater	NASA
crest	John Padour
crevasse	Information Canada Photothèque Ottawa, Canada
crocus	Gretchen Garner
crossbow	Royal MS. 14E. IV. f. 23 Reproduced by permission of the British Library Board
cupboard	Index of American Design National Gallery of Art, Washington
cupid	From the collection of Lois Metcalf
curtsy	Jean-Claude Lejeune
cutter	"The Road-Winter," N. Currier, 1853 The Harry T. Peters Collection Museum of The City of New York
dam	Ben Glaha, U.S. Department of the Interior
dangle	Photographer, Jonathan Wright © National Geographic Society from their film "Journey to the Outer Limits"
dazzling	Steve White / Photo Design
debris	Thomas W. Putney / Putney Photo Library
decoration	Library of Congress
decoy	Hand-carved decoy of a drake made during the Colonial period Index of American Design National Gallery of Art, Washington, D.C.
deface	Don Bronstein
dejected	"Employment Office," Isaac Soyer, 1937 Collection of the Whitney Museum of American Art, New York
delicate	Lynn M. Stone
deluge	Thomas W. Putney / Putney Photo Library
demolish	John Gordon
demonstration	United Press International
design	From the collection of Dr. Regina Holloman
desolate	Cecil W. Stoughton, National Park Service
dew	Dr. E. R. Degginger
diminutive	From the collection of G. Russell-Dempsey
dinosaur	Courtesy of the American Museum of Natural History
dirigible	U.S. Navy Photograph
disaster	Thomas W. Putney / Putney Photo Library
disdainful	From the collection of G. Russell-Dempsey
dismal	Thomas W. Putney / Putney Photo Library
doff	"General Washington on a White Charger" Unknown American Artist, National Gallery of Art, Washington, D.C., Gift of Edgar William and Bernice Chrysler Garbisch
dome	Abbie Rowe, National Park Service
domesticate	From the collection of G. Russell-Dempsey
dory	Information Canada Photothèque
dove	K. W. Fink / Bruce Coleman, Inc.
dragonfly	Lynn M. Stone
driftwood	Lynn M. Stone
dromedary	Jacques Jangoux
drought	Library of Congress
drum	Civil War Drum Index of American Design National Gallery of Art, Washington, D.C.

dubious "Their Pride," Thomas Hovenden, Courtesy of the Union League Club, New York City Photograph by Robert S. Crandall

duck Lynn M. Stone

dumbbell "Country Fair Athlete," Camille Bombois Musée National d'Art Moderne, Paris

dunes Cecil W. Stoughton, National Park Service

dwarf Courtesy of the Holsten Bonsai Collection, Brooklyn Botanic Garden

earthquake Library of Congress

elevator Charles Phelps Cushing

elk Information Canada Photothèque

elongate John Tenniel illustration from Lewis Carroll's Alice's Adventures in Wonderland

endanger "Whooping Crane," Audubon, Courtesy of The New York Historical Society

engross "Nearing the Issue at the Cockpit" Horace Bonham In the collection of the Corcoran Gallery of Art

equilibrium Courtesy of The New York Historical Society

erosion U.S.D.A. / SCS Photo by Erwin W. Cole

erupt "Pacayo Volcano" by Alfredo MacKenney, M.D. Reproduced, with permission, from Natural History Magazine, Copyright © The American Museum of Natural History, 1968

estate By courtesy of the Marquess of Bath

etching Scala / New York / Florence

everglade Lynn M. Stone

exhibit "Staircase of the Old British Museum, Montague House," George Scharf, The Elder The Trustees of the British Museum

exotic © A. Visage / Jacana / Liaison

expedition Photographer, Jonathan Wright © National Geographic Society from their film "Journey to the Outer Limits"

experimental General Motors Corporation

extricate The Bettmann Archive

eye "Queer Fish," Mabel Dwight, Collection of the Philadelphia Museum of Art: Purchased: The Harrison Fund

fad Wide World Photos

fanciful From the collection of G. Russell-Dempsey

fashionable By courtesy of The Victoria and Albert Museum

feat Keystone Press Agency, Inc.

feathery NASA

ferocious Japanese Buddhist Guardian Figure Kamakura period 1185–1192 A.D. Courtesy of The Art Institute of Chicago, Clarence Buckingham Collection

ferris wheel Courtesy of The Chicago Historical Society

festive UNICEF Collection

fife "Heroes of '76,' Marching to the Fight" Lithograph by Currier & Ives, 1876 Library of Congress

figurehead Index of American Design National Gallery of Art, Washington, D.C.

fingerprint F.B.I.

fiord Walter S. Clark, Jr.

firefly S. Kuribayashi / Katherine Young

flamingo Lynn M. Stone

flexible From the collection of G. Russell-Dempsey

flicker From the collection of Cynthia Zilliac

ford Savage and Savage Studio

forge "Trotting Cracks at the Forge" Currier and Ives, 1869 The Harry T. Peters Collection Museum of The City of New York

forlorn Leonard Freed / Magnum Photos

fracas "Farmers Attacking Officials at the Springfield Arsenal under Daniel Sharp's Leadership in 1786," American History Division, The New York Public Library, Astor, Lenox and Tilden Foundation

frame Photograph courtesy of owner/developer The John Hancock Mutual Life Insurance Company

freak Wide World Photos

frigate "A View of the American Frigate Constellation Capturing the French Frigate L'Insurgente"; 2-9-1799 The Franklin D. Roosevelt Library

frond Gretchen Garner

furrow F.A.O.

galaxy © California Institute of Technology & Carnegie Institution of Washington

gape H. Armstrong Roberts

gazelle Lynn M. Stone

geometric Navajo blanket Museum of the American Indian

geyser William B. Parker

glacier U.S. Department of the Interior Geological Survey

gleeful Gretchen Garner

golden Gold Mask, National Museum, Mycenae Scala / New York / Florence

gondola Adam Woolfitt / Woodfin Camp

gossamer S. Kuribayashi / Katherine Young

grimace Marble bust by F. X. Messerschmidt Courtesy Österreichische Galerie, Vienna

ground UNICEF Collection

gymnastics Wide World Photos

haggard Library of Congress

halo "The Adoration of the Magi," Gentile da Fabriano, detail from a tempera on wood painting, 1423. Scala / New York / Florence

harmony "Peaceable Kingdom," 1848, by Edward Hicks Collection of the Philadelphia Museum of Art: Bequest of Lisa Norris Elkins

harp Musée Instrumental, Brussels, Belgium

hawk From the collection of Cynthia Zilliac

hazardous United Press International

headdress Dr. Phillip Kahl / Black Star

headless Heraklion Museum of Archaeology, Greece

hedgehog H. Reinhard / Bruce Coleman, Inc.

helicopter Sikorsky Aircraft

helmet (right) Iron Helmet from the Anglo-Saxon Period: Courtesy of The Trustees of the British Museum

herald From the collection of Cynthia Zilliac

heron From the collection of Cynthia Zilliac

hideous Boris Karloff in "The Mummy," Universal Pictures. Photograph Courtesy of Film Stills Archive, The Museum of Modern Art

hippopotamus John Padour

hogan Diane M. Lowe

honeybee © Fred Winner / Jacana / Liaison

hooked Lynn M. Stone

horn Library of Congress

horned toad Robert L. Dunne / Bruce Coleman, Inc.

horror Tragic Mask Representing King Priam of Troy. Terra Cotta. c. 400 B.C. Staatliche Museen zu Berlin, Antikensammlung

hummingbird Anthony Mercieca / Root Resources

hurdle Gerry Cranham / Rapho Guillumette Photo Researchers

hyena Frederic / Jacana / Liaison

iceberg U.S. Coast Guard Official Photo

iceboat William B. Parker

icebreaker U.S. Coast Guard Official Photo

identical Harvey Stein

igloo Information Canada Photothèque

imaginative From the collection of G. Russell-Dempsey

immense C. Bonington / Woodfin Camp and Associates

Inca Shostal Associates

inedible The Museum of Modern Art Film Stills Archive

infancy National Air and Space Museum, Smithsonian Institution

inspect Hughes Aircraft Corp.

interference Vernon J. Biever

irrigate Monsanto Co., St. Louis, Missouri

isthmus Fairchild Aerial Surveys, Inc.

ivory Ivory Mask of the King of Benin, Nigeria 16th cent. Courtesy of The Trustees of the British Museum

jackal Lynn M. Stone

jaguar Kenneth W. Fink / Root Resources

jellyfish Al Giddings / Sea Library TOM STACK & ASSOCIATES

jerkin Folger Shakespeare Library

jester From the collection of Carol Hatcher

jewel Folger Shakespeare Library

joust The British Library

jumbo The American Antiquarian Society

junk Shostal Associates

jupiter Lick Observatory

jute United Press International

kangaroo Walter S. Clark, Jr.

katydid Lynn M. Stone

kayak Information Canada Photothèque

kilt Shostal Associates

kitten Allan Roberts

knight Royal MS. 6E. IX. f. 24. Reproduced by permission of the British Library Board

koala Walter S. Clark, Jr.

lacrosse Thomas W. Putney / Putney Photo Library

ladybug Lynn M. Stone

larva Turtox / Cambosco, MacMillan Science Company, Chicago, Illinois 60620 U.S.A.

lasso "Cowboy Roping a Steer," Charles Russell, 1904, The Woolaroc Museum

launching pad NASA

laurel From the collection of Cynthia Zilliac

lava Cecil Stoughton, National Park Service

leap Wide World Photos

leopard Carlton C. McAvey

lichen William B. Parker

litter Rare Book Division The New York Public Library Astor, Lenox and Tilden Foundation

lizard Z. Leszcynski / Animals, Animals © 1973

llama Jacques Jangoux

lock By Ewing Galloway, New York

loon Information Canada Photothèque

low tide Diane M. Lowe

lubricate Metro Goldwyn Mayer Production

ludicrous Harry Benson

lute From the collection of G. Russell-Dempsey

lyre "Music and Reading Lessons," detail from a cup by Douris. Staatliche Museen zu Berlin, Antiken-Abteilung

magnificent Carlton C. McAvey

mall The Metropolitan Museum of Art, Bashford Dean Memorial Collection, Purchase, 1929, Funds from Various Donors

Mars International Planetary Patrol Photograph

mask Rook Island Mask Field Museum of Natural History, Chicago

maxim White House Collection

maze Colonial Williamsburg Photo

meadowlark From the collection of Cynthia Zilliac

medal   Courtesy of Georgia Pacific Hopper Paper Division

megaphone   Shostal Associates

melancholy   "At The Front," Lambdin, George C. Detroit Institute of Art

mill wheel   H. Armstrong Roberts

mimic   Lynn M. Stone

minaret   Shostal Associates

misty   William B. Parker

moccasin   E.R. Degginger / Bruce Coleman, Inc.

mollusk   From the collection of G. Russell-Dempsey

monorail   William B. Parker

moon   NASA

moose   Information Canada Photothèque

mosaic   Bust of Theodora Scala / New York / Florence

mosque   Walter S. Clark, Jr.

moth   Lynn M. Stone

mountain goat   Jerry Hennen

muff   The Franklin D. Roosevelt Library

mule   David Salinger

mural   Hal A. Franklin

nape   Walter Chandoha

natural   National Park Service

neglect   Bill Owens / BBM

nerve   The Minnesota Historical Society

nestle   The Metropolitan Museum of Art, Rogers Fund, 1905

newborn   Tom Myers

newt   E.R. Degginger / Bruce Coleman, Inc.

nomad   An Exxon Photo Courtesy of Exxon Corporation

northern lights   N.O.A.A.

noteworthy   Union Pacific Railroad Museum Collection

notorious   Rare Book Division The New York Public Library Astor, Lenox and Tilden Foundation

novel   Shostal Associates

nucleus   Arnold H. Sparrow and R. F. Smith

nugget   Museum of Natural History, Smithsonian Institution. Photograph by Lee Boltin

nuzzle   The Museum of Modern Art Film Stills Archive

obelisk   Walter S. Clark, Jr.

obsolete   Bettmann Archives

obstinate   "Bucking Bronco," Frederic Remington Century Magazine, March, 1888

octopus   Jane Burton / Bruce Coleman, Inc.

ogre   From the collection of G. Russell-Dempsey

old-fashioned   From the collection of Lois Metcalf

ominous   "Grey and Gold," John Rogers Cox, 1942 The Cleveland Museum of Art Mr. and Mrs. William H. Marlatt Fund

opossum   John H. Gerard

orangutan   © Grossa / Jacana / Liaison

orchid   Maurice B. Cook

ornate   Ken Heyman

otter   William B. Parker

outrigger   John Padour

owl   From the collection of Cynthia Zilliac

pack animal   Jacques Jangoux

paddy   Walter S. Clark, Jr.

pagoda   Courtesy of the Consulate General of Japan, N.Y.

palm   Walter S. Clark, Jr.

palmetto   Lynn M. Stone

palomino   Kenneth W. Fink / Root Resources

panda   The Smithsonian Institution

parachute   U.S. Army Photograph

passenger pigeon   Watercolor by John Audubon The New York Historical Society

pasture   Lynn M. Stone

patchwork   Detail of the Mosaic or Honeycomb Quilt, c. 1840. The Art Institute of Chicago

patio   J. Lochridge

peace pipe   Carlton C. McAvey

pearl   Robert Joslin / Root Resources

peccary   Lynn M. Stone

pelican   Lynn M. Stone

penguin   © Suinot / Jacana / Liaison

pentagon   Official U.S. Navy Photo

perform   Library of Congress

perpendicular   H. Woodridge Williams U.S. Geological Survey

perplex   © Richard Feiner and Company, Inc., by permission of Hal Roach Studios, Inc.

pheasant   © A. Duchot / Jacana / Liaison

pier   Lynn M. Stone

pincer   Lynn M. Stone

pioneer   Thomas Hart Benton's Mural, "Independence and the Opening of the West" The Harry S. Truman Library

placid   Lynn M. Stone

plow   Courtesy of the Caterpillar Tractor Co.

plumage   Walter S. Clark, Jr.

poison ivy   Maurice B. Cook

polar bear   © J. Stoll / Jacana / Liaison

polygon   By Jean Seisser and France DeRanchin From the Harlin Quist book, Book of Amazements

polyp   From the collection of G. Russell-Dempsey

porcelain   Birthday Group, German Porcelain c. 1771 Artist: Frankenthal after a model by K. G. Luck. Courtesy of The Trustees of the British Museum

portico   Virginia Conservation Commission Richmond, Virginia

portrait   Pocahontas. National Portrait Gallery, The Smithsonian Institution, Washington, D.C.

pose   Franklin McMahon

potter   United Nations

prairie dog   Lynn M. Stone

prairie schooner   Settlers Wagon. Index of American Design. National Gallery of Art, Washington, D.C.

precise   Michael Mauney

predatory   From the collection of Cynthia Zilliac

preen   Lynn M. Stone

prickly pear   Lynn M. Stone

procession   Procession to a tomb of Ramose, 18th Dynasty, 1411–1375 B.C. The Oriental Institute, The University of Chicago

profile   Carlton C. McAvey

promontory   "Distant View of Village," Artist: George Catlin. U.S. National Museum, The Smithsonian Institution

propeller   Newport News Shipbuilding & Dry Dock Co.

proportion   John Tenniel illustration from Lewis Carroll's Alice's Adventures in Wonderland

provocation   The Museum of Modern Art Film Stills Archive

ptarmigan   Lynn M. Stone

pucker   Culver Pictures

puff   Lynn M. Stone

pupa   Lynn M. Stone

pussy willow   Lynn M. Stone

pyramid (upper)   Courtesy of Transamerica Corporation

pyramid (lower)   Walter S. Clark, Jr.

quartz   William B. Parker

quench   United Nations

raccoon   Lynn M. Stone

rage (top)   U.S. Dept. of the Interior Bureau of Land Management

rage (bottom)   U.P.I. Photo by Dennis Connor

rapid   Ernst Haas

rapt   Jerry Howard / Pioneer Press

rattlesnake   Lynn M. Stone

ravage   Thomas W. Putney / Putney Photo Library

rear   Walter R. Aguiar

recreation   UNICEF Collection

reef   Walter S. Clark, Jr.

reflection   J. Lochridge

refuge   Anthony Mercieca / Root Resources

regatta   From the collection of G. Russell-Dempsey

relay race   Thomas Hopker / Woodfin Camp

relief   Roman Emperor in a triumphal chariot drawn by four horses. Capitoline Museum Alinari / Art Reference Bureau

resemble   Edwin Smith

reservoir   Courtesy of Chicago Bridge & Iron Co.

resplendent   "Sun King, Louis XIV," Photo Bibliothèque Nationale, Paris

reunite   United Press International

rhea   Lynn M. Stone

rib   Information Canada Photothèque

rice   Walter S. Clark, Jr.

ride   UNICEF Collection

robot   United Press International

rodent   H. Reinhard / Bruce Coleman, Inc.

rodeo   Carlton C. McAvey

rose   South Rose Window, Notre Dame, Paris Scala / New York / Florence

rotor   U.S. Navy Photograph

ruff   Folger Shakespeare Library

russet   Lynn M. Stone

sacrifice   Raymond V. Schoder, S.J.

salamander   Lynn M. Stone

salmon   Lynn M. Stone

sandpiper   From the collection of Cynthia Zilliac

sari   Jean-Claude Lejeune

satellite   NASA

scaffold   Uris Building Corporation

scene   UNICEF Collection

scepter   Cecil Beaton / London

schooner   "Hudson River Schooner," George S. Wood The Smithsonian Institution

scooter   Richard L. Capps

scrap   From the collection of G. Russell-Dempsey

scribe   Add. MS. 39943, f. 2 Reproduced by permission of the British Library Board

sculpture   "Walking Man," Bronze, 1960, Alberto Giacometti; Grant J. Pick Purchase Fund The Art Institute of Chicago

seaplane   Shostal Associates

secretary   Sheraton Style Secretary, Index of American Design, National Gallery of Art Washington, D.C.

sedan chair   Messrs. Mallett and Son, London

seine   F.A.O.

settee   Sheraton Style Settee, Index of American Design, National Gallery of Art, Washington, D.C.

severe   United Press International

shark   Peter Lake / Sea Library TOM STACK & ASSOCIATES

sheer	Philip Hyde	swamp	Lynn M. Stone	urn	The Metropolitan Museum of Art, Rogers Fund, 1905
shimmer	William B. Parker	swan	Lynn M. Stone	valentine	From the collection of Lois Metcalf
shrew	Jerry Hennen	swept-back	William B. Parker	vane	H. Armstrong Roberts
silo	William B. Parker	symbol	Sternboard Eagle, Index of American Design, National Gallery of Art, Washington, D.C.	vase	Pottery Wine Jar, Landscape and Sages China, Ming Dynasty; The University Museum Philadelphia, Pennsylvania
single-handed	Carlton C. McAvey				
skeleton	The Metropolitan Museum of Art, Gift of Dr. Alfred E. Cohn, Dedicated to the Honor of William M. Ivins, Jr., 1953	symmetry (bottom)	William B. Parker	vault¹	Folger Shakespeare Library
		tablet	"Moses Breaking the Tables of the Law," detail from an illustration by Gustave Doré, 1866	vault²	United Press International
sleigh	"The Sleigh Race," Currier and Ives Library of Congress			vein	Lynn M. Stone
		tapestry	"The Woodpecker Tapestry," (1885–1887) by William Morris. William Morris Gallery and Brangwyn Gift	velocity	Monogram Models, Inc.
slug	Lynn M. Stone			vendor	"Root Beer Seller," Nicolino Calyo The Museum of The City of New York
snail	Lynn M. Stone				
snoop	From the collection of G. Russell-Dempsey	tarantula	J. McDonald / Bruce Coleman, Inc.	veranda	Walter S. Clark, Jr.
snowflake	N.O.A.A.	team	Courtesy of the Caterpillar Tractor Co., Peoria, Ill.	view	UNICEF Collection
soccer	Gerhard Gscheidle / Magnum Photos			vine	From the collection of Cynthia Zilliac
sod	Solomon D. Butcher Collection Nebraska State Historical Society	telescope (top)	© California Institute of Technology & Carnegie Institution of Washington	virus	Gene M. Milbrath, Department of Plant Pathology, University of Illinois
solemn	"Tea Time," Gift of Edgar William and Bernice Chrysler Garbisch, The Columbus Gallery of Fine Arts, Columbus, Ohio	tempest	Etching for "The Rime of the Ancient Mariner," by Gustave Doré, first published in 1875 by the Doré Gallery, London	vivid	South African Travel Bureau
				vulture	Lynn M. Stone
sop	Allan Roberts	tepee	Lynn M. Stone	walrus	F. Erize / Bruce Coleman, Inc.
		thatch	Diane M. Lowe		
sordid	Photograph by Jacob A. Riis The Jacob A. Riis Collection Museum of The City of New York	thistle	From the collection of Cynthia Zilliac	wampum	Museum of the American Indian
		thoroughbred	H. Reinhard / Bruce Coleman, Inc.	warbler	From the collection of Cynthia Zilliac
sow	"Sowing Grain at Bishop Hill" Olaf Krans; Department of Conservation Bishop Hill, Illinois	tide	Nova Scotia Information Service	wasp	R. E. Pelham / Bruce Coleman, Inc.
		tiger	Carlton C. McAvey	water buffalo	Walter S. Clark, Jr.
span	Janet Beller	tightrope	Shostal Associates	watercolor	PRENDERGAST, Maurice. The East River, 1901. Watercolor, 13¾ × 19¾" Collection, The Museum of Modern Art, New York. Gift of Abby Aldrich Rockefeller
spectacular	William B. Parker	timberline	Lynn M. Stone		
sperm whale	"Capturing a Sperm Whale," Engraving by John Hill, 1835; Courtesy of The New York Historical Society, New York City	toad	Lynn M. Stone		
		toil	"The Gleaners," by Jean F. Millet, Louvre, Paris. Scala / New York / Florence	waterlily	Lynn M. Stone
spider	Lynn M. Stone			way	From the collection of G. Russell-Dempsey
spin	Walter S. Clark, Jr.	tomahawk	Museum of the American Indian	weathercock	Index of American Design National Gallery of Art, Washington, D.C.
spine	Lynn M. Stone	tornado	E.S.S.A.		
spire	Library of Congress	torrent	UNICEF Collection	weave	Walter S. Clark, Jr.
splash	U.S. Department of Agriculture Photograph	tortoise	Lynn M. Stone	web	Lynn M. Stone
squire	Pierpont Morgan Library	towboat	Shostal Associates	weightless	NASA
stamen	Lynn M. Stone	track (top)	Information Canada Photothèque	weld	United Nations
stare	Information Canada Photothèque	track (bottom)	Caterpillar Tractor Co.	wharf	Shostal Associates
starfish	William B. Parker	train	From the collection of Cynthia Zilliac	whelk	Lynn M. Stone
statue	Courtesy of Braun and Company, Paris, New York	transform	From the motion picture "THE WEREWOLF" Courtesy of Universal Pictures	whippoorwill	From the collection of Cynthia Zilliac
				willful	From the collection of G. Russell-Dempsey
steamboat	"Great Mississippi Steamboat Race" Currier and Ives Museum of The City of New York	trapper	Illustration by courtesy of National Life Insurance Company, Montpelier, Vermont	wing	Lynn M. Stone
		treadmill	Library of Congress	wintry	R. Kluge / Bruce Coleman, Inc.
stork	Lynn M. Stone	trophy	Robert Farbin	withdraw	Lynn M. Stone
strain	George Silk, LIFE Magazine © Time, Inc.	turban	Walter S. Clark, Jr.	wolverine	Information Canada Photothèque
streamlined	Wide World Photos	ugly	E.S.S.A.	woodpecker	From the collection of Cynthia Zilliac
stunt	Syndication International	umpire	United Press International	wren	From the collection of Cynthia Zilliac
sublime	"Kindred Spirits, 1849," Asher Durand Collection of The New York Public Library Astor, Lenox and Tilden Foundation	unaware	From the collection of G. Russell-Dempsey	wrinkle	William B. Parker
		underdeveloped	F.A.O.	writhe	"The Wrestlers," by George Luks Courtesy of the Museum of Fine Arts, Boston. Charles Henry Hayden Fund
suffrage	Brown Brothers	ungainly	Tom Myers		
sugar maple	Information Canada Photothèque	unicorn	French or Flemish, Late 15th or early 16th century, "The Hunt of the Unicorn" Silk and Wool, Silver and Silver gilt threads, From the Chateau of Verteiu; The Metropolitan Museum of Art, The Cloister Collection, Gift of John D. Rockefeller, Jr.; 1937	X ray	Picken X-Ray Corporation
summit	Royal Geographical Society			yak	F.A.O.
sundial	The Metropolitan Museum of Art, Gift of Mrs. Stephen D. Tucker, 1903			yoke	"Haying Time-The First Load" Currier & Ives; Library of Congress
supple	Martha Swope			zebra	Carlton C. McAvey
surfboard	SPORTS ILLUSTRATED Photograph by Neil Leifer © Time, Inc.	unison	UNICEF Collection	zebu	Norman Owen Tomalin / Bruce Coleman, Inc.
		unwieldy	Republic Aviation Corporation Farmingdale, Long Island, New York	zigzag	Gretchen Garner
swallow	From the collection of Cynthia Zilliac				

Scott, Foresman staff photos:

Using This Dictionary p. 34 (left), p. 49 (top). abacus, absorb, affection, agate, algae, altar, andiron, architect, baboon, bagpipe, balance, balcony, banjo, barge, barometer, bassoon, bellows, bias, binoculars, boomerang, brocade, brooch, butte, butterfly, calculator, camel, camouflage, catkin, cello, chess, churn, clarinet, clown, cogs, coil, comfort, commemorate, companion, comparative, compass, competition, contrast, cornet, counterclockwise, crane, crinkle, croquet, cruet, cylinder, cymbal, daisy, dally, dawn, derrick, diagonal, dilapidated, display, distort, downcast, earthenware, eerie, elaborate, embroidery, embryo, enamel, engage, entangle, explore, face, fashioned, float, flute, fly, foal, fossil, fountain, fulcrum, fungus, gable, gargoyle, garter snake, gear, gerbil, glide, goblet, gourd, guinea pig, guitar, gull, gyroscope, halter, hamster, harmonica, helmet (left), hitch, hobbyhorse, iguana, incline, indiscreet, inflammable, ingenuity, inlaid, inscription, insignia, instep, insulator, intent, interlace, interlock, intricate, iris, ivy, jack, kettledrum, kimono, knocker, knot, lace, lantern, level, lighthouse, lion, loop, magnet, makeup, mango, marigold, marionette, menorah (from the collection of Rabbi Hillel Gamoran), meteorite, metric system, microscope, miscellaneous, movement, neckerchief, negative, neon, net, obi, oboe, oddity, onlooker, pansy, parallel, parrot, peer, perspective, piccolo, plaid, plumb line, prehistoric, prism, prohibit, project, puppet, puzzle, rare (from the collection of Rabbi Hillel Gamoran), recorder, recycle, refinery, refract, relic (from the collection of Rabbi Hillel Gamoran), renovate, repose, represent, resourceful, rhinoceros, rink, ripple, rooster, rubble, saddle, saxophone, score, sidelong, silhouette (lower), skein, snare drum, sombrero, spectrum, sphere, spiral, sprocket, square, stalactite, stethoscope, stirrup, stratum, subway, sunflower, suspension bridge, telescope (bottom), tempt, terrarium, thermometer, thoughtful, torch, toxic, translucent, transparent, triangle (bottom), trombone, trowel, trumpet, tuba, tug-of-war, tuning fork, tweed, twirl, veterinarian, viola/violin, vise, visor, volleyball, winch, wistful, xylophone, zinnia, zither

Answer Key

to

Using This Dictionary

page 11 **TEACH YOURSELF**
1. anteater, cobra, elephant
2. hyena, kangaroo, ostrich
3. turtle, walrus

page 12 **Exercise 1**
1. Ilno   4. Egirt   7. Celoot
2. Flow   5. Art   8. Korst
3. Aber   6. Low   9. Alrsuw

Exercise 2
1. call my name
2. see the whale
3. find her toy
4. give him some toast
5. don't go home now
6. every giraffe is tall
7. he lent me the wagon
8. let me play with you
9. feed my nice pet rabbit

page 13 **TEACH YOURSELF**
1. dr
2. the third letter
3. yes
4. the fourth letter
5. first
6. she, shed, sheep, shell, shepherd, sheriff

Exercise 3
2. cage   13. car
5. call   15. cardboard
8. can   17. carefree
10. cane   20. cash
12. cape   23. catch

page 14 **TEACH YOURSELF**
1. no   4. unhitch
2. no   5. unkind
3. unhitch/unkind

page 15 **Exercise 4**
1. b 3. b 5. c
2. c 4. b 6. a

page 16 **TEACH YOURSELF**
1. yes 5. yes
2. e 6. y
3. yes 7. yes
4. y 8. m

page 16   **Exercise 5**

1. thrush   6. aviary
2. fierce   7. grizzly
3. animal   8. cage
4. graze   9. swim
5. rhinoceros   10. hibernate

page 17   *TEST YOURSELF*

A. 1. both have many pages
   2. get gray hare spray
   3. an astronaut gets missile toe
   4. a coat of oozing orange paint
   5. finding four halves of white worms
   6. just like short skinny skunks
   7. holding the thin tiger tightly together

B. 1. airway/alfalfa
   2. ample/anchor
   3. actor/adjacent
   4. anticipation/apart
   5. allege/aloft
   6. adjective/adore
   7. April/arctic
   8. anchorage/angry

C. 1. moose   6. hippopotamuses or
   2. ostriches   hippopotami
   3. flamingos or   7. dormice
      flamingoes   8. canaries
   4. geese   9. walruses or walrus
   5. mongooses   10. grizzlies

page 18   **TEACH YOURSELF**

1. place where an animal or plant lives (or similar wording)
2. Answers will vary.

page 19   **Exercise 6**

1. b   5. c   9. b
2. a   6. a   10. a
3. a   7. c   11. b
4. a   8. c   12. b

page 20   **Exercise 7**

1. The winner of the debate was a peerless speaker.
2. The tiger's paw will heal in a few days.
3. Hilarious sounds of laughter came from the next room.
4. See how the jewels in the crown sparkle.
5. People at the movie screamed when the hideous monster attacked the hero.
6. We must not squander our natural resources.

page 21 **TEACH YOURSELF**
1. four
2. Answers will vary. The following are possibilities:
The donkey was in a dangerous position.
The donkey was in an uncertain position.

Exercise 8
1. b	3. c	5. c
2. a	4. a	6. c

page 22 **TEACH YOURSELF**
1. definition 6	3. definition 1
2. definition 3	4. definition 5

Exercise 9
1. definition 1	6. definition 2
2. definition 2	7. definition 1
3. definition 1	8. definition 5
4. definition 2	9. definition 1
5. definition 1	10. definition 2

page 23 **TEACH YOURSELF**
1. cricket^2
2. cricket^1

Exercise 10
1. last^1	6. kind^2
2. fly^2	7. shot^2
3. found^1	8. net^1
4. saw^2	9. plight^1
5. long^1	10. fast^1

page 24 *TEST YOURSELF*
A.
1. no	6. no
2. either no or yes	7. yes
3. no	8. no
4. yes	9. yes
5. no	10. yes

B. 1. definition 1
2. definition 17
3. definition 5

C. 1. definition 1
2. definition 1
3. definition 2
4. definition 3

D.
1.	a. bear^2	b. bear^1
2.	a. calf^1	b. calf^2
3.	a. quail^1	b. quail^2
4.	a. duck^2	b. duck^1
5.	a. bat^2	b. bat^1

page 25 **Crossword puzzle**

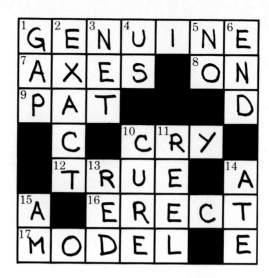

page 26 **Challenge**

Laura's idea was that the code was the letters of the alphabet written backwards, using *z* for *a*, *y* for *b*, *x* for *c*, and so on.

page 28 **TEACH YOURSELF**

1. bet 2. ridge

Exercise 11

1. man	6. cut
2. lab	7. get
3. got	8. met
4. pin	9. laugh
5. can't	10. hiss

page 29 **TEACH YOURSELF A**

1. bait 3. kite
2. feel 4. note

TEACH YOURSELF B

1. farm 3. book 5. cube
2. born 4. pool

page 30 **Exercise 12**

1. lark	7. loon
2. crow	8. teal
3. kite	9. snipe
4. rook	10. quail
5. goose	11. hawk
6. stork	12. jay

page 31 **TEACH YOURSELF A**

1. toy 2. count

TEACH YOURSELF B

1. think, breath, throw
2. this, breathe, those

page 32 **Exercise 13**

1. a	4. a	7. b	10. b
2. a	5. b	8. b	11. a
3. b	6. a	9. a	12. b

TEST YOURSELF

A.
1. laugh	6. pile	11. car
2. pill	7. look	12. all
3. rock	8. phone	13. these
4. says	9. luck	14. chew
5. rough	10. think	15. cave

page 33 B.
1. mile	4. purr	7. rain
2. through	5. trough	8. feet
3. pad	6. bear	

TEACH YOURSELF
1. one   2. two   3. three

page 34 **Exercise 14**

1. two; first	6. two; first
2. two; second	7. one
3. one	8. two; first
4. two; first	9. two; second
5. three; first	10. two; first

Exercise 15

fav<u>o</u>r	p<u>u</u>rsue	leop<u>a</u>rd
<u>gi</u>raffe	tow<u>e</u>r	mount<u>ai</u>n
tort<u>oi</u>se	buff<u>a</u>lo	curi<u>ou</u>s

page 35 *TEST YOURSELF*

1. b	3. c	5. c	7. c
2. a	4. b	6. b	8. b

page 36 **TEACH YOURSELF**
1. the first syllable   2. the third syllable

Exercise 16

1. hippopotamus	4. orangutan
2. peacock	5. copperhead
3. ladybug	6. salamander

TEACH YOURSELF
Answer: b

page 37 **Exercise 17**

1. b	3. a	5. a	7. a
2. a	4. b	6. a	

page 38 **Exercise 18**
Answers will vary.

page 39 **Exercise 19**

1. raining cats and dogs—cat
   smelled a rat—rat
   horsing around—horse
   let the cat out of the bag—cat
   got my goat—goat
   cook his goose—goose
   gone to the dogs—dog
   made a monkey out of him—monkey
   horse of a different color—horse
   talked turkey—turkey
   eat crow—crow²
2. Answers will vary.

page 40 **TEACH YOURSELF**

1. scoff
2. -er¹
3. yes
4. A person who scoffs makes fun of something or mocks something.
5. Answers will vary.

page 41 **Exercise 20**

Answers will vary.

page 43 **Exercise 21**

1. Any ten of the answers listed below would be correct.

lilac—Arabic	hippopotamus—Greek
pajamas—Hindu	yak—Tibetan
journey—French	moose—North American Indian
robot—Czech	alligator—Spanish
sky—Norse	walrus—Dutch
gumbo—Bantu	orangutan—Malay
yams—Senegalese	elephant—Greek
spaghetti—Italian	ambulance—French
yacht—Dutch	muscles—Latin
typhoon—Chinese	panic—Greek
dinosaur—Greek	foil—French
spaniel—French	clock—Latin
dachshund—German	barbecue—Spanish,
rhinoceros—Greek	Central American Indian

2. Answers will vary.

page 44 **Exercise 22**

1. field	5. weather	9. environment
2. usually	6. enemies	10. alter
3. affect	7. weasels	11. extinct
4. influence	8. increase	12. species

page 45 **Exercise 23**

1. grey	5. altho
2. fulfil	6. thru
3. enclose	7. quartette
4. skilful	8. OK

page 46 **Exercise 24**
1. o pos sum
2. mus<u>k</u> rat
3. a dult
4. b<u>i</u> son
5. co<u>t</u> t<u>on</u> tail
6. four-foo<u>t</u> ed
7. a<u>l</u> l<u>i</u> <u>ga</u> tor
8. co<u>p</u> per head

page 47 *TEST YOURSELF*

A.
1. one millimeter
2. China, Japan, and Korea
3. no
4. Julius Caesar
5. about 10 feet or 3 meters long
6. Sequoya was a Cherokee Indian who invented a way of writing his own language.
7. 1454 feet or 443 meters
8. at the Chicago world's fair in 1893
9. Yes, you need a microscope.
10. eight
11. I clear the thicket.
12. a bald eagle

B.
1. No. A machine shop is a workshop for repairing machines.
2. No. Low spirits means sadness or depression.
3. No. A magnetic field is the space around a magnet in which its power of attraction is effective.
4. Yes. They are sandwiches made of hot frankfurters enclosed in buns.
5. No. A square foot is a unit of area.
6. No. A spinning wheel is used to spin cotton, flax, or wool into thread or yarn.
7. No. A monkey wrench is a wrench with a movable jaw.
8. No. Ill will means dislike or spite.
9. No. A lymphatic vessel is a tube or canal in the body.
10. No. An oxygen tent is used in treating sick people who have difficulty breathing.
11. No. A nose cone is the front section of a missile or rocket.
12. No. A mountain range is a row or large group of mountains.
13. No. A magnifying glass is a lens that causes things to look larger than they really are.
14. No. Sweet peas are climbing plants with flowers.
15. No. A sea horse is a small fish.
16. No. A tuning fork is a small steel instrument that makes a musical tone of a certain pitch.
17. No. A running mate is a candidate in an election.
18. No. A powder horn is a flask used to carry gunpowder.
19. No. A prairie schooner is a large covered wagon.

page 47 **Step puzzle**

P	L	A	Y

1. 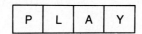 C L A Y

2. C L A D

3. G L A D

4. G O A D

G	O	A	L

Word square

¹E	²C	³H	⁴O
²C	H	O	P
³H	O	M	E
⁴O	P	E	N

Full pronunciation key

The pronunciation of each word is shown just after the word, in this way:
ab bre vi ate (ə brē′vē āt).

The letters and signs used are pronounced as in the words below.

The mark ′ is placed after a syllable with primary or heavy accent, as in the example above.

The mark ′ after a syllable shows a secondary or lighter accent, as in
ab bre vi a tion (ə brē′vē ā′shən).

a	hat, cap	**p**	paper, cup
ā	age, face	**r**	run, try
ä	father, far	**s**	say, yes
		sh	she, rush
b	bad, rob	**t**	tell, it
ch	child, much	**th**	thin, both
d	did, red	**ŦH**	then, smooth
e	let, best	**u**	cup, butter
ē	equal, be	**u̇**	full, put
ėr	term, learn	**ü**	rule, move
f	fat, if	**v**	very, save
g	go, bag	**w**	will, woman
h	he, how	**y**	young, yet
		z	zero, breeze
		zh	measure, seizure
i	it, pin		
ī	ice, five		
j	jam, enjoy	**ə**	represents:
k	kind, seek		a in about
l	land, coal		e in taken
m	me, am		i in pencil
n	no, in		o in lemon
ng	long, bring		u in circus
o	hot, rock		
ō	open, go		
ô	order, all		
oi	oil, voice		
ou	house, out		